Tolley's
Capital Gains Tax
1995–96

Gary B Mackley-Smith FFA FIAB ATT AIMgt
and
Patrick Noakes MA FCA ATII

Tolley Publishing Company Limited

un A United News & Media publication

Published by
Tolley Publishing Company Ltd
Tolley House
2 Addiscombe Road
Croydon Surrey CR9 5AF
England
Tel: 0181–686 9141

Typeset by
Interactive Sciences, Gloucester

Printed in Great Britain by The Bath Press, Avon

About This Book

This is the eighteenth edition of Tolley's Capital Gains Tax—a sister publication to Tolley's Income Tax, Tolley's Corporation Tax and Tolley's Inheritance Tax. The book is published annually and contains the latest legislation, relevant case law and other important information relating to capital gains tax. This edition contains the provisions of the Finance Act 1995.

The book includes the law and practice relating to capital gains tax and the charge to corporation tax in respect of chargeable gains for at least the past six years as well as the current year (i.e. for 1989/90 onwards and sometimes earlier) and so provides comprehensive information for claims, late assessments etc.

Tolley's Capital Gains Tax is arranged alphabetically for ease of reference and contains a comprehensive subject index and tables of cases and statutes. Worked examples are given within the text.

Comments and suggestions for improvement are always welcome.

TOLLEY PUBLISHING COMPANY LTD

Consolidation of Tax Enactments

With effect generally for 1992/93 and subsequent years of assessment (and for companies' accounting periods beginning after 5 April 1992) the *Taxes Acts* provisions relating to the taxation of chargeable gains are consolidated in the *Taxation of Chargeable Gains Act 1992 (TCGA 1992)*. The consolidation does not affect the application of the provisions concerned, but references to provisions which ceased to have effect before 6 April 1992 are omitted, as is the commencement date of the consolidated provisions (unless still relevant to the application of the current provisions).

The provisions for the six years before 1995/96, i.e. for 1989/90 to 1994/95, continue to be set out in this book. In strictness, the legislation applicable to the years before 1992/93 etc. is that in force prior to the consolidation referred to above, and the Revenue (while acknowledging that 'on previous consolidation, inspectors, Commissioners and taxpayers alike got used to the new references in dealing with previous periods'), have indicated that claims etc. for those years should refer to the statute then applicable.

Accordingly, the approach which has been adopted to statutory references in this book is as follows.

(i) References to current legislation invariably quote the *TCGA 1992* reference in the familiar form, i.e. '*TCGA 1992, s XXX*' to identify a section thereof and '*TCGA 1992, XX Sch*' to identify a Schedule thereto. Remaining references to pre-consolidation legislation are in the same form. Where there has been no change in the legislation in the last six years, no statutory reference other than that for *TCGA 1992* is quoted.

(ii) Where the legislation has changed during the last six years, the earlier provisions continue to be described in the text, and the appropriate earlier statutory reference is quoted. Legislation current during those six years but now repealed is similarly dealt with. Where any part of the current legislation was introduced during those six years, the commencement date is quoted, but the statutory reference for that date is generally omitted.

(iii) In any case where a claim or election for a year before 1992/93 may be involved, the appropriate earlier statutory reference is quoted.

(iv) Where a full pre-consolidation statutory reference is required, this may be obtained from Tolley's Capital Gains Tax 1991/92 or an earlier edition.

Contents

Contents

Notes

Years of Assessment run from 6 April. Thus '1995/96' or 'the year 1995/96' means the year from 6 April 1995 to 5 April 1996.

Inland Revenue explanatory pamphlets may be obtained from local tax enquiry offices (except where otherwise stated, see list in Chapter 26) and are free.

Retention of Tolley's. Subscribers should preserve each year's issue of 'Tolley's' because the necessity to include each year considerable new material involves the omission of some of the outdated matter.

Tolley's Income Tax 1995/96 is a comprehensive detailed guide to income tax and includes the provisions of the Finance Act 1995. £32.95.

Tolley's Corporation Tax 1995/96 is the companion publication to Tolley's Income Tax and is a comprehensive detailed guide to corporation tax and includes the provisions of the Finance Act 1995. £28.95.

Tolley's Inheritance Tax 1995/96 is a comprehensive detailed guide to inheritance tax and includes the provisions of the Finance Act 1995. £25.95.

Tolley's Tax Cases 1995 contains over 2,500 summaries of cases up to 1 January 1995 relevant to current legislation. £32.95.

Tolley's Tax Computations 1995/96 contains copious worked examples covering income tax, corporation tax, capital gains tax, inheritance tax and value added tax. £35.95.

Tolley's Official Tax Statements 1995/96 contains the full text of all Inland Revenue Statements of Practice and Extra-Statutory Concessions, together with important Inland Revenue Press Releases and statements made in Tax Bulletin and other non-Revenue material. Annotations are included where relevant. £39.95.

Tolley's Practical Tax is an eight-page fortnightly newsletter, containing news, articles and items of practical use to all involved with UK tax. By subscription only.

Tolley's Roll-over, Hold-over and Retirement Reliefs (fifth edition) is a practical and comprehensive guide to the calculation and operation of the three main capital gains tax reliefs, containing all the information required in one single reference work and includes the provisions of the Finance Act 1995. £39.95.

Tolley's Tax Planning 1995/96 pinpoints clear, practical taxation strategies across the whole range of financial decision-making required of individuals, partnerships and corporate bodies. Two volumes £69.50.

Tolley's Estate Planning 1995/96 provides detailed guidance on how to formulate a plan for the provision, holding and transfer of personal and family resources at the lowest tax cost. £34.95.

Tolley's UK Taxation of Trusts (fifth edition) is written by specialists in the field to provide a detailed explanation of the impact of income tax, capital gains tax and inheritance tax on the various types of trusts, including chapters covering the UK taxation of offshore trusts, and includes the provisions of the Finance Act 1995. £37.95.

Tolley's Self-Assessment (second edition) (formerly Simplified Assessing) is an in-depth review of the self-assessment rules and the change to the current year basis of assessment for businesses, and includes the provisions of the Finance Act 1995. £35.95.

Abbreviations and References

ABBREVIATIONS

A-G	Attorney-General.
CA	Court of Appeal.
CAA	Capital Allowances Act.
CCA	Court of Criminal Appeal.
CCAB	Consultative Committee of Accountancy Bodies.
Ch D	Chancery Division.
CES	Court of Exchequer (Scotland).
Cf.	compare.
CGT	Capital Gains Tax.
CGTA	Capital Gains Tax Act.
CJEC	Court of Justice of the European Communities.
CIR	Commissioners of Inland Revenue ('the Board' or 'the Revenue').
Commrs	Commissioners of Income Tax (General or Special).
CTT	Capital Transfer Tax.
ESC	Inland Revenue Extra-Statutory Concession.
Ex D	Exchequer Division (now part of Chancery Division).
FA	Finance Act.
Fam D	Family Division (formerly Probate, Divorce and Admiralty Division).
HC	House of Commons.
HC	High Court.
HL	House of Lords.
I	Ireland.
ICAEW	Institute of Chartered Accountants in England and Wales.
ICTA	Income and Corporation Taxes Act.
IHT	Inheritance Tax.
IHTA	Inheritance Tax Act.
KB	King's Bench Division.
NI	Northern Ireland.
PC	Privy Council.
PDA	Probate, Divorce and Admiralty Division (now Family Division).
QB	Queen's Bench Division.
R	Regina or Rex (i.e. The Crown).
RI	Republic of Ireland (Eire).
RPI	Retail Prices Index.
s	Section.
SCd	Special Commissioners' decisions.
SC	Supreme Court.
SCS	Scottish Court of Session.
Sch	Schedule [4 Sch 10 = 4th Schedule, paragraph 10].
SI	Statutory Instrument.
SP	Inland Revenue Statement of Practice.
TCGA	Taxation of Chargeable Gains Act.
TMA	Taxes Management Act.

REFERENCES (*denotes a series accredited for citation in court).

All E R	All England Law Reports (Butterworth & Co. (Publishers) Ltd, Halsbury House, 35 Chancery Lane, London WC2A 1EL).

Abbreviations and References

AC	*Law Reports, Appeal Cases (Incorporated Council of Law Reporting for England and Wales, 3 Stone Buildings, Lincoln's Inn, London, WC2A 3XN).
ATC	*Annotated Tax Cases (publication discontinued).
Ch	*Law Reports, Chancery Division.
CMLR	Common Market Law Reports.
Ex D	*Law Reports, Exchequer Division (1875–1880; see also below).
Fam D	*Law Reports, Family Division.
KB	*Law Reports, King's Bench Division (1900–1952).
IR	*Irish Reports (Law Reporting Council, Law Library, Four Courts, Dublin).
ITC	*Irish Tax Cases (Government Publications, 1 and 3, G.P.O. Arcade, Dublin 1).
LR Ex	*Law Reports, Exchequer Division (1865–1875; see also above).
NILR	Northern Ireland Law Reports.
[Year] QB	*Law Reports, Queen's Bench Division (1891–1901 and 1952 onwards).
QBD	Law Reports, Queen's Bench Division (1875–1890).
SLT	Scots Law Times.
STC	*Simon's Tax Cases (Butterworth & Co. (Publishers) Ltd, as above).
STI	Simon's Tax Intelligence (Butterworth & Co. (Publishers) Ltd, as above).
TC	*Official Reports of Tax Cases (H.M. Stationery Office, P.O. Box 276, London, SW8 5DT).
TR	Taxation Reports (publication discontinued).
WLR	*Weekly Law Reports (Incorporated Council of Law Reporting above).

The first number in the citation refers to the volume, and the second to the page, so that *[1978] 2 WLR 10* means that the report is to be found on page ten of the second volume of the Weekly Law Reports for 1978. Where no volume number is given, only one volume was produced in that year. Some series have continuous volume numbers.

Where legal decisions are very recent and in the lower courts, it must be remembered that they may be reversed on appeal. However, references to the official Tax Cases ('*TC*') and to the Appeal Cases ('*AC*') may be taken as final.

In English cases, Scottish and Northern Irish decisions (unless there is a difference of law between the countries) are generally followed but are not binding, and Republic of Ireland decisions are considered (and vice versa).

Acts of Parliament, Command Papers, 'Hansard' Parliamentary Reports and Statutory Instruments (SI) are obtainable from H.M. Stationery Office, (bookshops at 49 High Holborn, London, WC1V 6HB and elsewhere; orders to P.O. Box 276, London, SW8 5DT). Fax orders should be made to 0171–873 8200. General enquiries should be made to 0171–873 0011. Telephone orders should be made to 0171–873 9090. **Hansard** (referred to as HC Official Report or H L Official Report) references are to daily issues and do not always correspond to the columns in the bound editions. **N.B.** Statements in the House, while useful as indicating the intention of enactments, have no legal authority except in the limited circumstances mentioned in 4.9 APPEALS.

1 Introduction

1.1 GENERAL

Capital gains tax was introduced by the *Finance Act 1965* and commenced on 6 April 1965. It relates to chargeable gains in a 'year of assessment' accruing to individuals, personal representatives and trustees. *'Year of assessment'* is a year ending on 5 April. Thus '1993/94' indicates the year of assessment ending on 5 April 1994 (and so on). [*TCGA 1992, s 288(1)*]. For the position of companies (and other bodies), see 1.2 below.

The legislation was consolidated by the *Capital Gains Tax Act 1979* and subsequently by the *Taxation of Chargeable Gains Act 1992*. TCGA 1992 has effect in relation to capital gains tax for 1992/93 and subsequent years of assessment, to corporation tax for accounting periods beginning after 5 April 1992 and to certain other tax purposes after 5 April 1992. [*TCGA 1992, ss 289–291*].

An allowance, known as the indexation allowance (see 23 INDEXATION), was introduced by the *Finance Act 1982* with the intention of adjusting for the effects of inflation. The provisions for it were substantially modified by the *Finance Act 1985* but such modifications were largely removed by the *Finance Act 1994*. Subject to this, a gain is computed by reference to the excess of the disposal (or deemed disposal) consideration over the acquisition (or deemed acquisition) consideration, received and given, for an asset (see 16 DISPOSAL).

Major changes in the scope of the tax were introduced by the *Finance Act 1988*. The original base date of 6 April 1965 was replaced by 31 March 1982 subject to the detailed provisions of 8 ASSETS HELD ON 31 MARCH 1982.

The *Finance Act 1988* also introduced rates of tax for 1988/89 and subsequent years that, in broad terms, are equivalent to the rates of income tax that would apply if gains were treated as the top slice of taxable income. Before 1988/89, tax was charged at a rate of 30%. See 2 ANNUAL RATES AND EXEMPTIONS.

1.2 THE CHARGE TO TAX

Subject to exceptions and special provisions, a person is chargeable to capital gains tax in respect of chargeable gains accruing to him in a year of assessment during any part of which he is resident in the UK, or during which he is ordinarily resident in the UK. [*TCGA 1992, ss 1, 2(1)*].

Special rules apply to persons not resident or individuals not domiciled in the UK and to temporary visitors to the UK. See 39 OVERSEAS MATTERS, 46 REMITTANCE BASIS and 47 RESIDENCE AND DOMICILE.

For 1990/91 and subsequent years, married persons are taxed independently. For years before 1990/91, the gains of a husband and wife who were living together were, except in the year of marriage, aggregated and assessed on the husband unless an election for separate assessment was made. See 37 MARRIED PERSONS.

Persons may be assessed in a representative capacity. See 5 ASSESSMENTS, 11 CHILDREN, 15 DEATH and 52 SETTLEMENTS.

There are special rules for UK resident or ordinarily resident shareholders of certain overseas resident companies. See 39.5 OVERSEAS MATTERS. See 39.6–39.11 for the provisions applying to trustees, settlors and beneficiaries of settlements which are or become overseas resident.

1

Companies and other corporate bodies within the scope of corporation tax are not chargeable to capital gains tax. The chargeable gains of such bodies are assessed to corporation tax. The computation of their gains is in accordance with the general principles applying for capital gains tax contained in *TCGA 1992* and subsequent legislation which is to be construed as one with it. In addition, *TCGA 1992* contains further provisions relating to corporation tax on chargeable gains. Previously these provisions had not been included within *CGTA 1979* but had been contained within the *Income and Corporation Taxes Acts 1970* and *1988*. Assessments on companies are made by reference to accounting periods instead of years of assessment. Although *TCGA 1992, s 2(1)* refers to a 'person' (i.e. including a company) and ordinary residence, the key factor in charging companies is residence in the UK. See 13 COMPANIES, 39.12 OVERSEAS MATTERS, and 47.5 RESIDENCE AND DOMICILE.

For unit and investment trusts, see 57 UNIT AND INVESTMENT TRUSTS.

See Tolley's Corporation Tax under Friendly Societies and Life Insurance Companies for provisions of *TCGA 1992* (and related provisions) which are integral with the corporation tax regime applicable to life assurance business carried on by such entities.

TCGA 1992, ss 194–198, which deal with matters relating to oil exploration taxed under the *Oil Taxation Act 1975* and in practice apply mainly to companies, are not dealt with in this book.

---

2   Annual Rates and Exemptions

Cross-references. See 13.2 COMPANIES for the rate of corporation tax in respect of chargeable gains.

2.1   RATES OF TAX FOR 1988/89 ONWARDS

General. Subject to the further provisions for individuals, married persons and settlements below, the rate of capital gains tax for 1988/89 and subsequent years of assessment is equivalent to the basic rate of income tax for the year. For 1988/89 to 1995/96 (both years inclusive) this rate is **25%**. [*TCGA 1992, s 4(1); ICTA 1988, s 1; FA 1988, s 23; FA 1989, s 30(1); FA 1990, s 17(1); FA 1991, s 21(1); FA 1992, s 10(1)(b); FA 1993, s 51(1)(b); FA 1994, s 75(1)(b); FA 1995, s 35(1)(b)*].

Individuals. If income tax is chargeable at the higher rate in respect of any part of an individual's income for a year of assessment, the rate of capital gains tax is equivalent to the higher rate. [*TCGA 1992, s 4(2)*]. If no income tax is chargeable at the higher rate in respect of his income, but the amount on which he is chargeable to capital gains tax exceeds 'the unused part of his basic rate band', the rate of capital gains tax on the excess is equivalent to the higher rate of income tax for the year. [*TCGA 1992, s 4(3)*].

'The unused part of an individual's basic rate band' is the amount by which (ignoring any reduction made under *TCGA 1992, s 4(3B)(a)* below) the basic rate limit exceeds his total income (as reduced by any deductions made under the *Income Tax Acts*). [*TCGA 1992, s 4(4); FA 1993, s 79, 6 Sch 22(2)*].

For 1988/89 to 1995/96 (both years inclusive) the higher rate of income tax is **40%**.

For 1995/96 the basic rate limit is £24,300; for 1991/92 to 1994/95 (both years inclusive) it is £23,700; for 1989/90 and 1990/91 it is £20,700; and for 1988/89 it is £19,300. [*ICTA 1988, s 1; FA 1988, s 24(1)(2); SI 1989 No 467; FA 1989, s 30(2); FA 1990, s 17(1); FA 1991, s 21(1); FA 1992, s 10(1)(c)(2); FA 1993, s 51(1)(c)(2)(b); FA 1994, s 75(1)(c)(2)(b); SI 1994 No 3012; FA 1995, s 35(1)(c)*].

For 1992/93 and subsequent years of assessment, if an individual's income is such that there is an unused part (including the whole) of his lower rate band (i.e. the amount by which the lower rate limit exceeds his total income after this income has been reduced by any deductions made under the *Income Tax Acts*), then if the amount on which he is chargeable to capital gains tax exceeds the amount of that unused part, the rate of capital gains tax on that part of the amount chargeable to capital gains tax as corresponds to the amount of the unused part of the lower rate band is equivalent to the lower rate. Where there is no such excess, the rate of capital gains tax applying to all of the amount chargeable to capital gains tax is equivalent to the lower rate. [*TCGA 1992, s 4(1A)(1B); F(No 2)A 1992, s 23(1)(3)*].

For 1992/93 to 1995/96 (both years inclusive) the lower rate is 20%.

For 1995/96 the lower rate is £3,200; for 1994/95 it is £3,000, for 1993/94 it is £2,500 and for 1992/93 it is £2,000. [*ICTA 1988, s 1; FA 1992, ss 9, 10(1)(a); FA 1993, s 51(1)(a)(2)(a); FA 1994, s 75(1)(a)(2)(a); FA 1995, s 35(1)(a)(2)*].

In effect, therefore, but with one exception applying for 1993/94 and subsequent years, an individual's chargeable gains are taxed as if they constituted the top slice of taxable income. In addition, where an income tax relief is given by way of a reduction in income tax liability rather than by way of reduction of total income (e.g. for 1994/95 and subsequent years, married couple's allowance, certain interest payable (see further below for years before 1994/95), medical insurance premiums and enterprise investment scheme relief), the reduction in income tax liability has no effect on the marginal rate of capital gains tax.

The exception mentioned above relates to 1993/94 and subsequent years when, in determining the amount of an individual's taxable gains to be charged at the lower rate under *TCGA 1992, s 4(1A)(1B)* above, any Schedule F income (distributions from UK resident companies inclusive of tax credits) or any income treated as Schedule F income (broadly, distributions from non-UK resident companies taxed under Schedule D Case V other than on a remittance basis) of that individual, being income chargeable to income tax at the lower rate under *ICTA 1988, s 207A*, is disregarded in ascertaining the individual's total income for the year or whether he has any income. (Under *ICTA 1988, s 207A(2)(3)*, Schedule F income is treated as the highest part of a person's income subject to certain exceptions.) The same disregard applies even if the Schedule F income etc. is chargeable at the higher rate. [*TCGA 1992, s 4(3A); FA 1993, s 79, 6 Sch 22(1)*]. Any amount of gains chargeable at the lower rate only as a result of *TCGA 1992, s 4(3A)* is called '*the amount of the lower rate gains*'. The amount (if any) of income comprised in the individual's total income which is chargeable to income tax at the higher rate is determined, both for the purposes of the *Income Tax Acts* and *TCGA 1992, s 4*, as if the basic rate limit for the year were reduced in relation to the individual by the amount of the lower rate gains. [*TCGA 1992, s 4(3B)(a); FA 1993, s 79, 6 Sch 22(1)*]. The amount (if any) on which the individual would otherwise be chargeable under *TCGA 1992, s 4(2)* above to capital gains tax at a rate equivalent to the higher rate is treated as reduced by the amount of the lower rate gains or, if the amount to be reduced is not more than the amount of those gains, to nil. [*TCGA 1992, s 4(3B)(b); FA 1993, s 79, 6 Sch 22(1)*].

The Revenue has acknowledged that, because of a subsequent reduction in the level of taxable income by reason of a claim for income tax relief, a capital gains tax assessment may charge gains at too high a rate. In such circumstances, *TMA 1970, s 31* (appeal against assessment to be made within thirty days of the date of notice) or *s 42(7)* (Revenue to give effect to claim by discharge or repayment of tax) can be invoked, as appropriate, by the individual (Revenue Tax Bulletin August 1993 p 87).

Example

In 1995/96 an individual receives Schedule F income of £21,700 (inclusive of tax credits at 20% of £4,340). His other income for that year is untaxed and, after all deductions under the *Income Tax Acts* (e.g. personal allowance under *ICTA 1988, s 257*), amounts to £1,700. There are no income tax reliefs which operate by way of reduction in income tax liability. After deduction of the annual exempt amount, losses etc., the amount on which the individual is chargeable to capital gains tax amounts to £4,000.

The lower rate limit for 1995/96 is £3,200, so, ignoring the Schedule F income, £1,500 of the lower rate band is unused. £1,500 ('*the amount of the lower rate gains*') of the gains are therefore charged at a rate equivalent to the lower rate of 20%. The basic rate limit for that year is otherwise £24,300 but this is reduced to £22,800 (both for income tax purposes as well as capital gains tax purposes) after deduction of the amount of the lower rate gains of £1,500. Total income amounts to £23,400, so £600 (all represented by Schedule F income as forming the top slice of income) is charged to income tax at the higher rate of 40%. The balance of the gains, £2,500 (£4,000 less £1,500), is charged to capital gains tax at a rate equivalent to the higher rate of 40% (*TCGA 1992, s 4(2)* applies because income tax is already chargeable at the higher rate).

Income tax payable:	£
£ 1,700 of other income at 20%	340
£21,100 of Schedule F income at 20%	4,220
£ 600 of Schedule F income at 40%	240
	4,800
£21,700 of Schedule F income tax credits at 20%	(4,340)
Income tax payable	£ 460

Capital gains tax payable:	£
£1,500 at 20%	300
£2,500 at 40%	1,000
Capital gains tax payable	£1,300

For years before 1995/96 references in the above to income tax chargeable at the higher rate included references to tax chargeable under *ICTA 1988, s 683(1)* or *684(1)* (income arising under a settlement treated as income of settlor) in respect of excess liability.

Where for any year of assessment income is treated under either of those provisions as the income of the settlor for excess liability then, whether or not he is chargeable to tax otherwise than at the lower and basic rates, it is also treated as his income for the purposes of ascertaining the unused part of the lower and basic rate bands referred to above.

References in the above to income tax chargeable at the higher rate also included references to tax chargeable under *ICTA 1988, s 353(4)* or *369(3A)* (restriction to basic rate relief on interest paid before 6 April 1994 (whenever falling due) and relevant loan interest paid before 30 November 1993 (where due before 6 April 1994)) in respect of excess liability; and where for any year of assessment a deduction was denied by either of those provisions in computing total income for excess liability purposes then, whether or not he was chargeable to tax otherwise than at the lower and basic rates, that deduction was also denied for the purposes of ascertaining the unused part of the lower and basic rate bands.

References in the above to the lower rate apply for 1992/93 and subsequent years.

'*Excess liability*' for 1988/89 to 1991/92 (both years inclusive) is liability to income tax over what it would be if all income tax were charged at the basic rate to the exclusion of any higher rate; for 1992/93 it is liability to income tax over what it would be if all income tax not chargeable at the lower rate were charged at the basic rate to the exclusion of any higher rate; and for 1993/94 and subsequent years it is liability to income tax over what it would be if all income tax not chargeable at the lower rate under *ICTA 1988, s 1(2)(aa)* (lower rate of income tax in lower rate band) were charged at the basic rate, or (so far as applicable under *ICTA 1988, s 207A* above) the lower rate, to the exclusion of any higher rate. [*TCGA 1992, s 6(1); F(No 2)A 1992, s 22(2)(3); FA 1993, s 79, 6 Sch 24; FA 1994, 26 Sch Pt V*].

Where for any year of assessment

(*a*)   under *ICTA 1988, s 427(4)* (apportionment of close company income in relation to accounting periods ending before 1 April 1989) an amount is deemed not to form part of a person's income for the purposes of excess liability, or

(*b*)   under *ICTA 1988, s 549(2)* (gains under life policy or life annuity contract) a deduction of an amount is made from a person's total income for those purposes, or

(*c*)   for years before 1995/96 under *ICTA 1988, s 683(1)* or *684(1)* an amount of a person's income is treated as not being his income for those purposes, or

(*d*)   under *ICTA 1988, s 699(1)* (income accruing before death) the residuary income of an estate is treated as reduced so as to reduce a person's income by any amount for the purposes of excess liability,

the ascertainment of the unused part of the basic rate band referred to above has effect as if his income for the year were reduced by that amount. [*TCGA 1992, s 6(2); FA 1988, s 102(2)(a); FA 1989, 17 Sch Pt V*].

Where under *ICTA 1988, s 547(1)(a)* (gains from insurance policies etc.) a person's total income for a year of assessment is deemed to include any amount or amounts,

(i)   the ascertainment of the unused part of the basic rate band referred to above has effect as if his total income included not the whole of the amount or amounts concerned but only the appropriate fraction within the meaning of *ICTA 1988, s 550(3)*, and

(ii)   if relief is given under *ICTA 1988, s 550* and the calculation required by *section 550(2)(b)* does not involve the higher rate of tax, the ascertainment of the rate of tax applicable under *TCGA 1992, s 4(2)(3)* above is to have effect as if no income tax were chargeable at the higher rate in respect of his income.

[*TCGA 1992, s 6(3); FA 1995, 29 Sch Pt VIII(B)*].

Nothing in *TCGA 1992, s 6(1)-(3)* above is to be taken to reduce or increase (as the case may be), the amount of a deduction which a person is entitled to make from his total income under any provision of *ICTA 1988, Pt VII, Ch I* (personal reliefs) which limits any allowance by reference to the level of his total income. [*TCGA 1992, s 6(4)*].

5

2.2   Annual Rates and Exemptions

See Tolley's Income Tax for the income tax provisions mentioned above.

Married persons and settlements. Special provisions apply as regards the rate of tax for MARRIED PERSONS (37.4(*a*)) for 1988/89 and 1989/90 only and SETTLEMENTS (52.1 and 52.3) for 1988/89 and subsequent years.

2.2   **RATES OF TAX BEFORE 1988/89**

The rate of tax for all years of assessment from 1965/66 to 1987/88 (both inclusive) was 30%. [*CGTA 1979, s 3; FA 1988, 14 Sch Pt VII*].

2.3   **ANNUAL EXEMPTIONS**

For 1995/96 an individual is exempt from capital gains tax on the first £6,000 of his '*taxable amount*' (i.e. chargeable gains of the year less allowable losses). This exempt part of the taxable amount is termed the '*exempt amount for the year*'. Losses for the year are deducted in full but losses brought forward, or carried back from a subsequent year in which the taxpayer dies (see 15.5 DEATH), are deducted only insofar as is necessary to reduce the resulting net gains to the level of the exempt amount for the year. Any balance of losses is carried forward to subsequent years (or back to earlier ones) as necessary. This exemption also applies to personal representatives for the year of death and the following two years (see 15.7 DEATH). [*TCGA 1992, ss 2(2), 3(1)(2)(5)(7); SI 1983, No 402; SI 1984, No 343; SI 1985, No 428; SI 1986, No 527; SI 1987, No 436; FA 1988, s 108; FA 1989, s 122; FA 1990, s 72; SI 1991 No 736; SI 1992 No 626; FA 1993, s 82; FA 1994, s 90; SI 1994 No 3008*]. Similar rules applied for earlier years but with exemption limits of

1994/95	£5,800
1993/94	£5,800
1992/93	£5,800
1991/92	£5,500
1990/91	£5,000
1989/90	£5,000
1988/89	£5,000
1987/88	£6,600
1986/87	£6,300
1985/86	£5,900
1984/85	£5,600
1983/84	£5,300

The exempt amount for the year (see above), unless Parliament determines otherwise, is the previous year's exempt amount as increased by a percentage which is the same as the percentage increase in the retail prices index for the September preceding the year of assessment over the index for the previous September. The resulting figure is rounded up to the nearest £100 and is announced before the relevant year of assessment in a Treasury statutory instrument. For years of assessment prior to 1994/95, the percentage increase in the previous year's exempt amount was the same as the percentage increase in the retail prices index for the December preceding the year of assessment over the index for the previous December, rounded up to the nearest £100 and announced as above. [*ICTA 1988, s 833(2); TCGA 1992, ss 3(3)(4), 288(2); FA 1993, s 83*].

See 37.3 MARRIED PERSONS for years before 1990/91, and 52.4 and 52.5 SETTLEMENTS, for further applications of the above rules. See also 23.2 INDEXATION for transitional relief for 1993/94 and 1994/95 in respect of 'indexation losses' in the case of individuals and trustees of settlements made before 30 November 1993.

The exemption under *TCGA 1992, s 3* is available regardless of the residence, ordinary residence or domicile status of the individual and, for years after 1989/90, is available separately to husband and wife.

3 Anti-Avoidance

Cross-references. See 14 CONNECTED PERSONS; 39.12 and 39.13 OVERSEAS MATTERS for interests in controlled foreign companies and in offshore funds respectively; 52.3 SETTLEMENTS for charge on settlors with interests in settlements.

3.1 APPROACH OF THE COURTS

For the general approach of the Courts to transactions entered into solely to avoid or reduce tax liability, leading cases are *Duke of Westminster v CIR HL 1935, 19 TC 490; W T Ramsay Ltd v CIR; Eilbeck v Rawling HL 1981, 54 TC 101; CIR v Burmah Oil Co Ltd HL 1981, 54 TC 200; Furniss v Dawson (and related appeals) HL 1984, 55 TC 324.* See also *Coates v Arndale Properties Ltd HL 1984, 59 TC 516; Reed v Nova Securities Ltd HL 1985, 59 TC 516; Magnavox Electronics Co Ltd (in liquidation) v Hall CA 1986, 59 TC 610; Commissioner of Inland Revenue v Challenge Corporation Ltd PC, [1986] STC 548; Craven v White; CIR v Bowater Property Developments Ltd; Baylis v Gregory HL 1988, 62 TC 1; Dunstan v Young Austen Young Ltd CA 1988, 61 TC 448; Shepherd v Lyntress Ltd; News International plc v Shepherd Ch D 1989, 62 TC 495; Ensign Tankers (Leasing) Ltd v Stokes HL, [1992] STC 226; Moodie v CIR and another (and related appeals) HL, [1993] STC 188; Countess Fitzwilliam and others v CIR (and related appeals) HL, [1993] STC 502; Pigott v Staines Investments Co Ltd Ch D, [1995] STC 114.*

The classical interpretation of the constraints upon the Courts in deciding cases involving tax avoidance schemes is summed up in Lord Tomlin's statement in the *Duke of Westminster* case that 'every man is entitled if he can to order his affairs so that the tax attaching . . . is less than it otherwise would be'. The judgment was concerned with the tax consequences of a single transaction, but in *Ramsay*, and subsequently in *Furniss v Dawson*, the House of Lords has set bounds on the ambit within which this principle can be applied in relation to modern sophisticated and increasingly artificial arrangements to avoid tax. *Ramsay* concerned a complex 'circular' avoidance scheme at the end of which the financial position of the parties was little changed but it was claimed that a large capital gains tax loss had been created. It was held that where a preconceived series of transactions is entered into to avoid tax and with the clear intention to proceed through all stages to completion, once set in motion, the *Duke of Westminster* principle does not compel a consideration of the individual transactions and of the fiscal consequences of such transactions in isolation. The opinions of the House of Lords in *Furniss v Dawson* are of outstanding importance, and establish, *inter alia*, that the *Ramsay* principle is not confined to 'circular' devices, and that if a series of transactions is 'preordained', a particular transaction within the series, accepted as genuine, may nevertheless be ignored if it was entered into solely for fiscal reasons and without any commercial purpose other than tax avoidance, even if the series of transactions as a whole has a legitimate commercial purpose.

However, in *Craven v White* the House of Lords indicated that for the *Ramsay* principle to apply all the transactions in a series have to be preordained with such a degree of certainty that, at the time of the earlier transactions, there is no practical likelihood that the transactions would not take place. It is not sufficient that the ultimate transaction is simply of a kind that was envisaged at the time of the earlier transactions. In the unanimous decision of the House of Lords in *Ensign Tankers (Leasing) Ltd v Stokes*, the lead judgment drew a clear distinction between 'tax avoidance' and 'tax mitigation', it being said that the *Duke of Westminster* principle is accurate as far as the latter is concerned but does not apply to the former.

Fitzwilliam involved five transactions entered into over a short period of time to avoid capital transfer tax on appointments from a will trust, the last four transactions being determined by the Revenue to form a preordained series of transactions subject to the *Ramsay* principle but which the taxpayers claimed should be viewed separately with the result that by reason of a number of available reliefs no liability to capital transfer tax arose. The House of Lords stated that the correct approach to a consideration of steps 2 to 5 was to ask whether realistically they constituted a single and indivisible whole in which one or more of the steps was simply an element without independent effect and whether it was intellectually possible so to treat them. It was held that both questions should be answered in the negative. The case put by the Revenue did not depend on disregarding for fiscal purposes any one or more of steps 2 to 5 as having been introduced for fiscal purposes only and as having no independent effect, nor on treating the whole of steps 2 to 5 as having no such effect. Each of the four steps had a fiscal effect of giving rise to an income tax charge on two of the taxpayers for a period of time, and there was a potential capital transfer tax charge should either have died whilst in enjoyment of the income associated with the transactions. Although steps 2 to 5 were 'preordained', in the sense that they formed part of a pre-planned tax avoidance scheme and that there was no reasonable possibility that they would not all be carried out, the fact of preordainment in that sense was not sufficient in itself to negative the application of an exemption from liability to tax which the series of transactions was intended to create, unless the series was capable of being construed in a manner inconsistent with the application of the exemption. In the particular circumstances of the case, the series of transactions could not be so construed. Two or more transactions in the series could not be run together, as in *Furniss v Dawson*, nor could any one or more of them be disregarded. There was no rational basis on which the four separate steps could be treated as effective for the purposes of one provision which created a charge to tax on a termination of an interest in possession but ineffective for the purposes of two other provisions which gave exemptions from that charge where the interest was disposed of for a consideration and where the interest reverted to the settlor. Accordingly, the case was one to which the *Ramsay* principle, as extended by *Furniss v Dawson*, did not apply.

For an indication of Revenue practice as to the application of the principles established in decided cases up to and including *Furniss v Dawson* to certain types of transactions which may still be relevant, (e.g. 'bed and breakfasting' and transfers between spouses for retirement or rollover relief purposes), see ICAEW Guidance Note TR 588, 25 September 1985.

3.2   LEGISLATION

Anti-avoidance legislation is intended to counteract transactions designed to avoid taxation but bona fide transactions may sometimes be caught also. The provisions relating to capital gains tax are covered below and as further indicated in the cross-references given above at the beginning of the chapter.

3.3	UK domiciled and UK resident or ordinarily resident shareholder in overseas resident company. [*TCGA 1992, s 13*]. See 39.5 OVERSEAS MATTERS for full coverage.
3.4	Value shifting. [*TCGA 1992, s 29*].
3.6–3.9	Value shifting to give tax-free benefit. [*TCGA 1992, ss 30-34*].
3.10	Connected persons. [*TCGA 1992, s 18*].
3.11	Assets disposed of in a series of transactions. [*TCGA 1992, ss 19, 20*].
3.12	Close company transferring asset at undervalue. [*TCGA 1992, s 125*].

3.3 Anti-Avoidance

3.13–3.14	Restrictions on company reconstructions and amalgamations. [*TCGA 1992, ss 137, 138*]. For schemes involving the transfer of a business owned by a company under *TCGA 1992, s 139*, see 13.6 COMPANIES for full coverage.
3.15	Groups of companies. See 3.6–3.9, 3.16 and 3.17 below and 13.10–13.30 COMPANIES for full coverage.
3.16	Depreciatory transactions within groups of companies. [*TCGA 1992, s 176*].
3.17	Dividend stripping. [*TCGA 1992, s 177*].
3.18	Transactions in land. [*ICTA 1988, ss 776-778*]. See 33.4 LAND for full coverage.
3.19	Land sold and leased back. [*ICTA 1988, s 780*]. See 33.23 LAND for full coverage.
3.20	Restrictions on, and clawbacks of, hold-over reliefs and reinvestment in shares relief. See 22 HOLD-OVER RELIEFS and 45 REINVESTMENT IN SHARES RELIEF for full coverage.
3.21	Overseas resident settlements etc. See 39.6–39.11 OVERSEAS MATTERS and 52.8 SETTLEMENTS for full coverage.

For a detailed book on the subject, see Tolley's Anti-Avoidance Provisions by Robert W Maas FCA.

3.3   **UK SHAREHOLDER IN OVERSEAS RESIDENT COMPANY** [*TCGA 1992, s 13*]

A shareholder in a non-resident company, which would be a close company if it were resident in the UK, is assessable on a part of any chargeable gain made by the company which is not distributed by it to its shareholders within two years after the time when the gain accrues provided that, at that time, the person is

(*a*)   resident or ordinarily resident in the UK; and

(*b*)   if an individual, domiciled in the UK.

See 39.5 OVERSEAS MATTERS.

3.4   **VALUE SHIFTING** [*TCGA 1992, s 29*]

Without prejudice to the generality of *TCGA 1992*, any of the following transactions are to be treated as giving rise to a disposal of an asset for capital gains tax purposes and, if made gratuitously or at an undervalue, the consideration (or additional consideration) for the disposal which could have been obtained in an arm's length transaction is treated as having been actually received. This also applies to the corresponding acquisition of an interest in the asset, the arm's length consideration being treated as the market value of what is acquired. [*TCGA 1992, s 29(1)*].

(*a*)   If a person having control of a company exercises his control so that value passes out of shares in the company owned by him (or by CONNECTED PERSONS (14)) or out of rights over the company exercisable by him (or by connected persons) and passes into other shares in or rights over the company, a disposal is deemed to have been made out of those shares or rights. Losses arising from such a deemed disposal are not allowable. [*TCGA 1992, s 29(2)(3)*]. An omission to act may be treated as an exercise of control and 'person' includes the plural i.e. the provisions apply where two or more persons have control (*Floor v Davis HL 1979, 52 TC 609*).

(*b*) Where an owner of property enters into a transaction whereby he becomes the lessee of that property (e.g. a sale and lease-back) and there is a subsequent adjustment of the rights and liabilities under the lease (whether or not including the grant of a new lease) which is as a whole favourable to the lessor, such an adjustment is a disposal by the lessee of an interest in the property. [*TCGA 1992, s 29(4)*].

(*c*) If an asset is subject to any right or restriction, the extinction or abrogation, in whole or part, of that right, etc. by the person entitled to enforce it is treated as a disposal thereof. [*TCGA 1992, s 29(5)*].

3.5 *Example*

J owns the whole £1,000 £1 ordinary shares of K Ltd. The shares were acquired on subscription in 1967 for £1,000 and had a value of £99,000 on 31 March 1982. In December 1995, the trustees of J's family settlement subscribed at par for 3,000 £1 ordinary shares in K Ltd, thereby acquiring 75% of the voting power in the company. It is agreed that the price an unconnected party would have paid for 75% of the equity in a transaction at arm's length is £150,000. J's remaining 25% holding is valued at £15,000.

J will have a capital gain for 1995/96 as follows (subject to indexation allowance)

	£
Proceeds of deemed disposal	150,000
Allowable cost $\dfrac{150,000}{150,000 + 15,000} \times £99,000$	90,000
Unindexed gain	£60,000

3.6 **VALUE SHIFTING TO GIVE TAX-FREE BENEFIT** [*TCGA 1992, ss 30–34*]

These provisions apply to the disposal of an asset if a scheme has been effected or arrangements have been made (whether before or after the disposal) whereby the value of the asset or, for disposals after 13 March 1989, of a 'relevant asset' has been materially reduced after 29 March 1977 and a 'tax-free benefit' is conferred at any time on

(*a*) the person making the disposal or a person connected with him (see 14 CONNECTED PERSONS), or

(*b*) any other person unless it is shown that tax avoidance was not a main purpose of the scheme or arrangement.

Where the disposal of an asset precedes its acquisition, references to a reduction include references to an increase.

The inspector may notionally increase the consideration for the disposal in his calculations of the chargeable gain or allowable loss (subject to appeal) by an amount that appears to him to be 'just and reasonable' having regard to the scheme or arrangement and the tax-free benefit. Where such an increase of consideration has been made for one asset and the tax-free benefit was an increase in value of another asset, the consideration for the first disposal of that other asset may be notionally reduced by the inspector (subject to appeal) by such an amount as appears to him to be 'just and reasonable'.

(There is no provision for the acquirer's cost of the asset to be correspondingly increased or reduced.)

These provisions do not apply to disposals by personal representatives to legatees (see 15.9 DEATH), or between spouses living together (see 37.6 MARRIED PERSONS) or between companies in a group (see 13.11 COMPANIES). [*TCGA 1992, s 30(1)(4)-(7)(9), 11 Sch 10*].

An asset ('the second asset') is a '*relevant asset*' if

(1)   the disposal of an asset (here called 'the first asset') is made by a company ('the disposing company'),

(2)   the first asset comprises shares in, or securities (within *TCGA 1992, s 132* as in 18.5 EXEMPTIONS AND RELIEFS) of, a company, and

(3)   the second asset is owned at the time of disposal of the first asset by a company 'associated' (see 3.8 below) with the disposing company.

A reduction in value of a relevant asset is not taken into account except in a case where

(A)   during the period from the reduction in value to the time immediately before the disposal of the first asset there is no disposal of it other than one within *TCGA 1992, s 171* (intra-group transfers at no gain/no loss price as in 13.11 COMPANIES),

(B)   no disposal of that asset is treated as occurring during that period under *TCGA 1992, s 178 or 179* (company ceasing to be member of group as in 13.17 COMPANIES), and

(C)   if the reduction had not occurred, but any consideration given for the relevant asset and any other material circumstances (including any consideration given before the disposal for the first asset disposed of) were unchanged, the value of the first asset would have been materially greater at the time of its disposal.

Where the disposal of an asset precedes its acquisition, references to a reduction include references to an increase. [*TCGA 1992, s 30(2)(9)*].

A '*tax-free benefit*' arises to a person if he becomes entitled to money or money's worth or his interest in the value of any asset is increased or he is wholly or partly relieved from any liability to which he is subject *and* none of the foregoing benefits when conferred is otherwise liable to income tax, capital gains tax or corporation tax. [*TCGA 1992, s 30(3)*].

The Revenue do not regard ordinary commercial group relief transactions (e.g. the purchase of group relief) as falling within *TCGA 1992, s 30*. A lease of a farm at a rack-rent by a retiring farmer to his son, followed by a sale of the reversion at market value to an outside investor, would likewise be outside it (29.D18 INLAND REVENUE STATEMENTS OF PRACTICE).

Where a disposal within *TCGA 1992, s 30* would otherwise form the basis for a claim for loss relief against income under *ICTA 1988, s 573 or 574* these provisions apply if *any* benefit is conferred, whether tax-free or not. [*ICTA 1988, s 576(2)*]. See also 35.12 and 35.14 LOSSES.

The Revenue has confirmed that where a person was caught by the value-shifting provisions, the deemed gain could be held over under *FA 1980, s 79* (when extant after 5 April 1980 and before 14 March 1989 and provided that the other conditions were satisfied). This may also apply to the other reliefs mentioned in 22 HOLD-OVER RELIEFS which are still current.

Any reduction in value of shares disposed of before 14 March 1989 by one company in another company was disregarded if attributable to the payment of a dividend by the second company whilst both were in the same group (as in 13.10 COMPANIES), or the disposal of an asset by the second company as an intra-group transfer (see 13.11 COMPANIES). [*TCGA 1992, s 30(8)*]. For such disposals after 13 March 1989, see 3.7 below.

3.7   **Certain disposals of shares by companies.** The following provisions apply where a disposal within 3.6 above ('the *section 30* disposal') occurs after 13 March 1989 and is of shares ('the principal asset') which are owned by a company ('the first company') in another company ('the second company'). [*TCGA 1992, s 30(8)*].

Distributions within a group followed by a disposal of shares. If a reduction in the value of an asset is attributable to the payment, after 13 March 1989, of a dividend by the second company while the two companies are 'associated' (see 3.8 below), it is not treated as a reduction for the purposes of 3.6 above except to the extent (if any) that the dividend is attributable (see below) to 'chargeable profits' of the second company; and, in such a case, the tax-free benefit is ascertained without regard to any part of the dividend that is not attributable to such profits.

'Chargeable profits' are

(*a*)   the 'distributable profits' of a company, to the extent that they arise from a 'transaction caught by this *section*', and

(*b*)   the distributable profits of a company, to the extent that they represent so much of a distribution received from another company as was attributable to chargeable profits of that company (including ones similarly representing a distribution).

'Distributable profits' are such profits computed on a commercial basis as, after allowance for any provision properly made for tax, the company is empowered, assuming sufficient funds, to distribute to persons entitled to participate in its profits. So far as possible in ascertaining distributable profits, losses and other amounts to be set against profits must be set against profits other than ones which could be chargeable profits.

Profits arising on a *'transaction caught by this section'* are profits of a company (here called 'company X') where the three conditions in (1)-(3) below are met but the three exceptions to them (see (A)-(C) below) do not apply.

(1)   The transaction is

(i)   a no gain/no loss disposal by company X to another group company within *TCGA 1992, s 171(1)* (see 13.11 COMPANIES), or

(ii)   an exchange, or a transaction treated as an exchange for *TCGA 1992, s 135(2)* and *(3)* (see 53.8 SHARES AND SECURITIES), of shares in or debentures of a company held by company X for shares in or debentures of another company which immediately after the transaction is associated with company X, and which is treated as a reorganisation by *TCGA 1992, s 135(3)*, or

(iii)   a revaluation of an asset in the accounting records of company X.

(2)   No disposal of the 'asset with enhanced value'

(i)   occurs, other than one within *TCGA 1992, s 171(1)*, during the period beginning with the transaction within (1) above and ending immediately before the *section 30* disposal, or

(ii)   is treated as having occurred during that period by virtue of *TCGA 1992, s 178* or *179* (company ceasing to be member of group as in 13.17 COMPANIES).

(3)   Immediately after the *section 30* disposal the asset with enhanced value is owned by a person other than the disposing company or a company associated with it.

'*Asset with enhanced value*' is defined as follows, according to which transaction within (1)(i), (1)(ii) or (1)(iii) above occurs respectively: the asset acquired from company X; the shares or debentures acquired by company X as a result of the exchange; and the revalued asset.

The three exceptions to the foregoing three conditions are as follows.

(A)   At the time of the transaction within (1) above, company X carries on a trade, and a profit on a disposal of the asset with enhanced value would form part of the trading profits.

(B)   By reason of the nature of the asset with enhanced value, there could be no chargeable gain or allowable loss on its disposal.

(C)   Immediately before the *section 30* disposal, the company owning the asset with enhanced value carries on a trade, and a profit on disposal would form part of the trading profits.

Attribution of profits to a distribution is made by determining the total distributable profits and chargeable profits which remain at the time of distribution, after allowing for all earlier distributions and distributions to be made then or subsequently in respect of other classes of shares etc. and so far as possible by attributing distributable profits other than chargeable profits.

Chargeable profits are treated as arising to shareholders, etc. proportionately to their holdings of shares, etc. [*TCGA 1992, s 31*].

Disposals within a group followed by a disposal of shares. A reduction in the value of an asset is not treated as a reduction for the purposes of 3.6 above if it is attributable to the disposal, after 13 March 1989, of any asset ('the underlying asset') by the second company while the two companies are 'associated' (see 3.8 below) and the disposal is within *TCGA 1992, s 171(1)* (no gain/no loss disposals in a group as in 13.11 COMPANIES), unless

(*aa*)   the actual consideration for the disposal of the underlying asset is less than both its market value and its 'cost',

(*bb*)   the disposal is not effected for bona fide commercial reasons and forms part of a scheme or arrangements of which the main purpose, or one of the main purposes, is the avoidance of a corporation tax liability, and

(*cc*)   the first company is not treated as disposing of an interest in the principal asset by virtue of a distribution in a dissolution or winding up of the second company.

For the purpose of (*aa*) above, the '*cost*' of an asset is the aggregate of any capital expenditure incurred by the company in acquiring or providing it, or in respect of it while owned after its acquisition.

In the case of a part disposal of an underlying asset,

(AA)   the market value in (*aa*) above is the market value of the asset acquired by the transferee, and

(BB)   the amounts attributed to the cost of the underlying asset are reduced to the '*appropriate proportion*' thereof; i.e.,

   (i)   the proportion of capital expenditure properly attributed in the company's accounting records to the asset acquired by the transferee; or

(ii)   if (i) does not apply, such proportion as appears to the inspector (subject to appeal) to be just and reasonable.

[*TCGA 1992, s 32*].

3.8   **Interpretation of 3.6 and 3.7 above.** For disposals after 13 March 1989 the following interpretational provisions apply.

As regards any asset ('the original asset'), the provisions in (1)-(5) below apply in relation to the enactments mentioned in (*a*) and (*b*) below.

(*a*)   The enactments concerning relevant assets in *TCGA 1992, s 30(2)*: namely, in 3.6 above, (1)-(3) and (A)-(C).

(*b*)   The enactments concerning distributions within a group followed by a disposal of shares in *TCGA 1992, s 31(7)-(9)*: namely, in 3.7 above, the second and third conditions ((2) and (3)) and the three exceptions ((A)-(C)) to the three conditions.

The provisions mentioned above which apply as regards the original asset and in relation to the enactments mentioned in (*a*) and (*b*) above are as follows.

(1)   In (A) and (B) in 3.6 above and in the second condition ((2)) in 3.7 above, references to the disposal of an asset do not include a part disposal.

(2)   References to an asset are to the original asset; except that if subsequently one or more assets are treated under (4) or (5) below as the same as the original asset,

(i)   if there has been no disposal falling within (A) or (B) in 3.6 above or (2) in 3.7 above, the references are to the asset(s) so treated; and

(ii)   in any other case, the references are to the asset(s) representing that part of the value of the original asset remaining after allowance for earlier disposals within the relevant provision.

For these purposes a disposal includes a part disposal which would have been within (A) or (B) in 3.6 above or (2) in 3.7 above if it had not been excluded by (1) above.

(3)   If, by virtue of (2) above, a reference to an asset is treated as a reference to two or more assets,

(i)   the assets are treated as a single asset,

(ii)   a disposal of any of them is a part disposal, and

(iii)   the reference to the second asset in (3) in 3.6 above and the asset in the third condition mentioned in (3) in 3.7 above is to all or any of such assets.

(4)   If there is a part disposal of an asset, that asset and the asset acquired by the transferee are treated as the same.

(5)   Where

(i)   the value of an asset is derived from another asset owned by the same or an 'associated company' (see below), and

(ii)   assets have been merged or divided or have changed their nature, or rights or interests in or over assets have been created or extinguished,

the two assets are treated as the same.

Where a reduction in the value of a relevant asset is to be taken into account under *TCGA 1992, s 30(2)* (see (1)–(3) and (A)–(C) in 3.6 above) and at the time of the disposal of the first asset in 3.6(1) by the disposing company

3.9 Anti-Avoidance

(A) references to the relevant asset are treated under (1)-(5) above as references to two or more assets treated as a single asset, and

(B) one or more, but not all, of those assets is owned by a company 'associated' (see below) with the disposing company,

the amount of the reduction in the value of the relevant asset to be taken into account is reduced as the inspector thinks just and reasonable (subject to appeal).

For the provisions in TCGA 1992, s 31 concerning distributions within a group followed by a disposal of shares (see 3.7 above), the reduction in value of the principal asset is the amount which the inspector thinks just and reasonable (subject to appeal) if

(*aa*) a dividend paid by the second company is attributable to that company's chargeable profits, and

(*bb*) the criterion in (2), (3) or (C) in 3.7 above is satisfied by reference to an asset, or assets treated as a single asset, treated under (2)(ii) above as the same as the asset with enhanced value.

The definitions relating to groups of companies in *TCGA 1992, s 170(2)-(11)* apply as in 13.10 COMPANIES; and companies are '*associated*' if they are members of the same group. [*TCGA 1992, s 33*].

3.9 **Transactions treated as a reorganisation of share capital.** If the following conditions apply, a 'disposing company' is treated as receiving the amount specified in (*b*) below on a part disposal within *TCGA 1992, s 128(3)* (see 53.5 SHARES AND SECURITIES) of the 'original holding'.

(*a*) But for the rules whereby shares, etc. held after a reorganisation, reconstruction, etc. are treated as the same as those held beforehand (see 53.5, 53.8 SHARES AND SECURITIES), *TCGA 1992, s 30* in 3.6 above would apply on an exchange by a company (the 'disposing company') of shares, etc. in another company (the 'original holding') for shares, etc. in a third company which immediately afterwards is not in the same group (as defined in *TCGA 1992, s 170(2)-(11)* as in 13.10 COMPANIES) as the disposing company.

(*b*) If *TCGA 1992, s 30* had applied, and the reduction in value causing them to apply had occurred after 13 March 1989, any allowable loss or chargeable gain on the disposal would have been calculated as if the consideration had been increased by an amount.

These provisions are interpreted as if *TCGA 1992, s 136* (see 53.9 SHARES AND SECURITIES) had effect generally for the capital gains tax legislation. [*TCGA 1992, s 34*].

3.10 **CONNECTED PERSONS** [*TCGA 1992, s 18*]

A transaction between CONNECTED PERSONS (14) is treated as having been made by way of a non-arm's length bargain so that acquisition and disposal are treated as being made at market value in most cases (see 36.1 MARKET VALUE). [*TCGA 1992, s 18(1)(2)*]. There are restrictions on losses in such circumstances. See 35.4 LOSSES.

Where the asset disposed of is subject to a right or restriction enforceable by the person making the disposal or a person connected with him, then if the acquisition consideration is treated as being the market value of the asset, that value is ascertained by deducting from the market value of the unencumbered asset either the market value of the right or restriction or, if less, the amount by which its extinction would enhance the value of the asset to its owner. Rights or restrictions the enforcement of which might effectively destroy or substantially impair the value of the asset without bringing any countervailing advantage either to the person making the disposal or to a person connected with him are disregarded, e.g. rights to extinguish incorporeal assets by way of forfeiture or merger (but see below). Options and other rights to acquire assets are also disregarded.

The valuation provisions outlined above do not apply to rights of forfeiture etc. exercisable on the breach of a covenant in a lease, nor to any right or restriction under a mortgage or other charge. [*TCGA 1992, s 18(6)-(8)*].

3.11 ASSETS DISPOSED OF IN A SERIES OF TRANSACTIONS

Position after 19 March 1985. Where by way of two or more 'material transactions' which are linked (a '*series of linked transactions*')

(*a*)   a person disposes of assets to another person with whom he is connected (or to two or more other persons with each of whom he is connected) (see 14 CONNECTED PERSONS); and

(*b*)   the 'original market value' of the assets disposed of by any of the transactions in the series is less than the appropriate portion of the 'aggregate market value' of the assets disposed of by all the transactions in the series,

the disposal effected by the linked transaction in (*b*) is deemed to be for a consideration equal to the appropriate portion referred to in that paragraph. The above is not, however, to affect the consideration for any disposals between MARRIED PERSONS (37) living together.

A '*material transaction*' is a transaction taking place after 19 March 1985, and two or more such transactions are linked if they occur within the period of six years ending on the date of the last of them.

The provisions apply *both* when a second material transaction causes a series of linked transactions to come into being *and* when an existing series is extended by a further material transaction (whether or not an earlier transaction ceases to form part of the series). Assessments and adjustments are made accordingly.

In consequence of the provisions above applying after 19 March 1985, previous provisions for assets disposed of in a series of transactions (see below) were repealed for transactions after 19 March 1985. If any transaction(s) occurred before 20 March 1985, and any after 19 March 1985, such of the former as occurred not more than two years before the first of the latter will be treated as material transactions within the provisions applying after 19 March 1985 if all the transactions would have been within the previous provisions if they had not been repealed and all the transactions would have been within the provisions applying after 19 March 1985 if they had all occurred after that date. See also below for the Revenue attitude to the making of elections for 6 April 1965 value out of time which presumably still applies under provisions applying after 19 March 1985. The Revenue's practice might also apply to 31 March 1982 re-basing elections.

'*Original market value*'. If a transaction is the most recent in the series, the original market value of the assets disposed of by it is the market value which would otherwise be deemed to be the consideration for it under the general capital gains tax rules (e.g. 36 MARKET VALUE). In the case of any other transaction in the series, the original market value of the assets disposed of by it is the value which, prior to the occurrence of the most recent transaction in the series, was or would have been deemed to be the consideration, whether under the general capital gains tax rules or by the previous operation of the provisions applying after 19 March 1985.

'Aggregate market value'. Subject to further provisions below, aggregate market value is the amount which would have been the market value of all the transactions in the series under the general capital gains tax rules if, 'considering all the assets together', they had been disposed of by one disposal occurring at the time of the transaction concerned. The appropriate portion of the aggregate market value is that portion which it is reasonable to apportion to those of the assets which were actually disposed of by the transaction concerned.

'Considering all the assets together' is to include not only to considering them as a group or holding or collection of assets retaining their separate identities but also (if it gives a higher market value) to considering them as brought together, physically or in law, so as to constitute either a single asset or a number of assets which are distinct from those which were comprised in each of the transactions concerned.

Groups of companies. Intra-group transfers of assets which are treated as taking place on a no gain, no loss basis (see 13.11 COMPANIES and called here an 'intra-group transfer') are not material transactions. In a case where

(*a*)   a company ('company A') disposes of an asset by way of a material transaction; and

(*b*)   company A acquired the asset after 19 March 1985 by way of an intra-group transfer; and

(*c*)   the disposal by company A is to a person who is connected with another company ('company B') which at some time after 19 March 1985 disposed of the asset by way of an intra-group transfer; and

(*d*)   either the disposal by way of intra-group transfer which is referred to in (*c*) above was the occasion of the acquisition in (*b*) above or, between that disposal and acquisition, there has been no disposal of the asset which was not an intra-group transfer,

then, in determining whether the new provisions apply in relation to a series of linked transactions, the disposal by company A is treated as having been made by company B; but any increase in the consideration for that disposal resulting from the application of the new provisions has effect with respect to company A.

Disposal preceding acquisition. If any of the assets disposed of by all the transactions in a series of linked transactions were acquired after the time of the first of those transactions, then, in considering aggregate market value in relation to each of the transactions in the series, no account is taken of any assets which were acquired after the time of that transaction (unless they were acquired by way of an intra-group transfer). Further, the number of assets taken into account is limited to the maximum number held at any time in the period beginning immediately before the first transaction and ending immediately before the last; and in arriving at this figure any intra-group transfers prior to the first transaction are treated as taking place after that transaction. For identification purposes fungible assets are treated as disposed of on a 'first in, first out' basis. [*TCGA 1992, ss 19, 20, 11 Sch 1, 2(1)(2)(4)*].

Example

L purchased a set of 6 antique chairs in 1979 at a cost of £3,600. He gave 2 chairs to his daughter in February 1990, another pair to his son in November 1993, and sold the final pair to his brother for their market value in August 1995.

The market value of the chairs at the relevant dates were

	2 chairs £	4 chairs £	6 chairs £
February 1990	3,000	7,000	13,000
November 1993	3,900	9,000	17,100
August 1995	5,200	12,000	23,100

The market value of the set of 6 chairs at 31 March 1982 was £6,000. L has elected under *TCGA 1992, s 35(5)* for all his assets held at 31 March 1982 to be regarded as having been disposed of and re-acquired at market value on that date.

Indexation factors are

March 1982 – February 1990	0.513
March 1982 – November 1993	0.782
March 1982 – August 1995 (assumed)	0.890

The capital gains tax computations are as follows

February 1990
Disposal to daughter

Deemed consideration	£3,000

As the consideration does not exceed £3,000, the disposal is covered by the chattel exemption (see note (1)).

November 1993
(i) *1989/90 disposal to daughter recomputed*

Original market value (deemed disposal consideration at February 1990)	£3,000
Reasonable proportion of aggregate market value as at February 1990 of all assets disposed of to date £7,000 × $\frac{2}{4}$	£3,500

	£
Deemed consideration (greater of £3,500 and £3,000)	3,500
31.3.82 value $\dfrac{3,000}{3,000 + 7,000}$ × £6,000	1,800
Unindexed gain	1,700
Indexation allowance £1,800 × 0.513	923
Chargeable gain 1989/90	£777

(ii) *1993/94 disposal to son*

Original market value (deemed disposal consideration)	£3,900
Reasonable proportion of aggregate market value as at November 1993 of all assets disposed of to date £9,000 × $\frac{2}{4}$	£4,500

3.11 Anti-Avoidance

	£
Deemed consideration (greater of £4,500 and £3,900)	4,500
31.3.82 value $\dfrac{3,900}{3,900 + 3,900} \times (£6,000 - £1,800)$	2,100
Unindexed gain	2,400
Indexation allowance £2,100 × 0.782	1,642
Chargeable gain 1993/94	£758

August 1995

(i) *Gain on 1989/90 disposal to daughter recomputed*

Original market value (deemed consideration in recomputation at November 1993)	£3,500
Reasonable proportion of aggregate market value as at February 1990 of all assets disposed of to date £13,000 × $\frac{2}{6}$	£4,333

	£
Deemed consideration (greater of £4,333 and £3,500)	4,333
31.3.82 value (as before)	1,800
Unindexed gain	2,533
Indexation allowance (as before)	923
Revised chargeable gain 1989/90	£1,610

(ii) *Gain on 1993/94 disposal to son recomputed*

Original market value (deemed consideration in computation at November 1993)	£4,500
Reasonable proportion of aggregate market value as at November 1993 of all assets disposed of to date £17,100 × $\frac{2}{6}$	£5,700

	£
Deemed consideration (greater of £4,500 and £5,700)	5,700
31.3.82 value (as before)	2,100
Unindexed gain	3,600
Indexation allowance (as before)	1,642
Revised chargeable gain 1993/94	£1,958

(iii) *Gain on 1995/96 disposal to brother*

Original market value (actual consideration)	£5,200
Reasonable proportion of aggregate market value as at August 1995 of all assets disposed of to date £23,100 × $\frac{2}{6}$	£7,700

	£
Deemed consideration (greater of £5,200 and £7,700)	7,700
31.3.82 value (£6,000 − £1,800 − £2,100)	2,100
Unindexed gain	5,600
Indexation allowance £2,100 × 0.890	1,869
Chargeable gain 1995/96	£3,731

Notes to the example

(1) The disposal in February 1990 is at first covered by the chattel exemption (£6,000 for disposals after 5 April 1989). As the second disposal in November 1993 is to a person connected with the recipient of the first disposal, the two must then be looked at together for the purposes of the chattel exemption, and, as the combined proceeds exceed the chattel exemption limit, the exemption is not available. [*TCGA 1992, s 262*].

(2) The three disposals are linked transactions within *TCGA 1992, s 19* as they are made by the same transferor to persons with whom he is connected, and take place within a six-year period.

(3) It is assumed in the above example that it is 'reasonable' to apportion the aggregate market value in proportion to the number of items. In other instances a different basis may be needed to give the 'reasonable' apportionment required by *TCGA 1992, s 20(4)*.

Position before 20 March 1985. If a person 'is given or acquires' from one or more persons with whom he is connected by way of more than one transaction, assets of which the aggregate of their market values is less than their total market value when considered together, the market value of each shall be the appropriate portion of their total value. [*TCGA 1992, 11 Sch 2(1)(3)*].

Prior to 27 December 1984 the Revenue took the view that connected transactions could be taken into consideration without time limit (even before 6 April 1965) (CCAB Statement June 1968). But in a Revenue Press Release of 27 December 1984 it was declared (without reasons being given) that the legislation applied only to those transactions which occurred within the two-year period preceding the latest transaction in the series and that this practice would be followed henceforth. Subject to this the values attributed to assets at the time of any previous acquisition (or acquisitions) since 6 April 1965 and (subject to the BACK DUTY (9) provisions) within the normal time limits for making assessments, were reconsidered on the footing that the value of the assets acquired on each such occasion was a proportionate part of the value of the total asset acquired up to the time of the last acquisition. Insofar as this reconsideration produced a larger value for the acquisition, a recomputation of the liability on the corresponding disposal had to be made. The Revenue regarded the making of additional assessments under these provisions as sufficient reason for allowing an election to be made for valuation at 6 April 1965 outside the normal time limits. Where, however, an election had already been made, it could not be withdrawn (CCAB Statement June 1968).

3.12   **CLOSE COMPANY TRANSFERRING ASSET AT UNDERVALUE** [*TCGA 1992, s 125*]

Where a close company (as defined by *ICTA 1988, ss 414, 415*) transfers (other than within a group of companies under *TCGA 1992, s 171(1)*, see 13.11 COMPANIES) an asset to any person otherwise than at arm's length and for a consideration of an amount or value less than the market value of the asset, an amount equal to the difference is apportioned among the issued shares of the company. On a disposal of the shares by the person who owned them at the date of transfer, an amount equal to the amount so apportioned is not treated as allowable expenditure. Where the owner of such shares is itself a close company, an amount equal to the amount apportioned to those shares is apportioned among the issued shares of that close company, the owners thereof being treated as above, and so on through any number of close companies.

Where re-basing at 31 March 1982 applies to disposals after 5 April 1988, only transfers after 31 March 1982 (rather than 6 April 1965) are taken into account for the purposes of the above.

Where the asset is transferred to a settlement for the benefit of employees, etc. (see 18.75 EXEMPTIONS AND RELIEFS), the amount apportioned is the difference between the market value of the asset or the amount of the allowable expenditure attributable to the asset, whichever is the less, and the consideration. [*TCGA 1992, s 239(3)*].

TCGA 1992, s 125 is not in practice applied where the amount of the undervalue is treated as a distribution under *ICTA 1988, s 209(4)* (CCAB Statement June 1967).

3.13 RESTRICTIONS ON COMPANY RECONSTRUCTIONS AND AMALGAMATIONS [*TCGA 1992, ss 137, 138*]

TCGA 1992, s 135 applies to the takeover of one company by another wholly or partly for shares or debentures and provides that the original holding and the new holding are to be treated as the same asset. See 53.8 SHARES AND SECURITIES. *TCGA 1992, s 136* deals with company reconstructions where a company issues shares or debentures to another company's shareholders whose original holdings are either retained or cancelled. The original and new holdings are likewise treated as the same asset. See 53.9 SHARES AND SECURITIES. Neither of these provisions applies, however, unless the exchange, reconstruction, or amalgamation is for 'bona fide commercial reasons', and not part of a scheme or arrangement for the main or only purpose of avoiding capital gains tax or corporation tax. This restriction does not apply where a recipient of the shares, etc. holds 5% or less of, or of any class of, the relevant shares, etc. (including holdings by connected persons) in the company being acquired etc., or where the Board, on written application by either company, has indicated its satisfaction with the transfer before it is made. Such application must contain particulars of operations contemplated and the Board may, within thirty days of receipt, call for further particulars (to be supplied within thirty days, or longer if the Board allows). If the particulars are not supplied, the application lapses. Subject to this, the Board must indicate its decision within a further thirty days. If not so notified, or if dissatisfied with the decision, the applicants may within a further thirty days require the Board to refer the particulars to the Special Commissioners for their decision. All material facts and considerations must be disclosed, otherwise any decision is void. Applications should be made to Inland Revenue, Capital and Valuation Division (CGT), Sapphire House, 550 Streetsbrook Road, Solihull, West Midlands, B91 1QU. Tel. 0121-711 3232.

The above provisions also apply to interests in a company without share capital and certain quoted options.

Tax assessed on the chargeable person and not paid within six months of the date when it is payable may be recovered, in whole or in part, from certain third parties, in the name of the chargeable person, within two years of that date. There is a right of recourse to the chargeable person for the tax so paid. The third parties are restricted to persons holding the shares, etc. issued to the chargeable person who acquired them as a result of one or more disposals within *TCGA 1992, s 58(1)* (spouses living together) or *171(1)* (companies within same group) without any intervening disposals not within those provisions. In the case of a chargeable person who is a company, the rights of recovery and recourse are suitably adapted for accounting periods ending after 30 September 1993 (Pay and File) so that, in particular, the right of recourse also extends to any interest on unpaid tax which the third party has paid in respect of the outstanding tax.

Seeking to retain family control of a company may be a 'bona fide commercial reason', see *CIR v Brebner HL 1967, 43 TC 705; Clark v CIR Ch D 1978, 52 TC 482* and *CIR v Goodwin HL 1976, 50 TC 583*, which deal with the similar phrase in *ICTA 1988, s 703(1)*.

Strictly speaking, the reconstructed company or amalgamated companies should carry on substantially the same business and have substantially the same members as the original company or companies, but in practice the latter requirement may be waived if the scheme was carried out for bona fide commercial reasons. Where new companies are formed to take over separate parts of the original company's business, this provision may be applied even if the new companies have no common shareholder, provided that there is an actual segregation of trades or businesses which can be carried on in their own right, and not merely a segregation of assets (Revenue Statement of Practice SP 5/85).

For the Revenue's response to a number of concerns regarding aspects of clearances under *TCGA 1992, s 138*, see ICAEW Guidance Note TR 657, 10 April 1987. For the possibility of the Revenue expediting a reply by such means as facsimile transmission, see Law Society's Gazette 27 March 1991 practice note (reproduced at 1991 STI 389).

Prior to the commencement of *TCGA 1992*, the above provisions were contained in *CGTA 1979, ss 87, 88*.

3.14   **Schemes involving the transfer of a business owned by companies.** [*TCGA 1992, s 139*]. See 13.6 COMPANIES where a scheme of reconstruction involves the transfer of a UK resident company's business to another UK resident company for no consideration other than the assumption of liabilities of the business.

3.15   **GROUPS OF COMPANIES**

There are a number of anti-avoidance provisions relating to groups of companies generally. See 13.10–13.30 COMPANIES and in particular 13.17 for a company ceasing to be a member of a group. In addition, see 3.6–3.9 above for value shifting to give a tax-free benefit which may involve groups, 3.16 below for depreciatory transactions within groups of companies and 3.17 for dividend stripping treated as a depreciatory trans-action.

3.16   **DEPRECIATORY TRANSACTIONS WITHIN GROUPS OF COMPANIES**
[*TCGA 1992, s 176*]

Where (after 5 April 1965 or, where re-basing at 31 March 1982 takes effect in relation to disposals after 5 April 1988, after 30 March 1982) two or more members of a 'group of companies' are parties to a 'disposal of assets' at other than market value which has the effect of materially reducing the value of the shares or 'securities' of one of those companies ('a depreciatory transaction'), any loss arising on the ultimate disposal of those shares or securities by a member or a former member of the group (having been a member when the transaction took place) is to be allowable only so far as appears to the inspector to be 'just and reasonable'. The inspector will take into account any other transaction (after 5 April 1965 or, where re-basing at 31 March 1982 takes effect as above, after 30 March 1982) which may have

(i)   enhanced the value of the assets of the company the shares in which are being disposed of, and

(ii)   depreciated the assets of any other group member.

Where such a loss has been wholly or partly disallowed, any chargeable gain accruing within six years of the depreciatory transaction on the disposal of shares or securities of another company which was a party to it is reduced as appears to be just and reasonable (but not so as to exceed the reduction in the allowable loss). The inspector is to have regard to the effect of the depreciatory transaction on the value of the shares at the date of disposal. All adjustments, by discharge or repayment of tax, or otherwise, as are required to give effect to these provisions may be made at any time.

The inspector's decision on either point is subject to appeal to the Commissioners.

A *'depreciatory transaction'* also includes any other transaction where

(*a*)   the company, the shares or securities in which are the subject of the ultimate disposal, or any '75% subsidiary' of that company, was party to that transaction; and

(*b*)   the parties to the transaction were, or included, two or more companies which, when the transaction occurred, were in the same group.

A transaction is not depreciatory to the extent that it is a payment which is required to be, or has been, brought into account in computing a chargeable gain or allowable loss of the company making the ultimate disposal. Cancellation within *Companies Act 1985, s 135* of shares or securities of one member of a group which are owned by another is deemed to be a depreciatory transaction unless it falls within this exemption. The deemed disposal arising under a claim that shares or securities have become of negligible value under *TCGA 1992, s 24(2)* (see 35.8 LOSSES) may constitute a depreciatory transaction.

References to *'disposal of assets'* include appropriation by one member of a group of the goodwill of another member.

'Securities' includes loan stock or similar securities whether secured or unsecured.

'Group of companies' includes member companies not resident in the UK. Subject to this, see 13.10 COMPANIES for this definition as well as that for 'company' and '75% subsidiary'.

Where a subsidiary company pays dividends to its parent out of post-acquisition profits, the Revenue do not regard the payment as being a depreciatory transaction (ICAEW Guidance Note TR 588, 25 September 1985).

3.17   **DIVIDEND STRIPPING** [*TCGA 1992, s 177; F(No 2)A 1992, s 46(1)(6)*]

Where a company (the 'first company') holds 10% or more of a class of shares in another company (the 'second company') otherwise than as a dealing company, and a distribution is or has been made to the first company which materially reduces or has reduced the value of the holding, the distribution is to be treated as a depreciatory transaction under *TCGA 1992, s 176* (see 3.16 above) in relation to any disposal of the shares. This applies whether the disposal is by the first company or any other company to which the holding has been transferred under the provisions of *TCGA 1992, ss 140A* (transfer of UK trade between companies in different EC member States, see 39.15 OVERSEAS MATTERS), *171* (transfers within a group, see 13.11 COMPANIES) or *172* (transfer of UK branch or agency, see 39.3 OVERSEAS MATTERS). If the first and second companies are not members of the same group, they are deemed to be so.

For these purposes, a company's holding of different classes in another company are treated as separate holdings and holdings of the same class which differ in the entitlements or obligations they confer are treated as holdings of different classes. Subject to this, all of a company's holdings of the same class in another company must be treated as a single holding and other holdings of the same class held by connected persons are aggregated in determining whether the 10% test is satisfied. For the meaning of connected persons, see 14 CONNECTED PERSONS. For the above provisions only, the persons mentioned in 14.6 specifically include persons acting together to secure or acquire a holding in a company (and not just control).

A distribution need not be treated as a depreciatory transaction under these provisions to the extent that it consists of a payment which is required to be, or has been, brought into account in calculating a chargeable gain or allowable loss by the person making the ultimate disposal.

3.18 TRANSACTIONS IN LAND [*ICTA 1988, ss 776-778*]

Where land in the UK is acquired or developed with the sole or main object of realising a gain from disposing of it or is held as trading stock, any capital gain from 'disposal' of the land is, subject to certain exemptions, treated as *income* of the person realising the gain (or the person who transmitted to him the opportunity of making that gain). See 33.4 LAND.

3.19 LAND SOLD AND LEASED BACK [*ICTA 1988, s 780*]

As regards certain arrangements within *ICTA 1988, s 779*, part of the consideration received by the lessee for giving up the original lease (or undertaking to pay an increased rent) is treated as an income receipt and not a capital one. See 33.23 LAND.

3.20 RESTRICTIONS ON, AND CLAWBACKS OF, HOLD-OVER RELIEFS AND REINVESTMENT IN SHARES RELIEF

See 22 HOLD-OVER RELIEFS and 45 REINVESTMENT IN SHARES RELIEF for full coverage of provisions which either deny the granting of relief or provide for the clawback of relief previously given in certain circumstances.

3.21 OVERSEAS RESIDENT SETTLEMENTS ETC.

See 39.6–39.11 OVERSEAS MATTERS and 52.8 SETTLEMENTS.

3.22 RESTRICTIONS ON, AND CLAWBACKS OF, RELIEF ON INVESTMENTS IN VENTURE CAPITAL TRUSTS

See VENTURE CAPITAL TRUSTS (58) for full coverage of provisions which either deny the granting of relief or provide for the clawback of relief previously given in certain circumstances.

4 Appeals

Cross-references. See 5 ASSESSMENTS; 9.8 BACK DUTY for investigatory powers of the Revenue; 12.3 CLAIMS for appeals in respect of claims; 32 INTEREST ON UNPAID TAX; 41 PAYMENT OF TAX; 42.8 and 42.9 PENALTIES; 47.7 RESIDENCE AND DOMICILE; 51 SELF-ASSESSMENT for future changes broadly from 1996/97.

4.1   The majority of appeals are against assessments, the right of appeal being conferred by *TMA 1970, s 31*, but, with unimportant exceptions, the taxpayer may appeal against any formal decision by the inspector or the Board. In particular a decision on CLAIMS (12) may be appealed. [*TMA 1970, s 42*]. An appeal against an assessment to corporation tax is an appeal against the total amount of profits charged to tax in the assessment (*Owton Fens Properties Ltd v Redden Ch D 1984, 58 TC 218*).

4.2   **SPECIAL REGULATIONS**

These regulations make certain provisions in relation to capital gains tax appeals which are not covered by the general statutory provisions on appeals (see 4.3 *et seq.* below). In particular, they lay down procedures under which a question of market value or apportionment which affects the liability of two or more persons (e.g. a donor and donee, or a vendor and purchaser in a transaction not at arm's length) can be settled. The regulations, authorised by *TMA 1970, s 57*, are contained in *The Capital Gains Tax Regulations 1967 (SI 1967 No 149)*. Following the introduction of regulations governing the jurisdiction of the General and Special Commissioners and the procedure for proceedings before them with effect from 1 September 1994 (see 4.8 below), the regulations relating to capital gains tax appeals summarised below were subject to consequential amendments. For details of the earlier rules, see Tolley's Capital Gains Tax 1994/95 or earlier edition.

(*a*)   **Joinder of third parties in appeals.** Where the market value of an asset on a particular date or the apportionment of any amount or value is a material question in an appeal, any person whose liability to capital gains tax for any period may be affected by that market value may apply to be joined in the appeal. Application is in writing to the inspector and should state, *inter alia*, how the applicant's liability may be affected and his contention in relation to the matters under appeal. A copy of the application is sent by the inspector to the appellant and any other party to the appeal. If the application is received more than thirty days before the date of the appeal hearing, or before that date is set, then if the inspector is satisfied with the propriety of the applicant's case, the applicant will be joined as a third party and appropriate notice given to the other parties. Otherwise, the inspector will refer the application to the Commissioners who may allow or refuse the application at their discretion. Insofar as his interest is being considered, the third party has the same rights as the appellant. [*Para 8*].

(*b*)   **Applications for determination of market value.** Where the market value of an asset or the apportionment of any amount or value may affect the liability to capital gains tax of two or more persons, either or any of them may apply to the Commissioners (General or Special) for a ruling if the point is not, nor has been, a material question in an appeal brought by any of them. The inspector is a party to such proceedings. [*Para 9*].

(*c*)   **Conclusive effect of determination on appeal.** The values as determined are conclusive between the Revenue, the parties to the appeal and any third party who was given notice of the appeal in reasonable time unless that person's application (made without undue delay) to be joined as a party to the appeal was refused. [*Para 11*].

(*d*) **Agreements in writing.** There can be no binding agreement on the value of an asset between the Revenue and the taxpayer unless the agreement is joined by any proper third party to the appeal. A written agreement will be effective against the taxpayer's personal representatives, trustee in bankruptcy, etc. An agreement conclusive against trustees of a settlement will be effective against any person becoming absolutely entitled to the settled property. [*Paras 12, 13*].

4.3 GENERAL RIGHT OF APPEAL

Unless otherwise stated or required by the context, the paragraphs 4.4 to 4.11 below apply to all appeals and matters treated as appeals, and not only to appeals against assessments.

An appeal once made cannot be withdrawn unilaterally (see *R v Special Commissioners (ex p. Elmhirst) CA 1935, 20 TC 381* and *Beach v Willesden General Commissioners Ch D 1981, 55 TC 663*) but see 4.6 below for the withdrawal of appeals by agreement and 4.9 below regarding appeals to the High Court.

4.4 TIME LIMIT FOR APPEALS, ETC.

An appeal *against an assessment* must be made within 30 days of the date of *issue* of the notice of assessment or of the making of the disputed decision and state the grounds of appeal, but grounds not stated may be advanced at any hearing of the appeal if the Commissioners so allow. [*TMA 1970, s 31(1)(5); F(No 2)A 1975, s 67(1)*]. An appeal *against a decision on a claim* must be made within 30 days of *receipt* of written notice of the decision, except for matters relating to residence, ordinary residence and domicile (see 47.7 RESIDENCE AND DOMICILE). [*TMA 1970, s 42(3)*].

A late appeal may be accepted by the inspector if there is reasonable excuse for the delay and, if he does not accept it, he must refer the application to the Commissioners for their decision. [*TMA 1970, s 49*]. If they refuse, their decision is not subject to appeal by way of stated case (*R v Special Commrs (ex p. Magill) QB (NI) 1979, 53 TC 135*, but is subject to judicial review (see *R v Hastings and Bexhill General Commrs and CIR (ex p Goodacre) QB, [1994] STC 799*, in which a refusal was quashed and the matter remitted to a different body of Commissioners).

4.5 JURISDICTION OF APPEAL COMMISSIONERS

An appeal is made to the General or Special Commissioners. Notice of the appeal is given in writing to the appropriate inspector or officer of the Board. If not settled by agreement (4.6 below) it is heard by the Commissioners. Except in the circumstances outlined below regarding unquoted shares and land in the UK, the appeal is to the General Commissioners, unless the taxpayer elects for the Special Commissioners, either when the appeal is made or separately but within the time limit for making the appeal. See also 12.3 CLAIMS. After 31 December 1984, such an election is, however, disregarded if the appellant and the inspector so agree in writing before the appeal is determined, or if before the appeal is determined the inspector refers the election to the General Commissioners (after notifying the appellant) and they so direct. They must give such a direction unless satisfied that the appellant has arguments to present or evidence to adduce on the merits of the appeal. Such a direction may be revoked at any time before determination of the appeal if that condition is subsequently satisfied. The decision to give or revoke a direction is final. [*TMA 1970, ss 31(5A)-(5E), 46(1), 2 Sch 1A-1E; FA 1984, s 127, 22 Sch 3; SI 1984, No 1836*]. In deciding when the appeal should be listed for hearing, inspectors of taxes are to treat appeals to the Special Commissioners no differently from appeals to the General Commissioners. Inspectors are only to ask taxpayers to agree that an election for hearing by the Special Commissioners should be disregarded when a decision is needed to arrange the listing, and then only where the inspector is satisfied that it is a delay appeal as opposed to a contentious appeal. A contentious appeal does not become a delay appeal by reason of the fact that the inspector may still be seeking further information (Revenue Press Release, 26 February 1990).

Appeals to the General Commissioners may, if the parties so apply and the Commissioners consent, be transferred to the Special Commissioners (and vice versa) despite the expiry of the time limit for election as above or the making of such an election. [*TMA 1970, s 44(3)*]. In addition, after 31 December 1984, the General Commissioners may arrange that an appeal brought before them be transferred to the Special Commissioners, with the Special Commissioners' consent, if, after considering any representations made to them by the parties to the appeal, the General Commissioners consider that, because of the complexity of, or likely time required to hear, the appeal, it should be so transferred. [*TMA 1970, s 44(3A); FA 1984, s 127, 22 Sch 5; SI 1984, No 1836*].

Where the General Commissioners have jurisdiction, rules for prescribing the appropriate Division are in *TMA 1970, 3 Sch* as amended, although the parties may come to an agreement that the proceedings be brought before any body of General Commissioners specified in the agreement. [*TMA 1970, s 44(1)(2); FA 1988, s 133(2)*]. In general, inspectors will agree to transfer jurisdiction for an appeal to be heard in a Division more convenient for the taxpayer (Revenue Tax Bulletin May 1993 p 70; comments made there about Schedule E appeals are understood to apply also to capital gains tax appeals).

In relation to proceedings instituted after 31 December 1988, the Board may, however, direct that specified proceedings be brought before the General Commissioners for a specified division, provided that the inspector notifies the other party of the effect of that direction, unless

(A) the other party objects to the direction within 30 days of the service of the inspector's notice, or, in the case of an appeal, has elected for a hearing in the place where he ordinarily resides (see below), or

(B) the proceedings are subject to the special rules applicable where more than one taxpayer may be a party to the proceedings.

Any such direction may be superseded by an agreement between the parties (as above). [*TMA 1970, s 44(1A)(1B); FA 1988, s 133(1)*]. The power to make a direction is used broadly where the inspector has no expectation that the taxpayer will appear at the hearing of the appeal, but as a direction is made well in advance the inspector will withdraw it if the taxpayer objects because of an inconvenient journey (Revenue Tax Bulletin May 1993 p 70; comments made there about Schedule E appeals are understood to apply to capital gains tax appeals, and for both such types of appeal, even though the taxpayer's objection is made outside the 30-day time limit (provided it is made before the case is set down for hearing in the Division directed by the inspector)).

For appeals against *assessments* the broad effect of *TMA 1970, 3 Sch* is to designate the Division in which the appellant's trade etc. is carried on, or if he has no trade etc., the Division in which he is employed, *or (in either case) at his election by notice in writing given not later than the notice of appeal*, the Division in which he ordinarily resides. If he has no trade etc. or employment, the Division of ordinary residence applies. Although the election for a hearing in the Division of the ordinary place of residence should be given not later than the notice of appeal, in practice inspectors will accept such an election at any time before the case is set down for hearing in the Division determined as above

(Revenue Tax Bulletin May 1993 p 70; comments there made about Schedule E appeals are understood to apply also to capital gains tax appeals).

Corporation tax appeals are heard in the Division in which the company carries on its trade or where its head office is situate.

The above rules are, however, directory and not mandatory (*CIR v Adams CA 1971, 48 TC 67; Murphy v Elders Ch D 1973, 49 TC 135*) and a decision of the Commissioners cannot be invalidated for want of jurisdiction if there was no objection to jurisdiction before the decision. [*TMA 1970, s 44(4)*]. See also *R v Kingston & Elmbridge Commrs (ex p. Adams) QB 1972, 48 TC 75; R v St Pancras Commrs (ex p. Church of Scientology of California) QB 1973, 50 TC 365; Parikh v Birmingham North Commrs CA, [1976] STC 365*.

The Special Commissioners go on circuit to the chief provincial towns, but appeals to them may generally by arrangement be heard in London, which is usually more convenient if it is intended to engage counsel.

Insofar as an appeal involves a question of the value of unquoted shares, etc., of a company resident in the UK, that question is to be determined by the Special Commissioners. [*TMA 1970, s 47(3); FA 1975, s 54*]. Insofar as an appeal involves the question of the value of any land, or of a lease of land, in the UK, that question is to be determined by the Lands Tribunal (in England and Wales, Scotland or Northern Ireland as appropriate). [*TMA 1970, s 47(1)(2)*].

The Lord Chancellor has powers, by regulation, to provide for the transfer of appeals between the General and Special Commissioners or between General Commissioners for different divisions, and for varying the number of General or Special Commissioners required or permitted to hear appeals. Different provision may be made for different cases and different circumstances. [*TMA s 46A; F(No 2)A 1992, 16 Sch 3*]. See now *SI 1994 Nos 1811–1813* and 4.8 below.

In **Northern Ireland** all appeals were previously heard by the Special Commissioners except where the taxpayer elected (under *TMA 1970, s 59*) for private hearing by a single judge in the County Court. However, from 3 April 1989 this procedure ceased, and the provisions under which appeals elsewhere in the UK are heard by General Commissioners or Special Commissioners apply from that date. Proceedings which

(*a*)   were instituted but not determined before 3 April 1989 (the appointed day), and

(*b*)   might have been instituted before the General Commissioners if they had been in Great Britain,

were transferred to the General Commissioners unless either

(i)   within 30 days after the appointed day any party so elected, and gave written notice to the other parties, or

(ii)   the proceedings were under *TMA 1970, s 100* (see 42.9 PENALTIES).

If such a transfer occurred, the right to elect under *TMA 1970, 3 Sch* for the hearing to be in the Division of residence (see above) was exercisable for 30 days after the appointed day. [*FA 1988, s 134;* Revenue Press Release, 15 March 1989].

4.6   **SETTLEMENT OF APPEALS BY AGREEMENT**

Where agreement, written or otherwise, has been reached at any time between the Revenue and the appellant or his agent on any appeal to the Commissioners against any assessment or decision, the assessment or decision as upheld, varied, discharged, or cancelled by that agreement, is treated as if it had been determined on appeal, provided that

(*a*)   the taxpayer may withdraw from the agreement by giving written notice within 30 days of making it, and

(*b*)   oral agreements are ineffective unless confirmed in writing by either side (the date of such confirmation then being the effective date of agreement).

[*TMA 1970, s 54*].

The agreement must specify the figure for assessment or a precise formula for ascertaining it (*Delbourgo v Field CA 1978, 52 TC 225*). The inspector has no power unilaterally to withdraw ('vacate') an assessment (*Baylis v Gregory CA, [1987] STC 297*). See *Gibson v General Commissioners for Stroud Ch D 1989, 61 TC 645* for a case where there was held not to have been a determination and *R v Inspector of Taxes, ex p. Bass Holdings Ltd; Richart v Bass Holdings Ltd QB 1992, [1993] STC 122* for one where rectification of an agreement was ordered where a relief had been deducted twice contrary to the intention of Revenue and taxpayer. See *CIR v West CA, [1991] STC 357* for a case where the taxpayer was unsuccessful in seeking leave to defend a Crown action for payment of tax on the ground that the accountant who had entered into an agreement had no authority to do so given him by the taxpayer. For the extent to which further assessments are permissible if an appeal has been determined by agreement, see 5.2 ASSESSMENTS.

A taxpayer cannot withdraw an appeal made to the Commissioners (see 4.3 above), but if, having appealed, he or his agent gives the inspector oral or written notice of his desire not to proceed, then unless the inspector gives written notice of objection within 30 days thereof, the appeal is treated as if settled by agreement, as above. Agreement is effective from the date of the taxpayer's notification that the assessment, etc. be upheld without variation. [*TMA 1970, s 54(4)*].

In *Tod v South Essex Motors (Basildon) Ltd Ch D 1987, 60 TC 598*, the taxpayer company's agent and the inspector agreed in 1974 that a disposal by the company in 1968 (details of which had been fully disclosed) had resulted in an allowable loss available for carry forward. However, neither party had appreciated that a correct application of the law would have resulted in the disposal being treated as giving rise to neither a gain nor a loss. In 1977 a new inspector and new agent agreed that part of the previously agreed loss should be allowed against gains arising in 1975. In 1981 the company made a substantial gain against which it claimed to set the balance of the loss but the then inspector's refusal to allow the claim was upheld. The binding effect of an agreement under *TMA 1970, s 54(1)* could be no wider than the binding effect of a determination by Commissioners or by a court on appeal. There was nothing to prevent the parties agreeing under *TMA 1970, s 54* to correct a previous agreement (as was done here); the corrected agreement became operative both for the ordinary law of contract as well as this taxing statute. Provided that full disclosure had been made, the fact that the correction proceeded upon an erroneous view of fact or law made no difference.

4.7   **THE HANDLING OF TAXPAYERS' APPEALS**

Appeal meetings must be notified to the appellant and the inspector (or other Revenue party) (see 4.8 below). In practice the inspector normally gives details of appeals ready for hearing to the Clerk who, after consulting the inspector and, in important appeals, the taxpayer or his agent as appropriate, makes the necessary arrangements, notifies the inspector and issues notices of the hearing to the appellant. In some Divisions he may, by arrangement, also notify the appellant's agent.

In January 1983, the Revenue announced a change of practice as regards the handling of appeals, in an effort to reduce the number of 'delay' hearings. See Tolley's Income Tax for details. The change did *not* apply to capital gains tax appeals.

The procedural changes previously introduced in 1976 presumably still apply to capital gains tax assessments. Under these, inspectors will, in general, bring to the Appeal Meetings during the first half of the calendar year only the following types of case.

(a)   *Cases of gross delay* i.e. where there are unsettled appeals for more than one year and also where the reckonable date for interest purposes has passed (but some corporation tax assessments may be listed before the reckonable date where there is a long interval between the end of the accounting period and the due and payable date) and priority will be given where material amounts of interest on unpaid tax are likely to arise. At these hearings the inspector may be seeking the Commissioners' determination of the liability and will be unlikely to acquiesce in continued delay.

(b)   *Contentious cases.*

(c)   *Applications for postponement of tax pending appeal.* Inspectors will normally be selective and concentrate on worthwhile cases and will then usually contest any request for an adjournment pending production of accounts.

(d)   *Appeals where the taxpayer is not professionally advised or represented.* (CCAB Statement TR 181, 2 April 1976).

Under the above procedures, at least 15 months will usually elapse between the taxpayer's accounting date and the first listing for a Commissioners' hearing. At such hearings the onus is on the taxpayer or his agent to show cause for continued delay. (CCAB Statement TR 181a, 4 November 1976).

4.8   **APPEALS HEARD BY APPEAL COMMISSIONERS**

The Lord Chancellor has wide regulatory powers in relation to the practice and procedure to be followed in connection with appeals, including the power to make different provision for different cases and different circumstances. [*TMA 1970, ss 56B–56D; F(No 2)A 1992, 16 Sch 4; FA 1994, s 254*]. With effect from 1 September 1994, regulations are brought in governing the jurisdiction of the General Commissioners and the procedure for proceedings before them. [*SI 1994 No 1812*]. Similar regulations apply in relation to the Special Commissioners [*SI 1994 No 1811*], and *SI 1994 No 1813* makes consequential and complementary amendments to other enactments.

In relation to the General Commissioners, these regulations do not apply to any proceedings set down (or first set down) for hearing by notice given before 1 September 1994 if any party to those proceedings so elects (by notice to the Clerk to the Commissioners) prior to commencement of the hearing (or to the recommencement of adjourned proceedings which were commenced before 1 September 1994). They also do not apply to any proceedings under *TMA 1970, s 100c* (see 42.10 PENALTIES) in respect of which a summons was issued prior to 1 September 1994 to the defendant to appear before them at a time and place stated in the summons. Where these regulations *do* apply to proceedings set down (or first set down) for hearing by notice given before 1 September 1994, anything done in relation to those proceedings before that date which, if the proceedings had commenced on or after that date, could have been done pursuant to these regulations, is to have effect as if done pursuant to these regulations. [*SI 1994 No 1812, reg 1*].

4.8 Appeals

In relation to the Special Commissioners, these regulations do not apply to any proceedings set down for hearing by notice given before 1 September 1994, or in respect of which a summons was issued before that date. [*SI 1994 No 1811, reg 1*].

Where these regulations do not apply, the jurisdictional and procedural rules were broadly similar, the most significant difference being the absence of the powers of the Special Commissioners to hear cases in public, to publish their decisions and to award costs in certain cases. For details of the earlier rules, see Tolley's Capital Gains Tax 1994/95 or earlier edition.

The remainder of this section deals with the rules applicable from 1 September 1994, and with the general and case law which is of continuing application.

(*a*)   **General Commissioners.**

Constitution of Tribunal. Two or more, but not more than five, General Commissioners for a division may hear any proceedings. [*SI 1994 No 1812, reg 2*]. They will themselves decide which one of them will preside at the hearing. Where possible at least three will sit, and, with the consent of all the parties, proceedings may be continued by any one or more of them. [*SI 1994 No 1812, reg 11*]. For the effect of personal business connection between a Comissioner and a party to proceedings, see *R v Holyhead Commrs (ex p Roberts) QB 1982, 56 TC 127*.

The Clerk to the Commissioners, who is frequently a local solicitor, normally attends the meeting to take minutes and to advise them as required, but a meeting without the Clerk would not be invalid (*Venn v Franks CA 1958, 38 TC 175*).

Preparation for hearing. *Listing and notice of hearing.* Except in relation to proceedings under *TMA 1970, s 100C* (see 42.10 PENALTIES), any party to the proceedings may serve notice on the Clerk to the Commissioners that he wishes a date for the hearing to be fixed, on receipt of which the Clerk must send notice to each party of the place, date and time of the hearing. Unless the parties otherwise agree, or the Commissioners otherwise direct, the date must not be earlier than 28 days after the date of the Clerk's notice. [*SI 1994 No 1812, reg 3*].

Witnesses. A General Commissioner, on the application of any party to the proceedings, may issue a witness summons (in Scotland, a witness citation) requiring any person in the UK either to attend the hearing of those proceedings to give evidence or to produce any relevant document in his possession, custody or power. The party applying for issue of the summons is responsible for its service (for which see *reg 4(3)*), and attendance may not be required within seven days of service unless the witness informs the Clerk that he accepts shorter notice. That party must also agree to meet the witness's reasonable travelling expenses. The witness may apply, by notice served on the Clerk, for the Commissioner to set aside the summons (in whole or part), on which application the party on whose application the summons was issued is entitled to be heard.

Except in Scotland, a witness so summoned to give evidence may only be cross-examined by the party on whose application the summons was issued if the Commissioners decide that the witness is a hostile witness and give leave.

A witness cannot be compelled to give evidence or produce documents which he could not be compelled to give or produce in an action in a court of law. An auditor or tax adviser (within *TMA 1970, s 20B(10)*) cannot be compelled to produce any document which he would not be obliged to deliver or make available by notice under *TMA 1970, s 20(3)* or *(8A)* (having regard to *TMA 1970, s 20B(9)–(13)*), and copies of, or of parts of, documents may similarly be produced in certain cases (see 9.8 BACK DUTY).

In the event of failure by a witness to attend in obedience to the summons, or refusal to be sworn or to affirm, or refusal to answer any lawful question or to produce a document he is required to produce by the summons, the Commissioners may summarily determine a penalty not exceeding £1,000, to be treated as tax charged by an assessment and due and payable. [*SI 1994 No 1812, reg 4*].

Joint hearings. The Commissioners have powers to direct that two or more proceedings, in one or more divisions, with common issues be heard at the same time or consecutively within one division, either of their own motion or on an application by any of the parties to any of those proceedings. All the parties must be notified, and are entitled to be heard before such a direction is given. On the giving of a direction, the Clerk must send notice of its date and terms to all parties. [*SI 1994 No 1812, reg 6*]. The Commissioners have an inherent power to deal with two or more appeals simultaneously where the appellants' affairs are so intermingled as to be incapable of separation, and where they are satisfied that it would result in no injustice to either party (*Johnson v Walden; King v Walden Ch D 1993, [1994] STC 124*).

Postponements and adjournments. The Commissioners may postpone or adjourn the hearing of any proceedings, the Clerk being responsible for notifying all parties of the place, date and time of the postponed or adjourned hearing (unless announced before an adjournment in the presence of all parties). Where a hearing is adjourned for the obtaining of further information or evidence, the Commissioners may direct the parties regarding the disclosure of such information or evidence prior to resumption. [*SI 1994 No 1812, reg 8*]. In *Packe v Johnson Ch D 1991, 63 TC 507*, a determination was quashed because of the Commissioners' refusal to consider all relevant information in deciding to refuse an adjournment at a second hearing.

Other matters in preparation for hearing. There are also regulations dealing with the agreement of documents [*reg 5*], the joinder of additional parties to the proceedings [*reg 7*] and the admission of expert evidence [*reg 9*].

Hearing and determination of proceedings. Hearings are in private, except that certain persons with official responsibilities may be present, and may remain present during, but not take part in, the Commissioners' deliberations. With the consent of the parties, the Commissioners may permit any other person to attend the hearing. [*SI 1994 No 1812, reg 13*].

Power to obtain information. The Commissioners may, at any time before final determination of the proceedings, serve on any party to the proceedings (other than the Revenue) notice requiring that party, within a specified time,

(i)   to deliver such particulars as may be required to determine any issue of the proceedings, and

(ii) to make available for inspection by the Commissioners or by an officer of the Board such specified or described books, accounts, etc. in his possession or power as may, in their opinion, contain information relevant to the proceedings.

The Commissioners may summarily determine a penalty (to be treated as tax charged in an assessment and due and payable) of up to £300 for failure to comply with such a notice, plus up to £60 per day for continuing failure after such a penalty is determined. Any officer of the Board (and the Commissioners in the case of (ii)) may, at all reasonable times, take copies of, or extracts from, any such particulars, books, etc.. [*SI 1994 No 1812, reg 10*].

4.8 Appeals

Representation at hearing. A party to the proceedings may be represented by any person, except that the Commissioners may, if satisfied that there are good and sufficient reasons for doing so, refuse to permit a party to be represented by a particular person, not being a legally qualified person or a member of an incorporated society of accountants. In practice, most bodies of Commissioners permit the taxpayer to be representated by any person who they are satisfied is competent to present the appellant's case. The Revenue may be represented by a barrister, advocate, solicitor or any officer of the Board. [*SI 1994 No 1812, reg 12*]. The Revenue representative is normally an inspector. The secretary or 'other proper officer' represents a company (the liquidator if in liquidation). [*TMA 1970, s 108*].

Failure to attend hearing. Where a party fails to attend or be represented at a hearing of which he has been duly notified, the Commissioners may postpone or adjourn a hearing or (unless satisfied that there is good and sufficient reason for such failure, and after considering any written or other representations) hear and determine the proceedings. [*SI 1994 No 1812, reg 14*]. Determinations in the absence of the taxpayer or his agent have been upheld where notice of the meeting was received by the appellant (*R v Tavistock Commrs (ex p Adams) QB 1969, 46 TC 154; R v Special Commr (ex p Moschi) CA, [1981] STC 465* and see *Fletcher & Fletcher v Harvey CA 1990, 63 TC 539*), but Commissioners were held to have acted unreasonably in refusing to re-open proceedings when the taxpayer's agent was temporarily absent when the appeal was called (*R & D McKerron Ltd CS 1979, 52 TC 28*). Where the taxpayer was absent through illness, a determination was quashed because the Commissioners, in refusing an adjournment, had failed to consider whether injustice would thereby arise to the taxpayer (*R v Sevenoaks Commrs (ex p Thorne) QB 1989, 62 TC 341* and see *Rose v Humbles CA 1971, 48 TC 103*). See also *R v O'Brien (ex p Lissner) QB, 1984 STI 710* where the determination was quashed when the appellant had been informed by the inspector that the hearing was to be adjourned.

Procedure and evidence at hearing. The Commissioners have wide discretion as to the manner in which the proceedings are conducted, and should seek to avoid inappropriate formality. They may require any witness to give evidence on oath or affirmation, and may admit evidence which would be inadmissible in a court of law. Evidence may be given orally or, if they so direct, by affidavit or statement recorded in a document (and they may, on their own motion or on the application of any party, at any stage require the personal attendance as a witness of the maker of such a statement or affidavit or the person who recorded the statement). They may take account of the nature and source of any evidence, and the manner in which it is given, in assessing its truth and weight. The parties may be heard in any order, but are entitled to give evidence, to call witnesses, to question witnesses (including other parties who give evidence), and to address the Commissioners both on the evidence and on the subject matter of the proceedings. [*SI 1994 No 1812, reg 15*]. A party to the proceedings cannot insist on being examined on oath (*R v Special Commrs (in re Fletcher) CA 1894, 3 TC 289*). False evidence under oath would be perjury under criminal law (*R v Hood Barrs CA, [1943] 1 All ER 665*). A taxpayer was held to be bound by an affidavit he had made in other proceedings (*Wicker v Fraser Ch D 1982, 55 TC 641*). A remission to Commissioners to hear evidence directed at the credit of a witness was refused in *Potts v CIR Ch D 1982, 56 TC 25*. Rules of the Supreme Court under which evidence can be obtained from a witness abroad cannot be used in proceedings before the Commissioners (*In re Leiserach CA 1963, 42 TC 1*). As to hearsay evidence under *Civil Evidence Act 1968*, see *Forth Investments Ltd Ch D 1976, 50 TC 617* and *Khan v Edwards Ch D 1977, 53 TC 597*.

The Commissioners are under no obligation to adjourn an appeal for the production of further evidence (*Hamilton v CIR CS 1930, 16 TC 28; Noble v Wilkinson Ch D 1958, 38 TC 135*), and were held not to have erred in law in determining assessments in the absence abroad of the taxpayer (*Hawkins v Fuller Ch D 1982, 56 TC 49*).

The taxpayer has no general right to conduct his appeal in writing without attending the hearing (*Banin v Mackinlay CA 1984, 58 TC 398*), although written pleadings may, at the Commissioners' discretion, be taken into account (*Caldicott v Varty Ch D 1976, 51 TC 403*).

In reaching their decision, the Commissioners may not take into account matters appropriate for application for judicial review (*Aspin v Estill CA 1987, 60 TC 549*). They do not generally have the power to review on appeal the exercise of a discretion conferred on the Revenue by statute (see *Slater v Richardson & Bottoms Ltd Ch D 1979, 53 TC 155; Kelsall v Investment Chartwork Ltd Ch D 1993, [1994] STC 33*).

For the extent to which Commissioners may use their local knowledge, see *Forest Side Properties (Chingford) Ltd v Pearce CA 1961, 39 TC 665*.

Onus of proof. The onus is on the appellant to displace an assessment (but see 9.2 BACK DUTY for onus on Crown to prove fraud or wilful default to support extended time limit assessments). See *Brady v Group Lotus Car Companies plc CA 1987, 60 TC 359* where the onus of proof remained with the taxpayer where the amount of normal time limit assessment indicated contention of fraud. The general principle emerges in appeals against estimated assessments in 'delay cases' (see 4.7 above) which are the bulk of appeals heard by the General Commissioners. For examples of cases in which the Commissioners have confirmed estimated assessments in the absence of evidence that they were excessive, see *T Haythornthwaite & Sons Ltd v Kelly CA 1927, 11 TC 657; Stoneleigh Products Ltd v Dodd CA 1948, 30 TC 1; Rosette Franks (King St) Ltd v Dick Ch D 1955, 36 TC 100; Pierson v Belcher Ch D 1959, 38 TC 387*. In a number of cases, the Courts have supported the Commissioners' action in rejecting unsatisfactory accounts (e.g. *Cain v Schofield Ch D 1953, 34 TC 362; Moll v CIR CS 1955, 36 TC 384; Cutmore v Leach Ch D 1981, 55 TC 602; Coy v Kime Ch D 1986, 59 TC 447*) or calling for certified accounts (e.g. *Stephenson v Waller KB 1927, 13 TC 318; Hunt & Co v Jolly KB 1928, 14 TC 165; Wall v Cooper CA 1929, 14 TC 552*). In *Anderson v CIR CS 1933, 18 TC 320*, the case was remitted where there was no evidence to support the figure arrived at by the Commissioners (which was between the accounts figure and the estimated figure assessed), but contrast *Bookey v Edwards Ch D 1981, 55 TC 486*. The Commissioners are entitled to look at each year separately, accepting the appellant's figures for some years but not all (*Donnelly v Platten CA(NI) 1980, [1981] STC 504*). Similarly, the onus is on the taxpayer to substantiate his claims to relief (see *Eke v Knight CA 1977, 51 TC 121; Talib v Waterson Ch D, [1980] STC 563*).

For the standard of proof required in evidence, see *Les Croupiers Casino Club v Pattinson CA 1987, 60 TC 196*.

The Commissioners' decision. The Revenue representative must not be present while the Commissioners are deliberating their decision unless the other party or parties (or their representative(s)) are also present (*R v Brixton Commrs KB 1912, 6 TC 195*). The Commissioners' determination was quashed where the Clerk had discussed the case with Revenue representatives between hearing and announcement of determination (*R v Wokingham Commrs (ex p Heron) QB, 1984 STI 710*).

4.8   Appeals

If it appears to the Commissioners that the appellant has been over- or under-charged by any assessment under appeal, they must reduce or increase that assessment accordingly, but otherwise the assessment stands good. A determination of gains assessable determines the appeal; if the Commissioners alter the assessment, they are not obliged to determine the revised tax payable. [*TMA 1970, s 50(6)–(8); SI 1994 No 1813*]. Only the assessment by which the taxpayer was overcharged may be reduced under *TMA 1970, s 50(6)*. Any decision is by a majority of the Commissioners hearing the proceedings, with the presiding Commissioner having a casting vote where necessary. The final determination may be announced orally at the end of the hearing or may be reserved. In either case, the Clerk to the Commissioners must send to each party a notice (including details of the procedure for appeals from the General Commissioners) setting out the determination, and unless the determination was given at the hearing, the date of such notice is the date of the determination. [*SI 1994 No 1812, reg 16*]. Where the Clerk announced the decision wrongly, it was held that the correct decision stood good (*R v Morleston & Litchurch Commrs KB 1951, 32 TC 335*) (and see below under *Miscellaneous: Irregularities*).

Where Commissioners determined appeals in principle and held a further hearing to adjust assessments, their action in refusing to admit further evidence for the taxpayer at the later hearing was upheld (*R v St Marylebone Commrs (ex p Hay) CA 1983, 57 TC 59*). They are entitled, however, to alter their decision in principle at a later hearing (*Larner v Warrington Ch D 1985, 58 TC 557*). See also *Gibson v Stroud Commrs Ch D 1989, 61 TC 645*.

A decision of the Commissioners is not legally binding on them or any other Commissioners in any other proceedings, even on appeal by the same taxpayer against a similar assessment for another year (*CIR v Sneath CA 1932, 17 TC 149* and cf. *Edwards v 'Old Bushmills' Distillery HL 1926, 10 TC 285; Abdul Caffoor Trustees PC 1961, 40 ATC 93*).

Review of the Commissioners' final determination. A decision of the Commissioners is generally final and conclusive [*TMA 1970, s 46(2)*], but the Commissioners may review and set aside or vary their final determination on the application of any party or of their own motion where they are satisfied that either

(1)   it was wrongly made as a result of administrative error, or

(2)   a party entitled to be heard failed to appear or be represented for good and sufficient reason, or

(3)   relevant information had been supplied to the Clerk or to the appropriate inspector or other Revenue officer prior to the hearing but was not received by the Commissioners until after the hearing.

A written application for such a review must be made to the Commissioners not later than 14 days after the date of the notice of the determination (or by such later time as the Commissioners may allow), stating the grounds in full. Where the Commissioners propose of their own motion to review a determination, they must serve notice on the parties not later than 14 days after the date of the notice of the determination.

The parties are entitled to be heard on any such review or proposed review. If practicable, the review is to be determined by the Commissioners who decided the case, and if they set aside the determination, they may substitute a different determination or order a rehearing before the same or different Commissioners.

A decision to vary or substitute a final determination is to be notified in the same way as the original determination (see above). [*SI 1994 No 1812, reg 17*].

See 4.10 below as regards application for judicial review where the Commissioners have acted unfairly or improperly.

Special procedure. *Proceedings relating to tax on chargeable gains.* Where material, the market value of an asset or the apportionment of an amount or value is, if so required by any party, to be recorded in the final determination. They may be proved in any proceedings relating to tax on chargeable gains by a certificate signed by the Clerk to the Commissioners (in certain cases the clerk or registrar of another tribunal), or by the inspector where the appeal was settled by agreement, stating the material particulars. [*SI 1994 No 1812, reg 18*].

Reference to other tribunals. Certain questions relating to the value of land or of an interest in land may be referred to the appropriate Lands Tribunal, and similarly in relation to unquoted shares to the Special Commissioners (see *TMA 1970, s 47*). The instant proceedings may be determined without awaiting the outcome of such referral. [*SI 1994 No 1812, reg 19*].

Miscellaneous. *Irregularities.* Any irregularity resulting from failure to comply with regulations or with any Commissioners' direction given before a final determination is reached, shall not, of itself, render the proceedings void, and before reaching that determination the Commissioners may, and if they consider that any person has been prejudiced by the irregularity must, give such direction as they think just to cure or waive any irregularity which comes to their attention. Clerical errors in any document recording a direction or decision of the Commissioners may be corrected by any of the Commissioners concerned (or by the Clerk if all the Commissioners have died or ceased to be Commissioners) by certificate under his hand. [*SI 1994 No 1812, reg 24*].

Notices must be in writing unless the Commissioners authorise them to be given orally. [*SI 1994 No 1812, reg 25*].

Service of any notice or document (other than a witness summons, see above) may be by post, by (legible) facsimile transmission etc. or by delivery at the proper address. [*SI 1994 No 1812, reg 26(1)*]. The persons and addresses to whom and which a document may be sent or delivered are set out in *reg 26(2)(3)*, and the provisions for substituted or waived service in certain cases in *reg 27*.

Penalties. Any appeal against summary penalties determined under regulations as above lies to the High Court (in Scotland, the Court of Session). [*TMA 1970, s 53; SI 1994 No 1813*].

(*b*)   **Special Commissioners**

The provisions applicable to the General Commissioners (see (*a*) above) apply equally to the Special Commissioners, with the following variations.

Constitution of Tribunal. Any one, two or three of the Special Commissioners may hear any proceedings. If two or three Commissioners are sitting, the Presiding Special Commissioner, or, if he is not sitting, the Commissioner nominated by him, shall preside at the hearing. With the consent of all parties, proceedings may be continued by any one or two of the Commissioners unless the Presiding Special Commissioner otherwise directs. [*SI 1994 No 1811, regs 2, 13*].

Preparation for hearing. *Listing and notice of hearing.* Before notifying the parties of the place, date and time of a hearing, the Clerk to the Commissioners must satisfy himself that the Special Commissioners have jurisdiction over the proceedings and that he has sufficient particulars for determination. The Presiding Special Commissioner may direct that such notifications are not to be sent. [*SI 1994 No 1811, reg 3*].

General power to give directions. The Commissioner(s) have wide direction-giving powers, on the application of any of the parties to proceedings or of their own motion. Applications by the parties (otherwise than during the hearing) must be in writing to the Clerk, and if not made with the consent of all the parties, must be served by the Clerk on any affected party, who may object. [*SI 1994 No 1811, reg 4*].

Witnesses. The maximum penalty which the Commissioner(s) may summarily determine for failure to attend or refusal to be sworn or affirm, to answer any lawful question or to produce documents as required is £10,000. [*SI 1994 No 1811, regs 5, 24(2)*].

Preliminary hearing. Where it appears to a Special Commissioner that any proceedings would be facilitated by holding a preliminary hearing, he may, on the application of a party or of his own motion, give directions for such a hearing to be held. The Clerk to the Special Commissioners must give to all the parties 14 days' notice (or such shorter time as the parties agree or the Commissioner sees fit to impose) of the time and place of the hearing. On a preliminary hearing, the Commissioner has wide direction-giving powers, and may, if the parties so agree, determine the proceedings without any further hearing. [*SI 1994 No 1811, reg 9*]. See below as regards powers of Commissioner to obtain information on preliminary hearing of any proceedings.

Hearing and determination of proceedings. *Hearings in public or private.* Hearings before the Special Commissioner(s) are in public, unless any party applies by notice to the Clerk for the hearing (or any part) to be in private. A Revenue application for a private hearing requires in addition a direction by a Special Commissioner. The rules for attendance at a private hearing follow those before the General Commissioners (as above). [*SI 1994 No 1811, reg 15*].

Power to obtain information. The powers of General Commissioners to obtain information apply to both a preliminary hearing before a Special Commissioner and to the hearing of the proceedings, except that the specific penalty provisions for failure to comply with a notice do not apply (although the general penalty for failure to comply with Commissioner's direction, see below, *does* apply). [*SI 1994 No 1811, regs 10, 24(1)*].

The Commissioners' decision. The recording of the Commissioner(s)' decision must contain a statement of the facts found and the reasons for the determination. After reserving the final determination, the Commissioner(s) may give a written decision in principle on one or more of the issues arising, and adjourn the making of the final determination until after that decision has been issued and any further questions arising from it have been agreed by the parties or decided by the Commissioner(s) after hearing the parties. A decision in principle must contain a statement of the facts and the reasons for the decision, and these need not be repeated in the document recording the final determination. [*SI 1994 No 1811, reg 18*].

Review of the Commissioners' decision in principle may proceed in the same way as a review of a final determination. [*SI 1994 No 1811, reg 19*].

Publication of decisions in principle or final determinations. The Presiding Special Commissioner may arrange for the publication of such reports of decisions in principle and final determinations as he considers appropriate. If the proceedings (or any part) were held in private, he must ensure that the report is in a form which, so far as possible, prevents the identification of any person whose affairs are dealt with. [*SI 1994 No 1811, reg 20*].

Orders for costs. The Commissioner(s) may make an order awarding costs (in Scotland expenses) of, or incidental to, the hearing of any proceedings against any party who has, in their opinion, acted wholly unreasonably in connection with the hearing, but not without giving that party the opportunity of making representations against the award. The award may be of all or part of the costs of the other party or parties, such costs to be taxed in the county court (in Scotland the sheriff court) if not agreed. In Northern Ireland, the Commissioners may determine the costs. [*SI 1994 No 1811, reg 21*].

Penalty for failure to comply with Commissioner(s)' direction. The Commissioner(s) may summarily determine a penalty of up to £10,000 for any such failure, to be treated as if it were tax charged in an assessment and due and payable. [*SI 1994 No 1811, reg 24(1)(3)*].

4.9   APPEALS TO THE HIGH COURT

Prior to the determination of an appeal by the Commissioners, the Court may be prepared to consider an application seeking a determination as to whether the Revenue may make use of certain 'tax-altering' provisions in relation to the assessments under appeal (*Balen v CIR Ch D 1976, 52 TC 406; Beecham Group plc v CIR Ch D, [1992] STC 935*).

Case stated procedure—General Commissioners. Within 30 days of the date of final determination of an appeal (or of the variation or substitution of such a determination, see above) any party dissatisfied with the determination as being erroneous in point of law (for which see e.g. *Billows v Robinson CA, [1991] STC 127*) may serve notice on the Clerk requiring the Commissioners to state and sign a case for the opinion of the High Court (in Scotland the Court of Session, in Northern Ireland the Court of Appeal (NI)), setting forth the facts and final determination of the Commissioners. See *Grainger v Singer KB 1927, 11 TC 704* as regards receipt of the case. The 30 day time limit for requesting a case does not apply to the payment of the fee (*Anson v Hill CA 1968, 47 ATC 143*). The Commissioners may serve notice on the person who required the stated case requiring him, within 28 days, to identify the question of law on which he requires the case to be stated. They may refuse to state a case until such notice is complied with, or if they are not satisfied that a question of law is involved, or if the requisite fee (see below) has not been paid. A requirement for a case to be stated becomes invalid if the determination to which it relates is set aside or varied. [*SI 1994 No 1812, regs 20, 23*].

A fee of £25 is payable to the Clerk by the person requiring the case before he is entitled to have it stated. [*TMA 1970, s 56(3); SI 1994 No 1813*]. A single case may have effect as regards each of a number of appeals heard together (*Getty Oil Co v Steele and related appeals Ch D 1990, 63 TC 376*).

If the taxpayer dies, his personal representatives stand in his shoes (*Smith v Williams KB 1921, 8 TC 321*).

Although the case stated procedure envisages the determination of the proceedings before the Commissioners, where an appeal has been decided in principle but there may be considerable delay in reaching figures for the formal determination, the Court will accept a case stated in principle (see e.g. *Rank Xerox Ltd v Lane HL 1979, 53 TC 185*).

The case stated procedure is not open to a successful party to an appeal (*Sharpey-Schafer v Venn Ch D 1955, 34 ATC 141*), but where another party requires a case, the successful party may invite the Commissioners to include in the case an additional question relating to another ground on which the Commissioners had found against it (*Gordon v CIR CS, [1991] STC 174*). In the case of a partnership, the procedure is available to any one of the partners, with or without the consent of the others (*Re Sutherland & Partners appeal CA, [1994] STC 387*).

Consideration of draft case. Within 56 days of receipt of a notice requiring a stated case (or of the Commissioners being satisfied as to the question of law involved), the Clerk must send a draft of the case to all the parties. Written representations thereon may be made to the Clerk by any party within 56 days after the draft case is sent out, with copies to all the other parties, and within a further 28 days further representations may similarly be made in response. Any party to whom copies of representations are not sent may apply to the Clerk for a copy. The validity of a case after it has been stated and signed (see below), and of any subsequent proceedings, is not affected by a failure to meet these time limits or by a failure to send copies of representations to all parties. [*SI 1994 No 1812, reg 21*].

An application for the taxpayer's name to be withheld was refused (*In re H Ch D 1964, 42 TC 14*) as was an application for the deletion of a passage possibly damaging the taxpayer (*Treharne v Guinness Exports Ltd Ch D 1967, 44 TC 161*). An application for judicial review on the ground that the case did not cover all matters in dispute was refused in *R v Special Commrs (ex p Napier) CA 1988, 61 TC 206*. In *Danquah v CIR Ch D 1990, 63 TC 526*, an application for the statement of a further case was refused where the case did not set out all the questions raised by the taxpayer in the originating motion by which he had sought an order directing the Commissioners to state a case. The proper course was for the taxpayer to apply for remission of the case for amendment under *TMA 1970, s 56(7)*. See also *Consolidated Goldfields plc v CIR Ch D 1990, 63 TC 333* (dealt with further below) in which a request to remit a case to the Commissioners for further findings of fact was refused.

Preparation and submission of final case. As soon as may be after the final date for representations (see above), the Commissioners, after taking into account any representations, must state and sign the case. In the event of the death of a Commissioner, or of his ceasing to be a Commissioner, the case is to be signed by the remaining Commissioner(s) or, if there are none, by the Clerk. The case is then sent by the Clerk to the person who required it to be stated, and the other parties notified accordingly.

In England, Wales and Scotland, the party requiring the case must transmit it to the High Court (in Scotland, the Court of Session) within 30 days of receiving it, and at or before the time he does so must notify each of the other parties that the case has been stated on his application and send them a copy of the case. The 30 day time limit (under the similar earlier provisions of *TMA 1970, s 56(4)*) is mandatory (*Valleybright Ltd (in liquidation) v Richardson Ch D 1984, 58 TC 290; Petch v Gurney CA, [1994] STC 689*), and may run from the date the case is received by the taxpayer's authorised agent (*Brassington v Guthrie Ch D 1991, [1992] STC 47*). The notification (and copy) to the other parties is required only to give 'adequate notice' of the appeal and not to be 'too long delayed' (*Hughes v Viner Ch D 1985, 58 TC 437*). In Northern Ireland, slightly different rules apply (and see *CIR v McGuckian CA(NI), [1994] STC 888*).

[*SI 1994 No 1812, regs 22, 23*].

The High Court (or Court of Session or Court of Appeal (NI)) hears and determines any question(s) of law arising on the case, and may reverse, affirm or amend the determination of the Commissioners, or may remit the matter to the Commissioners with the opinion of the Court thereon, or may make such other order as seems to it fit. It may also cause the case to be sent back for amendment. An appeal from the decision of the High

Court lies (in England and Wales) to the Court of Appeal and thence (with leave) to the House of Lords. In certain cases, 'leap-frog' appeals direct from the High Court to the House of Lords may be permitted under *Administration of Justice Act 1969, s 12* (see e.g. *Fitzleet Estates Ltd v Cherry HL 1977, 51 TC 708*). In the case of an appeal against a decision on an appeal against an assessment, tax must be paid in accordance with the Commissioners' decision. Following the decision on appeal, any tax overpaid is refunded with such interest as the Court may allow, and any amount undercharged is due and payable 30 days after the inspector issues a notice of the amount due. [*TMA 1970, s 56(6)–(9)*].

Once set down for hearing, a case cannot be declared a nullity (*Way v Underdown CA 1974, 49 TC 215*) or struck out under *Order 18, rule 19 of the Rules of the Supreme Court* (*Petch v Gurney CA, [1994] STC 689*), but the appellant may withdraw (*Hood Barrs v CIR (No 3) CA 1960, 39 TC 209*, but see *Bradshaw v Blunden (No 2) Ch D 1960, 39 TC 73*). Where the appellant was the inspector and the taxpayer did not wish to proceed, the Court refused to make an order on terms agreed between the parties (*Slaney v Kean Ch D 1969, 45 TC 415*).

The Court may, however, return a case for amendment. [*TMA 1970, s 56(7)*]. In *Consolidated Goldfields plc v CIR Ch D 1990, 63 TC 333*, the taxpayer company's request that the High Court remit a case to the Commissioners for further findings of fact was refused. Although the remedy was properly sought, it would only be granted if it could be shown that the desired findings were (*a*) material to some tenable argument, (*b*) reasonably open on the evidence adduced, and (*c*) not inconsistent with the findings already made. However, in *Fitzpatrick v CIR CS 1990, [1991] STC 34*, a case was remitted where the facts found proved or admitted, and the contentions of the parties, were not clearly set out, despite the taxpayer's request for various amendments and insertions to the case, and in *Whittles v Uniholdings Ltd Ch D, [1993] STC 671*, remission was appropriate in view of the widely differing interpretations which the parties sought to place on the Commissioners' decision (and the case was remitted a second time (see *[1993] STC 767*) to resolve misunderstandings as to the nature of a concession made by the Crown at the original hearing and apparent inconsistencies in the Commissioners' findings of fact). If a case is remitted, the taxpayer has the right to attend any further hearing by the Commissioners (*Lack v Doggett CA 1970, 46 TC 497*) but the Commissioners may not, in the absence of special circumstances, admit further evidence (*Archer-Shee v Baker CA 1928, 15 TC 1; Watson v Samson Bros Ch D 1959, 38 TC 346; Bradshaw v Blunden (No 2) Ch D 1960, 39 TC 73*), but see *Brady v Group Lotus Car Companies plc CA 1987, 60 TC 359* where the Court directed the Commissioners to admit further evidence where new facts had come to light suggesting the taxpayers had deliberately misled the Commissioners. Errors of fact in the case may be amended by agreement of the parties prior to hearing of the case (*Moore v Austin Ch D 1985, 59 TC 110*). See *Jeffries v Stevens Ch D 1982, 56 TC 134* as regards delay between statement of case and motion for remission.

A new question of law may be raised in the Courts on giving due notice to the other parties (*Muir v CIR CA 1966, 43 TC 367*) but the Courts will not admit evidence not in the stated case (*Watson v Samson Bros Ch D 1959, 38 TC 346; Cannon Industries Ltd v Edwards Ch D 1965, 42 TC 625; Frowd v Whalley Ch D 1965, 42 TC 599*, and see *R v Great Yarmouth Commrs (ex p Amis) QB 1960, 39 TC 143*).

Following the decision in *Pepper v Hart HL, [1992] STC 898*, the Courts are prepared to consider the parliamentary history of legislation, or the official reports of debates in Hansard, where all of the following conditions are met.

4.9 Appeals

(*a*) Legislation is ambiguous or obscure, or leads to an absurdity.

(*b*) The material relied upon consists of one or more statements by a Minister or other promotor of the Bill together if necessary with such other parliamentary material as is necessary to understand such statements and their effect.

(*c*) The statements relied upon are clear.

Any party intending to refer to an extract from Hansard in support of any argument must, unless otherwise directed, serve copies of the extract and a brief summary of the argument intended to be based upon the extract upon all parties and the court not less than five clear working days before the first day of the hearing (Supreme Court Practice Note, 20 December 1994) (*[1995] STI 98*).

Many Court decisions turn on whether the Commissioners' decision was one of fact supported by the evidence, and hence final. The Courts will not disturb a finding of fact if there was reasonable evidence for it, notwithstanding that the evidence might support a different conclusion of fact. The leading case is *Edwards v Bairstow & Harrison HL 1955, 36 TC 207*, in which the issue was whether there had been an adventure in the nature of trade. The Commissioners' decision was reversed on the ground that the *only* reasonable conclusion from the evidence was that there had been such an adventure. For a recent discussion of the application of this principle, see *Milnes v J Beam Group Ltd Ch D 1975, 50 TC 675*.

A Court decision is a binding precedent for itself or an inferior Court except that the House of Lords, while treating its former decisions as normally binding, may depart from a previous decision should it appear right to do so. For this see *Fitzleet Estates Ltd v Cherry HL 1977, 51 TC 708*. Scottish decisions are not binding on the High Court but are normally followed. Decisions of the Privy Council and of the Irish Courts turning on comparable legislation are treated with respect. A Court decision does not affect other assessments already final and conclusive (see 5.4 ASSESSMENTS) but may be followed, if relevant, in the determination of any open appeals against assessments and in assessments made subsequently irrespective of the years of assessment or taxpayers concerned (*Re Waring decd Ch D, [1948] 1 All ER 257; Gwyther v Boslymon Quarries Ltd KB 1950, 29 ATC 1; Bolands Ltd v CIR SC(I) 1925, 4 ATC 526*). Further, a Court decision does not estop the Crown from proceeding on a different basis for other years (*Hood Barrs v CIR (No 3) CA 1960, 39 TC 209*). A general change of practice consequent on a Court decision may affect error or mistake relief (see 12.4 CLAIMS).

For joinder of CIR in non-tax disputes, see *In re Vandervell's Trusts HL 1970, 46 TC 341*.

Special Commissioners. In the case of an appeal to the Special Commissioners, if the appellant or the Revenue is dissatisfied in point of law with a decision (whether in principle or on final determination) or with a decision varying or substituting such a decision, appeal may be made to the High Court. Further appeal may be made to the Court of Appeal and thence (with leave) to the House of Lords. A 'leap-frog' appeal to the Court of Appeal may be made if all the parties agree, the Commissioners certify that a point of law is involved relating wholly or mainly to the construction of an enactment which was fully argued and considered before them, and the leave of the Court of Appeal has been obtained. In Scotland appeals are to the Court of Session, in Northern Ireland to the Court of Appeal (NI), and thence in either case to the House of Lords. When a decision against which an appeal has been made is set aside or varied (see above), the appeal is treated as withdrawn.

In the case of an appeal against a decision on an appeal against an assessment, tax must be paid in accordance with the Commissioners' decision. Following the decision on appeal, any tax overpaid is refunded with such interest as the Court may allow, and any amount undercharged is due and payable 30 days after the inspector issues a notice of the amount due. [*TMA 1970, ss 56A, 58; SI 1994 No 1813*].

For the general statutory provisions and case law applicable equally to Special Commissioners, see above in relation to General Commissioners.

4.10   JUDICIAL REVIEW (PREROGATIVE ORDERS)

A taxpayer who is dissatisfied with the exercise of administrative powers may in certain circumstances (e.g. where the Revenue has exceeded or abused its powers or acted contrary to the rules of natural justice, or where the Appeal Commissioners have acted unfairly or improperly) seek a remedy in one of the prerogative orders of mandamus, prohibition and certiorari. This is now done by way of application for judicial review under *Supreme Court Act 1981, s 31* and *Order 53* of the *Rules of the Supreme Court*.

The issue on an application for leave to apply for judicial review is whether there is an arguable case (*R v CIR (ex p. Howmet Corporation and another) QB, [1994] STC 413*). The procedure is generally used where no other, adequate, remedy, such as a right of appeal, is available. See *R v Special Commr (ex p. Stipplechoice Ltd) (No 1) CA, [1985] STC 248* and *(No 3) QB 1988, 61 TC 391, R v HMIT (ex p. Kissane and Another) QB, [1986] STC 152* and *R v CIR (ex p. Goldberg) QB 1988, 61 TC 403*.

There is a very long line of cases in which the courts have consistently refused applications where a matter should have been pursued through the ordinary channels as described above. See, for example, *R v Special Commrs (ex p. Morey) CA 1972, 49 TC 71; R v Special Commrs (ex p. Emery) QB 1980, 53 TC 555; R v Walton General Commrs (ex p. Wilson) CA, [1983] STC 464; R v Special Commrs (ex p. Esslemont) CA, 1984 STI 312; R v Brentford General Commrs (ex p. Chan and Others) QB 1985, 57 TC 651; R v Special Commr (ex p. Napier) CA, [1988] STC 573*. See, however, *R v HMIT and Others (ex p. Lansing Bagnall Ltd) CA 1986, 61 TC 112* for a successful application where the inspector issued a notice under a discretionary power on the footing that there was an obligation to do so, and *R v CIR (ex p. J Rothschild Holdings plc) CA 1987, 61 TC 178* where the Revenue were required to produce internal documents of a general character relating to their practice in applying a statutory provision. See also *R v CIR (ex p. Taylor) (No 1) CA 1988, 62 TC 562* where an application for discovery of a document was held to be premature, and *R v Inspector of Taxes, Hull, ex p. Brumfield and others QB 1988, [1989] STC 151*, where the court was held to have jurisdiction to entertain an application for judicial review of a failure by the Revenue to apply an established practice not embodied in an extra-statutory concession (cf. *R v CIR (ex p. Fulford-Dobson) QB 1987, 60 TC 168* at 24.4 INLAND REVENUE: ADMINISTRATION, which see for 'care and management' powers of the Revenue). It was held that there had been no unfairness by the Revenue when it refused to assess on the basis of transactions that would have been entered into by the applicants had a Revenue Statement of Practice been published earlier (*R v CIR, ex p. Kaye QB, [1992] STC 581*). A similar view was taken in *R v CIR (ex p. S G Warburg & Co. Ltd) QB, [1994] STC 518* where the Revenue declined to apply a previously published practice because not only was it not clear that the taxpayer's circumstances fell within its terms but also the normal appeal procedures were available.

The first step is to obtain leave to apply for judicial review from the High Court. Application for leave is made ex parte to a single judge who will usually determine the application without a hearing. The Court will not grant leave unless the applicant has a sufficient interest in the matter to which the application relates. See *CIR v National Federation of Self-Employed and Small Businesses Ltd HL 1981, 55 TC 133* for what is meant by 'sufficient interest' and for discussion of availability of judicial review generally.

4.11 Appeals

Time limit. Applications must be made **within three months** of the date when the grounds for application arose. The Court has discretion to extend this time limit where there is good reason, subject to conditions, but is generally very reluctant to do so. Grant of leave for review does not amount to a ruling that application is made in good time (*R v Tavistock Commrs (ex p. Worth) QB 1985, 59 TC 116*).

4.11 COSTS

Costs may be awarded by the Courts in the usual way. In suitable cases, e.g. 'test cases', the Revenue may undertake to pay the taxpayer's costs. There is no provision for the award of costs of appearing before General Commissioners or, for hearings notified before 1 September 1994, Special Commissioners. Costs awarded by the Courts may include expenses connected with the drafting of the Stated Case (*Manchester Corporation v Sugden CA 1903, 4 TC 595*). Costs of a discontinued application for judicial review were refused where the Revenue were not informed of the application (*R v CIR (ex p. Opman International UK) QB 1985, 59 TC 352*). Law costs of appeals are not allowable for tax purposes generally (*Allen v Farquharson KB 1932, 17 TC 59; Smith's Potato Estates Ltd v Bolland HL 1948, 30 TC 267; Rushden Heel Co. v. Keene HL 1948, 30 TC 298; Spofforth & Prince v Golder KB 1945, 26 TC 310*).

See 4.8 above as regards costs of Special Commissioners' hearings notified after 31 August 1994.

5   Assessments

Cross-references. See 4 APPEALS; 9 BACK DUTY; 11 CHILDREN; 37.4 MARRIED PERSONS for assessments of gains of husband and wife on husband and election for separate assessment before 1990/91; 39.3 OVERSEAS MATTERS; 40.4 PARTNERSHIPS; 51 SELF-ASSESSMENT for future changes broadly from 1996/97; 56 UNDERWRITERS.

5.1   ASSESSMENTS

These are made by inspectors, or their delegates [*TMA 1970, s 113(1A)(1B)*] on the chargeable gains (less allowable losses) realised by the taxpayer in the year of assessment. Companies are assessed by reference to accounting periods as in 13.1 COMPANIES. Notices of assessment are served which must also state the date of issue and the time limit for making APPEALS (4). [*TMA 1970, s 29(1)(2)(5); F(No 2)A 1975, s 44(5)*]. The assessment must include a statement of the tax actually payable (*Hallamshire Industrial Finance Trust Ltd v CIR Ch D 1978, 53 TC 631*). A taxpayer may request the inspector (on Form 64-8 (New)) to provide a copy of any assessment to any agent (Revenue Press Release 18 December 1973). As the inspector will calculate the amount of the assessment from the return forms, and the assessment becomes binding if not appealed against within 30 days after the date of the notice of assessment [*TMA 1970, s 31; F(No 2) A 1975, s 67(1)*], it is most important that the taxpayer should make accurate RETURNS (49) and at once check any assessment received. If assessments are not dealt with promptly, INTEREST ON UNPAID TAX (32) may arise and APPEALS (4.4) may be out of time. The inspector's power of assessment is not limited to persons (or sources of income) within the area of his tax office (*R v Tavistock Commrs (ex p. Adams) (No 2) CA 1971, 48 TC 56*). See 4.5 APPEALS for jurisdiction of Commissioners on appeal.

In the absence of a satisfactory return the inspector may make an assessment to the best of his judgment. [*TMA 1970, s 29(1)(b)*]. As to this see *Blackpool Marton Rotary Club v Martin CA 1989, 62 TC 686, Phillimore v Heaton Ch D 1989, 61 TC 584* and *Van Boeckel v Customs & Excise Commissioners QB 1980, [1981] STC 290* (which related to the comparable value added tax provision of *VATA 1983, 7 Sch 4(1)*).

An assessment defective in form or containing errors may be validated by *TMA 1970, s 114(1)* but this provision does not extend to integral fundamental parts of the assessment such as the year of assessment for which it is made (*Baylis v Gregory HL 1988, 62 TC 1*). The courts may amend an assessment on appeal under *TMA 1970, s 56(6)* (*Pickles v Foulsham HL 1925, 9 TC 261; Bath & West Counties Property Trust Ltd v Thomas Ch D 1977, 52 TC 20*). For cases where it is sought to make an assessment out of time (see 5.5 below) by virtue of the taxpayer's fraudulent or negligent conduct etc., see 9.4 BACK DUTY. [*TMA 1970, s 41*].

Following the introduction of the 'Pay and File' system of corporation tax returns and payments (see Tolley's Corporation Tax under Returns for a synopsis) for accounting periods ending after 30 September 1993, corporation tax assessments (including those charging corporation tax on chargeable gains) will in general be issued in agreed figures, as they will still be needed to finalise the position (unless no liability arises). Subject to this, the power of the inspector to make an assessment (e.g. where there is no return made by a company or he is dissatisfied with its return, there is a dispute which he or the company wishes to take to appeal or he makes a 'discovery' as in 5.2 below) is broadly unaffected save that revised assessing procedures apply in relation to determinations of claims for trading losses, capital allowances and group relief. See Tolley's Corporation Tax under Capital Allowances, Groups of Companies and Losses.

5.2 Assessments

5.2 DISCOVERY

If an inspector or the Board 'discovers' that insufficient gains have been assessed, insufficient tax assessed or excessive relief has been given, a corrective assessment can be made. [*TMA 1970, s 29(3)*]. The existence of an assessment under appeal capable of being increased and determined in the correct amount does not preclude the making of a further assessment and the consequent determination of both the original and further assessment (*Duchy Maternity Ltd v Hodgson Ch D 1985, 59 TC 85*). 'Discovery' has been given a very wide meaning by the courts. There is a discovery by the inspector if he comes to the honest conclusion that there has been under-assessment (*R v St Giles & St George Commrs (ex p. Hooper) KB 1915, 7 TC 59*). It has been established in a number of cases that a change of opinion or rectification of an error by the Revenue, including an arithmetical error in calculating the tax, without the ascertainment of any new fact amounts to discovery and this is so notwithstanding that the taxpayer had been notified of the former opinion. However, *if in the determination of an appeal (including a determination by agreement under TMA 1970, s 54)* (see 4.6 APPEALS) a specific matter has been adjudicated upon or agreed, the Revenue cannot re-open the matter by making a further assessment (*Cenlon Finance Co Ltd v Ellwood HL 1962, 40 TC 176*). The matter must have been dealt with specifically or clearly have been raised by implication, so that an inspector of average experience must have appreciated it was being raised (*Scorer v Olin Energy Systems Ltd HL 1985, 58 TC 592*). A further assessment may be made on incomplete information supplied on behalf of the taxpayer (*Gray v Matheson Ch D, [1993] STC 178*) and successive further assessments are permissible.

For other cases concerning discovery, see Tolley's Income Tax above and/or Tolley's Tax Cases below.

The Revenue have issued a Statement of Practice (SP 8/91) setting out their view of the application in practice of the case law outlined above. The following are listed as circumstances in which there are clearly no grounds for *not* making discovery assessments:

(*a*)   profits, gains or income have not earlier been charged to tax because of any form of fraudulent or negligent conduct;

(*b*)   the inspector has been misled or misinformed in any way about the particular matter at issue;

(*c*)   there is an arithmetical error in a computation which had not been spotted at the time agreement was reached, and which can be corrected by the making of an in date discovery assessment;

(*d*)   an error is made in accounts and computations which it cannot be reasonably alleged was correct or intended, e.g. the double deduction from a capital gains tax computation of a particular item (say, retirement relief).

The Statement of Practice also makes it clear that, by concession, the principles determining the making of a further assessment following settlement of an appeal by agreement will also be applied where agreement is reached prior to the issue of an assessment. Also by concession, whether or not there has been an appeal, a discovery assessment will not be made where, although the matter in question may not have been the subject of a specific agreement within the case law principles outlined above, the inspector's decision was based on full and accurate disclosure and was a tenable view, so that the taxpayer could have reasonably believed the inspector's decision to be correct (Revenue Statement of Practice SP 8/91, 26 July 1991).

See 12.2 CLAIMS for extended time limits for claims where fraudulent or negligent conduct is not involved.

5.3 DOUBLE ASSESSMENT

Where there has been 'double assessment' for the same cause and for the same chargeable period, a claim may be made to the Board for the assessment reflecting the overcharge to be vacated. An appeal on a claim may be made to the Commissioners having jurisdiction to hear an appeal against the assessment, or the later of the assessments, to which the claim relates. [*TMA 1970, s 32*]. See 12.4 CLAIMS for error or mistake relief and 30.1 INTERACTION WITH OTHER TAXES as regards alternative income tax and capital gains tax assessments.

5.4 FINALITY OF ASSESSMENTS

An assessment cannot be altered after the notice has been served except in accordance with the express provisions of the *Taxes Acts* [*TMA 1970, s 29(6)*], e.g. where the taxpayer appeals (see 4 APPEALS). Where over-assessment results from an *error or mistake* in a return, see 12 CLAIMS. An assessment as determined on appeal or not appealed against is final and conclusive.

5.5 TIME LIMITS

An assessment or additional assessment cannot be made later than six years from the end of the tax year to which it relates (or accounting period in the case of a company) [*TMA 1970, s 34*] except in cases of fraudulent or negligent conduct (for 1982/83 and earlier years, cases of fraud, wilful default, or neglect) or where there is specific statutory provision for later assessment. Assessments on personal representatives in respect of the deceased's chargeable gains before death must be made within three years after the end of the tax year in which death occurred and those arising from the fraudulent or negligent conduct (or fraud, wilful default, or neglect) of the deceased are restricted to years of assessment ending not earlier than six years before the death. [*TMA 1970, s 40; FA 1989, s 149(4)*]. In certain cases, specific provisions extend these time limits. See also 9.4 and 9.5 BACK DUTY; 41.10 and 41.12 PAYMENT OF TAX; 54 TIME LIMITS—5 APRIL 1996; 55 TIME LIMITS—MISCELLANEOUS and 56.1 and 56.5 UNDERWRITERS.

An assessment is made on the date on which the inspector authorised to make it signs a certificate in the appropriate assessments volume that he made certain assessments including the assessment in question (*Honig v Sarsfield CA 1986, 59 TC 337*).

5.6 TRUSTEES AND PERSONAL REPRESENTATIVES

Trustees and personal representatives are assessed and charged in the name of any one or more of them in respect of disposals etc. made by them, but if an assessment is raised otherwise than on all of them, any person who is not resident or ordinarily resident in the UK may not be included. Unless the assets are held by the trustees or personal representatives as nominees or bare trustees for another person absolutely (see 52.2 SETTLEMENTS), chargeable gains accruing to, and capital gains tax chargeable on, the trustees or personal representatives are not to be regarded as accruing to, or chargeable on, any other person. No trustee or personal representative is to be regarded as an individual for the purposes of the capital gains tax legislation. [*TCGA 1992, s 65*]. See also 52.3 SETTLEMENTS.

5.7 NON-CORPORATE BODIES, PERSONAL REPRESENTATIVES AND RECEIVERS

Assessments may be made on the treasurer etc. of bodies which are not corporations; on personal representatives in respect of disposals made *by the deceased person* (cf. 5.6 above); and receivers appointed by a court. [*TMA 1970, ss 71, 74, 75, 77*].

6 Assets

Cross-references. See 7 ASSETS HELD ON 6 APRIL 1965; 8 ASSETS HELD ON 31 MARCH 1982; 18 EXEMPTIONS AND RELIEFS for assets exempt from capital gains tax; 19 FURNISHED HOLIDAY ACCOMMODATION; 21 GOVERNMENT SECURITIES; 33 LAND; 35.8 LOSSES for assets of negligible value; 38 MINERAL ROYALTIES; 43 PRIVATE RESIDENCES; 44 QUALIFYING CORPORATE BONDS; 53 SHARES AND SECURITIES; 57 UNIT AND INVESTMENT TRUSTS; 59 WASTING ASSETS.

6.1   Capital gains tax is charged in respect of chargeable gains accruing to a person on the disposal of 'assets'. [*TCGA 1992, s 1(1)*].

'Assets' comprise all forms of property, wherever situated, including incorporeal property (goodwill, options, debts, etc.), currency other than sterling, and any form of property created by the disposer, or otherwise coming to be owned without being acquired. [*TCGA 1992, s 21(1)*]. Sovereigns minted after 1837 are still sterling currency and as such are not within this definition.

For the treatment of currency other than sterling when disposed of by a 'qualifying company' in certain circumstances, see 18.5 and 18.8 EXEMPTIONS AND RELIEFS.

There is no general principle that assets must have a market value or that they must be transferable or assignable (*O'Brien v Benson's Hosiery (Holdings) Ltd HL 1979, 53 TC 241*). A right to share in a statutory fund for compensation to owners of expropriated foreign property is a form of property and therefore an asset (*Davenport v Chilver Ch D 1983, 57 TC 661*). (To a great extent this decision was superseded by Revenue Press Release 19 December 1994 (see 16.7 below)). Tax is only chargeable in relation to an asset which existed at the time of disposal and not to an asset coming into existence only on a disposal which created it. 'Property' has the meaning of that which is capable of being owned in a normal legal sense and thus does not extend to include the right of freedom to trade and compete in the market place, but such a right must be distinguished from the goodwill in respect of the trade in question and which is an asset for capital gains tax purposes (*Kirby v Thorn EMI plc CA 1987, 60 TC 519*). The right to unquantified and contingent future consideration on the disposal of an asset is itself an asset (*Marren v Ingles HL 1980, 54 TC 76*).

The right to bring an action to enforce a bona fide claim, and which can be turned to account by negotiating a compromise yielding a capital sum, constitutes an asset. Such a right is acquired otherwise than by way of a bargain made at arm's length and at the time when the cause of action arises. Any capital sum received derives only from the right and not from other assets which may have been associated with the existence of the right (*Zim Properties Ltd v Proctor Ch D 1984, 58 TC 371*). However, by concession the Revenue now treat damages and compensation payments as derived from any underlying asset (and therefore exempt or taxable like that asset), and as exempt if there is no underlying asset. Entitlement to other reliefs is also determined on this basis, and the Revenue are prepared to consider extending time limits for claims where there has been a delay in obtaining compensation (Revenue Pamphlet IR 1 D 33).

See also 16.7 DISPOSAL regarding capital sums derived from assets.

6.2   **LOCATION OF ASSETS ('SITUS')**

Where liability depends on where the assets are actually situated (e.g. a non-resident trading in the UK or individuals not domiciled here, see 39 OVERSEAS MATTERS) the following provisions apply to determine the location of assets.

(a)   The situation of rights or interests (otherwise than by way of security) in or over *immovable property* is that of the immovable property.

(b)   Subject to the following provisions, the situation of rights or interests (otherwise than by way of security) in or over *tangible movable property* is that of the tangible movable property.

(c)   Subject to the following provisions, *a debt*, secured or unsecured, is situated in the UK if, and only if, the creditor is resident in the UK.

(d)   *Shares or securities issued by any municipal or governmental authority*, or by any body created by such an authority, are situated in the country of that authority.

(e)   Subject to paragraph (d) above, *registered shares or securities* are situated where they are registered and, if registered in more than one register, where the principal register is situated.

(f)   A *ship or aircraft* is situated in the UK if, and only if, the owner is then resident in the UK, and an interest or right in or over a ship or aircraft is situated in the UK if, and only if, the person entitled to the interest or right is resident in the UK.

(g)   The situation of *goodwill* as a trade, business or professional asset is at the place where the trade, business or profession is carried on.

(h)   *Patents, trade-marks and registered designs* are situated where they are registered, and if registered in more than one register, where each register is situated, and rights and licences to use a patent, trade-mark or registered design are situated in the UK if they, or any rights derived from them, are exercisable in the UK.

(j)   *Copyright, design right and franchises*, and rights or licences to use any copyright work or design in which design right subsists, are situated in the UK if they or any right derived from them are exercisable in the UK.

(k)   A *judgment debt* is situated where the judgment is recorded.

(l)   A *non-sterling debt owed by a bank* and represented by a sum standing to the credit of an individual not domiciled in the UK is situated in the UK if, and only if, that individual is resident in the UK and the branch or other place of business of the bank where the account is maintained is itself situated in the UK.

[*TCGA 1992, s 275; Trade Marks Act 1994, 5 Sch*].

Under the general law, *bearer shares and securities* transferable by delivery are situated where the certificate, etc. is kept. (*Winans v A-G (No 2) HL, [1910] AC 27*).

See also *Standard Chartered Bank Ltd v CIR Ch D, [1978] STC 272* where share certificates lodged in the UK by a person who was resident and domiciled abroad were held to be situated abroad, being registered in South Africa and effectively transferable only in that country. Renounceable letters of allotment of registered shares in a company are documents evidencing rights against the company and are only enforceable (and thus situated) where the register is kept. (*Young and Another v Phillips Ch D 1984, 58 TC 232*).

Securities issued by designated European Communities or international organisations (e.g. The Asian Development Bank, The African Development Bank and The European Bank for Reconstruction and Development) or the European Investment Bank are taken for the purposes of capital gains tax to be situated outside the UK. Organisations are designated by Treasury order. [*TCGA 1992, s 265*]. A similar treatment applies to securities issued by the Inter-American Development Bank [*TCGA 1992, s 266*] and by the OECD Support Fund [*OECD Support Fund Act 1975, s 4*].

6.3 Assets

6.3 APPROPRIATIONS TO AND FROM TRADING STOCK

Where an asset acquired by a person otherwise than as trading stock is appropriated by him for the purposes of his trade as trading stock (whether on the commencement of the trade or otherwise) and a chargeable gain or allowable loss would have accrued to him if he had then sold the asset for its market value, he is treated as having then disposed of the asset at its then market value. Where the asset is appropriated for the purposes of a trade chargeable to income tax under Schedule D, Case I, the person may alternatively elect (under *TCGA 1992, s 161(3)*) that, in computing the assessable profits of the trade, the market value of the asset is reduced by the amount of the chargeable gain or increased by the allowable loss that would otherwise arise (i.e. he may treat the gain or loss as subject to income tax rather than capital gains tax). A partner must have the agreement of all his co-partners to make the election effective. [*TCGA 1992, s 161(1)(3)(4)*].

Prior to the commencement of *TCGA 1992*, an election was made under *CGTA 1979, s 122(3)*.

Where an asset forming part of a person's trading stock is

(*a*)   appropriated by him for any other purpose, or

(*b*)   retained by him on his ceasing to carry on the trade,

he is treated as having acquired it at the time for a consideration equal to the amount brought into the accounts of the trade for tax purposes. [*TCGA 1992, s 161(2)*]. For the valuation of trading stock in such circumstances, see Tolley's Income Tax under Schedule D, Cases I and II.

See 13.9 COMPANIES for appropriations of gilt-edged securities and qualifying corporate bonds and see also 13.12 COMPANIES for intra-group transfers of assets which are trading stock of one of the companies but not of the other and for acquisition 'as trading stock' generally.

See 33.4 LAND for deemed appropriation as trading stock where transactions in land are within *ICTA 1988, s 776(2)(c)*.

See 23.2 INDEXATION for transitional relief for 1993/94 and 1994/95 in respect of 'indexation losses' referable to appropriations to trading stock in the case of individuals and trustees of settlements made before 30 November 1993.

6.4 KNOW-HOW

Consideration for a disposal of know-how used in a trade which continues to be carried on by the disposer after the disposal is treated, for all purposes, as a trading receipt unless

(i)   the consideration is otherwise chargeable as a revenue or income receipt; or

(ii)   the buyer is a body of persons (this term, here and in (iii) and (iv) below, includes a partnership), exercising control over the seller; or

(iii)   the seller is a body of persons exercising control over the buyer; or

(iv)   the buyer and seller are bodies of persons together controlled by a third person.

Where a person disposes of know-how in connection with the disposal of part or the whole of the trade in which it was used, any consideration for the know-how is treated as a payment for goodwill. These provisions do not apply to

(*a*)   both parties where a written joint election is made within two years of the disposal; or (*b*)   the acquirer only where the trade concerned was, before the acquisition, carried on wholly outside the UK.

If the consideration is, under (*a*) or (*b*), not regarded as a payment for goodwill, the acquirer is treated, for the purpose of claiming writing-down allowances, as if he had acquired the know-how for use in a trade previously carried on by him. However, the exclusion at (*a*) or (*b*) does not apply where any of (ii)-(iv) above applies.

Where consideration for the disposal of know-how is not taxed as a deemed trading receipt, or otherwise as an income or revenue receipt, or as a payment for goodwill, it is taxed under Schedule D, Case VI unless any one of (ii)-(iv) above applies. The consideration received is subject to the deduction of expenditure wholly and exclusively incurred in the acquisition or disposal of the know-how concerned. [*ICTA 1988, ss 530, 531*].

6.5   **PATENTS**

Capital sums received from the sale of patent rights are specifically taxable as income under Schedule D, Case VI. See Tolley's Income Tax under Patents. [*ICTA 1988, s 524*].

7   Assets held on 6 April 1965

Cross-reference. See 8 ASSETS HELD ON 31 MARCH 1982 for the restricted circumstances in which disposals after 5 April 1988 of such assets will be assessed by reference to the provisions of this chapter.

7.1   Assets held on 6 April 1965 (the original base date for the purposes of capital gains tax) are still subject to special provisions contained in *TCGA 1992, s 35(9), 2 Sch* and for this purpose may be divided into three categories.

(i)   Quoted securities (see 7.2-7.7 below).

(ii)   Land subsequently disposed of at a price including development value (see 7.8 below).

(iii)   Other assets and miscellaneous aspects (see 7.9-7.14 below).

Married persons. The provisions relating to assets held on 6 April 1965 apply in relation to the disposal of an asset by one spouse, and who acquired it from the other spouse in a year of assessment when they were living together, as if the other's acquisition or provision of the asset had been the acquisition etc. of the asset by the spouse making the disposal. [*TCGA 1992, 2 Sch 22*].

Groups of companies. The provisions relating to assets held on 6 April 1965 apply in relation to the disposal of an asset by a company which is or has been a member of a group of companies (within 13.10 COMPANIES), and which acquired the asset from another member of the group at the time when both were members of the group, as if all members of the group for the time being were the same person, and as if the acquisition or provision of the asset by the group, taken as a single person, had been the acquisition or provision of it by the member disposing of it. *After 31 March 1980*, this does not apply where the disposing company is an investment trust or acquired the asset after that date from an investment trust. [*TCGA 1992, s 174(4)(5)*].

7.2   **QUOTED SECURITIES: GENERAL RULES**

The provisions apply to 'quoted securities', namely

(i)   Shares and securities which on 6 April 1965, or at any time within six years prior to that date, had quoted market values on a 'recognised stock exchange' in the UK or elsewhere.

(ii)   Interests in unit trusts (see 57 UNIT AND INVESTMENT TRUSTS), the prices of which are published regularly by the scheme's managers.

Shares or securities issued to an employee on terms restricting his right to dispose of them are excluded. [*TCGA 1992, 2 Sch 1*].

'Recognised stock exchange' means, for disposals after 13 March 1989 (and, in practice, previously), The Stock Exchange and any other overseas stock exchange designated by an order of the Board under *ICTA 1988, s 841*. [*TCGA 1992, s 288(4)*].

Subject to the election in 7.3 below, on a disposal of such assets after 5 April 1965, computation of the gain or loss accruing is made

(*a*)   by reference to allowable expenditure computed according to the normal rules (i.e. cost/value at the *actual* date of acquisition and other allowable expenditure) (see 16.3 DISPOSAL), *and* (*b*)   by reference to allowable expenditure, etc. calculated according to identical rules, except that market value at 6 April 1965 is treated as the acquisition cost. Market value at 6 April 1965 (except where special circumstances may affect the value, see *Hinchcliffe v Crabtree HL 1971, 47 TC 419*) is the greater of

  (i)   a price half-way between the prices quoted in The Stock Exchange Daily Official List (or, for unit trusts, those published by the managers) and

  (ii)   for shares and securities, the average of the highest and lowest prices for normal bargains, if any, on that day.

Of the computations under (*a*) and (*b*), the one which prevails is that which produces (after, if available, any indexation allowance) the smaller gain or the smaller loss. But if one computation produces a gain and the other a loss, the disposal is treated as giving rise to neither a chargeable gain nor an allowable loss. [*TCGA 1992, 2 Sch 2(1), 11 Sch 6*].

Where the original cost of the shares is not known and no election (see 7.3 below) has been made, it is the Revenue's practice to compute gains by reference to the value of the shares at 6 April 1965 and to disallow losses (computed on the same basis) altogether.

The inspector will on request, give details of the market value of quoted shares and securities held on 6 April 1965 (adjusted for bonus and rights issues, etc).

7.3 **Elections.** The taxpayer (or his personal representatives) may, however, elect (under *TCGA 1992, 2 Sch 4*) that in respect of *all* disposals after 19 March 1968 (including those made before the election) of

(*a*)   fixed interest securities and preference shares, or

(*b*)   other quoted securities etc., or

(*c*)   both kinds of securities etc. under (*a*) and (*b*),

their actual cost be ignored and computations made by reference to their market value at 6 April 1965 only. The election, which is irrevocable, must be made, by notice in writing, within two years after the end of the year of assessment or accounting period in which the first post-19 March 1968 disposal (the 'first relevant disposal') is made of shares or securities of the kind covered by the election or within such further time as the Board allow.

Prior to the commencement of *TCGA 1992*, elections were made under *CGTA 1979, 5 Sch 4*.

After 5 April 1985 (31 March 1985 for companies), another opportunity is available for an election to be made where the time limit given above has expired by reference to the first relevant disposal after 19 March 1968. The time limit is extended so as to apply by reference to the first relevant disposal after 5 April 1985 (31 March 1985 for companies).

'*Fixed interest security*' is as defined in 53.10 SHARES AND SECURITIES.

'*Preference share*' means any share the holder of which has a right to a dividend at a fixed rate but no other right to share in the profits of the company. Fixed rate dividends include those payable before 6 April 1973 and which varied at a rate fluctuating in accordance with the standard rate of income tax.

Married persons. An election does not cover quoted securities which the holder acquired from his spouse on a disposal after 19 March 1968 (or, again, after 31 March 1985) but such securities continue to be covered by an election which the transferor may have

7.3 Assets held on 6 April 1965

made. Where it is necessary to identify securities disposed of, earliest acquisitions are deemed to be disposed of first.

Example

H acquired 3,000 U plc ordinary shares in 1962 for £15,000. Their market value was £10 per share on 6 April 1965 and £12 per share on 31 March 1982. In September 1995, H sells 2,000 of the shares for £25 per share. The indexation factor for March 1982 to September 1995 is assumed to be 0.860.

	£	£	£
Sale proceeds	50,000	50,000	50,000
Cost	10,000		
6 April 1965 value		20,000	
31 March 1982 value			24,000
Unindexed gain	40,000	30,000	26,000
Indexation allowance			
£24,000 × 0.860	20,640	20,640	20,640
Indexed gain	£19,360	£9,360	£5,360
Chargeable gain			£5,360

Notes to the example

(1)   The comparison is firstly between the gain arrived at by deducting cost and that arrived at by deducting 6 April 1965 value. The smaller of the two gains is taken. If, however, an election had been made under either *TCGA 1992, 2 Sch 4* or *TCGA 1992, s 109(4)* for 6 April 1965 value to be used in computing all gains and losses on quoted shares held at that date, this comparison need not be made and the taxable gain, subject to (*b*) below, would be £9,360.

(2)   The second comparison is between the figure arrived at in (*a*) above and the gain using 31 March 1982 value. As the latter is smaller, it is substituted for the figure in (*a*) above by virtue of *TCGA 1992, s 35(2)*. If, however, an election had been made under *TCGA 1992, s 35(5)* for 31 March 1982 value to be used in computing all gains and losses on assets held at that date, neither this comparison nor that in (*a*) above need be made and the taxable gain would still be £5,360.

(3)   Indexation is based on 31 March 1982 value in all three calculations as this gives the greater allowance.

(4)   All comparisons are between gains *after* indexation.

Groups of companies. An election does not cover quoted securities which a company acquired from another group company (see 13.10 COMPANIES) on a disposal after 19 March 1968 (or, again, after 31 March 1985) but such securities continue to be covered by an election which the transferor company may have made. Where it is necessary to identify securities disposed of, earliest acquisitions are deemed to be disposed of first. An election by a company which is at the 'relevant time' the principal company of the group has effect as an election by any other company which at that time is a member of the group. No election may be made by any other company which is a member of the group at that time. The *'relevant time'* is the first occasion after 19 March 1968 (or, again, after 31 March 1985) when any company which is then a member of the group disposes of quoted securities of a kind covered by the election. These provisions apply notwithstanding that a company ceases to be a member of the group at any time after the relevant time. They do not apply to securities owned by a company which, after 19 March 1968 (or, again, after 31 March 1985) and before the relevant time, was not a member of the group and in relation to which either an election was made or no election was made within the time limit following a disposal. [*TCGA 1992, s 109(4)(5), 2 Sch 3, 4(1)(2)(8) – (13), 5, 8*].

Partnerships. Each partner has a separate right of election for his share of partnership securities as well as for his personal holding. The time limit for making the election runs from the earlier of

(i)   the first relevant disposal of shares or securities by the partnership; and

(ii)   the first reduction of the particular partner's share in the partnership assets after 19 March 1968 (or, again, after 31 March 1985).

(29.D12 INLAND REVENUE STATEMENTS OF PRACTICE).

Underwriters. An election does not apply to quoted securities comprised in an underwriter's premiums trust fund, premiums trust fund deposits or personal reserves, being securities comprised in funds to which *TCGA 1992, s 206* applies. [*TCGA 1992, 2 Sch 7*]. As *TCGA 1992, s 206(1)*, which mentions *all* trust funds required or authorised by Lloyd's, was repealed after 1991/92 by *FA 1993, 23 Sch Pt III*, this provision, already defunct for practical purposes, would appear otiose after 1991/92.

7.4   **QUOTED SECURITIES: IDENTIFICATION RULES**

Where quoted securities of the same class are held on 6 April 1965, the identification rules for matching acquisitions with disposals depend on whether an election for 6 April 1965 market values under 7.3 above has been made or not. In addition, the rules are further governed by the general and special identification rules for securities etc. applying under the indexation provisions. Consequently this paragraph (dealing with the situation on or after the '1985 date') and 7.5 below (covering the period before the '1985 date' but on or after the '1982 date') should be read with the general rules at 23.9-23.16 INDEXATION. The position before the '1982 date' is dealt with at 7.6 below. For the position where there has been a reorganisation or exchange etc. of quoted securities following an election under 7.3(*a*) or (*b*) but not both, see 7.7 below.

After the '1985 date', the identification rules given in (*a*) or (*b*) below apply to quoted securities held on 6 April 1965 but excluding any 'relevant securities' so held. The full definition of 'relevant securities' is given at 23.12 INDEXATION. So far as concerns quoted securities held on 6 April 1965, this definition is only relevant to securities within the accrued income provisions (bondwashing) of *ICTA 1988, ss 710-728* (broadly any government, public authority, or company loan stock). The identification rules for such bondwashing securities are given separately at (A) and (B) below. GOVERNMENT SECURITIES (21) retain their own identification rules for disposals before 2 July 1986, being exempt for disposals on or after that date.

(*a*)   Where *no* election has been made, pre-7 April 1965 acquisitions are treated as disposed of on a 'last-in, first-out' basis and only identified with disposals after all post-6 April 1965 acquisitions have been identified under the general identification rules. See 23.9-23.11 INDEXATION. Such acquisitions comprise

(i)   the '1982 holding' i.e. acquisitions before the '1982 date' as they exist immediately before the '1985 date'; and

(ii)   any 'new holding' i.e. acquisitions on or after the '1982 date' as, where relevant, they exist immediately before the '1985 date'.

A holding within (ii) is treated as disposed of before a holding within (i).

7.5   Assets held on 6 April 1965

(*b*)   Where an election *is* made, pre-7 April 1965 acquisitions (at 6 April 1965 market values) form part, or the whole, of the '1982 holding' which is treated as a single asset (but one which cannot grow by further acquisitions). See 23.11 INDEXATION. Disposals are only identified with the '1982 holding' after all of any 'new holding' has been previously identified.

The '*1985 date*' is 6 April 1985 (1 April 1985 for companies). Similarly the '*1982 date*' should be read as 6 April 1982 (1 April 1982 for companies) although the legislation does not specifically use the latter definition.

Accrued income provisions. For securities within the accrued income provisions (other than government securities) the identification rules in (A) or (B) below apply.

(A)   Where *no* election has been made disposals are identified in the following order

    (i)   on a 'first-in, first-out' basis with acquisitions made within the twelve months preceding the disposal;

    (ii)   on a 'last-in, first-out' basis with other acquisitions made on or after the '1982 date';

    (iii)   with the '1982 holding' (see (*a*)(i) above); and

    (iv)   on a 'last-in, first-out' basis with pre-7 April 1965 acquisitions.

(B)   Where an election *is* made disposals are identified in the order of (A)(i)-(iii) above but (iv) is not required as pre-7 April 1965 acquisitions will form all or part of the '1982 holding' as at (*b*) above.

[*TCGA 1992, ss 104(3), 105, 108, 2 Sch 2(2), 3, 4(3)–(7)*].

For disposal consideration and allowable expenditure applicable to securities subject to the accrued income provisions, see 53.19 SHARES AND SECURITIES. For indexation provisions applicable, see 23.1 INDEXATION.

7.5   **Position on or after the 1982 date but before the 1985 date.** The identification rules given in (*a*) or (*b*) below applied to quoted securities held on 6 April 1965 (but not GOVERNMENT SECURITIES (21)) and are subject to the general rules at 23.13-23.16 INDEXATION.

(*a*)   Where *no* election had been made, pre-7 April 1965 acquisitions were treated as disposed of on a 'last-in, first-out' basis and were only identified with disposals after all post-6 April 1965 acquisitions had been identified. Such post-6 April 1965 acquisitions forming a holding in existence immediately before the '1982 date' (see 7.4 above), subject to transitional provisions, continued to be treated as a single asset (but one which could not grow by further acquisitions). In general, disposals were identified, on a 'first-in, first-out' basis, with acquisitions within the twelve months preceding the disposal. Otherwise, disposals were to be identified on a 'last-in, first-out' basis.

(*b*)   Where an election *was* made, pre-7 April 1965 acquisitions (at 6 April 1965 values) and any acquisitions post-6 April 1965 *and* before the '1982 date' and which together formed a holding in existence before the '1982 date', subject to transitional provisions, continued to be treated as a single asset (but one which could not grow by further acquisitions). Otherwise, disposals were identified as under the general rules in (*a*) above.

[*TCGA 1992, ss 104(3), 105, 2 Sch 2(2), 3, 4(3)–(7); FA 1982, ss 88, 89, 13 Sch Pt II*].

7.6   **Position before the 1982 date.** The identification rules given in (*a*) or (*b*) below applied to quoted securities held on 6 April 1965 (but not GOVERNMENT SECURITIES (21)).

(*a*)   Where *no* election had been made, pre-7 April 1965 acquisitions were treated as disposed of on a 'first-in, first-out' basis and post-6 April 1965 acquisitions formed a 'holding' which was treated as a single asset. Disposals were treated as made out of pre-7 April 1965 acquisitions before those in the holding. This rule also applied to determine how securities held on 6 April 1965 were to be identified with previous acquisitions where there had been disposals pre-7 April 1965. Disposals out of the holding were identified on a 'pool' basis, see 53.4 SHARES AND SECURITIES.

(*b*)   Where an election had been made, pre-7 April 1965 acquisitions and any acquisitions post-6 April 1965 together formed a 'holding' which was treated as a single asset.

[*TCGA 1992, ss 104(3), 105, 2 Sch (2), 3, 4(3)–(7)*].

7.7   **Reorganisation, exchange etc. following partial election.** Where an election has been made under 7.3(*a*) *or* under 7.3(*b*) above *but not both* and there is a disposal out of a 'new holding' (see definition below and *not* the one given in 7.4 above) following a reorganisation or exchange etc. of quoted securities held on 6 April 1965, the election applies according to the nature of the securities in the new holding, notwithstanding that it is to be treated as one with the 'original holding' and that the election would have applied differently to the original holding. Where the election does cover the disposal out of the new holding, but does not cover quoted securities of the kind comprised in the original holding, the question of how much of the new holding derives from securities held on 6 April 1965, and how much derives from other quoted securities is decided by the rules in 7.4(*a*) and (A), 7.5(*a*) and 7.6(*a*) above as appropriate.

Where the election does not cover a disposal out of the new holding, but does cover quoted securities of the kind comprised in the original holding, then, in computing the gain accruing on the disposal out of the new holding, the question of what remained undisposed of on any disposal out of the original holding is to be decided by the rules given in 7.4(*a*) and (A), 7.5(*a*) and 7.6(*a*) above, notwithstanding the fact that following an election the rules given in 7.4(*b*) and (B), 7.5(*b*) and 7.6(*b*) applied on a disposal out of the original holding. [*TCGA 1992, 2 Sch 6*].

'*Original holding*' means securities held before and concerned in the reorganisation etc. and '*new holding*' means, in relation to any original holding, the shares in and debentures of the company which, following the reorganisation etc., represent the original holding, together with any remaining original holding. [*TCGA 1992, ss 126, 127*]. See 53.5 SHARES AND SECURITIES for full coverage of reorganisations etc. generally.

Note. Where (i) disposals are made on or after the '1982 date' (see 7.4 above) out of the new holding and (ii) there were disposals out of the original holding before the '1982 date', the legislation does not make clear whether the 'last-in, first-out' basis applying on or after the '1982 date' in respect of original shares held on 6 April 1965 (as under 7.4(*a*) and (A) and 7.5(*a*) above) is the appropriate identification procedure for disposals in (ii) or if it is the 'first-in, first-out' basis applying before the 1982 date as under 7.6(*a*) above. In addition it should be noted that there is no provision to adjust the original *computation* of any gain arising on a disposal out of the original shares.

7.8 Assets held on 6 April 1965

7.8 LAND REFLECTING DEVELOPMENT VALUE

If land in the UK held on 6 April 1965 is disposed of after 17 December 1973 either

(i) at a price exceeding 'current use value' (as defined and see *Morgan v Gibson Ch D 1989, 61 TC 654*) at the time of the disposal, or

(ii) if any 'material development' (as defined) has been carried out after 17 December 1973 by the disposer,

on the disposal, computations of the gain or loss accruing are made

(*a*) by reference to the original cost, or market value when acquired if appropriate—see 36 MARKET VALUE, and

(*b*) by reference to market value on 6 April 1965.

Of these two computations, the one which produces the smaller gain or the smaller loss prevails, but if one computation produces a gain and the other a loss, the result is treated as giving rise to neither gain nor loss. The provisions apply only if before 6 April 1965, expenditure was *incurred* which would otherwise have been deductible in computing the gain on the disposal. A deemed acquisition cost by virtue of *TCGA 1992, s 17* (or similar previous legislation) is 'expenditure incurred' for this purpose. See *Mashiter v Pearmain CA 1984, 58 TC 334*. [*TCGA 1992, 2 Sch 9–15*].

Example

K sells a building plot, on which planning permission has just been obtained, in November 1995 for £200,000. He acquired the plot by gift from his father in 1953 when its value was £2,000. The market value was £5,000 at 6 April 1965 and £10,000 at 31 March 1982, and the current use value in November 1995 is £15,000. The indexation factor for March 1982 to November 1995 is assumed to be 0.870.

	£	£	£
Sale proceeds	200,000	200,000	200,000
Cost	2,000		
Market value 6.4.65		5,000	
Market value 31.3.82			10,000
Unindexed gain	198,000	195,000	190,000
Indexation allowance			
£10,000 × 0.870	8,700	8,700	8,700
Gain after indexation	£189,300	£186,300	£181,300
Chargeable gain			£181,300

Notes to the example

(1) Time apportionment would have substantially reduced the gain of £189,300, using cost, such that re-basing to 31 March 1982 would have given a greater gain than that based on cost and would not therefore have applied. However, as the plot has been sold for a price in excess of its current use value, no time apportionment can be claimed.

(2) Gains are compared after applying the indexation allowance, which is based on 31 March 1982 value, this being greater than either cost or 6 April 1965 value.

See 33.10 LAND for part disposals with development value of an estate of land acquired before 6 April 1965. See 33.6–33.9 LAND for disposals of development land generally before 19 March 1985.

7.9   OTHER ASSETS AND MISCELLANEOUS ASPECTS

Special provisions apply to other assets not falling within 7.2–7.8 above (including unquoted shares and land not covered by 7.8 above) held on 6 April 1965.

Gains on disposals of such assets which are held on 6 April 1965 are apportioned (on the basis of relative costs) between the original asset and any additions to it, and are deemed to have arisen evenly over the period from acquisition (or addition), or from 6 April 1945 if later, to the date of disposal. Only the part of the gain or loss attributable, on this basis, to the period from 6 April 1965 to disposal is taxable or allowable. [*TCGA 1992, 2 Sch 16*]. This basis is known as **time apportionment**. According to Revenue Pamphlet IR 131, SP 3/82, 24 November 1982, indexation allowance, where available, is calculated and deducted before applying such apportionment, and the case of *Smith v Schofield HL, [1993] STC 268* subsequently confirmed this practice.

Example

On 6 April 1955, A acquires 5,000 shares in C Ltd, an unquoted company, for £15,000. He sells these shares (his entire holding in the company) on 6 April 1988 for £65,000. The retail prices index for March 1982 is 79.44 and for April 1988 it is 105.8. No election for universal 31 March 1982 re-basing is made but the market value of the holding on that date is agreed at £27,000.

The chargeable gain is computed thus

Total period of ownership   : 33 years

Period after 6 April 1965   : 23 years

Unindexed gain
£(65,000 − 15,000)   : £50,000

Indexation allowance

$$\frac{105.8- 79.44}{79.44} \times £27,000$$: £8,964 (indexation factor 0.332)

Overall gain £(50,000 − 8,964) : £41,036

Chargeable gain   : £41,036 × 23/33 = £28,601

The gain by reference to 31 March 1982 value is
£(65,000 − 27,000 − 8,964)   : £29,036

31 March 1982 re-basing does not apply as a higher gain would thereby result.

Assume, however, that in April 1960, A, having discovered a defect in his title to the shares, incurred legal costs of £3,000 in order to correct it.

The gain would then be computed as follows

Overall gain (as revised)

£65,000 − £(15,000 + 3,000 + 8,964) : £38,036

Proportion of gain attributable to original expenditure (E(0)) : $\dfrac{£15,000}{£18,000} \times £38,036$ $= £31,697$

Proportion of gain attributable to enhancement expenditure (E(1)) : $\dfrac{£3,000}{£18,000} \times £38,036$ $= £6,339$

$$\dfrac{\text{Period of ownership since 6 April 1965}}{\text{Total period of ownership}} \times E(0)$$

$$= \dfrac{23}{33} \times £31,697 = £22,092$$

$$\dfrac{\text{Period of ownership since 6 April 1965}}{\text{Total period of ownership since enhancement}} \times E(1)$$

$$= \dfrac{23}{28} \times £6,339 = £5,207$$

Total chargeable gain £22,092 + £5,207 = £27,299

The gain by reference to 31 March 1982 value is again £29,036 so re-basing at that date does not apply.

The formulae for apportionment of gains are contained in *TCGA 1992, 2 Sch 16* (whence the designations 'E(0)' and 'E(1)' are taken).

Where the original expenditure (compared with the enhancement expenditure) is disproportionately small having regard to the value of the asset immediately before the enhancement expenditure was incurred (or where there is no original expenditure) the *actual gain* attributable to the enhancement expenditure is substituted for the figure arrived at under the formula, and the balance is treated as attributable to original expenditure. This is done in practice by establishing as a fact what the proceeds for the asset would have been without any of the enhancement expenditure in question.

The Revenue are prepared to accept a period of tenancy prior to a period of ownership as part of the time apportionment denominator e.g. where farm land was gifted by a father to his son in 1956 and subsequently sold by the son in 1980, if the son had been a tenant since 1945 a time apportionment factor of 15/(20+15) would apply rather than 15/(15+9). The existence of an ordinary tenancy is sufficient to allow the extended time apportionment formulae to apply even though no formal lease or tenancy agreement was in existence, provided sufficient rent was paid. Any sale of land, including buildings, follows the same pattern but any 'wasted cost' of a lease has to be added to the cost of the 'freehold reversion'. (CCAB Statement TR 500, 10 March 1983).

For the circumstances in which the Inland Revenue will require a valuation of the asset transferred where a claim for hold-over relief is made, see 22.1 HOLD-OVER RELIEFS.

7.10   **Election.** Alternatively (except in the case of an asset which has been the subject of a previous part disposal after 5 April 1965; see 16.6 DISPOSAL) the taxpayer may elect, by notice in writing, within two years from the end of the year of assessment, or accounting period of a company, in which the disposal is made, that the gain should be computed by reference to the market value at 6 April 1965 of the asset disposed of. The Board has discretion to extend the two-year time limit for instances of which see *Whitaker v Cameron Ch D 1982, 56 TC 97*, 3.11 ANTI-AVOIDANCE and 13.17 COMPANIES. The election (made on Form CG21) is irrevocable and the Inland Revenue will not normally discuss a valuation before an election is made. On a part disposal, an election will affect all later such disposals, or the ultimate disposal, made by the same person. [*TCGA 1992, 2 Sch 17(1)(3)–(5)*].

If the election to use 6 April 1965 value results in a gain, it is valid irrespective of all other figures (and the election will thus be to the detriment of the taxpayer if the time apportionment basis would have produced a smaller gain or a loss). If the election results in a loss, that loss is allowable, unless

(i)   there is a smaller loss by reference to cost in which case that smaller loss is taken (and this means that the full loss by reference to cost is taken instead of the time apportionment loss, so that the election has been beneficial to the taxpayer), or

(ii)   there is a gain by reference to cost, in which case the disposal will be treated as producing neither a gain nor a loss.

[*TCGA 1992, 2 Sch 17(2)*].

Prior to the commencement of *TCGA 1992*, elections were made under *CGTA 1979, 5 Sch 12*.

Part disposals out of an estate of land may be able to be treated as disposals of separate assets and thus allow 6 April 1965 value to be used in relation only to parts. See 33.10 LAND.

7.11   **Identification rules for unquoted securities, commodities etc. where no election under 7.10 above.** *After 5 April 1982 (31 March 1982 for companies)* on the realisation of part of an unquoted shareholding or other fungible assets, any shares held on 6 April 1965 are not pooled but are identified with shares disposed of on a last-in, first-out basis. *Before 6 April 1982 (1 April 1982 for companies)* the part sold was identified on a first-in, first-out basis with shares held on 6 April 1965 which again were not pooled. [*TCGA 1992, 2 Sch 18; CGTA 1979, 5 Sch 13*].

Post-6 April 1965 acquisitions are treated as in 23 INDEXATION and 52 SHARES AND SECURITIES.

7.12   **Time apportionment restrictions.** Where, after the date of acquisition and before 6 April 1965,

(*a*)   there was a *reorganisation* of a company's share capital (see 53.5 SHARES AND SECURITIES), time apportionment is not available. In such a case, 6 April 1965 value must be used. [*TCGA 1992, 2 Sch 19(1)*], or

(*b*)   a *part disposal* was made, time apportionment is calculated from the date of that part disposal by reference to market value at that time. [*TCGA 1992, 2 Sch 16(7)*].

Where, after 5 April 1965,

(i)   there is a *reorganisation* of a company's share capital, the new holding is treated as having been sold and immediately re-acquired at that time by the owner at the then market value. The amount of any gain on the disposal of the new holding, or part thereof, is computed by time apportioning any gain or loss over the period ending at that time and bringing into account the full gain or loss from that time to the date of disposal, computed by reference to the ultimate disposal value and the aforesaid market value. [*TCGA 1992, 2 Sch 19(2)*], or

(ii)   there is a *part disposal*, the asset is treated as having been sold and immediately re-acquired at that time by the owner at the then market value. The amount of any gain on the disposal is calculated as under (i) above. [*TCGA 1992, 2 Sch 16(8)*].

7.13 Assets held on 6 April 1965

The provisions under (*a*) and (i) above do not apply (i.e. normal time apportionment applies) in relation to a reorganisation of a company's share capital if the new holding differs only from the original shares in being a different number of shares of the same class as the original shares. [*TCGA 1992, 2 Sch 19(3)*]. Following the decision in *CIR v Beveridge CS 1979, 53 TC 178*, in all cases where liability is finalised after 19 July 1979, the Revenue do not consider this provision to apply where the shares comprised in the new holding are in a different company from the old shares. Previously, the practice of the Revenue had been to apply the wording to such a reorganisation (Revenue Statement of Practice SP 14/79, 1 December 1979).

Where (*a*) or (i) above has applied, gains chargeable on the disposal of the entire new holding are limited to the actual gains realised. Separate transactions in the year or accounting period are treated as a single disposal provided the entire holding is so disposed of (Revenue Pamphlet IR 1 (1992) D10).

Where the provisions in (ii) above would normally apply to unquoted shares in a winding-up, the time apportionment fraction determined at the date of the first distribution may be able to be used to calculate the gain on each additional distribution without further adjustment (29.D3 INLAND REVENUE STATEMENTS OF PRACTICE). See also 53.14 SHARES AND SECURITIES.

Part disposals out of an estate of land may be able to be treated as disposals of separate assets and so prevent the operation of (*b*) and (ii) above. See 33.10 LAND.

7.13   **Capital allowances.** Where the gain on the disposal of an asset is calculated by reference to its value on 6 April 1965, the restriction of relief given for losses accruing on assets which have qualified for capital allowances (*TCGA 1992, s 41*, see 16.5(*i*) DISPOSAL) and the provisions relating to wasting assets qualifying for capital allowances (*TCGA 1992, s 47*, see 59.1 WASTING ASSETS) apply as if the capital allowances for 1965/66 and subsequent years were allowances in respect of expenditure incurred on the asset on 6 April 1965. [*TCGA 1992, 2 Sch 20*].

7.14   **Assets transferred to close companies.** Where, at any time, a person who has 'control' of a 'close company', or a person 'connected' with him, transfers an asset to the company, and subsequently the first person (or any person with a 'substantial holding' of shares in the company) disposes of shares in circumstances such that the chargeable gain is to be determined by time apportionment, to the extent that the gain accruing on the disposal is attributable to a profit on the asset transferred, the shares are deemed to have been acquired at the date when the asset was transferred. The provisions do not apply where a loss accrues on the disposal. [*TCGA 1992, 2 Sch 21*].

'*Control*' is as given by *ICTA 1988, s 416*. '*Close company*' has the meaning given by *ICTA 1988, ss 414, 415*. '*Connected*' is as given at CONNECTED PERSONS (14). '*Substantial holding*' is not defined.

8   Assets held on 31 March 1982

Cross-references. See 23.11 and 23.16 INDEXATION for identification of certain share pools held by companies at 31 March 1982 and by others at 5 April 1982; 40.5 PARTNERSHIPS for partnership transactions involving assets held on 31 March 1982.

8.1   RE-BASING TO 31 MARCH 1982

Subject to certain exceptions, disposals after 5 April 1988 of assets which were held on 31 March 1982 by the person making the disposal are re-based by reference to the market value of the assets on the last-mentioned date; see 8.2 below. However, the taxpayer may irrevocably (with one exception mentioned in 8.3 below), subject to the modification in 8.2 below concerning certain disposals of 'oil industry assets', elect for such re-basing to apply to all assets held on 31 March 1982 regardless of the exceptions; see 8.3 below. Subject to certain exceptions and such election, re-basing applies to both the unindexed gain and the indexation allowance.

A 50% reduction is made in taxing certain deferred gains (except, in certain cases, where the deferred gain is never deemed to accrue at all) which arise after 5 April 1988 where such gains are wholly or partly attributable to an increase in value of an asset before 31 March 1982; see 8.12 below.

In addition, disposals after 5 April 1985 (31 March 1985 for companies) and before 6 April 1988 of assets held on 31 March 1982 could, on a claim, be the subject of a similar re-basing treatment as regards indexation allowance only; see 8.13 below.

8.2   GENERAL RE-BASING RULE

The general re-basing rule is that on a disposal after 5 April 1988 of an asset held on 31 March 1982 it is to be assumed that the asset was sold on the last-mentioned date by the person making the disposal and immediately reacquired by him at its market value on that date. [*TCGA 1992, s 35(1)(2)*].

Subject to the irrevocable (with one exception mentioned in 8.3 below) election in 8.3 below and subject to the modification below concerning certain disposals of 'oil industry assets', the general re-basing rule is not applied to a disposal where

(*a*)   a gain would accrue on the disposal if the general rule applied, and either a smaller gain or a loss would accrue if it did not, or

(*b*)   a loss would accrue if the general rule applied, and either a smaller loss or a gain would accrue if it did not, or

(*c*)   either on the facts of the case or by virtue of the provisions for ASSETS HELD ON 6 APRIL 1965 (7) in *TCGA 1992, 2 Sch*, neither a gain nor a loss would accrue if the general rule did not apply, or

(*d*)   the disposal is a 'no gain/no loss disposal' as in 8.7 below.

[*TCGA 1992, s 35(3)*].

Where the effect of the general re-basing rule would be to substitute a loss for a gain or a gain for a loss, but under (*a*)-(*d*) the application of that rule is excluded, it is to be assumed in relation to the disposal that the asset was acquired for a consideration such that, on the disposal, neither a gain nor a loss accrues. [*TCGA 1992, s 35(4)*].

8.2 Assets held on 31 March 1982

Indexation allowance on the disposal after 5 April 1988 of an asset held on 31 March 1982 is calculated, without need for a claim, on the assumption that the asset was sold on the last-mentioned date by the person making the disposal and immediately reacquired by him at its market value on that date. [*TCGA 1992, s 55(1)*]. Except where an irrevocable (with one exception mentioned in 8.3 below) election as in 8.3 below has effect and subject to the modification below concerning certain disposals of 'oil industry assets', neither this provision nor the general re-basing rule of *TCGA 1992, s 35(1)(2)* above is to apply for the purposes of calculating indexation allowance in a case where that allowance would be greater if they did not apply. [*TCGA 1992, s 55(2)*].

Modifications apply to the above provisions in respect of certain disposals after 21 January 1990 and before 30 November 1993 of 'oil industry assets'. These apply where the person making the disposal held the asset on 31 March 1982 (or is deemed to have done so because of previous no gain/no loss disposals as in 8.7 below), a loss would accrue on the disposal (disregarding the modifications below), and the general re-basing rule of *TCGA 1992, s 35(1)(2)* is disapplied by (*b*) above, i.e. because a smaller loss accrues if re-basing is not applied. For the purpose of the modifications, the loss or gain on the disposal (to be known as the '*non-rebased loss*' or '*non-rebased gain*') is calculated on the assumption that neither the general re-basing rule of *TCGA 1992, s 35(1)(2)* nor the equivalent rule for indexation allowance of *TCGA 1992, s 55(1)* applies. The non-rebased loss or gain is then compared with the loss arising but for the modifications below, i.e. the loss computed on the basis that the general re-basing rule of *TCGA 1992, s 35(1)(2)* does not apply but that the equivalent rule of *TCGA 1992, s 55(1)* does apply. If there is a non-rebased loss which is less than the loss arising but for the modifications below, the allowable loss is modified so as to be restricted to the non-rebased loss. If there is a non-rebased gain, or if there is neither a non-rebased gain nor a non-rebased loss, the modification is that it is to be assumed that the person making the disposal acquired the asset for a consideration such that neither a gain nor a loss accrues on the disposal. For the purposes of these provisions, the following are '*oil industry assets*': a licence under *Petroleum (Production) Act 1934* or *Petroleum (Production) Act (Northern Ireland) 1964*; shares of the kind excluded under 8.4 below from global re-basing elections under *TCGA 1992, s 35(5)*; 'oil exploration or exploitation assets' as mentioned in 8.4 but with suitable modifications; and any interest in an asset falling within these categories. These modifications do not apply to disposals on or after 30 November 1993. [*TCGA 1992, s 200; FA 1994, s 93(7)(11), 26 Sch Pt V*].

Where, for the purposes of the re-basing provisions in *TCGA 1992, s 35* and the indexation provisions in *TCGA 1992, s 55*, it is necessary to determine the market value of shares or securities of the same class in any company on 31 March 1982, all the shares or securities held at that date will be valued as a single holding whether they were acquired on or before 6 April 1965 or after that date. If the shares or securities in the relevant disposal represent some but not all of those valued at 31 March 1982 then the allowable cost or indexation allowance as appropriate will be based on the proportion that the shares or securities disposed of bears to the total holding at 31 March 1982 (Revenue Pamphlet IR 1 D34 (1992)). See also 8.7 below for the Revenue's practice as to the valuation of shares deemed held on 31 March 1982 by reason of 'no gain/no loss disposals' since that date.

Where a valuation at 31 March 1982 of unquoted shares is required for a number of shareholders, all of whom agree to be bound by the valuation, the Inland Revenue's Shares Valuation Division may initiate valuation procedures before receiving a formal request to do so from the inspector, provided that a full list of the company's shareholders and the size of their holdings, both at 31 March 1982 and at the date of disposal, is supplied, together with details of the tax offices involved, if available. It should be noted that entering into negotiations with Shares Valuation Division does not constitute a return for taxation purposes (Revenue Press Release 18 November 1991).

(*Note*. The examples below take no account of transitional relief for 'indexation losses' which may be due for 1993/94 and 1994/95 as in 23.2 INDEXATION.)

Example 1

An asset (which is neither tangible movable property nor otherwise exempt) was acquired for £900 in 1980 and, after having been held continuously by the same owner, is disposed of after 29 November 1993 in a month for which the increase in the retail prices index over that for March 1982 is 80%. The disposal proceeds are £1,900. The capital gains tax consequences, for differing 31 March 1982 values, are as follows. 'N/A' means that indexation allowance is not applicable and 'NGNL' means that the disposal is treated as giving rise to neither a gain nor a loss.

Example 1A

	(1)	(2)
	£	£
Sale proceeds	1,900	1,900
(1) Cost; (2) 31.3.1982 value	900	1,000
Unindexed gain	1,000	900
Indexation allowance at 80% of higher of (1) and (2)	800	800
Gain arising	£200	£100
Chargeable gain		£100

Example 1B

	(1)	(2)
	£	£
Sale proceeds	1,900	1,900
(1) Cost; (2) 31.3.1982 value	900	1,200
Unindexed gain	1,000	700
Indexation allowance at 80% of higher of (1) and (2)	960	N/A
Gain/NGNL arising	£40	£NGNL

The disposal is treated as giving rise to neither a gain nor a loss. Any corresponding acquisition is unaffected by this treatment.

8.2 Assets held on 31 March 1982

Example 1C

	(1)	(2)
	£	£
Sale proceeds	1,900	1,900
(1) Cost; (2) 31.3.1982 value	900	800
Unindexed gain	1,000	1,100
Indexation allowance at 80% of higher of (1) and (2)	720	720
Gain arising	£280	£380
Chargeable gain	£280	

Example 1D

	(1)	(2)
	£	£
Sale proceeds	1,900	1,900
(1) Cost; (2) 31.3.1982 value	900	3,000
Unindexed gain/(Loss)	1,000	(1,100)
Indexation allowance at 80% of higher of (1) and (2)	N/A	N/A
NGNL/(Loss) arising	NGNL	£(1,100)

The disposal is treated as giving rise to neither a gain nor a loss. Any corresponding acquisition is unaffected by this treatment.

Example 2

An asset (which is neither tangible movable property, land with development value, quoted securities nor otherwise exempt) was acquired in 1960 for £500. After having been held continuously by the same owner, the asset is completely destroyed after 29 November 1993 in a month for which the increase in the retail prices index over that for March 1982 is 80%. The asset was under-insured and later in the month of disposal only £1,900 was recovered from the insurers. The owner elects for valuation at 6 April 1965, which value is later agreed with the Revenue to be £2,000. The value at 31 March 1982 was similarly agreed at £1,700.

	(1)	(2)
	£	£
Insurance proceeds	1,900	1,900
(1) Cost; (2) 6.4.1965 value	500	2,000
	1,400	(100)

	(1)	(2)
	£	£
Indexation allowance at 80% of 31.3.1982 value (£1,700) for (1) only	1,360	N/A
Gain/(Loss) arising	£40	£(100)

Re-basing at 31 March 1982 does not apply since, under *TCGA 1992, 2 Sch 17(2)* (see 7.10 ASSETS HELD ON 6 APRIL 1965), the disposal is deemed to have given rise to neither a gain nor a loss. Any corresponding acquisition is unaffected by this treatment.

8.3   ELECTION FOR UNIVERSAL RE-BASING AT 31 MARCH 1982

If a person so elects (under *TCGA 1992, s 35(5)*), disposals made by him (including any made by him before the election) after 5 April 1988 of assets which he held on 31 March 1982 will all have the general re-basing rule of *TCGA 1992, s 35(1)(2)* in 8.2 above applied to them regardless of the exclusion of that rule that might otherwise apply under *TCGA 1992, s 35(3)*. Similarly in such a case, indexation alowance will always be calculated under the equivalent provision of *TCGA 1992, s 55(1)* as in 8.2 above regardless of the exclusion of that provision that might otherwise apply under *TCGA 1992, s 55(2)*. [*TCGA 1992, ss 35(5), 55(2)*].

An election is, with one exception as below, irrevocable and must be made by notice in writing to the inspector at any time before 6 April 1990 or at any time during the period beginning with the time of the first disposal after 5 April 1988 of an asset held on 31 March 1982 or treated (see 8.7 below) as so held (*'the first relevant disposal'*) and ending two years (or such longer period as may be allowed by the Board) after the end of the year of assessment or accounting period in which that disposal is made. An election made by a person in one capacity does not cover disposals made by him in another capacity. Adjustments as required may be made, whether by way of discharge or repayment of tax, the making of assessments or otherwise, to give effect to an election. [*TCGA 1992, s 35(6)-(8)*].

Where an election under *TCGA 1992, s 35(5)* (previously *FA 1988, s 96(5)* before the commencement of *TCGA 1992*) was made before 22 January 1990 which would otherwise apply to the disposal of assets which include assets mentioned in 8.4 below (unquoted shares deriving their value from oil assets etc.) which cannot be the subject of an election for disposals after 21 January 1990, the election could be revoked by the person by whom it was made, providing notice in writing to that effect was given to the inspector before 1 January 1991. [*FA 1990, s 63(4)*].

The Revenue will always exercise their discretion to extend the time limit for an election to at least the date on which the statutory time limit would expire if certain disposals, which do not count as a first relevant disposal, are made. There are three such kinds of disposal, as follows.

(1)   Disposals on which the gain would not be chargeable by virtue of a particular statutory provision. The main examples of these provisions are as follows.

(*a*)   Private cars (see 18.17 EXEMPTIONS AND RELIEFS).

(*b*)   Chattels, except commodity futures and foreign currency, worth less than the chattel exemption (see 18.4 EXEMPTIONS AND RELIEFS).

(*c*)   Chattels which are wasting assets, except plant and machinery used in business and commodity futures (see 18.4 EXEMPTIONS AND RELIEFS).

8.3   Assets held on 31 March 1982

(*d*)   Non-marketable government securities (see 18.3 EXEMPTIONS AND RELIEFS).

(*e*)   Gilt-edged securities and qualifying corporate bonds, except ones received in exchange for shares or other securities (see 21 GOVERNMENT SECURITIES and 44 QUALIFYING CORPORATE BONDS).

(*f*)   Life assurance policies and deferred annuity contracts, unless purchased from a third party (see 18.10 EXEMPTIONS AND RELIEFS).

(*g*)   Foreign currency acquired for personal or family expenditure abroad (see 18.8 EXEMPTIONS AND RELIEFS).

(*h*)   Rights of compensation for a wrong or injury suffered by an individual in his person, profession or vocation (see 18.19 EXEMPTIONS AND RELIEFS).

(*j*)   Debts, not on a security, held by the original creditor, his personal representative or his legatee (see 18.5 EXEMPTIONS AND RELIEFS).

(*k*)   Business expansion scheme shares issued after 18 March 1986 for which relief has been given and not withdrawn (see 53.18 SHARES AND SECURITIES).

(*l*)   Personal equity plan shareholdings (see 53.20 SHARES AND SECURITIES).

(*m*)   Gifts of eligible property, including works of art, for the benefit of the public (see 18.25 and 18.31 EXEMPTIONS AND RELIEFS).

(*n*)   Decorations for valour or gallantry (see 18.6 EXEMPTIONS AND RELIEFS).

(*o*)   Betting winnings (see 18.17 EXEMPTIONS AND RELIEFS).

(*p*)   A right to or to any part of an allowance, annuity or capital sum from a superannuation fund or any other annuity (but not under a deferred annuity policy) or annual payments received under a covenant which is not secured on property (see 18.3 EXEMPTIONS AND RELIEFS).

(2)   Disposals which, in practice, do not give rise to a chargeable gain or allowable loss. The main examples of these disposals are as follows.

(*a*)   Withdrawals from building society accounts.

(*b*)   The disposal of an individual's private residence where the whole of the gain is exempt under *TCGA 1992, s 223(1)* (see 43.1 PRIVATE RESIDENCES).

(*c*)   Disposals which give rise to neither a chargeable gain nor an allowable loss by virtue of the statutory 'no gain/no loss' provisions listed at *TCGA 1992, s 35(3)(d)* (see 8.7 below).

(3)   Excluded disposals (see 8.4 below).

As sterling is not an asset for capital gains tax purposes (see 6.1 ASSETS), a disposal of it cannot be a first relevant disposal.

Where a person holds assets in more than one capacity (for example, as an individual, trustee, partner or member of a European Economic Interest Grouping), there will be a first relevant disposal and a separate time limit for each group of assets which the person holds in a different capacity. An individual who holds assets in different capacities should indicate at the time an election under *TCGA 1992, s 35(5)* is made in what capacity it should be regarded as applying.

Where a person who is non-UK resident on 6 April 1988 makes a disposal which would otherwise count as a first relevant disposal between that date and the date on which they first become UK resident, the Revenue will give sympathetic consideration to extending the time limit to the end of the second year of assessment (for companies, the second accounting period) after the year in which the first disposal is made subsequent to becoming UK resident. In other words, the disposal made while non-resident may be disregarded at the discretion of the Board. The extension will not be available where the assets are within *TCGA 1992, s 10* (non-resident with UK branch or agency: see 39.3 OVERSEAS MATTERS).

Where, after 5 April 1988, an individual who is resident but not domiciled in the UK disposes of an asset situated outside the UK, the date of the first relevant disposal will be the date on which the proceeds of an overseas gain are remitted to the UK or the date of the first disposal of a UK asset, whichever is earlier.

Where an individual who was resident in the UK on 6 April 1988 has a period of non-residence before resuming UK residence, the first relevant disposal will be the first disposal made after 5 April 1988 on which the individual is chargeable to UK capital gains tax.

There are a variety of other circumstances where, having regard to the facts of each case, the Inland Revenue will or may exercise their discretion to extend the statutory time limit. (Revenue Pamphlet IR 131, SP 4/92, 14 May 1992. SP 4/92 replaces SP 2/89, 1 March 1989, but does not reflect any formal change of practice.)

8.4   **Excluded disposals.** An election does not cover a disposal of (or of an interest in): plant or machinery; an asset which the person making the disposal held at any time for the purposes of or in connection with a trade or part of a trade involving the working of a 'source of mineral deposits' (within *CAA 1990, s 121*); a licence under the *Petroleum (Production) Act 1934* or the *Petroleum (Production) Act (Northern Ireland) 1964*; or, for disposals after 21 January 1990, 'shares' which, on 31 March 1982, were 'unquoted' and derived their value, or the greater part thereof, directly or indirectly from 'oil exploration or exploitation assets' situated in the UK or a 'designated area' or from such assets and 'oil exploration or exploitation rights' taken together (the quoted terms having the meanings given by the legislation). However, disposals within the first two of these four categories are not excluded unless a capital allowance in respect of any expenditure attributable to the asset has been made to the person making the disposal or would have been made to him had he made a claim. Where that person acquired the asset on a 'no gain/no loss disposal' (see 8.7 below), references in the foregoing to the person making the disposal are references to that person, the person who last acquired the asset other than on a no gain/no loss disposal or any person who subsequently acquired the asset on such a disposal. [*TCGA 1992, 3 Sch 7*].

8.5   **Married persons.** Where a spouse disposes of an asset acquired by him from the other spouse after 5 April 1988 and the no gain/no loss basis of *TCGA 1992, s 58* applied to the acquisition (see 37.6 MARRIED PERSONS and 8.7 below), an election made by the transferee spouse does not apply to the disposal, and, whether or not an election is made by that spouse, the making of such an election by the transferor spouse applies to the ultimate disposal made by the transferee spouse. Where the transferor spouse also acquired the asset after 5 April 1988 and *TCGA 1992, s 58* applied to that acquisition, an election made by him does not have effect on the ultimate disposal, but an election made by the last person by whom the asset was acquired after 5 April 1988 otherwise than on an acquisition to which *TCGA 1992, s 58* applied or, if there is no such person, the person who held the asset on 5 April 1988, does have effect on the ultimate disposal. [*TCGA 1992, 3 Sch 2*].

8.6   **Groups of companies.** Where a member of a group of companies disposes of an asset acquired by it from another group member after 5 April 1988 and the no gain/no loss basis of *TCGA 1992, s 171* applied to the acquisition (see 13.11 COMPANIES and 8.7

below), an election made by the transferee company does not apply to the disposal, and, whether or not an election is made by that company, the making of such an election by the transferor company applies to the ultimate disposal made by the transferee company. Where the transferor company also acquired the asset after 5 April 1988 and *TCGA 1992, s 171* applied to that acquisition, an election made by it does not have effect on the ultimate disposal, but an election made by the last company by which the asset was acquired after 5 April 1988 otherwise than on an acquisition to which *TCGA 1992, s 171* applied or, if there is no such company, the company which held the asset on 5 April 1988, does have effect on the ultimate disposal. [*TCGA 1992, 3 Sch 2*].

Election by principal company. Only a company which is the 'principal company' of a 'group' (for which see 13.10 COMPANIES) may make an election unless the company did not become a group member until after the 'relevant time'. For this purpose the time limit for the making of an election (see 8.3 above) applies with the modification that a reference to 'the first relevant disposal' is a reference to the first disposal after 5 April 1988 of an asset held on 31 March 1982 by a company which is *either* a group member but not an 'outgoing company' in relation to the group *or* an 'incoming company' in relation to the group. An election made by the principal company also has effect as one made by any other company which is a group member at the relevant time; but this treatment does not extend to a company which, in some period after 5 April 1988 and before the relevant time, is not a member of the group if during that period the company makes a disposal of an asset which it held on 31 March 1982 and the time limit for the making of an election expires without an election having been made. However, the effect of an election continues to extend to a company notwithstanding that it ceases to be a group member after the relevant time except where it is an outgoing company in relation to the group and the election relating to the group is made after it ceases to be a group member. [*TCGA 1992, 3 Sch 8, 9(3)*].

'*The relevant time*', in relation to a group, is the earliest of: the first time when any company which is then a group member, and is not an outgoing member in relation to the group, makes a disposal after 5 April 1988 of an asset which it held on 31 March 1982; the time immediately following the first occasion when a company which is an incoming company in relation to the group becomes a group member; and the time when an election is made by the principal company. [*TCGA 1992, 3 Sch 9(1)*].

'*Incoming company*', in relation to a group, means a company which makes its first disposal after 5 April 1988 of an asset which it held on 31 March 1982 at a time when it is not a group member, and which becomes a group member before the expiry of the time limit for the making of an election which would apply to it and at a time when no such election has been made.

'*Outgoing company*', in relation to a group, means a company which ceases to be a group member before the expiry of the time limit for the making of an election which would apply to it and at a time when no such election has been made. [*TCGA 1992, 3 Sch 9(2)*].

8.7   SUPPLEMENTARY PROVISIONS FOR RE-BASING AT 31 MARCH 1982

Previous no gain/no loss disposals. Where

(*a*)   a person makes a disposal, other than a 'no gain/no loss disposal', after 5 April 1988 of an asset which he acquired after 31 March 1982, and

(*b*)   the disposal by which he acquired the asset and any previous disposal of the asset after 31 March 1982 was a no gain/no loss disposal,

he is treated for the purposes of the re-basing provisions of *TCGA 1992, s 35* and the equivalent provisions for indexation allowance of *TCGA 1992, s 55(1)* in 8.2 and 8.3 above as having held the asset on 31 March 1982. The Inland Revenue has confirmed that where a person is treated as having held an asset on 31 March 1982 under these provisions, enhancement expenditure on the asset incurred after 31 March 1982 by a previous owner may be taken into account for indexation and rebasing purposes on a disposal by the current owner (Revenue Tax Bulletin, August 1992, p.32).

A '*no gain/no loss disposal*' is one under the following enactments (being enactments by virtue of which neither a gain nor a loss accrues).

(i)   *TCGA 1992, s 58* (transfers between spouses living together, see 37.6 MARRIED PERSONS), *s 73* (reversion of settled property to settlor on death of person entitled to life interest, see 52.11 SETTLEMENTS), *s 139* (company reconstruction or amalgamation, see 13.6 COMPANIES), *s 140A* (transfer of UK trade between companies in different EC member States, see 39.15 OVERSEAS MATTERS), *s 171* (intra-group disposals of assets, see 13.11 COMPANIES), *s 172* (transfer of UK branch or agency, see 39.3 OVERSEAS MATTERS), *s 215* (amalgamation of building societies, see 13.6 COMPANIES), *s 216* (transfer of building society's business to company, see 13.6 COMPANIES), *s 217A* (transfer of assets on incorporation of registered friendly society, see 18.40 EXEMPTIONS AND RELIEFS), *ss 218–220* (housing associations, see 18.42 EXEMPTIONS AND RELIEFS), *s 221* (harbour authorities, see 18.63 EXEMPTIONS AND RELIEFS), *s 257(2)* (gifts to charities etc., see 10.5 CHARITIES), *s 257(3)* (gifts to charities etc. out of settlements, see 10.6 CHARITIES), *s 258(4)* (gifts of national heritage property, see 18.70 EXEMPTIONS AND RELIEFS), *s 259(2)* (gifts to housing associations, see 18.42 EXEMPTIONS AND RELIEFS), *s 264* (transfers between constituency associations, see 18.59 EXEMPTIONS AND RELIEFS) and *s 267(2)* (sharing of transmission facilities, see 13.6 COMPANIES);

(ii) *CGTA 1979, s 148* (assets transferred to maintenance funds for historic buildings, see 18.68 EXEMPTIONS AND RELIEFS);

(iii) *FA 1982, s 148* (transfers by Hops Marketing Board, see 18.65 EXEMPTIONS AND RELIEFS);

(iv) *Trustee Savings Banks Act 1985, 2 Sch 2* (see 13.6 COMPANIES);

(v)   *Transport Act 1985, s 130(3)* (see 13.6 COMPANIES);

(vi) *ICTA 1988, s 486(8)* (amalgamation of industrial and provident societies, see 13.6 COMPANIES);

(vii) *FA 1990, 12 Sch 2(1)* (broadcasting undertakings, see 13.6 COMPANIES);

(viii) *F(No 2)A 1992, 17 Sch 5(3)* (privatisation of Northern Ireland Electricity, see 13.6 COMPANIES);

(ix) *FA 1994, 24 Sch 2(1), 7(2), 11(3)(4), 25(2)* (provisions relating to *Railways Act 1993*, see 13.6 COMPANIES); and

(x)   *FA 1994, 25 Sch 4(2)* (Northern Ireland Airports Ltd, see 13.6 COMPANIES).

[*TCGA 1992, ss 35(3)(d)(10), 55(5)(6)(a), 3 Sch 1; F(No 2)A 1992, ss 46(1)(2), 56, 77, 9 Sch 21(1)(2), 17 Sch 5(9); FA 1994, ss 252, 253, 24 Sch 2(2), 25 Sch 4(3)*].

(*Note*. Neither *TCGA 1992, s 257(2)* nor *s 259(2)* is in strictness included as no gain/no loss provisions for the purposes of re-basing under *TCGA 1992, s 35* although they are for the equivalent provisions for indexation allowance under *TCGA 1992, s 55(1)*. However, both provisions deem (for the purposes of *TCGA 1992*) the original acquisition by the transferor making the disposal to which the provision concerned applies to be the acquisition of the transferee on the occasion of the transferee making a subsequent disposal. Consequently it seems that in practice both provisions are no gain/no loss provisions for the purposes of re-basing under *TCGA 1992, s 35*. It appears that the reason that both provisions have to be specifically included as no gain/no loss provisions for the purposes of *TCGA 1992, s 55(1)* is because of the effect of *TCGA 1992, s 56(2)* (see further below).)

Certain disposals of a share in partnership assets may be treated as if they were no gain/no loss disposals. See 40.5 PARTNERSHIPS.

Where (*a*) and (*b*) above apply on the disposal of an asset so that, as stated above, the person making the disposal is treated for the purposes of computing the indexation allowance on the disposal as having held the asset on 31 March 1982 [*TCGA 1992, s 55(6)(a)*], then for the purpose of determining any gain or loss on the disposal, the consideration which otherwise that person would be treated as having given for the asset is reduced by the amount of indexation allowance brought into account under *TCGA 1992, s 56(2)* (consideration on disposal treated as giving rise to neither a gain nor a loss to be computed on assumption that on the disposal an unindexed gain accrues equal to the indexation allowance on the disposal; see 23.4 INDEXATION) on any disposal falling within (*b*) above. [*TCGA 1992, s 55(6)(b)*].

Further rules as below apply (after the application of the computation of any indexation allowance under *TCGA 1992, s 53* (see 23.1 INDEXATION) but before the application of the provisions of *TCGA 1992, s 35(3)* or *(4)* (which disapply or amend the general re-basing rule of *TCGA 1992, s 35(1)(2)* in certain cases; see 8.2 above) in relation to disposals on or after 30 November 1993. The rules apply where (*a*) and (*b*) above apply to the disposal ('*the disposal in question*') of an asset by any person ('*the transferor*') and, but for *TCGA 1992, s 55(6)(b)* above, the consideration the transferor would be treated as having given for the asset would include an amount or amounts of indexation allowance brought into account under *TCGA 1992, s 56(2)* on any disposal made before 30 November 1993. [*TCGA 1992, s 55(7); FA 1994, s 93(4)(11)*]. The rules are that

(A)   where otherwise there would be a loss, an amount equal to the 'rolled-up indexation' is added to it so as to increase it,

(B)   where otherwise the unindexed gain or loss would be nil, a loss is deemed to accrue equal to the rolled-up indexation, and

(C)   where otherwise there would be an unindexed gain and the gain or loss would be nil but the amount of the indexation allowance used to extinguish the gain would be less than the rolled-up indexation, the difference is deemed to constitute a loss.

[*TCGA 1992, s 55(8); FA 1994, s 93(4)(11)*].

For the purposes of the above, the '*rolled-up indexation*' means, subject to *TCGA 1992, s 55(10)* and *(11)* below (which provisions, as well as applying on the disposal in question, are also treated as having applied on any previous part disposal by the transferor), the amount or, as the case may be, the aggregate of the amounts of indexation allowance which, but for *TCGA 1992, s 55(6)(b)* above, would be brought into account under *TCGA 1992, s 56(2)* on any disposal made before 30 November 1993. [*TCGA 1992, s 55(9); FA 1994, s 93(4)(11)*].

Where, for the purposes of any disposal of the asset made by the transferor on or after 30 November 1993, any amount, amounts or combination of amounts within *TCGA 1992, s 38(1)(a)–(c)* (acquisition consideration etc., enhancement expenditure etc. and incidental disposal costs respectively; see 16.3 DISPOSAL) is required to be excluded, reduced or written down, the amount or amounts constituting the rolled-up indexation (or so much of it as remains after the application of this provision and *TCGA 1992, s 55(11)* below on a previous part disposal) are reduced in proportion to any reduction made in the amount falling within one or any combination of *TCGA 1992, s 38(1)(a)–(c)*. [*TCGA 1992, s 55(10); FA 1994, s 93(4)(11)*].

Where the transferor makes a part disposal of the asset at any time on or after 30 November 1993, then, for the purposes of that and any subsequent part disposal, the amount or amounts constituting the rolled-up indexation (or so much of it as remains after the application of this provision and *TCGA 1992, s 55(10)* above on a previous part disposal by him or after the application of *TCGA 1992, s 55(10)* on the part disposal) is apportioned between the property disposed of and the property which remains in the same proportions as the amounts within *TCGA 1992, s 38(1)(a)* and *(b)*. [*TCGA 1992, s 55(11); FA 1994, s 93(4)(11)*].

(*Note.* In the example below transitional relief for 'indexation losses' is not applicable as only disposals by companies are involved. However, such relief may be due for 1993/94 and 1994/95 as in 23.2 INDEXATION in the case of disposals by individuals and trustees of settlements made before 30 November 1993.)

Example

X Ltd, Y Ltd and Z Ltd are all members of the same group within *TCGA 1992, s 170* (see 13.10 COMPANIES), all three companies having joined the group before 1 April 1987 (see 13.20 COMPANIES) and making up annual accounts for calendar years. No election under *TCGA 1992, s 35(5)* (universal re-basing; see 8.3 and 8.6 above) is in force. An asset was acquired by X Ltd from outside the group for £90,000 in 1980 and at 31 March 1982 the value of the asset is £100,000. The asset was transferred to Y Ltd in October 1985 such that the no gain/no loss basis of *TCGA 1992, s 171* (see 13.11 COMPANIES) applied. X Ltd made the appropriate election under *FA 1985, s 68(4)(5)* (indexation allowance to be calculated by reference to value at 31 March 1982 rather than original cost; see 8.13 and 8.14 below) before 1 January 1988. In January 1994 Y Ltd transferred the asset to Z Ltd such that *TCGA 1992, s 171* again applied. Z Ltd sells the asset outside the group in March 1995 for £80,000. The relevant retail prices indices are

| March 1982 | 79.44 | January 1994 | 141.3 |
| October 1985 | 95.59 | | |

	£
Original cost of asset to X Ltd in 1980	90,000

Indexation allowance: March 1982 – October 1985
on 31 March 1982 value under *FA 1985, s 68(4)(5)*

$$\frac{95.59 - 79.44}{79.44} \times £100,000 \text{ (indexation factor 0.203)} \qquad 20,300$$

Deemed consideration under *TCGA 1992, s 56(2)*	£110,300

Deemed cost of asset to Y Ltd in October 1985	110,300

Indexation allowance: October 1985 – January 1994

$$\frac{141.3 - 95.59}{95.59} \times £110,300 \text{ (indexation factor 0.478)} \qquad 52,723$$

Deemed consideration under *TCGA 1992, s 56(2)*	£163,023

8.7 Assets held on 31 March 1982

Under *TCGA 1992, ss 35(10), 55(6)(a), 3 Sch 1* Z Ltd is treated as having held the asset on 31 March 1982 for the purposes of re-basing under *TCGA 1992, s 35* and calculating indexation allowance.

	Cost £	Re-base £
Proceeds received by Z Ltd	80,000	80,000
Deemed consideration under *TCGA 1992, s 55(6)(b)* (£163,023 – £52,723 – £20,300)	90,000	
Market value at 31 March 1982		100,000
Loss before *TCGA 1992, s 55(8)* adjustment	10,000	20,000
Rolled-up indexation under *TCGA 1992, s 55(9)*	20,300	20,300
Loss after *TCGA 1992, s 55(8)* adjustment	£30,300	£40,300

TCGA 1992, s 35(3) applies, so the allowable loss arising is £30,300.

It should be noted that the effect of the legislation in force for disposals before 30 November 1993 meant that Z Ltd would not have been prejudiced on the ultimate disposal outside the group if X Ltd had not made a valid claim under *FA 1985, s 68(4)(5)* within the time limit in respect of the transfer of the asset to Y Ltd in October 1985. However, the legislation in force for disposals on or after 30 November 1993 means that, in the absence of such an election in respect of that disposal, the rolled-up indexation in the above example would have to be computed by reference to the original cost to X Ltd (i.e. $0.203 \times £90,000 = £18,270$). The allowable loss would then be £28,270 (i.e. £18,270 + £10,000). It is not known whether the Revenue would use the discretion it had in similarly affected cases to extend the time limit of two years after the end of the year of assessment or accounting period in which the disposal fell.

Shares or securities of the same class in any company which are *treated* as above as held on 31 March 1982 by a person will be treated as a single holding with any shares or securities of the same class in the same company *actually* held by that person in determining the market value for re-basing purposes of the shares or securities. If the shares or securities in the relevant disposal represent some but not all of those valued at 31 March 1982 then the allowable cost or indexation allowance as appropriate will be based on the proportion that the shares or securities disposed of bears to the total holding (Revenue Pamphlet IR 131, SP 5/89, 25 May 1989). See also 8.2 above regarding the concessionary valuation of a holding of shares or securities at 31 March 1982 where part of the holding was held on 6 April 1965.

Where SP 5/89 above applies, the Revenue will also apply the following concessional valuation treatment where shares or securities of the same class are acquired by way of no gain/no loss transfer under *TCGA 1992, s 58* (spouses living together) or *s 171* (intra-group disposals). The concessional treatment applies to disposals within the scope of SP 5/89 made before 16 March 1993 in relation to which a claim is made before liabilities are finally determined, and all such disposals made after 15 March 1993 provided that a claim is made within two years (or such further time as the Board may allow) of the end of the year of assessment or accounting period in which the disposal is made. Under the concessional valuation treatment the value of a single holding may be regarded as the appropriate proportion of the value of any larger holding of shares or securities of the same class which were held by a spouse or another company at 31 March 1982 and from which part or all of the single holding was derived by one or more transfers within *TCGA 1992, s 58* or *s 171* respectively (Revenue Pamphlet IR 1, D44).

8.8   **Capital allowances.** If, under either the re-basing provisions of *TCGA 1992, s 35* or the equivalent provisions for indexation allowance of *TCGA 1992, s 55(1)* (see 8.2 and 8.3 above), it is to be assumed that any asset was on 31 March 1982 sold by the person making the disposal and immediately reacquired by him, *TCGA 1992, s 41* (restriction of losses by reference to capital allowances, see 16.5(*i*) DISPOSAL) and *s 47* (wasting assets qualifying for capital allowances, see 59.1 WASTING ASSETS) apply with suitable modifications on the assumed reacquisition at 31 March 1982. [*TCGA 1992, s 55(3), 3 Sch 3*].

8.9   **Part disposals etc.** Where, on a disposal to which the general re-basing rule of *TCGA 1992, s 35(1)(2)* in 8.2 above applies, *TCGA 1992, s 42* (allowable expenditure on a part disposal, see 16.6 DISPOSAL) has effect by reason of an earlier disposal made after 31 March 1982 and before 6 April 1988, the sums to be apportioned under that provision on the later disposal are to take the general re-basing rule into account. [*TCGA 1992, 3 Sch 4(1)*].

If in relation to disposals after 5 April 1989 the general re-basing rule of *TCGA 1992, s 35(1)(2)* applies, and if that rule did not apply expenditure would under specified enactments not be allowable in computing a gain arising on the disposal, and the disallowance would be attributable to the reduction of the amount of the consideration for a disposal made after 31 March 1982 but before 6 April 1988, the amount otherwise allowable as a deduction on the disposal is reduced by the amount of the disallowance that would have been made if the general re-basing rule had not applied. The enactments specified are

(i)   *TCGA 1992, s 23(2)* (disallowance of allowable expenditure where allowance already given against receipts of compensation or insurance money, see 16.8 DISPOSAL);

(ii)   *TCGA 1992, s 122(4)* (disallowance where allowance already given against capital distribution, see 53.13 SHARES AND SECURITIES);

(iii)   *TCGA 1992, s 133(4)* (disallowance where allowance already given against premium on conversion of securities, see 53.10 SHARES AND SECURITIES); and

(iv)   *TCGA 1992, s 244* (disallowance where allowance already given against gain from small part disposal of land, see 33.11 and 33.13 LAND).

[*TCGA 1992, 3 Sch 4(2)*].

8.10   **Assets derived from other assets.** The re-basing provisions of *TCGA 1992, s 35* in 8.2 and 8.3 above apply with the necessary modifications in relation to a disposal of an asset which was not held on 31 March 1982, if its value is derived from another asset which is taken into account under *TCGA 1992, s 43* (assets derived from other assets, see 16.6 DISPOSAL). [*TCGA 1992, 3 Sch 5*]. For indexation allowance purposes, where, after 31 March 1982, an asset which was held on that date has been merged or divided or has changed its nature or rights in or over the asset have been created, then *TCGA 1992, s 55(1)(2)* (re-basing for indexation allowance purposes) in 8.2 above has effect to determine for the purposes of *TCGA 1992, s 43* the amount of the consideration for the acquisition of the asset which was so held. [*TCGA 1992, s 55(4)*].

8.11   **Time apportionment of pre-6 April 1965 gains and losses.** If *TCGA 1992, 2 Sch 16* (time apportionment of gains and losses accruing on ASSETS HELD ON 6 APRIL 1965; see 7.9) applies so that only part of a gain or loss is a chargeable gain or an allowable loss, the exclusion of the general re-basing rule of *TCGA 1992, s 35(1)(2)* under 8.2 (*a*) and (*b*) above has effect as if the amount of the gain or loss that would accrue if the general re-basing rule did not apply were equal to that part. [*TCGA 1992, 3 Sch 6*].

8.12   **DEFERRED CHARGES ON GAINS BEFORE 31 MARCH 1982**

Where, before 6 April 1988, a gain was deferred in respect of one or more disposals which related in whole or in part to an asset acquired before 31 March 1982, and the deferred gain is brought into charge on a disposal or other occasion after 5 April 1988, the deferred gain will, subject to conditions and on a claim, be halved (except, in certain cases, where the deferred gain is never deemed to accrue at all) when the charge to tax is computed in respect of it.

The provisions under which a gain can be deferred effectively fall into two groups for this purpose. In the first group (*TCGA 1992, 4 Sch 2*), which includes the hold-over provisions for gifts made before 14 March 1989 and rollover relief on the replacement of business assets, the deferred gain is deducted from the expenditure allowable in computing the gain on a later disposal. In the second group (*TCGA 1992, 4 Sch 3, 4*), the deferred gain is brought into charge on the occurrence of a subsequent event. For both groups, the deferred gain will be half of what it would otherwise be. [*TCGA 1992, s 36, 4 Sch 1*].

As regards the first group of provisions, both of the following circumstances must be fulfilled in order to bring about the halving of the deferred gain.

(*a*)   There is a disposal, other than a 'no gain/no loss disposal' (see 8.7 above), after 5 April 1988 of an asset acquired after 31 March 1982 by the person making the disposal.

(*b*)   A deduction from allowable expenditure falls to be made under any of the first group of provisions in computing the gain on that disposal and is attributable directly or indirectly, in whole or in part, to a chargeable gain accruing on the disposal before 6 April 1988 of an asset acquired before 31 March 1982 by the person making that disposal.

No relief is given under *TCGA 1992, 4 Sch* where, by reason of the previous operation of it, the amount of the deduction in (*b*) is less than it otherwise would be. Where the disposal takes place after 18 March 1991, no relief under *TCGA 1992, 4 Sch* is available if the amount of the deduction would have been less had relief by virtue of a previous application of it been duly claimed. (In effect, for disposals after 18 March 1991, the relief for the first group of provisions (*TCGA 1992, 4 Sch 2*) cannot be claimed twice for the same gain and must be claimed in respect of the earliest possible occasion. For disposals after 5 April 1988 and before 19 March 1991, it was possible to claim other than on the earliest possible occasion. See below as regards time limits for claims affected by this change.) [*TCGA 1992, 4 Sch 2(1)-(3)*].

Where the asset was acquired after 18 March 1991, the deduction is partly attributable to a claim under *TCGA 1992, s 154(4)* (rollover into non-depreciating asset instead of into depreciating asset, see 50.6 ROLLOVER RELIEF), and the claim applies to the asset, no relief under *TCGA 1992, 4 Sch* is available by virtue of its application in respect of the first group of provisions below (*TCGA 1992, 4 Sch 2*) (but see below as regards the relief available in respect of the second group of provisions). [*TCGA 1992, 4 Sch 2(4)*].

In the case of rollover relief on the replacement of business assets and subject to the usual time limits, the disposal of the old asset may be before 31 March 1982, and the replacement asset may be acquired afterwards (Revenue Press Release 8 July 1988).

For the circumstances in which the Inland Revenue will require a valuation of the asset transferred where a hold-over relief claim is made, see 22.1 HOLD-OVER RELIEFS.

The first group of provisions mentioned above is as follows.

(i)   *TCGA 1992, s 23(4)(5)* (rollover where replacement asset acquired after receipt of compensation or insurance money, see 16.9 DISPOSAL);

(ii)   *TCGA 1992, s 152* (rollover where replacement asset acquired on disposal of business asset, see 50 ROLLOVER RELIEF);

(iii)   *TCGA 1992, s 162* (hold-over where shares acquired on disposal of business to company, see 22.7 HOLD-OVER RELIEFS);

(iv)   *TCGA 1992, s 165* (hold-over where business asset acquired by gift, see 22.1–22.3 HOLD-OVER RELIEFS);

(v)   *TCGA 1992, s 247* (rollover where replacement land acquired on compulsory acquisition of other land, see 33.14 LAND);

(vi)   *FA 1980, s 79* (hold-over where asset acquired by gift after 5 April 1980 and before 14 March 1989, see 22.6 HOLD-OVER RELIEFS).

[*TCGA 1992, 4 Sch 2(5)*].

As regards the second group of provisions and subject to the exception below, both of the following circumstances must be fulfilled in order to bring about the halving of the deferred gain.

(A)   Under any of the second group of provisions a gain is treated as accruing in consequence of an event occurring after 5 April 1988.

(B)   The gain is attributable directly or indirectly, in whole or in part, to the disposal before 6 April 1988 of an asset acquired before 31 March 1982 by the person making that disposal.

[*TCGA 1992, 4 Sch 4(1)*].

Where a gain is treated as accruing in consequence of an event after 18 March 1991, relief under *TCGA 1992, 4 Sch* does not apply if the gain is attributable directly or indirectly, in whole or in part, to the disposal of an asset after 5 April 1988, or the amount of the gain would have been less had relief by virtue of a previous application of *TCGA 1992, 4 Sch* been duly claimed. [*TCGA 1992, 4 Sch 4(4)*]. (In effect, for events after 18 March 1991, the relief for the second group of provisions (*TCGA 1992, 4 Sch 3, 4*, and see below as regards *TCGA 1992, 4 Sch 3*) cannot be claimed twice for the same gain and must be claimed in respect of the earliest possible occasion. For events after 5 April 1988 and before 19 March 1991, it was possible to claim other than on the earliest possible occasion and more than once. See below as regards time limits for claims affected by this change.)

The second group of provisions mentioned above is as follows (and see also below).

(I)   *TCGA 1992, s 116(10)(11)* (postponement of charge on reorganisation etc. involving acquisition of qualifying corporate bonds, see 44.3 QUALIFYING CORPORATE BONDS).

(II)   *TCGA 1992, s 134* (postponement of charge where gilts acquired on compulsory acquisition of shares, see 53.10 SHARES AND SECURITIES);

(III)   *TCGA 1992, s 140* (postponement of charge where securities acquired in exchange for business acquired by overseas resident company until transferor company disposes of securities as mentioned in *s 140(4)* or transferee company within six years of exchange disposes of assets acquired on exchange as mentioned in *s 140(5)*, see 39.14 OVERSEAS MATTERS);

(IV)   *TCGA 1992, s 154(2)* (postponement of charge where depreciating asset acquired as replacement for business asset, see 50.6 ROLLOVER RELIEF) (and see below as regards *TCGA 1992, 4 Sch 3*);

(V)   *TCGA 1992, s 168* (as modified by *TCGA 1992, s 67(6)*) (activation of charge held over under *FA 1980, s 79* on emigration of donee in relation to a gift after 5 April 1981 and before 14 March 1989, see 22.6 HOLD-OVER RELIEFS);

(VI)   *TCGA 1992, s 178(3)* or *179(3)* (charge on company leaving group of companies in respect of asset acquired from another member of same group within previous six years, see 13.17 COMPANIES, but only if the asset was acquired by the chargeable company before 6 April 1988);

(VII)   *TCGA 1992, s 248(3)* (postponement of charge where depreciating asset acquired on compulsory acquisition of land, see 33.14 LAND);

[*TCGA 1992, 4 Sch 4(2)(3)*].

Where relief under *TCGA 1992, 4 Sch* would have applied on a disposal but for the effect of *TCGA 1992, 4 Sch 2(4)* (exclusion of relief under *TCGA 1992, 4 Sch 2* where deduction partly attributable to claim under *TCGA 1992, s 154(4)*) above, then such relief (on the same lines as for the second group of provisions above) is available (under *TCGA 1992, 4 Sch 3*) if the relief for the second group of provisions (*TCGA 1992, 4 Sch 4*) would have applied had *TCGA 1992, s 154(2)* (see (IV) above) continued to apply to the gain carried forward as a result of the claim under *TCGA 1992, s 154(4)*, and the time of disposal been the time when that gain was treated as accruing by virtue of *TCGA 1992, s 154(2)*. [*TCGA 1992, 4 Sch 3*].

There is an exception to the bringing about of the halving of the deferred gain in respect of certain provisions contained in the second group. None of *TCGA 1992, ss 134, 140(4), 154(2)* and *248(3)* (see (II)-(IV) and (VII) above) is to apply in consequence of an event occurring after 5 April 1988 if its application would be *directly* attributable to the disposal of an asset before 1 April 1982. [*TCGA 1992, 4 Sch 4(5)*]. In effect the deferred gain is in such circumstances never deemed to accrue. See also below regarding views expressed by the Revenue.

Relief is available as regards both groups of provisions where a person makes a disposal of an asset which he acquired after 30 March 1982 where the disposal by which he acquired it and any previous disposal of it after that date was a 'no gain/no loss disposal' (see 8.7 above). In such a case, the person is treated for the purposes of (*b*) and (B) above as having acquired the asset before 31 March 1982. [*TCGA 1992, 4 Sch 5, 7*].

Where deferral has been claimed under one of the first group of provisions and there is a subsequent no gain/no loss disposal (or continuous series of such disposals) as in 8.7 above, relief is available (subject to the conditions in (*a*) and (*b*) above) in computing the gain on the first later disposal which is not a no gain/no loss disposal. [*TCGA 1992, 4 Sch 6, 7*].

Relief is available as regards both groups of provisions for an asset which was not acquired before 31 March 1982 if its value was derived from another asset which was so acquired and which is taken into account under *TCGA 1992, s 43* (see 16.6 DISPOSAL). [*TCGA 1992, 4 Sch 8*].

No relief is available under *TCGA 1992, 4 Sch* unless a claim is made within two years (or such longer period as is allowed by the Board in a written notice) of the end of the accounting period or year of assessment in which, for the first group of provisions, the disposal to which the claim relates is made, or for the second group of provisions, the deferred gain is treated as accruing (except where (VI) above applies where the claim must be made within two years of the end of the accounting period in which the chargeable company ceases to be a member of a group of companies). A claim must be supported by any particulars the inspector may require for establishing the validity and quantum of any relief. [*TCGA 1992, 4 Sch 9*]. As regards the changes for disposals and other events after 18 March 1991 mentioned above, a person whose right to make a claim would otherwise have expired before the Royal Assent to *FA 1991* (25 July 1991) (e.g. because the person did not claim on the first possible occasion on the assumption a claim would be made on a later occasion) was allowed to make the relevant claim before 6 April 1992 (Revenue Press Release 19 March 1991).

Prior to the commencement of *TCGA 1992*, claims were made under *FA 1988, 9 Sch 8*.

It is understood that the Revenue accept that the crystallisation under *TCGA 1992, s 67(4)(5)* of a gain deferred by *FA 1980, s 79* (as extended by *FA 1981, s 78* and *FA 1982, s 82*) (clawback of deferred gain on death of life tenant, see 22.2 and 22.6 HOLD-OVER RELIEFS) can by concession be treated as if it were amongst the second group of provisions in (I)-(VII) above. In addition, a gain deferred on a transfer into settlement occurring before 1 April 1982 and which would otherwise crystallise on the death after 5 April 1988 of a life tenant will by concession be deemed never to accrue (and so treated in the same way as for the exception given by *TCGA 1992, 4 Sch 4(5)* above).

Example

1980   A acquires an asset for £10,000

1983   The asset is gifted to B with a hold-over election under *FA 1980, s 79* when worth £12,000. Indexation allowance is taken to be £500 for illustration purposes only.

Gain held over £12,000 − £10,000 − £500 = £1,500

B's cost of the asset £12,000 − £1,500 = £10,500

1985   B sells the asset for £15,000 and replaces it by one costing £17,000 at the same time. Indexation allowance is taken to be £750 by reference to the reduced base cost of £10,500. Full rollover under *TCGA 1992, s 152* (formerly *CGTA 1979, s 115*) is available and claimed.

Gain rolled over £15,000 − £10,500 − £750 = £3,750

Base cost of second asset £17,000 − £3,750 = £13,250

1987   B sells the replacement asset for £20,000 replacing it by one costing £22,000 at the same time. Indexation allowance is taken to be £1,250 by reference to the reduced base cost of £13,250. Full rollover as in 1985 is claimed.

Gain rolled over £20,000 − £13,250 − £1,250 = £5,500

Base cost of third asset £22,000 − £5,500 = £16,500 (but see below)

1995   B sells the third asset for £30,000 and does not replace it. The increase in the retail prices index between the month of sale in 1995 and the month of acquisition in 1987 is assumed to be 40%.

On a claim the deduction (£5,500) otherwise taken into account in arriving at the base cost of the third asset is reduced by half because it is partly attributable to the gain arising in 1983 in respect of the asset acquired in 1980.

Revised base cost of third asset £22,000 − £2,750 = £19,250

Chargeable gain £30,000 − £19,250 − 40% × £19,250 = £3,050

8.13   INDEXATION ALLOWANCE: CLAIM BEFORE 6 APRIL 1988 FOR RE-BASING AT 31 MARCH 1982

For disposals on or after the '1985 date' (1 April 1985 for companies and 6 April 1985 for others) and before 6 April 1988, a claim could be made for the indexation allowance (but not the unindexed gain or loss) arising on a disposal of an asset held on 31 March 1982 by the person making the disposal to be calculated on the assumption that on that date the asset was sold by the person concerned and immediately reacquired by him at its market value on that date. Such a claim had to be made within two years of the end of the year of assessment or accounting period in which the disposal occurred or within such longer period as the Board by notice in writing allowed. [*FA 1985, s 68(4)(5) (as originally enacted)*].

Although allowable expenditure relating to an asset held on 31 March 1982 may have been reduced (e.g. by rollover relief), there was no corresponding restriction applied to the market value on that date for the purposes of any deemed reacquisition on that date.

The Revenue in practice allowed a claim to be withdrawn within the time limit for making the claim provided the relevant assessment had not become final and conclusive (Tolley's Practical Tax 1986 pp 33, 88).

8.14   Previous no gain/no loss disposals. Where

(*a*)   a person made a disposal, other than a 'no gain/no loss disposal', of an asset which he acquired after 31 March 1982, and

(*b*)   the disposal by which he acquired the asset and any previous disposal of the asset after 31 March 1982 was a no gain/no loss disposal,

he was treated for the purposes of the re-basing provisions of *FA 1985, s 68(4)(5)* in 8.13 above as having held the asset on 31 March 1982.

A '*no gain/no loss disposal*' was one under the following enactments (being enactments by virtue of which neither a gain nor a loss accrues): *TCGA 1992, ss 58, 139, 171* and *264*; and *FA 1982, s 148*. See 8.7 above for details of these enactments and note the wider definition given there to a no gain/no loss disposal.

In computing the gain or loss on a person's disposal (not being a no gain/no loss disposal) of an asset which he was treated as having held on 31 March 1982, the no gain/no loss acquisition value which otherwise would have been deductible as allowable expenditure (see 23.4 INDEXATION) was reduced by any indexation allowance given on the disposal to him or any previous no gain/no loss disposal. [*FA 1985, s 68(7)(8) (as originally enacted)*].

8.15   Assets derived from other assets. For indexation allowance purposes, where, after 31 March 1982, an asset which was held on that date was merged or divided or changed its nature or rights in or over the asset were created, then the re-basing provisions of *FA 1985, s 68(4)(5)* in 8.13 above had effect to determine for the purposes of *TCGA 1992, s 43* (assets derived from other assets, see 16.6 DISPOSAL) the amount of the consideration for the acquisition of the asset which was so held. [*FA 1985, s 68(6)*].

9   Back Duty

Cross-reference. See 5 ASSESSMENTS; 12 CLAIMS; 32 INTEREST ON UNPAID TAX; 41 PAYMENT OF TAX; 42 PENALTIES; 51 SELF-ASSESSMENT for future changes broadly from 1996/97.

9.1   BACK DUTY CLAIMS

These are made by the Revenue where they consider tax to have been lost by a taxpayer's fraudulent or negligent conduct (or by his fraud, wilful default or neglect). In such cases, the normal time limits for assessments are extended (see 9.4 below) and INTEREST ON UNPAID TAX (32.4 and 32.6) and PENALTIES (42) are incurred, which the Board may mitigate in appropriate circumstances. For cases relating to back duty, see Tolley's Tax Cases.

9.2   FRAUD OR WILFUL DEFAULT

See 9.4 below as regards the replacement of 'fraud, wilful default or neglect' assessments by 'fraudulent or negligent conduct' assessments. The later expression is not defined, and the following cases may be of continued assistance in this respect.

The onus of proving fraud or wilful default is on the Crown but the onus then shifts to the taxpayer to prove the revised assessments incorrect if he wishes to do so (*Johnson v Scott CA 1978, 52 TC 383; Jonas v Bamford Ch D 1973, 51 TC 1; Nicholson v Morris CA 1977, 51 TC 95* and cf. *Barney v Pybus Ch D 1957, 37 TC 106; R v Special Commrs (ex p. Martin) CA 1971, 48 TC 1* and *Arumugam Pillai v Director General of Inland Revenue PC, [1981] STC 146*). For the standard of proof required, see *Les Croupiers Casino Club v Pattinson CA 1987, 60 TC 196*.

Unexplained capital increases or admitted omissions may be held evidence of fraud or wilful default (*Amis v Colls Ch D 1960, 39 TC 148; Woodrow v Whalley Ch D 1964, 42 TC 249; Hudson v Humbles Ch D 1965, 42 TC 380; Hillenbrand CS 1966, 42 TC 617; Young v Duthie Ch D 1969, 45 TC 624; James v Pope Ch D 1972, 48 TC 142;* and cf. *Brimelow v Price Ch D 1965, 49 TC 41*). Fraud or wilful default may be by an agent (*Clixby v Pountney Ch D 1967, 44 TC 515; Pleasants v Atkinson Ch D 1987, 60 TC 228*).

9.3   NEGLECT

See 9.4 below as regards the replacement of 'fraud, wilful default or neglect' assessments by 'fraudulent or negligent conduct' assessments.

'Neglect' means negligence or a failure to give any notice, make any return, or produce or furnish any document or other information required by or under the Taxes Acts. [*TMA 1970, s 118; FA 1989, 17 Sch Pt VIII*]. Neglect may be by an agent (*Mankowitz v Special Commrs Ch D 1971, 46 TC 707*).

9.4   EXTENDED TIME LIMITS

The normal time limit for making assessments is six years after the chargeable period concerned. [*TMA 1970, s 34*]. In certain cases, however, extended limits apply to assessments for the purpose of making good a loss of tax, subject to the overriding provision that an assessment may not be made on personal representatives later than three years after that in which the deceased died (see 9.5 below). See 5.5 ASSESSMENTS as regards the date on which an assessment is made.

Assessments made after 26 July 1989 relating to 1983/84 and subsequent years (or to accounting periods ending after 31 March 1983). Where the loss of tax arises due to the fraudulent or negligent conduct of a person (or of a person acting on his behalf), an assessment may be made at any time not later than 20 years after the end of the chargeable period to which it relates. If the person assessed so requires, the assessment may give effect to reliefs or allowances to which he would have been entitled had he made the necessary claims within the relevant time limits. [*TMA 1970, s 36(1)(3); FA 1989, s 149*].

Assessments made before 27 July 1989 or relating to 1982/83 and earlier years (or to accounting periods ending before 1 April 1983). *Fraud or wilful default.* An assessment to make good tax lost through fraud or wilful default may be made at any time. [*TMA 1970, s 36*]. The leave of a single General or Special Commissioner must be obtained, and the Commissioner must be satisfied that there are reasonable grounds for believing that tax may have been so lost. [*TMA 1970, s 41*]. There is no hearing, and the taxpayer is not entitled to appear or to present his case (*Day v Williams CA 1969, 46 TC 59; Pearlberg v Varty HL 1972, 48 TC 14* and *Nicholson v Morris CA 1977, 51 TC 95*) but contrast *R v Spec Commrs (ex p. Stipplechoice Ltd) (No 1) CA, [1985] STC 248* where a judicial review was granted in the absence of any other adequate remedy. The taxpayer may, of course, appeal against the assessment in the normal way. The Commissioner who gave leave to issue the assessment is not allowed to be present at the hearing of such an appeal. [*TMA 1970, s 41(2)*].

Neglect. Where, for the purpose of recovering tax lost due to fraud, wilful default, or neglect, an assessment has been made not later than six years after the end of the year for which the tax was lost (the '*normal year*'), the Revenue may make assessments for any of the six years prior to that normal year to make good a loss of tax attributable to neglect. Leave of a General or Special Commissioner is required. Such an assessment must be made not later than the end of the year of assessment following that in which the normal year assessment is finally determined. [*TMA 1970, s 37(1)-(3)*]. Thus an assessment made in 1988/89 to recover tax lost for the year 1982/83 may support assessments for 1976/77 onwards. The decision in *O'Mullan v Walmsley QB (NI) 1965, 42 TC 573* that such assessments are invalid unless the assessment for the 'normal year' was expressly stated to be for making good tax lost by fraud, default or neglect was not followed in *Thurgood v Slarke Ch D 1971, 47 TC 130*. 'What matters is not the purpose of the assessor but of the assessment.' See also *R v Spec Commrs (ex p. Rogers) CA 1972, 48 TC 46; Knight v CIR CA 1974, 49 TC 179* and *R v Holborn Commrs (ex p. Frank Rind Settlement Trustees) QB 1974, 49 TC 656*.

The Revenue may go back further if an assessment for any year has been made more than six years after the end of that year. The year for which the assessment has been made is called the '*earlier year*'. One of the following conditions must be satisfied.

(*a*)   The assessment has been made under *TMA 1970, s 37(3)* (see above).

(*b*)   The assessment is one of a number made under *TMA 1970, s 36* (see above) for years which are not more than six years apart and of which the latest is within six years prior to the normal year.

If (*a*) or (*b*) above applies, the Revenue may make an assessment for any of the six years immediately preceding the earlier year (and so on for other earlier years) with the leave of the General or Special Commissioners. The Commissioners must be satisfied that reasonable grounds exist for believing that tax for that year may have been lost through the taxpayer's neglect. The taxpayer is entitled to appear (or to be represented) and be heard. [*TMA 1970, s 37(4)-(7)*]. The Revenue must apply to the Commissioners not later than the end of the year following that in which liability under the assessment for the earlier year is finally determined.

In determining the tax to be charged for any year, the taxpayer is to be given the reliefs and allowances to which he would have been entitled for that year. [*TMA 1970, s 37(8)*].

The making of an assessment to income tax will not affect the time allowed for the making of a capital gains tax assessment under these provisions, and vice versa. [*TMA 1970, s 37(9)*].

For companies, similar provisions apply, by reference to accounting periods instead of tax years. [*TMA 1970, s 39*].

9.5 **Deceased persons.** Assessments on a deceased's capital gains arising or accruing before death must be made within three years after the end of year of assessment in which he dies and those made as a result of the deceased's fraudulent or negligent conduct (or fraud, wilful default or neglect) are restricted to years of assessment ending not earlier than six years prior to the death. A fraudulent or negligent act or omission under *TMA 1970, s 98B* (failure etc. to render return relating to European Economic Interest Groupings; see 39.20 OVERSEAS MATTERS, 42.7 PENALTIES and 49.8 RETURNS) on the part of a grouping or a member thereof is deemed to be the act or omission of each member. [*TMA 1970, s 40; FA 1989, s 149(4), 17 Sch Pt VIII; FA 1990, 11 Sch 4(2), 5*]. See 5.5 ASSESSMENTS as regards the date on which an assessment is made.

9.6 **EVIDENCE**

Statements made or documents produced by or on behalf of a taxpayer are admissible as evidence in proceedings against him, notwithstanding that reliance on the Board's practice in cases of full disclosure may have induced him to make or produce them. [*TMA 1970, s 105; FA 1989, s 168(1)(5)*]. See 9.7 and 9.9 and 42.6 PENALTIES below.

9.7 **CERTIFICATES OF FULL DISCLOSURE**

A certificate of full disclosure may be required by the Revenue from a taxpayer during a back duty enquiry stating that complete disclosure has been made of, inter alia, all banking, savings and loan accounts, deposit receipts, building society and co-operative society accounts; all investments including savings certificates and premium bonds and loans (whether interest-bearing or not); all other assets, including cash and life assurance policies, which the taxpayer and his spouse now possess, or have possessed, or in which they have or have had any interest or power to operate or control during the stated period; all gifts in any form, by the taxpayer or his spouse to their children or to other persons during the stated period; all sources of income and all income derived therefrom; and all facts bearing on liability to income tax, capital gains tax and other duties for the stated period. Great care must be exercised before signing such a certificate, since subsequent discovery of an omission could lead to heavy penalties. See 42 PENALTIES.

9.8 **INVESTIGATORY POWERS**

With effect from 27 July 1989, the Revenue's powers to obtain the production of accounts, books and other information were materially altered. The revised powers are described below. See 1988/89 or an earlier edition of Tolley's Capital Gains Tax for details of the previous powers.

For these purposes, '*document*' has the same meaning as in *Civil Evidence Act 1968, Pt I* (or Scottish or Northern Ireland equivalent), but does not include personal records or journalistic material (within *Police and Criminal Evidence Act 1984, ss 12, 13*) (and those exclusions apply also to particulars contained in such records or material). The documents concerned are those in the possession or power of the person receiving the notice. Photographic, etc. facsimiles may be supplied provided the originals are produced if called for, and documents relating to any pending tax appeal need not be delivered. There are special provisions relating to computer records (see *FA 1988, s 127*). Documents in a person's 'possession or power' are those actually in existence at the time the notice is given, and not any which would have to be brought into existence in order to satisfy the notice.

(*a*)   Where an inspector is of the reasonable opinion that documents contain, or may contain, information relevant to the tax liability of a person, he may (with the Board's authority and the consent of a General or Special Commissioner) by notice in writing require that person to deliver such documents to him (but only after that person has been given reasonable opportunity to produce them).

After 2 May 1994, the inspector must give a written summary of his reasons for applying for consent to the giving of the notice. He is not required to identify any informant in the summary and no summary need be provided if the Special or General Commissioner giving consent so directs, and the Commissioner concerned must not so direct unless he is satisfied that the inspector has reasonable grounds for believing that disclosure of the information in question would prejudice the assessment or collection of tax. The Commissioner concerned must not take part in or be present at any subsequent proceedings concerning an appeal made by the person if the Commissioner concerned has reason to believe that any of the documents which were the subject of the notice is likely to be adduced in evidence in those proceedings.

For an unsuccessful challenge to the validity of a notice, see *Kempton v Special Commrs & CIR Ch D, [1992] STC 823*.

(*b*)   An inspector may similarly by notice in writing require a person to furnish him with such particulars as he may reasonably require as being relevant to any tax liability of that person.

The notice is subject to the same authority and giving of consent requirements as at (*a*) above, and the requirements there relating to the giving of a written summary and the obligation imposed on the Special or General Commissioner giving consent apply similarly in relation to particulars as they do there to documents.

For an unsuccessful challenge to the validity of a notice, see *Kempton v Special Commrs & CIR Ch D, [1992] STC 823*.

(*c*)   An inspector may similarly by notice in writing require any other person (including the Director of Savings) to deliver to him (or, if the person so elects, make available for inspection by a named officer of the Board) documents relevant to any tax liability of a 'taxpayer'. A copy of the notice must be given to the taxpayer concerned unless, in a case involving suspected fraud, a General or Special Commissioner so directs. Production of documents originating more than six years before the notice cannot be required (unless the Commissioner who gave consent to the notice specifically allows it on being satisfied that there is reasonable ground for believing loss of tax through fraud).

'*Taxpayer*' includes an individual who has died (but any notice must be given no more than six years after the death) and a company which has ceased to exist.

The notice is subject to the same authority and giving of consent requirements as at (*a*) above, and the requirements there relating to the giving of a written summary and the obligation imposed on the Special or General Commissioner giving consent apply similarly, except that the summary must be given to, and the obligation imposed relates to an appeal brought by, the taxpayer rather than the person to whom the notice is given, and no summary need be given if the taxpayer is not, as above, given a copy of the notice.

A notice cannot require the production by a statutory auditor of his audit papers, nor by a tax adviser of communications with a client (or with any other tax adviser of his client) relating to advice about the client's tax affairs. This exemption does not, however, apply to explanatory documents concerning any other documents prepared with the client for, or for delivery to, the Revenue, unless the Revenue already has access to the information contained therein in some other document. Where the exemption is so disapplied, either the document must be delivered or made available to the Revenue or a copy of the relevant parts must be supplied (which parts must be available if required for inspection).

The Revenue's application of these provisions relating to papers of a statutory auditor or client communications of a tax adviser is set out in Statement of Practice SP 5/90 (11 April 1990). In particular, it is made clear that accountants' working papers will be called for only where voluntary access has not been obtained and it is considered absolutely necessary in order to determine whether a client's accounts or returns are complete and correct. Requests for access may on occasion extend to the whole or a particular part of the working papers, rather than just to information explaining specific entries, and the Revenue will usually be prepared to visit the accountants' or clients' premises to examine the papers and to take copies or extracts.

For guidance on the question of whether documents and records are the property of a statutory auditor or tax adviser, or of the client of such a person, see ICAEW Memorandum TR 781, 23 February 1990.

For an unsuccessful challenge to the validity of a notice, see *R v CIR (ex p. TC Coombs & Co.) HL, [1991] STC 97.*

(*d*)   An inspector may similarly (on an application authorised by the Board) give a notice in writing as under (*c*) above without naming the taxpayer concerned. Consent to the application must be obtained from a Special Commissioner, who must be satisfied that: it relates to a taxpayer or class of taxpayers whose identity(ies) is (are) not known; there are reasonable grounds to believe the taxpayer(s) to have failed to comply with the *Taxes Acts*, with the likelihood of serious prejudice to the assessment or collection of tax; and the information is not reasonably available from elsewhere. The recipient can object (with a right of appeal to the Special Commissioners), by notice in writing, within 30 days on the ground that it would be onerous for him to comply.

The requirements at (*a*) above relating to the giving of a written summary and the obligation imposed on the Special or General Commissioner giving consent do not apply. The exemption, and disapplication of the exemption, from the requirements of a notice under (*d*) above relating to the production of the papers of a statutory auditor or client communications of a tax adviser apply similarly, except that the exemption does not apply to any document giving the identity or address of any taxpayer to whom the notice relates or of any person who has acted on behalf of any such person, unless the Revenue already has access to the information contained therein in some other document.

(*e*)   An officer may similarly (with the Board's authority and the consent of a Circuit judge in England and Wales, a sheriff in Scotland or a county court judge in Northern Ireland) by notice in writing require a '*tax accountant*' (i.e. a person who assists another in the preparation of returns, etc. for tax purposes) who has been convicted by or before any UK court of a tax offence or incurred a penalty under *TMA 1970, s 99* (see 42.5 PENALTIES) to deliver documents in his possession or power relevant to any tax liability of any of his clients. The notice must be issued within twelve months of the final determination of the conviction or penalty award.

Neither the requirements at (*a*) above relating to the giving of a written summary nor the exemption from the requirements of a notice under (*d*) above relating to the production of the papers of a statutory auditor or client communications of a tax adviser apply to the giving of a notice as above.

(*f*)   The Board may require, by notice in writing, a person to deliver or furnish to a named officer of theirs documents or information as specified in (*a*) and (*b*) above relevant to the tax liability of that person.

The requirements at (*a*) above relating to the giving of consent and a written summary do not apply. However, notices cannot be given on or after 26 July 1990 under this power unless there are reasonable grounds for believing that that person may have failed, or may fail, to comply with any provision of the *Taxes Acts*, and that any such failure is likely to have led, or to lead, to serious prejudice to the proper assessment or collection of tax.

For procedural matters in relation to such a notice, see *R v CIR (ex p. Taylor) (No 1) CA 1988, 62 TC 562; (No 2) CA 1990, 62 TC 578.*

The notice must specify or describe the documents or particulars required, the time limit for production (generally not less than 30 days) and, except as above, the name of the taxpayer or client, as appropriate; and the person to whom they are delivered may take copies.

The penalty for failure to comply with a notice is given by *TMA 1970, s 98* (see 42.7 PENALTIES for this and the penalty for failure to allow access to computers). In addition there are severe penalties (in summary proceedings, a fine of the statutory maximum, and on indictment, imprisonment for two years and/or an unlimited fine) for the falsification, concealment, destruction or disposal of a document which is the subject of a notice, unless strict conditions and time limits are observed. [*TMA 1970, ss 20, 20A, 20B(1)(1A)(1B)(2)(4)–(7)(9)–(14), 20BB, 20D; FA 1976, 6 Sch; FA 1988, s 126(2)(3); FA 1989, ss 142–145, 148, 168(1)(2); FA 1990, s 93; FA 1994, s 255].*

Notices given on or after 26 July 1990 (other than those under (*d*) and (*e*) above) may relate to tax liabilities in EEC member States other than the UK. [*FA 1990, s 125(1)(2)(6)*].

Search and seizure. Where there is a reasonable suspicion of serious tax fraud, the Board may apply to a Circuit judge (a sheriff in Scotland or a county court judge in Northern Ireland) for a warrant to enter premises within 14 days to search and seize any things which may be relevant as evidence. There are detailed procedural rules governing searches and the removal of documents, etc. [*TMA 1970, ss 20C(1)(1A)(1B)(2)(3)(5)–(8), 20CC, 20D; FA 1976, 6 Sch; FA 1989, ss 146–148*].

The taxpayer is not entitled to be told the nature of the offence, the ground of suspicion, or the person suspected (*CIR and Another v Rossminster Ltd and Others HL 1979, 52 TC 160*).

Barristers, advocates or solicitors. A notice under (*a*), (*b*), (*c*) or (*e*) above to a barrister, advocate or solicitor can be issued only by the Board. The requirements at (*a*) above relating to the giving of consent and a written summary do not apply. The barrister etc. cannot (without his client's consent) be required to deliver under (*c*), (*d*) or (*e*) documents protected by professional privilege but, subject to that, the exemption, and disapplication of the exemption, from the requirements of a notice under, as the case may be, (*c*), (*d*) or (*e*) above relating to the production of the papers of a statutory auditor or client communications of a tax adviser apply similarly. Documents protected by professional privilege are not subject to the power of search and seizure. [*TMA 1970, ss 20B(3)(8), 20C(4), 20D; FA 1976, 6 Sch; FA 1988, s 126(4); FA 1989, s 146(4)*].

See *R v CIR (ex p. Goldberg) QB, 1988, 61 TC 403* and cf. *Dubai Bank Ltd v Galadari CA, [1989] 3 WLR 1044* (a non-tax case).

9.9 OFFERS BY TAXPAYER

Where back duty arises, the taxpayer may be invited to offer a sum in settlement of liability of tax, interest and penalties and such offers are often accepted by the Board without assessment of all the tax. A binding agreement so made cannot be repudiated afterwards by the taxpayer or his executors. Where the liability is agreed and the tax etc. paid, this cannot afterwards be set aside, notwithstanding any alleged overcharge and no formal assessment (see cases at 42.10 PENALTIES and *CIR v Nuttall CA 1989, 63 TC 148* and *CIR v Woollen CA, [1992] STC 944*). See generally Revenue Pamphlet IR 73 regarding negotiation of settlements.

The practice of the Board in cases of tax fraud is as follows.

(*a*) The Board may accept a money settlement instead of instituting criminal proceedings in respect of fraud alleged to have been committed by a taxpayer.

(*b*) They can give no undertaking that they will accept a money settlement and refrain from instituting criminal proceedings (even if the taxpayer has made a full disclosure and fully facilitated the investigation of the facts) and reserve to themselves full discretion in all cases as to the course they pursue.

(*c*) But in considering whether to accept a money settlement or to institute criminal proceedings, it is their practice to be influenced by the fact that the taxpayer has made a full disclosure and fully facilitated the investigation of his affairs.

(Revenue Press Release of 18 October 1990 reproducing a Parliamentary statement (HC Written answer 18 October 1990 Vol 177 col 882) and replacing the 'Hansard leaflet' statement of 5 October 1944). See also 9.6 above and 42.6 PENALTIES.

10   Charities

10.1   DEFINITIONS AND GENERAL PRINCIPLES

For certain income tax purposes, *'charity'* means any body of persons or trust established for charitable purposes only. [*ICTA 1988, s 506(1)*]. The meaning of charity is also governed by general law. These meanings apply for capital gains tax for all practical purposes.

Under *Recreational Charities Act 1958, s 1*, the provision, in the interests of social welfare, of facilities for recreation or other leisure occupation is deemed to be charitable (subject to the principle that, unless the trust is for the relief of poverty (*Dingle v Turner HL, [1972] 1 All E R 878*) a trust or institution to be charitable must be for the public benefit). See in this connection *Guild v CIR HL, [1992] STC 162*.

Charities are regulated under the *Charities Acts 1992* and *1993* in England and Wales by the Charity Commissioners. In Scotland, charities recognised as such by the Inland Revenue are regulated by the Scottish Charities Office, on behalf of the Lord Advocate, under the *Law Reform (Miscellaneous Provisions) (Scotland) Act 1990*. Registers of charities are kept by the Charity Commissioners and the Financial Intermediaries and Claims Office (Scotland), Trinity Park House, South Trinity Road, Edinburgh EH5 3SD (Tel. 0131 552 6255), as appropriate. A leaflet CB(1), available from the address quoted, provides further information on how to apply for recognition in Scotland and the tax reliefs available. Under *Charities Act 1993, s 10* and *Law Reform (Miscellaneous Provisions) (Scotland) Act 1990, s 1*, the Revenue may disclose information regarding charities to the Charity Commissioners and the Lord Advocate, as appropriate.

Subject to the above, what is a charity rests largely on judicial interpretation. A leading case is *Special Commrs v Pemsel HL 1891, 3 TC 53* in which Lord Macnaghten laid down that 'charity' should be given its technical meaning under English law and comprises 'four principal divisions; trusts for the relief of poverty, trusts for the advancement of education, trusts for the advancement of religion and trusts beneficial to the community and not falling under any of the preceding heads. The trusts last referred to are not the less charitable . . . because incidentally they affect the rich as well as the poor'. In the same case it was held that, in relation to tax, the English definition should be applied to Scottish cases (and cf. *Jackson's Trustees v Lord Advocate CS 1926, 10 TC 460* and *CIR v Glasgow (City) Police Athletic Assn HL 1953, 34 TC 76*). The concept of 'charity' may change with changes in social values (cf. *CIR v Trustees of Football Association Youth Trust HL 1980, 54 TC 413*).

The charity reliefs are not available to charities established overseas (*CIR v Gull KB 1937, 21 TC 374; Dreyfus Foundation Inc v CIR HL 1955, 36 TC 126*). The *Charitable Trusts (Validation) Act 1954* provides for validating as charitable a pre-1953 trust if its property was in fact applied for charitable purposes only, notwithstanding that the trust also authorised its application for non-charitable purposes (cf. *Vernon & Sons Ltd Employees Fund v CIR Ch D 1956, 36 TC 484; Buxton v Public Trustees Ch D 1962, 41 TC 235*).

10.2   CHARITY, CHARITABLE PURPOSES — EXAMPLES

Relevant cases are summarised below under appropriate headings.

(*a*)   **Almshouse.** Inmates need not be destitute (*Mary Clark Home Trustees v Anderson KB 1904, 5 TC 48*).

(b)   **Arts.** A musical festival association and the Royal Choral Society have been held to be charitable (*Glasgow Musical Festival Assn CS 1926, 11 TC 154; Royal Choral Socy v CIR CA 1943, 25 TC 263*) but not companies formed to produce plays in association with the Arts Council (*Tennent Plays Ltd v CIR CA 1948, 30 TC 107*) or with the aim of furthering the theatre and dramatic taste (*Associated Artists Ltd v CIR Ch D 1956, 36 TC 499*).

(c)   **Benevolent funds, etc.** for the relief of widows and orphans of members were held charitable (*Society for the Relief of Widows and Orphans of Medical Men KB 1926, 11 TC 1; Baptist Union, etc. Ltd v CIR KB (NI) 1945, 26 TC 335*) but not a death benefit fund (*Royal Naval etc. Officers' Assn Ch D 1955, 36 TC 187*) nor a fund set up to promote the formation of mutual provident associations (*Nuffield Foundation v CIR; Nuffield Provident Guarantee Fund v CIR KB 1946, 28 TC 479*).

(d)   **Education.** A trust for the advancement of education does not require an element of poverty to be charitable (*R v Special Commrs (ex p. University College of N. Wales) CA 1909, 5 TC 408*). The technical college of a trade association was held to be charitable (*Scottish Woollen Technical College v CIR CS 1926, 11 TC 139*) as was the Students' Union of a medical college (*London Hospital Medical College Ch D 1976, 51 TC 365*) and a trust to promote sports in schools, etc. (*CIR v Trustees of Football Association Youth Trust HL 1980, 54 TC 413*). See also *Educational Grants Assn Ltd CA 1967, 44 TC 93; Abdul Caffoor Trustees v Ceylon Income Tax Commr PC 1961, 40 ATC 93*. For 'public school' see (h) below.

(e)   **Hospital.** A friendly society's convalescent home was exempted (*Royal Antediluvian Order of Buffaloes v Owens KB 1927, 13 TC 176*).

(f)   **Political and similar objects** (including the reform of the law) are not charitable purposes. Objects held not to be charitable include the reform of the law on vivisection (*National Anti-Vivisection Socy HL 1947, 28 TC 311*) and temperance (*Temperance Council etc. of England KB 1926, 10 TC 748*), simplified spelling (*Hunter 'C' Trustees v CIR KB 1929, 14 TC 427*), fostering Anglo-Swedish relations (*Anglo-Swedish Socy v CIR KB 1931, 16 TC 34*), Jewish resettlement (*Keren Kayemeth Le Jisroel Ltd v CIR HL 1932, 17 TC 27*) and a memorial fund for Bonar Law (*Bonar Law Memorial Trust v CIR KB 1933, 17 TC 508*).

(g)   **Professional associations etc.** Professional associations are generally not admitted to be established for charitable purposes; they benefit their members, any wider public advantage being incidental (*R v Special Commrs (ex p. Headmasters' Conference) KB 1925, 10 TC 73; General Medical Council v CIR CA 1928, 13 TC 819; Geologists' Assn v CIR CA 1928, 14 TC 271; Midland Counties Institution of Engineers v CIR KB 1928, 14 TC 285; General Nursing Council for Scotland v CIR CS 1929, 14 TC 645; Master Mariners (Honourable Company of) v CIR KB 1932, 17 TC 298*). But contrast *Institution of Civil Engineers v CIR CA 1931, 16 TC 158*, where the Institution was held to be charitable, any benefit to members being incidental. Members' clubs and social clubs are not charitable (*Scottish Flying Club v CIR CS 1935, 20 TC 1; Sir H J Williams's Trustees v CIR HL 1947, 27 TC 409*). An agricultural society for the general promotion of agriculture was held charitable (*CIR v Yorkshire Agricultural Socy CA 1927, 13 TC 58*) but not a statutory pig marketing board (*Pig Marketing Board (Northern Ireland) v CIR KB (NI) 1945, 26 TC 319*) nor a society to promote foxhound breeding (*Peterborough Royal Foxhound Show Socy v CIR KB 1936, 20 TC 249*) (but it was given relief under *ICTA 1988, s 510* on its annual show).

(h)   **Public school.** A school may be for the public benefit and qualify for the relief notwithstanding that it derives substantial receipts from fees (*Blake v Mayor etc. of London CA 1887, 2 TC 209; Ereaut v Girls' Public Day School Trust Ltd HL 1930,*

10.3   Charities

15 TC 529, and contrast *Birkenhead School Ltd v Dring KB 1926, 11 TC 273).* A Quaker school exclusively for children of members of the Society of Friends was refused relief (*Ackworth School v Betts KB 1915, 6 TC 642*) but a Roman Catholic school which admitted non-Catholic pupils qualified for relief (*Cardinal Vaughan Memorial School Trustees v Ryall KB 1920, 7 TC 611*).

(*i*)   **Religion.** Charitable relief was refused for trusts to advance the 'religious, moral, social and recreative life' of Presbyterians in Londonderry (*Londonderry Presbyterian Church House Trustees v CIR CA (NI) 1946, 27 TC 431*), for the promotion and aiding of 'Roman Catholicism' in a particular district (*Ellis v CIR CA 1949, 31 TC 178*) and for the 'religious, educational and other parochial requirements' of the Roman Catholic inhabitants of a parish (*Cookstown Roman Catholic Church Trustees v CIR QB (NI) 1953, 34 TC 350*). In each case, the objects included non-charitable elements which prevented the whole being charitable. Relief was also refused to the Oxford Group (*Oxford Group v CIR CA 1949, 31 TC 221*).

(*j*)   **Miscellaneous.** A nursing home (*Peebleshire Nursing Assn CS 1926, 11 TC 335*) and a holiday home (*Roberts Marine Mansions Trustees CA 1927, 11 TC 425*) providing services for members etc. at reduced fees were held to be charitable, as was a non-profit making company for publishing law reports (*Incorpd. Council of Law Reporting v A-G CA 1971, 47 TC 321*). Relief was refused to a trust to maintain an historic building because it also had a non-charitable object (*Trades House of Glasgow v CIR CS 1969, 46 TC 178*) and to a Society established mainly with philanthropic objects which, in the event, were not achieved (*Hugh's Settlement Ltd v CIR KB 1938, 22 TC 281*).

10.3   EXEMPTION AVAILABLE

Subject to the restriction in 10.4 below, a gain accruing to a charity is not a chargeable gain provided it is 'applicable and applied for charitable purposes only'. [*TCGA 1992, s 256(1)*]. For the scope of 'applicable and applied for charitable purposes only', see *Lawrence v CIR KB 1940, 23 TC 333, Slater (Helen) Charitable Trust Ltd CA 1981, 55 TC 230* and *Guild and others v CIR CS, [1993] STC 444.*

Where property held on charitable trusts ceases to be subject to those trusts, the trustees are deemed to have disposed of, and immediately reacquired, the property at its market value at that time. Any gain arising is not treated as accruing to a charity. Furthermore, insofar as the property represents, directly or indirectly, the consideration for the disposal of assets by the trustees, any gain accruing on that earlier disposal (and previously exempt) is treated as not having accrued to a charity and capital gains tax is chargeable as if the exemption had never applied. A cumulative liability may therefore arise and an assessment may be made within three years of the end of the year of assessment in which the property ceases to be subject to charitable trusts. [*TCGA 1992, s 256(2)*]. Such an assessment seems to be able to be made even where the gain arising on an earlier disposal is outside the normal time limit for assessment.

By concession, where land given for educational and certain other charitable purposes ceases after 16 August 1987 to be used for such purposes and, under *Reverter of Sites Act 1987*, is held by the trustees on a trust for sale for the benefit of the revertee, then unless the revertee is known to be a charity, there is a deemed disposal and reacquisition for capital gains purposes under *TCGA 1992, s 256(2)* above, which may give rise to a chargeable gain. Any income arising from the property will be liable to income tax, and a chargeable gain may also arise on a subsequent sale of the land. By concession, where the revertee is subsequently identified as a charity or disclaims all entitlement to the property (or where certain orders are made by the Charity Commissioners or the Secretary of State), provided that charitable status is re-established within six years of the date on which the land ceased to be held on the original charitable trust, any capital gains tax paid as above in the interim period will be discharged or repaid (with repayment supplement where appropriate) as will any income tax (provided that the income charged was used for charitable purposes). Partial relief will be given where the above conditions are only satisfied in respect of part of the property concerned. A request by the trustees for postponement of the tax payable will be accepted by the Revenue where the revertee has not been identified and this concession may apply (Revenue Press Release 9 March 1994).

10.4   **Restriction after 11 June 1986.** For chargeable periods ending after 11 June 1986 a restriction of the exemption in 10.3 above will occur in certain circumstances. Where a chargeable period spans 11 June 1986 the charity may, by written election, treat that period as two separate periods for the purposes of the restriction, so that the second period begins on 12 June 1986.

If in any chargeable period (ending after 11 June 1986) a charity

(*a*)   has 'relevant income and gains' of £10,000 or more (but see below); and

(*b*)   has relevant income and gains exceeding the amount of its 'qualifying expenditure'; and

(*c*)   incurs, or is treated as incurring 'non-qualifying expenditure',

exemption under *TCGA 1992, s 256* (and *ICTA 1988, s 505(1)* for income tax) is not available for so much of the excess at (*b*) as does not exceed the non-qualifying expenditure incurred in that period. Where the exemption is not so available, the charity may, by notice in writing, specify which items of its relevant income and gains are wholly or partly to be attributed to the amount concerned. Covenanted payments to the charity (within *ICTA 1988, s 347A(7)*) are treated as a single item. If, within thirty days of a request to do so, the charity does not give notice, the Board determines the attribution.

The £10,000 limit in (*a*) above is proportionately reduced where a chargeable period is less than twelve months, and does not apply where two or more charities acting in concert are engaged in transactions aimed at tax avoidance and where the Board, by notice in writing, so direct. An appeal, as against a decision on a claim, may be made against such a notice.

'*Relevant income and gains*'. This means the aggregate of

(i)   income which, apart from *ICTA 1988, s 505(1)*, would not be exempt from tax, together with any income which is taxable notwithstanding *ICTA 1988, s 505(1)*; and

(ii)   gains which, apart from *TCGA 1992, s 256*, would be chargeable gains, together with any gains which are chargeable gains notwithstanding *TCGA 1992, s 256*.

'*Non-qualifying expenditure*'. This is expenditure other than 'qualifying expenditure'. If the charity invests any funds in an investment which is not a 'qualifying investment' or makes a loan (not as an investment) which is not a 'qualifying loan', the amount invested or lent is treated as non-qualifying expenditure. Where the investment or loan is realised or repaid in whole or in part in the period in which it was made, any further investment or lending of the sum realised or repaid in that period is, to the extent that it does not exceed the sum originally invested or lent, ignored in arriving at non-qualifying expenditure of the period.

Where the aggregate of the qualifying and non-qualifying expenditure incurred in a chargeable period (the '*primary period*') exceeds the relevant income and gains of that period, so much of the excess as does not exceed the non-qualifying expenditure constitutes '*unapplied non-qualifying expenditure*'. Except to the extent (if any) that it represents the expenditure of 'non-taxable sums' received in the primary period, the unapplied non-qualifying expenditure may be treated as non-qualifying expenditure of an '*earlier period*' (a chargeable period ending not more than six years before the end of the primary period). (It is presumed an earlier period must also end after 11 June 1986.) '*Non-taxable sums*' are donations, legacies and other sums of a similar nature which, apart from *ICTA 1988, s 505(1)* and *TCGA 1992, s 256*, are not within the charge to tax.

Where an amount of unapplied non-qualifying expenditure (the '*excess expenditure*') falls to be treated as non-qualifying expenditure of earlier periods, it is attributed only to those periods in which, apart from the attribution in question but taking account of any previous attribution, the relevant income and gains exceed the aggregate of the qualifying and non-qualifying expenditure in that period; and such attribution is not to be greater than the excess. Attributions are made to later periods in priority to earlier periods. Any excess expenditure which cannot be attributed to an earlier period is ignored for attribution purposes altogether. Adjustments by way of further assessment etc. are made in consequence of an attribution to an earlier period.

'*Qualifying expenditure*'. This is expenditure incurred for charitable purposes only. A payment made (or to be made) to a body situated outside the UK is not qualifying expenditure unless the charity concerned has taken such steps as may be reasonable in the circumstances to ensure that the payment will be applied for charitable purposes.

Expenditure incurred in a particular period may be treated as incurred in another period if it is properly chargeable against income of that other period and is referable to commitments (contractual or otherwise) entered into before or during that other period.

'*Qualifying investments*'. These are the following.

(A) Investments within *Trustee Investments Act 1961, 1 Sch Pts I, II* (*para 13* excepted; mortgages etc.) and *III*.

(B) Investments in a common investment fund established under *Charities Act 1993, s 24* (or NI equivalent), a common deposit fund established under *Charities Act 1960, s 25* or similar funds under other enactments.

(C) Any interest in land other than a mortgage, etc.

(D) Shares or securities of a company quoted on a recognised stock exchange (within *ICTA 1988, s 841*) or dealt in on the Unlisted Securities Market.

(E) Units in unit trusts (as statutorily defined).

(F) Deposits with a recognised bank or licensed institution in respect of which interest is payable at a commercial rate but excluding a deposit made as part of an arrangement whereby the bank, etc. makes a loan to a third party.

(G) Certificates of deposit within *ICTA 1988, s 56(5)*.

(H) Loans or other investments as to which the Board are satisfied, on a claim, that the loans or other investments are made for the benefit of the charity and not for tax avoidance purposes (whether by the charity or by a third party). Loans secured by mortgage etc, over land are eligible.

'*Qualifying loans*'. A loan which is not made by way of investment is a qualifying loan if it is one of the following.

(1) A loan made to another charity for charitable purposes only.

(2) A loan to a beneficiary of the charity which is made in the course of carrying out the purposes of the charity.

(3)   Money placed on a current account with a recognised bank or licensed institution otherwise than under arrangements as in (F) above.

(4)   A loan, not within (1)-(3) above, as to which the Board are satisfied, on a claim, that the loan is made for the benefit of the charity and not for tax avoidance purposes (whether by the charity or by a third party).

[*ICTA 1988, ss 505, 506, 20 Sch; Charities Act 1993, 6 Sch 25; FA 1995, 17 Sch 7*].

10.5   GIFTS TO CHARITIES

Where a disposal of an asset is made otherwise than under a bargain at arm's length to a charity, the normal MARKET VALUE (36) provisions (which deem the acquisition and disposal as being made at market value) do not apply.

If the disposal is by way of gift (including a gift into settlement) or for a consideration not exceeding the allowable expenditure which would be available on a disposal of the asset (see 16.3 DISPOSAL) the transaction is treated as made for a consideration producing neither a gain nor a loss. Where the asset is subsequently disposed of by the charity, its acquisition by the person making the original disposal is treated as the acquisition by the charity. See 8.7 ASSETS HELD ON 31 MARCH 1982 and 23.4 INDEXATION for consequential re-basing and indexation provisions.

If the disposal to the charity is for a consideration exceeding the allowable expenditure, the market value is not substituted for the actual consideration.

These provisions do not apply to disposals in relation to which venture capital trust relief is available (see VENTURE CAPITAL TRUSTS (58)).

The above provisions do apply to disposals made otherwise than under a bargain at arm's length to any of the bodies mentioned in *IHTA 1984, 3 Sch.* [*TCGA 1992, s 257(1)(2)(4); FA 1995, s 72(5)(8)*].

The bodies listed in *IHTA 1984, 3 Sch* (as amended) comprise

The National Gallery.

The British Museum.

The National Museum of Scotland.

The National Museum of Wales.

The Ulster Museum.

Any other similar national institution which exists wholly or mainly for the purpose of preserving for the public benefit a collection of scientific, historic or artistic interest and which is approved for this purpose by the Board.

Any museum or art gallery in the UK which exists wholly or mainly for that purpose and is maintained by a local authority or university in the UK.

Any library the main function of which is to serve the needs of teaching and research at a university in the UK.

The Historic Buildings and Monuments Commission for England.

The National Trust for Places of Historic Interest or Natural Beauty.

The National Trust for Scotland for Places of Historic Interest or Natural Beauty.

The National Art Collections Fund.

The Trustees of the National Heritage Memorial Fund.

10.6 Charities

The Friends of the National Libraries.

The Historic Churches Preservation Trust.

Nature Conservancy Council for England.

Scottish National Heritage.

Countryside Council for Wales.

Any local authority.

Any Government department (including the National Debt Commissioners).

Any university or university college in the UK.

A health service body within *ICTA 1988, s 519A*.

10.6   **Gifts out of settlements.** Where, subject to below, a charity becomes absolutely entitled to any assets (or part thereof) which were previously settled property and those assets are deemed to be disposed of and reacquired by the trustees on that occasion (under *TCGA 1992, s 71*) then, if no consideration is received by any person for or in connection with the transaction, the disposal is deemed to take place on a no gain, no loss basis. This does *not* apply where the charity becomes absolutely entitled to the assets on the termination of a life interest (within the meaning of *TCGA 1992, s 72*, see 52.7 SETTLEMENTS) by the death of the person entitled to it. (On such an event, because of the interaction of *TCGA 1992, ss 71* and *72*, the assets are revalued to market value at that date but no chargeable gain accrues; see 52.9, 52.11 SETTLEMENTS.)

The above provisions also apply to a gift to any of the bodies mentioned in *IHTA 1984, 3 Sch* (gifts for national purposes). See 10.5 above. [*TCGA 1992, s 257(3)*].

In *Prest v Bettinson Ch D 1980, 53 TC 437*, the residue of an estate was held on trust for five institutions, four of which were charities, subject to the payment of annuities to six individuals. No specific fund was set aside, but distributions of capital and income were made annually to the five institutions, the income of the residuary fund being more than sufficient to pay the annuities. The trustee failed in his claim that four-fifths of any capital gain arising was exempt as accruing for charitable purposes. Since no fund had been set aside to pay the annuities, the trustee retained full control of the trust property until the distribution of the proceeds of sale, and any gain from a disposal thereof had accrued to him as trustee and not to the charities.

11   Children

Cross-reference. See 47.6 RESIDENCE AND DOMICILE for domicile of children.

11.1   GENERAL

There is no general bar to the chargeable gains made by an infant (i.e. an individual under 18 years of age) being assessed and charged on him personally (see *R v Newmarket Commissioners (ex p. Huxley) CA 1916, 7 TC 49*). The Revenue can, therefore, resort directly to the infant, whether or not there is a guardian etc. to charge. Whether or not, in practice, they will do so will depend on particular circumstances.

A child is entitled to the same capital gains tax reliefs and exemptions as an adult (subject to specific exclusions).

11.2   NOMINEES AND BARE TRUSTEES

Where assets are held by a person as nominee, or as trustee for any person who would be absolutely entitled against him but for being an infant, the provisions of *TCGA 1992* apply as if the acts of the nominee or trustee are the acts of the infant. Acquisitions from or to the trustee or nominee to or from the infant are accordingly disregarded. References in *TCGA 1992* to a person being absolutely entitled against the trustee mean that the person has the exclusive right (subject only to satisfying any outstanding charge, lien or other right of the trustee to resort to the relevant asset(s) for payment of duty, taxes, costs or other outgoings) to direct how the asset(s) shall be dealt with. [*TCGA 1992, s 60*]. For the wider implications of nominees and bare trustees generally, see 52.2 SETTLEMENTS.

11.3   ASSESSMENT OF GUARDIANS ETC.

In practice, the Revenue often makes use of the machinery of *TMA 1970*, which enables it to charge and assess the tax due from an 'incapacitated person' (this term includes an 'infant': see *TMA 1970, s 118*), on the trustee, guardian, tutor, curator or committee, having the direction, control or management of that person's property. Such machinery applies whether or not the incapacitated person resides in the UK. The person chargeable in this way is answerable for all matters required to be done under the capital gains tax provisions, for the purpose of assessment of that tax, but is given a right of retention and indemnity in respect of tax charges or payments made on the incapacitated person's behalf. [*TMA 1970, ss 72, 77*].

11.4   DEFAULT OF INFANT

Where the person chargeable to tax is an infant, then his parent, guardian, or tutor is liable for the tax in the event of the infant's default. On neglect or refusal of payment, the parent etc. may be proceeded against for sums due to the Revenue. [*TMA 1970, ss 73, 77*].

12 Claims

Cross-reference. See 51 SELF-ASSESSMENT for future changes broadly from 1996/97.

12.1 Claims may be made to the local Inspector of Taxes (or to the Board of Inland Revenue in certain specified cases) whenever the *Taxes Acts* provide for relief to be given or other thing to be done. Any error or mistake in a claim may be rectified by a supplementary claim. [*TMA 1970, s 42(1)(2)(8)*]. See 12.4 below.

For accounting periods ending after 30 September 1993 (Pay and File), companies will not make certain claims under *TMA 1970, s 42* but instead in a corporation tax return required under *TMA 1970, s 11* (see 49.3 RETURNS).

Claims are personal matters and (except in the case of trustees for persons under disability etc.) can be made only by the person entitled to the relief (cf. *Fulford v Hyslop Ch D 1929, 8 ATC 588*). See 49.2 RETURNS for the signing of claims by an attorney.

12.2 TIME LIMITS FOR CLAIMS

See 54 TIME LIMITS—5 APRIL 1996 and 55 TIME LIMITS—MISCELLANEOUS for checklists of claims and elections.

Unless otherwise prescribed, a claim must be made within six years of the end of the tax year to which it relates (or the end of the accounting period in the case of a company). [*TMA 1970, s 43(1)*]. By concession, where an overpayment of tax arises because of an error by the Inland Revenue or another Government department and where there is no dispute as to the facts, claims to repayment of the tax overpaid made outside of the statutory period will be allowed (Revenue Pamphlet IR 1, B41).

A claim (including a supplementary claim) which could not have been allowed but for the making of an assessment to capital gains tax after the year of assessment to which it relates, may be made at any time before the end of the year of assessment following that in which the assessment was made. [*TMA 1970, s 43(2)*].

If an assessment made after 26 July 1989 for 1983/84 or later (or for an accounting period ending after 31 March 1983) makes good loss of tax arising from fraudulent or negligent conduct (see 9.4 BACK DUTY), the person assessed can require it to give effect to reliefs or allowances to which he would have been entitled had he made the necessary claims within the relevant time limits. [*TMA 1970, s 36; FA 1989, s 149*].

Discovery. In the case of a 'discovery' assessment (see 5.2 ASSESSMENTS) which is made after 26 July 1989, or an assessment to recover excess group relief under *ICTA 1988, s 412(3)* which is made after 26 July 1993, and is not for making good loss of tax attributable to fraudulent or negligent conduct (see 9.4 BACK DUTY),

(a) any 'relevant' claim, election, application or notice which could have been made or given within the normal time limits of the *Taxes Acts* may be made or given within a year of the end of the chargeable period in which the assessment is made, and

(b) any 'relevant' claim, etc. previously made or given, except an irrevocable one, can, with the consent of the person(s) by whom it was made or given (or their personal representatives), be revoked or varied in the manner in which it was made or given.

A claim, etc. is '*relevant*' to an assessment for a chargeable period if

(i) it relates to, or to an event occurring in, the chargeable period, and

(ii)   it, or its revocation or variation, reduces, or could reduce,

(A)   the increased tax liability resulting from the assessment, or

(B)   any other liability of the person for that chargeable period or a later one ending not more than one year after the period in which the assessment is made.

The normal APPEALS (4) provisions apply, with any necessary modifications.

If the making, etc. of a claim, etc. would alter another person's tax liability, the consent of that person (or his personal representatives) is needed. If such alteration is an increase, the other person cannot make, etc. a claim, etc. under the foregoing provisions.

If the reduction in tax liability resulting from one or more claims, etc. would exceed the additional tax assessed, relief is not available for the excess. If the reduction involves more than one period, or more than one person, the inspector will specify by notice in writing how it is to be apportioned; but within 30 days of the notice being given, or the last notice being given if there is more than one person, the person (or persons jointly) can specify the apportionment by notice in writing to the inspector. [*TMA 1970, ss 43A, 43B; FA 1989, s 150; FA 1993, s 120, 14 Sch 2*].

12.3   APPEALS IN RESPECT OF CLAIMS

An unfavourable decision by the inspector, or Board, on a claim, may be appealed against in writing within 30 days of *receipt* of written notice of the decision or within 3 months on matters relating to residence, ordinary residence or domicile.

Appeals from decisions of the inspector are to the General Commissioners or (at the taxpayer's option) to the Special Commissioners, and those from decisions of the Board to the Special Commissioners. [*TMA 1970, s 42, 2 Sch; FA 1984, s 127, 22 Sch 3*]. See under 4 APPEALS for this and for appeals to the High Court.

12.4   ERROR OR MISTAKE RELIEF

Relief may be claimed in writing, within six years after the end of the year of assessment in which the assessment was made, against any over-assessment due to an error or mistake (including an omission) in any return or statement. [*TMA 1970, s 33(1)*]. The relief is given because the return etc. was wrong and hence does not apply where the assessment is not on the basis of the return. No relief (except by concession) is allowed if the return or statement was made in accordance with the basis or practice generally prevailing at the time, or, in the opinion of the Board, if the relevant circumstances of the case render relief inequitable. [*TMA 1970, s 33(2)(3)*].

The relief is determined by the Board with appeal from them to the Special Commissioners and from them, but only on a point of law *arising in connection with the computation of the chargeable gains*, to the High Court. [*TMA 1970, s 33(4)(5)*]. (See *Rose Smith & Co Ltd v CIR KB 1933, 17 TC 586; Carrimore Six Wheelers Ltd v CIR CA 1944, 26 TC 301; R v Special Commrs (ex p. Carrimore Six Wheelers Ltd) CA 1947, 28 TC 422* and *Arranmore Investment Co Ltd v CIR CA (NI) 1973, 48 TC 623*.)

For relief for double assessment, see 5.3 ASSESSMENT.

13   Companies

Cross-references. See 7.1 and 7.3 ASSETS HELD ON 6 APRIL 1965 and 8.3 and 8.6 ASSETS HELD ON 31 MARCH 1982 for irrevocable election by principal company of a group; 23.17 INDEXATION for parallel pooling provisions before 1 April 1985; 47.5 RESIDENCE AND DOMICILE for company residence; 51 SELF-ASSESSMENT for future changes in respect of accounting periods ending on or after an appointed day (which cannot be earlier than 1 April 1986); 53 SHARES AND SECURITIES; 57 UNIT AND INVESTMENT TRUSTS.

13.1   LIABILITY OF COMPANIES TO CORPORATION TAX ON THEIR CHARGEABLE GAINS

Companies resident in the UK (and non-resident companies in respect of UK branch or agency assets, see 39.3 OVERSEAS MATTERS) are liable to corporation tax on their chargeable gains. These gains are included in their profits liable to corporation tax as described in 13.2 below. [*ICTA 1988, ss 6, 11(2); TCGA 1992, s 10(3)*].

Companies accordingly do not pay 'capital gains tax' as such, but their chargeable gains less allowable losses are computed in accordance with provisions relating to capital gains tax, except that

(i) computations are made by reference to accounting periods instead of years of assessment [*TCGA 1992, s 8(3)*],

(ii) provisions in the legislation confined to individuals do not apply to companies [*TCGA 1992, s 8(4)(5)*],

(iii) the indexation allowance and share identification rules apply (subject to transitional provisions) to disposals after 31 March 1982 and again after 31 March 1985 instead of 5 April 1982 and 5 April 1985 respectively,

(iv) an alternative method was available of identifying particular shares and securities which were disposed of after 31 March 1982 and before 1 April 1985 ('parallel pooling'; see 23.17 INDEXATION),

(v) for disposals by companies after 14 March 1988 and before 30 November 1993, indexation allowance was restricted or excluded in certain cases involving a debt on a security owed by, or shares in, a 'linked company' (see Tolley's Corporation Tax under Capital Gains), and

(vi) certain provisions, as contained in this chapter, apply only to companies.

See Tolley's Corporation Tax under Friendly Societies and Life Insurance Companies for provisions of *TCGA 1992* (and related provisions) which are integral with the corporation tax regime applicable to life assurance business carried on by such entities.

See also 5 ASSESSMENTS; 31 INTEREST ON OVERPAID TAX; 32 INTEREST ON UNPAID TAX; 41 PAYMENT OF TAX; 42 PENALTIES; and 49 RETURNS for matters applicable to companies generally (including the 'Pay and File' system of corporation tax payments and returns).

The definition of 'company' includes any body corporate or unincorporated association but does not include a partnership. [*TCGA 1992, s 288(1)*]. References to 'persons' in the capital gains tax legislation generally include unincorporated associations (*CIR v Worthing Rugby Football Club Trustees CA 1987, 60 TC 482*).

13.2   RATE OF CORPORATION TAX IN RESPECT OF CHARGEABLE GAINS

For accounting periods beginning after 16 March 1987 the whole of the chargeable gains (net of allowable losses under 13.3 below) of a company is included in the profits chargeable to corporation tax. The rate of corporation tax applicable will be dependent upon, inter alia, the residence position of the company, its status, the number of associated companies and the level of the chargeable profits and certain franked investment income but the rate so determined applies to both income and chargeable gains included in the chargeable profits. If the company's accounting period straddles different financial years, chargeable profits are apportioned on a time basis between the years. [ICTA 1988 s 8(3); TCGA 1992, s 8(1)]. For the level and applicability of the small companies rate of corporation tax, marginal relief and the full corporation tax rate, see Tolley's Corporation Tax.

Alternative rules apply as in 57 UNIT AND INVESTMENT TRUSTS.

13.3   CAPITAL AND INCOME LOSSES

The amount of chargeable gains to be taken into account for an accounting period is the amount of the chargeable gains accruing to the company in that period less the aggregate amount of the allowable losses in that period and allowable losses brought forward from any previous period. Allowable losses include short-term losses accruing under Schedule D, Case VII for years before 1971/72 which remain unrelieved. [TCGA 1992, s 8(1), 11 Sch 12]. It is expressly provided for the purposes of corporation tax on chargeable gains that an allowable loss does not include any loss which, if it had been a gain, would have been exempt from corporation tax in the hands of the company. [TCGA 1992, s 8(2)]. Allowable losses for the purposes of corporation tax on chargeable gains cannot normally be offset against trading profits or other income but see 35.14 LOSSES. Since chargeable gains are included in profits chargeable to corporation tax as in 13.1 above, claims under ICTA 1988, s 393A to set trading losses against such profits mean that, assuming accounting periods of twelve months' duration, the trading losses can be set against chargeable gains arising in the same and, if unexhausted, the three immediately preceding accounting periods (gains of a later period being relieved before those of an earlier period). See further Tolley's Corporation Tax under Losses for the detailed conditions which apply. Management expenses of an investment company may be offset against chargeable gains within the same or succeeding accounting periods. [ICTA 1970, s 304(2); ICTA 1988, s 75(3)].

See 13.20 below for the restriction on set-off of pre-entry losses where a company joins a group.

13.4   LIQUIDATION

The vesting of a company's assets in a liquidator is disregarded. All the acts of the liquidator in relation to such assets are treated as acts of the company. [TCGA 1992, s 8(6)].

Corporation tax on chargeable gains arising from the disposal of assets on a winding-up is a 'necessary disbursement' of the winding-up within the meaning of Insolvency Act 1986, s 156 (Re Mesco Properties Ltd CA 1979, 54 TC 238).

See also 53.13 and 53.14 SHARES AND SECURITIES.

13.5   RECOVERY FROM SHAREHOLDERS

Where a person connected with a UK resident company (see 14 CONNECTED PERSONS) receives, or becomes entitled to receive, in respect of shares in that company, a capital

13.6   Companies

distribution within *TCGA 1992, s 122* (see 53.13 SHARES AND SECURITIES) which is not a reduction of capital but which constitutes, or is derived from, a disposal of assets from which a chargeable gain accrues to the company, and the company does not pay, within six months after its due date, the corporation tax due for the accounting period in which the gain accrued, the recipient of the distribution may be required (by assessment within two years of the due date) to pay so much of that corporation tax as relates to chargeable gains but not exceeding the lesser of

(i)   part of that tax, at the rate in force when the gain accrued, proportionate to his share of the total distribution made by the company, and

(ii)   the value of the distribution he received or became entitled to receive.

The person then has a right of recovery against the company. These provisions do not affect any liability of the person in respect of a chargeable gain accruing to him as a result of the capital distribution. For accounting periods ending after 30 September 1993 (Pay and File) the provisions relating to the assessment of the person and the right of recovery are suitably adapted so that, in particular, the right of recovery also extends to any interest on unpaid tax which the person has paid in respect of the outstanding tax. [*TCGA 1992, s 189*].

For coverage of *ICTA 1988, ss 767A, 767B*, which broadly allow the Revenue to recover any corporation tax unpaid by a company from persons controlling the company in certain circumstances where there has been a change of ownership of the company after 29 November 1993 (other than under a contract entered into before 30 November 1993), see Tolley's Corporation Tax under Payment of Tax.

13.6   RECONSTRUCTIONS, AMALGAMATIONS ETC.

See also 53.8 and 53.9 SHARES AND SECURITIES and 13.33 below.

Subject to the following, where a 'scheme of reconstruction or amalgamation' (meaning a scheme for the reconstruction of any company or companies or the amalgamation of any two or more companies) involves the transfer of a UK resident company's business to another UK resident company for no consideration (other than the assumption of liabilities of the business), capital assets (not used as trading stock by either company) are regarded as being transferred at a 'no gain, no loss' disposal value and the acquiring company takes over the disposing company's acquisition date for the purposes of ASSETS HELD ON 6 APRIL 1965 (7). [*TCGA 1992, s 139(1)(2)(9)*].

Strictly, the second company should carry on substantially the same business and have substantially the same members as the first, but in practice the identity of shareholdings is not insisted upon where the scheme is for bona fide commercial reasons or where there is segregation of trades or businesses into identifiable parts which are capable of being carried on in their own right (Revenue Pamphlet IR 131, SP 5/85).

Anti-avoidance and disapplication of relief. *TCGA 1992, s 139* will not apply to any transfer unless the scheme is for bona fide commercial reasons and not to avoid corporation tax, capital gains tax or income tax, or the Board, on written application by the acquiring company, has notified its satisfaction with the scheme before the transfer is made. The Board may, within 30 days of receipt, call for further particulars to be supplied within 30 days, or longer if the Board allows; if the information is not supplied, the application lapses. Subject to this, the Board must notify its decision within a further 30 days. If not so notified, or if dissatisfied with the decision, the applicant may within a further 30 days require the Board to refer the application to the Special Commissioners for their decision. All material facts and considerations must be disclosed, otherwise any decision is void. [*TCGA 1992, ss 138(2)-(5), 139(5)*].

Where, if the disposing company had not been wound up, tax could have been assessed on it because of the effect of *TCGA 1992, s 139(5)* above, that tax can be assessed and charged (in the name of the disposing company) on the acquiring company. Subject to this, tax assessed on either company which is unpaid six months after the date when it is payable, may, within two years of that date, be similarly assessed and charged on certain third parties. The third parties are restricted to any person holding all or any part of the assets in respect of which the tax is charged and who either is the acquiring company or subsequently acquired them as a result of one or more disposals within *TCGA 1992, s 139* or *171(1)* (companies within same group) without any intervening disposals not within those provisions. Tax assessed on the third party is restricted to the proportion held of the assets in respect of which the tax was originally charged and may be recovered from the company originally assessed. The right of recovery is suitably adapted for accounting periods ending after 30 September 1993 (Pay and File) so that, in particular, the right of recovery also extends to any interest on unpaid tax which the third party has paid in respect of the outstanding tax. [*TCGA 1992, s 139(6)-(8)*].

Written application for clearance should be made (by either company) to Inland Revenue, Capital and Valuation Division (CGT), Sapphire House, 550 Streetsbrook Rd, Solihull, West Midlands, B91 1QU. Tel. 0121–711 3232. It should give full details of the transactions and of all the companies directly involved, their tax districts and references. Copies of accounts for the last two years for which accounts have been prepared should accompany the application, which should be cross-referenced to (though made separately from) any clearance or consent which is being sought under *ICTA 1988, ss 215, 225,* or *707* in respect of the same scheme. See also 3.13 ANTI-AVOIDANCE above.

Prior to the commencement of *TCGA 1992*, clearance was made under *ICTA 1970, s 267*.

The provisions of *TCGA 1992, s 139* do not apply in the case of a transfer of the whole or part of a company's business to a unit trust scheme within *TCGA 1992, s 100(2)* or which is an authorised unit trust or to an investment trust. See 57 UNIT AND INVESTMENT TRUSTS. Where *TCGA 1992, s 139* has applied in relation to a transfer to a company which was not then an investment trust but which subsequently becomes one for an accounting period, then any assets transferred and still owned by the company at the beginning of that accounting period are deemed to have been sold immediately after the transfer, and immediately reacquired, at their market value at that time. Notwithstanding the normal time limits, a corporation tax assessment in respect of any resulting liability can be made within six years of the end of the accounting period mentioned. Recomputations of gains and adjustments of tax liabilities may also be made in consequence of the above. [*TCGA 1992, ss 101, 139(4)*].

In respect of disposals after 19 March 1990, the provisions of *TCGA 1992, s 139* did not apply in relation to an asset acquired before 30 November 1993 (the latter date being the date of the coming into force of *FA 1994, s 249*; companies otherwise regarded as UK resident but under double tax relief arrangements already regarded as non-UK resident to be treated as non-UK resident for *Taxes Acts* purposes after 29 November 1993; see 47.5 RESIDENCE AND DOMICILE) if the company which acquired it, though resident in the UK, was regarded as resident elsewhere by virtue of DOUBLE TAX RELIEF (17.2) arrangements such that it would not under those arrangements be taxable in the UK on any gain arising on a disposal of the asset immediately after its acquisition. [*TCGA 1992, s 139(3); FA 1994, s 251(1)(5), 26 Sch Pt VIII*].

The following applies where there is a disposal or acquisition of currency; a 'qualifying asset' consisting of the right to settlement under a debt which is not a debt on a security (within *TCGA 1992, s 132*; see 18.5 EXEMPTIONS AND RELIEFS); a 'qualifying asset' consisting of the right to settlement under a debt on a security; or an obligation which by virtue of *TCGA 1992, s 143* (futures contracts; see 16.11 DISPOSAL) is regarded as an asset to the disposal of which *TCGA 1992* applies and which is a duty under a currency contract. Where the disposal or acquisition is by a 'qualifying company' and is made on or after the company's 'commencement day', and immediately before the disposal or after the acquisition, as the case may be, the asset is held wholly for 'qualifying purposes', and *TCGA 1992, s 139* would otherwise apply, the last-mentioned provision does not apply as regards the disposal or acquisition and the corresponding acquisition or disposal. '*Qualifying purposes*' are purposes of long term or mutual insurance business. [*FA 1993, s 169, 17 Sch 7*]. See 13.34 below for a note of the terms quoted and not otherwise defined.

Life assurance business. The provisions of *TCGA 1992, s 139* are adapted for certain transfers of an insurance company's long term business. See Tolley's Corporation Tax under Life Insurance Companies.

Privatisations etc. In connection with privatisations, and reorganisations of public corporations, various specific provisions have been enacted, mainly to cause transfers of assets to be treated on a 'no gain, no loss' basis, and to preclude a liability from arising under *TCGA 1992, s 178* or *179* (see 13.17 below) when a company leaves a group. See, for example, *British Telecommunications Act 1981, s 82*; *Telecommunications Act 1984, s 72*; *Trustee Savings Bank Act 1985, 2 Sch 2-6*; *Transport Act 1985, s 130(3)(4)*; *Airports Act 1986, s 77*; *Gas Act 1986, s 60*; *ICTA 1988, s 513*; *Water Act 1989, s 95*; *Electricity Act 1989, 11 Sch*; *FA 1990, 12 Sch* (broadcasting undertakings); *TCGA 1992, s 267* (sharing of transmission facilities); *F(No 2)A 1992, 17 Sch* (privatisation of Northern Ireland Electricity); *FA 1994, 24 Sch* (provisions relating to *Railways Act 1993*); and *FA 1994, 25 Sch* (Northern Ireland Airports Ltd).

Building society's business etc. transferred to a company or other building society. Similar provisions apply as for privatisations etc. above where there is a transfer of the whole of a building society's business to a successor company in accordance with the relevant provisions of *Building Societies Act 1986* [*TCGA 1992, s 216*] and where there is a disposal by one society to another as part of an amalgamation etc. of societies. [*TCGA 1992, s 215*].

Industrial and provident societies etc. Similar provisions apply as for privatisations etc. above where there is a union or amalgamation of two or more registered industrial and provident societies or a transfer of engagements from one society to another. This treatment also applies to certain co-operative associations established and resident in the UK, the primary purposes of which are to assist members in carrying on husbandry in the UK or fishery operations. [*ICTA 1988, s 486(8)(9)*].

13.7 OVERSEAS MATTERS

See 39.3 OVERSEAS MATTERS for the transfer of a UK branch or agency owned by a non-UK resident company to a UK resident company.

Various provisions apply where a UK resident company has an interest in a controlled foreign company. See 39.12 OVERSEAS MATTERS.

Where a UK resident company transfers all or part of a trade carried on by it outside the UK to a company not resident in the UK in exchange, wholly or partly, for shares, see 39.14 OVERSEAS MATTERS. Where the transferee company is resident in an EC member state, see 39.16 OVERSEAS MATTERS. Where the UK company's trade is carried on in the UK and is transferred to a company resident in another EC member state, see 39.15 OVERSEAS MATTERS.

There are 'exit charges' and provisions for the recovery of unpaid tax where a company ceases to be UK resident etc., is (before 30 November 1993) a dual resident company or is not resident in the UK. See 39.17 and 39.18 OVERSEAS MATTERS.

13.8   INTEREST CHARGED TO CAPITAL

For interest paid in accounting periods beginning after 31 March 1981, interest on money borrowed by a company for the construction of any building, structure or works, and referable to a time before disposal of it, may be added to the expenditure allowable as a deduction under *TCGA 1992, s 38* in computing the gain on the disposal of the building etc. by the company, provided the expenditure on the construction was itself so allowable. No relief is given for interest which has been treated as a charge on income under *ICTA 1988, s 338* (formerly *ICTA 1970, s 248 as amended*) or which is allowable as a deduction in computing income, profits, gains or losses for corporation tax purposes (or would be so but for an insufficiency of profits or gains) or which would be allowable if the building etc. was held as a fixed asset of a trade. For such accounting periods the practical effect of these provisions is that a payment of interest is unlikely to qualify as allowable expenditure in computing a chargeable gain.

For interest paid in accounting periods ending before 1 April 1981, the provisions and comment made in the last two sentences above do not apply. Instead, interest had to be charged to capital in order to qualify as allowable expenditure, which treatment prevented it being treated as a charge on income by virtue of *ICTA 1970, s 248(5)(a) as originally enacted*. [*TCGA 1992, s 40*].

13.9   GOVERNMENT SECURITIES AND QUALIFYING CORPORATE BONDS

See 21 GOVERNMENT SECURITIES and 44 QUALIFYING CORPORATE BONDS for the exemption available for gilt-edged securities and qualifying corporate bonds.

If gilt-edged securities are appropriated by a company *from* trading stock in such circumstances that any gain accruing on their disposal would be exempt from corporation tax on chargeable gains, there is a deemed disposal and re-acquisition at market value immediately before the appropriation. Where the securities are appropriated *to* trading stock, any trading loss arising on a subsequent disposal cannot exceed the loss which would have arisen if the securities had been acquired at their market value at the time of the appropriation. After 1 July 1986 the foregoing also applies to qualifying corporate bonds. [*ICTA 1988, s 126A; TCGA 1992, 10 Sch 14(6)*].

See 6.3 ASSETS for appropriations to and from trading stock generally and see also 13.12 below for intra-group transfers of assets which are trading stock of one of the companies but not of the other.

13.10   GROUPS OF COMPANIES

The following applies for the purposes of this paragraph, and of paragraphs 13.11–13.30 below.

Definition of company. '*Company*' means a company within the meaning of the *Companies Act 1985* or the corresponding enactment in Northern Ireland or which is constituted under any other Act, Royal Charter, or letters patent or under the law of a country outside the UK. It also includes a registered industrial and provident society and, from 21 November 1982, a trustee savings bank and, from 23 July 1987, a building society. In all cases, except those referred to in 13.18 below, 13.19 below (the latter being dealt with under 3.16 ANTI-AVOIDANCE (depreciatory transactions: groups of companies)) and 39.3 and 39.5 OVERSEAS MATTERS, the company must be resident in the UK. [*TCGA 1992, s 170(2)(a)(9)*].

Definition of group. *After 13 March 1989*, the following definitions apply, subject to the transitional provisions mentioned below.

A *'group'* comprises

(*a*)   a company ('the principal company of the group') and

(*b*)   that company's '75 per cent subsidiaries' (as in *ICTA 1988, s 838* i.e. where not less than 75 per cent of the 'ordinary share capital' (see below under 'General') is beneficially owned directly or indirectly by the principal company), and those subsidiaries' 75 per cent subsidiaries (and so on), except that any 75 per cent subsidiary which is not 'an effective 51 per cent subsidiary' of the principal company is excluded.

This definition is subject to the following rules.

(1)   A company ('the subsidiary') which is a 75 per cent subsidiary of another company cannot be a principal company of a group, unless

    (i)   because of the exclusion in (*b*) above, the two companies are not in the same group,

    (ii)   the requirements of the definition of a group in (*a*) and (*b*) are otherwise satisfied, and

    (iii)   no further company could, under this provision, be the principal company of a group of which the subsidiary would be a member.

(2)   If a company would otherwise belong to more than one group (the principal company of each of which is called the 'head of a group' below), it belongs only to the group which can first be determined under the following tests.

    (i)   The group to which it would belong if the exclusion of a company which is not an effective 51 per cent subsidiary in (*b*) above were applied without the inclusion of any amount to which the head of a group is entitled of any profits available for distribution to equity holders of a head of another group or would be entitled of any assets of a head of another group available for distribution to its equity holders on a winding up.

    (ii)   The group the head of which is entitled to a greater percentage than any other head of a group of its profits available for distribution to equity holders.

    (iii)   The group the head of which would be entitled to a greater percentage than any other head of a group of its assets available for distribution to equity holders on a winding-up.

    (iv)   The group the head of which owns (as in *ICTA 1988, s 838(1)(a)*) directly or indirectly more of its ordinary share capital than any other head of a group.

A company ('the subsidiary') is '*an effective 51 per cent subsidiary*' of another company ('the parent') at any time if and only if

(A)   the parent is entitled to more than 50 per cent of any profits available for distribution to equity holders of the subsidiary, and

(B)   the parent would be entitled to more than 50 per cent of any assets available for distribution to the equity holders on a winding up.

ICTA 1988, 18 Sch as amended (group relief: equity holders and profits or assets available for distribution) applies with suitable modifications for the purposes of (2) and (A) and (B) above with effect from 14 March 1989. One modification for these purposes disapplies the requirement that certain arrangements for changes in profit or asset shares are assumed to take place in applying the 50 per cent tests above. Although this change is made retrospectively with effect from 14 March 1989, an election was available for this disapplication not to apply in relation to the period from 14 March 1989 to 25 January 1990 inclusive. [*TCGA 1992, s 170(2)(b)(3)-(8); ICTA 1988, s 838; FA 1990, s 86; F(No 2)A 1992, s 24, 6 Sch 5, 10*]. For consideration of beneficial ownership of a company's shares where they are subject to cross-options by shareholders, see *J Sainsbury plc v O'Connor CA, [1991] STC 318*. Although legislation overturning the *Sainsbury* decision in respect of arrangements entered into after 14 November 1991 was introduced by *F(No 2)A 1992* for group relief purposes, it does not apply for the purposes of the taxation of chargeable gains.

A group remains the same group so long as the same company remains the principal company of the group, and if at any time the principal company of a group becomes a member of another group, the first group and the other group are regarded as the same, and the question whether or not a company has ceased to be a member of a group is determined accordingly. [*TCGA 1992, s 170(10)*].

The passing of a resolution, or the making of an order, or any other act for the winding-up of a member of a group is not treated as an occasion on which any company ceases to be a member of the group. [*TCGA 1992, s 170(11)*].

Transitional provisions. If, under a compromise or arrangement (within *Companies Act 1985, s 425*) agreed to before 14 March 1989 and sanctioned by the court, a company acquires, directly or indirectly, an interest in ordinary share capital of another company, and immediately afterwards

(*aa*)   under the 'old definition' (i.e., *ICTA 1970, s 272* before amendment by *FA 1989*) the two companies are, by virtue of the acquisition, members of a group for the purposes of the 'group provisions' (i.e. *TCGA 1992, ss 170-181* less *s 180(3)-(6)*) but

(*bb*)   the second company is not an effective 51 per cent subsidiary of the first,

the following provisions apply to those companies and any other members of the group (the 'relevant companies').

(AA)   For the period from the time of acquisition until six months afterwards, or, if earlier, the date when the other company ceases to be a member of the group under the old definition, the old definition applies to the relevant companies for the purposes of the group provisions.

(BB)   For those companies the commencement day for the purposes of 13.17(A) below is the day after that period ends.

[*TCGA 1992, s 180(5)-(7)*].

Before 14 March 1989, a *'group'* consisted of a principal company and all its '75 per cent subsidiaries' (as above) and where a principal company was a member of a group as being itself a 75 per cent subsidiary, this second group was to include all the members of the first group. [*ICTA 1970, s 272(1); ICTA 1988, s 838*]. See *Wood Preservation Ltd v Prior CA 1968, 45 TC 112* and *Burman v Hedges & Butler Ltd Ch D 1978, 52 TC 501*.

A group remained the same group so long as the same company remained the principal company of the group, and if at any time the principal company of a group became a 75 per cent subsidiary of another company the group of which it was the principal member before that time was regarded as the same as the group of which that other company, or one of which it was a 75 per cent subsidiary, was the principal company, and the question whether or not a company had ceased to be a member of a group was determined accordingly. [*ICTA 1970, s 272(3)*].

The passing of a resolution, or the making of an order, or any other act for the winding-up of a company was not regarded as an occasion on which it, or any of its 75 per cent subsidiaries, ceased to be a member of the group. [*ICTA 1970, s 272(4)*].

General. '*Ordinary share capital*' means all issued share capital of a company except that carrying a fixed rate of dividend only. Any share capital of a registered industrial and provident society is treated as ordinary share capital.

'*Group*' and '*subsidiary*' are construed with any necessary modifications where applied to a company incorporated outside the UK.

'*Profits*' means income and gains. '*Trade*' includes a vocation, office or employment (including the occupation of UK woodlands before 6 April 1993).

[*TCGA 1992, s 170(1)(2)(c)(d)*].

As regards nationalised industries, etc., see *TCGA 1992, s 170(12)-(14)*.

See also 39.5, 39.14, 39.19 OVERSEAS MATTERS.

13.11 **Disposals of capital assets by one member of a group to another member are treated as if made at a 'no gain, no loss' disposal value except for the following.**

(i) Assumed (as opposed to actual) disposals.

(ii) A disposal of a debt due from a group member effected by satisfying it (or part of it).

(iii) A disposal on redemption of redeemable shares.

(iv) A disposal of an interest in shares in consideration of a capital distribution within *TCGA 1992, s 122* whether or not involving a reduction of capital.

(v) The receipt of compensation for destruction etc. of assets (in that the disposal is treated as being to the insurer or other person who ultimately bears the burden of furnishing the compensation).

(vi) A disposal after 31 March 1980 by or to an investment trust within *ICTA 1988, s 842*.

(vii) A disposal after 31 March 1987 to a 'dual resident investing company' within *ICTA 1988, s 404*.

(viii) An exchange, etc., after 14 March 1988, of shares, etc. in a reorganisation, takeover, etc. which is treated by *TCGA 1992, ss 127, 135* as not involving a disposal by the member of the group first mentioned above (see 53.5 and 53.8 SHARES AND SECURITIES).

The position for exchanges of shares before 14 March 1988 in reorganisations within a group was examined in *Westcott v Woolcombers Ltd CA 1987, 60 TC 575* and *NAP Holdings UK Ltd v Whittles HL, [1994] STC 979*. The decision in the former case, which involved consideration of the original *FA 1965* legislation and a reorganisation occurring prior to the introduction by *FA 1968* of certain anti-avoidance provisions was approved in the judgments given in the latter case, which involved a reorganisation which occurred when the provisions of *ICTA 1970* and *CGTA 1979* were extant and subsequent to further anti-avoidance provisions introduced by *FA 1977*.

(ix) A disposal after 19 March 1990 and before 30 November 1993 (the latter date being the date of the coming into force of *FA 1994, s 249*; companies otherwise regarded as UK resident but under double tax relief arrangements already regarded as non-UK resident to be treated as non-UK resident for *Taxes Acts* purposes after 29 November 1993; see 47.5 RESIDENCE AND DOMICILE) to a company which, though resident in the UK, was regarded as resident elsewhere by virtue of DOUBLE TAX RELIEF (17.2) arrangements such that it would not under those arrangements be taxable in the UK on any gain arising on a disposal of the asset immediately after its acquisition.

[*TCGA 1992, s 171; FA 1994, s 251(1)(7), 26 Sch Pt VIII*].

The following applies where there is a disposal or acquisition of currency; a 'qualifying asset' consisting of the right to settlement under a debt which is not a debt on a security (within *TCGA 1992, s 132*; see 18.5 EXEMPTIONS AND RELIEFS); a 'qualifying asset' consisting of the right to settlement under a debt on a security; or an obligation which by virtue of *TCGA 1992, s 143* (futures contracts; see 16.11 DISPOSAL) is regarded as an asset to the disposal of which *TCGA 1992* applies and which is a duty under a currency contract. Where the disposal or acquisition is by a 'qualifying company' and is made on or after the company's 'commencement day', and immediately before the disposal or after the acquisition, as the case may be, the asset is held wholly for 'qualifying purposes', and *TCGA 1992, s 171* would otherwise apply, the last-mentioned provision does not apply as regards the disposal or acquisition and the corresponding acquisition or disposal. '*Qualifying purposes*' are purposes of long term or mutual insurance business. [*FA 1993, s 169, 17 Sch 7*]. See 13.34 below for a note of the terms quoted and not otherwise defined.

As regards (iv), the assets acquired in the capital distribution are nevertheless transferred at a 'no gain, no loss' price (see *Innocent v Whaddon Estates Ltd Ch D 1981, 55 TC 476*).

For the Revenue's views as to the application of the principles established by *Furniss v Dawson HL 1984, 55 TC 324* with regard to the use of 'capital loss' companies within a group, see ICAEW Guidance Note TR 588, 25 September 1985 (but note the provisions in 13.20 below).

13.12   **Intra-group transfers of assets which are trading stock of one of the companies but not of the other.**

(i)   *Transfer from a 'capital asset' company to a 'trading stock' company.* The acquiring company is treated as cquiring the asset as a capital asset (at a 'no gain, no loss' price under 13.11 above) and then immediately appropriating it to trading stock (leading to a chargeable gain or allowable loss of the difference between the market value and that 'no gain, no loss' price), under *TCGA 1992, s 161(1)* unless election is made under *TCGA 1992, s 161(3)*.

(ii)   *Transfer from a 'trading stock' company to a 'capital asset' company.* The disposing company is treated as having appropriated the asset as a capital asset immediately before the transfer (and thus having acquired it for that purpose at the amount brought into the accounts of the trade for tax purposes), under *TCGA 1992, s 161(2)*.

[*TCGA 1992, s 173*].

Acquisition 'as trading stock' implies a commercial justification for the acquisition, see *Coates v Arndale Properties Ltd HL 1984, 59 TC 516* and *Reed v Nova Securities Ltd HL 1985, 59 TC 516*. For appropriations from or to trading stock generally under *TCGA 1992, s 161*, see 6.3 ASSETS.

13.13 Companies

13.13 **Intra-group transfers: indexation allowances.** See 8.7 ASSETS HELD ON 31 MARCH 1982 and 23.4 INDEXATION for re-basing and indexation provisions on 'no gain, no loss' disposals.

13.14 **Disposal or acquisition outside a group etc.** Where there is a disposal of an asset after 19 March 1990 which was acquired in circumstances in which *TCGA 1992, ss 140A* (see 39.15 OVERSEAS MATTERS), *171* (see 13.11 above) or *172* (see 39.3 OVERSEAS MATTERS) applied or in which *TCGA 1992, s 171* would have applied but for the exclusions mentioned in 13(ii)–(iv)(vi)(vii)(ix) above, restriction of allowable losses by reference to capital allowances (see 16.5(*i*) DISPOSAL) applies in relation to capital allowances made to the person from whom it was acquired (so far as not taken into account in relation to a disposal by that person) and so on as respects previous such acquisitions. For disposals before 20 March 1990, the restriction applied only where a company which was or had been a group member disposed of an asset which it acquired from another group member when both were members of the group. These provisions do not affect the 'no gain, no loss' consideration deemed by *TCGA 1992, s 171* or *172*.

For disposals at any time, where a company which is or has been a group member disposes of an asset which it acquired from another group member when both were members of the group, the provisions relating to ASSETS HELD ON 6 APRIL 1965 (7) apply as if all group members were one person (except for disposals after 31 March 1980 where made by an investment trust within *ICTA 1988, s 842* or by a company which acquired the asset after that date from an investment trust). [*TCGA 1992, s 174; F(No 2)A 1992, s 46(1)(5)*].

13.15 **Rollover relief on the replacement of business assets** is granted by *TCGA 1992, ss 152–158*. See 50.4 ROLLOVER RELIEF for provisions relating to groups of companies.

13.16 **Collection of unpaid tax from other members of the group.** If corporation tax on a chargeable gain of a group member is not paid within six months of the time when it becomes payable, then, within two years of when it became so payable, the tax may be assessed on (*a*) the principal company of the group when the gain accrued or (*b*) any other company which at any time in the two years preceding the time the gain accrued was a group member and owned the asset disposed of (or the right, interest, etc. therein). The company paying the tax then has a right of recovery from the company to which the gain accrued, or from the principal company of the group when the gain accrued, if that is a different company. In the latter instance, a right is given to that principal company of recovery from the company to which the gain accrued and, insofar as the tax is not so recovered, of a just proportion from any present member of the group which has previously owned, whilst still a group member, the asset disposed of. These rights of recovery are suitably adapted for accounting periods ending after 30 September 1993 (Pay and File) so that, in particular, the right of recovery also extends to any interest on unpaid tax which has been charged in respect of the outstanding tax. [*TCGA 1992, s 190*].

For coverage of *ICTA 1988, ss 767A, 767B*, which broadly allow the Revenue to recover any corporation tax unpaid by a company from persons controlling the company in certain circumstances where there has been a change of ownership of the company after 29 November 1993 (other than under a contract entered into before 30 November 1993), see Tolley's Corporation Tax under Payment of Tax.

13.17 Broadly, where **a company ceasing to be a member of a group** owns a capital asset which has been transferred to it by another group member (such status being determined at the time of transfer) within the preceding six years, that company is treated as if, immediately after its acquisition of the asset, it had sold, and immediately reacquired, the asset at its then market value. There will thus be a gain or loss by reference to the market value of the asset at that time and its 'no gain, no loss' acquisition consideration under 13.11 above. The time limit for electing for 6 April 1965 value (normally two years from the end of the accounting period in which the disposal took place) is concessionally extended (29.D21 INLAND REVENUE STATEMENTS OF PRACTICE).

The provision applies to a company (*'the chargeable company'*) leaving a group which acquired an asset as described above where it or an 'associated' company also leaving the group at the same time owns (otherwise as trading stock) the asset at that time, property to which a gain on the disposal of the original asset has been carried forward under ROLLOVER RELIEF (50) or an asset the value of which is wholly or partly derived from the original asset.

Companies are *'associated'* if they would form a group by themselves.

If the accounting period in which the company ceases to be a member of the group ends after 30 September 1993 (Pay and File), any gain or loss on the deemed sale is treated as accruing at whichever is the later of the time immediately after the beginning of the accounting period in which or, as the case may be, at the end of which it so ceases and the time it is deemed to reacquire the asset concerned above.

An apportionment under *ICTA 1988, s 409(2)* (profits and losses for group relief etc. when two or more companies join or leave a group) is to take the timing of the gain or loss on the deemed sale into account but not so as to require any reference in that provision to an accounting period to have effect for any of the purposes mentioned in *ICTA 1988, s 409(3)* (surrendering and claimant companies) as a reference to any accounting period other than a true accounting period. Where the company ceases to be a member of the group in an earlier accounting period, any gain or loss on the deemed sale is treated, under general principles, as having accrued immediately after the date of acquisition of the original asset by the company.

The provision does not apply in relation to transfers of assets between associated companies which cease to be members of the group at the same time. [*TCGA 1992, ss 178(1)–(3)(8)(b)(c), 179(1)–(4)(9A)(10)(b)(c), 180(1); FA 1993, s 89; FA 1995, s 49*].

However, where a company in a group transfers an asset inter-group and both transferor and recipient then leave that group to form a second group 'connected' with the first, with one of those companies then departing from the second group after 28 November 1994, the provision will apply if the inter-group transfer, which is deemed for this purpose to have taken place in the second group, occurred within the preceding six years. The two groups are *'connected'* for this purpose if, broadly, at the time the chargeable company ceases to be a member of the second group, the second group is under the control of the first group or both groups are under the common control of a company which controls or has controlled the first group at any time since the chargeable company left the first group. The general definitions of *ICTA 1988, s 416(2)–(6)* (meaning of 'control') apply for this purpose (except for banking businesses). See Tolley's Corporation Tax under Close Companies.

'Ceasing to be a member of a group' does not apply to cases where a company ceases to be a member of a group in consequence of another member of the group ceasing to exist. For a company ceasing to be a member of a group before 15 November 1991, the phrase did not apply to cases where a company ceased to be a member of a group by being wound up or dissolved or in consequence of another member of the group being wound up or dissolved. [*TCGA 1992, ss 178(1), 179(1); F(No 2)A 1992, s 25*]. For events after 14 November 1991, the Revenue takes the view that this 'liquidation let out' only applies to

the case of a two company group where one company is liquidated (Taxation Practitioner April 1993 p 25). For a case relating to events before 15 November 1991 in which this provision was used to avoid a deemed sale and reacquisition, see *Burman v Hedges & Butler Ltd Ch D 1978, 52 TC 501*. The Revenue's practice for events before 15 November 1991 was not to apply the deemed sale and reacquisition where the company receiving the asset ceased to be a group member as a result of its only subsidiary leaving the group except where the parent company emigrated, thereby causing the group to break up (CCAB Statement TR 386, 14 April 1980). For such events its view was that a company did not leave a group until its or the relevant group member's winding-up or dissolution was complete (Taxation 7 November 1989 p 688).

In addition to the above, *'ceasing to be a member of a group'* does not apply to cases where the company ceases to be a member of a group by virtue of that company, or another company, ceasing to be UK resident on 30 November 1993 solely by virtue of the coming into force of *FA 1994, s 249* (companies otherwise regarded as UK resident but under double tax relief arrangements already regarded as non-UK resident to be treated as non-UK resident for *Taxes Acts* purposes after 29 November 1993; see 47.5 RESIDENCE AND DOMICILE). [*FA 1994, s 250(2)*].

Subject to the transitional provisions described below, if, **after 13 March 1989,**

(*a*)   a company ceases to be a member of a group only through the principal company becoming a member of another group (e.g. it is not an 'effective 51 per cent subsidiary' of the principal company of the other group as in 13.10 above), and

(*b*)   under the provisions described above, it would be treated as selling an asset at any time,

the following provisions apply.

(1)   The company in question is not treated as selling the asset at that time.

(2)   If

(i)   within six years of that time the company in question ceases at any time ('*the relevant time*') to satisfy the following conditions: namely that it is a '75 per cent subsidiary' (as defined in 13.10 above) of one or more members of the other group mentioned in (*a*) above and an 'effective 51 per cent subsidiary' (as defined in 13.10 above) of one or more of those members; and

(ii)   at the relevant time the company in question or a company in the same group, owns (otherwise than as trading stock) the asset, or property to which a chargeable gain has been rolled over from the asset, or an asset the value of which is wholly or partly derived from the original asset,

the company in question is treated as if, immediately after acquiring the asset, it had sold and reacquired it at its market value at the time of acquisition.

(3)   If the accounting period in which the first company ceases to be a member of the group ends after 30 September 1993 (Pay and File), any gain or loss on the deemed sale is treated as arising at the relevant time. If not, any gain or loss is treated, under the general rules, as having arisen at the date of acquisition by the company.

[*TCGA 1992, ss 178(4)-(6), 179(5)-(8), 180(2)*].

Under transitional provisions, if

(A)   at the beginning of the 'commencement day' (i.e. 14 March 1989 but see 13.10(BB) above) a company ceases to be a member of a group only because of the new definition in *ICTA 1970, s 272* (now *TCGA 1992, s 170*) resulting from the amendments made by *FA 1989* (see 13.10 above), and

(B) because of ceasing to be a member it would otherwise be treated by *ICTA 1970, s 278(3)* (now *TCGA 1992, s 178(3) or 179(3)*) (see above) as selling an asset at any time,

it is not treated as selling the asset then unless, if the old definition of a group under *ICTA 1970, s 272* before the amendments made by *FA 1989* still applied, the following conditions would be satisfied.

(*aa*) For the purposes of *ICTA 1970, s 278* (*now TCGA 1992, ss 178, 179*) the company ceases at any time ('the relevant time') to belong to the group mentioned in (A) above.

(*bb*) At the relevant time the company, or an associated company also leaving the group then, owns (otherwise than as trading stock) the asset, or property to which a chargeable gain has been rolled over from the asset or an asset the value of which is wholly or partly derived from the original asset.

(*cc*) The no gain/no loss acquisition from a group member (see 13.11 above) occurred within six years before the relevant time.

[*TCGA 1992, s 180(3)(4)(7)*].

If, **after 13 March 1989**, under any of the foregoing provisions a deemed sale arises at any time, and if on an actual sale at market value at that time any loss or gain would, under the value shifting provisions (see 3.6–3.9 ANTI-AVOIDANCE), have been calculated as if the consideration were increased by an amount, the market value at the time of the deemed sale is treated as having been greater by that amount. [*TCGA 1992, ss 178(4)-(7), 179(5)-(9), 180(1)(2)*].

If any corporation tax assessed on a company in consequence of the above is still unpaid six months after the later of the date when the tax becomes due and payable by the company and the date when the assessment was made on the chargeable company, it may instead be assessed and charged (in the name of the chargeable company), within two years from the date determined above, on the principal company of the group on that date or immediately after the time the chargeable company ceased to be a member of the group, or on a company which owned the asset on that date or immediately after that time. A company paying tax and interest under such an assessment is given a right of recovery against the chargeable company. For cases where the chargeable company ceases to be a member of a group in an accounting period ending before 1 October 1993 (pre-Pay and File), these provisions are similar save that all assessments have to be made within six years from the time the chargeable company ceases to be a member of the group, unpaid tax can be assessed on another company if it is still unpaid six months from the date it becomes payable, and there was no specific mention of interest on unpaid tax. In all cases, any adjustment of tax or recomputation of liability on a disposal may be made by assessment or otherwise as a result of any deemed disposal and reacquisition mentioned above. [*TCGA 1992, ss 178(9)(10), 179(11)-(13)*].

13.18 **Exemption from charge on company ceasing to be member of group.** Neither *TCGA 1992, s 178* nor *179* in 13.17 above apply, subject to conditions, where, as part of a 'merger', a company ('company A') ceases to be a member of a group ('the A group'), and it is shown that the merger was carried out for bona fide reasons and that the avoidance of a liability to tax was the not the main or one of the main purposes of the merger.

13.19   Companies

'*Merger*', in broad terms, means an arrangement whereby one or more companies ('the acquiring compan(y)(ies)') not in the A group acquire interests in the business previously carried on by company A, and one or more members of the A group acquire interests in the business or businesses previously carried on either by the acquiring company or companies or by a company at least 90 per cent of the ordinary share capital of which is owned by two or more of the acquiring companies. For this purpose a group member is treated as carrying on as one business the activities of that group. 25% of the value of the interests acquired must take the form of ordinary share capital, whilst the remainder of the interests acquired by the A group must consist of share capital or debentures or both. The value of the interests acquired must be substantially the same, and the consideration for the interests acquired by the acquiring companies must substantially consist of the interests acquired by the A group.

For the above purposes, references to a company include references to a company resident outside the UK. [*TCGA 1992, s 181*].

See also 13.33 below regarding demergers.

13.19   **Value shifting to give tax-free benefit, depreciatory transactions and dividend stripping.** See 3.6–3.9 ANTI-AVOIDANCE for value shifting to give a tax-free benefit where groups may be involved. See 3.16 ANTI-AVOIDANCE for depreciatory transactions within a group. See 3.17 ANTI-AVOIDANCE for dividend stripping.

13.20   **Restriction on set-off of pre-entry losses where a company joins a group.** *General outline and commencement.* Under *TCGA 1992, 7A Sch* ('*7A Sch*') a restriction applies to the deduction of allowable losses accruing to a company before the time it becomes a member of a group of companies and losses accruing on assets held by any company at such a time. The restriction is further described in 13.21–13.30 below.

The restriction applies for the calculation of the amount to be included in respect of chargeable gains in a company's total profits for any accounting period ending after 15 March 1993 (including one beginning before 6 April 1992 where the provisions of *TCGA 1992* are applied to the pre-consolidation legislation then in force). However, the restriction applies only in relation to the deduction from chargeable gains accruing after 16 March 1993 of amounts in respect of, or of amounts carried forward in respect of,

(*a*)   'pre-entry losses' accruing before it became a member of the 'relevant group' to a company whose membership of that group began or begins after 31 March 1987, and

(*b*)   losses accruing on the disposal of any assets so far as it is by reference to such a company that the assets fall to be treated as being or having been 'pre-entry assets' or assets incorporating a part referable to pre-entry assets.

[*TCGA 1992, s 177A; FA 1993, s 88, 8 Sch*].

The restriction is widely drawn, and whilst its stated principal intention is to prevent the fiscal effectiveness of an acquisition of a 'capital loss' company (i.e. a company that has a *realised* allowable loss as its only commercial feature), it may also impinge on an acquisition of a company solely for commercial reasons where it becomes a member of a group whilst holding an asset which is later disposed of (whether by the company or another group member to whom the asset has been transferred) outside the group at a loss. Further restrictions were imposed by *FA 1994, s 94* in relation to the deduction of a loss from a chargeable gain where either the gain or the loss accrues after 10 March 1994.

13.21   *Application and construction of 7A Sch. 7A Sch* has effect, in the case of a company which or has been the member of a group of companies ('*the relevant group*'), in relation to any pre-entry losses. A '*pre-entry loss*', in relation to a company, means any allowable loss that accrued to it at a time before it became a member of the relevant group or the 'pre-entry proportion' (see 13.22–13.25 below) of any allowable loss accruing to it on the disposal of any 'pre-entry asset'. [*TCGA 1992, 7A Sch 1(1)(2)*].

A '*pre-entry asset*', in relation to any disposal, means any asset that was held, at the time immediately before it became a member of the relevant group, by any company (whether or not the one which makes the disposal) which is or has at any time been a member of that group. [*TCGA 1992, 7A Sch 1(3)*]. However, subject to 13.23 below, an asset is not a pre-entry asset if the company which held the asset at the time it became a member of the relevant group is not the company which makes the disposal and since that time the asset has been disposed of otherwise than on the no gain/no loss basis of *TCGA 1992, s 171* (general provisions for transfers within a group; see 13.11 above) except where the company making the disposal retains an interest in or over the asset (when the interest is treated as a pre-entry asset). [*TCGA 1992, 7A Sch 1(4)*].

Subject to 13.23 below, an asset ('*the second asset*') which derives wholly or partly its value from another asset ('*the first asset*') acquired or held by a company at any time is treated as the same asset if the second asset is held subsequently by the same company, or by any company which is or has been a member of the same group of companies as that company (e.g. a freehold derived from a leasehold where the lessee acquires the reversion). Where this treatment applies, whether under this provision or not (*TCGA 1992, s 43* is similar; see 16.6 DISPOSAL), the second asset is treated as a pre-entry asset in relation to a company if the first asset would have been. [*TCGA 1992, 7A Sch 1(8)*].

In relation to a pre-entry asset, references to '*the relevant time*' are references to the time when the company in relation to which the asset is a pre-entry asset became a member of the relevant group. Where a company has become a member of the relevant group more than once, an asset is a pre-entry asset in relation to that company if it would be a pre-entry asset in relation to that company in respect of any of the entries into the group, but in these circumstances any reference to the time when a company became a member of the relevant group is a reference to the last time the company entered the group. [*TCGA 1992, 7A Sch 1(5)*].

Subject to so much of *7A Sch 9(6)* (see 13.29 below) as requires groups of companies to be treated as separate groups for the purposes of *7A Sch 9*, if

(a)   the principal company of a group of companies ('*the first group*') has at any time become a member of another group ('*the second group*') so that the two groups are treated as the same under *TCGA 1992, s 170(10)* (see 13.10 above), and

(b)   the second group, together in pursuance of *TCGA 1992, s 170(10)* with the first group, is the relevant group,

then, except where the circumstances are as in *7A Sch 1(7)* below, the members of the first group are treated for the purposes of *7A Sch* as having become members of the relevant group at that time, and not by virtue of *TCGA 1992, s 170(10)* at the times when they became members of the first group. [*TCGA 1992, 7A Sch 1(6)*].

The circumstances mentioned in *7A Sch 1(6)* are where

(1)   the persons who immediately before the time when the principal company of the first group became a member of the second group owned the shares comprised in the issued share capital of the principal company of the first group are the same as the persons who, immediately after that time, owned the shares comprised in the issued share capital of the principal company of the relevant group; and

(2)   the company which is the principal company of the relevant group immediately after that time

(i)   was not the principal company of any group immediately before that time; and

(ii)   immediately after that time had assets consisting entirely, or almost entirely, of shares comprised in the issued share capital of the principal company of the first group.

[*TCGA 1992, 7A Sch 1(7)*].

Where an allowable loss accrues to a company under *TCGA 1992, s 116(10)(b)* (gain or loss on shares exchanged on reorganisation, conversion or reconstruction for qualifying corporate bonds to crystallise when bonds sold; see 44.3 QUALIFYING CORPORATE BONDS and 13.27 below), that loss is deemed to accrue at the time of the reorganisation etc. for the purposes of deciding whether a loss accrues before a company becomes a member of the relevant group. [*TCGA 1992, 7A Sch 1(9)*]. Likewise, the annual deemed disposals of unit trust etc. holdings of a life assurance company's long term business fund under *TCGA 1992, s 212* (see Tolley's Corporation Tax under Life Insurance Companies) are deemed to occur for this purpose without regard to the 'spreading' provisions of *TCGA 1992, s 213*. [*TCGA 1992, 7A Sch 1(10)*].

13.22   *Pre-entry proportion of losses on pre-entry assets.* Subject to 13.23–13.25 below, the '*pre-entry proportion*' of an allowable loss accruing on the disposal of a pre-entry asset is the allowable loss that would accrue on that disposal if that loss were the sum of the amounts determined, for every item of relevant allowable expenditure (within *TCGA 1992, s 38(1)(a)* or *(b)*; see 16.3 DISPOSAL), according to the following formula:

$$A \times \frac{B}{C} \times \frac{D}{E} \text{ where}$$

A   is the total amount of the allowable loss;

B   is the sum of the amount of the item of relevant allowable expenditure concerned and, for disposals before 30 November 1993, the '*indexed rise*' (as in *TCGA 1992, s 54* (see 23.1 INDEXATION) but ignoring the effect of *TCGA 1992, s 110* (see 23.10 INDEXATION)) where the above formula is applied for the purposes of 13.23 below) in that item;

C   is the sum of the total amount of all such expenditure and, for disposals before 30 November 1993, the indexed rises in each of the items comprised in that expenditure;

D   is the length of the period beginning with 'the relevant pre-entry date' and ending with the relevant time or, if that date is after that time, nil (i.e. there is no pre-entry proportion if the relevant time precedes the relevant pre-entry date); and

E   is the length of the period beginning with the relevant pre-entry date and ending with the day of disposal.

[*TCGA 1992, 7A Sch 2(1)(9); FA 1994, s 93(8)(a)(d)(11), 26 Sch Pt V*].

'*The relevant pre-entry date*', in relation to any item referred to above, is the later of 1 April 1982 and the date the asset was acquired or provided or, as the case may be, improvement expenditure became due and payable (such date being subject to the assumptions provided for by *7A Sch 2(4)(5)(6A)(6B)* below in relation to the deduction of a loss from a chargeable gain where either the gain or the loss accrues after 10 March 1994 and subject to the assumptions provided for by *7A Sch 2(4)(5)* in relation to the deduction of a loss from a chargeable gain where both the gain and loss accrue before 11 March 1994). [*TCGA 1992, 7A Sch 2(3); FA 1994, s 94(1)(2)(4)*].

Where any 'original shares' are treated as the same asset as a 'new holding' (within *TCGA 1992, s 127*; see 53.5 SHARES AND SECURITIES), the above formula and (where applicable) the provisions in 13.23 below are applied (except, for disposals before 30 November 1993, in relation to the calculation of any indexed rise):

(*a*)   as if any item referred to above consisting in consideration given for the acquisition of the new holding had been incurred at the time the original shares were acquired; and

(*b*)   where there is more than one such time as if that item were incurred at those different times in the same proportions as the consideration for the acquisition of the original shares.

[*TCGA 1992, 7A Sch 2(4); FA 1994, s 93(8)(b)(d)(11), 26 Sch Pt V*].

Without prejudice to (*a*) and (*b*) above, the formula is applied to any asset which

(A)   was held by a company at the time when it became a member of the relevant group, and

(B)   is treated as having been acquired by that company on *any* no gain/no loss corresponding disposal,

as if the company and every person who acquired that asset or 'the equivalent asset' (see below) at a 'material time' had been the same person and, accordingly, as if the asset had been acquired by the company when it or the equivalent asset was acquired by the first of those persons to have acquired it at a material time and the time at which any expenditure had been incurred were to be determined accordingly. [*TCGA 1992, 7A Sch 2(5)*].

A '*material time*' is any time before an acquisition of an asset in circumstances as in (B) above and is, or is after, the last occasion before the occasion on which any person acquired that asset or the equivalent asset otherwise than on an acquisition which is within (B) above or is an acquisition by virtue of which any asset is treated as the equivalent asset; and the formula is applied in relation to any asset within (A) and (B) above without regard to *TCGA 1992, s 56(2)* (consideration on no gain/no loss disposal deemed to include indexation allowance; see 23.4 INDEXATION). [*TCGA 1992, 7A Sch 2(6)*].

In relation to the deduction of a loss from a chargeable gain where either the gain or the loss accrues after 10 March 1994, and notwithstanding anything in *TCGA 1992, s 56(2)* (see above), where in the case of the disposal of any pre-entry asset any company has, between the relevant time and the time of the disposal, acquired that asset or the equivalent asset, and the acquisition was either an acquisition in pursuance of a no gain/no loss disposal under *TCGA 1992, s 171* (general provisions for no gain/no loss transfers within a group; see 13.11 above) or an acquisition by virtue of which an asset is treated as the equivalent asset, the items of relevant allowable expenditure in the above formula, and the times they are treated as having been incurred, are determined on the assumption that the company by reference to which the asset in question is a pre-entry asset, and the company which acquired the asset or the equivalent asset as above (and every other company which has made such an acquisition), were the same person and, accordingly, that the pre-entry asset had been acquired by the company disposing of it at the time when it or the equivalent asset would have been treated as acquired by the company by reference to which the asset is a pre-entry asset. [*TCGA 1992, 7A Sch 2(6A)(6B); FA 1994, s 94(1)(2)(4)*].

In relation to the deduction of a loss from a chargeable gain where either the gain or the loss accrues after 10 March 1994, for the purposes of the provisions in *7A Sch*

2(5)(6)(6A)(6B) above, '*the equivalent asset*', in relation to another asset acquired or disposed of by any company, is any asset which falls in relation to that company to be treated (whether under *7A Sch 1(8)* in 13.21 or otherwise) as the same as the other asset or which would fall to be so treated after applying, as respects other assets, the assumptions for which those provisions provide. In relation to the deduction of a loss from a chargeable gain where both the gain and the loss accrue before 11 March 1994, for the purposes of the provisions in *7A Sch 2(5)(6)* above, '*the equivalent asset*', in relation to the acquisition of any asset by any company, is any asset which (whether under *7A Sch 1(8)* or otherwise) would be treated in relation to that company as the same as the asset in question. [*TCGA 1992, 7A Sch 2(7); FA 1994, s 94(1)(2)(4)*].

The above provisions and (where applicable) those in 13.23 below have effect where a loss accrues to a company under *TCGA 1992, s 116(10)(b)* (see *7A Sch 1(9)* in 13.21 above), and the shares exchanged for qualifying corporate bonds are treated under 13.23 below as including pre-entry assets, as if the disposal on which the loss accrues were the disposal of the shares assumed to be made by *s 116(10)(a)* at the time of reorganisation etc. [*TCGA 1992, 7A Sch 2(8)*].

In relation to disposals on or after 30 November 1993, where, under *TCGA 1992, s 55(8)* (rolled-up indexation on no gain/no loss disposals after 31 March 1982 and before 30 November 1993; see 8.7 ASSETS HELD ON 31 MARCH 1982), the allowable loss (or part) accruing on the disposal of a pre-entry asset is attributable to an amount of rolled-up indexation, the total relevant allowable expenditure is treated for the purposes of *7A Sch 2* above as increased by that rolled-up amount, each item of expenditure being treated as increased by the attributable proportion of the total. [*TCGA 1992, 7A Sch 2(8A); FA 1994, s 93(8)(c)(11)*].

Also in relation to disposals on or after 30 November 1993, where *TCGA 1992, s 56(3)* (disapplication of *TCGA 1992, s 56(2)* on any no gain/no loss disposal on or after 30 November 1993; see 23.4 INDEXATION) applies to reduce the total allowable expenditure on the disposal of a pre-entry asset on which an allowable loss accrues, the amount of each item of relevant allowable expenditure is treated for the purposes of *7A Sch 2* as reduced by so much of that reduction as is attributable to it. [*TCGA 1992, 7A Sch 2(8B); FA 1994, s 93(8)(c)(11)*].

13.23   *Disposals of pooled assets.* Subject to 13.24 and 13.25 below, the provisions below apply where any assets acquired by a company fall to be treated with other assets as indistinguishable parts of the same asset ('*a pooled asset*') and the whole or part of that asset is referable to pre-entry assets.

For the purposes of *7A Sch*, where a pooled asset has at any time contained a pre-entry asset, the pooled asset is treated, until on the assumptions below all the pre-entry assets included in the asset have been disposed of, as incorporating a part which is referable to pre-entry assets, the size of that part being determined as below. [*TCGA 1992, 7A Sch 3(1)(2)*].

Where there is a disposal of any part of a pooled asset and the proportion of the asset which is disposed of does not exceed the proportion of that asset which is represented by any part of it which is not, at the time of disposal, referable to pre-entry assets, that disposal is treated as confined to assets which are not pre-entry assets. Consequently, no part of any loss accruing on that disposal is treated as a pre-entry loss (except where *7A Sch 4(2)* in 13.24 below applies), and the part of the pooled asset which after the disposal is treated as referable to pre-entry assets is correspondingly increased (without prejudice to the effect of any subsequent acquisition of assets to be added to the pool in determining whether, and to what extent, any part of the pooled asset is to be treated as referable to pre-entry assets). [*TCGA 1992, 7A Sch 3(3)(11)*].

Where there is such an excess as postulated above, the disposal is treated as relating to pre-entry assets only so far as required for the purposes of the excess. Consequently

(*a*)   any loss accruing on that disposal is treated for the same purposes as an allowable loss on a pre-entry asset,

(*b*)   the pre-entry proportion of that loss is deemed (except where *7A Sch 4(3)* in 13.24 below applies) to be the amount (insofar as it does not exceed the amount of the loss actually accruing) which would have been the pre-entry proportion under 13.22 above of any loss accruing on the disposal of the excess if the excess were a separate asset, and

(*c*)   the pooled asset is treated after the disposal as referable entirely to pre-entry assets (with the same qualification as appears in parentheses at the end of the previous paragraph regarding any subsequent acquisition).

[*TCGA 1992, 7A Sch 3(4)(11)*].

Where there is a disposal of the whole or part of a pooled asset at a time when the asset is referable entirely to pre-entry assets, (*a*) and (*b*) above apply to the disposal of the asset or the part as they apply in relation to the assumed disposal of the excess mentioned in the preamble to (*a*) and (*b*) but, where the whole of an asset only part of which is referable to pre-entry assets is disposed of, the reference in (*b*) above to the excess is taken as a reference to that part. [*TCGA 1992, 7A Sch 3(5)*].

In applying (*b*) above, it is assumed that none of the assets treated as comprised in the separate asset mentioned in (*b*) has ever been comprised in a pooled asset with any assets other than those which are taken to constitute that separate asset for the purposes of determining what would have been the pre-entry proportion of any loss accruing on the disposal of any assets as that separate asset. [*TCGA 1992, 7A Sch 3(6)*].

Assets comprised in any asset which is treated as separate are identified on the following assumptions:

(A)   that assets are disposed of in the order of the relevant pre-entry dates for the acquisition consideration as under 13.22 above;

(B)   subject to (A), that assets with earlier relevant times are disposed of before those with later ones;

(C)   that disposals made when a company was not a member of the relevant group are made according to the provisions in *7A Sch 3(1) – (6)* and (A) and (B) above, as they have effect in relation to the group of companies of which the company was a member at the time of disposal or, as the case may be, of which it had most recently been a member before that time; and

(D)   subject to (A) – (C) above, that a company disposes of assets in the order in which it acquires them.

[*TCGA 1992, 7A Sch 3(7)*].

Where there is more than one pre-entry date in relation to acquisition consideration, the date in (A) above is the earlier or earliest of those dates if any such date relating to an option to acquire the asset is disregarded. [*TCGA 1992, 7A Sch 3(8)*].

Where a second asset falls to be treated as acquired at the same time as a first asset was earlier acquired (whether under *7A Sch 1(8)* in 13.21 above or otherwise), and the second asset is either comprised in a pooled asset partly referable to pre-entry assets or is, or includes, an asset which is to be treated as so comprised, (A)–(D) above apply not only in relation to the second asset as if it were the first asset but also, in the first place, for identifying the asset which is to be treated as the first asset under the above provisions. [*TCGA 1992, 7A Sch 3(10)*].

Where the formula in 13.22 above is applied to an asset treated as above as a separate asset, the amount or value of the asset's acquisition or disposal consideration and any related incidental costs are determined not under *TCGA 1992, s 129 or 130* (see 53.5 SHARES AND SECURITIES) but by apportioning the consideration or costs relating to both that asset and other assets acquired or disposed of at the same time according to the proportion that is borne by that asset to all the assets to which the consideration or costs related. [*TCGA 1992, 7A Sch 3(9)*].

13.24 *Rules to prevent pre-entry losses on pooled assets being treated as post-entry losses.* The provisions below apply if

(*a*) there is a disposal of any part of a pooled asset which under 13.23 above is treated as including a part referable to pre-entry assets;

(*b*) the assets disposed of are or include assets ('*the post-entry element of the disposal*') which for the purposes of 13.23 are treated as having been included in the part of the pooled asset which is not referable to pre-entry assets;

(*c*) an allowable loss ('*the actual loss*') accrues on the disposal; and

(*d*) the amount which in computing the allowable loss is allowed as a deduction of relevant allowable expenditure ('*the expenditure actually allowed*') exceeds such expenditure attributable to the post-entry element of the disposal.

[*TCGA 1992, 7A Sch 4(1)*].

Subject to *7A Sch 4(6)* below, where the post-entry element of the disposal comprises all of the assets disposed of the actual loss is treated for *7A Sch* purposes as a loss accruing on the disposal of a pre-entry asset, and the pre-entry proportion of that loss is treated as being the amount (insofar as it does not exceed the amount of the actual loss) of the excess referred to in (*d*) above. [*TCGA 1992, 7A Sch 4(2)*].

Subject to *7A Sch 4(6)* below, where the actual loss is treated under 13.23 above as a loss accruing on a pre-entry asset, and the expenditure actually allowed exceeds the actual cost of the assets to which the disposal is treated as relating, the pre-entry proportion of the loss is treated as being the amount which (insofar as it does not exceed the amount of the actual loss) is equal to the sum of that excess and what would, apart from the provisions in 13.25 and these provisions, be the pre-entry proportion of the loss accruing on the disposal. [*TCGA 1992, 7A Sch 4(3)*].

For the purposes of *7A Sch 4(3)* above, the actual cost of the assets to which the disposal is treated as relating is taken to be the sum of

(A) the relevant allowable expenditure attributable to the post-entry element of the disposal; and

(B) the amount which, in computing the pre-entry proportion of the loss under *7A Sch 3(4)(b)* (13.23(*b*) above) and *7A Sch 3(6)* (13.23 above), would be treated for the purposes of 'C' in the formula in 13.22 above as the total amount allowable as a deduction of relevant allowable expenditure in respect of such of the assets disposed of as are treated as having been incorporated in the part of the pooled asset referable to pre-entry assets.

[*TCGA 1992, 7A Sch 4(4)*].

Without prejudice to *7A Sch 4(6)* below, where *7A Sch 4(2)* or *(3)* above applies for the purpose of determining the pre-entry proportion of any loss, no election can be made

118

under 13.25 below for the purpose of enabling a different amount to be taken as the pre-entry proportion of that loss. [*TCGA 1992, 7A Sch 4(5)*].

Where

(*aa*)   the pre-entry proportion of the loss accruing to any company on the disposal of any part of a pooled asset falls to be determined under *7A Sch 4(2)* or *(3)* above,

(*bb*)   the amount determined thereunder exceeds the amount determined under *7A Sch 4(7)* below ('*the alternative pre-entry loss*'), and

(*cc*)   the company makes an election for the purpose,

the pre-entry proportion of the loss determined as specified in (*aa*) above is reduced to the amount of the alternative pre-entry loss. [*TCGA 1992, 7A Sch 4(6)*]. For this purpose '*the alternative pre-entry loss*' is whatever apart from these provisions would have been the pre-entry proportion of the loss on the disposal in question, if for the purposes of *7A Sch* the identification of the assets disposed of were to be made disregarding the part of the pooled asset which was not referable to pre-entry assets, except to the extent (if any) by which the part referable to pre-entry assets fell short of what was disposed of. [*TCGA 1992, 7A Sch 4(7)*].

The election mentioned in (*cc*) above must be made by the company incurring the loss by notice to the inspector given within the period of two years beginning with the end of its accounting period in which the disposal giving rise to the loss is made, or within such longer period as the Board may by notice allow. The provisions in 13.25 below may be taken into account under *7A Sch 4(7)* above in determining the amount of the alternative pre-entry loss as if an election had been made under 13.25 below but only if the election under (*cc*) above contains an election corresponding to the election that otherwise might have been made under 13.25 below. [*TCGA 1992, 7A Sch 4(8)*].

As the rules for pre-entry losses can operate in relation to losses which arise on disposals of assets by companies which became members of the relevant group after 31 March 1987, they may apply in situations where elections would be beneficial but the normal two year time limit has already passed. The Revenue will extend the period for elections for these cases, and others where the time limit would expire less than two years after 27 July 1993. Elections will be accepted as made in time in all cases where made by 27 July 1995. Queries concerning elections can be addressed to Capital & Valuation Division (CGT), Sapphire House, 550 Streetsbrook Road, Solihull B91 1QU (tel. 0121 711 3232 ext 2220) (Revenue Tax Bulletin, May 1994 p 129).

For the purposes of the above the relevant allowable expenditure attributable to the post-entry element of the disposal is the amount which, in computing any allowable loss accruing on a disposal of that element as a separate asset, would have been allowed as a deduction of relevant allowable expenditure if none of the assets comprised in that element had ever been comprised in a pooled asset with any assets other than those which are taken to constitute that separate asset for the purposes of this provision. [*TCGA 1992, 7A Sch 4(9)*]. To identify the assets which are to be treated for this purpose as comprised in the post-entry element of the disposal, a company is taken to dispose of assets in the order in which it acquired them. [*TCGA 1992, 7A Sch 4(10)*].

7A Sch 3(9) in 13.23 above is applied *mutatis mutandis* for the purposes of *7A Sch 4(9)* above, as is *7A Sch 3(10)* in 13.23 for the purposes of this provision in relation to *7A Sch 4(10)* above. [*TCGA 1992, 7A Sch 4(11)*].

In the above references to an amount allowed as a deduction of relevant allowable expenditure are references to the amount falling to be so allowed in accordance with *TCGA 1992, 38(1)(a)* and *(b)* and (so far as applicable) *s 42*, together (for disposals before 30 November 1993) with the indexed rises (as in 13.22 above) in the items comprised in that expenditure or, as the case may be, in the appropriate portions of those items. Nothing in the above provisions affects the operation of the rules contained in 13.23 above for determining, for any purposes other than those of *7A Sch 4(7)* above, how much of any pooled asset at any time consists of a part which is referable to pre-entry assets. [*TCGA 1992, 7A Sch 4(12)–(14); FA 1994, s 93(9)(11), 26 Sch Pt V*].

13.25 *Alternative calculation by reference to market value.* Subject to *7A Sch 4(5)* in 13.24 above and the following provisions, if an otherwise allowable loss accrues on the disposal by any company of any pre-entry asset, and that company makes an election accordingly, the pre-entry proportion of that loss (instead of being any amount arrived at under the above provisions of *7A Sch*) is whichever is the smaller of [*TCGA 1992, 7A Sch 5(1)*]

(*a*) the amount of any loss which would have accrued if that asset had been disposed of at the relevant time at its market value at that time; and

(*b*) the amount of the otherwise allowable loss accruing on the actual disposal of that asset.

[*TCGA 1992, 7A Sch 5(2)*].

In relation to disposals on or after 30 November 1993, in determining the amount of any notional loss under (*a*) above, it is assumed that the prohibition (and its consequences) of indexation allowance creating or increasing a loss introduced by *FA 1994, s 89(1)–(5)* with effect generally in relation to disposals on or after 30 November 1993 (see 8.7 ASSETS HELD ON 31 MARCH 1982 and 23.1 and 23.4 INDEXATION) has effect for disposals on or after the day on which the relevant time falls. [*TCGA 1992, 7A Sch 5(2A); FA 1994, s 93(10)(11)*].

Where no loss would have accrued on the deemed disposal in (*a*) above, the loss mentioned in (*b*) above is deemed not to have a pre-entry proportion. [*TCGA 1992, 7A Sch 5(3)*]. The election mentioned above must be made by the company incurring the loss by notice to the inspector given within the period of two years beginning with the end of its accounting period in which the disposal giving rise to the loss is made, or within such longer period as the Board may by notice allow. [*TCGA 1992, 7A Sch 5(8)*]. See 13.24 above regarding comments made about adherence to the similar two-year time limit mentioned there which apply equally here.

The provisions in *7A Sch 5(5)* below apply where an election as above is made in relation to any loss accruing on the disposal ('*the real disposal*') of the whole or any part of a pooled asset, and the case is one in which (but for the election) the provisions in 13.23 above would apply for determining the pre-entry proportion of a loss accruing on the real disposal. [*TCGA 1992, 7A Sch 5(4)*]. In these circumstances, these provisions have effect as if the amount specified in (*a*) above were to be calculated

(A) on the basis that the disposal which is assumed to have taken place was a disposal of all the assets falling within (*aa*)-(*cc*) below; and

(B) by apportioning any loss that would have accrued on that disposal between

(i) such of the assets falling within (*aa*)-(*cc*) below as are assets to which the real disposal is treated as relating, and

(ii) the remainder of the assets so falling,

according to the proportions of any pooled asset whose disposal is assumed which would have been, respectively, represented by assets mentioned in (i) above and by assets mentioned in (ii) above.

Where assets falling within (*aa*)-(*cc*) below have different relevant times there is assumed to have been a different disposal at each of those times. [*TCGA 1992, 7A Sch 5(5)*].

Assets fall to be included within (A) and (B) above if

(*aa*)   immediately before the time which is the relevant time in relation to those assets, they were comprised in a pooled asset which consisted of or included assets which fall to be treated for the purposes of 13.23 above as

    (i)   comprised in the part of the pooled asset referable to pre-entry assets; and

    (ii)   disposed of on the real disposal;

(*bb*)   they were also comprised in such a pooled asset immediately after that time; and

(*cc*)   the pooled asset in which they were so comprised immediately after that time was held by a member of the relevant group.

[*TCGA 1992, 7A Sch 5(6)*].

Where

(AA)   an election is made under *7A Sch 4(6)* (see 13.24 above) requiring the determination by reference to these provisions of the alternative pre-entry loss accruing on the disposal of any assets comprised in a pooled asset, and

(BB)   under that election any amount of the loss that would have accrued on an assumed disposal is apportioned in accordance with (A) and (B) above to assets ('*the relevant assets*') which

    (i)   are treated for the purposes of that determination as assets to which the disposal related, but

    (ii)   otherwise continue after the disposal to be treated as incorporated in the part of that pooled asset which is referable to pre-entry assets,

then, on any further application of these provisions for the purpose of determining the pre-entry proportion of the loss accruing on a subsequent disposal of assets comprised in that pooled asset, that amount (without being apportioned elsewhere) is deducted from so much of the loss accruing on the same assumed disposal as, apart from the deduction, would be apportioned to the relevant assets on that further application of these provisions. [*TCGA 1992, 7A Sch 5(7)*].

13.26   *Restrictions on the deduction of pre-entry losses.* In the calculation of the amount to be included in respect of chargeable gains in any company's total profits for any accounting period

(*a*)   if in that period there is any chargeable gain from which the whole or any part of any pre-entry loss accruing in that period is deductible in accordance with the provisions in 13.27 below, the loss or, as the case may be, that part of it is deducted from that gain;

(*b*)   if, after all the deductions in (*a*) above have been made, there is in that period any chargeable gain from which the whole or any part of any pre-entry loss carried forward from a previous accounting period is deductible in accordance with the provisions in 13.27, the loss or, as the case may be, that part of it is deducted from that gain;

(*c*)   the total of chargeable gains (if any) remaining after all the deductions in (*a*) or (*b*) above is subject to deductions in accordance with *TCGA 1992, s 8(1)* (chargeable gains less allowable losses of company to be included in chargeable profits; see 13.2 above) in respect of any allowable losses that are not pre-entry losses; and (*d*)   any pre-entry loss which has not been the subject of a deduction under (*a*) or (*b*) above (as well as any other losses falling to be carried forward under *section 8(1)*) are carried forward to the following accounting period of that company.

[*TCGA 1992, 7A Sch 6(1)*].

Subject to (*a*)-(*d*) above, any question as to which or what part of any pre-entry loss has been deducted from any particular chargeable gain is decided

(A)   where it falls to be decided in respect of the setting of losses against gains in any accounting period ending before 16 March 1993 as if

(i)   pre-entry losses accruing in any such period had been set against chargeable gains before any other allowable losses accruing in that period were set against those gains;

(ii)   pre-entry losses carried forward to any such period had been set against chargeable gains before any other allowable losses carried forward to that period were set against those gains; and

(iii)   subject to (i) and (ii) above, the pre-entry losses carried forward to any accounting period ending after 15 March 1993 were identified with those losses which are determined in accordance with elections made by the company to which they accrued;

and

(B)   in any other case, in accordance with such elections as may be made by the company to which the loss accrued;

and any question as to which or what part of any pre-entry loss has been carried forward from one accounting period to another is decided accordingly. [*TCGA 1992, 7A Sch 6(2)*].

An election under (A)(iii) above must be made by the company by notice to the inspector given before the end of the period of two years beginning with the end of its accounting period which was current on 16 March 1993. An election under (B) above must similarly be made before the end of the period of two years beginning with the end of the company's accounting period in which the gain in question accrued. [*TCGA 1992, 7A Sch 6(3)*].

For the purposes of *7A Sch* where any matter falls to be determined under the above provisions by reference to an election but no election is made, it is assumed, so far as consistent with any elections that have been made that losses are set against gains in the order in which the losses accrued, and that the gains against which they are set are also determined according to the order in which they accrued with losses being set against earlier gains before they are set against later ones. [*TCGA 1992, 7A Sch 6(4)*].

13.27   *Gains from which pre-entry losses are to be deductible.* A pre-entry loss that accrued to a company before it became a member of the relevant group is deductible from a chargeable gain accruing to that company if the gain is one accruing

(*a*)   on a disposal made by that company before the date on which it became a member of the relevant group ('*the entry date*');

(*b*)   on the disposal of an asset which was held by that company immediately before the entry date; or

(*c*)   on the disposal of any asset which

(i) was acquired by that company on or after the entry date from a person who was not a member of the relevant group at the time of the acquisition; and

(ii) since its acquisition from that person has not been used or held for any purposes other than those of a trade which was being carried on by that company at the time immediately before the entry date and which continued to be carried on by that company until the disposal.

[*TCGA 1992, 7A Sch 7(1)*].

The pre-entry proportion of an allowable loss accruing to any company on the disposal of a pre-entry asset is deductible from a chargeable gain accruing to that company if

(A) the gain is one accruing on a disposal made, before the date on which it became a member of the relevant group, by that company and that company is the one ('*the initial company*') by reference to which the asset on the disposal of which the loss accrues is a pre-entry asset;

(B) the pre-entry asset and the asset on the disposal of which the gain accrues were each held by the same company at a time immediately before it became a member of the relevant group; or

(C) the gain is one accruing on the disposal of an asset which

(i) was acquired by the initial company (whether before or after it became a member of the relevant group) from a person who, at the time of the acquisition, was not a member of that group; and

(ii) since its acquisition from that person has not been used or held for any purposes other than those of a trade which was being carried on, immediately before it became a member of the relevant group, by the initial company and which continued to be carried on by the initial company until the disposal.

[*TCGA 1992, 7A Sch 7(2)*].

Where two or more companies become members of the relevant group at the same time and those companies were all members of the same group of companies immediately before they became members of the relevant group, then, without prejudice to the provisions in 13.29 below

(*aa*) an asset is treated for the purposes of (*b*) above as held, immediately before it became a member of the relevant group, by the company to which the pre-entry loss in question accrued if that company is one of those companies and the asset was in fact so held by another of those companies;

(*bb*) two or more assets are treated for the purposes of (B) above as assets held by the same company immediately before it became a member of the relevant group wherever they would be so treated if all those companies were treated as a single company; and

(*cc*) the acquisition of an asset is treated for the purposes of (*c*) and (C) above as an acquisition by the company to which the pre-entry loss in question accrued if that company is one of those companies and the asset was in fact acquired (whether before or after they became members of the relevant group) by another of those companies.

[*TCGA 1992, 7A Sch 7(3)*].

TCGA 1992, 7A Sch 1(4) in 13.21 above is applied *mutatis mutandis* for determining for the purposes of the above provisions whether an asset on the disposal of which a chargeable gain accrues was held at the time when a company became a member of the relevant group. [*TCGA 1992, 7A Sch 7(4)*].

Subject to *7A Sch 7(6)* below, where a gain accrues on the disposal of the whole or any part of

(1)   any asset treated as a single asset but comprising assets only some of which were held at the time mentioned in (*b*) or (B) above, or

(2)   an asset which is treated as held at that time by virtue of a provision requiring an asset which was not held at that time to be treated as the same as an asset which was so held (see 13.21 above),

a pre-entry loss is deductible under (*b*) or (B) above from the amount of that gain to the extent only of such proportion of that gain as is attributable to assets held at that time or, as the case may be, represents the gain that would have accrued on the asset so held. [*TCGA 1992, 7A Sch 7(5)*].

Where

(AA)   a chargeable gain accrues under *TCGA 1992, s 116(10)* on the disposal of a qualifying corporate bond which has been exchanged for shares etc. (see 44.3 QUALIFYING CORPORATE BONDS and 13.21 above),

(BB)   that bond was not held as required by (*b*) or (B) above at the time mentioned respectively in (*b*) or (B), and

(CC)   the whole or any part of the asset which is the 'old asset' for the purposes of *TCGA 1992, s 116* was so held,

the question whether that gain is one accruing on the disposal of an asset the whole or any part of which was held by a particular company at that time is determined for the purposes of *7A Sch 7* as if the bond were deemed to have been so held to the same extent as the old asset. [*TCGA 1992, 7A Sch 7(6)*].

13.28   *Change of a company's nature.* If

(*a*)   within any period of three years, a company becomes a member of a group of companies and there is (either earlier or later in that period, or at the same time) 'a major change in the nature or conduct of a trade' carried on by that company, or

(*b*)   at any time the scale of the activities in a trade carried on by a company has become small or negligible, and before any considerable revival of the trade, that company becomes a member of a group of companies,

the trade carried on before that change, or which has become small or negligible, is disregarded for the purposes of 13.27 (*c*) and (C) above in relation to any time before the company became a member of the group in question.

'*A major change in the nature or conduct of a trade*' includes a reference to a major change in the type of property dealt in, or services or facilities provided, in the trade, or a major change in customers, markets or outlets of the trade. This applies even if the change is the result of a gradual process which began outside the period of three years mentioned in (*a*) above.

Where the operation of the above provisions depends on circumstances or events at a time after the company becomes a member of any group of companies (but not more than three years after), an assessment to give effect to the provisions may be made within six years from that time or the latest such time. [*TCGA 1992, 7A Sch 8*].

The above provisions are identical *mutatis mutandis* with those in *ICTA 1988, s 768* regarding the disallowance of trading losses on a change in ownership of a company. See Tolley's Corporation Tax under Losses for the appropriate case law and Revenue practice applying to that provision which may apply to the above.

13.29   *Identification of the 'relevant group' and application of 7A Sch to every connected group.* The provisions below apply where there is more than one group of companies which would be the relevant group in relation to any company.

Where any loss has accrued on the disposal by any company of any asset, *7A Sch* does not apply by reference to any group of companies in relation to any loss accruing on that disposal unless

(*a*)   that group is a group in relation to which that loss is a pre-entry loss because it is an allowable loss that accrued to that company at a time before it became a member of the group or, if there is more than one such group, the one of which that company most recently became a member;

(*b*)   that group, in a case where there is no group falling within (*a*) above, is either

(i)   the group of which that company is a member at the time of the disposal, or

(ii)   if it is not a member of a group of companies at that time, the group of which that company was last a member before that time;

(*c*)   that group, in a case where there is a group falling within paragraph (*a*) or, in relation to the deduction of a loss from a chargeable gain where either the gain or the loss accrues after 10 March 1994, paragraph (*b*) above, is a group of which that company was a member at any time in the accounting period of that company in which it became a member of the group falling within that paragraph;

(*d*)   that group is a group the principal company (see 13.10 above) of which is or has been, or has been under the control (within *ICTA 1988, s 416*) of

(i)   the company by which the disposal is made, or

(ii)   another company which is or has been a member of a group by reference to which *7A Sch* applies in relation to the loss in question under (*a*), (*b*) or (*c*) above; or

(*e*)   that group is a group of which either

(i)   the principal company of a group by reference to which *7A Sch* applies, or

(ii)   a company which has had that principal company under its control,

is or has been a member.

In the case of a loss accruing on the disposal of an asset where, under (*a*)-(*e*) above there are two or more groups ('*connected groups*') by reference to which *7A Sch* applies, the further provisions in *7A Sch 9(3)-(5)* below apply. [*TCGA 1992, 7A Sch 9(1)(2); FA 1994, s 94(1)(3)(4)*].

7A Sch is applied separately in relation to each of the connected groups (so far as they are not groups in relation to which the loss is a pre-entry loss because it is a loss that accrued to a company at a time before it became a member of the group) for the purpose of determining whether the loss on the disposal of an asset is a loss on the disposal of a pre-entry asset, and calculating the pre-entry proportion of that loss. [*TCGA 1992, 7A Sch 9(3)*].

Subject to *7A Sch 9(5)* below, the provisions in 13.26 above have effect

(A)   as if the pre-entry proportion of any loss accruing on the disposal of an asset which is a pre-entry asset in the case of more than one of the connected groups were the largest pre-entry proportion of that loss as calculated under *7A Sch 9(3)* above; and

(B)   so that, where the loss accruing on the disposal of an asset is a pre-entry loss because it is an allowable loss that accrued to a company at a time before it became a member of a group in the case of any of the connected groups, that loss is the pre-entry loss for the purposes of 13.26 above, and not any amount which is the pre-entry proportion of that loss in relation to any of the other groups.

[*TCGA 1992, 7A Sch 9(4)*].

Where, on the separate application of *7A Sch* in the case of each of the groups by reference to which *7A Sch* applies, there is, in the case of the disposal of any asset, a pre-entry loss by reference to each of two or more of the connected groups, no amount in respect of the loss accruing on the disposal is to be deductible under the provisions in 13.27 above from any chargeable gain if any of the connected groups is a group in the case of which, on separate applications of those provisions in relation to each group, the amount deductible from that gain in respect of that loss is nil. [*TCGA 1992, 7A Sch 9(5)*].

Notwithstanding that the principal company of one group (*'the first group'*) has become a member of another (*'the second group'*), those two groups are not under *TCGA 1992, s 170(10)* (see 13.10 above) treated for the purposes of the above provisions as the same group if the principal company of the first group was under the control, immediately before it became a member of the second group, of a company which at that time was already a member of the second group. [*TCGA 1992, 7A Sch 9(6)*].

Where, in the case of the disposal of any asset

(*aa*)   two or more groups which but for *7A Sch 9(6)* above would be treated as the same group are treated as separate groups because of that provision; and

(*bb*)   one of those groups is a group of which either

(i)   the principal company of a group by reference to which *7A Sch* applies by virtue of (*a*), (*b*) or (*c*) above in relation to any loss accruing on the disposal, or

(ii)   a company which has had that principal company under its control,

is or has been a member,

the above provisions have effect as if that principal company had been a member of each of the groups mentioned in (*aa*) above. [*TCGA 1992, 7A Sch 9(7)*].

13.30   *Miscellaneous.* Where, but for an election under *TCGA 1992, s 161(3)* (appropriation of asset to trading stock; see 6.3 ASSETS), there would be deemed to have been a disposal at any time by a company of an asset the amount by which the market value of it may be treated as increased under the election does not include the amount of any pre-entry loss that would have accrued on that disposal, and *7A Sch* has effect as if the pre-entry loss of the last mentioned amount had accrued to the company at that time. [*TCGA 1992, 7A Sch 10*].

The provisions of *7A Sch* are prevented from applying where a loss arises, or a company joins a group, as a result of any enactment under which transfers of property etc. are made from a statutory body, a subsidiary of such a body or a company wholly owned by the Crown. [*TCGA 1992, 7A Sch 11*].

For the purposes of *7A Sch*, and without prejudice to the provisions in *7A Sch 11* above, where

(*a*)   a company which is a member of a group of companies becomes at any time a member of another group of companies as the result of a disposal of shares in or other securities of that company or any other company; and

(*b*)   that disposal is one of the no gain/no loss disposals mentioned in *TCGA 1992, s 35(3)(d)* (see 8.7 ASSETS HELD ON 31 MARCH 1982),

7A Sch has effect in relation to the losses that accrued to that company before that time and the assets held by that company at that time as if any time when it was a member of the first group were included in the period during which it is treated as having been a member of the second group. [*TCGA 1992, 7A Sch 12*].

13.31   SHARES—ACQUISITIONS AND DISPOSALS WITHIN SHORT PERIOD

The ordinary rules for matching disposals with 'acquisitions' are modified for disposals by a company of shares (including securities and, for disposals before 2 July 1986, qualifying corporate bonds but excluding gilt-edged securities) if (i) the company (or a fellow member of a group as in 13.10 above) acquired shares of the same kind after that date *and* within one month before or after the disposal where the disposal was through a stock exchange or ARIEL (Automated Real-Time Investments Exchange Limited), or within six months otherwise, and (ii) the number of that kind of shares held by the company (or group) during the prescribed period before the disposal was not less than 2% of the number issued. Such acquisitions are called *'available shares'*.

Disposals are matched with available shares before other shares and with available shares acquired by the disposing company before those acquired by a fellow group member, and then with acquisitions before the disposal (latest ones first) rather than after (when earlier ones are taken first). Where disposals are identified with acquisitions of another group member, the cost to that member will be allowed to the disposing company plus the usual incidental costs of disposal. Shares identified with one disposal are precluded from further identification with a later disposal.

'*Acquisitions*' do not include shares acquired as trading stock or acquired from another group member.

For disposals after 31 March 1985, the above identification rules have priority over those pertaining to the INDEXATION (23) provisions generally, but not where shares acquired and disposed of on the same day are matched under *TCGA 1992, s 105(1)* (see 23.9 INDEXATION). For disposals after 31 March 1982 and before 1 April 1985 the above rules had priority over the then identification rules pertaining to the indexation provisions. For disposals before 1 April 1982 the above rules were subject to *TCGA 1992, s 105(1)* solely. [*TCGA 1992, s 106*].

13.32   CLOSE COMPANY TRANSFERRING ASSET AT UNDERVALUE

See 3.12 ANTI-AVOIDANCE where a close company transfers an asset otherwise than at arm's length for a consideration less than market value.

13.33   DEMERGERS

The provisions of *ICTA 1988, ss 213-218* have effect for facilitating certain transactions whereby trading activities carried on by a single company or 'group' are divided so as to be carried on by two or more companies not belonging to the same group or by two or more independent groups. '*Group*' means a company and all of its 75 per cent subsidiaries

13.34 Companies

(with the effect of direct and indirect ownership of shares held as trading stock being ignored in deciding whether one company is a 75 per cent subsidiary of another).

An exempt distribution (as in *ICTA 1988, s 213(2)*) within *ICTA 1988, s 213(3)(a)* (transfer by company of shares in one or more 75 per cent subsidiaries) is not a capital distribution within *TCGA 1992, s 122* (see 53.13 SHARES AND SECURITIES). *TCGA 1992, ss 126-130* (see generally 53.5 SHARES AND SECURITIES) are applied as if that company and the subsidiary whose shares are transferred were the same company and the distribution were a reorganisation of share capital.

A charge under *TCGA 1992, s 178* or *179* (see 13.17 above) on a company ceasing to be a member of a group does not apply where the cessation is by reason only of an exempt distribution. However, this exemption does not apply if there is a chargeable payment (within *ICTA 1988, s 214(2)*: payment not made for bona fide reasons or made for tax avoidance purposes) within five years of the exempt distribution, and will result in the *TCGA 1992, s 178* or *179* charge being able to be the subject of an assessment made within three years of the chargeable payment. [*TCGA 1992, s 192*].

For full details of the provisions see Tolley's Corporation Tax under Groups of Companies.

13.34 EXCHANGE GAINS AND LOSSES

The main elements of the provisions in *FA 1993, ss 60, 92–96, 125–170, 15–18 Schs* (as amended), which are described in detail in Tolley's Corporation Tax under Exchange Gains and Losses (wherein the terms referred to in the following are defined), are as below.

(*a*) The provisions apply, subject to transitional rules, to 'qualifying companies' (broadly all companies excepting charities, authorised unit trusts and investment trusts) becoming entitled to 'qualifying assets', subject to 'qualifying liabilities', or entitled or subject to 'currency contracts', on or after the company's 'commencement day'.

(*b*) Exchange gains and losses in respect of qualifying assets and liabilities and currency contracts are recognised as they accrue between set 'translation times'.

(*c*) Trading exchange gains and losses are treated as trading items within Schedule D, Case I, net non-trading exchange gains are assessed under Schedule D, Case VI, and there are special provisions for the relief of net non-trading exchange losses.

(*d*) Certain unrealised exchange gains on long-term capital items may be deferred.

(*e*) Exchange differences are generally calculated in sterling, although trading profits or losses (excluding capital allowances) may in certain circumstances be calculated in non-sterling currencies.

(*f*) Regulations may provide for the matching of borrowings with certain non-qualifying assets (it being envisaged that such regulations will have an effect as regards the deeming of a chargeable gain or allowable loss). See Tolley's Corporation Tax for details.

(*g*) The charge of corporation tax in respect of chargeable gains will cease to apply to qualifying assets (subject to transitional rules made under future regulations).

(*h*) Anti-avoidance rules operate to prevent abuse of the provisions.

There are a number of exclusions from the operation of the provisions, and special rules in relation to insurance companies and cases where assets or contracts are held, or liabilities owed, in *'exempt circumstances'* (broadly, for the purposes of long term insurance business; for the purposes of mutual insurance business; for the purposes of the occupation for profit of commercial woodlands in the UK; by an approved housing association; or by an approved self-build society).

The principal provisions consequential to (*g*) above are mentioned at 13.6 and 13.11 above; 18.5 and 18.8 EXEMPTIONS AND RELIEFS; 39.3 OVERSEAS MATTERS and 44.2 QUALIFYING CORPORATE BONDS.

13.35   **FINANCIAL INSTRUMENTS INVOLVING INTEREST RATE AND CURRENCY CONTRACTS**

The corporation tax provisions in *FA 1994, Pt IV Ch II* (i.e. *sections 147–177, 18 Sch*) relating to the treatment of financial instruments to manage interest rate and currency risk are given in Tolley's Corporation Tax under Financial Instruments (wherein the following quoted terms are defined). For the purposes of those provisions, an 'interest rate contract' or 'interest rate option', or a 'currency contract' or 'currency option', is a 'qualifying contract' as regards a 'qualifying company' if the company becomes entitled to rights or subject to duties under the contract or option on or after its 'commencement day'.

Any amount which under or by virtue of the above provisions is chargeable to corporation tax as profits of a qualifying company, or which falls to be taken into account as a receipt in computing for the purposes of those provisions (which are deemed to include certain provisions in 13.34 above dealing with non-trading exchange gains) the profits or losses of such a company, is excluded for the purposes of *TCGA 1992* from the consideration for a disposal of assets taken into account in the computation of the gain. Similarly, any amount (irrespective of whether effect is or would be given to the deduction of it in computing the amount of tax chargeable or by discharge or repayment of tax or in any other way), which is allowable as a deduction in computing for the above purposes (as similarly extended) the profits or losses of a qualifying company, or which under or by virtue of the above provisions is allowable as a deduction in computing any other income or profits or gains or losses of such a company for the purposes of the *Tax Acts*, or which, although not so allowable as a deduction in computing any losses, would be so allowable as a deduction but for an insufficiency of income or profits or gains, is excluded from the sums allowable under *TCGA 1992, s 38* (allowable expenditure on disposal) as a deduction in the computation of the gain. [*FA 1994, s 173*].

14 Connected Persons

[*ICTA 1988, s 839; TCGA 1992, s 286*]

Cross-references. See 3.10, 3.11 ANTI-AVOIDANCE for certain disposals between connected persons; 35.4 LOSSES for losses on disposals to connected persons; 40.10 PARTNERSHIPS for transactions between partners; and 52.6 SETTLEMENTS for settlors and trustees being connected persons.

14.1   An **individual** is connected with his spouse, any 'relative' (see 14.7 below) of himself or of his spouse, and with the spouse of any such relative. It appears that a widow or

14.2 Connected Persons

widower is no longer a spouse (*Vestey's Exors and Vestey v CIR HL 1949, 31 TC 1*). Spouses divorced by decree nisi remain connected persons until the divorce is made absolute (*Aspden v Hildesley Ch D 1981, 55 TC 609*).

14.2   A **trustee of a 'settlement'**, in his capacity as such, is connected with

(*a*)   the 'settlor' (if an individual) (see 14.7 below),

(*b*)   any person connected with the settlor, and

(*c*)   a 'body corporate connected with the settlement' (see 14.7 below).

The Revenue has confirmed (*a*) above applies as regards the time when a settlement is created and property first transferred to it. On the death of the settlor, neither (*a*) nor (*b*) apply (Revenue Tax Bulletin February 1993 p 56).

14.3   **Partners** are connected with each other and with each other's spouses (see 14.1 above) and relatives (see 14.7 below), except in connection with acquisitions and disposals of partnership assets made pursuant to bona fide commercial arrangements. See also 14.5 below.

14.4   A **company is connected with another company** if

(*a*)   the same person 'controls' both (see 14.7 below), or

(*b*)   one is controlled by a person who has control of the other in conjunction with persons connected with him, or

(*c*)   a person controls one company and persons connected with him control the other, or

(*d*)   the same group of persons controls both, or

(*e*)   the companies are controlled by separate groups which can be regarded as the same by interchanging connected persons.

14.5   A **company is connected with another person who** (either alone or with persons connected with him) **has control of it.** It is understood that the Revenue will accept that a partnership and a company under common control are connected for some purposes (see Tolley's Practical Tax 1981 p 142).

14.6   **Persons acting together to secure or exercise control of a company** are treated in relation to that company as connected with each other and with any other person acting on the direction of any of them to secure or exercise such control (see *Steele v European Vinyls Corp (Holdings) BV Ch D 1994, [1995] STC 31*). Control may be 'exercised' passively. See *Floor v Davis HL 1979, 52 TC 609*. See 3.17 ANTI-AVOIDANCE for an extension of this provision in connection with dividend stripping.

14.7   '*Company*' includes any body corporate, unincorporated association or unit trust scheme but does not include a partnership.

'*Control*' is as defined in *ICTA 1988, s 416*. [*TCGA 1992, s 288(1)*]. See Tolley's Corporation Tax under Close Companies.

'*Relative*' means brother, sister, ancestor or lineal descendant. [*TCGA 1992, s 286(8)*].

'*Settlement*' includes any disposition, trust, covenant, agreement, arrangement or transfer of assets. [*ICTA 1988, s 660G(1); FA 1995, 17 Sch 1*]. It must contain an element of bounty. It does not include a transfer of assets for full consideration (*CIR v Plummer HL 1979, 54 TC 1*).

'*A body corporate connected with the settlement*' is a close company (or one which would be so if resident in the UK) the participators in which include the trustees of the settlement, or a company controlled by such a close company. Control for these purposes is as under *ICTA 1988, s 840*: namely, the power of a person by shareholding or voting power (whether directly or through another company), or under Articles of Association, to secure that the company's affairs are conducted according to his wishes. Prior to 27 July 1981 it was defined as a close company (or one which would be so if resident in the UK), the participators in which include the trustees of, or a beneficiary under, the settlement. [*ICTA 1988, s 682A; FA 1995, 17 Sch 11*].

'*Settlor*' is any person by whom the settlement was made or who has directly or indirectly (or by a reciprocal arrangement) provided, or undertaken to provide, funds for the purpose of the settlement. [*ICTA 1988, s 660G(1)(2); FA 1995, 17 Sch 1*]. See *Countess Fitzwilliam and others v CIR (and related appeals) HL, [1993] STC 502*.

15 Deaths

Cross-references. See 30.2 INTERACTION WITH OTHER TAXES for inheritance tax (or capital transfer tax); 32.7 INTEREST ON UNPAID TAX for relief given if probate is delayed; 36 MARKET VALUE; 52.2 SETTLEMENTS for death of a bankrupt etc. and 52.9–52.11 for termination of a life interest by the death of the person entitled thereto; 53.19 SHARES AND SECURITIES.

15.1 GENERAL PROVISIONS

All 'assets of which a deceased person was competent to dispose' are deemed to have been acquired on his death by his personal representatives (or other person on whom they devolve) for a consideration equal to their market value at the date of death. However, they are not deemed to be disposed of by the deceased on his death (whether or not they were the subject of a testamentary disposition), i.e. no chargeable gain or allowable loss arises on death and any gain or loss arising on the disposal of the asset by the personal representatives, etc. after the death is calculated by reference to the market value of the asset at the date of death (subject to the further provisions in this chapter).

'Assets of which the deceased was competent to dispose' are those assets which (otherwise than in right of a power of appointment or of the testamentary power conferred by statute to dispose of entailed interests) he could, if of full age and capacity, have disposed of by his will, assuming that all the assets were situated in England and, if he was not domiciled in the United Kingdom, that he was domiciled in England, and include references to his severable share in any assets to which, immediately before his death, he was beneficially entitled as joint tenant. [*TCGA 1992, s 62(1)(10)*].

15.2 **Scotland.** So far as the provisions in *TCGA 1992* relate to the consequences of the death of

(*a*) an heir of entail in possession of any property in Scotland subject to an entail (whether *sui juris* or not), or

(*b*) a proper liferenter of any property,

then, on the death of any such heir or liferenter, the heir next entitled or, as the case may be, the person (if any) who, on the death of the liferenter, becomes entitled to possession of the property as fiar, is deemed to have acquired all the assets forming part of the property at the date of the deceased's death for a consideration equal to their market value at that date. [*TCGA 1992, s 63*].

15.3 **Valuation.** Where on the death of any person, inheritance tax (or capital transfer tax or estate duty) is chargeable on the value of his estate immediately before his death and the value of an asset forming part of his estate has been ascertained for those purposes, that value is taken to be the market value at the date of death for capital gains tax purposes. [*TCGA 1992, s 274, 11 Sch 9*]. However, in practice, the Capital Taxes Office follows the capital gains tax valuation in the case of quoted shares, as in 36.2 MARKET VALUE (Revenue Pamphlet IHT 1, para 8.9). See also 30.2 INTERACTION WITH OTHER TAXES.

Where, in consequence of a death before 31 March 1971 (when death *was* an occasion of charge), capital gains tax was chargeable or an allowable loss accrued, then if the market value of any property on the date of death which was subject to charge has been depreciated *by reason of the death*, then any later estimate of the market value is to take that depreciation into account. [*TCGA 1992, 11 Sch 8*]. This provision may still, therefore, be relevant in computing allowable expenditure on a first disposal subsequent to the date of death. The legislation now refers to deaths before 31 March 1973 but the reasoning for this is not clear; see *FA 1965, s 44(2) proviso* as repealed by *FA 1971, 14 Sch Pt V* for deaths occurring after 30 March 1971 and cf. *CGTA 1979, 6 Sch 2(2)*).

15.4   **Donatio mortis causa.** No chargeable gain arises on the making of a disposal by way of *'donatio mortis causa'* i.e. a gift of personal property made in 'contemplation of the conceived approach of death' (see *Duffield v Elwes Ch D 1827, 1 Bligh's Reports (New Series) 497*), and the recipient is treated as a legatee acquiring it at the date of death. [*TCGA 1992, ss 62(5), 64(2)*].

15.5   **Allowable losses** in excess of chargeable gains incurred by the deceased in the year of assessment in which death occurs can be carried back and set off against chargeable gains of the deceased (but not those of a spouse even where accruing in a year before 1990/91) in the preceding three years of assessment so as to reduce net gains for those earlier years to the exempt amount for each year (see 2.3 ANNUAL RATES AND EXEMPTIONS). Chargeable gains accruing in a later year are taken before those of an earlier year. [*TCGA 1992, s 62(2)*]. Any unused losses cannot be carried forward and set off against gains made by the personal representatives. For years of assessment before 1990/91 and unless an election was made to the contrary, losses of the deceased spouse in the year of assessment in which death occurred were apparently available against the gains of the surviving spouse for that year whether those gains arose before or after the date of death. See 37.3 MARRIED PERSONS.

15.6   **DEEDS OF FAMILY ARRANGEMENT, ETC.**

Variations or disclaimers of the dispositions (whether effected by will, under the intestacy rules or otherwise) of the 'property of which the deceased was competent to dispose' (see 15.1 above) which are made by deed of family arrangement (or similar instrument in writing) within two years of death do not constitute disposals but are related back to the date of death. However, in the case of a variation, an appropriate election (under *TCGA 1992, s 62(7)*) is required for this treatment to apply. Such treatment does not apply in respect of variations or disclaimers made for any consideration in money or money's worth other than consideration consisting of the making of a variation or disclaimer in respect of another of the dispositions. The election in respect of a variation must be made to the Board in writing by the parties to the instrument within six months after the date of the instrument or such longer time as the Board may allow. The provisions apply whether or not the administration of the estate is complete or the property has been distributed in accordance with the original dispositions. [*TCGA 1992, s 62(6)-(9)*].

In a case based upon the original *FA 1965* legislation, it was held that the equivalent provisions to *TCGA 1992, s 62(6)* above and *s 62(4)* (see 15.9 below), although deeming provisions, were to be given their normal and natural meaning. But, where such construction would lead to an injustice or absurdity, the application of the statutory fiction should be limited to the extent needed to avoid such injustice or absurdity. Thus, nothing in *TCGA 1992, s 62(6)* requires one to assume something which is inconsistent with the legatee under an original will, who then varies dispositions under *TCGA 1992, s 62(6)* to a third party, as having been the actual settlor of the arrangement. The deeming provisions apply only to assets of which the testator was competent to dispose at his death. However, the property settled by the legatee comprised, not the assets in the deceased's estate which eventually came to be vested in the third party, but a separate chose in action, i.e. the right to due administration of the estate, and this could only have been settled by the legatee and not by the deceased (*Marshall v Kerr HL, [1994] STC*

15.7 Deaths

638). Where, in the rare event, the administration of an estate has been completed before a deed of variation is made, a different analysis may follow.

Prior to the commencement of *TCGA 1992*, the election was made under *CGTA 1979, s 49(7)*.

For cases bearing on the effectiveness of similar deeds used for inheritance tax purposes, see Tolley's Inheritance Tax under Deeds Varying Dispositions on Death.

15.7 **PERSONAL REPRESENTATIVES**

Personal representatives are treated as a single and continuing body (distinct from persons who may from time to time be the personal representatives) which has the deceased's residence, ordinary residence and domicile at the date of death. [*TCGA 1992, s 62(3)*].

They are liable to capital gains tax on disposals of assets made by them by reference to the disposal proceeds and the market value at the date of death (but see 15.8 below). They may be assessed in respect of disposals made by the deceased prior to death as well as in respect of their own disposals. See 5.6, 5.7 ASSESSMENTS.

For the year of assessment in which death occurs and the following two years of assessment, the personal representatives are entitled to the same 'exempt amount for the year' as individuals. [*TCGA 1992, s 3(7)*]. See 2.3 ANNUAL RATES AND EXEMPTIONS.

Losses made by personal representatives during the administration period cannot be passed on to the legatees. The position should be compared with that for losses made by trustees as in 52.9 SETTLEMENTS.

15.8 **Allowable expenditure.** The decision in *Richards' Executors HL 1971, 46 TC 626* enables personal representatives, in computing chargeable gains on the disposal of assets, to add to the cost of acquiring the assets from the testator (i.e. the market value at the date of death) those legal and accountancy costs that are involved in preparing the inheritance tax or capital transfer tax account and obtaining the grant of probate etc. See also 16.3 DISPOSAL.

Because of the practical difficulty of identifying the costs applicable to individual assets comprised in the estate, the Board of Inland Revenue has agreed expenditure based on the following scales

Personal representatives

Deaths after 5 April 1993

	Gross value of estate	Allowable expenditure
A	Up to £40,000	1.75% of the probate value of the assets sold by the personal representatives.
B	Between £40,001 and £70,000	A fixed amount of £700, to be divided between all the assets in the estate in proportion to the probate values, and allowed in those proportions on assets sold by the personal representatives.
C	Between £70,001 and £300,000	1% of the probate value of the assets sold.
D	Between £300,001 and £400,000	A fixed amount of £3,000, to be divided as at B above.
E	Between £400,001 and £750,000	0.75% of the probate value of the assets sold.

Deaths before 6 April 1993

	Gross value of estate	Allowable expenditure
(a)	Up to £20,000	1.5% of the probate value of the assets sold by the personal representatives.
(b)	Between £20,001 and £30,000	A fixed amount of £300 to be divided among all the assets in the estate in proportion to their probate values, and allowed in those proportions on assets sold by the personal representatives.
(c)	Between £30,001 and £150,000	1% of the probate value of the assets sold.
(d)	Between £150,001 and £200,000	A fixed amount of £1,500, to be divided as in (b) above.
(e)	Between £200,001 and £400,000	0.75% of the probate value of the assets sold.

Deaths before 6 April 1981

(A)	Up to £13,000	1.5% of the probate value of the assets sold by the personal representatives.
(B)	Between £13,001 and £20,000	A fixed amount of £200 to be divided among all the assets in the estate in proportion to their probate values, and allowed in those proportions on assets sold by the personal representatives.
(C)	Between £20,001 and £100,000	1% of the probate value of the assets sold.
(D)	Between £100,001 and £135,000	A fixed amount of £1,000 to be divided as in (B) above.
(E)	Between £135,001 and £250,000	0.75% of the probate value of the assets sold.

The scales do not extend to gross estates that exceed £750,000 for deaths after 5 April 1993 (or £400,000 for deaths before 6 April 1993, or £250,000 previously). In those cases, the allowable expenditure has to be negotiated by the inspector and the personal representatives, according to the facts of the particular case.

In practice, the Board will accept computations based either on these scales or on the actual expenditure incurred (Revenue Pamphlet IR 131, SP 8/94, 16 September 1994).

Corporate trustees

The Board of Inland Revenue have also agreed the following scale of allowable expenditure for expenses incurred by corporate trustees in the administration of estates and trusts. The Board will accept computations based either on this scale or on the *actual* allowable expenditure incurred.

Acquisitions and disposals, or deemed disposals, after 5 April 1993

(a) *Transfers of assets to beneficiaries etc.*

(1) Quoted stocks and shares

    (A) One beneficiary   £20 per holding.

15.9 Deaths

(B)	More than one beneficiary between whom a holding must be divided	As (A), to be divided in equal shares between the beneficiaries.
(2)	Unquoted shares	As (1) above, with the addition of any exceptional expenditure.
(3)	Other assets	As (1) above, with the addition of any exceptional expenditure.

(b) *Actual disposals and acquisitions*

(1)	Quoted stocks and shares	The investment fee as charged by the trustee.
(2)	Unquoted shares	As (1) above, plus actual valuation costs.
(3)	Other assets	The investment fee as charged by the trustee, subject to a maximum of £60, plus actual valuation costs.

Where a comprehensive annual management fee is charged, covering both the cost of administering the trust and the expenses of actual disposals and acquisitions, the investment fee for (1)–(3) above will be taken to be £0.25 per £100 on the sale or purchase moneys.

(c) *Deemed disposals by trustees*

(1)	Quoted stocks and shares	£6 per holding.
(2)	Unquoted shares	Actual valuation costs.
(3)	Other assets	Actual valuation costs.

15.9 LEGATEES

A *'legatee'* includes any person taking under a testamentary disposition or an intestacy or partial intestacy, whether he takes beneficially or as trustee. [*TCGA 1992, s 64(2)*].

On a 'person acquiring any asset as legatee', no chargeable gain accrues to the personal representatives, and the legatee is treated as if the personal representatives' acquisition of the asset had been his acquisition of it. [*TCGA 1992, s 62(4)*]. The consequences of this are that the asset is taken as acquired at either the market value at the date of death or, if the asset was acquired subsequent to death, the allowable expenditure incurred by the personal representatives in providing etc. the asset. See also 15.6 above.

For the purposes of *'legatee'* and *'person acquiring an asset as legatee'*, property taken under a testamentary disposition or on an intestacy or partial intestacy includes any asset appropriated by the personal representative in or towards satisfaction of a pecuniary legacy or any other interest or share in the property devolving. [*TCGA 1992, s 64(3)*].

Where a legatee disposes of an asset acquired from personal representatives, all expenditure within *TCGA 1992, s 38(2)* (see 16.3 DISPOSAL) incurred both by the legatee and by the personal representatives in relation to the transfer of the asset to him is an allowable deduction in computing his gain arising on disposal. [*TCGA 1992, s 64(1)*].

16   Disposal

Cross-references. See 2.3 ANNUAL RATES AND EXEMPTIONS; 3.4 ANTI-AVOIDANCE for transactions treated as disposals; 7 ASSETS HELD ON 6 APRIL 1965; 8 ASSETS HELD ON 31 MARCH 1982; 23 INDEXATION; 30 INTERACTION WITH OTHER TAXES; 33 LAND for disposals of land and leases; 34.2 LIFE ASSURANCE POLICIES AND DEFERRED ANNUITIES; 35 LOSSES; 36 MARKET VALUE; 53 SHARES AND SECURITIES; 59 WASTING ASSETS.

16.1   GENERAL

Gains and losses accruing on disposals of assets are computed by deducting allowable expenditure (see 16.3–16.5 below) from the amount realised or deemed to be realised on the disposal (i.e. the actual or deemed consideration). [*TCGA 1992, ss 15, 38*]. No deduction is allowable more than once from any sum or from more than one sum. [*TCGA 1992, s 52(1)*]. See 16.2 below for date of disposal. See 16.6 below for part disposals.

There is a disposal of assets where a capital sum is derived from them. See 16.7–16.9 below. Options are dealt with at 16.10, commodity and financial futures at 16.11 and forfeited deposits of purchase money at 16.12.

'*Disposal*' is not defined in the legislation. It does not, however, include a conveyance or transfer of an asset or of a right therein *by way of security* (e.g. a mortgage), but if the creditor or any person appointed as receiver, manager, etc. deals with the asset in order to enforce the security, his activities are imputed to the giver of the security. The existence of a security is ignored for both acquisition and disposal of an asset save that the amount of liability assumed forms part of the acquisition and disposal consideration in addition to any other consideration. [*TCGA 1992, s 26*]. Relief is available if there has been a sale of an asset at arm's length in circumstances such that the vendor granted the purchaser a mortgage (in full or in part) in order for the purchaser to buy and where there has later been a default on the mortgage loan. If, as a result, the vendor regains beneficial ownership of the asset he has contracted to sell he may elect that the gain realised by him on that sale be taken as limited to the net proceeds (after incidental costs of disposal) retained by him and the loan be treated as never coming into existence (although interest on the loan would be subject to income tax in the usual way). On any subsequent disposal of the asset concerned, the computation will be by reference to the original date and costs of acquisition etc. (Revenue Pamphlet IR 1 (1992) D18).

For disposals after 29 November 1993, the gain (if any) arrived at as above is termed the '*unindexed gain*'. Any indexation allowance due is deducted from the unindexed gain to give the gain for the purposes of *TCGA 1992* unless otherwise provided. If the allowance equals or exceeds the unindexed gain, no gain or loss arises. If a loss arises as above, no indexation allowance is available. See 23.1 INDEXATION and note the transitional relief for 'indexation losses' which may be due for 1993/94 and 1994/95 as in 23.2 INDEXATION in the case of disposals by individuals and trustees of settlements made before 30 November 1993.

For disposals after 5 April 1985 (31 March 1985 for companies) and before 30 November 1993, the gain or loss (if any) arrived at by deducting allowable expenditure from disposal consideration received was termed the '*unindexed gain or loss*'. Any indexation allowance due was deducted from the unindexed gain (and so as to create a loss if greater than the unindexed gain) or was added to the unindexed loss. If the unindexed gain or loss was nil, the indexation allowance itself was the loss arising. The resulting net figure was the gain or loss for the purposes of *TCGA 1992* unless otherwise provided. See 23.1 INDEXATION.

16.2 Disposal

For disposals after 5 April 1982 and before 6 April 1985 (after 31 March 1982 and before 1 April 1985 for companies), the gain (if any) arrived at by deducting allowable expenditure from disposal consideration received was termed the 'gross gain'. Any indexation allowance due was deducted from the gross gain to arrive at the gain for the purposes of *CGTA 1979* unless otherwise provided. If the allowance exceeded or was equal to the gross gain, no gain or loss arose. If a loss was produced by deducting allowable expenditure from disposal consideration received, no indexation allowance was available. See 23.1 INDEXATION.

For disposals before 6 April 1982 (1 April 1982 for companies), indexation allowance did not apply. The gain, if any, arrived at above, was, unless the legislation provided otherwise, the chargeable gain.

16.2 **DATE OF DISPOSAL**

Contracts. Where an asset is disposed of and acquired under a contract, the disposal and acquisition are made at the time the contract is made (and not, if different, the time at which the asset is conveyed or transferred, e.g. on a contract for the sale of land). This rule applies even if the contract is unenforceable, provided that the disposal is actually completed (*Thompson v Salah Ch D 1971, 47 TC 559*). If the contract is conditional (and, in particular, if it is conditional on the exercise of an option), the disposal and acquisition are made at the time the condition is satisfied. [*TCGA 1992, s 28*]. See *Eastham v Leigh London & Provincial Properties Ltd CA 1971, 46 TC 687* and *Johnson v Edwards Ch D 1981, 54 TC 488*. See also under hire purchase below.

Gifts. A gift is treated as having been made when the donor has done everything within his power to transfer the property to the donee (*Re Rose, Rose and Others v CIR CA, [1952] 1 All ER 1217*).

Hire purchase. A transaction under which the assets may pass to the hirer at the end of the hire is treated as a disposal of the whole asset at the beginning of that period, with subsequent adjustments if the agreement terminates without the hirer acquiring the asset. [*TCGA 1992, s 27*]. For consideration of hire-purchase and conditional contracts (see above), see *Lyon v Pettigrew Ch D 1985, 58 TC 452*.

Capital sums. Deemed disposals covered by 16.7 below take place on the receipt of the capital sum. [*TCGA 1992, s 22(2)*].

Options. See 16.10 below.

Assets lost or destroyed are deemed to be disposed of at the time of loss etc. [*TCGA 1992, s 24(1)*]. It seems that this provision does not override *TCGA 1992, s 22(2)* above where an actual capital sum is received subsequent to the loss etc. (see comments by Hoffman J in the Ch D in *Powlson v Welbeck Securities Ltd CA 1987, 60 TC 269*).

Assets becoming of negligible value. See 35.8 LOSSES.

Land compulsorily acquired. See 33.12 LAND for acquisition of land by an authority possessing any power of compulsory purchase.

Rollover relief. See 50.1 ROLLOVER RELIEF.

16.3 **ALLOWABLE EXPENDITURE—GENERAL PROVISIONS**

Except as otherwise expressly provided, the sums allowable as a deduction from the consideration in the computation of any gain accruing to a person on the disposal of an asset are restricted to the following.

(a) **The amount or value of the consideration, in money or money's worth, given wholly and exclusively for the acquisition of the asset** (plus 'incidental costs') or expenditure incurred wholly and exclusively in providing the asset [*TCGA 1992, s 38(1)(a)*]. See *Cleveleys Investment Trust Co v CIR (No 2) CS 1975, 51 TC 26; Allison v Murray Ch D 1975, 51 TC 57.*

'*Incidental costs*' of acquisition are (strictly) limited to expenditure wholly and exclusively incurred for the purposes of the acquisition, being

(i) fees, commission or remuneration for the professional services of a surveyor, valuer, auctioneer, accountant, agent or legal adviser;

(ii) transfer/conveyancing charges (including stamp duty); and

(iii) advertising to find a seller.

[*TCGA 1992, s 38(2)*].

Where the purchaser is a company, and the purchase price is satisfied by the issue of fully paid-up shares in the company, the consideration is the shares and their value is normally that placed on them by the parties, i.e. the purchase price satisfied by the issue. 'Value' in *TCGA 1992, s 38(1)(a)* (see above) does not mean 'market value' (*Stanton v Drayton Commercial Investment Co Ltd HL 1982, 55 TC 286*). Disposals which are deemed to take place at market value will, generally speaking, give rise to an equivalent base cost in the acquirer's hands (but see 36.1 MARKET VALUE). No allowance is given for notional costs of disposal or reacquisition, where there is a deemed disposal and reacquisition. [*TCGA 1992, ss 17, 38(4)*].

Where the cost (or deemed cost) of an asset is in foreign currency, it is converted into sterling at the exchange rate ruling at the time of acquisition. Similarly, consideration is converted at the date of disposal. (*Bentley v Pike Ch D 1981, 53 TC 590; Capcount Trading v Evans CA 1992, [1993] STC 11*). However, the principle laid down by these cases is superseded in the case of a 'qualifying company' where the taxation regime for exchange gains and losses noted at 13.34 COMPANIES has effect.

See (b) below for capital contributions by shareholders.

A company with an annual turnover of not less than £5 million may round incidental costs of acquisition to the nearest £1,000 subject to certain conditions and exceptions (Revenue Press Release 18 May 1993).

(b) **Expenditure wholly and exclusively incurred for the purpose of enhancing the value of the asset being expenditure reflected in the state or nature of the asset at the time of disposal.** [*TCGA 1992, s 38(1)(b)*]. Expenditure on initial repairs (including decoration) to a property, undertaken to put it into a fit state for letting, and not allowable for Schedule A purposes, is regarded as allowable expenditure under this heading (29.D24 INLAND REVENUE STATEMENTS OF PRACTICE). The Revenue consider that capital contributions made to a company by shareholders are not allowable expenditure under this heading, but that if made at the time of issue of the shares they might be treated as in the nature of a share premium (ICAEW Guidance Note TR 713, 23 August 1988). See also 16.5(a) below.

'*Expenditure*' does not include the value of personal labour and skill (*Oram v Johnson Ch D 1980, 53 TC 319*). However, it may be in the form of providing money's worth and may be first reflected in the state or nature of the asset before completion even if this is after the time of disposal (*Chaney v Watkis Ch D 1985, 58 TC 707*).

(c)   **Expenditure wholly and exclusively incurred in establishing, preserving or defending title to, or to a right over, the asset.** [*TCGA 1992, s 38(1)(b)*]. This includes resealing Scottish confirmation and other probate etc. expenses incurred to establish the title of the personal representatives (*Richards' Executors HL 1971, 46 TC 626* and see 15.8 DEATH) and see 52.9 SETTLEMENTS.

(d)   **Incidental costs of disposal.** [*TCGA 1992, s 38(1)(c)*]. Strictly, such costs are limited to expenditure wholly and exclusively incurred for the purposes of the disposal, being

(i)   fees, commission or remuneration for the professional services of a surveyor, valuer, auctioneer, accountant, agent or legal adviser;

(ii)   transfer/conveyancing charges (including stamp duty);

(iii)   advertising to find a buyer; and

(iv)   any other costs reasonably incurred in making any valuation or apportionment for capital gains tax purposes, including, in particular, expenses reasonably incurred in ascertaining market value where this is required under *TCGA 1992*.

[*TCGA 1992, s 38(2)*].

Stamp duty and other expenses of terminating a settlement incurred to bring about a chargeable occasion within *TCGA 1992, s 71* are allowable (*Chubb's Trustee CS 1971, 47 TC 353*).

Costs within (iv) above only extend, in the Revenue's opinion, to costs reasonably incurred in making the valuation, but not to any subsequent costs incurred in negotiating a value with the Revenue or in litigation with it concerning the value (Revenue Tax Bulletin February 1994 p 116).

A company with an annual turnover of not less than £5 million may round incidental costs of disposal to the nearest £1,000 subject to certain conditions and exceptions (Revenue Press Release 18 May 1993).

16.4   ALLOWABLE EXPENDITURE—SPECIAL CASES

In addition to the general provisions relating to allowable expenditure in 16.3 above, specific items of expenditure are allowed as follows.

(a)   **Interest in certain circumstances** on money borrowed by a *company* for financing allowable expenditure on the construction of a building, structure, or work. There is no such provision for individuals, trustees, etc. See 13.8 COMPANIES.

(b)   **Income tax paid by a close company participator** on income which has been apportioned to him (broadly in relation only to accounting periods ending before 1 April 1989) but which remains undistributed is an allowable deduction. [*TCGA 1992, s 124*]. Alternatively, the Revenue will restrict a participator's 'excess liability' on an apportionment for a period after commencement of winding-up to the excess, if any, over capital gains tax paid on distributions made in respect of the participator's share by the liquidator during that period. Where post liquidation income is apportioned to trust beneficiaries or residuary legatees, account will be taken of any relevant capital gains tax paid by the trustees or personal representatives (see Revenue Pamphlet IR 1, A36). Where tax on the apportioned income is borne by a beneficiary under a trust or by a residuary legatee, the relief is extended to a disposal of the relevant shares by the trustees or by the personal representatives (see Revenue Pamphlet IR 1, D12). The reliefs in IR 1, A36 and

D12 are in the alternative. See also 3.12 ANTI-AVOIDANCE regarding *TCGA 1992, s 125* (close company transferring assets at undervalue).

(*c*) **Foreign tax** borne by the disposer on the disposal is deductible. See 17.5 DOUBLE TAX RELIEF.

(*d*) **Inheritance tax (or capital transfer tax)** is a deduction in some circumstances. See 30.2 INTERACTION WITH OTHER TAXES.

(*e*) **Acquisitions from persons neither resident nor ordinarily resident in the UK.** Where, *after 9 March 1981 and before 6 April 1983,*

    (i) a person acquired an asset for no valuable consideration, or for a consideration lower than the asset's market value, and no other amount or value was imputed to the consideration by operation of *CGTA 1979* (e.g. under the MARKET VALUE (36) rules); and

    (ii) there was a corresponding disposal of the asset by a person neither resident nor ordinarily resident in the UK; and

    (iii) a charge to income tax, corporation tax or capital gains tax arose in respect of the acquisition in (i) above;

a deduction is given on the subsequent disposal of the asset by the acquirer, equal to the amount in respect of which the charge in (iii) above arises. The condition in (iii) above was taken to be satisfied where, under *FA 1981, s 80(3)* (now *TCGA 1992, s 87(4)*; see 39.8 OVERSEAS MATTERS), in any year of assessment, gains were attributed to a beneficiary of a non-resident settlement, by reason of that beneficiary's acquisition of an asset in that or an earlier fiscal year. In such circumstances, the deduction is the amount of the gains attributed to the beneficiary because of the acquisition of the said asset.

After 5 April 1983, the market value rules were amended so that, subject to the election below, an acquisition under the circumstances in (i) to (iii) is treated as being made at market value and the above provisions do not apply. Where, however, the corresponding disposal under (ii) is made *after 5 April 1983 and before 6 April 1985* the persons acquiring and disposing of the asset may jointly elect that both the acquisition and disposal are excepted from the amended market value rules in which case the above provisions still apply. [*CGTA 1979, s 32(5)(6); FA 1981, s 90(2); FA 1984, s 66(3)*]. See 36.1 MARKET VALUE for further details.

(*f*) **Stock dividends.** The 'appropriate amount in cash' relating to a stock dividend is deductible. See 53.12 SHARES AND SECURITIES.

(*g*) **Offshore funds and deep discount securities.** Certain sums charged to income tax on the disposal of interests in offshore funds and on the disposal of deep discount securities. See 39.13 OVERSEAS MATTERS and 53.19 SHARES AND SECURITIES.

(*h*) **Shares acquired by employees.** See 53.16 SHARES AND SECURITIES for allowable expenditure.

(*i*) **Legatees and beneficiaries.** Where a person disposes of an asset to which he became absolutely entitled as legatee or as against the trustees of settled property, any expenditure incurred by that person, the personal representatives or the trustees in relation to the transfer of the asset to him, is allowable. [*TCGA 1992, s 64(1)*].

16.5 Disposal

(*j*) **Devaluation of sterling in November 1967.** In computing gains on the disposal of foreign securities purchased out of foreign currency borrowed before 19 November 1967 for that purpose (by permission given, subject to specified conditions, under *Exchange Control Act 1947*) the deduction under 16.3(*a*) above is increased by one-sixth. A similar increase applies to disposals after 18 November 1967 of foreign securities which at that date formed part of a trust fund established abroad by a Lloyd's underwriter, etc., or a company engaged in marine protection or indemnity assurance on a mutual basis, which consists of premiums received and used mainly for meeting business liabilities arising in the country in which the fund is set up. [*TCGA 1992, 11 Sch 13, 14*].

16.5   NON-ALLOWABLE EXPENDITURE

In no case is allowance given for the following.

(*a*) Expenditure which is deductible in computing profits or losses for income tax purposes [*TCGA 1992, s 39(1)*] or would be so deductible if the asset were held as a fixed asset of a trade [*TCGA 1992, s 39(2)*]. See *Emmerson v Computer Time International Ltd CA 1977, 50 TC 628.*

(*b*) Premiums paid to cover the risk of damage to, or loss or depreciation of, the asset. [*TCGA 1992, s 205*].

(*c*) Any expenditure recoverable from any government or public or local authority in the UK or elsewhere. [*TCGA 1992, s 50*].

(*d*) Interest, except as under 16.4(*a*) above. [*TCGA 1992, s 38(3)*].

(*e*) Income tax chargeable on shares acquired under certain employee schemes. See 53.16 SHARES AND SECURITIES.

(*f*) Liabilities remaining with, or assumed by, the disposer contingent upon the default of the assignee of a lease, or upon the breach of covenants in a conveyance or lease of land, or of warranties, or representations made on the sale or lease of other property. If the contingent liability subsequently becomes enforceable and is enforced, relief is given by way of discharge or repayment. [*TCGA 1992, s 49*]. An amount received under a warranty or indemnity is deductible from acquisition cost. Revenue Pamphlet IR 1, D33. See further 33.26 LAND.

(*g*) Any discount for postponement of receipt of the consideration and, in the first instance, for any risk of non-recovery, or for any contingency in the right to receive any part of the consideration. If, however, any part of the consideration is subsequently shown to the satisfaction of the inspector to be actually irrecoverable, the tax liability will be adjusted accordingly. [*TCGA 1992, s 48*]. (See *Marson v Marriage Ch D 1979, 54 TC 59.*) See also 16.7 below and 41.5 PAYMENT OF TAX for the possibility of payment by instalments.

(*h*) Notional expenses on deemed disposals and acquisitions. [*TCGA 1992, s 38(4)*].

(*i*) Where a 'loss' would otherwise be shown, expenditure otherwise allowable as a deduction is reduced to the extent that capital allowances have been made in respect of it. The capital allowances taken into account are those granted (less any balancing charge) to the disposer. Where the asset was treated for capital allowance purposes as acquired at written-down value, allowances granted to any former owner which were not taken into account in restricting his loss are also deducted from allowable expenditure. '*Loss*' seemed to refer to the unindexed loss for disposals before 30 November 1993 and after 5 April 1985 (after 31 March 1985 for companies), when the restriction of allowable expenditure above also applied in the calculation of the indexation allowance so that, broadly, the allowable loss was the indexation allowance arising. The Revenue appear to maintain that '*loss*' is the indexed loss, ie the loss after indexation (Revenue Manual CG17450), though this is arguable. Where the loss-making disposal is of machinery or plant in relation to expenditure on which allowances or charges have been made for capital allowance purposes and which has been used solely for trade purposes and has not attracted wear and tear subsidies which would deny capital allowances, the capital allowances (if any) are deemed to be the difference between the expenditure incurred (or treated as incurred) by the disposer, and the disposal value. [*TCGA 1992, ss 41, 53(3)*]. See also 7.13 ASSETS HELD ON 6 APRIL 1965 and 8.8 ASSETS HELD ON 31 MARCH 1982 for further applications of these rules.

16.6 PART DISPOSALS

References to a disposal for the purposes of the capital gains tax legislation include, unless otherwise required, references to a part disposal. There is a part disposal of an asset where an interest or right in or over the asset is created by the disposal, as well as where it subsists before the disposal, and generally, there is a part disposal of an asset where, on a person making a disposal, any description of property derived from the asset remains undisposed of. [*TCGA 1992, s 21(2)*].

Where a disposal is partial, those deductions which are not wholly attributable either to the part retained or to the part disposed of are apportioned over the total value of the asset, including the part retained, and only the portion relative to the part disposed of is deductible from the consideration received for it. This apportionment also applies for indexation allowance purposes. The apportioned allowable expenditure is calculated by reference to the formula

$$\frac{A}{A + B}$$

where

A is the consideration received or deemed to have been received; and

B is the market value of the part retained.

Any such apportionment is to be made before applying the following provisions.

(a)   *TCGA 1992, s 41* (restriction of losses by reference to capital allowances, see 16.5(*i*) above). (If after the part disposal there is a subsequent disposal of the asset, the capital allowances to be taken into account on that subsequent disposal are those referable to the expenditure incurred under 16.3(*a*)-(*c*) above whether before or after the part disposal, but those allowances are reduced by the amount, if any, by which the loss on the earlier disposal was restricted under *TCGA 1992, s 41*.)

(b)   *TCGA 1992, s 58(1)* (transfers between husband and wife, see 37.6 MARRIED PERSONS).

(c)   *TCGA 1992, ss 152-158* (replacement of business assets, see 50 ROLLOVER RELIEF).

(d)   *TCGA 1992, ss 171(1)* (transfers within a group of companies, see 13.11 COMPANIES).

(e)   Any other provision making an adjustment to secure that neither a gain nor a loss occurs on disposal.

(*f*)   The computation of any indexation allowance. [*TCGA 1992, s 56(1); FA 1994, 26 Sch Pt V*].

[*TCGA 1992, s 42*].

Similar apportionments of allowable deductions are made where assets have been merged or divided, have changed their nature, or have had interests created out of them, etc. [*TCGA 1992, s 43*].

See 8 ASSETS HELD ON 31 MARCH 1982 for further applications of *TCGA 1992, ss 42* and *43*.

Any other necessary apportionment is to be made as may be 'just and reasonable'. [*TCGA 1992, s 52(4), 11 Sch 11*].

Example

X buys a piece of land in 1984 for £180,000. He subsequently sells half of it to Y in May 1995 for £150,000. The remainder of the land, because of its better position, is estimated to be then worth £200,000.

X's unindexed gain is computed as follows

A = £150,000

B = £200,000

Allowable expenditure attributable to the part disposed of

$$\frac{150,000}{(150,000 + 200,000)} \times £180,000 = \underline{£77,143}$$

Unindexed gain: £150,000 − £77,143   = £72,857

The allowable expenditure on a disposal of the remaining land will be £102,857 i.e. £180,000 less £77,143.

In *Anders Utkilens Rederi A/S v O/Y Lovisa Stevedoring Co A/B and Another Ch D 1984, [1985] STC 301*, a plaintiff had initially obtained judgment for a liquidated sum against a defendant, but the action was then compromised by an agreement for the defendant's property to be sold and the proceeds divided between the parties. It was held that there had been a part disposal of an interest in the property by the defendant to the plaintiff followed by a disposal by each party of his interest then held to the final purchaser.

See 33.10 LAND for relief for certain part disposals of land and 33.19 where part of the premium received for a lease is liable to income tax.

16.7   CAPITAL SUMS DERIVED FROM ASSETS

Subject to 16.8 and 16.9 below, there is a disposal of assets by their owner where any 'capital sum' is *derived from* them, 'notwithstanding that no asset is acquired by the person paying the capital sum' (which means 'whether or not an asset is acquired', see *Marren v Ingles HL 1980, 54 TC 76*, and thus not following *CIR v Montgomery Ch D 1974, 49 TC 679*). See also *Zim Properties Ltd v Proctor Ch D 1984, 58 TC 371* (which has been superseded by extra-statutory concession; see 6.1 ASSETS) and *Kirby v Thorn EMI plc CA 1987, 60 TC 519*.

For general consideration of what constitutes an 'asset' for tax purposes, see 6.1 ASSETS.

'Capital sum' means any money or money's worth which is not otherwise excluded from the computation of chargeable gains.

The provisions apply in particular to capital sums received as follows (other than those brought into charge to income tax).

(*a*)   By way of compensation for any kind of damage or injury to assets or for the loss, destruction or dissipation of assets or for any depreciation or risk of depreciation of an asset.

Compensation received by milk producers for cuts in the amount of milk quota they hold or for complete cessation of milk production is chargeable in the first year of receipt (Revenue Tax Bulletin, May 1994, p 128).

Where compensation is paid for the acquisition of business property by an authority possessing powers of compulsory acquisition, any amount included for temporary loss of profits was formerly treated as part of the consideration for the premises for capital gains tax purposes (Revenue Press Release 13 December 1972). However, following *Stoke-on-Trent City Council v Wood Mitchell & Co Ltd CA 1978, [1979] STC 197*, any element of such compensation representing temporary loss of profits is treated as a trading receipt after 27 July 1978. Compensation for losses on trading stock and to reimburse revenue expenditure, such as removal expenses and interest, are similarly treated (Revenue Pamphlet IR 131, SP 8/79, 18 June 1979). See also *Lang v Rice CA (NI) 1983, 57 TC 80* and 30.1 INTERACTION WITH OTHER TAXES.

In *Pennine Raceway Ltd v Kirklees Metropolitan Borough Council CA, 1988, [1989] STC 122*, to which the Revenue was not a party, the company held a licence to conduct motor racing in accordance with existing planning permission. Compensation under *Town and Country Planning Act 1971* paid by the local authority for revoking the planning permission was held to be derived from the licence, the value of which had been depreciated.

(*b*)   Under a policy of insurance of the risk of any kind of damage or injury to, or the loss or depreciation of, assets.

(*c*)   In return for the forfeiture or surrender of rights or for refraining from exercising rights.

Compensation under *Agricultural Holdings Act 1948, s 34* for disturbance of a tenant is excluded (*Davis v Powell Ch D 1976, 51 TC 492*). (Grants for giving up agricultural land may be specifically exempt. See 18.16 EXEMPTIONS AND RELIEFS.) Compensation under *Landlord and Tenant Act 1954, Part II* to a tenant giving up possession is similarly excluded (*Drummond v Austin Brown CA 1984, 58 TC 67*).

(*d*)   As consideration for use or exploitation of assets.

Time of disposal under (*a*) to (*d*) above is when the capital sum is received. [*TCGA 1992, s 22*].

A right to unquantified and contingent future consideration on the disposal of an asset is itself an asset and the future consideration, if received, is a capital sum derived from that asset (*Marren v Ingles* above and *Marson v Marriage Ch D 1979, 54 TC 59*) but see 53.8 SHARES AND SECURITIES for extra-statutory mitigation of this principle in the case of 'earn-outs'.

The *entire* loss, destruction, dissipation or extinction of an asset (whether or not any capital sum is received as above) constitutes a disposal of that asset (with certain exceptions for options as in 16.10 below). For this purpose, land and buildings may be regarded as separate assets so that where there is a deemed disposal of a building, the land comprising the site of the building (including any land occupied for purposes

16.8 Disposal

ancillary to the use of that building) is treated as if it were sold and immediately reacquired at its then market value. [*TCGA 1992, s 24(1)(3)*]. Cf. the concessional treatment under *TCGA 1992, s 23(4)(5)* in 16.9 below. For relief where the value of an asset becomes *negligible*, see 35.8 LOSSES.

Subject to certain conditions (see below), a gain will be treated as exempt where it arises on compensation received after 18 December 1994 (or where appeals are not determined by 19 December 1994) deriving from an overseas government for property lost or confiscated which is paid under the *Foreign Compensation Act 1950*, or under circumstances directly analogous thereto (including certain arrangements with Germany, Uganda and Iraq) other than where the compensation arises from a right to payment under the law of the country concerned at the time the property is confiscated or destroyed or under contractual or similar arrangements. This concession applies to a person entitled to compensation:

(1)   who was the owner of the property at the time it was confiscated, expropriated or destroyed, or

(2)   who has since acquired their title, directly or otherwise from the owner of the property at that time.

This concession will not apply to a person who is not the owner of the relevant property and who has acquired directly or otherwise the right to receive compensation in money or money's worth. Transfers within the no gain/no loss provisions of *TCGA 1992, s 58* (inter-spouse transfers) and *TCGA 1992, s 171* (inter-group transfers) are to be ignored in deciding whether the concession applies. Claims for the concessionary treatment should be made to the Capital and Valuation Division, CGT (Foreign Compensation), Duchy Rooms, Somerset House, WC2R 2LL (Revenue Press Release 19 December 1994).

16.8   **Capital sums applied in restoring assets and small capital sums.** Where a capital sum within 16.7 (*a*)–(*d*) above is derived from an asset (other than a wasting asset) which is not lost or destroyed, the recipient may claim under *TCGA 1992, s 23(1)* that the asset is not treated as disposed of provided the capital sum is

(*a*)   wholly applied in restoring the asset; or

(*b*)   (subject to below) applied in restoring the asset except for a part which is not reasonably required for the purpose *and* which is 'small' compared with the whole capital sum; or

(*c*)   'small' as compared with the value of the asset.

'*Small*' for the purposes of (*b*) and (*c*) above is taken by the Revenue to be not exceeding 5% (withdrawn Revenue Pamphlet CGT 8, para 118). Additionally, for small part disposals of land, see 33.11 and 33.13 LAND.

If the receipt is not treated as a disposal, the capital sum is deducted from the allowable expenditure on a subsequent disposal. [*TCGA 1992, s 23(1)(6)*]. Prior to the commencement of *TCGA 1992*, claims were made under *CGTA 1979, s 21(1)*.

Where the *allowable expenditure* immediately prior to the receipt of the capital sum (including any restoration work before that time) *is less than the capital sum (or is nil)*, (*b*) and (*c*) above do not apply but the recipient may elect to reduce the capital sum by the amount of any allowable expenditure. The balance of the capital sum is treated as a part disposal. The capital sum so utilised cannot be deducted again either on the part disposal or on any subsequent disposal of the asset. [*TCGA 1992, s 23(2)*]. Prior to the commencement of *TCGA 1992*, claims were made under *CGTA 1979, s 21(2)*. If, however, the capital sum received is subsequently wholly applied in restoring the asset, the recipient may alternatively make a claim as under (*a*) above for the asset not to be treated as disposed of.

If part only of the capital sum is applied in restoring the asset (but not sufficient so as to fall within (*b*) above) the recipient may claim to have the part so applied deducted from any allowable expenditure on a subsequent disposal. The balance of the capital sum is treated as a part disposal of the asset. [*TCGA 1992, s 23(3)*]. In the part disposal computation, the Revenue take the market value after any restoration work. Prior to the commencement of *TCGA 1992*, claims were made under *CGTA 1979, s 21(3)*.

Examples

An Old Master painting belonging to X and worth £100,000 (in its undamaged state) is damaged in 1995. Subsequently X successfully claims £20,000 from his insurance company. The picture cost X £40,000 in 1990 and in its damaged state in 1995 is valued at £60,000. The following possibilities arise, the capital gains tax calculations being as shown.

(i) X retains the insurance moneys and does nothing to restore the picture. He is treated as having made a part disposal, and the unindexed gain is computed according to the formula described in 16.6 above. The allowable expenditure apportioned to the disposal is thus £10,000.

(ii) X subsequently expends the whole of the sum on restoration of the picture, but *does not* make a claim under (*a*) above. He will be treated as having made a part disposal as in (i) above, and his allowable expenditure on a future disposal is computed as follows.

	£
Original allowable expenditure	40,000
Deduct: apportioned allowable expenditure	10,000
	30,000
Add: Expenditure on restoration	20,000
Revised allowable expenditure	£50,000

(iii) X expends the whole of the sum on restoration of the asset *and* makes a claim under (*a*) above. The position is as follows

	£
Original allowable expenditure	40,000
Deduct: compensation moneys received	20,000
	20,000
Add: Expenditure incurred on the asset after compensation received	20,000
Revised allowable expenditure	£40,000

(iv) X expends £19,800 on restoration of the asset and makes a claim under (*b*) above. The shortfall of £200 is small in relation to the compensation moneys received, and will effectively be treated as a deferred capital gain.

147

	£
Original allowable expenditure	40,000
Deduct: compensation	20,000
	20,000
Add: Expenditure out of compensation	19,800
Revised allowable expenditure	£39,800

(v)   X manages to have the asset restored for £15,000. The shortfall is not small in relation to the compensation moneys received. X makes a claim under *TCGA 1992, s 23(3)*. The market value of the restored asset is £95,000.

	£
Consideration deemed to have been received for the part disposal (£20,000 − £15,000)	5,000
Deduct: Allowable expenditure on that disposal $\dfrac{5,000}{(5,000 + 95,000)} \times £(40,000 + 15,000)$	2,750
Unindexed gain	£2,250

The allowable expenditure on a future disposal is as follows

	£
Allowable expenditure after part disposal £(40,000 + 15,000 − 2,750)	52,250
Deduct: Compensation expended on asset	15,000
Revised allowable expenditure	£37,250

Indexation allowance will be computed at (i), (ii) and (v) above in respect of the expenditure attributable to the part disposed of as in 23.3 INDEXATION.

16.9   **Assets lost and replaced out of compensation.** Where an asset (other than a wasting asset) is lost or destroyed and a capital sum is received in compensation, there is a disposal of the asset under *TCGA 1992, s 22(1)* as in 16.7 above. Where, however, within one year of receipt (or such longer period as the inspector allows) the whole capital sum is applied in acquiring a replacement asset, the owner may claim under *TCGA 1992, s 23(4)* to have the disposal of the old asset (if otherwise greater) treated as made at a consideration giving rise to neither a gain nor a loss. The consideration for the acquisition of the new asset is then reduced by the amount of the excess of the capital sum received plus any residual or scrap value of the old asset over that allowable expenditure. [*TCGA 1992, s 23(4)(6)*]. Where all of the gain on the disposal of the original asset is not chargeable as it was acquired before 6 April 1965, the amount of the reduction in the acquisition cost of the new asset is the amount of the chargeable gain and not the whole amount of the gain. [*TCGA 1992, 2 Sch 23*]. Prior to the commencement of *TCGA 1992*, claims were made under *CGTA 1979, s 21(4)*.

If part only of the capital sum is applied in acquiring the new asset, the relief above cannot be claimed. However, provided that the amount not used is less than the gain (whether chargeable or not) accruing on the disposal of the old asset, the owner can claim to reduce the gain arising to the amount not used (and if not all chargeable, with a proportionate reduction in the amount of the chargeable gain). The amount of the consideration for the acquisition of the new asset is reduced by the same amount as the original gain. [*TCGA 1992, s 23(5)*]. Where all of the gain on disposal of the original asset is not chargeable as it was acquired before 6 April 1965, the amount of the reduction in acquisition cost is the amount by which the chargeable gain is reduced and not the amount by which the original gain is reduced. [*TCGA 1992, 2 Sch 23*]. Prior to the commencement of *TCGA 1992*, claims were made under *CGTA 1979, s 21(5)*.

Where a building is destroyed or irreparably damaged and a capital sum received by way of compensation is wholly or partly applied in constructing or otherwise acquiring a replacement building elsewhere, both the original and replacement buildings may, for the purposes of *TCGA 1992, s 23(4)(5)* above, be treated as distinct assets separate from the land on which they stand, any necessary apportionments of consideration or expenditure being made as is just and reasonable. This relief is not available where the interest in the land on which the old building stood is a wasting asset (Revenue Pamphlet IR 1 (1992) D19). Cf. the statutory treatment under *TCGA 1992, s 24(1)(3)* in 16.7 above.

Examples

(a) A bought an asset for £50,000 in February 1987. It is subsequently destroyed by fire in a later calendar month and A receives £90,000 compensation later in that month. A buys a new asset six months later for £100,000 and makes a claim under *TCGA 1992, s 23(4)*. The retail prices index for February 1987 is 100.4. Assume that for the month of destruction it is 140.0.

	£
Cost of destroyed asset	50,000
Indexation allowance	
$\dfrac{140.0 - 100.4}{100.4} \times £50,000$ (indexation factor 0.394)	19,700
Deemed consideration	£69,700
Compensation received	90,000
Deemed consideration	69,700
Excess (i.e. the gain otherwise accruing)	£20,300
Consideration for acquisition of new asset	100,000
Excess as above	20,300
Reduced allowable expenditure on new asset	£79,700

16.10 Disposal

(b) Facts as in *Example* (*a*) above except that A buys another asset to replace the old at a cost of £80,000 and makes a claim under *TCGA 1992, s 23(5)*.

	£	
Gain on disposal (see above)		£20,300
Compensation moneys received	90,000	
Compensation moneys expended	80,000	
Excess (being less than the gain of £20,300)	£10,000	
The chargeable gain is treated as reduced to the balance arrived at as above i.e.		£10,000
Amount by which the gain otherwise chargeable is reduced (£20,300 − £10,000)		£10,300

The allowable expenditure on the new asset is reduced as follows

	£
Actual expenditure	80,000
Amount by which chargeable gain is reduced	10,300
Total allowable expenditure	£69,700

16.10 OPTIONS

The grant of an option is the disposal of an asset (i.e. the option). This applies in particular to the grant of an option under which the grantor binds himself to sell what he does not own, and because the option is abandoned, never has occasion to own, and the grant of an option under which the grantor binds himself to buy what, because the option is abandoned, he does not acquire. This treatment is without prejudice to *TCGA 1992, s 21* (see 6.1 ASSETS and 16.6 above) and is subject to the provisions below as to treating the grant of an option as part of a larger transaction. [*TCGA 1992, s 144(1)*]. A grant of an option is not a part disposal of an asset which was the subject of the option even though the grantor possessed that asset at the time of the grant (*Strange v Openshaw Ch D 1983, 57 TC 544*).

Subject to the treatment of cash-settled options below, if an option is exercised, the grant of the option and the transaction entered into by the grantor in fulfilment of his obligations under the option are treated as a single transaction, so if a sale by the grantor can be called for under the option, the option consideration is part of the consideration for the sale, and if the grantor can be called on to buy, the option consideration is deducted from the acquisition cost incurred by him in buying in accordance with his option obligations. The exercise of an option by the grantee is not a disposal, but on that event the acquisition of the option (whether directly from the grantor or not) and the transaction entered into by the grantee (or his assignee etc.) on the exercise are treated as a single transaction, so if a sale by the grantor can be called for under the option, the option cost is part of the cost of acquiring what is sold, and if the grantor can be called on to buy, the option cost is treated as an incidental cost of disposal of what is bought by the grantor. [*TCGA 1992, s 144(2)(3)*]. Although not explicit, the time of the 'single transaction' is taken to be the time the option is exercised.

If an option binds the grantor both to sell and to buy, it is treated as two separate options with half the consideration attributable to each. [*TCGA 1992, s 144(5)*]. Any reference to an 'option' includes a reference to an option binding the grantor to grant a lease for a premium, or enter into any other transaction which is not a sale, so that references to 'buying' and 'selling' under an option are construed accordingly. [*TCGA 1992, s 144(6)*].

In relation to an option granted *after 29 November 1993*, alternative provisions to those in *TCGA 1992, s 144(2)(3)* above apply to a 'cash-settled' option, i.e. an option which is exercised where the nature of the option (or its exercise) is such that the grantor is liable to make, and the grantee is entitled to receive, a payment in full settlement (for partial settlement, see below) of all obligations under the option. [*TCGA 1992, s 144A(1); FA 1994, s 96*].

Under the alternative provisions, the grantor of a cash-settled option is treated as having disposed of an asset consisting of the liability to make the payment, the payment being treated as an incidental cost of making the disposal, and the grant of the option and the disposal are treated as a single transaction, the consideration for the option being treated as the consideration for the disposal. The grantee of the cash-settled option is treated as having disposed of an asset consisting of the entitlement to receive the payment, the payment received being treated as the consideration for the disposal, and the acquisition of the option and the disposal are treated as a single transaction, the cost of acquiring the option being treated as allowable expenditure deductible under *TCGA 1992, s 38(1)(a)* (acquisition and incidental costs; see 16.3 above). [*TCGA 1992, s 144A(2)(3)(a)(b); FA 1994, s 96*].

Where a payment is only in partial settlement of all obligations under a cash-settled option, *TCGA 1992, ss 144(2)(3)* and *144A(2)(3)* above both apply subject to the modification that, in those provisions, any reference to the grant or acquisition of an option is replaced by a reference to the grant or acquisition of so much of the option as relates to the making and receipt of the payment or, as the case may be, the sale or purchase by the grantor, and any reference to the consideration for, or the cost of or of acquiring, the option is replaced by a reference to a just and reasonable proportion of that consideration or cost. [*TCGA 1992, s 144A(4)(5); FA 1994, s 96*].

Despite the treatment above of the 'single transaction', the legislation fails to provide any proper mechanism for dealing with the discharge of any initial assessment raised in respect of the grant of an option or setting-off of any tax paid under such an assessment. The practice seems to be to allow a set-off of tax paid previously although there seems doubt whether repayment supplement will be allowed in respect of it (Tolley's Practical Tax 1986 p 159). Another practice seems to be to 'vacate' the initial assessment although, without the taxpayer's agreement, this is strictly wrong; see 4.6 APPEALS and 5.4 ASSESSMENTS. Again there would appear to be doubt about repayment supplement.

The above applies generally but the further treatment of options depends on the circumstances as under.

(*a*)   **Options to acquire assets for trading use.** An option to acquire an asset exercisable by a person intending to use it, if acquired, for the purpose of a trade carried on by him, is not a wasting asset, and abandonment of such an option constitutes a disposal of it. [*TCGA 1992, ss 144(4)(c), 146(1)(c)*].

(*b*)   **Quoted options to subscribe for shares.** An option to *subscribe* for shares in a company, which option is itself quoted on a 'recognised stock exchange', is not a wasting asset and an abandonment of such an option constitutes a disposal of it. [*TCGA 1992, ss 144(4)(a)(8)(a), 146(1)(a)(4)(a)*].

16.10 Disposal

'*Recognised stock exchange*' means The Stock Exchange (see also 36.2 MARKET VALUE) and any non-UK stock exchange designated by an order made by the Board. [*ICTA 1988, s 841; TCGA 1992, s 288(4)*].

(*c*)   **Traded options.** *After 5 April 1984* a 'traded option', i.e. an option quoted on a recognised stock exchange (see (*b*) above) or on a 'recognised futures exchange', is not a wasting asset, and an abandonment of such an option constitutes a disposal of it. [*TCGA 1992, ss 144(4)(b)(8)(b), 146(1)(b)(4)(a)*].

'*Recognised futures exchanges*' means the London International Financial Futures Exchange and any other UK or non-UK futures exchange designated by an order made by the Board. [*TCGA 1992, s 288(6)(7)*].

After 24 July 1991, where a person ('the grantor') who has granted a traded option ('the original option') closes it out by acquiring a traded option of the same description ('the second option'), any disposal by the grantor involved in closing out the original option is disregarded for the purposes of capital gains tax. The allowable expenditure attributable to the incidental costs to the grantor of making the disposal constituted by the original option is treated as increased by the aggregate of the amount or value of the consideration, in money or money's worth, given by him or on his behalf wholly and exclusively for the acquisition of the second option and the incidental costs of that acquisition. [*TCGA 1992, s 148*].

After 5 April 1985, gains arising in the course of dealing in traded options, which would previously have been chargeable to income tax under Schedule D otherwise than as profits of a trade are instead brought within the scope of capital gains tax. Losses are treated similarly. [*TCGA 1992, s 143(1)(2)(b)*]. See also 16.11 below.

(*d*)   **Financial options.** *After 28 April 1988*, 'financial options' are treated in the same way as traded options in (*c*) above except that *TCGA 1992, s 148* does not apply to financial options. A '*financial option*' is an option, other than a traded option, which

(i)   relates to currency, shares, securities or an interest rate and is granted (otherwise than as agent) by a member of a recognised stock exchange, an 'authorised person' (as in *Financial Services Act 1986*) or a 'listed institution' (as in *Financial Services Act 1986, s 43*); or

(ii)   relates to shares or securities which are quoted on a recognised stock exchange (see (*b*) above) and is granted by a member of such an exchange, acting as agent; or

(iii)   relates to currency, shares, securities or an interest rate and is granted to an authorised person or listed institution and concurrently and in association with an option falling within (i) above which is granted by the authorised person or listed institution concerned to the grantor of the first-mentioned option; or

(iv)   relates to shares or securities which are quoted on a recognised stock exchange and is granted to a member of such an exchange, including such a member acting as agent; or

(v)   is of a description specified in a Treasury order.

[*TCGA 1992, ss 144(4)(b)(8)(c)(9), 146(1)(b)(4)(a)*].

(e)   **Options to acquire or dispose of gilt-edged securities and qualifying corporate bonds.** *After 1 July 1986* disposals of any such options are exempt. [*TCGA 1992, s 115(1)(b)*].

(f)   **Options not within (a)-(e) above.** Such options are WASTING ASSETS (59) and the abandonment of such an option is not a disposal. Options (other than those in (b), (c) or (d) above) to buy or sell quoted shares and securities being shares or securities which have a quoted market value on a recognised stock exchange in the UK or elsewhere are regarded as wasting assets, the life of which ends when the right to exercise the option ends, or when the option becomes valueless, whichever is the earlier. [*TCGA 1992, ss 144(4), 146(2)(3)(4)(b)*].

Example

On 1 February 1992 F granted an option to G for £10,000 to acquire freehold land bought by F for £50,000 in September 1988. The option is for a period of 5 years, and the option price is £100,000 plus 1% thereof for each month since the option was granted. On 1 February 1994, G sold the option to H for £20,000. On 30 June 1995, H exercises the option and pays F £141,000 for the land. Neither G nor H intended to use the land for the purposes of a trade.

Indexation factors September 1988 to June 1995 (assumed)   0.375
                     February 1992 to February 1994   0.043

1992 Grant of option by F

	£
Disposal proceeds	10,000
Allowable cost	—
Chargeable gain	£10,000

1994 Disposal of option by G

Disposal proceeds	20,000
Allowable cost $\dfrac{5-2}{5} \times £10,000$	6,000
Unindexed gain	14,000
Indexation allowance £6,000 × 0.043	258
Chargeable gain	£13,742

1995 Exercise of option

(i) Earlier assessment on F vacated	
(ii) Aggregate disposal proceeds (£10,000 + £141,000)	151,000
Allowable cost of land	50,000
Unindexed gain	101,000
Indexation allowance £50,000 × 0.375	18,750
Chargeable gain (on F)	£82,250

16.10 Disposal

H's allowable expenditure is

	£	£
Cost of option	20,000	
Deduct Wasted up to date exercised $\left(\dfrac{1y5m}{3y}\right)$	9,444	
	10,556	
Cost of land	141,000	
	£151,556	

A sum paid to a person to relinquish his rights to call on another person to buy property from him (a put option) is a capital sum derived from an asset (the option) and can bring about a chargeable event as regards gains although such a transaction is not able to give rise to an allowable loss. Properly construed, the provision above that an abandonment of an option is not to be treated as a disposal is a specific exception to the general rule that the extinction of an asset constitutes a disposal of it (see 16.7 above) for the purpose of allowable losses but it does not exempt a gain made from such a transaction (*Golding v Kaufman Ch D 1984, 58 TC 296; Powlson v Welbeck Securities Ltd CA, 1987, 60 TC 269*). The consideration to be taken into account in respect of the receipt of a contingently repayable sum in return for the grant of an option to purchase land is valued subject to the contingency provided the contingency is not within 16.5(*f*) and (*g*) above (*Randall v Plumb Ch D 1974, 50 TC 392*).

If, under *Building Societies Act 1986*, the whole of a building society's business is transferred to a successor company, and in connection therewith rights are conferred on members to acquire shares in priority to other persons, at a discount or for no payment, the rights are treated as options within *TCGA 1992, s 144* having no value and granted for no consideration. [*TCGA 1992, ss 216(1), 217(1)(6)*]. See also 53.24 SHARES AND SECURITIES. Similar provisions apply where a building society confers on its members or former members (or any class of them) similar acquisition rights after 24 July 1991 over 'qualifying shares' in the society (see 44.2 QUALIFYING CORPORATE BONDS for definition). [*TCGA 1992, s 149*].

The Revenue have expressed their views on whether transactions in financial futures and options amount to trading where carried out by: investment trusts; unauthorised unit trusts; charities; companies; non-resident collective investment vehicles and non-resident pension funds, which either do not trade or whose principal trade is outside the financial area.

In general, while an individual is unlikely to be regarded as trading as a result of speculative transactions in futures or options, case law suggests that a corporate body cannot speculate and that transactions by it must be either trading or capital in nature. Transactions in futures or options by a company may be treated as giving rise to trading profits if they are ancillary to a trading transaction on current account or, if they are not clearly ancillary to another transaction, they may be treated as trading transactions in their own right. A transaction may be regarded as capital when it is clearly ancillary to a transaction which is not a trading transaction on current account.

A number of factors must be considered in determining whether an ancillary relationship exists between a futures or options transaction and another transaction.

(1) There must actually be another transaction which has been undertaken, or there must be a firm intention to undertake it in the future.

(2) The futures or options transaction must be

(i)   undertaken to reduce or eliminate risk, or to reduce costs, in respect of the other transaction, and

(ii)   'economically appropriate' to the reduction of those risks or costs.

An 'economically appropriate' futures or options transaction is one which, by virtue of the fluctuations in its price and the value of the other transaction, may reasonably be regarded as appropriate to the reduction of risk. Futures or options transactions which are based on an index of some kind are not necessarily considered inappropriate in this connection. However, in general, the amount of principal on which the futures or options transaction is based should not materially exceed the principal of the other transaction.

(3)   One futures and options transaction may be ancillary to a number of other transactions and, similarly, a number of futures and options transactions may be ancillary to one other transaction.

(4)   Where the value of the assets or liabilities resulting from the other transaction varies, it may be necessary to terminate existing futures or options transactions or to enter into new ones.

(5)   Where a financial futures transaction to buy or sell currency forward is entered into, the taxpayer's 'base currency' may be relevant in determining whether or not that futures transaction is ancillary to a capital transaction. The 'base currency' is the currency in which value is measured and, for UK resident taxpayers, that will normally be sterling. Where the Revenue is called on to determine whether there is a non-sterling currency base, they will have regard to the following factors:

(i)   the currency in which accounts are prepared;

(ii)   the currency in which share capital is denominated; and

(iii)   evidence of the taxpayer's intentions (in a published prospectus, for example).

(Revenue Pamphlet IR 131, SP 14/91, 21 November 1991 which superseded SPs 1/ 88 and 4/88). See also 18.48 EXEMPTIONS AND RELIEFS (in the case of pension funds) and 57.1 UNIT AND INVESTMENT TRUSTS (in the case of unit trusts).

For the Revenue's views on whether transactions in financial futures and options constitute investment transactions for the purposes of *TMA 1970, s 78(3)* (relief for agents carrying out investment transactions) see Statement of Practice 15/91, 29 November 1991.

See also 53.11 and 53.16 SHARES AND SECURITIES for quoted options granted following a reorganisation and options granted to employees respectively.

See 50.2 ROLLOVER RELIEF for options over land as regards that relief.

See 23.8 INDEXATION for indexation allowance provisions relating to options generally.

See 13.34 and 13.35 COMPANIES for, respectively, exchange gains and losses, and financial instruments involving interest rate and currency contracts, for certain provisions which may supersede those above in the case of certain companies.

16.11   FUTURES CONTRACTS

Commodity and financial futures. *After 5 April 1985,* gains arising in the course of dealing in '*commodity or financial futures*' (which here means commodity futures or financial futures which are for the time being dealt in on a 'recognised futures exchange'

16.11 Disposal

(as in 16.10(*c*) above)) which would otherwise (apart from *ICTA 1988, s 128*; corresponding treatment for Schedule D) have been chargeable to income tax under Schedule D otherwise than as profits of a trade are instead brought within the scope of capital gains tax. Losses are treated similarly. In addition, *after 28 April 1988*, the following transactions, not being entered into in the course of dealing on a recognised futures exchange and except in so far as any gain or loss arising to any person from any such transaction arises in the course of a trade, are regarded as being so dealt in.

(*a*)   A transaction under which an 'authorised person' (as in *Financial Services Act 1986*) or 'listed institution' (as in *Financial Services Act 1986, s 43*) enters into a commodity or financial futures contract with another person.

(*b*)   A transaction under which the outstanding obligations under a commodity or financial futures contract to which an authorised person or listed institution is a party are brought to an end by a further contract between the parties to the futures contract.

[*TCGA 1992, s 143(1)(2)(a)(3)(4)(8); FA 1994, s 95, 26 Sch Pt V*].

For the purposes of *TCGA 1992*, where, *after 5 April 1985*, in the course of dealing in commodity or financial futures (whether or not, it seems, ones dealt in on a recognised futures exchange) a person who has entered into a futures contract closes out that contract by entering into another futures contract with reciprocal obligations to those of the first contract, the transaction is regarded as the disposal of an asset consisting of the outstanding obligations under the first contract, and any money's worth received or paid by him on the transaction is treated, respectively, as consideration for the disposal or as incidental costs of the disposal. [*TCGA 1992, s 143(5)*].

In any case where, in the course of dealing in commodity or financial futures (whether or not, it seems, ones dealt in on a recognised futures exchange) a person has entered into, *after 29 November 1993*, a futures contract and has not closed out that contract as above, and he becomes entitled to receive or liable to make a payment, whether under the contract or otherwise, in full or partial settlement of any obligations under the contract, he is treated for the purposes of *TCGA 1992* as having disposed of an asset consisting of that entitlement or liability, and the payment received or made is treated, respectively, as consideration for, or as incidental costs of, the disposal. Previously, in any case where a person who, in the course of dealing in financial futures (whether or not, it seems, ones dealt in on a recognised futures exchange) had entered into, *after 5 April 1985 and before 30 November 1993*, a futures contract did not close out that contract as above, and the nature of the futures contract was such that, at its expiry date, he was entitled to receive or liable to make a payment in full settlement of all obligations under the contract, was treated for the purposes of *TCGA 1992* as having disposed of an asset consisting of the outstanding obligations under the futures contract, and the payment received or made was treated, respectively, as consideration for, or as incidental costs of, the disposal. [*TCGA 1992, s 143(6); FA 1994, s 95*].

In relation to contracts entered into *after 29 November 1993*, *TCGA 1992, s 46* (WASTING ASSETS (59)) does not apply to obligations under a commodity or financial futures contract which is entered into by a person in the course of dealing in such futures on a recognised futures exchange, or a commodity or financial futures contract to which an authorised person or listed institution is a party. [*TCGA 1992, s 143(7)(8); FA 1994, s 95*].

See 16.10 above for the further tax treatment of transactions in commodity and financial futures in certain cases.

Case VI losses arising from transactions in futures before 6 April 1985 cannot be set against chargeable gains arising from similar transactions carried out after 5 April 1985.

Instead another Case VI source of income may be used to offset the losses (Tolley's Practical Tax 1986 pp 96, 112).

See 18.48 EXEMPTIONS AND RELIEFS and 57.1 UNIT AND INVESTMENT TRUSTS for futures contracts entered into by pension schemes etc. and unit trusts respectively.

See 13.34 and 13.35 COMPANIES for, respectively, exchange gains and losses, and financial instruments involving interest rate and currency contracts, for certain provisions which may supersede those above in the case of certain companies.

Gilt-edged securities and qualifying corporate bonds. *After 1 July 1986*, the disposal of the outstanding obligation under any contract to acquire or dispose of such securities and bonds is exempt. Without prejudice to the provisions within *TCGA 1992, s 143(5)* above regarding the closing out of futures contracts generally, where a person closes out a contract for gilts or bonds as above by entering into another, reciprocal, contract, that transaction is treated as a disposal of the outstanding obligation under the first-mentioned contract. [*TCGA 1992, s 115(1)(b)(2)(3)*].

16.12   FORFEITED DEPOSIT OF PURCHASE MONEY

A forfeited deposit of purchase money or other consideration money for a prospective purchase or other transaction which is abandoned is treated in the same way as consideration given for an option to purchase which is not exercised. [*TCGA 1992, s 144(7)*]. There is no disposal for capital gains tax purposes by the person who abandons his deposit and no loss relief is available. There is, however, a disposal of an asset to which no allowable expenditure attaches by the person receiving the forfeited deposit the amount of which is treated as the consideration received. See 16.10 above.

17   Double Tax Relief

(See also Revenue Pamphlets IR 6 and IR 20.)

Cross-references. See 39 OVERSEAS MATTERS; 40.4 PARTNERSHIPS; 46 REMITTANCE BASIS; and 47 RESIDENCE AND DOMICILE.

17.1   Where the same gains are liable to be taxed in both the UK and another country, relief may be available as follows.

(*a*)   Under the specific terms of a double tax agreement between the UK and that other country—see 17.2 below.

(*b*)   Under special arrangements with Eire—see 17.3 below.

(*c*)   Under the unilateral double tax relief provisions contained in UK tax legislation—see 17.4 below.

(*d*)   By deduction—see 17.5 below.

17.2   **DOUBLE TAX AGREEMENTS** [*TCGA 1992, s 277; ICTA 1988, ss 788, 789, 791–816, 828*].

A list is given below of the bilateral agreements made by the UK which are currently operative. Under these agreements, exemption from taxes in the country where they arise may be granted for gains realised by UK residents, whether individuals or companies. Reciprocal relief is given to overseas residents from UK capital gains tax and corporation tax.

The specific provisions of the particular agreement concerned must be examined carefully. For relevant court decisions, see Tolley's Tax Cases. Where tax on overseas gains is not relieved, or is only partly relieved, under an agreement, unilateral relief (see 17.4 below) will normally apply.

Where double tax relief by agreement applies, no deduction for foreign tax is allowed in assessing the foreign gains. [*ICTA 1988, s 795(2)*]. If a taxpayer elects not to take credit allowable by an agreement any foreign tax paid on those gains is treated as allowable expenditure for the purposes of the UK assessment. See 17.5 below.

Reciprocal agreements with the following countries supersede the provisions of *ICTA 1988, s 790* (unilateral relief) to the extent, and as from the operative dates, specified therein (SI numbers in round brackets).

Antigua and Barbuda (1947/2865; 1968/1096), **Australia** (1968/305; 1980/707), **Austria** (1970/1947; 1979/117; 1994/768), **Azerbaijan** (1995/762),

Bangladesh (1980/708), **Barbados** (1970/952; 1973/2096), **Belgium** (1970/636; 1987/2053), **Belize** (1947/2866; 1968/573; 1973/2097), **Botswana** (1978/183), **Brunei** (1950/1977; 1968/306; 1973/2098), **Bulgaria** (1987/2054), **Burma** (see Myanmar below),

Canada (1980/709; 1980/780; 1980/1528; 1985/1996; 1987/2071), **China** (1981/1119; 1984/1826), **Cyprus** (1975/425; 1980/1529), **Czechoslovakia** (1991/2876. The old treaty between the UK and Czechoslovakia is still to be regarded as in force between the UK and, respectively, the Czech Republic and the Slovak Republic (Revenue Pamphlet IR 131, SP 5/93, 19 March 1993)),

Denmark (1980/1960; 1991/2877),

Eire (see 17.3 below), Egypt (1980/1091), Estonia (1994/3207),
Falkland Islands (1984/363; 1992/3206), Faroe Islands (1950/1195; 1961/579;
     1969/1068; 1971/717; 1973/1326; 1975/2190), Fiji (1976/1342), Finland
     (1970/153; 1980/710; 1985/1997; 1991/2878), France 1968/1869; 1973/1328;
     1987/466; 1987/2055),
Gambia (1980/1963), Germany (1967/25; 1971/874), Ghana (1947/2868; 1978/
     785; 1993/1800) (A Revenue Press Release of 31 January 1991 announced that
     the second-mentioned agreement had never officially come into force although its
     provisions had been applied since 1977. Details were given of the claims that
     could be made by taxpayers to apply the first-mentioned agreement if it was to
     their advantage.), Greece (1954/142), Grenada (1949/361; 1968/1867),
     Guernsey (1952/1215; 1994/3209), Guyana (1992/3207),
Hungary (1978/1056),
Iceland (1991/2879), India (1981/1120; 1993/1801), Indonesia (1975/2191; 1994/
     769) (notice given in June 1983 of termination of 1975/2191 but continues in
     force), Isle of Man (1955/1205; 1991/2880; 1994/3208), Israel (1963/616;
     1971/391), Italy (1962/2787; 1973/1763; 1990/2590), Ivory Coast (1987/169),
Jamaica (1973/1329), Japan (1970/1948; 1980/1530), Jersey (1952/1216; 1994/
     3210),
Kenya (1977/1299), Kiribati (as Tuvalu), Korea, Republic of (South) (1978/786),
     Kazakhstan (1994/3211),
Lesotho (1949/2197; 1968/1868), Luxembourg (1968/1100; 1980/567; 1984/364),
Malawi (1956/619; 1964/1401; 1968/1101; 1979/302), Malaysia (1973/1330; 1987/
     2056), Malta (1962/639; 1975/426; 1995/763), Mauritius (1981/1121; 1987/
     467), Mexico (1994/3212), Montserrat (1947/2869; 1968/576), Morocco
     (1991/2881), Myanmar (1952/751),
Namibia (1962/2352; 1962/2788; 1967/1489; 1967/1490), Netherlands (1967/
     1063; 1980/1961; 1983/1902; 1990/2152), Netherlands Antilles (1968/577;
     1970/1949) (terminated from 1 April 1989 in the UK), New Zealand (1984/
     365), Nigeria (1987/2057), Norway (1985/1998),
Pakistan (1961/2467; 1987/2058), Papua New Guinea (1991/2882), Philippines
     (1978/184), Poland (1978/282), Portugal (1969/599),
Romania (1977/57),
St. Christopher (St. Kitts) and Nevis (1947/2872), Sierra Leone (1947/2873;
     1968/1104), Singapore (1967/483; 1978/787), Solomon Islands (1950/748;
     1968/574; 1974/1270), South Africa (1969/864), Spain (1976/1919; 1995/
     765), Sri Lanka (1980/713), Sudan (1977/1719), Swaziland (1969/380),
     Sweden (1984/366), Switzerland (1978/1408; 1982/714; 1994/3215),
Thailand (1981/1546), Trinidad and Tobago (1983/1903), Tunisia (1984/133),
     Turkey (1988/932), Tuvalu (1950/750; 1968/309; 1974/1271),
Uganda (1952/1213; 1993/1802), Ukraine (1993/1803), U.S.A. (1946/1331; 1955/
     499; 1961/985; 1980/568; 1980/779), U.S.S.R. (1974/1269; 1986/224; 1994/
     3213. The old treaty between the UK and the USSR is still to be regarded as in
     force between the UK and the Russian Federation. Other former states of the
     USSR, namely Armenia, [Azerbaijan—see subsequent agreement mentioned
     under that country], Belarus, Georgia, [Kazakhstan—see subsequent agreement
     mentioned under that country] Kyrgystan, Moldova, Tajikistan, Turkmenistan,
     [Ukraine—see subsequent agreement mentioned under that country] and
     [Uzbekistan—see subsequent agreement mentioned under that country], are said
     to be committed to maintaining the provisions of the old treaty. The position with
     regard to the Baltic States (Lithuania and Latvia) will be clarified in due course by
     a further statement of practice (Revenue Pamphlet IR 131, SP 3/92, 1 May
     1992)), Uzbekistan (1994/770),
Vietnam (1994/3216),

Yugoslavia (1981/1815. The old treaty between the UK and Yugoslavia is still to be regarded as in force between the UK and, respectively, Croatia and Slovenia. The position relating to Bosnia-Hercegovina and the remaining Yugoslav republics is uncertain and will be clarified in a future statement of practice (Revenue Pamphlet IR 131, SP 6/93, 19 March 1993)),

Zambia (1972/1721; 1981/1816), **Zimbabwe** (1982/1842).

Shipping & Air Transport only—Algeria (Air Transport only) (1984/362), Argentina (1949/1435), Brazil (1968/572), Cameroon (Air Transport only) (1982/1841), Ethiopia (Air Transport only) (1977/1297), Iran (Air Transport only) (1960/2419), Jordan (1979/300), Kuwait (Air Transport only) (1984/1825), Lebanon (1964/278), Saudi Arabia (Air Transport only) (1994/767), Venezuela (1979/301; 1988/933), Zaire (1977/1298).

Representations about new double tax treaties, or suggestions about desirable changes in existing ones, should be made to Inland Revenue, International Division, Room 314, Strand Bridge House, 138–142 Strand, London WC2R 1HH (Tel. 0171 438 6333). Questions about a particular double tax treaty and its effects on an individual's own tax affairs should be addressed to the local tax office.

Representations for new or revised double tax treaties in connection with estates, inheritances and gifts should be made to Inland Revenue, Capital and Valuation Division, Room 306, Duchy Rooms, Somerset House, London WC2R 1LB (Tel. 0171 438 7741). Questions regarding a particular treaty on estates, inheritances and gifts should be addressed to Inland Revenue, Capital Taxes Office, Ferrers House, PO Box 38, Castle Meadow Road, Nottingham NG2 1BB (Tel. 0115 974 2416).

Revenue pamphlet IR 146 contains a full list of foreign taxes whose admissibility for tax credit relief the Inland Revenue have considered up to 31 December 1994. The Revenue Tax Bulletin April 1995 p 214 contains details of agreements under negotiation or concluded but not yet in force.

17.3   **EIRE** [*TCGA 1992, s 277; ICTA 1988, ss 788, 789, 791–816, 828; SI 1976, Nos 2151, 2152; SI 1995, No 764*].

Capital gains on immovable property (and assets of a permanent establishment or fixed base) are taxed in the country where it is situate with provision for a tax credit where the taxpayer is chargeable on the same gain as a resident of the other country. Gains on other property are taxed in the taxpayer's country of residence. See also 47.9 RESIDENCE AND DOMICILE.

17.4   **UNILATERAL RELIEF BY UK** [*TCGA 1992, s 277; ICTA 1988, ss 790, 794*].

Tax on chargeable gains, *other than that for which credit is available under the bilateral double tax agreements in* 17.2 *above,* payable under the law of any territory outside the UK (and see 17.3 above for Eire) and computed by reference to gains *arising in that territory* are allowed (to the extent defined below) as a credit against UK tax paid on those gains by *UK residents.* The machinery and limits (with modifications as below) are substantially the same as those under which the bilateral agreements operate and the credit given is, basically, such as would be allowable were a double taxation agreement in force with the territory concerned.

The modifications are as follows.

(a)   The foreign taxes must be charged on gains and correspond to capital gains tax in the UK but may include similar taxes payable under the law of a province, state or part of a country, or a municipality or other local body. See *Yates v GCA International Ltd (and cross-appeal) Ch D, [1991] STC 157.* Following that decision, the

Revenue issued Statement of Practice SP 7/91 (26 July 1991), amending their practice from 13 February 1991. For claims made on or after that date, and earlier claims unsettled at that date, foreign taxes will be examined to determine whether, in their own legislative context, they serve the same function as UK taxes, and are thus eligible for unilateral relief. Information on overseas taxes which the Board considers admissible for relief is obtainable from Foreign Intelligence Section, Inland Revenue, Room 7, New Wing, Somerset House, Strand, London WC2R 1LB. Tel 0171–438 6643.

(b) The restriction to tax on *'income arising in the territory'* does not apply in the case of the Channel Islands or the Isle of Man, and credit is given for CI or IOM tax if the claimant is resident for the particular year of assessment or accounting period *either in the UK or the Channel Islands or IOM*, as the case may be.

17.5 RELIEF BY DEDUCTION

Subject to 17.2–17.4 above, foreign tax on the disposal of an asset which is borne by the disposer is an *allowable deduction* in computing UK chargeable gains. [*TCGA 1992, s 278*].

17.6 SPECIFIC MATTERS

(a) (i) **Amounts assessable in UK on the remittance basis.** Where double tax credit for foreign tax is allowable in respect of it, any gain which is assessable on the basis of remittance is treated, for UK assessment purposes, as increased by the foreign tax on that gain. [*ICTA 1988, s 795(1)(3)*].

(ii) **Amounts assessable in UK on the arising basis.** Where gains are assessable to capital gains tax on the basis of the full amount arising (not on remittances as in (i) above) and double tax credit is allowable in respect of foreign tax suffered on a gain, no deduction may be made for foreign tax on that, or any other gain. [*ICTA 1988, s 795(2)*].

(b) **Claims** for credit under double tax arrangements must be made within six years after the end of the chargeable period for which the gain falls to be charged to capital gains tax. [*ICTA 1988, s 806(1)*]. Claims for credit are made to the inspector responsible for the relevant assessment but other claims for relief are to the Board. [*ICTA 1988, s 788(6)*]. Pending final agreement, a provisional allowance can usually be obtained on application to the inspector.

(c) **Limit of relief.** Where gains are chargeable to UK capital gains tax, credit for foreign tax suffered on a gain is set against the capital gains tax chargeable in respect of the double-taxed gain. [*ICTA 1988, ss 790(4), 793*]. See *George Wimpey International Ltd v Rolfe Ch D 1989, 62 TC 597* and *Yates v GCA International Ltd (and cross-appeal) Ch D, [1991] STC 157*. But the relief is limited to the *difference* between the capital gains tax (before double tax relief) which would be payable by the claimant

(i) if he were charged on his total capital gains (as computed under (a) above), and

(ii) if he were charged on those gains excluding the gains in respect of which the credit is to be allowed.

Where double tax relief is due from more than one source, the above limitation is applied successively to each source, but so that on each successive application, (i) above applies to the total capital gains exclusive of the capital gains to which the limitation has already been applied. [*ICTA 1988, s 796(1)(2)*].

In no case may total double tax credits exceed the total capital gains tax payable by the claimant for the year of assessment. [*ICTA 1988, s 796(3)*].

17.7   The standard credit article in double tax agreements provides for overseas tax to be allowed as a credit against UK tax on the gain in respect of which the overseas tax was computed. Unilateral relief operates similarly. There is no requirement for the two liabilities to arise at the same time or on the same persons; and therefore the Revenue consider that relief is available in the following situations.

(*a*)   A capital gain is taxed overseas as income.

(*b*)   Tax is charged overseas on a no gain, no loss transfer within a group of companies, and a UK liability arises on a subsequent disposal (see 13.11, 13.17 COMPANIES).

(*c*)   An overseas trade carried on through a branch or agency is transferred to a local subsidiary, with an immediate overseas tax charge; and a UK tax charge arises on a subsequent disposal of the securities or on a disposal of the assets by the subsidiary within six years (see 39.14 OVERSEAS MATTERS).

(*d*)   UK liability arises on a disposal of assets after overseas tax has become payable by reference to an increase in value without a disposal.

This relief is not available where a gain is rolled over in the UK (see 50 ROLLOVER RELIEF); but the overseas tax can be deducted from the gain (see 17.5 above). (Revenue Pamphlet IR 131, SP 6/88, 4 November 1988).

18   Exemptions and Reliefs

Cross-references. See 7 ASSETS HELD ON 6 APRIL 1965; 8 ASSETS HELD ON 31 MARCH 1982; 10 CHARITIES; 15 DEATH; 17 DOUBLE TAX RELIEF; 21 GOVERNMENT SECURITIES; 22 HOLD-OVER RELIEFS; 23 INDEXATION (including, in particular, the transitional relief for 'indexation losses' which may be due for 1993/94 and 1994/95 as in 23.2 INDEXATION in the case of disposals by individuals and trustees of settlements made before 30 November 1993); 35 LOSSES; 39 OVERSEAS MATTERS; 43 PRIVATE RESIDENCES; 44 QUALIFYING CORPORATE BONDS; 45 REINVESTMENT IN SHARES RELIEF; 47 RESIDENCE AND DOMICILE; 48 RETIREMENT RELIEF; 50 ROLLOVER RELIEF; 53 SHARES AND SECURITIES; 57 UNIT AND INVESTMENT TRUSTS; 58 VENTURE CAPITAL TRUSTS.

18.1   INTRODUCTION

A person is chargeable to capital gains tax on chargeable gains accruing to him on the disposal of assets in any year of assessment during any part of which he is resident in the UK, or during which he is ordinarily resident in the UK. [*TCGA 1992, ss 1(1), 2(1)*]. All forms of property except sterling are regarded as assets for these purposes [*TCGA 1992, s 21(1)*] and every gain, except as otherwise expressly provided, is a chargeable gain. [*TCGA 1992, s 28(2)*]. There are, however, a number of exemptions and reliefs. These may broadly be classified as follows.

(*a*)   Exempt assets (see 18.2–18.14 below).

(*b*)   Exempt gains and transactions (see 18.15–18.31 below).

(*c*)   Exempt organisations and individuals (see 18.32–18.54 below).

In addition, a number of reliefs are available to reduce or defer the amount of capital gains tax payable. See 18.55–18.77 and certain provisions in 18.42 and 18.50 below.

18.2   EXEMPT ASSETS

Gains accruing on the disposal of certain assets are exempt from capital gains tax. The exemption (total or partial) of the various types of asset is examined in 18.3–18.14 below. Losses arising from such disposals are similarly not allowable unless expressly provided otherwise. [*TCGA 1992, s 16(2)*].

18.3

Annuities and annual payments. A gain accruing on the disposal of a right to or to any part of an allowance, annuity, or capital sum from a *superannuation fund* or any other annuity (not under a deferred annuity policy, but see 18.10 below), or annual payments receivable under a 'covenant' not secured on property, is exempt. [*TCGA 1992, s 237*].

'Covenant' means a gratuitous promise enforceable solely due to the form in which it is evidenced (i.e., in England, in a document under seal). It does not include contracts enforceable as such (*Rank Xerox Ltd v Lane HL 1979, 53 TC 185*).

18.4

Chattels. A tangible movable asset (other than a commodity disposed of by or through a dealer on a terminal market) is entirely exempt, provided that the asset is not 'currency of any description' and that the disposal is for a consideration of £6,000 or less (£3,000 for disposals before 6 April 1989). If the consideration exceeds £6,000 (£3,000 for disposals before 6 April 1989), the chargeable gain is limited to five-thirds of the excess. [*TCGA 1992, s 262(1)(2)(6)*]. Sovereigns minted before 1838 are not legal tender and are thus within the exemption.

18.4   Exemptions and Reliefs

Examples

(i)   A chattel which cost £5,000 in 1990 is disposed of in 1995 for £8,000. Assume an indexation allowance of £565 and expenses of disposal of £135. The chargeable gain is ascertained as follows.

Excess of consideration over £6,000	£2,000
£2,000 × 5/3	= £3,333

Actual gain (after indexation) is £2,300 which is less than £3,333

Chargeable gain	= £2,300

(ii)   A chattel which cost £2,000 in 1990 is disposed of in 1995 for £8,000. Assume an indexation allowance of £226 and expenses of disposal of £135.

Excess of consideration over £6,000	£2,000
£2,000 × 5/3	= £3,333

Actual gain (after indexation) is £5,639 which is more than £3,333

Chargeable gain	£3,333

Part disposal. Where the disposal is of a right or interest in or over a tangible movable asset, and the sum of the consideration received plus the value of what remains exceeds £6,000, a similar limitation of the chargeable gain applies but the excess for this purpose is computed as follows.

$$(\text{consideration received} + \text{value of remainder} - £6,000) \times \frac{\text{consideration received}}{\text{total value}}$$

For disposals before 6 April 1989 the above also applied with the substitution of '£3,000' for '£6,000' in each place where it occurs. [*TCGA 1992, s 262(5)*].

Losses. For the purposes of loss relief, a disposal of a tangible movable asset for a consideration of less than £6,000 is deemed to be made for a consideration of £6,000. In the case of a partial disposal of an asset the total value of which is less than £6,000, the deemed consideration for loss relief purposes is computed as follows.

$$(£6,000 - \text{total value}) \times \left(\frac{\text{consideration received}}{\text{total value}}\right) + \text{consideration received}$$

Simplified, this becomes (£6,000 x consideration/total value). For disposals before 6 April 1989 the above also applied with the substitution of '£3,000' for '£6,000' in each place where it occurs. [*TCGA 1992, s 262(3)*].

Assets forming a set. Where these are owned by the same disposer they are to be treated as a single asset where they are disposed of, whether on the same or on different occasions, to the same person or to persons acting in concert, or to CONNECTED PERSONS (14). [*TCGA 1992, s 262(4)*].

Wasting assets. Tangible movable assets which are WASTING ASSETS (59) are exempt whatever the consideration received, but this exemption is restricted or eliminated to the extent that the asset, by reason of its having been used in trade or otherwise, has been or could have been the subject of a capital allowance. This exemption is not applicable to a disposal of commodities on a terminal market. [*TCGA 1992, s 45*]. Where capital allowances were initially granted in respect of qualifying expenditure on movable machinery but were later withdrawn because the machinery was sold without it having been brought into use by the taxpayer, it was held that the taxpayer should be treated as if the allowance had never been made with the result that the disposal on sale was exempt (*Burman v Westminster Press Ltd Ch D 1987, 60 TC 418*). If a restriction by reference to capital allowances would otherwise arise, relief as under *TCGA 1992, s 262* above may be available. See also 18.11 below as regards motor cars etc.

18.5   **Debts.** A debt, other than a 'debt on a security' (see below), disposed of by the original creditor or his personal representative or legatee is exempt. Where the original creditor is a trustee and the debt, when created, is settled property, a person becoming absolutely entitled to the debt is treated as a personal representative or legatee as is his own personal representative or legatee. [*TCGA 1992, s 251(1)(5)*].

The foregoing does not apply to the disposal of a bank balance in foreign currency (unless exempted similarly to *TCGA 1992, s 269* or under *FA 1993, 17 Sch 1–3*; see 18.8 below). [*TCGA 1992, s 252*]. A taxpayer may treat all bank accounts in his name containing a particular foreign currency as one account and so disregard direct transfers among such accounts which would otherwise constitute disposals and acquisitions under this last provision. The practice, once adopted, must be applied to all future direct transfers among bank accounts in the taxpayer's name designated in that currency until such time as all debt represented in the accounts has been repaid to the taxpayer. The practice may be applied to all cases where computations have not been settled as at 19 December 1984. Accounts held as in 6.2(*k*) ASSETS (non-domiciled individuals) do not qualify for this treatment. (Revenue Pamphlet IR 131, SP 10/84).

No chargeable gain or allowable loss accrues on the disposal by a 'qualifying company', on or after its 'commencement day', of a debt the right to settlement under which is a 'qualifying asset' see (13.34 COMPANIES for a note of these terms), and the settlement currency of which is a currency other than sterling, provided that immediately before the disposal the company did not hold the debt in 'exempt circumstances', and that the debt is not a debt on a security. '*Exempt circumstances*' are when the debt is held

(*a*)   for the purposes of long term insurance business;

(*b*)   for the purposes of mutual insurance business;

(*c*)   for the purposes of the occupation for profit of commercial woodlands in the UK;

(*d*)   by an approved housing association; or

(*e*)   by an approved self-build society.

No chargeable gain or allowable loss accrues on the disposal of a foreign currency debenture issued on a reorganisation or other transaction which meets the above conditions.

[*FA 1993, s 169, 17 Sch 3, 4; FA 1995, 24 Sch 5*]. See also 18.8 below.

Loss relief is available to the maker of a 'qualifying loan' or a guarantor of a qualifying loan. See 35.9 LOSSES. See 35.10 LOSSES for a corresponding relief where the borrower's debt is a debt on a security which is a qualifying corporate bond.

A right possibly to receive an unidentifiable sum at an unascertainable date is not a 'debt' (*Marren v Ingles HL 1980, 54 TC 76; Marson v Marriage Ch D 1979, 54 TC 59*).

Subject to the foregoing, the satisfaction of a debt (including a debt on a security) or part of it is treated as a disposal of the debt by the creditor made at the time when the debt is satisfied. Where a debt on a security is involved this rule is subject to the provisions in

TCGA 1992, ss 132, 135 covering the reorganisation of share capital (see 53.8 and 53.10 SHARES AND SECURITIES). [*TCGA 1992, s 251(2)*].

Where property is acquired by a creditor in satisfaction of a debt then, subject to any reorganisation of share capital as above, the property is not treated as disposed of by the debtor or acquired by the creditor for a consideration greater than its market value at the time of the creditor's acquisition of it. But if no chargeable gain accrues as regards the debt either because the creditor is the original creditor or under the share capital reorganisation rules *and* a chargeable gain accrues to the creditor on a disposal by him of the property, then any resulting chargeable gain is reduced so as not to exceed the chargeable gain that would have accrued if he had acquired the property for a consideration equal to the amount of the debt. [*TCGA 1992, s 251(3)*].

Where the original creditor and a subsequent creditor are CONNECTED PERSONS (14), a loss incurred by the subsequent creditor on the disposal of a debt is not an allowable loss. See 35.4 LOSSES.

A *'debt on a security'* is defined by reference to *TCGA 1992, s 132(3)(b)*, *'security'* thereby including any loan stock or similar security of any government or public or local authority in the UK or elsewhere, or of any company, and whether secured or unsecured. The existence of a document may be indicative of a 'debt on a security', but it cannot be concluded from the absence of a document that the debt is not 'on a security' (*Aberdeen Construction Group Ltd v CIR HL 1978, 52 TC 281; W T Ramsay Ltd v CIR HL 1981, 54 TC 101; Cleveleys Investment Trust Co v CIR (No 1) CS 1971, 47 TC 300*).

In the opinion of the Revenue the following characteristics must be satisfied before a debt can qualify as a debt on security.

(A)   The debtor should be a government, a public or a local authority, or a company.

(B)   The debt should be capable of being marketed, sold or assigned.

(C)   Interest should be payable to the lender (or at least the terms of the debt must be such that it is capable of being held as an investment, e.g. it would be so capable if it were issued at a discount or repayable at a premium).

(D)   There should be stated terms for the repayment of the debt.

(E)   The debt should be for a specified amount and for a definite term (normally for a period of years rather than months or days).

(F)   The debt should be capable of being issued or subscribed for (even if the procedure involved is simple, and if only one lender is involved).

(Tolley's Practical Tax 1983 p 119).

In relation to any chargeable period ending after 15 March 1993, a debenture issued by any company after 15 March 1993 is deemed to be a security within *TCGA 1992, s 132(3)(b)* above if

(1)   it is issued on a reorganisation or reduction of a company's share capital or in pursuance of its allotment on any such reorganisation or reduction;

(2)   it is issued in exchange for shares in or debentures of another company and in a case unaffected by *TCGA 1992, s 137* (restriction on application of share reorganisation rules in *TCGA 1992, ss 135, 136*; see 3.13 ANTI-AVOIDANCE and 53.8 and 53.9 SHARES AND SECURITIES) where one or more of the conditions mentioned in *s 135(1)(a)-(c)* (25% of ordinary share capital, view to control or greater part of the voting power) is satisfied in relation to the exchange;

(3)   it is issued under any such arrangements as are mentioned in *TCGA 1992, s 136(1)(a)* (arrangement between company and share or debenture holders in

connection with a scheme of reconstruction or amalgamation) and in a case unaffected by *s 137* where *s 136* requires shares or debentures in another company to be treated as exchanged for, or for anything that includes, that debenture; or

(4)   it is issued in pursuance of rights attached to any debenture issued after 15 March 1993 and falling within (1), (2) or (3) above.

[*TCGA 1992, s 251(6); FA 1993, s 84(2)(3)*]. See also 44.2 QUALIFYING CORPORATE BONDS for a corresponding provision regarding the definition of 'corporate bond', so that combined the two provisions prevent, in the circumstances stated, the issue of a debenture which neither represents a debt on a security nor is a qualifying corporate bond.

18.6   **Decorations.** A decoration for valour or gallantry (unless acquired by the vendor for money or money's worth) is exempt. [*TCGA 1992, s 268*].

18.7   **Dwelling-houses.** A gain accruing to an individual on the disposal of (or of an interest in) a dwelling-house which has been his only or main residence during his period of ownership is exempt (or partly exempt). See 43 PRIVATE RESIDENCES for this exemption which is also extended, in certain circumstances, to trustees and personal representatives.

18.8   **Foreign currency** acquired for an individual's (or his dependant's) personal expenditure outside the UK (including the provision or maintenance of his residence outside the UK) is exempt. [*TCGA 1992, s 269*].

No chargeable gain or allowable loss accrues on the disposal by a 'qualifying company', on or after its 'commencement day' (see 13.34 COMPANIES for a note of these terms), of currency other than sterling, provided that immediately before the disposal the company did not hold the currency in 'exempt circumstances'. '*Exempt circumstances*' are when the currency is held

(*a*)   for the purposes of long term insurance business;

(*b*)   for the purposes of mutual insurance business;

(*c*)   for the purposes of the occupation for profit of commercial woodlands in the UK;

(*d*)   by an approved housing association; or

(*e*)   by an approved self-build society.

[*FA 1993, s 169, 17 Sch 1–3*].

See also 18.5 below.

18.9   **Government securities.** After 1 July 1986 disposals of specified government and public corporation securities are exempt whatever the period of ownership. This also applies to options or contracts to acquire or dispose of such securities. See 21 GOVERNMENT SECURITIES and also 16.10 and 16.11 DISPOSAL as regards options and contracts.

18.10   **Insurance policies.** The disposal of rights under any insurance policy (other than a life policy) *by the insurer* is exempt, but the disposal of rights *of the insured* under any policy for damage to, or loss or depreciation of, assets is chargeable so far as the rights relate to assets which on a disposal could give rise to a chargeable gain. (Sums received under such policies for loss, damage, etc. to assets are chargeable; see 16.7–16.9 DISPOSAL.) [*TCGA 1992, s 204(1)(2)(4)*].

See also 34 LIFE ASSURANCE POLICIES AND DEFERRED ANNUITIES.

18.11 **Motor cars etc.** A mechanically propelled road vehicle constructed or adapted for the carriage of passengers, except for a vehicle of a type not commonly used as a private vehicle and unsuitable to be so used, is not a 'chargeable asset' and no chargeable gain or allowable loss accrues on its disposal. [*TCGA 1992, s 263*]. This exemption applies even if the vehicle was eligible for capital allowances (see 18.4 above). For the interpretation of 'commonly used as a private vehicle' in relation to capital allowances, see cases mentioned in Tolley's Capital Allowances. No provision of *TCGA 1992* defines 'chargeable asset' but the subsequent words of the provision seem to put the position beyond doubt. See also Revenue Tax Bulletin, October 1994, pp 166–167 for further discussion on motor vehicles.

18.12 **Qualifying corporate bonds.** After 1 July 1986 qualifying corporate bonds are exempt whatever the period of ownership. This also applies to options or contracts to acquire or dispose of such bonds. See 44 QUALIFYING CORPORATE BONDS and 16.10 and 16.11 DISPOSAL as regards options and contracts. For loans to traders evidenced by qualifying corporate bonds, see 35.10 LOSSES.

18.13 **Savings certificates, savings schemes and savings accounts etc.** Savings certificates, and non-marketable securities issued under the *National Loans Acts 1939 and 1968* and corresponding NI enactments are not 'chargeable assets' and accordingly no chargeable gain accrues on their disposal. Bonuses resulting from certified contractual savings schemes and tax-exempt special savings accounts are ignored for capital gains tax purposes. [*TCGA 1992, ss 121, 271(4)*]. No provision of *TCGA 1992* defines 'chargeable asset' but the subsequent words of the provision seem to put the position beyond doubt.

18.14 **Settlements.** With certain exceptions, no chargeable gain accrues on the disposal of an interest created by or arising under a settlement by the original beneficiary or any other person (other than one who acquired, or derives his title from one who acquired, his interest for money or money's worth). See 52.8 SETTLEMENTS.

18.15 **EXEMPT GAINS AND TRANSACTIONS**

The gains or transactions detailed in 18.16–18.31 below do not give rise to a liability to capital gains tax.

18.16 **Agricultural grants.** Grants made to an individual under *Agriculture Act 1967, s 27* (grants for relinquishing occupation of uncommercial agricultural units) are not treated as part of the consideration obtained, or otherwise accruing, on the disposal of any asset. [*TCGA 1992, s 249*]. See also 16.7(c) DISPOSAL.

18.17 **Betting, lottery etc.** Winnings from betting, including pool betting, or lotteries or games with prizes are not chargeable gains, and no chargeable gain or allowable loss accrues on the disposal of rights to such winnings obtained by participating. [*TCGA 1992, s 51(1)*]. Included is the betting on future price movements of precious and base metals, soft commodities and currencies etc. (see Tolley's Practical Tax 1982 p 59).

18.18   **Business expansion scheme.** In respect of shares issued after 18 March 1986 and before 1 January 1994, any gain or loss arising on a disposal of shares in respect of which such relief has been given and not totally withdrawn is exempt. In respect of such shares issued before 19 March 1986 there was no such exemption but a reduction was made in the amount of allowable expenditure where that amount exceeded the disposal consideration. See 53.18 SHARES AND SECURITIES.

18.19   **Damages and compensation.** Sums received by way of compensation or damages for any wrong or injury suffered by an individual 'in his person' or in his profession or vocation are not chargeable gains. [*TCGA 1992, s 51(2)*]. The words 'in his person' contrast with 'in his finances', but are construed widely. The exemption given in relation to vocation is extended by concession to an individual's trade or employment. See Revenue Pamphlet IR 1, D33. If the compensation relates to an asset (e.g. insurance recoveries), payment does constitute a disposal; see 16.7–16.9 DISPOSAL.

18.20   **Enterprise investment scheme.** In respect of shares issued after 31 December 1993, any gain arising on a disposal more than five years after the issue of them where an amount of such relief is attributable to them is totally or partly exempt. If a loss would otherwise arise on a disposal of shares where an amount of such relief is attributable to them, a reduction is made in the amount of allowable expenditure equal to the amount of relief. See 53.17 SHARES AND SECURITIES.

18.21   **Venture Capital trusts.** In respect of shares issued after 5 April 1995, any gain arising on a disposal of them where an amount of such relief is attributable to them is totally or partially exempt. A loss arising on a disposal of shares is not an allowable loss. See 58.9 VENTURE CAPITAL TRUSTS.

18.22   **Compensation from foreign governments.** Gains on sums received by individuals from foreign governments by way of compensation for assets confiscated, destroyed or expropriated are exempt provided certain conditions are met. See 16.7 DISPOSAL above.

18.23   **Exempt amount for the year.** A specified amount of the taxable amount of gains for a year of assessment is exempt. See 2.3 ANNUAL RATES AND EXEMPTIONS.

18.24   **Gains arising partly before 6.4.1965 or 31.3.1982.** Assets held on, and gains arising partly before, these dates are subject to special provisions. See 7 ASSETS HELD ON 6 APRIL 1965 and 8 ASSETS HELD ON 31 MARCH 1982.

18.25   **Gifts for public benefit.** Gifts of 'eligible property' to bodies not established or conducted for profit will, if the Board so direct (whether before or after the transfer), be exempt from capital gains tax.

'Eligible property' is

(*a*)   land which in the opinion of the Board is of outstanding scenic, historic or scientific interest;

(*b*)   a building for the preservation of which special steps should in the opinion of the Board be taken by reason of its outstanding historic, architectural or aesthetic interest and the cost of preserving it;

(*c*)   land used as the grounds of a building within (*b*) above;

(*d*)   an object which at the time of the transfer is ordinarily kept in, and is given with, a building within (*b*) above;

(*e*)   property given as a source of income for the upkeep of property within these sub-paragraphs;

(*f*)   a picture, print, book, manuscript, work of art or scientific collection which in the opinion of the Board is of national, scientific, historic or artistic interest. (*'National interest'* includes interest within any part of the UK.)

The Board must not give a direction (i) unless in their opinion, the body who receives the property is an appropriate one to be responsible for its preservation; or (ii) in relation to property within (*e*) above, if or to the extent that the property will, in their opinion, produce more income than is needed (with a reasonable margin) for the upkeep of the other property in question.

Before giving a direction, the Board may require undertakings (which may be varied by agreement) concerning the use, disposal, and preservation of the property and reasonable access to it for the public. [*TCGA 1992, s 258(1); IHTA 1984, s 26*].

See also 22.4 HOLD-OVER RELIEFS for relief for gifts for public benefit.

18.26   **Legatees.** No chargeable gain accrues to the personal representatives where a person acquires an asset from them as legatee, and the legatee is treated as if the personal representatives' acquisition of the asset had been his acquisition of it. See 15.9 DEATH.

18.27   **Personal equity plans.** An individual may, from 1 January 1987, make, subject to conditions, investments under a plan and obtain exemption from capital gains tax (as well as income tax) in respect of transactions covered by the plan. See 53.20 SHARES AND SECURITIES.

18.28   **Settled property.** No charge to capital gains tax arises

(*a*)   where a person disposes of an interest in settled property provided the interest either was created for his benefit or was not acquired for money or money's worth (see 52.8 SETTLEMENTS); or

(*b*)   when a person becomes absolutely entitled to settled property on the termination of a life interest by the death of the person entitled to it (see 52.9 and 52.11 SETTLEMENTS); or

(*c*)   on the termination, on the death of the person entitled to it, of a life interest in possession in settled property where the property does not cease at that time to be settled property (see 52.10 SETTLEMENTS).

18.29   **Special reserve funds of individual Lloyd's underwriters.** Disposals of assets held in an individual underwriter's special reserve fund set up in respect of the 1992 or a subsequent underwriting year of account are exempt. See 56.1 UNDERWRITERS.

18.30   **Woodlands.** Where woodlands are managed by the occupier on a commercial basis and with a view to the realisation of profits (before 6 April 1988, where land is assessed to either income tax or corporation tax under Schedule B)

(*a*)   any consideration for the disposal of trees (whether standing, felled or cut thereon) and saleable underwood; and

(b)   any capital sum received under an insurance policy in respect of the destruction of, or damage or injury to, trees or saleable underwood by fire or other hazard thereon

is excluded from any capital gains tax computation on the disposal if the person making the disposal is the occupier (before 6 April 1988, the person assessed under Schedule B).

In *any* capital gains tax computation on the sale of woodlands in the UK, there is excluded so much of the cost of the woodlands and/or consideration for the disposal as is attributable to trees, including saleable underwood, growing on the land. [*TCGA 1992, s 250*].

From 29 November 1994, the cultivation of 'short rotation coppice' is regarded as farming for capital gains purposes and not as forestry, and any land on which such activity takes place is regarded as farm land or agricultural land, as the case may be, and not as woodlands. '*Short rotation coppice*' means a perennial crop of tree species at high density, the stems of which are harvested above ground level at intervals of less than ten years. [*FA 1995, s 154*].

18.31   **Works of art etc.** A gain is not a chargeable gain if it accrues on the disposal of an asset with respect to which an undertaking has been given and where the disposal is

(a)   by way of sale by private treaty to a body mentioned in *IHTA 1984, 3 Sch* (see 10.5 CHARITIES); or

(b)   to such a body as in (a) above otherwise than by sale; or

(c)   to the Board in satisfaction of the payment of inheritance tax or capital transfer tax.

[*TCGA 1992, s 258(2)*].

See 18.70 (a)-(e) below for types of national heritage property which may be sold by private treaty within (a) above and also the undertakings required generally. See also 22.4 HOLD-OVER RELIEFS for relief for gifts of works of art etc.

The standard of objects which can be accepted under (c) above is very much higher. They have to satisfy a test of 'pre-eminence' either in the context of a national, local authority, or university collection, or through association with a particular building.

18.32   **EXEMPT ORGANISATIONS AND INDIVIDUALS**

The organisations and individuals detailed in 18.33–18.54 below are completely exempt from capital gains tax except where otherwise indicated.

18.33   **Atomic Energy Authority.** The authority is exempt from corporation tax in respect of chargeable gains. In addition, gains arising from investments or deposits held by a pension scheme provided and maintained by the Authority are exempt. [*TCGA 1992, s 271(7)*].

18.34   **Bare trustees and nominees.** Where assets are held by bare trustees or nominees for another person, capital gains tax is chargeable as if the assets were held by that other person. Consequently, there is no liability where the assets are transferred from the bare trustees etc. to that other person. [*TCGA 1992, s 60*].

18.35 Exemptions and Reliefs

18.35 **British Museum** and the **Natural History Museum** are entitled, on a claim to the Board, to exemption from tax on chargeable gains. [*TCGA 1992, s 271(6)(a); Museums and Galleries Act 1992, 8 Sch 1(8)(9)*].

18.36 **Central banks.** Non-resident central banks as specified by Order in Council and the issue departments of the Reserve Bank of India and the State Bank of Pakistan are exempt from tax on chargeable gains. [*ICTA 1988, s 516(3)-(5); TCGA 1992, s 271(8)*].

18.37 **Charities.** Subject to restrictions after 11 June 1986, a gain is not a chargeable gain if it accrues to a charity and is applicable and applied for charitable purposes. See 10.3 and 10.4 CHARITIES.

18.38 **The Crown** is not liable to tax unless statute otherwise provides; see *Bank voor Handel v Administrator of Hungarian Property HL 1954, 35 TC 311* and *Boarland v Madras Electric Supply Corporation HL 1955, 35 TC 612*. In addition, gains arising on the disposal of stock belonging to the Crown, or in the name of the Treasury or National Debt Commissioners under statutory schemes under which transfers are made in accounts at the Bank of England, are not chargeable gains. [*TCGA 1992, s 271(1)(a)*]. Property held under trusts contained in *Chevening Estate Act 1959* is exempt from capital gains tax. [*TCGA 1992, s 270*].

18.39 **Diplomatic agents** (i.e. heads of mission or members of the diplomatic staff) of foreign states are exempt from capital gains tax except on gains arising from private investments or immovable property in the UK. [*Diplomatic Privileges Act 1964*]. Similar exemption is given to agents-general and to their personal staffs. Consular officers and their personal staffs are exempt from gains arising out of disposals of assets which are situated outside the UK at the time of disposal. [*TCGA 1992, ss 11(2)-(4), 271(1)(f); ICTA 1988, ss 320, 322*].

An order made *Arms Control and Disarmament (Privileges and Immunities) Act 1988, s 1(2)* can extend a similar exemption to the above to persons designated by states other than the UK.

18.40 **Friendly societies.** A friendly society registered under *Friendly Societies Act 1974* (a registered friendly society) is an unincorporated society of individuals. Under *Friendly Societies Act 1992*, societies are able to incorporate, take on new powers and form subsidiary companies. Legislation introduced by *F(No 2)A 1992* provides continuity of tax treatment between registered societies and incorporated societies and removes adverse tax consequences which would otherwise arise as a result of incorporation.

Friendly societies which are neither registered nor incorporated, the incomes of which do not exceed £160 per annum, are wholly exempt from corporation tax on chargeable gains, but a claim must be made. Exemption for other friendly societies is broadly restricted in respect of life or endowment business to the assurance of gross sums under contracts under which the total premiums payable in any period of twelve months do not exceed £200 (£150 for contracts before 25 July 1991 and £100 for contracts before 1 September 1990 except that, for contracts after 31 August 1987 and before 25 July 1991, these limits can be increased by a variation made after 24 July 1991 and before 1 August 1992 so that the increased limit of £200 applies) or the granting of annuities not exceeding £156. For contracts before 1 September 1987 the restriction was by reference to the assurance of gross sums not exceeding £750 and of annuities not exceeding £156. The limits were £500 for gross sums and £104 for annuities for contracts before 14 March 1984. Exemption also applied before that date provided that the society's rules did not enable it to write business above £2,000 and £416 respectively for years of account ending after 31 May 1980. Some policies made before 20 March 1991 were written on the mistaken assumption that they fell outside the required conditions for the tax-exempt policies above. A society may treat the policies as not being tax-exempt by election made before 1 August 1992, but a member surrendering or allowing a policy to mature will not be affected (see Revenue Press Release 12 June 1991). [ICTA 1970, ss 331–337; FA 1976, s 48; FA 1980, s 57; FA 1984, s 73; Friendly Societies Act 1984, s 2(4); FA 1985, s 41, 8 Sch; FA 1987, s 30; F(No 2)A 1987, 2 Sch 2; ICTA 1988, ss 459–466; FA 1990, ss 49, 50; FA 1991, s 50, 9 Sch; TCGA 1992, ss 217A–217C; F(No 2)A 1992, s 56, 9 Sch; SI 1993 No 236]. See also Tolley's Corporation Tax under Friendly Societies.

18.41   **The Historic Buildings and Monuments Commission for England** is exempt from tax in respect of chargeable gains. [TCGA 1992, s 271(7)].

18.42   **Housing associations** approved under ICTA 1988, s 488 (see Tolley's Corporation Tax under Housing Associations Etc.) may make a claim to the inspector (within two years of the end of the relevant accounting period) for exemption from corporation tax on chargeable gains arising from the sale of property which is, or has been, occupied by a tenant of the association. [ICTA 1988, s 488(5)].

Relief from corporation tax generally by specific grant made by the Secretary of State for the Environment may also be obtainable under Housing Act 1988, s 54 for registered non-profit making housing associations which are approved as above. See Tolley's Corporation Tax under Housing Associations Etc.

Disposals of land and other assets by a housing association (as defined) to the Housing Corporation (or Housing for Wales or Scottish Homes) under certain statutory schemes, and subsequent disposals of those assets by the Corporation etc. to a single housing association, are treated as taking place on a no gain/no loss basis. The same applies to

(a)   transfers of land between the Housing Corporation etc. and registered housing associations (as defined and see 18.50 below regarding self-build societies);

(b)   transfers of land between such associations; and

(c)   transfers under a direction from the Corporation etc. of property other than land between such associations.

Similar relief applies to NI housing associations. [TCGA 1992, ss 218–220].

The disposal and corresponding acquisition of an estate or interest in land in the UK made after 13 March 1989 otherwise than under a bargain at arm's length to a registered housing association (as defined) is treated as being made for a no gain/no loss consideration (or for the actual consideration if the latter exceeds the disposer's allowable expenditure; see 16.3 DISPOSAL) if a joint claim for such relief is made. On a subsequent disposal of the land by the association after a no gain/no loss acquisition its acquisition by the original donor is treated as the acquisition of the association. [TCGA 1992, s 259]. See 8.7 ASSETS HELD ON 31 MARCH 1982 and 23.4 INDEXATION for the consequential re-basing and indexation provisions which apply.

18.43   **International organisations** (e.g. the United Nations) may be specified by Order in Council as exempt from certain taxes [International Organisations Act 1968], as may certain financial bodies under the Bretton Woods Agreement Act 1945 (e.g. the International Monetary Fund). Also exempt are the International Development Association [International Development Association Act 1960, s 3 and SI 1960 No 1383]; the

International Finance Corporation [*International Finance Corporation Act 1955, s 3* and *SI 1955 No 1954*]; and signatories to the Convention on the International Maritime Satellite Organisation in respect of capital gains tax on any payment received by the signatory from the Organisation in accordance with the Convention. [*TCGA 1992, s 271(5)*]. Bodies may be specified by Order as exempt under *European Communities Act 1972, s 2(2)*.

Securities issued by designated international organisations are treated as situated outside the UK. See 6.2 ASSETS.

18.44   **Local authorities, local authority associations and health service bodies** (as defined) are exempt from capital gains tax. [*TCGA 1992, s 271(3)*].

18.45   **National Debt.** Gains accruing to trustees of a settlement the property of which is for the reduction of the National Debt and which qualifies under statute are not chargeable. [*TCGA 1992, s 271(1)(e)*].

18.46   **The National Heritage Memorial Fund** is exempt from tax on chargeable gains. [*TCGA 1992, s 271(7)*].

18.47   **The National Radiological Protection Board** is exempt from tax on chargeable gains. [*TCGA 1992, s 271(7)*].

18.48   **Pension schemes, i.e. exempt approved schemes, retirement annuity schemes, approved personal pension schemes and pension business funds of life assurance companies and registered friendly societies.** Subject to the following, such schemes or the person deriving the benefit from them together with parliamentary pension schemes, National Insurance supplementary benefit schemes and certain overseas pension funds are exempt on gains arising from investments forming part of the fund or from the disposal of units in an authorised unit trust which is also an approved personal pension scheme. For disposals after 26 July 1990, futures contracts and options contracts are included as investments (notwithstanding that one party to the contract will not be involved with a transfer of assets other than money) as regards exempt approved schemes and approved personal pension schemes. (Income arising after 26 July 1990 from transactions relating to such contracts is regarded as income derived from, or income from, such contracts (and therefore exempt from income tax).) For disposals after 25 July 1984 and before 27 July 1990 a contract entered into by exempt approved schemes or approved personal pension schemes in the course of dealing in financial futures or 'traded options' is regarded as an investment. A *'traded option'* means an option which is for the time being quoted on a recognised stock exchange (within *ICTA 1988, s 841*) or on the London International Financial Futures Exchange. For the Revenue's treatment of options and futures in other cases, see 16.10 DISPOSAL. [*TCGA 1992, s 271(1)(b)(c)(d)(g)(h)(j)(10)(11); FA 1984, s 45; F(No 2)A 1987, ss 39(2), 40(2), 2 Sch 1, 2, 5, 3 Sch 5; ICTA 1988, ss 438(1), 460(1)(2), 461(1), 463, 466, 659; FA 1990, s 81(3)(4)(6)(8)*]. Before 26 July 1984, in the case of a covered option, the sale of the shares was normally treated as a disposal of an investment, and any gain was exempt under this provision. In the case of an uncovered option, whether the shares used to fulfil the obligation were regarded as an investment depended on the circumstances and, in particular, on whether they were acquired solely for resale. For consideration of whether *FA 1970, s 21(7)* (re-enacted as *CGTA 1979, s 149B(1)(g)*, and again as *TCGA 1992, s 271(1)(g)*) permits losses on disposals of investments to be allowable due to a drafting error, see Taxation 8 July 1988 p 299.

Pension scheme surpluses. From 6 April 1987, the exemption provided by *TCGA 1992, s 271(g)* will apply only to a prescribed percentage of any gain accruing on a disposal where an exempt approved scheme of a prescribed kind fails to carry out a reduction of its actuarial surplus. [*ICTA 1988, s 603, 22 Sch; SI 1987 No 412*]. For full coverage, see Tolley's Income Tax under Retirement Schemes for employees.

Non-approved pension schemes. The rules for non-approved or 'top-up' pension schemes introduced by *FA 1989* are explained in an Inland Revenue explanatory booklet, 'The Tax Treatment of Non-approved Pension Schemes'. Copies are available, price £1.50, from the Inland Revenue Reference Room, Room 8, New Wing, Somerset House, London WC2R 1LB.

Where a retirement benefits scheme ceases to be tax approved after 1 November 1994 (other than one which had its approval removed before that date), assets of the scheme are treated as having been acquired at their market value immediately before the date of cessation of approval, ensuring that on a future disposal of assets, only the gain accruing on these assets since approval was withdrawn will be brought into account. [*TCGA 1992, 239A; FA 1995, s 61(2)(3)*].

18.49   **Scientific research associations,** provided that in each case its object is research in the fields of natural or applied science which may lead to an extension of trade and which is approved by the Secretary of State for Industry, and that it is prohibited by its Memorandum or similar instrument from distributing its income or property in any form other than that of reasonable payments for supplies, labour, power, services, interest and rent. [*TCGA 1992, s 271(6)(b); ICTA 1998, s 508*].

18.50   **Self-build society.** An approved self-build society (as defined) may claim relief from corporation tax on chargeable gains arising on the disposal of any land to a member, provided that none of its land is occupied by a non-member. Claims must be made to the inspector within two years of the end of the accounting period. [*ICTA 1988, s 489*]. Disposals of land by unregistered self-build societies (as defined) to the Housing Corporation (or Housing for Wales or Scottish Homes) are treated as made at a no gain/no loss price. [*TCGA 1992, s 219*]. See Tolley's Corporation Tax under Housing Associations Etc. and 18.42 above.

18.51   **Superannuation funds.** Approved superannuation funds which, immediately before 6 April 1980, enjoyed exemption under *ICTA 1970, s 208* (repealed after 5 April 1980 by *FA 1971, 3 Sch 1*) may claim exemption for chargeable gains arising from the disposal of investments (for which see 18.48 above) held for the purposes of the fund. The following conditions must be satisfied.

(*a*)   The fund has not been approved under *FA 1970, Pt II Chapter II* or *ICTA 1988, Pt XIV Chapter I*.

(*b*)   No contribution has been made to it since 5 April 1980.

(*c*)   The terms on which benefits are payable from the fund have remained unaltered since 5 April 1980.

[*TCGA 1992, s 271(2)(10)(11); FA 1980, s 36; FA 1984, s 45; FA 1987, 16 Sch Part VI; ICTA 1988, ss 431(5), 608, 659, 29 Sch 26; FA 1990, s 81(3)(4)(6)(8); FA 1994, s 146, 17 Sch 4*].

18.52   **Trade unions.** Registered trade unions, provided that they are precluded from assuring more than £4,000 by way of gross sum or £825 by way of annuity (excluding approved annuities under *ICTA 1988, s 620(9)*) in respect of any one person. (Prior to 1 April 1991 the appropriate sums were £3,000 and £625 respectively, and before 17 March 1987 they were £2,400 and £500 respectively. Following the enactment of *FA 1991, s 74*, the Treasury has power to increase the limits by order.) Exemption is granted in respect of chargeable gains which are applicable and are applied to 'provident benefits' i.e. sickness, injury and superannuation payments, payment for loss of tools, etc. [*ICTA 1988, s 467; FA 1991, s 74*]. Provident benefits also include legal expenses incurred in representing members at Industrial Tribunal hearings of cases alleging unfair dismissal, or incurred in connection with a member's claim in respect of accident or injury suffered, and general administrative expenses of providing provident benefits (Revenue Statement of Practice SP1/84, 17 February 1984). This treatment as to provident benefits did not previously extend to legal and administrative costs of representing members in unfair dismissal cases or general administrative expenses of providing benefits (see above and Revenue Pamphlet IR 131, SP 6/78, 13 November 1978) but a supplementary claim for relief for a chargeable period in respect of any kind of expenditure mentioned in SP 1/84 may be made within normal time limits notwithstanding any prior agreement of liability (Revenue Press Release 1 August 1985).

The above exemption also applies to employers' associations registered as trade unions [*ICTA 1988, s 467(4)(b)*], and to the Police Federations for England and Wales, Scotland, and Northern Ireland and other police organisations with similar functions. [*ICTA 1988, s 467(4)(c)*].

18.53   **Unit and investment trusts.** Authorised UNIT AND INVESTMENT TRUSTS (57) are exempt from tax on chargeable gains. See also VENTURE CAPITAL TRUSTS (58).

18.54   **Visiting forces etc.** A period during which a member of a visiting force to whom *ICTA 1988, s 323(1)* applies is in the UK solely because of such membership is not treated either as a period of residence here or as creating a change in his residence or domicile. [*TCGA 1992, s 11(1); ICTA 1988, s 323*].

18.55   **RELIEFS AND DEFERRALS**

In addition to the exemption from capital gains tax detailed in 18.2–18.1 above, a number of reliefs are available to reduce or defer the amount of tax payable. The more common of these are outlined in 18.56–18.77 below as well as in certain provisions in 18.42 and 18.50 above. For reasons of space, less common reliefs cannot be mentioned below as well as in context in the other chapters of this book.

18.56   **Amalgamations and reconstructions.** These do not normally constitute disposals, the original holding and the new holding being treated as the same asset acquired at the same date as the original shares. See 53.8 and 53.9 SHARES AND SECURITIES and 13.6 COMPANIES.

18.57   **Capital distributions and sale of rights.** If small as compared with the value of the shares in respect of which it is made, a capital distribution may be treated not as a disposal but the proceeds deducted from the acquisition cost of the shares on a subsequent disposal. See 53.13 SHARES AND SECURITIES. This treatment also applies to any consideration received for the disposal of rights. See 53.7 SHARES AND SECURITIES.

18.58   **Companies.**

(a)   *Intra-group transfers of capital assets* are treated as if made at a no gain, no loss consideration (with certain exceptions). See 13.11 COMPANIES.

(b)   *Transfers of assets to non-UK resident company.* Where a UK resident company carrying on a trade outside the UK through a branch or agency transfers that trade and its assets to a non-UK resident company partly or wholly for shares in that company, a proportion of the net chargeable gains relating to those shares may be claimed by the transferor company as being deferred. See 39.14 OVERSEAS MATTERS.

(c)   *Transfers of UK trades between companies resident in different EC member States* are treated as if made at a no gain, no loss consideration. See 39.15 OVERSEAS MATTERS.

18.59   **Constituency associations.** Where, as a result of the redistribution of parliamentary constituencies, an existing constituency association in a former parliamentary constituency disposes, after 5 April 1983, of any land

(a)   to a new association which is its successor, or

(b)   to a body which is an organ of the political party (within *IHTA 1984, s 24*) and which, as soon as practicable thereafter, disposes of the land to a new association which is a successor to the existing association,

the disposal is treated as being made for such consideration as would secure that neither a gain nor loss accrues on disposal.

If the asset was originally held on 6 April 1965, time apportionment will be available (see 7.9 ASSETS HELD ON 6 APRIL 1965) to the new association as if it had held the land from the original date of acquisition.

Where, as a result of the redistribution of parliamentary constituencies, an existing constituency association in a former parliamentary constituency disposes, after 5 April 1983, of any land used and occupied by it for the purposes of its functions and transfers the whole or part of the proceeds to a new association which is its successor, ROLLOVER RELIEF (50) may be claimed as if the land disposed of had been the property of the new association since its acquisition. Where only part of the proceeds is transferred, rollover relief may be claimed on a corresponding share. [*TCGA 1992, s 264*].

18.60   **Disposals: capital sums received as compensation etc.** Where such a sum is received in respect of an asset which is damaged or, alternatively, lost or destroyed, a number of reliefs are available provided the capital sum is expended on restoration of, or a replacement for, the asset. See 16.8 and 16.9 DISPOSAL.

18.61   **Gifts of business assets and assets on which inheritance tax is chargeable etc.** A form of holdover relief applies to

(a)   gifts of business assets before 14 March 1989 (see 22.3 HOLD-OVER RELIEFS);

(b)   gifts of business assets after 13 March 1989 (see 22.1 HOLD-OVER RELIEFS); and

(c)   gifts after 13 March 1989 of assets on which inheritance tax is chargeable etc. (see 22.4 HOLD-OVER RELIEFS).

18.62   **Gifts to charities etc.** Disposals (otherwise than under a bargain at arm's length), by way of gift or at a consideration not exceeding the allowable expenditure, to charities or any of the bodies mentioned in *IHTA 1984, 3 Sch* are deemed to have been made for a consideration giving neither a gain nor a loss. See 10.5 CHARITIES.

18.63   **Harbour reorganisation schemes.** Where the trade of any body corporate, other than a limited company, is transferred to a harbour authority by or under a certified harbour reorganisation scheme which provides for the dissolution of the transferor, any assets transferred on the transfer of trade are treated as giving rise to neither gain nor loss and, for the purposes of any assets acquired before 6 April 1965, the transferor's acquisition of the asset is treated as the transferee's acquisition of it. The transferee is also entitled to relief for any amount for which the transferor would have been entitled to claim relief in respect of allowable losses if it had continued to trade. [*TCGA 1992, s 221; ICTA 1988, s 518*].

18.64   **Hold-over: general relief for gifts.** After 5 April 1980 and before 14 March 1989, a general relief for gifts applied to the disposal of an asset otherwise than at arm's length. Any gain otherwise chargeable could be deferred by deduction from the transferee's acquisition cost. For full details of the relief and claims required, together with the possible clawback of relief, see 22.6 HOLD-OVER RELIEFS.

18.65   **Hops Marketing Board.** Certain transfers of assets by the Hops Marketing Board were deemed to be for a consideration which gives rise to neither a gain nor a loss and the Board's period of ownership is imputed to the transferee for the purposes of applying (where relevant) the provisions relating to ASSETS HELD ON 6 APRIL 1965 (7). [*FA 1982, s 148; TCGA 1992, 12 Sch*].

18.66   **Land — compulsory acquisition.** Where *part* of a holding of land is transferred under a compulsory acquisition order, in certain circumstances the transferor may claim not to treat the transfer as a disposal and the consideration is then deducted from the allowable expenditure on a subsequent disposal. See 33.13 LAND for this and 33.14 for deferral of any gain arising on the compulsory purchase of land by means of a claim for rollover relief where the proceeds are re-invested in new land.

18.67   **Land — part disposals.** Where the value of the consideration for a part disposal of a larger holding of land does not exceed £20,000, in certain circumstances the transferor may claim that the transfer is not treated as a disposal and the consideration is then deducted from the allowable expenditure on a subsequent disposal. See 33.10 LAND.

18.68   **Maintenance funds for historic buildings.** After 5 April 1982 and before 6 April 1984, assets disposed of by a person to trustees for the purposes of maintenance, repair, preservation or reasonable improvement of, or for making provision for public access to, property of historic, scientific, etc. interest (see 18.70 below) where the transfer was exempt from capital transfer tax were deemed to be made for a consideration which gave neither a gain nor a loss for capital gains tax purposes. These provisions also applied in certain other circumstances. [*CGTA 1979, s 148; FA 1980, s 82; FA 1982, s 85; FA 1984, s 68*]. Broadly similar capital gains tax provisions existed for disposals after 30 July 1980 and before 6 April 1982, except that there was no provision for *improvement* of the buildings concerned. [*CGTA 1979, s 148; FA 1980, s 82*]. The still earlier provisions applying for disposals after 2 May 1976 and before 31 July 1980 were very restrictive and of negligible practical importance. [*FA 1976, s 55*].

In view of the general relief for gifts (see 22.6 HOLD-OVER RELIEFS but note that relief in turn was abolished for gifts after 13 March 1989) the above relief was abolished for disposals after 5 April 1984. For gifts after 13 March 1989, a specific deferral relief is again introduced in the form of the hold-over relief for gifts on which inheritance tax is chargeable etc. See 22.4 HOLD-OVER RELIEFS.

18.69 **Married persons.** Transfers between married persons are regarded as made on a no gain, no loss basis where the spouses are living together. See 37.6 MARRIED PERSONS.

18.70 **National heritage property.** The following types of property are within the terms 'national heritage property' provided they are so designated by the Board.

(a) Pictures, prints, books, manuscripts, works of art, scientific collections and other things not yielding income, which appear to the Board to be of national, scientific, historic or artistic interest. '*National interest*' includes interest within any part of the UK;

(b) Land which in the opinion of the Board is of outstanding scenic or historic or scientific interest;

(c) A building for the preservation of which special steps should in the opinion of the Board be taken by reason of its outstanding historic or architectural interest;

(d) Any area of land which in the opinion of the Board is essential for the protection of the character and amenities of such a building as is mentioned in (c) above. For events before 19 March 1985 the land had to *adjoin* the building;

(e) An object which in the opinion of the Board is historically associated with such a building as is mentioned in (c) above.

[*IHTA 1984, s 31(1)(5); FA 1985, s 94, 26 Sch 2(1)(2)*].

Where any of the above assets, which have been (or could be) designated by the Board under *IHTA 1984, s 31*, are disposed of by gift (including a gift into settlement) or deemed to be disposed of by trustees on a person becoming absolutely entitled to settled property (other than on the death of the life tenant), then the person making the disposal and the person acquiring the asset are treated for capital gains tax purposes as making the transaction for a consideration giving neither gain nor loss. [*TCGA 1992, s 258(3)(4)*].

Certain undertakings must be given by such persons as the Board think appropriate in the circumstances of the case that, until the person beneficially entitled to the property dies or the property is disposed of, certain conditions regarding the property are kept, e.g. reasonable access to the public. [*TCGA 1992, s 258(9); IHTA 1984, ss 30(1), 31(2) (4); FA 1985, s 94, 26 Sch 2(2)-(4)*].

If the asset is sold and inheritance tax (or capital transfer tax) is chargeable under *IHTA 1984, s 32* (or would be chargeable if an undertaking under that provision had been given), the person selling the asset is treated as having sold the asset for its market value. Similarly, if the Board are satisfied that at any time during the period for which any undertaking was given that it has not been observed in a material respect, the owner is treated as having sold and immediately reacquired the asset for its market value. An undertaking for the purposes of these provisions is given for the period until the person beneficially entitled to the asset dies or disposes of the asset (whether by sale, gift or otherwise). [*TCGA 1992, s 258(5)(6)*].

If the asset subject to the undertaking is disposed of otherwise than on sale and without a further undertaking being given, the asset is treated as having been sold to an individual for its market value. [*TCGA 1992, s 258(6)*].

Where a person is treated as having sold for market value any asset within (*c*), (*d*) or (*e*) above, he is also treated as having sold and immediately reacquired at market value any asset 'associated' with it (unless the Board directs otherwise). '*Associated*' assets are a building within (*c*) above and land or objects which, in relation to that building, fall within (*d*) or (*e*) above. [*TCGA 1992, s 258(7)*].

Where a person is treated as having sold an asset under these provisions and inheritance tax (or capital transfer tax) becomes chargeable on the same occasion, any capital gains tax payable is deductible in determining the value of the asset for capital transfer tax purposes. [*TCGA 1992, s 258(8)*].

See also 22.4 HOLD-OVER RELIEFS for relief for gifts of works of art etc.

Exceptions. The above provisions do not apply where the disposal is by way of gift or sale by private treaty to a body within *IHTA 1984, 3 Sch* or if the disposal is to the Board in satisfaction of inheritance tax (or capital transfer tax). Such disposals are exempt. See 18.31 above.

18.71   **Reinvestment in shares relief.** An individual or trustees disposing of shares etc. in a trading company can claim, subject to conditions, to defer the gain arising by deducting an amount equal to the gain from the consideration given for the acquisition of shares etc. in another trading company. See 45 REINVESTMENT IN SHARES RELIEF. Similar provisions apply for venture capital trusts and the enterprise investment scheme. See 53.17 SHARES AND SECURITIES and 58.10 VENTURE CAPITAL TRUSTS.

18.72   **Reorganisation of share capital.** Reorganisations do not normally constitute disposals, the original holding and the new holding being treated as the same asset acquired at the same date as the original shares. See 53.5 SHARES AND SECURITIES. See also 53.10 for conversion of securities into shares where the same principles apply.

18.73   **Retirement relief.** Subject to certain conditions, where an individual who has attained the age of 55 (or at a lesser age through ill-health) makes, at a gain, a 'material disposal of business assets', the gains qualifying for relief are reduced in accordance with the provisions in 48 RETIREMENT RELIEF.

18.74   **Rollover relief: replacement of business assets.** A person disposing of certain qualifying assets used exclusively for the purposes of a trade who used the proceeds to purchase other qualifying assets so used may claim to defer the capital gains tax payable by deducting the otherwise chargeable gain on the old asset from the cost of the newly acquired one. See 50 ROLLOVER RELIEF.

18.75   **Settlements for the benefit of employees.** Where the circumstances surrounding a disposal are as in one of (*a*)-(*c*) below, the MARKET VALUE 36.1 rules do not apply to it; and if made gratuitously or for a consideration of an amount not exceeding the allowable expenditure attributable to the asset, the disposal, and the corresponding acquisition by the trustees, is treated as taking place on a no gain/no loss basis and the transferor's acquisition of the asset is imputed to the trustees.

The circumstances mentioned above are as follows.

(*a*)   A close company (as in *ICTA 1988, ss 414, 415* but additionally including a non-UK resident company which would be close as defined by those provisions) disposes of an asset to trustees in circumstances such that the disposition is not a transfer of value for IHT purposes by virtue of *IHTA 1984, s 13* (employee trusts).

(b)   An individual disposes of an asset to trustees in circumstances such that the disposal is an exempt transfer for IHT purposes by virtue of *IHTA 1984, s 28* (employee trusts).

(c)   A company other than a close company (as in (*a*) above) disposes of property to trustees otherwise than under a bargain at arm's length in circumstances such that, broadly, had the disposition been made by a close company it would not be a transfer of value by virtue of *IHTA 1984, s 13*.

[*TCGA 1992, s 239(1)(2)(4)-(8)*].

For coverage of *IHTA 1984, s 13* and *28* (each of which refers to the provisions of *IHTA 1984, s 86*), see Tolley's Inheritance Tax under Trusts for Employees.

If the trustees of an 'employee trust' transfer an asset to a beneficiary for no payment, no charge under *TCGA 1992, s 71* will, by concession, be levied on the trustees provided there is a Schedule E income tax charge of the full market value of the asset on the employee. For this purpose, '*employee trust*' means a trust within *IHTA 1984, s 86* but ignoring the restriction in *s 86(3)* (class defined by employment with a particular body to include all or most employees), and the employee must not be a person of the kind described in *IHTA 1984, s 28(4)* (participators, connected persons etc.) and not excluded by *s 28(5)* (participators with 5% or more of a class of shares, etc.). The concession does not apply where special statutory rules restrict either the liability to capital gains tax or the Schedule E liability (Revenue Pamphlet IR1, D35).

For the position of the shareholders in a close company transferor which makes a transfer within (*a*)-(*c*) above at less than market value, see 3.12 ANTI-AVOIDANCE.

See also 22 HOLD-OVER RELIEFS and 53.25 SHARES AND SECURITIES for alternative reliefs which may be available in respect of transfers to settlements for the benefit of employees.

18.76   **Transfer of a business to a company.** Where a person transfers a business and its assets to a company in return for shares in that company, any chargeable gain on disposal of the assets is deferred by reducing the amount otherwise chargeable in the proportion of the value of the shares received to the value of the overall consideration received by the transferor in exchange for the business. See 22.7 HOLD-OVER RELIEFS.

18.77   **Unremittable overseas gains.** On a claim, such gains may be treated as gains of the year in which conditions preventing remittance cease to apply. See 39.4 OVERSEAS MATTERS. See also 32.5 INTEREST ON TAX OVERDUE.

19 Furnished Holiday Accommodation

19.1 DEFINITIONS

Special provisions apply to the treatment for the purposes of tax on chargeable gains of the commercial letting of furnished holiday accommodation in the UK.

'*Commercial letting*' is letting (whether or not under a lease) on a commercial basis and with a view to the realisation of profits, and accommodation is let '*furnished*' if the tenant is entitled to the use of furniture.

'*Holiday accommodation*' is accommodation which

(*a*)   must be available for commercial letting to the public generally as holiday accommodation for at least 140 days in a twelve month period (see below), and

(*b*)   is so let for at least 70 such days.

It must, however, not normally be in the same occupation for more than 31 consecutive days at any time during a period (although not necessarily a continuous period) of seven months in that twelve month period which includes any months in which it is let as in (*b*) above. In the case of an individual or partnership, these conditions must be satisfied in the year of assessment in which the profits or gains arise, unless

(i)   the accommodation was not let furnished in the preceding year of assessment but is so let in the following year of assessment, in which case they must be satisfied in the twelve months from the date such letting commenced in the year of assessment, or

(ii)   the accommodation was let furnished in the preceding year of assessment but is not so let in the following year of assessment, in which case they must be satisfied in the twelve months ending with the date such letting ceased in the year of assessment.

In the case of a company, the conditions must be satisfied in the twelve months ending on the last day of the accounting period in which the profits or gains arise, with similar variations as in (i) and (ii) above where the accommodation was not let furnished in the twelve months preceding or following the period in question.

In satisfying the 70 day test ((*b*) above) averaging may be applied to letting periods of holiday accommodation already treated as such ('*qualifying accommodation*') and letting periods of any or all of other accommodation let by the same person which would be holiday accommodation if it satisfied the 70 day test. Any such other accommodation is then treated as holiday accommodation if the average of the days let in the twelve month period is at least 70. A claim under *ICTA 1988, s 504(6)* for averaging must be made within two years of the end of the year of assessment or accounting period to which it is to apply. Only one such claim may be made in respect of qualifying accommodation in any year of assessment or accounting period.

Where there is a letting of accommodation only part of which is holiday accommodation, apportionments are made as is just and reasonable (subject to appeal). [*TCGA 1992, s 241(1)(2)(7); ICTA 1988, s 504*].

Furnished holiday accommodation may include caravans (Revenue Press Release 17 May 1984).

See Tolley's Income Tax regarding income tax provisions in respect of furnished holiday accommodation.

19.2   CAPITAL GAINS TAX TREATMENT

After 5 April 1982, for the purposes of the following provisions, the commercial letting of furnished holiday accommodation in the UK in respect of which the profits or gains are chargeable under Schedule A for 1995/96 onwards (previously Schedule D, Case VI) is treated as a trade and all such lettings made by a particular person, partnership or body of persons are treated as one trade.

(a)   RETIREMENT RELIEF (48).

(b)   ROLLOVER RELIEF (50).

(c)   Relief for gifts of business assets (see 22.1–22.3 HOLD-OVER RELIEFS).

(d)   Relief for loans to traders (see 35.9 LOSSES).

A notable omission from (a)-(d) above, which may be of advantage to the taxpayer, are the provisions applying in respect of a non-UK resident trading in the UK through a branch or agency (see 39.3 OVERSEAS MATTERS).

Where, in any chargeable period, a person makes a commercial letting within these provisions, the let property is to be taken for the purposes of (a)-(d) above as being used throughout that period only for the purposes of the deemed trade of making such lettings except for any period when it is neither commercially let nor available to be so let (unless it is only works of construction or repair that make this the case).

For the purposes of (b) above, the replacement asset must be acquired after 5 April 1982. However, where the only or main residence exemption in *TCGA 1992, s 222* (see 43 PRIVATE RESIDENCES) is also available to any extent, the gain to which *TCGA 1992, s 222* applies is reduced by the amount of the rolled-over gain. [*TCGA 1992, s 241(3)–(6)(8); FA 1995, 6 Sch 36*].

The Revenue consider that the relief at (a) or (b) is available if the holiday accommodation is sold within three years of its ceasing to be let so long as the owner does not occupy it or use it for some other non-qualifying purpose (CCAB Statement TR 551, June 1984). Where periods before 6 April 1982 need to be considered, then, for the purposes of (a)-(d) above, those periods would be judged by the Revenue on the basis of the actual activity carried on and whether that activity would have qualified in relation to the period after 5 April 1982 (Tolley's Practical Tax 1985 p 96).

20   Gifts

Cross-references. See 30.2 INTERACTION WITH OTHER TAXES for inheritance tax (or capital transfer tax) interaction on lifetime gifts; and 41.5 PAYMENT OF TAX for payment by instalments on certain gifts etc.

20.1   GENERAL

The fact that no proceeds are received on a disposal of an asset does not mean that capital gains tax will not apply. With certain exceptions, where a person acquires or disposes of an asset, otherwise than by way of a bargain made at arm's length *and in particular where he acquires or disposes of it by way of gift,* his acquisition or disposal of the asset is deemed to be for a consideration equal to the market value of the asset. [*TCGA 1992, s 17(1)(a)*]. See 36 MARKET VALUE for the full market value rules and the exceptions where the provisions do not apply.

Thus, the donor of an asset is normally treated as incurring a chargeable gain computed by reference to market value at the date of disposal. For the purposes of gifts, the date of disposal is the time when the donor has done everything within his power to transfer the property to the donee (see *Re Rose, Rose and Others v CIR CA, [1952] 1 All E R 1217*).

20.2 GENERAL RELIEF FOR GIFTS FROM 1980 TO 1989

After 5 April 1980 and before 14 March 1989, a general relief for gifts applied to the disposal of an asset otherwise than at arm's length. Any gain otherwise chargeable could be deferred by deduction from the transferee's acquisition cost. For full details of the relief and claims required, together with the possibility of clawback of relief, see 22.6 HOLD-OVER RELIEFS.

20.3 SPECIAL EXEMPTIONS RELATING TO GIFTS

Once the market value of a gift has been established, the ordinary capital gains tax provisions relating to exemptions apply to that gift. See 18 EXEMPTIONS AND RELIEFS. For example, the gift of a chattel with a market value of £6,000 (£3,000 for gifts before 6 April 1989) or less is exempt. The following gifts are expressly exempt.

(*a*)   Gifts for public benefit (see 18.25 EXEMPTIONS AND RELIEFS).

(*b*)   Gifts of property to bodies mentioned in *IHTA 1984, 3 Sch* for national purposes (see 18.31 EXEMPTIONS AND RELIEFS).

(*c*)   Donatio mortis causa (see 15.3 DEATH).

20.4 SPECIAL RELIEFS RELATING TO GIFTS

Apart from the general relief for gifts from 1980 to 1989 outlined in 20.2 above, reliefs are also available for

(*a*)   gifts of business assets before 14 March 1989 (see 22.3 HOLD-OVER RELIEFS);

(*b*)   gifts of business assets after 13 March 1989 (see 22.1 HOLD-OVER RELIEFS);

(*c*)   gifts to charities (see 10.5 CHARITIES);

(*d*)   gifts after 13 March 1989 of assets on which inheritance tax etc. is chargeable (see 22.4 HOLD-OVER RELIEFS);

(*e*)   gifts to housing associations after 13 March 1989 (see 18.42 EXEMPTIONS AND RELIEFS);

(*f*)   gifts to maintenance trusts for historic buildings before 6 April 1984 (see 18.68 EXEMPTIONS AND RELIEFS);

(*g*)   gifts of national heritage property subject to certain undertakings (see 18.70 EXEMPTIONS AND RELIEFS); and

(*h*)   gifts to settlements for the benefit of employees (see 18.75 EXEMPTIONS AND RELIEFS).

20.5 RECOVERY OF TAX FROM DONEE

Where capital gains tax arising on a disposal made by way of gift (including any transaction otherwise than at arm's length) is not paid by the donor (or, if he being an individual has died, his personal representatives) within twelve months from the date it became payable, it may be recovered, subject to the coverage below, from the donee within two years after the date on which it became payable. The donee then has a right of recovery from the donor or his personal representatives. The recovery is done by assessment and the donee is assessed and charged (in the name of the donor) to capital gains tax on an amount not exceeding the amount of the chargeable gain arising on the disposal, and not exceeding the grossed-up amount of the capital gains tax unpaid at the time such assessment is made, grossing up at the marginal rate of tax (i.e. by taking capital gains tax on a chargeable gain at the amount which would not have been chargeable but for that chargeable gain). [*TCGA 1992, s 282*].

21   Government Securities

21.1   EXEMPTION RULES

After 1 July 1986, disposals of any of the UK government and public corporation stocks ('gilts') specified in 21.2 below are exempt whatever the period of ownership. [*TCGA 1992, s 115(1)(a)*].

After 1 July 1986 disposals of options or contracts to acquire or dispose of gilts are also exempt. See 16.10 and 16.11 DISPOSAL.

See 13.9 COMPANIES for appropriations of gilts to and from trading stock by companies.

See 53.10 SHARES AND SECURITIES regarding government stock issued as compensation for shares compulsorily acquired.

21.2   EXEMPT SECURITIES

Government (and certain public corporation securities guaranteed by the Treasury) are specified as exempt in the circumstances described in 21.1 above by the Treasury in the form of a statutory instrument. In practice, all UK government securities charged on the National Loans Fund are so specified but there may be a period of time between the issue of such a security and the issue of the statutory instrument specifying it as exempt. [*TCGA 1992, s 288(8), 9 Sch Pt I*].

Those securities specified as exempt of which the latest redemption date falls after 31 December 1991 are now listed in *TCGA 1992, 9 Sch Pt II* as amended by *SI 1993 No 950* and *SI 1994 No 2656*. The position of securities with an earlier redemption date is protected by *TCGA 1992, 11 Sch 15*.

22   Hold-Over Reliefs

Cross-references. See 8.12 ASSETS HELD ON 31 MARCH 1982 for 50% relief etc. on held-over gains relating to an asset acquired before 31 March 1982; 13.6 COMPANIES for the relief available on a scheme of reconstruction or amalgamation and 13.11 for relief on disposals within a group; 16.8, 16.9 DISPOSAL for reliefs available where capital sums received as compensation are expended on restoration or replacement; 18 EXEMPTIONS AND RELIEFS generally; 20.4 GIFTS for summary of special reliefs relating to gifts; 33.11, 33.13, 33.14 LAND for reliefs available on small part disposals and compulsory purchase of land; 39.3 OVERSEAS MATTERS for transfer of UK branch or agency to UK resident company, 39.14 for transfers of assets to a non-UK resident company, 39.15 for transfer of trade between companies in different EC member States and 39.16 for transfer of non-UK trade between companies in different EC member States; 45 REINVEST-MENT IN SHARES RELIEF for a relief which may be able to be used as an alternative to the reliefs in this chapter in relation to disposals after 29 November 1993; 50 ROLLOVER RELIEF.

22.1   RELIEF FOR GIFTS OF BUSINESS ASSETS AFTER 13 MARCH 1989

Where, after 13 March 1989,

(*a*)   an individual ('*the transferor*') makes a disposal not at arm's length (e.g. a gift) of an asset specified below, and

(*b*)   a joint claim for relief is made by him and the transferee, or, where the transferee is a trustee of a settlement, by him alone,

then, subject to *TCGA 1992, s 165(3)* below and the provisions in 22.2 below, the hold-over relief described below is to apply. [*TCGA 1992, s 165(1)*]. Prior to the commence-ment of *TCGA 1992*, claims were made under *CGTA 1979, s 126(1)*.

An asset is within (*a*) above if

(i)   it is, or is an interest in, an asset used for the purposes of a trade, profession or vocation carried on by the transferor, his 'personal company' ('family company' for disposals before 16 March 1993) or a member of a 'trading group' of which the 'holding company' is his personal company (family company for disposals before 16 March 1993), or

(ii)   it consists of shares or securities of a 'trading company', or of the holding company of a trading group, where *either* the shares etc. are neither quoted on a recognised stock exchange (within *ICTA 1988, s 841*) nor dealt in on the Unlisted Securities Market *or* the trading company or holding company is the transferor's personal company (family company for disposals before 16 March 1993).

[*TCGA 1992, s 165(2)*; *FA 1993, s 87, 7 Sch 1, 23 Sch Pt III*].

There is nothing in the legislation to deny relief if consideration for the use of the asset passes between an individual and a company, e.g. under a lease or tenancy agreement, and similarly there is no requirement that the individual need be a 'full-time working officer or employee' ('full-time working director' for disposals before 16 March 1993) (see 48.3 RETIREMENT RELIEF). It is understood that the Revenue will apply SP D11 (see 50 ROLLOVER RELIEF) *mutatis mutandis* for this hold-over relief as it applies to rollover relief (Tolley's Practical Tax 1990 p 143). As a claim applies separately to each asset, the comments made about the general relief for gifts from 1980 to 1989 in 22.6 below regarding the treatment of property as separate assets would seem also to apply to the above relief.

Hold-over relief does not apply on a disposal if

(A)   the gain arising is wholly relieved by RETIREMENT RELIEF (48); or

(B)   the gain arising relates to shares or securities where the 'appropriate proportion' of it is wholly relieved by retirement relief (see 48.8 RETIREMENT RELIEF); or

(C)   the gain arises by virtue of *TCGA 1992, s 116(10)(b)* (disposal of qualifying corporate bonds derived from shares giving rise to deferred gain, see 44.3 QUALIFYING CORPORATE BONDS); or

(D)   hold-over relief is available (or would be if a claim were made) under *TCGA 1992, s 260* in 22.4 below for gifts after 13 March 1989 on which inheritance tax is chargeable etc.

[*TCGA 1992, s 165(3)*].

Where there is no actual consideration for the disposal (as opposed to a deemed MARKET VALUE (36.1) consideration under *TCGA 1992, s 17(1)*), or where an actual consideration does not exceed the allowable expenditure within *TCGA 1992, s 38* (see 16.3 DISPOSAL) relating to the asset, the effect of a claim is that the gain otherwise chargeable on the transferor apart from this relief and the transferee's acquisition cost are each reduced by the '*held-over gain*', i.e. the gain otherwise chargeable apart from this relief and, where relevant, retirement relief (termed the '*unrelieved gain*') but subject to the reductions described below. Where actual consideration exceeds the allowable expenditure, the held-over gain is the unrelieved gain less that excess but again subject to the reductions below. (*Note.* Indexation allowance is deductible in arriving at the gain otherwise chargeable but it is not allowable expenditure within *TCGA 1992, s 38*.) [*TCGA 1992, s 165(4)(6)(7)*].

In certain circumstances the Inland Revenue may require a valuation at the date of transfer of the asset transferred, notably where there is an interaction between hold-over relief and other relieving provisions. For example: where the gain attracts retirement relief; where relief in respect of deferred charges on gains arising before 31 March 1982 is available; and where the gain on an asset held at 6 April 1965 is time apportioned. The Inland Revenue have stated that, in these circumstances, a valuation will not usually be required before a subsequent disposal of the asset by the transferee (Revenue Statement of Practice SP 8/92, 26 October 1992).

The definitions of '*family company*' (for disposals before 16 March 1993), '*holding company*', '*personal company*' (for disposals after 15 March 1993), '*trading company*' and '*trading group*' have the meanings given by *TCGA 1992, 6 Sch 1* (see 48.3 RETIREMENT RELIEF). '*Trade*', '*profession*' and '*vocation*' generally have the same meanings as in the *Income Tax Acts* but the commercial letting of FURNISHED HOLIDAY ACCOMMODATION (19) in the UK in respect of which the profits, etc. are chargeable under Schedule D, Case VI is treated as a trade for relief purposes; and for the same purposes in determining whether a company is a trading company, '*trade*' includes the occupation of woodlands managed on a commercial basis by the occupier with a view to profit. [*TCGA 1992, ss 165(8)(9), 241(3); FA 1993, s 87, 7 Sch 1, 23 Sch Pt III*].

Where a hold-over relief claim is made, the transferee may deduct for capital gains tax purposes on a subsequent disposal made by him any inheritance tax attributable to the value of the asset on the transfer to him which qualified for relief and which is either a chargeable transfer or a potentially exempt transfer which proves to be a chargeable transfer. The tax deductible may be varied on the subsequent death of the transferor within seven years or otherwise but it cannot in any circumstances give rise to an allowable loss on the subsequent disposal. [*TCGA 1992, s 165(10)(11)*]. See also 30.2 INTERACTION WITH OTHER TAXES.

Reductions in the held-over gain. If the qualifying asset disposed of was not used for the purposes of the trade, profession or vocation concerned throughout the period of its ownership by the transferor, the held-over gain is reduced by multiplying it by the fraction of which the denominator is the total period of ownership and the numerator the number of days in the period during which the asset was so used. (*Note.* In the determination of the period of ownership there is no exclusion of any period before 31 March 1982, cf. 50.5 ROLLOVER RELIEF.) Where the qualifying asset disposed of is a building or structure part only of which has been used for the trade etc. concerned over all or a 'substantial' part of the period of its ownership, the held-over gain is reduced as is 'just and reasonable'. [*TCGA 1992, 7 Sch 4, 5(1), 6(1)*].

If the disposal of shares or securities of a company qualifies for relief and the company or group (as appropriate) then has 'chargeable assets' which are not 'business assets' and *either* at any time in the twelve months before the disposal the transferor could exercise 25% or more of the company's voting rights (as exercisable in general meeting) *or* the company is the personal company (family company for disposals before 16 March 1993) (see above) of an individual transferor at any time within that period of twelve months, the held-over gain is reduced by multiplying it by the fraction of which the denominator is the then market value of all of the company's or group's chargeable assets and the numerator is the then market value of the company's or group's business assets. In considering a group, a holding in the ordinary share capital of one group member by another is ignored, and if a 51% subsidiary is not wholly owned directly or indirectly by the holding company the values of its chargeable and business assets are reduced in proportion to the share capital owned; and for both purposes the expressions used are as in *ICTA 1988, s 838*. An asset is a *'business asset'* if it is or is an interest in an asset used for the purposes of a trade etc. carried on by the company or another group member, and an asset is a *'chargeable asset'* if a gain accruing on its disposal by the company or another group member would be a chargeable gain. [*TCGA 1992, 7 Sch 4, 7; FA 1993, s 87, 7 Sch 1, 23 Sch Pt III*].

If the asset disposed of is a 'chargeable business asset' for the purposes of retirement relief (see 48.8 RETIREMENT RELIEF) and the held-over gain (as reduced under the above) would exceed the gain otherwise chargeable (ignoring hold-over relief itself but allowing for any deduction of retirement relief), the held-over gain is reduced by the amount of the excess. In the case of a disposal of shares or securities qualifying for retirement relief where the held-over gain (as reduced under the above) would exceed an amount equal to the 'appropriate proportion' of the gain otherwise chargeable (ignoring hold-over relief itself but allowing for any deduction of retirement relief), the held-over gain is reduced by the amount of the excess. [*TCGA 1992, 7 Sch 4, 8*].

Agricultural property. If an asset, or an interest in an asset,

(I)   is 'agricultural property' within the inheritance tax provisions of *IHTA 1984, Pt V Chapter II* and *either* qualifies for an inheritance tax reduction in value in relation to a chargeable transfer made simultaneously with the disposal *or* would so qualify if there were a chargeable transfer on the disposal *or* would so qualify but for *IHTA 1984, s 124A* (additional conditions for transfers within seven years before death of transferor) (assuming, where there is no chargeable transfer, that there were); but

(II)   it fails to qualify for hold-over relief solely because the agricultural property is not used for the purposes of a trade etc. carried on as in (i) above,

then, notwithstanding (II) above, hold-over relief is granted to the individual transferor. Hold-over relief is also granted *mutatis mutandis* to trustees (see under settled property below) where the agricultural property would not otherwise qualify for relief solely because it is not used for the purposes of a trade etc. carried on as in (1) below. In these circumstances *TCGA 1992, 7 Sch 4, 5(1), 6(1)* above do not apply. [*TCGA 1992, s 165(5), 7 Sch 1, 3, 5(2), 6(2)*]. Where development value over and above the agricultural value of the land is inherent in the property transferred, hold-over relief is available in respect of the whole of the gain, i.e. not just that part which reflects the land's agricultural value (Revenue Tax Bulletin November 1991 p 5).

Settled property. If

(*aa*)   trustees of a settlement make a non-arm's length disposal of an asset specified below, and

(*bb*)   a claim for relief under *TCGA 1992, s 165* is made by the trustees and the transferee or, if trustees are also the transferee, by the trustees making the disposal alone,

then, subject to *TCGA 1992, s 165(3)* (see above) and the provisions in 22.2 below, hold-over relief given by *TCGA 1992, s 165(4)* (see above) applies to the disposal.

An asset is within (*aa*) above if

(1)   it is, or is an interest in, an asset used for the purposes of a trade, profession or vocation carried on by the trustees making the disposal or a beneficiary who had an interest in possession in the settled property immediately before the disposal, or

(2)   it consists of shares or securities of a trading company, or of the holding company of a trading group, where *either* the shares etc. are neither quoted on a recognised stock exchange nor dealt in on the Unlisted Securities Market *or* not less than 25% of the voting rights as exercisable in general meeting are held by the trustees at the time of disposal.

Where hold-over relief is granted to trustees in this way, references to the trustees are substituted for references to the transferor in *TCGA 1992, s 165(4)(a)* above and *CGTA 1979, s 126C* in 22.2 below; and where hold-over relief is granted on a disposal deemed to occur by virtue of *TCGA 1992, s 71(1)* or *72(1)* (see 52.9–52.11 SETTLEMENTS and 22.2 below), no reduction in the held-over gain is made under *TCGA 1992, s 165(7)* above (reduction by excess of actual consideration over allowable expenditure). [*TCGA 1992, s 165(5), 7 Sch 2; CGTA 1979, 4 Sch 2; FA 1989, 14 Sch 3(3)*]. See also under agricultural property above.

Example

S has carried on his antique dealing business for 10 years. The assets of the business are valued as follows

	£
Freehold shop and office	285,000
Goodwill	90,000
Stocks	50,000
Debtors	9,500
Cash	4,500

Before the business began, S let the shop premises for one year. In October 1995, S transfers the business as a going concern to a company which he has formed with share capital of £1,000, held wholly by him. The transfer consideration is £1. At the time of the transfer S is 56. The gain arising in respect of the freehold is £250,000 and on goodwill it is £83,000 (both after deducting indexation allowance).

22.2 Hold-Over Reliefs

	£	£
Gains eligible for retirement relief		
(£250,000 + £83,000)		333,000
Relief £250,000 × 100%	250,000	
£83,000 × 50%	41,500	291,500
Chargeable gain		£41,500

If S and the company jointly claim relief under *TCGA 1992, s 165*, part of the chargeable gain may be rolled over, as follows

	Freehold	Goodwill	
	£	£	£
Total gain	250,000	83,000	
Reduction for non-trade use [*TCGA 1992,*			
7 Sch 5] ($\frac{1}{11}$)	22,727		
	£227,273	£83,000	
Held-over gain before adjustment			310,273
Retirement relief [*TCGA 1992, 7 Sch 8*]			291,500
Held-over gain			£18,773

Notes to the example

(a) The chargeable gain neither relieved nor held over is therefore £22,727 (£333,000 – £291,500 – £18,773).

(b) There is no statutory formula for apportioning retirement relief between different assets for the purpose of calculating hold-over relief under *TCGA 1992, s 165*. The following is one possible method of computing the revised base costs in the hands of the company.

Freehold

Gain held over $\dfrac{227,273}{310,273} \times £18,773$ £13,751

Revised base cost (£285,000 – £13,751) £271,249

Goodwill

Gain held over $\dfrac{83,000}{310,273} \times £18,773$ £5,022

Revised base cost (£90,000 – £5,022) £84,978

(c) If S had transferred the business to the company in consideration for the issue of shares, *TCGA 1992, s 162* would have applied, but business assets relief under *TCGA 1992, s 165* would not. Retirement relief would still have applied in priority, so that the chargeable gain would have been £41,500. This gain would then have been rolled over against the base cost of the shares acquired by S.

22.2 **Restrictions on, and clawback of, hold-over relief under TCGA 1992, s 165, 7 Sch as applicable to disposals after 13 March 1989.** *Gifts to non-residents.* The hold-over relief of *TCGA 1992, s 165(4)* in 22.1 above is not to apply where the transferee is neither resident nor ordinarily resident in the UK. It also does not apply where the transferee is an individual or, for disposals before 30 November 1993 (this date being the date of the coming into force of *FA 1994, s 249*; companies otherwise regarded as UK resident but under double tax relief arrangements already regarded as non-UK resident to be treated as non-UK resident for *Taxes Acts* purposes after 29 November 1993; see 47.5 RESIDENCE AND DOMICILE), a company if that individual or, for disposals before 30 November 1993, company, though resident or ordinarily resident in the UK, is regarded as resident elsewhere by virtue of DOUBLE TAX RELIEF (17.2) arrangements such that it would not under those arrangements be taxable in the UK on a gain arising on a disposal of the asset immediately after its acquisition. [*TCGA 1992, s 166; FA 1994, s 251(1)(7), 26 Sch Pt VIII*].

Gifts to foreign-controlled companies. Relief under *TCGA 1992, s 165(4)* is also denied where the transferee is a company which is controlled by a person who, or by persons each of whom, is neither UK-resident nor ordinarily resident and is connected (see 14 CONNECTED PERSONS) with the person making the disposal; and in determining a person's residence status, a person who either alone or with others controls a company by virtue of holding assets relating to that or any other company and who is UK-resident or ordinarily resident is regarded as neither UK-resident nor ordinarily resident if he is regarded under a double tax agreement as resident overseas in circumstances in which he would not be liable to a UK tax charge on a gain arising on a disposal of the assets. [*TCGA 1992, s 167*].

Emigration of controlling trustees before 19 March 1991. If relief under *TCGA 1992, s 165* (formerly *CGTA 1979, s 126*) was given on a disposal of an asset to a company which was controlled by trustees of a settlement ('the relevant disposal') at a time when the person making the disposal was connected with the trustees, and at a time when the company had not disposed of the asset and the trustees still controlled the company the trustees became before 19 March 1991 neither UK-resident nor ordinarily resident (determined as above for *TCGA 1992, s 167*), then a gain equal to the held-over gain was deemed to accrue to the trustees immediately before the change in residence status. Provision was made for a corresponding reduction in the gain deemed to accrue to the trustees where before the change in residence status some of the held-over gain had been brought into charge on a disposal within the UK tax charge, e.g. on a part disposal, but this did not include a disposal under *TCGA 1992, s 171* (transfers within a group, see 13.11 COMPANIES) or *TCGA 1992, s 172* (transfer of UK branch or agency, see 39.3 OVERSEAS MATTERS) although the first subsequent disposal of the asset to which neither of these provisions applied was taken into account as if it had been made by the company. If tax assessed on the trustees as a result of the above was not paid within twelve months of the date when it became payable, the transferor could be assessed, within six years after the end of the year of assessment in which the relevant disposal was made, and he was then given a right of recovery against the trustees. Where an amount was assessed in this way, the consideration deemed to have been given for the asset in question was no longer deemed to have been reduced by the amount of the held-over gain. [*CGTA 1979, s 126C: FA 1989, 14 Sch 2; FA 1990, s 70(5)(9); FA 1991, s 92(1)(5)*]. For changes in residence status after 18 April 1991, see 39.6 OVERSEAS MATTERS et seq.

Gifts into dual resident trusts. Hold-over relief under *TCGA 1992, s 165* is not available where the transferees are trustees who fall to be treated as UK-resident although the general administration of the trust is carried on overseas, and where, on a notional disposal of the asset by the trustees immediately after the disposal of it to them, the trustees would be regarded for double tax relief arrangements as resident overseas and as not liable to UK tax arising on the notional disposal. Where relief has been allowed under *TCGA 1992, s 165* in respect of a disposal made after 13 March 1989 and subsequently the trustees' circumstances become before 19 March 1991 such that a disposal to them would not then qualify for relief in view of the above, a clawback of relief under *TCGA 1992, s 168* (formerly *FA 1981, s 79*) (see under emigration of transferee below) is to have effect (subject to any previous clawback under that provision) as if the trustees had become neither resident nor ordinarily resident in the UK. [*FA 1986, s 58; FA 1989, 14 Sch 6(4); FA 1991, s 92(4)(7)*]. For trustees becoming dual resident after 18 March 1991, see 39.6 OVERSEAS MATTERS et seq.

Emigration of transferee. Subject to the exception mentioned below, a gain held over under *TCGA 1992, s 165* will be clawed back if the individual transferee concerned becomes neither resident nor ordinarily resident in the UK or if the transferee trustees concerned become neither resident nor ordinarily resident in the UK before 19 March 1991. If the transferee is an individual the clawback may be made within six years after the end of the year of assessment in which the disposal for which hold-over relief was claimed was made; otherwise (e.g. where trustees are the transferee) no time limit is specified. The charge, which is on a gain deemed to have accrued just prior to the cessation of UK residence and ordinary residence, is reduced to the extent that the held-over gain has already been taken into account in a disposal by the transferee (e.g. on a part disposal). For the latter purpose, a disposal does not include a no gain/no loss disposal between MARRIED PERSONS (37.6) under *TCGA 1992, s 58*. If such an inter-spouse transfer occurs, a disposal by the acquiring spouse is treated as made by the spouse who originally acquired the asset to which the held-over gain related. If not paid within twelve months from the due date of payment, tax on the deemed gain assessed on the transferee can be assessed on the transferor within six years after the end of the year of assessment in which the disposal for which hold-over relief was claimed was made, although the transferor then has the right to recover any tax so paid from the transferee.

Where a deemed gain relating to a previously held-over gain has been assessed under the above, then on a subsequent disposal of the asset in question the allowable expenditure relating to it is not reduced by the held-over gain.

An exception to the above applies where the disposal for which relief was claimed was made to an individual, and

(a)   the reason for his becoming neither resident nor ordinarily resident in the UK is that he works in an employment or office, all of the duties of which are performed abroad, and

(b)   he again becomes UK-resident or ordinarily resident within three years of ceasing to be so, and

(c)   in the meantime, the asset which is the subject of the hold-over relief has not been subject to a disposal by him in connection with which the allowable expenditure attaching to the asset, if the individual had been UK-resident, would have been reduced by the held-over gain; for this purpose the same provisions as above for inter-spouse transfers apply.

Where (a) applies, and (b) and (c) *may* apply, no assessment under the main provisions outlined above will be made before the end of the three-year period. [*TCGA 1992, s 168; FA 1991, s 92(2)(6)*]. For changes of residence of trustees after 18 March 1991, see 39.6 OVERSEAS MATTERS et seq.

Clawback of relief on life tenant's death. The exemption otherwise available for gains arising on deemed disposals under *TCGA 1992, s 71(1)* or *72(1)(a)* (formerly *CGTA 1979, s 54(1)* or *55(1)(a)*) on the death of a life tenant etc. (see 52.9–52.11 SETTLEMENTS) does not apply to an asset (or part asset) where a claim for hold-over relief was made under *TCGA 1992, s 165* in relation to an original disposal of that asset after 13 March 1989 to the trustees. Any chargeable gain accruing to the trustees will, however, be restricted to the held-over gain (or corresponding part) on the original disposal of the asset. Where the life tenant's interest was in part only of the settled property, and that property is subject to a deemed disposal under *TCGA 1992, s 71(1)*, the clawback is proportional to the life tenant's interest. [*TCGA 1992, s 74*]. By analogy with the position when *FA 1980, s 79* (general relief for gifts) was extant before 14 March 1989, it seems to be possible for the trustees to claim hold-over relief under *TCGA 1992, s 165* (provided all the conditions are met) in respect of any gain arising from this clawback provision (Tolley's Practical Tax 1983 p 142).

22.3   RELIEF FOR GIFTS OF BUSINESS ASSETS BEFORE 14 MARCH 1989

As a result of the availability of the general relief for gifts in 22.6 below, the rules relating specifically to gifts of business assets were of restricted application for gifts after 5 April 1980 and before 14 March 1989. The scope of the provisions is given at the end of the coverage below. None of the provisions in 22.2 above applied to the hold-over relief described below.

If an individual ('*the transferor*') made a disposal not at arm's length (e.g. a gift) to a person resident or ordinarily resident in the UK ('*the transferee*') of

(*a*)   an asset which was, or was an interest in, an asset which was used for the purposes of a trade, profession or vocation carried on by the transferor or by a company which was his 'family company', or

(*b*)   shares or securities of a 'trading company' which was the transferor's family company,

then, subject to *CGTA 1979, s 126(2)* below, the hold-over relief described below applied on a joint claim made by the transferor and transferee. [*CGTA 1979, s 126(1)*].

Hold-over relief did not apply on a disposal if

(A)   the gain arising was wholly relieved by RETIREMENT RELIEF (48), or

(B)   it related to shares or securities where the 'appropriate proportion' of the gain arising was wholly relieved by RETIREMENT RELIEF (48).

Where there was no actual consideration for the disposal (as opposed to a deemed MARKET VALUE (36.1) consideration under *TCGA 1992, s 17(1)*), or where an actual consideration does not exceed the allowable expenditure within *TCGA 1992, s 38* (see 16.3 DISPOSAL) relating to the asset, the effect of a claim was that the gain otherwise chargeable on the transferor apart from this relief and the transferee's acquisition cost were each reduced by the '*held-over gain*', i.e. the gain otherwise chargeable apart from this relief and, where relevant, retirement relief (termed the '*unrelieved gain*' for the provision mentioned in the next sentence) but subject to the reductions described below. Where actual consideration exceeded the allowable expenditure, the held-over gain was the unrelieved gain less that excess but again subject to the reductions below. (*Note*. Indexation allowance was deductible in arriving at the gain otherwise chargeable but it was not allowable expenditure within *TCGA 1992, s 38*.) [*CGTA 1979, s 126(3)(5)(6)*].

The definition of '*family company*' had the meaning given by *TCGA 1992, 6 Sch 1* (see 48.3 RETIREMENT RELIEF). '*Trade*', '*profession*' and '*vocation*' generally have the same meanings as in the *Income Tax Acts* but the commercial letting of FURNISHED HOLIDAY ACCOMMODATION (19) in the UK in respect of which the profits, etc. were chargeable under Schedule D, Case VI was treated as a trade for relief purposes in relation to disposals after 5 April 1982. A '*trading company*' was any company which exists wholly or mainly for the purpose of carrying on a trade, and any other company whose income does not consist wholly or mainly of investment income, i.e. income which, if the company were an individual, would not be earned income; and for the purpose of determining whether a company is a trading company, '*trade*' includes the occupation of woodlands managed on a commercial basis by the occupier with a view to profit.[*CGTA 1979, s 126(7)(8); FA 1984, 11 Sch 1; ICTA 1988, 19 Sch 7*].

Reductions in the held-over gain. If the qualifying asset disposed of was not used for the purposes of the trade, profession or vocation concerned throughout the period of its ownership by the transferor, the held-over gain was reduced by multiplying it by the fraction of which the denominator was the total period of ownership and the numerator the number of days in the period during which the asset was so used. (*Note.* In the determination of the period of ownership there was no exclusion of any period before 31 March 1982 in relation to disposals after 5 April 1988, cf. 50.5 ROLLOVER RELIEF.) Where the qualifying asset disposed of was a building or structure part only of which has been used for the trade etc. concerned over all or a 'substantial' part of the period of its ownership, the held-over gain was reduced as was 'just and reasonable'. [*CGTA 1979, 4 Sch 5, 6*].

If the disposal of shares or securities of a company qualified for relief and the company then had 'chargeable assets' which were not 'business assets' the held-over gain was reduced by multiplying it by the fraction of which the denominator was the then market value of the whole of the company's chargeable assets and the numerator was the then market value of the company's business assets. An asset was a '*business asset*' if it was or was an interest in an asset used for the purposes of a trade etc. carried on by the company; and an asset was a '*chargeable asset*' if on its disposal a chargeable gain would accrue. [*CGTA 1979, 4 Sch 7*].

If the asset disposed of was a 'chargeable business asset' for the purposes of retirement relief (see 48.8 RETIREMENT RELIEF) and the held-over gain (as reduced under the above) would exceed the gain otherwise chargeable (ignoring hold-over relief itself but allowing for any deduction of retirement relief), the held-over gain was reduced by the amount of the excess. In the case of a disposal of shares or securities qualifying for retirement relief where the held-over gain (as reduced under the above) would exceed an amount equal to the 'appropriate proportion' of the gain otherwise chargeable (ignoring hold-over relief itself but allowing for any deduction of retirement relief), the held-over gain was reduced by the amount of the excess. [*CGTA 1979, 4 Sch 8*].

Agricultural property. If an asset, or an interest in an asset,

(I)   was 'agricultural property' within the inheritance tax (previously capital transfer tax) provisions of *IHTA 1984, Pt V Ch II* and either qualified for 50% inheritance tax relief in relation to a chargeable transfer made simultaneously with the disposal or would have qualified if there were a chargeable transfer on the disposal; but

(II)   it failed to qualify for hold-over relief solely because the agricultural property was not used for the purposes of a trade etc. carried on as in (*a*) above,

then, notwithstanding (II) above, hold-over relief was granted to the individual transferor. Hold-over relief was also granted *mutatis mutandis* to trustees (see under settled property below) on deemed disposals under *TCGA 1992, s 71(1)* after 5 April 1982 where the agricultural property would not otherwise qualify for relief solely because it was not used for the purposes of a trade etc. carried on as in (*aa*) below. Before 10 March 1981, hold-over relief was not restricted to cases where 50% capital transfer tax relief was given. [*CGTA 1979, 4 Sch 1, 3; FA 1981, s 96(3)(e)(4), 19 Sch Pt VIII; FA 1989, 17 Sch Pt VII*].

Settled property. If a trustee was deemed under *TCGA 1992, s 71(1)* (see 52.9 and 52.11 SETTLEMENTS) after 5 April 1982 to have disposed of, and immediately reacquired (*aa*)   an asset which was, or was an interest in, an asset used for the purposes of a trade carried on by the trustee or by a 'relevant beneficiary', or

(*bb*)   shares or securities of a trading company which conferred on the trustee not less than 25 per cent of the total voting rights then exercisable,

then hold-over relief given by *CGTA 1979, s 126(3)* (see above) applied to the disposal on a claim made by the trustee.

Where hold-over relief was granted to trustees in this way, references to the trustees were substituted for references to the transferor and transferee in *CGTA 1979, s 126(3)* above and no reduction in the held-over gain was made under *CGTA 1979, s 126(6)* above (reduction of excess of actual consideration over allowable expenditure). A '*relevant beneficiary*' was a beneficiary having an interest in possession in the settled property immediately before the deemed disposal. [*CGTA 1979, 4 Sch 2; FA 1982, 22 Sch Pt VI*]. See also under agricultural property above.

Disposals after 5 April 1982 and before 14 March 1989. Hold-over relief as described above under *CGTA 1979, s 126, 4 Sch* did not apply to any disposals or deemed disposals from individuals or trustees to individuals or trustees resident or ordinarily resident in the UK. [*FA 1982, s 82*]. The relief could therefore in practice only cover gifts by individuals to companies.

Disposals after 5 April 1981 and before 6 April 1982. Hold-over relief as described above under *CGTA 1979, s 126, 4 Sch* did not apply to any disposals by individuals to individuals or trustees resident or ordinarily resident in the UK. *CGTA 1979, 4 Sch 2* (see agricultural property and settled property above) additionally applied to deemed disposals under *CGTA 1979, s 55(1)* (as originally enacted) in relation to terminations of life interests in settled property. [*FA 1981, s 78*].

Disposals after 5 April 1980 and before 6 April 1981. Hold-over relief as described above under *CGTA 1979, s 126, 4 Sch* did not apply to any disposals by individuals to individuals resident or ordinarily resident in the UK. *CGTA 1979, 4 Sch 2* additionally applied to deemed disposals under *CGTA 1979, s 55(1)* (as originally enacted). [*FA 1980, s 79*].

22.4   **GIFTS ON WHICH INHERITANCE TAX IS CHARGEABLE ETC. AFTER 13 MARCH 1989**

After 13 March 1989, if

(*a*)   an individual or trustees ('the transferor') make a specified disposal of an asset,

(*b*)   the asset is acquired by an individual or trustees ('the transferee'), and

(*c*)   a claim for relief is made by the transferor and transferee or, where trustees are the transferee, by the transferor alone,

then, subject to the conditions below and in 22.5 below, hold-over relief is available as under *TCGA 1992, s 260(3)* below. [*TCGA 1992, s 260(1)*]. Prior to the commencement of *TCGA 1992*, claims were made under *CGTA 1979, s 147A(1)*.

A disposal is within (*a*) above if it is made otherwise than under a bargain at arm's length (e.g. a gift) and it

(i)   is a chargeable transfer within *IHTA 1984* (or would be but for annual exemptions under *IHTA 1984, s 19*) and is not a potentially exempt transfer within the meaning of *IHTA 1984*, or

(ii)   is an exempt transfer by virtue of *IHTA 1984, ss 24, 26, 27* or *30* (political parties, public benefit (see also 18.25 EXEMPTIONS AND RELIEFS), maintenance funds for

195

historic buildings (see also 18.68 EXEMPTIONS AND RELIEFS) and designated property), or

(iii) is a disposition to which *IHTA 1984, s 57A* applies and by which the property disposed of becomes held on trusts referred to in *IHTA 1984, s 57A(1)(b)* (maintenance funds for historic buildings), or

(iv) by virtue of *IHTA 1984, s 71(4)* (accumulation and maintenance trusts) does not constitute an occasion on which tax is chargeable under that provision, or

(v) by virtue of *IHTA 1984, s 78(1)* (works of art etc., see also 18.31 and 18.70 EXEMPTIONS AND RELIEFS) does not constitute an occasion on which tax is chargeable under *IHTA 1984, Pt III Ch III*, or

(vi) is a disposal of an asset comprised in a settlement where, as a result of the asset or part of it becoming comprised in another settlement, there is no charge, or a reduced charge, to inheritance tax by virtue of *IHTA 1984, 4 Sch 9, 16 or 17* (maintenance funds for historic buildings).

[*TCGA 1992, s 260(2)*].

The '*held-over gain*' on a disposal is the chargeable gain otherwise accruing and relief is given by deducting this amount from the gain otherwise accruing to the transferor and from the consideration otherwise regarded as being given by the transferee. [*TCGA 1992, s 260(3)(4)*].

Hold-over relief is reduced or eliminated to nil on a disposal where there is actual consideration (as opposed to any deemed MARKET VALUE (36) consideration) which exceeds the allowable expenditure under *TCGA 1992, s 38* (see 16.3 DISPOSAL), any such excess being deducted from the held-over gain; but no deduction is made of any such excess where *TCGA 1992, s 260(3)* above applies to a deemed disposal under *TCGA 1992, s 71(1)* or *72(1)* (see 52.9–52.11 SETTLEMENTS). (*Note.* Indexation allowance is deductible in arriving at the gain otherwise chargeable but it is not allowable expenditure within *TCGA 1992, s 38*.) Where part of a gain is relieved by RETIREMENT RELIEF (48), the held-over gain is reduced by so much, if any, of the excess of actual consideration over allowable expenditure as exceeds the part so relieved. [*TCGA 1992, s 260(5)(9)*].

Hold-over relief does not apply to a disposal if it arises by virtue of *TCGA 1992, s 116(10)(b)* (disposal of qualifying corporate bonds derived from shares giving rise to deferred gain, see 44.3 QUALIFYING CORPORATE BONDS). [*TCGA 1992, s 260(6)*].

Hold-over relief does not apply, so far as any gain accruing in accordance with *TCGA 1992, 5B Sch 4, 5* (crystallisation of a deferred gain on the happening of a chargeable event in relation to enterprise investment scheme shares, see 53.17 SHARES AND SECURITIES) is concerned. [*TCGA 1992, s 260(6A); FA 1995, 13 Sch 4(2)*].

Where hold-over relief is claimed on a transfer within (i) above, the transferee may deduct for capital gains tax purposes on a subsequent disposal made by him any inheritance tax attributable to the value of the asset on the transfer to him which qualified for hold-over relief. The tax deductible may be varied if the inheritance tax itself is varied but it cannot in any circumstances give rise to an allowable loss. [*TCGA 1992, s 260(7)(8)*]. See also 30.2 INTERACTION WITH OTHER TAXES.

Where a disposal is only partly within (i)-(v) above, or is a disposal within (vi) above on which there is a reduced charge as mentioned therein, the foregoing provisions apply to an appropriate part of the disposal. [*TCGA 1992, s 260(10)*].

As a claim applies separately to each asset, the comments made about the general relief for gifts from 1980 to 1989 in 22.6 below regarding the treatment of property as separate assets would seem also to apply to the above relief.

22.5   **Restrictions on, and clawback of, hold-over relief under TCGA 1992, s 260.** *Gifts to non-residents.* Relief is denied under *TCGA 1992, s 260* where the transferee is neither UK-resident nor ordinarily resident. Relief is also denied where the transferee is an individual who though UK-resident or ordinarily resident is regarded under a double tax agreement as resident overseas in circumstances where he would not be liable to a UK tax charge on a gain arising on a disposal of an asset immediately after its acquisition. [*TCGA 1992, s 261*].

Gifts into dual resident trusts. TCGA 1992, s 169 (formerly *FA 1986, s 58*) (see 22.2 above) operates *mutatis mutandis* for hold-over relief claimed under *TCGA 1992, s 260* in respect of gifts after 13 March 1989 as it does for hold-over relief under *TCGA 1992, s 165* in respect of gifts made after that date. [*TCGA 1992, s 169*].

Emigration of transferee. TCGA 1992, s 168 (formerly *FA 1981, s 79*) (see 22.2 above) operates *mutatis mutandis* for hold-over relief claimed under *TCGA 1992, s 260* in respect of gifts after 13 March 1989 as it does for hold-over relief under *TCGA 1992, s 165* in respect of gifts made after that date. [*TCGA 1992, s 168*].

Clawback of relief on life tenant's death. TCGA 1992, s 74 (see 22.2 above) operates *mutatis mutandis* for hold-over relief claimed under *TCGA 1992, s 260* in respect of gifts after 13 March 1989 as it does for hold-over relief under *TCGA 1992, s 165* in respect of gifts made after that date. [*TCGA 1992, s 74*].

22.6   **GENERAL RELIEF FOR GIFTS FROM 1980 TO 1989**

A general relief for gifts applied after 5 April 1980 and before 14 March 1989.

After 5 April 1982 and before 14 March 1989, relief could be claimed where the transferor, who could be either

(*a*)   an individual; or

(*b*)   the trustees of a settlement

disposed of an asset otherwise than at arm's length to

(i)   an individual resident or ordinarily resident in the UK; or

(ii)   trustees resident or ordinarily resident in the UK (but see under gifts into dual resident trusts).

The effect of a claim was that the gain otherwise chargeable (less any RETIREMENT RELIEF (48)), and the transferee's acquisition cost, were each reduced by the *'held-over gain'* i.e. the gain otherwise chargeable (less any retirement relief) less any excess of actual consideration over the aggregate of allowable expenditure within *TCGA 1992, s 38* and any retirement relief.

Whilst indexation allowance was deductible in arriving at the gain otherwise chargeable, it was not allowable expenditure within *TCGA 1992, s 38* (see 16.3 DISPOSAL). Ignoring cases involving retirement relief this meant that where there was no consideration or where the consideration was not greater than the allowable expenditure, the whole of the gain otherwise chargeable could be held over. In other cases not involving retirement relief a gain was left in charge equal to the lower of the excess of consideration over the allowable expenditure and the gain otherwise chargeable.

A claim had to be made jointly by the transferor and transferee unless the transfer was to trustees when only the transferor needed to claim.

In computing any chargeable gain accruing on the subsequent disposal of the asset, the transferee may deduct any inheritance tax (or capital transfer tax) attributable to the value of the asset on the original transfer, being either a chargeable transfer or a potentially exempt transfer which proves to be a chargeable transfer. The tax deductible may be varied on the subsequent death of the original transferor or otherwise but cannot create an allowable loss on the subsequent disposal. See also 30.2 INTERACTION WITH OTHER TAXES.

Gifts into dual resident trusts. TCGA 1992, s 169 (formerly *FA 1986, s 58*; see 22.2 above and note certain changes for trustees becoming dual resident after 18 March 1991) operated (and continues to operate after 13 March 1989) *mutatis mutandis* for hold-over relief claimed under the above provisions in respect of gifts made after 17 March 1986 and before 14 March 1989 as it does to hold-over relief under *TCGA 1992, s 165* in respect of gifts made after 13 March 1989. However, the clawback of relief when trustees became dual resident after 17 March 1986 and before 18 March 1991 operated in respect of gifts made before, on or after 18 March 1986.

Emigration of transferee. TCGA 1992, s 168 (see 22.2 above and note certain changes for trustees emigrating after 18 March 1991) operated (and continues to operate after 13 March 1989) *mutatis mutandis* for hold-over relief claimed under the above provisions in respect of gifts made after 5 April 1981 and before 14 March 1989 as it does to hold-over relief under *TCGA 1992, s 165* in respect of gifts made after 13 March 1989.

Clawback of relief on life tenant's death. TCGA 1992, s 74 (see 22.2 above) operated (and continues to operate after 13 March 1989) *mutatis mutandis* for hold-over relief claimed under the above provisions in respect of interests terminating after 5 April 1982 and where the original gift to the trustees was after 5 April 1981 and before 14 March 1989 as it does to hold-over relief under *TCGA 1992, s 165* in respect of gifts made after 13 March 1989. See 8.12 ASSETS HELD ON 31 MARCH 1982 for the treatment by the Revenue of the clawback in relevant cases occurring after 5 April 1988.

After 5 April 1981 and before 6 April 1982, (*b*) above did not apply.

Before 6 April 1981, neither (*b*) nor (ii) above applied.

[*TCGA 1992, ss 67, 74, 168, 169; CGTA 1979, s 56A; FA 1980, s 79; FA 1981, ss 78, 79; FA 1982, ss 82, 84(3); FA 1986, ss 58, 101(2); FA 1989, 124(1)(3), 17 Sch Pt VII; FA 1991, s 92(2)(4)(6)(7)*].

Where the property transferred consisted in law of two or more separate assets, the claim applied separately to each asset, and so some gains could be left in charge to be covered by annual exemptions or losses etc. Similarly, where freehold land was transferred to two or more joint tenants or tenants in common, a claim could be made individually in relation to the interest transferred to each recipient (Tolley's Practical Tax 1983 p 178, 1984 p 2 and 1985 p 195).

22.7   TRANSFER OF BUSINESS TO A COMPANY

Where a person who is not a company transfers to a company a business as a going concern, together with the whole assets of the business (or together with the whole of such assets other than cash) ('the old assets') and the transfer is made wholly or partly in exchange for shares issued by the company to the transferor ('the new assets'), the chargeable gain on the disposal of the old assets (or part thereof) is deferred by reducing the amount otherwise chargeable, by the fraction A/B, where 'A' is the 'cost of the new assets' and 'B' the value of the overall consideration received by the transferor in exchange for the business.

'The cost of the new assets' means the total allowable expenditure under *TCGA 1992, s 38(1)(a)* if the new assets were disposed of as a whole in circumstances giving rise to a chargeable gain. (See 16.3 DISPOSAL.) The total expenditure otherwise allowable on the new assets is reduced by the amount of the chargeable gain deferred, and if the new assets comprise different classes of share, the reduction is apportioned by reference to the market value of each class of share at the time of their acquisition by the transferor.

Deferment on part of the gain on the old assets therefore remains until the new assets are disposed of. [*TCGA 1992, s 162*].

The only point of time at which the test should be made as to whether a business is being transferred 'as a going concern' is at the time of transfer, so that if the business continues without interruption past that time relief will be available notwithstanding the existence of a planned move of the entire assets of the business from one place to another (*Gordon v CIR (and cross-appeal) CS, [1991] STC 174*).

The Revenue are prepared not to treat the assumption of liabilities by the transferee company as consideration for the transfer, and the relief is not precluded if some or all of the liabilities of the business are not taken over by the company (Revenue Pamphlet IR 1, D32; previously 29 D22 INLAND REVENUE STATEMENTS OF PRACTICE). However, it seems that the Revenue treat the assumption of provisions for partnership income tax liabilities as denying relief. (Tolley's Practical Tax 1984 p 26). If some of the assets are retained by the original owner, relief under *TCGA 1992, s 162* above is not available and liability to capital gains tax arises by reference to the market value of any chargeable assets transferred, e.g. goodwill. If the market value of such an asset exceeds the consideration given by the company, the Revenue will accept that the excess represents a gift and that the capital gain may be deferred by means of a joint election under *TCGA 1992, s 165* (see 22.1–22.3 above). (Tolley's Practical Tax 1983 pp 24, 188). Where a partner is a company, *TCGA 1992, s 162* strictly cannot apply because individual partners are not transferring the whole business but only their collective shares. However, the Revenue will view each partner separately thus enabling individual, but not company, partners to obtain relief. In addition, relief will be granted to individual partners taking shares even though others take purely cash. In all cases the whole of the business must be exchanged wholly or partly for shares. (Tolley's Practical Tax 1986 p 23).

Although the above relief is mandatory, the Revenue is prepared to allow rollover relief as an alternative if appropriate. See 50.1 ROLLOVER RELIEF. However, it is not clear whether the Revenue will allow the above relief *not* to apply in the absence of a rollover relief claim (e.g. so as to utilise allowable losses, annual exempt amount etc.).

Example

W carries on an antiquarian bookselling business. He decides to form an unquoted company, P Ltd, to carry on the business. He then transfers, in August 1995, the whole of the business undertaking, assets and liabilities to P Ltd, in consideration for the issue of shares, plus an amount left outstanding on interest-free loan. The business assets and liabilities transferred are valued as follows

	Value		Chargeable gain (after indexation)
	£	£	£
Freehold shop premises		80,000	52,000
Goodwill		36,000	26,000
Fixtures and fittings		4,000	—
Trading stock		52,000	—
Debtors		28,000	—
		200,000	
Mortgage on shop	50,000		
Trade creditors	20,000	70,000	—
		£130,000	£78,000

199

22.7 Hold-Over Reliefs

The company issues 100,000 £1 ordinary shares, valued at par, to W in August 1995, and the amount left outstanding is £30,000. In December 1996, W sells 20,000 of his shares for £45,000 to X. W's remaining shareholding is then worth £155,000. The indexation factor from August 1995 to December 1996 is assumed to be 0.038.

(i) Amount of chargeable gain rolled over on transfer of the business

$$\frac{100,000}{130,000} \times £78,000 \qquad\qquad £60,000$$

Of the chargeable gain, £18,000 (£78,000 − £60,000) remains taxable.

The allowable cost of W's shares is £40,000 (£100,000 − £60,000).

(ii) On the sale of shares to X, W realises a chargeable gain

	£	£
Disposal consideration		45,000
Allowable cost £40,000 × $\dfrac{45,000}{45,000 + 155,000}$		9,000
Unindexed gain		36,000
Indexation allowance £9,000 × 0.038		342
Chargeable gain		£35,658

23   Indexation

Cross-references. See 7 ASSETS HELD ON 6 APRIL 1965; 8 ASSETS HELD ON 31 MARCH 1982; 16 DISPOSAL; 33.16 LAND for concessionary treatment of indexation allowance on the merger of leases; 56 UNDERWRITERS; 57.1 and 57.2 UNIT AND INVESTMENT TRUSTS for Revenue practice in the case of unit trust units and investment trust shares acquired under monthly savings schemes.

23.1   INDEXATION ALLOWANCE

General. In respect of disposals after 5 April 1982 (31 March 1982 for companies) an indexation allowance is deductible under certain circumstances from the 'unindexed' or 'gross' gain, or is added, for disposals on or after the '1985 date' and before 30 November 1993, to the 'unindexed' loss.

Special provisions apply to the calculation of the allowance in relation to disposals involving ASSETS HELD ON 31 MARCH 1982 (8) where made on or after the '1985 date' or, again, on or after 6 April 1988. See that chapter for details.

Disposal on or after 30 November 1993. For disposals on or after 30 November 1993 the gain (if any) arrived at by deducting an amount of allowable expenditure from the amount of consideration realised (see 16 DISPOSAL), or deemed to be realised, on the disposal is termed an '*unindexed gain*'. There is to be allowed against the unindexed gain an 'indexation allowance', which is the aggregate of the 'indexed rise' in each item of 'relevant allowable expenditure', so as to give the gain for the purposes of *TCGA 1992*.

An indexation allowance is only allowed against an unindexed gain. If the disposal gives rise to a loss, no indexation allowance is allowed notwithstanding anything in *TCGA 1992, s 16* (computation of losses; see 35.2 LOSSES), and if the indexation allowance equals or exceeds the unindexed gain on a disposal so as to extinguish it, the disposal is one on which, after taking account of the indexation allowance, neither a gain nor a loss accrues.

The rules outlined above are subject to the special provisions in 23.3–23.8 below. In addition, a transitional relief applies as in 23.2 below for 1993/94 and 1994/95 in respect of 'indexation losses' in the case of individuals and trustees of settlements made before 30 November 1993.

'*Relevant allowable expenditure*' is allowable expenditure within *TCGA 1992, s 38(1)(a)* and *38(1)(b)*, i.e. basically acquisition cost or value, taken for these purposes as incurred when the asset is acquired or provided, and expenditure on enhancement and on establishing, preserving and defending title and rights to the asset, such expenditure being taken for these purposes as incurred when it becomes due and payable (see 16.3(*a*)-(*c*) DISPOSAL). Disposal costs are excluded. In determining relevant allowable expenditure, account is taken of any provision of any enactment which, for the purpose of computing gains, increases, excludes or reduces any item of expenditure, or provides for it to be written down.

The '*indexed rise*' in each item of relevant allowable expenditure is computed by multiplying that item by a figure (rounded to the nearest third decimal place) calculated by the formula

$$\frac{RD - RI}{RI}, \text{ where}$$

RD =   retail prices index for the month in which the disposal occurs; and

RI =   retail prices index for March 1982 or the month in which the expenditure was incurred, whichever is the later.

23.1 Indexation

If, in relation to any item of expenditure, RD in the formula is equal to, or less than, RI, there is no indexed rise for that item. [*TCGA 1992, ss 53, 54, 288(1); ICTA 1988, s 833(2); FA 1994, s 93(1)–(3)(11)*].

The figure given by the formula is commonly called the '*indexation factor*'. The consistent calculation of the indexation factor to more than three decimal places is generally accepted.

The Revenue publishes the retail prices index and the associated indexation factors in a monthly press release. Yearly tables of indexation factors are contained in Tolley's Tax Data and Tolley's Official Tax Statements.

Values of the retail prices index for March 1982 and subsequent months are as follows.

	1982	1983	1984	1985	1986	1987	1988	1989	1990	1991
January	—	82.61	86.84	91.20	96.25	100.0	103.3	111.0	119.5	130.2
February	—	82.97	87.20	91.94	96.60	100.4	103.7	111.8	120.2	130.9
March	79.44	83.12	87.48	92.80	96.73	100.6	104.1	112.3	121.4	131.4
April	81.04	84.28	88.64	94.78	97.67	101.8	105.8	114.3	125.1	133.1
May	81.62	84.64	88.97	95.21	97.85	101.9	106.2	115.0	126.2	133.5
June	81.85	84.84	89.20	95.41	97.79	101.9	106.6	115.4	126.7	134.1
July	81.88	85.30	89.10	95.23	97.52	101.8	106.7	115.5	126.8	133.8
August	81.90	85.68	89.94	95.49	97.82	102.1	107.9	115.8	128.1	134.1
September	81.85	86.06	90.11	95.44	98.30	102.4	108.4	116.6	129.3	134.6
October	82.26	86.36	90.67	95.59	98.45	102.9	109.5	117.5	130.3	135.1
November	82.66	86.67	90.95	95.92	99.29	103.4	110.0	118.5	130.0	135.6
December	82.51	86.89	90.87	96.05	99.62	103.3	110.3	118.8	129.9	135.7

	1992	1993	1994	1995
January	135.6	137.9	141.3	146.0
February	136.3	138.8	142.1	146.9
March	136.7	139.3	142.5	147.5
April	138.8	140.6	144.2	149.0
May	139.3	141.1	144.7	149.6
June	139.3	141.0	144.7	
July	138.8	140.7	144.0	
August	138.9	141.3	144.7	
September	139.4	141.9	145.0	
October	139.9	141.8	145.2	
November	139.7	141.6	145.3	
December	139.2	141.9	146.0	

Re-referencing of retail prices index. The index is calculated by the Central Statistical Office and was re-referenced so as to make January 1987 = 100.0 and equivalent to 394.5 on the former index where January 1974 = 100.0. In the above table, all the index figures for months before January 1987 have been re-indexed to the January 1987 base. This has been done by dividing the index on the January 1974 base for such a month by 3.945 (i.e. 394.5 divided by 100.0) and rounding to two places of decimals (e.g. the index for December 1985 is 393.0 on the January 1974 base, which would have been the figure announced at the time, and is 96.05 on the January 1987 base). By so rounding the re-indexed figures, the same level of accuracy (to 1 in 10,000) is maintained compared with the figures quoted for months after December 1986.

(*Note*. The examples below take no account of transitional relief for 'indexation losses' which may be due for 1993/94 and 1994/95 as in 23.2 below.)

Examples

(1)   X acquired an asset in November 1983 for £30,000. He disposes of the asset on 11 January 1995 for £99,000. The retail prices index for November 1983 is 86.67 and for January 1995 it is 146.0.

	£
Sale consideration	99,000
Cost of asset	30,000
Unindexed gain	69,000
Indexation allowance	

$$\frac{146.0 - 86.67}{86.67} = 0.685$$

	£
0.685 × £30,000	20,550
Chargeable gain	£48,450

(2)   Facts as in (1) above except that X receives consideration of £18,000.

	£
Sale consideration	18,000
Cost of asset	30,000
Allowable loss (no indexation allowance available)	£20,400

(3)   Facts as in (1) above except that X received consideration of £50,000.

	£
Sale consideration	50,000
Cost of asset	30,000
Unindexed gain	£20,000

Indexation allowance is as in (1) above (£20,550) but as this exceeds the amount of the unindexed gain, the disposal gives rise neither to a gain nor to a loss.

Disposal on or after the '1985' date and before 30 November 1993. Subject to below, for disposals on or after 6 April 1985 or, for companies, 1 April 1985 (the '1985 date') and before 30 November 1993, the gain or loss arrived at by deducting allowable expenditure from the amount realised, or deemed to be realised, on the disposal was termed the '*unindexed gain or loss*'. There was to be deducted from the unindexed gain or, as the case may have been, added to the unindexed loss, an 'indexation allowance' which was the aggregate of the indexed rise in each item of 'relevant allowable expenditure'.

The indexation allowance was set against the unindexed gain or, as the case may have been, added to the unindexed loss. If the allowance exceeded any unindexed gain, the excess constituted an allowable loss. Where there was no unindexed gain or loss, there was an allowable loss equal to the indexation allowance. [*TCGA 1992, ss 53, 54, 288(1); ICTA 1988, s 833(2)*].

See above for 'relevant allowable expenditure', 'indexed rise', 'indexation factor' and values of the retail prices index for March 1982 and subsequent months.

The rules outlined above are subject to the special provisions in 23.3 – 23.8 below. In addition, a transitional relief applies as in 23.2 below for 1993/94 and 1994/95 in respect of 'indexation losses' in the case of individuals and trustees of settlements made before 30 November 1993.

For disposals after 3 July 1987 and before 30 November 1993, the allowance was not available in respect of disposals of shares in a building society (within *Building Societies Act 1986*) or shares in a registered industrial and provident society (as defined by *ICTA 1988, s 486*). [*TCGA 1992, ss 111, 288(1); FA 1994, s 93(7)(11), 26 Sch Pt V*].

For disposals by companies after 14 March 1988 and before 30 November 1993, the allowance was restricted or excluded in certain cases involving a debt on a security owed by, or shares in, a 'linked company'. [*TCGA 1992, ss 182–184; F(No 2)A 1992, s 46(1)(7); FA 1994, s 93(7)(11), 26 Sch Pt V*]. Full details are given in Tolley's Corporation Tax under Capital Gains.

For disposals after 19 March 1990 and before 30 November 1993, the allowance was not available in respect of disposals of rights in property to which '*collective investment arrangements*' (i.e. arrangements constituting a 'collective investment scheme' within *Financial Services Act 1986*) related where at some time in the 'relevant ownership period' at least 90 per cent of the then market value of all of the property (except cash awaiting investment) then within the arrangements was represented by assets (including currency and debts other than securities disposed of as in *FA 1993, 17 Sch 2* and *4*) gains on the disposal of which at the time the rights were disposed of by a UK resident person would not be chargeable gains, shares in a building society (within *Building Societies Act 1986*), or both such assets and such shares. If under the arrangements the participants' contributions, and the profits etc. out of which payments were to be made to the participants, were pooled in relation to separate parts of the property, and the disposal was of rights in property falling within a separate part, this 90 per cent test applied only to that part. The '*relevant ownership period*' was the period beginning on 1 April 1982 or, if later, the earliest date on which any 'relevant consideration' was given for the rights, and ending on the date of the disposal. '*Relevant consideration*' was consideration which would be taken into account as allowable expenditure on the disposal, including consideration given by or on behalf of a predecessor in title whose acquisition cost represented (directly or indirectly) the whole or any part of the acquisition cost of the disposer. [*TCGA 1992, s 103; FA 1993, s 169, 17 Sch 8; FA 1994, s 93(7)(11), 26 Sch Pt V*].

In respect of disposals on or after the '1985 date' (see above) and before 2 July 1986, there was no indexation allowance in respect of a disposal of 21 GOVERNMENT SECURITIES or 44 QUALIFYING CORPORATE BONDS. Disposals after 27 February 1986 and before 30 November 1993 of securities within the accrued income scheme (see 23.12 below) had indexation allowance calculated and allowed as above for assets generally but, for disposals on or after the '1985 date' and before 27 February 1986, the indexation provisions which applied generally for disposal on or after the '1982' date and before the '1985 date' (see below) applied. [*FA 1985, s 68(2)*].

Disposals on or after the '1982 date' and before the '1985 date'. For disposals on or after 6 April 1982 or, for companies, 1 April 1982 (the '1982 date') and before the '1985 date' (see above), the gain (if any) arrived at by deducting allowable expenditure from the amount realised, or deemed to be realised, on the disposal was termed a '*gross gain*'.

There was to be deducted from it an 'indexation allowance' which was the aggregate of the 'indexed rise' in each item of 'relevant expenditure', provided the asset had been held for the 'qualifying period'.

The *'qualifying period'* was twelve months, beginning on the date on which the asset in question was acquired or provided.

See above for *'relevant allowable expenditure'*.

The *'indexed rise'* in each item of relevant allowable expenditure was computed by multiplying that item by a figure (rounded to the nearest third decimal place) calculated by the formula

$$\frac{RD - RI}{RI}, \text{ where}$$

RD =   retail prices index for the month in which the disposal occurred; and

RI =   retail prices index for the later of March 1982 or for the twelfth month after the expenditure was incurred.

If, in relation to any particular expenditure item, the month in which that item was incurred was less than thirteen months before the month of disposal, or RD in the above formula was equal to, or less than, RI, there was no indexed rise for that item.

An indexation allowance was only given where there was a gross gain (see above). Where there was a loss, there was no indexation allowance and no allowable loss could be created by such an allowance. Where the allowance exceeded the gross gain, there was to be neither a chargeable gain nor an allowable loss. [*FA 1982, ss 86, 87*].

See above for 'indexation factor' and values of the retail prices index for March 1982 and subsequent months.

The rules outlined above are subject to the special provisions in 23.3 – 23.8 below.

23.2   **Indexation losses: transitional relief in respect of 1993/94 and 1994/95 for individuals and trustees of settlements made before 30 November 1993.** (1) *Introduction.* Consequent to, inter alia, the provisions in 23.1 above which, broadly, for disposals after 29 November 1993 deny the giving of indexation allowance where it would otherwise create or increase a loss, a transitional form of relief applies to mitigate this denial for 1993/94 and 1994/95 in relation to chargeable gains and allowable losses accruing to an individual or trustees of a settlement made before 30 November 1993 (*'the taxpayer'*). Companies and personal representatives are excluded from the relief. [*FA 1994, s 93(11), 12 Sch 1*].

(2) *Determinations of indexation losses under old indexation rules.* If

(a)   an allowable loss accrues on a disposal made after 29 November 1993 and, under 'the old indexation rules', a greater allowable loss would have accrued, there is an *'indexation loss'* in respect of the disposal equal to the amount by which the allowable loss which would have accrued under the old indexation rules exceeds the allowable loss accruing on the disposal; or

(b)   a disposal made after 29 November 1993 is one on which neither a gain nor a loss accrues and, under the old indexation rules, an allowable loss would have accrued, there is an indexation loss in respect of the disposal equal to the amount of the allowable loss that would have accrued under the old indexation rules.

23.2 Indexation

If the total amount of chargeable gains accruing to the taxpayer in either 1993/94 or 1994/95 exceeds the allowable losses accruing in that year, there is a *'relevant gain'* for that year equal to the excess.

The foregoing determinations of any amount of indexation loss and relevant gain are made without regard to *FA 1994, 12 Sch 4–7* below. [*FA 1994, 12 Sch 2*].

'The old indexation rules' means *TCGA 1992* as it would have effect if *FA 1994, s 93(1)–(5)* (see 23.1 above for *subsections (1)–(3)*, 8.7 ASSETS HELD ON 31 MARCH 1982 for *subsection (4)* and 23.4 below for *subsection (5)*) and the repeal of *TCGA 1992, ss 103* and *111* by *FA 1994, s 93(7)* (see 23.1 above; collective investment schemes and building society shares) had not come into force. [*FA 1994, 12 Sch 8(1)(2)*]. In broad terms, the old indexation rules therefore means the provisions of *TCGA 1992* pertaining for disposals immediately before 30 November 1993 (when indexation allowance could increase or create a loss).

(3) *Appropriation of capital asset to trading stock and capital loss on disposal of shares treated as deduction from income.* The cases in which the appropriation of an asset by the taxpayer is treated under *TCGA 1992, s 161(1)* (appropriation of capital asset to trading stock; see 6.3 ASSETS) as a disposal of the asset include cases in which, if he sold the asset for its market value, an allowable loss would have accrued to him under the old indexation rules. Where, but for an election under *TCGA 1992, s 161(3)* (gain or loss treated as arising under *TCGA 1992, s 161(1)* taken into account for Schedule D, Case I rather than capital gains tax; see 6.3 ASSETS), an asset appropriated (an event called a *'relevant appropriation'*) by the taxpayer would have been treated as disposed of under *TCGA 1992, s 161(1)* and (2)(*a*) or (*b*) above would have applied on the disposal, *FA 1994, 12 Sch 1* and *2* (above) and *FA 1994, 12 Sch 6* and *7* (see below) apply as if the asset had been so treated, to determine for the purposes of *TCGA 1992, s 161(3)* any increase (references to an increase in any loss, where (2)(*b*) above applies, include a reference to the creation of the loss for the purposes of this provision (*FA 1994, 12 Sch 3*) and *FA 1994, 12 Sch 6* and *7* below) to be made in the amount of any allowable loss.

ICTA 1988, ss 574–576 (loss incurred by individual on shares subscribed for in unquoted trading companies treated as income deduction; see 35.12 LOSSES) apply if an individual who has subscribed for shares as mentioned in *ICTA 1988, s 574(1)* disposes of them in circumstances where (2)(*b*) above applies as they apply in other cases. Where an individual makes a claim for relief under *ICTA 1988, s 574(1)* in the case of a disposal in respect of which there is an indexation loss (a *'section 574 disposal'*), *FA 1994, 12 Sch 6* and *7* below apply to determine any increase to be made, for the purposes of that provision, in the amount of the allowable loss, and *FA 1994, 12 Sch 4* and *5* below apply to so much only of the indexation loss as is not relieved under *ICTA 1988, s 574*. [*FA 1994, 12 Sch 3*].

(4) *Relief against chargeable gains for 1993/94.* Where in the case of any taxpayer,

(*a*)   there is a relevant gain (see (2) above) for 1993/94,

(*b*)   the relevant gain exceeds the exempt amount for that year (i.e. £5,800 for individuals and settlements for the disabled and £2,900 for other settlements, subject to reduction for 'grouping' of both kinds of settlement as in 52.4 and 52.5 SETTLEMENTS), and

(*c*)   there are indexation losses (see (2) above) in respect of any disposals made in that year (which, by definition, would have to be disposals made after 29 November 1993),

then, for the purposes of *TCGA 1992*, the amount by which the total amount of chargeable gains accruing to the taxpayer in that year exceeds the allowable losses accruing in that year (i.e. such excess being the amount of the relevant gain although not so stated in the legislation) is reduced (including reducing an amount to nil) by the amount mentioned below, and is so reduced before the deduction of any allowable losses carried forward from any previous year or carried back under *TCGA 1992, s 62* (losses of year of death carried back against gains of previous three years; see 15.5 DEATH) from any subsequent year. [*FA 1994, 12 Sch 4(1), 8(3)*].

The amount of the reduction referred to above is so much of the total of indexation losses in respect of disposals made in 1993/94 as does not exceed £10,000 or the amount by which the relevant gain exceeds the exempt amount, whichever is the smaller. [*FA 1994, 12 Sch 4(2)*].

(5) *Relief against chargeable gains for 1994/95.* Where in the case of any taxpayer,

(*a*)   there is a relevant gain for 1994/95,

(*b*)   the relevant gain exceeds the exempt amount for that year (i.e. the same amounts mentioned in (4)(*b*) above for 1993/94 but subject to the same conditions as regards 'grouping' of settlements), and

(*c*)   there are indexation losses in respect of any disposals made in 1994/95 or 'unused indexation losses' for 1993/94,

then, for the purposes of *TCGA 1992*, the amount by which the total amount of chargeable gains accruing to the taxpayer in 1994/95 exceeds the allowable losses accruing in that year is reduced by the amount mentioned below, and is so reduced before the deduction of any allowable losses carried forward from any previous year or carried back under *TCGA 1992, s 62* from any subsequent year. [*FA 1994, 12 Sch 5(1)*].

The amount of the reduction referred to above is so much of the total of indexation losses in respect of disposals made in 1994/95, plus any unused indexation losses for 1993/94, as does not exceed

(A)   £10,000 less the aggregate of

(i)   the amount of any reduction made under *FA 1994, 12 Sch 4(1)* above for 1993/94, and

(ii)   any increase made under *FA 1994, 12 Sch 6(2)* below for 1993/94,

or

(B)   the amount by which the relevant gain exceeds the exempt amount for 1994/95,

whichever is the smaller. [*FA 1994, 12 Sch 5(2)*].

For the purposes of *FA 1994, 12 Sch 5(1)* and *(2)* above, if the total amount of indexation losses in respect of disposals made by the taxpayer in 1993/94 exceeds the aggregate of the amount of any reduction made under *FA 1994, 12 Sch 4(1)* for that year and any increase made under *FA 1994, 12 Sch 6(2)* for that year, there are *'unused indexation losses'* for that year of an amount equal to the excess. [*FA 1994, 12 Sch 5(3)*].

(6) *Relief against chargeable gains and income for 1993/94 where there is an appropriation of a capital asset to trading stock or a capital loss on a disposal of shares is treated as a deduction from income.* The following provisions apply where, at any time in the period beginning with 30 November 1993 and ending with 5 April 1994, the taxpayer makes any relevant appropriation or any *section 574* disposal, and for the purposes of those provisions the following amounts must be determined:

(*a*)   the amount of any reduction for the year 1993/94 which (disregarding relevant appropriations and *section 574* disposals) would be made under *FA 1994, 12 Sch 4(1)* above, and

(b)   the amounts of any indexation losses in respect of relevant appropriations or *section 574* disposals made in that period.

[*FA 1994, 12 Sch 6(1)*].

If the aggregate of the amounts in (a) and (b) above does not exceed £10,000, the amount of any allowable loss referable to such an appropriation or disposal is increased by any indexation loss in respect of it. [*FA 1994, 12 Sch 6(2)*].

In any other case, notwithstanding anything in *FA 1994, 12 Sch 4* and *5* above,

(A)   the aggregate of

   (i)   the amount of any reduction for the year 1993/94 to be made under *FA 1994, 12 Sch 4(1)* above, and

   (ii)   the amount of any indexation losses in respect of relevant appropriations or *section 574* disposals made in the period beginning with 30 November 1993 and ending with 5 April 1994,

   is deemed to be equal to £10,000 and is allocated as the taxpayer determines between that reduction and increases in allowable losses referable to such appropriations or disposals, and

(B)   no reduction is made for the year 1994/95 under *FA 1994, 12 Sch 5* (above) or *7* (below).

[*FA 1994, 12 Sch 6(3)*].

(7) *Relief against income and chargeable gains for 1994/95 where there is an appropriation of a capital asset to trading stock or a capital loss on a disposal of shares is treated as a deduction from income.* The following provisions apply where, at any time in 1994/95, the taxpayer makes any relevant appropriation or any *section 574* disposal, and for the purposes of those provisions the following amounts must be determined:

(a)   the amount of any reduction for the year 1994/95 which (disregarding relevant appropriations and *section 574* disposals) would be made under *FA 1994, 12 Sch 5(1)* above, and

(b)   the amounts of any indexation losses in respect of relevant appropriations or *section 574* disposals made in that year.

[*FA 1994, 12 Sch 7(1)*].

If the aggregate of the amounts in (a) and (b) above does not exceed the limit for 1994/95 (that limit being £10,000 less the aggregate of the amount of any reduction made under *FA 1994, 12 Sch 4(1)* above for the year 1993/94 and of any increases made under *FA 1994, 12 Sch 6(2)* above for that year), the amount of any allowable loss referable to such an appropriation or disposal is increased by any indexation loss in respect of it. [*FA 1994, 12 Sch 7(2)*].

In any other case, notwithstanding anything in *FA 1994, 12 Sch 5* above, the aggregate of any reduction for the year 1994/95 to be made under *FA 1994, 12 Sch 5(1)* above and of the amount of any indexation losses in respect of relevant appropriations or *section 574* disposals made in that year is deemed to be equal to the limit for 1994/95 and is allocated as the taxpayer determines between that reduction and increases in allowable losses referable to such appropriations or disposals. [*FA 1994, 12 Sch 7(3)*].

Example

At the beginning of 1993/94 individual G had allowable losses of £1,000 available to carry forward against general chargeable gains. In May 1993, he disposes of Asset 1 which gives rise to a chargeable gain of £9,000. In January 1994 he disposes of Asset 2 for a consideration of £26,000 which he had originally acquired in September 1985 for a consideration of £20,932. The retail prices index is 95.44 for September 1985 and 141.3 for January 1994. The computation of the gain or loss arising on the disposal of Asset 2 proceeds as follows.

	£
Disposal proceeds of Asset 2	26,000
Acquisition consideration of Asset 2	20,932
Unindexed gain arising on disposal	£5,068

Indexation allowance otherwise available:

$$\frac{141.3 - 95.44}{95.44} = 0.481$$

$0.481 \times £20,932$	£10,068

An indexation allowance of £10,068 would extinguish the unindexed gain of £5,068, so the disposal is treated as giving rise to neither a gain nor a loss. However, the indexation loss is £5,000 in respect of the January 1994 disposal because, under the old indexation rules, G would have had an allowable loss of that amount (i.e. £10,068 – £5,068).

If the May 1993 and January 1994 disposals are the only ones occurring in 1993/94, the relevant gain (because there are no allowable losses arising in that year) is £9,000. This is greater than the annual exempt amount of £5,800 by £3,200. The amount of £3,200 is less than £10,000 so, as the indexation losses for 1993/94 amount to £5,000, £3,200 is deducted from the net chargeable gains (ignoring, at this stage, the brought forward allowable losses of £1,000) of 1993/94 (£9,000) to give net chargeable gains for that year of £5,800, such net gains being exempt by virtue of the exempt amount of the year. There are unused indexation losses of £1,800 (£5,000 – £3,200) available for utilisation in 1994/95 only and unused allowable losses of £1,000 available for utilisation generally.

Suppose, for 1994/95, G has chargeable gains less allowable losses (ignoring, at this stage, the brought forward allowable losses of £1,000) of £20,000 (i.e. the relevant gain) and indexation losses of £7,600. As the relevant gain exceeds the exempt amount for the year of £5,800, the excess being £14,200, relief is available as follows.

	£
Indexation losses of 1994/95	7,600
Unused indexation losses of 1993/94	1,800
Aggregate of available indexation losses	£9,400

However, this aggregate is limited to the lower of:

£10,000 – £3,200 = £6,800
£20,000 – £5,800 = £14,200

	£
Net chargeable gains of 1994/95 before reduction	20,000
Restricted reduction for indexation losses	6,800
	13,200
Allowable losses brought forward	1,000
	12,200
Exempt amount for the year	5,800
Net chargeable gains for 1994/95	£6,400

23.3 Indexation

Indexation losses of £2,600 (£9,400 – £6,800) remaining unutilised in 1994/95 cannot be carried forward.

The example illustrates that all three conditions mentioned above, at (4)(*a*)–(*c*) for 1993/94 and (5)(*a*)–(*b*) for 1994/95, have to be fulfilled before relief is available for the year concerned.

23.3 **Part disposals.** Apportionment of relevant allowable expenditure is to take place before computing the indexation allowance. The allowance is then only calculated for relevant allowable expenditure attributable to the part disposed of. [*TCGA 1992, s 56(1); FA 1994, 26 Sch Pt V*].

Example

X sells part of a plot of land on 18 January 1995 for £100,000. The market value on the date of sale of the part of the plot is £30,000. The cost, in September 1982, of the whole plot was £25,000. The retail prices index at September 1982 is 81.85 and for January 1995 it is 146.0.

	£
Allowable expenditure attributable to the part disposed of	
$\dfrac{100,000}{(100,000 + 30,000)} \times £25,000$	£19,231
Unindexed gain: £100,000 – £19,231	80,769
Indexation allowance	
$\dfrac{146.0 - 81.85}{81.85} = 0.784$	
0.784 × £19,231	15,077
Chargeable gain	£65,692

No indexation allowance is calculated at this stage on the balance of expenditure to be carried forward of £5,769 (£25,000 – £19,231).

23.4 **Disposals on a no gain/no loss basis.** *Disposals on or after 30 November 1993.* On a 'no gain/no loss disposal' on or after 30 November 1993, both the disposal consideration of the transferor and the corresponding acquisition consideration of the transferee are calculated for the purposes of *TCGA 1992* on the assumption that, on the disposal, an unindexed gain accrues to the transferor which is equal to the indexation allowance on that disposal, and so that after taking account of the indexation allowance the disposal is one on which neither a gain nor a loss accrues.

For the purposes of calculating indexation allowance under *TCGA 1992, ss 53, 54* (see 23.1 above), any enactment is disregarded to the extent to which it provides that, on a subsequent disposal of an asset by the transferee which was acquired by him on a no gain/no loss disposal as above, the transferor's acquisition of the asset is to be treated as the transferee's acquisition of it. [*TCGA 1992, s 56(2); FA 1994, s 93(5)(11)*]. For further applications of this provision, see 8.7 ASSETS HELD ON 31 MARCH 1982 and 23.10 below.

Where otherwise a loss would accrue on the disposal of an asset, and the sums allowable as a deduction in computing the loss would include an amount attributable to the application of the assumption contained in *TCGA 1992, s 56(2)* above on any no gain/no loss disposal on or after 30 November 1993, those sums are determined as if *TCGA 1992, s 56(2)* had not applied on any such disposal made on or after that date and the loss is reduced accordingly or, if those sums are then equal to or less than the consideration for the disposal, the disposal is to be one on which neither a gain nor a loss accrues. [*TCGA 1992, s 56(3); FA 1994, s 93(5)(11)*].

For the purposes of *TCGA 1992, s 56(1)* (part disposals; see 23.3 above) and *TCGA 1992, s 56(2)(3)* above, a '*no gain/no loss disposal*' is one which, by virtue of any enactment other than *TCGA 1992, s 35(4)* (no gain/no loss disposal where the general re-basing rule of *TCGA 1992, s 35(1)(2)* would otherwise convert a gain into a loss and vice versa; see 8.2 ASSETS HELD ON 31 MARCH 1982), *s 53(1)* (no gain/no loss disposal where indexation allowance equals or exceeds indexation allowance; see 23.1 above) or *s 56* itself, is treated as a disposal on which neither a gain nor a loss accrues. [*TCGA 1992, s 56(4); FA 1994, s 93(5)(11)*]. For these purposes the definition is not therefore confined to those no gain/no loss disposals mentioned in *TCGA 1992, s 35(3)(d)* (see 8.7 ASSETS HELD ON 31 MARCH 1982), being disposals to which the general re-basing rule of *TCGA 1992, s 35(1)(2)* does not apply.

Disposals on or after the '1985 date' and before 30 November 1993. On a 'no gain/no loss disposal' on or after the '1985 date' and before 30 November 1993, the provisions of *TCGA 1992, s 56(2)* applied similarly as above but *TCGA 1992, s 56(3)(4)* did not apply. A '*no gain/no loss disposal*' was, in effect, a disposal which, by virtue of any enactment (other than, in practice, *TCGA 1992, s 35(4)* (as above), *s 53(1) (as originally enacted)* (indexation allowance equal to unindexed gain so as to produce neither gain nor loss) or *s 56* itself) was treated as one on which neither a gain nor a loss accrued. [*TCGA 1992, s 56(2)*].

Examples

(1) In January 1993, Y gives his wife X an asset which is worth £170,000. The asset was purchased from a third party in May 1983 for £80,000. The retail prices index for May 1983 is 84.64 and for January 1993 it is 137.9.

	£
Cost of asset	80,000
Indexation allowance	

$$\frac{137.9 - 84.64}{84.64} = 0.629$$

0.629 × £80,000

	£
	50,320
Deemed consideration	£130,320

X is deemed to acquire the asset for a consideration of £130,320.

(2) Facts in (1) above but Y and X subsequently divorce, with X retaining the asset. X later marries Z to whom the asset is transferred in February 1996 when it is worth £120,000. In May 1997 the asset is sold by Z to a third party for £130,000. The retail prices index for February 1996 is assumed to be 148.7.

	£
Cost of asset	130,320
Indexation allowance	

$$\frac{148.7 - 137.9}{137.9} = 0.078$$

0.078 × £130,320

	£
	10,165
Deemed consideration (X to Z)	£140,485

23.5 Indexation

	£
Sale consideration	130,000
Cost of asset	140,485
Loss (indexation allowance unavailable)	10,485
Less: Reduction under *TCGA 1992, s 56(3)* of £10,165 which was the indexation uplift on the no gain/no loss disposal of February 1996	10,165
Allowable loss accruing to Z	£320

Disposals on or after the '1982 date' and before the '1985 date'. On any no gain/no loss disposal (other than one occurring only by reason of the indexation provisions on the disposal of an asset outside the twelve month qualifying period) the consideration (and corresponding base cost) was adjusted so that after such adjustment, the transaction still gave rise to neither a gain nor a loss. In effect the disposal consideration (and corresponding base cost) was uplifted by the indexation allowance.

Except as provided below, for indexation purposes, any enactment was disregarded which provided that, on the subsequent disposal by the transferee of an asset acquired by him on a no gain/no loss disposal, the transferor's acquisition of the asset was imputed to the transferee.

If a *loss* accrued on a subsequent disposal of the same asset (a 'subsequent disposal'), the loss was to be reduced by the lesser of

(*a*)   the indexation allowance on the initial disposal; and

(*b*)   the amount required to secure that, on the subsequent disposal, neither a gain nor a loss accrued.

If a *gain* accrued on a subsequent disposal, the indexation allowance (if any) was calculated in the normal way, unless the no gain/no loss position on the initial disposal arose only by reason of any of the following enactments, viz. *TCGA 1992, s 139* (transfer of assets on amalgamation, see 13.6 COMPANIES); *TCGA 1992, s 171* (intra-group asset transfers, see 13.11 COMPANIES); *TCGA 1992, s 58* (inter-spouse transfers, see 37.6 MARRIED PERSONS); *FA 1982, s 148* (certain transfers of assets of the Hops Marketing Board, see 18.65 EXEMPTIONS AND RELIEFS); or *TCGA 1992, s 264* (certain transactions by local constituency associations, see 18.59 EXEMPTIONS AND RELIEFS). In those circumstances, if the transferor on the initial disposal had held the asset for at least the usual twelve month qualifying period, the requirement that the transferee must have held the asset for twelve months was removed, and the indexed rise in the deemed acquisition cost was taken from the month in which the expenditure was incurred (or March 1982 if later), and not the twelfth month thereafter. This provision applied both where the initial disposal took place on or after the '1982 date' and, in the Revenue's view, where it took place before that date (Revenue Pamphlet IR 131, SP 3/82, 24 November 1982). If the initial no gain/no loss disposal was within the above enactments, and was within the usual twelve-month qualifying period and thus ineligible for indexation allowance, the original transferor's acquisition was imputed to the second or subsequent transferee on further no gain/no loss disposals occurring within the twelve months of the initial no gain/no loss disposal. [*FA 1982, 13 Sch 2, 3*].

23.5   **Receipts affecting allowable expenditure.** Where account is to be taken, in determining relevant allowable expenditure (see 23.1 above) of any provision which, for the purposes of computing gains, reduces such expenditure by reference to a *'relevant event'* (i.e. any event which is not treated as a capital gains tax disposal), the computation of the indexation allowance proceeds in three stages.

(i)   The 'indexed rise' (see 23.1 above) is calculated for each item of expenditure ignoring the reduction.

(ii)   The 'indexed rise' is calculated of a notional item of expenditure equal to the amount of the reduction, as if that notional amount had actually been incurred on the date of the 'relevant event'.

(iii) The figure calculated in (ii) above is deducted from that in (i) above.

[*TCGA 1992, s 57*]. Examples of such 'relevant events' are small part disposals of land as in 33.11 LAND and the sale of rights nil paid where the consideration received is small as in 53.5 SHARES AND SECURITIES.

For disposals on or after the '1982 date' and before the '1985 date', the above provisions also applied, subject to the twelve month qualifying period, i.e. no adjustment under (ii) above was required if the asset was sold within twelve months of the 'relevant event'. [*FA 1982, 13 Sch 4*].

Example

Z purchases a large area of land in April 1989 for £800,000. In June 1992, he sells a small part of that land at arm's length for £750. In January 1995, he sells all the remaining land for £4,500,000. The retail prices index for April 1989 is 114.3, for June 1992 it is 139.3 and for January 1995 it is 146.0.

		£
Sale consideration		4,500,000
Cost	800,000	
Small sale not treated as a disposal	750	
	799,250	
Unindexed gain		£3,700,750

Indexation allowance on cost

$$\frac{146.0 - 114.3}{114.3} = 0.277$$

0.277 × £800,000	221,600

Indexation allowance on notional expenditure equal to small sale consideration

$$\frac{146.0 - 139.3}{139.3} = 0.048$$

0.048 × £750	36
Reduced indexation allowance	£221,564
Chargeable gain = £(3,700,750 − 221,564)	£3,479,186

23.6   **Reorganisation, reconstructions, etc.** In computing indexation allowance, any consideration given for 'the new holding' (treated under *TCGA 1992, s 127* as the same asset as 'the original shares' on a reorganisation or reduction of a company's share capital) is to be treated as an item of relevant allowable expenditure incurred when the consideration was, or was liable to be, given, i.e. not related back to the acquisition date of 'the original shares', as would normally be the case under *TCGA 1992, s 128(1)*.

'Reorganisation', the *'original shares'* and *'the new holding'* are as defined in *TCGA 1992, s 126(1)*. In addition the above provisions also apply where the treatment under *TCGA 1992, s 127* is adapted for a conversion of securities and company reconstructions and amalgamations. See 53.5–53.10 SHARES AND SECURITIES. [*TCGA 1992, ss 131, 132(1), 135(3)*].

Example

In November 1985, Y purchases 5,000 shares in A plc for £3,500. In June 1987, he acquires, for £960, 1,000 further shares by way of a 1 for 5 rights issue. In January 1995, he sells all his holding for £8,000. The retail prices index for November 1985 is 95.92, for June 1987 it is 101.9 and for January 1995 it is 146.0.

	£	£
Sale consideration		8,000
Original cost	3,500	
Cost of rights	960	
		4,460
Unindexed gain		£3,540

Indexation allowance on original cost

$$\frac{146.0 - 95.92}{95.92} = 0.522$$

$0.522 \times £3,500$		1,827

Indexation allowance on cost of taking up rights

$$\frac{146.0 - 101.9}{101.9} = 0.433$$

$0.433 \times £960$		416
Total indexation allowance		£2,243
Chargeable gain $= £(3,540 - 2,243)$		£1,297

23.7 **Calls on shares.** Where the whole or part of the consideration for the issue of shares, securities or debentures is given after the period of twelve months beginning on the date of the issue of the shares etc., that consideration (or part) is treated as a separate item of expenditure for indexation purposes, incurred at the time it is given and not at the time at which the shares etc. were acquired or provided. [*TCGA 1992, s 113*]. Any calls paid within the twelve month period are thus treated as incurred at the time the shares etc. were acquired or provided.

23.8 **Options.** Where, on a disposal, relevant allowable expenditure includes both

(*a*) the cost of acquiring an option binding the grantor to sell ('*the option consideration*'); and

(*b*) the cost of acquiring what was sold as a result of the exercise of the option ('*the sale consideration*')

the option consideration and sale consideration are regarded as separate items of expenditure incurred when the option was acquired and when the sale took place respectively.

An option binding the grantor both to sell and to buy is treated for these purposes as two separate options with one half of the consideration attributable to each. [*TCGA 1992, s 145*]. See also 23.10 below.

In the case of the grantee of a 'cash-settled' option granted *after 29 November 1993* (see 16.10 DISPOSAL), the cost of the option is treated as incurred when the option was acquired for the purposes of calculating any indexation allowance. [*TCGA 1992, s 144A(3)(c); FA 1994, s 96*].

Disposals on or after the '1982 date' and before the '1985 date'. The above provisions of what is now *TCGA 1992, s 145* applied to such disposals but the qualifying period did not begin until the date of the sale resulting from the exercise of the option, i.e. it began with the date of acquisition of the asset and not, for example, the date of the grant of the option. [*FA 1982, 13 Sch 7*].

23.9   IDENTIFICATION RULES FOR SHARES AND SECURITIES ON OR AFTER THE '1985 DATE'

For disposals on or after 6 April 1985, or, for companies, 1 April 1985 (the *'1985 date'*) the identification rules for securities are as follows.

Special rules apply to the following.

(*a*)   Shares to which enterprise investment scheme relief is attributable and shares in respect of which relief has been given (and not withdrawn) under the business expansion scheme. Disposals of such shares retain their own identification rules; see 53.17 and 53.18 SHARES AND SECURITIES.

(*b*)   *'Relevant securities'*, i.e. securities within the accrued income ('bondwashing') provisions, deep discount securities and securities which are, or have been, material interests in non-qualifying offshore funds. See 23.12 below for further details.

For shares and securities not falling within (*a*) and (*b*) above and any other assets dealt in without identifying the particular assets disposed of or acquired, then, subject to the rules for

(i)   disposals on or before the day of acquisition (see below);

(ii)   acquisitions and disposals of securities within a short period by companies (see 13.31 COMPANIES); and

(iii) acquisitions and disposals within a ten day period (see below)

securities disposed of are identified, in order of priority, with

(A)   securities acquired on or after the '1982 date' and forming part of a *'new holding'* (see 23.10 below);

(B)   securities forming part of a *'1982 holding'* (see 23.11 below); and then

(C)   other securities on a 'last-in, first-out' basis. (Broadly, those held on 6 April 1965, see 7.4 and 7.11 ASSETS HELD ON 6 APRIL 1965 for quoted and unquoted securities respectively.)

Securities held by a person in one capacity cannot be identified with similar securities which he holds or can dispose of only in some other capacity (e.g. as a trustee). [*TCGA 1992, ss 104(1)–(3), 107(1)(2)(7)–(9), 150(5), 150A(5); FA 1994, s 137, 15 Sch 30*].

Disposals on or before the day of acquisition. Securities disposed of on a particular day are matched with securities acquired on the same day by the same person in the same capacity and the pooling rules do not apply for this purpose. Where more securities are disposed of than are acquired, and the excess can neither be identified with previous acquisitions or a 'new holding' (see 23.10 below), that excess is matched with a subsequent acquisition or acquisitions, taking the earliest first. [*TCGA 1992, s 105*].

Acquisitions and disposals within a ten day period. Subject to the rules for disposals on or before the day of acquisition (see above) if, within a ten day period, a number of securities are acquired which would otherwise increase or constitute a 'new holding' (see 23.10 below) and subsequently a number of securities are disposed of, which would otherwise decrease or extinguish the same new holding, then the securities disposed of are identified with those acquired and are not regarded as forming part of, or constituting, a new holding. If the number of securities acquired exceeds the number disposed of, the excess is regarded as forming part of, or constituting, a new holding and where the security acquired was acquired at different times within the ten day period, securities disposed of are first identified with those acquired at an earlier time. If the number of securities disposed of exceeds the number acquired, the excess is not identified under this rule. Any securities which are identified under this rule do not qualify for indexation allowance. [*TCGA 1992, s 107(3)–(6)*].

'Bed and breakfasting'. The Revenue have stated, in connection with the application of the principles established in decided cases up to and including *Furniss v Dawson*, that the indexation provisions applying on and after the 1985 date are clearly not designed to make bed and breakfast share etc. transactions more difficult as compared to the position before the 1982 date but it will remain necessary to make sure that the transactions involved are effective in (for instance) transferring beneficial ownership of the shares. (ICAEW Guidance Note TR 588, 25 September 1985).

23.10   **'New holdings' of securities acquired on or after the '1982 date'.** Securities acquired on or after 6 April 1982, or, for companies, 1 April 1982 (the *'1982 date'*) are pooled. Thus any securities of the same class acquired on or after the '1982 date' and held by the same person in the same capacity immediately before the '1985 date' are pooled as a single asset which grows or diminishes as acquisitions and disposals are made on or after that date. Securities of the same class acquired for the first time on or after the '1985 date' are pooled as a single asset in the same way. This treatment has no effect on any market value that has to be ascertained.

Shares and securities of a company are not to be treated as being of the same class unless they are so treated by the practice of the Stock Exchange or would be so treated if dealt with on the Stock Exchange.

The single asset is referred to as the *'new holding'* and the part disposal rules apply on any disposal other than one of the whole holding.

A separate new holding applies in relation to any securities held by a person to whom they were issued as an employee of the company or of any other person on terms which restrict his rights to dispose of them, so long as those terms are in force, and while such a separate new holding exists the owner of it is treated as holding it in a different capacity to that in which he holds any other securities of the same class.

Indexation allowance. On any disposal from a new holding (other than the whole of it) the 'qualifying expenditure' and the 'indexed pool of expenditure' are apportioned between the part disposed of and the remainder in the same proportions as, under the normal capital gains tax rules for part disposals, the relevant allowable expenditure is apportioned (see 16.6 DISPOSAL). The indexation allowance on the disposal is the amount by which the part of the indexed pool of expenditure apportioned to the part disposed of exceeds the equivalent part of the qualifying expenditure. On a disposal of the whole of the new holding, the indexation allowance is the amount by which the indexed pool of expenditure at the time of disposal exceeds the qualifying expenditure at that time.

The *'qualifying expenditure'* is, at any time, the amount which would be the aggregate of the 'relevant allowable expenditure' in relation to a disposal of the whole of the holding at that time. See 23.1 above for *'relevant allowable expenditure'*.

The *'indexed pool of expenditure'* in the case of a new holding in existence immediately before the '1985 date' comes into existence immediately before that date. It consists of the aggregate of the qualifying expenditure at that time and the indexation allowance which would have been available if all the securities in the holding were disposed of at that time on the assumption that the twelve month qualifying period and restrictions on loss-making disposals (which applied before the '1985 date') had never applied. In the case of any other new holding, the indexed pool of expenditure is created at the same time as the holding (or, if earlier, when any of the qualifying expenditure is incurred) and is equal, at that time, to the qualifying expenditure.

Where a disposal on or after 30 November 1993 to a person acquiring or adding to a new holding is treated under any enactment as one on which neither a gain nor a loss accrues to the person making the disposal, *TCGA 1992, s 56(2)* (general treatment on no gain/no loss disposal; see 23.4 above) does not apply to the disposal (so that the amount of the consideration on the disposal is not calculated on the assumption that an unindexed gain of an amount equal to the indexation allowance accrues to the person making the disposal). However, an amount equal to the indexation allowance on the disposal is added to the indexed pool of expenditure for the holding acquired or, as the case may be, held by the person to whom the disposal is made, and in such a case where there is an addition to the indexed pool of a new holding already held, the addition is made after any increase required by (*a*) below.

Whenever there is an event, called an *'operative event'*, which has the effect of increasing or reducing the qualifying expenditure, a change is made to the indexed pool of expenditure.

(*a*)   The indexed pool of expenditure is increased by the 'indexed rise' since the last operative event or, if none, since the pool came into being. This is done before the calculation of the indexation allowance on a disposal.

(*b*)   If the operative event increases the qualifying expenditure, the indexed pool of expenditure is increased by the same amount.

(*c*)   If there is a disposal resulting in a deduction in the qualifying expenditure, the indexed pool of expenditure is reduced in the same proportion. This is done after the calculation of the indexation allowance on the disposal.

(*d*)   If the qualifying expenditure is reduced but there is no disposal, the indexed pool of expenditure is reduced by the same amount.

The *'indexed rise'* is the sum obtained by multiplying the value of the indexed pool of expenditure immediately before the operative event by a figure (expressed as a decimal but without any clarification as to the number of decimal places to be calculated) calculated by the formula

$$\frac{RE - RL}{RL}, \text{ where}$$

RE =   the retail prices index for the month in which the operative event occurs; and

RL =   the retail prices index for the month of the immediately preceding operative event or, if none, that in which the indexed pool of expenditure came into being.

If RE is equal to or less than RL, the indexed rise is nil.

23.10   Indexation

See 23.1 above for values of the retail price index for March 1982 and subsequent months.

Note. Reorganisations of shares do not normally constitute disposals or acquisitions but they may constitute an operative event as above; e.g. an issue of shares of the same class for payment under a rights issue would be an operative event as the qualifying expenditure is increased, but a bonus issue of shares of the same class would not be. Where the reorganisation involves shares of a different class this would seem automatically to give rise to an operative event as the qualifying expenditure attributable to the new holding consisting of the original class of shares is decreased. It is also thought that an additional new holding is created as only shares of the same class can be pooled in the original new holding. The rules in 53.5 SHARES AND SECURITIES determine the proportions of qualifying expenditure to be attributed to holdings of shares following a reorganisation and this is believed to apply to the indexed pool of expenditure.

Consideration for options. Where an increase in qualifying expenditure under (*b*) above is wholly or partly attributable to the cost of acquiring an option binding the grantor to sell, then the indexed pool of expenditure is additionally increased by a sum obtained by multiplying the consideration for the option by a figure (expressed as a decimal but without any clarification as to the number of decimal places to be calculated) calculated by the formula

$$\frac{RO - RA}{RA}, \text{ where}$$

RO =   the retail prices index for the month in which the option is exercised; and

RA =   the retail prices index for the month in which the option was acquired, or March 1982 if later.

If RO is equal or less than RA, the indexed rise is nil. [*TCGA 1992, ss 104(1)(3)–(6), 110, 114; FA 1994, s 93(6)(11)*].

For disposals before 30 November 1993, it was possible in practice not to keep a running total of the amount of qualifying expenditure because the chargeable gain or allowable loss on a disposal was the difference (positive or negative respectively) between the disposal proceeds and the amount by which the indexed pool was reduced. The denial of indexation allowance creating or increasing a loss on a disposal after 29 November 1993 requires the ascertainment of such a running total. It may be possible to arrive at the correct amount if the requisite records have been retained.

Example

At 6 April 1985, B owned 5,000 securities in REG plc purchased at a cost of £7,500 in June 1983. Subsequently B carried out the following transactions in those securities.

Date	No. of shares bought/(sold)	Cost/ (proceeds)
		£
May 1985	1,000	1,250
October 1985	400	500
December 1986	(2,000)	(5,000)
December 1992	(440)	(900)
January 1995	(2,000)	(4,700)

In addition, in January 1994 B acquired from a spouse (i.e. a gain/no loss disposal) 1,000 further such securities which had hitherto comprised the total holding of the spouse and been purchased originally in July 1985 at a cost of £1,500.

Relevant values of the retail prices index are

June 1983	84.84	December 1986	99.62
April 1985	94.78	December 1992	139.2
May 1985	95.21	January 1994	141.3
July 1985	95.23	January 1995	146.0
October 1985	95.59		

	No. of shares	Qualifying expenditure	Indexed pool
		£	£
Pool at 6.4.85	5,000	7,500	7,500

Indexation allowance
to initial pool: June 1983–April 1985

$$\frac{94.78 - 84.84}{84.84} \times £7,500$$

			878
			8,378

May 1985
Indexed rise: April 1985–May 1985

$$\frac{95.21 - 94.78}{94.78} \times £8,378$$

			38
			8,416
Additional shares	1,000	1,250	1,250
	6,000	8,750	9,666

October 1985
Indexed rise: May 1985–Oct 1985

$$\frac{95.59 - 95.21}{95.21} \times £9,666$$

			39
			9,705
Additional shares	400	500	500
	6,400	9,250	10,205

December 1986
Indexed rise: Oct 1985–Dec 1986

$$\frac{99.62 - 95.59}{95.59} \times £10,205$$

			430
			10,635
Disposal	(2,000)	(i)(2,891)	(ii)(3,323)
	4,400	6,359	7,312

December 1992
Indexed rise: Dec 1986–Dec 1992

$$\frac{139.2 - 99.62}{99.62} \times £7,312$$

			2,905
			10,217
Disposal	(440)	(636)	(1,022)
	3,960	5,723	9,195

23.10 Indexation

January 1994
Indexed rise: Dec 1992–Jan 1994

$$\frac{141.3 - 139.2}{139.2} \times £9,195$$

			139
Additional shares from spouse	1,000	1,500	1,500

Indexation allowance on such shares:
Jul 1985–Jan 1994

$$\frac{141.3 - 95.23}{95.23} \times £1,500$$

			725
	4,960	7,223	11,559

January 1995
Indexed rise: Jan 1994–Jan 1995

$$\frac{146.0 - 141.3}{141.3} \times £11,559$$

			381
	4,960	7,223	11,940
Disposal	(2,000)	(2,912)	(4,855)
Pool carried forward	2,960	£4,311	£7,085

Computation

			£
Disposal December 1986			
Proceeds			5,000
Cost		(i)2,891	
Indexation allowance		(iii) 432	
			(ii) 3,323
Chargeable gain			£1,677
Disposal December 1992			
Proceeds			900
Cost		636	
Indexation allowance		386	
			1,022
Allowable loss			£122

Disposal January 1995

Proceeds of £4,700, although greater than the qualifying expenditure attributable to the securities disposed of (£2,912) and so producing an unindexed gain of the excess (£1,788), are less than the indexed pool of expenditure attributable to the securities disposed of (£4,855). The indexation allowance on the disposal of £1,943 (i.e. £4,855 − £2,912) therefore extinguishes the unindexed gain with the result that the disposal is one on which neither a gain nor a loss accrues (see 23.1 above).

Notes.

The figure at (i) is given by $\quad \dfrac{2,000}{6,400} \times £9,250 = £2,891$

The figure at (ii) is given by $\quad \dfrac{2,000}{6,400} \times £10,635 = £3,323$

The figure at (iii) is given by the difference between (ii) and (i) i.e. £432.

The corresponding figures for the disposals in December 1992 and January 1995 are arrived at in a similar way.

The result of the January 1995 disposal (neither a gain nor a loss) may be able to be taken into account for transitional relief for 'indexation losses' which may be due for 1993/94 and 1994/95 as in 23.2 above.

23.11   **'1982 holding'.** On the introduction of indexation, pools of securities in existence before the '1982 date' continued to be treated as pools which were to be reduced where subsequent disposals were identified with them but which could not grow by acquisitions of additional securities of the same class. There were, however, special rules for adjustments to such pools where the relevant allowable expenditure at the '1982 date' exceeded such expenditure one year previously. All securities acquired between those dates were excluded from the pool in so far as they were not identified with disposals before the '1982 date'. See 23.16 below for full details.

The '1982 holding' comprises the following.

(*a*)   Any pooled holding of securities under the above provisions which is retained at the '1985 date'. The pooled holding includes quoted securities held on 6 April 1965 where an election had been made that their actual cost be ignored and computations made by reference to their market value at 6 April 1965 only. A further opportunity is available for an election to be made where the original time limit has expired by extending the time limit so as to apply by reference to the first relevant disposal on or after the '1985 date'. See 7.3 and 7.4 ASSETS HELD ON 6 APRIL 1965.

(*b*)   Any securities treated as separate assets under the special rules outlined above which have not been disposed of before the '1985 date'.

The '1982 holding', as determined above, continues, or starts, to be a single asset but one which cannot grow by the acquisition of additional securities of the same class. The relevant allowable expenditure attributable to it for capital gains tax purposes is the aggregate of that for the assets of which it is comprised. [*TCGA 1992, s 109*]. The treatment as a single asset as regards reorganisations of shares is believed to follow that in 23.16(*a*) below.

Where securities forming part of a 1982 holding were acquired between 1 and 5 April 1982 inclusive, they may be treated for the purposes of re-basing indexation allowance before 6 April 1988 under 8.13 ASSETS HELD ON 31 MARCH 1982 as held on 31 March 1982 if the taxpayer so wishes. (Tolley's Practical Tax 1986 p 39). Presumably this treatment also applies for the general re-basing rules of 8 ASSETS HELD ON 31 MARCH 1982 after 5 April 1988.

23.12   **Relevant securities.** The identification rules in 23.9 to 23.11 above do not apply to disposals of 'relevant securities' on or after the '1985 date'.

'Relevant securities' and their identification rules for such disposals are as follows.

(*a*)   *Government securities.* The then identification rules for such securities continued to apply to disposals on or after the '1985 date' and before 2 July 1986. *Disposals after 1 July 1986* are exempt from capital gains tax (whether held for twelve months or more or not) and, accordingly, after 1 July 1986 the identification rules cease to have any significance.

(b) *Qualifying corporate bonds.* The then identification rules for such securities continued to apply to disposals on or after the '1985 date' and before 2 July 1986. The rules were those outlined in 23.13 to 23.15 below subject to additional rules regarding acquisitions and disposals within a short period. Disposals *after 1 July 1986* are exempt from capital gains tax (whether held for twelve months or more or not) and, accordingly, the identification rules cease to have any significance.

(c) *Securities within the accrued income ('bondwashing') provisions other than those within (a) or (b) above.* These comprise any loan stock or similar security of any government, public or local authority in the UK or elsewhere or any company or other body other than

  (i)   shares in a company (except qualifying shares in a building society);

  (ii)   securities on which the whole of the return is a distribution by virtue of *ICTA 1988, s 209(2)(e)(iv)(v)*;

  (iii) national savings and war savings certificates;

  (iv)   certificates of deposit; and

  (v)   any security which is redeemable, for which the amount payable on redemption exceeds the issue price and in respect of which no return other than the amount of that excess is payable.

For disposals on or after the '1985 date' and before 28 February 1986, the identification rules in 23.13 to 23.15 below continue to apply, with the addition of the rule relating to the '1982 holding' under 23.11 above.

For disposals after 27 February 1986, the identification rules in 23.13 and 23.14 (but not 23.15) below apply, with the addition of the rule relating to the '1982 holding' under 23.11 above.

(d) *Deep discount securities.* The existing identification rules in 23.13 and 23.14 (but not 23.15) below continue to apply. See 53.19 SHARES AND SECURITIES.

(e) *Non-qualifying offshore funds.* Securities which are, or at any time have been, material interests in a non-qualifying offshore fund continue to be identified under the rules in 23.13 and 23.14 (but not 23.15) below.

Where any of the securities within (c) to (e) above are disposed of on or after the '1985 date' and within a period of ten days beginning on the day on which the expenditure was incurred, no indexation allowance is due. [*TCGA 1992, ss 54(2), 108*].

23.13   **IDENTIFICATION RULES FOR DISPOSALS OF SHARES AND SECURITIES ON OR AFTER THE '1982 DATE' AND BEFORE THE '1985 DATE'**

For disposals on or after 6 April 1982 or, for companies, 1 April 1982 (the *'1982 date'*) and before 6 April 1985, or, for companies, 1 April 1985 (the *'1985 date'*) 'securities' acquired on or after the '1982 date' are not subject to pooling. The identification rules directed how such disposals of securities were to be identified with acquisitions of securities of the same class held by the same person in the same capacity. As adapted by additional provisions, they also applied to disposals from pools of securities acquired before, and held on, the '1982 date'. Where securities were held on 6 April 1965, special rules apply. See 7.4 and 7.11 ASSETS HELD ON 6 APRIL 1965 for quoted and unquoted securities respectively.

The identification rules still apply to disposals of certain 'relevant securities' after the '1985 date'. See 23.12 above.

For companies, an alternative method ('parallel pooling') was available for identifying particular securities disposed of after 31 March 1982 and before 1 April 1985. See 23.17 below.

'*Securities*' meant company shares or securities (including qualifying corporate bonds) or any other asset (other than gilt-edged securities) of a type to be dealt in without identifying the particular assets disposed of or acquired (i.e. fungible assets).

The general rules were subject to

(i)   the special rules for acquisitions and disposals of securities within a short period by companies (see 13.31 COMPANIES),

(ii)   special rules for 'contangos' (see 23.14 below), and

(iii)   anti-avoidance provisions for married persons and groups of companies (see 23.15 below).

The general rules, in order of priority, were as follows.

(*a*)   For identification purposes, disposals were to be taken in chronological order. The identification of securities comprised in an earlier disposal therefore determine (by elimination) which securities could be comprised in a later disposal.

(*b*)   Securities disposed of for transfer or delivery on a particular date (e.g. a stock exchange settlement date) or in a particular period (e.g. a stock exchange account) were not to be identified with securities acquired for transfer or delivery on a later date or in a later period. They had to be identified with acquisitions of securities for transfer or delivery on or before that date, or, in or before that period, but, subject to this, they had to be first identified with acquisitions for *transfer or delivery* on or after the contract disposal date. (The 'transfer or delivery', i.e. settlement, date is generally different from the contract date. See also *Macpherson v Hall Ch D 1972, 48 TC 210.*)

(*c*)   Disposals were to be identified, on a 'first-in, first-out' basis, with acquisitions within the twelve months preceding the disposal. Otherwise, disposals were to be identified with acquisitions on a 'last-in, first-out' basis.

(*d*)   Disposals were to be identified with acquisitions at different times on the same day in as nearly as may be equal proportions.

[*TCGA 1992, s 108(1)–(6); FA 1982, s 88(1)–(6), (9)*].

23.14   **Contangos.** Where, under arrangements designed to postpone the transfer or delivery of securities disposed of, a person by a *single bargain* acquired securities for transfer or delivery on a particular date or in a particular period (the 'earlier date' or 'earlier period'), and disposed of them for transfer or delivery on a later date or in a later period, then the disposal and acquisition covered by the single bargain were matched. Any previous disposal which, apart from the above matching provisions, would have been identified with the acquisition under the contango arrangement had to (subject to the general rule that disposals must be taken in chronological sequence) be identified with any 'available securities' acquired for transfer or delivery on the earlier date or in the earlier period. '*Available securities*' were securities which had not been matched under the above 'single bargain' rule, or under the general identification rules, with disposals for transfer or delivery on the earlier date or in the earlier period. Insofar as the previous disposal could not be identified with 'available securities', the disposal was to be treated as being for transfer or delivery on the later date, or in the later period. [*TCGA 1992, s 108(7); FA 1982, s 88(7)*].

Inter-spouse and intra-group transfers. If such a transfer resulted in securities of the same kind transferred to a third party, which would otherwise be 'unindexed', becoming 'indexed', the usual identification was reversed, so that the whole or a corresponding part of the indexed securities transferred to the third party became 'unindexed'. *'Indexed'* securities, for this purpose, were shares acquired or provided more than twelve months before the date of the disposal concerned and the meaning of *'unindexed'* was construed accordingly. Where there were multiple inter-spouse, intra-group, or third party disposals, the reversal of identification was applied to such disposals in chronological sequence. By a process of elimination, the 're-identification' of earlier disposals thus determined how these provisions were to apply to later disposals. [*FA 1982, s 89*].

23.16 **Share pools in existence before the operative date.** The relevant allowable expenditure (see 23.1 above) of the holding of shares treated as a single asset ('pool') on 5 April 1982 (31 March 1982 for companies) was deemed the '1982 amount'. The relevant allowable expenditure on 5 April 1981 (31 March 1981 for companies) was deemed the '1981 amount'.

Where the '1982 amount' did not exceed the '1981 amount'

(a)   The pool (in the legislation termed 'the holding') held immediately before the '1982 date' continued to be treated as a pool, but one which could not grow by the *acquisition* of additional securities of the same class. However, this overrode neither the reorganisation provisions of *TCGA 1992, s 127,* as qualified by the special indexation rules of *TCGA 1992, s 131* concerning reorganisations (see 23.6 above), nor the effects of an election under *TCGA 1992, 2 Sch 4* (see 7.3 ASSETS HELD ON 6 APRIL 1965). Thus the pool could increase by the addition of shares of the same class from bonus and rights issues, from other reorganisations not constituting acquisitions, and from a 6 April 1965 pooling election, but any additional consideration given on a reorganisation was treated, for indexation allowance purposes, as incurred on the *actual* date on which the person concerned gave, or was liable to give, the consideration. Where a reorganisation involved shares of a different class but did not constitute an acquisition it is thought that the relevant allowable expenditure required apportionment as under 53.5 SHARES AND SECURITIES.

(b)   For indexation allowance purposes, the pool was regarded as having been acquired on 6 April 1981 (1 April 1981 for companies).

(c)   All relevant allowable expenditure on a disposal out of the pool on or after the '1982 date' and before the '1985 date' was to be regarded for indexation allowance purposes as incurred at such time that the month which determines RI in the general formula for computing indexation allowance (see 23.1 above) is March 1982. Thus the indexation allowance was given for March 1982 onwards (subject to the reorganisation consideration provisions in (a) above).

Where the '1982 amount' did exceed the '1981 amount', the rules were modified. Firstly, a separate set of identification rules was applied to all acquisitions and disposals after 5 April 1981 (31 March 1981 for companies) but before the '1982 date', which, apart from these provisions, would have increased or decreased the pool. The separate rules were, in order of priority, as follows.

(i)   Disposals of securities were identified in chronological order and the identification of the securities first disposed of accordingly determined the securities which could be comprised in a later disposal.

(ii)   Disposals were identified with securities acquired on a later date rather than with securities acquired on an earlier date. The Inland Revenue were prepared to apply the rules to the twelve-month period as a whole (i.e. to the period ending on 5 April 1982 or 31 March 1982) rather than to the period ending with each disposal. As a result it was possible in some cases for a disposal to be identified with a subsequent acquisition and thus give an earlier acquisition date for indexation purposes (Revenue Pamphlet IR 131, SP 3/82, 24 November 1982).

(iii)   Disposals were identified with acquisitions at other times on any one day in as nearly as may be equal proportions.

Only so much of the pool on 5 April 1981 (31 March 1981 for companies) (if any) which was not treated as disposed of before the '1982 date' by the rules in (i)–(iii) above was treated as constituting the pool on the '1982 date'. The pool, as adjusted (if at all) by these provisions, was termed the 'reduced holding', i.e. the reduced pool. All securities acquired after 5 April 1981 (31 March 1981 for companies), but before the '1982 date', were excluded from the pool, insofar as they were not identified under the rules in (i)–(iii) above with disposals before the '1982 date'. The acquisitions excluded from the pool in this manner were treated as separate assets. The rules in (*a*)–(*c*) above applied to the reduced pool but, for the purpose of computing the indexation allowance (if any) on a disposal after the '1982 date' of the reduced pool, or of the excluded acquisitions, the '1982 amount' was apportioned between the reduced pool and the excluded acquisitions pro rata to the number of securities comprised in each of those two categories on the operative date. The apportioned parts of the '1982 amount' were to be regarded for all capital gains tax purposes as the relevant allowable expenditure attributable to the pool, or to the excluded acquisitions, respectively. Such expenditure was deemed, for the purpose of the computing the indexation allowance, to be expenditure falling within *TCGA 1992, s 38(1)(a)* (see I3501 above). [*FA 1982, s 88(8), 13 Sch Part II*].

23.17   **ELECTION FOR 'PARALLEL POOLING' BY COMPANIES FOR DISPOSALS AFTER 31 MARCH 1982 AND BEFORE 1 APRIL 1985**

For companies, an alternative method was available, by election, to identify particular shares and securities which were disposed of after 31 March 1982 and before 1 April 1985 with shares etc. of the same kind which had been previously acquired. Following the abolition of the general twelve-month qualifying period for indexation allowance to apply and the general reintroduction of a form of pooling for disposals after 31 March 1985 under 23.1–23.11 above, any 'parallel pooling' election made ceases to apply to such disposals. An opportunity was given to revoke any election previously made, by written notice before 1 April 1987 (or within such longer period as the Board may allow), with the effect that the gains on all disposals which were subject to the election were recomputed under the normal rules in 23.13–23.16 above. If an election was not so revoked, no adjustment was to be made to the gains on disposals which were subject to the election, and further provisions enable the rules given in 23.9–23.12 above to apply to the pooled holding in respect of disposals after 31 March 1985. [*TCGA 1992, s 112; FA 1983, s 34, 6 Sch; FA 1985, 19 Sch Part V; SI 1986 No 387*].

For full coverage of the above, see Tolley's Capital Gains Tax 1986/87.

24   Inland Revenue: Administration

24.1   The levying and collection of capital gains tax is administered by the **Commissioners of Inland Revenue** (normally referred to as 'the Board'), Somerset House, London WC2R 1LB. [*TMA 1970, s 1(1)*].

Under them are local **inspectors of taxes** who are permanent civil servants responsible for making most assessments and dealing with claims and allowances and to whom all enquiries should be addressed.

24.2   **Collectors of Taxes** are also permanent civil servants and their duties for the most part relate only to the collection of tax. [*TMA 1970, ss 60–70*].

24.3   **Commissioners**. Except as otherwise provided, assessments are made by inspectors [*TMA 1970, s 29*] and appeals against such assessments are heard by

(*a*)   the *General Commissioners* (local people appointed on a voluntary basis by the Lord Chancellor for divisions in England and Wales and, from 3 April 1989, Northern Ireland or, for divisions in Scotland, by the Secretary of State) [*TMA 1970, s 2; FA 1975, s 57; FA 1988, s 125*], or

(*b*)   the *Special Commissioners* (full-time civil servants, being barristers, advocates or solicitors of at least ten years' standing) [*TMA 1970, s 4; FA 1984, s 127, 22 Sch 1*], or

(*c*)   a county court (in Northern Ireland and before 3 April 1989) [*TMA 1970, s 59; FA 1988, s 125*].

The Lord Chancellor has powers, by regulation, to change the appellations 'General Commissioners' and 'Special Commissioners' to something different. [*F(No 2)A 1992, s 75*].

See 4.5 and 4.8 APPEALS as regards jurisdiction of appeal Commissioners and the conduct of appeals before them.

24.4   **'Care and management' powers**. For the validity of amnesties by the Board, see *R v CIR (ex p. National Federation of Self-Employed and Small Businesses Ltd)* HL 1981, 55 TC 133. INLAND REVENUE EXTRA-STATUTORY CONCESSIONS (27) have been the subject of frequent judicial criticism but their validity has never been directly challenged in the Courts. In *R v CIR (ex p. Fulford-Dobson)* QB 1987, 60 TC 168, it was held that there had been no unfair treatment by the Revenue when it failed to apply a published extra-statutory concession because it was clear from the facts of the case that it was one of tax avoidance and this was a clearly stated general circumstance in which concessions would not be applied (cf. *R v Inspector of Taxes, Hull, ex p. Brumfield and others* QB 1988, 61 TC 589 at 4.10 APPEALS). For a general discussion of the Board's care and management powers and an example of a ruling by the Court that the Board had acted reasonably, see *R v CIR (ex p. Preston)* HL 1985, 59 TC 1. See also *R v Attorney-General (ex p. ICI plc)* CA 1986, 60 TC 1, *R v CIR (ex p. MFK Underwriting Agencies Ltd and others)* QB 1989, 62 TC 607 and *Matrix-Securities Ltd v CIR* HL, [1994] STC 272. See also 4.10 APPEALS regarding judicial review of Revenue powers.

The Revenue policy of selective prosecution for criminal offences (see 42.6 PENALTIES) in connection with tax evasion does not render a decision in a particular case unlawful or *ultra vires*, provided that the case is considered on its merits fairly and dispassionately to see whether the criteria for prosecution were satisfied, and that the decision to prosecute is then taken in good faith for the purpose of collecting taxes and not for some ulterior, extraneous or improper purpose (*R v CIR (ex p. Mead and Cook) QB, [1992] STC 482*).

24.5   **Mistakes by the Revenue.** If the Revenue makes a 'serious' mistake in dealing with a taxpayer's affairs, it will pay any costs he incurs as a direct result of the mistake. This practice is now embodied in the Revenue's Code of Practice 1 'Mistakes by the Inland Revenue' issued in February 1993 but appears to be a restatement of 29A31 INLAND REVENUE STATEMENTS OF PRACTICE which dates from 1975. Under the Code, the same practice also applies in relation to 'persistent' Revenue errors. The Code of Practice provides examples of what the Revenue envisage by the terms 'serious' and 'persistent'.

Further practices relating to Revenue mistakes are mentioned at 31.4 INTEREST ON OVERPAID TAX, 32.7 INTEREST ON UNPAID TAX and 41.8 PAYMENT OF TAX.

24.6   **Taxpayer's Charter.** The Board of Inland Revenue and HM Customs and Excise have jointly produced a Taxpayer's Charter setting out the principles they try to meet in their dealings with taxpayers, the standards they believe the taxpayer has a right to expect, and what people can do if they wish to appeal or complain. Copies are available from local tax or collection offices and from local VAT offices. The Revenue version is contained in Pamphlet IR 120.

A series of codes of practice, available from local tax offices from March 1993, setting out the standards of service people can expect in relation to specific aspects of the Revenue's work, was announced in a Revenue Press Release of 17 February 1993 to support the Taxpayer's Charter. The codes are not meant to represent any change of practice although some practices mentioned in them were not previously publicly available.

24.7   **Revenue Adjudicator.** A taxpayer who is not satisfied with the Revenue response to a complaint has the option of putting the case to a Revenue Adjudicator. The Adjudicator's office opened on 1 July 1993, and considers complaints about the Revenue's handling of a taxpayer's affairs, e.g. excessive delays, errors, discourtesy or the exercise of Revenue discretion, where the events complained of occurred after 5 April 1993 (31 March 1993 for companies). Matters subject to existing rights of appeal are excluded.

Complaints will normally go to the Adjudicator only after they have been considered by the Controller of the relevant Revenue office, and where the taxpayer is still not satisfied with the response received. The alternatives of pursuing the complaint to the Revenue's Head Office, to an MP, or (through an MP) to the Parliamentary Ombudsman continue to be available. The Adjudicator will review all the facts, consider whether the complaint is justified, and, if so, make recommendations as to what should be done. The Revenue will normally accept the recommendations 'unless there are very exceptional circumstances'.

The Adjudicator publishes an annual report to the Board. (Revenue Press Release 17 February 1993 and Tax Bulletin May 1993 p 75), the first of which was published on 13 September 1994. Contact should be made with Revenue Adjudicator, 3rd Floor, Haymarket House, 28 Haymarket, London SW1Y 4SP. Tel: 0171–930 2292. Fax: 0171–930 2298. An explanatory leaflet is available from the Adjudicator which describes the actions a taxpayer should take and how the Adjudicator will respond to complaints.

24.8   **Open Government.** Under the Government's 'Code of Practice on Access to Government Information', the Revenue (in common with other Government departments) is to make information about its policies and decisions more widely available. Revenue Pamphlet IR 141 ('Open Government') sets out the information to be made available, and how it may be obtained, and the basis on which a fee may be charged in certain circumstances to offset the cost of providing the information. Copies of the Code of Practice may be obtained by writing to Open Government, Room 417b, Office of Public Service and Science, 70 Whitehall, London SW1A 2AS (tel. 0345 223242).

---

25   Inland Revenue: Confidentiality of Information

25.1   The Revenue consider that the confidentiality of information maintained by their Department 'is essential to their traditional approach to their task and is deeply embedded in their practice'. (*Royal Commission on Standards of Conduct in Public Life 1976, para 111*). All officers of the Inland Revenue, together with General and Special Commissioners, are required to make declarations that information received in the course of their duty will not be disclosed except for the purposes of such duty or for the purposes of the prosecution of revenue offences or as may be required by law. [*TMA 1970, s 6, 1 Sch*]. As to production in Court proceedings of documents in the possession of the Revenue or copies of documents previously submitted to the Revenue which are held by a party to the proceedings, see *Brown's Trustees v Hay CS 1897, 3 TC 598; In re Joseph Hargreaves Ltd CA 1900, 4 TC 173; Shaw v Kay CS 1904, 5 TC 74; Soul v Irving CA 1963, 41 TC 517; H v H Fam D 1980, 52 TC 454; R v CIR (ex p. J Rothschild Holdings plc) CA 1987, 61 TC 178; Lonrho plc v Fayed and Others (No 4) CA, 1993 STI 1364.*

25.2   The Inland Revenue are authorised to disclose information to the following (and see also written reply in HC Official Report, 20 February 1990, col 685).

(*a*)   **Charity Commissioners for England and Wales.** The Revenue is authorised to disclose certain information to the Charity Commissioners regarding bodies which are or have been charities. Similar provisions apply in Scotland as regards disclosure to the Lord Advocate. [*Charities Act 1993, s 10; Law Reform (Miscellaneous Provisions) (Scotland) Act 1990, s 1*].

(*b*)   **Business Statistics Office of the Department of Trade and Industry or the Department of Employment.** The Revenue are authorised to disclose, for the purposes of statistical surveys, the names and addresses of employers and information concerning the number of persons employed by individual concerns. [*FA 1969, s 58; F(No 2)A 1987, s 69*].

(*c*)   **Tax authorities of other countries.** The Revenue are authorised to disclose information concerning individual taxpayers where it is necessary to do so for the operation of double taxation agreements. After 14 May 1987, provision is made for double taxation agreements to include arrangements for the exchange of information relating to the taxes covered by an agreement including, in particular, those concerned with the prevention of fiscal evasion. The Board may also be required to disclose information to an advisory commission set up under the Arbitration Convention (*90/436/EEC*). [*TCGA 1992, s 277(4); FA 1975, 7 Sch 7(5); IHTA 1984, s 158; ICTA 1988, ss 788(2), 816; F(No 2)A 1992, s 51(2)*]. Disclosure may also be made to the tax authorities of other member states of the

EEC which observe similar confidentiality and use the information only for taxation purposes. [*FA 1978, s 77; EEC Directive 19 December 1977 No 77/799 EEC*]. See also the working arrangement between USA and UK in Revenue Press Release 2 March 1978.

(d)   **Customs and Excise.** The Revenue and the Customs and Excise are authorised to disclose information to each other for the purpose of their respective duties. [*FA 1972, s 127*].

(e)   **Occupational Pensions Board.** The Revenue are authorised to disclose information about pension schemes. [*Social Security Act 1973, s 89(2)*].

(f)   **Social Security Departments.** The Revenue may disclose information obtained in connection with the assessment or collection of income tax but for self-employed persons they may only disclose the fact that a person has commenced or ceased self-employment together with the identity of that person and information relating to earners employed by that person. [*Social Security Administration Act 1992, s 122*]. Information under this authority will be disclosed in connection with the tracing of absent parents liable to maintain lone-parent families receiving income support (Revenue Press Release 9 May 1990).

(g)   **Police.** To assist investigation into suspected murder or treason. (*Royal Commission on Standards of Conduct in Public Life 1976, para 93*).

(h)   **Non-UK resident entertainers and sportsmen.** In connection with the deduction of sums representing income tax from certain payments to such persons after 5 April 1987, the Board may disclose relevant matters to any person who appears to the Board to have an interest. [*ICTA 1988, s 558(4)*].

25.3   After 28 February 1990 it is a criminal offence for a person to disclose tax information of an identifiable person held by him in the exercise of 'tax functions' or as a member of an advisory commission set up under the Arbitration Convention (*90/436/EEC*). '*Tax functions*' include functions relating to the General and Special Commissioners, the Board and their officers and any other persons providing, or employed in the provision of, services to the aforementioned persons. This does not apply if the person has (or believes he has) lawful authority or the information has lawfully been made available to the public, or if the person involved has consented. The maximum penalty for an offence is imprisonment for up to two years, a fine, or both. [*FA 1989, ss 182, 182A; F(No 2)A 1992, s 51(3)*].

26 Inland Revenue Explanatory Pamphlets

The Board publish explanatory pamphlets (with supplements from time to time) on Inland Revenue taxes. Those having a bearing on capital gains tax and corporation tax on chargeable gains are listed below, with the date of the latest edition in brackets, and are obtainable free of charge from local tax enquiry offices or, where unobtainable locally, the Public Enquiry Room, Inland Revenue, West Wing, Somerset House, Strand, London WC2R 1LB (Tel. 0171–438 6420/6425/7772), unless otherwise stated at the end of the list.

IR 1	Extra-Statutory Concessions in operation as at 31 December 1993 (June 1994).
IR 6	Double taxation relief for companies (December 1994).
IR 16	Share acquisitions by directors and employees: Explanatory notes (March 1994).
IR 17	Share acquisitions by directors and employees: An outline for employees (March 1994).
IR 20	Residents and Non-residents: Liability to Tax in the United Kingdom (November 1993).
IR 37	Income Tax and Capital Gains Tax: Appeals (June 1990).
IR 45	What happens when someone dies (May 1995).
IR 64	Giving to Charity: How businesses can get tax relief (November 1993).
IR 65	Giving to Charity: How individuals can get tax relief (November 1993).
IR 73	Inland Revenue Investigations: How Settlements are Negotiated (January 1994).
IR 75	Tax Reliefs for Charities (June 1987).
CB(1)	Setting up a charity in Scotland (see 10.1 CHARITIES for address).
IR 83	Independent Taxation: A guide for Tax Practitioners (January 1990).
IR 87	Income Tax; Capital Gains Tax: Rooms to Let (January 1991 and September 1992 insert).
IR 89	Personal Equity Plans (PEPs): A guide for potential investors (June 1992).
IR 95	Approved profit sharing schemes: An outline for employees (March 1994).
IR 96	Approved profit sharing schemes: Explanatory notes (March 1994).
IR 97	Approved SAYE share option schemes: An outline for employees (March 1994).
IR 99	Approved executive share option schemes: An outline for employees (March 1994).
IR 120	You and the Inland Revenue: Tax, Collection and Accounts Offices (May 1993).
IR 126	Corporation Tax Pay and File: A General Guide (June 1993).
IR 128	Corporation Tax Pay and File: Company Leaflet (June 1993).
IR 131	Statements of Practice in operation as at 31 December 1993 (July 1994).
IR 137	Guide to the Enterprise Investment Scheme (October 1994).
IR 141	Open Government (October 1994).
IR 142	Self-Assessment: An introduction (September 1994).
IR 146	Double Taxation Relief: Admissible and Inadmissible Taxes (March 1995).
CGT 4	Capital Gains Tax: Owner-occupied houses (November 1989).
CGT 6	Capital Gains Tax: Retirement Relief on Disposal of a Business (May 1992).
CGT 11	Capital Gains Tax and Small Businesses (February 1990).
CGT 13	The Indexation Allowance for Quoted Shares (January 1991).
CGT 14	Capital Gains Tax: An Introduction (May 1992).
CGT 15	Capital Gains Tax: A Guide for Married Couples (November 1990).
CGT 16	Capital Gains Tax: Indexation Allowance; Disposals after 5 April 1988 (August 1989).
IHT 1	Inheritance Tax (January 1991).
COP 1	Mistakes by the Inland Revenue (February 1993).
COP 2	Investigations (February 1993).
RAO	How to complain about the Inland Revenue (August 1993).

SAT 2   Self-Assessment: the legal framework (October 1994).

IR 83 is available from the Public Enquiry Room (see above).

IR 120 is also available in Bengali, Chinese, Greek, Gujarati, Hindi, Punjabi, Turkish, Urdu, Vietnamese and Welsh (from tax offices in Wales only) versions. Braille, large print and audio tape versions in English are also available although the first and last of these must be ordered and will be sent by post. Alternatively the Royal National Institute for the Blind can be requested (Tel: 0345–023153 at local call rates) to supply any one of these three versions.

IHT 1 is obtainable from the Capital Taxes Office at the following addresses:

England and Wales: Ferrers House, PO Box 38, Castle Meadow Road, Nottingham NG2 1BB;

Scotland: Mulberry House, 16 Picardy Place, Edinburgh EH1 3NF;

Northern Ireland: Dorchester House, 52–58 Great Victoria Street, Belfast BT2 7BB.

27 Inland Revenue Extra-Statutory Concessions

Below are summarised the concessions relating to tax on capital gains published (or to be published) in Revenue Pamphlet IR 1 (June 1994 being the latest edition thereof). Concessions announced in Press Releases but not yet designated by a formal prefix (see below) are summarised in date order at the end of the chapter. In the pamphlet it is stated: 'The concessions described within are of general application, but it must be borne in mind that in a particular case there may be special circumstances which will require to be taken into account in considering the application of the concession. A concession will not be given in any case where an attempt is made to use it for tax avoidance'. See also 24.4 INLAND REVENUE: ADMINISTRATION. Fuller coverage in context is normally given in the appropriate chapter referred to below. Except where the context otherwise requires, each concession relates to both individuals and companies. The full text of all current Extra-Statutory Concessions is reproduced in Tolley's Official Tax Statements.

D 1 **Insurance recoveries: short leases.** Such receipts will not be subject to tax if applied in pursuance of an obligation to make good damage to the property. See 33.24 LAND.

D 2 **Residence in the UK: year of commencement or cessation of residence.** Where a person's UK residence status is determined by reference to the period of actual residence in the UK, tax will only be charged on disposals made during the period of residence. (See also A11 below). This concession does not apply in certain cases. It was amended for disposals after 5 April 1989. See 47.2 RESIDENCE AND DOMICILE.

D 3 **Private residence exemption: periods of absence (a).** Periods of absence are ignored where husband and wife are living together and the conditions are satisfied by the spouse who is not the owner. See 43.2 PRIVATE RESIDENCES.

D 4 **Private residence exemption: periods of absence (b).** Resumption of occupation after certain periods of absence will not be necessary if the terms of his employment require the taxpayer to work elsewhere. See 43.2 PRIVATE RESIDENCES.

D 5 **Private residence exemption** is extended to cover a residence disposed of by personal representatives and occupied before and after the death of the deceased as an only or main residence by an individual entitled to the whole or a substantial part of the proceeds of sale either absolutely or for life. See 43.4 PRIVATE RESIDENCES.

D 6 **Private residence exemption: separated couples.** If, as the result of a breakdown of the marriage, one spouse ceases to occupy the matrimonial home and later transfers it (or part of it) as part of a financial settlement to the other spouse who has continued in occupation, no gain will be chargeable unless election has been made for some other house to be the main residence of the transferring spouse. See 43.2 PRIVATE RESIDENCES.

D10 **Unquoted shares acquired before 6 April 1965: disposals following reorganisation of share capital.** Tax is not charged on a disposal of the entire new shareholding on more than the actual gains realised. See 7.12 ASSETS HELD ON 6 APRIL 1965.

D12 **Close companies: apportionment of income and consequential capital gains.** Tax borne by a beneficiary under a trust, or residuary legatee on apportioned income of a company, is allowed as a deduction in computing the gain or loss arising to the trustees or administrators on the disposal of the relevant shares. Relief may not be claimed under both this concession and that in A36 below. See 16.4 DISPOSAL.

D15 **Rollover relief: unincorporated associations.** Where property is held via the medium of a company whose shares are held by the association, the relief is available provided the other conditions are satisfied. This concession was revised in a Revenue Press Release of 18 October 1994. See 50.4 ROLLOVER RELIEF.

D16   **Rollover relief: repurchase of the same asset.** An asset which is repurchased for purely commercial reasons after having been sold as part of a business may be treated as the 'new asset' for the purposes of the relief. See 50.2 ROLLOVER RELIEF.

D17   **Unit trusts for exempt unit holders.** The exemption available to the unit trust is not withdrawn because of the intermittent holding of units by the trust managers under statutory arrangements. See 57.3 UNIT AND INVESTMENT TRUSTS.

D18   **Mortgage granted by vendor: subsequent default by purchaser as mortgagor.** In such circumstances and where the vendor regains beneficial ownership of the asset and so elects, the original sale is ignored and the chargeable gain arising is limited to the net proceeds obtained from the transactions. See 16.1 DISPOSAL.

D19   **Replacement of buildings destroyed.** Where a capital sum received by way of compensation for a destroyed building is wholly or partly applied in constructing or acquiring a replacement building elsewhere, both the original and replacement buildings may, for the purposes of a claim under *TCGA 1992, s 23(4)* or *(5)*, be treated as distinct assets separate from the land on which they stand. See 16.9 DISPOSAL.

D20   **Private residence exemption: residence occupied by dependent relative.** The dependent relative may make certain payments in respect of his occupation without the exemption being lost. (It should be noted, however, that, subject to transitional provisions, the exemption for a residence occupied by such a relative is removed for periods of ownership falling after 5 April 1988.) This concession was revised in a Revenue Press Release of 18 August 1993. See 43.5 PRIVATE RESIDENCES.

D21   **Private residence exemption: late claims in dual residence cases.** The two-year time limit will be extended in cases where the capital value of each of the residences, or each of them except one, is negligible. See 43.3 PRIVATE RESIDENCES.

D22   **Rollover relief: expenditure on improvements to existing assets.** Such expenditure is treated as incurred in acquiring other assets provided certain conditions are met. See 50.2 ROLLOVER RELIEF.

D23   **Rollover relief: partition of land and other assets on the dissolution of a partnership.** Partitioned assets are treated as 'new assets' for the purposes of the relief provided that the partnership is dissolved immediately thereafter. See 50.1 ROLLOVER RELIEF.

D24   **Rollover relief: assets not brought immediately into trading use.** The 'new asset' will qualify for relief even if not immediately taken into use for the purposes of the trade provided certain conditions are met. Land to be used for the site of a qualifying building will also qualify as the 'new asset' for the purposes of this concession subject to conditions. See 50.2 ROLLOVER RELIEF.

D25   **Rollover relief: acquisition of a further interest in an existing asset.** The further interest is treated as a 'new asset' for the purposes of the relief. See 50.2 ROLLOVER RELIEF.

D26   **Exchange of joint interests in land: form of rollover relief.** A form of rollover relief as on the compulsory purchase of land (see 33.14 LAND) is allowed on a disposal caused by the exchange of interests in land which is in the joint beneficial ownership of two or more persons. This relief is not confined to traders. After 29 October 1987 the relief applies also to certain exchanges of milk or potato quota associated with such land. This concession was revised in a Revenue Press Release of 18 October 1994. See 33.15 LAND.

D27   **Earn-outs.** *TCGA 1992, s 135* may be applied to a takeover which includes an 'earn-out' element. This concession was revised by Revenue Press Release of 20 October 1994. See 53.8 SHARES AND SECURITIES.

D28   **Asset of negligible value: time limit for claim.** 29 D13 INLAND REVENUE STATEMENTS OF PRACTICE is revised for clarification and reclassified as an extra-statutory concession.

Amendments have been made to the concession where negligible value claims are made after 29 November 1993. See 35.8 LOSSES.

D30 **Groups of companies: rollover relief.** Rollover relief is available to a non-trading company on assets held for use in the trade of another group company. This concession has been replaced by legislation. See 50.4 ROLLOVER RELIEF.

D31 **Retirement relief: date of disposal.** If business activities continue beyond the date an unconditional contract is made, the date of completion will be accepted as the date of disposal. See 48.2 RETIREMENT RELIEF.

D32 **Transfer of a business to a company.** 29. D22 INLAND REVENUE STATEMENTS OF PRACTICE is reclassified as an extra-statutory concession. See 22.7 HOLD-OVER RELIEFS.

D33 **Compensation and damages.** These are treated as derived from any underlying asset, and exempt or taxable accordingly, and as exempt if there is no underlying asset. See 6.1 ASSETS and 18.19 EXEMPTIONS AND RELIEFS.

D34 **Rebasing and indexation: shares held on 31 March 1982.** A single holding treatment will apply even if the shares were acquired on or before 6 April 1965. See 8.2 ASSETS HELD ON 31 MARCH 1982.

D35 **Employee trusts.** Concessional treatment will apply where an asset is transferred to a beneficiary who as a result suffers a Schedule E income tax charge. See 18.75 EXEMPTIONS AND RELIEFS.

D36 **Loans to traders and loans to traders evidenced by qualifying corporate bonds: time limit for loss relief claims.** Revenue Statement of Practice SP 3/83 is revised for clarification, re-classified as an extra-statutory concession and extended to cover loans evidenced by qualifying corporate bonds. See 35.9 and 35.10 LOSSES.

D37 **Relocation of employees.** The exemption for a gain arising on the disposal of an employee's private residence is extended similarly to his right to share in any profits made by a relocation business or his employer to whom he sells property and which later sells it to a third party. See 43.2 PRIVATE RESIDENCES.

D38 **Loans to traders evidenced by qualifying corporate bonds.** A further concessional relief will apply in certain circumstances where the bonds concerned only became qualifying corporate bonds because of a change in definition even though they are not evidenced by a qualifying loan. See 35.10 LOSSES.

D39 **Extension of leases.** No capital gains tax is payable where a lessee surrenders an existing lease and is granted, in an arm's length transaction, a new, longer lease on the same property at a different rent, but otherwise on the same terms. This concession was revised in a Revenue Press Release of 18 October 1994. See 33.17 LAND.

D40 **Non-resident trusts.** The definition of 'participator' in *ICTA 1988, s 417(1)* is concessionally restricted for the purposes of *TCGA 1992, ss 86–98, 5 Sch.* This concession was revised by Revenue Press Release of 7 October 1994. See 39.7, 39.8 OVERSEAS MATTERS.

D41 **Non-resident trusts.** Certain loans repayable on demand which were made on non-commercial terms before 19 March 1991 will not be caught by the condition in *TCGA 1992, 5 Sch 9(3)* if they are either repaid in full or made subject to commercial terms before 31 July 1992. See 39.7 OVERSEAS MATTERS.

D42 **Mergers of leases.** Where a superior interest in leasehold land is acquired (being either a superior lease or the reversion of freehold), and the land is disposed of after 28 June 1992, indexation allowance on the expenditure incurred on the inferior lease will be calculated by reference to the date of its acquisition. See 33.16 LAND.

D43 **Settled property.** Interests in possession which are not life interests are afforded treatment which would otherwise only apply to life interests. See 52.7, 52.10 and 52.11 SETTLEMENTS.

D44 **Re-basing and indexation: shares derived from larger holdings held at 31 March 1982.** In certain circumstances a valuation of a shareholding held or treated as having been held at 31 March 1982 can be calculated by reference to the size of the shareholding held by a spouse or group member at that date. See 8.7 ASSETS HELD ON 31 MARCH 1982.

D45 **Rollover into depreciating assets.** Where an asset employed in a trade carried on by a claimant to rollover relief ceases to be used due to the claimant's death, no charge to tax will arise under *TCGA 1992, s 154(2)(b)*. See 50.6 ROLLOVER RELIEF.

D46 **Relief against income for capital losses on the disposal of unquoted shares in a trading company.** Where an unquoted trading company devoid of assets is wound up, a holder of shares in that company who has not made a negligible value claim under *TCGA 1992, s 24(2)* and did not receive a distribution during the course of winding up will, by concession, be able to claim relief under either *ICTA 1988, s 573* or *s 574* despite the requirements of *ICTA 1988, s 575(1)* not being met, provided all other conditions for relief are met. See 35.12 and 35.14 LOSSES.

D47 **Temporary loss of charitable status due to reverter of school and other sites.** A temporary loss of charitable status will in general be ignored for tax purposes. See 10.3 CHARITIES.

D48 **Retirement relief: final business period of less than one year allowed to be aggregated with earlier business periods.** The requirement that a final business period must be a minimum of one year is relaxed subject to conditions. See 48.9 RETIREMENT RELIEF.

The following income tax concessions are also relevant for the purposes of capital gains tax.

A11 **Residence in the UK: year of commencement or cessation of residence.** Although there is no provision for splitting a tax year in relation to residence, liability to UK tax which is affected by residence is computed by reference to the period of actual residence in the UK during the year. This concession was revised by Revenue Press Release of 14 September 1993. (See also D2 above). See 47.2 RESIDENCE AND DOMICILE.

A17 **Death of taxpayer before due date for payment of tax.** For notices of assessment issued after 31 July 1975, personal representatives unable to pay tax before obtaining probate may have concessional treatment so that interest on tax falling due after the date of death runs from the later of the expiration of thirty days after the grant of probate and the statutory date for interest to run. See 32.7 INTEREST ON UNPAID TAX.

A19 **Arrears of tax arising through official error.** Arrears of tax arising due to the Revenue's failure to make proper and timely use of information supplied by an *individual* taxpayer will be waived in certain cases. See 41.8 PAYMENT OF TAX.

A36 **Close companies in liquidation: distributions in respect of share capital.** Where income for a period ending after commencement of winding-up is apportioned to a participator, the resulting 'excess liability' (if any) will be restricted to the excess (if any) over the capital gains tax paid by him which is shown to be attributable to that income when received as a distribution in respect of share capital. Where such income of a company is apportioned to a beneficiary of a trust, or to a residuary legatee, account will be taken of any relevant capital gains tax paid by the trustees or personal representatives. (This relief is an alternative to that in D12 above.) See 16.4 DISPOSAL.

A78 **Residence in the UK—accompanying spouse.** Where an employee leaving the UK to work abroad satisfies the conditions of A11 above, the residence treatment of the employee may be extended to an accompanying spouse in certain circumstances. This concession was revised by Revenue Press Release of 14 September 1993. See 47.2–47.4 RESIDENCE AND DOMICILE.

A82   **Repayment supplement paid to individuals etc. resident in EC member states.** Residents of EC member states other than the UK will be treated on the same basis as UK residents in relation to a repayment supplement on a repayment of income tax. It is understood that this concession will also apply to repayments of capital gains tax. See 31.1 INTEREST ON OVERPAID TAX.

B15   **Borrowing and lending of securities** with repayment in other securities of the same description is not a disposal where it is standard practice designed to preserve a market in securities etc. After 17 August 1989 this concession is superseded by legislation. See 53.23 SHARES AND SECURITIES.

B36   **Stock lending.** The existing statutory provisions are concessionally extended. See 53.23 SHARES AND SECURITIES.

B41   **Claims to repayment of tax.** Where an overpayment of tax arises because of an error by the Inland Revenue or another Government department and where there is no dispute as to the facts, claims to repayment of the tax overpaid made outside of the statutory period will be allowed. See 41.8 PAYMENT OF TAX.

The following concessions have been announced by the Revenue in Press Releases as dated below and will be included in IR 1 in due course.

Private residence exemption: short delay by owner occupier in taking up residence. Restriction of relief is removed in certain circumstances where an individual acquires a property but does not immediately use it as his only or main residence. See 43.2 PRIVATE RESIDENCES (18 October 1994).

Compensation from foreign governments. Exemption from tax is granted for gains arising on compensation from foreign governments in certain circumstances. See 16.7 DISPOSAL (19 December 1994).

28   Inland Revenue Press Releases

The following is a summary, in date order, of Press Releases referred to in this Part other than those designated as containing Extra-Statutory Concessions or Statements of Practice. Certain pre-18 July 1978 Press Releases have been reissued as Statements of Practice on 18 June 1979 or subsequently (see 29 INLAND REVENUE STATEMENTS OF PRACTICE).

Copies of any individual Press Release may be obtained from: Inland Revenue, Public Enquiry Room, Somerset House, Strand, London WC2R 1LB (Tel. 0171–438 6420/6425/7772). A charge (currently £75) is made for Press Releases (including Extra-Statutory Concessions and Statements of Practice) mailed weekly throughout a calendar year. To receive Press Releases, application can be made to Tolley Publishing Co Ltd, Tolley House, 2 Addiscombe Road, Croydon, Surrey CR9 5AF (Tel. 0181–686 9141). A separate application is needed to subscribe to the Revenue's Tax Bulletin for an annual charge of £18, which should be made to Inland Revenue, Finance Division, Barrington Road, Worthing, West Sussex, BN12 4XH. See also Tolley's Official Tax Statements.

13.12.72	**Compensation for acquisition of property under compulsory powers.** Compensation for temporary loss of profits included in overall compensation on compulsory purchase is treated as part of the consideration on disposal for capital gains tax purposes. This practice ceased with effect from 28 July 1978 and the present provisions are to be found in Revenue Pamphlet IR 131, SP 8/79, 18 June 1979. See 16.7 DISPOSAL.
18.12.73	**Forms 64-8 (New).** This form may be used by a taxpayer to request the inspector to provide his agent with a copy of any assessment. See 5.1 ASSESSMENTS.
1.8.77	**Investigation of incorrect business accounts and tax returns.** The Board may mitigate penalties where the taxpayer shows a willingness to co-operate. See 42.10 PENALTIES.
2.3.78	**Double taxation: exchange of information with the USA.** Terms of a working arrangement between the USA and UK for the examination of the affairs of taxpayers with substantial operations in both countries. See 25.2 INLAND REVENUE: CONFIDENTIALITY OF INFORMATION.
25.6.82	**Deep discounted stock.** The Revenue indicate their view of the tax treatment of deep discounted stock, including zero-coupon bonds. The treatment of certain indexed stocks is also clarified. Subsequent legislation has modified this statement. See 53.19 SHARES AND SECURITIES.
23.2.84	**Building societies and the taxation of gains on the disposal of gilt-edged securities.** The Revenue indicate their view of the tax treatment of such disposals. See 30.1 INTERACTION WITH OTHER TAXES.
17.5.84	**Furnished holiday lettings and caravans.** The Revenue indicate their practice as to the tax treatment of such accommodation. See 19.1 FURNISHED HOLIDAY ACCOMMODATION.
27.12.84	**Assets disposed of in a series of transactions.** The Revenue give their views on anti-avoidance legislation applying before 20 March 1985. See 3.11 ANTI-AVOIDANCE.
16.4.85	**Retirement relief and ill-health.** The Revenue explain the procedures they will adopt in obtaining evidence of ill-health. See 48.3 RETIREMENT RELIEF.

1.8.85   **Trade unions: provident benefits.** Following the issue of Revenue Pamphlet IR 131, SP 1/84, 17 February 1984, claims for past chargeable periods may be made for exemption for gains applied to certain payments which were not previously regarded as provident benefits. See 18.52 EXEMPTIONS AND RELIEFS.

8.7.88   **Capital gains deferred between 1982 and 1988.** Guidance is given as to the availability of the 50% relief where rollover relief was claimed in respect of the disposal of the old asset before 31 March 1982, and the replacement asset was acquired afterwards. See 8.12 ASSETS HELD ON 31 MARCH 1982.

11.7.88   **Rollover relief: milk and potato quotas, satellites and spacecraft.** Guidance is given as to the effect of the law in certain transitional cases. See 50.2 ROLLOVER RELIEF.

15.3.89   **Appeals in Northern Ireland.** Information is given about the change whereby appeals are heard by General Commissioners. See 4.5 APPEALS.

3.5.89   **Personal equity plans.** The requirements that unit trusts and authorised unit trusts have to meet will be relaxed. See 53.20 SHARES AND SECURITIES.

28.7.89   **Stock lending.** New statutory provisions replace the previous concessional arrangements. See 53.23 SHARES AND SECURITIES.

6.10.89   **Personal equity plans.** New issue shares generally on offer to the public will not be disqualified from being transferred to a plan even though concurrent separate offers are made on slightly different terms to, for example, employees of the company concerned. See 53.20 SHARES AND SECURITIES.

19.12.89 **Business expansion scheme: shares issued before 19 March 1986.** An unintended change in the law made by *ICTA 1988* is to be corrected. See 53.18 SHARES AND SECURITIES.

26.2.90   **Elections for an appeal to be heard by the Special Commissioners.** The procedure to be adopted by inspectors of taxes is explained. See 4.5 APPEALS.

20.3.90   **Value added tax capital goods scheme: implication for capital gains tax.** See 30.3 INTERACTION WITH OTHER TAXES.

9.5.90   **Confidentiality of information.** The Revenue will disclose details of absent parents liable to support lone-parent families. See 25.2 INLAND REVENUE: CONFIDENTIALITY OF INFORMATION.

9.5.90   **Clearance procedure for employee share ownership trusts.** The Revenue are prepared to give an opinion whether a trust qualifies for relief. See 53.26 SHARES AND SECURITIES.

17.10.90 **Personal equity plans.** Pending the issue of revised regulations, certain changes to the rules for qualifying investments are applied by concession. See 53.20 SHARES AND SECURITIES.

18.10.90 **Tax fraud: 'Hansard' extract.** The Board's policy as to whether they will accept a money settlement instead of instituting fraud proceedings is explained. See 9.9 BACK DUTY.

21.11.90 **Married persons owning jointly held property.** The Revenue explain how gains should be allocated between spouses under independent taxation. See 37.1 MARRIED PERSONS.

14.12.90 **Clearance procedure for employee share ownership trusts.** The Revenue are prepared to give an opinion whether a draft trust deed (as well as any substantive one) qualifies for relief. See 53.26 SHARES AND SECURITIES.

19.12.90   **Revenue practice regarding validity of trust deeds for general and tax law purposes.** From 6 April 1991 new trust deeds will not normally be examined by the Revenue to check their validity. See 52.6 SETTLEMENTS.

31.1.91   **Double taxation: Ghana.** Details of claims able to be made by taxpayers are given following the discovery that an earlier agreement was still in force because a later agreement, which had been operated in practice for many years, had never been formally ratified. See 17.2 DOUBLE TAX RELIEF.

19.3.91   **Qualifying corporate bonds: definition of normal commercial loan.** The Revenue are prepared concessionally to extend the strict definition before 1 April 1991. See 44.2 QUALIFYING CORPORATE BONDS.

19.3.91   **Assets held on 31 March 1982: deferred charges on gains before 31 March 1982.** The time limit for claiming relief is extended in certain cases affected by legislative changes effective for disposals and other events after 18 March 1991. See 8.12 ASSETS HELD ON 31 MARCH 1982.

12.6.91   **Friendly societies: tax-exempt policies.** A mistaken assumption that certain policies were not tax-exempt is provided for by statute and extra-statutory concession. See 18.40 EXEMPTIONS AND RELIEFS.

18.11.91   **Valuation of unquoted shares at 31 March 1982.** Shares Valuation Division may initiate valuation procedures, in certain circumstances, before receiving a formal request to do so from the inspector. See 8.2 ASSETS HELD ON 31 MARCH 1982.

15.9.92   **Rollover relief and groups of companies.** Depending on the outcome of a court case, steps may be taken to ensure that the established practice in relation to roll-over relief and groups of companies will continue to apply. See 50.4 ROLLOVER RELIEF.

7.12.92   **Pay and File starting date.** For provisions other than those relating to filing of returns, the Pay and File system for corporation tax will come into effect in relation to accounting periods ending after 30 September 1993. As regards provisions relating to the filing of returns, the system will apply to notices to file returns given after 31 December 1993. See generally 41.1 PAYMENT OF TAX, 42.3 PENALTIES and 49.3 RETURNS.

17.2.93   **Revenue Adjudicator and Codes of Practice.** The appointment of the Adjudicator and publication of a series of Codes of Practice are announced. See 24.6 and 24.7 INLAND REVENUE: ADMINISTRATION.

16.3.93   **Temporary residents in the UK: available accommodation.** Available accommodation in the UK, though ignored for certain temporary visitors to the UK after 1992/93, will still be taken into determining an individual's residence or ordinary residence status in other circumstances. See 47.2–47.4 RESIDENCE AND DOMICILE.

1.4.93   **Payment of tax by electronic funds transfer.** An effective date of payment of tax is provided. See 41.4 PAYMENT OF TAX.

18.5.93   **Incidental acquisition and disposal costs rounded to nearest £1,000.** Larger companies may round such costs to reduce administrative effort. See 16.3 DISPOSAL.

23.7.93   **Tax repayments to EC resident companies.** Such companies can qualify for repayment supplement in respect of accounting periods ending before 1 October 1993 in certain circumstances. See 31.2 INTEREST IN OVERPAID TAX.

9.2.94   **European Economic Area Agreement.** The coming into force of the European Economic Area Agreement from 1 January 1994 affects European Economic Interest Groupings. See 39.20 OVERSEAS MATTERS.

28 Inland Revenue Press Releases

7.4.94 **Repayments of overpaid tax made automatically.** From 5 April 1994, the Revenue will use computer systems that identify and repay overpayments automatically in most cases. See 41.10 PAYMENT OF TAX.

29.11.94 **Claims for rollover relief.** After 28 November 1994 claims for rollover relief must be made in writing specifying certain details. See 50.1 ROLLOVER RELIEF.

27.3.95 **Double tax relief.** Revenue announce publication of IR 146 which lists foreign taxes admissible for relief. See 17.2 DOUBLE TAX RELIEF.

29   Inland Revenue Statements of Practice

The following is a summary of those Statements of Practice published in Revenue Pamphlet IR 131 (first published July 1994), or subsequently announced for inclusion therein, which are referred to in this book.

Statements are divided into those originally published before 18 July 1978 (which are given a reference letter (according to the subject matter) and consecutive number, e.g. E11) and later Statements (which are numbered consecutively in each year, e.g. SP 10/86).

Certain statements marked in IR 131 as obsolete will continue to be referred to in the text (having been relevant in the last six years), and the original source is quoted in such cases, as it is where the Statement awaits inclusion in IR 131.

Copies of individual SP-denominated Statements are available free of charge from Public Enquiry Room, West Wing, Somerset House, Strand, London WC2R 1LB (large SAE to accompany postal applications).

The full text of all Statements of Practice is published in Tolley's Official Tax Statements.

A8   **Stock dividends.** The interpretation of *ICTA 1988, s 251(2)* is clarified. See 53.12 SHARES AND SECURITIES.

A13   **Completion of return forms by attorneys.** In cases of age and infirmity of the taxpayer the Revenue will accept the signature of an attorney who has full knowledge of the taxpayer's affairs. See 49.2 RETURNS.

A14   **Delay in rendering tax returns.** The Revenue draws attention to the relevant provisions of *TMA 1970*. (Revenue Press Release 10 May 1977; British Tax Review 1977 pp 504-506; Taxation Vol 99 p 129). See 49.2 and 49.4 RETURNS. Subsequently superseded by SP 3/88 and SP 6/89 below.

A31   **Reimbursement of taxpayer's expenses.** Where there is serious error on the part of the Revenue itself, the facts of each case will be considered with a view to compensation being paid by the Revenue for any loss or expenditure incurred as a result of the error. (Letter from Chairman of the Board to the Clerk of the Select Committee on the Parliamentary Commissioner for Administration 16 June 1975). The scope of this practice has been superseded subsequently. See 24.5 INLAND REVENUE: ADMINISTRATION.

B1   **Treatment of VAT.** The position of partly exempt persons is considered (Revenue Press Release 7 May 1973; British Tax Review 1973 p 417; Taxation Vol 91 p 105). See 30.3 INTERACTION WITH OTHER TAXES.

D1   **Part disposals of land.** Where part of an estate is disposed of, the Revenue will accept that that part can be treated as a separate asset and the total cost apportioned accordingly (i.e. on an alternative basis to the usual part disposal formula). See 33.10 LAND.

D3   **Company liquidations: shareholders' capital gains tax.** Special rules can be applied where a shareholder receives more than one distribution in the liquidation. See 7.12 ASSETS HELD ON 6 APRIL 1965 and 53.14 SHARES AND SECURITIES.

D4   **Short delay by owner-occupier in taking up residence.** The period of occupation of a house will, in certain circumstances, include one year prior to taking up residence. This statement was replaced by a new extra-statutory concession D4 on 18 October 1994. See 43.2 PRIVATE RESIDENCES.

D6   **Replacement of business assets: time limit.** Where land is acquired under a compulsory purchase order and leased back to the vendor, the Revenue will, under certain conditions, extend the time limit for replacement. See 33.14 LAND.

D7   **Treatment of VAT.** See 30.3 INTERACTION WITH OTHER TAXES.

D8   **Houses owned by occupants of tied accommodation.** In certain circumstances, where the occupant owns another house he may nominate that house as his main residence. (Revenue Press Release 27 September 1973; British Tax Review 1973 p 415; Taxation Vol 92 p 11). This statement is, to some extent, superseded by legislation but may still be relevant where pre-31 July 1978 or pre-6 April 1983 periods of ownership need to be considered. See 43.2 PRIVATE RESIDENCES.

D11   **Partnership: assets owned by a partner.** Rollover relief may be available. See 40.12 PARTNERSHIPS and 50.1 ROLLOVER RELIEF.

D12   **Partnerships.** This statement sets out a number of points of general practice agreed in discussions with the Law Society and the Allied Accountancy Bodies on the capital gains tax treatment of partnerships. See 40 PARTNERSHIPS.

D13   **Assets of negligible value: time limit for claims** is extended to two years. This practice has been revised and is now reclassified as an extra-statutory concession. See 35.8 LOSSES.

D15   **Accommodation let by owner-occupiers.** The Revenue state their practice. (Revenue Press Release 6 November 1975). This statement has been substantially superseded by SP 14/80 below. But see 43.3 and 43.6 PRIVATE RESIDENCES where letting amounts to a trade.

D18   **Value-shifting: TCGA 1992, s 30, 11 Sch 10(1).** These provisions do not apply when a farmer retires, leases the farm to his son, and sells the freehold, subject to the lease, to an outside investor. See 3.6 ANTI-AVOIDANCE.

D19   **Replacement of business assets in groups of companies.** To obtain rollover relief, the Revenue do not insist that a company be a member of the group at the time of the transaction carried out by the other company. See 50.4 ROLLOVER RELIEF.

D21   **Time limit for an election for valuation on 6 April 1965 under TCGA 1992, 2 Sch 17: company leaving a group: TCGA 1992, ss 178, 179.** See 13.17 COMPANIES.

D22   **Transfer of a business to a company—TCGA 1992, s 162.** Liabilities taken over by a company on the transfer of a business are not treated as consideration and, provided other conditions are met, no gain arises. This practice has been reclassified as an extra-statutory concession. See 22.7 HOLD-OVER RELIEFS.

D23   **Overseas resident company.** The appropriate proportion of any overseas tax payable by a non-resident company is deductible in computing the gain chargeable on a UK shareholder under *TCGA 1992, s 13*. See 39.5 OVERSEAS MATTERS.

D24   **Initial repairs to property.** Such expense, including the cost of decorating, not allowable for Schedule A purposes, is regarded as allowable for capital gains tax purposes. See 16.3(*b*) DISPOSAL.

SP 1/79   **Partnerships: extension of SP D12 above.** The practice whereby the capitalised value of an annuity paid to a retired partner is not treated as consideration for the disposal of his share in the partnership assets in certain circumstances is extended to cases where a lump sum is paid in addition. See 40.8 PARTNERSHIPS.

SP 8/79   **Compensation for acquisition of property under compulsory powers.** As from 28 July 1978, any compensation for temporary loss of profits is taxable under Schedule D, Case I or II. See 16.7 DISPOSAL.

SP 10/79   **Power for trustees to allow a beneficiary to occupy a dwelling-house.** Depending upon the circumstances, this may be treated as giving rise to an interest in possession. See 52.7 SETTLEMENTS.

SP 14/79   **Unquoted shares or securities held on 6 April 1965: computation of chargeable gains where there has been a reorganisation of share capital.** (Revenue Press Release 21 December 1979). See 7.12 ASSETS HELD ON 6 APRIL 1965.

SP 14/80   **Relief for owner-occupiers.** This statement explains the relief for owner-occupiers who let living accommodation in their homes. See 43.6 PRIVATE RESIDENCES.

SP 18/80   **Securities dealt in on The Stock Exchange Unlisted Securities Market: status and valuation for tax purposes.** Such securities are not regarded as 'quoted' or 'listed' but are 'authorised to be dealt in'. See 36.4 MARKET VALUE.

SP 3/81   **Individuals coming to the UK: ordinary residence.** The ordinary residence position is further explained, regarding individuals coming to, or leaving, the UK who have, or acquire, accommodation for their use in the UK. See 47.3 RESIDENCE AND DOMICILE.

SP 7/81   **Allowable expenditure: expenses incurred by personal representatives under TCGA 1992, s 38(1)(b).** For deaths after 5 April 1981, a revised scale of expenditure is allowable for costs of establishing title in computing gains or losses of personal representatives on the sale of assets in a deceased person's estate. This statement was superseded by SP 8/94 below. See 15.8 DEATH.

SP 8/81   **Rollover relief for replacement of business assets: trades carried on successively.** The Board's practice in deciding whether trades are carried on successively, how acquisitions in the interval between trades are to be regarded, and how this treatment is to be applied to groups of companies, is explained. This statement was superseded by legislation. See 50.3 ROLLOVER RELIEF.

SP 3/82   **Capital gains tax indexation before the 1985 date.** The Revenue gives guidance on the practice that will be adopted in relation to (*a*) the identification of securities disposed of during the twelve months before indexation came into effect (see 23.16 INDEXATION); (*b*) the time apportionment rules for assets acquired before 6 April 1965 (see 7.9 ASSETS HELD ON 6 APRIL 1965); and (*c*) disposals of assets on a no gain/ no loss basis (see 23.4 INDEXATION). This practice is of limited application for disposals after 5 April 1985 (31 March 1985 for companies).

SP 3/83   **Relief for losses on loans to traders: time limit for claims.** The Revenue practice in relation to the time limits within which it is prepared to accept claims for relief is explained. This practice has been revised and is now classified as an extra-statutory concession. See 35.9 LOSSES.

SP 5/83   **Use of schedules in making personal tax returns.** Schedules supporting a return are acceptable provided the taxpayer signs the official declaration and all material in the schedules is clearly linked to the official return form. See 49.2 RETURNS.

SP 1/84   **Trade unions: provident benefits** include legal expenses in connection with a member's accident or injury claim or unfair dismissal. See 18.52 EXEMPTIONS AND RELIEFS.

SP 6/84   **Leasing of mobile drilling rigs etc. by overseas residents.** The Revenue indicate their practice. See 39.19 OVERSEAS MATTERS.

SP 7/84   **Exercise of a power of appointment over settled property.** The Revenue indicate how they will decide whether a new settlement has been created. See 52.6 SETTLEMENTS.

SP 10/84 **Foreign bank accounts.** The Revenue give their practice regarding direct transfers from one foreign bank account to another. See 18.5 EXEMPTIONS AND RELIEFS.

SP 5/85 **Division of a company on a share for share basis.** The special treatment accorded to a company reconstruction under *TCGA 1992, s 136(1)(2)* and *139* is extended to cover a division, for bona fide commercial reasons, of a company's undertakings into two or more companies owned by different sets of shareholders. See 3.13 ANTI-AVOIDANCE; 13.6 COMPANIES and 53.9 SHARES AND SECURITIES.

SP 5/86 **Rollover relief for employees and office-holders.** In certain circumstances relief is available to such persons where the land or building owned is in general use in the trade carried on by the employer. See 50.3 ROLLOVER RELIEF.

SP 2/88 **Civil tax penalties and criminal prosecution cases.** The Revenue explain a change of practice on seeking civil money penalties from certain taxpayers whom they have prosecuted. See 42.6 PENALTIES.

SP 3/88 **Delay in rendering tax returns; interest on unpaid tax.** The Revenue clarify their practice (see A14 above) on charging interest where a taxpayer has substantially delayed sending in his tax return. This practice has been replaced by SP 6/89 from 27 July 1989. See 49.4 RETURNS.

SP 6/88 **Double taxation relief.** The Revenue describe some situations where double taxation relief is available. See 17.7 DOUBLE TAX RELIEF.

SP 1/89 **Partnerships.** The practice concerning changes in partnership sharing ratios (see D12 above) is extended to cover the 1988 re-basing provisions. See 40.5 PARTNER-SHIPS.

SP 3/89 **Authorised unit trusts: monthly savings schemes.** A simplified method of calculating the chargeable gain arising on a disposal can be used. See 57.1 UNIT AND INVESTMENT TRUSTS.

SP 4/89 **Company purchasing own shares.** The Revenue's practice where a purchase gives rise to a distribution is explained. See 53.15 SHARES AND SECURITIES.

SP 5/89 **Capital gains re-basing and indexation: shares held at 31 March 1982.** A single holding treatment will apply if some shares were held on 31 March 1982 and the remainder are treated as held on that date. See 8.7 ASSETS HELD ON 31 MARCH 1982.

SP 6/89 **Delay in rendering tax returns: interest on unpaid tax.** This statement of the Revenue's practice replaces that in 3/88 above for failures after 26 July 1989. See 49.4 RETURNS.

SP 1/90 **Company residence.** The Revenue's approach to the determination of a company's residence is explained. See 47.5 RESIDENCE AND DOMICILE.

SP 2/90 **Company migration: notice and arrangements under FA 1988, s 130.** Guidance is given on the procedure, information and arrangements the Revenue will require under the provision. See 39.18 OVERSEAS MATTERS.

SP 5/90 **Accountants' working papers.** The Revenue's investigatory powers as regards the disclosure of accountants' working papers are explained. See 9.8 BACK DUTY.

SP 8/90 **Loans to traders evidenced by qualifying corporate bonds.** Loss relief will still be available where the security concerned ceases to have any value because it is redeemed early. See 35.10 LOSSES.

SP 2/91 **Residence in the UK: visits extended because of exceptional circumstances.** In deciding a person's residence status, days spent in the UK because of exceptional circumstances beyond the person's control will be ignored in certain cases. See 47.2 RESIDENCE AND DOMICILE.

SP 4/91   **Tax returns.** The principles adopted by the Revenue are explained. See 49.2 RETURNS.

SP 7/91   **Double taxation: business profits: unilateral relief.** The practice as regards admission of foreign taxes for unilateral relief is revised. See 17.4 DOUBLE TAX RELIEF.

SP 8/91   **Discovery assessments.** The Revenue practice as regards the making of further assessments following 'discovery' is explained. See 5.2 ASSESSMENTS.

SP 14/91   **Tax treatment of transactions in financial futures and options.** The Revenue give their views. See 16.10 DISPOSAL and 57.2 UNIT AND INVESTMENT TRUSTS.

SP 15/91   **Treatment of investment managers and their overseas clients.** The Revenue give their views. See 16.10 DISPOSAL.

SP 17/91   **Ordinary residence in the UK.** The practice regarding the commencement of ordinary residence where the period to be spent in the UK is less than three years is explained. See 47.3 RESIDENCE AND DOMICILE.

SP 3/92   **Double taxation agreement with the USSR.** The Revenue clarify the position following the disintegration of the old Soviet Union. See 17.2 DOUBLE TAX RELIEF.

SP 4/92   **Capital gains tax re-basing elections.** The Revenue describe the three kinds of disposal which will not be treated as the first relevant disposal for a re-basing election. See 8.3 ASSETS HELD ON 31 MARCH 1982.

SP 5/92   **Non-resident trusts.** The Revenue give their views on a number of detailed matters in connection with: the residence of trustees; past trustees' liabilities; the settlor's right to repayment from the trustees; trusts created before 19 March 1991; transactions entered into at arm's length; close companies; transactions with wholly-owned companies; loans made to settlements; loans made by trustees; failure to exercise rights to reimbursement; administrative expenses; life tenants; indemnities and guarantees; variations; *ultra vires* payments; and intra-group transfers. See 39.7 OVERSEAS MATTERS.

SP 8/92   **Hold-over relief: valuation of assets.** The circumstances in which the Inland Revenue will require a valuation of assets in respect of which a claim to hold-over relief is made are described. See 22.1 HOLD-OVER RELIEFS and 48.2 RETIREMENT RELIEF.

SP 5/93   **Double taxation agreement with Czechoslovakia.** The Revenue clarify the position following the split of Czechoslovakia into separate Czech and Slovak republics. See 17.2 DOUBLE TAX RELIEF.

SP 6/93   **Double taxation agreement with Yugoslavia.** The Revenue clarify the position following the disintegration of the former Yugoslavia into separate republics. See 17.2 DOUBLE TAX RELIEF.

SP 9/93   **Corporation tax Pay and File: corporation tax returns.** The Revenue explain how its statutory powers will be exercised in relation to corporation tax returns under Pay and File. See 49.3 RETURNS.

SP 10/93   **Corporation tax Pay and File: special arrangement for groups of companies.** For companies dealt with mainly in one tax district simplified procedures can operate regarding claims to group relief and giving consents to surrender such relief. See 49.3 RETURNS.

SP 11/93   **Corporation tax Pay and File: claims to capital allowances and group relief made outside the normal time limit.** The Revenue's power to exercise a discretion with regard to such late claims is explained. See 49.3 RETURNS.

29　Inland Revenue Statements of Practice

SP 13/93　**Compulsory acquisition of freehold by tenant.** The Revenue will accept a rollover relief claim from a landlord whose tenant has exercised his statutory rights to acquire the freehold reversion under the Leasehold Reform Act 1967 or the Housing and Urban Development Act 1993. See 33.14 LAND.

SP 4/94　**Enhanced stock dividends received by trustees of interest in possession trusts.** Revenue set out their view on tax treatment. See 53.12 SHARES AND SECURITIES.

SP 7/94　**Investment trusts investing in authorised unit trusts.** The Revenue express their views of the tax implications of such investment. See 57.2 UNIT AND INVESTMENT TRUSTS.

SP 8/94　**Allowable expenditure: expenses incurred by personal representatives and corporate trustees under TCGA 1992, s 38(1)(b).** For deaths after 5 April 1993, a revised scale of expenditure is allowable for costs of establishing title in computing gains or losses of personal representatives on the sale of assets in a deceased person's estate. See 15.8 DEATH.

30   Interaction with Other Taxes

Cross-references. See 2 ANNUAL RATES AND EXEMPTIONS for rates applicable to gains by reference to lower, basic and higher rates of income tax; 16 DISPOSAL for acquisition and disposal consideration taken into account for capital gains tax purposes generally; 13.34 COMPANIES as regards the taxation regime for exchange gains and losses of a 'qualifying company' whereby such transactions are only taken into account for the charge of corporation tax on income; 13.35 COMPANIES as regards the taxation regime for financial instruments involving interest rate and currency contracts of a 'qualifying company' whereby such transactions are only taken into account for the charge of corporation tax on income; 22.4 HOLD-OVER RELIEFS for relief given to gifts after 13 March 1989 on which inheritance tax is chargeable etc; 33.18–33.21 LAND for premiums on leases of land charged to income tax; 53 SHARES AND SECURITIES for interaction with income tax provisions; 56.1 UNDERWRITERS for treatment of assets in premiums trust funds.

30.1   GENERAL AND INCOME TAX

Any money or money's worth charged to income tax as income of, or taken into account as a receipt in computing income or profits or gains or losses of (except in relation to the computation under *ICTA 1988, s 76(2)* of management expenses of life assurance companies), the person making the disposal is excluded from the consideration for the disposal of the asset for capital gains tax purposes. However,

(a)   this is not to be taken as excluding any money or money's worth taken into account in making a balancing charge for capital allowance purposes or brought into account as the disposal value of machinery or plant for such purposes (see *Hirsch v Crowthers Cloth Ltd Ch D 1989, 62 TC 759*);

(b)   the capitalised value of a rentcharge (as in the case where a rentcharge is exchanged for another asset), ground annual or feu duty, or of a right of any other description to income or to payments in the nature of income over a period, or to a series of payments in the nature of income may be taken into account for capital gains tax purposes; and

(c)   amounts chargeable to tax under *ICTA 1988, s 348* or *349* (deduction of basic rate income tax from annual payments) are not excluded from the disposal consideration for capital gains tax purposes.

[*TCGA 1992, ss 37, 52(2)(3)(5), 8 Sch 5(6)*].

For income tax matters relating to know-how and patents (and which have a capital gains tax effect), see 6.4, 6.5 ASSETS. See also 39.13 OVERSEAS MATTERS for offshore funds.

Expenditure which is deductible in computing profits or losses for income tax purposes (or would be so deductible if the asset were held as a fixed asset of a trade) is excluded from being allowable expenditure for capital gains tax purposes. [*TCGA 1992, s 39(1)(2)*]. See 16.5 DISPOSAL.

Any assessment to income tax or decision on a claim under the *Income Tax Acts*, and any decision on an appeal in connection therewith, is conclusive for capital gains tax purposes where liability to tax depends on the provisions of the *Income Tax Acts*. [*TCGA 1992, s 284*]. Where *alternative* income tax and capital gains tax assessments are made in respect of the same transactions, the fact that the capital gains tax assessment becomes final does not preclude the income tax assessment taking effect instead (*Bye v Coren CA 1986, 60 TC 116*). See also *Lord Advocate v McKenna CS 1989, 61 TC 688* and *CIR v Wilkinson Ch D, [1992] STC 454*.

30.2   Interaction with Other Taxes

Income or capital? Whether the gain arising on the disposal of an asset is of income or capital nature has been tested in the courts on numerous occasions and the outcome is likely to be one of fact and degree. In particular, see 33.3 LAND for isolated and speculative transactions in land. 'No part of our law of taxation presents such almost insoluble conundrums as the decision whether a receipt or outgoing is capital or income for tax purposes' (Lord Upjohn in *Strick v Regent Oil Co Ltd HL 1965, 43 TC 1* which see for a comprehensive review of the law). A widely used test is the 'enduring benefit' one given by Viscount Cave in *Atherton v British Insulated & Helsby Cables Ltd HL 1925, 10 TC 155.*

Building societies and gilts. In the light of legal advice received, the Inland Revenue decided to treat gains of building societies arising from the realisation of gilt-edged securities and similar stock after 23 February 1984 as part of trading profits and not as chargeable gains subject to the rules of capital gains tax (Revenue Press Release 23 February 1984).

Dairy farmers. Under the Milk Supplementary Levy (Outgoers) Scheme 1984, any farmer claiming payment under that scheme may apply either for compensation for loss of profits in the five years immediately after ceasing to produce milk, or for compensation for the surrender of his milk quota. Payments in respect of loss of profits will be treated as receipts of the farming business and therefore liable to tax as income. Payments in respect of surrender of quota will be treated as capital and liable to capital gains tax (Hansard 18 July 1984, col 218 and 15 April 1985, col 27). Similar comments apply to the Milk (Community Outgoers) and Milk (Partial Cessation of Production) Schemes (Hansard 13 February 1987, col 384).

Investment trusts and the tax treatment of forward currency transactions. See 57.2 UNIT AND INVESTMENT TRUSTS.

Transactions in certain options and futures by certain taxpayers. See 16.10 and 16.11 DISPOSAL.

30.2   INHERITANCE TAX (OR CAPITAL TRANSFER TAX)

A lifetime disposal which contains an element of gift may incur liability to inheritance tax (IHT) (or capital transfer tax (CTT)) as well as capital gains tax. For the purposes of IHT or CTT, no account is taken of any capital gains tax borne by the transferor in determining the reduction in value in his estate. [*IHTA 1984, s 164*].

Example

A makes a gift of land to a non-UK resident discretionary trustee, B, and which is valued at £20,000 and on which there is a capital gains tax liability of £3,000. The value for IHT or CTT purposes (subject to grossing-up for the IHT or CTT payable) is £20,000 (i.e. the same as if A had sold the land and given the £20,000 proceeds to B).

Relief for CGT against IHT or CTT. Capital gains tax paid will be taken into account for IHT or CTT purposes in the following instances.

(a)   If the transferor fails to pay all or part of the capital gains tax within twelve months of the due date, an assessment may be made on the donee (see 20.5 GIFTS) and the amount of such tax borne by the donee is treated as reducing the value transferred. There is a similar effect when the transfer is from a settlement but, after 8 March 1982, this only applies if the capital gains tax is borne by a person who becomes absolutely entitled to the settled property concerned. [*IHTA 1984, s 165(1)(2)*].

Example

In the *Example* above, if A fails to pay the £3,000 capital gains tax and it is borne by B, the value transferred by A is £17,000 for the purposes of IHT or CTT (again subject to grossing-up for the IHT or CTT payable).

(*b*)   Where a person sells, or is treated as having sold, national heritage property on the breach or termination of an undertaking (see 18.70 EXEMPTIONS AND RELIEFS) any capital gains tax payable is deductible in determining the value of the asset for IHT or CTT purposes. [*TCGA 1992, s 258(8)*].

Relief for IHT or CTT against CGT. Where hold-over relief is granted under

(i)   *TCGA 1992, s 165* in relation to gifts made after 13 March 1989 (see 22.1 HOLD-OVER RELIEFS),

(ii)   *TCGA 1992, s 260* in relation to gifts after 13 March 1989 (see 22.4 HOLD-OVER RELIEFS), or

(iii)   *FA 1980, s 79* in relation to gifts after 5 April 1980 and before 14 March 1989 (see 22.6 HOLD-OVER RELIEFS),

the transferee may deduct on a subsequent disposal any IHT or CTT attributable to the value of the asset on the original transfer (being either a chargeable transfer or a potentially exempt transfer which proves to be a chargeable transfer). The tax deductible may be varied on the subsequent death of the transferor or otherwise but it cannot in any circumstances create an allowable loss on the subsequent disposal. [*TCGA 1992, ss 67(1)–(3), 165(10)(11), 260(7)(8)*].

There is no relief for IHT or CTT if hold-over relief is *not* claimed, so that even where the gain otherwise arising is negligible or covered by reliefs a hold-over relief claim may still be beneficial overall (Tolley's Practical Tax 1984 p 198). A hold-over relief claim can be made even if an allowable loss arises on the original gift and so give rise to an IHT or CTT deduction on a subsequent disposal by the donee whilst not affecting the loss relief position of the donor. Where only part of the asset gifted is subsequently disposed of, the Revenue accept that any IHT or CTT paid on the original gift can still be deducted in full on the part disposal (subject to the size of the gain arising) and there is no need to apportion IHT or CTT paid between the part disposed of and the part retained (Taxation 5 October 1989 pp 12, 14). There is no provision for indexation allowance to be calculated by reference to the IHT or CTT able to be deducted.

Valuation of assets. Valuations of assets made *at death* for the purpose of an inheritance tax (or capital transfer tax) charge on the value of a person's estate immediately before death are, in theory, binding for capital gains tax purposes. [*TCGA 1992, s 274; IHTA 1984, s 168*]. However, in practice, in the case of quoted securities, the Capital Taxes Office follow the capital gains tax position. (Revenue Pamphlet IHT 1 para 8.9). See 36.2 MARKET VALUE. The bases of valuation are not necessarily the same for capital gains tax and inheritance tax e.g. the related property provisions for inheritance tax do not apply to capital gains tax.

30.3   **VALUE ADDED TAX**

If VAT is suffered on the purchase of an asset, but is available for set-off in full in the purchaser's VAT account (e.g. a capital asset purchased by a trader who is registered for VAT), then the cost of the asset for capital gains tax purposes is the cost exclusive of VAT. Where no VAT set-off is available, the cost is inclusive of VAT borne. On the disposal of an asset, VAT chargeable is disregarded in computing the disposal consideration for capital gains tax purposes (29.D7 INLAND REVENUE STATEMENTS OF PRACTICE).

A person whose output is partly exempt and partly taxable may set off only part of his VAT on inputs against his VAT on outputs. In such a case, although the computation of disposal proceeds is as above, it will be necessary to allocate the VAT ultimately suffered to the various expense payments made. Inspectors will be prepared to consider any reasonable arrangements made to carry out this apportionment. A taxable person making both taxable and exempt supplies may therefore treat as part of the capital gains tax cost of an asset the input tax that was not available for credit in respect of the acquisition (29.B1 INLAND REVENUE STATEMENTS OF PRACTICE).

The above practices should be read in the light of a Revenue Press Release of 20 March 1990 which mentioned that VAT on certain inputs (broadly land, buildings and computers with values above certain levels) after 31 March 1990 may require annual adjustment for a period of up to ten years after the input concerned. In certain circumstances a VAT adjustment may reduce the amount of expenditure on an asset qualifying for ROLLOVER RELIEF (50). Where a VAT adjustment is made after a claim to rollover relief has been determined, the Revenue will not normally seek to reopen the claim.

---

31 Interest on Overpaid Tax

Cross-references. See 41 PAYMENT OF TAX; 51 SELF-ASSESSMENT for future changes broadly from 1996/97.

31.1 PERSONS OTHER THAN COMPANIES

A repayment (or set-off) after 31 July 1975 to an individual by the Revenue of capital gains tax (amounting to £25 or more where the repayment is made before 6 April 1993) and repaid more than twelve months after the end of the year of assessment to which it relates, carries interest ('*a repayment supplement*'), provided that the individual was resident in the UK for that year. However, repayment supplement will also be paid by concession where the individual was resident elsewhere in the European Community for that year provided all the other conditions are met. The Revenue will also accept claims on a similar basis from persons who were resident elsewhere in the EC for a year of assessment for which a repayment without supplement has been made since 12 July 1987 (Revenue Pamphlet IR 1, A82). (*Note.* Although stated by the Revenue to be a concession, there may be legal requirement not to discriminate against individuals resident elsewhere in the EC; see 31.2 below regarding company accounting periods ending before 1 October 1993. Although phrased in terms of income tax and repayment supplement under *ICTA 1988, s 824*, it is understood that the concession applies equally to capital gains tax and repayment supplement under *TCGA 1992, s 283*.)

The repayment supplement will not constitute income of the recipient for any tax purpose. The interest will run to the end of the tax month (i.e. 6th day of one calendar month to 5th day of following month) in which the repayment order is issued, and will commence as follows.

Tax originally paid	*Interest commences*
More than twelve months after year of assessment	From end of year of assessment in which tax was paid
In any other case	From end of twelve months following year of assessment

Rates of interest are:

7.00% from 6 March 1995
6.25% p.a. from 6 October 1994 to 5 March 1995
5.50% p.a. from 6 January 1994 to 5 October 1994
6.25% p.a. from 6 March 1993 to 5 January 1994
7.00% p.a. from 6 December 1992 to 5 March 1993
7.75% p.a. from 6 November 1992 to 5 December 1992
9.25% p.a. from 6 October 1991 to 5 November 1992
10.00% p.a. from 6 July 1991 to 5 October 1991
10.75% p.a. from 6 May 1991 to 5 July 1991
11.50% p.a. from 6 March 1991 to 5 May 1991
12.25% p.a. from 6 November 1990 to 5 March 1991
13.00% p.a. from 6 November 1989 to 5 November 1990
12.25% p.a. from 6 July 1989 to 5 November 1989
11.50% p.a. from 6 January 1989 to 5 July 1989
10.50% p.a. from 6 October 1988 to 5 January 1989
9.75% p.a. from 6 August 1988 to 5 October 1988
7.75% p.a. from 6 May 1988 to 5 August 1988
8.25% p.a. from 6 December 1987 to 5 May 1988
9.00% p.a. from 6 September 1987 to 5 December 1987
8.25% p.a. from 6 June 1987 to 5 September 1987
9.00% p.a. from 6 April 1987 to 5 June 1987
9.50% p.a. from 6 November 1986 to 5 April 1987
8.50% p.a. from 6 August 1986 to 5 November 1986
11.00% p.a. from 6 May 1985 to 5 August 1986
8.00% p.a. from 6 December 1982 to 5 May 1985
12.00% p.a. from 6 January 1980 to 5 December 1982
9.00% p.a. from 6 April 1974 to 5 January 1980
6.00% p.a. previously

From 18 August 1989 the interest rate is determined by criteria contained in Treasury regulations made by statutory instrument so that when such criteria change so as to alter the rate, the Board must specify in an order the new rate and the day from which it has effect. Prior to 18 August 1989 each interest rate change had to be made by Treasury order contained in a statutory instrument.

Where a repayment relates to tax paid in two or more years of assessment, it is treated, as far as possible, as representing payments made in later rather than earlier years.

Trustees of a 'United Kingdom trust' (within *ICTA 1988, s 231(5)*), 'personal representatives' (within *ICTA 1988, s 701(4)*) of a deceased person whose estate is a 'United Kingdom estate' (within *ICTA 1988, s 701(9)*) and partnerships are treated similarly to individuals (including the concessional practice mentioned above (Revenue Pamphlet IR 1, A82).

The above provisions do not apply to companies (see 31.2 below) or to payments or repayments made by order or judgment of a court having power to allow interest (for which see 41.3 PAYMENT OF TAX). [*TCGA 1992, s 283; ICTA 1988, s 824(8); SI 1974, No 966; SI 1979, No 1687; SI 1982, No 1587; SI 1985, No 563; SI 1986, Nos 1181,*

31.2 Interest on Overpaid Tax

1832; SI 1987, Nos 513, 898, 1492, 1988; SI 1988, Nos 756, 1278, 1621, 2185; SI 1989 No 1000; FA 1989, ss 158(2)(5)(6), 178, 179(1)(4), 17 Sch Pt IV; SI 1989, Nos 1297, 1298; SI 1993 No 753].

For the above purposes and for those in 31.2 below for accounting periods ended before 1 October 1993, the Board publish ready-reckoner tables of interest factors which may be used in calculating repayment supplement.

Example

L realised net chargeable gains (after the annual exemption) of £20,000 in 1992/93. An assessment was raised on 15 January 1994, charging tax of £8,000. L paid the tax on 30 January 1994. In December 1994, L made a claim under *TCGA 1992, s 152* (rollover relief) and the 1992/93 assessment was reduced to £8,000, with tax payable of £3,200. A repayment of £4,800 was made by payable order issued on 15 January 1995.

Repayment supplement is		£
6.4.94 – 5.10.94	£4,800 × 5.5% × $\frac{6}{12}$	132.00
6.10.94 – 5.2.95	£4,800 × 6.25% × $\frac{4}{12}$	100.00
		£232.00

Note to the example

(*a*) The calculation may be made, or checked, using the interest factor tables published from time to time by the Revenue.

Factor for February 1995	3.1584
Factor for April 1994	3.1101
Difference	0.0483
£4,800 × 0.0483 =	£231.84

31.2 COMPANIES

Accounting periods ending after 30 September 1993. Where a repayment of corporation tax falls to be made to a company for an accounting period ending after 30 September 1993 (Pay and File), the repayment carries interest (under *ICTA 1988, s 826*) from the 'material date' until the order for repayment is issued.

The *'material date'* is the later of the date the corporation tax was paid and the date on which it became (or would have become due and payable, i.e. the day following the expiry of nine months from the end of the accounting period (see 41.1 PAYMENT OF TAX)).

The interest rate is determined by criteria contained in Treasury regulations made by statutory instrument so that when such criteria change so as to alter the rate, the Board must specify in an order the new rate and the day from which it has effect.

Rates of interest are:

   4.00% p.a. from 6 March 1995
   3.25% p.a. from 6 October 1994 to 5 March 1995
   2.50% p.a. from 6 January 1994 to 5 October 1994
   3.25% p.a. from 1 October 1993 to 5 January 1994

There are restrictions on the amount of the interest where surplus advance corporation tax of a later accounting period displaces mainstream corporation tax paid in respect of an earlier accounting period, or trading losses or non-trading exchange losses of a later accounting period are offset against profits of an earlier period or there is a combination of such events.

Interest is paid without deduction of income tax and is not brought into account in computing profits or income. Corporation tax repayments are as far as possible treated as repayments of tax paid on a later date rather than an earlier date. [*ICTA 1988, s 826; FA 1989, ss 178, 179(1)(c)(ii), 180(6); FA 1991, 15 Sch 23; FA 1993, ss 120, 170, 14 Sch 10, 18 Sch 5; SI 1989 No 1297; SI 1993 No 2212*].

Accounting periods ending before 1 October 1993. A repayment after 31 July 1975 to a company by the Revenue of corporation tax on chargeable gains (amounting to £100 or more for repayments prior to 6 April 1993) and repaid more than twelve months after the 'material date' carries interest (*'a repayment supplement'*), which is disregarded for all tax purposes. Rates of interest are as under 31.1 above. The interest will run to the end of the tax month (i.e. 6th day of one calendar month to 5th day of the following month) in which the order for repayment is issued and will commence as follows. (Where a repayment relates to corporation tax paid on different dates, it is treated, as far as possible, as being for a later rather than an earlier date.)

Tax originally paid	*Interest commences*
On or after the first anniversary of the 'material date'	At the beginning of the tax month following the next anniversary of the 'material date' after the tax was paid.
In any other case	At the beginning of the tax month following the first anniversary of the 'material date'.

'Material date' means the earliest due date for payment of corporation tax for the accounting period in question (for which see 41.1 PAYMENT OF TAX).

In order to qualify for the repayment supplement, the company must have been resident in the UK for the accounting period in connection with which the repayment is made. However, the Revenue, following the case of *R v CIR (ex p. Commerzbank AG) CJEC, [1993] STC 605* decided on 13 July 1993 in which it was held that refusal to pay repayment supplement on a tax repayment to a company resident elsewhere in the European Community was discriminatory and breached the Treaty of Rome, has invited claims for repayment supplement from companies resident elsewhere in the EC in an accounting period for which a repayment without supplement has been made more than twelve months after the end of the accounting period and within the six years before 13 July 1993 (Revenue Press Release 23 July 1993). This practice presumably applies to subsequent accounting periods ending before 1 October 1993.

The provisions do not apply to amounts paid by order of a court having power to allow interest (for which see 41.3 PAYMENT OF TAX). There are restrictions on the amount of the supplement where surplus advance corporation tax of a later accounting period displaces mainstream corporation tax of an earlier period, or trading losses of a later accounting period are offset against profits of an earlier period, or there is a combination of such events. [*ICTA 1988, s 825; FA 1989, ss 158(2)(5)(6), 178, 179(1)(4); FA 1991, 15 Sch 22; FA 1993, s 120, 14 Sch 10; SI 1993 No 753*].

31.3   OVER-PAYMENTS

See 41.10 PAYMENT OF TAX as regards assessment of repayment supplement or interest overpaid.

31.4 Interest on Overpaid Tax

MISCELLANEOUS

31.4 **Unauthorised demands for tax.** There is a general right to interest under *Supreme Court Act 1981, s 35A* in a case where the taxpayer submits to an unauthorised demand for tax, provided that the payment is not made voluntarily to close a transaction (*Woolwich Equitable Building Society v CIR HL, [1992] STC 657*).

Mistakes by the Revenue. Where there is no good reason for a delay in excess of six months, over and above the 28-day target set by itself, before the Revenue replies to a letter or enquiry, it will: not charge interest on tax unpaid during the period of the delay; pay repayment supplement or interest (as appropriate) on tax overpaid during that period; and pay any reasonable costs the taxpayer has incurred as a direct result of the delay (Revenue Code of Practice 1).

32 Interest on Unpaid Tax

Cross-references. See 5 ASSESSMENTS; 9 BACK DUTY; 41 PAYMENT OF TAX; 42 PENALTIES; 51 SELF-ASSESSMENT for future changes broadly from 1996/97.

32.1 For notices of assessment issued after 31 July 1975 (but subject to the treatment for companies under Pay and File arrangements as in 32.4 below), if tax is not paid on the date it becomes due and payable (see 41 PAYMENT OF TAX), interest is chargeable from that date (even if it is a non-business day) on each assessment. This applies to all assessments but additional rules apply where an appeal is entered against the assessment (see 32.2 below). The Board could remit interest of £30 or less arising on any assessment notice of which was issued before 19 April 1993 (although it is understood an administrative de minimis limit applies subsequently). [*TMA 1970, s 86(1)(2)(5)(6); F(No 2)A 1975, s 46(1); FA 1980, s 62; FA 1989, s 158(1)(3)(6); SI 1993 No 753*].

Rates of interest are:
   7.00% from 6 March 1995
   6.25% p.a. from 6 October 1994 to 5 March 1995
   5.50% p.a. from 6 January 1994 to 5 October 1994
   6.25% p.a. from 6 March 1993 to 5 January 1994
   7.00% p.a. from 6 December 1992 to 5 March 1993
   7.75% p.a. from 6 November 1992 to 5 December 1992
   9.25% p.a. from 6 October 1991 to 5 November 1992
   10.00% p.a. from 6 July 1991 to 5 October 1991
   10.75% p.a. from 6 May 1991 to 5 July 1991
   11.50% p.a. from 6 March 1991 to 5 May 1991
   12.25% p.a. from 6 November 1990 to 5 March 1991
   13.00% p.a. from 6 November 1989 to 5 November 1990
   12.25% p.a. from 6 July 1989 to 5 November 1989
   11.50% p.a. from 6 January 1989 to 5 July 1989
   10.50% p.a. from 6 October 1988 to 5 January 1989

9.75% p.a. from 6 August 1988 to 5 October 1988
7.75% p.a. from 6 May 1988 to 5 August 1988
8.25% p.a. from 6 December 1987 to 5 May 1988
9.00% p.a. from 6 September 1987 to 5 December 1987
8.25% p.a. from 6 June 1987 to 5 September 1987
9.00% p.a. from 6 April 1987 to 5 June 1987
9.50% p.a. from 6 November 1986 to 5 April 1987
8.50% p.a. from 6 August 1986 to 5 November 1986
11.00% p.a. from 1 May 1985 to 5 August 1986
8.00% p.a. from 1 December 1982 to 30 April 1985
12.00% p.a. from 1 January 1980 to 30 November 1982
9.00% p.a. from 1 July 1974 to 31 December 1979

From 18 August 1989 the interest rate is determined by criteria contained in Treasury regulations made by statutory instrument so that when such criteria change so as to alter the rate, the Board must specify in an order the new rate and the day from which it has effect. Prior to 18 August 1989 each interest rate change had to be made by Treasury order contained in a statutory instrument. [*TMA 1970, s 89; F(No 2)A 1987, s 89; SI 1974, No 966; SI 1979, No 1687; SI 1982, No 1587; SI 1985, No 563; SI 1986, Nos 1181, 1832; SI 1987, Nos 513, 898, 1492, 1988; SI 1988, Nos 756, 1278, 1621, 2185; SI 1989 No 1000; FA 1989, ss 178, 179(1)(4); SI 1989 Nos 1297, 1298*].

See 41 PAYMENT OF TAX for collection.

Interest is payable gross and recoverable (as if it were tax charged and due and payable under the assessment to which it relates) as a Crown debt; it is not deductible from profits or income [*TMA 1970, ss 69, 90*] and is refundable to the extent that the tax concerned is subsequently cancelled. [*TMA 1970, s 91*].

32.2   TAX BECOMING DUE AFTER APPEAL AGAINST ASSESSMENT

For notices of assessment issued after 30 July 1982, on application by the taxpayer, the inspector may agree (or the Commissioners, or county court in NI before 3 April 1989, may determine) that part of the tax charged by an assessment may be postponed (see 41 PAYMENT OF TAX). Any tax which is *not postponed* then becomes due and payable as if it were tax charged by an assessment notice of which was issued on the date of the determination or agreement and in respect of which there had been no appeal, or, if later, on the due date had there been no appeal. On the determination of the substantive appeal, any *postponed tax* and/or *extra tax* (the latter being the tax additional to that charged by the original assessment) which then becomes payable is due and payable as if it were tax charged by an assessment notice of which was issued on the date on which the inspector issues to the appellant a notice of the total amount payable in accordance with the determination, or, if later, on the due date for the original assessment had there been no appeal. [*TMA 1970, s 55(3)(6)(9); F(No 2)A 1975, s 45(1); FA 1989, s 156(2)(4)*]. Interest on non-postponed and any postponed or extra tax will then run from a '*reckonable date*', which is the *later* of

(a)   the due date if there had been no appeal (i.e. under the original assessment, see 41.1 PAYMENT OF TAX), and

(b)   the *earlier* of

    (i)   the date on which the tax actually becomes due and payable (see 41 PAYMENT OF TAX), and

    (ii)   1 June in the year next following that for which the assessment is made— e.g. 1 June 1992 for a 1990/91 assessment. [*TMA 1970, s 86(3)(3A)(4); FA 1989, s 156(1)*].

32.3 Interest on Unpaid Tax

General. Adequate payments made on account of assessments under dispute or the use of certificates of tax deposit (see 41.11 PAYMENT OF TAX) may help prevent or reduce a charge to interest.

Example

Mr X makes his annual return of income and gains for 1993/94 in June 1994. He has substantial chargeable gains which become the subject of dispute with the inspector. On 10 October 1994 an assessment for 1993/94 is raised on Mr X showing tax due of £15,000. He appeals on 1 November 1994 and requests postponement of £5,000. On 8 November 1994 he and the inspector agree postponement of £4,000.

The appeal is determined by the Commissioners on 7 August 1995 and Mr X receives notice of the tax outstanding—£5,000—dated 14 August 1995.

The dates of consequence are as follows (for due dates of payment and further examples, see also 41.3 PAYMENT OF TAX):

(i) Due date of payment had there been no appeal:	1 December 1994
(ii) Revised due date of payment of non-postponed tax—£11,000:	8 December 1994 (30 days after agreement)
(iii) Date from which interest will run on non-postponed tax—£11,000:	8 December 1994 (30 days after agreement—due date)
(iv) Due date of payment of postponed and extra tax—£5,000:	13 September 1995 (30 days after notice of sum payable)
(v) Date from which interest will run on postponed and extra tax—£5,000:	1 June 1995 (the 'reckonable date')

Thus, although the postponed and extra tax is not due and payable until 13 September 1995, Mr X will have to pay interest on that tax from 1 June 1995 to the day of payment.

32.3 **INTEREST ON TAX BECOMING DUE AFTER DETERMINATION OF AN APPEAL BY THE COURTS**

Any outstanding tax charged in accordance with a Commissioners' decision must be paid before an appeal can be heard by the High Court, and if, on the determination of the appeal, further tax is found to be chargeable, it becomes due and payable thirty days from the date on which the inspector issues to the taxpayer a notice of the total amount payable. Interest under *TMA 1970, s 86*, however, runs from the later of 1 June in the year next following that for which the assessment was made and the date on which the tax would have become due and payable if charged by the original assessment (without an appeal being made). [*TMA 1970, ss 56(9), 86(3A); F(No 2)A 1975, s 45(3); FA 1989, s 156(1)(3)(4)*]. If a taxpayer in Northern Ireland exercised his right to appeal to the county court instead of to the Commissioners (which right ended after 2 April 1989), the same rule applied if a case was stated for the opinion of the Court of Appeal in Northern Ireland. [*TMA 1970, s 59(6); F (No 2)A 1975, s 45(3); FA 1988, s 134*]. See 41.3 PAYMENT OF TAX.

32.4 **COMPANIES**

Accounting periods ending after 30 September 1993. In relation to accounting periods ending after 30 September 1993 (Pay and File), corporation tax carries interest (under *TMA 1970, s 87A*) from the due and payable date (see 41.1 PAYMENT OF TAX), even if it is a non-business day, until payment. Where corporation tax assessed on a company may be assessed on other persons in certain circumstances, the due and payable date is that which refers to the company's liability.

The interest rate is determined by criteria contained in Treasury regulations made by statutory instrument so that when such criteria change so as to alter the rate, the Board must specify in an order the new rate and the day from which it has effect.

Rates of interest are:

> 7.00% p.a. from 6 March 1995
> 6.25% p.a. from 6 October 1994 to 5 March 1995
> 5.50% p.a. from 6 January 1994 to 5 October 1994
> 6.25% p.a. from 1 October 1993 to 5 January 1994

Interest on tax subsequently discharged is adjusted or repaid so as to secure that the total is as it would have been had the tax discharged never been charged. However, where surplus advance corporation tax of a later accounting period displaces mainstream corporation tax paid in respect of an earlier accounting period, or trading losses or non-trading exchange losses of a later accounting period are offset against profits of an earlier period, or there is a combination of such events, any such adjustment or repayment of interest is restricted. In considering an adjustment or repayment of interest, then, where relief for tax paid for an accounting period is given by way of repayment of tax, the amount repaid is, as far as possible, treated as if it were a discharge of the corporation tax charged for that period.

Interest is paid without deduction of income tax and is not brought into account in computing profits or income. It is recoverable (as if it were tax charged and due and payable under an assessment) as a Crown debt. [*TMA 1970, ss 69, 87A, 90, 91(1A)(2A); F(No 2)A 1987, ss 85, 86(5)(6); FA 1989, s 178; FA 1991, 15 Sch 2; FA 1993, ss 120, 170, 14 Sch 4, 5, 18 Sch 1; SI 1989 No 1297; SI 1993 No 2212*].

Accounting periods ending before 1 October 1993. The provisions in 32.1 to 32.3 above generally apply to corporation tax (including that in respect of chargeable gains) except that the '*reckonable date*' in 32.2 above is the *later* of

(*a*)   the due date if there had been no appeal (see 41.1 PAYMENT OF TAX), and

(*b*)   the *earlier* of

> (i)   the date on which the tax becomes due and payable, and

> (ii)   the last day of the six months following the payment interval given in 41.1 PAYMENT OF TAX.

As a transitional measure, where

(1)   a notice is served under *TMA 1970, s 11* (return of profits; see 49.3 RETURNS) after 31 December 1993 (post-Pay and File),

(2)   the notice relates to an accounting period ending before 1 October 1993 (pre-Pay and File), and

(3)   the tax charged by any corporation tax assessment for that accounting period does not become due and payable until after the date nine months after the end of that accounting period,

the reckonable date is the date mentioned in (3) above rather than the date determined under (*a*) and (*b*) above. The Board are given power to mitigate any interest falling due as a result of this provision and to stay or compound any proceedings for its recovery (see Revenue Tax Bulletin August 1993 pp 83–85 for guidance on the approach to be taken as regards mitigation etc.). [*TMA 1970, s 86; F(No 2)A 1975, s 46(1); FA 1980, ss 61(3)(5), 62; FA 1982, s 69; FA 1987, 6 Sch 6, 12; ICTA 1988, s 478(6), 30 Sch 1(7); FA 1989, s 156(1)(4); FA 1993, s 170, 18 Sch 3].*

Where surplus advance corporation tax of a later accounting period displaces mainstream corporation tax paid in respect of an earlier accounting period, or trading losses of a later accounting period are offset against profits of an earlier period, any adjustment or repayment of interest under *TMA 1970, s 91* is restricted. *[FA 1989, s 157; FA 1991, 15 Sch 1].*

32.5   EXCHANGE RESTRICTIONS AND DELAYED REMITTANCES

Where gains arising overseas cannot be remitted to the UK due to government action in the country of origin etc., and the Revenue agree to defer collection of the tax, interest ceases to run from the date on which the Board were first in possession of information necessary to enable them to agree to deferment. If that date is three months or less from the due and payable date, no interest is payable. But where a demand is later made for payment of the deferred tax, interest (from the date of demand) is only assessable if the tax is not paid within three months of that demand. *[TMA 1970, s 92; F(No 2)A 1987, s 86(2)(a)].* The Board may defer collection indefinitely. See 39.4 OVERSEAS MATTERS for an alternative relief under *TCGA 1992, s 279.*

32.6   FAILURE OR ERROR, AND FRAUD, WILFUL DEFAULT OR NEGLECT

Where an assessment is made for making good 'tax' lost, **after 26 July 1989,** through

(a)   a 'failure' to give a notice, make a return, or provide a document or other information, or

(b)   an error in any information, return, etc. supplied,

the tax attributable to that failure or error is chargeable with interest if an inspector or the Board so determines.

'*Tax*' includes capital gains tax and, with respect to accounting periods ending before 1 October 1993 (pre-Pay and File), corporation tax (including that in respect of chargeable gains). (For accounting periods ending after 30 September 1993 (Pay and File), corporation tax will carry a *TMA 1970, s 87A* interest charge if paid late; see 32.4 above).

'*Failure*' includes failure to do something at a particular time or within a particular period; and the exclusion in *TMA 1970, s 118(2)* (see 49.1 RETURNS) does not apply to it. *[TMA 1970, s 88(1)(7); F(No 2)A 1987, s 86(4); FA 1989, ss 159, 160(1)].*

Determination. A determination under these provisions can be made at any time within six years of the end of the chargeable period for which the tax is charged or within three years of the final determination of the amount of that tax. It must specify

(i)   the date of issue,

(ii)   the amount of tax carrying interest, and the assessment by which it was charged,

(iii)   the date when, for *section 88*, it ought to have been paid, and

(iv)   the time within which an appeal against the determination may be made.

The general APPEALS (4) provisions apply, except *TMA 1970, s 50(6)-(8)* (see 4.8 (*b*)-(*e*) APPEALS). On appeal, the Commissioners can set aside or confirm the determination, or alter it in respect of the amount of tax or the date. *[TMA 1970, ss 70, 88A(1)-(5); FA 1989, s 160(2)(3)].*

Where an assessment is made for making good tax lost by fraud, wilful default or neglect (see 9.4 BACK DUTY) **which occurred before 27 July 1989**, the tax attributable to that fraud, etc. is chargeable with interest. [*TMA 1970, s 88(1)*]. The amount of interest is certified by the General or Special Commissioners under *TMA 1970, s 70(3)*, following an application by the Revenue at which the taxpayer is entitled to appear and be heard (*Nicholson v Morris CA 1977, 51 TC 95*). There is no appeal by way of case stated (*R v Holborn Commissioners (ex p. Frank Rind Settlement Trustees) QB 1974, 49 TC 656*).

Tax carrying interest under these provisions does not also carry interest under *TMA 1970, s 86* (see 32.1, 32.2 and 32.4 above). It is payable gross (and not deductible for tax purposes) from the date when the tax ought originally to have been paid (but without the alternative of thirty days from the date of the issue of the notice of assessment, see 41.1 PAYMENT OF TAX) to the date of actual payment. The Board have power to mitigate interest payable and stay or compound any proceedings for recovery. Interest is refundable to the extent that the tax concerned is subsequently cancelled. [*TMA 1970, ss 88-91; F(No 2)A 1975, s 46(4); FA 1980, s 61(4)(5); FA 1987, 6 Sch 7; ICTA 1988, 30 Sch 1(8); FA 1989, s 161*]. See also 9.9 BACK DUTY, 42 PENALTIES and 49.4 RETURNS.

Rates of interest are the same as in 32.1 above except that a rate of 4% p.a. applied from 19 April 1967 to 30 June 1974 and a rate of 3% p.a. applied for periods up to and including 18 April 1967. [*TMA 1970, s 89; F(No 2)A 1987, s 89; FA 1989, ss 178, 179(1)(4)*].

The Board publish ready-reckoner tables of interest factors which may be used in calculating interest in BACK DUTY (9) investigation settlements.

Where a *TMA 1970, s 88* interest charge arises as regards one assessment and there is an amount of overpaid tax on a different assessment, a set-off will be given where requested (HC Official Report Standing Committee H col 746, 2 July 1975). It seems the set-off will only apply from the date of the request but in relation to non-corporate taxpayers, and corporate taxpayers before the introduction of Pay and File, it would usually be advantageous because of the disparity in the rules for INTEREST ON OVERPAID TAX (31) and *TMA 1970, s 88* interest.

The Revenue has pointed out that there is no element of culpability regarding the charging of interest under *TMA 1970, s 88* as it has effect **after 26 July 1989**. *Any* error in a return etc. which delays the payment of tax is sufficient for the provision to be operated. This may cover the case where a chargeable gain is returned based upon a valuation which is subsequently agreed or determined in such an amount as to increase the gain returned. Interest can be mitigated in such circumstances by making appropriate payments on account (specifying to the Collector precisely what liability it is intended to cover) or by purchasing a certificate of tax deposit in an appropriate amount before the normal due date of the tax. An assessment issued before the normal due date of the tax payment will not carry *section 88* interest (though it may carry *section 86* interest). Where such an assessment has been made which has not been appealed, a further assessment carrying *section 88* interest will normally be made on the basis that the return contained an error (subject to the restrictions on discovery assessments contained in Revenue Statement of Practice SP 8/91; see 5.2 ASSESSMENTS). Where an appeal is lodged against such an assessment, any interest charge will normally be under *section 86*, although exceptionally the power to make a further assessment carrying *section 88* interest whilst an original assessment is under appeal (see 5.2 ASSESSMENTS) will be used. The decision to make such a further assessment will be operated centrally, the main factor being the possible loss of interest to the public revenue. Where no assessment has been made before the earliest due date, any subsequent assessment based on an incomplete, misleading or erroneous return, even one submitted within the time limits specified by Revenue Statement of Practice 6/89 (late returns and charging

32.7   Interest on Unpaid Tax

of interest and penalties; see 49.4 RETURNS), will carry *section 88* interest as regards the tax lost due to the error etc. but will not carry such interest where, following the submission of a fully completed return within the time limits mentioned, the delay in issuing the assessment is due to the operation of the Revenue's procedures (Revenue Tax Bulletin May 1993 p 61).

See *Billingham v Myers Ch D [1994] STC 1016* where regard was had to events occurring after the issue of an assessment in deciding whether it was made for the purpose of making good a loss of tax.

32.7   MISCELLANEOUS

Mistakes by the Revenue. Where there is no good reason for a delay in excess of six months, over and above the 28-day target set by itself, before the Revenue replies to a letter or enquiry, it will: not charge interest on tax unpaid during the period of the delay; pay repayment supplement or interest (as appropriate) on tax overpaid during that period; and pay any reasonable costs the taxpayer has incurred as a direct result of the delay (Revenue Code of Practice 1).

Personal representatives. For notices of assessment issued after 31 July 1975, personal representatives unable to pay tax before obtaining probate may have concessional treatment so that interest on tax falling due after the date of death runs from the expiration of thirty days after the date of grant of probate or letters of administration (if this is later than the date arrived at under 32.1 or 32.2 above). (Revenue Pamphlet IR 1, A17).

33 Land

Cross-references. See 7.8 ASSETS HELD ON 6 APRIL 1965 for land reflecting development value and 7.9–7.14 for other land held at that date; 16.7 DISPOSAL for treatment of statutory compensation received by tenants of land, 16.9 for buildings destroyed and replaced out of compensation and 16.10 for granting of options; 18.16 EXEMPTIONS AND RELIEFS for certain agricultural grants; 18.30 for woodlands, 18.42 for housing associations, 18.50 for self-build societies and 18.70 for disposal by gift of national heritage property; 35.8 LOSSES for buildings becoming of negligible value; 36.5 MARKET VALUE; 38 MINERAL ROYALTIES; 41.5 PAYMENT OF TAX for payment by instalments on gifts of land before 6 April 1984; 43 PRIVATE RESIDENCES with land attached; 50 ROLLOVER RELIEF for a claim on disposal of land occupied for trade purposes.

33.1 INTRODUCTION

There are a number of special provisions in the capital gains tax legislation relating to land. For disposals of land generally, see 33.2–33.15 below. For provisions relating to leases of land, see 33.16–33.25. For contingent liabilities on the disposal of land, see 33.26 below.

33.2 GENERAL

The general principles of capital gains tax apply to disposals of land. There are, however, particular problems concerning land transactions.

(*a*)   An isolated or speculative transaction may be liable to income tax rather than to capital gains tax as amounting to an adventure or concern in the nature of trade (see 33.3 below).

(*b*)   Even where (*a*) above does not apply, capital gains from certain transactions in land may be treated as income (see 33.4 and 33.5 below).

(*c*)   The definition of 'land' for the purposes of *TCGA 1992* is not exclusive and may lead to difficulties of interpretation, especially where property derives its existence from the existence of the physical land. '*Land*' includes for such purposes, except where the context otherwise requires, messuages, tenements and hereditaments, houses and buildings of any tenure. [*TCGA 1992, s 288(1)*]. This should be compared with the *Interpretation Act 1978* definition which is that '*land*' includes buildings and other structures, land covered with water, and any estate, interest, easement, servitude or right in or over land. Apart from the specific definition for certain transactions in land under *ICTA 1988, ss 776–778* in 33.4 below, the definition of land under *Interpretation Act 1978* applies, by default, to *ICTA 1988*. That said, many provisions in *TCGA 1992* refer to 'land' as including any interest in or right over land or to an interest in an asset which can include land or buildings etc. (e.g. *TCGA 1992, s 152* (ROLLOVER RELIEF (50), although *TCGA 1992, s 155* treats buildings and the underlying land as separate) and *s 247* (33.14 below)). Deciding whether property is an interest or right over land can thus depend on general legal principles and the surrounding facts. The Revenue do not consider that milk quota constitutes such an interest or right (Revenue Tax Bulletin February 1993 p 49).

33.3 ISOLATED OR SPECULATIVE TRANSACTIONS

A line is drawn between realisations of property held as investment or as a residence and transactions amounting to an adventure or concern in the nature of a trade. Whether the surplus on the purchase and resale of land, otherwise than in the course of an established commercial enterprise, is derived from an adventure or concern in the nature of trade depends upon the facts.

Para. 116 of the Final Report of the Royal Commission on the Taxation of Profits and Income (1955 HMSO Cmd. 9474) lists six 'badges of trade'.

(*a*)   The subject matter of the realisation.

(*b*)   The length of period of ownership.

(*c*)   The frequency or number of similar transactions.

(*d*)   Supplementary work on assets sold.

(*e*)   Reason for the sale.

(*f*)   Motive.

Other relevant factors may be the degree of organisation, whether the taxpayer is or has been associated with a recognised business dealing in similar assets and how the purchases were financed.

In *Leeming v Jones HL 1930, 15 TC 333* an income tax assessment on the acquisitions and disposal of options over rubber estates was confirmed by Commissioners. The Crown had defended the assessment under both Schedule D, Case I and Case VI. In a Supplementary Case the Commissioners found there had been no concern in the nature of trade. The Court held there was no liability. Per Lawrence LJ 'in the case of an isolated transaction . . . there is really no middle course open. It is either an adventure in the nature of trade, or else it is simply a case of sale and resale of property.' See also *Pearn v Miller KB 1927, 11 TC 610* and *Williams v Davies* below.

Property transactions by companies were held to be trading in *Californian Copper Syndicate v Harris CES 1904, 5 TC 159* (purchase of copper bearing land shortly afterwards resold); *Thew v South West Africa Co CA 1924, 9 TC 141* (numerous sales of land acquired by concession for exploitation); *Cayzer, Irvine & Co v CIR CS 1942, 24 TC 491* (exploitation of landed estate acquired by shipping company); *Emro Investments v Aller* and *Webb (Lance) Estates v Aller Ch D 1954, 35 TC 305* (profits carried to capital reserve on numerous purchases and sales); *Orchard Parks v Pogson Ch D 1964, 42 TC 442* (land compulsorily purchased after development plan dropped); *Parkstone Estates v Blair Ch D 1966, 43 TC 246* (industrial estate developed—land disposed of by sub-leases for premiums); *Eames v Stepnell Properties Ltd CA 1966, 43 TC 678* (sale of land acquired from associated company while resale being negotiated). See also *Bath & West Counties Property Trust Ltd v Thomas Ch D 1977, 52 TC 20*. Realisations were held to be capital in *Hudson's Bay Co v Stevens CA 1909, 5 TC 424* (numerous sales of land acquired under Royal Charter—contrast *South West Africa Co* above); *Tebrau (Johore) Rubber Syndicate v Farmer CES 1910, 5 TC 658* (purchase and resale of rubber estates—contrast *Californian Copper* above); *Mamor Sendirian Berhad v Director-General of Inland Revenue PC, [1985] STC 801* (sales of timber in the course of developing forest land into an oil palm plantation). See also *Lim Foo Yong Sendirian Berhad v Comptroller-General of Inland Revenue PC, [1986] STC 255* where it was held that a company may hold property on both trading and capital account and the fact that acquisitions and disposals have taken place on the former does not automatically determine for all time the company's intention in acquiring, holding and developing other property; and contrast *Richfield International Land and Investment Co Ltd v Inland Revenue Commissioner PC, [1989] STC 820* where an initial finding that a property sale had been on trading account was upheld, such finding only being inferred from previous property sales which had either been taxed or accounted for as trading transactions.

In *Rand v Alberni Land Co Ltd KB 1920, 7 TC 629* sales of land held in trust were held not to be trading but contrast *Alabama Coal etc. Co Ltd v Mylam KB 1926, 11 TC 232; Balgownie Land Trust v CIR CS 1929, 14 TC 684; St Aubyn Estates v Strick KB 1932, 17 TC 412; Tempest Estates Ltd v Walmsley Ch D 1975, 51 TC 305.* Sales of property after a period of letting were held to be realisations of investments or not trading in *CIR v Hyndland Investment Co Ltd CS 1929, 14 TC 694; Glasgow Heritable Trust v CIR CS 1954, 35 TC 196; Lucy & Sunderland Ltd v Hunt Ch D 1961, 40 TC 132* but were held to be trading in *Rellim Ltd v Vise CA 1951, 32 TC 254* (notwithstanding that the company was previously admitted as an investment company); *CIR v Toll Property Co CS 1952, 34 TC 13; Forest Side Properties (Chingford) v Pearce CA 1961, 39 TC 665.* But sales by the liquidator of property owned by companies following the abandonment of a plan for their public flotation were held to be not trading in *Simmons v CIR HL 1980, 53 TC 461* (reversing Commissioners' decision).

Property transactions by individuals and partnerships. Profits were held assessable as income in *Reynold's Exors v Bennett KB 1943, 25 TC 401; Broadbridge v Beattie KB 1944, 26 TC 63; Gray & Gillitt v Tiley KB 1944, 26 TC 80; Laver v Wilkinson KB 1944, 26 TC 105, Foulds v Clayton Ch D 1953, 34 TC 382* and *Kirkby v Hughes Ch D 1992, [1993] STC 76*; in all of which the taxpayers were or had been associated with building or estate development, and contrast *Williams v Davies KB 1945, 26 TC 371* in which the taxpayers were closely associated with land development but a profit on transactions in undeveloped land belonging to their wives was held not assessable as income. The acquisition and resale of land for which planning permission had been or was obtained was held as trading in *Cooke v Haddock Ch D 1960, 39 TC 64; Turner v Last Ch D 1965, 42 TC 517* and *Pilkington v Randall CA 1966, 42 TC 662* (and cf. *Iswera v Ceylon Commr PC 1965, 44 ATC 157*), but contrast *Taylor v Good CA 1974, 49 TC 277* (in which a house bought as a residence was found unsuitable and resold to a developer after obtaining planning permission) and *Kirkham v Williams CA, [1991] STC 342* (in which a site was acquired principally as a capital asset to be used in the taxpayer's trade but which was later developed and sold), in both of which cases it was held that there had not been an adventure. In *Burrell v Davis Ch D 1948, 38 TC 307; Johnston v Heath Ch D 1970, 46 TC 463; Reeves v Evans, Boyce & Northcott Ch D 1971, 48 TC 495* and *Clark v Follett Ch D 1973, 48 TC 677* the short period of ownership or other evidence showed an intention to purchase for resale at a profit and not for investment, and contrast *CIR v Reinhold CS 1953, 34 TC 389, Taylor v Good* above and *Marson v Morton Ch D 1986, 59 TC 381.* For other cases in which profits were held assessable as income see *Hudson v Wrightson KB 1934, 26 TC 55, MacMahon v CIR CS 1951, 32 TC 311* and *Eckel v Board of Inland Revenue PC 1989, 62 TC 331.*

33.4   **TRANSACTIONS IN LAND** [*ICTA 1988, ss 776-778*]

The following provisions apply to all persons, whether UK residents or not, if all or any part of the 'land' in question is in the UK.

Where

(a)   land (or any 'property deriving its value from land') is acquired with the sole or main object of realising a gain from disposing of it, or

(b)   land is held as trading stock, or

(c)   land is developed with the sole or main object of realising a gain from disposing of it when developed,

any capital gain from 'disposal' of the land or any part of it (i.e. any amount not otherwise able to be included in any computation of income for tax purposes) which is realised (for himself or for any other person) by the person acquiring, holding or developing it (or by CONNECTED PERSONS (14), or a person party to, or concerned in, any arrangement or scheme to realise the gain indirectly or by a series of transactions) is, subject as below, treated for all tax purposes as income of the person realising the gain (or the person who transmitted to him, directly or indirectly, the opportunity of making that gain) assessable, under Schedule D, Case VI, for the chargeable period in which the gain is realised. See *Yuill v Wilson HL 1980, 52 TC 674* and its sequel *Yuill v Fletcher CA 1984, 58 TC 145, Winterton v Edwards Ch D 1979, 52 TC 655* and *Sugarwhite v Budd CA 1988, 60 TC 679*. Bona fide transactions, not entered into with tax avoidance in view, may be caught by the legislation. See *Page v Lowther and Another CA 1983, 57 TC 199*.

'*Land*' includes buildings, and any estate or interest in land or buildings.

'*Property deriving its value from land*' includes any shareholding in a company, partnership interest, or interest in settled property, deriving its value, directly or indirectly, from land, and any option, consent or embargo affecting the disposition of land. But see 'Exemptions' below.

'*Disposal*' of land occurs for the above purposes if, by any one or more transactions or by any arrangement or scheme (whether concerning the land or any property deriving its value therefrom), the property in, or control over, the land is effectively disposed of. Any number of transactions may be treated as a single arrangement or scheme if they have, or there is evidence of, a common purpose. For the date of disposal where instalments are involved see *Yuill v Fletcher* above. See also under 'General' below.

Exemptions.

(i)   An individual's gain made from the sale, etc., of his residence exempted from capital gains tax under *TCGA 1992, ss 222–226* or which would be so exempt but for *TCGA 1992, s 224(3)* (acquired for purpose of making a gain, see 43.3 PRIVATE RESIDENCES).

(ii) A gain on the sale of shares in a company holding land as trading stock (or a company owning, directly or indirectly, 90% of the ordinary share capital of such a company) *provided that* the company disposes of the land by normal trade and makes all possible profit from it, and the share sale is not part of an arrangement or scheme to realise a land gain indirectly. See *Chilcott v CIR Ch D 1981, 55 TC 446*.

(iii) If the liability arises solely under (*c*) above, any part of the gain fairly attributable to a period before the intention was formed to develop the land.

Gains are to be computed 'as is just and reasonable in the circumstances', allowance being given only for expenses attributable to the land disposed of, and the following may be taken into account.

(A)   If a leasehold interest is disposed of out of a freehold, the Schedule D, Case I treatment in such a case of a person dealing in land.

(B)   Any adjustment under *ICTA 1988, s 99(2)(3)* for the amount of any lease premium charged to income tax under Schedule A by *ICTA 1988, s 34* (see Tolley's Income Tax).

Where the computation of a gain in respect of the development of land (as under (*c*) above) is made on the footing that the land or property was appropriated as trading stock, that land, etc., is also to be treated for purposes of capital gains tax (under *TCGA 1992, s 161*; see 6.3 ASSETS) as having been transferred to stock.

Where, under *ICTA 1988, s 776*, tax is assessed on, and paid by, a person other than the one who actually realised the gain, the person paying the tax may recover it from the other party (for which purpose the Revenue will, on request, supply a certificate of income in respect of which tax has been paid).

Clearance. The person who made or would make the gain may (if he considers that (a) or (c) above may apply), submit to his inspector particulars of any completed or proposed transactions. If he does so, the inspector must, within 30 days of receiving those particulars, notify the taxpayer whether or not he is satisfied that liability under above does not arise. If the inspector is so satisfied no assessment can thereafter be made on that gain under the provisions above, provided that all material facts and considerations have been fully and accurately disclosed.

General. There are also provisions to prevent avoidance by the use of indirect means to transfer any property or right, or enhance or diminish its value, e.g., by sales at less, or more, than full consideration, assigning share capital or rights in a company or partnership or an interest in settled property, disposal on the winding-up of any company, partnership or trust etc. For ascertaining whether, and to what extent, the value of any property or right is derived from any other property or right, value may be traced through any number of companies, partnerships and trusts, at each stage attributing property held by the company etc. to its shareholders etc., 'in such manner as is appropriate to the circumstances'.

For the above purposes the Revenue may require, under penalty, any person to supply them with any particulars thought necessary, including particulars of

(I)   transactions, etc., in which he acts, or acted, on behalf of others, and

(II)   transactions, etc., which in the opinion of the Revenue should be investigated, and

(III) what part, if any, he has taken, or is taking, in specified transactions, etc. (Under this heading a *solicitor* who has merely acted as professional adviser is not compelled to do more than state that he acted and give his client's name and address.)

The transactions of which particulars are required need not be identified transactions (*Essex v CIR CA 1980, 53 TC 720*).

33.5   LAND SOLD WITH RIGHT OF RECONVEYANCE

Where an interest in land is sold on terms requiring it to be subsequently *reconveyed* two years or more after the sale (or leased back one month or more after the sale) *to the vendor*, or a person connected with him, and the price at which the interest is sold exceeds that at which it is to be reconveyed (or, in the case of a lease-back, the value of the reversionary interest plus any premium for the lease), the excess less 1/50th for each full year (minus one) between the sale and the date of the earliest possible reconveyance (or lease-back) is assessed on the vendor as income under Schedule A (before 1995/96 Schedule D, Case VI). [*ICTA 1988, s 36; FA 1995, 6 Sch 11*].

Any amount (as adjusted under *ICTA 1988, s 36(2)(b)*; price on reconveyance varying with time) as a receipt of a Schedule A business subject to income tax under these provisions is excluded from the consideration brought into account in the computation for capital gains tax purposes *except* in the denominator of the part disposal fraction (A/(A+B); see 16.6 DISPOSAL). This does not apply where what is disposed of is the remainder of a lease or a sub-lease out of a lease the duration of which does not exceed 50 years. See 33.20 below for the alternative provisions which apply. [*TCGA 1992, 8 Sch 5(3)(4), 6(3); FA 1995, 6 Sch 37(1)(2)*].

33.6   DEVELOPMENT GAINS BEFORE 19 MARCH 1985

When a gain accrued to a person on a disposal of any interest in land situated in the UK on or after 18 December 1973 but before 19 March 1985, a calculation had to be made to determine whether any part of the gain was to be deemed to be a 'development gain'. Such a development gain was then taxable as income under Schedule D, Case VI. The balance of the gain (i.e. total gain as calculated under normal capital gains tax provisions less development gain) was liable to capital gains tax. [*FA 1974, s 38(1)(2)*].

In addition, tax charges could arise on a first letting or occupation on or after 18 December 1973 (and in most cases before 1 August 1976 and in all cases before 19 March 1985) of a building in the UK (except private dwellings) in which case there was deemed to have been a disposal and re-acquisition of the property at market value for the purposes of both capital gains tax and the tax on development gains mentioned above. [*FA 1974, s 45*].

33.7   **Note.** The development gains income tax charge was replaced by development land tax (see 33.8 below) after 31 July 1976 and so after that date these earlier provisions continued only where material development started before 1 August 1976. The development gains income tax charge was abolished for disposals after 18 March 1985. [*FA 1985, s 93, 25 Sch*].

33.8   **DEVELOPMENT LAND TAX BEFORE 19 MARCH 1985**

For disposals of land on or after 1 August 1976 and before 19 March 1985 (except in certain circumstances referred to in 33.6 above), development land tax could be chargeable. The rules of DLT were contained in *Development Land Tax Act 1976*, as amended and extended. The charge to DLT was abolished in respect of disposals or deemed disposals after 18 March 1985, and no event occurring after that date will cause a DLT liability to arise although relief for contingent liabilities or irrecoverable consideration continues to be available. Tax deferred or postponed immediately before 19 March 1985 is remitted. [*FA 1985, s 93, 25 Sch*].

33.9   **BETTERMENT LEVY**

Betterment levy paid in respect of certain development land is deductible as expenditure wholly and exclusively incurred in enhancing the value of the asset in the CGT computation arising on the disposal or part disposal of that land. [*TCGA 1992, 11 Sch 17*]. (For disposals of land in the UK after 17 December 1973 and before 19 March 1985, see 33.6–33.8 above.)

33.10   **PART DISPOSALS**

The general provisions for part disposals in *TCGA 1992, s 42* apply to disposals of land. See 16.6 DISPOSAL. These require the use of the market value of the part retained. The Revenue will, however, accept an alternative basis of calculation in the case of land. Under this, the part disposed of will be treated as a separate asset and any fair and reasonable method of apportioning part of the total cost to it will be accepted — e.g. a reasonable valuation of that part at the acquisition date. Where the market value at 6 April 1965 is to be taken as the cost, a reasonable valuation of the part at that date will similarly be accepted.

The cost of the part disposed of will be deducted from the total cost of the estate (or the balance of total cost) to determine the cost of the remainder of the estate; thus the total of the separate amounts adopted for the parts will not exceed the total cost. The cost attributed to each part must also be realistic in itself and the Board reserves the right to apply the general rule if not satisfied that apportionments are fair and reasonable. The taxpayer can always require that the general rule should be applied (except in cases already settled on the alternative basis). If he chooses the general rule it will normally be necessary to apply this rule to all subsequent disposals out of the estate; but where the general rule has been applied for a part disposal before the introduction of the alternative basis and it produced a result broadly the same as under the alternative basis, the alternative basis may be used for subsequent part disposals out of the estate.

So long as disposals out of an estate acquired before 6 April 1965 are dealt with on the alternative basis, each part disposal will carry a separate right to elect for acquisition at market value on 6 April 1965. Similarly where part is sold with development value the mandatory valuation at 6 April 1965 will apply only to that part. Even where the part is to be treated as acquired at market value on 6 April 1965, however, it will still be necessary to agree how much of the actual cost should be attributed to the part disposed of: first, to ensure that any allowable loss does not exceed the actual loss, and second, to produce a balance of total cost for subsequent disposals.

Adoption of the alternative basis is without prejudice to the treatment of small disposals set out in 33.11 below (29.D1 INLAND REVENUE STATEMENTS OF PRACTICE).

For provisions which apply to land held on 6 April 1965 generally, see 7.8–7.14 ASSETS HELD ON 6 APRIL 1965. Although the Revenue have yet to confirm it, it seems the above practice could be applied to land held on 31 March 1982 with suitable modifications. See generally, 8 ASSETS HELD ON 31 MARCH 1982.

33.11   **Small part disposals.** Where there is a transfer of land forming part only of a holding of land (or an estate or interest therein) and the amount or value of the consideration does not exceed one-fifth of the market value of the holding as it existed immediately before the disposal, the transferor may claim under *TCGA 1992, s 242(2)* that the transfer is not treated as a disposal. The consideration which would have been brought into account in the capital gains tax computation is then treated as a reduction of allowable expenditure in relation to any subsequent disposal of the remaining holding.

The consideration for the transfer or, if the transfer is not for full consideration, the market value of the land transferred, must not exceed a limit of £20,000. Where the transferor has made other disposals of land in the year of assessment, the total amount or value of the consideration for all such disposals of land (other than those within 33.13 below) must not exceed the limit.

The provisions do not apply to

(*a*)   transfers treated as giving rise to neither a gain nor a loss between husband and wife (see 37.6 MARRIED PERSONS) or between companies in the same group (see 13.10 COMPANIES); or

(*b*)   an estate or interest in land which is a wasting asset (e.g. a short lease under 33.17 below).

Where the allowable expenditure is less than the consideration for the part disposal (or is nil) the claim referred to above cannot be made but, if the recipient elects under *TCGA 1992, s 244(2)* and there is allowable expenditure, the consideration for the part disposal is reduced by the amount of the allowable expenditure. None of that expenditure is then allowable as a deduction in computing the gain accruing on the part disposal or any subsequent disposal. [*TCGA 1992, ss 242, 244*].

Prior to the commencement of *TCGA 1992*, the above claim and election were made under *CGTA 1979, s 107(2)* and *109(2)* respectively.

33.11 Land

Example

C owns farmland which cost £134,000 in May 1982. In February 1990, a small plot of land is exchanged with an adjoining landowner for another piece of land. The value placed on the transaction is £18,000. The value of the remaining estate excluding the new piece of land is estimated at £250,000. In March 1996, C sells the whole estate for £300,000.

Indexation factors May 1982 to February 1990   0.473
                  February 1990 to March 1996 (assumed)   0.222
                  May 1982 to March 1996 (assumed)   0.800

(i) No claim made under what is now *TCGA 1992, s 242(2)*

		£	£
(a)	*Disposal in February 1990*		
	Disposal proceeds		18,000
	Allowable cost $\dfrac{18,000}{18,000 + 250,000} \times £134,000$		9,000
	Unindexed gain		9,000
	Indexation allowance £9,000 × 0.473		4,257
	Chargeable gain 1989/90		£4,743
(b)	*Disposal in March 1996*		
	Disposal proceeds		300,000
	Allowable cost		
	Original land £(134,000 − 9,000)	125,000	
	Exchanged land	18,000	143,000
	Unindexed gain		157,000
	Indexation allowance		
	Original land £125,000 × 0.800	100,000	
	Exchanged land £18,000 × 0.222	3,996	103,996
	Chargeable gain 1995/96		£53,004

(ii) Claim made under what is now *TCGA 1992, s 242(2)*

		£	£
(a)	*No disposal in February 1990*		
	Allowable cost of original land		134,000
	Deduct disposal proceeds		18,000
	Adjusted allowable cost		£116,000
	Allowable cost of additional land		£18,000
(b)	*Disposal in March 1996*		
	Disposal proceeds		300,000
	Allowable cost		
	Original land	116,000	
	Additional land	18,000	134,000
	Unindexed gain		166,000
	Indexation allowance		
	Original land £134,000 × 0.800	107,200	
	Additional land £18,000 × 0.222	3,996	
		111,196	
	Receipt set-off £18,000 × 0.222	3,996	107,200
	Chargeable gain 1995/96		£58,800

Notes to the example

(a)   If the second disposal had also been made in 1989/90 no claim under *TCGA 1992, s 242(2)* could have been made on the part disposal as proceeds of all disposals of land in the year would have exceeded £20,000.

(b)   If the original land had been held at 31 March 1982 and the part disposal took place after that date, the disposal proceeds, on a claim under *TCGA 1992, s 242(2)*, would be deducted from the 31 March 1982 value for the purpose of the re-basing provisions.

33.12   **COMPULSORY PURCHASE**

The transfer of an interest in land to an 'authority exercising or having compulsory powers' (see 33.13 below) is a disposal for capital gains tax purposes. If the land is acquired under a contract, the date of disposal is the time the contract is made (and not, if different, the time at which the asset is conveyed or transferred). If the contract is conditional, the date of disposal is the time when the condition is satisfied. See also 16.2 DISPOSAL. Otherwise, the disposal and acquisition are made at whichever is the earlier of

(a)   the date when compensation for the acquisition is agreed or otherwise determined (any variation on appeal against the original determination being disregarded); and

(b)   the date when the authority enters on the land in pursuance of its powers.

[*TCGA 1992, ss 28, 246*].

Relief is available for small part disposals (see 33.13 below). Rollover relief may be claimed in certain circumstances (see 33.14 below). In addition, where land or an interest in or right over land is acquired and the acquisition is (or could have been) made under compulsory powers, then the existence of the compulsory powers and any statutory provision treating the purchase price, compensation or other consideration as exclusively paid in respect of the land itself is disregarded in considering whether, under *TCGA 1992, s 52(4)* (just and reasonable apportionments), the purchase price etc. should be apportioned on a just and reasonable basis and treated in part as a capital sum within *TCGA 1992, s 22(1)(a)* (whether as compensation for loss of goodwill, for disturbance or otherwise) or should be apportioned in any other way. [*TCGA 1992, s 245(1)*]. The effect of this is that, where it is just and reasonable, part of the proceeds may be treated as a capital sum derived from an asset. See 16.7(a) DISPOSAL.

The receipt of severance compensation or compensation for injurious affection where part of a holding of land is or could have been compulsorily purchased is treated as a part disposal of the remaining land. [*TCGA 1992, s 245(2)*]. Where the conditions are satisfied, a claim for rollover relief may be made (see 33.14 below) in which case the consideration rolled over will include such compensation and there will be no deemed disposal of the remaining land. [*TCGA 1992, s 247(6)*].

Example

(i) Rollover not claimed
D owns freehold land purchased for £10,000 in 1967. Part of the land is made the subject of a compulsory purchase order. The compensation of £70,000 is agreed on 10 April 1995. The market value of the remaining land is £165,000. The value of the total freehold land at 31 March 1982 was £125,000. The indexation factor for the period March 1982 to April 1995 is assumed to be 0.819.

	£	£
Disposal consideration	70,000	70,000
Cost £10,000 × $\dfrac{70,000}{70,000 + 165,000}$	2,979	
Market value 31.3.82		
£125,000 × $\dfrac{70,000}{70,000 + 165,000}$		37,234
Unindexed gain	67,021	32,766
Indexation allowance £37,234 × 0.819	30,495	30,495
Gain after indexation	£36,526	£2,271
Chargeable gain		£2,271

(ii) Rollover claimed under *TCGA 1992, s 247*

If, in (i), D acquires new land costing, say, £80,000 in December 1995, relief may be claimed as follows.

	£
Allowable cost of land compulsorily purchased	37,234
Indexation allowance	30,495
Deemed consideration for disposal	67,729
Actual consideration	70,000
Chargeable gain rolled over	£2,271
Allowable cost of new land (£80,000 − £2,271)	£77,729

33.13   **Small part disposals.** Where a part of a holding of land (or an interest therein) is transferred to an 'authority exercising or having compulsory powers', the transferor may claim under *TCGA 1992, s 243(2)* that the transfer is not treated as a disposal, in which case the consideration which would have been brought into account is treated as a reduction of allowable expenditure in relation to any subsequent disposal of the remaining holding. A holding of land for these purposes comprises only the land in respect of which allowable expenditure would be apportioned under *TCGA 1992, s 42* if the transfer had been treated as a part disposal. The consideration for the transfer (or, if the transfer is not for full consideration, the market value of the land transferred) must be 'small' as compared with the market value of the holding immediately before the transfer.

The Revenue interpret small as normally being 5% or less (withdrawn Revenue Pamphlet CGT 8 para 127). The transferor must not have taken any steps, by advertising or otherwise, to dispose of any part of the holding or to make his willingness to dispose of it known to anyone. The provisions do not apply to wasting interests in land (e.g. a short lease under 33.17 below) but subject to this any estate or interest in land is included as a holding.

Where the allowable expenditure is less than the consideration for the part disposal (or is nil) the claim referred to above cannot be made but, if the recipient elects under *TCGA 1992, s 244(2)* and there is allowable expenditure, the consideration for the part disposal is reduced by the amount of the allowable expenditure. None of that expenditure is then allowable as a deduction in computing the gain accruing on the part disposal or any subsequent disposal.

'Authority exercising or having compulsory powers' means, in relation to the land transferred, a person or body of persons acquiring it compulsorily or who has or have been, or could be, authorised to acquire it compulsorily for the purposes for which it is acquired, or for whom another person or body of persons has or have been, or could be, authorised so to acquire it. *[TCGA 1992, ss 243, 244].*

Prior to the commencement of *TCGA 1992*, the above claim and election were made under *CGTA 1979, s 108(2)* and *109(2)* respectively.

Example

(i) No rollover relief claimed
T inherited land in June 1983 at a probate value of £290,000. Under a compulsory purchase order, a part of the land is acquired for highway improvements. Compensation of £32,000 and a further £10,000 for severance, neither sum including any amount in respect of loss of profits, is agreed on 15 April 1995. The value of the remaining land is £900,000. Prior to the compulsory purchase, the value of all the land had been £950,000. The indexation factor for the period June 1983 to April 1995 is assumed to be 0.703.

	£
Total consideration for disposal (£32,000 + £10,000)	42,000
Deduct allowable cost $\dfrac{42,000}{42,000 + 900,000} \times £290,000$	12,930
Unindexed gain	29,070
Indexation allowance £12,930 × 0.703	9,090
Chargeable gain	£19,980

(ii) Rollover relief claimed under *TCGA 1992, s 243*
Total consideration for disposal is £42,000, less than 5% of the value of the estate before the disposal (£950,000). T may therefore claim that the consideration be deducted from the allowable cost of the estate.

Revised allowable cost (£290,000 − £42,000)	£248,000

An indexation adjustment in respect of the amount deducted will be required on a subsequent disposal of the estate. *[TCGA 1992, ss 53(3), 57].*

33.14   **Rollover relief.** After 5 April 1982, ROLLOVER RELIEF (50) is extended to *any landowner* (i.e. not confined to land (or any interest in or right over land) which is used and occupied for the purposes of a trade) who disposes of land to an 'authority exercising or having compulsory powers' (see 33.13 above) where the landowner reinvests part or the whole of the proceeds in acquiring new land. Any land on which the whole or part of the gain on a subsequent disposal within six years would be covered by the exemptions for PRIVATE RESIDENCES (43) is excluded. Where any land is not so excluded at the time of its acquisition, but becomes so within six years, relief is withdrawn notwithstanding time limits for the making of assessments.

The effect of a claim (under *TCGA 1992, s 247(2)*) is to defer capital gains tax by deducting the otherwise chargeable gain on the original land from the acquisition cost of the newly acquired land. Relief is restricted where part only of the proceeds is reinvested in qualifying land. See 50.5 ROLLOVER RELIEF.

The following further matters should be noted.

(*a*)   The landowner must not have taken any steps, by advertising or otherwise, to dispose of the old land or to make his willingness to dispose of it known. The Revenue have said that, in practice, any event which occurred more than three years before the date of disposal is ignored. (CCAB Statements TR 476 and 477, May and June 1982).

(*b*)   The new land must be acquired in the period beginning twelve months before and ending three years after the disposal or such longer period as the Board may allow e.g. where it has not been practical to acquire new land within the time limit. New town corporations and similar authorities may purchase land for development and then grant the previous owner a lease or tenancy of the land until they are ready to commence building. Where land is so acquired under a compulsory purchase order or under the threat of such an order and is immediately leased back to the previous owner the Board is prepared, so long as there is a clear continuing intention that the sale proceeds will be used to acquire assets qualifying for rollover relief, to extend the time limit to a date three years after the land ceases to be used by him for his trade. An assurance to this effect will be given in appropriate cases subject to the reservation that it would be necessary to raise a protective assessment on the gain arising if exceptionally the lease or tenancy continued so long as to extend beyond the statutory six year time limit for making assessments (Revenue Pamphlet IR 131, D6). After 5 April 1982 the reference to 'trade' in the foregoing presumably extends to all activities.

(*c*)   Where the new land is a depreciating asset, similar provisions apply as in 50.6 ROLLOVER RELIEF except that the gain is held over for ten years or until the new asset is disposed of, whichever is the sooner. A gain previously held over is never deemed to accrue in consequence of an event occurring after 5 April 1988 if the application of this provision would be directly attributable to the disposal of an asset before 1 April 1982.

(*d*)   The normal treatment of severance compensation as a part disposal (see 33.12 above) is expressly excluded. Such compensation is treated as additional consideration for the old land.

(*e*)   Claims under these provisions and under *TCGA 1992, s 243* (see 33.13 above) are mutually exclusive.

(*f*)   Subject to all other conditions for the granting of relief being met, the Revenue will accept a claim after 28 October 1990 from a landlord whose leasehold tenant has exercised his statutory rights under the *Leasehold Reform Act 1967* or the *Housing and Urban Development Act 1993* to acquire the freehold reversion of a property (Revenue Pamphlet IR 131, SP 13/93, 17 September 1993, replacing SP 7/90, 29 October 1990).

(*g*)   In relation to a group of companies, where there is a compulsory purchase from one group member and acquisition of land by another, ROLLOVER RELIEF (50) is available where the compulsory purchase or the acquisition is after 28 November 1994. The previous ability to 'frank' a compulsory purchase from one group member to another by an intra-group acquisition was ended with effect to acquisitions after 28 November 1994.

[*TCGA 1992, ss 247, 248, 4 Sch 4(5); FA 1995, s 48(2)(6)*].

For a concessionary application of this relief to the exchange of joint interests in land, see 33.15 below.

Prior to the commencement of *TCGA 1992*, claims were made under *CGTA 1979, s 111A(2)*.

33.15 **CONCESSIONARY ROLLOVER RELIEF FOR EXCHANGE OF JOINT INTERESTS IN LAND**

A form of rollover relief is available by concession for exchanges made after 19 December 1984 on the lines provided in 33.14 above (i.e. not confined to land which is used and occupied for the purposes of a trade) where

(*a*)   a 'holding of land' is held jointly and as a result of the exchange each joint owner becomes sole owner of part of the 'land' formerly owned jointly; or

(*b*)   a number of separate holdings of land are held jointly and as a result of the exchange each joint owner becomes sole owner of one or more holdings.

The interest relinquished will be treated as the 'old land' and the interest acquired as the 'new land'. *'Land'* includes any interest or right over land and *'holding of land'* includes an estate or interest in a holding of land and is to be construed in accordance with *TCGA 1992, s 243(3)* (see 33.13 above).

Relief will be denied under the concession to the extent that the new land is, or becomes, a dwelling-house (or part) within the meaning of *TCGA 1992, ss 222–226* (see 43 PRIVATE RESIDENCES) but subject to this, relief will be restricted as in 33.14 above where there is only part re-investment or only part of the gain is chargeable because of time apportionment.

However, where individuals who are joint beneficial owners of dwelling-houses which are their respective residences become sole owners of those houses in consequence of an exchange of interests, an alternative concessionary relief may be claimed if the gain accruing on the disposal of each dwelling-house immediately after the exchange would be exempt under the provisions contained in 43.1–43.3 PRIVATE RESIDENCES. Each individual must undertake to accept that he is deemed to have acquired the other's interest in the dwelling-house at the original base cost and at the time at which that joint interest was acquired.

For the purposes of this concession, a married couple is treated as an individual, so that an exchange of interests which results in a married couple alone becoming joint owners of land or of a dwelling house will meet the terms of the concession.

Where

(i)   the concession applies to an exchange of interests in land after 29 October 1987,

(ii)   there is a parallel exchange of interests in milk or potato quota associated with the land, and

(iii)   each joint owner becomes sole owner of the part of the quota relating to the land he now owns,

the concession applies also to the exchange of interests in quota. (Revenue Pamphlet IR 1, D26, revised by Revenue Press Release of 18 October 1994).

The operation of the concession should be read in the light of the decision of *Warrington and others v Brown and others Ch D 1989, 62 TC 226*.

33.16 Land

For capital gains tax purposes, a *'lease'* in relation to land includes an underlease, sub-lease or any tenancy or licence, and any agreement for a lease, underlease, sub-lease or tenancy or licence. In the case of land outside the UK, any interest corresponding to a lease as so defined is included. *'Lessor'*, *'lessee'* and *'rent'* are construed accordingly. [*TCGA 1992, s 240, 8 Sch 10(1)*].

Where a leaseholder of land acquires a superior interest in that land (whether a superior lease or the freehold reversion) so that the first lease is extinguished, the two interests are merged within the meaning of *TCGA 1992, s 43* (assets derived from other assets). On a subsequent disposal the allowable expenditure relating to the merged interest will include the cost of the first lease, after exclusion, in the case of a lease with less than 50 years to run, of the part which was wasted under *TCGA 1992, 8 Sch* to the date of the acquisition of the superior interest (see 33.17 below) and the cost of the superior interest. Where the superior interest is itself a lease with less than 50 years to run, the total of these two amounts will also be wasted under *TCGA 1992, 8 Sch* down to the date of disposal. Strictly, indexation allowance should be calculated on the total of these two amounts by reference to the date of acquisition of the superior interest, but, by concession, for disposals after 28 June 1992, indexation on the expenditure on the earlier, inferior lease, will be calculated by reference to the date of its acquisition.

For disposals before 29 June 1992, indexation allowance for the total of the two amounts is, by concession, calculated by reference to the date of acquisition of the earlier interest (Revenue Press Release 29 June 1992).

33.17 LEASES AS WASTING ASSETS

A lease of land is not a wasting asset until the time when its duration does not exceed fifty years. [*TCGA 1992, 8 Sch 1(1)*]. The **duration** of a lease is to be decided by reference to the facts known or ascertainable at the time when the lease was acquired or created. In determining the duration, the following provisions apply.

(*a*) Where the terms of the lease include provision for the determination of the lease by notice given by the landlord, the lease is not to be treated as granted for a term longer than one ending at the earliest date on which it could be determined by notice given by the landlord.

(*b*) Where any of the terms of the lease or any other circumstances render it unlikely that the lease will continue beyond a date earlier than the expiration of the terms of the lease, the lease is not to be treated as having been granted for a longer term than one ending on that date. This applies in particular where the lease provides for rent to go up after a given date, or for the tenant's obligation to become more onerous after a given date, but includes provision for the determination of the lease on that date, by notice given by the tenant, and those provisions render it unlikely that the lease will continue beyond that date.

(*c*) Where the terms of the lease include provision for the extension of the lease beyond a given date by notice given by the tenant, the duration of the lease applies as if the term of the lease extended for as long as it could be extended by the tenant, but subject to any right of the landlord to determine the lease by notice.

[*TCGA 1992, 8 Sch 8*].

A lease granted under *Landlord and Tenant Act 1954* to follow on from another is not a continuation of the old lease and is to be treated as having been acquired on the date it was granted (*Bayley v Rogers Ch D 1980, 53 TC 420*).

A similar view was taken in *Lewis v Walters Ch D*, [*1992*] *STC 97* regarding the right of a tenant to be granted a lease under *Leasehold Reform Act 1967* to follow on from another and where it was also held that (*c*) above did not apply since such a right was not included in the terms of the original lease.

Where a lease is 'extended' by the surrender of an old lease and the grant of a new one for a longer term, a disposal of the old lease will in strictness occur, the consideration for it normally being the value, if any, of the new lease. By concession, a disposal is not treated as arising in these circumstances provided that: the parties are not connected and the transaction is at arm's length; the transaction is not part of or connected with a larger scheme or series of transactions; no capital sum is received by the lessee; the extent of the property in which the lessee has an interest is unchanged; and the terms of the leases remain the same except as regards the duration and amount of rent payable. For this purpose, trivial differences will be ignored. (Revenue Pamphlet IR 1, D39, revised by Revenue Press Release of 18 October 1994).

Computation. If a lease of land is a wasting asset, its original cost and any enhancement expenditure are not written off on a straight line basis (as would otherwise be required under *TCGA 1992, s 46*) but on a reducing basis as set out in the table below.

Table for depreciation of leases

Years	Percentage	Years	Percentage	Years	Percentage
50 (or more)	100	33	90.280	16	64.116
49	99.657	32	89.354	15	61.617
48	99.289	31	88.371	14	58.971
47	98.902	30	87.330	13	56.167
46	98.490	29	86.226	12	53.191
45	98.059	28	85.053	11	50.038
44	97.595	27	83.816	10	46.695
43	97.107	26	82.496	9	43.154
42	96.593	25	81.100	8	39.399
41	96.041	24	79.622	7	35.414
40	95.457	23	78.055	6	31.195
39	94.842	22	76.399	5	26.722
38	94.189	21	74.635	4	21.983
37	93.497	20	72.770	3	16.959
36	92.761	19	70.791	2	11.629
35	91.981	18	68.697	1	5.983
34	91.156	17	66.470	0	0

The fraction of the *original cost* which is not allowed is given by the fraction

$$\frac{P(1)-P(3)}{P(1)}$$

where

P(1) = the percentage derived from the table for the duration of the lease at acquisition

P(3) = the percentage derived from the table for the duration of the lease at the time of disposal

The fraction of any *enhancement expenditure* which is not allowed is given by the fraction

$$\frac{P(2)-P(3)}{P(2)}$$

where

P(2) =   the percentage derived from the table for the duration of the lease at the time when the item of expenditure is first reflected in the nature of the lease

P(3) =   as above

If the duration of the lease is not an exact number of years, the percentage is that for the whole number of years plus one twelfth of the difference between that and the percentage of the next higher number of years for each odd month, counting an odd 14 days or more as one month.

The provisions above apply even if the period of ownership of the lease exceeds 50 years. Accordingly, in such a case, any cost or enhancement expenditure incurred before the lease becomes a wasting asset is not reduced until the lease does become a wasting asset. [*TCGA 1992, 8 Sch 1(3)–(5)*]. In these circumstances P(1) and P(2) will each be 100 in the fractions given above.

Example

X purchases a 30-year lease of business premises in 1989 for £250,000. In 1992, when 27 years of the lease remain, he spends £25,000 on improvements which are at once reflected in the value of the lease and continue to be so until he disposes of it with 24 years remaining in 1995. His allowable expenditure is reduced as follows

$$\text{Original cost } (£250,000) \times \frac{(87.330 - 79.622)}{87.330} \qquad = \quad £22,066$$

$$\text{Additional cost } (£25,000) \times \frac{(83.816 - 79.622)}{83.816} \qquad = \quad £1,251$$

$$\underline{\qquad\qquad}$$
$$£23,317$$

The total allowable expenditure is then (£275,000 – £23,317)   = £251,683

Exceptions. The above provisions do not apply in the following circumstances.

(i)   If at the beginning of the period of ownership of a lease, it is subject to a *sub-lease not at a rackrent* and the value of the lease at the end of the sub-lease (estimated at the beginning of the period of ownership) exceeds the expenditure allowable in computing the gain accruing on the disposal of the lease (see 16.3(*a*) DISPOSAL), the lease is *not* a wasting asset until the end of the duration of the sub-lease. [*TCGA 1992, 8 Sch 1(2)*].

(ii)   Where the land, throughout the ownership of the person making the disposal, is used solely for the purposes of a trade, profession or vocation, and capital allowances have, or could have, been claimed in respect of its cost, or in respect of any enhancement expenditure. This also applies where the cost of land has otherwise qualified in full for any capital allowances. Where, however, the land disposed of has been used partly for non-business purposes, or has only partly qualified for capital allowances, the expenditure and consideration are apportioned and the restriction of allowable expenditure as above applies only to that portion of expenditure which has not qualified for capital allowances, or which relates to the period of non-business use. [*TCGA 1992, s 47, 8 Sch 1(6)*].

33.18   **PREMIUMS FOR LEASES**

Where the payment of a 'premium' is required under a lease (or otherwise under the terms subject to which the lease is granted) there is a part disposal of the freehold or other interest out of which that lease is granted. [*TCGA 1992, 8 Sch 2(1)*].

In the part disposal computation (which follows the normal rules in *TCGA 1992, s 42,* see 16.6 DISPOSAL) the property which remains undisposed of includes a right to any rent or other payments (other than a premium) payable under the lease, and that right is valued at the time of the part disposal. [*TCGA 1992, 8 Sch 2(2)*].

'*Premium*' includes any like sum, whether payable to the intermediate or superior landlord and includes any sum (other than rent) paid on or in connection with the granting of a tenancy except in so far as the other sufficient consideration for the payment is shown to have been given. In Scotland, '*premium*' includes in particular a *grassum* payable to any landlord or intermediate landlord on the creation of a sub-lease. [*TCGA 1992, 8 Sch 10(2)(3)*]. In addition, the following amounts are also to be regarded as premiums.

(*a*)   Where under the terms of a lease, the tenant must pay a sum in lieu of the whole or part of the rent for any period, or as consideration for the surrender of the lease, the lease is deemed to have required payment of a premium to the landlord (in addition to any other premium) of that amount for the period in relation to which it is payable.

Where the premium is deemed to have been received as consideration for the surrender of a lease, the surrender of the lease is not the occasion of any recomputation of the gain accruing on the receipt of any other premium, and the premium which is the consideration for the surrender of the lease is regarded as consideration for a separate transaction consisting of the disposal by the landlord of his interest in the lease.

(*b*)   Where, as consideration for the variation or waiver of any of the terms of a lease, the tenant must pay a sum otherwise than by way of rent, the lease is deemed to have required the payment to the landlord of a premium (in addition to any other premium) of that amount for the period from the time when the variation or waiver takes effect to the time it ceases. Where the transaction is not at arm's length or is entered into gratuitously, such a sum is deemed to be payable as if the transaction were at arm's length.

If under (*a*) or (*b*) above a premium is deemed to have been received by the landlord, otherwise than as consideration for the surrender of the lease then

(i)   subject to (ii) below, both the landlord and tenant are treated as if that premium were, or were part of, the consideration for the grant of the lease due at the time when the lease was granted, and the gain accruing to the landlord on the disposal by way of grant of the lease is recomputed and any necessary adjustments of tax made; and

(ii)   if the landlord is a tenant under a lease the duration of which does not exceed 50 years, the deemed premium is treated as allowable enhancement expenditure incurred by the sub-lessee.

[*TCGA 1992, 8 Sch 3*].

In *Clarke v United Real (Moorgate) Ltd Ch D 1987, 61 TC 353*, the taxpayer company contracted for a freehold site which it owned to be developed by a third party. Subsequently it entered into an 'agreement for a lease' with another third party ('A') under which A agreed to reimburse the company's development costs and the company was to grant A a long lease of the developed site at a rent below market value, which was to be ascertained by reference to A's reimbursement payments to the company. The granting of the lease was agreed to be a part disposal. The reimbursement payments were held to be a premium within *TCGA 1992, 8 Sch 2(1), 10(2)*, because they were made to the company in its capacity as landlord, and not to meet an obligation incurred by the company on behalf of A.

33.19 Land

33.19 **Premiums taxed under Schedule A.** Where a premium is received for a lease not exceeding 50 years and part of it is liable to income tax under *ICTA 1988, s 34* as a receipt of a Schedule A business (see Tolley's Income Tax) that part is excluded from the computation for capital gains tax purposes *except* in the denominator of the part disposal fraction of A/(A+B) given by *TCGA 1992, s 42*. '*Premium*' includes a deemed premium under *ICTA 1988, s 34(4)* or *(5)* (which correspond to a premium deemed to arise under *(a)* or *(b)* in 33.18 above. [*TCGA 1992, 8 Sch 5(1)(5); FA 1995, 6 Sch 37(1)(2)*].

Where the terms of a lease impose an obligation on the tenant to carry out work on the premises concerned, an amount equal to the increase in value of the landlord's interest occasioned by the work is treated as a premium under *ICTA 1988, s 34* above except insofar as the obligation relates to work which, had it been carried out by the landlord, would have been deductible as an expense of any Schedule A business carried on by the landlord. [*ICTA 1988, s 34(2)(3); FA 1995, 6 Sch 9(1)(2)*]. For capital gains tax purposes the consequential effect is that the landlord is treated as incurring enhancement expenditure of that amount on the premises at the time of the grant of the lease. [*TCGA 1992, 8 Sch 7, 7A; FA 1995, s 41(4), 6 Sch 37(4)*].

Example

X grants a 14-year lease of premises for a premium of £5,000 in 1995/96 and retains the freehold interest. The amount chargeable to income tax for that year is

	£
Premium	5,000
Deduct $\dfrac{14-1}{50} \times £5,000$	1,300
Chargeable to income tax	£3,700

If the allowable expenditure on the original unencumbered freehold (acquired in 1992) is £30,000 and the value of the reversion £47,000, the unindexed gain is computed as follows

	£
Consideration received (i.e. the premium)	5,000
Deduct amount chargeable to income tax	3,700
	£1,300

Allowable expenditure attributable to the part disposal

$$\frac{1,300}{(5,000 + 47,000)} \times £30,000 = \qquad \underline{£750}$$

Unindexed gain: £1,300 − £750 =	£550

33.20 **Sub-leases granted out of short leases.** Where a sub-lease is granted out of a head-lease with less than 50 years to run, the normal part disposal rules do not apply. Instead, subject to below, a proportion of the cost and enhancement expenditure attributable to the lease is apportioned to the part disposed of as follows

$$\frac{P(1)-P(3)}{P(2)}$$

where

P(1) = the percentage derived from the table in 33.17 above for the duration of the lease at the date of granting the sub-lease

P(3) = the percentage for the duration of the lease at the date of termination of the sub-lease

P(2) = the percentage for the duration of the lease at the date of acquisition (for apportionment of cost) *or* the date when expenditure is first reflected in the nature of the lease (for apportionment of enhancement expenditure)

If the amount of the premium is less than what would be obtainable by way of premium for the sub-lease if the rent payable under the sub-lease were the same as the rent payable under the lease, the percentage attributable to the sub-lease as calculated above must be multiplied by the premium received over the premium so obtainable before being applied to cost or enhancement expenditure. [*TCGA 1992, 8 Sch 4(1)(2)*].

Example

X purchases a 40-year lease of a flat in 1989 for £15,000. In 1995, he sub-lets the flat to Y for 20 years for a premium of £8,000. The premium obtainable on the basis of the rent paid under the head-lease is £10,000. X's original expenditure of £15,000 is apportioned as follows

$$\frac{91.981-61.617}{95.457} = 0.3180908 \times \frac{8,000}{10,000} = 0.2544726$$

0.2544726 × £15,000 = £3,817

The expenditure attributable to the part disposal is therefore £3,817 as against £4,771 (£15,000 x 0.3180908) if the premium had been the maximum obtainable, £10,000.

Where the sub-lease is a sub-lease of part only of the land comprised in the lease, the cost and enhancement expenditure of the head-lease must be apportioned between the sub-lease and the remainder in proportion to their respective values. [*TCGA 1992, 8 Sch 4(3)*].

Where a premium (including a deemed premium as in 33.19 above) is paid for the sub-lease, an amount of which is liable to income tax under *ICTA 1988, s 34* as a receipt of a Schedule A business, that amount is deducted from any *gain* accruing on the disposal for which the premium is consideration but not so as to convert the gain into a loss or to increase any loss. [*TCGA 1992, 8 Sch 5(2)(5); FA 1995, 6 Sch 37(1)(2)*]. Similar provisions apply where, under *ICTA 1988, s 36* (see L1005 above) what is disposed of is the remainder of a lease or a sub-lease out of a lease the duration of which does not exceed 50 years. [*TCGA 1992, 8 Sch 5(4)*].

33.21 **Allowances to payer for premiums paid.** Where a lease, granted for a premium which gave rise to a liability under *ICTA 1988, s 34* (see 33.19 above) or *35* (see 33.22 below) on the landlord, is sub-leased or sold for a premium, any potential liability on that latter event is compared with the 'appropriate fraction' of the liability on the first transaction (proportionate to the period covered by the sub-lease as compared with that covered by the first lease) and only the excess is chargeable. [*ICTA 1988, s 37(1)(2)(3)(7)*].

33.21 Land

Where the 'appropriate fraction' of the amount chargeable on the superior landlord exceeds the amount of the premium chargeable on the intermediate landlord, the surplus is treated under *ICTA 1988, s 37(4)* as 'additional rent' allowable against property income. In this event, if a *loss* accrues for capital gains tax purposes to the intermediate landlord on the disposal by way of the grant of the sub-lease, the loss is reduced by the total amount of the additional rent but not so as to convert the loss into a gain. Any adjustment under *ICTA 1988, s 36(2)(b)* (see 33.5 above) is taken into account. [*TCGA 1992, 8 Sch 6(1)(3)*].

(*Note.* The example below takes no account of transitional relief for 'indexation losses' which may be due for 1993/94 and 1994/95 as in 23.2 INDEXATION.)

Example

On 21 January 1988 C is granted a lease of a shop for 21 years for a rent and a premium of £12,800. On 21 January 1995 he grants a sub-lease for a period of 7 years for a premium of £1,000 and a rent equal to that payable under the terms of the head-lease.

	£	£
Schedule A		
Premium	1,000	
Deduct $\dfrac{7-1}{50} \times £1,000$	120	880
Allowances for premium paid		

$$\frac{\text{Duration of sub-lease}}{\text{Duration of head-lease}} = \frac{7}{21}$$

Amount chargeable on superior landlord

$$£12,800 - \left(\frac{21-1}{50} \times £12,800\right) = £7,680$$

Allowance $= £7,680 \times \dfrac{7}{21}$		2,560
Amount allowable under Schedule A against rent received		£1,680

	£	£
Capital gains tax		
Premium received		£1,000
Consideration given for lease	£12,800	
Percentage applicable to lease of 21 years	74.635	
Percentage applicable to lease of 14 years	58.971	
Percentage applicable to lease of 7 years	35.414	
Amount allowable		
$\dfrac{58.971 - 35.414}{74.635} \times £12,800$		£4,040
Loss £(1,000 − 4,040 − 2,424)		3,040
Deduct amount allowable under Schedule A		1,680
Allowable loss		£1,360

33.22   **Anti-avoidance provisions.** Where a lease not exceeding 50 years granted at *less than market value* is assigned for a consideration exceeding any premium for which it was granted (or the consideration on any previous assignment) the excess, up to the limit of the amount of any premium, or additional premium, which the grantor forwent when granting the lease, is assessed on him, but under Schedule A (before 1995/96 Schedule D, Case VI), to the same extent that an additional premium would have been assessed under *ICTA 1988, s 34(1)* (see 33.19 above). [*ICTA 1988, s 35; FA 1995, 6 Sch 10*].

Any assessment to income tax under these provisions is not taken into account in any capital gains tax computation. [*TCGA 1992, 8 Sch 6(2); FA 1995, 6 Sch 37(3)*]. There may, therefore, be a double charge to tax.

33.23   **LAND SOLD AND LEASED BACK — PROPORTION OF CAPITAL SUM RECEIVED IS TO BE TAXED AS INCOME IN CERTAIN CIRCUMSTANCES**

As regards arrangements within *ICTA 1988, s 779* (land sold and leased back), where the lease when sold has no more than 50 years still to run and the period for which the premises are leased back is *15 years or less*, any increased rent payable, so far as it does not exceed a commercial rent, is allowable as a deduction from profits, but of the consideration received by the lessee for giving up the original lease (or undertaking to pay an increased rent) a proportion equivalent to one-fifteenth of that consideration multiplied by the number of years by which the term of the lease-back falls short of 16 years will be treated as an income receipt instead of a capital one. Appropriate adjustment is made where the lease-back is of part only of the property previously leased. For the above purposes the term of the new lease is deemed to end on any date whereafter the rent payable is reduced, or, if the lessor or lessee has power to determine the lease or the lessee has power to vary its terms, on the earliest date on which the lease can be so determined or varied. [*ICTA 1988, s 780*].

33.24   **INSURANCE RECOVERIES: SHORT LEASES**

Where property is held on a lease which has 50 years or less to run, insurance payments received by the lessee in respect of the property will not be treated as a capital sum derived from the lease within the meaning of *TCGA 1992, s 22(1)* to the extent that they are applied by the lessee in discharging an obligation to restore any damage to the property. (Revenue Pamphlet IR 1, D1). See generally 16.7(*a*) DISPOSAL.

33.25   **VALUE SHIFTING — ADJUSTMENT OF LEASEHOLD RIGHTS**

Where an owner of land (or of any other description of property) enters into a transaction whereby he becomes the lessee of that property (e.g. a sale and lease-back) and there is a subsequent adjustment of rights and liabilities under the lease (whether or not involving the grant of a new lease) which is on the whole favourable to the lessor, such an adjustment is a disposal by the lessee of an interest in the property. [*TCGA 1992, s 29(4)*]. See 3.4 ANTI-AVOIDANCE for full coverage.

33.26   **CONTINGENT LIABILITIES**

In the first instance, no allowance is made in a capital gains tax computation for

(*a*)   in the case of a disposal by way of assigning a lease of land or other property, any liability remaining with, or assumed by, the person making the disposal which is contingent on a default in respect of liabilities thereby or subsequently assumed by the assignee under the terms and conditions of the lease; and (*b*)   any contingent liability of the person making the disposal in respect of any covenant for quiet enjoyment or other obligation assumed as vendor of land, or of any estate or interest in land, or as a lessor.

If it is subsequently shown to the satisfaction of the inspector that any such contingent liability has become enforceable, and is being or has been enforced, such adjustment is made as is required in consequence. [*TC.GA 1992, s 49(1)(a)(b)(2)(3)*].

The receipt of a contingently repayable deposit in return for the grant of an option to purchase land was valued subject to the contingency because on the facts the contingency was not within (*b*) above (*Randall v Plumb Ch D 1974, 50 TC 392*).

34 Life Assurance Policies and Deferred Annuities

34.1 The disposal of rights under, or of an interest in, a life assurance policy or deferred annuity does not give rise to a chargeable gain unless it is made by a person other than the original beneficial owner who has acquired the rights or interest for money or money's worth.

Subject to this, the payment of the sum assured by the policy or of the first instalment of the deferred annuity, the transfer of investments or other assets to the owner in accordance with the policy and the surrender of the policy or of rights thereunder, are each treated as a disposal of rights under the policy. The amount of the consideration for the disposal of a deferred annuity is deemed to be the then market value of the outstanding annuity payments. [*TCGA 1992, s 210*]. Any transfer of investments or other assets is deemed to be made at market value. [*TCGA 1992, s 204(3)*].

In computing any chargeable gain, allowable expenditure will be

(*a*) the base cost of the policy to the person to whom the gain accrues (normally, this will be what the purchaser paid for the policy), and

(*b*) any premiums paid by the purchaser.

34.2 *ICTA 1988, ss 539-554* provide for income tax to be charged on the profits arising on certain life policies and life annuity contracts. Before 26 June 1982, where such policies or contracts were assigned for money or money's worth, any profit subsequently arising was taken out of charge to income tax and was subject instead to capital gains tax. To counter the tax advantages previously gained by the use of such policies and contracts, any profit on policies etc. taken out after 25 June 1982 cease to escape the charge to income tax. The former provisions also cease to apply to policies etc. issued and assigned for money or money's worth before 26 June 1982 if, after 23 August 1982,

(i) the rights under the policy etc. are again assigned for money or money's worth; or

(ii) further capital is injected; or

(iii) subject to certain conditions, loans are taken against the security of the policy etc.

[*ICTA 1988, ss 540(3), 542(3), 544*].

For full details, see Tolley's Income Tax.

34.3 For gains made in connection with life assurance policies which are assessable to income tax or corporation tax, not capital gains tax, see Tolley's Income Tax or Tolley's Corporation Tax respectively.

34.4 For the treatment of other kinds of policy, see 18.10 EXEMPTIONS AND RELIEFS.

35 Losses

35.1 GENERAL

Assessment to capital gains tax is on all chargeable gains accruing to the taxpayer in the year of assessment, less any allowable losses accruing to him in that year and, so far as not allowed as a deduction from chargeable gains accruing in any previous year of assessment, any allowable losses, accruing to him in any previous year (but not earlier than 1965/66). [*TCGA 1992, s 2(2)*].

See 23.2 INDEXATION for transitional relief for 'indexation losses' in 1993/94 and 1994/95 only in the case of disposals by individuals and trustees of settlements made before 30 November 1993.

See 37.3 MARRIED PERSONS for the availability of a spouse's losses before 1990/91.

Short-term losses which accrued before 1971/72 but which were not relieved under Schedule D, Case VII may be brought forward against gains chargeable to capital gains tax. [*TCGA 1992, 11 Sch 12*]. This is the only instance where losses incurred before 6 April 1965 can be carried forward.

A person may be able to enjoy the benefit of unutilised losses of trustees which have accrued to them in respect of property to which the person has become absolutely entitled. See 52.9 SETTLEMENTS. This provision does not apply as regards personal representatives and legatees. See 15.7 DEATH.

Where a loss accrues on the disposal of an asset held on 6 April 1965 there are provisions (e.g. time apportionment), which may restrict the loss allowable. See 7 ASSETS HELD ON 6 APRIL 1965. Similar observations may apply to disposals after 5 April 1988 of assets held on 31 March 1982. See 8 ASSETS HELD ON 31 MARCH 1982. See also 16.5(*i*) DISPOSAL where an asset has qualified for capital allowances.

A loss accruing to a person in a year of assessment during no part of which he is resident or ordinarily resident in the UK is not allowable unless

(*a*) if there had been a gain instead of a loss, he would have been chargeable under *TCGA 1992, s 10* (see 39.3 OVERSEAS MATTERS), in respect of that gain; or

(*b*) it is a loss accruing to trustees in a year of assessment for which *CGTA 1979, s 17* or *TCGA 1992, s 84* (see 39.8–39.11 OVERSEAS MATTERS) applies to the settlement.

[*TCGA 1992, ss 16(3), 97(6)*].

A loss arising to an individual not domiciled in the UK but resident or ordinarily resident here in respect of the disposal of an asset overseas is not allowable. See 39.2 OVERSEAS MATTERS. [*TCGA 1992, s 16(4)*].

An agreement under *TMA 1970, s 54* (see 4.6 APPEALS) allied to the existence of a loss for a chargeable period does not preclude the Revenue from challenging its size or existence in a later chargeable period (*Tod v South Essex Motors (Basildon) Ltd Ch D 1987, 60 TC 598*).

35.2

Computation. Losses are computed as for gains except as in *FA 1991, s 72* (see 35.6 below) and where expressly provided otherwise (e.g. as in 23.1 INDEXATION). Wherever an exemption is given under *TCGA 1992* (or under any provision which is to be construed as one with it) so as to make a gain not a chargeable gain, that exemption applies similarly to losses so that they are not to be allowable losses. [*TCGA 1992, s 16(1)(2); ICTA 1988, s 834(1)*].

Losses are not deductible if, and so far as, other tax relief can be claimed in respect of them and may only be deducted once for capital gains tax purposes. They may not be deducted at all if already given relief for income tax (see 35.12 and 35.14 below regarding an election for capital losses arising on the disposal of certain shares in unquoted trading companies to be set off against general income). [*TCGA 1992, s 2(3)*].

Example

On 30 April 1995 Q sells for £40,000 a part of the land which he owns. The market value of the remaining estate is £160,000. Q bought the land for £250,000 in March 1987.

	£
Disposal consideration	40,000
Allowable cost $\dfrac{40,000}{40,000 + 160,000} \times £250,000$	50,000
Allowable loss	£10,000

35.3   **Carry-back**. Losses may not be carried back against the gains of an earlier year (except from the year of death, see 15.5 DEATH). [*TCGA 1992, s 2(3)*].

35.4   **Connected persons**. A loss on a disposal to a (14) CONNECTED PERSON is deductible only from chargeable gains arising on other disposals to that same person while he is still connected. A disposal, whereby capital and income are settled wholly or primarily for educational, cultural or recreational purposes, the beneficiaries being 'an association of persons' most of whom are *not* connected persons, is not subject to this restriction on losses. [*TCGA 1992, s 18(3)(4)*]. The restriction does not apply where a person becomes absolutely entitled as against the trustee to property in a settlement (see 52.9 SETTLEMENTS).

Where the disposal is of an option to enter into a transaction with the disposer, no loss accruing to a connected person who acquires the option is allowable unless it accrues on the disposal of the option at arm's length to a person unconnected with the acquirer. [*TCGA 1992, s 18(5)*].

See 3.10 ANTI-AVOIDANCE for special market value provisions for disposals between connected persons.

Debts. A loss accruing on the disposal of a debt by a person making the disposal (the 'subsequent creditor') who acquired it from the 'original creditor' at a time when the original creditor or his personal representative or legatee was connected with the subsequent creditor, is not an allowable loss. Purchases through persons all of whom are connected with the subsequent creditor are also included as are acquisitions from the original creditor's personal representative or legatee. Where the original creditor is a trustee and the debt, when created, is settled property, any loss accruing to the subsequent creditor is not allowable if he is connected with any person (or his personal representative or legatee) who becomes absolutely entitled to the debt on its ceasing to

35.5 Losses

be settled property. [*TCGA 1992, s 251(4)(5)*]. For debts generally, see 18.5 EXEMPTIONS AND RELIEFS.

35.5 **Anti-avoidance.** Where a deemed disposal arises under *TCGA 1992, s 29(2)* on the transfer of value between different shares or rights in a company by the person controlling it, no loss is allowable on such a disposal. See 3.4 ANTI-AVOIDANCE. Value-shifting to give a tax free benefit may result in losses being allowable only to such extent as is just and reasonable. See 3.6–3.9 ANTI-AVOIDANCE.

Where there are depreciatory transactions within a group of companies or where there is 'dividend stripping' by one company holding 10% or more of a class of shares in another company, any related loss is only allowable to the extent that it is just and reasonable. See 3.16, 3.17 ANTI-AVOIDANCE.

A restriction of a loss accruing to a company which is a member of a group of companies may occur where the loss is wholly or partly referable to a time before it joined the group or the disposal of an asset which was held by another group member when that member company joined the group. See 13.20 COMPANIES.

Trading losses effectively converted into allowable capital losses under 35.6 below cannot be carried forward as a deduction against chargeable gains after the time the trade concerned ceases.

35.6 **CAPITAL AND INCOME SET-OFFS**

General. A person other than a company cannot normally set off his allowable losses for capital gains tax purposes against his general income, and he could not set off his trading losses incurred in years before 1991/92 against his chargeable gains (see below for later years). A company, also, cannot normally set off its allowable losses for the purposes of corporation tax on chargeable gains against general income but trading losses or management expenses of a company can, in certain cases, be set off against profits chargeable to corporation tax, such profits including the whole or the appropriate fraction of chargeable gains. See 13.2, 13.3 COMPANIES. See, however, 35.12 and 35.14 below for the allowance of capital losses arising on the disposal of certain shares in unquoted trading companies against general income of *individuals* and *investment companies* respectively.

Set-off of trading losses against chargeable gains of a person other than a company. Where trading losses arise in 1991/92 and subsequent years of assessment and a person makes a claim for relief under *ICTA 1988, s 380* (set-off for income tax purposes of trading losses against general income; see Tolley's Income Tax under Losses) for a year of assessment in respect of an amount ('the trading loss') which is available for relief under that provision, he may in the notice by which the claim is made make a further claim (under *FA 1991, s 72(1)*) for 'the relevant amount for the year' to be determined. Where such a claim is finally determined (see below), the relevant amount for the year is treated (or the 'maximum amount' if lower) as an allowable loss for capital gains tax purposes accruing to the claimant in the year. (This means that in effect capital losses flowing from a claim are treated as current year losses rather than losses brought forward from prior years; see 35.1 above and 35.7 below.) However, an amount treated as an allowable loss under the foregoing is not allowed as a deduction from chargeable gains accruing to a person in any year of assessment beginning after he has ceased to carry on the trade, profession, vocation or employment in which the relevant trading loss was sustained. (The Revenue have indicated that a continuing partner in a partnership which has a technical discontinuance for income tax purposes under *ICTA 1988, s 113* will not be prejudiced by this restriction. However, this comment would appear otiose after 1993/94 in respect of trades set up after 5 April 1994 or after 1995/96 for other trades since, in such circumstances, the effect of the changes made by *FA 1994, s 216(1)(2), 26 Sch Pt V* to that provision is that only a total change in the persons carrying on the trade will bring about such a discontinuance.)

'*The relevant amount for the year*' is so much of the trading loss as

(*a*)   cannot be set off against the claimant's income for the year, and

(*b*)   has not already been taken into account for the purposes of giving relief (under *ICTA 1988, s 380*, this relief provision or otherwise) for any year.

'*The maximum amount*' is the amount on which the claimant would be chargeable to capital gains tax for the year, disregarding the annual exemption available under *TCGA 1992, s 3(1)* and the effect of this relief provision. In ascertaining the maximum amount, no account is taken of any event occurring after the date on which the claim for relief is finally determined, and in consequence of which the maximum amount is reduced by virtue of any capital gains tax provision (e.g. a claim for rollover relief in a later year having the effect of reducing the amount chargeable for the year for which this relief provision is claimed; in such a case the allowable capital losses flowing from a claim under this provision would be displaced by the effect of the rollover claim but would be available for carry forward to subsequent years). A claim for relief is not deemed finally to be determined until the relevant amount for the year can no longer be varied, whether by the Commissioners on appeal or on the order of any court.

Trading losses relieved under the above are treated similarly to losses relieved under *ICTA 1988, s 380* as regards *ICTA 1988, s 382(3)* (prevention of double allowances), *383(6)–(8)* (extension of right of set-off to capital allowances before 1994/95 in respect of trades set up after 5 April 1994 or before 1997/98 for other trades) and *385(1)* (carry-forward of trading losses against subsequent profits reduced by other set-offs claimed). [*FA 1991, s 72; FA 1994, ss 209(1), 211(2), 215(4)(5), 218(1)(5), 20 Sch 8, 26 Sch Pt V*].

Time limits for the making of claims under *ICTA 1988, s 380* are covered in Tolley's Income Tax under Losses and so the time limits for an effective claim under *FA 1991, s 72* above follow these. In broad terms, in respect of losses sustained in 1995/96 and earlier years in trades commenced before 6 April 1994, a claim under *section 380* in respect of a trading loss incurred in a particular year of assessment or (so far as not already relieved under that provision and provided the taxpayer carried on the trade) in the last preceding year of assessment, has to be made within two years of the end of the particular year of assessment if income tax relief is to be given for the particular year. In respect of losses sustained in 1994/95 and subsequent years in trades commenced after 5 April 1994 and in respect of losses sustained in 1996/97 and subsequent years in trades commenced on or before that date, a claim under *section 380* in respect of a trading loss incurred in a particular year of assessment has to be made within two years of the end of the particular year of assessment (for 1996/97 and later years, within twelve months after 31 January next following the particular year of assessment) if income tax relief is to be given for the particular year or the last preceding year.

Although in strictness the two claims should be made in the same notice, the Revenue are prepared to accept a separate claim under *section 72* where: the trader has previously made a *section 380* claim to which a *section 72* claim could have been added; a separate *section 72* claim is made within the time limits for the original *section 380* claim; after giving relief under *section 380* there is a balance of trading losses which have not otherwise been relieved; and all the other conditions for the relief are satisfied (Revenue Tax Bulletin August 1993 p 87).

See Tolley's Income Tax under Losses for the possible augmentation under *ICTA 1988, s 383* of a loss determined under *ICTA 1988, s 380* by an amount of capital allowances for years before 1994/95 in respect of trades set up after 5 April 1994 or for years before

1997/98 for other trades. In other circumstances, capital allowances will be treated as a trading expense. See Tolley's Income Tax under Capital Allowances.

Set-off of post-cessation expenditure of a trade against capital gains. Relief is available against both income and capital gains for individuals who incur qualifying business expenditure after 28 November 1994 in connection with a trade or profession which has ceased within seven years of its ceasing. Broadly, qualifying expenditure includes costs of remedying defective work or services rendered and damages in respect thereof, insurance premiums paid to insure against such costs and legal and other professional expenses incurred in connection therewith. Relief is also given for bad debts which prove to be bad or which are released in whole or in part after 28 November 1994, and for the costs of collecting debts which have been taken into account in the final accounts. The relief is reduced by accruals for costs in the final accounting period which remain unpaid. On a claim, the relief may be set against income and then against capital gains of the year of assessment in which the qualifying expenditure is incurred, otherwise it will have to be carried forward to be set only against any post-cessation receipts under *ICTA 1988, s 105*. Claims for relief in respect of 1994/95 and 1995/96 must be made within two years of the end of the year of assessment in which the expenditure is incurred. For 1996/97 onwards claims must be made within twelve months of 31 January following the year of assessment in which the expenditure was incurred. A claim for relief cannot exceed the capital gains available, disregarding losses brought forward, the annual exemption and trading losses set against gains under *FA 1991, s 72*. For full details of the provisions see Tolley's Income Tax under Post-Cessation Etc. Receipts and Expenditure. [*ICTA 1988, s 109A; FA 1995, s 90*].

Set-off of post-employment deductions against capital gains. For 1995/96 onwards relief against income or capital gains will be given to former employees who bear the costs of indemnity insurance or certain work-related uninsured liabilities relating to their former employment where such costs are incurred by them up to six years after the year in which the employment ended. On a claim, the relief may be set against income and then against capital gains of the year of assessment in which the qualifying expenditure is incurred, otherwise it will be lost. Claims for relief in respect of 1995/96 must be made before 6 April 2002. For 1996/97 onwards claims must be made within five years of 31 January following the year of assessment to which the claim relates. A claim for relief cannot exceed the capital gains available, disregarding losses brought forward, the annual exemption and trading losses set against gains under *FA 1991, s 72*. For full details of the provisions see Tolley's Income Tax under Schedule E-Emoluments. [*ICTA 1988, s 201AA; FA 1995, ss 91, 92*].

35.7 **INTERACTION WITH ANNUAL EXEMPT AMOUNT**

The '*taxable amount*' on which this relief is based is the total amount of chargeable gains for the year less allowable losses as arrived at for the purposes of *TCGA 1992, s 2(2)* (see 35.1 above) except that deductions for losses carried forward or back are limited so as not to reduce the taxable amount below the annual exemption. [*TCGA 1992, s 3(5)*]. See 2.3 ANNUAL RATES AND EXEMPTIONS; 37.3 MARRIED PERSONS; and 52.4 and 52.5 SETTLEMENTS for further application of this rule.

Example

U has the following chargeable gains and allowable losses

	Gains	Losses	Net
	£	£	£
1992/93	8,000	12,300	(4,300)
1993/94	2,800	2,100	700
1994/95	6,000	—	6,000
1995/96	14,500	2,200	12,300

1992/93	£
Net chargeable gains	—
Losses carried forward	£4,300

1993/94	
Net chargeable gains (covered by annual exemption)	£700
Losses brought forward and carried forward	£4,300

1994/95	£
Chargeable gains	6,000
Deduct losses brought forward (part)	200
Taxable amount (exempt)	£5,800
Losses carried forward (£4,300 − £200)	£4,100

1995/96	£
Net chargeable gains	12,300
Deduct losses brought forward	4,100
Taxable amount	8,200
Deduct exempt amount	6,000
Taxable gains	£2,200

Note to the example

(*a*)   'Indexation losses', for the purposes of this example, have been ignored.

35.8   **ASSETS OF NEGLIGIBLE VALUE**

If, on a claim by the owner of an asset, the inspector is satisfied that the value of an asset has become negligible, he may allow the claim and the asset will thereupon be treated as having been sold and immediately re-acquired at that value and a loss claim, where relevant, made on that basis. [*TCGA 1992, s 24(2)*]. For this purpose, land and buildings may be regarded as separate assets so that where there is a deemed sale of a building, the land comprising the site of the building (including any land occupied for purposes ancillary to the use of that building) is treated as if it were sold and immediately reacquired at its then market value. [*TCGA 1992, s 24(3)*]. See also 50.1 ROLLOVER RELIEF.

On a literal construction the word 'thereupon' relates back to the inspector's allowing of the claim but in practice the Revenue has construed it to relate back to the making of the claim. There is no ground for construing the notional sale and re-acquisition as taking place at an earlier date (*Williams v Bullivant Ch D 1982, 56 TC 159; Larner v Warrington Ch D 1985, 58 TC 557*). By concession, a claim for a particular date may be made within two years after the end of the tax year or accounting period in which that date falls, provided that the asset was of negligible value *both* on that date (whether or not it had become so before then) *and* when the claim is made. Claims within 35.12 and 35.14 below (losses on shares in unquoted trading companies) are treated similarly (Revenue Pamphlet IR 1, D28 replacing 29.D13 INLAND REVENUE STATEMENTS OF PRACTICE but with a revised text to make it clear that the asset must be of negligible value not only on the particular date but also when the claim is made). However, for negligible value claims made on or after 29 November 1993, the computation on the disposal will be made on the basis of the legislation in force at the date of claim, not at the date of the deemed disposal. This modification ensures that no advantage will be obtained arising out of the prohibition of indexation allowance creating or increasing a loss on a disposal on or after that date (Revenue Press Release, 31 May 1994).

'*Negligible*', in relation to the value of shares, is regarded as 'considerably less' than 5% of the nominal value, 5% of nominal value being regarded as 'small'. See CCAB Statement June 1971 and 53.13 SHARES AND SECURITIES.

For certain qualifying corporate bonds becoming of negligible value where evidencing a 'qualifying loan', see 35.10 below.

Prior to the commencement of *TCGA 1992*, claims were made under *CGTA 1979*, *s 22(2)*.

Quoted securities. The Inland Revenue have accepted that certain quoted securities have become of negligible value within the meaning of *TCGA 1992, s 24(2)*. For securities so accepted in recent years, see Tolley's Tax Data. For additional securities so accepted, see the quarterly list in Tolley's Practical Tax.

35.9 **LOANS TO TRADERS**

Relief for lender on loan becoming irrecoverable. Provided that the inspector is satisfied that the claimant and borrower were neither spouses living together nor companies in the same 'group' when the loan was made or at any subsequent time, and that the claimant has not assigned his right of recovery, loss relief is available to the extent that any outstanding amount of the principal of a 'qualifying loan' made by the claimant after 11 April 1978 has become irrecoverable otherwise than under the express terms of the loan or related arrangements, or by reason of any act or omission by the lender (or, as appropriate, the guarantor of a loan claiming the relief below). The loss is treated as accruing when the claim under *TCGA 1992, s 253(3)* is made (subject to the concessionary treatment below). [*TCGA 1992, s 253(3)(12)(14)(a)(15)*].

A '*qualifying loan*' is a loan to a UK resident borrower in the case of which the money lent is used by him wholly for the purposes of a trade, profession or vocation (not being a trade which consists of or includes the lending of money) carried on by him (and for this purpose money used by a borrower for setting up a trade which is subsequently carried on by him is treated as used for the purposes of that trade), and which is not a 'debt on a security'. However, for guarantees see below, and for loans evidenced by securities which are qualifying corporate bonds, see 35.10 below.

The 'commercial letting' of 'furnished holiday accommodation' in the UK is treated as a trade for losses arising after 5 April 1982. See 19 FURNISHED HOLIDAY ACCOMMODATION.

A '*debt on security*' is defined by reference to *TCGA 1992, s 132*, security thereby embracing any loan stock or similar security of any government or public or local authority in the UK or elsewhere, or of any company, and whether secured or unsecured. See further 18.5 EXEMPTIONS AND RELIEFS. [*TCGA 1992, s 253(1)(2)*].

Where a company re-lends money to a 'trading company' in the same group, the original loan is treated as having been used by the first company as it is used by the second while the second remains a member of the group. '*Trading company*' has the meaning given by *TCGA 1992, 6 Sch 1* as in 48.3 RETIREMENT RELIEF (for claims made before 1 April 1989 the meaning was given by *ICTA 1988, 19 Sch 7* (see 22.6 HOLD-OVER RELIEFS)) and '*group*' is as defined by *TCGA 1992, s 170* (see 13.10 COMPANIES). [*TCGA 1992, s 253(2)(14)(b)(c); FA 1989, 12 Sch 6*].

Relief is not available and nor is a clawback of relief made (see below) if the amount in question is taken into account for computing income for the purposes of income tax or corporation tax. [*TCGA 1992, s 253(10)*].

As stated above, any loss arises, in strictness, at the date of claim but it will, by concession, be treated as arising in a particular year of assessment (or accounting period in the case of a company) where the claim is made not later than two years after the end of that year of assessment (or accounting period) and provided that all the conditions for the relief are satisfied *both* at the date of claim *and* at the end of that year of assessment (or accounting period) (Revenue Pamphlet IR 1, D36; this concession replaces Revenue Pamphlet IR 131, SP 3/83 but with a revised text to make it clear that the conditions for relief must be met not only at an earlier specified time but also when the claim is made).

Prior to the commencement of *TCGA 1992*, claims were made under *CGTA 1979, s 136(3)*.

Relief for payment made under guarantee. The relief given above to a lender also applies to a guarantor of a qualifying loan who makes a claim under *TCGA 1992, s 253(4)* and who must prove additionally that he has made a payment under the guarantee to the lender or a co-guarantor. The claimant is treated as if an allowable loss of the amount of the payment had accrued to him when the payment was made. Where loss relief is given, no allowable loss and no chargeable gain (otherwise than on a clawback of relief as below) will accrue on the disposal of rights consequent on his having made a payment (which may include a payment in respect of interest as well as principal) under the guarantee. The guarantee must have been given after 11 April 1978. Relief is available to a guarantor even though the original loan is a 'debt on a security' (see above and 35.10 below). Relief is reduced to the extent that any contribution is 'payable' to the claimant by any co-guarantor. [*TCGA 1992, s 253(4)(11)(15)*].

'*Payable*' has its ordinary meaning, so that if under general legal principles the claimant could have made a recovery against one or more co-guarantors of part of a sum paid by him under a guarantee but chose not to do so, the relief given to him is reduced proportionately (*Leisureking Ltd v Cushing Ch D 1992, [1993] STC 46*).

'*Guarantee*' covers the case where a person's property is charged as security for a qualifying loan. It does not include an indemnity, which creates a primary liability. A guarantee can apply to the repayment of an overdraft but not a hire purchase agreement. (CCAB Memorandum TR 308, 4 October 1978). Presumably, therefore, an indemnity could itself be treated as a qualifying loan.

The Revenue have stated that they interpret the provision in *TCGA 1992, s 253(4)* concerning reduction of relief where any contribution is 'payable' by a co-guarantor as limiting the relief available to the level it would be if all *possible* recoveries had been made. (Tolley's Practical Tax 1986 p 40 and cf. the *Leisureking* case above which was heard subsequently). The Revenue ignore voluntary payments, only those being made as a consequence of the formal calling in of a guarantee being covered by the relief. (Tolley's Practical Tax 1987 p 147). The Revenue have confirmed that a trading debt arising from the supply of stock to a trading company is considered capable of being treated as a qualifying loan as regards a guarantee made in respect of the debt. (Tolley's Practical Tax 1988 p 40).

Prior to the commencement of *TCGA 1992*, claims were made under *CGTA 1979, s 136(4)*.

Clawback of relief. Where loss relief has been obtained by the person who made the loan or a guarantor of it, and all or part of the outstanding amount of, or of interest in respect of (in the case of a guarantor), the principal of the loan is recovered, a chargeable gain is deemed to accrue to him at the time of recovery equal to so much of the allowable

35.10 Losses

loss (for which relief was claimed) as corresponds to the amount recovered. Where a claimant has obtained loss relief in respect of a payment under a guarantee and recovers, at any time after 19 March 1990, the whole or any part of that payment, he will be treated as if there had accrued to him at that time a chargeable gain equal to so much of the allowable loss as corresponds to the amount recovered. A similar treatment will apply to a company ('the second company') which, at any time after 19 March 1990, recovers the whole or any part of the outstanding amount of the principal of a loan which has become irrecoverable in circumstances where a company ('the first company'), which made the loan originally and is in the same group as the second company when the loan was made or at any subsequent time, has obtained loss relief in respect of that loan becoming irrecoverable. Where the first company has obtained loss relief in relation to a payment made under a guarantee in respect of a loan which has become irrecoverable, a similar treatment of the second company applies if it recovers, at any time after 19 March 1990, the whole or any part of the outstanding amount of, or of interest in respect of, the principal of the loan, or the whole or any part of the guarantee payment made by the first company. An amount is treated as recovered if money or money's worth is received in satisfaction of the right of recovery. If this right is assigned otherwise than at arm's length, its full market value at that time is deemed to have been received. [*TCGA 1992, s 253(5)–(9)(13)*].

35.10 **LOANS TO TRADERS EVIDENCED BY QUALIFYING CORPORATE BONDS**

Relief to lender on loan becoming irrecoverable etc. If, on a claim under *TCGA 1992, s 254(4)* by a person who has made a 'qualifying loan', the inspector is satisfied that one of the three conditions given below is fulfilled, the claimant is treated as if an allowable loss equal to the 'allowable amount' had accrued to him when the claim was made. (However, the Revenue will apply their concessionary practice, as contained in Revenue Pamphlet IR 1, D36 and outlined in 35.9 above, regarding the time a loss may be treated as accruing in the same way for this relief as they do for the relief for irrecoverable loans to traders).

A '*qualifying loan*' means a loan in the case of which

(*a*) the borrower's debt is a debt on a security within *TCGA 1992, s 132* (see 35.9 above) which was issued after 14 March 1989, or issued before 15 March 1989 but held on 15 March 1989 by the person who made the loan,

(*b*) but for the borrower's debt being a debt on a security, the loan would be a qualifying loan within *TCGA 1992, s 253* (see 35.9 above), and

(*c*) the security is a qualifying corporate bond within *TCGA 1992, s 117* (as in 44.2 QUALIFYING CORPORATE BONDS but with modifications where applied for the purposes of this relief, certain of which have a consequential effect as regards the 'allowable amount' where the first or second condition below is fulfilled).

The first condition is that

(i) the value of the security has become negligible (but relief will still be available where the security ceases to have any value because it is redeemed early; Revenue Pamphlet IR 131, SP 8/90, 6 December 1990 and see (1) below for 'redemption date'),

(ii) the claimant has not assigned his right to recover any outstanding amount of the principal of the loan, and

(iii)   the claimant and the borrower are not companies which have been in the same group (within *TCGA 1992, s 170*, see 13.10 COMPANIES) at any time after the loan was made.

The second condition is that

(1)   the security's 'redemption date' (i.e. the latest date on which, under the terms under which the security was issued, the company or body which issued it can be required to redeem it) has passed,

(2)   all the outstanding amount of the principal of the loan was irrecoverable (taking the facts existing on that date) or proved to be irrecoverable (taking the facts existing on a later date), and

(3)   the requirements in (ii) and (iii) above are fulfilled.

The third condition is that

(A)   the security's redemption date (as at (1) above) has passed,

(B)   sub-condition (2) of the second condition above was fulfilled on a similar basis as regards part (rather than the whole) of the outstanding principal of the loan, and

(C)   the requirements in (ii) and (iii) above are fulfilled.

Where the inspector is satisfied that the first or second condition is fulfilled, '*the allowable amount*' is the lesser of the outstanding amount of the principal of the loan and the amount of the security's acquisition cost (i.e. the amount or value of the consideration in money or money's worth given, by or on behalf of the person who made the loan, wholly and exclusively for the acquisition of the security, together with the incidental costs to him of the acquisition). However, if any amount of the principal of the loan has been recovered the amount of the security's acquisition cost is for this purpose reduced (but not beyond nil) by the amount recovered. An amount is treated as recovered if money or money's worth is received in satisfaction of the right of recovery. If this right is assigned otherwise than at arm's length, its full market value at that time is deemed to have been received.

Where the inspector is satisfied that the third condition is fulfilled, then '*the allowable amount*' is an amount equal to the excess (if any) of the security's acquisition cost over the 'relevant amount' or nil (if there is no such excess). The '*relevant amount*' is the aggregate of the amount (if any) of the principal of the loan which has been recovered (as above) and the amount (if any) of the principal of the loan which has not been recovered but which in the inspector's opinion is recoverable.

Relief is not available and nor is a clawback of relief made (see below) if the amount in question is taken into account for computing income for the purposes of income tax or corporation tax. An amount is not treated as irrecoverable for the purposes of the relief if it becomes irrecoverable under the express terms of the loan or related arrangements, or by reason of any act or omission by the lender. [*TCGA 1992, ss 254(1)–(8)(12), 255(1)(2)(4)(5)*].

Prior to the commencement of *TCGA 1992*, claims were made under *CGTA 1979, s 136A(2)*.

Clawback of relief. Where an allowable loss has been treated under the above as accruing to any person and the whole or any part of the 'relevant outstanding amount' is at any time recovered (as above) by him, he is treated as if there had accrued to him at that time a chargeable gain equal to so much of the allowable loss as corresponds to the amount recovered. A similar treatment applies to a company ('the second company') where an allowable loss has been treated under the above as accruing to a company ('the first company'), and the whole or any part of the relevant outstanding amount is at any time recovered by the second company which is in the same group (as above) as the first company at any time after the loan was made. The '*relevant outstanding amount*' means, in a case where the inspector was satisfied that the first or second condition was fulfilled, the amount of the principal of the loan outstanding when the claim was allowed or, in a case where he was satisfied that the third condition was fulfilled, the amount of the part (or the greater or greatest part) arrived at by the inspector under sub-condition (B) of the third condition above. [*TCGA 1992, ss 254(9)–(11), 255(3)–(5)*].

35.11   **Qualifying corporate bonds: reorganisations etc. thereof and relief under 35.10 above.** *TCGA 1992, s 116(10)(11)* deals with the situation where, on a reorganisation etc. of shares (which are not qualifying corporate bonds), such shares ('the old asset') are replaced by securities ('the new asset') which are qualifying corporate bonds (and thus exempt from capital gains tax). The broad effect is to defer the chargeable gain or allowable loss that would have accrued on a disposal of the old asset at its market value immediately before the reorganisation until such time as a part or the whole of the new asset is disposed of, at which time the corresponding part or the whole of the deferred gain or loss is deemed to accrue. See 44.3 QUALIFYING CORPORATE BONDS for full details. In such a case and where the new asset is a qualifying corporate bond in respect of which an allowable loss is treated as accruing under *TCGA 1992, s 254(2)* in 35.10 above, and the loss is treated as so accruing at a time falling after the reorganisation but before any actual disposal of the new asset subsequent to the reorganisation, then, for the purposes of *TCGA 1992, s 116(10)(11)*, a disposal of the new asset is deemed to have occurred at (and only at) the time the loss is deemed to have accrued. This applies whatever the time the reorganisation occurs. [*TCGA 1992, s 116(15)*]. The effect is that the deferred gain or loss relating to the old asset will be deemed to accrue at the same time as the loss arising on a claim under *TCGA 1992, s 254(2)* above in respect of the new asset is deemed to accrue, and any later disposal of the new asset is ignored for the purposes of ascertaining when and in what amount the deferred gain or loss is treated as arising.

A concessional practice, contained in Revenue Pamphlet IR 1 (1992) D38, will apply as follows. Where a person acquired corporate bonds in respect of shares and securities and those bonds became, or would fall to be treated as, qualifying corporate bonds by virtue only of *FA 1989, s 139* (extension of definition to include a wider range of sterling bonds; see 44.2 and 44.3 QUALIFYING CORPORATE BONDS), an allowable loss, computed in accordance with the rules in *TCGA 1992, s 116* (see 35.10 above), will accrue if

(*a*)   the qualifying corporate bonds were issued in respect of shares or other securities before 14 March 1989 and were still retained at that date by the person to whom they were issued;

(*b*)   the bonds were acquired in a transaction within *TCGA 1992, s 116(10)(11)* (see above) and on disposal after 13 March 1989 fall to be treated as qualifying corporate bonds as a result of *FA 1989, s 139*;

(*c*)   relief under *TCGA 1992, s 254* would have been available had the loan been a qualifying loan within *TCGA 1992, s 254(1)*;

(*d*)   the taxpayer claiming the concessional relief agrees that if all or part of the amount relieved is subsequently recovered the relief will be clawed back in the same way as if *TCGA 1992, s 254* had applied, save that in all cases the chargeable gain will be treated as accruing to the claimant; and

(*e*)   when this concession applies, any gain or loss on the original shares or securities will be treated as accruing at the same time as the loss on the bonds in accordance with *TCGA 1992, s 116(15)* (see above and also 44.3 QUALIFYING CORPORATE

BONDS for an additional relief which may apply in such circumstances where the bonds are gifted to a charity).

Under the concession the allowable loss will be treated as arising when a claim is made but it will be treated as arising in an earlier year of assessment or accounting period provided the claim is made not later than two years after the end of that year of assessment or accounting period, all the conditions for relief are satisfied at the date of claim, and the relief would have been available at the end of the year of assessment or accounting period for which relief is claimed.

35.12   LOSSES ON SHARES IN UNQUOTED TRADING COMPANIES: INDIVIDUALS

In relation to losses incurred in 1994/95 and subsequent years, where an individual who has 'subscribed' for 'shares' in a 'qualifying trading company' incurs an allowable loss (for capital gains tax purposes) on the disposal of the shares in any year of assessment, he may, by written notice given within two years after that year (for 1996/97 and subsequent years, within twelve months from 31 January next following that year), make a claim for relief from income tax on

(1)   so much of his income for that year as is equal to the amount of the loss or, where it is less than that amount, the whole of that income; or

(2)   so much of his income for the last preceding year as is equal to the amount of the loss as remains after deducting that part of the loss utilised under (1) above or, where it is less than that remaining amount, the whole of that income.

Where such relief is given in respect of the loss or any part of it, no deduction from chargeable gains is available in respect of the loss or (as the case may be) that part. Relief claimed under (1) above in respect of any income is given in priority to any relief claimed under (2) in respect of that income; and relief claimed under either (1) or (2) in respect of any income is given in priority to relief claimed under *ICTA 1988, s 380* (trading losses set against general income) or *s 381* (further relief for trading losses to be set against general income in early years of a trade) in respect of that income.

The relief described above for 1994/95 and 1995/96 applied similarly for years before 1994/95, except that the relief applied to reduce income for the year of assessment in which the loss was incurred (here called the 'year of loss') and the *next following* year rather than the year of loss and the *last preceding* year. Where relief was claimed for a deduction to be made from income of a particular year (such a claim having to be made within two years of the end of that particular year) in respect of losses arising in that year and the last preceding year, relief in respect of losses arising in that last preceding year was given in priority to relief in respect of losses arising in the particular year. Where relief was given for years before 1990/91 relief was given first against the earned income of the claimant, then against his other income and then against the earned income, and then the other income, of his spouse provided they were living together, although the individual could require relief to be given against only his income.

There is no statutory order of priority between the relief due under the old rules and that due under the new rules. In practice, a claimant can choose the order in which these reliefs are given (Revenue Tax Bulletin, December 1994, p 184).

For all years of assessment, a claim for relief cannot be made unless the disposal is at arm's length for full consideration, by way of a distribution in the course of dissolving or winding up the company or a deemed disposal under *TCGA 1992, s 24(2)* (see 35.8 above and note certain concessionary treatment there under ESC D28 which is equally applicable to this relief) where the shares have become of negligible value. Despite this restriction, by concession, where an unquoted trading company devoid of assets is wound up, a holder of shares in that company who has not made such a negligible value claim and did not receive a distribution during the course of winding up is able to claim relief under these provisions in any case still open after 15 December 1993, provided all other conditions for relief are met (Revenue Pamphlet IR 1, D46).

Adjustments to capital gains tax liabilities may be made in consequence of a claim under these provisions.

An individual *'subscribes'* for shares if they are issued to him by the company for money or money's worth, or if they were so issued to his 'spouse', who transferred them to him by a transaction inter vivos. *'Spouse'* refers to one of two spouses who are living together (see 37.2 MARRIED PERSONS).

A *'qualifying trading company'* is a company none of the shares in which is, or has ever been, quoted on a recognised stock exchange (see *ICTA 1988, s 841*) and which

(*a*) either   (i)   is a 'trading company' at the date of disposal, or

          (ii)   has ceased to be a trading company within three years of that date and has not since that cessation been an 'excluded company' or an 'investment company', *and*

(*b*) either   (i)   has been a trading company for a continuous period at least six years prior to the disposal (or prior to the cessation, as the case may be), or

          (ii)   has been a trading company for a shorter continuous period ending with the disposal or cessation and has not previously been an excluded company or an investment company, *and*

(*c*)   has been resident in the UK throughout the period from incorporation to the disposal or cessation.

'Trading company' is any company (other than an excluded company—see below) whose business consists wholly or mainly of the carrying on of a trade or trades (for disposals before 1 April 1989, any company which exists wholly or mainly for the purpose of carrying on a trade, or the income of which does not consist wholly or mainly of investment income). The 'holding company' of a 'trading group' is also included.

'Excluded company' means a company the trade of which consists wholly or mainly of dealing in shares, securities, land, trades or commodity futures. A company which does not carry on its trade on a commercial basis and with a reasonable expectation of profit is within this definition, as are the holding company of a non-trading group, a building society or a registered industrial and provident society.

'Trading group' means a 'group' the business of the members of which, taken together, consists wholly or mainly in the carrying on of a trade or trades. Any trade carried on by a subsidiary which is non-resident or an excluded company is disregarded.

'Group' means a company and its 51% subsidiary or subsidiaries, and a *'holding company'* is one the business of which consists wholly or mainly in the holding of shares or securities in its 51% subsidiary or subsidiaries. 51% subsidiaries are as defined by *ICTA 1988, s 838*.

'Investment company' has the meaning given by *ICTA 1988, s 130* (i.e. any company the business of which consists wholly or mainly in the making of investments and the principal part of the income of which is derived therefrom but including banks and other banks for savings (except trustee savings banks)) except that it does not include the holding company of a trading group. In *Tintern Close Residents Society Ltd v Winter SC 3113/94 (SC000007), [1995] STI 574*, it was decided that property management

companies which collect income from residents for the upkeep of relevant properties are not investment companies within the meaning of *ICTA 1988, s 130*.

'Shares' (except in the definition of 'excluded company', when all shares and stock are covered) means 'ordinary share capital' as defined in *ICTA 1988, s 832(1)* (see 53.8 SHARES AND SECURITIES).

Where an individual who has subscribed for shares in a company has also acquired similar shares by other means, disposals are to be related to later, rather than earlier, acquisitions. Loss relief under these provisions on the disposal of qualifying shares forming part of a holding (broadly a pool as in 23.10 INDEXATION) is restricted to the sums that would be allowed as deductions in computing the loss if the qualifying shares had been acquired and disposed of as a separate holding (pool). Presumably these provisions are subject to the identification rules for shares applying after 5 April 1982 (31 March 1982 for companies). See 23 INDEXATION.

Relief is not available in respect of a 'new holding' (within *TCGA 1992, s 127*) unless relief could have been given (assuming the legislation to have been in force) on the disposal which would have occurred on the reorganisation but for *TCGA 1992, s 127* or unless the claimant gave 'new consideration' for the new holding, in which latter case the relief is restricted to such amount or value of the new consideration as represents allowable expenditure. See, generally, 53.5 SHARES AND SECURITIES.

'New consideration' means consideration in money or money's worth (other than the surrender of rights etc. and that met out of the company's assets).

An amalgamation or scheme of reconstruction which is undertaken for tax avoidance purposes or other than for bona fide commercial reasons, and therefore gives rise to a chargeable disposal under *TCGA 1992, s 137*, cannot support a claim under these provisions. See 3.13 ANTI-AVOIDANCE.

Where a claim is made under these provisions, *TCGA 1992, s 30* (value-shifting to give tax-free benefit, see 3.6 ANTI-AVOIDANCE) has effect in relation to the disposal if *any* benefit is conferred, whether tax-free or not. [*ICTA 1988, ss 574–576; FA 1988, 14 Sch Pt VIII; FA 1989, 12 Sch 14; FA 1994, ss 146, 210, 218(5) 17 Sch 6, 20 Sch 8; FA 1995, s 119*].

It is formally provided that the provisions given above apply on the disposal by an individual of shares issued after 31 December 1993 to which enterprise investment relief (see 53.17 SHARES AND SECURITIES) is attributable as they apply to a disposal by him of shares in a 'qualifying trading company' for which he has 'subscribed' (both terms having the same meaning as above). However, the provisions in the fourth and fifth paragraphs immediately preceding this one (matching of disposals with acquisitions, restriction of loss and relief not available on certain new holdings) do not apply to the application of the above relief to shares to which enterprise investment relief is attributable. [*ICTA 1988, s 305A; FA 1994, s 137, 15 Sch 20*].

There was no equivalent to *ICTA 1988, s 305A* in respect of a loss arising on shares issued after 18 March 1986 and before 1 January 1994 in respect of which business expansion scheme relief (see 53.18 SHARES AND SECURITIES) has been given and not withdrawn, because any loss so arising was not allowable for capital gains tax purposes. A complete withdrawal of relief would have meant that any loss was allowable for such purposes and, all conditions being met, there seemed nothing to prevent the above relief from applying. The position seems to be the same in respect of a loss arising on shares issued before 19 March 1986 in respect of which business expansion scheme relief has been given but completely withdrawn. A loss arising on shares issued before 19 March 1986 in respect of which business expansion scheme relief has been given and not

35.13   Losses

withdrawn, could give rise to an allowable (albeit reduced) loss so that, again, there seemed nothing to prevent the reduced loss from being similarly set against income.

See 23.2 INDEXATION for transitional relief for 1993/94 and 1994/95 in respect of 'indexation losses' referable to disposals of shares within the above provisions.

35.13   *Example*

P subscribed for 3,000 £1 ordinary shares in W Ltd, a new trading company, at par in June 1988. In September 1989, P acquired a further 2,000 shares at £1.60 from another shareholder. In December 1995, P sold 3,800 shares at 90p.

Indexation factors	June 1988 to September 1989		0.094
	June 1988 to December 1995 (assumed)		0.371
	September 1989 to December 1995 (assumed)		0.253

(i)   Establish new holding pool

	Shares	Qualifying expenditure £	Indexed pool £
June 1988 subscription	3,000	3,000	3,000
Indexation to September 1989 £3,000 × 0.094			282
September 1989 acquisition	2,000	3,200	3,200
	5,000	6,200	6,482
Indexed rise: September 1989 to December 1995 £6,482 × 0.253			1,640
	5,000	6,200	8,122
December 1995 disposal	(3,800)	(4,712)	(6,173)
Pool carried forward	1,200	£1,488	£1,949

(ii)   The overall loss is calculated as follows

	£
Disposal consideration 3,800 × £0.90	3,420
Allowable cost $\dfrac{3,800}{5,000} \times £6,200$	4,712
Allowable loss	£1,292

[See note (*a*) below]

(iii)   The loss allowable against income is calculated as follows

	£
Loss referable to 1,800 subscription shares $\dfrac{1,800}{3,800} \times £1,292$	£612

	£
Loss restricted to actual loss on the subscription shares	
Disposal consideration 1,800 × £0.90	1,620
Allowable cost 1,800 × £1.00	1,800
Allowable loss	£180

[See note (*a*) below]

(iv)   The loss not relieved against income remains a capital loss

£1,292 − £180 =	£1,112

Note to the example

(*a*)   For disposals after 29 November 1993, indexation allowance cannot increase or create a loss for CGT purposes (and therefore for losses on shares in unquoted trading companies also).

35.14   **LOSSES ON SHARES IN UNQUOTED TRADING COMPANIES: INVESTMENT COMPANIES**

Where, after 31 March 1981, an 'investment company' disposes of shares in a 'qualifying trading company' for which it has subscribed (i.e. not purchased in the open market), and thereby incurs an allowable capital loss in an accounting period, it may claim relief for the loss against income of that accounting period, instead of against gains chargeable to corporation tax. Additionally, if it was an investment company at that earlier time, it may claim to set off any balance of the loss remaining, after relief above, against income of the twelve months immediately preceding the accounting period in which the loss was incurred (income of the relevant accounting periods being time apportioned for this purpose).

The investment company must have been such on the date of the relevant disposal and must either

(*a*)   have been an investment company for a continuous period of six years ending on that date; or

(*b*)   have been an investment company for a shorter continuous period ending on that date, and must not have been, before the beginning of that period, a 'trading company' or an 'excluded company'.

It must also not have been 'associated' with, or have been a member of the same 'group' as, the qualifying trading company, at any time in the period beginning with the date of its (the investment company's) subscription for the shares, and ending with the date of disposal.

Companies are *'associated'* with each other, for this purpose, if one controls the other, or both are under the control of the same person or persons. The general definitions of *ICTA 1988, s 416(2)(6)* (meaning of 'control') apply for this purpose. See Tolley's Corporation Tax under Close Companies.

Subject to the above, the definitions of *'excluded company'*, *'group'*, *'investment company'*, *'qualifying trading company'*, *'trading company'*, and the other general definitions and provisions (including concessionary treatment under ESCs D28 and D46) relating to the similar relief for individuals outlined in 35.12 above, apply, *mutatis mutandis*, to this relief.

Relief must be claimed within two years of the end of the accounting period in which the loss arises and is given before any deduction for charges on income, expenses of management or other deductions. [*ICTA 1988, ss 573, 575, 576; FA 1989, 12 Sch 14; FA 1994, s 146, 17 Sch 6*].

Subject to the general provisions of the foregoing a capital loss may be relieved against surplus franked investment income, by means of a claim, under *ICTA 1988, s 242*, made within two years of the end of the accounting period in which the loss is incurred. See, generally, Tolley's Corporation Tax under Franked Investment Income.

35.15   **WRITE-OFF OF GOVERNMENT INVESTMENT**

Where, after 9 March 1981, any amount of an investment, by the Government, in a *corporate body*, is written off, an equal amount is to be set off against the body's tax

35.15 Losses

'losses', starting with losses available at the end of the accounting period ended before the write-off, and continuing for subsequent periods, until the investment is covered. The definition of *'losses'*, for this purpose, includes, inter alia, unrelieved allowable losses under *TCGA 1992, s 8* (capital losses of companies). It should be noted, however, that the investment is only written off against capital losses as a last resort, i.e. after the extinction of other losses, unrelieved capital allowances, management expenses and charges. The investment can also be written off against the losses of any member of the same 51% group within *ICTA 1988, s 838*. An investment is written off if the liability to repay any money lent is extinguished; if any shares subscribed for out of public funds are cancelled; or if 'commencing capital debts' (as defined) or 'public dividend capital' (as defined) is reduced otherwise than by being paid off or repaid. These provisions do not apply where the investment written off is replaced in some other form. [*ICTA 1988, s 400*]. See Tolley's Corporation Tax under Losses for further details.

36   Market Value

Cross-references. See 3.10–3.11 ANTI-AVOIDANCE for anti-avoidance provisions which may override or amend the general rules given below; 4.2 and 4.5 APPEALS for appeals relating to market values; 7.2 ASSETS HELD ON 6 APRIL 1965 for valuation of quoted shares and securities held on 6 April 1965; 15.3 DEATH for valuation at death; 16.3 DISPOSAL for allowable expenditure relating to acquisition of assets at market value; 35.8 LOSSES for loss relief where the market value of an asset has become negligible; 40 PARTNERSHIPS for further valuation rules which apply to partnership assets.

36.1   Market value is the price which assets might reasonably fetch in the open market, sold individually, with no allowance being made for any reduction in market value arising out of the whole of the assets being placed on the market at one and the same time. [*TCGA 1992, s 272(1)(2)*].

After 9 March 1981, acquisition and disposal are treated as being made at market value (subject to any other provision and the exception below) if the transaction is

(*a*)   not at arm's length (which includes, in particular, a transaction between CONNECTED PERSONS (14), or

(*b*)   by way of gift, or

(*c*)   on a transfer into settlement by a settlor, or

(*d*)   a distribution from a company in respect of shares in that company, or

(*e*)   wholly or partly for a consideration that cannot be valued (see *Fielder v Vedlynn Ltd Ch D, [1992] STC 553*), or

(*f*)   in connection with his own or another's loss of office or employment, diminution of emoluments, or in consideration for or recognition of his or another's services (in any office, employment or otherwise), past or future.

Exception. The market value provisions in (*a*)-(*f*) above do not apply to the *acquisition* of an asset if there is no corresponding disposal of it *and* there is no consideration in money or money's worth (or the consideration is of an amount or value lower than the market value of the asset). [*TCGA 1992, s 17*].

See Revenue Tax Bulletin, December 1994, pp 181, 182 for discussion on transfers at undervalue to employees or directors.

Special rules applied to disposals by 'excluded persons' after 9 March 1981 and before 6 April 1985. *'Excluded persons'* meant

(i)   a person neither resident nor ordinarily resident in the UK;

(ii)   a person wholly exempt from tax in respect of chargeable gains (or who would have been so exempt on making a claim for exemption);

(iii)   a charity;

(iv)   a registered friendly society; or

(v)   a person making the disposal for the purposes of a pension fund (as defined) which was exempt from tax.

Where the corresponding disposal (see the exception above) was made by an excluded person, the following provisions applied.

(A)   *For disposals after 9 March 1981 and before 6 April 1983,* the market value rules in (*a*)-(*f*) above did not apply (with one exception) to the *acquisition* or *disposal* of the asset. The exception was the *acquisition,* by an individual, of currency or tangible movable property (excluding commodities of a kind dealt with on a terminal market or a mere right in, or over, any property) in circumstances where there was a corresponding disposal by an individual who was neither resident nor ordinarily resident in the UK. In this case the acquisition was treated as being made at market value.

(B)   *For disposals after 5 April 1983 and before 6 April 1985* by an excluded person who would be chargeable in respect of any chargeable gain thereon, then provided there was no consideration in money or money's worth (or the consideration was of an amount or value lower than the market value of the asset), the person acquiring the asset and the excluded person could jointly elect that the deemed market value rules in (*a*)-(*f*) above did not apply to the acquisition and corresponding disposal. The election had to be made in writing within two years of the end of the chargeable period in which the corresponding disposal occurred. Any adjustments of capital gains tax (or corporation tax in respect of chargeable gains) in consequence of the election were to be made by way of assessment, discharge or repayment of tax.

[*CGTA 1979, s 29A(3)–(5); FA 1981, s 90(1); FA 1984, s 66(2)*].

See also 39.8 OVERSEAS MATTERS and 16.4 DISPOSAL.

Before 10 March 1981, (*c*) above was not expressly stated to apply and the exception to (*a*)-(*f*) above also did not apply (but see *CGTA 1979, s 76* regarding share option schemes). See *Harrison v Nairn Williamson Ltd CA 1977, 51 TC 135,* where the earlier provisions, found in *CGTA 1979, s 19(3) (as originally enacted),* were held to operate where there was an acquisition but no corresponding disposal.

36.2   **QUOTED SHARES AND SECURITIES**

The market value of shares and securities listed in The Stock Exchange Daily Official List is the lesser of

(*a*)   the lower of the two prices quoted in The Stock Exchange Daily Official List for the relevant date, plus a quarter of the difference between those prices ('*the quarter-up rule*'), and

(*b*)   the average of the highest and lowest prices for normal bargains recorded on that date, if any.

If the London trading floor is closed on the relevant date, the prices are to be taken by reference to the latest previous date or to the earliest subsequent date, whichever produces the lower figure.

The above method of valuation does not apply for computing the value of shares as at 6 April 1965 (see 7.2 ASSETS HELD ON 6 APRIL 1965), nor where special circumstances may affect the value. [*TCGA 1992, s 272(3)(4)(6), 11 Sch 6(1)(2)(4), 7(1)*]. See *Hinchcliffe v Crabtree HL 1971, 47 TC 419.*

From 23 July 1987, the Board may make regulations extending, inter alia, provisions relating to tax on chargeable gains and referring to The Stock Exchange to any or all other investment exchanges within the meaning of *Financial Services Act 1986.* [*TCGA 1992, ss 285, 287*].

Units in unit trusts, subject to similar valuation rules at 6 April 1965 (as above), are valued at the lower of the two prices published by the managers on the relevant date or if no price is published at that time, on the latest date before the relevant date. [*TCGA 1992, s 272(5)(6), 11 Sch 6(1)(3)*].

For securities dealt in on the Unlisted Securities Market see 36.4 below.

36.3   UNQUOTED SHARES

Market value of unquoted shares is determined on the assumption that all information is available which a prudent prospective purchaser might reasonably require before purchase by private treaty at arm's length from a willing vendor. [*TCGA 1992, s 273*]. This counteracts *In re Lynall HL 1971, 47 TC 375*.

This provision applies to disposals after 5 July 1973 and valuations are made on the present basis in connection both with acquisition (even if before 6 July 1973, or 6 April 1965) and disposal. Otherwise, the chargeable gain on a part disposal before 6 July 1973 is not itself affected but it is re-computed on the present basis for the purpose of calculating the gain on a subsequent disposal after 5 July 1973. As regards deemed acquisitions on death after 30 March 1971 and before 6 July 1973, the present basis does not apply if the shares constituted a controlling holding and were valued on the assets basis for estate duty purposes. [*TCGA 1992, 11 Sch 3–5*].

36.4   UNLISTED SECURITIES MARKET (USM)

Securities dealt in on the USM are not treated as 'listed' or 'quoted' for those provisions of the *Taxes Acts* which use such terms in relation to securities. Evidence of the open-market value of such securities will be suggested, initially, by details of the bargains done at, or near, the relevant date. Where other factors need to be weighed, the Shares Valuation Division of the Capital Taxes Office will consider whether a value offered on the basis of those bargains can be accepted as an adequate reflection of the open-market value. The Revenue states that securities dealt in on the USM will satisfy the tests of being 'authorised to be dealt in' and 'dealt in (regularly or from time to time)' on a recognised stock exchange (Revenue Pamphlet IR 131, SP 18/80, 23 December 1980). It appears that the Revenue apply similar criteria to securities covered by Rule 4.2 (formerly Rule 535.2) of The Stock Exchange. This may also be the position as regards the Third Market of The Stock Exchange.

The USM is to close at the end of 1996. Companies not wishing to apply for a full listing will have access to the Alternative Investment Market (AIM) launched on 19 June 1995. AIM replaces the existing Rule 4.2 dealing facility, and transitional provisions will be available to assist companies already under Rule 4.2 to migrate to the AIM at minimum cost. AIM companies are not treated as 'quoted' or 'listed' for those provisions of the *Taxes Acts* which use such terms in relation to securities (Inland Revenue Press Release 20 February 1995).

36.5   LAND

Where, at a certain date, freehold land was subject to a tenancy by a company controlled by the freeholder, the valuation had to be of the reversion in the land expectant on the determination of the tenancy and not of the unencumbered freehold (*Henderson v Karmel's Exors Ch D 1984, 58 TC 201*).

36.6   EXCHANGE CONTROL

In relation to assets of a kind the sale of which was subject to restrictions imposed under the *Exchange Control Act 1947*, a determination of market value at any time before 13 December 1979 is subject to adjustment for the premium which would have been payable by a purchaser but not receivable by a seller. [*TCGA 1992, 11 Sch 7(2)*].

37 Married Persons

Cross-references. See 2 ANNUAL RATES AND EXEMPTIONS; 7.1 and 7.3 ASSETS HELD ON 6 APRIL 1965; 8.5 ASSETS HELD ON 31 MARCH 1982; 22 HOLD-OVER RELIEFS; 23.4 INDEXATION for certain transfers between spouses before 6 April 1985 and after 5 April 1982; 35.9 LOSSES for loss relief restrictions on qualifying loans between spouses; 43.1 and 43.2 PRIVATE RESIDENCES; 47 RESIDENCE AND DOMICILE for treatment of spouses; 48.9 RETIREMENT RELIEF for reliefs applicable to spouses; 49.2 RETURNS for returns required by spouses.

37.1 INTRODUCTION

For 1990/91 and subsequent years of assessment, the spouses, whether or not 'living together' (see 37.2 below), are each treated as separate individuals so that

(*a*) each spouse is assessed and charged by reference only to their own gains and circumstances (e.g. the rate of tax applicable);

(*b*) losses of one spouse are not deductible from the gains of the other; and

(*c*) each spouse has a separate right to the whole of the annual exempt amount available to individuals generally.

Where a husband and wife have made a declaration under *ICTA 1988, 282B* in respect of their individual beneficial interests in, and in the income from, jointly held property (see Tolley's Income Tax under Married Persons) and the declaration is still effective at the time of disposal of the property, there is a presumption that the declared split of interests is effective for capital gains tax purposes. Where there is no declaration which has effect at the time of disposal but it is clear that there is a particular split of ownership (e.g. a separate agreement may provide for the spouses' respective rights or that one spouse is merely a nominee and has no beneficial interest in the property) any gain on a disposal should be reported to the Revenue on that basis. In other cases where the split of ownership is not clear the Revenue will normally accept that the spouses hold the property in equal shares (Revenue Press Release 21 November 1990).

For years of assessment before 1990/91, where the spouses were 'living together' (see 37.2 below), the chargeable gains less allowable losses of each spouse, although computed and aggregated separately for each year, were assessed in total on the husband (with certain exceptions). Spouses not living together were broadly treated as separate individuals. See 37.3–37.5 below.

Allowable losses of either the husband or wife which were not utilised at **6 April 1990** may only be carried forward against the future chargeable gains of the individual concerned.

General. Transfers of assets between spouses living together are treated as made on a 'no gain, no loss basis' as in 37.6 below.

Where

(i) the husband makes a claim under *TCGA 1992, s 279* (previously *CGTA 1979, s 13*; enforced delay in remitting gains from disposals of overseas assets, see 39.4 OVERSEAS MATTERS) in respect of gains accruing to the wife before 6 April 1990, and

(ii) under that provision the amount of the gains falls to be assessed as if it were an amount of gains accruing after 5 April 1990, the assessment is to be made on the wife (or her personal representatives). [*TCGA 1992, s 279(7)*].

Gains accruing to one spouse as trustee or personal representative cannot affect the position of the other spouse. [*TCGA 1992, s 65(2)*].

Spouses living together may claim exemption in respect of only one main residence. See 43.1 PRIVATE RESIDENCES.

37.2   'LIVING TOGETHER'

For 1990/91 and subsequent years of assessment, a husband and wife are treated as living together unless they are

(*a*)   separated under a court order or separation deed, or

(*b*)   in fact separated in circumstances which render permanent separation likely.

[*ICTA 1988, s 282; TCGA 1992, s 288(3)*].

For years of assessment before 1990/91, a married woman was treated as living with her husband unless (*a*) or (*b*) above applied but, if while still living together under this definition, one spouse was resident in the UK 'for a year' of assessment and one was not, or both were resident in the UK but one was absent abroad throughout the year, then for that year they were treated as if permanently separated. [*ICTA 1988, s 282(1)(2) as originally enacted; CGTA 1979, s 155(2); FA 1988, 3 Sch 11, 13 Sch 18*]. Although residence 'for a year' included residence for part of that year, *ICTA 1988, s 282(3)* (as originally enacted; substituted by FA 1988, 3 Sch 11) was solely a relieving provision applying to capital gains tax as well as income tax and so prevented more tax being charged than would have been the case if *ICTA 1988, s 282* had not applied (*Gubay v Kington HL 1984, 57 TC 601*). The Revenue took the view that in such a case the general position was as in 37.3(*d*) and 37.4(*d*) below and that, in particular, each spouse was eligible for the PRIVATE RESIDENCES (43) exemption. (Tolley's Practical Tax 1986 p 71).

37.3   TREATMENT OF GAINS AND LOSSES BEFORE 1990/91

(*a*)   **Spouses living together throughout the year.** Where a husband and wife were living together throughout the year the gains and losses of each spouse were computed separately and were also aggregated separately. The exempt amount for the year was divided between them in proportion to their respective taxable amounts (see 2.3 ANNUAL RATES AND EXEMPTIONS). For these purposes the provisions whereby losses brought forward or carried back are only deducted insofar as it is necessary to reduce the taxable amounts to the level of the exempt amount for the year were ignored. However, where the aggregate of the taxable amounts did not exceed the exempt amount for the year and there were allowable losses brought forward, the exempt amount could be divided in such other proportion as the spouses may have agreed.

Excess losses (including brought forward losses) of one spouse were available against net gains of the other, except that losses incurred by one spouse in the year of death could only be carried back against that spouse's gains of the three previous years. See 15.5 DEATH. It appeared that losses of one spouse incurred prior to the date of marriage could be set against gains of the other spouse incurred after the marriage. However, either spouse could elect in the prescribed manner for the losses of the one *not* to be set against the gains of the other. The election had to be made before 6 July in the year following the relevant year of assessment. Following an election, the net losses incurred in a year by one spouse could only be carried forward against the gains incurred by that spouse in a subsequent year. This position continued, it appeared, until the losses were fully utilised although the legislation did not make clear whether such losses, or the current losses of a later year, were identified first. See 35.1 LOSSES.

(b)   **Year of marriage.** Each party was treated as a separate individual *throughout* the year of marriage so that each spouse had a separate entitlement to the full exempt amount for the year unless the marriage took place on 6 April, when (a) above applied. Provided the spouses actually lived together for the part of the year following the marriage, the provisions in (a) above regarding the setting off of excess losses of one spouse against the gains of the other also appeared to apply even to the extent of allowing losses of one spouse to be utilised against gains of the other spouse where both gains and losses were incurred in the part of the year prior to the marriage.

(c)   **Year of separation etc.** The rules given in (a) above continued to apply except that the taxable amounts of the wife excluded gains or losses accruing to her in the part of the year following separation. The death of the husband or divorce (without an earlier period of separation) were similarly treated. The gains and losses of the wife accruing in the remainder of the year were treated as if they had accrued in a separate year of assessment so that the exempt amount for the year was available for this period in full. Despite this treatment the construction of the legislation appeared to allow the provisions in (a) above regarding excess losses of one spouse to apply to the whole of the year in which separation etc. took place.

(d)   **Spouses separated throughout the year.** Each spouse was treated as a separate individual having an entitlement to the full exempt amount for the year. Excess losses of one spouse were *not* available against gains of the other.

(e)   **Spouses recommencing living together.** Where this occurred in a year of assessment it appeared such a year was treated as if it were the year of marriage as in (b) above.

[*CGTA 1979, ss 4, 5(1)(4)(6), 1 Sch 1, 2; FA 1980, s 77(2); FA 1982, s 80(1)(3)(b); FA 1988, s 104(1)(a)(c)(2), 14 Sch Pt VIII*].

37.4   ASSESSMENT AND RATES BEFORE 1990/91

(a)   **Spouses living together throughout the year.** The amount of tax chargeable on the wife's net gains was assessed and charged on the husband. The total tax payable was to remain unchanged. By application made by either party in the prescribed manner before 6 July in the year following the year of assessment, *separate assessment* could be claimed. The application continued in force for subsequent years until notice was given revoking it within the period allowed for making an application i.e. before 6 July in the year following the year of assessment for which the application was withdrawn.

For 1988/89 and 1989/90 only, where

(i)   gains accrued to a woman in a year of assessment during which she was a married woman living with her husband, and

(ii)   if her 'chargeable amount' were added to, and constituted the highest part of, her husband's chargeable amount for the year, capital gains tax would be chargeable on it or any part of it at a rate equivalent to the higher rate of income tax for the year (see 2.1 ANNUAL RATES AND EXEMPTIONS),

the rate of capital gains tax on her chargeable amount or that part of it was equivalent to the higher rate.

A person's '*chargeable amount*' for these purposes was the amount on which he was (or would have been apart from the provision above whereby the wife's net gains were assessed and charged on the husband) chargeable to capital gains tax for the year. In effect, this amount was the taxable amount for each spouse less their respective share of the exempt amount for the year. See 37.3(*a*) above.

Where separate assessment had effect for 1988/89 or 1989/90, the amounts of tax payable by the husband and by the wife were determined by aggregating the amounts that would otherwise have been payable by each of them and dividing that aggregate between them in proportion to their chargeable amounts for the year.

(*b*) **Year of marriage.** Both husband and wife were assessed as separate individuals. However, if the marriage took place on 6 April the rules as in (*a*) above applied.

(*c*) **Year of separation etc.** The amount of tax chargeable on the wife's net gains accruing in the period from 6 April to the date of separation was assessed and charged on the husband subject to a separate assessment application as in (*a*) above. The death of the husband or divorce (without an earlier period of separation) was similarly treated. The wife was assessed to tax chargeable on her net gains accruing in the remainder of the year.

For 1988/89 and 1989/90 only, the provisions in (*a*) above applying only for such years applied similarly in relation to the part of the year prior to separation (except that references to a husband's chargeable amount were references to his chargeable amount for the whole year).

(*d*) **Spouses separated throughout the year.** Each spouse was assessed as a separate individual.

(*e*) **Spouses recommencing living together.** Where this occurred in a year of assessment it appeared such a year was treated as if it were the year of marriage as in (*b*) above.

[*CGTA 1979, s 45(1)(2)(5); FA 1988, ss 99, 104(1)(b)(2), 14 Sch Pt VIII*].

37.5 COLLECTION OF TAX FROM WIFE BEFORE 1990/91

(*a*) **Claim by Revenue.** If capital gains tax assessed on the husband (or his personal representatives) remained unpaid after 28 days from the due date, and the Board considered that under the separate assessment procedure in 37.4(*a*) above (although no such application had been made), an assessment could have been made on his wife (or former wife, or her personal representatives), they could require payment of that unpaid tax by the wife or her personal representatives, up to the amount so notionally assessable on her. [*ICTA 1988, s 285; CGTA 1979, s 45(4); FA 1988, s 104(1)(b)(2), 14 Sch Pt VIII*].

(*b*) **A widower** (or his personal representatives) **could disclaim liability** for unpaid tax relating to his deceased wife's gains while they were living together by giving notice to her personal representatives and the inspector within two months after the grant of probate or letters of administration (or later if the personal representatives consented), and the Revenue had then to collect from the deceased wife's estate tax calculated as under the separate assessment procedure. [*ICTA 1988, s 286; CGTA 1979, s 45(4); FA 1988, s 104(1)(b)(2), 14 Sch Pt VIII*].

(*c*) **Tax was also collectable from the wife** if a separate assessment election was made or if the wife was otherwise assessed separately as under 37.4 above.

37.6 Married Persons

TRANSFERS BETWEEN SPOUSES

Transfers of assets, in a year of assessment, between spouses who are living together (see 37.2 above) in any part of that year are regarded as made on a 'no gain, no loss' basis, both parties being treated as identical. This treatment also seems to apply for transfers between spouses in the part of a year following marriage and in the whole of the year in which separation takes place even though the spouses may not be 'living together' at the time of transfer. The no gain, no loss treatment does not apply to transfers (i) by way of *donatio mortis causa* (see 15.4 DEATH); (ii) to or from trading stock of either spouse; or (iii) after decree absolute. [*TCGA 1992, s 58*].

See 16.6 DISPOSAL for part disposals between spouses and 33.11 LAND for small part disposals of land.

Example

(A) No inter-spouse transfer
Paul and Heidi are a married couple with total income of £24,000 and £28,000 respectively for 1995/96. Of the total income, there is sufficient non-dividend income to fully utilise the lower rate band. On 4 April 1996, Heidi sells a painting which she had acquired in June 1992 at a cost of £5,000. Net sale proceeds amount to £17,000 and the indexation factor for the period June 1992 to April 1996 is assumed to be 0.110. Neither spouse disposed of any other chargeable assets during 1995/96.

Chargeable gain — Heidi

	£
Net proceeds	17,000
Cost	5,000
Unindexed gain	12,000
Indexation allowance £5,000 × 0.110	550
Chargeable gain	11,450
Annual exemption	6,000
Taxable gain	£5,450

Total income	28,000
Personal allowance	3,525
Taxable income	£24,475

Basic rate limit = £24,300, so gain of £5,450 is all taxed at 40%.

Tax payable £5,450 × 40%   £2,180.00

(B) Inter-spouse transfer
The facts are as in (A) above except that in January 1996, Heidi gives the painting to Paul who then makes the sale on 4 April 1996.
Indexation factors (assumed)

June 1992 to January 1996	0.089
January 1996 to April 1996	0.020

Chargeable gain — Heidi

	£
Deemed consideration (January 1996)	5,445
Cost	5,000
Unindexed gain	445
Indexation allowance £5,000 × 0.089	445
Chargeable gain	Nil

Chargeable gain — Paul

	£
Net proceeds (4.4.96)	17,000
Cost (January 1996)	5,445
Unindexed gain	11,555
Indexation allowance £5,445 × 0.020	109
Chargeable gain	11,446
Annual exemption	6,000
Taxable gain	£5,446

Total income	24,000
Personal allowance	(3,525)
Taxable income	£20,475

Taxable income falls short of the basic rate limit (£24,300) by £3,825, so gain of £5,446 is taxed as follows.

£3,825 at 25%	956.25
1,621 at 40%	648.40
Tax payable	£1,604.65
Tax saving compared with (A) above	£575.35

Notes to the example

(a)   The inter-spouse transfer is deemed to be for such consideration as to ensure that no gain or loss accrues. Effectively, the consideration is equal to cost plus indexation to date.

(b)   The fact that transfers of assets between husband and wife are no gain/no loss transfers enables savings to be made by ensuring that disposals are made by a spouse with an unused annual exemption and/or lower tax rates.

(c)   An inter-spouse transfer followed by a sale could be attacked by the Revenue as an anti-avoidance device. To minimise the risk, there should be a clear time interval between the two transactions and no arrangements made to effect the ultimate sale until after the transfer. The gift should be outright with no strings attached and with no 'arrangement' for eventual proceeds to be passed to the transferor.

Transfers whilst spouses separated or treated as separated. In a case in which spouses, after several years of separation, were divorced and the court order (by consent) on the decree nisi provided for the transfer of certain property (which was not otherwise exempt) it was held that the property had been disposed of at the time of the decree nisi. As the divorce was not then absolute, the spouses were still connected persons and the consideration was to be taken as the market value. See 14.1 CONNECTED PERSONS and 32.1 MARKET VALUE. The normal 'no gain, no loss' basis (see above) did not apply as the spouses were not living together (*Aspden v Hildesley Ch D 1981, 55 TC 609*). Such transfers after 5 April 1980 and before 14 March 1989 prima facie qualified for the general hold-over relief for gifts but the Revenue normally rejected a claim in the usual case where the transfer of an asset had been made in consideration of the giving up of rights to take action under the various provisions concerning matrimonial proceedings. See 22.6 HOLD-OVER RELIEFS and Tolley's Practical Tax 1984 p 145 and 1986 p 96. Other than in divorce proceedings, relief as in *Gubay v Kington* (see 37.2 above) may have been available for years of assessment before 1990/91 where one spouse was non-UK resident or absent abroad such that the spouses were treated as permanently separated.

38 Mineral Royalties

Cross-reference. See 33 LAND.

38.1   Where a person resident or ordinarily resident in the UK is entitled to receive mineral royalties (i.e. so much of any rents, tolls, royalties or periodical payments as relates to the winning and working of minerals other than water, peat, topsoil, etc.) under a lease, licence or agreement conferring a right to win and work minerals in the UK or under a sale or conveyance of such minerals, only one-half of any such royalties receivable, after 5 April 1970, in any year of assessment or accounting period is treated as income for the purposes of income tax or for corporation tax on profits other than chargeable gains (except for the deduction of income tax under *ICTA 1988, s 348* or *349* for payments before 1 May 1995). The other half of the royalties is treated as a chargeable gain to which no allowable expenditure attaches.

A 'terminal loss' which accrues on a 'relevant event' may (if the taxpayer so claims within six years of the event) be carried back and set against chargeable gains accruing in the years of assessment or accounting periods falling wholly or partly within a period of 15 years before the relevant event, taking later years first.

A '*relevant event*' occurs on the expiry or termination of the mineral lease or the disposal (or deemed disposal under any provision) of the interest held in the land to which the lease relates ('*the relevant interest*'). The taxpayer must have been entitled to receive mineral royalties under the mineral lease and held the interest immediately before the relevant event.

A '*terminal loss*' is an allowable loss for capital gains tax purposes which arises

(a)   on the expiry or termination of the mineral lease, and on an additional claim within the same time limit as above, by which the taxpayer is treated as if he had disposed of and immediately re-acquired the relevant interest at its market value; or

(*b*) on the actual disposal (or any other deemed disposal under any provision) of the relevant interest.

Relief in any one year or accounting period is restricted to the chargeable gains previously assessed by reason of the treatment above in respect of the mineral lease in question, except that any unrelieved balance is treated as accruing at the date of the relevant event and as allowable against general gains. If no claim is made for the terminal loss to be treated as above, the whole of such loss is treated as accruing at the date of the relevant event and as an allowable loss against general gains. Repayments of tax are made as may be necessary.

Regulations may be made by the Board to facilitate the above provisions. [*SI 1971, No 1035*]. These deal with apportionments of payments where they relate to other matters as well as mineral royalties.

Where, on the last disposal (before 23 July 1970) affecting a mineral lease, betterment levy was chargeable under Case B (as defined by *Land Commission Act 1967, Pt III*) the chargeable gain was limited to a fraction (base value of that disposition/consideration received) of one half of the royalties received. After 5 April 1988, this limitation applies only if it applied in a chargeable period ending before 6 April 1988. But if such a lease has been renewed, extended or varied after 22 July 1970, one half of any subsequent royalty receipt is treated as a chargeable gain. [*TCGA 1992, ss 201–203; ICTA 1988, s 122(1)(5)–(7); FA 1995, 29 Sch Pt VIII (22)*].

Example

L Ltd, an investment company preparing accounts to 31 December, is the holder of a lease of land acquired in 1984 for £66,000, when the lease had an unexpired term of 65 years. In January 1990, L Ltd grants a 10-year licence to a mining company to search for and exploit minerals beneath the land. The licence is granted for £60,000 plus a mineral royalty calculated on the basis of the value of any minerals won by the licensee. The market value of the retained land (exclusive of the mineral rights) is then £10,000. L Ltd receives mineral royalties as follows

		£
Year ended	31 December 1990	12,000
	31 December 1991	19,000
	31 December 1992	29,000
	31 December 1993	38,000
	31 December 1994	17,000
	31 December 1995	10,000

On 2 January 1996, L Ltd relinquishes its rights under the lease and receives no consideration from the lessor.

(i) Chargeable gains 1990

		£
(*a*)	Disposal proceeds	60,000
	Allowable cost $\dfrac{60,000}{60,000 + 10,000} \times £66,000$	56,571
	Chargeable gain before indexation	£3,429
(*b*)	$\frac{1}{2} \times £12,000$	£6,000

38.1 Mineral Royalties

(ii) Chargeable gains 1991 to 1995

		£
1991	$\frac{1}{2} \times £19,000$	9,500
1992	$\frac{1}{2} \times £29,000$	14,500
1993	$\frac{1}{2} \times £38,000$	19,000
1994	$\frac{1}{2} \times £17,000$	8,500
1995	$\frac{1}{2} \times £10,000$	5,000

(iii) Loss 1996

Proceeds of disposal of lease		Nil
Allowable cost £66,000 − £56,571	note (a)	9,429
Allowable loss		£9,429

(iv) The loss may be set off against the chargeable gains arising on the mineral royalties as follows

	£
1995 (whole)	5,000
1994 (part)	4,429
	£9,429

Notes to the example

(a)   Under *ICTA 1988, s 122* and *TCGA 1992, s 201*, one half of mineral royalties is taxed as income and one half as a chargeable gain. The gain is deemed to accrue in the year of assessment or company accounting period for which the royalties are receivable and is not capable of being reduced by any expenditure or by indexation allowance.

39   Overseas Matters

Cross-references. See 6.2 ASSETS for location of assets; 16.4 DISPOSAL for acquisitions from persons neither resident nor ordinarily resident in the UK after 9 March 1981 and before 6 April 1985; 17 DOUBLE TAX RELIEF for relief which may be claimable and for double tax agreements which may override or amend statutory provisions; 22 HOLD-OVER RELIEFS for clawback of relief where transferee becomes before 19 March 1991 neither resident nor ordinarily resident in the UK; 36.1 MARKET VALUE for special market value rules which apply to disposals by persons neither resident nor ordinarily resident in the UK after 9 March 1981 and before 6 April 1985; 37.2 MARRIED PERSONS for the position before 1990/91 where one spouse is not resident in, or is absent from, the UK; 40.4 PARTNERSHIPS for partnerships controlled and managed abroad; 47 RESIDENCE AND DOMICILE for the determination of a person's residence, ordinary residence and domicile status; 52.3 and 52.8 SETTLEMENTS for the residence status of settlements and provisions dealing with trustees neither resident nor ordinarily resident in the UK; and 56.7 UNDERWRITERS for overseas resident underwriters.

39.1   INTRODUCTION

As a general rule a person is chargeable to capital gains tax in respect of chargeable gains accruing to him in a year of assessment during any part of which he is resident in the UK, or during which he is ordinarily resident in the UK. [*TCGA 1992, s 2(1)*]. However, where an individual is not domiciled in the UK but resident or ordinarily resident here, and where a person neither resident nor ordinarily resident in the UK trades etc. in the UK through a branch or agency, alternative rules apply. See 39.2 and 39.3 below. See 39.3 also for the relief applying when a non-UK resident company transfers the trade of a UK branch or agency to a UK resident company.

Where a person is within the ambit of *TCGA 1992, s 2(1)* he may be unable to remit overseas gains to the UK. See 39.4 below for the special relief available in such circumstances.

Persons within *TCGA 1992, s 2(1)* may also be assessed by reference to chargeable gains accruing to non-UK resident persons with whom they have certain specified relationships. See 39.5 below for circumstances where a UK resident is a shareholder in a closely-held overseas resident company; and see 39.8–39.11 below where a UK domiciled individual is a beneficiary of an overseas resident settlement. See 39.6 below for the 'exit charge' on trustees of a settlement who become resident overseas and 39.7 where a UK domiciled settlor has an interest in an overseas resident settlement.

Where a UK resident company has an interest in a 'controlled foreign company' and where a UK resident has 'offshore income gains' arising out of certain interests in 'offshore funds', there may be a capital gains tax effect. See 39.12 and 39.13 below.

A special relief is available where a UK resident company transfers the assets of an overseas trading branch or agency to an overseas resident company in exchange for shares in that company. See 39.14 below.

See 39.15 below for the special relief claimable where a UK trade is transferred between companies in different EC member States and 39.16 for the claim and double taxation relief available where a non-UK trade is transferred between companies in different EC member States.

There are 'exit charges' and provisions for the recovery of unpaid tax where a company ceases to be UK resident etc., is a dual resident company (before 30 November 1993) or is not resident in the UK. See 39.17 and 39.18 below.

39.2 Overseas Matters

For exploration and exploitation rights to the UK territorial sea-bed, see 39.19 below.

For European Economic Interest Groupings, see 39.20 below.

For the collection of tax where an overseas element is involved, see 39.21 below.

39.2 INDIVIDUALS NOT DOMICILED IN THE UK DISPOSING OF OVERSEAS ASSETS

Individuals not domiciled in the UK, but resident or ordinarily resident here, are liable on gains arising in the UK, but gains accruing after 5 April 1965 from disposals of assets abroad are chargeable if, and only so far as, remitted here (with no allowance for losses arising abroad). [*TCGA 1992, ss 12(1), 16(4)*]. For this purpose, gains effectively transferred to the UK through loan, etc. transactions as under the REMITTANCE BASIS (46) are treated as if remitted here. [*TCGA 1992, s 12(2)*].

39.3 NON-UK RESIDENT TRADING ETC. IN THE UK THROUGH BRANCH OR AGENCY

Disposals and other events after 13 March 1989. Subject to transitional provisions and any other exceptions in the legislation, for disposals after 13 March 1989 a person is chargeable to capital gains tax in respect of chargeable gains accruing to him in a year of assessment in which he is not resident and not ordinarily resident in the UK and which are made at a time when he is carrying on a trade, profession or vocation in the UK through a 'branch or agency', and is so chargeable on chargeable gains accruing on the disposal

(*a*)   of assets situated in the UK and used in or for the purposes of the trade, profession or vocation at or before the time when the gain accrued, or

(*b*)   of assets situated in the UK and used or held for the purposes of the branch or agency at or before that time, or assets acquired for use by or for the purposes of the branch or agency.

These provisions are applied to companies not resident in the UK carrying on a trade or vocation through a UK branch or agency as for individuals not resident and not ordinarily resident in the UK in arriving at their chargeable profits for an accounting period. [*TCGA 1992, s 10(1)–(3)(5)*].

The commercial letting of FURNISHED HOLIDAY ACCOMMODATION (19.2) in the UK, although treated as a trade for certain capital gains tax provisions, is not so treated for the purposes of *TCGA 1992, s 10*.

Transitional provisions. Under transitional provisions, a person was chargeable under *TCGA 1992, s 10(1)* (formerly *CGTA 1979, s 12(1)*) above for 1988/89 in respect of a disposal made after 13 March 1989 if he ceased to carry on a *trade* (but not a *profession or vocation*) in the UK through a branch or agency before 14 March 1989 but a person is not to be chargeable under *TCGA 1992, s 10(1)* for 1988/89 and later years of assessment where he carries on a profession or vocation in the UK through a branch or agency in respect of chargeable gains accruing on the disposal of assets only used in or for the purposes of the profession or vocation before 14 March 1989 or only used or held for the purposes of the branch or agency before that date. [*TCGA 1992, s 10(5)*].

As a further transitional measure, where immediately before 14 March 1989 a person was not resident and not ordinarily resident in the UK but was carrying on a *profession* or *vocation* (but not a *trade*) in the UK through a branch or agency, he was deemed to have disposed immediately before 14 March 1989 of every specified asset and to have immediately reacquired every such asset, all such deemed transactions being treated as made at market value at that time. An asset was specified for this purpose if it was held by the person concerned immediately before 14 March 1989 and if at the beginning of 14 March 1989 it was a 'chargeable asset' in relation to him by virtue of his carrying on the profession or vocation. For this purpose an asset was at the beginning of 14 March 1989 a *'chargeable asset'* in relation to the person if, had it been disposed of at that time, any chargeable gains accruing would have been chargeable under *TCGA 1992, s 10(1)* above. [*FA 1989, s 126(3)–(5)*]. (No chargeable gain actually arose on the deemed disposal immediately before 14 March 1989 as professions and vocations were not then within the charge of *TCGA 1992, s 10(1)* (see below) and the broad effect was that the assets of a person carrying on a profession or vocation which became within the charge of *TCGA 1992, s 10(1)* were re-based to their market value on that date.)

Deemed disposals. Where an asset ceases after 13 March 1989 by virtue of becoming situated outside the UK to be a 'chargeable asset' (as below) in relation to a person, he is deemed to have disposed of the asset immediately before the time when the asset becomes situated outside the UK and immediately to have reacquired it, both such transactions being treated as made at market value. This does not apply where the asset becomes situated outside the UK contemporaneously with the person involved ceasing to carry on a trade, profession or vocation in the UK through a branch or agency (see below) or where the asset is an *'exploration or exploitation asset'* (i.e. an asset used in connection with 'exploration or exploitation activities' carried on in the UK or a 'designated area' as defined by *TCGA 1992, s 276* in 39.19 below; in this case comparable provisions apply).

Where an asset ceases to be a chargeable asset in relation to a person by virtue of his ceasing after 13 March 1989 to carry on a trade, profession or vocation in the UK through a branch or agency, he is deemed to have disposed of the asset immediately before the time when he ceased to carry on the trade, profession or vocation in the UK through the branch or agency and immediately to have reacquired it, both such transactions being treated as made at market value. The deemed disposal and reacquisition does not apply to an asset which is a chargeable asset in relation to the person concerned at any time after he ceases to carry on the trade, profession or vocation in the UK through a branch or agency and before the end of the chargeable period in which he does so. There is no deemed disposal and reacquisition of an asset to which a claim for relief under *TCGA 1992, s 172* applies (see below under transfer of UK branch or agency). The Revenue take a similar view as regards a claim for relief under *TCGA 1992, s 162* (see 22.7 HOLD-OVER RELIEFS) (Taxation Practitioner May 1990 p 232). There is also no deemed disposal and reacquisition of an asset by reason of a transfer of the whole or part of the long term business of an insurance company to another company if *TCGA 1992, s 139* has effect in relation to the asset by virtue of *TCGA 1992, s 211* (see Tolley's Corporation Tax under Life Insurance Companies). Similarly, there is no deemed disposal and reacquisition on a transfer within *TCGA 1992, s 140A* of a UK trade between companies in different EC member States (see 39.15 below).

For the purposes of the above, an asset is at any time a *'chargeable asset'* in relation to a person if, were it to be disposed of at that time, any chargeable gains accruing to him on the disposal either would be chargeable under *TCGA 1992, s 10(1)* or would form part of his chargeable profits for corporation tax purposes by virtue of *TCGA 1992, s 10(3)*. [*TCGA 1992, ss 25, 140A(4)(b), 172(2)(b); F(No 2)A 1992, s 44*].

Rollover relief. Where the disposal of the 'old assets' or the acquisition of the 'new assets' (or both) (within the meaning of *TCGA 1992, s 152*, see 50 ROLLOVER RELIEF) takes place after 13 March 1989, rollover relief under that provision is not to apply if the old assets are 'chargeable assets' (having the same meaning as in *TCGA 1992, s 25* above) in relation to the person concerned at the time of disposal unless the new assets are chargeable assets in relation to him immediately after the time they are acquired.

References to acquisition of the new assets include references to acquisition of an interest in them or to entering into an unconditional contract for the acquisition of them. However, rollover relief may apply where the acquisition of the new assets occurs before 14 March 1989 and the disposal of the old assets is after 13 March 1989 but within twelve months (or such longer period as is allowed by written notice given by the Board) of the acquisition of the new assets.

Rollover relief will, however, apply, where the acquisition of the new assets takes place after the disposal of the old assets and immediately after the time of acquisition the person concerned is resident or ordinarily resident in the UK, unless he is also then a 'dual resident' and the new assets are 'prescribed assets'. A *'dual resident'* is a person who is resident or ordinarily resident in the UK and falls to be regarded under any DOUBLE TAX RELIEF (17.2) arrangements as resident overseas. A *'prescribed asset'*, in relation to a dual resident, is one which under any double tax relief arrangements would not give rise to a UK tax charge on him in respect of a gain accruing to him on a disposal of it. [*TCGA 1992, s 159*].

Non-payment of tax attributable to TCGA 1992, s 10(3) by non-resident company. See 39.17 below.

Disposals and other events before 14 March 1989. Subject to the commencement and transitional provisions for disposals and other events after 13 March 1989 above and any other exceptions in the legislation, for disposals before 14 March 1989 a person was chargeable to capital gains tax in respect of chargeable gains accruing to him in a year of assessment in which he was not resident and not ordinarily resident in the UK but was carrying on a trade in the UK through a 'branch or agency', and was so chargeable on chargeable gains accruing on the disposal

(A)   of assets situated in the UK and used in or for the purposes of the trade at or before the time when the gain accrued, or

(B)   of assets situated in the UK and used or held for the purposes of the branch or agency at or before that time, or assets acquired for use by or for the purposes of the branch or agency.

These provisions were applied to companies not resident in the UK carrying on a trade or vocation through a UK branch or agency as for individuals not resident and not ordinarily resident in the UK in arriving at its chargeable profits for an accounting period. [*CGTA 1979, s 12(1); ICTA 1988, s 11(2)(b)*].

In effect, the charge to tax applied only to trades and not to professions or vocations, and could where relevant be avoided by removing an asset from the UK before disposal even though the UK trade continued or disposing of an asset situated in the UK in a chargeable period subsequent to that in which the UK trade ceased.

General provisions for disposals. No charge to tax under *TCGA 1992, s 10* applies to a person who, by virtue of any relevant double tax agreement, is exempt from income tax for the particular year in respect of profits or gains from the branch or agency. [*TCGA 1992, s 10(4)*].

'Branch or agency' means, for *TCGA 1992, s 10* and capital gains tax provisions generally, any factorship, agency, receivership, branch or management but excludes any general agents or brokers carrying on bona fide business as such who act for non-residents and are exempt under *TMA 1970, s 82*. [*TCGA 1992, s 10(6)*].

Losses accruing to a person in a year of assessment during no part of which he is resident or ordinarily resident in the UK are not allowable unless, under *TCGA 1992, s 10* above, he would be chargeable in respect of a chargeable gain if there had been a gain instead of a loss on that occasion. [*TCGA 1992, s 16(3)*].

Where a non-resident etc. person is chargeable under *TCGA 1992, s 10* he is assessable and chargeable in the name of the branch or agent. Any person so chargeable in the name of a non-resident is responsible for all matters required to be done by a taxpayer under the capital gains tax provisions. The person so chargeable may retain, out of money coming into his hands on behalf of the non-resident, any tax or interest on unpaid tax under *TMA 1970, s 87A* required to be paid and is indemnified for all such payments made. [*TMA 1970, ss 84, 85; F(No 2)A 1987, 6 Sch 7*].

See 47.2 RESIDENCE AND DOMICILE for the exclusion, after 5 April 1989, of extra-statutory concession D2 in respect of the period from the cessation of UK residence to the end of the year of assessment.

Transfer of UK branch or agency. For disposals after 19 March 1990 a relief for the purposes of corporation tax on chargeable gains applies where

(*a*)   there is a scheme for the transfer by a non-UK resident 'company' ('company A') which carries on a trade in the UK through a branch or agency of the whole or part of the trade to a UK resident company ('company B'),

(*b*)   company A disposes of an asset to company B in accordance with the scheme at a time when both companies are members of the same 'group', and

(*c*)   a claim under *TCGA 1992, s 172(1)* relating to the asset is made by both companies within two years after the end of the accounting period of company B during which the disposal is made.

'Company' and 'group' have the same meanings as in *TCGA 1992, s 170* (see 13.10 COMPANIES) but ignoring *subsections 2(a)* and *(9)* thereof (references to company only to include UK resident companies etc. incorporated under UK and overseas legislation etc.).

The relief given is that, firstly, the asset is treated as disposed of by company A and acquired by company B for a no gain, no loss consideration and, secondly, *TCGA 1992, s 25(3)* (deemed disposal by non-resident on ceasing to trade in the UK through a branch or agency; see above under disposals and other events after 13 March 1989) is not to apply to the asset by reason of the transfer.

The relief did not apply on a disposal before 30 November 1993 where company B was UK resident but under any double tax relief arrangements was regarded as resident elsewhere and would not have been liable to UK tax on a gain arising on the disposal of the asset occurring immediately after its acquisition. Relief is also denied if company B is a 'dual resident investing company' within *ICTA 1988, s 404* or an 'investment trust' within *ICTA 1988, s 842*. No relief is given unless any gain accruing to company A on the disposal of the asset in accordance with the scheme, or, where that disposal occurs after the transfer has taken place, on a disposal of the asset immediately before the transfer, would be a chargeable gain and would, under *TCGA 1992, s 10(3)* above, form part of its profits for corporation tax purposes. [*TCGA 1992, s 172; FA 1994, s 251(1)(7), 26 Sch Pt VIII*].

The following applies where there is a disposal or acquisition of currency; a 'qualifying asset' consisting of the right to settlement under a debt which is not a debt on a security (within *TCGA 1992, s 132*; see 18.5 EXEMPTIONS AND RELIEFS); a 'qualifying asset' consisting of the right to settlement under a debt on a security; or an obligation which by virtue of *TCGA 1992, s 143* (futures contracts; see 16.11 DISPOSAL) is regarded as an asset to the disposal of which *TCGA 1992* applies and which is a duty under a currency contract. Where the disposal or acquisition is by a 'qualifying company' and is made on or after the company's 'commencement day', and immediately before the disposal or after the acquisition, as the case may be, the asset is held wholly for 'qualifying purposes', and *TCGA 1992, s 172* would otherwise apply, the last-mentioned provision does not apply as regards the disposal or acquisition and the corresponding acquisition or disposal. '*Qualifying purposes*' are purposes of long term or mutual insurance business. [*FA 1993, s 169, 17 Sch 7*]. See 13.34 COMPANIES for a note of the terms quoted and not otherwise defined.

Prior to the commencement of *TCGA 1992*, claims were made under *ICTA 1970, s 273A(1)*.

39.4   RELIEF FOR UNREMITTABLE OVERSEAS GAINS

Where chargeable gains accrue from assets situated abroad and the taxpayer is unable with reasonable endeavour to transfer those gains to the UK due to the laws of the territory where the assets were situated at the time of disposal, or to the executive action of its government, or to the impossibility of obtaining foreign currency in that territory, he may claim under *TCGA 1992, s 279(1)* within six years after the year of assessment in which the gains arose that they be left out of account. They are then treated as gains of the year in which the conditions cease to apply. The claim is open to personal representatives. [*TCGA 1992, s 279(1)–(3)(5)(6)(8)*].

These provisions cannot be relied upon as a defence against an assessment under *TCGA 1992, s 13* (see 39.5 below) if the taxpayer's inability to transfer the gain to the UK is owing to the company's failure to distribute the gain. Relief can only be given if the gain is represented by money, or money's worth, in the hands of the taxpayer (*Van Arkadie v Plunket, Ch D 1982, 56 TC 310*).

See 32.5 INTEREST ON UNPAID TAX for an alternative relief given to interest on tax overdue, where collection of tax is deferred in similar circumstances. See also 37.1 MARRIED PERSONS where a claim for the relief above has effect before 1990/91 in respect of a wife's gains which would otherwise have been assessed on the husband.

Gains which are subject to payments made by the Export Credits Guarantee Department under statutory arrangements for export guarantees do not qualify for the relief above to the extent of such payments. [*TCGA 1992, s 279(4)*].

Prior to the commencement of *TCGA 1992*, claims for relief were made under *CGTA 1979, s 13(1)*.

39.5   UK RESIDENT SHAREHOLDER IN OVERSEAS RESIDENT COMPANY

A UK resident or ordinarily resident shareholder in an overseas resident company which would be a close company (under *ICTA 1988, ss 414, 415*; see Tolley's Corporation Tax under Close Companies) if it were UK resident, is assessable on a part of any chargeable gain made by the company which is not distributed by it to its shareholders, etc., within two years after it accrues. The part assessable is proportional to his interest in the assets of the company if it were liquidated but no assessment will be raised if such part is less than one-twentieth of the gain. The residence status of the shareholder is determined at the time the gain accrues and an individual is only liable if domiciled in the UK at that time. Notwithstanding any intention to distribute part of a gain within the two-year period mentioned, an assessment may be made on a shareholder, although it may be adjusted as necessary if the distribution is subsequently made within the two-year period.

For the above purposes, gains from tangible property (or a lease thereof) used solely for a trade outside the UK, gains chargeable to UK tax *under TCGA 1992, s 10(3)* by virtue of the company's trading through a UK branch or agency, and gains from disposals of foreign currency or of a debt within *TCGA 1992, s 252(1)* where the currency or debt is or represents money used solely for a trade outside the UK are ignored.

Any tax so paid by the shareholder, if not reimbursed by the company, may be deducted in computing the gain on disposal of his shares in the company. If the tax is paid by the company, that payment is not treated as a payment to the shareholder for purposes of income tax, capital gains tax or corporation tax.

Any loss arising on the disposal of assets by the company may be similarly apportioned, but only insofar as it reduces or extinguishes gains accruing in the same year of assessment to the shareholder under these provisions. Any part of a gain apportioned to a shareholder which is itself a company which is overseas resident but would be a close company if it were UK resident, is further apportioned through that company (and so on) before being treated as above.

Certain assets transferred within a group of overseas resident companies which would, if the companies were UK resident, be treated as giving rise to neither gain nor loss under *TCGA 1992, ss 171–174, 175(1)* (intra group transfers, etc. and rollover relief, see 13.11 COMPANIES, 39.3 above, 13.12 COMPANIES, 13.14 COMPANIES and 50.4 ROLLOVER RELIEF), are treated similarly for the purposes of the above provisions, as are *TCGA 1992, s 178–180* (companies leaving groups, see 13.17 COMPANIES) when a company leaves such a group. (The Revenue has stated that the foregoing provisions relating to the charge of corporation tax on chargeable gains are applied not only where the UK resident shareholder on whom gains are assessed is subject to a like charge but also where the shareholder is within the charge to capital gains tax (Revenue Tax Bulletin May 1993 p 74).)

In respect of gains accruing after 9 March 1981 to a company, the persons treated under the above as if part of those gains had accrued to them expressly include trustees owning shares in the company if, when the gains accrue to the company, the trustees are neither resident nor ordinarily resident in the UK. See further in 39.6–39.11 below. [*TCGA 1992, ss 13, 14*].

A person who holds shares in an overseas resident company can be required by notice from the Board to provide sufficient information to give effect to the above provisions. [*TMA 1970, s 28; TCGA 1992, 10 Sch 2(5)*].

The appropriate proportion of any overseas tax in respect of its gain which the company pays in its country of residence is deductible in computing the gain chargeable on the shareholder; alternatively, tax credit relief may be allowable for the overseas tax (29.D23 INLAND REVENUE STATEMENTS OF PRACTICE). The Revenue has confirmed that where the overseas resident company is a subsidiary of a UK resident parent company and the relevant double taxation agreement has an article exempting residents of the overseas territory from a charge to UK capital gains tax, then such an article may prevent the imposition of a charge under the above provisions (CCAB Statement TR 500 March 1983).

The relief for unremittable overseas gains (see 39.4 above) is not a defence to an assessment under the above provisions. See also 39.12 below for a UK resident company having an interest in a 'controlled foreign company'.

39.6   **OVERSEAS RESIDENT SETTLEMENTS ETC.**

Trustees ceasing to be resident in the UK. Where, at any time ('*the relevant time*') after 18 March 1991, trustees of a settlement become neither resident nor ordinarily resident in the UK (for which, see *TCGA 1992, s 69* at 52.3 SETTLEMENTS and also 47.2

RESIDENCE AND DOMICILE), they are deemed for capital gains tax purposes to have disposed of 'the defined assets' immediately before the relevant time, and immediately to have reacquired them, at their market value at that time.

'*The defined assets*' are all assets constituting settled property of the settlement immediately before the relevant time. However, if immediately after the relevant time the trustees carry on a trade in the UK through a branch or agency, and any assets are situated in the UK and either used in or for the purposes of the trade or used or held for the purposes of the branch or agency, those assets are not defined assets (see also 39.3 above). In addition, assets are not defined assets if they are of a description specified in any DOUBLE TAX RELIEF (17.2) arrangements, and were the trustees to dispose of them immediately before the relevant time, the trustees would fall to be regarded for the purposes of those arrangements as not liable in the UK to tax on gains accruing to them on the disposal (but see below under trustees ceasing to be liable to UK tax).

TCGA 1992, s 152 (50 ROLLOVER RELIEF) is not to apply where the trustees have disposed of, or their interest in, 'the old assets' before the relevant time, and acquire 'the new assets', or their interest in them, after that time. However, this denial of relief does not apply to new assets if, at the time they are acquired, the trustees carry on a trade in the UK through a branch or agency, and any new assets are situated in the UK and either used in or for the purposes of the trade or used or held for the purposes of the branch or agency. '*The old assets*' and '*the new assets*' have the same meanings as in *TCGA 1992, s 152*. [*TCGA 1992, s 80*].

For the Revenue's practice in this area, see Revenue Pamphlet IR 131, SP 5/92, 21 May 1992, paras 2 and 3.

Death of trustee: special rules. Special rules apply where *TCGA 1992, s 80* above applies as a result of the death of a trustee of the settlement, and within the period of six months beginning with the death, the trustees of the settlement become resident and ordinarily resident in the UK. In such circumstances, *TCGA 1992, s 80* is to apply as if the defined assets were restricted to such assets (if any) as would, apart from this special rule, be defined assets and are included in one or other of two specified descriptions. The first such description is of assets which are disposed of by the trustees in the period which begins with the death and ends when the trustees become resident and ordinarily resident in the UK. Assets fall within the second such description if they are of a description specified in any double tax relief arrangements, they constitute settled property of the settlement immediately after the trustees become resident and ordinarily resident in the UK, and were the trustees to dispose of them at that time, the trustees would fall to be regarded for the purposes of the arrangements as not liable in the UK to tax on gains accruing to them on the disposal.

Further special rules apply where at any time (whether before, on or after 19 March 1991) the trustees of a settlement become resident and ordinarily resident in the UK as a result of the death of a trustee of the settlement, and *TCGA 1992, s 80* above applies as regards the trustees of the settlement in circumstances where the relevant time (within the meaning of that provision) falls within the period of six months beginning with the death. In such circumstances, *TCGA 1992, s 80* is to apply as if the defined assets were restricted to such assets (if any) as would, apart from this special rule, be defined assets and are included in a further specified description. Assets fall within this description if the trustees acquired them in the period beginning with the death and ending with the relevant time, and they acquired them as a result of a disposal in respect of which relief is given under *TCGA 1992, s 165* (hold-over relief for gifts of business assets; see 22.1 HOLD-OVER RELIEFS) or in relation to which *TCGA 1992, s 260(3)* (hold-over relief for gifts on which inheritance tax is chargeable etc; see 22.4 HOLD-OVER RELIEFS) applies. [*TCGA 1992, s 81*].

Past trustees: liability for tax. Where *TCGA 1992, s 80* above applies as regards the trustees of a settlement (*'the migrating trustees'*), and any resulting capital gains tax which is payable by the migrating trustees is not paid within six months from the time when it became payable, the Board may act as below.

The Board may, at any time before the end of the period of three years beginning with the time when the amount of tax is finally determined, serve on any person who, at any time within 'the relevant period', was a trustee of the settlement (but not so as to include a person ceasing to be a trustee before the end of the relevant period who can show that at the time he ceased to be a trustee there was no proposal that the trustees might become neither resident nor ordinarily resident in the UK), a notice requiring the payment of outstanding tax and interest within 30 days from the service of the notice. The notified amount can be recovered from the person concerned as if it were tax due and payable; and he may recover from the migrating trustees any amount paid by him. No tax relief is given on any such payment in computing taxable profits etc.

Where the relevant time for the purposes of *TCGA 1992, s 80* above is within the period of twelve months beginning with 19 March 1991, *'the relevant period'* is the period beginning with that date and ending with that time, and in any other case, *'the relevant period'* is the period of twelve months ending with the relevant time. [*TCGA 1992, s 82*].

For the Revenue's practice in this area, see Revenue Pamphlet IR 131, SP 5/92, 21 May 1992, paras 4–6.

Trustees ceasing to be liable to UK tax. Where, at any time (*'the time concerned'*) after 18 March 1991, the trustees of a settlement, while continuing to be resident and ordinarily resident in the UK, become trustees who fall to be regarded for the purposes of any double tax relief arrangements as resident overseas and as not liable in the UK to tax on gains accruing on disposals of assets (*'relevant assets'*) which constitute settled property of the settlement and fall within descriptions specified in the arrangements, they are deemed for capital gains tax purposes to have disposed of the relevant assets immediately before the time concerned, and immediately to have reacquired them, at their market value at that time. [*TCGA 1992, s 83*].

Acquisition by dual resident trustees. Where 'new assets', within the meaning of *TCGA 1992, s 152* (see under *TCGA 1992, s 80* above), are, or the interest in them is, acquired after 18 March 1991, the first-mentioned provision does not apply where: the new assets are, or the interest in them is, acquired by the trustees of a settlement; at the time of acquisition the trustees are resident and ordinarily resident in the UK and fall to be regarded for the purposes of any double tax relief arrangements as resident overseas; the assets are of a description specified in the arrangements; and were the trustees to dispose of the assets immediately after the acquisition, the trustees would fall to be regarded for the purposes of the arrangements as not liable in the UK to tax on gains accruing to them on the disposal. [*TCGA 1992, s 84*].

Disposal of settled interest. Where *TCGA 1992, s 80* above applies as regards the trustees of a settlement, and after the relevant time (within the meaning of that provision) a person disposes of an interest created by or arising under the settlement and the circumstances are such that *TCGA 1992, s 76(1)* (exemption for disposal of interest in a settlement) is prevented from applying by *TCGA 1992, s 85(1)* (exemption under *TCGA 1992, s 76(1)* not to apply where trustees resident and ordinarily resident overseas; see 52.8 SETTLEMENTS), and the interest was created for his benefit, or he otherwise acquired it, before the relevant time, then, for the purpose of calculating any chargeable gain accruing on the disposal of the interest, he is treated as having disposed of it immediately before the relevant time, and immediately reacquired it, at its market value at that time. This treatment does not apply if *TCGA 1992, s 83* above applied as regards the trustees in circumstances where the time concerned (within the meaning of that provision) fell before the time when the interest was created for the benefit of the person disposing of it or when he otherwise acquired it.

The above treatment is also disapplied where *TCGA 1992, s 80* above applies as regards the trustees of a settlement, and after the relevant time (within the meaning of that provision) a person disposes of an interest created by or arising under the settlement and the circumstances are such that *TCGA 1992, s 76(1)* is prevented from applying by *TCGA 1992, s 85(1)*, and the interest was created for his benefit, or he otherwise acquired it, before the relevant time, and *TCGA 1992, s 83* above applied as regards the trustees in circumstances where the time concerned (within the meaning of that provision) fell in 'the relevant period'. In these circumstances, for the purposes of calculating any chargeable gain accruing on the disposal of the interest, the person disposing of it is treated as having disposed of it immediately before the time referred to below, and immediately reacquired it, at its market value at that time.

'*The relevant period*' is the period which begins when the interest was created for the benefit of the person disposing of it or when he otherwise acquired it, and ends with the relevant time. The time referred to above is the time concerned (where there is only one such time) or the earliest time concerned (where there is more than one because *TCGA 1992, s 83* above applied more than once). [*TCGA 1992, s 85*].

Information required to be returned in respect of settlements with a foreign element. With effect after 2 May 1994, there are extensive requirements for information relating to 'settlements with a foreign element' to be returned to the Revenue within certain time limits *without a notice to make a return having to be given by the Revenue*. PENALTIES (42.7) under *TMA 1970, s 98* apply for failure to comply although no failure will arise where information already has been returned or will be returned later under any other provision. In particular, the following requirements should be observed.

(*a*) Where property is transferred after 2 May 1994, otherwise than by way of an arm's length transaction or in pursuance of a liability incurred on or before that date, to a settlement created before 19 March 1991 which is non-UK resident at the time of transfer, a return of certain particulars must be made by the transferor within *twelve months* of the day ('*the relevant day*') of the transfer if he knows, or has reason to believe, the residence status of the settlement.

(*b*) Where a settlement is created at a time after 18 March 1991 which, at that time, is either non-UK resident or both UK resident and, under double tax relief arrangements, resident elsewhere, a return of certain particulars must be made by the settlor within *twelve months* of the day ('*the relevant day*') he first fulfils after 2 May 1994 the condition that he is UK domiciled and UK resident or ordinarily resident, not having met that condition at the time of the settlement's creation. Similarly, where such a settlement is created after 2 May 1994, a return of certain particulars must be made by the settlor who meets the above condition at the time of the settlement's creation within *three months* of the day ('*the relevant day*') on which the settlement was created.

(*c*) Where a settlement becomes at any time ('*the relevant time*') after 2 May 1994 non-UK resident or, whilst continuing to be UK resident becomes at any time ('*the relevant time*') after 2 May 1994, under double tax relief arrangements, resident elsewhere, a return of certain particulars must be made by a person who was a trustee immediately before the relevant time within *twelve months* of the day ('*the relevant day*') when the relevant time falls.

[*TCGA 1992, s 98A, 5A Sch; FA 1994, s 97(1)–(3)(6)*].

Returns of information should be made to Financial Intermediaries and Claims Office (Foreign Trusts Section), St John's House, Merton Road, Stanley Precinct, Bootle, Merseyside L69 9BB. Tel: 0151 472 6000.

In view of the introduction of the above requirements, the broadly equivalent provisions of *TCGA 1992, 5 Sch 11–14* (information powers for purposes of *TCGA 1992, s 86, 5 Sch*; settlor having interest in overseas resident settlement) in 39.7 below are repealed where the relevant day as above falls after 2 May 1994.

39.7   **Charge on settlor with interest in settlement.** (1) *Conditions for the charge.* The charge under (2) below on the settlor applies where

(*a*)   the settlement is a 'qualifying settlement' (see (9) below) in a particular year of assessment;

(*b*)   the trustees of the settlement fulfil a specified residence condition;

(*c*)   the person who is the settlor in relation to the settlement ('the settlor') is domiciled in the UK at some time in the year and is either resident in the UK during any part of the year or ordinarily resident in the UK during the year;

(*d*)   at any time during the year the settlor has an 'interest' (see (4) below) in the settlement;

(*e*)   by virtue of disposals of any of the settled property originating from the settlor (see (8) below), there is an amount on which the trustees would be chargeable to tax for the year under *TCGA 1992, s 2(2)* (chargeable gains less current and brought forward allowable losses to be assessable; see 35.1 LOSSES) if certain assumptions as to residence were made; and

(*f*)   the provisions in (5) below do not prevent a charge.

The specified residence condition in (*b*) is that *either* the trustees are not resident or ordinarily resident in the UK during any part of the year, *or* the trustees are resident in the UK during any part of the year or ordinarily resident in the UK during the year, but at any time of such residence or ordinary residence they fall to be regarded for the purposes of any DOUBLE TAX RELIEF (17.2) arrangements as resident overseas. Where the first alternative residence condition specified above applies, the assumption as to residence in (*e*) above is that the trustees are resident or ordinarily resident in the UK throughout the year; and where the second alternative residence condition specified above applies, the assumption as to residence in (*e*) above is that the double tax relief arrangements do not apply.

(2) *The charge.* Where the conditions in (1) above are fulfilled, chargeable gains of an amount equal to that referred to in (1)(*e*) above are treated as accruing in a particular year of assessment to 'the settlor' (see (7) below) of a settlement such that they are treated as forming the highest part of the amount on which he is chargeable to capital gains tax for the year.

(3) *Calculation of amount to be charged.* In arriving at the amount to be charged on the settlor for a particular year of assessment, the effects of *TCGA 1992, s 3* (annual exempt amount; see 52.4 and 52.5 SETTLEMENTS) and *TCGA 1992, ss 77–79* (settlor having interest in UK resident settlement chargeable instead of trustees in certain circumstances; see 52.3 SETTLEMENTS) are ignored. In addition, any deductions provided for by *TCGA 1992, s 2(2)* (current and brought forward allowable losses) are to be made in respect of disposals of any of the settled property originating from the settlor, and *TCGA 1992, s 16(3)* (losses of non-resident not to be allowable; see 39.3 above) is to

be assumed not to prevent losses accruing to trustees in one year of assessment from being allowed as a deduction from chargeable gains in a later year (so far as not previously set against gains). Where trustees hold shares in a company which originate from the settlor, and under *TCGA 1992, s 13* (gains of non-resident close company assessable on shareholder; see 39.5 above) gains or losses would be treated as accruing to the trustees in a particular year of assessment by virtue of the shares if the assumption in (1) above as to residence were made, the gains or losses are taken into account in arriving at the amount charged on the settlor as regards that year as if they had accrued by virtue of disposals of settled property originating from the settlor.

Where, as regards a particular year of assessment, there would otherwise be an amount to be charged on the settlor and the trustees fall within the second alternative residence condition specified in (1) above, the following assumptions and adjustments to the amount are made. It is to be assumed that references in the foregoing to settled property originating from the settlor were to such of it as constitutes 'protected assets' and that references in the foregoing to shares originating from the settlor were to such of them as constitute protected assets. The amount (if any) to be charged on the settlor is found on those assumptions, and if there is no amount found there is deemed to be no amount to be charged on the settlor, and if an amount is found on these assumptions it is compared with the amount which would otherwise be charged on the settlor, and the smaller of the two is taken to be the amount to be charged on the settlor.

Where the trustees fall within the first alternative residence condition specified in (1) above, further rules apply to arrive at the amount to be charged on the settlor as regards a particular year of assessment ('*the year concerned*'). If the conditions mentioned in (1) above for the charge to apply are not fulfilled as regards the settlement in any year of assessment falling before the year concerned, no deductions are made for losses accruing before the year concerned. If those conditions are fulfilled as regards the settlement in any year or years of assessment falling before the year concerned, no deductions are made for losses accruing before that year (or the first of the years) so falling. However, these two prohibitions on deductions being made for losses are not to prevent deductions being made in respect of losses accruing in a year of assessment in which the conditions mentioned in (1)(*a*) to (*d*) and (*f*) above are fulfilled as regards the settlement. As regards a particular year of assessment and in relation to a settlement created before 19 March 1991, no account is taken of disposals made before 19 March 1991 (whether for the purpose of arriving at gains or losses).

Assets are '*protected assets*' if they are of a description specified in the double tax relief arrangements mentioned in connection with the second alternative residence condition specified in (1) above, and were the trustees to dispose of them at any 'relevant time', the trustees would fall to be regarded for the purposes of the arrangements as not liable in the UK to tax on gains accruing to them on the disposal. For this purpose, the alternative assumptions as to residence in (1) above are ignored, the '*relevant time*' is any time, in the year of assessment concerned, when the trustees fall to be regarded for the purposes of the arrangements as resident overseas, and if different assets are identified by reference to different relevant times, all of them are protected assets.

(4) *Test whether settlor has an interest.* There are detailed rules for determining whether a settlor has an interest in a settlement. A settlor has an interest in a settlement if

(*a*)   any property originating from the settlor ('*relevant property*') which is or may at any time be comprised in the settlement is, or will or may become, applicable for the benefit of or payable to a 'defined person' in any circumstances whatever;

(*b*)   any income originating from the settlor ('*relevant income*') which arises or may arise under the settlement is, or will or may become, applicable for the benefit of or payable to a defined person in any circumstances whatever; or (*c*)   any defined person enjoys a benefit directly or indirectly from any relevant property which is comprised in the settlement or any relevant income arising under the settlement.

Each of the following is a '*defined person*': the settlor; the settlor's spouse; any child (which term includes stepchild) of the settlor or of the settlor's spouse; the spouse of any such child; a company controlled (construed as in *ICTA 1988, s 416* but for these purposes no rights or powers of (or attributed to) an associate or associates of a person are attributed to him under *ICTA 1988, s 416(6)* if he is not a participator (within *ICTA 1988, s 417(1)*) in the company) by a person or persons mentioned in the foregoing; a company associated (construed as in *ICTA 1988, s 416* but for these purposes where it falls to be decided whether a company is controlled by a person or persons, a similar relaxation to that for control applies as above) with any such company.

A settlor does not have an interest in a settlement at any time when none of the property or income concerned can become applicable or payable as mentioned above except in the event of: the bankruptcy of some person who is or may become beneficially entitled to that property or income; any assignment of or charge on the property or income being made or given by some such person; in the case of a marriage settlement, the death of both parties to the marriage and of all or any of the children of the marriage; or the death under the age of 25 or some lower age of some person who would be beneficially entitled to the property or income on attaining that age. He also does not have an interest in a settlement under (*a*) above at any time when some person is alive and under the age of 25 if during that person's life none of the property or income concerned can become applicable or payable as mentioned in (*a*) above except in the event of that person becoming bankrupt or assigning or charging his interest in the property or income concerned.

(5) *Exceptions to charge.* There is no charge on the settlor if he dies in the year. There is also no charge on him where one of the persons referred to below dies in the year and he has no interest in the settlement at any time in the year except for one of the following reasons: property is, or will or may become, applicable for the benefit of or payable to another person (referred to earlier in this sentence), being one of the settlor's spouse, the children (which term includes stepchildren) of the settlor or of the settlor's spouse, or the spouses of any such children; income is, or will or may become applicable for the benefit of or payable to another such person; or another such person enjoys a benefit from property or income. There is again no charge on the settlor where this condition is fulfilled by virtue of two or more of these reasons being satisfied by reference to the same person. Where the person concerned is the settlor's spouse or the spouse of any child (which term includes stepchild) of the settlor or of the settlor's spouse, there is no charge on the settlor if during the year the person concerned ceases to be married to the settlor or the child concerned (as the case may be). There is no charge on the settlor in the following circumstances: the settlor has no interest in the settlement at any time in the year except for the reason that there are two or more persons, each of whom is one of the settlor's spouse, the children (which term includes stepchildren) of the settlor or of the settlor's spouse, and the spouses of any such children and stands to gain for the reason mentioned below; and each of the persons concerned dies in the year. The reason mentioned is that property is, or will or may become, applicable for the person concerned's benefit or payable to him; the income is, or will or may become, applicable for his benefit or payable to him; he enjoys a benefit from property or income; or two or more of the foregoing reasons apply in his case.

(6) *Right of recovery.* Where a charge is made on a settlor, any tax he pays as a result may be recovered by him from any person who is a trustee of the settlement. For this purposes, the settlor may require certificated proof from the inspector of the amount of the gains concerned and the amount of tax paid.

For the Revenue's practice in this area, see Revenue Pamphlet IR 131, SP 5/92, 21 May 1992, paras 7–10 and ICAEW guidance note TAX 20/92, 14 December 1992, paras 5, 6 and 24–26.

(7) *Meaning of 'settlor'.* For the purposes of these provisions, a person is a '*settlor*' in relation to a settlement if the settled property consists of or includes property originating from him.

(8) *Meaning of 'originating'.* References to property originating from a person are taken as references to property provided by that person, property representing property provided by that person, and so much of any property provided by that person and other property as, on a just apportionment, can be taken to represent property provided by that person. References to income originating from a person are taken as references to income from property originating from that person and income provided by that person.

Where a person who is a settlor in relation to a settlement makes reciprocal arrangements with another person for the provision of property or income, then the property or income provided by the other person under the arrangements is treated as provided by the settlor, but property or income provided by the settlor under the arrangements is treated as provided by the other person (and not by the settlor).

Where property is provided by a '*qualifying company*' (i.e. a company which is a close company within *ICTA 1988, ss 414, 415* or which would be a close company if it were resident in the UK) controlled (construed as in *ICTA 1988, s 416* but with the same relaxation as in (4) above) by one person alone at the time it is provided, that person is taken to provide it. Where property is provided by a qualifying company controlled by two or more persons (taking each one separately) at the time it is provided, those persons are taken to provide the property in equal shares. Where property is provided by a qualifying company controlled by two or more persons (taking them together) at the time it is provided, the persons who are participators (construed as in *ICTA 1988, s 417(1)*) in the company at the time it is provided are taken to provide it in just proportions (save that where a person would otherwise be treated under this last provision as providing less than 5% of any property, he is not taken as providing any property). By concession, a beneficiary in the settlement is not to be regarded as a participator in the company solely by virtue of his status as beneficiary (Revenue Pamphlet IR 1, D40 as revised by Revenue Press Release of 7 October 1994).

References to property representing other property include references to property representing accumulated income from that other property. A person is treated as providing property or income if he provides it directly or indirectly. The above provisions for determining whether property of any kind originates from a person apply equally to determine whether shares held by the trustees of a company whose gains and losses are taken into account in arriving at the amount to be charged on the settlor (see (3) above) originate from the settlor.

(9) *Qualifying settlements, and commencement.* A settlement created after 18 March 1991 is a '*qualifying settlement*' for the purposes of these provisions in the year of assessment in which it is created and subsequent years of assessment. In addition, a settlement created before 19 March 1991 is a qualifying settlement in a year of assessment in which any of four conditions becomes fulfilled and subsequent years of assessment.

(*a*)   The first condition is that after 18 March 1991 property or income is provided directly or indirectly for the purposes of the settlement otherwise than under a transaction entered into at arm's length and otherwise than in pursuance of a liability incurred by any person before 19 March 1991. However, if the settlement's expenses relating to administration and taxation for a year of assessment exceed its income for the year, property or income provided towards meeting those expenses is ignored for the purposes of this condition if the value of the property or income so provided does not exceed the difference between the amount of those expenses and the amount of the settlement's income for the year. By concession, a repayable on demand loan which was made to a relevant trust on non-commercial terms before 19 March 1991 will not be caught by this condition provided that, before 31 July 1992, it is either repaid in full with any outstanding interest or made subject to fully commercial terms (Revenue Pamphlet IR 1, D41 – this concession contains further detailed notes on the treatment of amounts paid where the loan is put on a commercial basis. See also Revenue Tax Bulletin August 1993 p 83).

(*b*)   The second condition is that the trustees become after 18 March 1991 neither resident nor ordinarily resident in the UK, or the trustees, while continuing to be resident and ordinarily resident in the UK, become after 18 March 1991 trustees who fall to be regarded for the purposes of any double tax relief arrangements as resident overseas.

(*c*)   The third condition is that after 18 March 1991 the terms of the settlement are varied so that a defined person (see (4) above) becomes for the first time a person who will or might benefit from the settlement.

(*d*)   The fourth condition is that on or after 19 March 1991 a defined person enjoys a benefit from the settlement for the first time and the person concerned is not one who (looking only at the terms of the settlement immediately before 19 March 1991) would be capable of enjoying a benefit from the settlement on or after that date.

For the Revenue's practice in this area, see Revenue Pamphlet IR 131, SP 5/92, 21 May 1992, paras 11–37, Revenue Tax Bulletin August 1993 p 82 and April 1995 pp 204, 205, and ICAEW guidance note TAX 20/92, 14 December 1992, paras 7–23.

(10) *Information.* The inspector can require, under notice of at least 28 days, a return to be made by a trustee, beneficiary or settlor of particulars he thinks necessary for the purposes of these provisions. 42.7 PENALTIES under *TMA 1970, s 98* apply for failure.

There were also extensive requirements for information relating to these provisions to be returned, subject to the same penalties as above, to the Revenue within certain time limits *without a notice to make a return having to be given by the Revenue*. In view of the introduction of virtually identical but *general* information powers relating to 'settlements with a foreign element' (see *TCGA 1992, 5A Sch* in 39.6 above), the information powers relating solely to the above provisions were repealed where the 'relevant day' (see 39.6(*a*)-(*c*) above) falls after 2 May 1994. Prior to this repeal, these information powers were as in *TCGA 1992, 5A Sch* except that the following subparagraphs (*a*)-(*c*) should be substituted for the corresponding subparagraphs (*a*)-(*c*) in 39.6 above.

(*a*)   Where property was transferred after 18 March 1991, otherwise than by way of an arm's length transaction or in pursuance of a liability incurred on or before that date, to a settlement created on or before that date which was non-UK resident at the time of transfer, a return of certain particulars had to be made by the transferor within *twelve months* of the later of the day of the transfer and 25 July 1991 if he knew, or had reason to believe, the residence status of the settlement.

(*b*)   Where a settlement was created at a time after 18 March 1991 which, at that time, was either non-UK resident or both UK resident and, under double tax relief arrangements, resident elsewhere, a return of certain particulars had to be made by the settlor within *twelve months* of the later of the day he first fulfilled after the settlement was created the condition that he was UK domiciled and UK resident or ordinarily resident, not having met that condition at the time of the settlement's creation, and 25 July 1991. Similarly, where such a settlement was created after 18 March 1991, a return of certain particulars had to be made by the settlor who met the above condition at the time of the settlement's creation within *three months* of the day on which the settlement was created.

(c)   Where a settlement became at any time ('*the relevant time*') after 18 March 1991 non-UK resident or, whilst continuing to be UK resident became at any time ('*the relevant time*') after 18 March 1991, under double tax relief arrangements, resident elsewhere, a return of certain particulars had to be made by a person who was a trustee immediately before the relevant time within *twelve months* of the later of the day when the relevant time fell and 25 July 1991.

[*TCGA 1992, s 86, 5 Sch; FA 1994, s 97(4)(5), 26 Sch Pt V*].

(11) *Interaction with other provisions.* 'The trust gains for the year' of *TCGA 1992, s 87(2)* (gains of overseas resident settlements chargeable on beneficiaries; see 39.8 below) are reduced by the amount or the aggregate of the amounts chargeable on the settlor under the above provisions. [*TCGA 1992, s 87(3)*]. Both the above provisions and *TCGA 1992, ss 77–79* (settlor having interest in UK resident settlement chargeable instead of trustees in certain circumstances) contain a direction that the charge on the settlor is to be treated as the highest part of the amount on which he is chargeable to capital gains tax for a year of assessment. Where charges under both provisions apply to the same person in the same year, then the direction under *TCGA 1992, ss 77–79* takes effect subject to the similar direction under the above provisions. [*TCGA 1992, s 78(3)*].

39.8   **Charge on beneficiary in respect of capital payments received from settlement.** A 'beneficiary'of an overseas resident settlement is liable to capital gains tax for 1981/82 onwards on the gains of the settlement in the following circumstances.

(a)   The trustees must be neither resident nor ordinarily resident in the UK during any part of the year of assessment.

(b)   The 'settlor', or one of the settlors, either at some time during the year of assessment, or when the 'settlement' was made, must be, or have been, domiciled and either resident or ordinarily resident in the UK.

(c)   The beneficiary must be domiciled in the UK at some time during the year of assessment.

(d)   There must be 'trust gains for the year'.

(e)   The beneficiary must have received 'capital payments' from the trustees.

[*TCGA 1992, s 87(1)(2)(4)(7)(10)*].

'*Settlement*' and '*settlor*' after 5 April 1984 are defined by the references in *ICTA 1988, s 660G(1)(2)* (see 14.7 CONNECTED PERSONS) and 'settled property' is construed accordingly and as regards 'settlor' includes, in the case of a settlement arising under a will or intestacy, the testator or intestate. Before 6 April 1984 no definition was given. [*TCGA 1992, s 97(7); FA 1995, 17 Sch 30*]. In a case where a residuary legatee (who was domiciled, resident and ordinarily resident in the UK) settled the unadministered residue of the estate of a testator (who was domiciled, resident and ordinarily resident outside the UK) under a deed of family arrangement within *TCGA 1992, s 62(6)* (see 15.6 DEATH), it was held that the legatee was the settlor for the purposes of *TCGA 1992, s 87* above (*Marshall v Kerr HL, [1994] STC 638*).

'*Beneficiary*' is not otherwise defined, but in any case where:

(1)   at any time after 18 March 1991 a capital payment is received from the trustees of a settlement or is treated as so received by virtue of the *TCGA 1992, s 96(1)* below;

(2)   it is received by a person, or treated as received by a person by virtue of *TCGA 1992, s 96(2)–(6)* below:

(3)   at the time it is received or treated as received, the person is not otherwise a beneficiary of the settlement; and

(4)   certain exceptions do not apply;

then for the purposes of *TCGA 1992, ss 87–90* (for which see further below) the person is treated as a beneficiary of the settlement as regards events occurring on or after that time. The first exception is where a payment within (1) above is made in circumstances where it is treated (otherwise than under the provision in the last sentence) as received by a beneficiary. The second exception is where the trustees of the settlement concerned or trustees of any other settlement are beneficiaries of the settlement concerned. [*TCGA 1992, s 97(8)–(10)*].

For the purposes of (*b*) above, a settlement arising under a will or intestacy is treated as made by the testator or intestate at the time of his death. [*TCGA 1992, s 87(9)*].

The trust gains for a year of assessment are treated as chargeable gains accruing in that year to beneficiaries of the settlement who receive capital payments from the trustees in that year or have received such payments in any earlier year, such attribution being made in proportion to, but not exceeding, the amounts of capital payments received by them. A capital payment is left out of account for these purposes to the extent that chargeable gains have by reason of the payment been treated as accruing to the recipient in an earlier year. [*TCGA 1992, s 87(4)–(6)*].

'*Trust gains for the year*'. This is an amount which is the aggregate of

(i)   the amount of the gains for the current year which would have been chargeable on the trustees under *TCGA 1992, s 2(2)* (chargeable gains less current and brought forward losses to be assessable), had they been resident or ordinarily resident in the UK in the year in which the gains accrued; and

(ii) the corresponding amount, but as yet unattributed under *TCGA 1992, s 87(4)* above or *TCGA 1992, s 89(2)* (migrant settlements) below, for earlier years (but not prior to 6 April 1981).

[*TCGA 1992, s 87(2)*].

Example

T and M are the only beneficiaries under a Jersey settlement set up by their grandfather, who was then domiciled and resident in the UK. None of the trustees is resident in the UK.

T is resident in the UK but M is neither resident nor ordinarily resident in the UK. Both beneficiaries have a UK domicile. In 1994/95, the trustees sell shares realising a chargeable gain of £102,000. No disposals are made in 1995/96.

The trustees make capital payments of £60,000 to M in 1994/95. In 1995/96 they make capital payments of £60,000 to T and £10,000 to M.

1994/95	£
Trust gains	102,000
Capital payment	60,000
Trust gains carried forward	£42,000

M has chargeable gains of £60,000 but is not subject to CGT.

39.8   Overseas Matters

1995/96	£
Trust gains (brought forward)	42,000
Capital payments (£60,000 + £10,000)	70,000
Balance of capital payments carried forward	£28,000

The chargeable gains are apportioned as follows

		£
T	$\dfrac{60,000}{70,000} \times £42,000$	36,000
M	$\dfrac{10,000}{70,000} \times £42,000$ (not assessable)	6,000
		£42,000

The capital payments carried forward are apportioned as follows

	£
T £60,000 − £36,000	24,000
M £10,000 − £6,000	4,000
	£28,000

Where as regards the same settlement and for the same year of assessment chargeable gains, whether of one amount or of two or more amounts, are treated as accruing by virtue of *TCGA 1992, s 86(4)* (see (2) (the charge) in 39.7 (overseas resident settlement where settlor has interest) above), and an amount falls to be computed under *TCGA 1992, s 87(2)* above, the amount so computed is treated as reduced by the amount, or aggregate of the amounts, mentioned in 39.7 above. [*TCGA 1992, s 87(3)*]. In addition, in computing an amount under *TCGA 1992, s 87(2)* for years of assessment after 1990/91, the effect of *TCGA 1992, ss 77–79* (settlor having interest in UK resident settlement chargeable instead of the trustees in certain circumstances after 1987/88; see 52.3 SETTLEMENTS) is ignored. (The interaction between these two charging provisions is not explicitly stated for 1988/89, 1989/90 and 1990/91 but in *de Rothschild v Lawrenson CA, [1995] STI 639* it was held that a practically similar position applied for those years as it does for subsequent ones.) [*TCGA 1992, s 87(8)*].

Where a loss accrues to the trustees in a year of assessment for which these provisions apply, or *CGTA 1979, s 17* applied (see 39.10 below), the loss is allowable against gains accruing to the trustees in any later year beginning after 5 April 1981, insofar as it has not previously been set against gains for the purpose of a computation under either of the foregoing provisions or otherwise. [*TCGA 1992, ss 16(3), 97(6)*].

'*Capital payments*'. These are any 'payments' received after 9 March 1981 which either are not chargeable to income tax on the 'recipient' (formerly 'beneficiary' for payments etc. before 19 March 1991), or, in the case of a recipient neither resident nor ordinarily resident in the UK, are payments received otherwise than as income. However, payments received *after 9 March 1981 and before 6 April 1984* and which represent chargeable gains accruing to the trustees *before 6 April 1981* are dealt with under the previous legislation (see 39.10 below), subject to provisions which avoid double taxation. For payments received after 18 March 1991, a capital payment does not include a payment under a transaction entered into at arm's length. [*TCGA 1992, ss 87(10), 97(1); FA 1995, 17 Sch 30*].

The beneficiary is regarded as having received a capital payment from the trustees where

(A)   the beneficiary receives the payment from them, whether directly or indirectly; or

(B)   the trustees, directly or indirectly, apply the payment in settlement of any of the beneficiary's debts, or it is otherwise paid or applied for his benefit; or

(C)   a third party receives it at the beneficiary's direction.

[*TCGA 1992, s 97(5)*].

'*Payment*' includes the transfer of an asset and the conferring of any other benefit. It also includes any occasion where settled property becomes property to which *TCGA 1992, s 60* applies (e.g. property held by nominees or on bare trusts for persons absolutely entitled). [*TCGA 1992, s 97(3)*]. A benefit treated (in whole or in part), under *ICTA 1988, s 740(2)(b)* (transfer of assets abroad: liability of non-transferors on benefits received; see Tolley's Income Tax under Anti-Avoidance), as the recipient's income for a year of assessment *later* than the year of receipt, is not precluded from being treated as a capital payment in relation to any year *prior* to the year of assessment for which it is treated as income. It cannot, however, be treated as a capital payment in relation to the year for which it is treated as income, or in relation to any *subsequent* year. [*TCGA 1992, s 97(3)*].

The amount of capital payment made by way of loan, and of any other capital payment which is not an outright payment of money, is to be taken as the value of the benefit conferred by it. [*TCGA 1992, s 97(4)*].

In addition to (*c*) above, a beneficiary would not be chargeable if he was neither resident nor ordinarily resident in the UK for the year of assessment in question under the general rules of *TCGA 1992, s 2(1)* (see 39.1 above). Thus, in respect of capital payments received by a beneficiary in these circumstances, whilst trust gains are attributed to those capital payments, no charge to tax can be made in respect of them.

For allowable expenditure on a subsequent disposal of an asset transferred to a beneficiary, see 36.1 MARKET VALUE. Where beneficiaries resident or ordinarily resident in the UK became absolutely entitled to settled property (see 52.9 SETTLEMENTS) after 5 April 1982 and before 14 March 1989 hold-over relief was available as in 22.6 HOLD-OVER RELIEFS (Tolley's Practical Tax 1984 p 25). By analogy, the other current HOLD-OVER RELIEFS (22) would be available in such circumstances (provided all the conditions for the relief in question are met).

Dual-resident settlements. *TCGA 1992, s 87* above also applies to a settlement for years of assessment beginning after 1990/91 if: the trustees are resident in the UK during any part of the year or ordinarily resident in the UK during the year; at any time of such residence or ordinary residence they fall to be regarded for the purposes of any DOUBLE TAX RELIEF (17.2) arrangements as resident overseas; and the settlor or one of the settlors is at any time during that year, or was when he made his settlement, domiciled and either resident or ordinarily resident in the UK.

In the above circumstances, *TCGA 1992, s 87* is to have effect for every year of assessment as if the amount to be computed under *TCGA 1992, s 87(2)* were 'the assumed chargeable amount'; and the reference in *TCGA 1992, s 87(2)* to 'the corresponding amount' in respect of an earlier year is to be construed as a reference to the amount computed under *TCGA 1992, s 87(2)* apart from this provision (*TCGA 1992, s 88*) or (as the case may be) the amount computed under *TCGA 1992, s 87(2)* by virtue of this provision.

'*The assumed chargeable amount*' in respect of a year of assessment is the lesser of: the amount on which the trustees would be chargeable to tax for the year under *TCGA 1992, s 2(2)* on the assumption that the double tax relief arrangements did not apply; and the amount on which, by virtue of disposals of protected assets, the trustees would be chargeable to tax for the year under *TCGA 1992, s 2(2)* on the assumption that those arrangements did not apply. Assets are *'protected assets'* if they are of a description specified in the double tax relief arrangements, and were the trustees to dispose of them at any 'relevant time', the trustees would fall to be regarded for the purposes of the arrangements as not liable in the UK to tax on gains accruing to them on the disposal. For the purposes of this definition of protected assets: the second assumption in the first sentence of this paragraph is ignored; *'the relevant time'* is any time, in the year of assessment concerned, when the trustees fall to be regarded for the purposes of the arrangements as resident overseas; and if different assets are identified by reference to different relevant times, all of them are protected assets. In computing the assumed chargeable amount in respect of a particular year of assessment, the effect of *TCGA 1992, ss 77–79* is ignored. For the purposes of *TCGA 1992, s 87* as it applies by virtue of this provision, capital payments received before 6 April 1991 are disregarded. [*TCGA 1992, s 88*].

Migrant settlements. A capital payment (see above) made to a beneficiary in a period of one or more years of assessment 'for each of which *TCGA 1992, s 87* above does not apply to the settlement' (formerly 'in each of which the trustees were at some time resident or ordinarily resident in the UK' before 25 July 1991) (a *'resident period'*) is disregarded provided that the payment is not anticipatory of a disposal by the trustees in a succeeding period of one or more years of assessment for which *TCGA 1992, s 87* applies to the settlement (a *'non-resident period'*). Where a resident period follows a non-resident period and part or whole of the trust gains for the last year of the non-resident period have not yet been apportioned and charged to beneficiaries, the outstanding trust gains are, to the extent, each year, that the beneficiaries receive capital payments, apportioned and charged to them for the first year of the resident period and so on for successive years, until the outstanding gains are exhausted. [*TCGA 1992, s 89(2)*]. *TCGA 1992, s 87(5)(7)* is applied to *TCGA 1992, s 89(2)* as it applies to *TCGA 1992, s 87(4)*. [*TCGA 1992, s 89(3)*].

Transfers between settlements. There are provisions for the carry-over of unattributed trust gains under *TCGA 1992, s 87* or *89(2)* (apportioned where necessary), in cases where transfers of settled property are made from one settlement to another other than for consideration in money or money's worth. If neither of the last mentioned provisions would otherwise apply to the transferee settlement for the year of transfer, *TCGA 1992, s 89(2)* is deemed to apply to it as if the year were the first year of a resident period following a non-resident period, and the trust gains equal to the trust gains for the last year of the non-resident period. [*TCGA 1992, s 90*].

Payments by and to companies. In respect of capital payments received after 18 March 1981, where a capital payment is received from a *'qualifying company'* (i.e. a company which is a close company within *ICTA 1988, ss 414, 415* or which would be a close company if it was UK resident) which is controlled (as construed in accordance with *ICTA 1988, s 416* except that for this purpose no rights or powers of (or attributed to) an associate or associates of a person are attributed to him under *ICTA 1988, s 416(6)* if he is not a participator (within *ICTA 1988, s 417(1)*) in the company) by the trustees of a settlement at the time it is received, it is treated for the purposes of *TCGA 1992, ss 87–90* above as received from the trustees. For this purpose a company is controlled by the trustees of a settlement if it is controlled by the trustees alone or by the trustees together with a person who (or persons each of whom) is a settlor in relation to the settlement) or he is connected (see 14 CONNECTED PERSONS) with a settlor. By concession, a beneficiary in the settlement is not to be regarded as a participator in the company solely by virtue of his status as beneficiary (Revenue Pamphlet IR 1, D40 as revised by Revenue Press Release of 7 October 1994).

Where a capital payment is received from trustees of a settlement (or treated as so received under the foregoing) and it is received by a *'non-resident qualifying company'* (i.e. a company which is not resident in the UK and would be a close company if it were so resident), the following provisions apply for the purposes of *TCGA 1992, ss 87–90*. If the company is controlled by one person alone at the time the payment is received, and that person is then resident or ordinarily resident in the UK, it is treated as a capital payment received by that person. If the company is controlled by two or more persons (taking each one separately) at the time the payment is received, then: if one of them is then resident or ordinarily resident in the UK, it is treated as a capital payment received by that person; and if two or more persons are then resident or ordinarily resident in the UK (*'the residents'*) it is treated as being as many equal capital payments as there are residents and each of them is treated as receiving one of the payments.

If the company is controlled by two or more persons (taking them together) at the time the payment is received and each of them is then resident or ordinarily resident in the UK: it is treated as being as many capital payments as there are participators in the company at the time it is received; and each such participator (whatever his residence or ordinary residence) is treated as receiving one of the payments, quantified on the basis of just and reasonable apportionment. But where a participator would otherwise be treated as receiving less than 5% of the payment actually received by the company, he is not treated as receiving anything by virtue of the foregoing. [*TCGA 1992, s 96*].

For the Revenue's practice in this area, see SP 5/92, 21 May 1992, paras 38–40.

Powers to obtain information. The Board may, by notice in writing, require any person, within such time as it directs (not less than 28 days), to furnish it with such particulars as it thinks necessary for the purposes of *TCGA 1992, ss 87–90* above. The very wide powers of *ICTA 1988, s 745(2)–(5)*, suitably adapted, are also expressly stated to apply. [*TCGA 1992, s 98*].

39.9   **Further charge on beneficiary in respect of capital payments received from settlement.** (1) *Introduction.* Further provisions apply as regards the regime of provisions in 39.8 above for taxing beneficiaries of overseas resident settlements. They provide for an increased tax charge on the beneficiary in certain cases. For the purposes of the provisions below, *'trust gains for a year'* and *'capital payment'* are construed and have the same meaning (respectively) as in 39.8 above.

(2) *Qualifying amounts.* For the purposes of the provisions, if *TCGA 1992, s 87* applied to a settlement for the year 1990/91 the settlement had a *'qualifying amount'* for the year, and the amount was the amount constituting the trust gains for the year less so much of them as were by virtue of *TCGA 1992, s 87* treated as chargeable gains accruing in that year to the beneficiaries. If *TCGA 1992, s 87* applies to a settlement for the year 1991/92 or a subsequent year of assessment the settlement has a qualifying amount for the year, and that amount is the amount computed for the settlement in respect of the year concerned under *TCGA 1992, s 87(2)*.

A qualifying amount for 1990/91 is also determined where

(a)   there was a period (*'a non-resident period'*) of one or more years of assessment for each of which *TCGA 1992, s 87* applied to a settlement and each of which fell before the year 1990/91;

(b)   *TCGA 1992, s 87* did not apply to the settlement for the year 1990/91; and

(c)   there were trust gains for the last year of the non-resident period which were not (or were not wholly) treated by virtue of *TCGA 1992, s 87* or *89(2)* as chargeable gains accruing to beneficiaries before the year 1990/91.

In such a case the settlement had a qualifying amount for the year 1990/91 of the amount constituting the trust gains mentioned in (*c*) above (or the outstanding part of them) less so much of them as were by virtue of *TCGA 1992, s 87(2)* treated as chargeable gains accruing in that year to beneficiaries.

(3) *Matching capital payment.* For the purposes of the provisions, the following applies where capital payments are made by the trustees of a settlement after 5 April 1991 and the payments are made in a year or years of assessment for which *TCGA 1992, s 87* applies to the settlement or in circumstances where *TCGA 1992, s 89(2)* treats chargeable gains as accruing in respect of the payments. In these circumstances the payments are matched with qualifying amounts of the settlement for the year 1990/91 and subsequent years of assessment (so far as the amounts are not already matched with payments by virtue of this provision). Payments are matched with qualifying amounts so that: earlier payments are matched with earlier amounts; payments are carried forward to be matched with future amounts (so far as not matched with past amounts); a payment which is less than an unmatched amount (or part) is matched to the extent of the payment; and a payment which is more than an unmatched amount (or part) is matched, as to the excess, with other unmatched amounts.

Where part only of a capital payment is taxable, the part which is not taxable does not fall to be matched until taxable parts of other capital payments (if any) made in the same year of assessment have been matched, and the provisions in the paragraph above have effect accordingly. For this purpose a part of a capital payment is taxable if the part results in chargeable gains accruing under *TCGA 1992, s 87 or 89(2)*.

(4) *Increased tax: the main rule.* The following applies where

(*a*)   a capital payment is made by the trustees of a settlement after 5 April 1992;

(*b*)   the payment is made in a year of assessment for which *TCGA 1992, s 87* applies to the settlement or in circumstances where *TCGA 1992, s 89(2)* treats chargeable gains as accruing in respect of the payment;

(*c*)   the whole payment is matched with a qualifying amount of the settlement for a year of assessment falling at some time before that immediately preceding the one in which the payment is made; and

(*d*)   a beneficiary is charged to tax in respect of the payment by virtue of *TCGA 1992, s 87 or 89(2)*.

In the above circumstances the tax payable by the beneficiary in respect of the payment is increased (by an assessment made for the purpose), except that it cannot be increased beyond the amount of the payment. The amount is equal to the interest that would be yielded if an amount equal to the tax which would be otherwise payable by him in respect of the payment carried interest for 'the chargeable period' at the rate of 10% per annum. The Treasury are given powers to amend the percentage under the 'negative' statutory instrument procedure. '*The chargeable period*' is the period which begins with the later of 1 December in the year of assessment following that for which the qualifying amount mentioned in (*c*) above is the qualifying amount and 1 December falling six years before 1 December in the year of assessment following that in which the capital payment is made, and ends with 30 November in the year of assessment following that in which the capital payment is made.

(5) *More than one qualifying amount.* For the purposes of the provisions, the following applies where

(*a*)   a capital payment is made by the trustees of a settlement after 5 April 1992;

(*b*)   the payment is made in a year of assessment for which *TCGA 1992, s 87* applies to the settlement or in circumstances where *TCGA 1992, s 89(2)* treats chargeable gains as accruing in respect of the payment;

(c)   the whole payment is matched with qualifying amounts of the settlement for different years of assessment, each falling at some time before that immediately preceding the one in which the payment is made; and

(d)   the beneficiary is charged to tax in respect of the payment by virtue of *TCGA 1992, s 87* or *89(2)*.

In the above circumstances the capital payment ('*the main payment*') is treated as being as many payments ('*subsidiary payments*') as there are qualifying amounts; a qualifying amount is attributed to each subsidiary payment and each payment is quantified accordingly; and the tax in respect of the main payment is divided up and attributed to the subsidiary payment on the basis of a just and reasonable apportionment. The provisions in (4) above then apply in the case of each subsidiary payment, the qualifying amount attributed to it and the tax attributed to it.

(6) *Payment partly ignored.* For the purposes of the provisions, the following applies where

(a)   a capital payment is made by the trustees of a settlement after 5 April 1992;

(b)   the payment is made in a year of assessment for which *TCGA 1992, s 87* applies to the settlement or in circumstances where *TCGA 1992, s 89(2)* treats chargeable gains as accruing in respect of the payment;

(c)   part of the payment is matched with a qualifying amount of the settlement for a year of assessment falling at some time before that immediately preceding the one in which the payment is made, or with qualifying amounts of the settlement for different years of assessment each so falling; and

(d)   the beneficiary is charged to tax in respect of the payment by virtue of *TCGA 1992, s 87* or *89(2)*.

In the above circumstances only the tax in respect of so much of the payment as is matched as mentioned in (c) above is taken into account, and references below to the tax are to be construed accordingly; the capital payment is divided into two, the first part representing so much as is matched as mentioned in (c) above and the second so much as is not; the second part is ignored; and the first part is treated as a capital payment, the whole of which is matched with the qualifying amount or amounts mentioned in (c) above, and the whole of which is charged to tax. The provisions in (4) or (4) and (5) above (as the case may be) are then applied in the case of the capital payment divided as above, the qualifying amount or amounts, and the tax.

(7) *Parts of amounts matched.* The provisions in (4) to (6) above apply (with suitable modifications) where a payment or part of a payment is to any extent matched with part of an amount.

(8) *Transfers between settlements.* For the purposes of the provisions, the following applies if: in the year 1990/91 or a subsequent year of assessment the trustees of a settlement ('*the transferor settlement*') transfer all or part of the settled property to the trustees of another settlement ('*the transferee settlement*'), and looking at the state of affairs at the end of the year of assessment in which the transfer is made, there is a qualifying amount of the transferor settlement for a particular year of assessment ('*the year concerned*') and the amount is not (or not wholly) matched with capital payments.

In the above circumstances, if the whole of the settled property is transferred: the transferor settlement's qualifying amount for the year concerned is treated as reduced by so much of it as is not matched; and so much of that amount as is not matched is treated as (or as an addition to) the transferee settlement's qualifying amount for the year concerned. If, in the above circumstances, only part of the settled property is transferred: so much of the transferor settlement's qualifying amount for the year concerned as is not matched is apportioned on a just and reasonable basis, part being attributed to the transferred property and part to the property not transferred; the transferor settlement's qualifying amount for the year concerned is treated as reduced by the part attributed to the transferred property; and that part is treated as (or as an addition to) the transferee settlement's qualifying amount for the year concerned. If the transferee settlement did not in fact exist in the year concerned, then it is treated as having been made at the beginning of that year. If the transferee settlement did in fact exist in the year concerned, the foregoing provisions ((8)) are to apply whether or not *TCGA 1992, s 87* applies to the settlement for that year or for any year of assessment falling before that year.

(9) *Matching after transfer.* In the case of a transferee settlement within (8) above, matching is to be made in accordance with the provisions in (3) above by reference to the state of affairs existing immediately before the beginning of the year of assessment in which the transfer is made, and the transfer is not to affect matching so made. Subject to this, payments are matched with amounts in accordance with the provisions in (3) above and by reference to amounts arrived at under the provisions in (8) above. [*TCGA 1992, ss 91–95, 97(1)–(4)(6)(7); FA 1995, 17 Sch 30*].

39.10   **Charge on beneficiary in respect of settlement gains before 1981/82.** The provisions applied to chargeable gains accruing to the trustees of a settlement if the trustees were not resident and not ordinarily resident in the UK, and if the settlor (or any one of them) was domiciled and either resident or ordinarily resident in the UK when the gains accrued (or was domiciled and either resident or ordinarily resident in the UK when he made the settlement). Any beneficiary under the settlement who was domiciled and either resident or ordinarily resident in the UK during any year of assessment was treated as if an apportioned part of the amount, if any, on which the trustees would have been chargeable to capital gains tax (i.e. if domiciled and either resident or ordinarily resident in the UK in that year of assessment) had been chargeable gains accruing to the beneficiary in that year of assessment. The amount of such gains was apportionable in such manner as was 'just and reasonable' between persons having interests in the settled property, whether that interest was a life interest or an interest in reversion and so that, as near as maybe, the gains were apportioned according to the respective values of those interests, disregarding in the case of a defeasible interest the possibility of defeasance. [*CGTA 1979, s 17(1)(2)*].

Following *Ritchie v McKay Ch D 1984, 57 TC 719* it appears that losses accruing to trustees are treated similarly to the provisions outlined in 39.8 above.

Where in the three years ending with the year of the gain, a person had received a discretionary payment of income from the settlement, he was regarded as having an interest in the settled property of a value equal to that of an annuity of a yearly amount equal to one-third of the payments so received by him in that time. [*CGTA 1979, s 17(3)(a)*].

Where a person received at any time after the chargeable gain accrued (but before 6 April 1984) a capital payment out of the settled property in exercise of the trustee's discretion, insofar as it represented a chargeable gain which had accrued to the trustees before 6 April 1981 but which had not already been attributed to any other person domiciled and resident or ordinarily resident in the UK, that person (if domiciled and resident or ordinarily resident in the UK) was treated as if the chargeable gain (or part) represented by the capital payment had accrued to him at the time he received the capital payment. [*CGTA 1979, s 17(3)(b); FA 1984, s 70(2)*]. See *Ewart v Taylor Ch D 1983, 57 TC 401 and Jones v Lincoln-Lewis and others Ch D, [1991] STC 307.* Tax paid by the trustees was not regarded as a payment to the beneficiary. [*CGTA 1979, s 17(5)*]. Similar payments made after 5 April 1984 are dealt with under the present legislation (see 39.8 above) even where the payments represent chargeable gains which accrued to the trustees before 6 April 1981.

Where the settlement was made before 6 April 1965

(i)   payment of the capital gains tax apportioned to a beneficiary in respect of an interest in reversion in any part of the trust capital could be postponed until that beneficiary became absolutely entitled or disposed of all or part of his interest unless he could, with or without the consent of another person, obtain any of the capital at an earlier date. [*CGTA 1979, s 17(4)(b); TCGA 1992, 11 Sch 18(a)*].

(ii)   a beneficiary who had an interest in income only and who could not, whether with or without the consent of another person, obtain any part of the capital of the settlement, was not within these provisions. [*CGTA 1979, s 17(4)(a)*].

'Settlor' and *'settlement'* were as defined in *ICTA 1970, s 454(3)* and settled property was construed accordingly. [*CGTA 1979, s 17(7)*].

In *Leedale v Lewis HL 1982, 56 TC 501* it was held that a discretionary interest was an interest in settled property and the direction that the gain should be apportioned 'as near as may be, according to the respective values of the interests' envisaged not a strict apportionment by reference to actuarial valuations but a much looser apportionment by reference to what was just and reasonable in view of the real probabilities under the particular settlement.

To mitigate the effect of this decision, legislation as summarised in 39.11 below allows postponement of tax due in certain circumstances.

39.11   **Postponement of tax due from beneficiary in respect of settlement gains before 1981/82.** Under certain circumstances, the UK beneficiary of an overseas resident settlement who has been assessed under *CGTA 1979, s 17* to capital gains tax on trust gains arising before 6 April 1981 (see 39.10 above) may postpone payment of that tax, without incurring further INTEREST ON UNPAID TAX (32), until he or a *'close relative'* (i.e. spouse, child or remoter descendant) of his obtains some benefit from the trust.

For the rules to apply, the following conditions must be satisfied.

(*a*)   A chargeable gain accruing to an overseas resident settlement before 6 April 1981 falls within *CGTA 1979, s 17*.

(*b*)   Under *section 17* a beneficiary is assessed to capital gains tax on all or part of that gain for any year of assessment before 1984/85.

(*c*)   Any of the capital gains tax thereby due had not been paid at 29 March 1983.

A claim to postpone payment had to be made before 1 July 1985 or, if later, within 30 days of the date of issue of a notice of assessment requiring payment.

For full details of the relief see the 1984/85 edition of Tolley's Capital Gains Tax where full coverage is given of the relevant provisions viz. *FA 1984, s 70, 14 Sch* (which are preserved by *TCGA 1992, 11 Sch 18(b)*).

39.12   **UK RESIDENT COMPANY HAVING AN INTEREST IN A CONTROLLED FOREIGN COMPANY**

Legislation relating to controlled foreign companies ('CFC's') is contained in *ICTA 1988, ss 747–756, 24–26 Sch* (as amended). For full coverage of these provisions see Tolley's Corporation Tax under Controlled Foreign Companies. Broadly, the Board of Inland Revenue may direct that the provisions shall apply in relation to an accounting period beginning (or deemed to begin) after 5 April 1984 of a 'CFC'. A *'CFC'* is a company which is

(i)   resident outside the UK for the purposes of the provisions;

(ii)   'controlled' by persons resident in the UK; and

(iii)   subject to a 'lower level of taxation' in the territory in which it is 'resident'.

Following a direction, a UK resident company which has an 'interest' in the CFC at any time in the accounting period is then liable to be assessed to a sum as if it were corporation tax. Such sum is computed by multiplying the part of the 'chargeable profits' arising in an accounting period of the CFC that is proportionate to the interest held by the UK resident company and the 'appropriate rate' of UK corporation tax. The foregoing is subject to further detailed rules. See Tolley's Corporation Tax for these and the definitions assigned to the terms given above. Rules specifically relating to corporation tax on chargeable gains are given below.

(*a*)   **Gains on disposal of shares.** Relief may be claimed where

(i)   a direction is given in respect of a CFC's accounting period;

(ii)   a UK resident company (the *'claimant company'*) disposes of shares, acquired before the end of that accounting period, in either the CFC or another company whose shares give rise to the claimant company's interest in the CFC; and

(iii)   chargeable profits of the CFC are apportioned to the claimant company, and a sum is accordingly assessed on it as if it were corporation tax.

Where a claim is made, in the computation of the chargeable gain accruing on the disposal in (ii) above, a deduction is allowed of the sum assessed as in (iii) above, reduced to the proportion thereof that the average market value, in the period for which the direction was given, of the interest in the CFC in respect of which the charge as in (iii) above arose bears to the average market value in that period of the shares disposed of. A sum assessed as at (iii) above may only be relieved once in this way.

Relief may, however, be restricted where, before the disposal, a dividend is paid by the CFC out of profits from which the chargeable profits in (iii) above derived. If either

(1)   the effect of the payment of the dividend is to reduce the value of the shares disposed of as in (ii) above; or

(2)   the claimant company obtains relief (see (*b*) below) in respect of a dividend paid on the shares disposed of as in (ii) above, by reference to sums including that referred to in (iii) above,

then relief is denied in respect of so much of the sum assessed as corresponds to the part of the chargeable profits in (iii) above corresponding to the profits which the dividend represents.

Claims for relief must be made within three months of the later of the end of the accounting period in which the disposal occurs and the date the assessment in (iii) above becomes final and conclusive.

Identification of shares disposed of for this purpose is with those acquired earlier before those acquired later. [*ICTA 1988, 26 Sch 3*].

(*b*)   **Dividends from the CFC.** The total of assessments on UK resident companies under the provisions in respect of a CFC's chargeable profits (the *'gross attributed tax'*) is treated as underlying tax for double taxation relief purposes (see Tolley's Corporation Tax under Double Taxation Relief) where a dividend is paid by the

CFC wholly or partly out of profits from which those chargeable profits derive. The gross attributed tax is *not*, however, treated as increasing the amount of the dividend income in determining liability on that income.

If *ICTA 1988, s 796* or *797(1)* act to limit the foreign tax credit by reference to the UK tax on the dividends concerned, the amount so debarred from relief, insofar as it does not exceed the foreign tax *other than* underlying tax attributable to the dividend, is set against the gross attributed tax assessed on UK resident companies. On a claim by any of those companies, the tax so assessed on it is reduced and, if appropriate, repaid.

Any condition for double tax relief under *ICTA 1988, ss 788* or *789* (by agreement with other countries) or *s 790* (unilateral relief) (see 17 DOUBLE TAX RELIEF) requiring a particular degree of control of the company paying the dividend is treated as satisfied for these purposes.

Where the CFC dividend is paid out of unspecified profits, and any part of its chargeable profits is apportioned other than to UK resident companies, the gross attributed tax is attributed to the proportion of the chargeable profits apportioned to UK resident companies (the *'taxed profits'*). So much of the dividend as is received by, or by a 'successor in title' of, any such company is regarded as paid primarily out of the taxed profits. *'Successor in title'* for this purpose refers to a successor in respect of the whole or part of the interest in the CFC giving rise to a charge under these provisions.

If

(i) relief has been allowed for the purposes of corporation tax on chargeable gains, on a disposal of shares, in respect of a sum assessed under these provisions (see (*a*) above); and

(ii) that sum forms part of the gross attributed tax in relation to a dividend, as above; and

(iii) a person receiving the dividend in respect of the shares referred to in (i) above (the *'primary dividend'*), or any other dividend in respect of shares in a company resident outside the UK representing profits consisting directly or indirectly of or including the primary dividend, is entitled to relief by way of underlying tax (as above) by reference to the whole or part of the gross attributed tax,

then the relief available as in (iii) above is reduced or extinguished by deducting therefrom the amount allowed by way of relief as in (i) above. [*ICTA 1988, 26 Sch 4-6*].

39.13   **OFFSHORE FUNDS**

For disposals after 31 December 1983 'offshore income gains' arising out of certain interests in 'offshore funds' which are considered not to distribute sufficient income are charged to income tax or corporation tax under Schedule D, Case VI rather than to capital gains tax or corporation tax in respect of chargeable gains. Broadly, a capital gains tax treatment applies to any part of such a gain accruing before 1 January 1984 but the whole of the gain arising thereafter (without indexation allowance) is taxed as income. [*ICTA 1988, ss 437(2)(a), 441, 660B(4), 757-764, 27-28 Sch; FA 1990, 7 Sch 3; FA 1995, 17 Sch 1*]. Interests held were identified under the rules applicable to securities generally before 6 April 1985 (1 April 1985 for companies). After 5 April 1985 (31 March 1985 for companies) interests are designated 'relevant securities' and amended identification rules apply. See 23.12 INDEXATION. See Tolley's Income Tax under

Overseas Matters for general coverage and definitions assigned to terms used in the provisions. Rules relating to capital gains tax are given below.

Deduction of offshore income gain in determining capital gain. There are provisions in substitution of *TCGA 1992, s 37(1)* (deduction of consideration chargeable to tax on income) to prevent a double charge to tax when a disposal gives rise to both an offshore income gain and a chargeable gain for capital gains tax purposes.

(i)   Where an offshore income gain arises on a 'material disposal' that gain is deducted from the sum which would otherwise constitute the amount or value of the consideration in the calculation of the capital gain arising under *TCGA 1992* although the offshore gain is not to be deducted in calculating the figure 'A' in the A/(A + B) fraction under the rules relating to part disposal. See 16.6 DISPOSAL.

(ii)   Where a capital gains tax disposal forms part of a transfer within *TCGA 1992, s 162* (see 22.7 HOLD-OVER RELIEFS) the offshore income gain is taken into account to reduce 'B' in the A/B fraction determined under those provisions.

(iii)   Where a reorganisation of shares or securities (see 53.5 SHARES AND SECURITIES) constitutes a disposal of an interest in an offshore fund the amount of any offshore income gain to which the disposal gives rise is treated as consideration for the new holding.

[ICTA 1988, s 763(1)-(6)].

39.14   **UK RESIDENT COMPANY TRANSFERRING ASSETS TO OVERSEAS RESIDENT COMPANY**

Where, after 28 March 1977, a UK resident company carrying on a trade (which includes vocations, offices and employments) outside the UK through a branch or agency transfers the whole or part of that trade together with its assets, or its assets other than cash, to a company not resident in the UK in exchange, wholly or partly, for shares (or shares and loan stock) in that company, so that thereafter it holds one quarter or more of the transferee company's ordinary share capital, and the chargeable gains on the transfer exceed the allowable losses, a proportion of the resulting net chargeable gains relating to the shares (in the proportion that the market value of the shares at the time of the transfer bears to the market value of the whole consideration received) may be claimed by the transferor company as being deferred and not treated as arising until the happening of one of the following events.

(i)   The transferor company disposes of all or any of the shares received. The 'appropriate proportion' of the deferred gain (insofar as not already charged under this specific provision or under (ii) below) is then added to the consideration received on the disposal. The '*appropriate proportion*' is the proportion which the market value of the shares disposed of bears to the market value of the shares held immediately before the disposal. However, where the disposal of the shares received occurs after 5 April 1988 no addition to the consideration is made under this provision if its application would be directly attributable to the disposal of an asset before 1 April 1982.

(ii)   The transferee company disposes, within six years of the transfer, of the whole or part of the assets on which chargeable gains were deferred. The gain chargeable (insofar as it has not already been charged under this provision, or under (i) above) is the proportion which the deferred gain on the assets disposed of bears to the total deferred gain on assets held immediately before the disposal.

For the purposes of (i) and (ii) above, intra-group transfers are disregarded (including for (ii), those to overseas resident companies which would otherwise qualify under

TCGA 1992, s 171; see 13.11 COMPANIES) and a charge will arise when a subsequent group company makes a disposal outside the group. A claim under *TCGA 1992, s 140C* (transfer of non-UK trade between different EC member States; see 39.16 below) as regards a transfer precludes a claim under the above.

Prior to 29 March 1977, the chargeable gain on any asset transferred as above (in similar proportion) was deferred (without claim) for ten years after the transfer, or, if earlier, until

(*a*)   the transferor company was wound up, or disposed of all or any of the shares received (other than by intra-group transfer under *TCGA 1992, s 171*); or

(*b*)   the transferee company was wound up, or disposed or partly disposed of that asset or ceased to use it.

Where, under the earlier provisions, there were deferred chargeable gains at 29 March 1977, the provisions under (i) and (ii) above will apply for their subsequent charge. [*TCGA 1992, s 140, 4 Sch 4(5); F(No 2)A 1992, s 46(4)*].

Insurance companies. Where, after 28 March 1977, a UK resident insurance company (i.e. not confined to life assurance companies) transfers its foreign branch or agency business and assets to an overseas company in exchange wholly or partly for shares in that company in circumstances corresponding to those set out above any profit or loss on the assets transferred which would otherwise be included in the computation of profits or losses under Schedule D, Case I will be disregarded for that purpose (otherwise than in restricting management expenses under *ICTA 1988, s 76(2)*) and treated as chargeable gains or allowable losses. Any net chargeable gain may then be deferred as given above. [*ICTA 1988, s 442(1)-(3)*]. *ICTA 1988, s 442(3)* is ignored in calculating any relief given under *TCGA 1992, s 140C* (transfer of non-UK trade between different EC member States; see 39.16 below). [*TCGA 1992, s 140C(8); F(No 2)A 1992, s 45*].

39.15   **TRANSFER OF UK TRADE BETWEEN COMPANIES IN DIFFERENT EC MEMBER STATES**

A special relief may be claimed where, **after 31 December 1991**, a 'qualifying company' resident in one EC member State transfers the whole or part of a trade carried on by it in the UK to a qualifying company resident in another member State wholly in exchange for securities (including shares) in the latter company, provided that certain conditions (see below) are met. On such a claim made by both companies (under *TCGA 1992, s 140A*), any assets included in the transfer are treated for the purposes of corporation tax on chargeable gains as transferred for a no gain/no loss consideration, and *TCGA 1992, s 25(3)* (deemed disposal by non-resident on ceasing to trade in the UK through a branch or agency, see 39.3 above) does not apply to the assets by reason of the transfer.

A '*qualifying company*' is a body incorporated under the law of a member State.

A company is regarded for the above purposes as resident in a member State under the laws of which it is chargeable to tax because it is regarded as so resident (unless it is regarded under DOUBLE TAX RELIEF (17.2) arrangements entered into by the member State as resident in a territory not within any of the member States).

The conditions referred to above are:

(*a*)   (i)   if the transferee company is non-UK resident immediately after the transfer, any chargeable gain accruing to it on a disposal of the assets included in the transfer would form part of its corporation tax profits under *TCGA 1992, s 10(3)*, or

(ii)   if it is UK resident at that time, none of the assets included in the transfer is exempt from UK tax on disposal under double tax relief arrangements; and

(b)   the transfer is effected for *bona fide* commercial reasons and not as part of a scheme or arrangement a main purpose of which is avoidance of income, corporation or capital gains taxes.

Advance clearance in relation to (b) above may be obtained from the Board on the application of the companies, subject to the same conditions and appeal procedures as apply to clearances under *TCGA 1992, s 138* (see 3.13 ANTI-AVOIDANCE). [*TCGA 1992, ss 140A, 140B; F(No 2)A 1992, s 44*].

Prior to the commencement of *TCGA 1992*, claims were made under *ICTA 1970, s 269A*.

The above provisions were introduced to comply with EEC Directive No 90/434/EEC.

39.16   TRANSFER OF NON-UK TRADE BETWEEN COMPANIES IN DIFFERENT EC MEMBER STATES

Where, **after 31 December 1991**,

(a)   a 'qualifying company' resident in the UK transfers to a qualifying company resident in another member State the whole or part of a trade carried on by the UK company immediately before the transfer through a branch or agency in a member State other than the UK,

(b)   the transfer includes all the UK company's assets used in that trade or part (with the possible exception of cash),

(c)   the transfer is wholly or partly in exchange for securities (including shares) in the non-UK company,

(d)   the aggregate of the chargeable gains accruing to the UK company on the transfer exceeds the aggregate of the allowable losses so accruing, and

(e)   the transfer is effected for *bona fide* commercial reasons and not as part of a scheme or arrangement a main purpose of which is avoidance of income, corporation or capital gains taxes,

the UK company may claim that the transfer be treated as giving rise to a single chargeable gain of the excess at (d) above. No claim may, however, be made where a claim is made under *TCGA 1992, s 140* at 39.14 above in relation to the same transfer. As regards insurance companies, *ICTA 1988, s 442(3)* (also see 39.14 above) is ignored in arriving at the chargeable gains and allowable losses accruing on the transfer.

A '*qualifying company*' is a body incorporated under the law of a member State.

For the purposes of (a) above, a company is not regarded as resident in the UK if it is regarded under any DOUBLE TAX RELIEF (17.2) arrangements to which the UK is a party as resident in a territory not within any of the member States. A company is regarded as resident in another member State under the laws of which it is chargeable to tax because it is regarded as so resident (unless it is regarded under a double tax relief arrangement entered into by the member State as resident in a territory not within any of the member States).

Advance clearance in relation to (e) above may be obtained from the Board on the application of the UK company, subject to the same conditions and appeal procedures as apply to clearances under *TCGA 1992, s 138* (see 3.13 ANTI-AVOIDANCE). [*TCGA 1992, ss 140C, 140D; F(No 2)A 1992, s 45*].

Prior to the commencement of *TCGA 1992*, claims were made under *ICTA 1970, s 269C*.

The above provisions were introduced to comply with EEC Directive No 90/434/EEC.

Double tax relief. Where the above provisions apply, and the UK company produces to the inspector an 'appropriate certificate' from the tax authorities of the Member State in which the company carried on the trade immediately before the transfer, the amount stated in the certificate is treated for double tax relief purposes as tax paid in that other member State.

An *'appropriate certificate'* is one which states that gains accruing to the UK company on the transfer would, but for the Mergers Directive (*90/434/EEC*), have been chargeable to tax in the other member State, and which states the amount of tax which would, but for that Directive, have been payable in respect of the gains. The tax must be calculated after any permissible set-off of losses arising on the transfer and on the assumption that any available reliefs are claimed.

Where the UK company is unable to obtain an appropriate certificate and the Board is satisfied that this is the case, the company may make a claim to the Board to have the amount of tax computed which, in the opinion of the Board, would have been payable under the law of the relevant member State in respect of the gains accruing to it on the transfer but for the Mergers Directive. The company is required to provide such information and documents in connection with the claim as the Board may require. [*ICTA 1988, s 815A(3); F(No 2)A 1992, s 50*].

39.17 **COMPANY CEASING TO BE UK RESIDENT ETC., DUAL RESIDENT COMPANIES (BEFORE 30 NOVEMBER 1993) AND NON-RESIDENT COMPANIES**

Company ceasing to be UK resident etc. If, at any time (*'the relevant time'*) after 14 March 1988, a company ceases to be resident in the UK, except with Treasury consent under *ICTA 1988, s 765(1)(a)* on an application made before 15 March 1988, and does not cease to exist,

(*a*) it is deemed to dispose of, and immediately reacquire, all its 'assets' at market value, and

(*b*) ROLLOVER RELIEF (50) under *TCGA 1992, s 152* is not subsequently available by reference to disposals of old 'assets' made before the relevant time.

If at any later time the company carries on a trade in the UK through a branch or agency (as defined in 39.3 above), the foregoing does not apply

(i) for (*a*) above, to any assets which, immediately after the relevant time, or

(ii) for (*b*) above, to any new assets which, after the relevant time,

are situated in the UK and are used in or for a trade, or are used or held for the branch or agency. *'Assets'* include various assets and rights relating to exploration or exploitation activities in the UK or a designated area of the sea, within *TCGA 1992, s 276* in 39.19 below. [*TCGA 1992, s 185*].

Where the company concerned ceases to be resident in the UK on 30 November 1993 solely by virtue of the coming into force of *FA 1994, s 249* (companies otherwise regarded as UK resident but under double tax relief arrangements already regarded as non-UK resident to be treated as non-UK resident for *Taxes Acts* purposes after 29 November 1993; see 47.5 RESIDENCE AND DOMICILE) and a deemed disposal under (*a*) above occurs, further provisions apply. Where an actual disposal of the assets is made on or before the day when corporation tax would otherwise be due and payable in respect of the deemed disposal, the tax is due and payable on that day; otherwise the tax is due and payable on the earlier of the day the assets are actually disposed of and 30 November 1999. Interest on unpaid tax in respect of the deemed disposal will only run from the due and payable date as determined above. If an actual part disposal of the assets is made, these further provisions are applied separately to the different parts, and the tax apportioned (and carrying interest) accordingly. [*FA 1994, s 250(3)–(6)*].

Where, at any time after 14 March 1988 and before 30 November 1993 (the latter date being the date of the coming into force of *FA 1994, s 249* above), a company, while continuing to be UK resident, commenced to be regarded, for the purposes of any DOUBLE TAX RELIEF 17.2 arrangements, as resident in a territory outside the UK, and as not liable to UK tax on gains on disposals of assets specified in those arrangements, (*a*) and (*b*) above applied to those assets. [*TCGA 1992, s 186; FA 1994, s 251(1)(9), 26 Sch Pt VIII*].

If the deemed disposal described in paragraph (*a*) above includes any '*foreign assets*' (i.e. assets which are situated, and are used in or for a trade carried on, outside the UK), any charge to tax will be postponed, as described below, if

(A)   immediately after the relevant time the company was a '75% subsidiary' (see below) of a company ('*the principal company*') which was resident in the UK, and

(B)   both companies elect in writing within two years after that time.

The excess of gains over losses arising on the foreign assets included in the deemed disposal is treated as a single chargeable gain not accruing to the company on the disposal. An equal amount ('*the postponed gain*') is instead treated as follows.

If within six years after the relevant time the company disposes of any assets (the '*relevant assets*') capital gains on which were taken into account in arriving at the postponed gain, a chargeable gain equal to the whole, or 'the appropriate proportion', of the postponed gain, so far as this has not already been treated as a chargeable gain under these provisions, is deemed to accrue to the principal company. '*The appropriate proportion*' is the proportion which the chargeable gain taken into account in arriving at the postponed gain in respect of the part of the relevant assets disposed of bears to the aggregate of the chargeable gains so taken into account in respect of the relevant assets held immediately before the time of the disposal.

If at any time

(I)   the company ceases to be a 75% subsidiary of the principal company on a disposal by the principal company of ordinary shares in it, or

(II)   after the company otherwise ceases to be a 75% subsidiary, the principal company disposes of ordinary shares in it, or

(III)   the principal company ceases to be resident in the UK,

a chargeable gain, equal to so much of the postponed gain as has not previously been charged under these provisions, is deemed to arise.

If any part of the postponed gain becomes chargeable, and the subsidiary has unrelieved capital losses, the companies can elect within two years for part or all of the losses to be set against the amount chargeable.

For the purposes of the above provisions a company is a '*75% subsidiary*' of another company if and so long as not less than 75% of its ordinary share capital is owned *directly* by that other company. [*TCGA 1992, s 187; FA 1994, s 251(1)(9), 26 Sch Pt VIII*].

Dual resident companies. Where, at any time after 14 March 1988 and before 30 November 1993 (the latter date being the date of the coming into force of *FA 1994, s 249* above), an asset of a 'dual resident company' became a 'prescribed asset', the company was deemed immediately before that time to have disposed of and immediately reacquired it, both transactions being treated as carried out at the then market value. No deemed disposal and acquisition was to take place under this provision, however, where the asset became a prescribed asset on the company becoming to be regarded as a dual resident company as this already took place on such an event under *TCGA 1992, s 186* above. A company was a '*dual resident company*' if it was UK resident and fell to be regarded under any double tax relief arrangements as resident in another territory elsewhere. A '*prescribed asset*', in relation to a dual resident company, was an asset treated under any double tax relief arrangements as not giving rise to a UK tax charge on the company in respect of a gain arising on its disposal. [*TCGA 1992, s 188; FA 1994, s 251(1)(10), 26 Sch Pt VIII*].

Where either the disposal of the 'old assets' (or of the interest in them) or the acquisition of the 'new assets' is made (or the acquisition of the interest in them is made or the unconditional contract for their acquisition is entered into) (or both such events) occurred after 13 March 1989, then, if either such event occurred before 30 November 1993 (the latter date being the date of the coming into force of *FA 1994, s 249* above), ROLLOVER RELIEF (50) under *TCGA 1992, s 152* (the above quoted terms having the same meaning as in that provision) did not apply where a company was a 'dual resident company' (having the same meaning as in *TCGA 1992, s 188* above) at the time of disposal and at the time of acquisition, and the old assets were not 'prescribed assets' (defined as for in *TCGA 1992, s 188* above) at the time of disposal, unless the new assets were not prescribed assets immediately after the time of acquisition. However, rollover relief could apply where the acquisition of the new assets occurred before 14 March 1989 and the disposal of the old assets was after 13 March 1989 but within twelve months (or such longer period as is allowed by written notice given by the Board) of the acquisition of the new assets. [*TCGA 1992, s 160; FA 1994, s 251(1)(6), 26 Sch Pt VIII*].

39.18   **Company ceasing to be UK resident etc: compliance.** Before a company, after 14 March 1988, ceases to be resident in the UK, otherwise than with Treasury consent under *ICTA 1988, s 765(1)(a)*, it must give the Board

(*a*)   notice of its intention to cease to be resident, specifying the time when it intends to do so,

(*b*)   a statement of the amount of tax which it considers payable for periods beginning before that time, and

(*c*)   particulars of the arrangements which it proposes to make to secure the payment of that tax.

It must also make arrangements to secure the payment of that tax; and the arrangements must be approved by the Board.

References to tax payable are not defined but include specified liabilities such as certain income tax payments, sub-contractors' deductions and amounts payable under *FA 1973, 15 Sch 4* (territorial extension of charge of tax as in 39.19 below). Interest on unpaid tax is included in certain circumstances.

Any question as to the amount of tax payable is to be determined by the Special Commissioners. If any information provided by the company does not fully and accurately disclose all the material facts and considerations, any resulting approval is void. [*FA 1988, s 130*].

A person who is, or is deemed to be, involved in a failure to comply with the foregoing provisions is liable to a penalty not exceeding the amount of unpaid tax for periods beginning before the failure occurred. [*FA 1988, s 131*].

The requirements of *FA 1988, s 130* and the penalty that can be exacted under *FA 1988, s 131* above do not apply where the company concerned ceases to be resident in the UK on 30 November 1993 solely by virtue of the coming into force of *FA 1994, s 249* (companies otherwise regarded as UK resident but under double tax relief arrangements already regarded as non-UK resident to be treated as non-UK resident for *Taxes Acts* purposes after 29 November 1993; see 47.5 RESIDENCE AND DOMICILE). [*FA 1994, s 250(1)*].

Any tax in respect of accounting periods beginning before the cessation of UK residence which is still unpaid six months after the time when it became payable can (see also 39.17 above), within three years of final determination of the tax due, be recovered from a person who is, or in the twelve months before the cessation of UK residence (or, if less, the period after 14 March 1988) was, a member of the same group of companies (as in *TCGA 1992, s 170* but excluding any references to UK residence and substituting 51 per cent subsidiary for '75 per cent subsidiary') or a controlling director (as defined). [*FA 1988, s 132*].

Guidance on the procedure to be followed under these provisions is given in Revenue Pamphlet IR 131, SP 2/90. In particular, notice under (*a*) above should be sent to Inland Revenue, International Division (Company Migrations) (at Room 312, Melbourne House, Aldwych, London WC2B 4LL) to whom an initial enquiry may be made via the Inland Revenue Public Enquiry Room (Tel. 0171-438 6420/5).

Non-resident companies. Where a non-UK resident company makes a gain on the disposal after 13 March 1989 of an asset, the gain forms part of its chargeable profits for corporation tax purposes under *TCGA 1992, s 10(3)* (non-UK resident trading etc. in the UK, see 39.3 above), and any of the corporation tax assessed relating to the accounting period in which the gain accrued remains unpaid after six months from it becoming payable, then the unpaid tax (or an amount equal to corporation tax on the amount of the gain at the rate in force at the time when the gain accrued if lower) can be recovered by the Board within three years from the amount being determined from a person who is, or in the twelve months before the disposal occurred (or, if less, the period after 13 March 1989) was, a member of the same group of companies (as in *TCGA 1992, s 170* but excluding any references to UK residence and substituting '51 per cent subsidiary' for '75 per cent subsidiary') or a controlling director (as defined). [*TCGA 1992, s 191*].

39.19   **EXPLORATION AND EXPLOITATION RIGHTS TO TERRITORIAL SEA-BED AND CONTINENTAL SHELF**

Any gains accruing on the disposal of 'exploration or exploitation rights' are treated for the purposes of *TCGA 1992* as gains accruing on the disposal of assets situated in the UK. For this and all other purposes of the taxation of chargeable gains, the territorial sea of the UK is deemd to be part of the UK. (Under the *Territorial Sea Act 1987, s 1*, the breadth of the territorial sea adjacent to the UK is 12 nautical miles, a nautical mile being approximately 1,852 metres.)

Gains accruing on the disposal of 'exploration or exploitation assets' which are situated in a 'designated area', or 'unquoted shares' (i.e. not quoted on a recognised stock exchange) deriving their value or the greater part of their value directly or indirectly from exploration or exploitation assets situated in the UK or a designated area or from such assets and exploration or exploitation rights taken together, are treated for the purposes of *TCGA 1992* as gains accruing on the disposal of assets situated in the UK. Gains accruing to a person not resident in the UK on the disposal of such rights or of such assets (the latter including for this purpose unquoted shares of the description above) are treated for the same purposes as gains accruing on the disposal of assets used for the purposes of a trade carried on by that person in the UK through a branch or agency (for which see 39.3 above).

If exploration or exploitation rights or exploration or exploitation assets (the latter including for this purpose unquoted shares of the description above) are disposed of by a company resident in an overseas territory to a company resident in the same territory or a UK resident company, *TCGA 1992, ss 171–174, 178–181* are applied as if *TCGA 1992, s 170* excluded the requirement for a company to be UK resident (see generally 13.10–13.12 and 13.4 COMPANIES and 39.3 above).

'Exploration or exploitation rights' means rights to assets to be produced by 'exploration or exploitation activities' or to interests in or to the benefit of such assets. *'Exploration or exploitation activities'* means activities carried on in connection with the exploration or exploitation of so much of the seabed and subsoil and their natural resources as is situated in the UK or a designated area.

References in the above to the disposal of exploration or exploitation rights include references to the disposals of shares' deriving their value or the greater part of their value directly or indirectly from such rights, other than shares quoted on a recognised stock exchange. *'Shares'* includes stock and any security as defined in *ICTA 1988, s 254(1)*. *'Designated area'* means an area designated by Order in Council under the *Continental Shelf Act 1964, s 1(7)*.

For the above purposes, an asset disposed of is an *'exploration or exploitation asset'* if either

(*a*)   it is not a mobile asset and it is being or has at some time (for disposals before 14 March 1989, being a time within the period of two years ending at the date of disposal) been used in connection with exploration or exploitation activities carried on in the UK or a designated area; or

(*b*)   it is a mobile asset which has at some time (for disposals before 14 March 1989, being a time within the period of two years ending at the date of disposal) been used in connection with exploration or exploitation activities so carried on and is dedicated to an oil field in which the person making the disposal, or a person connected with him, is or has been a participator;

and expressions used in (*a*) and (*b*) above have the same meanings there as if those paragraphs were included in *Oil Taxation Act 1975, Pt I. [TCGA 1992, s 276; FA 1989, ss 130, 17 Sch Pt VII]*.

There are comprehensive information and enforcement powers in relation to tax assessed by virtue of *TCGA 1992, s 276* above. In particular, unpaid tax so assessed on an overseas resident person may be recovered together with interest thereon from the holder of a licence granted under *Petroleum (Production) Act 1934* in respect of chargeable gains accruing on the disposal of exploration or exploitation rights connected with activities authorised, or carried on in connection with activities authorised, by the licence. An overseas resident liable to charge and who the Board are satisfied will meet his obligations under the *Taxes Acts* may apply for a certificate to be issued to the licence holder exempting him (subject to detailed conditions) from a charge on the default of the applicant. *[FA 1973, s 38(2)(8), 15 Sch]*.

Where an 'exploration or exploitation asset' (for this purpose, an asset used in connection with 'exploration or exploitation activities' carried on in the UK or a 'designated area', both expressions having the same meanings as in *TCGA 1992, s 276* above) ceases to be 'chargeable' in relation to a person by virtue of ceasing after 13 March 1989 to be 'dedicated to an oil field' in which he, or a person connected with him, is or has been a 'participator' (these last two expressions having the same meanings as in *Oil Taxation Act 1975, Pt I*), he is deemed for all purposes of *TCGA 1992* to have disposed of the asset immediately before the time when it ceased to be so dedicated, and immediately to have reacquired it, at its market value at that time.

An asset is a *'chargeable'* asset at any time in relation to a person if, were it to be disposed of at that time, any chargeable gains accruing to him on the disposal would be brought into charge for capital gains tax or corporation tax by virtue of *TCGA 1992, s 10(1)* or *(3)* respectively.

A similar deemed disposal and acquisition takes place where a person who is not resident or ordinarily resident ceases after 13 March 1989 to carry on a trade through a branch or agency in respect of any exploration or exploitation asset, other than a mobile asset, used in or for the purposes of the trade at or before the time of the deemed disposal. No such deemed disposal and reacquisition takes place if, immediately after the cessation of the trade carried on through the UK branch or agency, the asset is used in or for the purposes of exploration or exploitation activities carried on by him in the UK or a designated area. However, on a person ceasing after 13 March 1989 so to use the asset, there will be a deemed disposal and reacquisition. [*TCGA 1992, s 199*].

As regards leasing of mobile drilling rigs and other assets by overseas resident companies, see Revenue Pamphlet IR 131, SP 6/84, 31 July 1984.

See also 47.8 RESIDENCE AND DOMICILE for the territorial extent of the UK.

39.20 EUROPEAN ECONOMIC INTEREST GROUPINGS

With retrospective effect after 30 June 1989, new provisions are introduced governing the tax treatment of European Economic Interest Groupings ('groupings'), wherever registered, within *EEC Council Regulation No 2137/85* dated 25 July 1985. For the purposes of charging tax in respect of gains and subject to exceptions as below, a grouping is regarded as acting as the agent of its members. Its activities are regarded for such purposes as those of its members acting jointly, each member being regarded as having a share of its property, rights and liabilities, and a person is regarded as acquiring or disposing of a share of its assets not only where there is an acquisition or disposal by it while he is a member but also where he becomes or ceases to be a member or there is a change in his share of its property. A member's share in a grouping's property, rights or liabilities is that determined under the contract establishing the grouping or, if there is no provision determining such shares, it will correspond to the profit share to which he is entitled under the provisions of the contract (or if the contract makes no such provision, members are regarded as having equal shares). Where the grouping carries on a trade or profession, the members are regarded for the purposes of tax on gains as carrying on that trade or profession in partnership.

There are also provisions regarding requirements to make a return in connection with the above provisions, penalties for failure to make such a return and the making of back duty assessments. [*ICTA 1988, s 510A; FA 1990, s 69, 11 Sch*].

The EEC provision of 25 July 1985 mentioned above covers all groupings established within the European Economic Area on the coming into force of the European Economic Area Agreement on 1 January 1994 (Revenue Press Release 9 February 1994).

39.21   COLLECTION OF TAX

Although tax is legally assessable by notice served abroad, there are difficulties in collection. The UK courts will not enforce the revenue laws of other countries, see *Government of India v Taylor (re Delhi Electric Supply & Traction Co. Ltd) HL*, *[1955] AC 491* and *Brokaw v Seatrain UK Ltd, CA, [1971] 2 All E R 98*. See also 39.3 above for the assessment of UK resident agents of overseas resident traders, 39.6 for the arrangements where trustees become non-resident and 39.18 above for arrangements required to secure payment of tax by a company ceasing to be UK resident or by a non-UK resident company.

40 Partnerships

Cross-references. See 39.20 OVERSEAS MATTERS for European Economic Interest Groupings deemed to carry on a trade in partnership; 48 RETIREMENT RELIEF; 49 RETURNS for returns by partnerships; and 50 ROLLOVER RELIEF.

40.1   A partnership is defined in *Partnership Act 1890, s 1* as 'the relation which subsists between persons carrying on a business in common with a view of profit'. This does not include purely capital transactions, e.g. the sale of a house by joint tenants.

40.2   An English partnership or firm is not a legal entity distinct from the partners themselves, but a collection of separate persons (which may be companies or individuals). In Scotland a firm is a legal person, but in general this does not affect the application of the *Taxes Acts*. A partnership cannot be a company for the purposes of *TCGA 1992*. [*TCGA 1992, s 288(1)*].

40.3   The taxation of partnership gains is based on a body of Revenue practice superimposed on the general capital gains rules. There are few specific references to partnerships in the capital gains legislation. For a useful codification of Revenue practice, following discussions with the Law Society and the Allied Accountancy Bodies, reference should be made to the Revenue Statements of Practice set out in Revenue Press Releases dated 17 January 1975 and 12 January 1979 (see 29.D12, SP 1/79 and SP 1/89 INLAND REVENUE STATEMENTS OF PRACTICE) on which much of this chapter is based. See also 29.D5, 29.D11 INLAND REVENUE STATEMENTS OF PRACTICE regarding retirement relief and rollover relief respectively.

Unless otherwise stated paragraph references in the remainder of this chapter are to Statement of Practice D12.

40.4   **TREATMENT AND ASSESSMENT GENERALLY**

Where two or more persons carry on a trade or business in partnership, tax is assessed and charged on them separately in respect of chargeable gains accruing to them on the disposal of any partnership assets. (The treatment of partnerships in Scotland as a legal person is ignored for this purpose.) Any partnership dealings are treated as dealings by the partners and not by the firm as such. [*TCGA 1992, s 59(a)(b)*].

An income tax provision, *ICTA 1988, s 112(1)(2)* (partnerships controlled abroad), is also applied for the purposes of *TCGA 1992*. [*TCGA 1992, s 59(c)*]. The rules, as applied, are by no means clear in their treatment of residence as regards partnerships controlled abroad. The interpretation believed to be held by the Revenue is that they have no effect as regards partners *per se* because of the separate assessment and charging procedure of capital gains tax given above. If this is so, it will be the circumstances of the partner alone that will dictate the basis of charge, e.g. a partner who is UK-resident or ordinarily resident and UK-domiciled will be assessable wherever partnership gains arise and whether remitted to the UK or not. A partner neither resident nor ordinarily resident in the UK would only be liable in respect of partnership assets under *TCGA 1992, s 10* (UK branch or agency; see 39.3 OVERSEAS MATTERS). Further to the foregoing, it is specifically provided that, if, under a double tax agreement, any income or capital gains of a partnership residing, or deemed to reside, outside the UK is relieved from tax in the UK, such relief is not to affect the liability of any UK resident partner's share (including the share attributed to a company which is a partner) of the income or capital gains. Such treatment is always deemed to have applied, except as regards

(*a*)   any Commissioners' determination or the judgment of any court made or given before 17 March 1987; or

(*b*)   the law applicable in an appeal to the Court of Appeal or House of Lords where the judgment of the High Court or the Court of Session which is in issue was given before that date.

[*ICTA 1988, ss 112(4), 115(5)*]. Where applicable this provision overrules *Padmore v CIR CA 1989, 62 TC 352.*

Each partner is regarded as owning a fractional share of each asset which is calculated by reference to his asset-surplus-sharing ratio. Where no such ratio is specified, the share will follow the treatment in the accounts, subject to any external agreement. Failing that, regard will be had to the normal profit-sharing ratios. For appeals regarding apportionments of amounts etc., see 4 APPEALS.

The fraction is applied to the value of the total partnership interest in the asset disposed of, and no discount is allowed against market value for the size of an individual partner's share.

Expenditure on the acquisition of partnership assets will be allocated for capital gains tax purposes, in similar fashion to gains/losses, at the time of acquisition, subject to adjustment on any subsequent change in partnership sharing ratios (*paragraphs 1 and 2*).

Examples

Each of the following partnerships disposes of its offices to outside parties at arm's length at a chargeable gain of £30,000. No reliefs (e.g. rollover) are otherwise claimed. The gain is apportioned among the partners in the manner shown.

(*a*)   *A & Co.* The partnership agreement states that each of the three partners shall be entitled to share equally in any surplus arising from assets disposed of by the partnership. Each partner is therefore treated as if he had made a gain of £10,000.

(*b*)   *B & Co.* The three partners in B & Co have no formal agreement, but interest on capital contributed to the partnership is shown in the accounts at the same sum for each. The inference is that the capital has been equally contributed and can be equally withdrawn, so that the apportioned gain is £10,000 to each partner.

(*c*)   *C & Co.* The three partners in C & Co, X, Y, and Z, have no formal agreement and the capital is shown in the accounts as a global sum. The profit-sharing ratio is 3:2:1, so that the apportioned gain is X-£15,000, Y-£10,000, and Z-£5,000.

40.5   CHANGES IN SHARING RATIOS

Where changes occur in partnership sharing ratios (including partners joining or leaving the firm), each partner is treated as acquiring or disposing of part or the whole of a share in each of the partnership assets, insofar as his share increases or decreases. Subject to certain qualifications (see below) the disposal consideration of each chargeable asset is regarded as being equal to the relevant fraction of the *current balance sheet value*. The balance sheet value could therefore be less than, equal to (i.e. on a no loss/no gain basis subject to any indexation allowance as below), or more than the cost for capital gains tax purposes, depending on what adjustments, if any, have been made in the accounts since acquisition of the assets. The cost of any part disposal under these provisions is calculated as a corresponding fraction of the total acquisition cost, and not by way of apportionment under *TCGA 1992, s 42* as in 16.6 DISPOSAL (*paragraph 4*).

40.5 Partnerships

A figure other than balance sheet value may have to be used in the following cases.

(a) Where a direct payment is made in connection with the change in sharing ratios (see 40.7 below).

(b) Where the change in sharing ratios results from a transaction made otherwise than at arm's length or made between CONNECTED PERSONS (14). The meaning of connected persons for these purposes is narrowed. See 40.10 below.

Re-basing to 1982, deferred charges and indexation allowance. The Revenue have agreed that a disposal of a share of partnership assets which is treated under *paragraph 4* above as on a no gain/no loss basis (before indexation, for disposals before 6 April 1988) may be treated as if it were a no gain/no loss disposal within *TCGA 1992, s 35(3)(d)* (see 8.7 ASSETS HELD ON 31 MARCH 1982). Such a disposal may also be treated as if it were a no gain/no loss disposal within that provision for the purposes of *TCGA 1992, s 36, 4 Sch* (deferred charges; see 8.12 ASSETS HELD ON 31 MARCH 1982). Where such a disposal occurs after 5 April 1988, the amount of the consideration will be calculated on the assumption that an unindexed gain will accrue to the transferor equal to the indexation allowance, so that after taking into account the indexation allowance due, neither a gain nor a loss accrues. Where under the above a partner is treated as having owned the asset on 31 March 1982 in relation to a disposal after 5 April 1988 of all or part of his share of partnership assets, the indexation allowance on the disposal may be calculated as if he had acquired the share on 31 March 1982. A disposal of a share in a partnership asset after 30 March 1982 which is treated under *paragraph 4* above as on a no gain/no loss basis may be treated for the purposes of *TCGA 1992, s 55(5)(6)* as if it were a no gain/no loss disposal within those provisions (see 8.7 ASSETS HELD ON 31 MARCH 1982). A special rule will however apply where the share changed hands after 5 April 1985 (31 March 1985 in the case of an acquisition from a company) and before 6 April 1988: in these circumstances the indexation allowance will be calculated by reference to the 31 March 1982 value *but* from the date of the last disposal of the share before 6 April 1988 (Revenue Pamphlet IR 131, SP 1/89, 1 February 1989). This practice should be read in the light of the changes made regarding indexation allowance for disposals on or after 30 November 1993.

Example

J and K have traded in partnership for several years, sharing capital and income equally. The acquisition costs and 31 March 1982 values of the chargeable assets of the firm are as follows

	Cost	31.3.82 value
	£	£
Premises	60,000	150,000
Goodwill	10,000	50,000

The assets have not been revalued in the firm's balance sheet. On 1 June 1995, J and K admit L to the partnership, and the sharing ratio is J 35%, K 45% and L 20%. The indexation factor for March 1982 to June 1995 is assumed to be 0.824.

J and K are regarded as disposing of part of their interest in the firm's assets to L as follows

	£	£
J		
Premises		
Deemed consideration		
£60,000 × (50% − 35%)	9,000	
Add indexation allowance (see below)	18,540	
Total deemed consideration	27,540	
Allowable cost	9,000	
Unindexed gain	18,540	
Indexation allowance (50% − 35%) × £150,000 × 0.824	18,540	—
Goodwill		
Deemed consideration		
£10,000 × (50% – 35%)	1,500	
Add indexation allowance (see below)	6,180	
Total deemed consideration	7,680	
Allowable cost	1,500	
Unindexed gain	6,180	
Indexation allowance (50% − 35%) × £50,000 × 0.824	6,180	—
Chargeable gain/allowable loss		Nil
K		
Premises		
Deemed consideration		
£60,000 × (50% − 45%)	3,000	
Add indexation allowance (see below)	6,180	
Total deemed consideration	9,180	
Allowable cost	3,000	
Unindexed gain	6,180	
Indexation allowance (50% − 45%) × £150,000 × 0.824	6,180	—
Goodwill		
Deemed consideration		
£10,000 × (50% − 45%)	500	
Add indexation allowance (see below)	2,060	
Total deemed consideration	2,560	
Allowable cost	500	
Unindexed gain	2,060	
Indexation allowance (50% − 45%) × £50,000 × 0.824	2,060	—
Chargeable gain/allowable loss		Nil

The allowable costs (inclusive, in L's case, of indexation allowance to June 1995) of the three partners are now

		Freehold land £	Goodwill £
J		21,000	3,500
K		27,000	4,500
L	note *(b)*	36,720	10,240

40.6 Partnerships

Notes to the example

(a) The treatment illustrated above is taken from Revenue Pamphlet IR 131, SP D12 (17.1.75), para. 4 as extended by SP 1/89. Each partner's disposal consideration is equal to his share of current balance sheet value of the asset concerned plus, for disposals after 5 April 1988, indexation allowance, and each disposal treated as producing no gain and no loss.

(b) L's allowable costs comprise 20% of original cost, plus indexation allowance to date based on 20% of 31 March 1982 value.

General rules. Where a partner is treated as making a disposal it may also qualify for HOLD-OVER RELIEFS (22), RETIREMENT RELIEF (48) or ROLLOVER RELIEF (50). As regards an acquisition, this may be used to cover a chargeable gain as in ROLLOVER RELIEF (50). A partner treated as disposing of a partnership asset (or share) seems to be able to roll over any chargeable gain arising against an acquisition in another trade carried on, whether as sole trader or in another partnership trade, and vice versa.

40.6 ACCOUNTING ADJUSTMENTS

An upward revaluation of a partnership asset with the consequent credit to a partner's current or capital account does not give rise to a chargeable gain, but if after such a revaluation, a change occurs in a partner's sharing ratio (see 40.5 above), the disposal which he is thereby treated as making takes place at the increased value and may therefore give rise to a chargeable gain. Any acquisition is similarly treated.

Examples (ignoring indexation)

(a) X, Y and Z are partners in D & Co and share both capital and income profits and losses in the ratio 3:2:1. X wishes to take a less active part in the business, and Z to devote more time to it. The asset-surplus-sharing ratio is then amended to 2:2:2. X is treated as having disposed of a one-sixth interest in each chargeable asset belonging to the partnership for a consideration equal to one-sixth of their respective book values, and Z as having acquired that interest for the same consideration.

(b) The facts are as (a) above, save that before the ratio is altered, the partnership premises are written up in the books from £120,000 to £180,000. No charge arises on this occasion. On the change in sharing ratio, however, X is treated as having made a gross or unindexed gain of £10,000 (one-sixth of the book gain) and this forms part of Z's acquisition cost.

A downward revaluation, even if following an upward revaluation, is similarly not treated as giving rise to an allowable loss, but a change in partnership shares following such a revaluation may do so (*paragraph 5*).

40.7 CONSIDERATION OUTSIDE THE ACCOUNTS

Where actual consideration is given in connection with an alteration in partnership sharing ratios (see 40.5 above), it is added to the consideration deemed to have been received under the rules in 40.5 and 40.6 above, and may therefore give rise to a chargeable gain or increased gain, the payer's acquisition cost being adjusted accordingly. Where such an extraneous payment is expressed to be in respect of goodwill not included in the balance sheet, it is only deductible by the payer from a subsequent disposal (including a reduction in his share) of the goodwill, or on the payer's leaving the partnership (*paragraph 6*). It is understood that the Revenue do not accept that the writing down to nil of the value of goodwill by a professional partnership is able to form the basis of a 'negligible value' loss claim (see 35.8 LOSSES) by a partner who has previously given consideration for goodwill.

Example

D, E and F are partners in a firm of accountants who share all profits in the ratio 7:7:6. G is admitted as a partner in May 1995 and pays the other partners £10,000 for goodwill. The new partnership shares are D $\frac{3}{10}$, E $\frac{3}{10}$, F $\frac{1}{4}$ and G $\frac{3}{20}$. The book value of goodwill is £18,000, its cost on acquisition of the practice from the predecessor in 1985.

The partners are treated as having disposed of shares in goodwill as follows

D	£	£
$\frac{7}{20} - \frac{3}{10} = \frac{1}{20}$		
Disposal consideration		
Notional $\frac{1}{20} \times$ £18,000	900	
Actual $\frac{7}{20} \times$ £10,000	3,500	
		4,400
Allowable cost $\frac{1}{20} \times$ £18,000		900
Unindexed gain		£3,500

E		
$\frac{7}{20} - \frac{3}{10} = \frac{1}{20}$		
Disposal consideration (as for D)		4,400
Allowable cost (as for D)		900
Unindexed gain		£3,500

F		
$\frac{6}{20} - \frac{1}{4} = \frac{1}{20}$		
Disposal consideration		
Notional $\frac{1}{20} \times$ £18,000	900	
Actual $\frac{6}{20} \times$ £10,000	3,000	
		3,900
Allowable cost		900
Unindexed gain		£3,000

G's allowable cost of his share of goodwill is therefore	
Actual consideration paid	10,000
Notional consideration paid $\frac{3}{20} \times$ £18,000	2,700
	£12,700

Note to the example

(*a*)   In practice, the above calculations must be adjusted for indexation allowance which is added to the notional consideration and deducted from the unindexed gain (see *Example* at 40.5 above).

40.8   **ANNUAL PAYMENTS**

Insofar as **annual payments** (whether under covenant or not) **to a retired partner** exceed an amount regarded as reasonable in view of the partner's past work for the firm, the capitalised value of the annuity is treated as consideration for the disposal of his partnership share (and as allowable expenditure by the remaining partners). If he had been a partner for at least ten years, the maximum 'reasonable' annuity is two-thirds of his average share of the partnership profits (before capital allowances or charges on income) in the best three of the last seven years in which he was required to devote substantially the whole of his time to the partnership. The ten-year period includes any period during which the partner was a member of another firm which has been merged with the existing firm. For periods less than ten years, the relevant fractions are as follows.

Complete years	Fraction
1-5	1/60 for each year
6	8/60
7	16/60
8	24/60
9	32/60

This treatment applies to certain cases in which a lump sum is paid as well as the annuity (*paragraph 8*). Where the aggregate of the annuity and one-ninth of the lump sum does not exceed the appropriate fraction of the retired partner's average share of the profits (as above), the capitalised value is not treated as consideration in his hands. The lump sum continues to be treated as consideration (Revenue Pamphlet IR 131, SP 1/79, 12 January 1979).

40.9   **SHARES ACQUIRED IN STAGES**

Position before 6 April 1982 (1 April 1982 for company partners). Where a share in a partnership asset was acquired in stages wholly after 5 April 1965 then, on a part disposal (e.g. on a decrease in a partner's asset-surplus-sharing ratio) the pooling rules for shares and other fungible assets applied in the usual way. Where a share built up in stages was acquired wholly or partly before 6 April 1965 the rules given in 7 ASSETS HELD ON 6 APRIL 1965 normally applied on a disposal or part disposal to identify the acquisition cost of the share in each asset i.e. the disposal was normally identified firstly with shares held on 6 April 1965 on a 'first in, first out basis' and then on a 'pool' basis with shares acquired after 6 April 1965. The Revenue gave special consideration to situations where this rule appeared to produce an unreasonable result when applied to temporary changes in the shares of a partnership, e.g. those occurring when a partner's departure and a new partner's arrival did not exactly coincide (*paragraph 10*). Presumably each partner has a separate right of election for 6 April 1965 value in addition to the election in 40.13 below as regards quoted shares and securities.

Position after 5 April 1982 (31 March 1982 for company partners). Although the Revenue have not indicated any change, it seems that their practice given above for earlier disposals requires amendment in the light of the identification rules for fungible assets applying under the INDEXATION (23) provisions applying at the date of disposal. Disposals after 5 April 1988 of assets held on 31 March 1982 may be affected by the provisions in 8 ASSETS HELD ON 31 MARCH 1982 (and see also the Revenue's practice mentioned in 40.5 above).

Example

Q is a partner in a medical practice. The partnership's only chargeable asset is a freehold house used as a surgery. The cost of the house to the partnership was £3,600 in 1960 and it was revalued in the partnership accounts at £50,000 in 1985. Q was admitted to the partnership in June 1963 with a share of $\frac{1}{6}$ of all profits. As a result of partnership changes, Q's profit share altered as follows

1968 $\frac{1}{5}$
1979 $\frac{1}{4}$
1995 $\frac{3}{10}$

For capital gains tax, Q's allowable cost of his share of the freehold house is calculated as follows

		£	
1963 $\frac{1}{6} \times £3,600$			£600
1968 $(\frac{1}{5}-\frac{1}{6}) \times £3,600$	120		
1979 $(\frac{1}{4}-\frac{1}{5}) \times £3,600$	180		
1995 $(\frac{3}{10}-\frac{1}{4}) \times £50,000$	2,500	£2,800	

Notes to the example

(*a*)   The pre- and post-6.4.65 costs are not pooled.

(*b*)   On Q's acquisition of an increased share of the property in 1995, any partner with a reduced share will be treated as having made a disposal and thus a chargeable gain. The re-basing rules will apply to the disposal (subject to the usual comparison with the gain or loss without re-basing).

40.10   TRANSACTIONS BETWEEN PERSONS NOT AT ARM'S LENGTH

Transactions within the partnership are not treated as made between CONNECTED PERSONS (14), provided they are pursuant to bona fide commercial arrangements, unless the partners are otherwise connected. Market value will be substituted for actual consideration only if the consideration would have been different had the parties been at arm's length. Where market value is applied, the deemed disposal proceeds are treated as in 40.7 above (*paragraph 7*).

40.11   PARTNERSHIP ASSETS DISTRIBUTED IN KIND

The disposal of a partnership asset to one or more of the partners is treated as being made at market value which is apportioned among all the partners as in 40.5 above. Chargeable gains thus attributable to partners receiving no asset are taxed at the time of the disposal. Any gain notionally accruing to a receiving partner is treated as reducing his allowable expenditure on a subsequent disposal of the asset. The same principle applies where a loss arises (*paragraph 3*).

Example

R, S and T are partners sharing all profits in the ratio 4:3:3. Farmland owned by the firm is transferred in 1995 to T for future use by him as a market gardening enterprise separate from the partnership business. No payment is made by T to the other partners but a reduction is made in T's future share of income profits. The book value of the farmland is £5,000, its cost in 1985, but the present market value is £15,000.

		£
R		
Deemed disposal consideration	$\frac{4}{10} \times £15,000$	6,000
Allowable cost	$\frac{4}{10} \times £5,000$	2,000
Unindexed gain		£4,000

40.12 Partnerships

S

Deemed disposal consideration	$\frac{3}{10} \times £15,000$	4,500
Allowable cost	$\frac{3}{10} \times £5,000$	1,500
Unindexed gain		£3,000

T

Partnership share	$\frac{3}{10} \times £5,000$	1,500
Market value of R's share		6,000
Market value of S's share		4,500
Allowable cost of land for future disposal		£12,000

40.12 MERGERS

Mergers of existing partnerships are treated as in 40.5–40.7 above. If gains arise for reasons similar to 40.6 and 40.7 above, a continuing partner may claim ROLLOVER RELIEF (50) insofar as he disposes of his share of assets of the old firm and acquires a share in other assets of the new firm (*paragraph 9*).

40.13 6 APRIL 1965 AND 31 MARCH 1982 ELECTIONS

Each partner has a separate right of election for his share of partnership securities and equities as well as for his personal holdings (*paragraph 11*). See 7.3 ASSETS HELD ON 6 APRIL 1965. It is understood that a similar separate right will apply in relation to a share in partnership assets and assets owned personally which were held on 31 March 1982, disposed of after 5 April 1988, and can be covered by an election under *TCGA 1992, s 35(5)*. See 8.3 ASSETS HELD ON 31 MARCH 1982.

40.14 COMPANIES

The above rules apply, mutatis mutandis, to company partners.

41   Payment of Tax

Cross-references. See 4 APPEALS; 5 ASSESSMENTS; 9 BACK DUTY; 32 INTEREST ON UNPAID TAX; 39.4 OVERSEAS MATTERS for relief for unremittable overseas gains, 39.6 as regards the liability of migrating trustees of a settlement and 39.18 for companies ceasing to be UK resident and non-resident companies; 51 SELF-ASSESSMENT for future changes broadly from 1996/97.

41.1   **Capital gains tax.** This becomes due and payable on 1 December following the end of the year of assessment to which it relates, or thirty days after the issue of the notice of assessment, whichever is the later. [*TCGA 1992, s 7*].

Corporation tax in respect of chargeable gains. The following applies *for accounting periods ending after 30 September 1993* (Pay and File). Corporation tax (including that in respect of chargeable gains) is due and payable without assessment on the day following the expiry of nine months from the end of the period. The amount shown in the return for the period under *TMA 1970, s 11* (see 49.3 RETURNS) as the corporation tax due for the period is treated for collection purposes as tax charged and due and payable under an assessment on the company.

If the company subsequently has grounds for believing that a change in circumstances has rendered payment for a period excessive, it may, by notice to the inspector stating the grounds and the amount it considers should be repaid, claim repayment of the excess. Such notice may not be given before the date on which the tax became (or would have become) due and payable as above, or after an assessment for the period has become final. If the company wishes to claim repayment at a time when an assessment for the period is under appeal, the company must apply to the Appeal Commissioners concerned for a determination of the amount to be repaid pending determination of the appeal. Such an application may be combined with an application for postponement of tax pending an appeal (see 41.2 below). [*ICTA 1988, s 10; FA 1990, s 106; SI 1992 No 3066*].

There are provisions to allow two companies within a group (as defined for group relief purposes under *ICTA 1988, Pt X Ch IV*) to jointly give notice to the inspector that a 'tax refund relating to an accounting period' which falls to be made to one of them should be surrendered in whole or part to the other. The surrendering company is then treated as having received on the 'relevant date' a payment equal to the refund (or part), and the recipient company as having paid on that date corporation tax equal to the amount of the refund (or part). [*FA 1989, s 102; FA 1993, s 120 14 Sch 11*]. These provisions are designed to enable group members to rearrange their tax liabilities without suffering a disadvantage because of the higher rates for interest on unpaid tax as compared with those for interest on overpaid tax. See Tolley's Corporation Tax under Groups of Companies for full coverage of the provisions.

See Tolley's Corporation Tax under Advance Corporation Tax, Groups of Companies and Income Tax in relation to a Company for set-offs available for advance corporation tax paid or surrendered and income tax suffered on payments received.

The following applies *for accounting periods ending before 1 October 1993*. Corporation tax (including that in respect of chargeable gains) assessed for an accounting period is due and payable within nine months from the end of the period or, if later, within 30 days from the date of issue of the notice of assessment. [*ICTA 1988, s 10(1)(b)*].

For accounting periods beginning before 17 March 1987, certain companies trading before 1 April 1965 had an extended payment period of up to 21 months following the end of an accounting period. Transitional provisions applied in such cases to reduce the payment period to nine months over the first accounting period beginning after 16 March 1987 and accounting periods beginning before the end of the two years following the start of that period. [*ICTA 1970, s 244(1); FA 1987, s 36, 6 Sch Pt I*].

For accounting periods ending before 6 April 1990, separate payment dates applied to a building society which had entered into special arrangements with the Revenue for the year of assessment 1965/66 and which would, but for those arrangements, have been assessed for that year by reference to a basis period ending before that year, but which under the arrangements (and without any election thereunder) was assessed by reference to a basis period ending in that year. A transitional provision applied for an accounting period ending in 1989/90. [*ICTA 1988, s 478; ICTA 1970, s 344; FA 1987, s 36, 6 Sch Pt II*].

41.2   POSTPONEMENT OF TAX PENDING APPEAL

If a taxpayer has grounds for believing that he is overcharged to tax by an assessment, he (or his agent) may, by notice in writing stating those grounds and given to the inspector within thirty days after the issue of the notice of assessment, apply for postponement of a specified amount of tax. Application may be made outside the normal thirty-day time limit if there is a change in circumstances giving grounds for belief that the appellant is overcharged by the assessment. The Revenue have said that a 'change in circumstances' is not just a 'change of mind' but a change in the circumstances in which the decision not to apply for postponement was made. Two examples cited by the Revenue are (*a*) where further work on the preparation of accounts indicates that the estimated assessment is 'wide of the mark' and (*b*) where it has become apparent that further relief (e.g. loss or group relief) is due (CCAB Statement TR 477, 28 June 1982). The taxpayer and the inspector may then come to an agreement in writing as to the amount of tax to be postponed (if any), and the giving by either party to the other of written notice confirming the existence of an agreement and the terms thereof is treated as a written agreement for this purpose. Where the parties cannot (or do not attempt to) come to an agreement, the matter is referred to the Commissioners (though in Northern Ireland before 3 April 1989 the taxpayer had the option of the county court; see 4.5 APPEALS) who, if they consider that there are reasonable grounds for believing that an amount of tax has been overcharged, must postpone that amount pending determination of the substantive appeal (which consideration of the issue of postponement does not preclude them from hearing). [*TMA 1970, ss 55(1)(d)(3)(3A)(4)(8)(10), 59; F(No 2)A 1975, s 45(1); FA 1982, s 68; FA 1988, s 134; FA 1990, s 104(2)(4)*].

On the determination of (or agreement on) the amount of tax to be postponed, the balance which is *not postponed* becomes due and payable as if it had been charged by an assessment, notice of which was issued on the date of that determination or agreement (or on the date of notice of confirmation of the latter) and in respect of which there had been no appeal (see example at 41.3 below). [*TMA 1970, s 55(6)(a); F(No 2)A 1975, s 45(1); FA 1989, s 156(2)(4)*].

If, after the determination of an amount of tax to be postponed, the inspector or the taxpayer has grounds, as a result of a change in the circumstances of the case, for believing that that amount is excessive or insufficient, as the case may be, he may, by notice in writing given to the other party at any time before the determination of the substantive appeal, apply to the Commissioners for a further determination of that amount. The notice must state the amount in which the postponement is believed to be discrepant and the grounds for that belief. Any tax which then ceases to be postponed is treated as charged by an assessment, notice of which was issued on the date of the further determination and in respect of which no appeal is pending. Any tax overpaid is repaid. [*TMA 1970, s 55(4)(6)(b); F(No 2)A 1975, s 45(1); FA 1989, s 156(2)(4)*].

41.3   **PAYMENT OF TAX ON DETERMINATION OF APPEAL**

Any tax payable in accordance with the determination of the substantive appeal, the payment of which had been postponed (see 41.2 above), or which would not have been charged by the assessment if there had been no appeal (i.e. further tax found to be due on the appeal), becomes due and payable as if it were charged by an assessment, notice of which was issued on the date on which the inspector issued to the taxpayer a notice of the total amount payable in accordance with the determination and in respect of which there had been no appeal, and any tax overpaid is repaid. [*TMA 1970, s 55(9); F(No 2)A 1975, s 45(1); FA 1989, s 156(2)(4)*].

Any outstanding tax charged in accordance with the Commissioners' decision must be paid as above before an appeal can be heard by the High Court (or Court of Appeal in NI). If, on the determination of the appeal by the High Court, further tax is found to be chargeable, it becomes due and payable thirty days from the date on which the inspector issues to the taxpayer a notice of the total amount payable. [*TMA 1970, s 56(9); F(No 2)A 1975, s 45(3); FA 1989, s 156(3)(4)*]. If a taxpayer in NI before 3 April 1989 exercised his right to appeal to the county court instead of to the Special Commissioners, the same rule applied if a case was stated for the opinion of the Court of Appeal in NI. [*TMA 1970, s 59(6); F(No 2)A 1975, s 45(3); FA 1988, s 134*]. Tax overpaid consequent on the decision of the High Court (or Court of Appeal in NI) is repaid (with, at the Court's discretion, interest) even though further appeal is possible (*T & E Homes Ltd v Robinson CA 1979, 52 TC 567*). [*TMA 1970, s 55(9); FA 1989, s 156(2)(4)*]. See also 31 INTEREST ON OVERPAID TAX.

Example

On 5 October 1995, Y is assessed to capital gains tax for 1994/95 in the sum of £15,000. Y appeals against the assessment and applies for a postponement of £5,000, which is agreed by the inspector on 8 December 1995. The inspector then discovers that Y has mistakenly under-calculated his gains and successfully applies to the Commissioners on 6 January 1996 for the postponed sum to be reduced by £900. The substantive appeal is determined on 8 May 1996 and a revised notice of assessment, showing a total tax charge of £17,000, is issued on 12 May 1996. The due dates are as follows (each being thirty days after the notional notice of assessment)

£10,000 due on 7 January 1996
£900 due on 5 February 1996
£6,100 due on 11 June 1996

If Y makes the last payment due on 11 June 1996, he will be liable for interest, from 1 June 1996, on £6,100. See 32.2 INTEREST ON UNPAID TAX.

41.4   **DATE OF PAYMENT**

The Revenue consider that the effective dates of payment for the various methods by which tax may be paid are as follows.

(i)   In-date cheques tendered by post: the third working day before the day on which the Collector receives the cheque.

(ii)   Cash and in-date cheques (other than those returned to the drawer) tendered personally: the date of tender.

(iii) Post-dated cheques: the date of the cheque.

(iv)   Bank giro credit: the date stamped on the payslip by the bank's cashier.

(v)   National Giro bank in-payment: the date stamped on the payslip by the Post Office counter clerk.

(vi) National Giro bank transfer: the date of the Inland Revenue's National Giro bank statement on which the item appears.

(Tolley's Practical Tax 1981, p 42).

From 1 April 1993, where payment of tax is made by electronic funds transfer (BACS and CHAPS), an effective date of payment of the tax of one working day immediately before the date value is received by the Revenue will be allowed. The prior practice was to treat the date value was received as the effective date of payment (Revenue Press Release 1 April 1993).

41.5 **PAYMENT BY INSTALMENTS ETC.**

Where the whole or part of the consideration for a disposal is receivable by instalments over a period exceeding 18 months, beginning not earlier than the date of disposal, the tax arising may be paid by such instalments as the Revenue allows, over a period not exceeding eight years (and ending not later than the time at which the last of the instalments of the consideration is payable), if the person chargeable satisfies the Revenue that payment in one sum would cause him undue hardship. [*TCGA 1992, s 280*].

In other cases, where a satisfactory arrangement has been negotiated and the taxpayer requests it, agreed monthly payments by standing order are acceptable to the Revenue (Hansard 19 July 1984, col 311).

In the first situation (and presumably the second) INTEREST ON UNPAID TAX (32) will be charged only if an instalment is paid late. It will be charged on that instalment, and will run from the date when the instalment was due (Tolley's Practical Tax 1988, p 176 and 1989, p 5).

For postponed or contingent future consideration, see 16.5 and 16.7 DISPOSAL.

Gifts etc. Subject to the conditions below, capital gains tax chargeable on a gift made after 13 March 1989 may, on election in writing, be paid by ten equal yearly instalments. The first instalment is due on the ordinary due date and the unpaid tax will attract interest on unpaid tax in the usual way and which will be payable with each instalment. The outstanding balance together with accrued interest may be paid at any time. The deferral of payment is available where the whole or any part of specified assets is disposed of by way of gift or is deemed to be disposed of by trustees under *TCGA 1992, s 71(1)* or *72(1)* (see 52.9–52.11 SETTLEMENTS) and the disposal is *either* one to which neither *TCGA 1992, s 165(4)* nor *260(3)* (see 22.1 and 22.4 HOLD-OVER RELIEFS) applies (or would apply if a claim was made) *or* one to which either of those *sections* does apply but on which the held-over gain only partly reduces the gain otherwise arising or is nil. The assets specified for this purpose are: land or any interest or estate in land; any shares or securities of a company which, immediately before the disposal, gave control to the person making or deemed to be making the disposal; and any shares or securities of a company not falling within the foregoing and not quoted on a recognised stock exchange nor dealt in on the Unlisted Securities Market. Tax and any accrued interest is payable immediately if the disposal was by way of a gift to a person connected (see 14 CONNECTED PERSONS) with the donor or was deemed to be made under *TCGA 1992, s 71(1)* or *72(1)* and the assets are disposed of for a valuable consideration under a subsequent disposal (whether or not made by the original donee). [*TCGA 1992, s 281*].

For a summary of other reliefs available to disposals by way of gift etc., see 20.4 GIFTS.

41.6 **COLLECTION AND GENERALLY**

The Collector of Taxes may distrain (poind in Scotland). [*TMA 1970, ss 61–64; FA 1989, ss 152–155; SI 1994, Nos 87, 236*]. See also *Herbert Berry Associates Ltd v CIR HL*

1977, 52 TC 113. Where an amount due (or any instalment) is less than £1,000 (before 1 September 1991, £500, before 11 September 1989, £250 and before 26 July 1984, £50) the Collector may within six months of the due date take summary magistrates' court proceedings. The Collector may also recover the tax by proceedings in the county court. [*TMA 1970, ss 65, 66; FA 1984, s 57; SI 1989 No 1300; SI 1991 Nos 724, 1625, 1877*]. But for limitations in Scotland and NI see *TMA 1970, ss 65(4), 66(3)(4), 67; FA 1976, s 58,* and see *Mann v Cleaver KB 1930, 15 TC 367.* Unpaid tax (and arrears) may also be recovered (with full costs) as a *Crown debt in the High Court.* [*TMA 1970, s 68*]. The amount of an assessment which has become final cannot be re-opened in proceedings to collect the tax (*CIR v Pearlberg CA 1953, 34 TC 57; CIR v Soul CA 1976, 51 TC 86*), and it is not open to the taxpayer to raise the defence that the Revenue acted *ultra vires* in raising the assessment (*CIR v Aken CA 1990, 63 TC 395*).

For whether unpaid tax is a business liability for commercial etc. purposes, see *Conway v Wingate CA, [1952] 1 All E R 782; Stevens v Britten CA, [1954] 3 All E R 385; R v Vaccari CCA, [1958] 1 All E R 468; In re Hollebone's Agreement CA, [1959] 2 All E R 152.*

41.7   CROWN PRIORITY

After 28 December 1986 the previous priority granted to the Crown was ended, inter alia, as regards capital gains tax and corporation tax in respect of chargeable gains. [*Insolvency Act 1985, ss 235(3), 236, 10 Sch Pts II, III; Insolvency Act 1986, s 438, 12 Sch; SI 1986, No 1924* and similar legislation for Scotland and NI].

41.8   REMISSION AND REPAYMENT OF TAX IN CASES OF OFFICIAL ERROR

Arrears of tax arising due to the Revenue's failure to make proper and timely use of information supplied by an *individual* taxpayer (or, in certain circumstances, an employer or the Department of Social Security supplying information relating to the individual) about his income and personal circumstances so that he could reasonably believe that his affairs were in order will be waived as follows.

Taxpayer's Gross Annual Income	Remission
Up to £15,500	All
£15,501–£18,000	75%
£18,001–£22,000	50%
£22,001–£26,000	25%
£26,001–£40,000	10%
Over £40,000	Nil

The income to be considered is that for the year in which the arrears are to be met, although in practice the preceding year's income is considered. If this produces an anomaly, income of the current year may be estimated (ICAEW Technical Memorandum TR 627, August 1986).

All these limits apply to arrears where the actual or likely amount of which is notified after 16 February 1993.

Inspectors may give discretionary relief if the taxpayer's gross income (before personal allowances, deductions etc.) marginally exceeds the above limits and he has large or exceptional family responsibilities. Arrears notified by the end of the tax year following that in which they arose are not remitted except where the Revenue has made repeated errors within that period or the arrears have built up over two whole years in succession as a direct result of the Revenue's failure to make proper and timely use of information. The relief applies for income and capital gains tax purposes, and, for arrears notified after 5 April 1990, the income limits will apply only to the income of the spouse assessed rather than, as previously, to the joint incomes of a husband and wife (Revenue Press Releases 17 February 1993 and 26 April 1994 and Revenue Pamphlet IR 1 A19).

Under *TMA 1970*, unless a longer or shorter period is prescribed, no statutory claim for relief is allowed unless it is made within six years from the end of the tax year to which it relates.

However, repayments of tax will be made in respect of claims made outside the statutory time limit where an overpayment of tax has arisen because of an error by the Inland Revenue or another Government department, and where there is no dispute or doubt as to the facts (Revenue Pamphlet IR 1 B41).

41.9   RECOVERY OF TAX FROM OFFICERS

Tax which has fallen due may be recovered from the treasurer or acting treasurer (the 'proper officer') of a company which is not a body corporate or not incorporated under a UK enactment or by charter. That officer then has a right of reimbursement out of moneys coming into his hands on behalf of that company, and to be indemnified by the company for any balance. [*TMA 1970, s 108(2)(3)*].

41.10   REPAYMENTS AND OVER-REPAYMENTS

Repayments. From 5 April 1994, whilst the onus still seems to be on the taxpayer to claim any repayment that is due, either by reason of mistake, over-estimate or the settling of an appeal, the Revenue has brought into force computer systems that will identify and repay automatically, unless there is an outstanding liability in respect of the same taxpayer when in most cases there will be a set-off made, overpaid income tax under Schedules A and D, capital gains tax, higher rate tax, Class 4 national insurance contributions and associated interest. A letter will accompany the payable order setting out details of the overpayment and the way it has been dealt with. Although computations of revised and repaid interest and repayment supplement will not be produced with the letter they can be requested if desired. Taxpayers can still authorise the Revenue to make the repayment to an agent by sending the authority to the tax office dealing with their affairs (Revenue Press Release 7 April 1994).

Over-repayments. If not otherwise assessable under *TMA 1970, s 29* (see 5 ASSESSMENTS), tax over-repaid may be assessed under Schedule D, Case VI as if it were unpaid tax. Any associated excess repayment supplement (see 31 INTEREST ON OVERPAID TAX) may be included in the assessment. The time limit for such assessments is extended to the end of the year of assessment (chargeable period for a company) following that in which the repayment was made if it would otherwise have passed and is subject to the usual fraudulent or negligent conduct extensions.

Similar provisions to the above apply to companies to enable excess set-offs of advance corporation tax and excess set-offs or payments of tax credit to be recovered, including any INTEREST ON OVERPAID TAX (31).

Where an assessment on a company is to recover repayment of tax paid for an accounting period ending after 30 September 1993, or a repayment of tax received in such a period, the assessment is treated as being for that accounting period, and the sum assessed carries interest under *TMA 1970, s 87A* (see 32.4 INTEREST ON UNPAID TAX) from the date the payment being recovered was made until payment. For this purpose, and where appropriate, sums recovered in respect of repayments are as far as possible identified with later repayments in respect of the accounting period rather than earlier ones. [*TMA 1970, s 30; FA 1982, s 149; F(No 2)A 1987, s 88; ICTA 1988, s 252; FA 1989, s 149(3); FA 1990, s 105*].

41.11   CERTIFICATES OF TAX DEPOSIT

Such certificates, which enable money to be set aside for payment of future tax liability, may be used in payment of capital gains tax. Interest is received on these certificates from the date of purchase until the date on which the tax in respect of which they are surrendered falls due. Certificates may also be encashed (with interest to the date of encashment) but a lower rate of interest is then paid. Certificates for use against corporation tax liabilities ceased to be available for purchase after 30 September 1993 as a result of the introduction of Pay and File procedures. For further details, see Tolley's Income Tax.

41.12   RECOVERY OF TAX IN RESPECT OF DISPOSALS BY OTHERS

There are instances in the legislation whereby the Revenue can assess, and/or recover tax from, persons other than the person actually making the disposal which gives rise to the chargeable event. This right usually follows from the non-payment of tax by the person originally assessed in respect of the chargeable disposal by him but may also arise because of specific legislation (e.g. UK residents charged in respect of disposals made by certain overseas resident companies, see 39.5 OVERSEAS MATTERS). The person from whom tax is recovered is normally given a right of recovery from any person originally assessed.

Specific occurrences of the foregoing are to be found at: 3.13 ANTI-AVOIDANCE; 11.3 and 11.4 CHILDREN; 13.5, 13.6, 13.16, 13.17 and 13.18 COMPANIES; 20.5 GIFTS; 22.2, 22.5 and 22.6 HOLD-OVER RELIEFS; 33.4 LAND; 37.5 MARRIED PERSONS; 39.5–39.10, 39.18 and 39.19 OVERSEAS MATTERS; and 52.3 and 52.8 SETTLEMENTS.

42 Penalties

Cross-references. See 9 BACK DUTY; 32 INTEREST ON UNPAID TAX; 39.18 OVERSEAS MATTERS for companies ceasing to be UK resident; 41 PAYMENT OF TAX; 49 RETURNS; 51 SELF-ASSESSMENT for future changes broadly from 1996/97.

42.1 NOTIFICATION OF CHARGEABILITY

For failure to notify chargeability to capital gains tax or corporation tax as described in 49.1 RETURNS for a year of assessment after 1987/88, or accounting period ending after 31 March 1989, the following maximum penalties apply.

(i) For a person chargeable to capital gains tax: the tax liability on chargeable gains for the year under assessments made more than twelve months after the end of the year.

(ii) For a company where the accounting period ends after 30 September 1993 (Pay and File): the amount by which so much of the corporation tax chargeable on its profits for the period as remains unpaid twelve months after the end of the period exceeds any income tax which, under *ICTA 1988, s 7(2)* or *11(3)*, is to be set off against the corporation tax so chargeable. In relation to earlier accounting periods, the maximum penalty is the corporation tax liability for the period under assessments made more than twelve months after the end of the period. In both cases, the amount of the corporation tax outstanding is determined disregarding the discharge of any liability for that tax attributable to surplus advance corporation tax carried back under *ICTA 1988, s 239(3)*.

[*TMA 1970, ss 10, 11A(2); FA 1988, ss 121, 122; FA 1993, s 120, 14 Sch 1*].

For failure to notify chargeability for an earlier year of assessment or accounting period, there was a maximum penalty of £100. [*TMA 1970, ss 7, 10, 12*].

42.2 FAILURE TO RENDER CAPITAL GAINS TAX RETURN

Notices served after 5 April 1989. If a person other than a company fails to make a return when required to do so under *TMA 1970, s 8, 8A,* or *9* (as applied for capital gains tax purposes by *TMA 1970, s 12*), he incurs a maximum penalty of £300. If his failure continues beyond the end of the tax year following that in which notice was served under one of those provisions, he is liable to a further penalty not exceeding the amount of tax (no amount being taken into account more than once) charged under assessments made on him or his personal representatives after that year on gains which should have been included in the return. A further penalty of up to £60 per day, not continuing after the failure has been remedied, is incurred if the failure continues after the non-tax-based penalty has been imposed (but not for any day for which such a daily penalty has already been imposed). Except in cases where a tax-based penalty is incurred, the rendering of the return prevents the imposition of a penalty. In addition, if the person proves that there was no income or chargeable gain to be included in the return, the overall penalty under the foregoing cannot exceed £100. [*TMA 1970, s 93(1)(2)(5)–(8); FA 1988, 3 Sch 28; FA 1989, s 162; FA 1990, s 90(3)*].

Notices served before 6 April 1989. A person other than a company who fails to make a return when required to do so under *TMA 1970, s 8* or *9* (as applied for capital gains tax purposes by *TMA 1970, s 12*) incurs a maximum penalty of £50. If the failure continues beyond the end of the tax year following that in which notice was served under either provision, the amount of tax (no amount being taken into account more than once) charged under assessments made on him or his personal representatives after that year on gains which should have been included in the return is added, as a penalty and without prejudice to, the £50 maximum penalty. A further penalty of up to £10 per day is incurred if the failure continues after having been declared by a court or by Commissioners before whom proceedings have been commenced. However, if the person proves that there was no income or chargeable gain to be included in the return, the overall penalty under the foregoing cannot exceed £5. Except in cases where a tax-based penalty is incurred, the rendering of the return before proceedings are commenced will avoid a penalty. [*TMA 1970, s 93(1)(2)(5)–(8); FA 1988, 3 Sch 28*].

42.3   **FAILURE TO RENDER CORPORATION TAX RETURN**

Notices served after 31 December 1993. A company which fails to make a return for any period ('*the return period*') (normally limited in practice to a period ending after 30 September 1993; see Revenue Press Release 7 December 1992), when required to do so by a notice served under *TMA 1970, s 11* (see 49.3 RETURNS) after 31 December 1993 (Pay and File), is liable to penalty of £200 (£100 if the return is delivered within three months of the final day for delivery). (The Revenue will apply administrative transitional measures where a notice is served after 31 December 1993 requiring a return to be made for an accounting period ending before 1 October 1993 (Revenue Tax Bulletin August 1993 pp 83–85).) If the return period is one for which accounts are required under *Companies Act 1985*, these penalties do not apply provided that the return is delivered by the last day for delivery of those accounts. These penalties are increased to £1,000 and £500 respectively for failure in relation to a return for an accounting period where such a penalty or a tax-based penalty (see below) was incurred under these provisions for each of the two immediately preceding accounting periods, and the company was within the charge to corporation tax for the whole of the three accounting periods (each accounting period being a return period). A further penalty is imposed (without prejudice to the fixed penalties mentioned above) where the return has not been delivered before the later of the end of the final day for the delivery of the return and the end of the day falling 18 months after the end of the return period. This further penalty is 10% of 'the tax unpaid' at the end of the 18-month period referred to, increased to 20% of the tax unpaid at the end of that 18-month period if the return still has not been delivered before the end of the day falling two years after the end of the return period. '*The tax unpaid*' at any time is the unpaid corporation tax chargeable on the profits for the return period less any income tax which, under *ICTA 1988, s 7(2)* or *11(3)*, is to be set off against the corporation tax so chargeable, disregarding any discharge of liability by set-off of surplus advance corporation tax under *ICTA 1988, s 239(3)* arising in an accounting period ending more than two years after the end of the return period. [*TMA 1970, s 94; F(No 2)A 1987, s 83; FA 1993, s 120, 14 Sch 6*].

Notices served before 1 January 1994. In relation to notices served before 1 January 1994 (and, normally, accounting periods ending before 1 October 1993; see Revenue Press Release 7 December 1992), a company which fails to make a return when required to do so under *TMA 1970, s 11* incurs a maximum penalty of £50. If the failure continues beyond two years from the date of service of notice to make the return, there is an additional penalty of the total amount of tax charged under assessments made after the end of the two-year period on profits that should have been included in the return. In either case, a further penalty of £10 per day is incurred if the failure continues after having been declared by the Court or Appeal Commissioners before whom penalty proceedings have been commenced. If the company can show that there was no profit to be included in the return, the total penalty under these provisions cannot exceed £5. Except in cases where a tax-based penalty is incurred, the rendering of a return before proceedings for recovery are commenced will avoid a penalty. [*TMA 1970, s 94*].

42.4 Penalties

42.4 NEGLIGENCE OR FRAUD

The maximum penalty for negligently or fraudulently delivering, making or submitting an incorrect return or claim for allowance or relief etc., or incorrect accounts, is the amount of tax underpaid by reason of the incorrectness, for the tax year in which the return, etc. was delivered, the year after, and any preceding year, or, in the case of a company, for the chargeable period(s) covered. For returns, etc. before 27 July 1989, the maximum penalty is £50 plus, in the case of negligence, the amount of tax so underpaid, and, in the case of fraud, twice the latter amount.

In each case the amount is additional to any tax or interest actually chargeable.

'*Negligence*' for this purpose includes any innocent error not rectified without unreasonable delay after its discovery by the taxpayer. Accounts are deemed to have been submitted by the taxpayer unless he proves they were submitted without his consent or connivance. [*TMA 1970, ss 95, 96, 97; FA 1988, 3 Sch 28; FA 1989, s 163; FA 1990, s 90(4)*].

42.5   For the position if an agent is negligent or fraudulent, see *Mankowitz v Special Commrs Ch D 1971, 46 TC 707* and cf. *Clixby v Pountney Ch D 1967, 44 TC 515* and *Pleasants v Atkinson Ch D, [1987] STC 728*. **After 26 July 1989,** assisting in or inducing the preparation or delivery of any information, return, accounts or other document known to be incorrect and to be, or to be likely to be, used for any tax purpose carries a maximum penalty of £3,000. **Before 27 July 1989,** assisting in, or inducing, the making or delivery of a return or accounts known to be incorrect carried a maximum penalty of £500. [*TMA 1970, s 99; FA 1989, s 166*].

42.6 LIABILITY UNDER CRIMINAL LAW

'False statements to the prejudice of the Crown and public revenue' are criminal offences (*R v Hudson CCA 1956, 36 TC 561*). False statements in income tax returns, or for obtaining any allowance, reduction or repayment may involve liability to imprisonment for up to two years, under *Perjury Act 1911, s 5*, for 'knowingly and wilfully' making materially false statements or returns for tax purposes. Also, in Scotland, summary proceedings may be taken under *TMA 1970, s 107*.

For the Revenue's practice in considering whether to accept a money settlement or institute criminal proceedings for fraud, see 9.9 BACK DUTY.

In relation to any criminal prosecution case which comes to court after 10 May 1988, the Revenue will

(*a*)   refrain (as previously) from taking steps to recover civil money penalties on the basis of fraud in respect of an offence which has been before the criminal courts;

(*b*)   seek appropriate civil money penalties in respect of any offence which has not been brought before the courts; and

(*c*)   reserve the right to seek, where there are grounds to do so, a civil penalty in respect of negligence by a taxpayer who has been acquitted of criminal intent in respect of a prosecution for fraud.

Previously, when the Revenue prosecuted, the practice had been not to seek a civil money penalty, whether for fraud or negligence, in respect of any offence brought before the criminal courts and any other tax offence committed by the person concerned which was brought to light in the course of the same investigation but which, for some reason, it was not appropriate to bring before the criminal courts (Revenue Statement of Practice SP 2/88, 10 May 1988). See also 24.4 INLAND REVENUE: ADMINISTRATION.

Falsification etc. of documents after 26 July 1989 which are required to be produced as in 9.8 BACK DUTY is a criminal offence punishable, on summary conviction, by a fine of the statutory maximum or, on indictment, by a fine or imprisonment for up to two years or both. [*TMA 1970, s 20BB; FA 1989, s 145*].

42.7   OTHER RETURNS ETC.

Failure to render any information or particulars or any return, certificate, statement or other document which is required, whether by notice or otherwise, under the provisions listed in *TMA 1970, s 98* is the subject of a maximum penalty of £300, plus £60 for each day the failure continues after that penalty is imposed (but not for any day for which such a daily penalty has already been imposed). These penalties are increased by a factor of ten in the case of a failure under *ICTA 1988, s 765A* (movements of capital after 30 June 1990 between residents of EEC member States). (Before 27 July 1989 the penalties were £50 and £10 respectively, and the latter applied for each day the failure continued after having been declared by a court or Commissioners before whom penalty proceedings have been commenced.) The maximum penalty for an incorrect return, etc. given fraudulently or negligently is £3,000. (Before 27 July 1989 it was £250 for negligence and £500 for fraud). Penalties for failure to render information etc. required by notice cannot be imposed after the failure is rectified, and daily penalties can similarly not be imposed where the information etc. was required other than by notice. (Before 27 July 1989 penalties could not be imposed if the failure had been rectified before proceedings for the recovery of penalties had been commenced.) [*TMA 1970, s 98; FA 1980, s 121; FA 1989, s 164(1)-(4)(7); FA 1990, s 68(3)(4)*].

Failure to allow access to computers renders a person liable to a £500 penalty. [*FA 1988, s 127*].

Failure to render a return under *TMA 1970, s 12A* (European Economic Interest Groupings as in 39.20 OVERSEAS MATTERS) renders the grouping or a member of it liable to penalties similar to those imposed by *TMA 1970, s 98* above except that a limit of £100 applies if there is no income or gain to be included in a return and the maximum penalty for an incorrect return given fraudulently or negligently is £3,000 multiplied by the number of members of the grouping at the time of delivery. [*TMA 1970, s 98B; FA 1990, 11 Sch 3(1), 5*].

42.8   COMMISSIONERS' PRECEPTS

Summary penalties (to be treated as tax assessed and due and payable) may be determined by Commissioners against any party to proceedings before them who fails to comply with a precept, order for inspection etc. (see 4.8 APPEALS). The maximum penalty is £300 in the case of the General Commissioners, £10,000 in the case of the Special Commissioners (and in the case of the General Commissioners, a daily penalty up to £60 may also be imposed for continuing failure). A penalty up to £10,000 may similarly be imposed for failure to comply with any other direction of the Special Commissioners (including in relation to a preliminary hearing). [*SI 1994 No 1811, reg 24(1)(3); SI 1994 No 1812, reg 10(1)(3)(4)*]. If a person on whom a witness summons is served (see 4.8 APPEALS) fails to attend in obedience thereto, or attends but refuses to be sworn or to affirm, or refuses to answer any lawful question, or refuses to produce any document required by the summons, the Commissioners may summarily determine a penalty against that person, to be treated as tax assessed and due and payable. The maximum penalty is £1,000 in the case of the General Commissioners, £10,000 in the case of the Special Commissioners. [*SI 1994 No 1811, reg 24(2)(3); SI 1994 No 1812, reg 4(12)(13)*]. Before 1 September 1994, similar provisions applied under *TMA 1970, ss 51–53*, except that the maximum penalty for failure to comply with precepts etc. was in

42.9 Penalties

all cases £300 plus £60 per day (£3,000 in cases of fraudulently or negligently incorrect returns) under *TMA 1970, s 98* (see 42.7 above), and the maximum penalty in relation to a witness summons was £50 in all cases.

Appeal against such summary penalties lies to the High Court (or Court of Session). [*TMA 1970, s 53 (as inserted by SI 1994 No 1813)*]. For the procedure on such appeals, see *QT Discount Foodstores Ltd v Warley Commrs Ch D 1981, 57 TC 268* and, for a case in which penalties were quashed because the taxpayer's evidence that he was unable to supply the information in question was not properly tested, *Boulton v Poole Commrs Ch D 1988, 60 TC 718*.

For appeals against penalties for non-compliance with precepts etc. see *Shah v Hampstead Commrs Ch D 1974, 49 TC 651; Chapman v Sheaf Commrs Ch D 1975, 49 TC 689; Toogood v Bristol Commrs Ch D 1976, 51 TC 634 and [1977] STC 116; Campbell v Rochdale Commrs Ch D 1975, 50 TC 411; B & S Displays Ltd v Special Commrs Ch D 1978, 52 TC 318; Galleri v Wirral Commrs Ch D 1978, [1979] STC 216; Beach v Willesden Commrs Ch D 1981, 55 TC 663; Stoll v High Wycombe Commrs and CIR Ch D, [1992] STC 179; Wilson v Leek Commrs and CIR Ch D 1993, [1994] STC 147.*

42.9 PROCEDURE FOR OCCURRENCES AFTER 26 JULY 1989

Except in the case of

(a)   penalties instituted for suspected fraud (see 42.10 below),

(b)   penalties imposed for failure to comply with Commissioners' precepts (see 42.8 above), and

(c)   penalties (see 42.10 below) under

    (i)   *TMA 1970, s 93(1)* before amendment by *FA 1989, s 162*, or *TMA 1970, s 93(1)(a)* after such amendment (see 42.2 above),

    (ii)   *TMA 1970, s 94(1)* before the substitution made by *F(No 2)A 1987, s 83* (see 42.3 above), and

    (iii)   *TMA 1970, s 98(1)* before amendment by *FA 1989, s 164*, or *TMA 1970, s 98(1)(i)* after such amendment (see 42.7 above),

    (iv)   *TMA 1970, s 98B(2)(a)* (European Economic Interest Groupings as in 42.7 above),

an authorised officer of the Board may make a determination imposing a penalty of an amount which he considers correct or appropriate. The amendments referred to in (c) (i) and (c) (iii) above refer to notices served after 5 April 1989 and to failures etc. occurring after 26 July 1989 respectively, and in relation to such notices or failures etc. only the fixed penalty, and not the daily penalty, is excluded from imposition by determination by the Board's officer. The substitution referred to in (c)(ii) above refers to notices served after 31 December 1993.

The notice of determination must state the date of issue and the time within which an appeal can be made. It cannot be altered unless

(A)   there is an appeal (see 42.10 below), or

(B)   an authorised officer discovers that the penalty is or has become insufficient (in which case he may make a further determination), or

(C)   the penalty arises under *TMA 1970, s 94(6)*, and an authorised officer subsequently discovers that the amount of tax is or has become excessive (in which case it is to be revised accordingly).

370

A penalty under these provisions is due 30 days after the issue of the notice of determination, and is treated as tax charged in an assessment which is due and payable. A determination which could have been made on a person who has died can be made on his personal representatives, and is then payable out of his estate. [*TMA 1970, ss 100, 100A; FA 1989, s 167; FA 1990, 11 Sch 3(2); SI 1994 No 1813*].

42.10   **Appeals.** Subject to the following points, the general APPEALS (4) provisions apply to an appeal against a determination.

TMA 1970, s 50(6)-(8) (see 4.8(*b*)–(*e*) APPEALS) does not apply. Instead on appeal the Commissioners can

(*a*)   in the case of a penalty which is required to be of a particular amount, set the determination aside, confirm it, or alter it to the correct amount, and

(*b*)   in any other case, set the determination aside, confirm it if it seems appropriate, or reduce it (including to nil) or increase it as seems appropriate (but not beyond the permitted maximum, as above).

Without prejudice to *TMA 1970, s 56* (see 4.9 APPEALS), an appeal lies to the High Court (in Scotland, the Court of Session). [*TMA 1970, s 100B; FA 1989, s 167*].

Proceedings before Commissioners. For a penalty within 42.9(*c*) above, an authorised officer can commence proceedings before the General or Special Commissioners. The proceedings are by information in writing, upon summons to the defendant (or defender); and they are heard in a summary way. An appeal lies to the High Court (or Court of Session) on a question of law, or by the defendant (defender) against the amount. The court can set the determination aside, confirm it if it seems appropriate, or reduce it (including to nil) or increase it as seems appropriate. The penalty is treated as tax charged in an assessment and due and payable. [*TMA 1970, s 100C; FA 1989, s 167*].

Proceedings before court. If the Board considers that liability of any person for a penalty arises from fraud of any person, proceedings can be brought in the High Court (or Court of Session). If the court does not find fraud proved, it can nevertheless impose a penalty to which it considers the person liable. [*TMA 1970, s 100D; FA 1989, s 167*].

Interpretation. See 42.11 below for cases on the interpretation of earlier legislation.

Mitigation, etc. The Board may mitigate penalties before or after judgment. [*TMA 1970, s 102; FA 1989, s 168(1)(4)*]. In doing so they will give credit for co-operation by the taxpayer (Revenue Press Release 1 August 1977). A binding agreement by a taxpayer to pay an amount in composition cannot be repudiated afterwards by him or his personal representatives (*A-G v Johnstone KB 1926, 10 TC 758; A-G v Midland Bank Executor and Trustee Co Ltd KB 1934, 19 TC 136; CIR v Richards KB 1950, 33 TC 1*). Statements made or documents produced by or on behalf of a taxpayer are admissible evidence in proceedings against him, notwithstanding that reliance on the Board's practice in cases of full disclosure may have induced him to make or produce them. [*TMA 1970, s 105; FA 1989, s 168(1)(4)*].

If two or more penalties determined by reference to tax chargeable are incurred

(*a*)   by a person in respect of capital gains tax for 1988/89 or later, or

(*b*)   by a company in respect of corporation tax for an accounting period ending after 31 March 1989,

each one after the first is reduced so that the aggregate referable to any particular part of the tax does not exceed whichever penalty so far determined would otherwise have been the greatest. [*TMA 1970, s 97A; FA 1988, s 129*].

42.11 Penalties

In mitigating penalties, the Revenue regard the weight to be attached to specified circumstances (the amount of tax lost being 100%) as follows.

(i)   Disclosure (if any) and its completeness or otherwise, 20-30%.

(ii)   Co-operation by the taxpayer and production of information, up to 40%.

(iii) Size and gravity of the offence(s), up to 40%.

(Revenue Pamphlet IR 73).

See also 49.1 RETURNS as regards *TMA 1970, s 118(2)* (reasonable excuse for failure, etc.).

For the validity of tax amnesties see *R v CIR (ex p. National Federation of Self-Employed and Small Businesses Ltd) HL 1981, 55 TC 133.*

42.11   PROCEDURE FOR OCCURRENCES BEFORE 27 JULY 1989

In the case of a person's failure to make a capital gains tax return (and that of any person to make a special return or provide the documents or information required by the provisions listed in *TMA 1970, s 98* (see 42.7 above), the inspector may himself commence penalty proceedings before the General Commissioners (or, before 3 April 1989, the Special Commissioners in Northern Ireland), but the Commissioners then have no power to award a penalty based on tax due (see 42.2 above). Penalties for failure to comply with precepts etc. are awarded by Commissioners summarily. Penalties awarded are treated as tax charged by an assessment which is due and payable. Subject to this, penalty proceedings require an order of the Board and may be commenced before the General or the Special Commissioners, the High Court or the Court of Session in Scotland. From the Commissioners, an appeal lies to the High Court or the Court of Session on a point of law or (in the taxpayer's case only) against the amount of the penalty awarded. [*TMA 1970, s 100; FA 1988, 14 Sch Pt IX*].

Interpretation. Non-receipt of notice of the hearing at which the Commissioners awarded penalties is not a ground of appeal to the courts (*Kenny v Wirral Commrs Ch D 1974, 50 TC 405; Campbell v Rochdale Commrs Ch D 1975, 50 TC 411*). A mere denial of liability to penalties implies an intention by the taxpayer to set up a case in refutation, and details must be supplied (*CIR v Jackson CA 1960, 39 TC 357*).

For the validity of penalty proceedings while assessments remain open, see *A-G for Irish Free State v White SC (RI) 1931, 38 TC 666* and *R v Havering Commrs (ex p. Knight) CA 1973, 49 TC 161.* For other procedural matters, see *Collins v Croydon Commrs Ch D 1969, 45 TC 566; Bales v Rochford Commrs Ch D 1964, 42 TC 17; Sparks v West Brixton Commrs Ch D, [1977] STC 212; Moschi v Kensington Commrs Ch D 1979, 54 TC 403;* and for other appeals against penalties for failure to make returns, see *Dunk v Havant Commrs Ch D 1976, 51 TC 519; Napier v Farnham Commrs CA, [1978] TR 403; Garnham v Haywards Heath Commrs Ch D 1977, [1978] TR 303; Cox v Poole Commrs and CIR (No 1) Ch D 1987, 60 TC 445; Montague v Hampstead Commrs & Others Ch D 1989, 63 TC 145; Cox v Poole Commrs (No 2) Ch D 1989, 63 TC 277.*

Variation, mitigation or limitation of penalties. On appeal by the taxpayer, the court may confirm, reduce or increase any penalty imposed by Commissioners. [*TMA 1970, s 100(6)(7)*]. See *Dawes v Wallington Commrs Ch D 1964, 42 TC 200; Salmon v Havering Commrs CA 1968, 45 TC 77; Williams v Special Commrs Ch D 1974, 49 TC 670; Wells v Croydon Commrs Ch D 1968, 47 ATC 356; Taylor v Bethnal Green Commrs Ch D 1976, [1977] STC 44; Stableford v Liverpool Commrs Ch D 1982, [1983] STC 162; Sen v St. Anne, Westminster Commrs Ch D, [1983] STC 415; Jolley v Bolton Commrs Ch D, [1986] STC 414; Lear v Leek Commrs Ch D 1986, 59 TC 247; Brodt v Wells Commrs Ch D 1987, 60 TC 436; Walsh v Croydon Commrs Ch D 1987, 60 TC 442.*

See also 42.10 above: mitigation, etc.

42.12   BANKRUPTS

Penalties awarded after a bankruptcy are provable debts, but in practice the Revenue does not proceed for penalties during a bankruptcy where there are other creditors. The trustee may agree to compromise any penalties awarded but the compromise must also be agreed by the bankrupt (*Re Hurren Ch D 1982, 56 TC 494*).

42.13   TIME LIMITS

Occurrences after 26 July 1989. The time within which a penalty can be determined, or proceedings can be commenced, depends on the penalty, as follows.

(*a*)   If the penalty is ascertainable by reference to tax payable, the time is

    (i)   six years after the penalty was incurred, or

    (ii)   a later time within three years after the final determination of the amount of tax (except that this alternative does not apply if the tax was payable by a person who has died, it is charged in an assessment made more than six years after the chargeable period for which it is charged, and the determination would be made in relation to the personal representatives).

(*b*)   If the penalty arises under *TMA 1970, s 99* (in relation to provision of inaccurate information etc., see 42.5 above) the time is twenty years after the date when it was incurred.

(*c*)   In other cases the time is six years from the time when the penalty was, or began to be, incurred.

[*TMA 1970, s 103; FA 1989, s 169*].

Occurrences before 27 July 1989. Normally, penalty proceedings must be commenced within six years after the date the penalty was incurred [*TMA 1970, s 103(1)*], but, in cases of fraud or wilful default, this limit is extended to three years after final determination of tax liability. [*TMA 1970, s 103(2)*].

This time limit is also extended in cases where a penalty is calculated (e.g. under *TMA 1970, s 93(2)*) by reference to tax charged under an assessment for any chargeable period which is made within six years after the end of that chargeable period. Proceedings may be commenced within three years of the final determination of that tax. [*TMA 1970, s 103(3)*]. But where proceedings could not have been commenced but for this extension, tax on assessments under *TMA 1970, ss 37, 39* or *40(2)* (see 9 BACK DUTY) is left out of account in penalty calculations. [*TMA 1970, s 103(4)*].

The effect of the above provisions is to limit the recovery of a penalty attributable to neglect to years for which assessments can be made within normal time limits. For this reason (among others) the Revenue will usually make an assessment within the normal time limits for every year which goes out of date in the course of a back duty enquiry.

Deceased persons. Any proceedings under *TMA 1970, s 103* which were, or could have been, commenced against the deceased may be commenced or continued against his personal representatives, any fine or penalty thereunder being a debt of his estate. [*TMA 1970, s 100(5)*]. The extension of time referred to above for fraud and wilful default does not, however, apply. [*TMA 1970, s 103(2)*].

Provisional agreement of the amount due subject to the inspector being satisfied later with statements of assets, etc. is not final determination (*Carco Accessories Ltd v CIR CS 1985, 59 TC 45*).

43 Private Residences

Private Residences

Cross-references. See 33 LAND generally; 53.26 SHARES AND SECURITIES for restriction on rollover relief arising from disposal of shares to employee share ownership trust where replacement asset is or becomes exempt as a private residence.

43.1 EXEMPTION GENERALLY

Where a gain accrues to an individual so far as attributable to the disposal of, or of an interest in,

(*a*) a dwelling-house or part of a dwelling-house which is, or has at any time in his period of ownership been, his only or main residence, or

(*b*) land which he has for his own occupation and enjoyment with that residence as its garden or grounds up to the 'permitted area',

then either the whole or a fraction of the gain is exempt as below. [*TCGA 1992, s 222(1)*].

Any loss accruing is similarly treated as being wholly or partly a non-allowable loss. [*TCGA 1992, s 16(2)*].

The *'permitted area'* means an area of 0.5 hectares (i.e. 5,980 sq. yards or 5,000 sq. metres). For disposals before 19 March 1991, the permitted area was an area of one acre (i.e. 4,840 sq. yards; 4,047 sq. metres; or 0.4047 hectares). This area is inclusive of the site of the dwelling-house, but may, in any particular case, be a larger area if the appeal Commissioners concerned determine that, regard being had to the size and character of the dwelling-house, that larger area is required for the reasonable enjoyment of it (or the part in question) as a residence. Where part of the land occupied with a residence is and part is not within (*b*) above, then (up to the permitted area) the part that is to be taken within (*b*) is that part which would be most suitable for occupation and enjoyment with the residence if the remainder were separately occupied. [*TCGA 1992, s 222(2)–(4); FA 1991, s 93*].

There can only be one main residence in the case of a man and his wife living with him, so long as they are 'living together' (see 37.2 MARRIED PERSONS). [*TCGA 1992, s 222(6)*].

Total exemption (under *TCGA 1992, s 223(1)*) applies to a gain within *TCGA 1992, s 222(1)* above if the dwelling-house or part of a dwelling-house has been the individual's only or main residence throughout the period of ownership, or throughout the period of ownership except for all or any part of the last 36 months (24 months for disposals before 19 March 1991; however, the Treasury has the power under the 'negative' statutory instrument procedure to reduce the period to twenty-four months again, and then increase it again to thirty-six months, and so on down or up to these levels) of that period. The power cannot be used retrospectively and in practice reasonable notice of any variation will be given (HC Official Report Standing Committee B 7th sitting col 312, 13 June 1991).

Fractional exemption (under *TCGA 1992, s 223(2)*) applies where total exemption does not apply to a gain within *TCGA 1992, s 222(1)*. The fraction of the gain that is exempt is given by

(i)   the length of the part or parts of the period of ownership during which the dwelling-house (or part) was the individual's only or main residence, but inclusive of the last thirty-six months (twenty-four months for disposals before 19 March

1991; however, the above Treasury power applies) of the period of ownership in any event, divided by

(ii)   the length of the period of ownership.

In considering 'period of ownership' for the purposes of the total or fractional exemption (but *not* for determining for the purposes of *TCGA 1992, s 222(1)* above whether the dwelling-house (or part) has at any time in the period of ownership been the only or main residence), any period before 31 March 1982 (6 April 1965 for disposals before 6 April 1988) is ignored, and if time apportionment applies (see 7.9 ASSETS HELD ON 6 APRIL 1965 but subject to the rules in 8 ASSETS HELD ON 31 MARCH 1982), the resulting fraction is applied only to that part of the gain that would otherwise be chargeable after the time apportionment. [*TCGA 1992, s 223(1)(2)(5)–(7), 2 Sch 16(10); FA 1988, 8 Sch 8; FA 1991, s 94*].

See 43.2 below for certain periods of ownership that additionally qualify for the purposes of total and fractional exemption.

Where the individual has had different interests at different times, the period of ownership is taken for the purposes of *TCGA 1992, ss 222–226* generally (i.e. all the provisions contained in this chapter) to begin from the first acquisition taken into account in arriving at the amount of the allowable expenditure deductible in the computation of the gain to which *TCGA 1992, s 222(1)* above applies. In the case of a man and his wife living with him

(A)   if one disposes of, or of his interest in, the dwelling-house (or part) which is their only or main residence to the other, and in particular if it passes on death to the other as legatee, the other's period of ownership is treated as beginning with the beginning of the period of ownership of the one making the disposal, and

(B)   if (A) above applies, but the dwelling-house (or part) was not the only or main residence of both throughout the period of ownership of the one making the disposal, account is taken of any part of that period during which it was his only or main residence as if it was also that of the other.

For the purposes of *TCGA 1992, ss 222–226*, apportionments of consideration are to be made wherever required, and, in particular, where a person disposes of a dwelling-house only part of which is his only or main residence. [*TCGA 1992, s 222(7)(10)*].

An immobilised caravan with main services installed has been held to be a dwelling-house (*Makins v Elson Ch D 1976, 51 TC 437*) but one still on wheels and with no services installed was not so held (*Moore v Thompson Ch D 1986, 61 TC 15*). A houseboat will normally be an exempt asset in its own right (see 18.4 EXEMPTIONS AND RELIEFS regarding tangible movable wasting assets) but if this is not the case, it may, exceptionally, qualify as a dwelling-house (Hansard 21 March 1985 Col 597).

A lodge built for occupation rent-free by a caretaker/gardener and his wife, the housekeeper, and separated from the main house by the width of a tennis court (around nine yards) with the total area of land involved being around 1.1 acres, was held to be within the exemption (*Batey v Wakefield CA 1981, 55 TC 550*). A residence for exemption purposes was declared to be a dwelling-house and all of those buildings which are part and parcel of the whole, where each part is appurtenant to and occupied for the purposes of the building occupied by the taxpayer. However, this is a question of fact and degree.

Whereas *Batey v Wakefield* was concerned with buildings physically separate from the main dwelling-house, *Green v CIR CS 1982, 56 TC 10*, in contrast, involved the disposal of a mansion (occupied by the taxpayer) and its two wings. The Commissioners' finding that the wings were not part of his dwelling-house was upheld.

43.1 Private Residences

In *Markey v Sanders Ch D 1987, 60 TC 245*, a finding by Commissioners that a staff bungalow situated 130 metres away from the main dwelling-house and screened from it by a belt of trees, formed part of the taxpayer's residence was not accepted. It was held that *Batey v Wakefield* laid down two tests:

(1) the occupation of the building must increase the taxpayer's enjoyment of the main dwelling-house, and

(2) the building must be 'very closely adjacent to' the main dwelling-house.

Each of these was held to be a necessary, but not by itself sufficient, test and in the present case the first test was satisfied but not the second. The total area of land involved was around twelve acres.

However, *Markey v Sanders* was expressly not followed in *Williams v Merrylees Ch D 1987, 60 TC 297*, so that a finding by Commissioners that a lodge situated 200 metres from the main dwelling-house formed part of the taxpayer's residence during his occupation of the latter was upheld. The total area of the property was around four acres. In the latter case doubt was expressed whether the *Batey v Wakefield* decision did require the satisfaction of two distinct conditions and it was concluded that all the circumstances should be looked at to see whether there is 'an entity which could sensibly be described as being a dwelling-house though split up into different buildings performing different functions'.

The *Williams v Merrylees* decision was itself disapproved by the Court of Appeal in *Lewis v Rook CA, [1992] STC 171*. A finding by Commissioners that a gardener's cottage some 170 metres from the main dwelling-house formed part of the taxpayer's residence was initially upheld in the High Court, but was rejected in the Court of Appeal. The true test was declared to be whether the cottage was 'within the curtilage of, and appurtenant to [the main house], so as to be part of the entity which, together with [the main house], constituted the dwelling-house occupied by the taxpayer as her residence'. The curtilage concept was derived from a non-tax case, *Methuen-Campbell v Walters CA, [1979] QB 525* (and see also *Dyer v Dorset County Council CA, [1989] QB 346*), in which Buckley LJ stated that 'for one corporeal hereditament to fall within the curtilage of another, the former must be so intimately associated with the latter as to lead to the conclusion that the former in truth forms part and parcel of the latter'. The cottage in *Lewis v Rook* was not 'intimately associated' with the main house as it was some way off and separated from it by a large garden. The total area of land involved was around 10.5 acres and Balcombe LJ remarked that as 'the 'permitted area' of garden and grounds which is exempt from capital gains tax is limited to one acre [now 0.5 hectares] or such larger area as the [Appeal] Commissioners may determine as required for the reasonable enjoyment of the dwelling-house as a residence, it does seem to me to be remarkable that a separate lodge or cottage which by any reasonable measurement must be outside the permitted area can nevertheless be part of the entity of the dwelling-house'. It should also be noted that Counsel for the Inland Revenue reserved the right to argue in the House of Lords, had the case proceed that far, that the reference in *TCGA 1992, s 222(1)(a)* to a 'dwelling-house' in the singular meant that buildings which are separate from the main house cannot be included within the exemption if they form separate, self-contained dwelling-houses in their own right. See Revenue Tax Bulletin, August 1994, p 148 for further discussion of this matter.

In *Honour v Norris Ch D, [1992] STC 304* the taxpayer owned four separate, self-contained flats in a London square. Two of these were adjacent and were converted to form a single property, the other two being some way off and not adjacent to each other. Although the taxpayer and his wife had occasionally used the non-adjacent flats themselves, their main function was to provide sleeping accommodation for guests and a nanny. The Commissioners upheld the taxpayer's contention that one of the distant flats, which had been sold, was part of his main residence. However, the Revenue's appeal was upheld in the High Court, Vinelott J remarking that the proposition that the flat which had been sold formed part of the taxpayer's main residence was 'an affront to common sense'.

In *Varty v Lynes Ch D 1976, 51 TC 419*, the taxpayer owned and occupied a house and garden (together comprising an area less than one acre, the latter being the then 'maximum' permitted area subject to an appeal Commissioners' determination). He sold the house and part of the garden in June 1971. In May 1972, he sold at a substantial profit the rest of the garden for which he had meanwhile obtained planning permission. An assessment on the gain accruing on the disposal of the remainder of the garden was upheld. The exemption provided by (*b*) above related only to the actual moment of disposal of the land, and in relation to land formerly used as garden and grounds did not apply to a disposal subsequent to the disposal of the residence. The judgment of Brightman J pointed to anomalies in the legislation. In particular, he stated 'The anomaly which I find most striking [is] the disregard for the purposes of [the provisions providing for total exemption] of the last twelve months [this period being the then period disregarded above] of the period of ownership in respect of the dwelling-house. On the construction advanced by the Crown it must follow, I am disposed to think, that if the taxpayer goes out of occupation of the dwelling-house a month before he sells it, the exemption will be lost in respect of the garden. That, however, is merely my impression, and I do not intend so to decide because it is not a matter for decision before me'. The Revenue did say that they would not take this point unless the garden had development value (CCAB Statements TR 211 December 1976 and TR 233 June 1977). However, the Revenue no longer seek to apply arguments based on the dicta in this case, but will apply the decision itself, so that no relief is due on any sale of a garden taking place after a prior sale of the dwelling house (Revenue Tax Bulletin, August 1994, pp 148, 149).

For a useful summary of the considerations made by the Revenue in arriving at the 'permitted area' and whether a subsidiary building forms part of the residence as a whole, see Revenue Tax Bulletin, February 1992, p 10. The Revenue makes the point that land, other than that taken by the site of the dwelling-house, must be 'garden or grounds' at the time of sale if it is to be within the permitted area. In deciding whether an area of garden or grounds larger than 0.5 hectares is 'required for the reasonable enjoyment' of the dwelling-house as a residence, it considers the following words of Du Parcq J in the compulsory purchase case of *In Re Newhill Compulsory Purchase Order 1937, Payne's Application KB 1937, [1938] 2 All E R 163* to be useful guidance: ' "Required", I think, in this Section does not mean merely that the occupiers of the house would like to have it, or that they would miss it if they lost it, or that anyone proposing to buy the house would think less of the house without it than he would if it was preserved to it. "Required" means, I suppose that without it there will be such a substantial deprivation of amenities or convenience that a real injury would be done to the property owner.' However, it can be argued that the Revenue has taken the words spoken out of context since the case mentioned concerned legislation which prohibited compulsory purchase of 'any land . . . which . . . forms part of any park, garden or leisure ground, or is otherwise required for the amenity or convenience of any house'. The construction of this legislation suggests that, in interpreting it, a garden, park or leisure ground should automatically be considered as required for the amenity or convenience of a dwelling-house. The application of Du Parcq J's words may therefore be invalid in the context of capital gains tax and the private residence exemption.

See Taxation 5 January 1989, p 311 for a case where the Ombudsman considered the District Valuer to have been wrong in taking the view that the presence of a tennis court and swimming pool must be regarded as irrelevant in deciding what was the permitted area.

For the question of whether or not a dwelling-house is a 'main residence', see *Frost v Feltham Ch D 1980, 55 TC 10* which concerned mortgage interest relief for income tax purposes but note that that question may be determined, for capital gains tax purposes only, by election as in 43.3 below.

See 43.3 to 43.6 below for provisions supplementary to the above.

43.2 **PERIODS OF OWNERSHIP QUALIFYING FOR EXEMPTION**

For the purposes of the total or fractional exemption of a gain to which *TCGA 1992, s 222(1)* in 43.1 above applies the following provisions apply.

(*a*)   **Periods of absence.** A *'period of absence'* means a period during which the dwelling-house (or part) was not the individual's only or main residence and throughout which he had no residence or main residence eligible for relief under the provisions of *TCGA 1993, s 223* in 43.1 above. In applying the total or fractional exemption provided by *TCGA 1992, s 223(1)* and *(2)* respectively in 43.1 above (i.e. ignoring periods of ownership before 31 March 1982 (6 April 1965 for disposals before 6 April 1988))

  (i)   a period of absence not exceeding three years (or periods of absence which together did not exceed three years), and in addition

  (ii)   any period of absence throughout which the individual worked in an employment or office all the duties of which were performed outside the UK, and in addition

  (iii)   any period of absence not exceeding four years (or periods of absence which together did not exceed four years) throughout which the individual was prevented from residing in the dwelling-house (or part) in consequence of the situation of his place of work or in consequence of any condition imposed by his employer requiring him to reside elsewhere, being a condition reasonably imposed to secure the effective performance by the employee of his duties,

is treated as if in that period of absence the dwelling-house (or part) was the individual's only or main residence *provided* both before and after the period there was a time when the dwelling-house (or part) was the individual's only or main residence. [*TCGA 1992, s 223(3)(7)*].

The Revenue will view residence as a question of fact. A minimum period is not specified and the Revenue do not attempt to impose one. They take the view that it is quality of occupation rather than length of occupation which determines whether a dwelling house is its owner's residence. Miller J in *Moore v Thompson Ch D 1986, 61 TC 15* commented that 'the Commissioners were alive to the fact that even occasional and short residence in a place can make that a residence; but the question was one of fact and degree'. (Revenue Tax Bulletin, August 1994, p 149).

Where the periods of absence exceed the three or four years mentioned in (i) and (iii) above, it is only the excess which does not qualify for the exemption treatment (CCAB Statement TR 500, 10 March 1983). Where in the case of a husband and wife who are living together the conditions in (i) to (iii) above are satisfied as regards the spouse who is not the owner of the dwelling-house, they are deemed satisfied as regards the spouse who is the owner. Also, the condition requiring the dwelling-house to be the only or main residence after absence under (ii) and (iii) above will be treated as satisfied if the individual is unable to resume residence because the terms of his employment require him to work elsewhere (Revenue Pamphlet IR 1, D3, D4).

The requirement that the period of absence is a period throughout which the individual has no residence or main residence eligible for relief under *TCGA 1992, s 223* may be difficult to meet in practice given the view (see the ESC mentioned in Revenue Pamphlet IR 1, D21 in 43.3 below) of the Revenue that a 'weekly rented flat, or accommodation provided by an employer' (the latter not presumably being job-related as in (*d*) below) can constitute an individual's residence, albeit with a negligible capital value. Conversely, the Revenue, in providing an example of the operation of *TCGA 1992, s 223(3)(7)* in its explanatory pamphlet CGT 4 (1989), specifically contemplates a period within (iii) above where an 'employer moved [the individual] to another part of the UK that was so far away [the individual] needed to stay in rented accommodation'. If the latter view prevails, it would not seem necessary to consider a main residence election as in 43.3 below but such consideration would seem necessary, subject to the above ESC, if the former view is the valid one.

Example

P sold a house on 1 July 1995 realising an otherwise chargeable gain of £58,333. The house was purchased on 1 February 1980 and was occupied as a residence until 30 June 1985 when P moved to another residence, letting the house as residential accommodation. He did not re-occupy the house prior to its sale.

	£
Gain on sale	58,333
Deduct Exempt amount under main residence rules	
$\dfrac{\text{2y 3m} \times \text{3y}}{\text{12y 3m}} \times £58,333$	25,000
	33,333
Deduct Let property exemption	25,000
Net chargeable gain	£8,333

Notes to the example

(1) The period of ownership for the exemption calculation does not include any period before 31 March 1982. This applies regardless of whether the gain has been calculated by reference to cost or to 31 March 1982 value under the re-basing rules.

(2) The gain attributable to the letting (£33,333) is exempt to the extent that it does not exceed the lesser of £40,000 (£20,000 for disposals before 19 March 1991) and the gain otherwise exempt (£25,000 in this example) (see 43.1 above).

(3) See also 43.6 below.

(*b*) **Delay in taking up residence.** The treatment as the individual's only or main residence applies during the twelve months (or longer period up to a maximum of two years if a good reason can be shown) prior to taking up residence during which the dwelling-house was built, alterations etc. were made to it or the necessary steps were being taken to dispose of the individual's previous residence. (Revenue Press Release, 18 October 1994).

43.2 Private Residences

(c) **Separation or divorce of married persons.** Where a married couple separate or are divorced and one partner ceases to occupy the matrimonial home and subsequently, as part of a financial settlement, disposes of the home, or an interest in it, to the other partner, the home may be regarded for the purposes of the exemption as continuing to be a residence of the transferring partner from the date his or her occupation ceases until the date of transfer, provided that it has throughout this period been the other partner's only or main residence. Thus where a husband leaves the matrimonial home while still owning it, the exemption for the only or main residence would be given on the subsequent transfer to the wife, provided she has continued to live in the house and the husband has not elected that some other house should be treated as his main residence for this period (Revenue Pamphlet IR 1 D6). See also 37.6 MARRIED PERSONS.

(d) **'Job-related' accommodation.** If at any time (being a time after 30 July 1978 for disposals before 6 April 1988) during an individual's period of ownership (as for *TCGA 1992, s 222(1)* in 43.1 above so that a period before 31 March 1982 is *not* ignored) of part or the whole of a dwelling-house he resides in 'job-related' living accommodation and he intends in due course to occupy the dwelling-house (or part) as his only or main residence, he is deemed at that time to occupy the dwelling-house (or part) as a residence for the purposes of *TCGA 1992, ss 222–226* (i.e. all the provisions contained in this chapter). Living accommodation is 'job-related' for these purposes if it is provided for a taxpayer by reason of his (or for his spouse by reason of her) employment, in any of the following cases.

(i) Where it is necessary for the proper performance of the duties of the employment that the employee should reside in that accommodation.

(ii) Where the provision of such accommodation is customary and it is provided for the better performance of the duties of employment.

(iii) Where there is a special threat to the employee's security, special security arrangements are in force, and the employee resides in the accommodation as part of those arrangements.

With certain exceptions, (i) and (ii) above do not apply to accommodation provided to its directors by a company (or associated company).

In respect of residence after 5 April 1983, living accommodation is also job-related if either the person claiming the relief or his or her spouse is carrying on a trade, profession or vocation on premises or other land provided by another person, under tenancy or otherwise, and is bound under an arm's length contract to live in those premises or on other premises provided. Relief is not given if the accommodation is provided, in whole or in part, by a company in which the borrower, or his or her spouse, has a material interest (as defined) or by any person or persons with whom he or she is in partnership. [*TCGA 1992, s 222(8)(9); ICTA 1988, s 356; FA 1988, 14 Sch Pt VII*].

The above treatment still applies if the dwelling-house is disposed of without having been occupied by the individual (but subject to the test of intention to occupy being satisfied previously) or if the property has been let (see 43.6 below). It appears that the above provisions do not obviate the need to consider, subject to the ESC there mentioned as contained in Revenue Pamphlet IR 1 D21, a main residence election as in 43.3 below.

To some extent these provisions regarding 'job-related' accommodation supersede an earlier Revenue Statement of Practice set out in a Press Release dated 27 September 1973. The latter states that an occupant of tied accommodation who owns another house may nominate that other house as his main residence provided that it is both available to him for residential purposes, and that he does in fact reside there at regular intervals, each case being considered on its merits. Where such a person has been unaware of the need to make an election, inspectors are prepared to extend the time limit. (29.D8 INLAND REVENUE STATEMENTS OF PRACTICE). This treatment may still be of importance where pre-31 July 1978 or pre-6 April 1983 periods of ownership need to be considered.

(e)   **Relocation of employees.** Where liabilities are agreed after 13 January 1991, the Revenue are prepared concessionally to extend the exemption for a private residence where an employee sells his home to a relocation business or his employer and is given the right to share in any profits made when that business or his employer later sells the home, so that the right will generally be exempt to the same extent as the home itself. Relocation arrangements must be set up under arm's length agreements whereby the employee moves home because of the requirements of his place of work or employer and the right to a profit share by the employee must not exceed three years. The concession applies equally to office holders and any other joint owners of the home provided the employee qualifies for his interest in it (Revenue Pamphlet IR 1, D37 with a revised text published in a Revenue Press Release of 27 April 1994 to make clear the concession applies not only to the sale by an employee of his home to a relocation business but also to a similar sale to his employer).

43.3   **SUPPLEMENTARY PROVISIONS**

Exclusive part-business use, changes of use etc. If a gain accrues from the disposal of a dwelling-house or part of a dwelling-house part of which is used *exclusively* for the purposes of a trade or business, or of a profession or vocation, the gain is apportioned and *TCGA 1992, s 223* applied in relation to the part of the gain apportioned to the part which is not exclusively used for those purposes. If at any time in the period of ownership there is a change in what is occupied as the individual's residence, whether on account of a reconstruction or conversion of a building or for any other reason, or there have been changes as regards the use of part of the dwelling-house for the purpose of a trade etc. or for any other purpose, the relief given under *TCGA 1992, s 223* may be adjusted in such manner as the appeal Commissioners concerned may consider to be 'just and reasonable'. [*TCGA 1992, s 224(1)(2)*].

It appears the Revenue are prepared to accept a 'just and reasonable' basis by reference to one other than on a straight-line time apportionment (Taxation 21 February 1991 p 558). Their approach in cases falling within *TCGA 1992, s 224(2)* is to deal with each case on its merits, and to produce an adjustment which as far as possible reflects the extent to which, and the length of time over which, each part of the dwelling house has been used as part of residence. It is not normally considered appropriate to take into account intervening market values when apportioning gains to different periods in *TCGA 1992, s 224(2)* cases since *TCGA 1992, s 223* clearly provides for time apportionment as the appropriate method (Revenue Tax Bulletin August 1994 p 149).

ROLLOVER RELIEF (50) may be available in respect of any chargeable gain arising because of the foregoing provisions if a new dwelling-house is acquired, part of which will also be used *exclusively* for the purposes of a trade etc. so that relief will apply to the acquisition costs of that part. Although the treatment by the Revenue is not always consistent, it seems that where an individual, assessable to income tax under Schedule E, uses part of his home exclusively for the purposes of his employment, no restriction of the exemption can be made under the foregoing provisions (Tolley's Practical Tax 1981, p 178).

43.3 Private Residences

Letting the dwelling-house may restrict the exemption given by 43.1 and 43.2 above (but see 43.6 below) but there is no restriction where a lodger lives as part of a family, sharing their living accommodation and taking meals with them. See 29.D15 INLAND REVENUE STATEMENTS OF PRACTICE and Revenue Pamphlet IR 131, SP 14/80. In addition, participation in the 'rent a room' income tax relief scheme of *F(No 2)A 1992, s 59, 10 Sch* will not normally lead to any capital gains tax liability (HL Written Answers, 27 January 1993, Vol 514 col 94).

Exclusion of exemption where dwelling-house acquired for profit. The exemption given by *TCGA 1992, s 223* does not apply in relation to a gain if the acquisition of, or of the interest in, the dwelling-house (or part) was made wholly or partly for the purpose of realising a gain from the disposal of it, and does not apply in relation to a gain so far as attributable to any expenditure which was incurred after the beginning of the period of ownership and was incurred wholly or partly for the purpose of realising a gain from the disposal. [*TCGA 1992, s 224(3)*]. The Revenue give the example of the taxpayer already owning the lease of a house, and, before disposing of it, buying the freehold intending to make a larger gain; or the taxpayer converting some or all of his house into flats with the same intention (Revenue Pamphlet CGT 4). The Revenue's practice is not to take into account expenditure incurred in obtaining planning permission or in removing restrictive covenants when considering whether to apply the second leg of *TCGA 1992, s 224(3)* (see Revenue Tax Bulletin, August 1994, p 150).

Election for main residence. So far as it is necessary for the purposes of *TCGA 1992, s 222* to determine which of two or more residences is an individual's main residence for any period,

(*a*)   the individual may conclude that question by written notice to the inspector given within two years from the beginning of that period but subject to a right to vary that notice by a further written notice to the inspector as respects any period beginning not earlier than two years before the giving of the further notice,

(*b*)   subject to (*a*) above, the question is to be concluded by the determination of the inspector, which may be as respects the whole or specified parts of the period of ownership in question,

and written notice of any determination of the inspector under (*b*) above must be given to the individual who may appeal to the General Commissioners or the Special Commissioners against that determination within thirty days of service of the notice. [*TCGA 1992, s 222(5)*].

Any notice of election given under *TCGA 1992, s 222(5)* which relies on a residence occupied under licence for its effect and which is made after 16 October 1994 will not be regarded as valid. This does not affect the need for an election in the majority of cases where an individual owns one property and rents another property, since the rented property will normally be occupied under a tenancy rather than under a licence. Existing elections made in respect of residences occupied under licence are regarded as ceasing to have effect from 16 October 1994 (Revenue Tax Bulletin, October 1994, p 167).

In the case of a man and his wife living with him, there can only be one residence or main residence for both, so long as 'living together' (see 37.2 MARRIED PERSONS) and, where a notice specifying the main residence under (*a*) above affects both husband and wife, it must be given by both, and any notice of the inspector's determination of the main residence under (*b*) above must be given to each and either may appeal against such determination. [*TCGA 1992, s 222(6)*]. See Revenue Tax Bulletin, August 1994, pp 149, 150 for further discussion on elections by married couples.

The case of *Griffin v Craig-Harvey Ch D 1993, [1994] STC 54* upheld the Revenue's long-standing view (e.g. see withdrawn Pamphlet CGT 8 (1980), para 74 and currently

Pamphlet CGT 4 (1989), p 4) that, broadly and subject to the following, initial notice under (*a*) nominating the main residence must be given within two years of the time the individual first begins to have two or more residences if it is to be effective from that time. Further notice(s) of variation under (*a*) can then only be made subsequent to such an effective initial notice but not so as to vary the nomination of the main residence more than two years before the giving of the further notice. The *ratio decidendi* (supported by certain words to cover transitional cases at 6 April 1965 formerly contained in the equivalent of (*a*) above in the original *FA 1965* legislation and the *CGTA 1979* consolidation and, under principles established in *Pepper v Hart HL, [1992] STC 898*, a Minister's statement in the HC Official Report relevant to the enactment of the *FA 1965* legislation) of the judgment of Vinelott J appears to be that 'the reference to "any period" in the opening part of [*TCGA 1992, s 222(5)* as above] and to "that period" in para (*a*) [as above] are most naturally read as referring to "the whole or any part of the period of ownership in question" that being the period in relation to which in default of agreement or of any notice under para (*a*) the inspector's determination is to be made'. However, in the judgment the following hypothetical situations were put forward.

(1)   The taxpayer owns two houses, each of which he occupies as a residence. More than two years have elapsed since he began to have two residences. He then begins to use a third house as a residence. A new two-year period begins to run at that time so that he can make an election as between all three residences during that two-year period.

(2)   If on the same facts the taxpayer ceased, after acquiring a third residence, to use one of them as a residence a new period will begin at the time of cesser so that, again, he will have a period of two years during which he can elect between the remaining residences.

(3)   The taxpayer owns two houses which he occupies as residences. The taxpayer conveys one of the houses to the trustees of the settlement under which he has a beneficial interest and the trustees have power which they exercise to permit him to continue to reside in the residence. A new two-year period begins at the time when he creates the settlement and again an election can be made (jointly by the taxpayer and the trustees; see 43.4 below) within the subsequent two years.

(4)   The taxpayer has two residences, one owned by him and the other by the trustees of a settlement under which the trustees have power to permit the taxpayer to occupy it as a residence. No election is made during the two years following the inception of this state of affairs. If the trustees have and exercise a power to transfer the residence which they own to the taxpayer he can elect that that residence is to be his main residence at any time during the subsequent two years.

In *obiter dicta* comment on these examples, Vinelott J said (1) and (2) 'do no more than illustrate the inevitable consequence of [*TCGA 1992, s 222(5)*], namely that it becomes necessary to determine which of two or more residences is an individual's main residence whenever there is a change in the number of properties which he occupies as a residence; apart from an election under para (*a*) that question has to be determined afresh by the inspector (unless, of course, the disposal of one property occupied as a residence leaves him with only one residence)'. However, although not stated but crucial in the instant case, it appears implicit in the overall judgment that, in relation to examples similar to (1) and (2) above, an initial notice and a further notice under (*a*) above can only affect the position since the last change of circumstances in which the individual has two or more residences; they cannot change the main residence nomination for a previous combination of two or more residences which existed before that change even though such notices are made within the time limits. Vinelott J found it unnecessary to comment on a submission given in evidence that the taxpayer can give an initial notice of election and so preserve a right to vary an election even if at the time he has only one residence.

As regards the examples at (3) and (4) above, Vinelott J said they 'seem to be altogether unsurprising consequences of the legislation. If [there is a transfer as in (3) and (4) above], the transfer of the house to the trustees or from the trustees to the taxpayer is a disposal giving rise to a charge to capital gains tax on any gain so far as not exempt under [*TCGA 1992, s 222*]. The position is the same as if he had bought the house from or sold it to a stranger'. This statement, although *obiter dicta*, can be criticised if *TCGA 1992, s 222(5)* is concerned with *occupation* (or, perhaps, *use*) rather than *ownership*. It also seems at variance with the stated comment on (1) and (2) above ('. . . whenever there is a change in the number of properties which he *occupies* [emphasis added] . . .'). Indeed, allied to the Revenue's view mentioned above, is its further long-standing one that it is immaterial for the purposes of *TCGA 1992, s 222(5)* whether the individual owns any of the two or more residences which he occupies (or, perhaps, uses) (see withdrawn Pamphlet CGT 8 (1980), para 74). Furthermore, the extra-statutory concession mentioned below (which was announced on 17 May 1985) proceeds on that basis.

Example

S purchased the long lease of a London flat on 1 June 1986. He occupied the flat as his sole residence until 31 July 1988 when he acquired a property in Shropshire. Both properties were thereafter occupied as residences by S until the lease of the London flat was sold on 28 February 1995, realising an otherwise chargeable gain of £75,000.

The possibilities open to S are

(i) Election for London flat to be treated as main residence throughout

Exempt gain   £75,000

(ii) Election for Shropshire property to be treated as main residence from 31.7.88 onwards

Exempt gain $£75,000 \times \dfrac{\text{2y 2m} + \text{3y}}{\text{8y 9m}}$ £44,286

(iii) Election for London flat to be treated as main residence up to 28 February 1992, with election for the Shropshire property to be so treated thereafter

Exempt gain $£75,000 \times \dfrac{\text{5y 9m} + \text{3y}}{\text{8y 9m}}$ £75,000

Note to the example

(*a*)   The elections in (iii) are the most favourable, provided they could have been made by 31 July 1990 in respect of the London flat, and by 28 February 1994 in respect of the Shropshire property. Note that the last three years' ownership of the London flat is an exempt period in any case. The advantage of (iii) over (i) is that the period of ownership 1 March 1992 to 28 February 1995 of the Shropshire property will be treated as a period of residence as regards any future disposal of that property.

Where for any period an individual has, or is treated by the *Taxes Acts* as having, more than one residence but his interest in each of them, or in each of them except one, is such as to have no more than a negligible capital value on the open market (e.g. a weekly rented flat or accommodation provided by an employer (see 43.2(*a*) and (*d*) above)), the two-year time limit laid down by (*a*) above for nominating one of those residences as the individual's main residence will be extended where the individual was unaware that such a nomination could be made. In such cases the nomination may be made within a reasonable time of the individual becoming aware of the possibility of so doing, and it will be regarded as effective from the date on which the individual first had more than one residence (Revenue Pamphlet IR 1, D21). See Revenue Tax Bulletin October 1994 P167 with regard to residences occupied under licence.

43.4 OCCUPATION UNDER TERMS OF SETTLEMENT OR BY WILL OR INTESTACY

The provisions of *TCGA 1992, ss 222–224* (see 43.1–43.3 above) also apply in relation to a gain accruing to a trustee on a disposal of settled property being an asset within *TCGA 1992, s 222(1)* (see 43.1 above) where, during the period of ownership of the trustee, the dwelling-house (or part) has been the only or main residence of a person entitled to occupy it under the terms of the settlement. In the application of those provisions, references to the individual are taken as references to the trustee except in relation to the occupation of the dwelling-house. Any election for main residence treatment under 43.3 above is to be a joint notice by the trustee and the person entitled to occupy. [*TCGA 1992, s 225*].

A person is 'entitled' to occupy if he does so by permission of the trustees of a discretionary trust of which he is a beneficiary (*Sansom v Peay Ch D 1976, 52 TC 1*). See 52.7 SETTLEMENTS as to the Revenue's views on whether an 'interest in possession' is created in such circumstances.

Relief is given similarly to the above where personal representatives dispose of a dwelling-house which *before and after* the deceased's death has been used as their only or main residence by individuals who, under the will or intestacy, are entitled to the whole (or substantially the whole, interpreted by the Revenue as 75% or more) of the proceeds of the dwelling-house either absolutely or for life (Revenue Pamphlet IR 1, D5). See Revenue Tax Bulletin, August 1994, pp 150, 151 for further discussion on this point.

43.5 OCCUPATION BY DEPENDENT RELATIVE

If an individual so claims, relief as in 43.1 to 43.3 above is given to a gain accruing to him so far as attributable to the disposal of, or of an interest in, a dwelling-house (or part) which, on 5 April 1988 or at any earlier time in his period of ownership, was the *sole* residence of a 'dependent relative' of the individual, provided 'rent-free and without any other consideration'. Such relief is given in respect of the dwelling-house and its garden and grounds as would be given under *TCGA 1992, ss 222–224* if the dwelling-house had been the individual's only or main residence in the period of residence by the dependent relative; and any such relief is to be in addition to any relief already available under those provisions. Not more than one dwelling-house (or part) may qualify for relief as the residence of a dependent relative at any one time. In the case of a man and his wife living with him, no more than one dwelling-house may qualify as the residence of a dependent relative of the claimant or of the claimant's husband or wife at any one time. The inspector, before allowing a claim, may require the claimant to show that the giving of the relief claimed will not preclude the giving of relief to the claimant's spouse or that a claim for any such relief has been relinquished. [*TCGA 1992, s 226(1)(2)(4)(5)*].

If in a case within *TCGA 1992, s 226(1)* above the dwelling-house (or part) ceases, whether before 6 April 1988 or later, to be the sole residence (provided as mentioned above) of the dependent relative, any subsequent period of residence beginning after 5 April 1988 by that or any other dependent relative is disregarded for the purposes of the above relief. [*TCGA 1992, s 226(3)*]. If a dependent relative is obliged temporarily to live elsewhere (e.g. in a nursing home), the absence will not normally be treated as bringing this provision into play (ICAEW Statement TR 739, 13 February 1989).

For disposals before 6 April 1988, the dwelling-house (or part) merely had to be, or had to have been at some time in the period of ownership, the sole residence; and *TCGA 1992, s 226(3)* did not apply. [*FA 1988, s 111*].

The condition that the dwelling-house must have been provided 'rent-free and without any other consideration' will be regarded as satisfied where the dependent relative paid all or part of the occupier's rates or council tax and the cost of repairs to the dwelling-house attributable to normal wear and tear. In addition, the exemption will not be lost where the dependent relative made other payments in respect of the property either to the individual claiming the exemption or to a third party, provided that no net income was receivable by the individual, taking one year with another. For this purpose, the income receivable and allowable deductions will be computed in accordance with normal Schedule A income tax rules, except that account will be taken of mortgage payments (including both income and capital elements) and of other payments made by the dependent relative as consideration for the provision of the property, whether such payments were made directly to the mortgagee or other recipient or indirectly via the individual (Revenue Pamphlet IR 1, D20 with revision made in Revenue Press Release 18 August 1993).

'*Dependent relative*' means, in relation to an individual

(*a*) any 'relative' of the individual or of his spouse who is incapacitated by old age or infirmity from maintaining himself, or

(*b*) the mother of the individual or of his spouse who, whether or not incapacitated, is widowed, separated, or a single woman in consequence of dissolution or annulment of marriage.

[*TCGA 1992, s 226(5)(6)*].

This definition seems to exclude the mother of a child born out of wedlock (unless the mother either is incapacitated or has married subsequent to the child's birth and then become widowed etc.) but the Revenue have confirmed that such persons will in practice be included (Tolley's Practical Tax 1986 p 143). Also included, it seems in (*a*), is the incapacitated widowed stepmother of an individual, or of an individual's spouse, where the father has remarried and subsequently died. (Tolley's Practical Tax 1981 p 171 and 1984 p 198). '*Relative*' is undefined but may be compared with a specific meaning for other provisions as in 14.7 CONNECTED PERSONS i.e. brother, sister, ancestor or lineal descendant.

Old age, according to the Revenue, is reached at an age of 65 years in any case, and can be reached at an age greater than 54 years if the individual becomes, only because of age, not capable of working again 'in his own industry' (i.e. a man aged 57 years is not considered to have reached old age if he chooses not to work again or is unemployed because of a general lack of jobs). An individual is regarded as infirm if he is prevented by physical or mental illness from supporting himself by working (Revenue Pamphlet CGT 4, p 9).

43.6   **EXEMPTION FOR LETTING AS RESIDENTIAL ACCOMMODATION**

Where a gain to which *TCGA 1992, s 222* (see 43.1 above) applies accrues to an individual and the dwelling-house in question, or any part of it, is or has at any time in his period of ownership been wholly or partly let (thus including any tenancy or licence or agreement for a lease, tenancy or licence; see *TCGA 1992, 8 Sch 10*) by him as residential accommodation, the part of the gain, if any, which otherwise would be a chargeable gain by reason of the letting is exempt to the extent of the lower of

(*a*) £40,000 (£20,000 for disposals before 19 March 1991); and (*b*)   the amount of the gain otherwise exempt under *TCGA 1992, s 222(1)–(3)* (see 43.1 and 43.2 above) or those provisions as applied by *TCGA 1992, s 225* (see 43.4 above).

'Period of ownership' does not include any period before 31 March 1982 (6 April 1965 for disposals before 6 April 1988). [*TCGA 1992, s 223(4)(7); FA 1988, 8 Sch 8; FA 1991, s 94(3)(4)*].

The length of a letting is not determinative and the words 'residential accommodation' do not limit the above relief to accommodation which is used by a tenant etc. as his home (*Owen v Elliott CA 1990, 63 TC 319*). (In this case the taxpayer let short- and long-term accommodation in private hotel premises which he also occupied different parts of at different times of the year as his main residence in such a way that every part of the premises had at some time in his period of ownership been his main residence and it was agreed that on a disposal of the premises one-third of the gain arising was exempt under *TCGA 1992, ss 222–224*. The CA held that the above relief was also available in respect of the remaining non-exempt gain but Leggatt LJ indicated that it would not be available 'to a taxpayer the whole or part of whose dwelling-house is exclusively used as an hotel or boarding house. It will apply only where a dwelling-house has at any time been used wholly or partly for that or a like purpose by a person whose only or main residence it is'. Cf. the Revenue's practice below as to whether let accommodation forms part of the dwelling-house.)

Whether the let accommodation is part of the owner's dwelling-house, or is itself a separate dwelling-house, will depend on the facts of particular cases. In the Revenue's view, the relief will apply to the common case where the owner of a house, which was previously occupied as his or the family home, lets part as a flat or set of rooms without structural alteration, or with only minor adaptations. Whether or not the tenants have separate washing or cooking facilities will not affect the relief. Where a property, although part of the same building, forms a dwelling-house separate from that which is, or has been, the owner's dwelling-house, e.g. a fully self-contained flat with its own access from the road, relief will not be granted. (Revenue Pamphlet IR 131, SP 14/80, 14 November 1980).

Where the letting constitutes a trade (an 'unlikely event' according to the Revenue), it is open to the taxpayer to consider both the provisions given above or a claim for ROLLOVER RELIEF (50) if he uses the proceeds to buy another property where he will continue to provide similar accommodation and services (29.D15 INLAND REVENUE STATEMENTS OF PRACTICE).

Provided the conditions for relief are otherwise met (principally that the dwelling-house must have been, at some time in the period of ownership (including pre-31 March 1982 or pre-6 April 1965 periods as appropriate), the only or main residence), it seems that the relief provisions apply regardless of where the individual was living when the dwelling-house was let after 31 March 1982 or 6 April 1965 as appropriate, and that relief for more than one dwelling-house may be claimed contemporaneously.

The relief appears to be available separately to each spouse where married persons dispose of a dwelling-house which they have owned jointly. This seems to apply to disposals before 6 April 1990 as well as to those on and after that date (Taxation 14 March 1991 p 640).

See 43.2 above for an example on letting as residential accommodation.

For the capital gains tax consequences of eligibility for 'rent a room' income tax relief, see 43.3 above.

For reliefs applicable to the commercial letting of furnished holiday accommodation in the UK, see 19 FURNISHED HOLIDAY ACCOMMODATION.

44 Qualifying Corporate Bonds

44.1 EXEMPTION RULES

After 1 July 1986, disposals of qualifying corporate bonds are exempt whatever the period of ownership subject to the definition in 44.2 below. [*TCGA 1992, s 115(1)(a)*].

After 1 July 1986, disposals of options or contracts to acquire or dispose of qualifying corporate bonds are exempt. See 16.10 and 16.11 DISPOSAL.

See 35.10 LOSSES for allowable loss relief in respect of certain qualifying corporate bonds evidencing loans which become irrecoverable etc.

See 13.9 COMPANIES for appropriations of qualifying corporate bonds to and from trading stock by companies after 1 July 1986.

44.2 DEFINITION

Subject to the inclusion of certain other securities below, a '*corporate bond*' is a 'security' which fulfils all of the three following conditions.

(*a*)   It is a security which, for disposals before 14 March 1989, from the time of its issue has been quoted on a recognised UK stock exchange or dealt in on the Unlisted Securities Market or was issued by a body provided *any other* share, stock or security of the body was so quoted or dealt in at the time of issue.

(*b*)   The debt on the security represents, and has at all times represented, a 'normal commercial loan' as would be defined by *ICTA 1988, 18 Sch 1(5)* (as it has effect following amendments made to *ICTA 1988, 18 Sch* by *FA 1989, s 101* and *FA 1991, s 77*; see Tolley's Corporation Tax under Groups of Companies) if for *ICTA 1988, 18 Sch 1(5)(a)(i)–(iii)* there were substituted the words 'corporate bonds (within the meaning of *TCGA 1992, s 117*)'. The broad effect of the modification is that securities can be treated as corporate bonds if they carry conversion rights into other corporate bonds but not if the conversion rights relate to securities other than corporate bonds.

The above condition is strictly only extant for disposals and certain claims after 18 March 1991 and again after 31 March 1991 (see below) but in a Revenue Press Release of 19 March 1991 it was stated that the changes made subsequently by *FA 1991, s 77* would be recognised for such events etc. before 1 April 1991. The legislation for disposals etc. before 19 March 1991 still referred to the definition of a normal commercial loan in *FA 1973, 12 Sch 1(5)* even though that provision had been repealed by *ICTA 1988* and consolidated as *ICTA 1988, 18 Sch 1(5)* (as originally enacted).

(*c*)   The security is expressed in sterling and in respect of which no provision is made for conversion into, or redemption in, a currency other than sterling. However, a security is not treated as expressed in sterling if the amount of sterling falls to be determined by reference to the value at any time of any other currency or asset. A provision for redemption in a currency other than sterling is disregarded provided the rate of exchange is that prevailing at redemption.

After 28 November 1994 a security (whenever issued) will not be a '*corporate bond*' where it falls to be treated as a 'quoted index security' for the purposes of *FA 1989, 11 Sch 2(2)(c)*.

For disposals after 13 March 1989, a '*corporate bond*' also includes a security not qualifying under (*b*) and (*c*) above and which is a 'deep gain security' for the purposes of *FA*

1989, 11 Sch or falls to be treated as a deep gain security under *FA 1989, 11 Sch 21(2)* (non gilts: special rules) or *22(2)* (indexed securities: special rules). For disposals after 'the relevant time' (see below), a *'corporate bond'* also includes a security not qualifying under (*b*) and (*c*) above and which falls to be treated as a deep gain security under *FA 1989, 11 Sch 22A(2)* (convertible securities: special rules (1)) or *22B(3)* (convertible securities: special rules (2)). For disposals after 24 July 1991 (save in relation to the application of this definition for the purposes of *TCGA 1992, s 254* (loss relief for irrecoverable loans to traders evidenced by qualifying corporate bonds; see 35.10 LOSSES and also below)), a *'corporate bond'* also includes a share in a building society (within *Building Societies Act 1986*) which meets the condition in (*c*) above and which is a 'qualifying share' (i.e. a share which is either a 'permanent interest bearing share' (as defined in *Building Societies (Designated Capital Resources) (Permanent Interest Bearing Shares) Order 1991, SI 1991 No 702* or alternative Treasury regulations) or is of a description specified in Treasury regulations).

In relation to any chargeable period ending after 15 March 1993, *'corporate bond'* also includes, except in relation to a person who acquires it on or after a disposal in relation to which *TCGA 1992, s 115* has or has had effect in accordance with *TCGA 1992, s 116(10)(c)* (exempt disposal of qualifying corporate bonds derived from shares giving rise to deferred gain; see 44.3 below), any debenture issued after 15 March 1993 which is not a 'security' as defined below but is issued in circumstances such that under *TCGA 1992, s 251(6)* (see 18.5 EXEMPTIONS AND RELIEFS) it would fall to be treated for the purposes of *TCGA 1992, s 251* as such a security and would be a corporate bond if it were a security as so defined. (This provision and *TCGA 1992, s 251(6)* prevent, in certain circumstances, the issue of a debenture which neither represents a debt on a security nor is a qualifying corporate bond).

Subject to *TCGA 1992, s 251(6)* above, *'security'* includes any loan stock or similar security of any government or public or local authority in the UK or elsewhere, or of any company, and whether secured or unsecured. [*TCGA 1992, ss 132(3)(b), 117(1)–(6)(6A)(11)(b)(12)(13); FA 1989, ss 139(1)–(3); FA 1990, 10 Sch 28(1)(2), 29(2)(3); FA 1991, ss 51, 77, 98, 10 Sch 1; FA 1993, s 84(1)(3)*].

A corporate bond

(A) is a *'qualifying corporate bond'* if it is issued after 13 March 1984; and

(B) becomes a *'qualifying corporate bond'* if, having been issued before 14 March 1984, it is acquired by any person after 13 March 1984 unless

(i) the acquisition is as the result of *any* disposal treated as a 'no gain, no loss' transaction or a disposal where the consideration is reduced by an amount of held-over gain under *TCGA 1992, s 165* or *260* or, for disposals before 14 March 1989, *FA 1980, s 79* (see 22.1–22.6 HOLD-OVER RELIEFS); and

(ii) the bond was not a qualifying corporate bond before the disposal.

[*TCGA 1992, s 117(2A)(7)(8); FA 1989, s 124(1), 14 Sch 6; FA 1995, s 50*].

Example

B has the following transactions in 5% unsecured loan stock issued in 1983 by F Ltd.

		£
11.11.83	Purchase £2,000	1,800
10.7.85	Gift from wife £1,000 (original cost £900)	—
30.9.87	Purchase £2,000	1,700
5.6.95	Sale £4,000	(3,300)

44.2   Qualifying Corporate Bonds

Apart from the gift on 10.7.85, all acquisitions were arm's length purchases. B's wife acquired her £1,000 holding on 11.11.83. Indexation allowance of £89 arose on the transfer from wife to husband.

For the purposes of the accrued income scheme, the sale is without accrued interest and the rebate amount is £20. The stock is a corporate bond as defined by *TCGA 1992, s 117(1)* and a 'relevant security' as defined by *TCGA 1992, s 108(1)*.

Under the rules for matching relevant securities in *TCGA 1992, s 108*, the stock disposed of is identified with acquisitions as follows.

(i) Identify £2,000 with purchase on 30.9.87 (LIFO)

	£
Disposal consideration £3,300 × $\frac{2,000}{4,000}$	1,650
Add rebate amount £20 × $\frac{2,000}{4,000}$	10
	1,660
Allowable cost	1,700
Loss	£40

The loss is *not* allowable as the £2,000 stock purchased on 30.9.87 is a qualifying corporate bond (note (*a*)). [*TCGA 1992, s 115*].

(ii) Identify £1,000 with acquisition on 10.7.85

	£
Disposal consideration £3,300 × $\frac{1,000}{4,000}$	825
Add rebate amount £20 × $\frac{1,000}{4,000}$	5
	830
Allowable cost (including indexation to 10.7.85)	989
Allowable loss	£159

The loss is allowable as the stock acquired on 10.7.85 is not a qualifying corporate bond (note (*b*)).

(iii) Identify £1,000 with purchase on 11.11.83

	£
Disposal consideration £3,300 × $\frac{1,000}{4,000}$	825
Add rebate amount £20 × $\frac{1,000}{4,000}$	5
	830
Allowable cost £1,800 × $\frac{1,000}{2,000}$	900
Allowable loss	£70

The loss is allowable as the stock acquired on 11.11.83 is not a qualifying corporate bond (note (*c*)).

Notes to the example

(*a*)   The acquisition on 30.9.87 is a qualifying corporate bond as it was acquired after 13 March 1984 otherwise than as a result of an excluded disposal.

(*b*)   The acquisition on 10.7.85 was the result of an excluded disposal, being a no gain/no loss transfer between spouses where the first spouse had acquired the stock before 14 March 1984. It is therefore not a qualifying corporate bond.

(*c*)   Securities acquired before 14 March 1984 cannot be qualifying corporate bonds in the hands of the person who so acquired them.

TCGA 1992, s 117(7)(8) does not apply to a security which falls to be treated as a corporate bond by virtue of being, or being treated as, a deep gain security under *FA 1989, 11 Sch, 11 Sch 21(2)* or *11 Sch 22(2)* (see above) and such a corporate bond is a qualifying corporate bond whatever its date of issue except that where a security is treated as a corporate bond by the two last-mentioned provisions, a corporate bond is a qualifying corporate bond as regards a disposal made respectively after the time mentioned in *FA 1989, 11 Sch 21(1)(c)* or the time the agreement mentioned in *FA 1989, 11 Sch 22(1)(b)* is made. Where a security falls to be treated as a corporate bond by virtue of being treated as a deep gain security under *FA 1989, 11 Sch 22A(2)* or *22B(3)* (see above), such a corporate bond is a qualifying corporate bond as regards a disposal made after the time mentioned respectively in *FA 1989, 11 Sch 22A(1)(c)* or *22B(2)(b)*. Such a time is '*the relevant time*' (see above). [*TCGA 1992, s 117(9); FA 1989, s 139(4); FA 1990, 10 Sch 28(1)(3), 29(2)(3)*].

Where a right to a security is comprised in a provisional letter of allotment or similar instrument, the security is not deemed to be issued until acceptance has been made. A security issued by a member of a group (within *TCGA 1992, s 170*; see 13.10 COMPANIES) to another member of the same group is excluded from being a qualifying corporate bond except in relation to a disposal after 13 March 1989 by a person who (at the time of the disposal) is not a member of the same group as the company which issued the security. [*TCGA 1992, ss 117(10)(11)(a)(13), 288(5); FA 1989, s 139(5), 14 Sch 6(4)*].

In relation to disposals after 13 March 1989, the changes made by *FA 1989, s 139, 14 Sch 6* are to be regarded as always having had effect. In relation to disposals after the relevant time (see above), the changes made by *FA 1990, 10 Sch 28* are also to be regarded as always having had effect.

Subject to the concessionary practice mentioned in (*b*) above, *FA 1991, s 77* has effect, so far as concerns the application of *TCGA 1992, s 117(1)* (see formerly *FA 1984, s 64(2)*) for the purposes of *TCGA 1992, s 254*, in relation to claims after 31 March 1991, and so far as concerns any other application of *TCGA 1992, s 117(1)*, in relation to disposals on or after that date (and, in relation to such disposals is to be regarded as always having had effect). *FA 1991, s 98* has similar effect *mutatis mutandis* to *FA 1991, s 77* but in relation to the application of *TCGA 1992, s 117* (see formerly *FA 1984, s 64*) generally (rather than *TCGA 1992, s 117(1)*) and claims and disposals after 18 March 1991 (rather than 31 March 1991). [*TCGA 1992, 11 Sch 16(4); FA 1991, ss 77(2), 98(1)(4)*].

The capital element of a deep discount security within *ICTA 1988, 4 Sch* (see 53.19 SHARES AND SECURITIES) can be a qualifying corporate bond (CCAB Statement TR 551, July 1984).

The following applies where a 'qualifying asset' consists of a right to settlement under a debt on a security, and on or after its 'commencement day' a 'qualifying company' (see 13.34 COMPANIES for a note of these terms) disposes of the security (or engages in an event which would be a disposal of the security in the absence of *TCGA 1992, s 127* (reorganisations)) and immediately before the disposal the company did not hold the security in 'exempt circumstances'. '*Exempt circumstances*' are when the security is held for the purposes of long term insurance business; for the purposes of mutual insurance business; for the purposes of the occupation for profit of commercial woodlands in the UK; by an approved housing association; or by an approved self-build society. Where these conditions are fulfilled, then in applying *TCGA 1992, s 117* above or to a transaction to which the rules in *TCGA 1992, ss 127–130* apply (reorganisations) or would apply but for *TCGA 1992, s 116* (qualifying corporate bonds)

(1) the requirement that the security be expressed in sterling as in (*c*) above is ignored, and

44.3 Qualifying Corporate Bonds

(2) where the settlement currency of the debt is a currency other than sterling:

(i) the definition of 'normal commercial loan' in (*b*) above has effect as if *ICTA 1988, 18 Sch 1(5)(b)(c)* (which broadly requires the return on the security not to depend on results or exceed a commercial return and the repayment of the security not to exceed the new consideration lent or what is generally available on similar securities) were omitted; and

(ii) *TCGA 1992, s 117(10)* above (relating to securities issued within a group) is ignored.

[*FA 1993, s 169, 17 Sch 3, 5; FA 1995, 24 Sch 6*].

The following applies where a 'qualifying company' (see above) has made a loan under which the debt is a debt on a security, and the right to settlement under the debt is a 'qualifying asset' (see above). In these circumstances the following apply in relation to relief claims made on or after the company's commencement day.

(*aa*) In applying *TCGA 1992, s 117* above for the purposes of *TCGA 1992, s 254* (see above), the requirement that the security be expressed in sterling as in (*c*) above is ignored.

(*bb*) Where the settlement currency of the debt is a currency other than sterling, then in applying *TCGA 1992, s 117* for the purposes of *TCGA 1992, s 254*:

(i) the definition of 'normal commercial loan' in (*b*) above has effect as if *ICTA 1988, 18 Sch 1(5)(b)(c)* (see (2) above) were omitted; and

(ii) *TCGA 1992, s 117(10)* above (relating to securities issued within a group) is ignored.

(*cc*) In applying *TCGA 1992, s 254(6)* (allowable amount if first or second condition fulfilled) in a case where a security would not be a qualifying corporate bond but for (*aa*) or (*bb*) above, the 'allowable amount' under that provision is found by deducting from what the amount would otherwise be the amount of any exchange loss or losses (whether trading or non-trading) accruing to the company as regards the asset for a period or periods ending on or before the 'relevant date'. The '*relevant date*' is the date when the security's value became negligible or the outstanding amount of the principal of the loan was or proved to be irrecoverable. The amount of an exchange loss expressed in a currency other than the basic currency (i.e. the currency in which the allowable amount is expressed) is for these purposes treated as the basic currency equivalent on the day the related claim is made, calculated by reference to the London closing exchange rate for that day.

[*FA 1993, s 169, 17 Sch 6*].

44.3 REORGANISATION OF SHARE CAPITAL

Special provisions apply to a transaction ('*relevant transaction*') where otherwise *TCGA 1992, ss 127–130* (share reorganisation rules for 'original shares' and 'new holding'; see 53.5 SHARES AND SECURITIES) would otherwise apply under any provision contained in *TCGA 1992, Pt IV Ch II* (reorganisation of share capital, conversion of securities etc.), and either the original shares would consist of or include a qualifying corporate bond and the new holding would not, or the original shares would not and the new holding would consist of or include such a bond. Where the qualifying corporate bond would constitute the original shares it is referred to as '*the old asset*', the shares and securities constituting the new holding being referred to as '*the new asset*'. Where the qualifying corporate bond would constitute the new holding it is referred to as '*the new asset*', the shares and securities constituting the original shares being referred to as '*the old asset*'.

TCGA 1992, ss 127–130 do not apply to the relevant transaction so far as the latter relates to the old asset and the new asset. (The Revenue has stated that where shares (or other chargeable securities) are exchanged, converted etc. for a new holding consisting partly of qualifying corporate bonds and partly of shares etc., then *TCGA 1992, ss 127–130* are only disapplied to the extent that the consideration takes the form of qualifying corporate bonds, any apportionment of the base cost of the original shares being on a just and reasonable basis under *TCGA 1992, s 52(4)* by reference to the respective market values at the time of exchange etc. of the shares etc. and qualifying corporate bonds received in exchange etc. (Revenue Tax Bulletin February 1993 p 57).)

Where the qualifying corporate bond would constitute the old asset, the shares or securities which constitute the new asset are to be treated as being acquired on the date of the relevant transaction and for a consideration of the market value of the old asset immediately before the relevant transaction. Similar provisions apply where the qualifying corporate bond constitutes the new asset. Where a sum of money by way of consideration for the old asset is received, in addition to the new asset, that sum is to be deducted from the deemed market value consideration and where a sum of money is paid by way of consideration, in addition to the old asset, that sum is to be added to the deemed market value consideration. See also (ii) below.

Where the old asset consists of a qualifying corporate bond, then so far as it relates to the old and the new asset, the relevant transaction (being after 1 July 1986) is to be treated as a disposal of the old asset and an acquisition of the new asset. In all other cases (e.g. where the new asset consists of a qualifying corporate bond) then so far as it relates to the old asset and to the new asset the relevant transaction is *not* to be treated as a disposal of the old asset but

(*a*)   the chargeable gain or allowable loss is calculated that would have accrued had the old asset been disposed of at the time of the relevant transaction at its market value immediately before that time, and

(*b*)   subject to the exclusions below, the whole or a corresponding part of the calculated chargeable gain or allowable loss at (*a*) above is to be deemed to accrue on a subsequent disposal of the whole or part of the new asset. For events after 1 July 1986, the total exemption provided by 44.1 above is to apply only to the gain or loss actually accruing at the time of the event and *not* to any gain or loss deemed to accrue at the same time.

The following exclusions are made to the above provisions.

(i)   The provisions in (*b*) above do not apply to disposals falling within: *TCGA 1992, s 58(1)* (see 37.6 MARRIED PERSONS); *s 62(4)* (see 15.9 DEATH); *s 139* in respect of disposals after 13 March 1989 (see 13.6 COMPANIES); *s 140A* (see 39.15 OVERSEAS MATTERS); *s 171(1)* (see 13.11 COMPANIES); or *s 172* (see 39.3 OVERSEAS MATTERS). Where there is such a disposal (and without there having been a previous disposal other than such a disposal or a devolution on death) the person who has acquired the new asset is treated for the purposes of (*b*) above as if the new asset had been acquired by him at the same time and for the same consideration as it was acquired by the person making the disposal.

(ii)   Where a chargeable gain arises under (*a*) above *and* part of the consideration for the old asset is received as money, a proportion of the chargeable gain is deemed to accrue at that time. The proportion is the ratio which the sum of money bears to the market value of the old asset immediately before the relevant transaction. On a later disposal of a part or the whole of the new asset, the proportion already deemed to have accrued is to be deducted from the gain accruing under (*b*) above. However, if the sum of money is 'small' (not defined, but regarded by the Revenue as 5% or less of market value; see CCAB Statement TR 551 July 1984) in comparison with the market value of the old asset immediately before the relevant transaction, the Revenue may direct that no chargeable gain accrues at that time. The money consideration is then deducted from allowable expenditure on any subsequent disposal (see 16.8 DISPOSAL).

[*TCGA 1992, s 116(1)–(14); FA 1985, s 67(2)(c), 27 Sch Part VII; FA 1989, s 139(6); FA 1990, s 70(6)(9); F(No 2)A 1992, s 46(1)(3)*].

In relation to disposals after 13 March 1989, the changes made by *FA 1989, s 139* are to be regarded as always having had effect. [*TCGA 1992, 11 Sch 16*].

Where the new asset is a qualifying corporate bond which is subsequently gifted to a charity, the Revenue take the view that no deferred gain or loss will arise to the donor under (*b*) above (Revenue Tax Bulletin May 1992 p 21). This will be advantageous if the loss relief for loans becoming irrecoverable etc. and evidenced by qualifying corporate bonds is unavailable (see below).

See 53.26 SHARES AND SECURITIES for the interaction of the provisions above with those relating to certain disposals to employee share ownership trusts.

See 35.10 LOSSES for the interaction of the provisions above with those relating to loss relief by reference to certain qualifying corporate bonds evidencing loans which become irrecoverable etc.

Example

D holds 5,000 £1 ordinary shares in H Ltd. He acquired the shares in April 1982 by subscription at par. On 1 August 1985, he accepted an offer for the shares from J plc. The terms of the offer were one 25p ordinary share of J plc and £10 J plc 10% unsecured loan stock (a qualifying corporate bond) for each H Ltd ordinary share. Both the shares and the loan stock are listed on the Stock Exchange. In December 1995, D sells £20,000 loan stock at its quoted price of £105 per cent.

The value of J plc ordinary shares at 1 August 1985 was £3.52 per share and the loan stock was £99.20 per cent. The indexation factor for April 1982 to August 1985 is 0.178.

The cost of the H Ltd shares must be apportioned between the J plc ordinary shares and loan stock.

	£
Value of J plc shares	
5,000 × £3.52	17,600
Value of J plc loan stock	
£50,000 × 99.2%	49,600
	£67,200

Allowable cost of J plc shares

$$\frac{17,600}{67,200} \times £5,000 \qquad\qquad £1,310$$

Allowable cost of J plc loan stock

$$\frac{49,600}{67,200} \times £5,000 \qquad\qquad £3,690$$

Chargeable gain on H Ltd shares attributable to J plc loan stock to date of exchange

	£
Deemed disposal consideration	49,600
Allowable cost	3,690
Unindexed gain	45,910
Indexation allowance £3,690 × 0.178	657
Deferred chargeable gain	£45,253

Deferred chargeable gain accruing on disposal of loan stock

Loan stock sold (nominal)	£20,000
Total holding of loan stock before disposal (nominal)	£50,000

Deferred chargeable gain accruing in 1995/96

$$\frac{20,000}{50,000} \times £45,253 \qquad\qquad £18,101$$

Notes to the example

(a)   The gain on the sale of J plc loan stock is exempt (as the stock is a qualifying corporate bond) except for that part which relates to the gain on the previous holding of H Ltd shares. [*TCGA 1992, ss 115, 116(10)*]. There will also be income tax consequences under the accrued income scheme.

(b)   The qualifying corporate bond is treated as acquired at the date of the reorganisation, so even if the original shares had been held at 31 March 1982, re-basing could *not* apply on the subsequent disposal, after 5 April 1988, of the loan stock. However, where the original shares were acquired before 31 March 1982, the reorganisation took place before 6 April 1988, and the qualifying corporate bonds are disposed of after 5 April 1988, the deferred chargeable gain is halved. [*TCGA 1992, 4 Sch 4*].

(c)   The exchange of J plc ordinary shares for H Ltd shares is dealt with under *TCGA 1992, ss 127-130*, and no gain or loss will arise until the J plc shares are disposed of.

45 Reinvestment in Shares Relief

Cross-references. See 48 RETIREMENT RELIEF; 50 ROLLOVER RELIEF; 53 SHARES AND SECURITIES; (58) VENTURE CAPITAL TRUSTS.

45.1 INTRODUCTION

In respect of disposals after 15 March 1993, *Chapter IA* of *Part V* of *TCGA 1992* (referred to in this chapter as '*Chapter IA*'), as inserted by *FA 1993, s 87, 7 Sch 3*, provides, subject to conditions, for relief where reinvestment is made in shares in a company.

Chapter IA is entitled 'rollover relief on reinvestment', but in order to avoid confusion with the rollover relief for replacement of business assets (see ROLLOVER RELIEF (50)), the appellation 'reinvestment in shares relief' is adopted in this publication. The term 'entrepreneurial relief' has been used by the Revenue to identify the relief as originally enacted (although no like or similar term is mentioned in the legislation). However, subsequent changes to the relief (see below) would seem to make this appellation somewhat of a misnomer.

In its original form, which existed for disposals occurring after 15 March 1993 but before 30 November 1993, the relief required the gain which could be rolled over to arise, broadly, in respect of an individual's disposal of unquoted shares or other securities of a trading company in circumstances where the individual had throughout a minimum period of one year before the disposal both exercised at least 5% of the voting rights and worked full-time for the company as an officer or employee. However, for disposals after 29 November 1993, the main change to the relief made by *FA 1994, s 91(1)(2), 11 Sch* was to allow a gain on any asset arising to an individual to qualify for relief. Similarly, the original requirement to acquire, broadly, at least a 5% holding of the ordinary shares in the company in order for the acquisition cost of that shareholding to be reduced was removed.

Trustees of certain settlements are treated similarly to individuals in the claiming of relief.

The broad approach taken in the coverage below is to describe the relief as it relates to disposals after 29 November 1993, the relief for disposals after 15 March 1993 and before 30 November 1993 being explained by way of contrast in view of its restricted application and relatively short currency before amendment.

Where a qualifying corporate bond is redeemed or otherwise disposed of, that disposal does not give rise to a chargeable gain (*TCGA 1992, s 115*). So reinvestment relief cannot be available in respect of that disposal. However, in calculating any chargeable gains under *TCGA 1992, s 116(10)(a)* (gains deferred where shares exchanged for qualifying corporate bonds) a claim for reinvestment relief may be made on the basis of a disposal at the date that the chargeable gain is calculated, i.e. at the time of the relevant exchange. Reinvestment relief will be available in accordance with the *FA 1993* provisions where the exchange took place after 15 March 1993 and in accordance with the *FA 1994* provisions for exchanges after 29 November 1993 (Revenue Tax Bulletin May 1994 pp 128, 129).

45.2 RELIEF FOR INDIVIDUALS

Subject to the following provisions of *Chapter IA*, relief is available where a chargeable gain would otherwise accrue to any individual ('*the reinvestor*') on any disposal made

after 29 November 1993 by him of any asset ('*the asset disposed of*'), and that individual acquires a 'qualifying investment' at any time in the 'qualifying period' (these two terms being defined below). [*TCGA 1992, s 164A(1); FA 1993, 7 Sch 3; FA 1994, 11 Sch 2(a)*].

A reinvestor on claiming the relief is treated

(*a*)   as if the consideration for the disposal of the asset disposed of were reduced (including reducing an amount to nil) by whichever is the smallest of the following four amounts:

(i)   the amount of the chargeable gain which would otherwise accrue in the absence of a claim on the disposal of the asset disposed of, so far as that amount has not already been held over by way of reductions under this provision,

(ii)   the actual amount or value of the consideration for the acquisition of the qualifying investment,

(iii)   in the case of a qualifying investment acquired otherwise than by a transaction at arm's length, the market value of that investment at the time of its acquisition, and

(iv)   the amount specified for the purposes of this provision in the claim;

and

(*b*)   as if the amount or value of the consideration for the acquisition of the qualifying investment were reduced by the amount of the reduction made under (*a*) above.

Neither (*a*) nor (*b*) affects the treatment under *TCGA 1992* of the other party to the transaction involving the asset disposed of or of the other party to the transaction involving the qualifying investment. [*TCGA 1992, ss 164A(2), 164N(4); FA 1993, 7 Sch 3; FA 1994, 11 Sch 2(b)*].

In the normal case of the reinvestor acquiring the qualifying investment at arm's length and in the absence of other reliefs and time apportionment, the effect of (*a*)(i) and (ii) above is to provide full deferral of the gain otherwise accruing on the disposal of the asset disposed of where the acquisition consideration given for the qualifying investment is equal to or exceeds the amount of that gain (and *not* where it is equal to or exceeds the amount of the disposal consideration given for the asset disposed of, cf ROLLOVER RELIEF (50)). It was difficult to ascertain whether the legislation allowed relief under (*a*) (ii) above where the qualifying investment was acquired by way of gift (when other provisions in *TCGA 1992* would substitute a deemed consideration e.g. market value or at a no gain/no loss consideration). *FA 1995* removed any doubt by preventing excess relief being claimed in respect of shares acquired by way of gift if the qualifying investment was acquired after 19 June 1994, or a claim under *TCGA 1992, s 164A(2)* above relating to a disposal is made after that date. Thus, where a claim for the above relief is made after 19 June 1994 and the qualifying investment in respect of which the claim is made was acquired by the reinvestor through an inter-spouse (no gain/no loss) transfer under *TCGA 1992, s 58*, the relief claimed cannot exceed the transferor spouse's allowable base cost of the qualifying investment, after any reduction in that cost due to gains already rolled over into that investment, irrespective of the rebasing rules in *TCGA 1992, s 35, 3 Sch 1* or *TCGA 1992, s 55* in situations where the qualifying investment was held by the transferor spouse since 31 March 1982. Similarly, the rebasing provisions are disapplied where the claimant returns the qualifying investment to his spouse on a no gain/no loss basis. The reduction provided by (*a*)(iii) would only seem to be in point, having regard to *TCGA 1992, s 164A(10)* below, where the amount of the consideration deemed to be given for the qualifying investment (e.g. at a no gain/

no loss transfer consideration) is greater than its market value at the time of its acquisition. The reduction at (*a*)(iv) above is most likely to be useful in cases where the annual exempt amount, allowable losses or other reliefs (e.g. retirement relief; see 45.6 below) are available. In all cases, the reduction provided by (*a*) above is from the disposal consideration, again subject to *TCGA 1992, s 164A(10)* below, of the asset disposed of (and *not* from the gain otherwise arising on that disposal; see further in 45.6 below).

For the purposes of the relief, a person who acquires any 'eligible shares' (see below) in a 'qualifying company' (see 45.13 below) is regarded as acquiring a *'qualifying investment'* unless, where the asset disposed of consisted of shares in or securities of any company ('*the initial holding*'), the qualifying company

(1)   is the company in which the holding subsisted, or

(2)   is a company that was, at the time of the disposal of the initial holding, or is, at the time of the acquisition of the qualifying investment, a member of the same *'group of companies'* (as in *TCGA 1992, 6 Sch 1*; see 48.3 RETIREMENT RELIEF) as the company in which the initial holding subsisted.

[*TCGA 1992, ss 164A(8)(14), 164FF; FA 1993, 7 Sch 3; FA 1994, 11 Sch 7; FA 1995, s 47(1)(2)(4)(6)(8)*].

'*Eligible shares*' means (subject to *TCGA 1992, ss 164L, 164M* in 45.15 below) any 'ordinary shares' in a company which do not carry any present or future preferential rights to dividends or the company's assets on a winding up or right to be redeemed. '*Ordinary shares*' means shares forming part of a company's '*ordinary share capital*' (i.e. all the issued share capital of the company, other than capital the holders of which only have a right to a fixed rate of dividend). [*TCGA 1992, s 164N(1); FA 1993, 7 Sch 3*].

For the purposes of the relief the acquisition of a qualifying investment is taken to be in the '*qualifying period*' if, and only if, it takes place at any time in the period beginning twelve months before and ending three years after the disposal of the asset disposed of, or at such time before the beginning of that period or after it ends as the Board may by notice allow. [*TCGA 1992, s 164A(9); FA 1993, 7 Sch 3; FA 1994, 11 Sch 2(d)*].

The provisions of *TCGA 1992* fixing the amount of consideration deemed to be given for the acquisition or disposal of assets are applied before the relief given by the above provisions is applied; and without prejudice to the generality of this, *TCGA 1992, s 42(5)* (apportionment on part disposal to be operated before certain provisions including those deeming a no gain/no loss disposal consideration; see 16.6 DISPOSAL) is applied in relation to an adjustment by way of the above relief of the consideration for the acquisition of any shares as it applies to an adjustment in relation to a deemed no gain/no loss disposal consideration. [*TCGA 1992, s 164A(10); FA 1993, 7 Sch 3*].

Without prejudice to *TCGA 1992, s 52(4)* (apportionment of consideration or expenditure to be just and reasonable; see 16.6 DISPOSAL), where consideration is given for the acquisition of any assets some of which are shares to the acquisition of which a claim for relief relates and some of which are not, the consideration is to be apportioned in a just and reasonable manner. [*TCGA 1992, s 164A(12); FA 1993, 7 Sch 3; FA 1994, 11 Sch 2(e)*].

Where an acquisition is made after 28 November 1994, *TCGA 1992, s 164H* (interests in land rule, see 45.13 below) no longer applies in deciding whether it is an acquisition of a qualifying investment for the purposes of the above relief. [*TCGA 1992, s 164A(13); FA 1995, s 46(1)(2)*].

FA 1995 introduced rules with regard to the making of multiple claims for relief against the same qualifying investment to ensure that aggregate gains rolled over do not exceed the cost thereof. These rules have effect where a qualifying investment is acquired after

19 June 1994, or claims under *TCGA 1992, s 164A(2)* are made in respect of the same qualifying investment for disposals after that date. Where multiple reductions are claimed under the above relief in respect of the same qualifying investment, the reductions shall be treated as claimed separately in such order as the claimant elects or, in default, the Board determines. On the second and subsequent claims the amount of gain able to be rolled over will be limited to the remaining acquisition cost ((*a*)(ii) above) or market value ((*a*)(iii) above) of the qualifying investment left after any previous claims have been made. A claim that has become final (i.e. it may not be amended or is finally determined, whichever occurs first) will be treated as made earlier than any claim which is not final. [*TCGA 1992, ss 164A(14), 164FG; FA 1995, s 47(1)(2)(5)(7)(8)*].

Example

In April 1995 R sells a painting for £200,000 which he purchased in June 1985 for £65,000. In October 1995, R acquires 30,000 ordinary shares in A Ltd for £150,000. A Ltd is an unquoted company which exists wholly for the purpose of carrying on a manufacturing trade. R has no other chargeable gains in 1995/96. He wishes to make a claim under *TCGA 1992, s 164A* for reinvestment relief but so as to leave sufficient gains in charge to utilise £2,000 worth of capital losses brought forward and his annual exemption of £6,000. All transactions are at arm's length. The indexation factor for the period June 1985 to April 1995 is assumed to be 0.515.

The chargeable gain on the disposal of the painting is calculated as follows

	£
Disposal consideration	200,000
Cost	65,000
Unindexed gain	135,000
Indexation allowance £65,000 × 0.515	33,475
Gain after indexation	£101,525

The disposal consideration received is treated as reduced by the smallest of

(i)	the chargeable gain	£101,525
(ii)	the amount reinvested	£150,000
(iii)	the amount specified in the claim for relief (£101,525 − £(2,000 + 6,000))	£93,525

The chargeable gain is recalculated as follows

	£
Disposal consideration	200,000
Less reduction (see (iii) above)	93,525
	106,475
Cost	65,000
Unindexed gain	41,475
Indexation allowance as above	33,475
Gain after indexation	8,000
Less losses brought forward	2,000
Net gain (covered by annual exemption)	£6,000

The base cost of R's acquired shares in A Ltd is reduced by the same amount as above and thus becomes £56,475 (£150,000 − £93,525).

The cost of the painting in the hands of the purchaser is not affected by R's claim for reinvestment relief and is thus £200,000.

45.3   **Relief for disposals after 15 March 1993 and before 30 November 1993.** Subject to the following provisions of *Chapter IA*, relief was available where a chargeable gain would otherwise accrue to any individual ('*the reinvestor*') on any 'material disposal' by him of shares in or other securities of any company ('*the initial holding*)', and that individual acquires a 'qualifying investment' at any time in the 'qualifying period' (these three terms being defined below). [*TCGA 1992, s 164A(1); FA 1993, 7 Sch 3*].

The relief under *TCGA 1992, s 164A(2)* before amendment by *FA 1994, 11 Sch 2(b)* (see 45.2 above) operated similarly but by reference to the 'initial holding' instead of the 'asset disposed of' and was subject to *TCGA 1993, s 164C* in 45.8 below. The comments made about the operation of the reduction under 45.2(a) above also applied. [*TCGA 1992, ss 164A(2), 164N(4); FA 1993, 7 Sch 3*].

Subject to the following, the disposal of shares in or other securities of a company was a '*material disposal*' for these purposes if the conditions specified in (*a*)–(*d*) below were satisfied in relation to a period of one year ending with the date of disposal or, if the company ceased at any time in the '*permitted period*' (broadly, one year or such longer period as is allowed by the Board) before the disposal to be a '*trading company*' or the '*holding company*' of a '*trading group*' (these last four terms having the same meaning as in *TCGA 1992, 6 Sch 1*; see 48.3 RETIREMENT RELIEF), that time. [*TCGA 1992, ss 164A(3), 164N(3)(4); FA 1993, 7 Sch 3; FA 1994, 11 Sch 2(c), 26 Sch Pt V*].

The conditions mentioned above were satisfied in relation to any period if throughout that period

(*a*)   the company was a trading company or the holding company of a trading group;

(*b*)   the company was an '*unquoted company*' (being a company none of the shares in or other securities of which were quoted on any recognised stock exchange or were dealt in on the Unlisted Securities Market) (but see below for the relaxation of this condition in certain circumstances);

(*c*)   the company was the reinvestor's '*personal company*' (within *TCGA 1992, 6 Sch 1*; see 48.3 RETIREMENT RELIEF; broadly, he must have had a minimum of 5% of the voting rights in the company); and

(*d*)   the reinvestor was a '*full-time working officer or employee*' of the company or, if that company was a member of a '*group of companies*' or '*commercial association of companies*' (these three terms having the same meaning as in *TCGA 1992, 6 Sch 1*; see 48.3 RETIREMENT RELIEF), of one or more companies which were members of the group or association.

[*TCGA 1992, ss 164A(4), 164N(1)(3); FA 1993, 7 Sch 3; FA 1994, 11 Sch 2(c), 26 Sch Pt V*].

Where, throughout a period ending at the same time as the one-year period referred to in relation to the definition of 'material disposal' in *TCGA 1992, s 164A(3)* above and beginning at a time ('*the time of partial retirement*') when the reinvestor ceased to be such a full-time working officer or employee as is mentioned in (*d*) above

(1)   the conditions specified in (*a*)–(*c*) above were satisfied in relation to any company,

(2)   the reinvestor was an officer or employee of that company or, as the case may have been, of one or more companies of the group or association in question, and

(3)   in that capacity, the reinvestor devoted at least ten hours per week (averaged over the period) to the service of the company or companies in a technical or managerial capacity,

the disposal of shares in or other securities of that company was a material disposal for the purposes of the relief if the conditions specified in (a)–(d) above were satisfied in relation to the period of one year ending with the time of partial retirement. [*TCGA 1992, s 164A(5); FA 1993, 7 Sch 3; FA 1994, 11 Sch 2(c), 26 Sch Pt V*].

Where any company ceased to be an unquoted company and all of the conditions specified in (a)–(d) above were satisfied in relation to the period of one year ending with the time when the company ceased to be unquoted, *TCGA 1992, s 164A* had effect in relation to an initial holding acquired by the reinvestor at the time when the company in question was an unquoted company as if the company continued to be an unquoted company after that time until the disposal of that holding and as if the one-year period referred to in relation to the definition of 'material disposal' in *TCGA 1992, s 164A(3)* above included all such time (if any) as fell after the company's ceasing to be an unquoted company and before what would otherwise have been the beginning of that period. For the purposes of this treatment, to determine when the shares or other securities comprised in a pool which formed the initial holding were acquired, it had to be assumed that later acquisitions were disposed of before earlier acquisitions. [*TCGA 1992, s 164A(6)(7); FA 1993, 7 Sch 3; FA 1994, 11 Sch 2(c), 26 Sch Pt V*].

For the purposes of the relief a person was regarded as acquiring a '*qualifying investment*' where he acquired any 'eligible shares' (defined as in 45.2 above) in a 'qualifying company' (see 45.13 below) if

(A)   he held 5% or more of the eligible shares in that company

    (i)   at any time after making the acquisition and in the period of three years after the disposal of the initial holding, or

    (ii)   at such time after the end of that period as the Board by notice allowed;

(B)   that company did not cease to be a qualifying company between the acquisition of those shares and that time; and

(C)   that company was neither the company in which the initial holding subsisted nor a company that was a member of the same group of companies (as in (c) above) as that company at the time of disposal of the initial holding or of the acquisition of the qualifying investment.

[*TCGA 1992, ss 164A(8), 164N(1)(3); FA 1993, 7 Sch 3*].

TCGA 1992, s 164A(9) before amendment by *FA 1994, 11 Sch 2(d)* (see 45.2 above) operated similarly by reference to the 'initial holding' instead of the 'asset disposed of'. *TCGA 1992, s 164A(10)* (see 45.2) above also operated similarly. *TCGA 1992, s 164A(12)* although substituted by *FA 1994, 11 Sch 2(e)* (see 45.2 above) operated similarly *mutatis mutandis* but applied additionally in relation to consideration given for the disposal of any assets. [*TCGA 1992, s 164A(9)(10)(12); FA 1993, 7 Sch 3*].

For interaction of the above relief with retirement relief, see 45.7 below.

45.4   RELIEF FOR TRUSTEES

Subject to the following, *TCGA 1992, s 164A* in 45.2 above (after amendment by *FA 1994, 11 Sch*) applies, as it applies in the circumstances mentioned in *TCGA 1992, s 164A(1)* mentioned there, where there is

45.4   Reinvestment in Shares Relief

(a)   a disposal made **after 29 November 1993** by the trustees of a settlement of any asset comprised in any settled property of the kinds mentioned in (1) and (2) below, and

(b)   such an acquisition by those trustees of 'eligible shares' (as in 45.2 above) in a 'qualifying company' (see 45.13 below) as would under *TCGA 1992, s 164A* be an acquisition of a 'qualifying investment' at a time in the 'qualifying period' (these two last terms being defined as in 45.2 above).

[*TCGA 1992, s 164B(1); FA 1993, 7 Sch 3; FA 1994, 11 Sch 3*].

The kinds of settled property referred to in (a) above are

(1)   settled·property on discretionary trusts (i.e. settlements where the beneficiaries' interests are not interests in possession, an interest in possession for this purpose not including an interest for a fixed term; and see generally 52.7 SETTLEMENTS) where all of the beneficiaries are either individuals or charities, and

(2)   settled property on non-discretionary trusts (i.e. settlements where the beneficiaries' interests are interests in possession as in (1) above) where any of the beneficiaries is an individual or a charity.

[*TCGA 1992, s 164B(2); FA 1993, 7 Sch 3; FA 1994, 11 Sch 3*].

For the purposes of (1) and (2) above and *TCGA 1992, s 164B* generally, where there is at least one beneficiary holding a non-discretionary interest and at least one beneficiary holding a discretionary interest, all of the discretionary interests are treated as if they were a single interest in possession, and that interest held, where all the discretionary beneficiaries are individuals or charities, by an individual or charity, and in any other case, by a person who is not an individual or charity. [*TCGA 1992, s 164B(7); FA 1993, 7 Sch 3; FA 1994, 11 Sch 3*]. The broad effect for such 'mixed' settlements, is that the settled property will fall within (2) above if either any non-discretionary interest is held by an individual or charity or all discretionary interests are held by individuals or charities, or both such situations arise. This is subject to the provisions below (in particular, regarding the calculation of the 'relevant proportion').

If, at the time of the disposal of the asset in relation to which relief is to be claimed, the settled property comprising that asset is within (2) above but not all of the beneficiaries are individuals or charities, then

(A)   only the 'relevant proportion' of the gain which would accrue to the trustees on the disposal is taken into account for the purposes of 45.2(a)(i) above (reduction in disposal consideration of gain otherwise accruing), and

(B)   no reduction from disposal or acquisition consideration is made under 45.2(b) above for the whole or any part of the balance of the gain.

[*TCGA 1992, s 164B(3); FA 1993, 7 Sch 3; FA 1994, 11 Sch 3*].

At any time, the '*relevant proportion*' at that time is the proportion the aggregate amount of the income of the settled property interests in which are held by individuals or charities bears to the total amount of all of the income of the settled property. [*TCGA 1992, s 164B(6); FA 1993, 7 Sch 3; FA 1994, 11 Sch 3*].

If the settled property qualifies under (1) above at the time of the disposal of the asset comprised in it for which relief is to be claimed, relief under *TCGA 1992, s 164A* is not applied as above unless, immediately after the acquisition of the eligible shares, the settled property comprising the shares also qualifies under (1) above. This also applies *mutatis mutandis* to settled property qualifying under (2) above but, if not all the beneficiaries are individuals or charities, with the additional condition that the relevant proportion immediately after the acquisition of the shares must be not less than that proportion at the time of the disposal of the asset concerned. [*TCGA 1992, s 164B(4)(5); FA 1993, 7 Sch 3; FA 1994, 11 Sch 3*].

For interaction of the above relief with retirement relief, see 45.6 below.

45.5   **Relief for disposals after 15 March 1993 and before 30 November 1993.** Subject to the following, the provisions of *TCGA 1992, s 164A* in 45.3 above applied, as they applied to an individual, where there was

(a)   a disposal by trustees of a settlement of any shares in or other securities of a company which were part of the settled property; and

(b)   such an acquisition by those trustees of 'eligible shares' (see 45.3 above) in a 'qualifying company' (see 45.13 below) as would for the purposes of *TCGA 1992, s 164A* have been an acquisition of a 'qualifying investment' at a time in the 'qualifying period' (these two last terms being defined as in 45.3 above),

but as if the disposal were a 'material disposal' if, and only if, the conditions specified below were satisfied in relation to the one-year period ending with the date of the disposal or, if the case was as contemplated by *TCGA 1992, s 164A(3)* in 45.3 above, the date in the 'permitted period' before the disposal the company ceased to be a 'trading company' or the 'holding company' of a 'trading group'. [*TCGA 1992, s 164B(1); FA 1993, 7 Sch 3*].

The conditions mentioned above were satisfied *mutatis mutandis* in relation to any period and a 'relevant beneficiary' as they were in *TCGA 1992, s 164A(4)* in 45.3(*a*)–(*d*) above in relation to any period and a reinvestor. [*TCGA 1992, s 164B(2); FA 1993, 7 Sch 3*].

A '*relevant beneficiary*' was any beneficiary who, under the settlement concerned, had an interest in possession (other than, for this purpose, an interest for a fixed term; and see generally 52.7 SETTLEMENTS) in the whole of the settled property or, as the case may have been, in a part of it which consisted of or included the shares or securities that were disposed of by the trustees of the settlement. [*TCGA 1992, s 164B(3); FA 1993, 7 Sch 3*].

Where, in addition to the interest in possession held by a relevant beneficiary who satisfied the conditions *mutatis mutandis* in 45.3(*d*) above in relation to a reinvestor ('*the qualifying beneficiary*'), one or more other beneficiaries had such an interest at the 'relevant time' in the shares or securities being disposed of by the trustees, virtually identical provisions to *TCGA 1992, s 164B(3)* as substituted by *FA 1994, 11 Sch 3* (see 45.4(A) and (B) above) applied regarding the treatment of the 'relevant proportion' of the gain eligible for relief. [*TCGA 1992, s 164B(4); FA 1993, 7 Sch 3*].

The '*relevant proportion*' was the proportion of the qualifying beneficiary's interest at the relevant time in the income of the part of the settled property comprising the shares and securities bore to the interests at that time in that income of all the beneficiaries (including the qualifying beneficiary) who at that time had interests in possession in that part. For this purpose, the qualifying beneficiary's interest was only to take into account the interest by virtue of which he was a qualifying beneficiary and not any other interest he may have held. [*TCGA 1992, s 164B(5)(6); FA 1993, 7 Sch 3*].

Relief was unavailable to trustees unless, immediately after the acquisition by them of eligible shares in a qualifying company, the qualifying beneficiary had an interest in possession in the whole of the settled property, or in the part of it in which the acquired shares were comprised, which was the same as or, as the case may have been, was equivalent to the interest at the relevant time by virtue of which he was a qualifying beneficiary. [*TCGA 1992, s 164B(7); FA 1993, 7 Sch 3*].

The '*relevant time*', in relation to a disposal of shares or other securities, meant the time of disposal or, if the case was as contemplated by *TCGA 1992, s 164A(3)* in 45.3 above, the date in the 'permitted period' before the disposal the company ceased to be a 'trading company' or the 'holding company' of a 'trading group'. [*TCGA 1992, s 164B(8); FA 1993, 7 Sch 3*].

45.6   **RETIREMENT AND OTHER RELIEFS**

The provisions of *TCGA 1992, s 164A* in 45.2 above for making a reduction from disposal and acquisition consideration in respect of disposals made **after 29 November 1993** must be applied before any provisions for calculating the amount of, or giving effect to, any RETIREMENT RELIEF (48) under *TCGA 1992, s 163* or *164*. Accordingly, references in *TCGA 1992, s 164A* to a 'chargeable gain' must be construed ignoring retirement relief. However, if a claim is made under *TCGA 1992, s 164A* in respect of a chargeable gain (ignoring retirement relief), and apart from *Chapter IA* (reinvestment in shares relief), the whole or any part of the gain would be relieved by retirement relief, then further provisions apply. For the purpose of giving retirement relief, reinvestment in shares relief under *TCGA 1992, s 164A* is treated as having been made first against 'the unrelieved part of the chargeable gain'; and only the amount (if any) which is equal to the unrelieved part of the chargeable gain (ignoring retirement relief) after that reduction is treated as exceeding 'the amount available for relief'.

'*The unrelieved part of a chargeable gain*' is so much of a chargeable gain, ignoring retirement relief and apart from *Chapter IA*, as would constitute a chargeable gain after the application of the retirement relief provisions in, as the case may be, *TCGA 1992, 6 Sch 6, 7(1)(b)* or *8* (see 48.8 RETIREMENT RELIEF). '*The amount available for relief*' is in practical terms the amount of retirement relief given by way of deduction from chargeable gains. [*TCGA 1992, s 164BA; FA 1994, 11 Sch 8*].

The above provisions are intended to obviate some of the practical difficulties caused by the previous legislation relevant to the interaction of reinvestment in shares relief with retirement relief applying in respect of disposals after 15 March 1993 and before 30 November 1993 and which are mentioned in 45.7 below. The problem mentioned there caused by time apportionment of gains is not dealt with by the above provisions but re-basing to 1982 will in most cases mean that time apportionment is now rarely met.

In correspondence, the Revenue has indicated, that where reinvestment in shares relief is contemplated in circumstances where retirement relief is to be given (whether or not on a claim because of ill-health), the steps to be taken are illustrated by the Example below.

Example

F, on 10 October 1995 when aged 56, sells all of the 100% shareholding in a trading company (which has no subsidiaries) of which F has been a full-time working officer or employee since 1984. At the date of disposal, the proportion by value of chargeable business assets to chargeable assets held by the company was 80%. Subject to this, all of the other conditions for retirement relief are satisfied. The consideration received for the shares is £1,000,000 and their indexed cost to the date of disposal is £125,000. On 17 October 1995 F acquires for £1,200,000 shares in a company, the acquisition qualifying for reinvestment in shares relief in relation to the 10 October 1995 disposal. F has the 1995/96 annual exempt amount of £6,000 available as well as allowable losses of £94,000. F does not anticipate any further disposals in 1995/96 and there are no 'indexation losses' for that year.

In the absence of a claim under *TCGA 1992, s 164A* and before giving effect to retirement relief under *TCGA 1992, s 163* or *164*, the chargeable gain arising on the 10 October disposal is £875,000 (£1,000,000–£125,000). Under *TCGA 1992, 6 Sch 7(1)(b)*, only 80% of this gain can be eligible for retirement relief, the balance of £175,000 remaining chargeable and unaffected by retirement relief. Thus £700,000 of the gain is eligible for retirement relief. In the absence of a claim under *TCGA 1992, s 164A*, the amount of retirement relief to be given by way of deduction is as follows.

Chargeable gains eligible for retirement relief		£700,000

	£	£
Amount available for relief		
100% relief: 100% × £250,000		250,000
50% relief:	£	
Excess of eligible gains before retirement relief over £250,000	450,000	
100% × £750,000	750,000	
Half of lower of £450,000 and £750,000		225,000
Retirement relief given by way of deduction		£475,000

Thus chargeable gains remaining after deduction of retirement relief are:

£175,000+(£700,000 − £475,000)	*£400,000
Allowable losses and 1995/96 annual exempt amount (£94,000 + £6,000)	100,000
Chargeable gains assessable 1995/96	£300,000

* The amount of £400,000 is the amount referred to as '*the unrelieved amount of the chargeable gain*' above. If a claim is made under *TCGA 1992, s 164A* for a reduction of £300,000 (see 45.2(*a*)(iv) above), the position is as follows.

	£
Consideration received	1,000,000
Reinvestment in shares relief	300,000
	700,000
Indexed cost	125,000
Chargeable gains before retirement relief	575,000
Retirement relief given by deduction	**475,000
Chargeable gains after retirement relief	**100,000
Allowable losses and 1995/96 annual exempt amount	100,000
Chargeable gains assessable 1995/96	£Nil

** For the purposes of retirement relief only, the reinvestment in shares relief deduction of £300,000 is 'first' set against the £400,000 of unrelieved gains, so that there are only £100,000 of gains left in charge. This means that the retirement relief *actually given by deduction* is still £475,000, £250,000 having been given at the 100% relief level and £225,000 at the 50% relief level. This will be relevant if F makes a disposal in the future qualifying for retirement relief. The acquisition cost of the shares acquired is reduced by £300,000 from £1,200,000 to £900,000.

With regard to the classes of assets qualifying for ROLLOVER RELIEF (see 50.2), on a disposal after 29 November 1993 it is possible to dispose of an asset in such a class and, rather than claim rollover relief by reference to that disposal and an acquisition of an asset in such a class, claim reinvestment in shares relief in relation to that disposal and an acquisition of eligible shares. Shares are not within the classes of assets qualifying for rollover relief, so it is not possible to claim that relief where either the asset being disposed of or the one acquired consists of shares.

45.7 **Disposals after 15 March 1993 and before 30 November 1993.** The provisions of *TCGA 1992, s 164A* in 45.3 above for making a reduction from disposal and acquisition consideration had to be applied before any provisions for calculating the amount of, or giving effect to, any RETIREMENT RELIEF (48) under *TCGA 1992, s 163* or *164*. Accordingly, references in *TCGA 1992, s 164A* to a 'chargeable gain' had to be construed ignoring retirement relief. [*TCGA 1992, s 164A(11); FA 1993, 7 Sch 3; FA 1994, 11 Sch 8, 26 Sch Pt V*].

It was intended that those who were eligible both for retirement relief and reinvestment in shares relief should have been able to claim either relief or any combination of the two reliefs (HC Official Report, Standing Committee A, Sixth Sitting, 15 June 1993, Part III, col 423). This statement not only ignored the fact that retirement relief is not the subject of a claim unless ill-health grounds are involved but also the seemingly anomalous result the legislation produced. The operation of time apportionment or retirement relief at the 50% level (i.e. permanent but partial reliefs rather than reliefs by way of deferral) subsequent to a reduction of the disposal consideration by way of an amount of reinvestment in shares relief (i.e. a relief by way of deferral) meant that gains had to be left in charge, despite that latter relief, even though a greater amount of reinvestment in shares relief could have been claimed such as to reduce the gains left in charge to nil, so that no time apportionment or retirement relief could have been given (Taxation, 12 August 1993 p 469 and 11 November 1993 p 126). In correspondence, the Revenue indicated that it did not find this situation anomalous but merely a consequence of the way the legislation was drafted.

45.8 **RESTRICTION OF RELIEF: DISPOSALS AFTER 15 MARCH 1993 AND BEFORE 30 NOVEMBER 1993**

The following provisions applied to disposals made **after 15 March 1993 and before 30 November 1993.**

Subject to the following, where a claim was made under 45.3 above in respect of a disposal of shares in or other securities of a company

(*a*) the gains which (apart from RETIREMENT RELIEF (48) under *TCGA 1992, ss 163, 164* and relief under 45.3 and 45.5 above) would have accrued on the disposal to the individual or trustees concerned were aggregated,

(*b*) the amount available in respect of the disposal for retirement relief and for the making of deductions from disposal and acquisition consideration under 45.3 above was deemed to be confined to 'the appropriate proportion' of the aggregated gains, and

(*c*) the amount by which the aggregated gains exceeded the amount so available was disregarded for the reliefs mentioned in (*a*), so that that amount constituted chargeable gains.

In relation to a company which was not a holding company of a trading group (see 45.3 above), '*the appropriate proportion*' was the proportion that the value of the company's 'chargeable business assets' bore at the relevant time (as in 45.5 above) to the value at that time of the company's 'chargeable assets', and in any other case, it was the proportion that the value of the trading group's 'chargeable business assets' bore at the relevant time to the value at that time of the trading group's 'chargeable assets'. Where the company or trading group had no chargeable assets, the appropriate proportion was deemed to be the whole.

Every asset was a '*chargeable asset*' except one, on the disposal of which by the company at the relevant time, no gain accruing to the company would have been a chargeable gain. A '*chargeable business asset*' of a company meant a chargeable asset (including goodwill but not including any shares or other securities or any assets held as investments) of it which was, or was an interest in, an asset used for the purposes of a trade, profession, vocation, office or employment (these terms having the same meaning as in *ICTA 1988*) carried on by the individual concerned, the personal company (as in 45.3 above) of that individual, a member of a trading group of which the holding company was a personal company of that individual, or a partnership of which that individual was a member. References in the foregoing to the individual were taken as references to the qualifying beneficiary where trustees disposed of any shares or other securities.

A trading group's chargeable business assets and chargeable assets comprised those assets respectively of every member of a trading group, but for this purpose a holding by one member of the group of the ordinary share capital (see 45.2 above) of another member was not a chargeable asset. Where the whole of the ordinary share capital of a 51% subsidiary (within *ICTA 1988, s 838*) of a holding company was not owned directly or indirectly by that company, the value of the subsidiary's chargeable business assets and chargeable assets were reduced respectively according to the formula

$$A \times \frac{B}{C}, \text{ where}$$

'A' was the value falling to be reduced of the subsidiary's chargeable business assets or chargeable assets;

'B' was the amount of the subsidiary's ordinary share capital owned, directly or indirectly (as in *ICTA 1988, s 838*), by the holding company; and

'C' was the whole of the subsidiary's ordinary share capital.

The above provisions were without prejudice to *TCGA 1992, 6 Sch 7–11* (which apply a similar restriction to the above in the case of retirement relief; see 48.8 RETIREMENT RELIEF). [*TCGA 1992, ss 164C, 164N(1)(3); FA 1993, 7 Sch 3; FA 1994, 11 Sch 4, 26 Sch Pt V*].

45.9   **RELIEF CARRIED FORWARD INTO REPLACEMENT SHARES: DISPOSALS AFTER 15 MARCH 1993 AND BEFORE 30 NOVEMBER 1993**

The following provisions applied to disposals made **after 15 March 1993 and before 30 November 1993**.

Further provisions applied as below where a person acquired any eligible shares (see 45.3 above) in a qualifying company (see 45.13 below) ('*the acquired holding*') for a consideration which was treated as reduced, under 45.3 above or by the provisions below, by any amount ('*the held-over gain*').

If

(*a*) the person who acquired the acquired holding disposed of eligible shares in the company in question ('*the acquired shares*'),

(*b*) that person at any time in 'the relevant period' (see below) acquired other eligible shares ('*the replacement shares*') in a qualifying company which was not a 'relevant company' (see below),

(c)   the acquisition of the replacement shares would have, in relation to the disposal of the acquired shares, been treated (had the disposal been a material disposal) as an acquisition of a qualifying investment for the purposes of the provisions in 45.3 above, and

(d)   relief was not available under 45.3 above in relation to the acquisition of the replacement shares,

that person, on making a claim in respect of the acquisition of the replacement shares, was treated as below.

In relation to the acquisition, the person was treated

(1)   as if the disposal consideration of the acquired shares were reduced by the smallest of the following amounts:

(i)   the amount of the held-over gain on the acquisition of the acquired holding, so far as that amount had not already been carried forward under this provision from any disposal of eligible shares in the company in question or been charged (see below) on a disposal or under *TCGA 1992, s 164F* in 45.12 below,

(ii)   the actual amount or value of the consideration for the acquisition of the replacement shares,

(iii)   in the case of replacement shares acquired otherwise than by a transaction at arm's length, the market value of the replacement shares at the time of their acquisition, and

(iv)   the amount specified for the purposes of this provision in the claim;

and

(2)   as if the amount or value of the consideration for the acquisition of the replacement shares were reduced by the amount of the reduction made under (1) above.

Neither (1) nor (2) affected the treatment under *TCGA 1992* of the other party to the transaction involving the acquired shares or of the other party to the transaction involving the replacement shares.

In (1)(i) above, the reference to an amount which was carried forward from a disposal of eligible shares was a reference to the reduction by that amount under (1) above of the amount of the consideration for the disposal of those shares. Similarly in (1)(i), the whole or any part of any held-over gain on the acquisition of the acquired holding was treated

(A)   under (*aa*) and (*bb*) below as charged on any disposal in relation to which the whole or any part of the held-over gain was taken into account in determining the chargeable gain or allowable loss on the disposal; and

(B)   as charged under *TCGA 1992, s 164F* in 45.12 below so far as it fell to be disregarded in accordance with *TCGA 1992, s 164F(11)* which provided that an amount of the held-over gain was disregarded in certain circumstances.

In the case of a disposal within (A) above, the amount of the held-over gain charged on that disposal

(*aa*)   was, except for a part disposal, so much of the amount taken into account within (A) above as was not carried forward under this provision from the disposal in question; and

(*bb*)   for a part disposal, was calculated by multiplying so much of the amount of the held-over gain as was not carried forward under this provision from the disposal in question and had not already been either charged on a previous disposal or carried forward under this provision from a previous disposal by the $A/(A + B)$ fraction of *TCGA 1992, s 42(2)* (see 16.6 DISPOSAL) used, subject to any deductions under *Chapter IA*, in computing the apportioned allowable expenditure on the disposal in question.

Where *TCGA 1992, s 58* (transfers between spouses at no gain/no loss; see 37.6 MARRIED PERSONS) applied to any disposal of the whole or any part of the acquired holding to any individual, that individual was not regarded under the foregoing as acquiring eligible shares for a consideration which was treated as reduced, and the amount of the held-over gain that was to be treated under the above as charged on the disposal was the amount that would have been charged on the disposal if it had been a disposal at market value.

TCGA 1992, s 164A(10)(12) in 45.3 above, which concern deemed amounts of consideration and apportionment of expenditure, and *TCGA 1992, s 164A(11)* in 45.7 above, which concerns interaction with retirement relief, all apply similarly for these provisions as they do there.

A company was a '*relevant company*' for these purposes if it was

(AA)   the company in which the acquired holding subsisted or a company which was a member of the same group of companies (see 45.3 above) as that company at the time of the disposal of the acquired holding or of the acquisition of the replacement shares;

(BB)   a company in relation to the disposal of any shares in which there had been a claim under *Chapter IA* such that without that or an equivalent claim there would have been no held-over gain in relation to the acquired holding; or

(CC)   a company which, at the time of the disposal or acquisition to which the claim related, was a member of the same group of companies as a company falling within (BB) above.

For the above, '*relevant period*' meant the period (not including any period before the acquisition of the acquired holding) which began twelve months before and ended three years after the disposal of the acquired shares, together with any such further period after the disposal as the Board by notice allowed. [*TCGA 1992, ss 164D, 164N(1)(3); FA 1993, 7 Sch 3; FA 1994, 11 Sch 4, 26 Sch Pt V*].

45.10   RELIEF WHERE SHARES ARE EXCHANGED: DISPOSALS AFTER 15 MARCH 1993 AND BEFORE 30 NOVEMBER 1993

The following provisions applied to disposals made **after 15 March 1993 and before 30 November 1993**.

Where

(*a*)   there was a transaction involving the issue of any shares in or debentures of any company in exchange for any shares in or debentures of another company ('*the exchanged securities*'),

(*b*)   but for this provision, *TCGA 1992, s 127* would have had effect in pursuance of *TCGA 1992, s 135* for requiring the transaction to have been treated for the purposes of *TCGA 1992* as one that did not involve a disposal of the exchanged securities (see 53.5 and 53.8 SHARES AND SECURITIES),

(*c*)   any person would have been entitled, if the transaction had been treated as involving such a disposal, to make a claim for relief under *Chapter IA* by reference to that disposal and an acquisition of eligible shares in a qualifying company, and

(d)   that person made an election under this provision (*TCGA 1992, s 164E*) for the transaction to be treated as involving the disposal of the exchanged securities and claimed that relief,

Chapter IA and the other provisions of *TCGA 1992* had effect as if *TCGA 1992, s 127* did not apply in the case of that transaction and, accordingly, as if that transaction did involve such a disposal, together with an acquisition of the shares or debentures that were issued in exchange.

The election mentioned in (*d*) above had to be made by notice given to the Board not more than two years after the end of, as the case may have been, the qualifying period mentioned in 45.3 above or the relevant period mentioned in 45.9 above. Such an election made in connection with a claim for relief under 45.5 above had to be made jointly by the trustees of the settlement and the qualifying beneficiary.

Any adjustment by way of an assessment on any person to give effect to an election was not out of time if the assessment was made within one year of the final determination of the claim for relief in connection with which the election was made. For this purpose a claim for relief was not deemed to be finally determined until the amount of the relief allowed under the claim could no longer be varied, whether on appeal or by the order of any court or otherwise. [*TCGA 1992, ss 164E, 164N(1)(3); FA 1993, 7 Sch 3; FA 1994, 11 Sch 4, 26 Sch Pt V*].

45.11   WITHDRAWAL OF RELIEF

In certain circumstances and in relation to disposals **after 29 November 1993**, an effective withdrawal of relief applies as below where a person has acquired any eligible shares (see 45.2 above) in a qualifying company (see 45.13 below) ('*the acquired holding*') for a consideration which is treated as reduced, under *TCGA 1992, s 164A* in 45.2 above (consideration treated as reduced under *TCGA 1992, s 164D* in 45.9 above as extant for disposals after 15 March 1993 and before 30 November 1993 being treated as such a reduction) or the provisions below, by any amount ('*the held-over gain*'). [*TCGA 1992, ss 164F(1), 164N(1); FA 1993, 7 Sch 3; FA 1994, 11 Sch 9(1)(a)(2)(a)*].

Subject to the following, if at any time in the 'relevant period' (see below),

(a)   the shares forming the acquired holding cease to be eligible shares,

(b)   the company whose shares form the acquired holding ceases to be a qualifying company,

(c)   the person who acquired the acquired holding becomes neither resident nor ordinarily resident in the UK, or

(d)   any of the shares forming the acquired holding are, on a reorganisation, conversion or reconstruction, exchanged for qualifying corporate bonds so that the transaction is within *TCGA 1992, s 116* (gain on original shares not deemed to crystallise until bonds disposed of; see 44.3 QUALIFYING CORPORATE BONDS),

a chargeable gain equal to 'the appropriate proportion' of the held-over gain is treated as accruing to that person immediately before that time or, in a case within (*d*) above, immediately before the disposal that is hypothecated under *TCGA 1992, s 116(10)(a)* immediately before the transaction concerned. [*TCGA 1992, s 164F(2), 164N(1); FA 1993, 7 Sch 3*].

In deciding for the purposes of (*b*) above whether a company is a qualifying company at a time falling after 28 November 1994, *TCGA 1992, s 164H* (interests in land rule, see 45.13 below) no longer applies. [*TCGA 1992, s 164F(2A); FA 1995, s 40(1)(3)*].

'*The appropriate proportion*' of the held-over gain is so much, if any, of that gain as has not already been charged on any disposal (such reference to a gain having been charged on a disposal includes the amount of reduction made under *TCGA 1992, s 164D(3)(a)* in 45.9(1) above as extant for disposals after 15 March 1993 and before 30 November 1993 from the disposal consideration received for acquired shares) or under the provisions below. However, where (*d*) above applies, or where (*a*) or (*b*) above applies in accordance with (A)–(D) below, the proportion is a just and reasonable one having regard to the extent to which the acquired holding forms the original shares. [*TCGA 1992, s 164F(3); FA 1993, 7 Sch 3; FA 1994, 11 Sch 9(1)(b)(2)(b)(3)*].

The whole or a part of any held-over gain on the acquisition of the acquired holding is treated as below as charged on any disposal in relation to which the whole or any part of the held-over gain falls to be taken into account in determining the chargeable gain or allowable loss on the disposal, and as charged under these provisions so far as it falls to be disregarded under *TCGA 1992, s 164F(11)* below. For a disposal other than a part disposal, the amount of the held-over gain charged on that disposal is the amount taken into account in determining the amount of the chargeable gain etc. as above (but any such amount is reduced by the amount of any reduction made under *TCGA 1992, s 164D(3)(a)* in 45.9(1) above as extant for disposals after 15 March 1993 and before 30 November 1993 from the disposal consideration received for acquired shares). In the case of a part disposal, the corresponding amount charged on that disposal is calculated by multiplying so much of the amount of the held-over gain as has not already been charged on a previous disposal (as similarly reduced by any reduction made under *TCGA 1992, s 164F(3)(a)*) by the A/ (A + B) fraction of *TCGA 1992, s 42(2)* (see 16.6 DISPOSAL) used, subject to any deductions under *Chapter IA*, in computing the apportioned allowable expenditure on the disposal in question. [*TCGA 1992, s 164F(4)(4A); FA 1993, 7 Sch 3; FA 1994, 11 Sch 9(1)(c)(2)(c)(3)*].

Where the acquired holding or any asset treated as comprised in a single asset (e.g. a share pool) with the whole or any part of that holding has been disposed of under *TCGA 1992, s 58* (transfers between spouses at no gain/no loss; see 37.6 MARRIED PERSONS) by the individual who acquired that holding to another person ('*the spouse*')

 (I) the spouse is not (subject to below) treated for the purposes of these provisions as a person who has acquired eligible shares for a consideration which is treated as reduced under *TCGA 1992, s 164A* in 45.2 above;

 (II) the disposal is not included in the disposals on which the whole or any part of the held-over gain may be treated as charged for the purposes of these provisions;

 (III) disposals by the spouse, as well as disposals by that individual, are taken into account under *TCGA 1992, s 164F(4)(4A)* above;

 (IV) any charge under (*a*), (*b*) or (*d*) above is apportioned between that individual and the spouse according to the extent to which the appropriate proportion of the held-over gain would be charged on the disposal by each of them of their respective holdings (if any);

 (V) (*c*) above has effect as if the reference there to that individual included a reference to the spouse;

 (VI) a charge under (*c*) above is imposed only on a person who becomes neither resident nor ordinarily resident in the UK; and

 (VII) the amount of the charge imposed on any person under (*c*) above is that part of the charge on the appropriate proportion of the held-over gain which would be apportioned to that person under (4) above.

[*TCGA 1992, s 164F(5); FA 1993, 7 Sch 3; FA 1994, 11 Sch 9(1)(d)*].

45.11 Reinvestment in Shares Relief

Subject to (A)–(D) below, where the qualifying company in which the acquired holding subsists ceases to be an unquoted company (see 45.2 above) these provisions have effect as if the relevant period ended immediately before it so ceased. (Because, under 45.13 below, a company to be a qualifying company has to be unquoted, this provision seems to prevent a charge arising under (*b*) above because the cessation of qualifying status will not arise in the relevant period.) Subject to this, '*the relevant period*' means the period of three years after the acquisition of the acquired holding. [*TCGA 1992, ss 164F(6)(12), 164N(1); FA 1993, 7 Sch 3*].

Where there is a transaction involving shares in a company which applies *TCGA 1992, s 127* (see 53.5 SHARES AND SECURITIES) so that those shares are regarded as the same asset as the acquired holding or the whole or any part of an asset comprising that holding, no charge arises as a result of the event in (*a*) or (*b*) above except where

(A) those shares are not, or cease to be, eligible shares in that company;

(B) neither that company nor (if different) the company in which the acquired holding subsisted is or continues to be a qualifying company, or would be or continue to be a qualifying company if it were an unquoted company;

(C) the transaction is one resulting in the shares comprised in the acquired holding ceasing to be eligible shares under *TCGA 1992, s 164L* (anti-avoidance; see 45.15 below); or

(D) there is a transaction under which any shares at any time comprised in the acquired holding would have ceased to be eligible shares under *TCGA 1992, s 164L*.

[*TCGA 1992, ss 164F(7), 164N(1); FA 1993, 7 Sch 3*].

A charge (*a*) or (*b*) above does not apply where the company in which the acquired holding subsists is wound up or dissolved without winding up and

(*aa*) it is shown that the winding-up or dissolution is for bona fide commercial reasons and not part of a scheme or arrangement the main purpose of which, or one of the main purposes of which, is the avoidance of tax; and

(*bb*) the company's net assets (if any) are distributed to its members or dealt with as bona vacantia before the end of the period of three years from the commencement of the winding up or dissolution.

[*TCGA 1992, s 164F(8); FA 1993, 7 Sch 3*].

A charge will not apply under (*c*) above in relation to any person if

(AA) the reason for his becoming neither resident nor ordinarily resident in the UK is that he works in an employment or office all the duties of which are performed outside the UK, and

(BB) he again becomes resident or ordinarily resident in the UK within the period of three years from the time he ceases to be so, without having meanwhile disposed of any eligible shares in the company in question.

The Revenue are precluded from making an assessment under (*c*) above before the end of the three year period mentioned in (BB) above where the person has satisfied the condition in (AA) above and may satisfy that in (BB). A person is taken to have disposed of an asset under (BB) if there has been such a disposal as would, if the person making the disposal had been resident in the UK, have been a disposal on which the whole or any part of the held-over gain would have been charged. [*TCGA 1992, ss 164F(9)(10), 164N(1); FA 1993, 7 Sch 3*].

Where otherwise a chargeable gain would arise under (*a*)–(*d*) above but the person who acquired the acquired holding also acquires, within a specified period, a qualifying investment (as in 45.2 above), he is treated as respects the qualifying investment on making a claim

(1)   as if the amount of the gain were reduced by whichever is the smallest of the following amounts:

     (i)   the actual amount or value of the consideration for the acquisition of the qualifying investment,

     (ii)   in the case of a qualifying investment acquired otherwise than by a transaction at arm's length, the market value of that investment at the time of its acquisition,

     (iii)   the amount specified for these purposes in the claim;

     and

(2)   as if the amount or value of the consideration for the acquisition of the qualifying investment were reduced by the amount of the reduction made under (1) above (but without affecting the treatment for the purposes of *TCGA 1992* of the other party to the transaction involving the qualifying investment).

FA 1995 introduced measures to prevent excess relief being claimed in respect of shares acquired by way of gift if the qualifying investment was acquired after 19 June 1994, or a claim under the preceding paragraph is made in relation to a gain which would otherwise accrue after that date. Thus, where a claim for the above relief is made after 19 June 1994 and the qualifying investment in respect of which the claim is made was acquired by the reinvestor through an inter-spouse (no gain/no loss) transfer under *TCGA 1992, s 58*, the relief claimed cannot exceed the transferor spouse's allowable base cost of the qualifying investment, after any reduction in that cost due to gains already rolled over into that investment, irrespective of the rebasing rules in *TCGA 1992, s 35, 3 Sch 1* or *TCGA 1992, s 55* in situations where the qualifying investment was held by the transferor spouse since 31 March 1982. Similarly, the rebasing provisions are disapplied where the claimant returns the qualifying investment to his spouse on a no gain/no loss basis.

In addition, rules were introduced with regard to the making of multiple claims for relief against the same qualifying investment to ensure that aggregate gains rolled over do not exceed the cost thereof. These rules have effect where claims under the penultimate paragraph above are made in respect of gains which would otherwise accrue after 19 June 1994. Where multiple reductions are claimed under the above relief in respect of the same qualifying investment, the reductions shall be treated as claimed separately in such order as the claimant elects or, in default, the Board determines. On the second and subsequent claims the amount of gain able to be rolled over will be limited to the remaining acquisition cost ((1)(i) above) or market value ((1)(ii) above) of the qualifying investment left after any previous claims have been made. A claim that has become final (i.e. it may not be amended or is finally determined, whichever occurs first) will be treated as made earlier than any claim which is not final.

The specified period mentioned above is the period (not including any period before the acquisition of the acquired holding) beginning twelve months before and ending three years after the time the chargeable gain accrues or would otherwise accrue, together with any such further time after the disposal as the Board may by notice allow. [*TCGA 1992, ss 164F(10A–10C), 164FF, 164FG; FA 1993, 7 Sch 3; FA 1994, 11 Sch 9(1)(f); FA 1995, s 47(1)(3)–(8)*].

Gains on disposals made after a chargeable gain has been deemed to accrue under (*a*)–(*d*) above to any person in respect of the acquired holding are computed as if so much of the held-over gain as is equal to the amount of the chargeable gain were to be disregarded. [*TCGA 1992, ss 164F(11); FA 1993, 7 Sch 3*].

45.12   **Disposals after 15 March 1993 and before 30 November 1993.** In certain circumstances, an effective withdrawal of relief applied as below where a person had acquired any eligible shares (see 45.3 above) in a qualifying company (see 45.13 above) (*'the acquired holding'*) for a consideration which was treated as reduced, under *TCGA 1992, s 164A* in 45.3 or *TCGA 1992, s 164D* in 45.9 above by any amount (*'the held-over gain'*). [*TCGA 1992, ss 164F(1), 164N(1); FA 1993, 7 Sch 3*].

The provisions of *TCGA 1992, s 164F(2)* (see 45.11(*a*)–(*d*) above) applied similarly regarding 'the appropriate proportion' of the held-over gain. [*TCGA 1992, ss 164F(2), 164N(1); FA 1993, 7 Sch 3*].

'The appropriate proportion' of the held-over gain was so much, if any, of that gain as had not already been *either* charged on any disposal or under these provisions *or* carried forward under *TCGA 1992, s 164D* in 45.9 above. However, where 45.11(*d*) above applied, or where 45.11(*a*) and (*b*) applied in accordance with 45.11(A)–(D), the proportion was a just and reasonable one having regard to the extent to which the acquired holding represented the original shares. [*TCGA 1992, s 164F(3); FA 1993, 7 Sch 3*].

Subject to *TCGA 1992, s 164F(5)* below, references in the above to an amount carried forward from a disposal were as in 45.9 above, and the provisions contained there in (A) and (B) and (*aa*) and (*bb*) were applied to these provisions as they applied there. [*TCGA 1992, s 164F(4); FA 1993, 7 Sch 3*].

The provisions of *TCGA 1992, s 164F(5)* in 45.11 applied similarly, except that 45.10(I) above referred to a reduction under *TCGA 1992, s 164A* or *s 164D*, and 45.11(III) referred to disposals taken into account under 45.9(A) and (B) and (*aa*) and (*bb*) as applied above instead of disposals taken into account under *TCGA 1992, s 164F(4)(4A)*. [*TCGA 1992, s 164F(5); FA 1993, 7 Sch 3*].

TCGA 1992, s 164F(6)(12) in 45.11 above regarding the definition of 'relevant period' applied similarly. [*TCGA 1992, ss 164F(6)(12), 164N(1); FA 1993, 7 Sch 3*].

TCGA 1992, s 164F(7) in 45.11(A)–(D) above regarding the effect of *TCGA 1992, s 127* applied similarly. [*TCGA 1992, ss 164F(7), 164N(1); FA 1993, 7 Sch 3*].

TCGA 1992, s 164F(8) in 45.11(*aa*)–(*bb*) above regarding winding up and dissolution applied similarly. [*TCGA 1992, s 164F(8); FA 1993, 7 Sch 3*].

TCGA 1992, s 164F(9)(10) in 45.11(AA)–(BB) above regarding non-UK residents etc. applied similarly but by reference to a disposal on which (within the meaning of *TCGA 1992, s 164D*) the whole or any part of the held-over gain would have been charged. [*TCGA 1992, ss 164F(9)(10), 164N(1); FA 1993, 7 Sch 3*].

TCGA 1992, s 164F(11) in 45.11 above concerning the disregarding of an amount of the held-over gain applied similarly. [*TCGA 1992, ss 164F(11); FA 1993, 7 Sch 3*].

45.13   **DEFINITION OF QUALIFYING COMPANY**

Except where otherwise stated, the provisions below apply to disposals made after **15 March 1993**.

A company is a *'qualifying company'* for the purposes of *Chapter IA* if it complies with the following conditions.

Subject to the further provisions below a company is a qualifying company if it is

(a)   an unquoted company (being a company none of the shares in or other securities of which were quoted on any recognised stock exchange or were dealt in on the Unlisted Securities Market) which exists wholly for the purpose of carrying on one or more 'qualifying trades' (see 45.14 below) (but purposes capable of having no significant effect, other than in relation to incidental matters, on the extent of the company's activities are ignored). (The case of *Lord v Tustain; Lord v Chapple Ch D, [1993] STC 755* concerning interest relief had as its main issue the meaning of the phrase 'any company which exists wholly or mainly for the purpose of carrying on a trade' in a similar context.);

(b)   an unquoted company whose business consists entirely in the holding of shares in or other securities of, or the making of loans to, one or more 'qualifying subsidiaries' of the company; or

(c)   an unquoted company whose business consists entirely in the holding of such shares or securities, or the making of such loans, and the carrying on of one or more qualifying trades.

A company is not a qualifying company if

(1)   it controls (within *ICTA 1988, s 416*; see Tolley's Corporation Tax under Close Companies) (whether on its own or together with any persons connected (within *TCGA 1992, s 286*) with it) any company which is not a qualifying subsidiary or, without controlling it, has a 51% subsidiary (within *ICTA 1988, s 838*) which is not a qualifying subsidiary;

(2)   it is under the control of another company (or of another company and a person connected with the other company) or, without being controlled by it, is a 51% subsidiary of another company; or

(3)   arrangements are in existence under which the company could fall within (1) or (2) above.

In relation to a company ('*the holding company*') a '*qualifying subsidiary*' means a company which is a member of a 'group of companies' (within *TCGA 1992, s 170*; see 13.10 COMPANIES) of which the holding company is the 'principal company' (within *TCGA 1992, s 170*), and of which each of the members, or each of the members other than the holding company, is a company satisfying one of the following conditions, namely

(aa)   it is such a company as is mentioned in (a) above;

(bb)   it exists wholly for the purposes of holding and managing property used by the holding company or any of the holding company's other subsidiaries for the purposes of

    (i)   research and development (as defined) from which it is intended that a qualifying trade to be carried on by the holding company or any of those other subsidiaries will be derived, or

    (ii)   one or more qualifying trades so carried on;

(cc)   it would exist wholly for such a purpose apart from purposes capable of having no significant effect (other than in relation to incidental matters) on the extent of the company's activites; or

(dd)   it has no profits for the purposes of corporation tax and no part of its business consists in the making of investments.

Without prejudice to the generality of (a)–(c) above or *TCGA 1992, s 164F(8)* in 45.11 and 45.12 above, a company ceases to be a qualifying company if a resolution is passed or an order is made for its winding up, or any other act is done for a like purpose under foreign law or the company is dissolved without winding up. [*TCGA 1992, ss 164G, 164N(1)(2); FA 1993, 7 Sch 3*].

The following rules with regard to determining whether a company is a qualifying company do not apply where an acquisition is made after **28 November 1994** of shares in a company.

In determining whether a company is a qualifying company for the purposes of *Chapter IA* after **29 November 1993 and before 29 November 1994**, a company is not a qualifying company at any time when the value of the 'interests in land' held by the company exceeds the greater of half the value of the company's 'chargeable assets' and half the value of the company's assets as a whole (this latter value being determined *mutatis mutandis* as in *ICTA 1988, s 294(3)(4)* for the purposes of enterprise investment scheme relief or, before 1 January 1994, business expansion scheme relief). Under *ICTA 1988, s 294(3)(4)*, the value of a company's assets as a whole is arrived at by first aggregating the market value of each of those assets and then deducting the amount of the debts and liabilities of the company, for which purpose a debt includes the amount paid up in respect of any of the shares of the company which carry a present or future preferential right to the company's assets in a winding up and the company's other share capital, share premium account and reserves are not treated as debts or liabilities. In determining whether a company was a qualifying company for the purposes of *Chapter IA* before **30 November 1993**, a company was not a qualifying company at any time when the value of the interests in land held by the company was greater than half the value of the company's chargeable assets.

For disposals **after 29 November 1993**, a '*chargeable asset*' of a company at any time is every asset of that company, except one on the disposal of which by the company at that time no gain accruing to the company would be a chargeable gain. For disposals **after 15 March 1993 and before 30 November 1993**, the definition of the term was as in 45.8 above, although both definitions are virtually identical.

'*Interest in land*' is widely defined to include rights related to land, and rights to obtain an interest etc. from another which depend on that other's ability to grant the interest etc., but excludes the interest of a creditor secured by any mortgage or charge over land.

Valuation of an interest in land excludes any plant or machinery which is, in law, part of the land etc. An interest is valued on the assumption that there is no source of mineral deposits on the land exploitable other than by opencast mining or quarrying and that the existence of any oil exploration (as defined) borehole is disregarded.

Where a company is a member of a partnership, the value of any interest in land held by the partnership is apportioned as on a dissolution of the partnership. Where a company is a member of a group (within *TCGA 1992, s 170*) all the group members are treated as one company for the above purposes, but ignoring any debts and liabilities as between the members. [*TCGA 1992, ss 164A(13), 164H, 164N(1)(1A)(2); FA 1993, 7 Sch 3; FA 1994, s 91(3)(4), 11 Sch 5, 26 Sch Pt V; FA 1995, s 46(1)(2)*].

The legislation does not make clear whether a qualifying company has to be resident in the UK. Whilst *TCGA 1992, s 164N(2)* requires *TCGA 1992, s 170* to apply for the interpretation of *TCGA 1992, s 164G* above, it could be argued that the requirement in *TCGA 1992, s 170(2)(a)* (certain references to 'company' to include only a UK resident company) is only for the purposes of interpreting group relationships and does not require the qualifying company to be resident in the UK. The Revenue have stated their view that a company with no subsidiaries and which is not itself a subsidiary does not have to be UK resident in order to be a qualifying company, but a non-resident holding company will not qualify under the rules in (*a*)–(*c*) above. Nor will a non-resident trading company which has trading subsidiaries. A non-resident company which is itself a subsidiary will be excluded by the rule in (2) above. (Revenue Tax Bulletin, May 1994, p 128).

45.14 DEFINITION OF QUALIFYING TRADE

The provisions below apply to disposals made after **15 March 1993**.

A trade is a '*qualifying trade*' for the purposes of *Chapter IA* if it complies with the requirements below, and for this purpose the carrying on of any activities of research and development (as defined) from which it is intended that a trade meeting those requirements will be derived is treated as the carrying on of a qualifying trade. A trade cannot be a qualifying trade unless it is conducted on a commercial basis and with a view to profit realisation.

Subject to the following, a trade is a qualifying trade if neither that trade nor a substantial part of it consists in one or more of the following activities:

(*a*) dealing in land, in commodities or futures or in shares, securities or other financial instruments;

(*b*) dealing in goods, otherwise than in the course of an ordinary trade of wholesale or retail distribution;

(*c*) banking, insurance, money-lending, debt-factoring, hire-purchase financing or other financial activities;

(*d*) leasing (including letting ships on charter or other assets on hire) or receiving royalties or licence fees;

(*e*) providing legal or accountancy services;

(*f*) providing services or facilities for any trade which consists, to a substantial extent, in activities within (*a*)–(*e*) above and is carried on by another person (except the principal company of a group of companies, these terms being as defined in *TCGA 1992, s 170*; see 13.10 COMPANIES) who has a 'controlling interest' (see below) in both trades;

(*g*) property development (broadly land development for disposal when developed at a profit); this is treated as a qualifying trade for determinations after 28 November 1994;

(*h*) farming (broadly husbandry in the UK other than market gardening); this is treated as a qualifying trade for determinations after 28 November 1994.

In relation to (*b*) above

(1) a trade of wholesale distribution is one in which the goods are offered for sale and sold to persons for resale (with or without processing) by them to the general public;

(2) a trade of retail distribution is one in which the goods are offered for sale and sold to the general public; and

(3) a trade is not an ordinary trade within (1) or (2) above if it consists, to a substantial extent, in dealing in goods which are collected or held as an investment (or of that and any other activity in (*a*)–(*h*) above), and a substantial proportion of those goods is held for a significantly longer period than might reasonably be expected of a vendor trying to dispose of them at market value.

45.14   Reinvestment in Shares Relief

In determining whether a trade is an ordinary one within (1) and (2) above, regard is had to the extent the following features are present, with (A)–(C) below being regarded as indicative features whilst (D)–(H) are regarded as contra-indicative ones.

(A)   The breaking of bulk between purchase and resale.

(B)   The purchase and sale of goods in different markets.

(C)   The employment of staff and incurring of expenses in the course of a trade other than the cost of goods or, in the case of a company carrying on a trade, of remuneration of persons connected with it.

(D)   The purchase and sale of goods from persons connected with the trader.

(E)   The matching of purchases with sales.

(F)   The holding of goods for longer than normal for goods of the kind in question.

(G)   The carrying on of the trade at a place not commonly used for wholesale or retail trading.

(H)   No physical possession of the goods being taken by the trader.

As regards (*d*) above, a trade carried on by a company engaged in the production of films (as defined, and with or without the distribution of films within three years of their production) is not disqualified from being a qualifying trade by reason only of all royalties and licence fees received relating to films (or sound or other by-products arising therefrom) produced within the preceding three years. Similar comments apply to a trade carried on by a company engaged in research and development where all royalties and licence fees received are attributable to such activities it has carried out. Likewise, a trade is not disqualified by reason only of its consisting in the letting of ships, other than oil rigs or pleasure craft (as both defined), on charter if

(*aa*)   the company beneficially owns all the ships it so lets;

(*bb*)   every ship beneficially owned by the company is UK registered;

(*cc*)   the company is solely responsible for arranging the marketing of the services of its ships; and

(*dd*)   the further conditions below are satisfied in relation to every letting on charter.

If any of the conditions in (*aa*)–(*dd*) above are not satisfied for any lettings, only those lettings are taken into account, when taken together with any other activity within (*a*)–(*h*) above, in deciding whether a substantial part of the trade consists of activities within (*a*)–(*h*).

The conditions mentioned in (*dd*) above require, broadly, that each letting is for no more than twelve months and is by way of an arm's length bargain, and that chartering is conducted by the company as principal bearing the responsibility or making management decisions and paying expenses between voyages.

Under (*f*) above, a person has a '*controlling interest*' in a trade carried on by a company, or carried on by a person other than a company (when trade also includes any business, profession or vocation), if (AA) or (BB), or (CC), below applies respectively. For this purpose there is attributed to any person any rights or powers of any other person who is an '*associate*' (as in *ICTA 1988, s 417(3)(4)* except that, for the purposes of *Chapter IA*, a brother or sister is not treated as a relative) of his.

(AA)   The person controls (within *ICTA 1988, s 416*) the company.

(BB)   The company is a close company (within *ICTA 1988, ss 414, 415*) and he or an associate of his is a director (within *ICTA 1988, s 417(5)*) of the company and either the beneficial owner of, or able to control directly or in any indirect manner, more than 30 per cent. of the company, or not less than half the trade could be regarded under *ICTA 1988, s 344(2)* as belonging to him.

(CC) The person is entitled to not less than half the assets used for, or the income arising, from the trade.

As regards (*g*) and (*h*) above, these conditions no longer apply in deciding whether a company is conducting a qualifying trade after 28 November 1994.

[*TCGA 1992, ss 164I, 164J, 164N(1)(2); FA 1993, 7 Sch 3; FA 1995, s 46(1)(4)*].

See Tolley's Corporation Tax under Losses for *ICTA 1988, s 344(2)*, and under Close Companies for *ICTA 1988, ss 414, 415, 416, 417(3)(4)(5)*.

45.15   **DENIAL OF RELIEF**

General. The following provisions apply to disposals **after 15 March 1993 unless otherwise stated.**

Overseas residents. Relief under *Chapter IA* does not apply in relation to any person in respect of his acquisition of any eligible shares (see 45.2 and 45.3 above) in a qualifying company (see 45.13 above) if at the time when he acquires them he is neither resident nor ordinarily resident in the UK. The same restriction applies to a person who, though resident or ordinarily resident in the UK at the time of acquisition, is regarded under double taxation relief arrangements as resident outside the UK, and under the arrangements would not be liable in the UK to tax on a gain arising on a disposal of the shares immediately after their acquisition. [*TCGA 1992, s 164K; FA 1993, 7 Sch 3*].

Anti-avoidance. For the purposes of *Chapter IA* an acquisition of shares in a qualifying company (see 45.13 above) is not treated as an acquisition of eligible shares (see 45.2 and 45.3 above) if the arrangements (including any scheme, agreement or understanding, whether or not legally enforceable) for the acquisition of those shares, or any prior preliminary arrangements, include: arrangements with a view to the subsequent reacquisition, exchange or other disposal of the shares; arrangements for or with a view to the cessation of the company's trade or the disposal of all or a substantial part of its 'chargeable business assets'; or arrangements for the return of the whole or part of the value of an individual's investment.

For disposals **after 29 November 1993**, a '*chargeable business asset*' of a company means a 'chargeable asset' (including goodwill but not including any shares or other securities or any assets held as investments) which is, or is an interest in, an asset used for the purposes of a trade, profession, vocation, office or employment (these terms having the same meaning as in *ICTA 1988*) carried on by the individual acquiring the shares, any 'personal company' of that individual, a member of a 'trading group' of which the 'holding company' (these last three terms being defined as in *TCGA 1992, 6 Sch 1*; see 48.3 RETIREMENT RELIEF) is a personal company of that individual or a partnership of which that individual is a member. For disposals **after 15 March 1993 and before 30 November 1993**, the definition of the term was as in 45.8 above, although both definitions are virtually identical. Similarly, for disposals **after 29 November 1993**, a '*chargeable asset*' of a company at any time is every asset of that company, except one on the disposal of which by the company at that time no gain accruing to the company would be a chargeable gain. For disposals **after 15 March 1993 and before 30 November 1993**, the definition of the term was as in 45.8 above, although again both definitions are virtually identical.

If an individual, having acquired eligible shares in a qualifying company, has returned to him afterwards the whole or any part of the value of his investment, the shares are treated as ceasing to be eligible shares under *Chapter IA* (for the consequences of which event when it occurs in the relevant period, see 45.11 above). A return of the whole or part of the value of the investment of an individual who is to acquire or has acquired shares in a company is treated as being made if the company

(*a*)   repays, redeems or repurchases any of its shares or other securities belonging to that individual or makes any payment to him for giving up rights on the cancellation or extinguishment of any of the company's shares or securities;

(*b*)   repays any debt owed to that individual, other than a debt that was incurred by the company on or after the acquisition of the shares and otherwise than in consideration of the extinguishment of a debt incurred before the acquisition;

(*c*)   makes any payment to that individual for giving up his rights to any debt on its extinguishment;

(*d*)   releases or waives any liability of that individual to the company (which is deemed to occur if the liability remains undischarged twelve months after the time it should have been discharged) or discharges, or undertakes to discharge, any liability of his to a third party;

(*e*)   provides a benefit or facility for that individual;

(*f*)   disposes of an asset to that individual for no or an insufficient consideration;

(*g*)   acquires an asset from that individual for more than a sufficient consideration; or

(*h*)   makes any payment to that individual other than a 'qualifying payment'.

Similarly, a whole or partial return of the value of an individual's investment is treated as being made where there is a loan made (including the giving of credit and the assignment of debt) by any person to that individual such that either no loan would have been made or the terms of it would have been different had the individual not have acquired, or been proposing to acquire, the shares.

Debts and liabilities that could be discharged by the company making a qualifying payment are ignored for the purposes of the above, as are benefits or facilities provided in circumstances such that a payment made to the value of them would be a 'qualifying payment'. A '*qualifying payment*' means

(1)   reasonable payment by a company of remuneration to an officer or employee;

(2)   reimbursement by a company of an officer's or employee's travel or other expenses incurred wholly, exclusively and necessarily in the performance of his duties;

(3)   interest paid by a company on money lent to it on reasonable commercial terms;

(4)   payment by a company of a dividend etc. not exceeding a normal return on the investment in shares etc. of the company;

(5)   a payment not exceeding market value for the supply of goods;

(6)   a payment by a company, as rent for any property occupied by the company, of an amount not exceeding a reasonable and commercial rent for the property;

(7)   any reasonable and necessary remuneration paid by a company for services rendered to it in the course of a trade assessed under Schedule D, Case I or II;

(8)   a payment in discharge of an '*ordinary trade debt*' (meaning any debt for goods or services supplied in the ordinary course of trade or business where any credit given does not exceed six months and is not longer than that normally given to customers generally).

In relation to disposals **after 29 November 1993**, for the purposes of *Chapter IA*, where a person has acquired any eligible shares in a qualifying company (*'the acquired holding'*) for a consideration which is treated as reduced under *Chapter IA* by any amount (*'the held-over gain'*) and after that acquisition, he acquires eligible shares in a 'relevant company', his acquisition of the eligible shares in the relevant company is not regarded as the acquisition of a qualifying investment for the purposes of *TCGA 1992, s 164A* in 45.2 above. A company is a *'relevant company'* if

(A)   where that person has disposed of any of the acquired holding, it is the company in which the acquired holding has subsisted or a company which was a member of the same *'group of companies'* (as in *TCGA 1992, 6 Sch 1*; see 48.3 RETIREMENT RELIEF) as that company at any time since the acquisition of the acquired holding,

(B)   it is a company in relation to the disposal of any shares in which there has been a claim under *Chapter IA* such that, without that or an equivalent claim, there would have been no held-over gain in relation to the acquired holding, or

(C)   it is a company which, at the time of the disposal or acquisition to which the claim relates, was a member of the same group of companies as a company falling within (B) above.

In the above provisions, a payment or disposal made indirectly to an individual, or to his order or benefit, is treated as made to him, and any reference to an individual includes a reference to any associate (as in 45.14 above) of his, and any reference to a company includes a reference to any person connected (within *TCGA 1992, s 286*) with the company.

For disposals after **29 November 1993**, the above provisions have effect in relation to the acquisition of shares by the trustees of a settlement as if references to an individual acquiring the shares were references to those trustees or any individual or charity by virtue of whose interest, at the time of acquisition, the relief given under *TCGA 1992, s 164B* in 45.4 above applies to the settled property. For disposals **after 15 March 1993 and before 30 November 1993**, the above provisions had effect in relation to the acquisition of shares by the trustees of a settlement as if references to an individual acquiring the shares were references to those trustees or the individual who was the qualifying beneficiary (see 45.5 above) by reference to whom *Chapter IA* had or, as the case may have been, would have had effect in relation to the acquisition. [*TCGA 1992, ss 164L, 164N(1)(1A)(3); FA 1993, 7 Sch 3; FA 1994, 11 Sch 6, 10, 11*].

Relief excluded where enterprise investment scheme relief claimed. In relation to shares issued **after 31 December 1993**, if a person makes a claim for relief under *ICTA 1988, Pt VII, Ch III* in respect of any shares, those shares cannot be, or be treated as ever having been, eligible shares within 45.2 and 45.3 above. [*TCGA 1992, ss 164MA, 164N(1); FA 1994, s 137, 15 Sch 32, 33*]. This provision would seem to override *TCGA 1992, s 164F* in 45.11 and 45.12 above regarding the withdrawal of reinvestment in shares relief and so provide for denial or withdrawal of relief in all circumstances. Cf. *TCGA 1992, s 164M* regarding business expansion scheme relief below. See also 53.17 SHARES AND SECURITIES for the treatment of shares on which enterprise investment scheme relief has been given.

Relief excluded where business expansion scheme relief claimed. In relation to shares issued **before 1 January 1994**, where a person acquires any shares in a company those shares cannot be eligible shares within 45.2 and 45.3 above or, as the case may be, cease to be eligible shares if that person or any person connected (within *TCGA 1992, s 286*) with him has made or makes a claim for relief in relation to those shares under *ICTA 1988, Pt VII, Ch III*. [*TCGA 1992, ss 164M, 164N(1); FA 1993, 7 Sch 3; FA 1994, s 137, 15 Sch 31, 33*]. This provision seems to allow for the application

45.15 Reinvestment in Shares Relief

of *TCGA 1992, s 164F* in 45.11 and 45.12 above regarding the withdrawal of reinvestment in shares relief. If so, it is arguable that in certain unusual circumstances (e.g. company not beginning to trade until up to two years after issue of shares) a valid claim to business expansion scheme relief would not lead to the withdrawal of reinvestment in shares relief. If the former relief is not itself withdrawn, any gain arising on the shares is exempt (see 53.18 SHARES AND SECURITIES). However, the shares to be eligible shares must be in a qualifying company as in 45.13 above and it is not clear whether any delay between the issue of shares and the commencement of trading would prejudice such status.

See 53.17 SHARES AND SECURITIES for provisions on deferral of gains on re-investment in enterprise investment schemes, and 58.10 VENTURE CAPITAL TRUSTS for similar provisions.

46   Remittance Basis

Cross-references. See 6.2 ASSETS for the location of assets; 17.6 DOUBLE TAX RELIEF for relief available where remittance basis applies; 39.4 OVERSEAS MATTERS for relief available where overseas gains are unremittable to the UK; 47 RESIDENCE AND DOMICILE.

46.1   The remittance basis implies that assessments to UK capital gains tax on gains arising abroad are restricted to sums actually remitted (or deemed to have been remitted) into the UK out of those gains, such remittances being treated as gains accruing when received in the UK. Subject to any relevant double taxation agreement, it applies to disposals by individuals *resident or ordinarily resident but not domiciled* in the UK of assets situated abroad (with no allowance for losses arising abroad). [*TCGA 1992, ss 12(1), 16(4)*].

Revenue practice appears to be to leave out of account remittances made out of the proceeds of disposals made whilst a non-UK domiciled individual was neither resident nor ordinarily resident in the UK and, subject to this, to treat a remittance as taxable to the extent given by the proportion which represents chargeable gain on normal disposal principles (see 16.3 DISPOSAL for allowable expenditure and proceeds in foreign currency). This practice even seems to extend to the case where the taxpayer divides the proceeds of disposal but only makes remittances from that part which represents the original allowable expenditure and indexation allowance.

In an appeal to General Commissioners, the Revenue were successful in applying the provisions where the individual was at all material times resident and ordinarily resident in the UK but acquired a UK domicile between the realisation of the gains in question and the time, in a later year of assessment, when the proceeds of the gains were remitted to the UK (Taxation, 6 June 1991, p 257).

For the situation where an individual becomes, or ceases to be, resident or ordinarily resident in the UK, see 47.2 RESIDENCE AND DOMICILE.

46.2   **REMITTANCES GENERALLY**

By analogy with cases relating to income tax, a taxable remittance may include the repatriation of reinvested gains, provided those gains were made whilst the disposer was resident or ordinarily resident in the UK (*Scottish Provident Institution v Farmer CS 1912, 6 TC 34* and *Kneen v Martin CA 1934, 19 TC 33*). Similarly, a remittance from a foreign bank account into which overseas gains have been paid may be assessable, depending on the circumstances, see *Walsh v Randall KB 1940, 23 TC 55* (sterling draft on foreign bank received by UK resident drawer before handing to UK payee) and *Thomson v Moyse HL 1960, 39 TC 291* (dollar cheques on US bank sold to the Bank of England held to be remitted) but cf. *Carter v Sharon KB 1936, 20 TC 229* (drafts on foreign bank posted abroad by UK drawer for daughter's maintenance; held no remittance as, under relevant foreign law, gift to daughter complete on posting of draft). In *Harmel v Wright Ch D 1973, 49 TC 149* an amount received via two South African companies, ending as a loan from one of them, was held to be a remittance. An erroneous remittance by a bank, contrary to the customer's instructions, was held not liable in *Duke of Roxburghe's Exors v CIR CS 1936, 20 TC 711*.

46.3   **CONSTRUCTIVE REMITTANCES**

Gains arising abroad to a person ordinarily resident in the UK and which he applies abroad towards the satisfaction of

46.3 Remittance Basis

(a)   a debt (or interest thereon) for money lent to him in the UK, or

(b)   a debt for money lent to him abroad and brought here, or

(c)   a loan incurred to satisfy such debts,

are treated as received by him in the UK.

Where an ordinarily resident person imports money lent to him abroad, the debt for which has at that time already been wholly or partly satisfied, the imported money (up to the amount of the original loan) is treated as a remittance at the date of importation, and the provisions at (a) to (c) above apply accordingly.

Gains available in any form to the 'lender' so that the amount of a loan debt, or the time of its repayment, depends directly or indirectly on the amount of property so available to the lender, are treated as having been applied towards satisfaction of the loan.

'*Lender*' includes any person for the time being entitled to repayment. [*TCGA 1992, s 12(2); ICTA 1988, s 65(6)-(9)*].

Example

X, ordinarily resident but not domiciled in the UK, borrows £28,000 in the UK in order to buy a residence here. Out of a later loan of US $50,000 raised abroad, he uses $40,000 to repay the loan incurred in the UK. He repays the $50,000 loan out of the disposal proceeds of assets situated abroad but he uses the balance ($10,000) of the actual dollars borrowed in improving his UK residence. The disposal proceeds of the overseas assets were $140,000 and the disposal would have given rise to a chargeable gain of £60,000 on normal disposal principles. Subject to double taxation arrangements the gain arising abroad will be liable to UK capital gains tax as follows.

(i) $40,000 under (c) above, treated as remitted on the repayment of the dollar loan.

(ii) $10,000 treated as remitted at the date of importation, representing money lent abroad.

Thus for example, in (i) above the chargeable gain arising is

$$\frac{£60,000 \times 40,000}{140,000} = £17,143$$

The balance of the disposal proceeds $(140,000-50,000) will remain exempt unless and until it is remitted (or deemed remitted) to the UK.

(*Note.* Foreign currency and bank balances denominated therein are themselves chargeable assets in certain cases. See 6.2 ASSETS and 18.5 and 18.8 EXEMPTIONS AND RELIEFS.)

47   Residence and Domicile

Cross-references. See 15.7 DEATH for residence etc. status of personal representatives; 17 DOUBLE TAX RELIEF for double tax agreements which may override or amend statutory provisions or Revenue practice for the purposes of such agreements; 39 OVERSEAS MATTERS; 40.4 PARTNERSHIPS for overseas resident partners and partnerships; and 52.3 SETTLEMENTS for residence etc. status of trustees.

47.1   The legislation contains few specific directions as to the ascertainment of a person's 'residence' and 'ordinary residence' status in a particular year of assessment for general tax purposes and this is especially so of capital gains tax. Consequently it is a body of case law that has brought about the view that these terms are to be interpreted according to their normal meanings and that each case must rest on its own facts and particular circumstances. The Revenue have taken case decisions, *inter alia*, in formulating their own practice as to the determination of residence and ordinary residence (see 47.2–47.4 below for individuals and 47.5 for companies). The term 'domicile' is governed by the general legal meaning rather than any specific definitions for tax purposes but again, each case rests on its own facts. See 47.6 below. For appeals relating to residence and domicile generally, see 47.7 below.

The extent of the UK for tax purposes is given in 47.8 below and special rules relating to residence status in connection with the double taxation agreement between the UK and Eire are in 47.9 below.

47.2   **RESIDENCE**

An individual can be resident for a particular year of assessment in one or more countries for tax purposes so that a claim not to be UK resident merely because of resident status in another country will usually fail. Unusually, an individual may be regarded as not resident in any country.

Subject to the foregoing an individual is resident in the UK for a year of assessment if any one of the following applies.

(a)   He is in the UK for some temporary purpose only and not with any view or intent to establish his residence in the UK and if, and only if, the period (or the sum of the periods) for which he is resident (i.e. physically present) in the UK in the year of assessment exceeds six months. [*TCGA 1992, s 9(3)*]. After 1992/93, the question whether for the purposes of this provision an individual is in the UK for some temporary purpose only and not with any view or intent to establish his residence in the UK is decided without regard to any living accommodation available in the UK for his use. [*TCGA 1992, s 9(4); FA 1993, s 208(2)(4)*].

The six months' rule is rigidly applied, even in cases of force majeure, and in border-line cases hours may be significant. See *Wilkie v CIR Ch D 1951, 32 TC 495* where 'six months' was held to mean six calendar months. Otherwise, to be regarded by the Revenue as UK resident for a year of assessment an individual would normally have to be physically present in the UK at some time in the tax year and would also depend on the circumstances. The Revenue treat, *with no exceptions* (including years after 1992/93), an individual as resident if he is in the UK for six months or more during the year. Six months are regarded as 183 days and days of arrival and departure are normally ignored (Revenue Pamphlet IR 20, November 1993 edition, para 1.2).

(b)   He *visits the UK year after year* (so that his visits become in effect 'part of his habit of life') and the annual visits are for a substantial period or periods of time. The Revenue would normally regard an average annual period or periods which amount to 91 days or more as substantial. Where, after four years, the individual's visits average 91 days or more per year, he is treated as resident from the beginning of the fifth year. However, he will be treated as resident from the beginning of the first year if it is clear at the time of his first visit that he intends to make such visits. Also, if the individual decides that he will make such visits before the beginning of the fifth year, he will be treated as resident from the beginning of the year in which that decision is made (Revenue Pamphlet IR 20 para 3.3).

Where the Revenue apply the above averaging treatment it will exclude any days spent in the UK because of exceptional circumstances beyond the individual's control (e.g. illness of the individual or a member of his immediate family) although each case will be examined on its facts and the exclusion will not apply for the purposes of the six months' rule in (a) above (Revenue Pamphlet IR 131, SP 2/91, 19 March 1991 and Revenue Pamphlet IR 20 para 3.3).

For further discussion on the position of visitors to the UK see Revenue Tax Bulletin, May 1994, p 130.

(c)   For years prior to 1993/94, he has *accommodation* (e.g. a house or flat) available for his use in the UK and makes one visit to the UK, however short, in the tax year (Revenue Pamphlet IR 20 paras 2.5 and 3.3).

After 1992/93, the enactment of *TCGA 1992, s 9(4)* in (a) above (no regard to be had for the purposes of *TCGA 1992, s 9(3)* to any living accommodation available in the UK for an individual's use) means that this Revenue practice (which is based on case law prior to 1993/94) ceases. However, the Revenue have said that there will be no change in the practice of treating as resident and ordinarily resident an individual who comes to and remains in the UK where he owns or acquires on a lease of three years or more accommodation in the UK. Similarly, where an individual leaves the UK, the retention of a home here will continue to be a factor in considering whether he has left the UK permanently (Revenue Pamphlet IR 20 para 2.7 and Revenue Press Release 16 March 1993).

Subject to the above, if an individual works full-time in a trade, profession or vocation which does not have a branch or place of business in the UK, or in an office or employment the whole of the duties under which (apart from mere 'incidental' duties) are performed outside the UK, or in a combination of such activities, any accommodation maintained in the UK for his use is disregarded in determining whether or not he is resident in the UK (although the legislation is unclear whether this provision applies equally to capital gains tax as well as income tax). [*TCGA 1992, s 9(1); ICTA 1988, s 335*]. As to whether duties are 'incidental', see *Robson v Dixon Ch D 1972, 48 TC 527* where an airline pilot was employed abroad but occasionally landed in the UK where the family home was maintained. Held, the UK duties were more than incidental. See also Revenue Pamphlet IR 20 paras 6.7 and 6.8. In deciding whether an individual works full-time in the activities mentioned, the Revenue will consider the particular facts of the case, such as whether there is a standard or irregular number of hours to be worked, a formal job structure, concurrent part-time appointments or a mix of employments and self-employments (Revenue Tax Bulletin February 1993 p 57).

Where available accommodation in the UK is to be taken into account for the determination of an individual's residence or ordinary residence status, it does not depend on ownership, but on whether any accommodation is in fact available for use. Accommodation may be treated as not available for an individual's use if it is:

(i)   let on a lease which denies his right to stay in the property;

(ii) left unfurnished so that it is not possible to live in it;

(iii) only available for the individual's use when he is not in the UK;

(iv) too far away from the place visited to be reasonably used when the individual makes one brief business visit to the UK during the tax year;

(v)   owned purely for investment purposes and is neither used nor usable by the individual when he is in the UK;

(vi) rented furnished for the individual's use for a period of less than two years;

(vii) rented unfurnished for the individual's use for a period of less than one year.

A house owned or rented by one spouse will (subject to the above) normally be considered available for the use of the other. (Revenue Pamphlet IR 20 paras 4.1–4.4).

(*d*)   He is a *Commonwealth* or *Eire* citizen, having been ordinarily resident (see 47.3 below) in the UK, who has left the UK for the purpose only of 'occasional residence' abroad (although the legislation is unclear whether the provisions apply equally to capital gains tax as well as income tax). [*TCGA 1992, s 9(1); ICTA 1988, s 334*].

For a discussion of the meaning of 'occasional residence', see *Reed v Clark Ch D 1985, 58 TC 528.*

Married persons. A wife's residence is not governed by her husband's status but is determined by her own circumstances. (Revenue Pamphlet IR 20 para 1.6). For a particular application of this, see 37.2 MARRIED PERSONS and see also 47.3 and 47.4(*b*) below.

Change in residence status. In general, residence status in the UK for part of a year is taken to apply for a whole year (see *Neubergh v CIR Ch D 1977, 52 TC 79* and *Gubay v Kington HL 1984, 57 TC 601*) and, for capital gains tax in particular, disposals are chargeable where they accrue to a person in a year of assessment *during any part of which* he is resident in the UK. [*TCGA 1992, s 2(1)*]. Concessional treatment is, however, available where an individual

(1)   comes to the UK to take up permanent residence or to stay for at least three years (when he would otherwise be treated as resident and ordinarily resident in the UK from the date of arrival; see Revenue Pamphlet IR 20 para 3.1); or

(2)   comes to the UK to take up employment which is expected to last for a period of at least two years; or

(3)   ceases to reside in the UK if he has left for permanent residence abroad; or

(4)   goes abroad for full-time (see (*c*) above) service under a contract of employment, provided that: the individual's absence from the UK and the term of the employment both extend over a complete tax year; any interim visits to the UK do not amount to 183 days or more in any tax year, or an average of 91 days or more in a tax year over the period of absence (up to a maximum of four years); and, for years prior to 1993/94, all the duties of the employment (apart from 'incidental' duties; see (*c*) above) are performed abroad. See (*b*) above for the Revenue's practice in applying averaging treatment. (Where the employee satisfies these

conditions the concession may be extended to an accompanying spouse. See further 47.4(*b*) below.)

In such circumstances the individual will be liable to UK tax only by reference to the period of residence in the UK during the year of assessment, provided he is not ordinarily resident in the UK prior to his arrival or on departure (Revenue Pamphlet IR 1, A11 and A78 as revised by Revenue Press Release 14 September 1993 to reflect the enactment of *TCGA 1992, s 9(4)* mentioned in (*a*) and (*c*) above). This concession, although stated to be for income tax purposes, seems to be able to be read with a further capital gains tax concession. Under this, an individual who is *treated as* (e.g. under the A11 concession and see Revenue Pamphlet IR 20 para 1.5) resident in the UK for any year of assessment from the date of his arrival here, but who has not been regarded at any time during the period of three years immediately preceding the date of his arrival as resident or ordinarily resident here, is charged to capital gains tax only in respect of the chargeable gains accruing to him from disposals made after his arrival in the UK. Where an individual leaves the UK and is treated on his departure as not resident and not ordinarily resident in the UK he is not charged to capital gains tax on gains accruing to him from disposals made after the date of his departure (Revenue Pamphlets IR 1, D2 and IR 20 para 9.3).

The D2 concession does not apply to

(A)   any person in relation to gains accruing to him on the disposal after 5 April 1989 of assets in the UK which, at any time between his departure and the end of the year, are used for a trade, profession or vocation carried on by him in the UK through a branch or agency, or are used for or acquired for use by or for such a branch or agency (see also 39.3 OVERSEAS MATTERS);

(B)   trustees who commence or cease residence in the UK after 9 March 1981 (see 39.6–39.9 OVERSEAS MATTERS and 52.8 SETTLEMENTS);

(C)   a settlor after 5 April 1988 who commences or ceases UK residence during a year in relation to gains of a settlement which are assessed on him as in 52.3 SETTLEMENTS; or

(D)   a settlor on whom gains arising after 18 March 1991 are taxed under *TCGA 1992, s 86, 5 Sch* (see 39.7 OVERSEAS MATTERS).

As with all published extra-statutory concessions, the D2 concession will not be applied in cases where it would have been part of a tax avoidance arrangement (see Revenue Pamphlet IR 1 and *R v CIR (ex p. Fulford-Dobson) QB 1987, 60 TC 168*).

Where this split year basis is applied, the day of departure from, or arrival in, the UK is treated as falling into the period of UK residence or ordinary residence (Revenue Pamphlet IR 20 para 1.5).

For visits to the UK for educational purposes, see 47.3 below. For visits abroad generally, see 47.4 below.

Temporary employment in the UK. An individual coming to the UK to work for a period of *at least two years* is treated as resident for the whole period from the day of arrival to the day of departure. Otherwise the normal rules are applied e.g. the six months' or, before 1993/94, the accommodation available rule. (Revenue Pamphlet IR 20 para 3.6).

Examples

(*Note.* After 1992/93, the case law decisions below, which all predate 1993/94, should be read in the light of the enactment of *TCGA 1992, s 9(4)* mentioned in (*a*) and (*c*) above (no regard to be had for the purposes of *TCGA 1992, s 9(3)* to any living accommodation available in the UK for an individual's use) and the comments mentioned there made by the Revenue.)

A resident of Eire making monthly visits here as director of a British company, having no place of abode here, but a permanent one in Eire, was held to be resident and ordinarily resident (*Lysaght v CIR HL 1928, 13 TC 511*). However, compare *CIR v Combe CS 1932, 17 TC 405*. An officer succeeding to an Eire estate, intending to return there permanently but prevented by military duties in the UK, was held, on the facts, to be resident in both countries (*Inchiquin v CIR CA 1948, 31 TC 125*).

In *CIR v Brown KB 1926, 11 TC 292*, and *CIR v Zorab KB 1926, 11 TC 289*, it was held that retired Indian civil servants making periodical visits to, but having no business interests in, the UK, were not resident.

An American holding a lease of a shooting box in Scotland and spending two months there every year (*Cooper v Cadwalader CES 1904, 5 TC 101*), and a merchant physically present and carrying on business in Italy, but owning a house in the UK where he resided for less than six months (*Lloyd v Sulley C/E/S 1884, 2 TC 37*) have both been held to be resident.

A Belgian who had at his disposal for the visits he paid here a house owned not by him but by a company which he controlled, so that it was in fact available whenever he chose to come, was held to be taxable as a resident (*Loewenstein v De Salis KB 1926, 10 TC 424*). But in *Withers v Wynyard KB 1938, 21 TC 724*, an actress (after 18 months abroad) performing in the UK and occupying for $3\frac{1}{2}$ months in 1933/34 a leasehold flat (unable to be disposed of and sub-let when possible), was held not to be UK resident for that year.

A husband and wife who were not actually physically present during the year, although their children were in the UK, were held not to be UK resident (*Turnbull v Foster CES 1904, 6 TC 206*). In *Reed v Clark Ch D 1985, 58 TC 528* the taxpayer had left the UK with the intention to remain abroad throughout a year of assessment and, in the event, did so remain abroad. He was held not to be resident in the UK for the year of absence since his purpose was not only of 'occasional residence' abroad (see (*d*) above).

The taxpayer's presence in the UK need not be voluntary, see *In re Mackenzie decd Ch D 1940, 19 ATC 399* (taxpayer confined in a lunatic asylum).

47.3   ORDINARY RESIDENCE

The term 'ordinary residence' is not defined in the *Taxes Acts*. Broadly, it denotes greater permanence than the term 'residence' (see 47.2 above), and is equivalent to habitual residence; if an individual is resident year after year, he is ordinarily resident. An individual, whose home has been abroad, coming to the UK to live here permanently or intending to stay here for three years or more is treated as resident and ordinarily resident here from the date of his arrival (Revenue Pamphlet IR 20 para 3.1). An individual may be resident in the UK under the six months' rule of *TCGA 1992, s 9(3)* (see 47.2(*a*) above) without becoming ordinarily resident. Equally, he may be ordinarily resident without being resident in a particular year, e.g. because he usually lives in the UK but is absent on an extended holiday throughout a tax year. (Revenue Pamphlet IR 20 para 1.3).

Accommodation. The availability of accommodation (see 47.2(*c*) above) in the UK for the use of an individual has an important bearing on the determination of ordinary residence status. An individual who has accommodation available and who visits the UK regularly for only limited periods in one or more tax years is regarded as ordinarily resident for each of those years. If such accommodation is not available, he will only be so regarded after such visits have averaged 91 days or more per tax year for four consecutive years (although if he intends such visits from the start of the period, ordinary residence may commence earlier on the same basis as in 47.2(*b*) above). (Revenue Pamphlet IR 131, SP 3/81, 10 April 1981 and Revenue Pamphlet IR 20 paras 3.4 and 3.5).

If an individual regarded as ordinarily resident solely because of the availability of accommodation disposes of it and leaves the UK within three years of arrival, he is normally treated as not ordinarily resident for the duration of his stay (assuming this is to his advantage). (Revenue Pamphlet IR 131, SP 3/81, 10 April 1981 and Revenue Pamphlet IR 20 para 3.12).

After 1992/93, the above Revenue practices should be read in the light of the enactment of *TCGA 1992, s 9(4)* mentioned in 47.2(*a*) and (*c*) above (no regard to be had for the purposes of *TCGA 1992, s 9(3)* to any living accommodation available in the UK for an individual's use) and the comments mentioned there made by the Revenue.

Longer term visitors—commencement of ordinary residence. The Revenue practice is to treat an individual coming to the UK but not intending to stay more than three years (and not buying or leasing for three years or more accommodation for use in the UK), as ordinarily resident from the beginning of the tax year following the third anniversary of arrival. If, before the beginning of that tax year, either there is a change in the individual's intention (i.e. to an intention to stay in the UK for three years or more in all) or accommodation for use in the UK is bought (or leased for three years or more), ordinary residence is treated as commencing at the beginning of the tax year in which either of those events happens (or from the date of arrival in the UK if later). For individuals coming to the UK before 6 April 1988, this practice applied only to those coming to the UK for employment. For other visitors, ordinary residence was treated as commencing either from the beginning of the tax year which included the third anniversary of arrival or from the beginning of the following tax year, depending on the amount of time spent in the UK in the tax year of arrival. (Revenue Pamphlet IR 131, SP 17/91, 4 December 1991 and Revenue Pamphlet IR 20 paras 3.1 and 3.8–3.11). See above under 'Accommodation' for years after 1992/93.

Education. An individual who comes to the UK for a period of study or education which is not expected to exceed four years will be treated as not ordinarily resident provided that

(i) he does not own or buy accommodation here, or acquire it on a lease of three years or more; or

(ii) on leaving the UK he will not be returning regularly for visits which average 91 days or more in each tax year.

(Revenue Pamphlet IR 20 para 3.13). See above under 'Accommodation' for years after 1992/93.

Spouse accompanying employee working overseas. See 47.4(*b*) below.

Averaging of visits to UK over a period. Where this applies in the foregoing, see 47.2(*b*) above for the Revenue's practice in applying averaging treatment.

Examples

(*Note.* After 1992/93, the case law decisions below, all of which predate 1993/94, should be read in the light of the enactment of *TCGA 1992, s 9(4)* mentioned in 47.2(*a*) and (*c*) above (no regard to be had for the purposes of *TCGA 1992, s 9(3)* to any living accommodation available in the UK for an individual's use) and the comments mentioned there made by the Revenue.)

In *Reid v CIR CS 1926, 10 TC 673*, a British subject was held ordinarily resident in the UK although she had no fixed residence either here or abroad and was regularly absent abroad for $8\frac{1}{2}$ months every year. She had here an address, family ties, bank account and furniture in store. *Levene v CIR HL 1928, 13 TC 486*, was decided similarly (British subject abroad for health reasons since 1918, no fixed residence here since (or abroad until 1925), but having ties with this country and in the usual ordering of his life making habitual visits to the UK for 20 weeks yearly for definite purposes). The judgments in this case interpreted the meaning of 'ordinarily resident' by the following phrases: 'habitually resident', 'residence in a place with some degree of continuity' and 'according to the way a man's life is usually ordered'. In *Peel v CIR CS 1927, 13 TC 443*, although the taxpayer had his business and house in Egypt, he was held ordinarily resident in the UK because he also had a house here, and spent an average of 139 days of each year in the UK.

In *Kinloch v CIR KB 1929, 14 TC 736*, a widow living mainly abroad with a son at school in the UK, who had won an appeal in previous years but continued regular annual visits, was held to be resident and ordinarily resident. In *Elmhirst v CIR KB 1937, 21 TC 381* the taxpayer was held to have been ordinarily resident although denying any intention at the time of becoming so. See *Miesegaes v CIR CA 1957, 37 TC 493* (minor at school here for five years, spending the occasional vacation with his father in Switzerland, held ordinarily resident).

In *R v Barnet London Borough Council, ex p. Nilish Shah HL 1982, [1983] 1 All E R 226*, a non-tax case, the words 'ordinarily resident' were held to refer to a man's abode in a particular place or country which he has adopted voluntarily and for settled purposes (i.e. with a sufficient degree of continuity) as part of the regular order of his life for the time being, whether of short or long duration. In *Reed v Clark Ch D 1985, 58 TC 528*, ordinary residence was held to be the converse of 'occasional residence' (see 47.2(*d*) above).

See also the cases under 47.2 above.

47.4   **VISITS ABROAD AND CLAIMS TO NON-UK RESIDENCE AND TO NON-UK ORDINARY RESIDENCE**

Visits abroad are broadly differentiated by the Inland Revenue as follows.

(*a*)   **Visits abroad for short periods.** An individual who has been ordinarily resident in the UK is regarded as remaining resident and ordinarily resident in the UK if he only makes short visits abroad, i.e. for less than a complete tax year. (Revenue Pamphlet IR 20 paras 1.5, 2.1). See also 47.2(*d*) above.

(*b*)   **Going abroad for full-time service under a contract of employment.** In such circumstances, where the conditions set out at 47.2(4) above are satisfied, the employee is normally regarded as not resident and not ordinarily resident in the UK from the day following the date of his departure until the day preceding the day of return. On his return (if at all), the individual is treated as a new permanent resident. On both occasions (going abroad and eventual return) the year of assessment will be 'split' because of the change in ordinary residence as in 47.2 above (Revenue Pamphlet IR 1, A11 as revised by Revenue Press Release 14 September 1993 to reflect the enactment of *TCGA 1992, s 9(4)* mentioned in 47.2(*a*) and (*c*) above; see also Revenue Pamphlet IR 20 paras 2.2 and 2.3).

Although the residence status of each spouse is determined independently, the following concessional treatment applies where an individual going abroad for full-time employment meets the conditions set out in 47.2(4) above and is accompanied, or later joined, by his or her spouse who is not in full-time employment. Where the accompanying spouse is abroad for a complete tax year and interim visits to the UK do not amount to 183 days or more in any tax year, or an average of 91 days or more in a tax year over the period of absence (up to a maximum of four years), then the accompanying spouse's liability to UK tax which is affected by residence, for the years of departure and return at the beginning and end of the period spent abroad, is determined by reference to the period of his or her residence in the UK during the year. However, for this treatment to apply for years before 1993/94 in circumstances where accommodation in the UK was available for use by the accompanying spouse, the latter had to ensure that there were no visits to the UK between the date of departure and the following 5 April or, for the year of return, between 6 April and the date of return. In addition, for years before 1993/94, an accompanying spouse who had available accommodation in the UK was regarded as not ordinarily resident in the UK from the day after leaving the UK to the day before the date of return, provided that the absence was for three years or more and visits to the UK averaged less than 91 days in a tax year over the period of absence. If the absence abroad was expected to be for three years or more but was cut short because the period of the spouse's employment was terminated unexpectedly, the shorter absence 'might' (the Revenue do not specify further conditions so presumably 'would normally' is intended) qualify for this treatment provided that it included a complete tax year and any visits to the UK averaged less than 91 days in a tax year over the period of absence (Revenue Pamphlet IR 1, A78 as revised by Revenue Press Release 14 September 1993 to reflect the enactment of *TCGA 1992 s 9(4)* mentioned in 47.2(*a*) and (*c*) above; see also Revenue Pamphlet IR 20 paras 1.6 and 2.4). For the Revenue's practice in applying averaging treatment, see 47.2(*b*) above.

(*c*)   **Permanent emigration for reasons other than a full-time service contract abroad.** Despite *actual* permanent residence abroad, the taxpayer may still fall into one of the *tax* residence traps in 47.2(*a*)–(*c*) above. If, e.g. on retirement abroad, he claims that he has ceased residence and ordinary residence, and requires an immediate provisional Revenue ruling to that effect, he must show, in general terms, that he has completely cut his ties with the UK (e.g. that he has taken steps to acquire accommodation abroad to live in as a permanent home, and if he continues to own property in the UK, the reason is consistent with his stated aim of permanent residence abroad; see the comments made about available accommodation in the UK at 47.2(*c*) above). If he can do this, the claim is usually provisionally admitted with effect from the day after departure and the ruling is confirmed after absence for a period including a complete fiscal year during which any visits to this country have been for an annual average of less than 91 days (for the Revenue's practice in applying this averaging treatment, see 47.2(*b*) above). If the individual cannot produce sufficient evidence to the Revenue to obtain a ruling at the start of his absence, the Revenue adopt a 'wait and see' approach for a period of three years, during which the individual's tax liabilities are computed provisionally on the basis that the individual is UK resident. That liability is adjusted, if necessary, when a final Revenue decision is made at the end of the three-year period. Again a tax year may be split as in 47.2 above if a claim for a change of status is sustained (Revenue Pamphlet IR 20 paras 1.5, 2.7 and 2.8).

47.5   **COMPANIES**

Subject to *FA 1994, s 249* below, after 14 March 1988, a company incorporated in the UK is regarded for the purposes of the *Taxes Acts* as resident there, irrespective of any rule of law giving a different place of residence. [*FA 1988, s 66(1)*].

This 'incorporation' test does not, however, apply in the following circumstances.

(a)   Where, immediately before 15 March 1988, a company was carrying on business and was not UK resident, having ceased to be so resident in pursuance of a Treasury consent given under *ICTA 1970, s 482* or *ICTA 1988, s 765* (or any predecessor legislation), and, where the consent was a general consent, the company was liable, by reason of domicile, residence or place of management, to tax on income in a territory outside the UK. If, after 14 March 1988, the company ceases to carry on business or, where the consent was a general consent, ceases to be taxable in a territory outside the UK, the incorporation test applies after that time (or after 14 March 1993 if later).

(b)   Where a company which carried on business at any time before 15 March 1988 ceases to be UK resident after 14 March 1988 in pursuance of a Treasury consent, and immediately thereafter carries on business. If, after ceasing to be UK resident, the company at any time ceases to carry on business, the incorporation test applies after that time (or after 14 March 1993 if later).

(c)   Where a company not within (a) above carried on business at any time before 15 March 1988, and was not UK resident immediately before that date, the incorporation test applies only after 14 March 1993.

(d)   Where a company not within (b) above carried on business at any time before 15 March 1988, and ceases to be UK resident on or after that date in pursuance of a Treasury consent, the incorporation test applies only after 14 March 1993.

If a company within (a)-(d) above becomes UK resident at a time after 14 March 1988, the incorporation test applies to it after that time.

Residence for the purposes of (a)-(d) above is determined without reference to the incorporation test. [*FA 1988, 7 Sch*].

A company which is no longer carrying on any business, or is being wound up outside the UK, is treated as continuing to be resident in the UK if it was regarded as resident immediately before it ceased business or any of its activities came under the control of a person exercising the functions which in the UK a liquidator would exercise. [*FA 1988, s 66(2)*].

Revenue Statement of Practice 1/90, 9 January 1990, clarifies the Revenue's interpretation of three points in relation to *FA 1988, s 66, 7 Sch*.

(i)   As regards whether a company is 'carrying on business' at a particular time, 'business' has a wider meaning than 'trade', and can include, for instance, the purchase of stock prior to trading, or the holding of investments (which could include the holding of shares in a subsidiary company, or a holding consisting of a single non-income producing investment). A company (e.g. a 'shelf' company) whose transactions have been limited to those formalities necessary to maintain its registration is not regarded as carrying on business. Where, in terms of the application of general case law to the question of residence (see below), a company can demonstrate that it is or was resident outside the UK by reference to the place 'where its real business is carried on', it will have carried on business for the above purposes.

(ii)   As regards the requirement under (a) that a company be taxable in a territory outside the UK, the liability must be to tax on income, so that liability to a flat rate fee or lump sum duty does not fulfil the test. It is, however, satisfied where the company is within the charge to tax, even though it may pay no tax because, for example, it makes losses or claims double taxation relief.

(iii)   The exceptions granted to companies who have ceased to be resident in pursuance of a Treasury consent do not apply to companies who ceased to be resident without Treasury consent but who were subsequently informed by letter that no action would be taken against them.

The Revenue has set up a telephone helpline to assist companies becoming resident in the UK after 14 March 1993 under *FA 1988, s 66, 7 Sch* above. The telephone number is 071-438 7551. Alternatively contact should be made with Inland Revenue International Division, Melbourne House, Aldwych, London WC2B 4LL.

After 29 November 1993, a company which would otherwise be regarded as resident in the UK for the purposes of the *Taxes Acts*, and is regarded for the purposes of any double tax relief arrangements within *ICTA 1988, s 788* as resident in a territory outside the UK and not resident in the UK (on the assumption that a claim for relief under those arrangements has been made and under the claim it falls to be decided whether the company is to be so regarded for the purposes of those arrangements), is treated for the purposes of the *Taxes Acts* as resident outside the UK and not resident in the UK. This treatment applies whether the company would otherwise be regarded as resident in the UK for the purposes of the *Taxes Acts* under the 'incorporation test' of *FA 1988, s 66(1)* above or by virtue of some other rule of law. [*FA 1994, s 249*].

There is no statutory definition of residence; and before the enactment of the deeming provisions described above the courts had determined that a company resides where its real business is carried on, i.e. '*where its central management and control actually abide*'. This criterion continues to apply for companies incorporated outside the UK and for companies covered by the transitional provisions of *FA 1988, 7 Sch* above.

Although no general rules for determining company residence are laid down by statute, it is clear, as stated above, from case law that a company resides '*where its central management and control actually abide*' and therefore a company doing business abroad but controlled from the UK is resident in the UK subject to any overriding provisions contained in relevant double taxation agreements. In the following cases, the company was held to be managed and controlled from, and hence resident in, the UK; *Calcutta Jute Mills Co Ltd v Nicholson Ex D 1876, 1 TC 83* (UK company operating abroad but directors and shareholders meeting in UK); *De Beers Consolidated Mines Ltd v Howe HL 1906, 5 TC 198* (South African company operating there but important affairs controlled from UK where majority of directors resided); *New Zealand Shipping Co Ltd v Thew HL 1922, 8 TC 208* (New Zealand company with New Zealand directors, but overall control lay with separate London board); *American Thread Co v Joyce HL 1913, 6 TC 163* (UK company operating in USA with US directors in charge of current business, but overall control in London); *John Hood & Co Ltd v Magee KB (I) 1918, 7 TC 327* (company registered in both UK and USA, with the only director resident in USA, but general meetings and material trading activities in UK). But in *A-G v Alexander Ex D, [1874] 10 Ex 20*, a foreign state bank with a UK branch was held resident abroad, notwithstanding that shareholders' meetings were held in London.

The Revenue's approach to applying the basic test of the place of central management and control is first to ascertain whether the directors in fact themselves exercise central management and control; if so, to determine where that central management and control is exercised (not necessarily where they meet); if not, to establish where and by whom it is exercised. The concept of the place of central management and control is directed at the highest level of control of the company's business, rather than the place where the main business operations are to be found. This must always be a question of fact in any particular case, but the place of directors' meetings will usually be of significance if they are the medium through which central management and control is exercised. If, however, central management and control is in reality exercised by, for example, a single individual, the company's residence will be where that individual exercises his powers. With regard to the particular problem of residence of a subsidiary, the Revenue would not normally seek to impute to the subsidiary the residence of its parent unless the parent in effect usurps the functions of the Board of the subsidiary. Matters taken into account would include the extent to which the directors of the subsidiary take decisions on their own authority as to investment, production, marketing and procurement without reference to the parent (and see below).

In all cases, the Revenue will seek to determine whether a major objective of the existence of any particular factors bearing on residence is the obtaining of tax benefits from residence or non-residence, and to establish the reality of the central management and control (Revenue Pamphlet IR 131, 1/90, 9 January 1990 replacing SP 6/83, 27 July 1983).

Incorporation in the UK and compliance with the requirements of the *Companies Act 1985* did not in themselves render a company resident there before 15 March 1988. See *Todd v Egyptian Delta Land and Investment Co Ltd HL 1928, 14 TC 119* and cf. *Eccott v Aramayo Francke Mines Ltd HL 1925, 9 TC 445*. A company may be resident in more than one country. See *Swedish Central Railway Co Ltd v Thompson HL 1925, 9 TC 342*, and for an authoritative discussion of dual residence, *Union Corporation Ltd v CIR HL 1953, 34 TC 207*.

A company may have a domicile (see *Gasque v CIR KB 1940, 23 TC 210*), but it would seem from the *Union Corporation* case above that, for a company, ordinary residence and residence are synonymous. In the light of *ICTA 1988, s 11* and *TCGA 1992, s 10* it would seem, anyway, that ordinary residence is not relevant to the chargeable gains of companies.

47.6 DOMICILE

An individual may have only one domicile at any given time, denoting the country or state considered his natural home. Domicile does not necessarily correspond with either residence or nationality and is essentially a question of fact (*Earl of Iveagh v Revenue Commissioners SC (RI), [1930] IR 431*). A *domicile of origin* is acquired at birth (normally that of the taxpayer's father, see below), but may be replaced by a *domicile of choice* (to be proved by subsequent conduct). A domicile of choice may be replaced by another domicile of choice (if the necessary proof is forthcoming), but if a domicile of choice is lost without another being acquired, the domicile of origin immediately revives (*Fielden v CIR Ch D 1965, 42 TC 501*).

It is normally more difficult to show the displacement of a domicile of origin than that of a domicile of choice. See *CIR v Bullock CA 1976, 51 TC 522* where a taxpayer with a domicile of origin in Canada lived in England and intended to remain here during his wife's lifetime. He was held not to have acquired an English domicile of choice (the judgments in this case give a useful review of the law relating to domicile). In *Buswell v CIR CA 1974, 49 TC 334*, the taxpayer had a domicile of origin in South Africa. He came to England to school in 1928, and was called up into the British Army during the Second World War, serving in India. On his return, he signed a written declaration that he intended to remain permanently in the UK. In 1955, he took out a South African passport. In 1961, he married an English lady and their children were brought up in the UK, though registered as South African nationals. In 1968, he and his wife visited South Africa for the first time for 40 years and, with the intention of eventually settling there permanently, bought property there in which they spent three months in each year. He was held never to have abandoned his domicile of origin. In *Re Clore (decd.) (No 2), Official Solicitor v Clore and Others Ch D, [1984] STC 609*, it was held that an English domicile of origin was never lost as, on the evidence, the taxpayer never formed a settled intention to reside permanently elsewhere. Contrast *Qureshi v Qureshi Fam D, [1972]*

Fam D 173, and *In re Lawton Ch D 1958, 37 ATC 216*. Actual settlement abroad is necessary as well as intention; see *Plummer v CIR Ch D 1987, 60 TC 452*.

In *Steiner v CIR CA 1973, 49 TC 13*, a Jew who had acquired a German domicile of choice, but who fled to England in 1939 and obtained British naturalisation was held to have acquired an English domicile of choice.

Married women. Up to 31 December 1973, a woman automatically acquired the domicile of her husband on marriage. From 1 January 1974 onwards, the domicile of a married woman is ascertained in the same way as any other individual capable of having an independent domicile, except that a woman already married on that date will retain her husband's domicile until it is changed by acquisition or revival of another domicile. [*Domicile and Matrimonial Proceedings Act 1973, ss 1, 17 (5)*]. See *CIR v Duchess of Portland Ch D 1981, 54 TC 648*. But a woman who is a national of the USA and who married a man with UK domicile before 1974 will be treated (after 5 April 1976) in determining her domicile, as if the marriage had taken place in 1974. See Article 4(4) of the US/UK Double Tax Agreement and any similar provisions in double tax agreements with other countries. A widow retains her late husband's domicile unless she later acquires a domicile of choice (or reverts to a domicile of origin) (*In re Wallach PDA 1949, [1950] 1 All E R 199*).

Minors. The domicile of a minor follows that of a person on whom he is legally dependent (usually his father). Under *Domicile and Matrimonial Proceedings Act 1973, s 3* (which does not extend to Scotland), a person first becomes capable of having an independent domicile when he attains 16 (in Scotland, 14 for boys and 12 for girls) or marries under that age. Under *section 4* thereof, where a child's father and mother are living apart, his domicile is that of his mother if he has his home with her and has no home with his father.

47.7 APPEALS

Ordinary residence and domicile in relation to capital gains tax are determined by the Board. [*ICTA 1988, s 207; TCGA 1992, s 9(2)*]. Any appeal from a Board decision is to the Special Commissioners [*TMA 1970, 2 Sch 3; ICTA 1988, s 207*] and the normal time limit of thirty days from the receipt of written notice of the decision is extended to three months if the appeal concerns residence, ordinary residence or domicile. [*TMA 1970, s 42(3)(b); ICTA 1988, s 207*]. Other disputes regarding residence are settled by appeal against the relevant assessment in the ordinary way. See generally, 4 APPEALS.

47.8 UNITED KINGDOM

The United Kingdom for tax purposes comprises England, Scotland, Wales and Northern Ireland. The Channel Islands (Jersey, Guernsey, Alderney, Sark, Herm and Jethou) and the Isle of Man are excluded. Great Britain comprises England, Scotland and Wales only.

See 39.19 OVERSEAS MATTERS for the territorial extension of the UK in certain circumstances.

47.9 EIRE

For double taxation relief purposes a person cannot be resident in both the UK and Eire. The residence of an *individual* is first determined under normal tax rules relating to abode, domicile etc. If this results in him being technically resident in both States the question is decided by reference successively to permanent home, personal and economic ties, habitual abode, and nationality, and if necessary is decided by agreement between the States. A *company or body of persons* is deemed to be resident where its place of effective management is situated. [*SI 1976, Nos 2151, 2152; ICTA 1988, ss 68(1)-(4), 192(1), 3 Sch 15*]. See also 17.3 DOUBLE TAXATION RELIEF.

48   Retirement Relief

Cross-references. See 19.2 FURNISHED HOLIDAY ACCOMMODATION for application of retirement relief to such accommodation in the UK; 22 HOLD-OVER RELIEFS for interaction of retirement relief and those reliefs; 45.6, 45.7 and 45.8 REINVESTMENT IN SHARES RELIEF for interaction of retirement relief and that relief.

48.1   INTRODUCTION

In respect of disposals made after 5 April 1985, the retirement relief provisions in *CGTA 1979, ss 124, 125* ceased to apply and were replaced by the provisions of what are now *TCGA 1992, ss 163, 164, 6 Sch*. See also Revenue Pamphlet CGT 6 (1992).

Under transitional provisions, where a disposal took place after 5 April 1985 but the 'qualifying period' (as defined in the current provisions) relating to the disposal ended before 6 April 1985, the provisions of *CGTA 1979, ss 124, 125* applied to the disposal. [*TCGA 1992, 6 Sch 5(1); FA 1985, s 69(1), 27 Sch Pt VII*].

48.2   RELIEF FOR DISPOSALS AFTER 5 APRIL 1985

Relief is given for material disposals of business assets by individuals on retirement from their own, partnership or corporate personal (corporate family, for disposals before 16 March 1993) business provided the necessary conditions are met (see 48.4 below). In addition, relief may also be given for disposals, associated with retirement, of

(*a*)   assets used in an office or employment (see 48.5 below);

(*b*)   assets owned by a partner, or by an officer or employee (director only, for disposals before 16 March 1993) of a company, and used in the business of the partnership or, as the case may be, the company (see 48.6 below); and

(*c*)   settled property consisting of shares or assets used for business purposes if a beneficiary has an interest in possession in the settled property (see 48.7 below).

Except in the case of a disposal made by an individual who has attained the age of 55 (60 for disposals before 19 March 1991), relief is subject to a claim being made (under *TCGA 1992, 6 Sch 5(2)*) not later than two years after the end of the year of assessment in which the disposal occurred. In the case of a trustees' disposal, the claim (under *TCGA 1992, 6 Sch 5(3)*) must be made jointly by the trustees and the beneficiary concerned. Where a claim is dependent upon an individual having retired on ill-health grounds below the age of 55 (60 for disposals before 19 March 1991), the claim must be made to the Board. [*TCGA 1992, 6 Sch 5(2)–(4)*].

Prior to the commencement of *TCGA 1992*, the first claim mentioned above was made under *FA 1985, 20 Sch 5(2)* and the second under *FA 1985, 20 Sch 5(3)*.

Husband and wife. A husband and wife are each eligible for the relief if they individually meet the qualifying conditions. See also 48.9 below.

Date of disposal. For an unconditional contract this is strictly the date the contract is made but if business activities continue beyond that date pending completion of the contract, the date of completion will be accepted as the date of disposal for the purposes of calculating the relief (Revenue Pamphlet IR 1, D31). This treatment seems to apply even to the extent of allowing relief where the individual's 55th (60th for disposals before 19 March 1991) birthday falls in the intervening period (Tolley's Practical Tax 1986 p 175).

Valuation where hold-over relief also claimed. Where the gain arising on the disposal of an asset is partly relieved by retirement relief and partly by hold-over relief, the Inland Revenue will require a valuation of the asset. However, unless the claimants request otherwise, the valuation may be deferred until either:

(a)   it is necessary to determine the amount of retirement relief due, for example where the transferor makes another disposal which attracts retirement relief; or

(b)   it is necessary to determine the transferee's cost of the asset.

(Revenue Pamphlet IR 131, SP 8/92, 26 October 1992).

48.3   **Definitions.** The following definitions apply for the purposes of 48.4–48.9 below.

'*Business*' is not defined but is effectively limited to trades (which includes for retirement relief purposes commercial letting of FURNISHED HOLIDAY ACCOMMODATION (19) in the UK and the activities of both parties to a share farming agreement, provided the landowner takes an active part in the venture (see Country Landowners Association statement of 19 December 1991 reproduced at 1992 STI 189)), professions, vocations, offices or employments as in 48.8 below.

'*Commercial association of companies*' means a company together with such associated companies (within *ICTA 1988, s 416*, see Tolley's Corporation Tax under Close Companies) as carry on businesses of such a nature that the businesses of all the companies together may be reasonably considered to make up a single composite undertaking.

'*Family company*', in relation to disposals before 16 March 1993 and an individual, is a company where either (i) not less than 25% of the voting rights are 'exercisable' by the individual; or (ii) more than 50% of the voting rights are exercisable by the individual and his family (spouse and brother, sister, ancestor or lineal descendant of the individual or spouse) with not less than 5% being exercisable by the individual himself. '*Exercisable*' means capable of being exercised, whether in fact exercised (*Hepworth v Smith Ch D 1981, 54 TC 396*). Voting rights of trustees are included as those of a member of the family where the individual or a member of his family is a beneficiary of the settlement and no other person is for the time being entitled to receive any income or capital from the settlement or can become so entitled (otherwise than on the failure of the individual or a member of his family to become entitled).

'*Full-time working director*', in relation to disposals before 16 March 1993 and one or more companies, is a director required to devote substantially the whole of his time to the service of the company or companies in question in a managerial or technical capacity.

'*Full-time working officer or employee*', in relation to disposals after 15 March 1993 and one or more companies, is an officer or employee required to devote substantially the whole of his time to the service of the company or companies in question in a managerial or technical capacity.

'*Group of companies*' means a company which has one or more '51% subsidiaries' within *ICTA 1988, s 838(1)* together with those subsidiaries.

'*Holding company*' means a company whose business (disregarding any trade carried on by it) consists wholly or mainly of the holding of shares or securities of one or more companies which are its 51% subsidiaries (within *ICTA 1988, s 838*).

'*Ill-health grounds*'. A person is treated as having retired on ill-health grounds if the Board are satisfied, on production of reasonable evidence, that he has ceased to be engaged in the work previously undertaken, is incapable of engaging in that kind of work by reason of ill-health and is likely to remain permanently so incapable. In practice, the Board will in all cases require claimants to provide a medical certificate, signed by a qualified medical practitioner. The Board will themselves take advice from the Regional Medical Service of the Department of Health and in some cases a further medical examination by the Regional Medical Officer will be required. The Board will act on the basis of the advice they receive from the Regional Medical Service (Revenue Press Release 16 April 1985). A claim for retirement relief on these grounds must be due to the ill health of the claimant: the ill health of one party cannot force the retirement of another (Revenue Tax Bulletin November 1991 p 5).

'Permitted period' is a period of one year or such longer period as the Board may, in any particular case, by notice allow.

'Personal company', in relation to disposals after 15 March 1993 and an individual, is a company where not less than 5% of the voting rights are 'exercisable' by the individual. *'Exercisable'* means capable of being exercised, whether in fact exercised (*Hepworth v Smith Ch D 1981, 54 TC 396*).

'Trading company' and *'trading group'* mean a company or group whose business consists wholly or mainly of the carrying on of a trade or trades, i.e. including every trade, manufacture, adventure or concern in the nature of trade. [*TCGA 1992, s 163(9), 6 Sch 1, 3; FA 1993, s 87, 7 Sch 1, 2, 23 Sch Pt III*].

48.4   **Disposals by individuals on retirement from own, partnership or corporate personal (corporate family, for disposals before 16 March 1993) business.** Relief is given where an individual who has attained the age of 55 (60 for disposals before 19 March 1991) or has retired below that age on 'ill-health grounds' makes a 'material disposal of business assets'.

A *'material disposal of business assets'* is one of the following.

(*a*)   A disposal of the whole or part of a business (including an interest in the assets of a partnership carrying on a business) where throughout a period of at least one year ending with the date of disposal (the *'qualifying period'*) the business is owned by

　　(i)   the individual making the disposal; or

　　(ii)   a 'trading company' which is either the individual's 'personal company' ('family company' for disposals before 16 March 1993) or a member of a 'trading group' of which the 'holding company' is that individual's personal company (family company for disposals before 16 March 1993). The individual must be a 'full-time working officer or employee' ('full-time working director' for disposals before 16 March 1993) of that company or, if that company is a member of a 'group of companies' or 'commercial association of companies', of one or more companies which are members of the group or association.

Where the business is carried on by a partnership, it is treated as owned by each partner who is, at that time, a member of the partnership. [*TCGA 1992, s 163(1)–(3)(8), 6 Sch 4(1)(2); FA 1993, s 87, 7 Sch 1, 2, 23 Sch Pt III*].

Disposal of a part of a business must be distinguished from the disposal of assets of the business. See *McGregor v Adcock Ch D 1977, 51 TC 692* where a farmer sold part of his land for which outline planning permission had been obtained. This decision was followed in *Atkinson v Dancer; Mannion v Johnston Ch D 1988, 61 TC 598*, on the ground that after such a long time only the Court of Appeal should reconsider whether the case had correctly laid down that the test was the degree of 'interference' with the whole complex of activities and assets. In *Pepper v*

Daffurn Ch D, [1993] STC 466 it was doubted whether Fox J in *McGregor* had intended to lay down any such test at all. See also *Jarmin v Rawlings Ch D 1994, [1994] STC 1005* where *McGregor* was followed. With reference to similar cases, it is understood to be Revenue practice to allow relief if

(i) a distinct activity in a particular part of the farm ceases (e.g. a piggery is sold, or there is a cessation of dairying coupled with the sale of milk quota *and* land — although it has been suggested that the Revenue have allowed relief where there is a cessation of dairying coupled with the sale of milk quota *or* land), or

(ii) 50 per cent of the farm is disposed of.

(*b*) A disposal of one or more assets used for the purposes of a business at the time when the business ceased to be carried on, where throughout a period of at least one year ending with the date of cessation of business (the '*qualifying period*') either the business was owned by the individual making the disposal or the conditions in (*a*)(ii) above applied. The individual must have attained the age of 55 (60 for disposals before 19 March 1991), or retired below that age on 'ill-health grounds', on or before the date of cessation of business and the asset(s) must be disposed of within the '*permitted period*' (defined as a period of one year or such longer period as is allowed in a written notice by the Board) after that date. Where the business is carried on by a partnership, it is treated as owned by each partner who is, at the time, a member of the partnership. [*TCGA 1992, s 163(1)(2)(4)(8), 6 Sch 4(1)(2); FA 1993, s 87, 7 Sch 1, 2, 23 Sch Pt III*]. In practice the period allowed after cessation will be up to three years provided the asset or, in the case of a company, any chargeable business asset retained by it at the date of cessation, is not used or leased for any purpose during that period (Revenue Pamphlet CGT 6 (1992) p 3). See also Taxation 27 July 1989 p 516 for a possible further relaxation in certain cases where assets are retained for reasons beyond the control of the individual concerned.

(*c*) A disposal of shares or securities of a company (including a deemed disposal of an interest in shares under *TCGA 1992, s 122* as a result of a capital distribution; see 53.13 SHARES AND SECURITIES) where throughout a period of at least one year ending with the 'operative date' (the '*qualifying period*') either

(i) the individual owns the business which, at the date of disposal, is owned by the company, or, if the company is the 'holding company' of a 'trading group', by any member of the group; or

(ii) the company is the individual's 'personal company' ('family company' for disposals before 16 March 1993) and is either a 'trading company' or the 'holding company' of a 'trading group'. The individual must be a 'full-time working officer or employee' ('full-time working director' for disposals before 16 March 1993) of the company or, in the case of a member of a 'group of companies' or 'commercial association of companies', of one or more companies which are members of the group or association.

The '*operative date*' is normally the date of disposal but there are two exceptions.

(A) If within the year before disposal the company concerned ceased to be either a trading company or a member of a trading group (without becoming the other), and on or before the cessation, the individual making the disposal attained the age of 55 (60 for disposals before 19 March 1991) or retired earlier on 'ill-health grounds', then, subject to (B) below, the operative date is the date of cessation. In consequence, the reference in (*c*)(i) above to the date of disposal is to be read as referring to the date of cessation of trading.

(B) If the individual ceased to be a full-time working officer or employee (full-time working director for disposals before 16 March 1993) of the company (or, in the case of a member of a group or commercial association of companies, of one or more companies which are members of the group or association) but remained an officer or employee (a director for disposals before 16 March 1993) of the company concerned (or one or more members of the group or association) and worked an average of at least ten hours per week in a technical or managerial capacity until either the date of disposal or the date of cessation of trading where (A) above applies, the operative date is the date on which he ceased to be a full-time working officer or employee (full-time working director for disposals before 16 March 1993).

Where under *TCGA 1992, s 127* a new holding would be treated as the same asset as a previous holding after a reorganisation under *TCGA 1992, s 126* (including an exchange of shares or securities treated as such a reorganisation under *TCGA 1992, s 135(3)*) the individual may elect by notice in writing within two years of the end of the year of assessment in which the disposal occurred for *TCGA 1992, s 127* not to apply. [*TCGA 1992, s 163(1)(2)(5)–(7), 6 Sch 1, 2, 4(1)(2); FA 1993, s 87, 7 Sch 1, 2, 23 Sch Pt III*]. For reorganisation and exchanges of shares etc., see 53.5, 53.8 SHARES AND SECURITIES. In the Revenue's opinion an election cannot be made in respect of part only of the shares held before and concerned in the reorganisation (Tolley's Practical Tax 1986 p 166).

48.5 **Assets used in an office or employment.** Relief is given where an individual who has attained the age of 55 (60 for disposals before 19 March 1991) or has retired below that age on 'ill-health grounds' makes a 'relevant disposal' of the whole or part of the assets provided or held for the purposes of his office or employment.

A disposal is a *'relevant disposal'* if

(*a*) the office or employment was the individual's full-time occupation throughout a period of at least one year ending with the date of disposal (the *'qualifying period'*), or if the office etc. ceased earlier, before the cessation date; and

(*b*) the office or employment was not as officer or employee (as director for disposals before 16 March 1993) of his 'personal company' ('family company' for disposals before 16 March 1993) or a member of a 'trading group' of which the 'holding company' was his personal company (family company for disposals before 16 March 1993) (as this situation is covered by 48.4 above); and

(*c*) where the individual ceased office or employment before the disposal

(i) he either attained 55 (60 for disposals before 19 March 1991) on or before the date of cessation or retired on ill-health grounds on that date; and

(ii) the disposal took place within one year of ceasing office or employment (or such longer period as is allowed by the Board; see 48.4(*b*) above).

[*TCGA 1992, s 164(1)(2), 6 Sch 1, 4(1)(2); FA 1993, s 87, 7 Sch 1, 2, 23 Sch Pt III*].

48.6 **Assets owned by a partner, or by an officer or employee (director only, for disposals before 16 March 1993) of a company, and used in the business of the**

partnership or, as the case may be, the company. Where relief is available to partners, or to officers or employees of personal companies (to directors only of family companies for disposals before 16 March 1993), for a 'material disposal of business assets' (see 48.4 above) consisting of an interest in the assets of a partnership, or of shares etc. in a personal company (family company for disposals before 16 March 1993), relief is also available where the individual concerned makes an 'associated disposal' of assets.

A disposal is an *'associated disposal'* if

(*a*)   it takes place as part of a withdrawal of the individual from the business carried on by the partnership or company concerned;

(*b*)   the asset was in use for the purposes of the partnership or company business until immediately before the material disposal or, if earlier, the cessation of the business; and

(*c*)   the asset has been used for all or part of the period in which it has been owned by the individual for business purposes (including other previous businesses carried on by the individual whether alone or in partnership or by a personal company (family company for disposals before 16 March 1993)).

The *'qualifying period'* in the case of an associated disposal is the same as that for the material disposal of business assets with which it is associated. [*TCGA 1992, s 164(6)–(8), 6 Sch 4(1)(2); FA 1993, s 87, 7 Sch 1, 2, 23 Sch Pt III*].

In *Clark v Mayo Ch D [1994] STC 570* Evans-Lombe J held that the words 'immediately before . . . the cessation of the business' should not be construed in isolation, but in the context of *TCGA 1992, ss 163, 164* as a whole. The words 'immediately before' could be construed as meaning 'sufficiently proximate in time to the material disposal or cessation so as to justify the conclusion that the transaction formed part of it'.

A withdrawal may be partial and is a disposal of an interest in the partnership, or of shares in the company, concerned (Revenue Pamphlet CGT 6 (1992) p 5). There is no requirement that a member of a partnership should dispose of the whole of his interest in the partnership (Tolley's Practical Tax 1986 p 40).

48.7   **Disposal of assets by trustees.** Relief is given where trustees dispose of settled property consisting of shares or securities of a company, or of an asset used or previously used for business purposes, if a beneficiary has an interest in possession (excluding one for a fixed term) in the settled property and certain conditions are met. For consideration of the meaning of 'interest in possession', see 52.7 SETTLEMENTS.

In relation to a disposal of shares or securities of a company (including a deemed disposal of an interest in shares under *TCGA 1992, s 122* as a result of a capital distribution; see 53.13 SHARES AND SECURITIES), the conditions are that

(*a*)   the company was the beneficiary's 'personal company' ('family company' for disposals before 16 March 1993) and either a 'trading company' or the 'holding company' of a 'trading group' throughout a period of at least one year (the *'qualifying period'*) ending not earlier than one year (or longer if the Board allow; see 48.4(*b*) above) before the date of disposal; and

(*b*)   the beneficiary was a 'full-time working officer or employee' ('full-time working director' for disposals before 16 March 1993) of the company (or, if the company is a member of a 'group of companies' or 'commercial association of companies', of one or more companies which are members of the group or association) throughout a period of at least one year ending as in (*a*) above; and

(c)   the beneficiary ceased to be a full-time working officer or employee (full-time working director for disposals before 16 March 1993) on or within one year (longer if the Board allow; see 48.4(*b*) above) before the date of disposal, having attained the age of 55 (60 for disposals before 19 March 1991) or retired earlier on 'ill-health grounds'.

Where under *TCGA 1992, s 127* a new holding would be treated as the same asset as a previous holding after a reorganisation under *TCGA 1992, s 126* (including an exchange of shares or securities treated as such a reorganisation under *TCGA 1992, s 135(3)* the trustees and the individual may jointly elect in writing within two years of the end of the year of assessment in which the disposal occurred for *TCGA 1992, s 127* not to apply. For reorganisation and exchanges of shares etc., see 53.5, 53.8 SHARES AND SECURITIES. In the Revenue's opinion an election cannot be made in respect of part only of the shares held before and concerned in the reorganisation (Tolley's Practical Tax 1986 p 166).

In relation to a disposal of an asset, the conditions are that

(i)   the asset was used for the purposes of a business carried on by the beneficiary throughout a period of at least one year (the *'qualifying period'*) ending not earlier than one year (or longer if the Board allow, see 48.4(*b*) above) before the disposal;

(ii)   the beneficiary ceased to carry on that business on or within one year (or longer if the Board allow) before the date of disposal; and

(iii)   the beneficiary attained the age of 55 (60 for disposals before 19 March 1991) or retired earlier on 'ill-health grounds' on or before the date of disposal or, if earlier, the date he ceased to carry on the business.

[*TCGA 1992, s 164(3)–(5), 6 Sch 1, 2, 4(1)(2); FA 1993, s 87, 7 Sch 1, 2, 23 Sch Pt III*].

48.8   **GAINS QUALIFYING FOR RELIEF**

Subject to the provisions below relating to trustees' disposals, associated disposals and capital distributions

(a)   in the case of a qualifying disposal within 48.4–48.7 above, other than one of shares or securities of a company, the gains accruing on the disposal of 'chargeable business assets' comprised in the qualifying disposal are aggregated and only the excess of those gains over 'the amount available for relief' (see 48.9 below) is a chargeable gain [*TCGA 1992, 6 Sch 6*]; and

(b)   where the qualifying disposal is of shares or securities of a company, the gains accruing are aggregated, and of the 'appropriate proportion' of the aggregated gains, only the excess of that proportion over 'the amount available for relief' is a chargeable gain (but not so as to affect liability in respect of gains representing the balance of the aggregated gains).

The *'appropriate proportion'* is a proportion given as follows.

(i)   *For a trading company which is not a holding company*, the proportion is that which the value of the company's 'chargeable business assets' bears to the value of all its 'chargeable assets' immediately before the end of the qualifying period.

(ii)   *For a holding company*, the proportion is that which the value of the trading group's 'chargeable business assets' bears to the value of all the group's 'chargeable assets' immediately before the end of the qualifying period. If a 51% subsidiary of a holding company is not wholly owned, the values of its chargeable assets and chargeable business assets are reduced in proportion to the share capital owned.

See 48.4–48.7 above as appropriate for the qualifying period.

A *'chargeable asset'* is every asset except one where a gain accruing on a disposal immediately before the end of the qualifying period would not be a chargeable gain, but a holding by one member of a trading group of the ordinary share capital of another is not a chargeable asset.

If the company or group has no chargeable assets, the appropriate proportion is the whole. [*TCGA 1992, 6 Sch 7, 8*].

Where the qualifying disposal is a disposal which the individual is (or trustees are) treated as making under *TCGA 1992, s 122* (see 53.13 SHARES AND SECURITIES) in consideration of a capital distribution, the recipient of the distribution can elect, by notice in writing not later than two years after the end of the year of assessment in which he received the capital distribution, for any asset sold not more than six months before the end of the qualifying period to be treated as remaining the property of the company and in use for the purposes for which it was used before the sale. The proceeds of disposal are treated as not forming part of the assets of the company. [*TCGA 1992, 6 Sch 12(5)(6)*].

A *'chargeable business asset'* is an asset which is, or is an interest in, an asset used for the purposes of a trade, profession, vocation, office or employment carried on by the individual or beneficiary concerned, his personal company (family company for disposals before 16 March 1993), a member of a trading group of which the holding company is his personal company (family company for disposals before 16 March 1993) or a partnership of which he is a member. Goodwill is included but not shares or securities or other assets held as investments. An asset is not a chargeable business asset if, on the disposal of it, any gain which might accrue would not be a chargeable gain. [*TCGA 1992, 6 Sch 12(2)–(4); FA 1993, s 87, 7 Sch 1, 2, 23 Sch Pt III*].

In *Durrant v CIR SC 3114/93 (SC000024), [1995] STI 694*, it was decided that all shares or securities were excluded from being chargeable business assets within *TCGA 1992, 6 Sch 12(2)*, regardless of whether they were held as investments.

In arriving at the aggregate gains, the normal capital gains tax provisions fixing the amount of chargeable gains apply, and any allowable loss accruing on the qualifying disposal concerned is deducted. The retirement relief provisions do not affect the computation of the amount of any allowable loss. [*TCGA 1992, 6 Sch 12(1)*].

Example

P Ltd carries on a trade of printing and bookbinding. Its directors include C who owns 10% of the issued share capital and of the voting rights. In December 1995, on reaching the age of 63, C gives his shares to his sister. At the date of transfer, the company's assets are valued as follows

	£	£	Market value £	Cost £
Leasehold printing works			190,000	50,000
Goodwill			60,000	—
Stocks of materials			80,000	75,000
Plant				
Printing presses No 1	8,000			3,000
No 2	8,500			3,500
No 3	6,500	23,000		2,000
Typesetter		10,500		15,000

48.8   Retirement Relief

	Market value	Cost
	£	£	£
Binding machine	16,500		12,000
Small tools, type etc.	7,000		10,000
Motor cars	20,000		30,000
Office fixtures and fittings (items under £6,000)	9,000	86,000	15,000
Shares in associated publishing company		60,000	40,000
Cash at bank and in hand		7,500	—
Debtors		11,500	—

The chargeable gain arising on the shares given to C's sister is £75,000.

The value of the company's chargeable assets is as follows

	Business	Non-business
	£	£
Leasehold	190,000	—
Goodwill	60,000	—
Plant (£23,000 + £10,500 + £16,500)	50,000	—
Shares	—	60,000
	£300,000	£60,000

Gain eligible for retirement relief is therefore

$$£75,000 \times \frac{300,000}{300,000 + 60,000} \qquad £62,500$$

Note to the example

(a)   Chargeable assets are all assets other than those on which any gain accruing on a disposal immediately before the end of the qualifying period would not be a chargeable gain.

Trustees' disposals. Where the disposal is a trustees' disposal under 48.7 above, and at least one beneficiary other than the one carrying on the business etc. (the *'qualifying beneficiary'*) also has an interest in possession in the same property at the end of the qualifying period, only the 'relevant proportion' of the gain accruing to the trustees on disposal qualifies for relief, and the remainder is a chargeable gain. The *'relevant proportion'* is the proportion which the qualifying beneficiary's interest in the income from the settled property comprising the shares, securities or asset in question bears to the interests in the income of all the beneficiaries (including the qualifying beneficiary) who then have interests in possession in that part. [*TCGA 1992, 6 Sch 9*].

Associated disposals. Where the disposal is an associated disposal under 48.6 above, only part of the gain qualifies for relief if (i) the asset was not used for business purposes throughout the individual's period of ownership (*Note.* In the determination of the period of ownership there is no exclusion of any period before 31 March 1982, cf. 50.5 ROLLOVER RELIEF); or (ii) during part of the period of use in a business the individual was not concerned in the carrying on of that business (whether personally, in partnership or as a full-time working officer or employee (full-time working director for disposals before 16 March 1993)); or (iii) rent (including consideration in any form) was paid for use of the asset. The part which qualifies for relief is that which appears just and reasonable to the Board, having regard to the lengths of the periods in question and the extent to which any rent paid was less than the open market rent. [*TCGA 1992, 6 Sch 10*]. See Revenue Pamphlet CGT 6 (1992) p 6 for an example of the Revenue's interpretation of this provision.

Capital distributions. Where a material disposal of business assets (see 48.4 above) or a trustees' disposal (see 48.7 above) is a disposal deemed to be made under *TCGA 1992, s 122* in consideration of a capital distribution, the gain on which relief may be given is restricted if the capital distribution consists wholly or partly of chargeable business assets. If the distribution consists wholly of such assets, no relief is available. If the distribution consists partly of chargeable business assets, the aggregated gains are proportionately reduced and the appropriate proportion then applied to the reduced amount. Any question as to whether a capital distribution consists of chargeable business assets is determined by reference to the status of the assets immediately before the end of the qualifying period. [*TCGA 1992, 6 Sch 11*].

48.9   **AMOUNT OF RELIEF**

The basic rule. *For disposals after 5 April 1988*, 'the amount available for relief' (or more simply, the amount of relief) is the aggregate of

(a)   so much of the 'gains qualifying for relief' as does not exceed the 'appropriate percentage' of £250,000 (£150,000 for disposals before 30 November 1993 and £125,000 for disposals before 19 March 1991 and after 5 April 1988), and

(b)   one half of any excess of such gains, subject to a maximum excess equal to the appropriate percentage of £750,000 (£450,000 for disposals before 30 November 1993 and £375,000 for disposals before 19 March 1991 and after 5 April 1988).

'*Gains qualifying for relief*' is the aggregate amount of gains described in 48.8 above, after the application of the provisions mentioned there but before deduction of any retirement relief.

The '*appropriate percentage*' is a percentage determined according to the length of the qualifying period, rising arithmetically from 10% (the minimum) where the period is one year to 100% (the maximum) where it is ten years.

For the purposes of the above a trustees' disposal under 48.7 above is regarded as a qualifying disposal by the beneficiary. However, if, on the same day, an individual makes a material disposal of business assets under 48.4 above and is also the beneficiary in relation to a trustees' disposal, the amount available for relief is applied to the former disposal in priority to the latter.

For disposals before 6 April 1988, the amount of relief was a percentage of £125,000 (£100,000 before 6 April 1987), determined in the same way as the appropriate percentage described above. [*TCGA 1992, 6 Sch 4(3), 13; FA 1988, s 110(1)(2)(8); FA 1991, s 100(1)(3)(4); FA 1994, s 92*].

Example

X, who is aged 56, disposes in 1995 of a business which he has owned for 6 years, and realises gains qualifying for retirement relief amounting to £840,000. His entitlement to relief is calculated as follows.

		£
Appropriate percentage of £250,000: 60% of £250,000		150,000
Excess of gains over £150,000:	£690,000	
Appropriate percentage of £750,000:	£450,000	
Relief is available on £450,000		
Half thereof		225,000
Total relief		£375,000

447

Aggregation of earlier business periods. The amount available for relief may be increased where the qualifying period appropriate to a qualifying disposal (the *'original qualifying period'*) would be less than ten years but the individual or beneficiary was 'concerned in the carrying on of another' business (*'the previous business'*) in some earlier part (the *'earlier business period'*) of the ten-year period up to the end of the original qualifying period. There must be no more than a two-year gap between the end of the earlier business period and the beginning of the original qualifying period. For the purposes of calculating the increase, the previous business is assumed to be the same business as the 'business at retirement', and, in the first instance, any gap between the two businesses is ignored so that the two periods are assumed to be one continuous extended qualifying period. However, this extended qualifying period is not to begin earlier than the beginning of the ten-year period ending at the end of the original qualifying period, and is then to be reduced by the gap between the businesses. Where there is more than one earlier business (and, therefore, more than one earlier business period) the provisions are to be first applied to the latest of the earlier business periods and the original qualifying period, and then to the extended qualifying period so resulting and the next latest of the earlier business periods, and so on.

The reference to a person being *'concerned in the carrying on of another business'* above is a reference to his being so concerned personally or as a member of a partnership or, if the business was owned by a company, then as a 'full-time working officer or employee' ('full-time working director' for disposals before 16 March 1993) of that company or, as the case may be, of any member of the 'group' or 'commercial association of companies' of which it is a member.

The *'business at retirement'* is a reference to the business giving rise to the qualifying disposal being one within 48.4, 48.6 and 48.7 above (i.e. the length of an original qualifying period relating to employee disposals within 48.5 above cannot be the subject of an increase). [*TCGA 1992, 6 Sch 4(3), 14; FA 1993, s 87, 7 Sch 2(1)*].

In strictness, the original qualifying period must be a period of at least one year as in 48.4–48.7 above. However, with effect from 14 April 1994 for all new and still open cases, the Revenue by concession treats as a qualifying disposal a disposal which was not a qualifying disposal by reason only that the original qualifying period was less than one year. Hence any final business period can be aggregated with earlier business periods (presumably subject to the two-year gap limit mentioned above) irrespective of the length of the final business period. The concession does not mean that a final business period of less than one year is treated as a period of one year in calculating the length of the extended qualifying period (Revenue Press Release 14 April 1994).

There is no specific requirement for there to have been a material disposal of business assets, a trustees' disposal or an associated disposal in connection with the previous business. Similarly, in the case of a previous business carried on by a company, there is no stated condition that the company had to have been at any time the 'personal company' ('family company' for disposals before 16 March 1993) of the individual or individual beneficiary by reference to whom there is a qualifying disposal in relation to the business at retirement. (See Tax Journal, 25 November 1993, pp 12–14).

Example

A owns a business for 7 years before disposing of it in 1995 when he is 54 and in good health. After a break of exactly 2 years he buys another business and runs it for 5 years before disposing of it in 2002. The percentage of the maximum relief available on the 2002 disposal is 8/10 = 80% (and not 12/14 = 86%).

Relief on earlier disposals. Where qualifying disposals are made at different times, the relief available on a later disposal is restricted by reference to the relief given on any earlier disposals (including relief under the provisions of *FA 1965, s 34, CGTA 1979, s 124* and, in practice, *FA 1985, ss 69, 70, 20 Sch*).

For later disposals after 5 April 1988, relief is restricted to

(A)   the amount of relief which would otherwise have been available if

    (i)   the gains qualifying for relief on the disposal were increased by the amount of the 'underlying gains' relieved on earlier disposals, and

    (ii)   the qualifying period appropriate to this disposal (redetermined as above for aggregation of earlier business periods) were extended by the addition of periods equal to so much (if any) of previous qualifying periods appropriate to earlier disposals not already falling within the qualifying period appropriate to this disposal; over

(B)   the aggregate amount of relief given on all earlier disposals.

The amount of the 'underlying gains' is determined in one of the following ways, according to what disposal(s) occurred.

(I)   If the earlier disposal or all of the earlier disposals occurred before 6 April 1988, the amount of the underlying gains is the total relief obtained on that disposal or those disposals.

(II)   If there has only been one earlier disposal and it occurred after 5 April 1988, the amount of the underlying gains is the aggregate of the relief obtained by reference to the appropriate percentage of £250,000 (£150,000 for disposals before 30 November 1993 and £125,000 for disposals before 19 March 1991) and twice the relief obtained by reference to any excess.

(III)   In cases not within (I) and (II) above, the amount of the underlying gains is calculated as in (II) above, but on the assumption that

    (i)   the previous disposal was the only earlier disposal, and

    (ii)   the totals calculated for (A)(i) and (A)(ii) above on that disposal were the gains qualifying for relief on that disposal, and the qualifying period appropriate to that disposal, respectively.

For later disposals before 6 April 1988, relief was restricted to

(*aa*)   the amount of relief which would be available on the later disposal if the qualifying period appropriate to the later disposal (redetermined as above for aggregation of earlier business periods) were extended by the addition of periods equal to so much (if any) of previous qualifying periods appropriate to earlier disposals not already falling within the qualifying period appropriate to the later disposal; over

(*bb*)   the aggregate amount of relief given on all earlier disposals.

General. Where earlier disposals took place before 12 April 1978, the reference in (A)(ii) and (*aa*) above to the qualifying period appropriate to the later disposal is to be taken as the period of ten years ending with that disposal. [*TCGA 1992, 6 Sch 4(3), 15; FA 1988, s 110(3)–(6)(8)*].

Example

P, who was born in 1928, carried on businesses, and made gains qualifying for retirement relief on disposals of them, as follows.

Business A	1.7.1985–30.6.1989	£60,000
Business B	1.1.1992–31.12.1992	£100,000
Business C	1.1.1994–31.12.1995	£520,0000

His entitlement to retirement relief is calculated as follows.

48.9 Retirement Relief

Business A

Gains qualifying for relief	£60,000
Qualifying period	4 years
Maximum relief available:	

	£
40% × £125, 000	50,000

Excess of gains: £60,000 − £50,000 = £10,000		
50% of £375,000	£187,500	
Half of £10,000		5,000
Relief given, 1989/90		£55,000

Business B

Gains qualifying for relief on this disposal	£100,000
Underlying gains under (II) above: £50,000 + (2 × £5,000)	60,000
Gains qualifying for relief as increased	£160,000

	Years
Original qualifying period	1
Aggregation of earlier business periods under *TCGA 1992, 6 Sch 14* (more than 2-year gap)	Nil
	1
Extension in respect of earlier disposal under *TCGA 1992, 6 Sch 15*	4
Qualifying period as aggregated and extended	5

	£
Maximum relief available:	
50% × £150,000	75,000

Excess of gains: £160,000 − £75,000 = £85,000		
50% of £450,000	£225,000	
Half of £85,000		42,500
		117, 500
Deduct Relief given on earlier disposal		55,000
Relief given, 1992/93		£62,500

Business C

Gains qualifying for relief on this disposal	£520,000
Underlying gains under (III) above: £75,000 + (2×£42,500)	160,000
Gains qualifying for relief as increased	£680,000

	Years
Original qualifying period	2
Extension in respect of earlier disposals under *TCGA 1992, 6 Sch 15*	5
Qualifying period as extended	7

Maximum relief available:

	£
70% × £250, 000	175,000

Excess of gains: £680,000 − £175,000 = £505,000		
70% of £750,000	£525,000	

Half of £505,000	252,500
	427,500
Deduct Relief given on earlier disposals	117,500
Relief given, 1995/96	£310,000

Aggregation of spouse's interest in the business. Where an individual makes a material disposal of business assets (within 48.4 above) which, in whole or in part, he acquired either under the will or intestacy of his spouse or by way of lifetime gift from her, he may make a written election, within two years after the end of the year of assessment in which the material disposal occurs, for his qualifying period (which must be at least one year as in 48.4–48.7 above) to be extended by what would have been his spouse's qualifying period if the relevant conditions of ownership etc. had applied to the spouse. The individual and spouse must have been living together at the time of the spouse's death or lifetime gift and the whole of the spouse's interest in the business, assets, shares or securities concerned immediately before the acquisition or, as the case may be, the spouse's death, must be acquired.

Example

R acquired her late husband's 30% shareholding in X Ltd on his death in June 1987. She took over the office he had held for many years as a full-time working officer until, at the age of 63, she sold her shares in June 1995 incurring an otherwise chargeable gain of £264,000.

The chargeable gain is calculated as follows	£
Gain eligible for relief	264,000
Maximum available for 100% relief	

$$\frac{8 + 2}{10} \times £250,000 \times 100\% \qquad (250,000)$$

Maximum available for 50% relief

$$\frac{8 + 2}{10} \times £1 \text{ million} = £1 \text{ million} - £250,000 = £750,000$$

£264,000 − £250,000 = £14,000 × 50%	(7,000)
Chargeable gain	£7,000

48.9 Retirement Relief

For disposals after 5 April 1988, where the acquisition was by way of lifetime gift, the amount available for relief is not to exceed the amount that would be available for relief on the assumption that the lifetime transfer had not taken place and the material disposal had been made by the spouse (to whom is attributed anything done by the individual in relation to the business concerned after the lifetime gift). *For disposals before 6 April 1988,* an alternative restriction applied if lower: namely, £125,000 (£100,000 before 6 April 1987) less any relief (including relief under earlier legislation) given on the spouse's own disposals, or on trustees' disposals where the spouse was a beneficiary, up to and including the lifetime transfer. [*TCGA 1992, 6 Sch 16; FA 1988, s 110(7)(8)*].

For an indication of Revenue practice as to the application of the principles established in decided cases up to and including *Furniss v Dawson* to asset transfers between spouses made for retirement relief purposes, see ICAEW Guidance Note TR 588 25 September 1985.

49   Returns

Cross-reference. See 51 SELF-ASSESSMENT for future changes broadly from 1996/97.

49.1   GENERAL, NOTIFICATION OF CHARGEABILITY AND REASONABLE EXCUSE

The Revenue have considerable powers to obtain information and these are generally exercised initially by the requirement to complete and submit various returns, with PENALTIES and 32.6 INTEREST ON UNPAID TAX for non-compliance, omissions or incorrect statements. Explanatory notes are usually issued with returns, but the capital gains tax aspects are summarised below.

A person chargeable to capital gains tax or a company chargeable to corporation tax who has not already made a statutory return for that year of assessment or accounting period, or (for years after 1987/88 or accounting periods ending after 31 March 1989) has not received a notice requiring such a return, must, within twelve months after the end of that year or accounting period, notify the Revenue of the chargeability. This does not apply for years after 1987/88 to a person chargeable to capital gains tax if all his chargeable gains for the year have been assessed. [*TMA 1970, ss 7, 8, 10, 11A, 12(1); FA 1988, ss 120-122*]. See 42.1 PENALTIES regarding failure to meet this requirement.

It is generally provided for the purposes of *TMA 1970* that a person is deemed not to have failed to do anything required to be done where there was a reasonable excuse for the failure and, if the excuse ceased, provided that the failure was remedied without unreasonable delay after the excuse had ceased. Similarly, a person is deemed not to have failed to do anything required to be done within a limited time if he did it within such further time as the Board, or the Commissioners or officer concerned, may have allowed. [*TMA 1970, s 118(2); F(No 2)A 1987, s 94*]. For failures after 26 July 1989, this provision does not apply for 32.6 INTEREST ON UNPAID TAX (and see 49.4 below as regards late returns). [*TMA 1970, s 88(7); FA 1989, s 159(1)(3)(4)*]. Consideration of what constitutes a reasonable excuse was made in *R v Sevenoaks Commrs, ex p. Thorne; Thorne v Sevenoaks Commrs & CIR, Ch D & QB 1989, 62 TC 341* which was concerned with the provision in 32.6 INTEREST ON UNPAID TAX prior to 27 July 1989.

49.2   CAPITAL GAINS TAX RETURNS

Soon after the commencement of each tax year, return forms are normally issued to persons considered liable to capital gains tax and these must be completed within the time stipulated (30 days) although in practice further time is allowed. Returns must contain such information, and be accompanied by such related accounts and statements, as the inspector requires. [*TMA 1970, ss 8, 8A, 12(1); FA 1990, s 90*].

The Revenue have issued guidance on the principles adopted in designing tax returns and determining the information which is required in them (Revenue Pamphlet IR 131, SP 4/91, 1 May 1991).

The Revenue has indicated that returns or claims may, in cases of physical inability to sign, be signed by an attorney acting under a general or enduring power. The attorney must have full knowledge of the taxpayer's affairs and a copy of the original power or a certified copy will need to be provided when the return or claim is first made. The attorney will need to be appointed under an enduring power registered with the Court of Protection (except in Scotland, where there is no such registration, and a signature of an attorney or curator bonis will be accepted) where he acts in the case of a mentally incapacitated person, for whom any receiver or committee appointed by the Court may also sign. These criteria apply similarly to any other declaration required for tax purposes (e.g. an application for a personal equity plan). An attorney cannot sign in any case where the taxpayer is physically capable of signing (even though he may be unavailable abroad) (Revenue Pamphlet IR 131, A13 and Revenue Tax Bulletin February 1993 p 51).

Computations of any chargeable gain must be submitted with a return of income or profits, which is not complete without them. For example, an entry in the capital gains section such as 'to be advised' is insufficient, even though the return may be accompanied by an investment schedule giving particulars of changes in holdings and proceeds of sale (29.A14 INLAND REVENUE STATEMENTS OF PRACTICE).

A taxpayer may use schedules to support a return but must in all cases sign the official declaration. All material in the schedules must be clearly linked to the official return form (Revenue Pamphlet IR 131, SP 5/83, 28 April 1983).

The Revenue have issued a Statement of Practice (SP 5/87, 15 June 1987) concerning the acceptability of facsimile and photocopied tax returns. Whenever such a substitute form is used, it is important to ensure that it bears the correct taxpayer's reference.

A facsimile must satisfactorily present to the taxpayer the information which the Board have determined shall be before him when he signs the declaration that the return is correct and complete to the best of his knowledge. It should be readily recognisable as a return when received in the Revenue office, and the entries of taxpayers' details should be distinguishable from the background text. Copies of the return forms for which a facsimile is to be produced together with an information sheet on the production of substitute forms are available from Inland Revenue, Corporate Communications Office, 6th Floor (KB), North West Wing, Bush House, London WC2B 4PP. Approval must be obtained from Inland Revenue, Corporate Communications Office, Room 9/3A, 9th Floor, North West Wing, Bush House, London WC2B 4PP before a facsimile return is used, and the facsimile must bear an agreed unique imprint for identification purposes.

Photocopies must bear the actual, not photocopied, signature of the relevant person. They are acceptable provided that they are identical (except as regards use of colour) to the official form. Where double-sided copies are not available, it is sufficient that all pages are present and attached in the correct order. Although the copying of official forms is, in strictness, a breach of HMSO copyright, action will be taken only where forms are copied on a large scale for commercial gain.

Particulars must also be given of assets acquired (but only where requested) except

(*a*)   tangible movable assets (not part of a set, currency, or commodities on a terminal market) acquired for £6,000 (£3,000 for acquisitions before 6 April 1989) or less;

(*b*)   pool, betting or lottery winnings;

(*c*)   government non-marketable securities;

(*d*)   passenger vehicles;

(*e*)   decorations for valour;

(*f*)   foreign currency for personal expenditure; and

(*g*)   assets acquired as trading stock.

[*TMA 1970, s 12(2)(5); FA 1982, s 81(1); FA 1989, s 123*]. For the exemptions available for the assets at (*a*) to (*f*) above see 18 EXEMPTIONS AND RELIEFS.

Where the chargeable gains of an individual, or a settlement for the disabled (see 52.5 SETTLEMENTS), for any year, do not exceed the exempt amount for the year (i.e. £6,000 for 1995/96, £5,800 for 1994/95, 1993/94 and 1992/93, £5,500 for 1991/92 and

£5,000 for 1990/91, 1989/90 and 1988/89) and the total consideration for the disposal of chargeable assets does not exceed twice the exempt amount (i.e. £12,000 for 1995/96, £11,600 for 1994/95, 1993/94 and 1992/93, £11,000 for 1991/92 and £10,000 for 1990/91, 1989/90 and 1988/89), a statement by the taxpayer to this effect is a sufficient return unless the inspector otherwise requires. (The gains limit was £6,600 for 1987/88, £6,300 for 1986/87, £5,900 for 1985/86, £5,600 for 1984/85, £5,300 for 1983/84 and £5,000 for 1982/83. The restriction by reference to consideration was £13,200 for 1987/88, £12,600 for 1986/87, £11,800 for 1985/86, £11,200 for 1984/85, £10,600 for 1983/84 and £10,000 for 1982/83.)

In any year of assessment before 1990/91 during which, or during a part of which (being a part beginning on 6 April) the individual is a married man whose wife is living with him such that the man is assessable in respect of his wife's gains (see 37.4 MARRIED PERSONS) the limits given above for individuals apply as if all the chargeable gains and disposals of them both in that year (or part) accrued to him. This does not apply if the individual is a married man whose wife is living with him but who is not assessable in respect of her gains.

Where the 'grouping' anti-avoidance provisions apply to settlements for the disabled, the gains limit is reduced to the greater of ten per cent of the exempt amount for the year and the exempt amount divided by the number of settlements in the group (e.g. for 1995/96 the greater of £600 or £6,000 divided by the number of settlements in the group).

In respect of settlements (other than settlements for the disabled) set up before 7 June 1978, the relevant limits are one-half of the exempt amount (gains) and the exempt amount (consideration) (e.g. for 1995/96, £3,000 and £6,000 respectively). For settlements (other than settlements for the disabled) set up after 6 June 1978, these provisions do not apply at all. [*TCGA 1992, s 3(6)(8), 1 Sch; CGTA 1979, 1 Sch 3; FA 1988, s 104(1)(c), 14 Sch Pt VIII; SI 1992 No 626; FA 1993, s 82; FA 1994, s 90*].

A married woman could be required to make a separate return of her chargeable gains for years before 1990/91. Otherwise, if her husband was assessable in respect of her gains (see 37.4 MARRIED PERSONS), a return could be required from him in respect of her gains and, for 1988/89 and 1989/90 only, her gains had to be included in a notification of chargeability required from him as described in 49.1 above. [*TMA 1970, ss 8(1), 11A(3), 12(1); FA 1988, ss 104(1)(b)(2), 122, 14 Sch Pt VIII*].

49.3 **CORPORATION TAX RETURNS OF PROFITS**

Notices served after 31 December 1993. In relation to notices served after 31 December 1993 (and, in practice, relating to accounting periods ending after 30 September 1993; see Revenue Press Release 7 December 1992 regarding Pay and File) and if so required by the inspector, a company must make a return of such information, relevant to its corporation tax liabilities, as is required under the notice. Supporting accounts, statements and reports may also be required, although the accounts required of companies resident in the UK throughout the period to which the return relates ('*the return period*'), and required to prepare accounts under the *Companies Act 1985* (or NI equivalent) for any period consisting of or including the return period, are only those it is so required to prepare. Details of assets acquired on which chargeable gains or allowable losses may arise may also be required under *TMA 1970, s 12(2)(3)* (see 49.2 above).

The return must include a declaration to the effect that, to the best of the knowledge of the person making it, it is correct and complete. *TMA 1970, s 108(1)*, as amended by *FA 1993, s 120, 14 Sch 7*, requires that person to be '*the proper officer of the company*' (i.e. the secretary of a corporate body, except where a liquidator has been appointed when the latter is the proper officer, or the treasurer of a non-corporate body) or, except where a liquidator has been appointed, any authorised person. The return must be made by the later of

(*a*)   twelve months after the end of the period to which it relates,

(*b*)   twelve months after the end of the period for which the company makes up accounts ('*period of account*') in which falls the last day of the accounting period to which it relates (except that periods of account in excess of 18 months are treated as ending after 18 months for this purpose), and

(*c*)   three months after service of the notice requiring the return.

If the period specified by the notice for the making of a return ('*the specified period*') is not an accounting period of the company, but the company is within the charge to corporation tax for some part of the specified period, the notice is to be taken as referring to all company accounting period(s) ending in or at the end of the specified period. If there is no such accounting period, but there is a part of the specified period which does not fall within an accounting period, the notice is to be treated as requiring a return for that part of the period. Otherwise, the notice is of no effect, and the company is not required to make any return pursuant to it. For the determination of a company's accounting period, see Tolley's Corporation Tax under Accounting Periods.

Amendments to returns must be in such form, and accompanied by such information etc., as the Board may require. [*TMA 1970, s 11; F(No 2)A 1987, s 82; FA 1990, s 91; SI 1992 No 3066*].

Useful background information on the making of returns under Pay and File is contained in a Revenue consultative document published on 28 February 1991 and a Revenue Press Release of 7 December 1992. Reference should also be made to Revenue Pamphlets IR 126 and 128 and Revenue Tax Bulletin August 1993 pp 83–85. Subsequently three substantive Revenue Statements of Practice have been issued as follows (all dated 8 October 1993).

(i)   Revenue Pamphlet IR 131, SP 9/93 explains that, under Pay and File, an amended corporation tax return for an accounting period may be made by completing and delivering to the inspector an amended official corporation tax return form. Alternatively, a form or letter can be substituted which gives clear and sufficient information about the change, shows the tax effect of the change and includes a declaration that the information is correct and complete.

(ii)   Revenue Pamphlet IR 131, SP 10/93 provides an opportunity for companies to use a similar procedure under Pay and File for making or revising claims to group relief, and for giving and receiving notices of consent to surrender relief, where a group of companies is dealt with mainly in one tax district.

(iii)   Revenue Pamphlet IR 131, SP 11/93 explains the criteria the Board adopts in exercising its power to admit claims to capital allowances or group relief which are made outside the normal time limit.

Returns will also incorporate claims for group relief, capital allowances, payments of tax credits and repayments of income tax deducted from payments received. Such claims are covered in detail in Tolley's Corporation Tax under the appropriate subject heading.

Notices served before 1 January 1994. In relation to notices served before 1 January 1994 (and, in practice, accounting periods ending before 1 October 1993; see Revenue Press Release 7 December 1992) and if so required by the inspector, a company must make, for any period during which it was within the charge to corporation tax, a return of its profits computed for corporation tax purposes, including such particulars as disposals of assets giving rise to chargeable gains or allowable losses and details of those chargeable gains or losses. Details of assets acquired on which chargeable gains or allowable losses could arise could also be required under *TMA 1970, s 12(2)(3)* (see 49.2 above). [*TMA 1970, s 11; FA 1990, s 91(4)*].

49.4   LATE RETURNS

Before *TMA 1970, s 88* was amended by *FA 1989* with effect from 27 July 1989 (see 32.6 INTEREST ON UNPAID TAX) the Revenue stated that an interest charge would be considered where, without reasonable excuse or without having been allowed an extension of time, there was a 'substantial delay' in the submission of a return (or where an incomplete return was submitted and there was a substantial delay in providing details required to complete it) if, in consequence, an assessment was made after the normal time in order to make good capital gains tax which turned out to be due. As a separate matter, the Revenue may levy penalties under *TMA 1970, s 93* or *94* (see 42.2 and 42.3 PENALTIES). (Revenue Pamphlet IR 131, SP A14). For failures after 26 July 1989, the defence of reasonable excuse or extension of time does not apply to *TMA 1970, s 88* interest (see 49.1 above and Revenue Pamphlet IR 131, SP 6/89, 31 July 1989). For failures at any time, the Revenue have stated subsequently that in respect of chargeable gains, a delay is regarded as 'substantial' if the relevant tax return has not been made by the later of the end of the 30-day period immediately following the date on which it is issued and 31 October following the end of the tax year in which the gain arises. Where it is not possible to submit a return, no interest charge will be raised if the inspector is provided, within such time limits, with sufficient information to enable an adequate estimated assessment to be made, e.g. at least the sale price relating to the disposal of a chargeable asset (Revenue Pamphlet IR 131, SP 6/89, 31 July 1989 replacing Revenue Statement of Practice SP 3/88, 10 May 1988).

Companies are removed from the scope of *TMA 1970, s 88* for accounting periods ending after 30 September 1993 as a result of the introduction of *TMA 1970, s 87A* as part of 'Pay and File' for such periods (see 32.4 INTEREST ON UNPAID TAX). In relation to earlier periods, whilst the above Statements of Practice refer mainly to persons not chargeable to corporation tax, by analogy a company should provide sufficient information to enable an adequate estimated assessment to be made by the later of the end of the 30-day period immediately following the date of issue of the corporation tax return and the expiry of seven months from the end of the accounting period (Revenue Tax Bulletin August 1992 p 27).

49.5   HOTELS AND BOARDING HOUSES

Certain details of all lodgers and persons resident in any dwelling-house, hostel, hotel, etc. must be given by the proprietor, if required by notice from the inspector. [*TMA 1970, s 14*].

49.6   ISSUING HOUSES, STOCKBROKERS, AUCTIONEERS, NOMINEE SHAREHOLDERS, ETC.

Certain details of assets dealt with from issuing houses, members of stock exchanges (but not jobbers or market makers), commodity clearing houses and auctioneers must be given together with a return of the parties to the transaction, if required by notice from the inspector. [*TMA 1970, s 25; FA 1986, s 63, 18 Sch 8*].

In respect of shares, securities and loan capital registered in the name of a person, that person must, if required by notice from the inspector issued for the purpose of obtaining particulars of chargeable gains, state whether he is the beneficial owner thereof or otherwise provide the name and address of the persons on whose behalf he acts as nominee. [*TMA 1970, s 26*].

49.7 PARTNERSHIPS

Under a notice given to the partners of a trading partnership, such person as is identified under rules given with the notice must complete and deliver a return containing such information, and accompany it with such accounts and statements, as the inspector may require as well as the following information.

(*a*)   The chargeable gains relating to partnership property as if the partnership were itself liable to tax.

(*b*)   The names and addresses of the other partners.

(*c*)   The acquisition (including the name of the disposer and the consideration) of all assets as partnership property with the same exceptions as for individuals (see 49.2 above).

The inspector may, if he thinks fit, require a similar return to be made by any partner, any of the partners or all of the partners. [*TMA 1970, ss 9, 12(2)-(4); FA 1990, s 90*]. See, generally, 40 PARTNERSHIPS.

49.8 EUROPEAN ECONOMIC INTEREST GROUPINGS

For the purposes of making assessments, a European Economic Interest Grouping (see 39.20 OVERSEAS MATTERS) registered in the UK or having an establishment there must make and deliver a return (through its manager or the individual representative of its manager) containing such information and accompanied by such accounts and statements as may be required by a notice given by the inspector. In the case of any other grouping, a return is required from any member of it resident in the UK, or, if none is, from any member. [*TMA 1970, s 12A; FA 1990, 11 Sch 2, 5*].

49.9 FORM AND DELIVERY OF RETURNS

For the forms of return, see *TMA 1970, s 113* and 49.2 above. For delivery and service of documents, see *TMA 1970, s 115*.

50   Rollover Relief—Replacement of Business Assets

Cross-references. See 8.12 ASSETS HELD ON 31 MARCH 1982 for 50% relief on rolled over gains relating to an asset acquired before 31 March 1982; 19.2 FURNISHED HOLIDAY ACCOMMODATION for application of rollover relief to such accommodation in the UK; 22 HOLD-OVER RELIEFS generally; 33.14 and 33.15 LAND for rollover relief on compulsory purchase of land and exchanges of joint interests in land (including milk and potato quotas in certain cases) respectively; 39.3, 39.6, 39.17 and 39.19 OVERSEAS MATTERS for restriction on rollover relief in certain cases; 45.6 and 45.7 REINVESTMENT IN SHARES RELIEF for a possible alternative relief where a disposal is made of an asset qualifying for rollover relief; 53.26 SHARES AND SECURITIES for application of rollover relief in relation to certain disposals to employee share ownership trusts.

50.1   NATURE OF RELIEF

If the consideration which a person carrying on a trade obtains for the disposal of, or of his interest in, assets (*'the old assets'*) used, and used only, for the purposes of the trade throughout the 'period of ownership' (which, for disposals after 5 April 1988, excludes any period before 31 March 1982) is applied by him in acquiring other assets, or an interest in other assets (*'the new assets'*) which on the acquisition are taken into use, and used only, for the purposes of the trade, and the old assets and the new assets are within the classes of assets listed in *TCGA 1992, s 155* (see 50.2 below), then the person carrying on the trade is, on making a claim as respects the consideration which has been so applied, treated for the purposes of *TCGA 1992*

(*a*)   as if the consideration for the disposal of, or of the interest in, the old assets were (if otherwise of a greater amount or value) of such an amount as would secure that on the disposal neither a gain nor a loss accrues to him, and

(*b*)   as if the amount or value of the consideration for the acquisition of, or of the interest in, the new assets were reduced by the excess of the amount or value of the actual consideration for the disposal of, or of the interest in, the old assets over the amount of the consideration which he is treated as receiving under (*a*) above.

The treatment in (*a*) and (*b*) above does not affect the treatment for the purposes of *TCGA 1992* of the other party to the transaction involving the old assets, or of the other party to the transaction involving the new assets. [*TCGA 1992, s 152(1)(9)*].

The relief given under (*a*) and (*b*) above applies in relation to a person who, either successively or at the same time, carries on two or more trades as if both or all of them were a single trade. [*TCGA 1992, s 152(8)*]. For consideration of this provision and activities other than trades, see 50.3 below.

Where (*a*) above applies to exclude a gain which, in consequence of *TCGA 1992, 2 Sch* (ASSETS HELD ON 6 APRIL 1965 (7)), is not all chargeable gain, the amount of the reduction to be made under (*b*) above is the amount of the chargeable gain, and not the whole amount of the gain. [*TCGA 1992, s 152(2)*].

Prior to the commencement of *TCGA 1992*, the claim was made under *CGTA 1979, s 115(1)*.

Where a claim for relief is made after 28 November 1994 it must be made in writing, specifying:

(1)   the identity of the claimant;

(2)   the assets which have been disposed of;

(3)   the date of disposal of each of those assets;

(4)   the consideration received for the disposal of each of those assets;

(5)   the assets which have been acquired;

(6)   the date of acquisition of each of those assets or the dates on which unconditional contracts for the acquisition of each of those assets were entered into;

(7)   the consideration given for each of those assets; and

(8)   the amount of the consideration received for the disposal of each of the specified assets which has been applied in the acquisition of each replacement asset.

(Inland Revenue Press Release, 29 November 1994).

The old assets must actually be used for the trade in question, any original intention for such use being ignored. Relief was refused where land was purchased on which it was proposed to build a factory for use in the taxpayer's trade but was sold without the factory being built (*Temperley v Visibell Ltd Ch D 1973, 49 TC 129*). Subject to concessionary treatment as in 50.2 below, the new assets must be taken into trading use immediately on acquisition, and not as soon as reasonably practicable after acquisition, again any original intention to attempt at immediate use being ignored (*Campbell Connelly & Co. Ltd v Barnett CA 1993, [1994] STC 50*). In this case the taxpayer company (C Ltd) claimed relief in respect of a gain accruing from the sale in 1984 of its trading premises, the sale taking place shortly after C Ltd had become a wholly-owned subsidiary of M Ltd. C Ltd and M Ltd henceforth traded from premises already occupied by M Ltd. In January 1986 C Ltd acquired the freehold interest in a new property but it was not until September 1986 that C Ltd and M Ltd were able to occupy and use it for trading purposes because the property was subject to both a headlease and an underlease to two third parties. Occupation and use was only possible after M Ltd had acquired in September 1986 the underlease for a capital sum. During the period from January 1986 to September 1986 C Ltd received rent from the lessee whilst from September 1986 to November 1987, when the headlease was itself surrendered, M Ltd paid a slightly higher rent to the lessee. Although it had been the intention to acquire the freehold interest in, and vacant possession of, the new property at the same time, relief was refused in relation to C Ltd's claim to roll over the gain into the freehold interest acquisition. It was held that the words 'which on the acquisition are taken into use, and used only for the purposes of the trade' referred to the acquisition of the assets (and *not* to an interest in them) mentioned in the phrase which occurs earlier in *TCGA 1992, s 152(1)* 'If the consideration . . . is applied by him in acquiring other assets'. In addition *TCGA 1992, s 152* only covered one acquisition by one person; it could not be extended to cover two different interests in the same asset being acquired by two different legal persons at different times. *Obiter dicta* of Knox J in the *Ch D* suggests that the time of acquisition and disposal for the purposes of *TCGA 1992, s 152* is the date of transfer or conveyance, and not the date of the contract (cf. *TCGA 1992, s 28* at 16.2 DISPOSAL).

For convenience, references in the rest of this chapter to the acquisition or disposal of an asset can be taken to include references to the acquisition or disposal of an interest in that asset except where the context requires otherwise.

Part disposals seem to be included (see Tolley's Practical Tax 1981 p 99).

The Revenue has indicated that in its view the wording of *TCGA 1992, s 152(1)*, which states that 'if the consideration which a person . . . obtains for the disposal of . . . assets . . . is applied by him in acquiring other assets', simply requires the taxpayer to reinvest an amount equal to the proceeds received. It also sees no reason why in principle relief should not be available where the acquisition consideration is satisfied by the issue of shares by a company (Institute of Taxation TIR/11/91, 1991 STI 1097).

In *Tippett v Watton SC 3091/94 (SC000019), [1995] STI 576*, it was decided that the correct time to consider whether there were separate and identifiable 'new assets' and 'old assets' was immediately after the disposal. Only then was there any consideration to which the relief could be applied and in respect of which a claim could be made. Accordingly, a claim by a taxpayer to rollover the gain on a subsequent part disposal of a single, undivided business property against the acquisition cost of the remainder of that property unsold and acquired within the period of twelve months before the part disposal was allowed. The proceeds of sale of the part sold were 'applied by him in acquiring' the balance of the property ('other assets').

The Revenue have confirmed the relief is available where assets are exchanged (CCAB Statement TR 508 9 June 1983). Where land or other assets used for the purposes of a trade carried on in partnership are partitioned by the partners, the asset acquired is treated as a newly acquired asset provided the partnership is dissolved immediately thereafter (Revenue Pamphlet IR 1, D23).

Partial relief may be available in certain circumstances. See 50.5 below.

The acquisition of the new assets must take place within one year before, or three years after, the disposal of the old assets, though the Revenue may allow further time where the trader can show that there was a firm intention to acquire new assets within the time limit but was prevented from doing so by circumstances outside his control (Inland Revenue Tax Bulletin November 1991 p 5). The Revenue seems prepared to extend this treatment even though an asset qualifying for rollover relief is acquired within the statutory time limit but which the taxpayer chooses not to make the subject of a claim (Institute of Taxation TIR/11/91, 1991 STI 1097). It is sufficient if an unconditional contract for acquisition is entered into within the specified periods; but adjustments are made, without time limit, if the contract is not completed. [*TCGA 1992, s 152(3)(4)*]. See also the *obiter dicta* of Knox J in *Campbell Connelly & Co. Ltd v Barnett* above.

The Revenue has stated that inspectors have a duty to assess gains at the normal time even though the taxpayer has indicated that a rollover claim will be forthcoming once a qualifying asset is acquired. This protects the Revenue's position as regards interest on unpaid tax should no rollover claim be possible and ensures the gains are not overlooked entirely. On the making of the assessment, the taxpayer may apply for postponement of tax on production of satisfactory evidence of his intention to acquire a qualifying asset within the time limit. An inspector's refusal to agree to postponement is subject to appeal in the normal way (Institute of Taxation TIR/11/91, 1991 STI 1097).

Relief is denied if the acquisition of the new assets was made wholly or partly for the purpose of realising a gain from their subsequent disposal. [*TCGA 1992, s 152(5)*].

Example

L Ltd carries on a vehicle repair business. In December 1995 it sells a workshop for £90,000 net of costs. The workshop had cost £45,000 inclusive in April 1989. A new workshop is purchased for £144,000 (including incidental costs of acquisition) in January 1996 and sold for £168,000 in January 1998.

Indexation factors (assumed) April 1989 to December 1995   0.381
January 1996 to January 1998   0.100

50.1 Rollover Relief—Replacement of Business Assets

L Ltd claims rollover of the chargeable gain.

	£
Allowable cost of original workshop	45,000
Indexation allowance £45,000 × 0.381	17,145
	62,145
Actual disposal consideration	90,000
Chargeable gain rolled over	£27,855

Cost of new workshop	144,000
Deduct amount rolled over	27,855
Deemed allowable cost	£116,145

Disposal consideration, replacement workshop	168,000
Allowable cost	116,145
Unindexed gain	51,855
Indexation allowance £116,145 × 0.100	11,615
Chargeable gain	£40,240

In relation to a case where

(i) the person disposing of the old assets and acquiring the new assets is an individual, and

(ii) the trade or trades in question are carried on not by that individual but by a company, which, both at the time of disposal and at the time of the acquisition referred to in (i) above, is his 'personal company' ('family company' for disposals before 16 March 1993), within the meaning of *TCGA 1992, 6 Sch* (see 48.3 RETIREMENT RELIEF),

any reference in *TCGA 1992, ss 152–156* (see 50.2, 50.3, 50.5 and 50.6 below) to the person carrying on the trade includes a reference to that individual. [*TCGA 1992, s 157; FA 1993, s 87, 7 Sch 1, 23 Sch Pt III*].

In correspondence the Revenue have expressed the view that *TCGA 1992, s 157* does not extend to the acquisition of a new asset for use by a subsidiary of a personal company (family company for disposals before 16 March 1993) carrying on a trade or trades where the old asset was disposed of by the personal company (family company for disposals before 16 March 1993) (and vice versa). Assets must be disposed of and acquired by the individual for use by the same personal company (family company for disposals before 16 March 1993) (although relief in relation to use by such a company may not be precluded if contemporaneous use is made by one or more subsidiaries of the company) and the provisions of *TCGA 1992, s 175(1)* (see 50.4 below) do not extend to the position of regarding all companies within a group as one taxable entity. The payment of rent to the individual by the company concerned for the use of property will not debar relief under *TCGA 1992, s 157*. In addition, the occupancy test of *TCGA 1992, s 155* for land and buildings (see 50.2 below) may be met by either the individual or the company concerned, so the existence of a lease or tenancy (whether or not with consideration passing), or consideration passing, will not prevent relief under *TCGA 1992, s 157*. The position here should be contrasted with a claim under *TCGA 1992, s 158(1)(c)* by an employee to which Revenue Pamphlet IR 131, SP 5/86 applies (see 50.3 below). It is not possible to 'mix' claims under *TCGA 1992, ss 157 and 158(1)(c)* (e.g. the disposal of land owned by an individual but occupied and used exclusively for the purposes of a trade carried on by his personal company (family company for disposals before 16 March 1993) cannot be rolled over into his acquisition of land which is to be occupied and used by him exclusively as an employee of the same company). See also Institute of Taxation TIR/11/91, 1991 STI 1097, for confirmation of these points.

It should be noted that *TCGA 1992, s 157* does not require the individual to be a 'full-time working officer or employee' ('full-time working director' for disposals before 16 March 1993) (see 48.3 RETIREMENT RELIEF and 50.3 below).

Relief is available to the owner of assets let to a trading or professional partnership of which he is a member, provided they are used for the purposes of the partnership's trade or profession (29.D11 INLAND REVENUE STATEMENTS OF PRACTICE). See also 40.5 PARTNERSHIPS as regards disposals by partners and 40.12 as regards mergers of partnerships and 50.4 below for partnerships involving a member of a group of companies.

Any provision which fixes the amount of consideration deemed to be given for the acquisition or disposal of assets is applied before operating the relief. [*TCGA 1992, s 152(10)*]. The Revenue has been asked its views on whether relief can be claimed where a gain arises on a simple gift and where an asset is appropriated from 'capital' to 'trading stock' within *TCGA 1992, s 161(1)*. It replied that in its view gifts of assets were within *TCGA 1992, s 152(10)*. Where the other conditions for relief were met, relief will be available based on the amount of the consideration deemed to have been received under other provisions of *TCGA 1992*. It does not, however, regard relief as available where there is a deemed disposal and reacquisition of the same asset (Institute of Taxation TIR/11/91, 1991 STI 1097).

Where the disposal of an asset to a company qualifies for relief both under *TCGA 1992, s 152* and *s 162* (transfer of a business to a company; see 22.7 HOLD-OVER RELIEFS), the Revenue has stated that it will in practice ignore the mandatory nature of the latter relief and allow the former provided qualifying assets are acquired subsequently and within the usual time limits (Institute of Taxation TIR/11/91, 1991 STI 1097).

For the application of the relief to groups of companies, see 50.4 below.

For an indication of Revenue practice as to the application of the principles established in decided cases up to and including *Furniss v Dawson* to asset transfers between spouses made for rollover purposes, see ICAEW Guidance Note TR 588, 25 September 1985.

50.2   QUALIFYING ASSETS

Subject to the overriding requirement of use for the purposes of a trade as specified in *TCGA 1992, s 152(1)* in 50.1 above, qualifying assets, for the purpose of relief under that provision, are currently divided into six classes (although, after 26 July 1993, the Treasury is given power to add one or more additional classes). Both the old and the new assets must fall within these classes though not necessarily within the same class. The classes are as follows.

1.   (*a*)   Land, buildings (including parts thereof) and any permanent or semi-permanent structures in the nature of buildings, all such assets being occupied (as well as used) only for the purposes of the trade. A person who is a lessor of tied premises is treated as if he occupied (as well as used) those tied premises only for the purposes of the relevant trade (the foregoing being construed in accordance with *ICTA 1988, s 98(2)*). See also 50.3 below where the trade involves dealing in or developing land, etc.

    (*b*)   Fixed plant or machinery (see *Williams v Evans Ch D, 1982, 59 TC 509*, and Tolley's Practical Tax 1983 p 211) which does not form part of a building or of a permanent or semi-permanent structure in the nature of a building.

2. Ships, aircraft and hovercraft.

3. Satellites, space stations and spacecraft (including launch vehicles). This class qualifies where the disposal of the old assets or the acquisition of the new assets occurs after 27 July 1987; but it is accepted that the legislation gives relief where an asset in this class is disposed of or acquired before 28 July 1987 if the corresponding new asset acquired or old one disposed of after 27 July 1987 (but within the time limits of 50.1 above) falls within a class already qualifying at the date of the earlier transaction (Revenue Press Release 11 July 1988).

4. Goodwill.

5. (*a*) 'Milk quotas'; i.e. rights to sell dairy produce without liability to pay milk levy, or to deliver dairy produce without liability to pay a milk levy contribution.

   (*b*) 'Potato quotas'; i.e. rights to produce potatoes without liability to pay more than the ordinary contribution to the Potato Marketing Board's fund.

   This class qualifies where the disposal of the old assets or the acquisition of the new assets occurs after 29 October 1987 but the Revenue's comments made above concerning class 3 apply similarly by reference to 29 October 1987 rather than 27 July 1987.

6. 'Ewe and suckler cow premium quotas', i.e. rights in respect of any ewes or suckler cows to receive payments by way of any subsidy entitlement to which is determined by reference to limits contained in a European Community instrument. This class qualifies where the disposal of the old assets or the acquisition of the new assets occurs after 31 December 1992. Although the Revenue's comments made above concerning class 3 would otherwise apply similarly by reference to 31 December 1992 rather than 27 July 1987, it is understood that assets within this class only came into existence after 31 December 1992.

[*TCGA 1992, ss 155, 156(1)(4); FA 1993, s 86*].

Except as affects the determination of any Commissioners or the judgment of any court made or given before 14 May 1987, a licence under *Petroleum (Production) Act 1934* or *Petroleum (Production) Act (Northern Ireland) 1964* is not and is assumed never to have been an asset falling within any of the classes above. [*TCGA 1992, s 193*].

Where a building is rebuilt after having been destroyed by fire, gains on other assets may be rolled over into the cost of rebuilding (subject to any claim made under *TCGA 1992, s 23* in respect of insurance proceeds, see 16.8 and 16.9 DISPOSAL and CCAB Statement TR 508 9 June 1983). Capital expenditure to enhance the value of other assets already held is treated as incurred in *acquiring* other assets provided the other assets are used only for the purposes of the trade or, on completion of the enhancement work, the assets are immediately taken into use and used only for the purposes of the trade (Revenue Pamphlet IR 1, D22). Similar treatment is given where a *further* interest is acquired in another asset which is already in use for the purposes of the trade (Revenue Pamphlet IR 1, D25). An asset which is repurchased for purely commercial reasons after having been sold as part of a business will be treated as the 'new asset' for the purposes of the relief (Revenue Pamphlet IR 1, D16).

Where a new asset is not, on acquisition, immediately taken into use for the purposes of a trade it will nevertheless qualify for relief provided

(*a*) the owner proposes to incur capital expenditure for the purpose of enhancing its value;

(b)   any work arising from such capital expenditure begins as soon as possible after acquisition, and is completed within a reasonable time;

(c)   on completion of the work the asset is taken into use for the purpose of the trade and for no other purpose; and

(d)   the asset is not let or used for any non-trading purpose in the period between acquisition and the time it is taken into use for the purposes of the trade.

Where a person acquires land with a building on it, or with the intention to construct a building on it, the land is treated as qualifying for (a)–(d) above provided that the building itself qualifies for relief whether under (a)–(d) above or otherwise and provided that the land is not let or used for any non-trading purpose between its acquisition and the time that both it and the building are taken into use for the purposes of the trade (Revenue Pamphlet IR 1, D24). The Inland Revenue have stated that, in some circumstances, relief would not be denied where the asset is not ready to be taken into use immediately solely on the grounds that it was not brought into use as soon as acquired, provided that all reasonable steps are taken to make it ready and that it is then brought into use without unnecessary delay (Revenue Tax Bulletin November 1991 p 5). It is not clear to what extent, if any, this last statement extends the scope of IR 1, D24. It is difficult too, to reconcile both treatments with the Revenue's arguments in the case of *Campbell Connelly & Co. Ltd v Barnett CA 1993, [1994] STC 50* mentioned at 50.1 above.

Buildings and structures (but not normally including dwelling-houses) provided by a trader for the welfare of employees, though qualifying for industrial building allowances under *CAA 1990, s 18(1)(4)(5)* are technically outside the scope of rollover relief, not being used exclusively for the purposes of the trade. Similar observations can be made in respect of agricultural buildings (which may include dwellings) and agricultural building allowances under *CAA 1990, ss 122(1), 123*. It is understood that the Revenue may not always, in practice, take this point. (In *Anderton v Lamb Ch D 1980, 55 TC 1*, it was held that houses occupied by farm employees were not *occupied for the purposes of the business,* and, therefore, were not qualifying assets. The taxpayer appealed to the CA where the appeal was stayed on agreed terms: see *1982 STI 179.*)

Acquisitions of fixed plant and machinery under hire purchase agreements will qualify for relief as regards the capital element but lease purchase agreements are not considered by the Revenue to be equivalent to the rights which accrue under the former so that acquisitions under the latter will not be eligible for relief (Tolley's Practical Tax 1986 p 136).

Provided relief would be due on the disposal of the underlying land which is the subject of the grant of an option, the Revenue are prepared to ignore the separate disposal treatment of *TCGA 1992, s 144(1)* so that any gain arising on the grant of the option can be the subject of a rollover relief claim. The Revenue point out that relief will only be obtained if the land continues to be occupied and used for the claimant's trade (Revenue Tax Bulletin, February 1992, p 13). Presumably this treatment applies regardless of whether an option is exercised (such an event bringing into play the single transaction treatment of *TCGA 1992, s 144(2)*). The Revenue make no comment whether the cost of the option and the exercise price under it could frank a rollover relief claim where the grantee of an option subsequently exercises it (such an event bringing into play the single transaction treatment of *TCGA 1992, s 144(3)*) and brings the underlying land into trading use and occupation immediately on exercise. Relief would seem to be available on the exercise price but may not be for the option cost. For options generally, see 16.10 DISPOSAL.

50.3   **QUALIFYING UNDERTAKINGS**

TCGA 1992, ss 152–157 (see 50.1 and 50.2 above and 50.5 and 50.6 below) apply with necessary modifications in relation to the following activities as they apply in relation to a trade.

(*a*)   The discharge of the functions of a public authority.

(*b*)   The occupation of woodlands where the woodlands are managed by the occupier on a commercial basis and with a view to the realisation of profits.

(*c*)   A profession, vocation, office or employment.

(*d*)   Such of the activities of a body of persons whose activities are carried on otherwise than for profit and are wholly or mainly directed to the protection or promotion of the interests of its members in the carrying on of their trade or profession as are so directed.

(*e*)   The activities of an unincorporated association or other body chargeable to corporation tax, being a body not established for profit whose activities are wholly or mainly carried on otherwise than for profit, but in the case of assets within 1.(*a*) in 50.2 above only if they are both occupied and used by the body, and in the case of other assets only if they are used by the body.

'Trade', 'profession', 'vocation', 'office' and 'employment' have the same meanings as in the *Income Tax Acts* for the purposes of the above and *TCGA 1992, ss 152–157*, but not so as to apply the provisions of the *Income Tax Acts* as to the circumstances in which, on a change in the persons carrying on a trade, a trade is to be regarded as discontinued, or as set up and commenced. These provisions and *TCGA 1992, ss 152–157* are construed as one. [*TCGA 1992, s 158*]. '*Trade*' includes every trade, manufacture, adventure or concern in the nature of trade, but the other expressions are not directly defined. [*ICTA 1988, s 832(1)*].

For disposals after 5 April 1982 commercial letting of 'furnished holiday accommodation' in the UK is treated as a trade for the purposes of the relief. See 19 FURNISHED HOLIDAY ACCOMMODATION.

The Revenue have indicated that both parties to a share farming agreement may be considered to be carrying on a farming business for taxation purposes provided that the landowner takes an active part in the venture, e.g. by concerning himself with details of farming policy, etc. (1992 STI 189 reproducing statement of 19 December 1991 issued by Country Landowners Association).

If land or a building is owned by an employee or office-holder but is made available to the employer for general use in his trade, the employee etc. may nonetheless satisfy the occupation test of *TCGA 1992, s 155* (see 50.2 above at 1.) provided the employer does not make any payment (or give other consideration) for his use of the property nor otherwise occupy it under a lease or tenancy. The qualifying use of assets by an employee etc. for the purposes of *TCGA 1992, s 152* (see 50.1 above) will include any use or operation of those assets by him, in the course of performing the duties of his employment or office, as directed by the employer (Revenue Statement of Practice SP 5/86, 21 August 1986). The practice may be applied to all open cases as at 21 August 1986 and may be compared with the relief available under *TCGA 1992, s 157* (see 50.1 above) where the trade is carried on by the individual's 'personal company' ('family company' for disposals before 16 March 1993) although in relation to SP 5/86 consideration passing or the existence of a lease or tenancy would deny relief but would not under *TCGA 1992, s 157*. Provided such factors are absent it is understood that so long as a director is a 'full-time working director' or, presumably for disposals after 15 March 1993, an officer or employee is a 'full-time working officer or employee' (see 48.3

RETIREMENT RELIEF), then he can also qualify as an employee for the purposes of SP 5/86. Where relief under *TCGA 1992, s 157* is unavailable (e.g. where the individual as a partner disposes of an asset which has been used by the partnership and acquires an asset which is to be used by his personal or, as the case may be, family company or, possibly, where different such companies are involved) then, provided the factors mentioned previously are absent, relief may still be claimed (Tolley's Practical Tax 1986 p 183 and subsequent correspondence with the Revenue).

Lessors of tied premises are treated as occupying and using them solely for the purposes of a relevant trade. [*TCGA 1992, s 156(4)*]. Where the trade is one of dealing in or developing land or of providing services for the occupier of land in which the trader has an interest, the trader's disposal of the land does not qualify for relief. However, this does not apply where a profit on the sale of any land held for the purposes of a trade of dealing in or developing land would not form part of the trading profits. [*TCGA 1992, s 156(1)–(3)*]. However, it appears that the Revenue may allow relief on the disposal of a caravan site where the disposer's occupation of that site amounts to the carrying on of a trade, notwithstanding that that trade is one of providing services for the occupier(s). See also 19 FURNISHED HOLIDAY ACCOMMODATION for such accommodation in the UK.

The application of the relief in relation to a person who, either successively or at the same time, carries on two or more trades as if both or all of them were a single trade (see *TCGA 1992, s 152(8)* in 50.1 above) is not further qualified so that one or all the trades could be situated outside the UK and outside the scope of UK taxation because the taxpayer is neither resident nor ordinarily resident in the UK (see also Tolley's Practical Tax 1981 p 126 but note the restrictions in 39.3, 39.6, 39.17 and 39.19 OVERSEAS MATTERS in certain cases and note that 'furnished holiday accommodation' must be in the UK).

Where a trader ceases carrying on one trade and, within three years, commences carrying on another, they continue to be treated as a single trade. If the disposal or acquisition takes place in the intervening period, relief will be restricted in respect of the period during which the assets disposed of were not used for trade purposes, and will be conditional on the replacement assets not being used or leased for any purpose prior to commencement of the new trade, and on their being taken into use for the purposes of the new trade on its commencement (Revenue Statement of Practice SP 8/81, 18 September 1981). The Revenue generally has no difficulty in regarding a second or subsequent new trade as the successor trade for the purposes of *TCGA 1992, s 152(8)*. This means relief will be available where a gain arises from the old trade and new assets are acquired in the second or subsequent new trade, provided that the other conditions for the relief are met and the gap between the cessation of the old trade and the commencement of the new trade in question is within the limits of SP 8/81 (Institute of Taxation TIR/11/91, 1991 STI 1097).

50.4　**GROUPS OF COMPANIES**

For the purposes of *TCGA 1992, ss 152–158* (see 50.1–50.3 above and 50.5 and 50.6 below) all the trades carried on by members of a group of companies are, for the purposes of corporation tax on chargeable gains treated as a single trade (unless, for cases where the acquisition of the new assets was before 29 November 1994, it was a case of one member of the group acquiring the new assets from another or disposing of the old assets to another). [*TCGA 1992, s 175(1); FA 1995, 29 Sch Pt VIII(4)*].

TCGA 1992, s 154(2) (see 50.6 below) applies where the company making the claim is a member of a group of companies as if all members of the group for the time being were the same person (and, in accordance with *TCGA 1992, s 175(1)* above, as if all trades carried on by members were the same trade) and so that the gain accrues to the member of the group holding the asset concerned on the occurrence of the event mentioned in *TCGA 1992, s 154(2)* (i.e. the earlier of the disposal of the depreciating asset, cessation of its trading use or the expiry of ten years from its acquisition). [*TCGA 1992, s 175(3)*].

Acquisitions as a group member by a 'dual resident investing company' within *ICTA 1988, s 404* after 31 March 1987 are excluded from the treatment given by *TCGA 1992, s 175(1)* above. Where either the disposal of the old assets or the acquisition of the new assets (or both such events) occurred after 13 March 1989, then, if either such event occurred before 30 November 1993 (the latter date being the date of the coming into force of *FA 1994, s 249*; companies otherwise regarded as UK resident but under double tax relief arrangements already regarded as non-UK resident to be treated as non-UK resident for *Taxes Acts* purposes after 29 November 1993; see 47.5 RESIDENCE AND DOMICILE), a similar exclusion applied to a company which, though resident in the UK, was regarded as resident elsewhere by virtue of double tax relief arrangements in circumstances such that it would not under those arrangements have been taxable in the UK on any gain arising on a disposal of the new assets immediately after their acquisition. However, the exclusion in the second case did not apply where the acquisition of the new assets was before 20 March 1990 and the disposal of the old assets took place within twelve months beginning with the date of acquisition or such longer period as was allowed in writing by the Board. [*TCGA 1992, s 175(2)(4); FA 1994, s 251(1)(8), 26 Sch Pt VIII*].

'*Group*' is as defined in 13.10 COMPANIES. [*TCGA 1992, s 170(1)*]. Hence, subject to the above regarding events before 20 March 1990 in relation to certain dual resident companies etc., group members must be UK resident.

In *Campbell Connelly & Co. Ltd v Barnett CA 1993, [1994] STC 50* (see 50.1 above), an argument that *TCGA 1992, s 175(1)* should be construed such that not only should the trades carried on by members of a group of companies be treated as a single trade and thereby the same trade but that members of a group of companies should be treated as a single person and thereby the same person was rejected. It was pointed out that the wording of *TCGA 1992, s 175(3)* was an instructive contrast to that in *s 175(1)*. The words in parentheses at the end of *s 175(1)* 'unless it is a case . . . the old assets to another' were described *obiter* by Knox J in the Ch D as 'an anti-avoidance provision to prevent the shuffling of assets within a group of companies to postpone liability to . . . tax when a member of a group disposes of an asset outside the group'. Subject to this, one interpretation of *s 175(1)* would allow relief to a group member disposing of an asset outside the group at a gain if that member acquired an asset from another group member provided all other conditions for relief are fulfilled. By virtue of *TCGA 1992, s 171(1)* the acquisition cost to the group member would be limited to the cost to the group plus improvement costs, expenses of transfer (but less any reduction in respect of previous rollover relief claims) and any indexation allowance. This interpretation would not allow a claim for relief where one group member disposes of an asset outside the group and another group member acquires an asset from a third group member. In addition to this, the 'normal' use of *s 175(1)* has been accepted as being to frank the disposal of old assets by one group member outside the group by the acquisition of new assets by another group member from outside the group. However, the Inland Revenue indicated that, if necessary, steps would be taken to ensure that the established practice (see below) in relation to rollover relief and groups of companies would continue whatever the outcome of the *Campbell Connelly* case. This practice allowed 'one trading company in a group to obtain rollover relief even though the replacement asset was acquired by another trading member of the same group'. (Revenue Press Release, 15 September 1992).

Provisions were introduced by *FA 1995* to put into effect the long-standing Revenue practice (see below) in order that rollover relief would apply in the following circumstances:

(*a*)   where there is a disposal by a member of a group of companies and an acquisition by another member of the same group and both companies claim rollover relief after 28 November 1994 as if they were the same person (giving effect to the Revenue's concessionary practice in Revenue Pamphlet IR 131, SP 8/81, 18 September 1981, see below); or

(*c*)   where a non-trading member of a group makes a disposal or acquisition of assets after 28 November 1994 used only for trading purposes by other members of the same group (giving effect to Revenue Pamphlet IR 1, D30 which applied up to that date, see below).

With regard to (*a*) above, this is deemed always to have had effect.

However, rollover relief will not apply where there is an acquisition of new assets after 28 November 1994 by a member of a group from another member of that group resulting from a no gain/no loss disposal (see 8.7 ASSETS HELD AT 31 MARCH 1982 above). [*TCGA 1992, s 175(2A)–(2C); FA 1995, s 48(1)(3)–(5)*].

The remaining part of this section on groups should be read in the light of the *FA 1995* provisions, which replace the previous concessionary treatments in SP 8/81 and ESC D30 below.

The disposing company must be a member of a group at the time of disposal, and the acquiring company must be a member of the same group at the time of acquisition, but the Revenue does not insist that either company be a member of that group at the time of the transaction carried out by the other (Revenue Pamphlet IR 131, SP D19). Where this applies in a case before 29 November 1994 where one member of a group makes the disposal and a second the acquisition, it may happen that the disposal takes place after the first company has ceased to trade, or the acquisition takes place before the second company commences trading. Relief will then be restricted in respect of the period during which the assets disposed of were not used for business purposes, and will be conditional on the replacement assets not being used or leased for any purpose prior to the second company's commencing trading, and being taken into use for the purposes of the trade on its commencement (Revenue Pamphlet IR 131, SP 8/81, 18 September 1981 and see also 50.3 above). If an asset is sold by a member of a sub-group and a replacement asset is acquired by another member of that sub-group, but in the interval before replacement the sub-group leaves the main group and becomes part of a second main group, the Revenue take the view that rollover relief is not available (CCAB Statement TR 508, 9 June 1983).

Relief is extended to companies which hold assets used for trade purposes by trading companies in the same group. This treatment applies even if the company also holds assets used by non-group members although relief is only available in respect of those assets used by group members (Revenue Pamphlet IR 1, D30 (obsolete from 29 November 1994)).

The Revenue have confirmed that where an asset is transferred to another group company prior to disposal outside the group, entitlement to relief depends on its use during the final period of ownership (CCAB Statement TR 425, 3 April 1981).

If a qualifying unincorporated association uses property owned by a company, the shares in which at least 90% are held by or on behalf of the association or its members, rollover relief can be claimed subject to the usual conditions. (Revenue Pamphlet IR 1, D15, revised by Revenue Press Release of 18 October 1994).

See 33.14(*g*) LAND above with regard to rollover relief in cases of compulsory purchase of land.

50.5 Rollover Relief—Replacement of Business Assets

PARTIAL RELIEF

A modification of the relief under *TCGA 1992, s 152(1)* (see 50.1 above) is available where not all of the amount or value of the consideration received for the disposal of the old assets is applied in acquiring the new assets. Provided that the part of the disposal consideration *not* applied in acquiring the new assets is less than the amount of the gain (whether all chargeable gain or not; this presumably only applies when *TCGA 1992, 2 Sch* is in point for ASSETS HELD ON 6 APRIL 1965 (7)) otherwise accruing on the disposal of the old assets, the person carrying on the trade, on making a claim as respects the consideration applied in acquiring the new assets, is treated for the purposes of *TCGA 1992*

(a)   as if the gain accruing on the disposal of the old assets were reduced *to* the amount of the said part, and

(b)   as if the amount or value of the consideration for the acquisition of the new assets were reduced *by* the amount by which the gain is reduced in (a) above.

If not all the gain accruing on the disposal of the old assets is a chargeable gain, (a) above applies but with a proportionate reduction in the amount of the chargeable gain, and in (b) above the reduction in consideration is the amount by which the chargeable gain is proportionately reduced. Neither (a) nor (b) above affects the treatment for the purposes of *TCGA 1992* of the other party to the transaction involving the old assets, or of the other party to the transaction involving the new assets. *TCGA 1992, s 152(3)–(11)* (see 50.1 above and also see further below) are applied to the above provisions as if they formed part of *TCGA 1992, s 152*. [*TCGA 1992, s 153*].

If, over the 'period of ownership' (which, for disposals after 5 April 1988, excludes any period before 31 March 1982) or any substantial part of the period of ownership, part of a building or structure is, and part is not, used for the purposes of a trade, *TCGA 1992, s 152* applies as if the part so used, with any land occupied for purposes ancillary to the occupation and use of that part of the building or structure, were a separate asset, and subject to any necessary apportionments of consideration for an acquisition or disposal of the building or structure and other land. [*TCGA 1992, s 152(6)(9)*].

See Revenue Tax Bulletin, October 1994, p 166 for further discussion on partial relief.

If the old assets were not used for the purposes of the trade throughout the 'period of ownership' (which, for disposals after 5 April 1988, excludes any period before 31 March 1982) *TCGA 1992, s 152* applies as if a part of the asset representing its use for the purposes of the trade having regard to the time and extent to which it was, and was not, used for those purposes, were a separate asset which had been wholly used for the purposes of the trade, and this treatment applies in relation to that part subject to any necessary apportionment of consideration for an acquisition or disposal of the asset. [*TCGA 1992, s 152(7)(9)*].

Without prejudice to *TCGA 1992, s 52(4)* (just and reasonable apportionments of consideration and expenditure; see 16.6 DISPOSAL), where consideration is given for the acquisition or disposal of assets some or part of which are assets in relation to which a claim under *TCGA 1992, s 152* applies, and some or part of which are not, the consideration is apportioned in such manner as is just and reasonable. [*TCGA 1992, s 152(11)*].

For disposals before 6 April 1988, periods of ownership before 6 April 1965 were taken into account (whether time apportionment or 6 April 1965 value applied) following *Richart v J Lyons & Co Ltd CA 1989, 62 TC 261.*

Where the taxpayer acquires an undivided share in the new asset which is only partly used for trade purposes, relief is limited to the proportion so used of the individual's undivided share of the asset (*Tod v Mudd Ch D 1986, 60 TC 237*). Vinelott J noted in his judgment that a concession might be in existence as regards *TCGA 1992, s 156(6)(7)(9)(11)* above (although he was not required to consider the point further as it was not argued before him) because those provisions do not seem strictly to prevent relief being denied under *TCGA 1992, s 152(1)* in 50.1 above because the new asset is only partly used for trade purposes. For consideration of the difficulties that arise in such a case, see Taxation 18 November 1993, p 141.

Examples

(a) In 1989, X purchased a factory for £40,000. It was used and occupied entirely for carrying on his trade until sold for £100,000 in October 1996. In the same month X bought another factory for £120,000 which was immediately used and occupied for carrying on a new trade carried on by him. Assume indexation allowance of £14,000 is available as regards the sale. He claimed rollover relief, computed as follows.

	£
Proceeds of sale of factory 1	100,000
Allowable expenditure on factory 1	40,000
Unindexed gain on sale of factory 1	60,000
Indexation allowance	14,000
Chargeable gain eligible to be rolled over	£46,000
Cost of factory 2	120,000
Rolled-over gain	46,000
Base cost for factory 2 on subsequent disposal	£74,000

(b) Facts as in (a) above, except factory 2 is bought for £90,000. The part of the £100,000 disposal consideration of factory 1 which is not applied in acquiring factory 2 (acquired for £90,000) is £10,000. This is less than the gain otherwise arising on the disposal of factory 1 (£46,000). The gain deemed to arise on the disposal of factory 1 is therefore £10,000. The gain so arising has therefore been reduced by £36,000, with the result that this amount is deducted from the £90,000 consideration given for factory 2, and so producing a base cost of £54,000 on a subsequent disposal.

(c) In September 1995, Y purchased a new factory for £100,000, having sold his old one in the same month for £50,000. The original factory had been bought in September 1985 for £20,000 but had only been used for his trade since September 1987. He claimed rollover relief. It is accepted that one-quarter of the new factory is not used for trade purposes. It is assumed that the RPI rises by 60% between September 1985 and September 1995.

	£
Proceeds of sale of old factory	50,000
Cost of old factory	20,000
Unindexed gain	30,000
Indexation allowance: 60% × £20,000	12,000
Chargeable gain	£18,000

50.6 Rollover Relief—Replacement of Business Assets

$$\frac{\text{Period of trading use of old asset}}{\text{Period of ownership}} = \frac{8 \text{ years}}{10 \text{ years}}$$

Gain on old asset eligible for relief

$$\text{\pounds}18,000 \times \frac{8}{10} \qquad\qquad \text{\pounds}14,400$$

Cost of qualifying part of new factory	
($\frac{3}{4} \times \text{\pounds}100,000$)	75,000
Rolled-over gain	14,400
Base cost of qualifying part of new factory	£60,600

The unrelieved gain of £3,600 (£18,000 − £14,400) is brought into charge on the disposal of the old factory. The base cost of the non-qualifying part of the new factory, treated as separate, is £25,000.

50.6 **WASTING ASSETS**

For the purpose of relief under *TCGA 1992, ss 152, 153* (see 50.1 and 50.5 above), if the new asset is at the time of acquisition a WASTING ASSET (59) or will become so within ten years beginning at that time, it is known as a '*depreciating asset*'. In such cases, the gain on the disposal of the old asset is not deducted from the acquisition consideration of the new asset, but held over until ten years after the time of acquisition of the new asset, or until the new asset is disposed of, or until the new asset ceases to be used for the trade, whichever is the sooner, upon which event the held-over gain becomes chargeable to capital gains tax; but the held-over gain is not brought into charge under this provision in consequence of an event after 5 April 1988 if its application would be directly attributable to the disposal of an asset before 1 April 1982. [*TCGA 1992, s 154(1)(2)(7), 4 Sch 4(5)*].

However, if not later than the time when the held-over gain would be brought into charge a further asset is acquired which is not a depreciating asset, the trader may claim relief under *TCGA 1992, s 152 or 153* as if it had been acquired within the time limits of *TCGA 1992, s 152(3)* for the application of the proceeds of the disposal of the old asset, the depreciating asset being effectively disregarded. The trader may claim relief if only part of the proceeds can be treated in this way, the balance remaining held over until crystallisation by virtue of one of the events specified. [*TCGA 1992, s 154(4)–(6)*].

By concession, where a held-over gain would otherwise be brought into charge on a cessation of trading use due to the trader's death, no charge to tax will arise. This concession is stated to apply from 16 December 1993 for both new and open cases so could presumably apply where the case is not final even though death occurred before that date (Revenue Pamphlet IR 1, D45).

A gain which has been held over under *TCGA 1992, s 154* will crystallise on a disposal even where the disposal concerned is within *TCGA 1992, s 162* (hold-over on a transfer of a business to a company; see 22.7 HOLD-OVER RELIEFS) (Tolley's Practical Tax 1985 p 139).

A building constructed on leasehold land where the lease has less than 60 years to run at the time of construction is considered by the Revenue to be a depreciating asset. This is despite the treatment in *TCGA 1992, s 155* (see 50.2 above) which treats land and buildings as separate assets (and contrary to the general rule for land as in 33.2 LAND).

If, as contemplated by *TCGA 1992, s 155*, an item of fixed plant or machinery has effectively become a part of a building or structure, it will be so treated for rollover relief purposes, with the result that such assets acquired for installation in a building etc. then held freehold or on a lease with more than 60 years to run will not be treated as depreciating assets. Subject to this, because an item of plant and machinery is always to be treated as being a wasting asset (see 59.1 WASTING ASSETS), it will also be treated as a depreciating asset. Deciding whether an item of fixed plant or machinery has become part of a building etc. will normally be done by reference to the size and nature of the item in question, how it is attached to the building and whether damage to the fabric of the building would be caused if the item was removed (Revenue Tax Bulletin May 1993 p 73).

51   Self-Assessment

51.1   INTRODUCTION

Self-assessment will have effect generally for 1996/97 and subsequent years of assessment, although certain aspects of the system come into effect in earlier or later years of assessment. The term 'self-assessment' refers to the system whereby the annual tax returns filed by individuals and trustees should include a self-assessment of the taxpayer's liability for income tax and capital gains tax. Payment of tax will then be due automatically, based on the self-assessment. The main body of legislation introducing self-assessment is contained in *Finance Act 1994*, with further provisions in *Finance Act 1995*.

Although this work is concerned with capital gains tax, it is felt helpful to describe in this chapter the overall changes that will be brought about by self-assessment not only in relation to that tax but also in relation to income tax. For coverage of the latter in more depth, see Tolley's Income Tax under Self-Assessment and the further chapters of that part referred to in 51.2 below in regard to changes made to facilitate self-assessment. Similarly, the *Finance Act 1994* contains provisions extending, generally for accounting periods ending on or after an appointed day (which cannot be earlier than 1 April 1986), the principles of self-assessment to the existing Pay and File system for corporation tax payment and returns. These are covered briefly in this chapter and in more depth in the appropriate chapters of Tolley's Corporation Tax.

Provisions in *Finance Act 1995*, which are briefly covered in this chapter, include further rules on returns, surcharges and interest, liability of trustees, and other amendments to existing legislation to facilitate the introduction of self-assessment.

Returns. The first returns to be affected will be those covering the tax year 1996/97, normally sent out by the Revenue in April 1997. Such returns must normally be filed by 31 January following the year of assessment (see 51.5 below). Taxpayers who would prefer not to compute their own liabilities will not have to do so providing they file their return early, normally by 30 September following the year of assessment (see 51.6 below). Penalties will be imposed for late submission of returns, subject to appeal on the grounds of reasonable excuse (see 51.25 below). There are provisions for making amendments to self-assessments (see 51.7 below). The Revenue are given broadly one year from the filing date to give notice of their intention to enquire into the return (see 51.11 below). A formal procedure is laid down for such enquiries (see 51.11 to 51.13 below). If they do not give such notice, the return becomes final and conclusive, subject to any 'error or mistake' claim by the taxpayer (see 51.34 below) or 'discovery' assessment by the Revenue (see 51.15 below). In the event of non-submission of a return, the Revenue will be able to make a determination of the tax liability; there will be no right of appeal but the determination may be superseded upon submission of the return (see 51.14 below).

A new style of return will have to be filed by partnerships. This must include a statement of the allocation of partnership income between the partners. See 51.8 and 51.9 below.

Payment of tax. Income tax (on all sources of taxable income) for a year of assessment will be payable by means of two interim payments of equal amounts, based normally on the liability for the previous year of assessment and due on 31 January in the year of assessment and the following 31 July, and a final balancing payment due on the following 31 January (on which date any capital gains tax liability will also be due for payment). Taxpayers will have the right to reduce their interim payments if they believe their income tax liability will be less than that for the previous year of assessment or to dispense with interim payments if they believe they will have no liability. Interim payments will not in any case be required where substantially all of a taxpayer's income is subject to deduction of tax at source, including PAYE, or where the amounts otherwise due are below de minimis limits to be prescribed by regulations. See 51.17 to 51.19 below.

Interest on overdue payments will run from the due date to the date of payment (see 51.21 below). There will also be a 5% surcharge on any tax unpaid by 28 February following the year of assessment and a further 5% surcharge on any tax unpaid by the following 31 July, such surcharges being subject to appeal on the grounds of reasonable excuse (see 51.20 below). Interest on tax overpaid will run from the due date (or date of payment if later) to the date of repayment (see 51.22 below); the rate of interest is likely to be lower than that on overdue tax.

Miscellaneous. Numerous consequential amendments are made to the taxes management provisions and existing time limits. There is a new statutory requirement for taxpayers to keep records for the purpose of making returns and to preserve such records for specified periods (see 51.10 below).

The above changes are covered in this chapter, except for certain prospective changes to existing time limits which are dealt with at 35.6 and 35.12 LOSSES.

51.2   **Changes to facilitate self-assessment.** Fundamental changes are made by *Finance Act 1994* to the system of computing tax liabilities under Schedule D. The principal change involves a move from a preceding year basis of assessment to a current year basis, but they also involve amendments to the provisions on, for example, trading loss reliefs, capital allowances and to the means by which members of partnerships are charged to tax. The new provisions are summarised below and covered in detail in the appropriate chapters in Part 1 above.

As regards businesses commenced, and other sources of income first arising, after 5 April 1994, the new provisions have effect for 1994/95 and subsequent years of assessment. As regards businesses commenced, and other sources of income first arising, before 6 April 1994, they generally come into effect for 1996/97 and subsequent years of assessment. For such businesses, etc., there are transitional provisions to facilitate the changeover from the old system to the new. Some of the provisions affecting partnerships do not have effect until 1997/98 and subsequent years of assessment.

Detailed Revenue booklets 'The new current year basis of assessment – A guide for Inland Revenue officers and tax practitioners' and 'Self-Assessment – the legal framework' should have been sent by tax offices to all tax practices with which they deal during 1994. Further copies are available (price £3.00 each) from Inland Revenue Library, Mid-Basement, Somerset House, Strand, London WC2R 1LB. Also, a series of explanatory articles have appeared in the Revenue Tax Bulletin from August 1993 onwards, illustrating various aspects of the new regime.

Current year basis. Subject to special rules for opening years of assessment and the closing year of assessment, individuals carrying on a trade, profession or vocation will be taxed for a year of assessment on the profits made in the period of account ending in that year of assessment. There are statutory rules for determining the basis period in the event of a change of accounting date; these can produce a basis period of more than 12 months but not one of less than 12 months.

The broad intention is that over the lifetime of a business the profits taxed should equate to the profits earned (as adjusted for tax purposes). Profits will, in fact, sometimes be taxed twice (as a result of the rules for opening years of assessment or certain changes of accounting date). However, the amount taxed twice can be deducted (known as overlap relief) in computing profits for the year of assessment in which the trade ceases or for a year of assessment the basis period for which is longer than 12 months, i.e. as a result of a change of accounting date.

Income chargeable under Schedule D, Cases III to VI will be taxed for a year of assessment on the basis of the income arising in that year of assessment. See Tolley's Income Tax under Schedule D, Case III, Schedule D, Cases IV and V and Schedule D, Case VI.

Transitional provisions. For businesses commenced before 6 April 1994, 1996/97 will be a transitional year of assessment. The basis period will run from the end of the basis period for 1995/96 (on a preceding year basis) to the end of the basis period for 1996/97 (applying the current year basis). Assuming no change of accounting date, this will be a two-year period and the taxable profit will be one half of the profits for that period, the other half escaping tax. Where this transitional period is more or less than two years, the profits will be apportioned so that twelve months' profits are taxed and the balance escapes tax. A trading loss for the transitional period will qualify for relief in full, with no apportionment.

For businesses commenced before 6 April 1994, the current year basis and the transitional rules above will not apply if the business ceases before 6 April 1997. Special rules, based on the rules for closing years under the preceding year basis, may be applied as regards 1995/96 and 1996/97 where such a business ceases in 1997/98 and as regards 1996/97 only for a cessation in 1998/99.

See Tolley's Income Tax under Schedule D, Cases I and II for further details unless otherwise stated above.

Similar rules will apply to other sources of Schedule D income on the changeover to a current year basis. See Tolley's Income Tax under Schedule D, Case III and Schedule D, Cases IV and V.

Anti-avoidance provisions are included in the *Finance Act 1995* to counter attempts to exploit the transitional provisions for businesses, e.g. by shifting profits into the transitional basis period or manufacturing artificial losses. See Tolley's Income Tax under Self-Assessment.

Losses. Under the current year basis, trading losses will always be computed for a year of assessment by reference to the same period as would form the basis period for the charging of profits arising from that trade for that year of assessment (as was usually the case in practice under the preceding year basis of assessment) rather than by reference to the actual losses arising in the year of assessment. Loss relief under *ICTA 1988, s 380* (against other income) will be available against income of the year of assessment in which the loss is incurred and/or the previous year of assessment (see 35.6 LOSSES for an application of this). This will also apply, for 1994/95 onwards, to income tax relief for losses on unquoted shares (see 35.12 LOSSES). Other consequential changes are made to loss relief provisions.

See Tolley's Income Tax under Losses for further details unless otherwise stated above.

Capital allowances. Capital allowances are to be treated as trading expenses (and balancing charges as trading receipts) in the same way as has long since applied for corporation tax purposes. The chargeable period for capital allowances purposes will be the period of account rather than the year of assessment. For businesses commenced before 6 April 1994, these changes apply for 1997/98 and later years of assessment. Other consequential changes are made to capital allowances provisions.

See Tolley's Income Tax under Capital Allowances for further details.

Partnerships. A partnership will no longer be taxed as a separate entity. Instead, each individual partner's share of profits, after all partnership expenses and capital allowances, will fall to be included in his or her self-assessment. Profits will be allocated between partners by reference to the sharing ratios for the period of account (rather than those for the year of assessment). A change in the members of a partnership will no longer be regarded as a cessation for tax purposes (provided there is at least one continuing partner), and continuation elections under *ICTA 1988, s 113(2)* will thus be defunct. The commencement and cessation provisions will instead apply to partners individually. For partnership businesses commenced before 6 April 1994, these changes apply for 1997/98 and later years of assessment. A deemed cessation and recommencement after 5 April 1994 will bring the new rules into effect immediately as regards the new partnership.

See Tolley's Income Tax under Partnerships for further details.

Double taxation relief. Special rules are introduced to ensure that all relief available for foreign tax on business profits is given over the lifetime of a business.

See Tolley's Income Tax under Double Tax Relief for further details.

51.3   INTERPRETATION OF REFERENCES TO ASSESSMENTS, ETC.

Following the introduction of self-assessment, references to a person being assessed to tax, or being charged to tax by an assessment, are to be construed as including a reference to his being so assessed, or being so charged, by a self-assessment under *TMA 1970, s 9* or *11AA* (see 51.6 below) or by a determination under *TMA 1970, s 28C* (see 51.14 below) which has not been superseded by a self-assessment. [*FA 1994, ss 197, 199*].

51.4   NOTICE OF CHARGEABILITY

For 1995/96 and subsequent years of assessment, a person chargeable to income tax or capital gains tax for a year of assessment who has not received a notice under *TMA 1970, s 8* (see 49.1 RETURNS for 1995/96 and 51.5 below for later years of assessment) to deliver a return for that year of his total income and chargeable gains must, within six months after the end of that year, notify an officer of the Board that he is so chargeable. This also applies with the appropriate modification to trustees of settlements. The maximum penalty for non-compliance is the amount of tax in which the person is assessed for that year which is not paid on or before 31 January following that year. A person is not required to give notice under these provisions if his total income for the year consists of income from the sources below and he has no chargeable gains. The said sources are those in respect of which

(*a*)   all payments, etc. are dealt with under PAYE, or

(*b*)   all income has been or will be taken into account either in determining the chargeable person's liability to tax or under PAYE, or

(*c*)   the income is chargeable under Schedule F or is other income from which income tax has been, or is treated as having been, deducted, provided that the chargeable person is not liable for that year other than at the basic or lower rate, or

(*d*)   all income for that year is income for which the chargeable person could not become liable to tax under a self-assessment under *TMA 1970, s 9* (see 51.6 below) in respect of that year.

[*TMA 1970, s 7; FA 1994, ss 196, 199(2), 19 Sch 1; FA 1995, ss 103(7), 115(1)*].

TMA 1970, s 11A, which is the existing provision governing notification of chargeability to capital gains tax (see 49.1 RETURNS) is repealed with effect for 1995/96 and subsequent years of assessment. [*TMA 1970, s 11A; FA 1994, s 199(2), 26 Sch Pt V; FA 1995, s 115(3)(13)*].

TMA 1970, s 10 which is the existing provision governing notification of chargeability to corporation tax under Pay and File (see 49.1 RETURNS) remains unchanged on the inception of self-assessment. The maximum penalty is the amount by which so much of the corporation tax chargeable on the profits of the accounting period as remains unpaid twelve months after the end of the period exceeds any income tax deducted at source on certain annual payments, interest, etc. received by the company.

51.5   **ANNUAL RETURNS OF INCOME AND CHARGEABLE GAINS AND RETURNS OF PROFITS BY COMPANIES**

For the purposes of establishing the amounts in which a person is chargeable to income tax and capital gains tax for 1996/97 and subsequent years of assessment, an officer of the Board may by notice require that person to deliver a return on or before 31 January following the year of assessment or, if later, within three months beginning with the date of the notice. The return must contain such information and be accompanied by such accounts, statements and documents as may reasonably be required. This will include not only information relating to disposals on which chargeable gains or allowable losses arise but also may include under *TCGA 1992, s 12(2)* (see 49.2 RETURNS) details of acquisitions of assets. The return must include a declaration that, to the best of the knowledge of the person making it, it is complete and correct. The information, accounts and statements required by the notice may differ in relation to different periods, or different sources of income, or different descriptions of person. [*TMA 1970, ss 8, 12; FA 1994, ss 178(1), 199(2), 26 Sch Pt V; FA 1995, ss 103(7), 104(1)–(3)*]. Similar provisions apply in relation to returns by trustees. [*TMA 1970, ss 8A, 12; FA 1994, ss 178(2), 199(2), 26 Sch Pt V; FA 1995, ss 90(3)(4)(7), 91(1)*].

For 1996/97 and subsequent years of assessment or accounting periods ending on or after an appointed day (which cannot be earlier than 1 April 1996), minor consequential amendments are made to *TMA 1970, s 12A* (return by European Economic Interest Grouping; see 49.8 RETURNS). [*TMA 1970, s 12A; FA 1994, ss 196, 199(2)(3), 19 Sch 2*].

Subject to the changes in 51.9 below regarding a 'relevant statement' where a company carries on a trade in partnership, the present requirements under Pay and File for a company to make a return of profits under *TMA 1970, s 11* (see 49.3 RETURNS) remain virtually unaltered for any accounting period ending on or after an appointed day (which cannot be earlier than 1 April 1996). [*TMA 1970, ss 11(1)(1A), 12; FA 1994, ss 181(1)(2), 199(2)(3), 26 Sch Pt V*].

In the case of a person carrying on a profession, trade or business in partnership, a return under *TMA 1970, s 8* must include each amount, which according to any 'relevant statement' is his share of any income, loss, tax, credit or charge for the period covered by the statement. A *'relevant statement'* is a statement falling to be made, as respects the partnership, under *TMA 1970, s 12AB* (see 51.9 below) for a period which includes, or includes any part of, the year of assessment or its basis period. [*TMA 1970, s 8(1B)(1C); FA 1994, ss 178(1), 199(2); FA 1995, ss 103(7), 104(2)*].

See 51.25 below as regards penalties for non-compliance.

51.6   **SELF-ASSESSMENTS**

For 1996/97 and subsequent years of assessment, every return under *TMA 1970, s 8* or *8A* (see 51.5 above) must include, subject to the exception below, an assessment (a self-assessment) of the liability, based on the information in the return, of the person making the return to income tax and capital gains tax for the year of assessment. In the event of non-compliance, an officer of the Board *may* make the assessment on his behalf, based on the information in the return, and send the person a copy.

A person need not comply with this requirement if he makes and delivers his return on or before 30 September following the year of assessment or, if later, within two months beginning with the date of the notice to deliver the return. For returns submitted outside these time limits, the Revenue will still, if the taxpayer so requests, carry out the computations based on the return, but will not guarantee that the relevant filing date will be met.

In the event of a person making no self-assessment under this option, an officer of the Board *must* make the assessment on his behalf, based on the information in the return, and send the person a copy. If, by reason only of Revenue delay, the assessment is made less than 30 days before the due date for payment of the tax, the date from which any interest or surcharge is triggered (see 51.20, 51.21 below) is 30 days after the issue of the assessment. (ICAEW Technical Release Tax 9/94, 7 June 1994).

Assessments made as above by an officer of the Board are treated as self-assessments by the person making the return. [*TMA 1970, s 9(1)–(3); FA 1994, ss 179, 199(2); FA 1995, ss 103(7), 104(4), 115(2)*].

Similar provisions are applied for accounting periods ending on or after an appointed day (which cannot be earlier than 1 April 1996) to a company's corporation tax return made under *TMA 1970, s 11* (see 49.3 RETURNS) except that the company cannot opt not to complete the self-assessment. [*TMA 1970, s 11AA(1); FA 1994, ss 182, 199(2)(3); FA 1995, ss 103(7), 104(5)*].

51.7   **Amendments of self-assessments other than where enquiries made.** At any time within nine months beginning with the delivery of a person's return, an officer of the Board may by notice to that person amend his self-assessment to correct obvious errors (whether of principle, arithmetical or otherwise).

At any time within twelve months beginning with the filing date (i.e. the date by which the return must be delivered, as in 51.5 above), that person may by notice to an officer of the Board amend his self-assessment to give effect to any amendments to his return which he has notified to such an officer.

However, no such amendment of a self-assessment may be made (by the taxpayer or the Revenue) after an officer of the Board has given notice of intention to enquire into the return (see 51.11 below) and before his enquiries are completed. [*TMA 1970, s 9(4)–(6); FA 1994, ss 179, 199(2)*].

Similar provisions are applied for accounting periods ending on or after an appointed day (which cannot be earlier than 1 April 1996) to a company's corporation tax return made under *TMA 1970, s 11* (see 49.3 RETURNS). [*TMA 1970, s 11AA(2)(3); FA 1994, ss 182, 199(2)(3)*].

See 51.13 below for amendments to self-assessments where the Revenue make enquiries into the return.

51.8   **PARTNERSHIP RETURNS**

The following provisions apply for 1996/97 and subsequent years of assessment or accounting periods ending on or after an appointed day (which cannot be earlier than 1 April 1996).

51.9 Self-Assessment

Any partner may be required by notice to complete and deliver a return of the partnership profits together with accounts, statements, etc. (see also 51.9 below). The return must include the names, residences and tax references of all persons (including companies) who were partners during the period specified in the notice and such other information as may reasonably be required by the notice, which may include information relating to disposals and acquisitions of partnership property under *TCGA 1992, s 12(2)* (see 49.2 RETURNS). The general requirements are similar to those for personal returns under *TMA 1970, s 8* (see 51.5 above). The notice will specify the period (the relevant period) to be covered by the return (which is expected to be normally a period of account of the partnership) and the date by which the return should be delivered (the filing date). For a partnership including at least one individual, the filing date will be no earlier than 31 January following the year of assessment concerned (normally that in which the relevant period ends). For a partnership including at least one company, the filing date will be no earlier than the first anniversary of the end of the relevant period. In both cases, the filing date will be deferred until, at the earliest, the last day of the three-month period beginning with the date of the notice, if this is a later date than that given above. [*TMA 1970, s 12AA; FA 1994, ss 184, 199(2)(3); FA 1995, ss 103(7), 104(6), 115(4)*].

See 51.26 below as regards penalties for non-compliance.

51.9 PARTNERSHIP STATEMENTS

Subject to the same commencement provisions, every partnership return under 51.8 above must include a statement (a partnership statement) showing, in respect of each period of account ending within the period covered by the return, the partnership income or loss from each source plus the amount of each charge on partnership income and each partner's share of that income, loss or charge on income. Provisions similar to those in 51.7 above apply as regards amendments to partnership statements. Where a partnership statement is so amended, the partners' self-assessments will be amended by the Revenue accordingly, by notice to each partner concerned. [*TMA 1970, s 12AB; FA 1994, ss 185, 199(2); FA 1995, ss 103(7), 104(7)(8)*].

Subject to the same commencement provisions, where a company carries on a trade, etc. in partnership the company's corporation tax return made under *TMA 1970, s 11* (see 49.3 RETURNS) for any period must include amounts in respect of the company's share of any income, loss or charge stated in any relevant statement falling to be made by the partnership for a period which includes, or includes any part of, the period in respect of which the return is required. [*TMA 1970, s 11(2A)(2B); FA 1994, ss 181, 199(2)(3)*].

51.10 RECORDS

Subject to the same commencement provisions, any person who may be required (in practice, this would seem to exclude no one) make and deliver a return under 51.5 above (personal, trustee or company return) or 51.8 (partnership returns) for a year of assessment or other period will be statutorily required to keep all necessary records and to preserve them until, normally,

(a)   in the case of a person carrying on a trade (including, for these purposes, any letting of property), profession or business alone or in partnership or a company, the fifth anniversary of 31 January following the year of assessment or (as the case may be) the sixth anniversary of the end of the period covered by the return; and

(b)   in any other case, the first anniversary of 31 January following the year of assessment.

Where, however, a person's return is enquired into by the Revenue, he must preserve the records until, if later, the day the enquiries are treated as completed (see 51.13 below).

In the case of a person within (*a*) above, the records in question include records concerning business receipts and expenditure and, in the case of a trade involving dealing in goods, all sales and purchases of goods. All supporting documents (including accounts, books, deeds, contracts, vouchers and receipts) relating to such items must also be preserved. Copies of documents may be preserved instead of the originals and are admissible in evidence in proceedings before the Commissioners.

The maximum penalty for non-compliance in relation to any year of assessment or accounting period is £3,000. This does not apply to records only required for claims, elections or notices not included in the return. [*TMA 1970, s 12B; FA 1994, ss 196, 199(2)(3), 19 Sch 3; FA 1995, s 103(7), 105*].

51.11 **ENQUIRIES INTO RETURNS**

Power to enquire. An officer of the Board may enquire into a return (or amendment of a return) on the basis of which a person's self-assessment under *TMA 1970, s 9* (personal and trustee's return; see 51.6 above) has been made (or amended by that person). The officer must give notice in writing of his intention to so enquire, such notice to be given,

(*a*)   in the case of a return delivered or amendment made on or before the filing date (i.e. the date on or before which the return must be delivered; see 51.5 above), within twelve months beginning with that date; and

(*b*)   otherwise on or before the quarter day (meaning 31 January, 30 April, etc.) next following the first anniversary of the day of delivery or amendment.

A return or amendment cannot be enquired into more than once. [*TMA 1970, s 9A; FA 1994, ss 180, 199(2)*].

Similar provisions apply as regards a partnership return on the basis of which a partnership statement (see 51.9 above) was made. The notice of intention to enquire may be given to a 'successor' (as defined) of the person who made the return or amendment. The giving of such notice is deemed to include the giving of notice under *TMA 1970, s 9A* (see above) (or, where applicable, the equivalent corporation tax provision of *TMA 1970, s 11AB*) to each partner affected. [*TMA 1970, ss 12AC, 118(1)(3); FA 1994, ss 186, 196, 199(2)(3), 19 Sch 34, 26 Sch Pt V*].

Similar provisions are applied for accounting periods ending on or after an appointed day (which cannot be earlier than 1 April 1996) to a company's corporation tax return made under *TMA 1970, s 11* (see 49.3 RETURNS) in relation to which a self-assessment was made under *TMA 1970, s 11AA* (see 51.6 above). [*TMA 1970, s 11AB; FA 1994, ss 183, 199(2)(3)*].

51.12 **Power to call for documents.** At the same time as giving notice under 51.11 above to any person, or subsequently, an officer of the Board may by notice in writing require that person, within a specified period of at least 30 days, to produce to the officer such documents (as are in the person's possession or power) and such accounts or particulars as the officer may reasonably require to check the validity of the return or amendment. Copies of documents may be produced but the officer has power to call for originals, and may himself take copies of, or make extracts from, any document produced. A person is not obliged under these provisions to produce documents, etc. relating to the conduct of any pending appeal by him. There is provision for a person to appeal, within 30 days of the giving of the notice, against any requirement imposed by a notice as above. *[TMA 1970, s 19A; FA 1994, ss 187, 199(2)(3)]*.

See 51.28 below as regards penalties for non-compliance.

51.13 **Amendment of self-assessment or partnership statement where enquiries made.** Where notice has been given by an officer of the Board under 51.11 above of an intention to enquire into the taxpayer's return (or amendment), the officer's enquiries are treated as completed at such time as he, by notice, informs the taxpayer that he has completed his enquiries and states his conclusions as to the amount of tax which should be contained in the taxpayer's self-assessment. The taxpayer may before that time apply to the appeal Commissioners concerned for a direction that the officer shall give such notice within a period specified in the direction, such application to be heard and determined in the same way as an appeal and the Commissioners to give such a direction unless they are satisfied that the officer has reasonable grounds for not giving such notice.

The taxpayer is given 30 days beginning with the date of completion of the officer's enquiries to amend his self-assessment in accordance with the officer's conclusions. Where the enquiry was into a return rather than an amendment, and the return was made before the expiry of twelve months beginning with the due date for delivery (see 51.5 above), the taxpayer also has this 30-day period to amend his self-assessment in accordance with any amendments to the return which he has notified to the officer. The officer then has a further 30 days in which to amend the self-assessment himself.

If, in the officer's opinion, there is otherwise likely to be a loss of tax to the Crown, the officer may by notice amend the self-assessment before his enquiries are completed.

Where the enquiry is into an amendment by the taxpayer to the return, rather than into the return itself, any amendment by the officer of the self-assessment, whether before or after completion of the enquiry, must be restricted to any deficiency or excess of tax as is attributable to the taxpayer's amendment. *[TMA 1970, s 28A; FA 1994, ss 188, 199(2)(3)]*.

Similar provisions apply in the case of an enquiry into a partnership return (or amendment), taking references above to the self-assessment as references to the partnership statement (see 51.9 above) based on the return. However, there is no provision for the officer to amend the partnership statement before completion of his enquiries. Where a partnership statement is amended under these provisions, the officer will, by notice, make any necessary consequential amendments to the self-assessments of the partners (including company partners). *[TMA 1970, s 28B; FA 1994, ss 189, 199(2)(3)]*.

See 51.30 below for the right of appeal against an amendment by the Revenue to a self-assessment or partnership statement.

51.14 **DETERMINATION OF TAX WHERE NO RETURN DELIVERED**

Where a notice has been given under *TMA 1970, s 8* or *8A* (notice requiring an individual or trustee to deliver a return; see 51.5 above) for 1996/97 and subsequent years of assessment, or under *TMA 1970, s 11* (see 49.3 RETURNS) for accounting periods ending on or after an appointed day (which cannot be earlier than 1 April 1996), and the return is not delivered by the due date (the filing date), an officer of the Board may make a determination of the amounts of income tax and capital gains tax or (as the case may be) corporation tax which, to the best of his information and belief, he estimates to be due for the year of assessment or (as the case may be) accounting period concerned. The officer must serve notice of the determination on the person concerned. Tax is payable as if the determination were a self-assessment, with no right of appeal. No determination may be made after the expiry of five years beginning with the filing date.

A determination is automatically superseded by any self-assessment made (whether by the taxpayer or the Revenue), based on information contained in a return, within twelve months beginning with the date of the determination. Any recovery proceedings commenced before the making of such a self-assessment may be continued in respect of so much of the tax charged by the self-assessment as is due and payable and has not been paid. [*TMA 1970, s 28C; FA 1994, ss 190, 199(2)(3)*].

51.15 DISCOVERY ASSESSMENTS

If, as regards 1996/97 and subsequent years of assessment or accounting periods ending on or after an appointed day (which cannot be earlier than 1 April 1996), an officer of the Board or the Board 'discover', as regards any person (the taxpayer) and a chargeable period (i.e. for income tax and capital gains tax purposes, a year of assessment or for corporation tax, an accounting period), that

(*a*) any profits (i.e. income or chargeable gains) which ought to have been assessed to tax (see 51.3 above) have not been assessed, or

(*b*) an assessment is or has become insufficient, or

(*c*) any relief given is or has become excessive,

then with the exceptions below, an assessment (a discovery assessment) may be made to make good to the Crown the apparent loss of tax.

No discovery assessment may be made in respect of a chargeable period, where a return under *TMA 1970, s 8, 8A or 11* (see 51.5 above) has been delivered in respect of that period,

(1) if it would be attributable to an error or mistake in the return as to the basis on which the liability ought to have been computed and the return was, in fact, made on the basis, or in accordance with the practice, generally prevailing at the time when it was made; or

(2) unless either

(i) the loss of tax is attributable to fraudulent or negligent conduct by the taxpayer or a person acting on his behalf, or

(ii) at the time when an officer of the Board either ceased to be entitled to enquire (see 51.11 above) into the return or informed the taxpayer of the completion of his enquiries, he could not have been reasonably expected, on the basis of the information so far made available to him (see below), to be aware of the loss of tax.

For the purposes of (2)(i) above, information is regarded as having been made available to the officer if it has been included in

(A) the return (or accompanying accounts, statements or documents) for the chargeable period concerned or for either of the two immediately preceding it, or

(B) a partnership return (see 51.8 above), where applicable, in respect of the chargeable period concerned or either of the two immediately preceding it, or

(C) any claim for the chargeable period concerned, or

(D) documents, etc. produced for the purposes of any enquiries into such a return or claim, or is information the existence and relevance of which could reasonably be expected to be inferred from the above-mentioned information or are notified in writing to the Revenue.

An objection to a discovery assessment on the grounds that neither (i) nor (ii) in (2) above applies can be made only on an appeal against the assessment. (See 51.30 below for right of appeal.) An amendment is made to *TMA 1970, s 46(2)* (determination of appeal Commissioners; see 4.8 APPEALS) in consequence of the foregoing provisions. [*TMA 1970, ss 29, 46(2); FA 1994, ss 191(1), 196, 199(2)(3), 19 Sch 16*].

See 51.18 below as regards due date of payment. The above provisions supersede the existing discovery assessment provisions of *TMA 1970, s 29(3)* (see 5.2 ASSESSMENTS). As regards partnership businesses commenced (or deemed to commence) before 6 April 1994, the existing provisions continue to apply for all years of assessment before 1997/98. [*FA 1994, s 191(2)*].

51.16   **Amendment of partnership statement where loss of tax discovered.** Provisions broadly similar to those described in 51.15 above apply, for 1996/97 and subsequent years or accounting periods ending on or after an appointed day (which cannot be earlier than 1 April 1996), as regards an understatement of profits or excessive claim for relief or allowance in a partnership statement (see 51.9 above), although the Revenue's remedy in this case is to amend the partnership statement, with consequent amendment of partners' self-assessments. [*TMA 1970, s 30B; FA 1994, ss 196, 199(2)(3), 19 Sch 6; FA 1995, ss 103(7), 115(5)*].

See 51.30 below for the right of appeal.

51.17   **INTERIM PAYMENTS OF TAX ON ACCOUNT**

For 1997/98 and subsequent years of assessment (see below as regards 1996/97), where, as regards the year immediately preceding the year of assessment in question,

(*a*)   a person is assessed to income tax (including Class 4 national insurance contributions treated as income tax under *Social Security Contributions and Benefits Act 1992, s 16*) under *TMA 1970, s 9* (self-assessment in personal or trustee's return; see 51.6 above),

(*b*)   the assessed amount exceeds any income tax deducted at source (including tax deducted under PAYE, taking in any deduction in respect of that year but to be made in a subsequent year, tax treated as deducted from, or as paid on, any income, and tax credits on dividends),

(*c*)   the said excess (the relevant amount) and the proportion which the relevant amount bears to the assessed amount are not less than, respectively, a de minimis limit and a de minimis proportion, both to be prescribed by regulations,

the person must make two interim payments on account of his income tax liability (but not his capital gains tax liability) for the year of assessment in question, each payment being equal to 50% of the relevant amount (see (*c*) above), the first such payment being due on or before 31 January in the year of assessment, the second being due on or before the following 31 July.

At any time before 31 January following the year of assessment, the taxpayer may make a claim stating his belief that he will have no liability for the year or that his liability will be fully covered by tax deducted at source, and his grounds for that belief, in which case each of the interim payments is not, and is deemed never to have been, required to be made. Within the same time limit, the taxpayer may make a claim stating his belief that his liability for the year after allowing for tax deducted at source will be a stated amount which is less than the relevant amount, and stating his grounds for that belief, in which case each of the interim payments required will be, and deemed always to have been, equal to 50% of the stated amount. The maximum penalty for an incorrect statement fraudulently or negligently made in connection with either claim is the amount or additional amount he would have paid on account if he had made a correct statement. Interim payments of tax are subject to the same recovery provisions as any other payments of tax. An officer of the Board may direct, prior to 31 January following the year of assessment, that payments on account are not required. Any payments on account already made will be repaid. [*TMA 1970, s 59A; FA 1994, ss 192, 196, 199(2), 19 Sch 45; FA 1995, s 103(7), 108*].

Special provisions apply to determine the amount of interim payments in respect of 1996/97. Broadly, such payments are based on the excess (the relevant amount) of income tax assessed, disregarding tax charged at other than the basic rate on taxed investment income, for 1995/96 (the assessed amount) over tax deducted at source. It is then necessary to calculate the 'relevant proportion' of the relevant amount. The *'relevant proportion'* is the proportion which tax charged under Schedule A or any of Cases III to VI of Schedule D for 1995/96 bears to the assessed amount. The whole of the relevant proportion of the relevant amount is payable on or before 31 January 1997. The balance of the relevant amount is payable in equal instalments on or before 31 January 1997 and 31 July 1997. Claims may be made as above to forego interim payments or make reduced payments. [*TMA 1970, s 59A; FA 1994, ss 192, 198(1)(2), 199(2); FA 1995, s 116, 21 Sch 1, 2*].

51.18   FINAL PAYMENT (REPAYMENT) OF TAX

For 1996/97 and subsequent years of assessment, a final payment is due for a year of assessment if a person's combined income tax (including certain Class 4 national insurance contributions treated as income tax as in 51.17 above) and capital gains tax liabilities contained in his self-assessment (see 51.6 above) exceed the aggregate of any payments on account (whether under *TMA 1970, s 59A*, see 51.17 above, or otherwise) and any income tax deducted at source. If the second total exceeds the first, a repayment will be made. Tax deducted at source has the same meaning as in 51.17 (*b*) above, except that it does not include tax paid under PAYE in the year of assessment but in respect of a previous year of assessment (and see below as regards partnership income tax for 1996/ 97).

The due date for payment (or repayment) is 31 January following the year of assessment. The one exception is where the person gave notice of chargeability under *TMA 1970, s 7* (see 51.4 above) within six months after the end of the year of assessment, but was not given notice under *TMA 1970, s 8 or s 8A* (personal and trustee's return; see 51.5 above) until after 31 October following the year of assessment; in such case, the due date is the last day of the three months beginning with the date of the said notice. [*TMA 1970, s 59B(1)–(4)(7); FA 1994, ss 193, 196, 199(2), 19 Sch 45*].

As regards partnership businesses commenced (or deemed to commence) before 6 April 1994, each partner's share of income tax assessed on the partnership for 1996/97 is treated for the purposes of determining that partner's final payment or repayment for that year of assessment as if it were tax deducted at source. [*FA 1994, s 198(3); FA 1995, s 116, 21 Sch 1, 3*].

ICTA 1988, s 5 (date of payment of income tax) is repealed for 1996/97 and subsequent years of assessment in relation to partnership businesses such as are mentioned in the preceding paragraph, and for 1997/98 and subsequent years of assessment in any other case. For 1996/97 and subsequent years of assessment, the waiting period of one year from the end of the year of assessment before PAYE repaid by the Revenue carries

51.19 Self-Assessment

interest is removed. [*ICTA 1988, ss 5, 203(2)(dd); FA 1994, s 199(2), 26 Sch Pt V*]. *TCGA 1992, s 7* (date of payment of capital gains tax) is repealed for 1996/97 and subsequent years of assessment in order to correspond with the provisions in the preceding paragraphs.

For accounting periods ending on or after an appointed day (which cannot be earlier than 1 April 1996) a company will pay corporation tax and reclaim it if overpaid in broadly the same way as it does at present under Pay and File arrangements under *ICTA 1988, s 10* (corporation tax due and payable on day following expiry of nine months from end of accounting period; see 41.1 PAYMENT OF TAX). [*TMA 1970, s 59D; ICTA 1988, ss 10, 478; FA 1994, ss 195, 199(2)(3), 26 Sch Pt V; FA 1995, 29 Sch Pt VIII(14)*].

51.19   Where a person's self-assessment is amended under the relevant provisions in 51.7, 51.13 or 51.16 above, the due date for the final payment (or repayment) is normally as in 51.18 above but is deferred, as regards any tax payable (or repayable) by virtue of the amendment and subject to the appeal and postponement provisions in 51.30 below, until, if later, 30 days after the date of notice of the amendment (but note that this does not defer the date from which interest accrues on unpaid tax; see 51.21 below).

The due date for payment of tax charged by assessment otherwise than under *TMA 1970, s 9* (see 51.6 above) is unless otherwise directed 30 days after the date of the assessment (but see 51.21 below as regards interest on unpaid tax). [*TMA 1970, s 59B(5)(6); FA 1994, ss 193, 199(2)(3); FA 1995, ss 103(7), 115(6)*].

51.20   SURCHARGE ON UNPAID TAX

For 1996/97 and subsequent years of assessment, where income tax (including certain Class 4 national insurance contributions treated as income tax as in 51.17 above) or capital gains tax has become payable in accordance with *TMA 1970, s 59B* (see 51.18 and 51.19 above) or *TMA 1970, s 55* (payment and postponement of tax pending appeal; see 51.30 below) and any of the tax remains unpaid more than 28 days after the due date, the taxpayer will be liable to a surcharge of 5% of the unpaid tax. A further 5% surcharge will be levied on any tax still unpaid more than six months after the due date. Interest will accrue on an unpaid surcharge with effect from the expiry of 30 days beginning with the date of the notice imposing the surcharge. An appeal may be made, within that same 30-day period, against the imposition of a surcharge as if it were an assessment to tax. The appeal Commissioners concerned may, on appeal, set aside the surcharge if it appears to them that, throughout the period from the due date until payment, the taxpayer had a reasonable excuse for not paying the tax. Inability to pay the tax will not be regarded as a reasonable excuse.

There are provisions to prevent a double charge where tax has been taken into account in determining the tax-geared penalties of *TMA 1970, s 7* (see 51.4 above), *s 93(5)* (tax-geared penalty for failure to make return for income tax and capital gains tax; see 51.25 below), *s 95* (incorrect return etc. for income tax or capital gains tax; see 51.27 below) and *s 95A* (incorrect return etc. for partnerships; see 51.27 below). Any such tax will not be subject to a surcharge. The Board have discretion to mitigate, or to stay or compound proceedings for recovery of, a surcharge and may also, after judgment, entirely remit the surcharge. [*TMA 1970, s 59C; FA 1994, ss 194, 196, 199(2), 19 Sch 45; FA 1995, s 109*].

51.21   INTEREST ON UNPAID TAX

Interest will be charged on interim payments (see 51.17 above) and final payments (see 51.18 and 51.19 above) of income tax and capital gains tax which are made late. Interest will accrue normally from the due date (even if a non-business day) until the date of payment. Where the due date is deferred under the provisions in 51.19 above, interest will nevertheless accrue from what would have been the due date under 51.18 above (normally 31 January following the year of assessment). Interest on a discovery assessment under *TMA 1970, s 29* (see 51.15 above) will also accrue from that date, as will interest on tax becoming payable under *TMA 1970, s 55* (payment and postponement of tax pending appeal; see 51.30 below).

There are provisions to remit interest charged on interim payments to the extent that an income tax repayment is found to be due for the year of assessment. There are also complex provisions to cover the situation where a taxpayer makes a claim to dispense with or reduce interim payments and the total income tax liability for the year of assessment is such that interim payments should have been made or should have been greater. The taxpayer is effectively charged interest by reference to the payments he should have made. [*TMA 1970, s 86; FA 1994, ss 196, 199(2), 19 Sch 23(1); FA 1995, s 110*].

The above provisions replace the existing provisions of *TMA 1970, s 86* (see 32.1 to 32.3 INTEREST ON UNPAID TAX) which do, however, continue to apply for 1996/97 as regards partnerships whose trades commenced before 6 April 1994. [*FA 1994, s 196, 19 Sch 23(2); FA 1995, s 110(2)*].

Apart from a consequential amendment, the provisions for interest on unpaid corporation tax (see 32.4 INTEREST ON UNPAID TAX) under Pay and File and for setting rates of interest for general tax purposes remain unchanged. [*TMA 1970, s 87A; FA 1989, s 178; FA 1994, ss 196, 199(2)(3), 19 Sch 24, 44*].

51.22   INTEREST ON OVERPAID TAX

The provisions of *ICTA 1988, s 824* (see Tolley's Income Tax under Interest on Overpaid Tax) are amended for 1996/97 and subsequent years of assessment (for 1997/98 and subsequent years of assessment as regards partnerships whose trades commenced before 6 April 1994). A repayment of income tax (including an amount paid on account as in 51.17 above), or of a surcharge under *TMA 1970, s 59C* (see 51.20 above) or of a penalty incurred by an individual under any provision of *TMA 1970* will be increased by an amount (a repayment supplement) equal to interest on the amount repaid for the period (if any) between the 'relevant time' and the date of repayment. The '*relevant time*' is,

(*a*)   as regards interim payments (see 51.17 above), the due date,

(*b*)   as regards income tax (other than that paid by way of interim payment), 31 January following the year of assessment, and

(*c*)   as regards a penalty or surcharge, the date following the expiry of 30 days from the date it was incurred or imposed,

or, in all cases, if later than the date given above, the date of payment. Other amendments are made to *ICTA 1988, s 824* in consequence of the introduction of self-assessment. [*ICTA 1988, s 824; FA 1994, ss 196, 199(2), 19 Sch 41, 26 Sch Pt V*].

The provisions of *TCGA 1992, s 283* (see 31.1 INTEREST ON OVERPAID TAX) are amended for 1996/97 and subsequent years of assessment. A repayment of capital gains tax will be increased by an amount (a repayment supplement) equal to interest on the amount repaid for the period (if any) between the 'relevant time' and the date of repayment. The '*relevant time*' is the later of 31 January next following the year of assessment and the date on which the tax was paid. [*TCGA 1992, s 283; FA 1994, ss 196, 199(2), 19 Sch 46, 26 Sch Pt V*].

51.23 Self-Assessment

Apart from a consequential amendment, the provisions for interest on overpaid corporation tax (see 31.2 INTEREST ON OVERPAID TAX) under Pay and File remain unchanged. [*ICTA 1988, s 826; FA 1994, ss 196, 199(2), 19 Sch 42*].

51.23 DATE OF PAYMENT BY CHEQUE

For the purposes of *TMA 1970* generally, *ICTA 1988, ss 824* and *826* and *TCGA 1992, s 283* (see 51.22 above) as well as *ICTA 1988, s 825* (repayment supplement in respect of accounting period of a company ended before 1 October 1993; see 31.2 INTEREST ON OVERPAID TAX), where any payment to an officer of the Board or the Board is received by cheque after 5 April 1996 and the cheque is paid on its first presentation to the bank on which it is drawn, the payment is treated as made on the date of receipt of the cheque by the officer or the Board. [*TMA s 70A; FA 1994, s 196, 19 Sch 22*].

51.24 PENALTIES

The penalty provisions described below and at 51.25 to 51.28 below apply for 1996/97 and subsequent years of assessment or accounting periods ending on or after an appointed day (which cannot be earlier than 1 April 1996). See also 51.4 above for the penalty for failing to give notice of chargeability to tax, 51.17 for the penalty relating to incorrect payments on account and 51.20 for the surcharge imposed on unpaid tax. Penalties for other returns etc. under *TMA 1970, s 98* (see 42.7 PENALTIES) continue to apply as before, as do the statutory provisions of *TMA 1970, ss 97A, 102, 105* concerning mitigation and limitation of penalties described at 42.10 PENALTIES.

A penalty under *TMA 1970, s 7* or *10* (failure to give notice of chargeability for income tax and capital gains tax and corporation tax; see 51.4 above), *Pt IV* (assessments and claims), *s 59A* (payments on account of income tax; see 51.17 above) or any penalty under *TMA 1970, Pt X* (i.e. the following provisions mentioned in 42 PENALTIES unless otherwise stated: *ss 93* (see 51.25 below), *93A* (see 51.26 below), *94* (penalty for failure to make corporation tax return), *95* (see 51.27 below), *95A* (see 51.27 below), *96* (penalty for fraudulently or negligently making corporation tax return), *97AA* (see 51.28 below), *98* (see above), *98A* (PAYE and subcontractors; see Tolley's Income Tax under Construction Industry Tax Deduction Scheme and Penalties), *98B* (see 51.26 below), *99* (penalty for assisting in preparation of incorrect returns, etc.) and *99A* (incorrect certificates relating to non-deduction of income tax; see Tolley's Income Tax under Banks) carries interest, calculated from the due date (broadly, 30 days after issue of a determination of it by an officer of the Board or immediately on determination by appeal Commissioners or judgment of High Court; see 42.9 and 42.10 PENALTIES) to the date of payment. [*TMA 1970, s 103A; FA 1994, ss 196, 199(2)(3), 19 Sch 33; FA 1995, ss 103(7), 115(8)*].

Consequential amendments are made to *TMA 1970, s 100B* (appeals against penalty determinations; see 42.10 PENALTIES) and *Social Security Contributions and Benefits Act 1992, s 16* (Class 4 contributions treated as income tax). In addition, the disapplication of the three-year time limit within which tax-geared penalty proceedings must be commenced from final determination of tax in the case of a deceased person (see 42.13 PENALTIES) is to apply by reference to tax charged in an assessment made later than six years after 31 January next following the chargeable period (previously, after the end of the chargeable period) for which it was charged. [*TMA 1970, ss 100B, 103(2); FA 1994, ss 196, 199(2)(3), 19 Sch 31, 32, 45; FA 1995, ss 103(7), 115(7)*].

51.25

Failure to make return for income tax and capital gains tax. A person (the taxpayer) who fails to deliver a return when required to do so by notice under *TMA*

1970, s 8 or *8A* (personal or trustee's return; see 51.5 above) is liable to a penalty of £100 which can be determined by an authorised officer of the Board. For continuing failure, a further penalty of up to £60 per day may be imposed by the appeal Commissioners concerned (but not at any time after the failure has been remedied) on application by an officer of the Board, such daily penalty to start from the day after the taxpayer is notified of the Commissioners' direction (but not for any day for which such a daily penalty has already been imposed). If the failure continues for more than six months beginning with the filing date (i.e. the due date for delivery of the return; see 51.5 above), and no application for a daily penalty was made within those six months, the taxpayer is liable to a further £100 penalty determined as above. If failure continues after the anniversary of the filing date, and there would have been a liability under *TMA 1970, s 59B* (final payment of tax; see 51.18 above), based on a proper return promptly delivered, the taxpayer is liable to a further penalty determined as above of an amount not exceeding that liability.

If the taxpayer proves that his liability under *TMA 1970, s 59B*, based on a proper return promptly delivered, would not have exceeded a particular amount, his liability to penalties other than the daily and tax-geared penalties is reduced to that amount. On an appeal against either of the £100 penalties (reduced where appropriate), the Commissioners may either confirm the penalty or, if it appears to them that throughout the period of failure the taxpayer had a reasonable excuse for not delivering the return, set it aside. [*TMA 1970, s 93; FA 1994, ss 196, 199(2), 19 Sch 25*].

51.26 **Failure to make partnership return or return relating to European Economic Interest Grouping.** The same fixed penalties and daily penalties determined and imposed as in *TMA 1970, s 93* (see 51.25 above) apply in the case of failure to submit a partnership return as required by a notice under *TMA 1970, s 12AA* (see 51.8 above). However, there is no tax-geared penalty and no provision for reducing the £100 penalties. Each person who was a partner at any time during the period in respect of which the return was required is separately liable to the fixed and daily penalties. The penalties apply by reference to failure by the representative partner, i.e. the partner required by the notice under *TMA 1970, s 12AA* to deliver the return. Where penalties are imposed on two or more partners, an appeal cannot be made otherwise than by way of composite appeal by the representative partner. The same reasonable excuse provisions apply as under *TMA 1970, s 93* but by reference to the representative partner. [*TMA 1970, s 93A; FA 1994, ss 196, 199(2)(3), 19 Sch 26*].

The fixed penalty provided for by *TMA 1970, s 98B* (penalty for failure by European Economic Interest Grouping or member of it to make a return; see 51.5 above) is increased to £300 multiplied by the number of members of the grouping at the time of failure and this can be determined by an authorised officer of the Board. For continuing failure, there is a further daily penalty of up to £60 multiplied by the number of members of the grouping at the end of the day on which the grouping or member is notified of a direction to impose such a penalty by the appeal Commissioners concerned on an application by an officer of the Board, such daily penalty to start from the day after the taxpayer is so notified (but not for any day for which such a daily penalty has already been imposed). Neither the fixed nor the daily penalty can be imposed after the failure is remedied and the aggregate of any fixed and daily penalties cannot exceed £100 if there is no income or chargeable gain to be included in the return. [*TMA 1970, s 98B(1)(2)(2A)(2B)(3)(4); FA 1994, s 196, 199(2)(3), 19 Sch 30*].

51.27 **Fraud or negligence.** The provisions of *TMA 1970, s 95* (tax-geared penalty for fraudulently or negligently delivering an incorrect return, accounts etc. for income tax or capital gains tax; see 42.4 PENALTIES) continue to apply, with consequential amendments, under self-assessment. [*TMA 1970, s 95; FA 1994, ss 196, 199(2)(3), 19 Sch 27, 26 Sch Pt V*].

Similar provisions will apply as regards partnerships. They apply where a partner (the representative partner) delivers an incorrect partnership return (see 51.8 above), or, in connection with such a return, makes an incorrect statement or declaration or submits incorrect accounts, and either he does so fraudulently or negligently or his doing so is attributable to fraudulent or negligent conduct on the part of a 'relevant partner' (i.e. any person who was a partner at any time in the period covered by the return). Each relevant partner is liable to a penalty not exceeding the income tax (or corporation tax) underpaid by him as a result of the incorrectness. Where penalties are imposed on two or more partners, an appeal cannot be made otherwise than by way of composite appeal by the representative partner. [*TMA 1970, s 95A; FA 1994, ss 196, 199(2)(3), 19 Sch 28*].

51.28 **Failure to produce documents.** A new penalty applies where a person fails to comply with a notice or requirement under *TMA 1970, s 19A* (notice requiring production of documents, etc. for purpose of Revenue enquiry into a return; see 51.12 above). He is liable to a fixed penalty of £50 determinable by an authorised officer of the Board and, for each day of continuing failure (but not for any day for which such a daily penalty has already been imposed) after the fixed penalty is imposed, a further penalty not exceeding the 'relevant amount'. Neither the fixed nor the daily penalty may be imposed after the failure has been remedied. An officer of the Board may also determine the daily penalty under *TMA 1970, s 100* (see 42.9 PENALTIES), in which case the 'relevant amount' is £30, or instead may commence proceedings under *TMA 1970, s 100C* (see 42.10 PENALTIES) for determination of the penalty by the appeal Commissioners concerned, in which case the 'relevant amount' is £150. [*TMA 1970, s 97AA; FA 1994, ss 196, 199(2)(3), 19 Sch 29*].

51.29 **ASSESSMENTS: PROCEDURE AND TIME LIMIT**

The procedure for the raising of assessments other than self-assessments is set out in *TMA 1970, s 30A*. All income tax falling to be charged by such an assessment may, even if chargeable under more than one Schedule, be included in one assessment. These provisions apply for 1996/97 and subsequent years of assessment or accounting periods ending on or after an appointed day (which cannot be earlier than 1 April 1996) except that, in relation to partnerships whose trades were set up or commenced before 6 April 1994, they apply for 1997/98 and subsequent years of assessment. [*TMA 1970, s 30A; FA 1994, ss 196, 199(2)(3), 19 Sch 5*].

The normal time limit for the making of an assessment to income tax and capital gains tax for 1996/97 or a subsequent year of assessment is five years after 31 January following the year of assessment to which the assessment relates. The existing normal time limit of six years after the end of the accounting period for the making of a corporation tax assessment continues unchanged for accounting periods ending on or after an appointed day (which cannot be earlier than 1 April 1996). [*TMA 1970, s 34(1); FA 1994, ss 196, 199(2)(3), 19 Sch 10*]. For such chargeable periods, the extended time limit in cases of fraudulent or negligent conduct is twenty years after 31 January next following the year of assessment in the case of an income tax or capital gains tax assessment, and twenty-one years after the end of the accounting period in the case of a corporation tax assessment. Assessments under these extended time limits can be made on partners of the person in default. [*TMA 1970, s 36(1)(2); FA 1994, ss 196, 199(2)(3), 19 Sch 11*]. The latest time for assessing the personal representatives of a deceased person is three years after 31 January following the year of assessment. [*TMA 1970, s 40(1)(2); FA 1994, ss 196, 199(2), 19 Sch 12*]. (For time limits applying before 1996/97, see 5.5 ASSESSMENTS and 9.4, 9.5 BACK DUTY.)

51.30   APPEALS

For 1996/97 and subsequent years of assessment or accounting periods ending on or after an appointed day (which cannot be earlier than 1 April 1996), a right of appeal is conferred by *TMA 1970, s 31* against

(*a*)   any assessment other than a self-assessment,

(*b*)   an amendment by an officer of the Board of a self-assessment or partnership statement on enquiry into the return on which it is based (see 51.13 above), and

(*c*)   an amendment of a partnership statement where loss of tax is 'discovered' (see 51.16 above).

Written notice of appeal must be given within 30 days after the issue of the notice of assessment or amendment. An appeal within (*b*) above against an amendment to a self-assessment cannot be heard and determined before the officer gives notice that he has completed his enquiries, if he has not already done so (see 51.13 above). [*TMA 1970, s 31(1)–(3); F(No 2)A 1975, s 67(1); FA 1994, ss 196, 199(2)(3), 19 Sch 7, 26 Sch Pt V*].

Consequential amendments are made to *TMA 1970, s 50* (procedure on appeals heard by Commissioners; see 4.8 APPEALS). [*TMA 1970, s 50(6)–(9); FA 1994, ss 196, 199(2)(3), 19 Sch 17*]. Otherwise, the provisions in 4 APPEALS generally continue to apply.

Payment of tax pending appeal. The provisions of *TMA 1970, s 55* (payment and postponement of tax pending appeal; see 41.2 and 41.3 PAYMENT OF TAX) continue to apply in respect of

(i)   a 'discovery' assessment (see 51.15 above), and

(ii)   an amendment by an officer of the Board of a self-assessment on enquiry into the return on which it is based (see 51.13 above).

[*TMA 1970, s 55(1); FA 1994, ss 196, 199(2), 19 Sch 18*].

See 51.21 above as to the date from which interest on unpaid tax will accrue.

51.31   CLAIMS, ETC.

A new formal procedure applies for 1996/97 and subsequent years of assessment or accounting periods ending on or after an appointed day (which cannot be earlier than 1 April 1996) as regards the making of claims, elections and notices. Where notice has been given by the Revenue requiring the delivery of a return (see 51.5 and 51.8 above), a claim, etc. (other than one falling to be taken into account for PAYE) can only be made at any time by inclusion in such a return (or by virtue of an amendment to a return) *unless it could not be so included* either at that time or subsequently. In the case of a partnership business, a claim under any of numerous provisions specified in *TMA 1970, s 42(7)* must be made by a partner nominated by the partnership if it cannot be included in a partnership return (or amendment thereto). See 51.32 below for provisions applying where a claim, etc. is made otherwise than by inclusion in a return.

Where a claimant discovers that an error or mistake has been made in a claim (whether or not made in a return), he may make a supplementary claim within the time allowed for making the original claim. [*TMA 1970, s 42; FA 1994, ss 196, 199(2)(3), 19 Sch 13; FA 1995, ss 103(7), 107*].

51.32   Claims, etc. not included in returns. Subject to any specific provision requiring a claim, etc. to be made to the Board, a claim, election or notice made otherwise than in a return (see 51.31 above) must be made to an officer of the Board. The claim, etc. must include a declaration by the claimant that all particulars are correctly stated to the best of his information or belief. No claim requiring a tax repayment can be made unless the claimant has documentary proof that the tax has been paid or deducted. The claim must be made in a form determined by the Board and may require, inter alia, a statement of the amount of tax to be discharged or repaid. In the case of a claim by or on behalf of a person who is not resident (or who claims to be not resident or not ordinarily resident or not domiciled) in the UK, the Revenue may require a statement or declaration in support of the claim to be made by affidavit.

Provisions similar to those in 51.7 above (amendments of self-assessments) apply to enable a claimant (within twelve months of the claim) or officer of the Board (within nine months of the claim) to amend a claim, etc. The Revenue have power of enquiry into a claim, etc. (or amendment thereof) similar to that in 51.11 above (enquiries into returns), notice of intention to enquire to be given on or before the quarter day (meaning 31 January, 30 April, etc.) next following the first anniversary of the date of claim. In the event of such an enquiry, they have power to call for documents similar to that in 51.12 above. Provisions similar to those in 51.13 above apply as regards amendments of claims upon completion of an enquiry. The Revenue must give effect to such an amendment, by assessment if necessary, within 30 days after it is made. An appeal may be made against a Revenue amendment to a claim following an enquiry, written notice of appeal to be given normally within 30 days after the amendment is made (extended to three months where certain specified issues concerning residence are involved). If an amendment is varied on appeal, the Revenue have a further 30 days to give effect to the variation. [*TMA 1970, s 42(11), 1A Sch; FA 1994, ss 196, 199(2)(3), 19 Sch 13, 35; FA 1995, ss 103(7), 107(10)(11), 20 Sch*].

Jurisdiction of Commissioners. *TMA 1970, 2 Sch* (jurisdiction in appeals on claims; see 4.5 APPEALS) applies, with consequential amendments, to determine the appeal Commissioners (i.e. General or Special) to whom an appeal lies under the above provisions. [*TMA 1970, s 42(12), 2 Sch; FA 1994, ss 196, 199(2)(3), 19 Sch 13, 36*].

51.33   **General time limit for claims.** *Unless otherwise prescribed,* a claim relating to 1996/97 and subsequent years of assessment with respect to income tax or capital gains tax must be made within five years after 31 January immediately following the year of assessment to which it relates. For accounting periods ending on or after an appointed day (which cannot be earlier than 1 April 1996), the time limit remains as six years from the end of the period to which the claim relates. A corresponding amendment is made to *TMA 1970, s 43A* (further assessments: time limits for claims etc.; see 12.2 CLAIMS) in conse-quence of the changes made for discovery assessment under *TMA 1970, s 29* (see 51.15 above) so that the amendment does not apply in relation to a partnership whose trade commenced before 6 April 1994 until 1997/98 and subsequent years of assessment. [*TMA 1970, ss 43(1), 43A(1); FA 1994, ss 196, 199(2)(3), 19 Sch 14, 15*]. (See 12.2 CLAIMS and 54.4 TIME LIMITS – 5 APRIL 1995) for the position as regards earlier years of assessment and accounting periods.)

51.34   **ERROR OR MISTAKE RELIEF**

The error or mistake relief provisions of *TMA 1970, s 33* (see 12.4 CLAIMS) continue to apply for 1996/97 and subsequent years of assessment or accounting periods ending on or after an appointed day (which cannot be earlier than 1 April 1996). They apply by reference to an overcharge to tax under a self-assessment as well as under any other assessment. The time limit for claiming error or mistake relief, in the case of an income tax or capital gains tax assessment, is five years after 31 January immediately following the year of assessment to which the return in question relates, and, in the case of an assessment to corporation tax, six years after the end of the accounting period to which the return relates. No relief is available in respect of an error or mistake in a claim which is included in a return (but see 51.31 above as regards supplementary claims). [*TMA 1970, s 33; FA 1994, ss 196, 199(2)(3), 19 Sch 8, 26 Sch Pt V*].

51.35   **Error or mistake in partnership statement.** For 1996/97 and subsequent years of assessment or accounting periods ending on or after an appointed day (which cannot be earlier than 1 April 1996), error or mistake relief is extended to cover an error or mistake in a partnership statement (see 51.9 above) by reason of which the partners allege that their self-assessments were excessive. The claim to relief must be made by one of the partners within five years after the filing date for the partnership return (see 51.8 above). Where the claim results in an amendment to the partnership statement, the Board will, by notice, make any necessary amendments to the self-assessments of all persons who were partners at any time in the period covered by the partnership statement. Otherwise, provisions similar to those in 12.4 CLAIMS apply, with appropriate modifications. [*TMA 1970, s 33A; FA 1994, ss 196, 199(2)(3), 19 Sch 9*].

51.36   **OVER-REPAYMENTS OF TAX**

For 1996/97 and subsequent years of assessment or accounting periods ending on or after an appointed day (which cannot be earlier than 1 April 1996), *TMA 1970, s 30* (assessments to recover tax over-repaid; see 41.10 PAYMENT OF TAX) continues to apply but subject to the same exceptions (modified as appropriate) as in 51.15 above (discovery assessments). The normal time limit for such an assessment is extended, if necessary, to the later of the end of the chargeable period following that in which the repayment was made and, where relevant, the day on which an officer of the Board's enquiries into a return (or amendment of a return) delivered by the person concerned are treated as completed (see 51.13 above). [*TMA 1970, s 30(1B)(5); FA 1994, ss 196, 199(2)(3), 19 Sch 4*].

51.37   **COLLECTION AND RECOVERY**

For 1996/97 and subsequent years of assessment or accounting periods ending on or after an appointed day (which cannot be earlier than 1 April 1996), miscellaneous amendments are made to provisions covering the collection and recovery by the Revenue of tax, interest on tax, surcharges and penalties. The limit of £1,000 referred to in 41.6 PAYMENT OF TAX is raised to £2,000. [*TMA 1970, ss 65, 69, 70; FA 1994, ss 196, 199(2)(3), 19 Sch 19–21*].

51.38   **SETTLEMENTS AND TRUSTEES**

From 1996/97 new rules will be introduced for the assessment and collection of tax on trust income and gains where there is more than one trustee. Anything done by a liable trustee will be regarded as done by all the liable trustees, including the making of returns and self-assessment. Liability for penalties, interest or surcharge may be recovered (but only once) from any one or more of the trustees other than a trustee who was not a relevant trustee at the relevant time. [*TMA 1970, ss 7(2)(9), 8A(1)(5), 107A, 118; FA 1995, s 103, 29 Sch Pt VIII(14)*].

For 1996/97 onwards, chargeable gains which accrue to a trustee will be assessed on any trustee in the year in which they arise, and any subsequent trustee, with similar provisions for personal representatives of deceased persons. Where a trust ceases to be UK resident, an assessment under *TCGA 1992, s 80* (trustees ceasing to be resident in UK, see 39.6 OVERSEAS MATTERS) will not be made on a former trustee who can show that at the time he resigned there was no proposal that the trustees might migrate. [*TCGA 1992, ss 65(1)(3); FA 1995, ss 103(7), 114*].

51.39 ALLOWABLE CGT LOSSES

From 1996/97 (or from a date to be appointed in relation to companies) a capital loss will not be an allowable loss unless it is notified to the Revenue as if it was a claim under *TMA 1970, ss 42, 43* (see 51.31–51.33 above). A loss accruing in 1996/97 or later year is relieved before that relating to an earlier year. [*TCGA 1992, s 16(2A); FA 1995, ss 103(7), 113*].

51.40 UK REPRESENTATIVES OF NON-RESIDENTS

From 1996/97 (or from a date to be appointed in relation to companies) obligations and liabilities under self-assessment will fall upon UK representatives of non-residents carrying on a trade in the UK through a branch or agency. A business carried on wholly or partly overseas by a sole trader or partner who ceases to be UK resident will be treated as having ceased and recommenced. This will have effect for 1997/98 onwards for businesses established before 6 April 1994, otherwise it has effect for 1995/96 and 1996/97 also. Certain persons will not be regarded as UK representatives in order that certain professional services may be provided without risking the non-resident client to UK tax. [*FA 1995, ss 126, 127, 23 Sch*].

52 Settlements

Cross-references. See 2 ANNUAL RATES AND EXEMPTIONS; 5.6 ASSESSMENTS for assessments on trustees; 10 CHARITIES; 11.2 CHILDREN for bare trustees for children; 15 DEATH for provisions relating to death and to personal representatives; 18.75 EXEMPTIONS AND RELIEFS for settlements for the benefit of employees; 20 GIFTS and 22 HOLD-OVER RELIEFS for disposals not at arm's length and the availability of hold-over reliefs generally; 23.2 INDEXATION for transitional relief for 'indexation losses' in 1993/94 and 1994/95 only in the case of disposals by trustees of settlements made before 30 November 1993; 39.6–39.11 OVERSEAS MATTERS for overseas resident settlements etc.; 43.4 PRIVATE RESIDENCES for reliefs applicable to trustees; 45.5 REINVESTMENT IN SHARES RELIEF for relief available on disposals by trustees; 48.7 RETIREMENT RELIEF for relief available on disposals by trustees; 49.2 RETURNS for returns by trustees; 53.12 and 53.25 SHARES AND SECURITIES for stock dividends received by trustees and certain transfers of shares to employee share ownership trusts; 59.6 WASTING ASSETS for the situation where a disposal of a life interest in settled property gives rise to a chargeable event.

52.1 RATES OF TAX

For 1988/89 to 1995/96 (both years inclusive), the rate of capital gains tax applying to the trustees of a settlement (other than an 'accumulation or discretionary settlement') who are liable in respect of disposals of settled property (see 52.2 and 52.3 below) is equivalent to the basic rate of income tax for the year (but subject to the charge on settlors with interests in settlements as in 52.3 below). The rate throughout such years is 25%.

For 1988/89 to 1995/96 (both years inclusive) the rate of capital gains tax applying to the trustees of an accumulation or discretionary settlement who are similarly liable is equivalent to the sum of the basic and additional rates of income tax for the year (but again subject to the charge on settlors in 52.3 below). The rate throughout such years is 35%.

An *'accumulation or discretionary settlement'* is, for the above purposes, a trust where

(a)   all or any part of the income arising to the trustees in the year of assessment is income to which *ICTA 1988, s 686* (income tax rate applicable to discretionary or accumulating trust; prior to 1993/94, liability to income tax at the additional rate) applies, or

(b)   all the income arising to the trustees in the year is treated as the income of the settlor, but *section 686* would apply to it if it were not so treated, or

(c)   all the income arising to the trustees in the year is applied in defraying expenses of the trustees in that year, but *section 686* would apply to it if it were not so applied, or

(d)   no income arises to the trustees in the year, but *section 686* would apply if there were income arising to the trustees and none of it were treated as the income of the settlor or as applied in (c) above.

[*TCGA 1992, ss 4(1), 5; ICTA 1988, ss 1, 686(1)(1A), 832(1); FA 1993, s 79, 6 Sch 8, 15, 23*].

Before 1988/89, gains arising to the trustees of any settlement were charged at the rate of 30%. [*CGTA 1979, s 3; FA 1988, 14 Sch Pt VII*].

52.2 Settlements

52.2 MEANING OF 'SETTLED PROPERTY'

'Settled property' means any property held in trust other than property held by 'nominees' or 'bare trustees' (see below). Property held by a trustee or assignee in bankruptcy or under a deed of arrangement (see below) is not settled property. Property under a unit trust scheme (as defined) is also excluded from being settled property. [*TCGA 1992, ss 66(4), 68, 99*]. See also 57.1 UNIT AND INVESTMENT TRUSTS.

Nominees and bare trustees. Where assets are held by a person

(i)   as nominee for another or others, or

(ii)   as trustee for a person (or persons) 'absolutely entitled' as against him,

capital gains tax is chargeable as if the assets were held by that other person or persons and such property were not settled property.

A person is *'absolutely entitled'*, for these purposes, if he has the exclusive right (subject only to satisfying any outstanding charge, lien or other right of the trustee to resort to the property for the payment of duty, tax, costs or other outgoings) to direct how that asset shall be dealt with, or would have that right but for being an infant or under some other legal disability (e.g. a mentally handicapped person). [*TCGA 1992, s 60*]. The disability must arise from the general law, and not from the wording of the trust deed (see *Tomlinson v Glyn's Exor and Trustee Co Ltd CA 1969, 45 TC 600* where the trustees were held assessable to capital gains tax because the beneficiary's interest was contingent on his attaining majority, and could not be deemed to be vested in him). In *Booth v Ellard CA 1980, 53 TC 393*, several taxpayers by agreement transferred their shares in a company to trustees. The trusts were determinable by a majority of the beneficiaries (who were also the settlors), each beneficiary had a right of pre-emption over the others' shares, and the income was to be distributed in proportion to the number of shares to which each beneficiary was entitled (which corresponded with the number which he had settled). It was held that each beneficiary retained his interest in the same number of shares as he had settled (albeit not the identical shares). Despite the restraints, it was within the beneficiaries' collective power to terminate the trusts, and each beneficiary was therefore absolutely entitled as against the trustees. See also *Jenkins v Brown; Warrington v Sterland Ch D, [1989] STC 577*.

Kidson v Macdonald Ch D 1973, 49 TC 503 laid down that tenants in common of land held on trust for sale were jointly absolutely entitled. It is not necessary that particular assets to which the beneficiaries are entitled should be identifiable (*Stephenson v Barclays Bank Trust Co Ltd Ch D 1974, 50 TC 374*), but see *Cochrane's Exors v CIR CS 1974, 49 TC 299* (entitlement to residue) and *Crowe v Appleby CA 1975, 51 TC 457*.

Insolvents' assets. Assets held by a trustee or assignee in bankruptcy or under a 'deed of arrangement' are treated as if still owned by the bankrupt or debtor (the trustee's acquisitions from, or disposals to, the bankrupt being disregarded) and as if the trustee's acts in relation to those assets were acts of the bankrupt. But tax on chargeable gains arising from such acts is assessable on, and payable by, the trustee, etc. *'Deed of arrangement'* means a deed to which the *Deeds of Arrangement Act 1914* (or any corresponding Act in Scotland or NI) applies. [*TCGA 1992, s 66(1)(5)*].

When the bankrupt etc. dies, the assets held by the trustee are deemed for the purposes of *TCGA 1992, s 62(1)* (see 15.1 DEATH) to have then been acquired by the trustee as if he were a personal representative. The provisions above do not then apply after death. But if the bankrupt is dead before the trustee is appointed, the provisions above also do not apply, the assets being regarded as held by the deceased's personal representative. [*TCGA 1992, s 66(2)–(4)*].

In re McMeekin QB (NI) 1973, 48 TC 725 it was held that capital gains tax is an administration cost of bankruptcy.

52.3   **LIABILITY OF TRUSTEES, SETTLORS AND BENEFICIARIES**

Trustees of a settlement are liable to capital gains tax, under provisions relating to the tax generally, on disposals or deemed disposals of settled property (but subject to the charge on settlors with interests in settlements as below). The exempt amount for a year of assessment available to trustees is given in 52.4 and 52.5 below. Trustees are treated as a single and continuing body (distinct from the persons who may from time to time be trustees) which is resident and ordinarily resident in the UK unless the administration of the settlement is ordinarily carried on outside the UK and the trustees or a majority of them for the time being are not resident or not ordinarily resident in the UK. A person carrying on the business of managing settlements (and acting as trustee in the course of that business) is treated as not resident in relation to a settlement if the entire settled property consists of, or is derived from, property provided by a person not at the time (or, in the case of a will trust, at death) domiciled, resident or ordinarily resident in the UK. If, in such a case, the trustees or a majority of them are, or are treated as, not resident in the UK, the administration of the settlement is treated as ordinarily carried on outside the UK. [*TCGA 1992, s 69(1)(2)*].

Special rules apply to overseas resident settlements etc. See 39.6–39.11 OVERSEAS MATTERS.

Where part of the property comprised in a settlement is vested in one trustee or set of trustees and part in another (and in particular settled land within the meaning of the *Settled Land Act 1925* is vested in the tenant for life and investments representing capital money are vested in the trustees of the settlement), all the trustees are treated as together constituting and, insofar as they act separately, as acting on behalf of a single body of trustees. [*TCGA 1992, s 69(3)*].

The Board may by notice in writing require a person who is a 'party' to a settlement (within *ICTA 1988, s 660G(1)(2)*) to provide within not less than 28 days information it thinks necessary for the purposes of *TCGA 1992*. [*TMA 1970, s 27*].

Charge on settlors with interests in settlements. In certain circumstances gains accruing to trustees in a year after 1987/88 are not chargeable on them, but instead an equal amount of gains (as in (*b*) below) is treated as accruing to the settlor in the year. (See 39.6–39.11 OVERSEAS MATTERS for interaction between the provisions mentioned therein and those given below.)

The charge on the settlor arises if all of the following conditions are fulfilled.

(*a*)   Chargeable gains (including those arising under *TCGA 1992, s 13* as in 39.5 OVERSEAS MATTERS) accrue in a year to the trustees of a settlement from the disposal of any or all of the settled property.

(*b*)   The trustees would otherwise, after making deductions for losses (including those taken into account under *TCGA 1992, s 13*) under *TCGA 1992, s 2(2)* (see 35.1 LOSSES) but taking no account of the annual exemption under *TCGA 1992, s 3* (see 52.4 and 52.5 below), be chargeable to tax for the year in respect of those gains.

(*c*)   The settlor is, and the trustees are, either resident in the UK during any part of the year or ordinarily resident in the UK during the year.

(*d*)   The settlor is alive at the end of the year.

(*e*)   At any time during the year the settlor has an interest in the settlement.

(*f*)   The settlor is not excepted from the charge as below.

52.3   Settlements

A settlor has an interest in a settlement if

(i)   any property which may at any time be comprised in the settlement or any derived property is, or will or may become, payable to or applicable for the benefit of the settlor or his spouse in any circumstances whatsoever, or

(ii)   the settlor or his spouse, enjoys a benefit deriving directly or indirectly from any property which is comprised in the settlement or any derived property.

For 1995/96 onwards, references to the spouse of the settlor in (i) and (ii) above do not include a person to whom the settlor is not for the time being married but may marry later, or a spouse from whom the settlor is separated under a court order or similar arrangement that is likely to be permanent, or the widow or widower of the settlor.

A settlor does not have an interest under (i) above if and so long as

(A)   none of the property which may at any time be comprised in the settlement and no derived property can become applicable or payable as mentioned in (i) above except in the event of: the bankruptcy of some person who is or may become beneficially entitled to that property or any derived property; any assignment of or charge on that property or any derived property being made or given by some such person; in the case of a marriage settlement, the death of both the parties to the marriage and all or any of the children of the marriage; or the death of a child of the settlor who had become beneficially entitled to the property or any derived property at an age not exceeding 25; or

(B)   some person is alive and under the age of 25 during whose life the property or any derived property cannot become applicable or payable as mentioned in (i) above except in the event of that person becoming bankrupt or assigning or charging his interest in that property.

The settlor is excepted from the charge where

(I)   he has an interest in a settlement under (i) or (ii) above only because that property is, or will or may become, payable to or applicable for the benefit of his spouse *or* his spouse enjoys a benefit from property, or for both such reasons, and

(II)   his spouse dies, or he and his spouse cease to be married, during the year.

For these purposes, derived property means income from that property or any other property directly or indirectly representing proceeds of that property or income therefrom.

For years before 1995/96 the above provisions differed in some degree in their wording. For the previous wording see Tolley's Capital Gains Tax 1994/95 or earlier.

Where the trustees of a maintenance fund for an historic building elect under *ICTA 1988, s 691(2)* that income arising under the settlement or part of the settlement involved is not to be treated as income of the settlor for a year of assessment, no charge arises under these provisions in relation to the settlement or part for the year.

For these provisions a person is a '*settlor*' in relation to a settlement if the settled property consists of or includes property originating from him. Property originates from a settlor where he provides it directly or indirectly for the purposes (see *Countess Fitzwilliam and others v CIR (and related appeals) HL, [1993] STC 502*) of the settlement (including property provided by another person under reciprocal arrangements) and where property (or a proper part thereof) represents that property. In general, references to settled property (and to property comprised in a settlement), in relation to a settlor, are references only to property originating from that settlor.

A settlor has a right of recovery against any trustee for the amount of tax he is charged under these provisions. Such amount is identified by treating the gains that are deemed to accrue to him (or, for 1988/89 and 1989/90 only, his wife, if he is chargeable in respect of her gains) as forming the highest part of his chargeable amount for the year. There are provisions for 1988/89 and 1989/90 only to ascertain the amount where tax at a rate equivalent to the higher rate of income tax is charged in respect of gains assessed on a man who is chargeable in respect of his wife's gains and gains under these provisions accrue to either of them.

The inspector may require a settlor, trustee or former trustee to provide him with particulars for the purposes of these provisions. Failure to do so within a specified time (which cannot be less than 28 days) incurs penalties under *TMA 1970, s 98* (see 42.7 PENALTIES). [*TCGA 1992, ss 77, 78(1)(2), 79; FA 1988, 10 Sch 5(3)–(5), 14 Sch Pt VIII; FA 1995, 17 Sch 27–29*].

Collection of unpaid tax from beneficiaries etc. If tax assessed on trustees in respect of a chargeable gain accruing to them is not paid within six months from the date when it becomes payable *and* before or after that date the asset in respect of which the gain accrued, or any part of the proceeds of sale of that asset, is transferred to a person who becomes absolutely entitled to it, or the proceeds etc., that person may be assessed and charged in the name of the trustees within two years from the time when the tax became payable. The tax chargeable is not to exceed the tax chargeable on an amount equal to the chargeable gain and, where only a part of the asset or of the proceeds was transferred, is not to exceed a proportionate part of that amount. [*TCGA 1992, s 69(4)*].

52.4   **ANNUAL EXEMPTIONS**

An annual exempt amount is allowed to trustees in the same way as it is to individuals subject to a charge on the settlor with an interest in the settlement as in 52.3 above. Losses accruing to the trustees are treated as in the context of the annual exemption available to individuals. See 2.3 ANNUAL RATES AND EXEMPTIONS.

The level and availability of the exemption are subject to conditions. These are given below or, in the case of settlements for the disabled etc., in 52.5 below.

Settlements made before 7 June 1978. For 1980/81 onwards an outright exemption of *one-half* of the full annual exemption for individuals is available to trustees of such settlements. The exemption limits are thus £3,000 for 1995/96, £2,900 for 1992/93 to 1994/95 (both years inclusive), £2,750 for 1991/92, £2,500 for 1988/89, 1989/90 and 1990/91, £3,300 for 1987/88, £3,150 for 1986/87, £2,950 for 1985/86, £2,800 for 1984/85 and £2,650 for 1983/84.

Losses brought forward are deducted only insofar as is necessary to reduce the taxable amount to the level of the annual exemption above. If the taxable amount is not greater than the annual exemption no deduction is made from losses brought forward.

Settlements made after 6 June 1978. For 1980/81 and subsequent years of assessment the same exemption is available as for settlements made before 7 June 1978 above with the addition of special provisions for 'groups' of settlements. Where a settlement is one of two or more 'qualifying settlements' comprised in a group, the annual exemption is the amount given by dividing one-half of the full annual exemption for individuals (see above) by the number of settlements in the group. However, there is a minimum exemption per settlement of one-tenth of the full annual exemption for individuals.

A *'qualifying settlement'* is any settlement made after 6 June 1978 and which is not a settlement for the disabled, etc. (see 52.5 below) or an 'excluded settlement' (see below). A *'group'* of settlements constitutes all those qualifying settlements with the same 'settlor'. Where, in consequence of this, a settlement is comprised in two or more groups because that settlement was made by two or more settlors, then, in determining the level of annual exemption available as above, it is deemed to be in the group comprised of the greatest number of settlements.

'*Settlor*' has the meaning given by *ICTA 1988, s 660G(1)(2)* (see 14.7 CONNECTED PERSONS) and includes, in the case of a settlement arising under a will or intestacy, the testator or intestate. Settlements created by a deed of variation within 15.6 DEATH do not 'arise under' a will so that in the Revenue's view the testator is not the settlor of the settlements created (Tolley's Practical Tax 1986 p 48).

'*Excluded settlements*' are any of the following

(i)   Settlements, the trustees of which are not for the whole or any part of the year of assessment treated under *TCGA 1992, s 69(1)* (see 52.3 above) as resident and ordinarily resident in the UK.

(ii) Settlements, the property in which is held solely for charitable purposes and cannot become applicable for other purposes. See also 10.1 CHARITIES.

(iii) Settlements, the property in which is held for the purposes of certain retirement benefits and compensation funds which are exempt from a charge on capital gains.

The inspector may, by notice in writing, require any party to a settlement to provide, within a stipulated time (not less than 28 days), such information as the inspector thinks necessary for the application of the above provisions. [*TCGA 1992, s 3(1)–(5), 1 Sch 2; SI 1992 No 626; FA 1993, s 82; FA 1994, s 90; SI 1994 No 3008; FA 1995, 17 Sch 32*].

52.5   **Settlements for the disabled, etc.** Subject to the 'grouping' provisions below the same annual exemption as for individuals (e.g. £6,000 for 1995/96) (applied, in general, as for individuals: see 2.3 ANNUAL RATES AND EXEMPTIONS for this and exemptions for earlier years) is available to trustees of such settlements, provided that, during the whole or part of the year of assessment concerned, the settled property is held on trusts which secure that, during the lifetime of a 'mentally disabled person' or a person in receipt of 'attendance allowance' or of a 'disability living allowance' by virtue of entitlement to the care component at the highest or middle rate,

(*a*)   not less than half of the property which is applied, is applied for the benefit of the person concerned, and

(*b*)   that person is entitled to not less than half of the income arising from the property, or no such income may be applied for the benefit of any other person.

'*Mentally disabled person*' means a person who, by reason of mental disorder within the meaning of *Mental Health Act 1983*, is incapable of administering his property or managing his affairs.

'*Attendance allowance*' means an allowance under *Social Security Contributions and Benefits Act 1992, s 64* or *Social Security Contributions and Benefits (Northern Ireland) Act 1992, s 64*.

'*Disability living allowance*' means a disability living allowance under *Social Security and Benefits Act 1992, s 71* or *Social Security and Benefits (Northern Ireland) Act 1992, s 71*.

Losses brought forward are deducted only insofar as is necessary to reduce the taxable amount to the level of the annual exemption. If the taxable amount is not greater than the annual exemption no deduction is made from losses brought forward.

For the purposes of (*a*) and (*b*) above, powers of advancement conferred on the trustees under *Trustee Act 1925, s 32* or *Trustee Act (Northern Ireland) 1958, s 33* will not, as such, disqualify the trust from the relief, and requirements that income be applied for qualifying purposes 'during the lifetime' of a person are deemed satisfied if income is applied for such purposes, during a period where it is held for that person on protective trusts, as under *Trustee Act 1925, s 33*.

Groups. For 1981/82 and subsequent years of assessment, where a settlement is one of two or more 'qualifying settlements' made after 9 March 1981 comprised in a 'group', the annual exemption is the full annual exemption for individuals divided by the number of settlements in the 'group'. However, there is a minimum exemption of one-tenth of the full annual exemption.

A *'qualifying settlement'* is any settlement for a disabled person, etc. within the provisions above made after 9 March 1981 and which is not an 'excluded settlement'. A *'group'* of settlements constitutes all those qualifying settlements with the same 'settlor'. Where in consequence of this, a settlement is comprised in two or more groups because that settlement was made by two or more settlors, then, in determining the level of annual exemption available as above, it is deemed to be in the group comprised of the greatest number of settlements.

'Settlor' and *'excluded settlement'* are as defined in 52.4 above in relation to other settlements made after 6 June 1978 and there are similar powers to call for information. [*TCGA 1992, s 3(1)–(5), 1 Sch 1; SI 1992 No 626; FA 1993, s 82; FA 1994, s 90; SI 1994 No 3008*].

52.6 CREATION OF A SETTLEMENT

A transfer into settlement, whether revocable or irrevocable, is a disposal of the entire property settled even if the transferor is a beneficiary or trustee of the settlement. [*TCGA 1992, s 70*]. The acquisition and disposal are treated as being made at MARKET VALUE (36) subject to the exclusion therein mentioned. HOLD-OVER RELIEFS (22) may be available in respect of chargeable gains that would otherwise arise to the settlor. The settlor of a settlement and the trustees of that settlement are CONNECTED PERSONS (14) and further rules may operate as to valuation and losses (in particular see 3.10 and 3.11 ANTI-AVOIDANCE, 36.1 MARKET VALUE and 35.4 LOSSES).

Example

In December 1995, C transfers to trustees of a settlement for the benefit of his children 10,000 shares in W plc, a quoted company. The value of the gift is £80,000. C bought the shares in 1979 for £20,000 and their value at 31 March 1982 was £35,000. The indexation factor for March 1982 to December 1995 is assumed to be 0.839.

	£	£
Deemed disposal consideration	80,000	80,000
Cost	20,000	
Market value 31.3.82		35,000
Unindexed gain	60,000	45,000
Indexation allowance £35,000 × 0.839	29,365	29,365
Gain after indexation	£30,635	£15,635
Chargeable gain		£15,635
Trustees' allowable cost		£80,000

Note to the example

(*a*)   If the transfer is a chargeable lifetime transfer for inheritance tax purposes, or would be one but for the annual inheritance tax exemption, C could elect under *TCGA 1992, s 260* to roll the gain over against the trustees' base cost of the shares. The trustees do not join in any such election. This would normally cover only a transfer to a discretionary settlement.

Before 10 March 1981 the legislation used the term 'gift in settlement' rather than 'transfer into settlement'. [*CGTA 1979, s 53*]. For the position regarding the definition of 'gift' in this regard see *Berry v Warnett HL 1982, 55 TC 92*. Here the HL, by a majority, rejected the Crown's contention that 'gift in settlement' should be equated with 'transfer into settlement' but unanimously accepted the Crown's argument that, on a proper construction of the relevant agreement, there had been a disposal of the entirety of the trust fund to the trustee under a bargain other than at arm's length and accordingly MARKET VALUE (36) applied to the disposal. What are now *TCGA 1992, s 70* and *TCGA 1992, ss 71, 72* (see 52.9 and 52.10 below) are special cases of the assumption on which the legislation, in particular *TCGA 1992, s 69(1)(2)* (see 52.3 above) proceeded, namely that tax was chargeable on disposals to trustees.

Exercise of power of appointment or advancement. For the consequences of the exercise of such a power see *Hoare Trustees v Gardner; Hart v Briscoe Ch D 1977, 52 TC 53; Chinn v Collins HL 1980, 54 TC 311; Roome v Edwards HL 1981, 54 TC 359; Eilbeck v Rawling HL 1981, 54 TC 101; Bond v Pickford CA 1983, 57 TC 301; Swires v Renton Ch D, [1991] STC 490*. Following the decision in *Bond v Pickford* above, the Board of Inland Revenue issued Pamphlet IR 131, SP 7/84, 11 October 1984 to set out the Revenue's views on the capital gains tax implications of the exercise of a power of appointment or advancement when continuing trusts are declared. This Statement modified the earlier Statement of Practice SP 9/81, 23 September 1981 which was issued for a similar purpose following the decision in *Roome v Edwards* above and accordingly SP 9/81 was withdrawn from 11 October 1984.

The Board states in SP 7/84 that the judgments in *Roome v Edwards* emphasised that, in deciding whether or not a new settlement has been created by the exercise of a power of appointment or advancement, each case must be considered on its own facts, and by applying established legal doctrine to the facts in a practical and commonsense manner. The Court of Appeal judgments in *Bond v Pickford* explained that the consideration of the facts must include examination of the powers which the trustees purported to exercise, and the determination of the intention of the parties, viewed objectively.

The Board considers it now clear that a deemed disposal under *TCGA 1992, s 71(1)* (see 52.9 below) cannot arise unless the power exercised by the trustees, or the instrument conferring the power, expressly or by necessary implication, confers on the trustees authority to remove assets from the original settlement by subjecting them to trusts of a different settlement. Such powers (which may be powers of advancement or appointment) were referred to by the Court of Appeal in *Bond v Pickford* as 'powers in the wider form'. The Board considers that a deemed disposal will not arise when such powers are exercised and trusts are declared in circumstances such that

(*a*)   the appointment is revocable, or

(*b*)   the trusts declared of the advanced or appointed funds are not exhaustive so that there exists a possibility at the time when the advancement or appointment is made that the funds covered by it will, on the occasion of some event, cease to be held upon such trusts and once again come to be held upon the original trusts of the settlement.

The Board also considers it unlikely a deemed disposal will occur when trusts are declared following the exercise of such a power if the duties of trusteeship as regards the appointed assets fall to the trustees of the original settlement. This follows from the provision in *TCGA 1992, s 69(1)* that the trustees of a settlement form a single and continuing body (see 52.3 above).

In conclusion the Board accepts that a power of appointment or advancement can be exercised over only a part of settled property and that the foregoing would apply to that part.

Revenue practice regarding validity of trust deeds for general and tax law purposes. From 6 April 1991 new trust deeds (other than those for special types of trust such as unit trusts, charitable trusts and employee trusts) will not, as previously, be examined individually by the Revenue for their validity under general law as well as tax law. The Revenue will normally rely on the information shown in returns etc. made by the settlors, trustees and beneficiaries and will only seek further information where necessary, and only exceptionally will they ask to see deeds or other documents. Trustees will be asked to supply information about themselves and the settlor and whether the trustees have power to accumulate income or to distribute it at their discretion. This change of practice is for the purposes of income and capital gains tax but the examination of deeds for inheritance tax purposes is unaffected (Revenue Press Release 19 December 1990). It follows that great care should be exercised before executing a trust deed to ensure it is effective for the purposes desired.

52.7 **INTERESTS IN SETTLED PROPERTY**

Interests in settled property take a variety of forms as outlined below. Their treatment for capital gains tax purposes is given in 52.8 to 52.11 below.

Interests created by or arising under a settlement. These include, in particular, an annuity or life interest (see below), and the reversion to an annuity or life interest, but are otherwise not specifically defined. [*TCGA 1992, s 76*].

Life interests in relation to a settlement. The meaning of 'life interest' includes a right under the settlement to the income of, or the use or occupation of, settled property for the life of a person other than the person entitled to the right, or for lives. [*TCGA 1992, s 72(3)(a)*]. Any right which is contingent on the exercise of the discretion of the trustee or some other person is not a life interest. [*TCGA 1992, s 72(3)(b)*]. The ordinary meaning of 'life interest' (i.e. the right of a person to income etc. during his life) is also accepted as applying. Interests which are not primarily defined by reference to a life are not considered to be life interests, so that a beneficiary with an interest in possession (see below) in settled property which will come to an end on obtaining a specified age does not have a life interest (Revenue Pamphlet IR 1, D43). However, concessional treatment is available for such non-life interests which cease on the death of a beneficiary as in 52.10 and 52.11 below.

An annuity created by the settlement is included as a life interest if

(i) some or all of the settled property is appropriated by the trustees as a fund out of which the annuity is payable and

(ii) there is no right of recourse to settled property not so appropriated or to the income thereof.

While such an annuity is payable, and on the occasion of the death of the annuitant, the appropriated part of the settled property is treated as being settled property under a separate settlement. Annuities, other than those above, are not life interests notwithstanding that they are payable out of, or charged on, settled property or the income thereof. [*TCGA 1992, s 72(3)(c)(4)*]. However, where an annuity which is not a life interest is terminated by the death of the annuitant, certain provisions in 52.10–52.11 below apply as on the termination of a life interest by the death of the person entitled thereto.

Life interest in possession in all or part of settled property. The legislation gives no meaning to the term 'life interest in possession' although it seems regard must be made to the meaning of 'life interest' (as above) and to judicial interpretation of the term 'interest in possession'. Such interpretation arose in *Pearson and Others v CIR HL, [1980] STC 318* where the point at issue was the meaning of the term 'interest in possession' as used in certain capital transfer tax legislation dealing with settled property. The majority opinions of the HL indicated the following.

(a)   There must be a *present right to the present enjoyment* of something for there to be an interest in possession in settled property. So a person with an interest in possession will have an immediate right to trust income as it arises.

(b)   If the trustees have *any power to withhold income* as it arises there is no interest in possession. There is a distinction between a power to terminate a present right to present enjoyment and a power which prevents a present right of present enjoyment arising. It follows that

    (i)   a power to accumulate income is sufficient to prevent a beneficiary from having an interest in possession. The position is the same if there is a trust to accumulate. Whether or not income is in fact accumulated is irrelevant;

    (ii)   an overriding power of appointment which could be used to defeat the interest of a beneficiary does not prevent that interest from being in possession if it does not affect the right of the beneficiary to the income which has already arisen;

    (iii)   the possibility of future defeasance of an interest does not prevent it from being in possession until the occurrence of the relevant event; and

    (iv)   a power of revocation does not prevent an interest from being in possession until it is exercised.

(c)   There is a distinction between trustees' *administrative powers*, such as those to pay duties, taxes etc., and their *dispositive powers* to dispose of the net income of the trust. The existence of the former does not prevent an interest from being in possession. Any interest in possession will be in the net income of the trust after deduction of administrative expenses.

(d)   The fact that an interest in settled property is not in remainder or reversion or contingent does not automatically make it an interest in possession.

The Revenue had published their views on the meaning of 'interest in possession' prior to the HL decision in *Pearson* above. Their statement, although now withdrawn, is reproduced in Revenue Pamphlet IHT 1 (1991), p 88 and the Revenue regard the views expressed therein as 'not inconsistent' with the opinions given in *Pearson*.

If, in exercise of their powers under the settlement, the trustees grant a beneficiary an exclusive or joint right to occupy a dwelling-house which forms part of the settled property with the intention of providing the beneficiary with a permanent home, the Revenue regard this as creating an interest in possession, even if the right is revocable or for a limited period. A right granted for non-exclusive occupation or for full consideration is not so regarded (Revenue Pamphlet IR 131, SP 10/79, 15 August 1979). See 43.4 PRIVATE RESIDENCES for the exemption available on the disposal of a dwelling-house which has been occupied in the above circumstances.

52.8   **DISPOSAL OF AN INTEREST IN SETTLED PROPERTY**

Subject to the exclusion below for non-resident settlements, where there is a disposal of an interest created by or arising under a settlement, (see 52.7 above) no chargeable gain accrues if the disposal was made

(a)   by the person for whose benefit the interest was created by the terms of the settlement; or

(b)   by any other person except one who acquired, or derives his title from one who acquired, the interest for a consideration in money or money's worth, other than consideration consisting of another interest under the settlement.

Subject to the above, where a person who has acquired an interest in settled property becomes, as the holder of that interest, absolutely entitled (see 52.2 above) as against the trustee to any settled property, he is treated as disposing of the interest in consideration of obtaining the property so received (but without prejudice to any gain accruing to the trustee on the deemed disposal by the trustee under *TCGA 1992, s 71(1)* (see 52.9 below)). [*TCGA 1992, s 76*].

Where the disposal of a life interest in settled property does give rise to a chargeable event, the interest may be treated as a wasting asset in certain circumstances. See 59.6 WASTING ASSETS.

Exclusion for certain non-resident settlements. The exemption above does not apply to disposals of interests in settled property if, at the time of disposal (being after 9 March 1981), the trustees are neither resident nor ordinarily resident in the UK (see 52.2 above) except where the disposal arises on a person becoming absolutely entitled to settled property as against the trustees (see above). [*TCGA 1992, s 85(1)*].

If, however, after 9 March 1981 and before 19 March 1991, a disposal of an interest in settled property occurs while the trustees are still either resident or ordinarily resident in the UK, the exemption will be available as above, but a charge, equal to the amount of any gain exempted, will arise on the trustees, just before they become neither resident nor ordinarily resident in the UK. This charge does not apply, where, before the end of the year of cessation of their residence and ordinary residence in the UK, the trustees dispose of all the assets, which, at the time of the original disposal, constituted the settled property in which the interest subsisted. Extra-statutory concession D2 is not applied in these circumstances; see 47.2 RESIDENCE AND DOMICILE. If a charge does arise, it is not to exceed the market value, at the time of the charge, of such of those assets as are not disposed of at the end of the year of cessation of both residence and ordinary residence. For the above purposes trustees will be regarded as not having disposed of an asset if, and to the extent that, they retain part of it, an interest in or right over it, or property derived from it. Tax assessed on the trustees under these provisions and remaining unpaid twelve months after the payable date, may be assessed within six years of the original disposal, and charged, in the name of the trustees, on the person originally disposing of the exempted interest. The latter is given a right of recovery from the trustees. [*FA 1981, s 88(2)–(7); FA 1991, s 92(3)(5)*]. For trustees becoming neither resident nor ordinarily resident in the UK after 18 March 1991 and for the calculation of the gain arising on a disposal of a settled interest in such circumstances, see 39.6 OVERSEAS MATTERS et seq.

52.9   **PERSON BECOMING ABSOLUTELY ENTITLED TO SETTLED PROPERTY**

Subject to the exception below, where a person becomes absolutely entitled to any settled property as against the trustee, all the assets forming part of the settled property to which he becomes so entitled are deemed to have been disposed of by the trustee and immediately reacquired by him in the capacity of bare trustee or nominee within *TCGA 1992, s 60(1)* (see 52.2 above) for a consideration equal to the market value of the assets. [*TCGA 1992, s 71(1)*].

Any resulting net chargeable gain is assessed on the trustee in the usual way (subject to a claim for HOLD-OVER RELIEFS (22) but note the general relief for gifts in 22.6 was only extant after 5 April 1982 and before 14 March 1989).

On the occasion when a person becomes absolutely entitled to any settled property as against the trustees, any allowable loss which has accrued to the trustees in respect of property which is, or is represented by, the property to which the person becomes so entitled (including allowable losses brought forward from previous years of assessment) is treated (to the extent that it cannot be set against other chargeable gains arising to the trustee in that year of assessment but before that occasion) as an allowable loss accruing to that person at the time he became entitled. [*TCGA 1992, s 71(2)*]. The position should be contrasted with that of allowable losses made by personal representatives as in 15.7 DEATH.

For deemed disposals after 9 March 1981 it is made clear that references in the foregoing to the case where a person becomes absolutely entitled to settled property as against the trustee include references to the case where a person would become so entitled but for being an infant or other person under disability. [*TCGA 1992, s 71(3)*].

Where *TCGA 1992, s 71(2)* above applies, the Revenue do not restrict those losses under *TCGA 1992, s 18(3)* (see 35.4 LOSSES) where the trustees and the person becoming absolutely entitled are CONNECTED PERSONS (14) (Revenue Tax Bulletin February 1993 p. 57).

See 16.3 and 16.4 DISPOSAL for allowable expenditure.

Exception where a life interest is terminated by the death of the person entitled thereto. Where, as above, a person becomes absolutely entitled as against the trustee to assets forming part of settled property and that occasion is the termination of a life interest by the death of the person entitled to that interest then, subject to conditions and certain exceptions, *no* chargeable gain arises on the deemed disposal. See 52.11(*a*) below for full details.

52.10   **TERMINATION OF LIFE INTEREST IN POSSESSION ON DEATH OF PERSON ENTITLED: ASSETS REMAINING SETTLED PROPERTY**

The following provisions apply after 5 April 1982 and are subject to the exception below.

(*a*)   Where a life interest in possession in all or any part of settled property is terminated on the death of the person entitled to it (e.g. a life tenant), the whole or a corresponding part of each of the assets forming part of the settled property and not at that time ceasing to be settled property is deemed to be disposed of and immediately reacquired by the trustee at that time for a consideration equal to the whole or a corresponding part of the market value of the asset. However, any gain arising on such a deemed disposal is not a chargeable gain. [*TCGA 1992, s 72(1)*].

(*b*)   The provisions in (*a*) above also apply where the person entitled to a life interest in possession in all or part of settled property dies although the interest does not then terminate. [*TCGA 1992, s 72(2)*]. This situation could occur where the person for whose benefit the interest was created had previously disposed of his interest under 52.8 above to the deceased and was still living at the date of death. The foregoing also contemplates interests created *pur autre vie*, i.e based on the life of another.

Annuities which are not life interests. Sub-paragraph (*a*) above also applies where an annuity which is not a life interest within 52.7 above is terminated by the death of the annuitant. Similarly, sub-paragraph (*b*) above applies where the annuitant dies although the annuity does not then terminate. [*TCGA 1992, s 75*]. In the case where the annuity is not paid out of specified funds, the Revenue treat the 'corresponding part' (see (*a*) above) of the assets forming the settled property as being given by the proportion which the amount of the annuity bears to the whole of the settlement income arising in the year prior to the date of death.

Part interests and income interests. For the purposes of (*a*) and (*b*) above, a life interest which is a right to part of the income of settled property is treated as a life interest in a corresponding part of the settled property. If there is a life interest in income in a part of settled property such that there is no right of recourse to, or to the income from, the remainder of the settled property, then the part of the settled property in which the life interest subsists is similarly treated as being settled property under a separate settlement for so long as the life interest subsists. [*TCGA 1992, s 72(1)(5)*].

Interests in possession which are not life interests. For all cases which are settled after 16 February 1993, the Revenue will extend (subject to *TCGA 1992, ss 67* and *74* below) concessionally the treatment statutorily afforded by *TCGA 1992, s 72* above regarding life interests to interests in possession which are not life interests. Where the property remains settled property, the concession can be claimed on the subsequent disposal of that property (except where there is a charge on that disposal under *TCGA 1992, s 67* or *74* in respect of a held-over gain (see below)) but in cases where there is an amount of outstanding chargeable gain which was held over when the property was transferred to the trustees, that amount must be deducted from the market value of the property at the date of death. If the concession is claimed, it must apply to all of the assets in which the deceased had an interest in possession, other than any assets which are covered by agreements made before 17 February 1993 or subject to a charge under *TCGA 1992, s 67* or *74* (Revenue Pamphlet IR 1, D43).

Exception where hold-over relief under TCGA 1992, s 165 or 260 or FA 1980, s 79 claimed previously. In certain circumstances where a claim has been made for hold-over relief in respect of the disposal of an asset to the trustee and, subsequently, the trustee is deemed to dispose of and immediately reacquire the asset so that under *TCGA 1992, s 72* above there would otherwise be no chargeable gain arising, it is specifically provided by *TCGA 1992, s 67* or *74* that a chargeable gain, restricted to the amount of the held-over gain, is to accrue to the trustee. See 22.2, 22.5 and 22.6 HOLD-OVER RELIEFS.

52.11   **TERMINATION OF LIFE INTEREST ON DEATH OF PERSON ENTITLED: PERSON BECOMING ABSOLUTELY ENTITLED**

The following provisions apply after 5 April 1982 and are subject to the exception below.

(*a*)   Where, under 52.9 above, the assets forming part of any settled property are deemed to be disposed of and reacquired at market value by the trustee on the occasion when a person becomes, or would but for a disability become, absolutely entitled thereto as against the trustee then, if that occasion is the termination of a life interest by the death of the person entitled to that interest (e.g. a life tenant)

(i)   no chargeable gain accrues on the deemed disposal; and

(ii)   if on the death the property reverts to the disponer (e.g. the original settlor), the disposal and reacquisition by the trustee is treated as taking place on a 'no gain, no loss' basis, and if the acquisition by the trustee was at a time prior to 6 April 1965, the reversion is related back to that date.

52.11 Settlements

(b)   Where the life interest is an interest in part only of the settled property to which a person becomes absolutely entitled, (a)(i) above does not apply but although a chargeable gain will accordingly arise as under 52.9 above it is reduced by a proportion corresponding to that represented by the part in which the life interest subsisted. Any remaining chargeable gain may be the subject of a claim for HOLD-OVER RELIEFS (22) but note the general relief for gifts in 22.6 was only extant after 5 April 1982 and before 14 March 1989.

[*TCGA 1992, s 73(1)(2)*].

Annuities which are not life interests. The provisions in (*a*) and (*b*) above also apply where an annuity which is not a life interest within 52.7 above is terminated by the death of the annuitant. [*TCGA 1992, s 75*]. In a case where the annuity is not paid out of specified funds, the Revenue treat the 'proportion corresponding to that represented by the part in which the life interest subsisted' (see (*b*) above) as being given by the proportion which the amount of the annuity bears to the whole of the settlement income arising in the year prior to the date of death.

Part interests and income interests. For the purposes of (*b*) above, a life interest which is a right to part of the income of settled property is treated as a life interest in a corresponding part of the settled property. If there is a life interest in income in a part of the settled property such that there is no right of recourse to, or to the income from, the remainder of the settled property, then the part of the settled property in which the life interest subsists is treated as being settled property under a separate settlement for so long as the life interest subsists. [*TCGA 1992, s 73(3)*].

Interests in possession which are not life interests. For all cases which are settled after 16 February 1993, the Revenue will extend (subject to *TCGA 1992, ss 67* and *74* below) concessionally the treatment statutorily afforded by *TCGA 1992, s 73* above regarding life interests to interests in possession which are not life interests. If the concession is claimed, it must apply to all of the assets in which the deceased had an interest in possession, other than any assets which are covered by agreements made before 17 February 1993 or subject to a charge under *TCGA 1992, s 67* or *74* (Revenue Pamphlet IR 1, D43).

Exception where hold-over relief under TCGA 1992, s 165 or 260 or FA 1980, s 79 claimed previously. In certain circumstances where a claim has been made for hold-over relief in respect of the disposal of an asset to the trustee and, subsequently, the trustee is deemed to dispose of and immediately reacquire the asset so that under *TCGA 1992, s 73* above there would otherwise be no chargeable gain arising, it is specifically provided by *TCGA 1992, s 67* or *74* that a chargeable gain, restricted to the amount of the held-over gain, is to accrue to the trustee. See 22.2, 22.5 and 22.6 HOLD-OVER RELIEFS.

53 Shares and Securities

Cross-references. See 3 ANTI-AVOIDANCE for certain provisions which apply to share disposals; 4.5 APPEALS for appeals regarding values of unquoted shares; 6.2 ASSETS for location of shares; 7 ASSETS HELD ON 6 APRIL 1965 generally; 8 ASSETS HELD ON 31 MARCH 1982 generally; 13 COMPANIES generally; 16.10 DISPOSAL for options to acquire shares; 18.5 EXEMPTIONS AND RELIEFS for meaning of 'debt on a security'; 21 GOVERNMENT SECURITIES; 22 HOLD-OVER RELIEFS for relief in respect of gifts of shares in certain cases and transfers to companies in exchange for shares; 23 INDEXATION for detailed identification rules for shares after 5 April (or 31 March) 1982; 35 LOSSES for reliefs available for losses arising from certain share disposals and for negligible value claims for certain securities specifically and securities generally; 36 MARKET VALUE generally; 38 MINERAL ROYALTIES for shares in companies deriving their value from exploration etc. rights; 39 OVERSEAS MATTERS for shares in certain overseas resident companies and funds; 44 QUALIFYING CORPORATE BONDS; 45 REINVESTMENT IN SHARES RELIEF, 48 RETIREMENT RELIEF and 50 ROLLOVER RELIEF for relief where shares etc. are held in certain companies; and 57 UNIT AND INVESTMENT TRUSTS.

53.1   Share identification rules are given generally in 53.2–53.4 below. The reorganisation of share capital (e.g. bonus and rights issues, amalgamations, reconstructions and conversions) is covered in 53.5–53.12; capital distributions in 53.13 and 53.14; company purchasing own shares in 53.15; shares acquired by employees in 53.16; enterprise investment scheme in 53.17; business expansion scheme in 53.18; the accrued income scheme and certain financial instruments in 53.19; personal equity plans in 53.20 and miscellaneous aspects in 53.21 to 53.26.

53.2   **IDENTIFICATION RULES — DISPOSALS POST-FA 1985**

For disposals after 5 April 1985 (31 March 1985 for companies), the identification of 'securities' is governed by the provisions in 23.9–23.11 INDEXATION.

For the position where quoted and unquoted securities were held on 6 April 1965, see 7.2–7.7 and 7.9–7.12 ASSETS HELD ON 6 APRIL 1965.

Identification rules for disposals of 'relevant securities' are not as above but are as detailed in 23.12 INDEXATION.

53.3   **IDENTIFICATION RULES — DISPOSALS POST-FA 1982 AND PRE-FA 1985**

For disposals after 5 April 1982 (31 March 1982 for companies) but before 6 April 1985 (1 April 1985 for companies), the identification of 'securities' disposed of was governed by the provisions in 23.13–23.16 INDEXATION for securities generally.

For the position where quoted and unquoted securities were held on 6 April 1965, see 7.2–7.7 and 7.9–7.12 ASSETS HELD ON 6 APRIL 1965 respectively.

For companies, an alternative method ('parallel pooling') was available to identify 'qualifying securities' which are disposed of after 31 March 1982 and before 1 April 1985 with securities of the same kind acquired previously. See 23.17 INDEXATION.

53.4   **IDENTIFICATION RULES — DISPOSALS PRE-FA 1982**

Prior to 6 April 1982 (1 April 1982 for companies), any number of 'securities' of the same class acquired after 6 April 1965 and held by one person in one capacity was deemed to form a single asset. A disposal of some of the securities held was treated as a part disposal, the allowable expenditure of the securities disposed of being taken as a proportionate part of the total allowable expenditure of all the securities in the holding, i.e. a 'pooling' treatment applied. The proportion was given by the part disposal fraction, $A/(A + B)$, as in 16.6 DISPOSAL. Securities with restricted rights of disposal (e.g. those issued under a share option scheme) formed a separate pool for as long as the restrictions lasted. The pooling procedure was not to affect the manner in which market value was to be ascertained. [*CGTA 1979, s 65(1)-(3), (5)(6)*].

For the position where quoted and unquoted securities were held on 6 April 1965, see 7.2–7.7 and 7.9–7.12 ASSETS HELD ON 6 APRIL 1965 respectively.

Securities of a particular kind disposed of on a particular day were matched with securities of the same kind acquired on the same day by the same person in the same capacity, and the 'pooling' rules of *CGTA 1979, s 65* above did not apply for this purpose. If more securities were disposed of than acquired on a particular day, and the excess could neither be identified with securities held on or acquired before 6 April 1965, nor be treated as diminishing a holding under *CGTA 1979, s 65* above, that excess was matched pro rata with a subsequent acquisition or acquisitions, taking the earliest first. [*CGTA 1979, s 66(1)(2)*].

'*Securities*' for the above purposes meant shares (which included stock), or securities of a company, or any other assets (except GOVERNMENT SECURITIES (21)) where they were of a nature to be dealt in without identifying the particular assets disposed of or acquired. Securities were not treated as being of the same kind unless they were treated as being of the same class of any one company by a recognised UK or overseas stock exchange or would have been so treated if dealt with on such a stock exchange. Shares or debentures comprised in any letter of allotment or similar instrument were treated as issued unless the right to the shares or debentures thereby conferred remained provisional until accepted, and there was no acceptance. [*CGTA 1979, ss 64, 65(2)(7), 66(3)(4)*].

53.5   REORGANISATION OF SHARE CAPITAL

A '*reorganisation*' (i.e. a 'reorganisation' or 'reduction' of a company's share capital) does not normally constitute a disposal, the '*original shares*' and the '*new holding*' being treated as acquired at the same date as the original shares, any additional consideration given by the shareholder at the time of reorganisation (e.g. as a subscription for a rights issue: see 53.7 below) being added to the cost of the original holding for the purpose of computing the unindexed (or, before 6 April 1985 (1 April 1985 for companies), the gross gain). See 23.6 INDEXATION for the calculation of indexation allowance in respect of the additional consideration.

For this purpose

(a)   '*original shares*' means shares held before and concerned in the reorganisation, and

(b)   '*new holding*' means, in relation to any original shares, the shares in and debentures of the company which, following the reorganisation, represent the original shares and any remaining original shares.

[*TCGA 1992, ss 126(1), 127*].

The surrender, cancellation or alteration of the original holding or the rights attached thereto; and any consideration met out of the assets of the company (e.g. on a bonus issue) or represented by a dividend or other distribution declared but not paid are not regarded as 'additional consideration' for the above purpose. Similarly, in the case of a reorganisation occurring after 9 March 1981, any consideration given, otherwise than by way of a bargain made at arm's-length, for part or all of the new holding will be disregarded, to the extent that its amount or value exceeds the amount by which the market value of the new holding, immediately after the reorganisation, exceeds the market value of the original shares immediately before the reorganisation. (See also *CIR v Burmah Oil Co. Ltd HL 1981, 54 TC 200.*) [*TCGA 1992, s 128(1)(2)*].

The Revenue have expressed their views on when an open offer is treated as a share reorganisation. An open offer is where a company invites its shareholders to subscribe for shares subject to a minimum entitlement based on their existing holdings, and possibly enabling them to also subscribe for shares which other shareholders do not want. For capital gains tax purposes the Revenue will treat any subscription for shares, which is equal to or less than the shareholder's minimum entitlement, as a share reorganisation. Any shares subscribed for in excess of the minimum entitlement will be treated as a separate acquisition (Revenue Tax Bulletin, August 1994, p 148).

Where, on a reorganisation, a person receives (or is deemed to receive), or becomes entitled to receive, any consideration, other than the new holding, for the disposal of an interest in the original shares, and in particular

(i)   where under *TCGA 1992, s 122* he is to be treated as if he had in consideration of a capital distribution disposed of an interest in the original shares (see 53.13 below and note the procedure where the amount of the capital distribution is small or exceeds the allowable expenditure attaching to the original shares),

(ii)   where he receives (or is deemed to receive) consideration from other shareholders in respect of a surrender of rights derived from the original shares,

he is treated as if the new holding resulted from his having for that consideration disposed of an interest (but without prejudice to the original shares and the new holding being treated in accordance with *TCGA 1992, s 127* above as the same asset. [*TCGA 1992, s 128(3)*].

For transactions between companies in the same group, see 13.11 COMPANIES.

Reorganisations covered by the provisions. '*Reorganisation*' for the purposes above includes the making of bonus and rights issues of shares or debentures in proportion to the original holdings, the reduction of share capital and the alteration of rights attaching to the original shares. [*TCGA 1992, s 126(1)(2)*]. See also *Dunstan v Young Austen Young Ltd CA 1988, 61 TC 448*. Unit trusts schemes are treated similarly to companies but see 57.1 UNIT AND INVESTMENT TRUSTS for the disapplication of the above provisions as regards collective investment schemes entitling participants to exchange rights in one part of a scheme property for rights in another. [*TCGA 1992, s 99*].

'*Reduction*' of share capital for the purposes above does not include the paying off of redeemable share capital, and where shares in a company are redeemed by the company otherwise than by the issue of shares or debentures (with or without other consideration) and otherwise than in a liquidation, the shareholder is treated as disposing of the shares at the time of the redemption. [*TCGA 1992, s 126(3)*].

Alternative rules apply to the reorganisation of share capital involving qualifying corporate bonds. See 44.3 QUALIFYING CORPORATE BONDS.

In certain cases involving RETIREMENT RELIEF (48.4) or, for disposals after 15 March 1993 and before 30 November 1993, REINVESTMENT IN SHARES RELIEF (45.10) an election may be made for the reorganisation to be treated as an actual disposal and reacquisition.

53.5   Shares and Securities

See also 53.17 and 53.18 below for reorganisations where enterprise investment scheme relief or business expansion scheme relief has been given respectively.

Valuation of different classes of share on subsequent disposal. Where the new holding consists of more than one class of share, security, debenture, etc. none of which is quoted on a recognised stock exchange within three months of the reorganisation, the allowable acquisition cost is arrived at on the basis of the market value of the various classes at the date of a chargeable disposal of the new holding or part thereof. This also applies where consideration, other than the new holding, is received as in *TCGA 1992, s 128(3)* above. [*TCGA 1992, ss 128(4), 129*].

However, in the case of shares and securities any one class or more of which is or are quoted on a recognised stock exchange (within *ICTA 1988, s 841*) in the UK or elsewhere (or, in the case of unit trust rights, of which the prices were published daily by the managers) within three months after the reorganisation takes effect (or such longer time as the Board may allow), the base value is determined *once and for all* by reference to the respective market value, on the first day on which the market values or prices of the shares are quoted or published (whether published before or after the actual reorganisation). The provisions apply, mutatis mutandis, to the reorganisation of rights under unit trusts. See 57 UNIT AND INVESTMENT TRUSTS. A reorganisation which involves the allotment of holdings is deemed to take effect on the day following the day on which the right to renounce any allotment expires. [*TCGA 1992, s 130*].

For the application of the indexation provisions to holdings of shares arising out of these rules, see 23.6, 23.10, 23.11 and 23.16 INDEXATION.

Assets held on 6 April 1965. See 7.7 and 7.12 ASSETS HELD ON 6 APRIL 1965 for certain situations that may still arise in relation to reorganisations.

Example

A Ltd, an unquoted company, was incorporated in 1988 with an authorised share capital of £50 million denominated into 500 million Ordinary Shares of 10p each, of which 300 million were issued at par on incorporation. In 1995, the directors decide to reorganise the company's share capital by issuing the balance of the authorised share capital in the form of a bonus issue of 200 million Ordinary Shares of 10p so that two such shares are issued for every three of such shares already held. The 500 million Ordinary Shares of 10p each in issue are then consolidated into 50 million New Ordinary Shares of £1 each. A rights issue is then made on the basis of one 7% Cumulative Preference Share of £1 issued at par for every five New Ordinary Shares of £1 already held.

X was issued 90,000 Ordinary Shares of 10p on incorporation and has held them continually since then. Assuming he takes up the rights issue, his new holding after the reorganisation is as follows.

	No. of shares	Par value	Cost £
Original holding: 10p Ords	90,000	10p	9,000
Bonus issue: 10p Ords	60,000	10p	Nil
	150,000		£9,000
Consolidation: 10p Ords to £1			
New Ords	15,000	£1	9,000
Rights issue: £1 Prefs	3,000	£1	3,000
Cost of complete new holding			£12,000

X disposes of 1,500 £1 Prefs in 1995 when each such share is worth £3 and each £1 New Ord is worth £1.80. The apportionment is as follows

		£
Total value of £1 Prefs: (£3 × 3,000)	=	9,000
Total value of £1 New Ords: (£1.80 × 15,000)	=	27,000
		£36,000

Proportional value of £1 Prefs × original cost

$$\frac{9}{36} \times £12,000 \qquad = \qquad £3,000$$

Allowable cost of 1,500 £1 Prefs (£3,000 ÷ 2)	=	£1,500

Note. If X later disposes of the remainder (1,500) of the £1 Prefs when their value is £4 each and that of the £1 Ords is £2 each, the calculation will be made as follows

		£
Total value of £1 Prefs: (£4 × 1,500)	=	6,000
Total value of £1 Ords: (£2 × 15,000)	=	30,000
		£36,000

Original cost (as reduced by previous disposal)	=	£10,500

Proportional value of £1 Prefs × original cost

$$\frac{6}{36} \times £10,500 \qquad = \qquad £1,750$$

Allowable cost of 1,500 £1 Prefs	=	£1,750

53.6   **Bonus issues.** These are treated as a reorganisation within 53.5 above but see 53.12 below for stock dividends.

In practice, where a bonus issue follows a repayment of share capital (e.g. under *ICTA 1988, s 210*), and is treated as income of the recipient, the amount of that income net of basic rate tax is treated as the acquisition cost of the new shares (CCAB Statement June 1968).

Example

X plc, a quoted company, makes a bonus issue in September 1995 of one preference share for every eight ordinary shares held. On first trading after issue, the preference shares were valued at £10 and the ordinary shares at £6.

Mr A had purchased 1,000 ordinary shares in December 1994 for £7,000. After the issue of preference shares, the allowable expenditure on a subsequent disposal of the ordinary and preference shares is computed as follows.

	£
Initial value of preference shares (125 × £10)	1,250
Initial value of ordinary shares (1,000 × £6)	6,000
Total	£7,250

Allowable cost of 1,000 ordinary shares	$\dfrac{6,000}{7,250} \times £7,000$	=	£5,790
Allowable cost of 125 preference shares	$\dfrac{1,250}{7,250} \times £7,000$	=	£1,210

53.7 **Rights issues.** These are treated as reorganisations within 53.5 above.

Where a person receives or becomes entitled to receive in respect of any shares in or debentures of a company a provisional allotment or shares in or debentures of the company and he disposes of his rights, *TCGA 1992, s 122* applies as if the amount of consideration for the disposal were a capital distribution received by him from the company in respect of the first-mentioned shares or debentures, and as if he had, instead of disposing of the rights, disposed of an interest in those shares or debentures. [*TCGA 1992, s 123*].

See 53.13 below for *TCGA 1992, s 122* and note the procedure where the amount of the capital distribution is small or exceeds the allowable expenditure attaching to the original shares etc.

Example

W plc is a quoted company which in June 1988 made a rights issue of one £1 ordinary share for every eight £1 ordinary shares held, at £1.35 payable on allotment. V, who held 16,000 £1 ordinary shares purchased in May 1982 for £15,000, took up his entitlement in full, and was allotted 2,000 shares. In December 1995, he sells 6,000 of his shares for £12,000.

Indexation factors May 1982 to April 1985 (actual)	0.161
April 1985 to June 1988 (actual)	0.125
June 1988 to December 1995 (assumed)	0.371

New holding	Shares	Qualifying expenditure £	Indexed pool £
May 1982 acquisition	16,000	15,000	15,000
Indexed rise: May 1982 – April 1985 £15,000 × 0.161			2,415
Pool at 6.4.85	16,000	15,000	17,415
Indexed rise: April 1985 – June 1988 £17,415 × 0.125			2,177
June 1988 rights issue	2,000	2,700	2,700
	18,000	17,700	22,292
Indexed rise: June 1988 – December 1995 £22,292 × 0.371			8,270
			30,562
December 1995 disposal	(6,000)	(5,900)	(10,187)
Pool carried forward	12,000	£11,800	£20,375

Calculation of chargeable gain	£
Disposal consideration	12,000

Allowable cost $\dfrac{6,000}{18,000} \times £17,700$ — 5,900

Unindexed gain	6,100
Indexation allowance	

$$\dfrac{6,000}{18,000} \times £30,562 = £10,187$$

$£10,187 - £5,900$	4,287
Chargeable gain	£1,813

53.8   **Exchange of securities for those in another company.** (See also 13.6 COMPANIES).
The same treatment as under 53.5 above is applied to shares or debentures issued in
exchange for the shares or debentures of a company by another company which in consequence of the exchange will hold more than 25% of the 'ordinary share capital' or, in
relation to exchanges made after 31 December 1991, more than 50% of the voting
power of the first company. Similar treatment applies where the second company issues
the shares, etc. in exchange for those of the first company as the result of a general offer
made to the shareholders of the first company (or any class of them), provided that the
offer was initially made on a condition which, if satisfied, would give the first company
control of the second. This covers abortive takeover bids which become unconditional,
but which do not succeed. [*TCGA 1992, s 135; F(No 2)A 1992, s 35*].

See 57.1 UNIT AND INVESTMENT TRUSTS for the application of this provision as regards
collective investment schemes entitling participants to exchange rights in one part of a
scheme for rights in another.

For the tax consequences of a share exchange within a group of companies, see *Westcott v
Woolcombers Ltd CA 1987, 60 TC 575* and *NAP Holdings UK Ltd v Whittles HL [1994]
STC 979*. See 13.11 COMPANIES for a commentary on the position but note the law was
changed for intra-group transactions after 14 March 1988.

'Ordinary share capital' means all the issued share capital (by whatever name called) of a
company, other than that which produces a fixed rate of dividend and is non-participating. [*ICTA 1988, s 832(1)*].

Earn-outs. A concessionary treatment (published on 26 April 1988 and available in all
cases where liabilities had not then been finally determined) applies where a takeover,
etc. takes the form of an exchange of shares or securities but part of the deal consists of
an 'earn-out' element, i.e., of shares or securities issued at some future date, for example
if a profit target is met. Where such an agreement creates a right to an unascertainable
element (whether or not subject to a maximum) against the purchaser which is acquired
by the vendor at the time of disposal and that right falls, under the terms of the
agreement, to be satisfied wholly by the issue of shares or debentures, then, notwithstanding a concurrent right to consideration other than in the form of shares or
debentures, the Revenue are prepared to treat the right to shares or debentures in the
hands of the vendor as a security (within 53.10 below) issued by the purchasing
company, provided that

(*a*)   the vendor so claims before his liability in respect of the sale of the shares or
debentures is finally determined; and

(*b*) as a consequence of its being so treated *TCGA 1992, s 135* would apply to the disposal of the shares or debentures; and

(*c*) any vendor who so claims undertakes to accept this treatment for all capital gains tax purposes.

In determining whether *TCGA 1992, s 135* would apply, regard will be had to the anti-avoidance rules below. If a right falls to be treated as a security and subsequently is satisfied by shares or debentures issued, in accordance with the sale agreement, by the purchasing company to the vendor, the Revenue will treat that issue as a conversion of securities within 53.10 below.

As a transitional measure, where, before 26 April 1988 a right was acquired under which the vendor could receive cash or some other alternative, and a maximum amount for the consideration was specified in the agreement, it will be possible to treat the consideration as if it were ascertainable in that maximum amount even though the cash alternative exists. Subject to a claim by the vendor and to the anti-avoidance rules below, *TCGA 1992, s 135* will therefore be capable of applying to any shares or debentures issued to him by the purchasing company. This concession will also apply where the purchaser is itself subsequently purchased by another company not in the same group, and the vendor's rights against the purchaser are exchanged for similar rights against that other company, or where there is a subsequent variation in the terms of the original sale agreement, provided the conditions in this concession would have been met in either case had the change been part of the original arrangements (Revenue Pamphlet IR 1, D 27, revised by Revenue Press Release of 20 October 1994).

Notwithstanding the requirement in the concession for the element of deferred consideration to be wholly in 'paper' form, the Revenue are prepared to apply the concession to a separate part of the element of deferred consideration so long as that part is to be satisfied (and can only be satisfied) by the issue of paper without a cash option (Taxation 10 August 1989 p 571).

The above concessionary treatment mitigates the effect of the judgment in *Marren v Ingles HL 1980, 54 TC 76* (see 16.7 DISPOSAL).

Example

K owns 10,000 ordinary shares in M Ltd, which he acquired for £12,000 in December 1989. In July 1995, the whole of the issued share capital of M Ltd was acquired by P plc. Under the terms of the takeover, K receives £2 per share plus the right to further consideration up to a maximum of £1.50 per share depending on future profit performance. The initial consideration is receivable in cash, but the deferred consideration is to be satisfied by the issue of shares in P plc. In December 1996, K duly receives 2,000 ordinary shares valued at £6 per share in full settlement of his entitlement. The right to future consideration is valued at £1.40 per share in July 1995. The indexation factor for the period December 1989 to July 1995 is assumed to be 0.314.

Without a claim by K under Inland Revenue extra-statutory concession D27 the position would be

1995/96

	£	£
Disposal proceeds 10,000 × £2	20,000	
Value of rights 10,000 × £1.40	14,000	34,000
Cost	12,000	
Indexation allowance £12,000 × 0.314	3,768	15,768
Chargeable gain		£18,232

1996/97

	£
Disposal of rights to deferred consideration:	
Proceeds — 2,000 P plc shares @ £6	12,000
Deemed cost of acquiring rights	14,000
Allowable loss	£2,000
Cost for CGT purposes of 2,000 P plc shares	£12,000

On a claim under extra-statutory concession D27, the position would be

1995/96

	£
Proceeds (cash) (as above)	20,000
Cost £12,000 × $\dfrac{20,000}{20,000 + 14,000}$	7,059
Unindexed gain	12,941
Indexation allowance £7,059 × 0.314	2,217
Chargeable gain	£10,724
Cost of rights for CGT purposes (£12,000 − £7,059)	£4,941

1996/97

The shares in P plc stand in the place of the right to deferred consideration and will be regarded as having been acquired in July 1995 for £4,941. No further gain or loss arises until a disposal of the shares takes place.

An extension to the above concession (announced in a Revenue Press Release of 25 July 1990 and available in all cases where the liability for the relevant chargeable period had not then been finally determined) applies to financial concerns who hold shares or securities as trading stocks rather than as capital assets. (Such concerns cannot benefit from the unextended concession because any profits they make on the disposal of shares would be liable to tax as part of their trading profits rather than as a capital gain.) Where *ICTA 1988, s 473* (conversion etc. of securities held as circulating capital not to be treated as disposal of original holding) does not apply to an exchange of shares only because *TCGA 1992, ss 126–136* would not have applied, then, if the taxpayer so claims, it may apply by concession if *TCGA 1992, ss 126–136* would have applied by virtue of the unextended concession above, if it had been claimed. The vendor must claim the benefit of the extension to the concession before his trading profit or loss for the relevant chargeable period is finally determined, and must agree to accept this treatment for all tax purposes (Revenue Pamphlet IR 1, D 27).

Anti-avoidance. TCGA 1992, s 135 does not apply unless the exchange is made for bona fide commercial reasons and does not form part of a scheme or arrangements of which the main purpose, or one of the main purposes, is the avoidance of capital gains tax or corporation tax. In such cases, a chargeable disposal is treated as taking place except where a person to whom the new shares are issued owns (or he and persons connected with him together own) less than 5% of, or any class of, the shares or debentures of the acquired company. There are provisions for advance clearance of an exchange by the Revenue. [*TCGA 1992, ss 137, 138*]. For full coverage see 3.13 ANTI-AVOIDANCE.

53.9   **Schemes of reconstruction or amalgamation involving issue of securities.** Where, under an arrangement entered into for the purposes of such a scheme between a company and its share- or debenture-holders (or any class of them), another company issues shares or debentures to those holders in respect of, or in proportion to (or as nearly as may be in proportion to), their original holdings, which latter are then either 'retained' or cancelled, the new holding is treated as under 53.8 above (without the requirement that the issuing company hold more than 25% of the ordinary share capital, more than 50% of the voting power or have control of the other). [*TCGA 1992, s 136; F(No 2)A 1992, s 35*].

Anti-avoidance. The same anti-avoidance rules apply as in 53.8 above. These rules are fully detailed in 3.13 ANTI-AVOIDANCE.

Example

N Ltd carries on a manufacturing and wholesaling business. In 1989, it was decided that the wholesaling business should be carried on by a separate company. Revenue clearance under what is now *TCGA 1992, s 138* was obtained, and a company, R Ltd, was formed which, in consideration for the transfer to it by N Ltd of the latter's wholesaling undertaking, issued shares to the shareholders of N Ltd. Each holder of ordinary shares in N Ltd received one ordinary share in R Ltd for each N Ltd share he held. W, who purchased his 2,500 N shares for £10,000 in 1986, received 2,500 R shares. None of the shares involved is quoted. In August 1995, W sells 1,500 of his N shares for £6 each, a total of £9,000, agreed to be their market value. The value of W's remaining N shares is also £6 per share, and the value of his R shares is £4.50 per share.

	£
Disposal consideration	9,000

Allowable cost $£10,000 \times \dfrac{9,000}{9,000 + (1,000 \times £6) + (2,500 \times £4.50)}$ ⟶ 3,429

Unindexed gain	£5,571

Note to the example

(*a*)   If the original shares had been held on 31 March 1982, the above fraction would be applied to their 31 March 1982 value for the purposes of the re-basing calculation under *TCGA 1992, s 35*.

53.10   **Conversion of securities.** The provisions outlined in 53.5 above apply *mutatis mutandis* to the *'conversion of securities'*, which phrase includes a conversion of securities of a company into shares in that company; a conversion in lieu of redemption at the option of the holder of the securities; and any exchange of securities in pursuance of compulsory purchase powers.

'Security' includes any loan stock or similar security issued by national or local government or public authority in the UK or elsewhere, or by a company, and whether secured or unsecured. [*TCGA 1992, s 132*]. For 'debt on a security' see 18.5 EXEMPTIONS AND RELIEFS.

A premium in money (in addition to a new holding) on a conversion of securities is treated in virtually identical terms as under *TCGA 1992, s 122* for a capital distribution in 53.13 below. (It would appear that the case of *O'Rourke v Binks CA, [1992] STC 703* mentioned therein applies equally to premiums on conversion within this provision as it does to capital distributions within *TCGA 1992, s 122*.) [*TCGA 1992, s 133*].

Alternative rules apply to the conversion of securities of a company involving qualifying corporate bonds. See 44.3 QUALIFYING CORPORATE BONDS.

See also 57.1 UNIT AND INVESTMENT TRUSTS for the disapplication of *TCGA 1992, s 132* as regards collective investment schemes entitling participants to exchange rights in one part of a scheme for rights in another.

Example

N bought £10,000 8% convertible loan stock in S plc, a quoted company, in June 1986. The cost was £9,800. In August 1990, N exercised his right to convert the loan stock into B' ordinary shares of the company, on the basis of 50 shares for £100 loan stock, and acquired 5,000 shares. In June 1995, N sells 3,000 of the shares for £2.50 each. The indexation factor for June 1986 to June 1995 is assumed to be 0.518.

	£
Disposal consideration	7,500
Cost $\dfrac{3,000}{5,000} \times £9,800$	5,880
Unindexed gain	1,620
Indexation allowance £5,880 × 0.518 = £3,046	
but restricted to	1,620
Chargeable gain	Nil

Notes to the example

(a) The shares acquired on the conversion in 1990 stand in the shoes of the original loan stock. [*TCGA 1992, s 132*].

(b) The loan stock cannot be a corporate bond (and thus cannot be a qualifying corporate bond) as it is convertible into securities other than corporate bonds, i.e. into ordinary shares. [*ICTA 1988, 18 Sch 1(5); TCGA 1992, s 117(1)*].

Compensation stock. Instead of *TCGA 1992, s 132* above applying, gilt-edged securities issued on the compulsory acquisition after 6 April 1976 of shares or securities are treated as acquired on the date of issue (or, if earlier, of compulsory acquisition) at a cost equal to the value of the shares etc. as determined for the purposes of the exchange, which transaction is treated as not involving any disposal of the shares or securities. The gain that would have accrued had the shares or securities been disposed of at that value at that time is not treated as arising until the gilt-edged securities are disposed of, so that it is added to any actual chargeable gain (or deducted from any actual allowable loss) which may, before 2 July 1986, accrue at that time. However, where the gilt-edged securities received are disposed of after 5 April 1988 no addition or deduction is made under this provision if its application would be directly attributable to the disposal of an asset before 1 April 1982.

Before 2 July 1986 disposals were identified as far as possible with similar securities acquired within the preceding twelve months (otherwise than under the above provisions) and thereafter with securities so acquired, taking earlier issues before later ones. The then rules for identifying gilt-edged securities were disregarded for this latter purpose.

After 1 July 1986 (when disposals of gilt-edged securities are exempt *in all cases*) disposals are, so far as possible, identified with gilts issued under the above provisions rather than with other gilts of the same kind and subject to this, with gilts issued at an earlier time rather than with those issued at a later time.

The deferment of the gain otherwise arising on the issue of the gilt-edged securities is extended to the recipient where their later disposal is within *TCGA 1992, ss 58(1)* (spouses), *62(4)* (legatee acquiring asset from personal representatives) and *171(1)*

53.11 Shares and Securities

(groups of companies). [*TCGA 1992, s 134, 4 Sch 4(5); CGTA 1979, s 84; FA 1985, s 67(2)(b); 27 Sch Pt VII*].

53.11 **Quoted option granted following reorganisation.** If a quoted option (within *TCGA 1992, s 144(8)*; see 16.10 DISPOSAL) to subscribe for shares in a company (see 16.10 DISPOSAL) is dealt in (on the stock exchange where it is quoted) within three months after (or such longer period after as may be allowed in written notice by the Revenue) a reorganisation, reduction, conversion or amalgamation (within the provisions in 53.5–53.10 above) relating to the company granting the option, then

(*a*)   the option is regarded for those provisions as the shares which could be acquired following the reorganisation etc. by exercising the option, and

(*b*)   the ordinary market value rules for quoted securities apply (see 36.2 MARKET VALUE).

[*TCGA 1992, s 147*].

53.12 **Stock dividends.** *Individuals.* Issues of shares in lieu of dividend on or before 5 April 1975 were treated as bonus issues, and no allowance for capital gains tax purposes was made for the cash dividend forgone. Issues made by a UK resident company after 5 April 1975 are subject to income tax (see Tolley's Income Tax under Stock Dividends), and the 'appropriate amount in cash' is treated as allowable expenditure for capital gains tax purposes. Thereafter the issue is treated as a reorganisation within 53.5 above where additional consideration is given. [*TCGA 1992, s 141*].

The *'appropriate amount in cash'* is

(*a*)   where the shares are offered as an alternative to a cash dividend, the amount of that cash dividend;

(*b*)   where the shares are offered in a quantity which is determined by, or determines, the amount of a dividend in cash payable in respect of shares in the company of a different class, the amount of that cash dividend;

unless the amount arrived at under (*a*) or (*b*) above is substantially (i.e. 15% or more; 29.A8 INLAND REVENUE STATEMENTS OF PRACTICE) greater or less than the market value of the shares, when the latter is substituted. Market value is also used in any other case. [*ICTA 1988, ss 249(1), 251(2)-(4)*]. If two or more persons are entitled to the shares issued, those shares (and the appropriate amount in cash) are apportioned among them by reference to their interests in the shares at the date of issue. [*ICTA 1988, s 249(3)*].

Close companies. The appropriate amount in cash relating to shares issued in lieu of a dividend made by a UK resident company to a close company in accounting periods ending before 1 April 1989 were treated as part of its apportionable income for income tax purposes, and any income tax in respect of such income apportioned (but not paid) to a participator can be added to his allowable expenditure, for capital gains tax purposes, on a disposal of shares in the close company. The close company's allowable expenditure in respect of the shares was increased by the appropriate amount in cash. [*CGT 1979, s 89; TCGA 1992, s 124; ICTA 1988, 19 Sch 12; FA 1989, 17 Sch Pt V*]. See further in 53.21 below. There is no addition to allowable expenditure of the shares held for later accounting periods or, for any accounting period, where the shares are held by a non-close company.

Settlements and personal representatives. Where a beneficiary is to be treated as receiving income as a result of shares issued to the trustees of a discretionary or accumulation (and, in certain circumstances, in the view of the Revenue (see ICAEW Faculty of Taxation Memorandum Tax 17/93, 29 September 1993), an interest in possession) settlement, the appropriate amount in cash is added to the trustees' allowable expenditure, for capital gains tax purposes. A similar provision applies to personal representatives. In the case of nominees or bare trustees, the income and the allowable expenditure are treated as that of the person absolutely entitled. However, the stock dividend is not treated as a reorganisation, the shares represented by the dividend being treated as a new acquisition by that person. [*TCGA 1992, ss 141, 142; ICTA 1988, s 249(4)-(6)*].

There is some doubt as to whether the Revenue's view that *ICTA 1988, s 249* can apply to an interest in possession settlement is correct, such view proceeding on principles of both trust and tax law. See Taxation, 17 June 1993 p 261, 4 November 1993 p 104 and 6 January 1994, p 274 and Law Society's Gazette, 28 July 1993 p 17. The Revenue issued Statement of Practice SP 4/94 on 17 May 1994 setting out their views on the tax treatment of enhanced stock dividends received by trustees of interest in possession trusts. They are prepared to treat such dividends in accordance with the wishes of the trustees. Where the dividend is to be regarded as capital, the issue is a reorganisation within *TCGA 1992, s 126* and the trustees are not regarded as having made any payment for the shares. Where trustees pay compensation to a beneficiary in the form of shares for forgoing the cash dividend alternative, the transfer constitutes a part disposal of the new holding.

53.13   CAPITAL DISTRIBUTIONS

A capital distribution (other than of a new holding within 53.5 above), on liquidation or otherwise (defined as any distribution in money or money's worth by a company to a shareholder, which is not treated as income for tax purposes) is treated as accruing to him from the disposal of an interest in the shares. [*TCGA 1992, s 122(1)(5)*].

If the amount or value of the capital distribution is small (5% or less in the view of the Revenue; see withdrawn Revenue Pamphlet CGT 8, para 118, but in *O'Rourke v Binks* below it was said *obiter* that the comparison would have to be determined on the facts of each case but that 15% was excessive), as compared with the value of the shares in respect of which it is made, then the inspector may direct that the capital distribution not be treated as a disposal, in which case no immediate capital gains tax liability arises, but the proceeds are deducted from the acquisition cost of the shares on a subsequent disposal. [*TCGA 1992, s 122(2)*].

If the inspector refuses such a direction, the taxpayer may appeal. [*TCGA 1992, s 122(3)*]. Also, if it would be to the taxpayer's advantage for such a direction *not* to be made (for example, where the gain would be covered by the annual exemption), the Revenue will not insist on the application of *section 122(2)* (Revenue Tax Bulletin, November 1992 p 46).

Where the amount or value of the capital distribution exceeds any allowable expenditure on the shares, the taxpayer may elect to have *all* such expenditure set against the distribution with the balance of the distribution being treated as on a part disposal and the expenditure deducted not allowable on that or any subsequent disposal. [*TCGA 1992, s 122(4)*]. In *O'Rourke v Binks CA, [1992] STC 703* it was held that the right to make the election under *TCGA 1992, s 122(4)* was constrained by the requirement of *TCGA 1992, s 122(2)* that the amount or value of the capital distribution be small as compared with the value of the shares in respect of which it was made.

Income tax charges under *ICTA 1988, s 186(3)* (approved profit sharing schemes—see Tolley's Income Tax under Share Incentives and Options) are to be disregarded in determining whether a distribution is a capital distribution. [*TCGA 1992, s 238(2)(b)*].

Example

T holds 10,000 ordinary shares in a foreign company M SA. The shares were bought in April 1983 for £80,000. In February 1996, M SA has a capital reconstruction involving the cancellation of one-fifth of the existing ordinary shares in consideration of the repayment of £10 to each shareholder per share cancelled. T's holding is reduced to 8,000 shares, valued at £96,000. The indexation factor for April 1983 to February 1996 is assumed to be 0.848.

	£
Disposal consideration (2,000 × £10)	20,000
Allowable cost $\dfrac{20,000}{20,000 + 96,000} \times £80,000$	13,793
Unindexed gain	6,207
Indexation allowance £13,793 × 0.848 = £11,696	
but restricted to	6,207
Chargeable gain	Nil
The allowable cost of the remaining shares is £80,000 − £13,793	£66,207

53.14 **Distributions in a liquidation: unquoted shares.** Instead of requiring a strict valuation of unquoted shares for the purposes of the part disposal arising on a distribution, the Revenue are prepared to accept a reasonable estimate of the residual value of the shares if the liquidation is expected to be completed within two years of the first distribution. If the distribution takes longer, the valuations may be reopened. Where time apportionment (see 7.9 et seq. ASSETS HELD ON 6 APRIL 1965) applies, the Revenue are prepared to calculate the gain on each distribution by applying the time apportionment fraction as at the date of the first distribution (29.D3 INLAND REVENUE STATEMENTS OF PRACTICE).

53.15 **COMPANY PURCHASING OWN SHARES**

Any consideration given by a company for the redemption, repayment or purchase of its own shares, *except* insofar as it represents repayment of share capital, is normally treated as a distribution, and hence as income in the hands of the recipient (see Tolley's Corporation Tax under Distributions). Such payments after 5 April 1982 in respect of shares in certain unquoted trading companies (or holding companies) are *not* treated as distributions, and thus give rise to liability to capital gains tax (or corporation tax on chargeable gains) on the recipient in the normal way. See Tolley's Corporation Tax under Company Purchasing Own Shares for detailed conditions. [*ICTA 1988, ss 219-229*].

Where the recipient is a dealer in securities, any payment after 5 April 1982 by a company for the redemption, repayment or purchase of its own shares, or of rights to acquire those shares, is treated as trading income of the recipient. [*ICTA 1988, s 95*].

In relation to purchases after 19 April 1989, if the purchase of its own shares by a UK resident company gives rise to a distribution, and the shareholder receiving such a distribution is itself a company, the Revenue's practice is to include the distribution in the consideration for the disposal of the shares for the purposes of the charge to corporation tax on chargeable gains. In the Revenue's view the effect of *ICTA 1988, ss 208, 345(3)* is that the distribution does not suffer a tax charge as income within the terms of

TCGA 1992, s 37(1) (see 30.1 INTERACTION WITH OTHER TAXES) (Revenue Statement of Practice SP 4/89, 19 April 1989).

53.16   **SHARES ACQUIRED BY EMPLOYEES**

Legislation relating to income tax applies where there are arrangements to allow employees to acquire shares in their employing companies (as to which, see Tolley's Income Tax under Share Incentives and Options). Capital gains tax provisions specific to such arrangements are as follows.

See also 16.10 DISPOSAL and 59 WASTING ASSETS for treatment of options generally, which treatment may affect the expenditure relating to the consideration given for any option mentioned below.

See 53.25 below for employee share ownership trusts.

Share options generally. If a gain is realised by the exercise of a right to acquire shares and is subject to income tax under *ICTA 1988, s 135(1)* or *(6)*, the total allowable expenditure in respect of the shares for capital gains tax purposes (see 16.3 DISPOSAL) will consist of

(i)   the open market value of the option at the time the grant was given (as the option is in consideration for services; see 36.1*(f)* MARKET VALUE);

(ii)   the consideration given for the shares acquired on the exercise of the option; and

(iii)   the amount charged to income tax as above.

[*TCGA 1992, s 120(2)(4)(7)*].

Approved share option schemes. If by reason of a receipt of a right to acquire shares an income tax charge arises under *ICTA 1988, s 185(6A)* (*ICTA 1988, s 185(6)* for rights obtained before 1 January 1992) in respect of a right obtained after 5 April 1984 under an approved share option scheme, the allowable expenditure of the shares acquired on an exercise of that right is the sum of the consideration given for the right, the consideration given for the shares and the amount charged to income tax as above. Simplified, for options acquired before 1 January 1992 this normally equates to the market value of the shares at the date of granting the option. For options acquired after 31 December 1991, the allowable expenditure equates to the value at which shares are allowed to be acquired provided such value is not less than 85% of the market value of the shares at the date of granting the option and subject to certain conditions being fulfilled. This treatment applies whether or not the exercise of the right is within the provisions of an approved scheme or whether or not the scheme is approved at the time of the exercise. The ordinary MARKET VALUE (36) rules are removed subject to conditions. [*TCGA 1992, s 120(2)(6)(7); ICTA 1988, s 185; FA 1988, s 89; FA 1991, s 39(3)–(6); FA 1993, s 105*]. Where, under *ICTA 1988, 9 Sch 15*, schemes are allowed to make provision for the release of option rights over one company's shares in consideration of the grant of option rights over another company's shares, any such transaction is not treated as a disposal or acquisition, the new rights and the old rights being treated as the same asset. [*TCGA 1992, s 238(4); ICTA 1988, 9 Sch 15*]. The ordinary market value rules will not apply to tax a company on the market value of an option granted after 15 March 1993 to an employee under an approved scheme. The company will only be assessed to tax on any actual consideration received from the employee (whose capital gains tax treatment is unaffected), for which purpose any value put on his services to the company is to be ignored. [*TCGA 1992, s 149A; FA 1993, s 104*].

Share incentives. Where shares are acquired by employees for less than open market value an income tax charge arises under the normal rules of Schedule E by reference to the difference between the open market value of the shares at that time and the consideration given, if any, for the shares. For acquisitions by an employee of shares *issued* to him by the employer company etc. after 9 March 1981 the allowable expenditure is limited to the consideration given and the usual MARKET VALUE (36) rules do not apply as there is no corresponding disposal. For acquisitions before 10 March 1981 the market value rules did apply in such circumstances. For shares acquired *other than by issue* etc., the market value rules would normally operate whatever the date of acquisition. [*TCGA 1992, s 17(2); CGTA 1979, ss 19(3)(a), 29A(2); FA 1981, s 90(1)(3)(4)*]. There are no provisions to enable any income tax charge arising under Schedule E in the above circumstances to be treated as allowable expenditure so it is advantageous to structure the issue so as to include the grant of an option which is taxed under *ICTA 1988, s 135(1) or (6)* (see above and Tolley's Practical Tax 1991, p 87). If, at the same or a subsequent time, there is a charge to income tax under *FA 1988, ss 78-80* (or, for acquisitions before 26 October 1987, *FA 1972, s 79* or *ICTA 1988, s 138*) on the value of any special benefits conferred or on the difference between the market value of the shares at that subsequent time and their market value at acquisition, this charge *is* treated as allowable expenditure in respect of the shares. [*TCGA 1992, s 120(1)(2)(5)(7)*]. The same treatment also applies to a charge under *ICTA 1988, s 162(5)* (deemed release of notional loan in respect of shares acquired at undervalue). [*TCGA 1992, s 120(2)(3)(7)*].

Savings-related share option schemes. Similar comments to those stated above for approved share option schemes apply save that the value at which shares are allowed to be acquired is not less than 80% (90% for options granted after 14 November 1980 and before 27 July 1989) of the market value of the shares at the date of granting the option. In addition, as regards the treatment of arrangements under *ICTA 1988, 9 Sch 15*, the option had to have been obtained originally after 14 November 1980. [*TCGA 1992, ss 120(2)(6)(7), 149A, 238(4); ICTA 1988, s 185, 9 Sch 15; FA 1988, s 89; FA 1991, s 39(3)–(6); FA 1993, ss 104, 105*].

Profit sharing schemes. Notwithstanding any period of retention or other restriction imposed by an approved profit sharing scheme, the participant who has shares appropriated to him in pursuance of such a scheme is treated as absolutely entitled as against the trustees for capital gains tax purposes. [*TCGA 1992, s 238(1)(3)*]. The trustees following appropriation act as bare trustees (see 52.2 SETTLEMENTS) and consequently the allowable expenditure as regards the participant will be the market value of the shares at the appropriation date or such other date as may be agreed in writing between the Revenue and the trustees. [*ICTA 1988, 9 Sch 30(4)*]. Shares acquired by an employee to whose bare trustee they were *issued* under a profit sharing scheme on terms which restrict his rights to dispose of them are generally prevented from being pooled or identified with disposals of shares carrying unrestricted rights of transferability as long as those restrictions remain in force. In addition, acquisitions are only pooled where the person is acting in the same capacity. [*TCGA 1992, ss 104(1)(4), 107(1)*]. In practice, scheme shares are not pooled with non-scheme shares; see Tolley's Practical Tax 1983 p 16 and p 195. The provisions relating to identification of shares under such schemes do not affect the identification rules relating to the part disposal of such shares. [*TCGA 1992, s 238(2)(c)*]. No allowance is made against capital gains tax for any income tax payable in relation to shares acquired under a scheme. [*TCGA 1992, s 238(2)(a)*]. No chargeable gain (or allowable loss) will arise on the trustees if the shares are appropriated to a participant within eighteen months after the trustees' acquisition thereof. [*TCGA 1992, s 238(2)(d)*].

Priority share allocations in public offers. If a benefit derived by an employee from a priority allocation of shares in a public offer made after 22 September 1987 is exempted from income tax by *FA 1988, s 68*, the usual MARKET VALUE (36) rules do not apply and the allowable expenditure for capital gains tax of the shares will be the consideration given. [*FA 1988, s 68(4)*].

53.17   **ENTERPRISE INVESTMENT SCHEME**

Shares issued after 31 December 1993. For shares issued after 31 December 1993, an individual is able to claim enterprise investment scheme relief in accordance with *ICTA 1988, Pt VII Ch III* as it has effect after that date. The relief is given in the form of a deduction from the individual's income tax liability on his total income for the year of assessment in which the shares are issued. In broad terms, the deduction is an amount equal to the lower of an amount arrived at by multiplying the lower rate of income tax for that year by the amount or aggregate amounts (subject to certain limits) subscribed for '*eligible shares*' (new ordinary shares which throughout the five years from issue have no preferential rights etc.) in the year and the amount which would (ignoring the relief itself) reduce the above liability to nil.

For capital gains tax purposes, if on any disposal of eligible shares by an individual after the end of the period beginning with the incorporation of the company concerned (or, if the company was incorporated more than two years before the date on which the shares were issued, beginning two years before that date) and ending five years after the issue of the shares, then, where an amount of relief is attributable (such attribution and the amount thereof being decided under the provisions of *ICTA 1988, Pt VII Ch III*; in broad terms the relief attributable to any share is the numerical proportion of the reduction, after taking into account any bonus shares, made in the individual's income tax liability referable to the amount subscribed to the issue of shares of which the share is one, more than one issue on any day being treated as one issue, after taking account of any withdrawal or reduction of relief) to the shares and there would otherwise be a gain, that gain is not a chargeable gain (i.e. it is an exempt gain). (This treatment does not apply to a disposal on which a loss accrues, as mentioned below). However, where an individual's income tax liability has been reduced (or treated under *ICTA 1988, s 304* as reduced where eligible shares have been the subject of relief against one spouse's income but have been transferred to the other spouse) for a year of assessment in respect of an issue of shares, and the amount of the reduction is not because the investor's income tax liability was too small to enable the relief to be fully utilised, and the amount of the reduction ('A') is less than the amount ('B') which is equal to the amount arrived at by multiplying the lower rate of income tax for that year by the amount subscribed for that issue, then in respect of any disposal of the shares on which there is a gain, the exemption above only applies to a fractional amount of the gain, that fraction being A/B. The exemption is also restricted where relief attributable to any shares has been partially withdrawn as a result of value received after 28 November 1994, but before disposal, from the company by the investor or another shareholder. The restriction is computed by excluding from the exemption a proportion of the gain equal to the reduction in the relief resulting from the value received.

For the purposes of determining the gain or loss on a disposal of eligible shares by an individual where an amount of relief is attributable to the shares and there would otherwise be a loss, the consideration given for the shares is treated as reduced by the amount of the 'relief' (i.e. the net deduction given against income tax liability as above). If, after this reduction of original consideration, the disposal results in a gain the whole or a fraction of that gain will be exempt as above provided the disposal is after the end of the period specified. If a loss still results after such reduction, the resulting loss is allowable for capital gains tax and may be eligible for relief under *ICTA 1988, s 574* (capital gains tax loss accruing to individual in respect of unquoted shares in a trading company converted to an income tax loss; see 35.12 LOSSES).

Further rules dealing with identification and other matters apply as follows.

(*a*)   The identification rules applying for securities generally do not apply to shares to which relief is attributable. Instead, where any relief is attributable to shares of any class in a company which have been issued to an individual at different times, any disposal of shares of that class is related firstly to the earlier issue rather than the later issue. For this purpose and that in (*d*) below, shares are only treated as being of the same class if they would be so treated if dealt with on the Stock Exchange and the grant of an option the exercise of which would bind the grantor to sell shares is treated as a disposal of those shares.

(*b*)   Where an individual holds shares which form part of the ordinary share capital of a company, and relief is attributable to some of the shares but not others, then, if there is a reorganisation affecting those shares within *TCGA 1992, s 126*, the shares of each kind are treated as a separate holding of old shares and identified, under *TCGA 1992, s 127*, with a separate new holding. See 53.5 above for reorganisations under these provisions.

(*c*)   *TCGA 1992, ss 135, 136* in 53.8 and 53.9 above (company amalgamations and reconstructions) do not apply in respect of shares to which relief is attributable. These disapplications do not apply where the new holding comprises shares issued after 28 November 1994 by a company which had itself previously issued shares to which relief is attributable. The new holding of shares is treated as the same asset as the original holding, provided the new shares are ordinary shares carrying no preferential rights to dividends or assets, or preferential rights of redemption, and they must be issued at least five years after the issue of the original shares.

(*d*)   Where relief is attributable to any shares, a disposal of the whole or part of the new holding, allotted other than for payment as a result of a reorganisation affecting those shares within *TCGA 1992, s 126(2)(a)* (allotments in respect of, and in proportion to, existing holdings or of any class of shares, e.g. with payment, a rights issue or, without payment, a bonus issue) is treated, for the purposes of deciding whether relief is to be reduced or withdrawn, as a disposal of the whole or a corresponding part of those shares with which, by reason of *TCGA 1992, s 127*, the new holding is identified.

(*e*)   The general share reorganisation rules of *TCGA 1992, ss 127–130* (see 53.5–53.7 above) do not apply where

(i)   an individual holds shares which form part of the ordinary share capital of a company ('*the existing holding*'),

(ii)   there is, by virtue of an allotment for payment within *TCGA 1992, s 126(2)(a)*, a reorganisation affecting the existing holding, and

(iii)   immediately following the reorganisation, relief is attributable to the existing holding or the allotted shares.

Where (i) and (ii) above are satisfied, and immediately before the reorganisation for payment an amount of relief ('X') is attributable to the shares in the existing holding and both the amount subscribed for the shares ('Z') and the market value of the shares immediately before the reorganisation ('P') exceed their market value immediately after the reorganisation ('Q'), the relief attributable to the shares is reduced by the amount $(X \times Y)/Z$, where 'Y' is the smaller of the amounts $(Z - Q)$ and $(P - Q)$. This reduction also applies *mutatis mutandis* where the individual sells his rights instead of taking up his allotment. Where the relief is so reduced an amount equal to the reduction is treated as additional allowable expenditure for capital gains tax purposes on a disposal of the allotted shares or debentures and such expenditure is apportioned between the allotted shares in a just and reasonable manner. Where a disposal of any of the shares in the existing holding is not ultimately affected by any of the above provisions (e.g. a withdrawal of relief is made so no relief is attributable to those shares), the allowable expenditure relating to such shares is reduced by an amount equal to the above reduction and is again apportioned in a just and reasonable manner.

Where relief is granted or withdrawn, consequential adjustments may be made to the individual's capital gains tax position. [*TCGA 1992, s 150A–150C; ICTA 1988, ss 289, 289A, 289B, 299, 304, 305, 312(1A)(a); FA 1994, s 137, 15 Sch 2, 12, 18, 19, 27(b), 30; FA 1995, ss 66, 67, 13 Sch 1–3*].

For consideration of the determination of the time shares are issued under the forerunner business expansion scheme, see *National Westminster Bank plc v CIR; Barclays Bank plc v CIR CA 1993, [1994] STC 184.*

Deferred charge on re-investment. *TCGA 1992, s 150C, 5B Sch* (introduced as *FA 1995, 13 Sch 4(1)(3)* by *FA 1995, s 67* applies where:

(*a*)   a chargeable gain accrues to an individual after 28 November 1994 on the disposal of any asset (or on the occurrence of certain events in relation to venture capital trusts, see *TCGA 1992, 5C Sch 4, 5* introduced as *FA 1995, 16 Sch* (see 58.10 VENTURE CAPITAL TRUSTS), or under the current provisions, see below);

(*b*)   the individual makes a 'qualifying investment'; and

(*c*)   the individual is UK resident or ordinarily resident both when the chargeable gain accrues to him and when he makes the 'qualifying investment', and is not, at the latter time, regarded as resident outside the UK for the purposes of any double taxation arrangements the effect of which would be that he would not be liable to tax on a gain arising on a disposal, immediately after their acquisition, of the shares comprising the 'qualifying investment'.

A *'qualifying investment'* is a subscription for shares by reference to which relief is obtained under the enterprise investment scheme, within twelve months (extendible by the Board) before or within three years (extendible by the Board) after the time of the accrual of the chargeable gain in question, and, if before, provided that the shares are still held at that time. The shares are not deemed to be issued by reason only of a letter of allotment.

Broadly, the detailed provisions below allow a claim for the chargeable gain to be rolled over into shares under the enterprise investment scheme, and for the gain to become chargeable on certain events in relation to those shares (including, in particular, on their disposal).

Postponement of original gain. Where a chargeable gain would otherwise accrue to an individual ('the investor') and he acquires a qualifying investment, a claim can be made by him to defer the whole or part of that gain against a corresponding amount of his qualifying investment up to the amount of the gain, or for an amount so claimed, whichever is the smaller. The amount of qualifying investment available for set off is restricted to the amount on which relief has been given under *ICTA 1988, s 289A*, less any amount already utilised against other gains.

Chargeable event. The original gain deferred through the making of the above claim will subsequently crystallise (without any further relief) if one of the following circumstances arise:

(A)   the investor disposes of the shares in his qualifying investment ('the relevant shares') otherwise than under *TCGA 1992, s 58* (an inter-spouse transfer);

(B)   the relevant shares are disposed of by the spouse of the investor (otherwise than by a transfer back to him), the spouse having first acquired them from the investor under *TCGA 1992, s 58*;

(C)   the investor becomes neither resident nor ordinarily resident in the UK whilst holding the relevant shares and within the 'first relevant period';

(D)   an individual who acquired the relevant shares through an inter-spouse transfer under *TCGA 1992, s 58* becomes neither resident nor ordinarily resident in the UK whilst holding those shares and within the 'first relevant period';

(E)   the company which issued the shares ceases to be a 'qualifying company' within the 'second relevant period'; or

(F)   the relief given under *ICTA 1988, s 289A* by reference to relevant shares is withdrawn or reduced in circumstances not falling within (A) to (E) above.

The '*first relevant period*' with regard to relevant shares is that found by applying *ICTA 1988, s 312(1A)(a)* and the '*second relevant period*' is that found in *ICTA 1988, s 312(1A)(b)*. Whether a company is a '*qualifying company*' shall be determined in accordance with *ICTA 1988, s 293*.

In the case of (C) or (D) above, the original gain will not crystallise where the individual concerned became neither resident nor ordinarily resident in the UK through temporarily working abroad and he again becomes UK resident or ordinarily resident in the UK within three years of that event, without having disposed of any of the relevant shares in the meantime. An assessment will be issued by the Revenue when it is clear that the individual will not regain UK resident status within the three year period.

There is no crystallisation of the original gain where an event within (A)–(F) above occurs at or after the time of death of the investor or a person to whom the relevant shares were transferred under *TCGA 1992, s 58*.

Crystallisation of original gain. Where a chargeable event mentioned in (A)–(F) above relating to relevant shares occurs for the first time in connection with those shares, a chargeable gain is deemed to accrue at that time equal to so much of the expenditure on those shares which was set against the original gain.

Identification of shares. In determining whether any shares to which a chargeable gain relates are shares the expenditure on which has been set against the whole or part of any gain, disposals of shares (including transfers under *TCGA 1992, s 58*) are identified with those subscribed for earlier rather than later, and as between shares in a company acquired on the same day, those the expenditure on which has been set against a gain are treated as disposed of after any other shares in that company.

Assets. Where at the time of a chargeable event relevant shares are regarded as represented by assets which consist of or include assets other than relevant shares, the expenditure on those shares is apportioned between those assets on a just and reasonable basis. As between different assets regarded as representing the same relevant shares, the identification of those assets will be determined on a similar basis to the identification of shares.

Persons assessable. The chargeable gain is treated as accruing, as the case may be:

(i)   to the individual who makes the disposal;

(ii)   to the individual who holds the shares in question at the time when the company ceases to be a qualifying company;

(iii)   to the individual who becomes non-UK resident etc.; or

(iv)   to the individual who holds the shares in question when the circumstances arise in respect of which the relief is withdrawn or reduced.

A chargeable gain is computed separately for the investor without reference to any shares held at the time of the chargeable event by a recipient of the investor from a *TCGA 1992, s 58* transfer.

[*TCGA 1992, 5B Sch; FA 1995, 13 Sch 4(1)(3)*].

53.18   **BUSINESS EXPANSION SCHEME**

Shares issued after 18 March 1986 and before 1 January 1994. For shares issued after 18 March 1986 and before 1 January 1994 (from which date relief under the scheme is withdrawn), where an individual to whom relief has been given disposes of the shares and the relief is not withdrawn, the disposal is exempt for capital gains tax. Where *TCGA 1992, s 58* (see 37.6 MARRIED PERSONS) has applied to shares disposed of to a spouse, the exemption applies to a subsequent disposal by that spouse to a third party.

It seems that only a complete withdrawal of relief, and not a partial one, will affect the capital gains tax position, i.e. exemption for a gain, no allowance for a loss (Tolley's Practical Tax 1987, p 115). If relief is withdrawn completely, any allowable loss which results on a disposal of the shares may be eligible for relief under *ICTA 1988, s 574* (capital gains tax loss accruing to individual in respect of unquoted shares in a trading company converted to an income tax loss; see 35.12 LOSSES).

Further rules dealing with identification and other matters apply as follows.

(*a*)   The identification rules applying for securities generally do not apply to shares in respect of which any relief has been given and not withdrawn. Instead, where an individual holds ordinary shares of any class and relief has been given in respect of some shares of that class but not others, any disposal is related firstly to acquisitions of shares in respect of which relief has been given under the *FA 1981* provisions and then to those given relief under the *FA 1983* or *ICTA 1988* provisions. For this purpose and that in (*b*) and (*e*) below shares are only treated as being of the same class if they would be so treated if dealt with on the Stock Exchange and the grant after 18 March 1986 of an option the exercise of which would bind the grantor to sell shares is treated as a disposal of those shares.

(*b*)   Where relief has been given to an individual in respect of shares of any class which have been issued to him at different times, any disposal of shares of that class is related to earlier rather than later acquisitions. This rule is deemed to have been subject to (*a*) above since the original enactment of the *FA 1983* provisions.

(*c*)   Where an individual holds ordinary shares and relief has been given in respect of some but not others, then, if there has been a reorganisation affecting those shares within *TCGA 1992, s 126*, the shares of each kind are treated as a separate holding of old shares and identified, under *TCGA 1992, s 127*, with a separate new holding. For reorganisations generally see 53.5 above.

(*d*)   Where the provisions of *TCGA 1992, s 135* in 53.8 or of *TCGA 1992, s 136* in 53.9 above (company amalgamations and reconstructions) would otherwise apply in relation to eligible shares and in respect of which relief has been given, those provisions are only to apply if the relief is withdrawn. These disapplications do not apply where the new holding comprises shares issued after 28 November 1994 by a company which had itself previously issued shares to which relief is attributable. The new holding of shares is treated as the same asset as the original holding, provided the new shares are ordinary shares carrying on preferential rights to dividends or assets, or preferential rights of redemption, and they must be issued at least five years after the issue of the original shares.

(*e*)   Where an original holding has been subject to the relief, a disposal of the whole or part of a new holding, allotted other than for payment as a result of a reorganisation within *TCGA 1992, s 126(2)(a)* after 18 March 1986 (allotments in respect of, and in proportion to, existing holdings or of any class of shares, e.g. a bonus issue within 53.6 above), will be treated, for the purposes of deciding whether relief given is to be withdrawn, as a disposal of the whole or a corresponding part of the original holding with which, by reason of *TCGA 1992, s 127*, the new holding is identified. Also, for the purposes of (*a*) above, the new shares will be treated as shares in respect of which relief has been given.

(*f*)   The general share reorganisation provisions of *TCGA 1992, ss 127–130* (see 53.5–53.7 above) do not apply after 18 March 1986 to ordinary shares in respect of which relief has been given if

   (i)   there is, by virtue of an allotment for payment within *TCGA 1992, s 126(2)(a)* (see also (*e*) above), a reorganisation affecting those shares; and

   (ii)   immediately following the reorganisation, the relief has not been withdrawn in respect of those shares or relief has been given in respect of the allotted shares and not withdrawn.

On such a reorganisation where immediately before it the relief has not been withdrawn, and where both the amount of relief (or the amount remaining where it has been reduced) and the market value of the shares immediately before the reorganisation exceed their market value immediately after the reorganisation, the relief is reduced by an amount equal to whichever is the smaller of those excesses. This reduction also applies *mutatis mutandis* where the individual sells his rights instead of taking up his allotment. Where the relief is so reduced an amount equal to the reduction is treated as additional allowable expenditure for capital gains tax purposes on a disposal of the allotted shares or debentures and such expenditure is apportioned between the allotted shares etc. in a just and reasonable manner. Where a disposal of the original holding of ordinary shares is not ultimately exempt (e.g. because all relief has been withdrawn), the allowable expenditure relating to such shares is reduced by an amount equal to the above reduction and is again apportioned in a just and reasonable manner.

Shares issued before 19 March 1986. For shares issued before 19 March 1986 in computing any gains or losses arising on an individual's disposal of shares in respect of which any relief has been given and not withdrawn, any deductible expenditure for capital gains tax purposes is calculated without regard to 'that relief' (i.e. the relief given and not withdrawn), except that where that expenditure exceeds the consideration received, it is reduced by the lesser of that excess and the amount of 'that relief' (i.e. the relief given and not withdrawn). However, this foregoing provision does not apply to disposals falling within *TCGA 1992, s 58(1)* (but will apply on a subsequent disposal to a third party by the transferee spouse). In determining whether any sums are excluded under *TCGA 1992, s 39(1)(2)* (exclusion of expenditure allowable against income; see 16.5 DISPOSAL), the existence of any relief given and not withdrawn is ignored.

The provisions in (*a*) (except in relation to a grant of an option etc.), (*b*) and (*c*) above also apply to shares issued before 19 March 1986 as do those in (*e*) in respect of reorganisations before that date. The provisions in (*d*) do not apply to shares issued before 19 March 1986 and those in (*f*) do not apply to reorganisations before that date. (*Note.* A Revenue Press Release of 19 December 1989 announced that an unintended change in the law had been made by *ICTA 1988* so as to apply the provisions in (*d*) above to shares issued before 19 March 1986 where a reconstruction or amalgamation involving an exchange or cancellation of shares occurs after 5 April 1988 with the result that the exchange or cancellation would give rise to a disposal. *FA 1990, 14 Sch 17, 19* restored the position for exchanges etc. occurring after 5 April 1988 save that in respect of an exchange before 1 January 1990 the shareholder could irrevocably elect to have the exchange treated as a disposal by giving written notice at any time before 6 April 1991.)

Where an allowable loss still arose after the above reduction in consideration, the loss may have been eligible for relief under *ICTA 1988, s 574* (capital gains tax loss accruing to individual in respect of unquoted shares in a trading company converted to an income tax loss; see 35.12 LOSSES).

General. Where relief has been granted or withdrawn, consequential adjustments may be made to the individual's capital gains tax position. [*TCGA 1992, ss 39(3), 150; FA 1985, 19 Sch 16(3); ICTA 1988, ss 289, 299, 305; FA 1991, s 99(2)(4); F(No 2)A 1992, s 38; FA 1994, s 137, 15 Sch 29; FA 1995, ss 68, 69*]. It should be noted that 'relief' refers to the deduction falling to be made from a person's income and not to any amount of income tax which is not chargeable due to such a deduction.

For consideration of the determination of the time shares are issued under the scheme, see *National Westminster Bank plc v CIR; Barclays Bank plc v CIR CA 1993, [1994] STC 184.*

53.19   **ACCRUED INCOME SCHEME, DEEP DISCOUNT SECURITIES, INDEXED STOCK, DEEP GAIN SECURITIES AND CONVERTIBLE SECURITIES**

Accrued income scheme. The accrued income scheme provisions of *ICTA 1988, ss 710–728* apply, broadly, to transfers of any government, public authority or company loan stock after 27 February 1986. (See further 23.12 INDEXATION.) If a transfer is with accrued interest, the transferor is treated as entitled to the 'accrued amount' for income tax purposes, and the transferee is allowed similar relief for income tax purposes, for the interest period in which the settlement day falls. If the transfer is without accrued interest, the transferor is allowed relief on the 'rebate amount', and the transferee is treated as entitled to the same amount, for the relevant interest period.

Where a transfer within the accrued income provisions also constitutes a disposal for the purposes of *TCGA 1992*, neither *TCGA 1992, s 37* nor *39* applies (see 30.1 INTER-ACTION WITH OTHER TAXES). Instead, where a transfer is with accrued interest, an amount equal to the accrued amount is excluded for those purposes from the transferor's disposal consideration, and the same amount is excluded from the transferee's allowable expenditure when he makes a subsequent disposal. Where the transfer is without accrued interest, an amount equal to the rebate amount is added for those purposes to the transferor's disposal consideration, and the same amount is added to the transferee's allowable expenditure when he makes a subsequent disposal. Similar rules apply where there is a disposal (e.g. a deemed disposal) for the purposes of *TCGA 1992* without there being a contemporaneous transfer within the scope of the accrued income provisions. Where on a 'conversion' (being one within *TCGA 1992, s 132*; see 53.10 above) or an 'exchange' (being one which is not treated as a disposal: see generally 53.5 above) of securities, a person is treated as entitled to the accrued amount, an equal amount less any consideration received on the conversion or exchange (other than the new holding of securities) is treated for the purposes of *TCGA 1992* as consideration given on the conversion or exchange. Where the consideration received on the conversion or exchange (other than the new holding of securities) equals or exceeds an amount equal to the accrued amount, that consideration is treated for the purposes of *TCGA 1992* as reduced by that amount. If on a conversion or exchange of securities, a rebate amount is allowed for income tax purposes, an amount equal to the rebate amount is treated for the purposes of *TCGA 1992* as consideration received on the conversion or exchange.

Where a transfer of securities is made after 27 February 1986 with the right to receive interest ('unrealised interest') falling before the settlement day payable on them on an interest payment date, neither *TCGA 1992, s 37* nor *39* applies. Instead, an amount equal to any such unrealised interest charged to income tax on the transferor is excluded for the purposes of *TCGA 1992* from the transferor's disposal consideration. Where such a transfer is made after 18 March 1986, an amount equal to the unrealised interest left out of account in charging income tax on the transferee is excluded for those purposes from the transferee's allowable expenditure when he makes a subsequent disposal. [*TCGA 1992, s 119*].

See Tolley's Income Tax under Schedule D, Case VI for full details of the accrued income scheme.

The above procedures will not be required for the purposes of computing a chargeable gain where the security is otherwise exempt. See 21 GOVERNMENT SECURITIES and 44 QUALIFYING CORPORATE BONDS.

Deep discount securities issued after 13 March 1984. Income and corporation tax legislation relating to 'deep discount securities' is contained in *TCGA 1992, s 118; ICTA 1988, s 57, 4 Sch* (as amended). For the income tax charge on the holder of the security, see Tolley's Income Tax under Interest Receivable and for the relief from corporation tax received by companies issuing such securities, see Tolley's Corporation Tax under Profit Computations, and generally see both publications for coverage of the provisions. Broadly, a *'deep discount security'* is a redeemable security issued at a discount exceeding 15% of the amount payable on redemption overall or $\frac{1}{2}$% per annum of that amount for each complete year from issue to redemption. Shares, index-linked securities and share capital within *ICTA 1988, s 209(2)(c)* are excluded. Rules specifically dealing with chargeable gains relating to deep discount securities are given below.

(*a*)   *Disposals.* In computing the gain accruing on the disposal of a deep discount security the consideration for the disposal is treated as reduced by the amount which represents the accrued income attributable to the period of ownership and which is charged to income tax under Schedule D, Case III or IV. *TCGA 1992, s 37* (see 30.1 INTERACTION WITH OTHER TAXES) is excluded for this purpose. Where the amount charged to income tax exceeds the disposal consideration, the excess is treated as allowable expenditure within *TCGA 1992, s 38(1)(b)* (see 16.3 DISPOSAL) incurred immediately before disposal (and thus effectively resulting in an additional allowable loss equal to the excess).

(*b*)   *Occurrence of disposal.* There is a disposal for the purposes of the income and corporation tax provisions if there would be a disposal for the purposes of *TCGA 1992*. (It would therefore appear that there is a disposal under the income and corporation tax provisions, even when there is only a deemed disposal for the purposes of the charge to tax on chargeable gains.) In addition, death is also an occasion of disposal notwithstanding the general rule given at 15.1 DEATH but this provision appears only to apply for the purposes of assessment to income tax or corporation tax and not for the purposes of the charge to tax on chargeable gains. See also (*f*) below.

(*c*)   *Time of disposal.* The time of disposal of a deep discount security for the purposes of income or corporation tax is the contract date but if a contract is conditional, the time of disposal is the time when the condition is satisfied.

(*d*)   *'No gain, no loss' disposals.* After a 'no gain, no loss' disposal for the purposes of the charge to tax on chargeable gains of a deep discount security, the allowable expenditure of the acquirer is increased by the amount of accrued income arising in the previous owner's period of ownership.

(*e*)   *Identification of securities.* Deep discount securities are identified under the rules applicable to securities generally before 6 April 1985 (1 April 1985 for companies). After 5 April 1985 (31 March 1985 for companies) deep discount securities are designated 'relevant securities' and amended identification rules apply. See 23.12 INDEXATION. This applies for income and corporation tax purposes as well as for the purposes of the charge to tax on chargeable gains.

(*f*)   *Conversion or exchange of securities.* Where on the conversion or exchange of securities (within *TCGA 1992, s 132* or *135(3)* (including in the latter case the deemed treatment under *s 136(1)*; see 53.8–53.10 above) any money sum is received (in addition to the new holding) as consideration for the disposal of the deep discount securities, for the purposes of the charge to tax on capital gains, the disposal proceeds are treated as reduced by the amount of accrued income charged to income tax on a disposal deemed to occur for income or corporation tax purposes on the conversion or exchange. Where the accrued income exceeds the proceeds, the excess is treated as allowable expenditure as at (*a*) above.

(*g*)   UNDERWRITERS (56) are deemed for the income or corporation tax provisions to dispose of and reacquire securities held in a premiums trust fund at each 31 December date for 1989 and subsequent underwriting years prior to 1994. Such transactions are also treated for the purposes of the charge to tax on chargeable gains as disposals and acquisitions at market value.

[*TCGA 1992, s 118; ICTA 1988, 4 Sch; FA 1993, 23 Sch Pt III*].

The capital element of a deep discount security can be a qualifying corporate bond and thus totally exempt for disposals after 1 July 1986. See 44.2 QUALIFYING CORPORATE BONDS.

Where a deep discount security carries interest (in addition to a discount to redemption as above), the accrued income scheme provisions (see above) may apply to a disposal after 27 February 1986. In addition certain rules relating to indexation allowance and identification applying generally before 6 April 1985 (1 April 1985 for companies) were retained until after 27 February 1986 where this would not otherwise be the case, see 23.12 INDEXATION.

Deep discounted stock and indexed stock not within TCGA 1992, s 118. Companies registered in the UK were permitted to issue deep discounted stock (including zero coupon bonds) after 24 June 1982. However, there was no specific legislation applicable to such issues made before 14 March 1984 (but see below under deep gain securities) but the Revenue indicated their practice in relation to such stocks and also to indexed stock and this practice still has relevance where the specific provisions above do not apply. In the Revenue's view the discount on issue of a deep discounted stock was chargeable on redemption as rolled-up interest in the lender's hands and allowable against the borrower's profits for corporation tax purposes. This applied whether or not there had been intermediate transactions. As regards indexed stock issued by companies at a reasonable commercial rate of interest, if the indexed uplift on redemption merely took account of any fall in the real value of the stock, then the lender (provided it was not a bank or financial concern), was liable only to capital gains tax on the uplift. The borrowing company was not able to claim a deduction for the uplift against its corporation tax profits. If, however, the indexing applied to the interest element, and additional sums of interest were rolled up to be paid with the capital on redemption, then both indexed and rolled-up interest was, when paid, given the same tax treatment for borrower and lender as non-indexed interest (Revenue Press Release 25 June 1982).

Deep gain securities. *FA 1989, s 94, 11 Sch* introduces legislation for 'deep gain securities'. Broadly, a '*deep gain security*' is a security which, at whatever time it was issued and assuming redemption, is redeemable in an amount which exceeds the issue price by more than 15% of that amount or $\frac{1}{2}$% per annum of that amount for each complete year from issue to redemption. Deep discount securities, index-linked securities, shares and (subject to exceptions) gilt-edged securities issued before 14 March 1989 are excluded.

A transfer or redemption after 13 March 1989 of a deep gain security for an amount exceeding the acquisition cost results in an amount equal to the difference (net of transfer costs) being treated as income of the transferor. There are no specific consequential provisions for the purposes of the charge to tax on chargeable gains because, it seems, a deep gain security (or a security falling to be treated as a deep gain security) will be a gilt-edged security (see 21 GOVERNMENT SECURITIES) or, in some cases, a qualifying corporate bond (see 44.2 QUALIFYING CORPORATE BONDS) and thus exempt. If this is not the case it would seem the position is governed by *TCGA 1992, s 37* (see 30.1 INTER-ACTION WITH OTHER TAXES).

Convertible securities. *FA 1990, s 56, 10 Sch* introduces legislation for 'qualifying convertible securities'. Broadly, a *'qualifying convertible security'* is a quoted redeemable security other than a share which is issued by a company after 8 June 1989, which would otherwise be a deep discount or deep gain security (see above) but would not be such a security but for certain provisions as to redemption and which is convertible into ordinary share capital in the company.

A transfer or redemption after 8 June 1989 of a qualifying convertible security results in a 'chargeable amount' (calculated by reference to the length of ownership and the yield to redemption exclusive of interest) being treated as income of the transferor. There are no specific consequential provisions for capital gains tax and the position seems to be as for deep gain securities above except that, because of the condition that a qualifying convertible security must be convertible into ordinary share capital, such a security cannot be a qualifying corporate bond. Obviously, too, such a security cannot be a gilt-edged security.

53.20 PERSONAL EQUITY PLANS

From 1 January 1987, a 'qualifying individual' may subscribe a specified maximum to a personal equity plan to which no-one else may subscribe. New regulations came into force on 6 April 1989 (the *1989 Regulations*) (subsequently amended) and these modified the original provisions (the *1986 Regulations*) which continued to apply to existing plans until 31 December 1989 or such earlier date (which had to be after 5 April 1989) as was agreed either in writing or under the terms of the main agreement between the investor and the plan manager. A person who subscribed to a plan under the *1986 Regulations* after 31 December 1988 could not subscribe to one under the *1989 Regulations* until after the date determined as above.

A *'qualifying individual'* must be 18 years of age or over, and either resident or ordinarily resident in the UK or a non-resident Crown employee serving overseas whose duties are treated as performed in the UK. Subscriptions may be made to only one general plan and one 'single company plan' (see below) in any tax year.

Under the *1989 Regulations*, a maximum of £6,000 (£4,800 for 1989/90) may be invested in a personal equity plan in any tax year. For so long as the various conditions continue to be met, dividend income is tax-free (and the plan manager may reclaim the related tax credits). Before 6 April 1991, rights issues attracted special treatment, but on and after that date they must meet the usual conditions for plan investments and be within the overall investment limits. There is no capital gains tax liability (nor is there relief for losses) on the sale of an investment under the plan. All gains arising within the plan are exempt, even where a cash sum equivalent to the amount of the gain is withdrawn. Where plan investments are withdrawn *in specie*, the plan investor is deemed to have made a disposal and reacquisition at market value, thus exempting any gain or loss arising prior to withdrawal. The plan investor is treated as holding securities within the plan in a capacity other than that in which he holds any other securities of the same class so that plan investments are pooled separately and the normal share reorganisation rules are disapplied in respect of plan investments where there is a reorganisation of share capital. There is no deemed disposal when the plan investor transfers shares into a plan (see below under conditions applicable etc.) and the investor retains his beneficial ownership of plan investments even though legal ownership is held by the manager. From 27 July 1993, power is given to adapt the normal share pooling and other capital gains tax rules where such a transfer of shares into a plan is made. This will obviate the previous uncertainty in the calculation of gains relating to shares not in a plan which are of the same class as those which have been transferred to it.

From 1 January 1992, up to £3,000 per tax year (including 1991/92) may be invested in a 'single company plan' (often known as a 'corporate PEP') in addition to any investment in a general plan as described above. A *'single company plan'* allows investment only in shares of one designated company. An additional condition imposed is that substantially the whole of the cash subscribed to the plan, or from realisation of plan shares, must be reinvested in plan shares within 42 days, or transferred (with interest) to the investor within 14 days thereafter.

Regulations may provide that a European authorised institution, a European subsidiary or a person authorised under *FSA 1986, s 31* cannot be a plan manager unless arrangements have been made for certain prescribed duties to be complied with. Such arrangements may include the appointment of a UK tax representative responsible for ensuring compliance with the prescribed duties.

Conditions applicable to both 'general' and 'single company' plans. All transactions involving plan investments must be carried out at open market prices, and investments may not be purchased from the plan investor or spouse. Subscription to a plan must be by payment of cash to the plan manager for investment by him, except that

(*a*)   qualifying shares allotted under public offers, and

(*b*)   (in relation to single company plans, see below) certain shares acquired under employee share schemes,

may be transferred into plans. As regards (*a*) above, the shares must be transferred to the plan within 42 days of allotment and their cost included within the overall investment limit. This also applies to shares in a building society issued on conversion to plc status. The fact that a new issue may take the form of separate offers on slightly different terms (e.g. to employees or customers of the issuing company) does not prevent the shares being eligible for transfer into a plan. (Revenue Press Releases 6 October 1989, 17 October 1990).

Cash held in a plan must be within the overall limit, must be held in sterling and must be invested in a designated account with a deposit taker or building society. Interest is paid gross and will be exempt from tax altogether, so long as it is eventually invested in plan shares or unit trusts. (Revenue Press Release 17 October 1990).

Before 6 April 1991, cash had to be invested in a composite or reduced rate account, and the interest was exempt from higher rate tax. After 5 April 1991, if interest etc. exceeding £180 in a year is paid by the plan manager to or for the plan investor in respect of cash held within a plan, the plan manager must account for a sum representing basic rate tax on all such interest payments in the year; the interest payments are for all purposes treated as interest taxable under Schedule D Case III in the year in which they arise, the basic rate liability of which is satisfied as above.

53.20 Shares and Securities

General plans. The investments which may be purchased, made or held under a general plan are as follows.

(i) Ordinary shares in UK companies (other than investment trusts) listed on a recognised stock exchange (including, from 6 April 1993, any such exchange in another EC Member State) or dealt in on the Unlisted Securities Market.

(ii) 'Qualifying EC shares', provided that they form part of the authorised share capital of the company, carry no fixed, guaranteed or secured redemption rights or preferential rights to dividends or to company property in a liquidation, and are neither shares carrying no right to a profit share other than fixed dividends nor shares carrying no right to a profit share but carrying a right of conversion into shares which do carry such a right. The company must not be an open-ended investment company within *Financial Services Act 1986, s 75(8)*, and, after 5 April 1993, must not derive the principal part of its income from shareholdings each of which represents 10% or less of the voting power in the company concerned (before 6 April 1993, from shareholdings each of which represented 15% or less by value of its investments).

(iii) Investment trusts (including 'split-level' trusts, see Revenue Press Release 3 May 1989), authorised unit trusts (as specially defined and excluding, from 6 April 1993, certain pension schemes with restricted investment powers ('feeder funds') and schemes which may invest wholly in warrants ('warrant funds')) and 'funds of funds' (i.e. unit trust schemes investing in authorised unit trusts), subject either

 (*a*) to a limit (which is, however, abolished after 5 April 1992) of one-half of the subscription limit and, after 5 April 1990, to a condition that at least 50% in value of the investments held by the trust are either ordinary shares within (i) or, after 31 December 1991, (ii) above (or, in the case of an investment trust, units in an authorised unit trust meeting that condition), or (except in the case of funds of funds) shares in an investment trust where 50% of the value of the trust investments are such shares (although, in either case, an occasional inadvertent fall below 50% will generally be disregarded, see Revenue Press Release 3 May 1989), or

 (*b*) after 5 April 1990, to a limit of one-quarter of the subscription limit in any year on the amount which may be invested in authorised unit trusts, investment trusts (including new issues transferred in) and funds of funds without the 50% test being met but, from 6 April 1993, with a requirement that the trust holds at least one-half of its assets in ordinary shares, i.e. shares listed on a recognised stock exchange which satisfy the conditions applicable to qualifying EC shares under (ii) above.

(iv) Cash.

'Qualifying EC shares' are shares issued by a company incorporated in a Member State other than the UK and officially listed on a recognised stock exchange in a Member State.

After 5 April 1992, cash received by the plan manager from dividends, disposals etc. may be reinvested in any qualifying investments, provided that the market value of investments within (iii)(*b*) does not immediately thereafter exceed one-quarter of the market value of all plan investments. Before 6 April 1992, the restriction on cash investment was that, where cash received in respect of shares within (i) or (ii) was used to purchase investments within (iii) above, the market value of investments within (iii) above immediately after the purchase could not exceed one-half of the market value of all the plan investments.

Before 1 January 1992, 'paired' shares, where a UK and a foreign company have provided that no share in either company may be acquired other than as part of a unit comprising one share in each company (such units being offered for sale in both countries at a broadly equivalent price), may be held under a plan subject to a limitation of one-half of the subscription limit in any year on the total amount invested in paired shares, investment trusts, authorised unit trusts and funds of funds.

Where investments held on 5 April 1990 failed to meet the 50% test specified in (iii)(*a*) above for qualification ('non-qualifying investments'), those investments may continue to be held under a plan, provided that

(*a*)   the total of such investments made during 1989/90 and held at that date did not exceed £2,400, and

(*b*)   apart from the reinvestment of proceeds of sale of non-qualifying investments, the amount invested in non-qualifying investments in 1990/91 did not exceed £900, and

(*c*)   after 5 April 1991, the total amount invested in authorised unit trusts, funds of funds and investment trusts does not exceed one-quarter of the subscription limit.

Single company plans. The investments which may be purchased, made or held under a single company plan are as follows.

(i)   Where the company designated for the purposes of the plan is a UK company (other than an investment trust) quoted on a recognised stock exchange or dealt in on the Unlisted Securities Market, ordinary shares in the company, and ordinary shares or 'qualifying EC shares' 'representing' those shares.

(ii)   Provided that the designated company is not an open-ended investment company within *Financial Services Act 1986, s 75(8)*, and does not derive the principal part of its income from shareholdings each of which represents 15% or less by value of its investments, 'qualifying EC shares' issued by the company, and 'qualifying EC shares' or ordinary shares 'representing' those shares.

(iii)   Investments in units comprising ordinary shares or 'qualifying EC shares' in the designated company which are 'paired' either with ordinary shares in another company meeting the condition in (i) above or with 'qualifying EC shares' in another company meeting the condition in (ii) above.

(iv)   Cash.

In addition, the plan investor may subscribe to a plan by transferring to the plan manager shares in the designated company which were appropriated to the plan investor under an approved profit-sharing scheme or acquired by exercise of options under a SAYE share option scheme (see 53.16 above). Shares acquired under SAYE schemes must be transferred within 90 days of exercise of the option, and those appropriated under profit-sharing schemes within 90 days of the earlier of the date the plan investor directed the trustees of the scheme to transfer the shares to him and the 'release date' in relation to the shares. The sum of the market value of shares so transferred to a plan and of the cost of any new issue shares so transferred (see conditions applicable etc. above) must, together with any cash subscribed, be within the overall subscription limit for the single company plan.

'Qualifying EC shares' are shares issued by a company incorporated in a Member State other than the UK and officially listed on a recognised stock exchange in a Member State. Shares *'represent'* other shares when there is a company reorganisation under which, for capital gains tax purposes, they are (or would but for being plan investments be) equated with the other shares. Shares in two companies are *'paired'* where it is provided in their governing instruments that no share in either company may be

acquired otherwise than as part of a unit comprising one share in each company, such units being offered for sale at the same time and at the same price or, where sales are in more than one country, at a broadly equivalent price.

Cash received by the plan manager from dividends, disposals etc. may be reinvested in other shares within (i)-(iii) above. Where the cash arises in respect of shares transferred in from a profit-sharing or SAYE share option scheme (see above), it may be reinvested in similar shares even where they are not otherwise qualifying investments.

Pre-1990 plans. Plans under the *1986 Regulations* operated by reference to calendar years rather than tax years. There was an overall limit of £3,000 (£2,400 before 22 April 1988) per year of which the greater of £540 (£420 before 22 April 1988) and one quarter of the plan subscription could be invested in investment trusts and authorised unit trusts. There were restrictions on the amount of cash that could be held although interest on deposits of such cash was excluded from the composite rate scheme and payable gross by building societies. There was a minimum holding period of one year after the end of the calendar year in which the first subscription was made under the plan and any transfer of plan cash or investments to the subscriber before the expiry of that period resulted in the tax exemptions being rescinded. The death of a subscriber within that period did not result in a loss of exemptions. There was no provision for transferring new allotments of shares into a plan. Before 11 January 1989, plan managers were unable to reclaim tax credits on dividends not reinvested, but they are enabled to do so from that date by concession. Due to a drafting error losses incurred on plan investments before 18 January 1988 were allowable. [*TCGA 1992, ss 151, 287; ICTA 1988, ss 333, 333A, 828, FA 1988, s 116; SI 1986, No 1948; SI 1987, No 2128; SI 1988, Nos 657, 1348; SI 1989, No 469; FA 1991, s 70; SI 1990, No 678; SI 1991 Nos 733, 2774; SI 1992 No 623; SI 1993 No 756; FA 1993, s 85; FA 1995, s 64*].

General. A list of registered plan managers may be obtained by sending a self-addressed A4 size envelope to (or calling at) Inland Revenue, Public Enquiry Room, West Wing, Somerset House, London WC2R 1LB. The list is updated quarterly. An information pack on personal equity plans is available from the Inland Revenue Library, Room 8, New Wing, Somerset House, price £3.50.

See generally Revenue Pamphlet IR 89.

53.21   CLOSE COMPANIES

Income tax which has been charged on a participator as a result of an apportionment under *ICTA 1988, ss 423-430, 19 Sch* (broadly only in relation to accounting periods ending before 1 April 1989; see Tolley's Corporation Tax under Close Companies) and paid by him in respect of income of a close company which has not subsequently been distributed (including stock dividends; see 53.12 above), may be deducted, pro rata, in computing a gain on the disposal of any of his shares in that company. Apportioned income is treated as the top slice of income and shares are identified on a first in, first out basis. [*TCGA 1992, s 124*].

Tax paid which is referable to gains of a non-resident company charged on an individual UK shareholder under *TCGA 1992, s 13* (see 39.5 OVERSEAS MATTERS) is similarly deductible. See also 16.4 DISPOSAL for an alternative concessional treatment.

53.22   LIFE ASSURANCE POLICIES

Investments or other assets transferred to a policy holder by an insurance company after 5 April 1967, in accordance with a life assurance policy, are deemed to be transferred at market value. [*TCGA 1992, s 204(3)(4)*].

53.23   LOANS OF SECURITIES

After 17 August 1989 a transfer of securities (including stocks and shares) under either of the following types of arrangement is ignored for the purposes of the charge to tax on capital gains.

(i)   Where a person (A) enters into an arrangement under which another person (B) is to transfer securities to A or his nominee, and securities of the same kind and amount are to be transferred by someone to B or his nominee.

(ii)   Where, to enable B to make such a transfer to A or his nominee, similar arrangements are made between B or his nominee and another person (C) or his nominee; and where a similar arrangement is entered into after 30 September 1993 as part of a chain of arrangements for overseas securities, all having the effect of enabling B to make the transfer to A or his nominee.

Transfers within (i) or (ii) are also left out of account in computing income for tax purposes of any trade carried on by the transferor or transferee. The Treasury may make regulations by statutory instrument imposing further conditions. Except in so far as those regulations otherwise provide, the above provisions only apply if A enters into the arrangement mentioned in (i) above to enable him to fulfil a contract under which he is required to sell securities. [*TCGA 1992, s 271(9); ICTA 1988, ss 129, 828; FA 1991, s 57; SI 1989, No 1299; SI 1990, No 2552; SI 1992 No 572; SI 1993 No 2003; FA 1995, s 84*].

By concession, a loan of securities is also left out of account for income and capital gains tax purposes where it is made to enable a borrower to replace an existing loan of such securities rather than to meet a sale, provided the existing loan was within the above provisions (as extended by this concessional treatment if necessary) and the replacement loan would otherwise have been within them but for the requirement that it must be made to enable the transferee to fulfil a contract to sell securities (or to transfer the securities to a third party to enable him to fulfil a contract to sell securities) (Revenue Pamphlet IR 1 (1992) B36).

Before 18 August 1989 the borrowing and lending of securities with repayment in other securities of the same description is not a disposal for capital gains tax purposes where it is standard practice designed to preserve a market in securities, etc. (Revenue Pamphlet IR 1 (1992) B15 and subject to transitional provisions contained in Revenue Press Release 28 July 1989).

53.24   BUILDING SOCIETIES BECOMING COMPANIES

The following applies where there is a transfer of the whole of a building society's business to a successor company in accordance with the relevant provisions of the *Building Societies Act 1986*.

Subject to the operation of *TCGA 1992, s 217(1)* (rights to acquire shares in successor company treated as valueless options, see 16.10 (*f*) DISPOSAL), shares issued to members by the successor company, or disposed of to members by the society, are regarded as acquired for any new consideration given and as having at the time of acquisition a value equal to such new consideration (if any). Where shares are so issued or disposed of to trustees on terms providing for their transfer to members for no new consideration, and they constitute settled property in the trustees' hands, then

(*a*)   they are regarded as acquired by the trustees for no consideration;

(*b*)   a member's interest in the shares is regarded as acquired for no consideration and as having no value at the time of acquisition;

(c)   on the member becoming absolutely entitled to any shares, or where such entitlement would arise but for the member being an infant or otherwise under disability, the shares are treated as disposed of and reacquired by the trustees in a nominee capacity under *TCGA 1992, s 60(1)* and at a no gain/no loss price and *TCGA 1992, s 71* (see 52.9 SETTLEMENTS) does not then apply; and

(d)   on the member disposing of his interest in the settled property, any gain is a chargeable gain and *TCGA 1992, s 76(1)* (see 52.8 SETTLEMENTS) does not then apply.

Any gain on the disposal by the society of shares in the successor company in connection with the transfer is not a chargeable gain. [*TCGA 1992, ss 216(1), 217(2)–(7)*].

The conferring of any benefit under the above or *TCGA 1992, s 217(1)* on a member of a society in connection with a transfer, or any payment in lieu of such a benefit, or any distribution in pursuance of *Building Societies Act 1986, s 100(2)(b)*, is not regarded as either the making of a distribution for corporation tax purposes or the payment of a dividend by the society. However, any such disregarded benefit etc. may be taken into account as a capital distribution as in 53.13 above. [*FA 1988, 12 Sch 6*].

53.25   EMPLOYEE SHARE OWNERSHIP TRUSTS

Under provisions contained in *FA 1989, ss 67–74, 5 Sch*, payments made after 26 July 1989 by a UK resident company to a 'qualifying employee share ownership trust' (broadly, a trust set up to acquire shares in a company and distribute them to employees of that company) will, subject to conditions, be deductible for corporation tax purposes. On the happening of a 'chargeable event', any tax relief given to the company will be clawed back by means of a charge under Schedule D, Case VI on the trustees of the trust, and if they fail to pay the tax it can be recovered from the company. See Tolley's Income Tax under Schedule D, Cases I and II and Share Incentives and Options for the detailed provisions.

For disposals after 19 March 1990 of shares to a qualifying employee share ownership trust, a relief in the form of a deferral of the gain applies subject to the detailed conditions below.

The relief given under *TCGA 1992, s 229(1)* below is available where the following conditions are met.

(a)   The claimant makes a disposal after 19 March 1990 of, or of his interest in, shares to the trustees of a trust which is a 'qualifying employee share ownership trust' at the time of the disposal and which was established by a company (the 'founding company') which, immediately after the disposal, was a 'trading company' or the 'holding company' of a 'trading group'.

(b)   The shares are fully paid up, not redeemable, form part of the 'ordinary share capital' of the founding company, and are not subject to any restrictions other than those which attach to all shares of the same class or are authorised by *FA 1989, 5 Sch 7(2)*.

(c)   At any time in the 'entitlement period', the trustees are beneficially entitled to at least 10% of the 'ordinary share capital' of the founding company and of any 'profits available for distribution to equity holders' therein, and would be beneficially entitled to at least 10% of any of the founding company's 'assets available for distribution to equity holders' on a winding-up.

(d)   The claimant obtains consideration for the disposal and, at any time in the 'acquisition period', applies all (but see below under *TCGA 1992, s 229(2)(3)*) the consideration in acquiring assets ('replacement assets') (or an interest therein) which are, immediately thereafter, 'chargeable assets' in relation to the claimant and which are not shares in, or debentures issued by, the founding company or a company which, at the time of the acquisition, is in the same 'group' as the founding company. The requirement that the consideration be applied in the 'acquisition period' is satisfied if the acquisition is made pursuant to an unconditional contract entered into in that period.

(e)   At all times in the 'proscribed period', there are no 'unauthorised arrangements' under which the claimant or a person connected with him may be entitled to acquire any of the shares, or an interest in or right deriving from any of the shares, which are the subject of the disposal by the claimant.

(f)   No 'chargeable event' occurs in relation to the trustees in the chargeable period(s) in which the claimant makes the disposal and acquisition or in any other chargeable period between those of the disposal and the acquisition, 'chargeable period' meaning year of assessment or (if the claimant is a company) claimant company accounting period.

[*TCGA 1992, s 227*].

Where relief is available as above, the claimant may, within two years of the acquisition, claim that, for the purposes of *TCGA 1992*, the disposal be treated as made at a no gain/no loss consideration (if it otherwise would be greater), the consideration for the acquisition being treated as reduced by the excess of the actual consideration for the disposal over that no gain/no loss consideration. [*TCGA 1992, s 229(1)*].

Partial relief is available on a claim made within the same time limit where part only of the consideration for the disposal is applied as under (*d*) above and the amount of the consideration not so applied is less than the gain (whether all chargeable gain or not) accruing on the disposal. In such a case, the amount of the gain on the disposal is treated as reduced to the amount of the consideration not so applied, and the consideration for the acquisition is treated as reduced by the reduction so made to the amount of the gain. [*TCGA 1992, s 229(2)(3)*].

The other parties to the disposal and acquisition are not affected by such claims for relief. Any provision of *TCGA 1992* fixing deemed consideration for a disposal or acquisition is applied before the above adjustments are made. [*TCGA 1992, s 229(4)(5)*].

Prior to the commencement of *TCGA 1992*, the claim was made under *FA 1990, s 33*.

For the purposes of *TCGA 1992, s 227* above, the following applies.

(A)   The '*entitlement period*' is the period beginning with the disposal and ending twelve months after the date of the disposal.

(B)   The '*acquisition period*' is the period beginning with the disposal and ending six months after the date of the disposal or, if later, the date on which the condition at (*c*) above first becomes fulfilled.

(C)   The '*proscribed period*' is the period beginning with the disposal and ending on the date of the acquisition or, if later, the date on which the condition at (*c*) above first becomes fulfilled.

(D)   Arrangements are '*unauthorised arrangements*' unless either they arise wholly from a restriction authorised by *FA 1989, 5 Sch 7(2)*, or they only allow, as regards shares, interests or rights, acquisition by a beneficiary under the trust and/or appropriation under an approved profit sharing scheme (within *ICTA 1988, 9 Sch*).

(E)   An asset is a *'chargeable asset'* at a particular time in relation to the claimant if

 (i) he is at that time resident or ordinarily resident in the UK and, were the asset to be disposed of at that time, a gain accruing to him would be a chargeable gain; or

 (ii) were it to be disposed of at that time, any gain accruing to him would be a chargeable gain under *TCGA 1992, s 10(1)* or form part of his corporation tax profits under *ICTA 1988, s 11(2)(b)* (see 39.3 OVERSEAS MATTERS),

but not if, were he to dispose of it at that time, double tax relief arrangements under *ICTA 1988, s 788* (as extended to capital gains tax by *TCGA 1992, s 277*) would render him not liable to UK tax on any gain accruing to him on the disposal.

(F)   *'Qualifying employee share ownership trust'* has the same meaning as under *FA 1989, 5 Sch*, and *'chargeable event'* in relation to the trustees has the same meaning as under *FA 1989, s 69*.

(G)   *'Holding company'*, *'trading company'* and *'trading group'* have the same meanings as under *TCGA 1992, 6 Sch 1* (see 48.3 RETIREMENT RELIEF); and *'group'* (except in the expression 'trading group) is construed in accordance with *TCGA 1992, s 170* (see 13.10 COMPANIES).

(H)   *'Ordinary share capital'* means all issued share capital other than that carrying a right to a dividend at a fixed rate but with no other right to share in profits.

(J)   As regards the condition at (*c*) above, the provisions of *ICTA 1988, 18 Sch* (suitably adapted) apply as appropriate.

[*TCGA 1992, ss 228, 288(1)*].

53.26 **Chargeable event when replacement assets owned.** Where

(*a*) relief under *TCGA 1992, s 229(1)* or *(3)* is given as in 53.25 above,

(*b*) a 'chargeable event' in relation to the trustees (within *FA 1989, s 69* as amended) occurs on or after the date on which the disposal is made,

(*c*) the claimant was neither an individual who died before the occurrence of the chargeable event nor trustees of a settlement which ceased to exist before that occurrence, and

(*d*) at the time of the occurrence of the chargeable event, the claimant or a person connected with him (within *TCGA 1992, s 286*) is beneficially entitled to all the replacement assets acquired as under 53.25(*d*) above,

the claimant or the connected person (as the case may be) is deemed, immediately before the occurrence of the chargeable event, to have disposed of, and immediately reacquired, all the replacement assets at the 'relevant value'.

The *'relevant value'* is such value as secures on the deemed disposal a chargeable gain equal to the amount of the gain carried forward by virtue of *TCGA 1992, s 229(1)* or *(3)*, i.e. the amount by which the consideration for the acquisition was treated as reduced as a result of a claim for that relief to apply.

Where only a part of the replacement assets falls within 53.25(*d*) above, there is a deemed disposal and reacquisition of that part, the relevant value being reduced as is just and reasonable.

An adjustment may be made where there is a deemed disposal and reacquisition under these provisions, and before the occurrence of the chargeable event it can be said that, because of something which has happened as regards any of the replacement assets, a charge has accrued in respect of any gain carried forward as a result of relief having been given under *TCGA 1992, s 229(1)* or *(3)*. In these circumstances, the deemed disposal and reacquisition rules apply, if it is just and reasonable, as if the relevant value either were such value as secures that the deemed disposal produces neither gain nor loss (if that is just and reasonable), or, unless it produces a lower value, were reduced to whatever value is just and reasonable. [*TCGA 1992, s 232*].

Where a charge can be said, on a just and reasonable basis, to accrue by virtue of a deemed disposal as above in respect of any of the gain carried forward by virtue of *TCGA 1992, s 229(1)* or *(3)*, so much of the gain charged is not to be capable of being carried forward for the purposes of ROLLOVER RELIEF (50) under *TCGA 1992, ss 152–158*. For the purposes of ROLLOVER RELIEF (50.4) under *TCGA 1992, s 154* (new assets which are depreciating assets), a charge will arise under that provision by reference to the earlier of the disposal of the replacement asset, the deemed disposal of it under the above and the expiration of ten years beginning with the acquisition of the replacement asset. [*TCGA 1992, ss 154(3), 236(1)(2)*].

Chargeable event when replacement property owned. Where

(A)   the conditions described in (*a*)-(*c*) above are fulfilled,

(B)   before the time when the chargeable event occurs all the gain carried forward by virtue of *TCGA 1992, s 229(1)* or *(3)* (see 53.25 above) was in turn carried forward from all the replacement assets to other property by virtue of a claim for ROLLOVER RELIEF (50) to apply under *TCGA 1992, ss 152–158*, and

(C)   at the time of the occurrence of the chargeable event, the claimant or a person then connected with him (as above) is beneficially entitled to all the property,

the claimant or the connected person (as the case may be) is deemed, immediately before the occurrence of the chargeable event, to have disposed of, and immediately reacquired, all the property at the 'relevant value'.

The '*relevant value*' is as defined for *TCGA 1992, s 232* above.

Where the conditions at (B) and (C) above were satisfied as regards only part of the gain carried forward, the replacement assets from which it was in turn carried forward or the beneficial entitlement to the property into which it was further carried forward, there is a deemed disposal and reacquisition of the property concerned, the relevant value being reduced as is just and reasonable.

An adjustment may be made where there is a deemed disposal and reacquisition under these provisions, and before the occurrence of the chargeable event it can be said that, because of something which has happened as regards any of the replacement assets or any other property, a charge has accrued in respect of any gain carried forward by virtue of *TCGA 1992, s 229(1)* or *(3)*. In these circumstances, the deemed disposal and reacquisition rules apply, if it is just and reasonable, as if the relevant value either were such value as secures that the deemed disposal produces neither gain nor loss (if that is just and reasonable), or, unless it produces a lower value, were reduced to whatever value is just and reasonable. [*TCGA 1992, s 233*].

Where a charge can be said to accrue, on a just and reasonable basis, by virtue of a deemed disposal as above in respect of any of the gain carried forward by virtue of *TCGA 1992, s 229(1)* or *(3)*, so much of the gain charged is not to be capable of being carried forward for the purposes of ROLLOVER RELIEF (50) under *TCGA 1992, ss 152–158*. [*TCGA 1992, s 236(1)(2)*].

Chargeable event when qualifying corporate bonds owned. Where

(1)   the conditions described in (*a*)-(*c*) above are fulfilled,

(2)   all the replacement assets were shares in a company or companies (referred to below as 'new shares'),

(3)   there has been a transaction within *TCGA 1992, s 116(10)* (see 44.3 QUALIFYING CORPORATE BONDS) as regards which all the new shares constitute the 'old asset' and qualifying corporate bonds constitute the 'new asset', and

(4)   at the time of the occurrence of the chargeable event, the claimant or a person then connected with him (as above) is beneficially entitled to all the bonds,

a chargeable gain of the 'relevant amount' is deemed to have accrued to the claimant or the connected person (as the case may be) immediately before the time when the chargeable event occurs.

The '*relevant amount*' is the lesser of the 'first amount' and the 'second amount'.

The '*first amount*' is the amount of the chargeable gain that would be deemed to accrue under *TCGA 1992, s 116(10)(b)* if there were a disposal of all the bonds at the time the chargeable event occurs (or nil if an allowable loss would arise). The '*second amount*' is the relevant value as for *TCGA 1992, s 232* above.

Where the conditions at (2), (3) and (4) above were satisfied as regards only part of the replacement assets, the new shares constituting the old asset or the bonds to which there is beneficial entitlement, a chargeable gain is nevertheless deemed to arise as above, but the first amount is determined only by reference to the bonds concerned, the second amount is reduced as is just and reasonable, and the relevant amount is reduced accordingly.

An adjustment may be made where a chargeable gain arises as above, and before the occurrence of the chargeable event it can be said that, because of something which has happened as regards any of the new shares or any of the bonds, a charge has accrued in respect of any gain carried forward by virtue of *TCGA 1992, s 229(1)* or *(3)* (see 53.25 above). In these circumstances, the chargeable gain is, if it is just and reasonable, calculated as if the second amount were reduced as is just and reasonable (but not so as to reduce it below nil) and the relevant amount reduced (if appropriate) accordingly. [*TCGA 1992, s 234*].

Where a charge arises as above in the case of qualifying corporate bonds and subsequently a chargeable gain accrues under *TCGA 1992, s 116(10)(b)* on a disposal of them (see above), the chargeable gain is reduced by the relevant amount or (if the amount exceeds the gain) reduced to nil. The relevant amount is apportioned for this purpose where the subsequent disposal is of only some of the bonds. [*TCGA 1992, s 236(3)(4)*].

Dwelling-houses: special provisions. As regards 53.25(*d*) above, a replacement asset which is a dwelling-house (or part thereof) or land is not treated (where it would otherwise be so treated) as being a chargeable asset in relation to the claimant immediately after the asset's acquisition if on a disposal of it (or an interest in it) at some time in the period from its acquisition to the time a claim is made under *TCGA 1992, s 229(1)* or *(3)* the PRIVATE RESIDENCES (43.1) exemption of *TCGA 1992, s 222(1)* would apply to the asset (or interest in it) and the 'individual' (which includes references to a person entitled to occupy the dwelling-house etc. under the terms of a settlement; see 43.4 PRIVATE RESIDENCES) mentioned in *TCGA 1992, s 222(1)* would be the claimant or his spouse. A similar treatment applies retrospectively where the replacement asset is a dwelling-house etc. and which would otherwise be a chargeable asset in relation to the claimant immediately after its acquisition and the private residences exemption would apply similarly on a disposal at some time after a claim under *TCGA 1992, s 229(1)* or *(3)* is made, and adjustments can be made accordingly, but in such a case any gain treated as accruing is not deemed to accrue until the time (or the earliest time) on which a disposal of the dwelling-house would be within the private residences exemption. Similar provisions apply in relation to a replacement asset which is an option to acquire (or to acquire an interest in) a dwelling-house and the application of the private residences exemption in the period from the exercise of the option and the time of claim, and subsequent to the time of claim, respectively. [*TCGA 1992, s 230*].

Shares qualifying for enterprise investment or business expansion scheme relief: special provisions. As regards 53.25(*d*) above, a replacement asset which consists of shares is not treated (where it would otherwise be so treated) as being a chargeable asset in relation to the claimant immediately after the asset's acquisition if at some time in the period from its acquisition to the time a claim is made under *TCGA 1992, s 229(1)* or *(3)* enterprise investment or business expansion scheme relief (see 53.17 and 53.18 above) is claimed in respect of it. A similar treatment applies retrospectively where the replacement asset consists of shares and which would otherwise be a chargeable asset in relation to the claimant immediately after its acquisition and enterprise investment or business expansion scheme relief is claimed at some time after a claim under *TCGA 1992, s 229(1)* or *(3)* is made, and adjustments can be made accordingly. [*TCGA 1992, s 231; FA 1994, s 137, 15 Sch 34*].

Information. The inspector may, by notice in writing, require a return containing specified information by the trustees of an employee share ownership trust (within *FA 1989, 5 Sch*) where a disposal of shares (or an interest therein) has been made to them and a claim is made under *TCGA 1992, s 229(1)* or *(3)*. The information specified must be needed for the purposes of *TCGA 1992, ss 232–234* above, and may include information about: expenditure incurred by the trustees (including the purpose of the expenditure and the recipients); assets acquired by them (including the persons from whom the assets were acquired and the consideration); and transfers of assets made by them (including the persons to whom they were transferred and the consideration). Penalties under *TMA 1970, s 98* apply for failure to comply with a notice. Where relief has been given by virtue of *TCGA 1992, s 229(1)* or *(3)*, the inspector must send to the trustees a certificate that it has been given, stating the effect on the consideration for the disposal or on the gain accruing on the disposal. [*TCGA 1992, s 235*].

Clearance procedure. Trustees are able to seek and obtain confirmation that a particular trust is a qualifying employee share ownership trust and so facilitate a sale by a potential vendor who would be able to claim the relief in 53.25 above. A written request should be sent to Inland Revenue, Insurance and Specialist Division (Employee Share Schemes), Room 111A, New Wing, Somerset House, Strand, London WC2R 1LB. Tel: 071-438 7801 or 071-438 7803. The request should be accompanied by copies of the executed trust deed and any other relevant information that may be required by the Revenue (Revenue Press Release 9 May 1990). The Revenue will also examine and comment on draft trust deeds submitted to them (Revenue Press Release 14 December 1990).

54 Time Limits—5 April 1996

Cross-reference. See 55 TIME LIMITS—MISCELLANEOUS.

Note. Except where other time limits are prescribed in the statute, claims must normally be made within six years of the end of the year of assessment (accounting period in the case of companies) to which they relate. See 12 CLAIMS and 54.6 and 54.7 below. In some (but not all) cases given below, the periods can be extended at the discretion of the Board.

54.1 TIME LIMITS OF ONE YEAR OR LESS

(*a*) **Nine months**

In respect of accounting periods ending after 30 September 1993 (Pay and File), payment of corporation tax in respect of chargeable gains will be required in all cases by the day following the expiry of nine months from the end of the period if interest on unpaid tax is to be avoided. For earlier accounting periods, payment was generally required within nine months of the end of the accounting period. See 41.1 PAYMENT OF TAX.

(*b*) **Twelve months**

(i) Chargeability to tax. Any person who is chargeable to tax for a year of assessment must, unless he has made a return of his chargeable gains, give notice to the inspector that he is so chargeable within one year after the end of that year of assessment. See 42.1 PENALTIES and 49.1 RETURNS.

(ii) Claims following late assessments. A claim (including a supplementary claim) which could not have been allowed but for the making of an assessment to capital gains tax after the year of assessment to which it relates, may be made at any time before the end of the year of assessment following that in which the assessment was made; and one which arises from a discovery assessment not involving fraudulent or negligent conduct, and could not have been made within the normal time limits, can be made within a year of the end of the chargeable period in which the assessment was made. See 12.2 CLAIMS.

(iii) Tax over-repaid. This (and any associated excess repayment supplement) may be recovered by the end of the year of assessment following that in which the repayment was made. See 41.10 PAYMENT OF TAX.

(iv) Corporation tax returns under Pay and File. In respect of notices served after 31 December 1993, a company must generally comply with a notice to make a corporation tax return within twelve months of the end of the relevant accounting period or, if later, within three months of service of the notice. See 49.3 RETURNS.

54.2 TWO-YEAR TIME LIMITS

(*a*) **Quoted shares and securities.** Election for adoption of 6 April 1965 values for quoted securities (within either of the two categories) that were held on that date, where the first relevant disposal since 19 March 1968 took place during a year of assessment must be made within two years after the end of that year of assessment. With respect to disposals after 5 April 1985 (31 March 1985 for companies) the foregoing is to be read as if '5 April 1985' or '31 March 1985' (as relevant) was substituted for '19 March 1968'. The Revenue may allow extension of this time limit. See 7.3 ASSETS HELD ON 6 APRIL 1965. An election in respect of disposals after 5 April 1988 is only relevant if the rules for ASSETS HELD ON 31 MARCH 1982 (8) do not apply.

(b)   **Assets of negligible value, loans to traders becoming irrecoverable and loans to traders evidenced by qualifying corporate bonds.** A claim to this effect may be made by concession within two years after the end of the tax-year in which the relevant date falls. See 35.8–35.9 LOSSES.

(c)   **Loss relief for subscribing individual shareholders.** For 1994/95 and 1995/96 a claim for a loss arising in a particular year of assessment on the disposal of qualifying shares by a subscriber to be set against his income of that year or the last preceding year must be made within two years after that particular year. For years before 1994/95, a claim could be made for a loss arising in a year of assessment to be set against income of that year and the next following year, in each case having to be made within two years after the year for which relief was claimed. See 35.12 LOSSES.

(d)   **Loss relief for subscribing investment companies.** A claim for a loss arising on the sale of qualifying shares by a subscribing investment company to be set against income, or surplus franked investment income, must be made within two years of the end of the accounting period in which the loss arises. See 35.14 LOSSES.

(e)   **Miscellaneous disposals of assets held on 6 April 1965.** Election for adoption of 6 April 1965 value of miscellaneous assets (apart from quoted investments and UK land disposed of for a consideration including development value) disposed of must be made within two years of the end of the year of assessment in which the disposal was made. The Board may allow extension of this time limit. See 7.10 ASSETS HELD ON 6 APRIL 1965. An election in respect of disposals after 5 April 1988 is only relevant if the rules for ASSETS HELD ON 31 MARCH 1982 (8) do not apply.

(f)   **Assets held on, and gains arising before, 31 March 1982.** The latest time for making an irrevocable election for universal re-basing at 31 March 1982 is two years after the end of the year of assessment in which 'the first relevant disposal' occurs. The Board may allow an extension of this time limit. See 8.3 ASSETS HELD ON 31 MARCH 1982. A claim for 50% relief in taxing deferred charges on gains before 31 March 1982 must be made within two years of the end of the year of assessment in which the disposal or deferred gain in question occurs or accrues. See 8.12 ASSETS HELD ON 31 MARCH 1982.

(g)   **Furnished holiday accommodation.** A claim for 'averaging' of let periods of holiday accommodation must be made within two years of the end of the relevant year of assessment. See 19.1 FURNISHED HOLIDAY ACCOMMODATION.

(h)   **Retirement relief.** In respect of disposals after 5 April 1985, certain elections must be made within two years of the end of the year of assessment in which the disposal occurs. See 48.2, 48.4, 48.7 RETIREMENT RELIEF.

(i)   **Loss relief for trading losses against chargeable gains of a person other than a company.** See 35.6 LOSSES for the circumstances in which this time limit operates.

(j)   **Groups of companies: pre-entry losses.** Certain elections have to be made within two years of the end of the accounting period in which a loss or gain (as appropriate) is made. See 13.24–13.26 COMPANIES.

54.3   THREE-YEAR TIME LIMITS

(*a*)   **Deceased persons.** Assessments on gains arising or accruing before death must be made on the deceased's personal representatives within three years after the end of the tax-year in which death occurs. Assessment for any of the six years preceding death, to recoup tax lost by the deceased's fraudulent or negligent conduct (or fraud, wilful default or neglect), must be made within a similar period. See 5.5 ASSESSMENT.

(*b*)   **Charities.** Where property ceases to be held on charitable trusts in circumstances giving rise to a deemed disposal by the trustees, an assessment on the cumulative gains must be made within three years of the end of the tax-year in which the cessation occurred. See 10.3 CHARITIES.

54.4   SIX-YEAR TIME LIMITS

The more important six-year time limits are as follows.

(*a*)   **Error or mistake claims.** See 12.4 CLAIMS.

(*b*)   **Claim against double assessment** where the same person has been assessed 'for the same cause' in the same year. See 5.3 ASSESSMENTS.

(*c*)   **Relief against double taxation.** See 17 DOUBLE TAX RELIEF.

(*d*)   **Delayed remittances of overseas gains.** See 32.5 INTEREST ON UNPAID TAX and 39.4 OVERSEAS MATTERS.

(*e*)   **Disposals by way of gift etc.** See 41.5 PAYMENT OF TAX.

(*f*)   **Capital distributions in respect of shares etc.** Where allowable expenditure on shares etc. is less than the amount of a capital distribution, the taxpayer may make an election to set off all that expenditure against the distribution. See 53.13 SHARES AND SECURITIES.

(*g*)   **Private residence occupied by a dependent relative.** Subject to transitional provisions, exemption is available only for periods of ownership before 6 April 1988. See 43.5 PRIVATE RESIDENCES.

(*h*)   **Part disposal of land.** See 33.11 and 33.13 LAND.

(*j*)   **Appropriation to trading stock.** An election may be made to treat the transfer as taking place at cost instead of market value. See 6.3 ASSETS.

(*k*)   **Hold-over relief for gifts of business assets and assets on which inheritance tax is chargeable etc.** See 22.1–22.5 HOLD-OVER RELIEFS.

(*l*)   **Hold-over: general relief for gifts from 1980 to 1989.** See 22 HOLD-OVER RELIEFS.

(*m*)   **Rollover relief.** See 50 ROLLOVER RELIEF (and note that replacement assets must be acquired before this time limit).

(*n*)   **Relief on compulsory acquisition of land.** Proceeds must not be invested in land which would be exempt from capital gains tax on a disposal of it within six years of acquisition. See 33.14 LAND.

(*o*)   **Reinvestment in shares relief.** See REINVESTMENT IN SHARES RELIEF (45) (and note that reinvestment must be made before this time limit).

54.5   **OTHER ACTION BEFORE 6 APRIL 1996**

Tax-loss selling. Appropriate disposals should be made if it is desired to realise capital losses to set off against chargeable gains in the same year of assessment. See 23 INDEXATION; 35 LOSSES; and, with regard to companies, 13.31 COMPANIES.

Use of annual exempt amount. Action should be taken so as to utilise the exempt amount of chargeable gains for the year of assessment concerned. See 2.3 ANNUAL RATES AND EXEMPTIONS.

'Bed and Breakfasting'. See 23.9 INDEXATION.

54.6   **COMPANIES**

Claims and elections in respect of companies, where applicable, usually have the time limits similar to those above, save that the expiry date is by reference to the end of the company's accounting period instead of the year of assessment.

54.7   **LLOYD'S UNDERWRITERS**

Due to delay in establishing the results from Lloyd's underwriting, the Revenue may, in certain circumstances, extend the time limits for making elections as prescribed otherwise. Some time limits are extended statutorily. See 56.1 and 56.5 UNDERWRITERS.

55   Time Limits—Miscellaneous

Cross-reference. See 54 TIME LIMITS—5 APRIL 1996.

Note. Time limits other than by reference to 5 April or the end of a company's accounting period are set out below. In some (but not all) cases, the periods can be extended at the discretion of the Board.

55.1   **TIME LIMITS OF ONE YEAR OR LESS**

(*a*)   **Thirty days**

(i)   For appeals against assessments, formal notice of appeal must be lodged within thirty days of the date of issue of the assessment. See 4.4 APPEALS. For postponement of tax, see 32.2 INTEREST ON UNPAID TAX and 41 PAYMENT OF TAX.

(ii)   For appeals to the High Court, written notice requiring the Commissioners to state and sign a case must be sent to their Clerk within thirty days of the determination. The case stated must be transmitted to the High Court within thirty days of its receipt. See 4.9 APPEALS.

(iii)   Returns of income and chargeable gains must be completed within thirty days of issue. See 49.2 RETURNS.

(iv)   Capital gains tax generally becomes due and payable thirty days after the issue of the notice of assessment (if later than 1 December following the end of the year of assessment) and interest then begins to run. In certain cases interest may run on tax which is yet to be due and payable. See 32 INTEREST ON UNPAID TAX and 41 PAYMENT OF TAX.

(v)   A notice specifying the apportionment of a reduction in tax liability involving more than one period or person, in certain discovery cases, must be given within thirty days of the inspector issuing a notice apportioning it. See 12.2 CLAIMS.

(b)   **Two months**

By notice given to the personal representatives within two months of the grant of representation, a widower may disclaim liability for his deceased wife's capital gains tax in respect of years before 1990/91. See 37.5 MARRIED PERSONS.

(c)   **Three months**

(i)   Appeals against a decision of the Board relating to residence, ordinary residence or domicile. See 47.7 RESIDENCE AND DOMICILE.

(ii)   Certain reliefs in relation to a disposal of shares in a 'controlled foreign company' must be claimed within three months of the later of the end of the relevant accounting period and the date that an assessment made on the claimant company in respect of the apportioned profits of the controlled foreign company becomes final and conclusive. See 39.12 OVERSEAS MATTERS.

(iii)   Applications for judicial review must be made within three months of the date when the grounds for application arose. See 4.10 APPEALS.

(iv)   Certain particulars of a settlement with a foreign element etc. must be supplied within three months of the creation of it. See 39.6 and 39.7 OVERSEAS MATTERS.

(v)   In respect of notices served after 31 December 1993, a company must generally comply with a notice to make a return within three months of service or, if later, twelve months of the end of the accounting period. See 49.3 RETURNS.

(d)   **Six months**

In respect of the form of rollover relief available on a disposal of shares to an employee share ownership trust, the disposal consideration must be used to acquire replacement assets within six months (or longer period in certain cases) of the disposal. See 53.25 SHARES AND SECURITIES.

(e)   **Twelve months**

(i)   To qualify for rollover relief an acquisition must be made twelve months before the associated disposal (or three years after). See 50.1 ROLLOVER RELIEF. This applies also to the general relief for compulsory acquisition of land (see 33.14 LAND).

(ii)   Where, within twelve months of receipt, a capital sum, received as compensation is applied in replacing an asset lost or destroyed, a claim may be made for the deemed disposal arising on the loss etc. to be treated as made for a 'no gain, no loss' consideration. See 16.9 DISPOSAL.

(iii) Certain particulars of a settlement with a foreign element etc. must be supplied within twelve months of certain events. See 39.6 and 39.7 OVERSEAS MATTERS.

(iv) Reinvestment in shares relief is only available if the shares whose acquisition value is to be reduced are acquired within twelve months before (or three years after) the disposal of the asset (shares before 30 November 1993) the proceeds of which are to be similarly reduced. See 45.2, 45.3 and 45.9 REINVESTMENT IN SHARES RELIEF.

(v) Acquisition of ordinary shares of an approved venture capital trust, against which the deferral of a capital gain can be claimed, must take place within a qualifying period of twelve months before the chargeable event giving rise to the gain (but not before 6 April 1995) and twelve months after the chargeable event. See 58.10 VENTURE CAPITAL TRUSTS.

(vi) Acquisition of shares by reference to which relief is obtained under the enterprise investment scheme, against which the deferral of a capital gain accruing after 28 November 1994 can be claimed, must take place within a qualifying period of twelve months before the chargeable event giving rise to the gain (or three years after). See 53.17 SHARES AND SECURITIES.

(f) **On or before 1 December following year of assessment**

Tax becomes due and payable on 1 December following the end of the year of assessment to which it relates (if later than thirty days after the issue of the notice of assessment). See 41.2 PAYMENT OF TAX.

55.2 TWO-YEAR TIME LIMITS

(a) **Only or main residence.** The election by individuals with more than one private residence must be made within two years from the date from which it is to take effect subject to certain concessions. See 43.3 PRIVATE RESIDENCES.

(b) **Family arrangements and disclaimers after death** must take effect within two years of the death, and within six months of the making of the instrument. See 15.6 DEATH.

(c) **Distribution of gains by overseas companies** in order to avoid a charge under *TCGA 1992, s 13* on a UK shareholder must be made within two years of the accrual of the gain. See 39.5 OVERSEAS MATTERS.

(d) **Unpaid corporation tax.** Where a company fails to pay corporation tax on its chargeable gains within six months of the due date, any of that tax which is recoverable from certain third parties (including members or former group members and shareholders) must be assessed within two years of the due and payable date. See 13.5, 13.6, 13.16 COMPANIES.

(e) **Groups of companies.** A company leaving a group remains liable for unpaid corporation tax on a chargeable gain arising from the disposal by a group member of any asset formerly owned by that company while it was a member of the group for a period of two years following the time the gain accrues. See 13.16 COMPANIES.

(f) **Know-how.** An election for know-how not to be treated as goodwill must be made within two years of the disposal. See 6.4 ASSETS.

(g) **Company ceasing to be UK resident etc: postponement of charge on deemed disposal.** Subject to certain conditions an election may be made by the company concerned and the principal company within two years of the cessation of UK residence etc. so that postponement is obtained. If any part of the postponed gain becomes chargeable on the principal company, it and the company concerned can elect within two years of the time the gain becomes chargeable that any unrelieved capital losses of the company be set against the gain. See 39.17 OVERSEAS MATTERS.

(*h*)   **Transfer of UK branch or agency of overseas resident company to UK resident company.** Subject to conditions a form of hold-over relief is available on a joint claim within two years after the end of the accounting period of the transferee company in which the transfer was made. See 39.3 OVERSEAS MATTERS.

(*i*)   **Employee share ownership trust: rollover relief.** In respect of the form of rollover relief available on a disposal of shares to an employee share ownership trust, the relief must be claimed within two years of the acquisition of replacement assets. See 53.25 SHARES AND SECURITIES.

(*j*)   **Reinvestment in shares relief.** In respect of disposals before 30 November 1993, an election to disapply the normal share reorganisation rules so as to bring about a disposal and acquisition where shares etc. are exchanged for other shares must be made not more than two years after the end of two alternative specified periods related to the reinvestment in shares or replacement of a reinvestment. See 45.10 REINVESTMENT IN SHARES RELIEF

55.3   THREE-YEAR TIME LIMITS

(*a*)   **Rollover relief** is only available if the acquisition is made within three years after the disposal (or twelve months before). See 50.1 ROLLOVER RELIEF. This applies also to the general relief for compulsory acquisition of land (see 33.14 LAND).

(*b*)   **Company ceasing to be UK resident and non-resident company.** Any tax due by a company ceasing to be UK resident and not paid within six months of becoming payable can, within three years of the amount being determined, be recovered from a person who is, or in the twelve months before residence ceased (or if less, the period after 14 March 1988) was, a member of the same group or a controlling director. Similar provisions apply to non-UK resident companies in relation to disposals after 13 March 1989. See 39.18 OVERSEAS MATTERS.

(c)   **Reinvestment in shares relief** is only available if the shares whose acquisition value is to be reduced are acquired within three years after (or twelve months before) the disposal of the shares the gain on which is to be similarly reduced. Relief can be withdrawn if certain events occur within three years of the acquisition of shares whose acquisition value has been reduced by the relief. See 45.2, 45.9, 45.11 and 45.12 REINVESTMENT IN SHARES RELIEF.

(d)   Acquisition of shares by reference to which relief is obtained under the enterprise investment scheme, against which the deferral of a capital gain accruing after 28 November 1994 can be claimed, must take place within a qualifying period of three years after the chargeable event giving rise to the gain (or twelve months before). See 53.17 SHARES AND SECURITIES.

55.4   FOUR-YEAR TIME LIMITS

Underwriters. Capital gains tax payable for years before 1994/95 by underwriters in respect of disposals of assets within premiums trusts funds becomes due and payable on the fourth anniversary of the beginning of the underwriting year for which it is assessed. See 56.6 UNDERWRITERS.

55.5   **SIX-YEAR TIME LIMITS**

(*a*)   **Intra-group transfers: company ceasing to be a member of a group.** If a company leaves a group within six years of the transfer to it of a capital asset by another member of the group, it will be liable on the market value of the asset at the time of transfer less the 'no gain, no loss' transfer price. See 13.17 COMPANIES.

(*b*)   **Company ceasing to be UK resident etc: postponement of charge on deemed disposal.** If within six years after the cessation of residence etc. the company disposes of assets held at that time, the whole or the appropriate part of the postponed gain (insofar as not already so treated) is deemed to accrue to the principal company. See 39.17 OVERSEAS MATTERS.

56 Underwriters

56.1 1992/93 AND SUBSEQUENT YEARS

Individual underwriters. For 1992/93 (subject to special transitional provisions which allow for the 'closing' of an underwriting year (i.e. the calendar year) of Lloyd's at the end of the next but one underwriting year) and subsequent years of assessment, the main income tax provisions (*ICTA 1988, ss 450–457*), capital gains tax provisions (*TCGA 1992, ss 206–209*) and various ancillary provisions previously having effect in relation to the taxation of underwriters are repealed and replaced with a new regime of provisions contained in *FA 1993, ss 171–184, 19, 20 Schs; FA 1995, s 143*. See Tolley's Income Tax under Underwriters for the revised income tax treatment.

For 1992/93 and subsequent years, trust funds held by an underwriting member of Lloyd's are classified as to '*premiums trust funds*' (as referred to in *Insurance Companies Act 1982, s 83*), 'new-style special reserve funds' (see below) and 'ancillary trust funds'. An '*ancillary trust fund*', in relation to the member, does not include his premiums trust fund or new-style special reserve fund but otherwise means any trust fund (including an 'old-style special reserve fund' as below) required or authorised by Lloyd's rules, or required by a members' agent of his or, before 1994/95, the managing agent of a syndicate of which he is a member.

In general terms for 1992/93 and subsequent years, disposals of assets in a Lloyd's member's premiums trust fund are only taken into account for income tax purposes, consideration relating to acquisitions and disposals of those assets being left out of account for capital gains tax purposes. However, because of the special Lloyd's provisions relating to

(*a*)   the closing of an underwriting year (above),

(*b*)   the allocation of profits arising in one underwriting year over that year and the two previous years,

(*c*)   the profits assessed for a year of assessment before 1997/98 being treated as those arising in the corresponding underwriting year (an underwriting year and a year of assessment being deemed to correspond to each other if the underwriting year ends in the year of assessment), and

(*d*)   the deemed disposal at the end of an underwriting year of assets forming part of a member's premiums trust fund at their value at that time and their deemed reacquisition at the beginning of the next underwriting year at the same value,

this will not apply to acquisitions or disposals made, or deemed to be made, of assets before 1 January 1994. See 56.3 below for the previous treatment of assets in a premiums trust fund.

For 1997/98 and subsequent years, the profits assessed for a year of assessment (see (*c*) above) are to be treated as those of any previous underwriting year which are declared in the corresponding underwriting year (an underwriting year and a year of assessment again being deemed to correspond to each other if the underwriting year ends in the year of assessment). Profits for a particular underwriting year are declared in the underwriting year immediately following the underwriting year in which the particular year is closed (e.g. the profits of the underwriting year 1995 are declared in 1998 and taxed in 1998/99, the 1995 year closing at the end of 1997).

For 1992/93 and subsequent years, gains arising from the disposals of assets forming part of an ancillary trust fund are assessed in the normal way to capital gains tax (and losses are treated as allowable losses for that tax). No special basis of capital gains tax assessment applies. This represents no change of treatment for practical purposes from that pertaining previously as in 56.2 below.

For 1992/93 and subsequent years, a member is treated for capital gains tax purposes as absolutely entitled as against the trustees to the assets forming part of any of his premiums trust funds or ancillary trust funds. From 1994/95, money deposits required to be paid out of a premiums trust fund under overseas regulatory arrangements are still deemed to form part of the fund. [*ICTA 1988, s 450(6); FA 1993, ss 171, 172, 174(1), 176, 184, 23 Sch Pt III; FA 1994, s 228, 21 Sch 1(1)(3)(a), 2, 3, 8, 26 Sch Pt V*]. Both such funds are therefore not 'settled property' as in 52.2 SETTLEMENTS.

The reference above to a '*new-style special reserve fund*' is to the 'new-style' funds authorised by *FA 1993, s 175(1)* to be set up in respect of 1992 and subsequent underwriting years although the capital of '*old-style special reserve funds*' authorised under *ICTA 1988, s 452(1)* for underwriting years prior to 1992 may be transferred to a new style fund within certain time limits, any asset being so transferred being deemed for capital gains tax purposes to be disposed of by the member at its market value at the time of transfer. [*FA 1993, s 175(4), 20 Sch 14(1)*]. As regards a new-style special reserve fund, the member is treated for capital gains tax purposes as absolutely entitled as against the trustees to the assets forming part of his fund but, for 1994/95 and later years, this does not affect the normal capital gains tax treatment of a transfer by him of an asset to the trustees. Profits and losses arising from assets forming part of such a fund are excluded for all capital gains tax (and income tax) purposes. [*FA 1993, s 175, 20 Sch 8, 9(1); FA 1994, s 228, 21 Sch 13*]. On cessation of underwriting, whether on death or otherwise, the amount of a member's new style special reserve fund, so far as not required as cover for cash calls and syndicate losses, must be paid over to him. Where the payment out of the fund on cessation takes the form of or includes an asset, the asset is deemed for capital gains tax purposes to be acquired by the member at its market value as at the end of 'the penultimate underwriting year' (before 1994/95, 'the relevant year'). '*The penultimate underwriting year*' and '*the relevant year*' both mean, subject to any regulations made by the Board, the underwriting year immediately preceding that in which the member's Lloyd's deposit is paid over to him or his personal representatives or assigns. [*FA 1993, s 175, 20 Sch 11(4)(5); FA 1994, s 228, 21 Sch 15(2)(3)*].

Regulations made under *TCGA 1992, s 209(4)* (which allow the making of regulations to extend certain time limits; see 56.5 below) in force immediately before 6 April 1992 continue in force for 1992/93 and subsequent years and are deemed to have been validly made. The Board have power, for 1992/93 to 1996/97 (both inclusive), to make similar regulations and, for 1992/93 and subsequent years, to make certain other supplementary regulations. [*FA 1993, ss 182, 184(3); FA 1994, s 228, 21 Sch 7, 26 Sch Pt V; FA 1995, s 83(2)*]. See SI 1995 Nos 351–353.

Corporate underwriters. For accounting periods ending after 31 December 1993 or, as the case may require, for the underwriting year 1994 and subsequent years, *FA 1994, ss 219–227, 229, 230* (i.e. *FA 1994, Pt IV Ch V* except *sections 228* and *21 Sch*) broadly apply the above provisions *mutatis mutandis* to corporate members of Lloyd's except that there is no provision for a corporate member to set up a new-style special reserve fund.

56.2   **INDIVIDUALS: 1991/92 AND PRIOR YEARS**

As indicated in 56.1 above, the provisions below and in 56.3–56.6 below are repealed after 1991/92 (again subject to special transitional provisions which allow for the 'closing' of an underwriting year (i.e. the calendar year) of Lloyd's at the end of the next but one underwriting year).

56.3 Underwriters

For 1991/92 and prior years of assessment, an individual underwriting member of Lloyd's is treated for capital gains tax purposes as absolutely entitled as against the trustees to the investments of his *'premiums trust fund'* (as referred to in *Insurance Companies Act 1982, s 83*, his *'old-style special reserve fund'* (as authorised by *ICTA 1988, s 452(1)*) and any other trust fund required or authorised by Lloyd's rules or required by an underwriting agent through whom his business is carried on in whole or part. [*TCGA 1992, s 206(1); FA 1993, 23 Sch Pt III*]. Such funds are therefore not 'settled property' as in 52.2 SETTLEMENTS.

Despite this nominee status for the trustees of a member's premiums trust fund (who may be, and normally is, treated as such a trustee), they are assessed and charged to capital gains tax for years before 1994/95 (see 56.3 below as to the allocation of gains over three underwriting years) as if *TCGA 1992, s 206(1)* above (and *FA 1993, s 174(1)* in 56.1 for years after 1991/92) did not apply. For years after 1987/88 and before 1994/95, such capital gains tax is charged at a rate equivalent to the basic rate of income tax for the year of assessment concerned, an appropriate credit being given of the tax paid if the underwriter is assessed at a higher rate in respect of the same gains. Losses accruing in prior years of assessment are not taken into account in assessing the trustees, and if for that and any other reason the tax paid on behalf of a member under assessments for a year of assessment exceeds the tax for which he is liable, the member can claim (under *TCGA 1992, s 206(4)*) the excess be repaid. [*TCGA 1992, s 206(2)–(5); FA 1993, s 183(7), 23 Sch Pt III*]. Before 1988/89, the rate of tax was 30% and there were no stated circumstances whereby an additional assessment charging a higher rate would have been made. The claim mentioned previously was made under *CGTA 1979, s 142(3)* prior to the commencement of *TCGA 1992*. [*CGTA 1979, s 3; FA 1988, s 101, 14 Sch Pt VII*].

It follows that for 1991/92 and prior years of assessment, gains and losses arising from investments in a member's old-style special reserve fund and any other trust fund within *TCGA 1992, s 206(1)* above (other than his premiums trust fund) are assessed and charged personally on him. No special basis of capital gains tax assessment applies.

56.3   **Calculation of gains and losses in premiums trust fund.** For underwriting years before 1994, an allocation is made of the realised and *unrealised* unindexed gains and losses arising from assets forming part of a member's premiums trust fund in the underwriting year (i.e. calendar year). Such gains and losses are arrived at by taking the difference between the valuations at the beginning and at the end of the underwriting year of the assets forming part of the fund, the value at the beginning of the year of assets acquired in the year being taken as their acquisition cost and the value at the end of the year of assets disposed of during the year being taken as their disposal consideration. The allocation (on a percentage basis agreed with the Inland Revenue) is among three underwriting years of account, viz. the calendar year in which the gains and losses arose and the two immediately *preceding* calendar years. (*Note.* An underwriting year of account is kept open for at least two years after the end of that year of account.) Thus, each underwriting year of account will have apportioned to it a fraction of gains and losses arising in that year, and in the two subsequent years. The total of gains so apportioned to a particular underwriting year of account ('syndicate gains') is assessed for the year of assessment in which that year of account ends. The above rules do not apply to GOVERNMENT SECURITIES (21) and QUALIFYING CORPORATE BONDS (44) but apply broadly to deep discount securities (see 53.19 SHARES AND SECURITIES). Securities which have been lent within *TCGA 1992, s 271(9); ICTA 1988, s 129* (see 53.23 SHARES AND SECURITIES) are treated as still held if the lending is still current at the end of the underwriting year of account. [*ICTA 1988, s 450(6); TCGA 1992, ss 118(5)(6), 207; FA 1989, ss 91(2), 96(1)–(4); FA 1993, 23 Sch Pt III*].

It appears that the rules for ASSETS HELD ON 31 MARCH 1982 (8) cannot apply to premiums trust funds for underwriting years before 1994.

For underwriting years before 1994 and after 5 April 1985, the provisions relating to INDEXATION (23) generally after that date apply 'with any necessary modifications' in relation to assets forming part of a premium trust fund as they apply in relation to other assets. Assets within the fund are assumed to be disposed of and immediately reacquired on each 31 December and any indexation allowance computed is allocated on the same basis given above for realised and unrealised unindexed gains and losses. [*TCGA 1992, s 208; FA 1993, 23 Sch Pt III*].

Realised and unrealised unindexed gains and losses in any particular calendar year prior to 1994 in respect of run-off accounts of the premiums trust fund are imputed to the underwriting year of account which closes at the end of that calendar year, i.e. the underwriting account ending two years before the end of the calendar year in which the gain arises. (*Example*. Gains arise in 1991 in respect of the 1985 run-off account. In 1991 the 1989 account closes. The gains in respect of the 1985 run-off account will therefore be attributed to the 1989 account and be assessed for 1989/90.) [*TCGA 1992, s 209(1)(2)(4); FA 1993, s 183(8), 23 Sch Pt III; SI 1974 No 896, Reg 7(1)(b)*].

For the special deduction available on the disposal of foreign securities held in a trust fund established abroad, see 16.4 DISPOSAL.

56.4 **Retirement of underwriter.** Other than on death, retirement of an underwriting member of Lloyd's will normally take place at the end of an underwriting year so his share of syndicate gains for underwriting years prior to 1994 will be treated as in 56.3 above. On death, it is standard practice not to allow a member dying in such an underwriting year to share in the gains or losses of that year unless death occurs on 31 December. In either case, no adjustment is required to the general capital gains tax rules on death (see 15.1 DEATH).

56.5 **Time limits.** For years of assessment prior to 1992/93, due to delay in establishing the results from Lloyd's underwriting, the Revenue may, in certain circumstances, extend the time limits for making elections as prescribed otherwise. In particular, it extends statutorily the time limits under the following heads.

(*a*) **Error or mistake claim** (see 12.4 CLAIMS).

(*b*) **General six-year time limit for making assessments and the time limit for assessments made to make good fraudulent or negligent conduct of taxpayer** (see 5.5 ASSESSMENTS and 9.4 BACK DUTY).

(*c*) **Assessments on personal representatives** (see 5.6 ASSESSMENTS and 9.5 BACK DUTY).

(*d*) **General six-year time limit for making claims** (see 12.2 CLAIMS).

(*e*) **Set-off of trading losses against chargeable gains of a person other than a company** (see 35.6 LOSSES).

In the above cases, the time limit is extended to six years after the end of the year which is the closing year for the underwriting account in relation to the year of assessment i.e., in effect, a further two-year extension. In certain cases such an extension also applies to the making of a claim etc. by the spouse of the underwriting member. [*TCGA 1992, s 209(3)-(6); FA 1993, s 183(8), 23 Sch Pt III; SI 1974 No 896, Reg 4; SI 1989 No 421, Reg 3(2); SI 1990 No 627, Reg 3(2); SI 1991 No 851, Regs 3(2), 9; SI 1992 No 511, Regs 3(2), 9; SI 1993 No 415, Regs 3(2), 9; SI 1994 No 728, Regs 3(2), 9*]. See also 56.1 above for the position for 1992/93 and onwards.

56.6   **Payment of tax.** For years of assessment prior to 1994/95 the Revenue may make regulations for the assessment and collection of tax charged under *TCGA 1992, s 207* (see 56.3 above) on gains arising from disposals of assets forming part of an underwriting member's premiums trust fund. Such tax is due on or before the fourth anniversary of the beginning of the relevant underwriting year, e.g. capital gains tax payable for the underwriting year 1991 (1 January to 31 December) falls due on 1 January 1995. Tax charged by an assessment made after (or, for the 1986 underwriting year and onwards, within thirty days before) this time limit has expired is due on the day (for the 1986 underwriting year and onwards, thirtieth day) following the date of issue of the assessment. [*TCGA 1992, s 209(1)(2)(4); FA 1993, s 183(8), 23 Sch Pt III; SI 1974 No 896, Reg 5; SI 1989 No 421, Reg 4; SI 1990 No 627, Reg 4; SI 1991 No 851, Reg 4; SI 1992 No 511, Reg 4; SI 1993 No 415, Reg 4; SI 1994 No 728, Reg 4*].

Capital gains tax arising from Lloyd's trust funds other than a premiums trust fund (e.g. those held in an old-style special reserve fund as in 56.2 above) is due, as for non-underwriting investments, on 1 December following the end of the year of assessment (see 41.1 PAYMENT OF TAX). [*TCGA 1992, s 7*].

56.7   **OVERSEAS RESIDENTS**

Where a capital gains tax treatment, rather than an income tax, or corporation tax charging income, one (see 56.1 above in relation to the position for 1992/93 and onwards), would apply to assets held as part of an individual underwriter's or corporate underwriter's trust funds, then if the individual or company is neither resident nor, in the case of an individual, ordinarily resident in the UK, he or the company is still liable to capital gains tax or corporation tax on chargeable gains on such assets which are situate in the UK. See 6.2 ASSETS and 39.3 OVERSEAS MATTERS. For this purpose, investments comprised in the Lloyd's American and Canadian Trust Funds are regarded as not situate in the UK. Investments held in the Lloyd's Sterling Trust Fund are situate in the UK, except for non-UK equities. The double taxation arrangements between the UK and the relevant countries should be consulted, as well as the relevant domestic legislation of the overseas countries concerned. For overseas matters generally and for the determination of residence and domicile, see 39 OVERSEAS MATTERS and 47 RESIDENCE AND DOMICILE.

57 Unit and Investment Trusts

Cross-references. See 7.2 ASSETS HELD ON 6 APRIL 1965 and 36.2 MARKET VALUE for valuation of units in unit trusts; 13.6 and 13.11 COMPANIES for transfers of businesses to, and intra-group disposals of assets by, authorised unit trusts and investment trusts; 23.1 INDEXATION for exclusion of indexation allowance in respect of disposals before 30 November 1993 of certain collective investment schemes; 58.1 VENTURE CAPITAL TRUSTS.

57.1 AUTHORISED UNIT TRUSTS

These are 'unit trust schemes' designated by an order of the Department of Trade under *Prevention of Fraud (Investments) Act 1958, s 17* (or NI equivalent) or, after 28 April 1988, designated by an order under *Financial Services Act 1986, s 78*. *'Unit trust scheme'* has the meaning given by *section 26(1)* of the former *Act*, but after 28 April 1988 this is replaced by that given under the latter *Act*, save that the Treasury may after 10 March 1988 by regulation provide for any scheme of a specified description not to be treated as a unit trust scheme for capital gains purposes. [*TCGA 1992, s 99(2)(3); ICTA 1988, ss 468(6), 469(7), 832; SI 1988, Nos 179, 266, 745*]. Certain limited partnership schemes and employee profit sharing schemes have been excepted from treatment as unit trust schemes for such purposes.

For capital gains purposes, any unit trust scheme is treated as if the scheme were a company and the rights of the unit holders were shares in the company, and in the case of an authorised unit trust (as defined by *ICTA 1988, s 468(6)*) as if the company were resident and ordinarily resident in the UK. [*TCGA 1992, s 99(1)*].

Gains realised by authorised unit trusts are not chargeable gains. [*TCGA 1992, s 100(1)*].

Income derived after 26 July 1990 in an accounting period in which a unit trust scheme is an authorised unit trust from transactions relating to futures contracts or options contracts is exempt from income tax under Schedule D, Case I. A contract is included for this purpose notwithstanding that one party to it will not be involved with a transfer of assets other than money. [*ICTA 1988, s 468AA; FA 1990, s 81(1)(5)*]. In effect the legislation now prevents a Schedule D Case I or Case VI or capital gains tax assessment in respect of such income or gains. See 16.10 and 16.11 DISPOSAL for the Revenue's treatment of options and futures in other cases.

In relation to disposals after 5 April 1988, a person acquiring units in authorised unit trusts under a monthly savings scheme can opt for a simpler arrangement for computing any chargeable gains arising. Under the arrangements, a person will be treated in most cases as having made a single annual investment in the seventh month of the trust's accounting year. This will be made up of savings plus reinvested income less any small withdrawals in the year concerned (Revenue Pamphlet IR 131, SP 3/89, 20 March 1989).

If under a 'collective investment scheme' (within the meaning of *Financial Services Act 1986*) contributions to it and profits arising from it are pooled in relation to separate parts of the property in the scheme and the participants are entitled to exchange rights in one part for rights in another, then for such exchanges after 13 March 1989 *TCGA 1992, s 127* (reorganisation etc. of shares etc.) is not to prevent the exchange constituting a disposal and acquisition for capital gains tax purposes. For this purpose *TCGA 1992, s 127* includes a reference to that provision as applied by *TCGA 1992, s 132* (conversion of securities) but does not include a reference to that provision as applied by *TCGA 1992, s 135* (exchange of securities for those in another company); see 53.5, 53.8

and 53.10 SHARES AND SECURITIES. These provisions do not seem to have been affected by the enactment (by virtue of *FA 1994, s 113*), broadly from 1 April 1994 but subject to transitional provisions, of *ICTA 1988, s 468(7)–(9)* (umbrella schemes). For exchanges before 14 March 1989 and after 22 July 1987 any question as to whether arrangements of a multi-portfolio collective investment scheme which provided for pooling constituted a single collective investment scheme was determined for capital gains tax purposes without regard to any entitlement of the participants to exchange rights in one part of the property for rights in another. [*TCGA 1992, s 102; F(No 2)A 1987, s 78*]. As regards exchanges before 23 July 1987 the position may be governed by *Arbuthnot Financial Services Ltd v CIR Ch D, [1985] STC 211* (a stamp duty case in which it was decided that a participant had transferred his units in one fund of a multi-fund unit trust scheme to the managers in consideration for units in another fund of the scheme).

57.2   **INVESTMENT TRUSTS**

An investment trust is a 'company' fulfilling the following conditions. [*ICTA 1988, s 842; FA 1988, s 117; FA 1990, s 55; FA 1994, ss 146, 170, 17 Sch 8*].

(*a*)   It is not a close company.

(*b*)   It is resident in the UK.

(*c*)   It derives its income wholly or mainly from 'shares' or securities (in practice taken as 70% or more, although, if the income in an accounting period falls slightly below this figure as a result of the profit on an isolated financial futures or options transaction, the trust may retain its approved status at the Revenue's discretion per Revenue Pamphlet IR 131, SP 14/91, 21 November 1991).

(*d*)   No 'holding' in any one company represents more than 15% of the value of its investments, unless that company is itself an investment trust or would be so but for being unquoted. This requirement is waived in respect of investments which, when acquired, represented no more than 15% of the value of the investments, and in respect of an investment held on 6 April 1965 provided that the holding represented not more than 25% of the overall value of the investments at that date. There is no waiver in either case where there has been an 'addition' to the holding.

(*e*)   Its 'ordinary share capital' (and every class thereof, if there is more than one) is quoted on a recognised stock exchange in the UK.

(*f*)   Its Memorandum or Articles prohibit the distribution by way of dividend of gains arising from the sale of investments.

(*g*)   It does not retain more than 15% of its income derived from shares and securities in any accounting period. However, for accounting periods ending after 25 July 1990, this requirement does not apply if the excess over the 15% limit is less than £10,000 (or proportionately reduced amount if the period is less than twelve months) or the company is required by law to retain an amount of income for the period in excess of the 15% limit and in circumstances such that the aggregate of the excess of the amount of income retained for the period over the amount of income required to be retained for the period and any amount distributed in respect of the period is less than £10,000 (or proportionately reduced amount where the period is less than twelve months).

(*h*)   It is approved by the Board.

As regards (*c*) above, units in an authorised unit trust (see 57.1 above) are for this purpose treated as shares in a company. Where the condition at (*d*) above is then relevant, it is regarded as being satisfied *provided that*, during any accounting period in which units in the unit trust were held by the investment trust, the unit trust itself satisfied the condition at (*c*) above (and this will always be considered to be the case where the unit trust is a securities fund under the *Financial Services Act 1986*). (Revenue Pamphlet IR 131, SP 5/91, 15 July 1991, as superseded by SP 7/94, 15 September 1994).

'Company' includes any body corporate or unincorporated association, but not a partnership. [*TCGA 1992, s 288(1)*].

'Shares' includes stock.

'Holding' means the shares or securities of whatever class or classes held in any one company. Where, in connection with a scheme of reconstruction or amalgamation (see 13.6 COMPANIES; 53.8, 53.9 SHARES AND SECURITIES), a company issues shares or securities to persons holding shares or securities in another in respect of and in proportion to (or as nearly as may be in proportion to) such holdings, without the recipients becoming liable for any consideration, the old and the new holdings are treated as the same.

For accounting periods ending after 5 April 1988, if the investing company is a member of a group (i.e. a company and its 51% subsidiaries), money owed to it by another group member is treated as a security and, as such, as part of its holding in that other group member. Holdings in companies which are members of a group (whether or not including the investing company) are treated as holdings in a single company.

An *'addition'* is made to a holding whenever the investing company acquires further shares or securities in any company in which it already has a holding, otherwise than by being allotted them without liability for consideration (e.g. a bonus issue). The holding is deemed to have been acquired at the date of the latest addition.

'Ordinary share capital' means all the issued share capital (by whatever name called) of a company, other than that which produces a fixed rate of dividend and is non-participating. [*ICTA 1988, s 832(1)*].

See Tolley's Corporation Tax for the definition of a close company.

For the Revenue's views on whether forward currency transactions by investment trusts are on capital or income account and whether such a transaction on income account would breach the test in (*c*) above, see Revenue Pamphlet IR 131, SP 1/88, 3 February 1988.

See Revenue Pamphlet IR 131, SP 3/89, 20 March 1989 (as in 57.1 above), which applies to investment trusts as it does to authorised unit trusts.

Gains realised by investment trusts are not chargeable gains. [*TCGA 1992, s 100(1)*].

See 58.1 VENTURE CAPITAL TRUSTS.

57.3   **UNIT TRUSTS FOR EXEMPT UNIT HOLDERS**

If, for any reason other than non-residence, none of the holders of units in a unit trust scheme would be liable to capital gains tax (or to corporation tax on chargeable gains) on a disposal of units, gains accruing to the trust itself are not chargeable gains. [*TCGA 1992, s 100(2)*]. This exemption applies whenever the gains accrued, but is of practical importance only in relation to unit trust schemes which have not been designated as in 57.1 above. It is not withdrawn by reason of units being temporarily held by the trust's managers under the ordinary arrangements of the trust for the issue and redemption of units. (Revenue Pamphlet IR 1, D17.)

57.4   **COURT INVESTMENT FUNDS**

These are common investment funds established under *Administration of Justice Act 1982, s 42*. The Accountant General is deemed to hold the funds (together with other funds in court) as nominee or bare trustee as in 52.2 SETTLEMENTS. [*TCGA 1992, ss 61, 100(3)*].

Gains realised by court investment funds are not chargeable gains. [*TCGA 1992, s 100(1)*].

57.5   **INVESTMENT CLUBS**

Chargeable gains and allowable losses made by investment clubs are apportioned among the members, each individual being assessed on his share of the whole. The secretary may apply (on Form 185-1) for the gains and losses to be agreed by the inspector of the district in which he lives if

(*a*)   the club has not more than 20 members at any one time;

(*b*)   the annual subscription has a maximum rate of £1,000;

(*c*)   the annual net gains are less than £5,000;

(*d*)   the average investment per head based on cost price does not exceed £5,000; and

(*e*)   all members have agreed the division of the capital gains.

Each member's share can then be accepted by his own local inspector without further argument. Otherwise, the total gains and the member's share must be separately agreed.

57.6   **VENTURE CAPITAL TRUSTS**

For 1995/96 and subsequent years of assessment, chargeable gains of venture capital trusts are not chargeable gains. See 58.8 VENTURE CAPITAL TRUSTS below.

58 Venture Capital Trusts

Cross-references. See 57 UNIT AND INVESTMENT TRUSTS and 45 REINVESTMENT IN SHARES RELIEF.

58.1   From 6 April 1995, the venture capital trust scheme described at 58.2 *et seq.* below is introduced to encourage individuals to invest in unquoted trading companies through such trusts. The provisions dealing with the approval of companies as venture capital trusts, and with the reliefs for investors, are introduced in *FA 1995, ss 70–72, 14–16 Schs*. The Treasury has wide powers to make regulations governing all aspects of the reliefs applicable to venture capital trust investments, and for the tax credits attached to venture capital trust distributions to be claimed by and paid to the trust, and not set against income tax. [*FA 1995, s 73*].

58.2   **CONDITIONS FOR APPROVAL** [*ICTA 1988, s 842AA; FA 1995, s 70*]

A '*venture capital trust*' ('VCT') is a company approved for this purpose by the Board. Close companies (see Tolley's Corporation Tax under Close Companies) are excluded. The time from which an approval takes effect is specified in the approval, and may not be earlier than the time the application for approval was made or, for approvals given in 1995/96, 6 April 1995.

Except as detailed further below, approval may not be given unless the Board are satisfied that the following conditions are met.

(*a*)   The company's income in its most recent complete accounting period has been derived wholly or mainly from shares or securities, and not more than 15% of its income from shares and securities has been retained.

(*b*)   Throughout that period at least 70% by value of the company's investments has been represented by shares or securities in 'qualifying holdings' (see 58.3 below), at least 30% of which (by value) has been represented by holdings of '*eligible shares*', i.e. ordinary shares carrying no present or future preferential right to dividends, to assets on a winding up or to redemption.

(*c*)   The company's ordinary shares (or each class thereof) have been quoted on the Stock Exchange throughout that period.

(*d*)   No holding in any company other than a VCT (or a company which could be a VCT but for (*c*) above) has at any time in that period represented more than 15% of the value of the company's investments.

'Securities' includes liabilities in respect of certain loans not repayable within five years, and any stocks or securities relating to which are not re-purchasable or redeemable within five years of issue.

As regards the 15% limits in (*a*) and (*d*) above, the provisions which apply to the similar restrictions on investment trusts (see 57.2 UNIT AND INVESTMENT TRUSTS) apply with appropriate modification.

Where (*a*)–(*d*) above are met, the Board must also be satisfied that they will be met in the accounting period current at the time of application for approval. Where any of (*a*)–(*d*) above are not met, approval may nevertheless be given where the Board are satisfied that:

(i)   in the case of (*a*), (*c*) or (*d*), the condition will be met in the accounting period current when the application for approval is made or in the following accounting period;

(ii)   in the case of (*b*), the condition will be met in an accounting period beginning no more than three years after the earlier of the time approval is given and the time it takes effect; and

(iii)   in any case, that the condition will continue to be fulfilled in accounting periods following that referred to in (i) or (ii).

The value of any investment for the purposes of (*b*) and (*d*) above is the value when the investment was acquired, except that where it is added to by a further holding of an investment of the same description, or a payment is made in discharge of any obligation attached to it which increases its value, it is the value immediately after the most recent such addition or payment.

Approval may be **withdrawn** where there are reasonable grounds for believing that either:

(A)   the conditions for approval were not satisfied at the time the approval was given; or

(B)   a condition that the Board were satisfied (as above) would be met has not been or will not be met; or

(C)   where (ii) above applies, any other conditions prescribed by regulation in relation to the three-year period have not been met; or

(D)   in either the most recent complete accounting period or the current one, one of conditions (*a*)–(*d*) above has failed or will fail to be met (unless the failure was allowed for under (i)–(iii) above).

The withdrawal is effective from the time the company is notified of it, except that:

(1)   where approval is given under (i)–(iii) above, and is withdrawn before all the conditions in (*a*)–(*d*) above have been satisfied in relation to either a complete twelve-month accounting period or successive complete accounting periods constituting a continuous period of twelve months or more, the approval is deemed never to have been given; and

(2)   for the purposes of relief for capital gains accruing to a VCT under *TCGA 1992, s 100* (see 58.8 below), withdrawal may be effective from an earlier date, but not before the start of the accounting period in which the failure occurred (or is expected to occur).

An assessment consequent on the withdrawal of approval may, where otherwise out of time, be made within three years from the time notice of the withdrawal was given.

Applications for approval should be made to the Financial Intermediaries and Claims Office, St John's House, Merton Road, Bootle, Merseyside L69 9BB.

58.3   **QUALIFYING HOLDINGS** [*ICTA 1988, 28B Sch; FA 1995, 14 Sch*]

Shares or securities in a company are comprised in a VCT's '*qualifying holdings*' at any time if they were first issued to the VCT, and have been held by it ever since, and the following conditions are satisfied at that time.

(*a*)   The company is an '*unquoted company*' (whether or not UK resident), i.e. none of its shares, stocks, debentures or other securities is

(i)   listed on a recognised stock exchange, or a designated exchange outside the UK, or

(ii)   dealt in on the Unlisted Securities Market, or outside the UK by such means as may be designated for the purpose by order.

If the company ceases to be an unquoted company at a time when its shares are comprised in the qualifying holdings of the VCT, this condition is treated as continuing to be met, in relation to shares or securities acquired before that time, for the following five years. [*ICTA 1988, 28B Sch 2; FA 1995, 14 Sch 2*].

(*b*)   Either

(i)   the company must exist wholly for the purpose of carrying on one or more 'qualifying trades' (disregarding any purpose having no significant effect on the extent of its activities as a whole). (The case of *Lord v Tustain; Lord v Chapple Ch D, [1993] STC 755* concerned the question whether a company exists for the purposes of carrying on a trade), or

(ii)   its business must consist entirely in holding shares in or securities of, or making loans to, one or more 'qualifying subsidiaries', with or without the carrying on of one or more 'qualifying trades'.

In addition, the company, or a 'qualifying subsidiary', must, when the shares were issued to the VCT and ever since, have been carrying on a 'qualifying trade' wholly or mainly in the UK, or preparing to carry on such a trade intended to be carried on wholly or mainly in the UK. In the latter case, there is a time limit of two years from the issue of the shares for the trade to be commenced as intended.

A trade is a '*qualifying trade*' if it does not, or not substantially, consist of any of the activities at (A)–(F) below. Research and development (i.e. activity intended to result in a patentable invention or a computer program) from which it is intended that there will be derived a qualifying trade carried on wholly or mainly in the UK is treated as the carrying on of a qualifying trade.

(A)   Dealing in land, in commodities or futures or in shares, securities or other financial instruments.

(B)   Dealing in goods otherwise than in the case of an 'ordinary' trade of wholesale or retail distribution.

(C)   Banking, insurance, money-lending, debt-factoring, hire-purchase financing or other financial activities.

(D)   Leasing (including letting ships on charter or other assets on hire) or receiving royalties or licence fees.

(E)   Providing legal or accountancy services.

(F)   Providing services or facilities for any trade, profession or vocation within (A)–(E) above and which is carried on by another person (other than a parent company), where one person has a 'controlling interest' in both trades.

Adventures and concerns in the nature of trade, and trades not carried on commercially and with a view to the realisation of profits, are also excluded.

In relation to similar provisions under the Business Expansion Scheme, the Revenue are understood to have regarded as 'substantial' for the above purposes a part of a trade which gives rise to 20% or more of total turnover. (Tolley's Practical Tax 1987 p 162). Similarly, as regards (A) above, it is understood that it was not intended to exclude from relief what is mainly a building trade, despite the technical position that what the builder sells is the land with the buildings on it. (Tolley's Practical Tax 1984 p 206).

As regards (B) above, a trade of wholesale or retail distribution is a trade consisting of the offer of goods for sale either to persons for resale (or processing and resale) (which resale must be to members of the general public) by them ('*wholesale*') or to the general public ('*retail*') and a trade is not an ordinary wholesale or retail trade if it consists to a substantial extent of dealing in goods collected or held as an investment (or of that and any other activity within (A)–(F) above), and a substantial proportion of such goods is held for a significantly longer period than might reasonably be expected for a vendor trying to dispose of them at market value. Whether such trades are '*ordinary*' is to be judged having regard to the following features, those under (1) supporting the categorisation as 'ordinary', those under (2) being indicative to the contrary.

(1) (*a*) The breaking of bulk.

  (*b*) The purchase and sale of goods in different markets.

  (*c*) The employment of staff and incurring of trade expenses other than the cost of goods or the remuneration of persons connected (within *ICTA 1988, s 839*) with a company carrying on the trade.

(2) (*a*) The purchase or sale of goods from or to persons connected (within *ICTA 1988, s 839*) with the trader.

  (*b*) The matching of purchases with sales.

  (*c*) The holding of goods for longer than might normally be expected.

  (*d*) The carrying on of the trade at a place not commonly used for wholesale or retail trading.

  (*e*) The absence of physical possession of the goods by the trader.

As regards (D) above, the trade of a company engaged in the production of original master films, tapes or discs is not excluded by reason only of the receipt of royalties or licence fees, provided that all royalties and licence fees received by the company are in respect of films, etc. produced by it since the issue of the shares to the VCT or in respect of by-products arising therefrom. The company may also be engaged in the distribution of films produced by it since those shares were issued. Similarly the trade of a company engaged in research and development is not excluded by reason only of the receipt of royalties and licence fees attributable to that research and development.

Also as regards (D) above, a trade carried on by a company will not be excluded by reason only of its consisting of chartering ships, other than oil rigs or ships of a kind primarily used for sport or recreation, provided that

(I) the company beneficially owns all the ships it so lets,

(II) every ship beneficially owned by the company is UK-registered,

(III) the company is solely responsible for arranging the marketing of the services of its ships, and

(IV) in relation to every letting on charter, certain conditions as to length and terms of charter, and the arm's length character of the transaction, are met,

and if any of (I)–(IV) above is not met in relation to certain lettings, only those lettings (together with any other excluded activities) are taken into account in determining whether a substantial part of the trade consists of excluded activities.

As regards (F) above, a person has a '*controlling interest*' in a trade carried on by a company if he controls the company (within *ICTA 1988, s 416*, see Tolley's Corporation Tax under Close Companies); or if the company is close (see Tolley's Corporation Tax under Close Companies) and he or an 'associate' (within *ICTA 1988, s 417*, see Tolley's

Corporation Tax under Close Companies, but excluding a brother or sister) is a director of the company and the beneficial owner of, or able to control, more than 30% of its ordinary share capital; or if at least half of its ordinary share capital is directly or indirectly owned by him. In any other case, it is obtained by his being entitled to at least one-half of the assets used for, or income arising from, the trade. Rights and powers of 'associates' (as above) are taken into account for these purposes.

(c)   The money raised by the issue of shares to the VCT must have been employed wholly for the purposes of, or of preparing for the carrying on of, the qualifying trade (disregarding insignificant amounts used for other purposes), or be intended to be so employed. In the latter case, the money must actually be so employed within twelve months of the later of the issue of the shares to the VCT and the date the qualifying trade was commenced.

(d)   The aggregate of money raised from shares issued by the company to the VCT must not have exceeded the 'maximum qualifying investment' of £1 million in the period from six months before the issue in question (or, if earlier, the beginning of the year of assessment of the issue) to the time of the issue in question. Disposals are treated as far as possible as eliminating any such excess. The £1 million limit is proportionately reduced where, at the time of the issue, the qualifying trade is carried on, or to be carried on, in partnership or as a joint venture, and one or more of the other parties is a company.

(e)   The value of the company's assets as a whole did not exceed £10 million immediately before the issue and did not exceed £11 million immediately afterwards. For this purpose, value means the value of the gross assets of the company at a time when it did not have any qualifying subsidiaries, or the aggregate value of the gross assets of all the companies in the group where it does have such subsidiaries (but disregarding any rights against, or shares in or securities of, another group member).

(f)   The company must not control (within *ICTA 1988, s 416*, see Tolley's Corporation Tax under CLOSE COMPANIES, and with or without CONNECTED PERSONS) any company other than a 'qualifying subsidiary', nor must another company (or another company and a person connected with it) control it. Neither must arrangements be in existence by virtue of which such control could arise. These provisions do not, however, apply to control by a VCT attributable primarily to a change in the value of any shares in or securities of the company.

A company is a *'qualifying subsidiary'* for these purposes provided that:

(i)   it (and any fellow subsidiary) either:

(A)   satisfies the condition in (b)(i) above, or

(B)   exists wholly for the purpose of holding and managing property used by the parent or a fellow subsidiary or subsidiaries for the purposes of a qualifying trade (disregarding any purpose having no significant effect on the extent of its activities as a whole), or for research and development from which it is intended that a qualifying trade will be derived, or

(C)   has no corporation tax profits, and no part of its business consists in the making of investments;

(ii)   the parent or a fellow subsidiary possesses at least 90% of both its issued share capital and its voting power, and would be beneficially entitled to at least 90% of its assets available for distribution to equity holders on a winding-up, etc. and of any profits available for distribution to equity holders (see 13.10 COMPANIES);

(iii)   no person other than the parent or a fellow subsidiary has control of the company within *ICTA 1988, s 840* (i.e., no person has the power by shareholding or voting power (whether directly or through another company), or under Articles of Association, to secure that the company's affairs are conducted according to his wishes); and

(iv)   no arrangements are in existence which could result in failure to fulfil any of (i)–(iii).

Where

(A)   the subsidiary is being wound up, or

(B)   arrangements are in existence for the disposal of all the parent company's (or fellow subsidiary's) interest in the subsidiary,

it is not regarded as failing to meet conditions (i)–(iv) above provided that the winding up or disposal is for *bona fide* commercial reasons and not part of a scheme or arrangement a main purpose of which is the avoidance of tax and, in the case of (A), that it would meet those conditions apart from the winding up.

(g)   Where the company is being wound up, none of conditions (a)–(f) above are regarded on that account as not being satisfied provided that those conditions would be met apart from the winding up, and that the winding up is for *bona fide* commercial reasons and not part of a scheme or arrangement a main purpose of which is the avoidance of tax.

As regards (c) and (d) above, where either condition would be met as to only part of the money raised by the issue, and the holding is not otherwise capable of being treated as separate holdings, it is treated as two separate holdings, one from which that part of the money was raised, the other from which the rest was raised, with the value being apportioned accordingly to each holding. In the case of (c), this does not require an insignificant amount applied for non-trade purposes to be treated as a separate holding.

The Treasury have power by order to modify the requirements under (b) above as they consider expedient, and to alter the cash limits referred to in (d) and (e) above.

58.4   **INCOME TAX RELIEFS** [*ICTA 1988, s 332A, 15B Sch; FA 1995, s 71, 15 Sch*]

Relief from income tax is granted for 1995/96 and subsequent years in respect of both investments in VCTs and distributions from such trusts.

58.5   **Relief in respect of investments.** Subject to the conditions described below, an individual may claim relief for a year of assessment for the amount (or aggregate amounts) subscribed by him on his own behalf for 'eligible shares' issued to him in a year of assessment by a VCT (or VCTs) for raising money. There is a limit of **£100,000** on the relief which may be claimed for any year of assessment.

'*Eligible shares*' means new ordinary shares in a VCT which, throughout the five years following issue, carry no present or future preferential right to dividends or to assets on a winding up or to be redeemed.

Relief is given by a reduction in what would otherwise be the individual's income tax liability for the year of assessment by the lesser of

(i)   tax at the lower rate (currently 20%) on the amount(s) subscribed, and

(ii)   an amount sufficient to reduce that liability to nil.

In determining what would otherwise be the individual's income tax liability for the year of assessment for this purpose, no account is taken of:

(A)   any income tax reduction in respect of enterprise investment scheme investments, personal reliefs, qualifying maintenance payments, interest relief or medical insurance (see Tolley's Income Tax under Enterprise Investment Scheme, Allowances and Tax Rates, Married Persons, Interest Relief and Medical Insurance respectively);

(B)   any reduction of liability to tax by way of DOUBLE TAX RELIEF (17); or

(C)   any basic rate tax on income the tax on which the individual is entitled to charge against any other person or to deduct, retain or satisfy out of any payment.

Where relief is given by repayment of tax more than twelve months after the end of the year of assessment in which the shares were issued, interest under *ICTA 1988, s 824* (see Tolley's Income Tax under Interest on Overpaid Tax) is payable.

An individual is **not** entitled to relief where:

(*a*)   he was under 18 years of age at the time of issue of the shares;

(*b*)   circumstances have arisen which, had the relief already been given, would have resulted in the withdrawal or reduction of the relief (see 58.6 below);

(*c*)   the shares were issued or subscribed for other than for *bona fide* commercial purposes or as part of a scheme or arrangement a main purpose of which was the avoidance of tax; or

(*d*)   a loan is made to the individual (or to an 'associate' within *ICTA 1988, s 417*, see Tolley's Corporation Tax under Close Companies, but excluding a brother or sister) by any person at any time in the period beginning with the incorporation of the VCT (or, if later, two years before the date of issue of the shares) and ending five years after the date of issue of the shares, and the loan would not have been made, or would not have been made on the same terms, if he had not subscribed, or had not been proposing to subscribe, for the shares. The granting of credit to, or the assignment of a debt due from, the individual or associate is counted as a loan for these purposes.

[*ICTA 1988, 15B Sch 1, 2, 6; FA 1995, 15 Sch 1, 2, 6*].

Example

On 1 August 1995, A Ventura, a 44 year old married man and whose salary is £50,000 p.a. from UK employment, subscribes for 50,000 eligible £1 shares issued at par to raise money by VCT plc, an approved venture capital trust. On 1 March 1996 he purchases a further 90,000 £1 shares in VCT plc for £70,000 on the open market. The trust makes no distribution in 1995/96. Mr Ventura's other income for 1995/96 consists of dividends of £12,000 (net).

Mr Ventura's tax computation for 1995/96 is as follows.

		£
Earnings from UK employment		50,000
Dividends	12,000	
Add Tax credit	3,000	15,000
Total income		65,000
Deduct personal allowance		3,525
Taxable income		£61,475

Tax payable:

3,200 @ 20%	640
21,100 @ 25%	5,275
37,175 @ 40%	14,870
	20,785
Married Couple's Allowance £1,720 @ 15%	258
	20,527
Deduct Tax credit	3,000
	17,527
Deduct Relief for investment in VCT plc, 20% of £50,000 subscribed	10,000
Net tax payable	£7,527

58.6   **Withdrawal of relief on investment.** *Disposal of investment.* Where an individual disposes of eligible shares in respect of which relief has been claimed as under 58.5 above within five years of their issue (other than to a spouse when they are living together, see below), then:

(*a*)   if the disposal is otherwise than at arm's length, relief given by reference to those shares is withdrawn;

(*b*)   if the disposal is at arm's length, the relief given by reference to those shares is reduced by an amount equivalent to tax at the lower rate (for the year for which relief was given) on the consideration received for the disposal (or withdrawn if the relief exceeds that amount).

Relief is **not** withdrawn where the disposal is by one spouse to the other at a time when they are living together. However, on any subsequent disposal the spouse to whom the shares were transferred is treated as if he or she were the person who subscribed for the shares, as if the shares had been issued to him or her at the time they were issued to the transferor spouse, and as if his or her liability to income tax had been reduced by reference to those shares by the same amount, and for the same year of assessment, as applied on the subscription by the transferor spouse. Any assessment for reducing or withdrawing relief is made on the transferee spouse.

Identification of shares. For the above purposes, disposals of eligible shares in a VCT are identified with those acquired earlier rather than later. As between eligible shares acquired on the same day, shares by reference to which relief has been given are treated as disposed of after any other eligible shares.

Withdrawal of approval. Where approval of a company as a VCT is withdrawn (but not treated as never having been given) (see 58.2 above), relief given by reference to eligible shares in the VCT is withdrawn as if on a non-arm's length disposal immediately before the withdrawal of approval.

Assessments withdrawing or reducing relief, whether because relief is subsequently found not to have been due or under the above provisions, are made under Schedule D, Case VI for the year of assessment for which the relief was given. No such assessment is, however, to be made by reason of an event occurring after the death of the person to whom the shares were issued.

Information. Particulars of all events leading to the reduction or withdrawal of relief must be notified to the inspector by the person to whom the relief was given within 60 days of his coming to know of the event. Where the inspector has reason to believe that a notice so required has not been given, he may require that person to furnish him, within a specified time not being less than 60 days, with such information relating to the event as he may reasonably require. The requirements of secrecy do not prevent the inspector disclosing to a VCT that relief has been given or claimed by reference to a particular number or proportion of its shares. Penalties under *TMA 1970, s 98* apply for failure to comply with these requirements.

[*ICTA 1988, 15B Sch 3–5; FA 1995, s 71(3), 15 Sch 3–5*].

Example

On 1 August 1998, A Ventura in the *Example* at 58.5 above, who has since 1995/96 neither acquired nor disposed of any shares in VCT plc, gives 30,000 shares to his son. On 1 March 1999 he disposes of the remaining 110,000 shares for £95,000. The relief given in 58.5 above is withdrawn as follows.

Disposal on 1 August 1998

The shares disposed of are identified with 30,000 of those subscribed for, and, since the disposal was not at arm's length, the relief given on those shares is withdrawn.

$$\text{Relief withdrawn } \frac{30,000}{50,000} \times 10,000 = \qquad\qquad \text{£ } 6,000$$

Disposal on 1 March 1999

The balance of £4,000 of the relief originally given was in respect of 20,000 of the shares disposed of. The disposal consideration for those 20,000 shares is

$$95,000 = \frac{20,000}{110,000} = \qquad\qquad \text{£ } 17,273$$

The relief withdrawn is the lesser of the relief originally given and 20% of the consideration received, i.e.

£

20% of £17,273 = £3,455.

Relief withdrawn is therefore   3,455

The 1998/99 Schedule D, Case VI assessment is therefore   £9,455

58.7   **Relief on distributions.** A 'relevant distribution' of a VCT to which a 'qualifying investor' is beneficially entitled is not treated as income for income tax purposes.

A *'qualifying investor'* is an individual aged 18 or over who is beneficially entitled to the distribution either as the holder of the shares or through a nominee (including the trustees of a bare trust).

A *'relevant distribution'* is a dividend (including a capital dividend) in respect of ordinary shares in a company which is a VCT which were acquired at a time when it was a VCT by the recipient of the dividend, and which were not shares acquired in excess of the 'permitted maximum' for the year of assessment. It does not include any dividend paid in respect of profits or gains of any accounting period ending when the company was not a VCT.

Shares are acquired in excess of the *'permitted maximum'* for a year where the aggregate of the market values of ordinary shares acquired in VCTs by the individual or his nominee(s) in that year exceeds £100,000, disregarding shares acquired other than for *bona fide* commercial reasons or as part of a scheme or arrangement a main purpose of which is the avoidance of tax. Shares acquired later in the year are identified as representing the excess before those acquired earlier, and in relation to same-day acquisition of different shares, a proportionate part of each description of share is treated as representing any excess arising on that day. Shares acquired at a time when a company was not a VCT are for these purposes treated as disposed of before other shares in the VCT. Otherwise, disposals are identified with earlier acquisitions before later ones, except that as between shares acquired on the same day, shares acquired in excess of the permitted maximum are treated as disposed of before any other shares. There are provisions for effectively disregarding acquisitions arising out of share exchanges where, for capital gains purposes, the new shares are treated as the same assets as the old.

[*ICTA 1988, 15B Sch 7–9; FA 1995, 15 Sch 7–9*].

58.8   **CAPITAL GAINS TAX RELIEFS** [*TCGA 1992, ss 151A, 151B, 5C Sch; FA 1995, s 72, 16 Sch*]

From 6 April 1995, the capital gains of a VCT are not chargeable gains. [*TCGA 1992, s 100(1); FA 1995, s 72(2)*]. In addition, for 1995/96 and subsequent years, individual investors in VCTs are entitled to two reliefs:

(*a*)   on disposal of VCT shares (see 58.9 below); and

(*b*)   by deferral of chargeable gains on re-investment in VCT share issues (see 58.10 below).

Various provisions of *TCGA 1992* which are superseded for these purposes by specific provisions (as below) are disapplied or applied separately to parts of holdings which do not fall within the reliefs.

Withdrawal of approval. Where approval of a company as a VCT is withdrawn (but not treated as never having been given) (see 58.2 above), shares which (apart from the withdrawal) would be eligible for the relief on disposal (see 58.9 below) are treated as disposed of at their market value at the time of the withdrawal. For the purposes of the relief on disposal, the disposal is treated as taking place while the company is still a VCT, but the re-acquisition is treated as taking place immediately after it ceases to be so.

58.9   **Relief on disposal.** A gain or loss accruing to an individual on a 'qualifying disposal' of ordinary shares in a company which was a VCT throughout his period of ownership is not a chargeable gain or an allowable loss. A disposal is a *'qualifying disposal'* if:

(*a*)   the individual is 18 years of age or more at the time of the disposal;

(*b*)   the shares were not acquired in excess of the 'permitted maximum' for any year of assessment; and

(*c*)   the shares were acquired for *bona fide* commercial purposes and not as part of a scheme or arrangement a main purpose of which was the avoidance of tax.

The identification of those shares which were acquired in excess of the *'permitted maximum'* is as under 58.7 above, i.e. where the aggregate of the market values of ordinary shares acquired in VCTs by the individual or his nominee(s) in that year exceeds £100,000, disregarding shares acquired other than for *bona fide* commercial reasons or as part of a scheme or arrangement a main purpose of which is the avoidance of tax. Shares acquired later in the year are identified as representing the excess before those acquired earlier, and in relation to same-day acquisition of different shares, a proportionate part of each description of share is treated as representing any excess arising on that day. Shares acquired at a time when a company was not a VCT are for these purposes treated as disposed of before other shares in the VCT. Otherwise, disposals are identified with earlier acquisitions before later ones, except that as between shares acquired on the same day, shares acquired in excess of the permitted maximum are treated as disposed of before any other shares.

Share pooling. The normal rules for the pooling of shares and identification of disposals in *TCGA 1992, ss 104, 105, 107* (see 23.9 INDEXATION) are disapplied in respect of shares which are eligible for the above relief.

There are provisions (see below) for effectively disregarding acquisitions arising out of share exchanges where, for capital gains purposes, the new shares are treated as the same assets as the old.

Where an individual holds ordinary shares in a VCT which fall into more than one of the following groups:

(1)   shares eligible for relief on disposal (as above) and by reference to which he has been given or is entitled to claim relief under the provisions in 58.5 above (income tax relief on investments);

(2)   shares eligible for relief on disposal but by reference to which he has not been given or will be unable to claim relief under the provisions in 58.5 above;

(3)   shares by reference to which he has been given or is entitled to claim relief under the provisions in 58.5 above but which are not eligible for relief on disposal;

(4)   shares not within (1)–(3) above;

then, if there is a reorganisation under *TCGA 1992, s 126*, the provisions in *TCGA 1992, s 127* (equation of original shares with new holding) (see 53.5 SHARES AND SECURITIES above) will apply separately to each group of shares (if any) in order that they continue to be kept within their respective groups.

Where an individual holds ordinary shares in a company ('the existing holding') and there is, by virtue of an allotment for payment within *TCGA 1992, s 126(2)(a)* (e.g. a rights issue), a reorganisation affecting the existing holding immediately following which the shares or allotted holding are shares falling within (1)–(3) above, the provisions in *TCGA 1992, ss 127–130* will not apply in relation to that existing holding. The effect is that the rights issue will be treated as an acquisition.

Where holding consists of shares falling within (1) or (2) above and it is exchanged or is deemed to be exchanged for a second holding which does not consist of ordinary shares in a VCT, then the provisions in *TCGA 1992, ss 135, 136* will not apply (see 53.8 and 53.9 SHARES AND SECURITIES above). The effect is that there will be or deemed to be a disposal and acquisition.

[*TCGA 1992, ss 151A, 151B; FA 1995, s 72(3)*].

See 58.8 above as regards relief on withdrawal of approval of the VCT.

Example

On the disposals in the *Example* at 58.6 above, a chargeable gain or allowable loss arises only on the disposal of the shares acquired in excess of the permitted maximum for 1995/96. The shares in VCT plc were acquired in 1995/96 for £120,000, so that there is a £20,000 excess over the permitted maximum. The 50,000 shares first acquired for £50,000 are first identified, so that shares representing the excess are two-sevenths of the 90,000 shares subsequently acquired for £70,000 on 1 March 1996, i.e. 25,714 of those shares. The disposal identified with those shares is a corresponding proportion of the 110,000 shares disposed of for a consideration of £95,000 on 1 March 1999.

Mr Ventura's capital gains tax computation for 1998/99 is as follows.

Disposal consideration for 25,714 shares:

	£
$95,000 = \dfrac{25,714}{110,000} =$	22,207
Deduct Cost:	
$\dfrac{25,714}{110,000} \times (70,000 + \dfrac{20,000}{50,000} \times 50,000) =$	21,038
Unindexed gain	£1,169

58.10   **Deferred charge on re-investment.** *TCGA 1992, 5C Sch* (introduced as *FA 1995, 16 Sch* by *FA 1995, s 72(4)*) applies where:

(*a*)   a chargeable gain accrues to an individual after 5 April 1995 on the disposal of any asset (or on the occurrence of certain events in relation to enterprise investment scheme investments, see *TCGA 1992, 5B Sch 4, 5* introduced as *FA 1995, 13 Sch 4(3)* (see 53.17 SHARES AND SECURITIES), or under the current provisions, see below);

(*b*)   the individual makes a 'qualifying investment'; and

(*c*)   the individual is UK resident or ordinarily resident both when the chargeable gain accrues to him and when he makes the 'qualifying investment', and is not, at the latter time, regarded as resident outside the UK for the purposes of any double taxation arrangements the effect of which would be that he would not be liable to tax on a gain arising on a disposal, immediately after their acquisition, of the shares comprising the 'qualifying investment', disregarding the exemption under *TCGA 1992, s 151A(1)* (see 58.9 above).

A '*qualifying investment*' is a subscription for shares in a company which is a VCT, by reference to which relief is obtained under 58.5 above, within twelve months (extendible by the Board) before or after the time of the accrual of the chargeable gain in question, and, if before, provided that the shares are still held at that time. The shares are not deemed to be issued by reason only of a letter of allotment.

Broadly, the detailed provisions below allow a claim for the chargeable gain to be rolled over into the VCT shares, and for the gain to become chargeable on certain events in relation to those shares (including, in particular, on their disposal).

Postponement of original gain. Where a chargeable gain would otherwise accrue to an individual ('the investor') and he acquires a qualifying investment, a claim can be made by him to defer the whole or part of that gain against a corresponding amount of his qualifying investment up to the amount of the gain, or for an amount so claimed, whichever is the smaller. The amount of qualifying investment available for set off is restricted to the amount on which relief has been given under 58.5 above, less any amount already utilised against other gains.

Chargeable event. The original gain deferred through the making of the above claim will subsequently crystallise (without any further relief) if one of the following circumstances arise:

(A)   the investor disposes of the shares in his qualifying investment ('the relevant shares') otherwise than under *TCGA 1992, s 58* (an inter-spouse transfer);

(B)   the relevant shares are disposed of by the spouse of the investor (otherwise than by a transfer back to him), the spouse having first acquired them from the investor under *TCGA 1992, s 58*;

(C)   where shares falling within 58.9(3) above are exchanged or treated as exchanged for any non-VCT holdings and under *TCGA 1992, s 135* or *TCGA 1992, s 136* (see 53.8 and 53.9 SHARES AND SECURITIES above) there is a requirement (or, but for *TCGA 1992, s 116*) (see 44.3 QUALIFYING CORPORATE BONDS above) there would be a requirement) for those holdings to be regarded as the same assets as those shares;

(D)   the investor becomes neither resident nor ordinarily resident in the UK whilst holding the relevant shares and within five years of the making of the qualifying investment ('the relevant period');

(E)   an individual who acquired the relevant shares through an inter-spouse transfer under *TCGA 1992, s 58* becomes neither resident nor ordinarily resident in the UK whilst holding those shares and within the relevant period;

(F)   the company in which the relevant shares are held has its approval as a VCT withdrawn (in a case in which approval is not treated as never having been given) (see 58.2 above);

(G)   the relief given under 58.5 above by reference to relevant shares is withdrawn or reduced in circumstances not falling within (A)–(F) above.

In the case of (D) or (E) above, the original gain will not crystallise where the individual concerned became neither resident nor ordinarily resident in the UK through temporarily working abroad and he again becomes UK resident or ordinarily resident in the UK within three years of that event, without having disposed of any of the relevant shares in the meantime. An assessment will be issued by the Revenue when it is clear that the individual will not regain UK resident status within the three year period.

There is no crystallisation of the original gain where an event within (A)–(G) above occurs at or after the time of death of the investor or a person to whom the relevant shares were transferred under *TCGA 1992, s 58*.

Without prejudice to the following provisions in a case falling within (F) above, any reference above to a disposal excludes a reference to a disposal deemed to occur on a withdrawal of approval within 58.8 above.

Crystallisation of original gain. Where a chargeable event mentioned in (A)–(G) above relating to relevant shares occurs for the first time in connection with those shares, a chargeable gain is deemed to accrue at that time equal to so much of the expenditure on those shares which was set against the original gain.

Identification of shares. In determining whether any shares to which a chargeable gain relates are shares the expenditure on which has been set against the whole or part of any gain, disposals of shares are identified with those subscribed for earlier rather than later, and as between shares in a company acquired on the same day, those the expenditure on which has been set against a gain are treated as disposed of after any other shares in that company. This applies also to shares not eligible for relief under 58.9 above, notwithstanding anything in *TCGA 1992, ss 104, 105, 107*.

Assets. Where at the time of a chargeable event relevant shares are regarded as represented by assets which consist of or include assets other than relevant shares, the expenditure on those shares is apportioned between those assets on a just and reasonable basis. As between different assets regarded as representing the same relevant shares, the identification of those assets will be determined on a similar basis to the identification of shares.

Persons assessable. The chargeable gain is treated as accruing, as the case may be:

   (i)   to the individual who makes the disposal;

   (ii)   to the individual who holds the shares in question at the time of the exchange or deemed exchange;

   (iii) to the individual who becomes non-UK resident etc.;

   (iv) to the individual who holds the shares in question when the withdrawal of the approval takes effect; or

   (v)   to the individual who holds the shares in question when the circumstances arise in respect of which the relief is withdrawn or reduced.

A chargeable gain is computed separately for the investor without reference to any shares held at the time of the chargeable event by a recipient to the investor from a *TCGA 1992, s 58* transfer).

[*TCGA 1992, 5C Sch; FA 1995, 16 Sch*].

Example

The facts are as in the *Example* at 58.5 above except that Mr Ventura sells a painting on 1 November 1995, realising a capital gain (after indexation) of £25,000. In addition to the relief against income tax he receives, he also claims deferral of the gain against his subscription for shares in VCT plc up to an amount of £19,000, leaving £6,000 to be covered by his annual exemption of £6,000.

When the shares in VCT plc are subsequently disposed of in 1998/99 (see *Example* at 58.6 above), the gain of £19,000 deferred on the disposal of the painting crystallises and forms part of his gains for 1998/99.

59 Wasting Assets

Cross-references. See 18.4 EXEMPTIONS AND RELIEFS for tangible movable assets generally and 18.11 for private passenger motor vehicles; 33.16–33.25 LAND for leases of land which are wasting assets; and 50.6 ROLLOVER RELIEF for the relief available where assets are, or will within ten years, become wasting assets.

59.1   Subject to the following, where an asset disposed of is a 'wasting asset'

(a)   the original cost, etc. (see 16.3 DISPOSAL) less predictable residual value, is treated as diminishing evenly day by day over the asset's life, and

(b)   additional expenditure (see 16.3 DISPOSAL) is similarly treated as diminishing evenly over the remaining life of the asset as from the date the expenditure was first reflected in the state or nature of the asset

and only so much of the original cost and additional expenditure as, on the above basis, remains at the date of disposal is then deductible. If additional expenditure under (b) above creates or increases a residual value, then the new residual value is taken into account in (a) above. [*TCGA 1992, s 46*].

A '*wasting asset*' is an asset with a predictable 'life' not exceeding fifty years and, in relation to tangible movable property, '*life*' means 'useful life', having regard to the purpose for which the tangible assets were acquired or provided by the person making the disposal. However, plant and machinery are always regarded as having a predictable life of less than fifty years and that life is to be based on normal usage. Freehold land is never a wasting asset, whatever its nature and whatever the nature of the building or works on it. The predictable life and predictable residual value, if not immediately ascertainable by the nature of the asset, are to be taken on a disposal as they were known or ascertainable at the time when the asset was acquired by the person making the disposal. [*TCGA 1992, s 44*].

No restriction of allowable expenditure as above occurs where an asset, throughout the ownership of the person making the disposal, is used solely for the purposes of a trade, profession or vocation, and capital allowances have, or could have, been claimed in respect of its cost, or in respect of any enhancement expenditure. This also applies where an asset has otherwise qualified in full for any capital allowances. Where, however, the asset disposed of has been used partly for non-business purposes, or has only partly qualified for capital allowances, the expenditure and consideration are apportioned and the restrictions imposed above applied to that portion of expenditure which has not qualified for capital allowances, or which relates to the period of non-business use. [*TCGA 1992, s 47*].

Tangible movable assets (chattels) which are wasting assets are exempt subject to certain conditions. See 18.4 EXEMPTIONS AND RELIEFS. Chattels such as antique clocks and certain motor vehicles may be 'machinery' and thus exempt subject to those conditions (which broadly correspond to those of *TCGA 1992, s 47* above). See Revenue Tax Bulletin, October 1994, pp 166, 167 for the Revenue's meaning of machinery.

Example

V bought an aircraft on 31 May 1991 at a cost of £90,000 for use in his air charter business. It has been agreed that V's non-business use of the aircraft amounts to one-tenth, on a flying hours basis, and capital allowances and running costs have accordingly been restricted for income tax purposes. On 1 February 1996, V sells the aircraft for

£185,000. The aircraft is agreed as having a useful life of 20 years at the date it was acquired. The indexation factor for May 1991 to February 1996 is assumed to be 0.163.

	£
Amount qualifying for capital allowances	
Relevant portion of disposal consideration $\frac{9}{10} \times$ £185,000	166,500
Relevant portion of acquisition cost $\frac{9}{10} \times$ £90,000	81,000
Unindexed gain	85,500
Indexation allowance £81,000 × 0.163	13,203
Chargeable gain	£72,297

Amount not qualifying for capital allowances		
Relevant portion of disposal consideration $\frac{1}{10} \times$ £185,000		18,500
Relevant portion of acquisition cost		
$\frac{1}{10} \times$ £90,000	9,000	
Deduct wasted £9,000 × $\dfrac{\text{4y 8m}}{\text{20y}}$	2,100	6,900
Gain		£11,600

The whole of the £11,600 is exempt.

The total chargeable gain is therefore	£72,297

59.2   OPTIONS AND FUTURES CONTRACTS

Generally speaking, options are treated as wasting assets and are subject to the rules outlined in 59.1 above. However, there are specific statutory exceptions to this and these, together with further rules relating to options generally, are covered in 16.10 DISPOSAL. For employee share options, see 53.16 SHARES AND SECURITIES. See 18.48 EXEMPTIONS AND RELIEFS and 57.1 UNIT AND INVESTMENT TRUSTS for options held by pension schemes and authorised unit trusts respectively.

See 16.11 DISPOSAL for certain commodity and financial futures which are excepted from wasting asset treatment.

59.3   LEASES OF PROPERTY OTHER THAN LAND

In accordance with the definition of a wasting asset given in 59.1 above a 'lease of property other than land' may be or become a wasting asset. Such a lease which is a wasting asset is subject to the rules in 59.1 above, and in particular those regarding allowable expenditure. This treatment should be compared with leases of land which are wasting assets where, instead of allowable expenditure being written off at a uniform rate, a special basis is used (see 33.17 LAND). Despite this, the legislation regarding leases of property other than land is mainly by direct reference to that covering leases of land with 'necessary modifications'. [TCGA 1992, ss 44, 46, 47, 240, 8 Sch 9(1)].

A *'lease of property other than land'* means any kind of agreement or arrangement under which payments are made for the use of, or otherwise in respect of, property and *'lessor'*, *'lessee'* and *'rent'* are construed accordingly. [TCGA 1992, 8 Sch 10(1)(b)].

Duration of a lease. The duration of a lease is to be decided by reference to the facts known or ascertainable at the time when the lease was acquired or created. In determining the duration, the following provisions apply.

(a)   Where the terms of the lease include provision for the determination of the lease by notice given by the lessor, the lease is not to be treated as granted for a term longer than one ending at the earliest date on which it could be determined by notice given by the lessor.

(b)   Where any of the terms of the lease or any other circumstances rendered it unlikely that the lease will continue beyond a date earlier than the expiration of the terms of the lease, the lease is not to be treated as having been granted for a longer term than one ending on that date. This applies in particular where the lease provides for rent to go up after a given date, or for the lessee's obligation to become more onerous after a given date, but includes provision for the determination of the lease on that date, by notice given by the lessee, and those provisions render it unlikely that the lease will continue beyond that date.

(c)   Where the terms of the lease include provision for the extension of the lease beyond a given date by notice given by the lessee, the duration of the lease applies as if the term of the lease extended for as long as it could be extended by the lessee, but subject to any right of the lessor to determine the lease by notice.

(d)   In the case of a lease of an asset which itself is a wasting asset and also movable property, the lease is assumed to terminate not later than the end of the life of the wasting asset.

[*TCGA 1992, 8 Sch 8, 9(3)*].

59.4   **Premiums for leases.** Where the payment of a 'premium' is required under a lease (or otherwise under the terms subject to which the lease is granted) there is a part disposal of the asset or other interest out of which that lease is granted.

In the part disposal computation (which follows the normal rules in *TCGA 1992, s 42*, see 16.6 DISPOSAL) the property which remains undisposed of includes a right to any rent or other payments (other than a premium) payable under the lease, and that right is valued at the time of the part disposal. [*TCGA 1992, 8 Sch 2*].

'*Premium*' includes any like sum, whether payable to the intermediate or superior lessor and includes any sum (other than rent) paid on or in connection with the granting of a lease except in so far as the other sufficient consideration for the payment is shown to have been given. In addition, the following amounts are also to be regarded as premiums.

(a)   Where under the terms of a lease, the lessee must pay a sum in lieu of the whole or part of the rent for any period, or as consideration for the surrender of the lease, the lease is deemed to have required payment of a premium to the lessor (in addition to any other premium) of that amount for the period in relation to which it is payable.

Where the premium is deemed to have been received as consideration for the surrender of a lease, the surrender of the lease is not the occasion of any recomputation of the gain accruing on the receipt of any other premium, and the premium which is the consideration for the surrender of the lease is regarded as consideration for a separate transaction consisting of the disposal by the lessor of his interest in the lease.

(b)   Where, as consideration for the variation or waiver of any of the terms of a lease, the lessee must pay a sum otherwise than by way of rent, the lease is deemed to have required the payment to the lessor of a premium (in addition to any other premium) of that amount for the period from the time when the variation or waiver takes effect to the time it ceases. Where the transaction is not at arm's length or is entered into gratuitously, such a sum is deemed to be payable as if the transaction were at arm's length.

If under (a) or (b) above a premium is deemed to have been received by the lessor, otherwise than as consideration for the surrender of the lease then

(i)   subject to (ii) below, both the lessor and lessee are treated as if that premium were, or were part of, the consideration for the grant of the lease due at the time when the lease was granted, and the gain accruing to the lessor on the disposal by way of grant of the lease is recomputed and any necessary adjustments of tax made; and

(ii)   if the lessor is a tenant under a lease the duration of which does not exceed 50 years, the deemed premium is treated as allowable enhancement expenditure incurred by the sub-lessee.

[*TCGA 1992, 8 Sch 3*].

Where by reference to any capital sum within the meaning of *ICTA 1988, s 781* (assets leased to traders and others) any amount of that capital sum is charged to income tax then that amount is deducted from the consideration for capital gains tax purposes but not so as to convert a gain into a loss or increase a loss. [*TCGA 1992, 8 Sch 9(2)*].

59.5   **Sub-leases granted out of short leases.** Where a sub-lease is granted out of a head-lease with less than fifty years to run, the normal part disposal rules do not apply. Instead, subject to below, a proportion of the cost and enhancement expenditure attributable to the lease is apportioned to the part disposed of as follows

P(1)

P(2)

where

P(1) =   the duration of the sub-lease

P(2) =   the duration of the lease at the date of acquisition (for apportionment of cost) or the duration of the lease at the date when expenditure is first reflected in the nature of the lease (for apportionment of enhancement expenditure).

If the amount of the premium is less than what would be obtainable by way of premium for the sub-lease if the rent payable under the sub-lease were the same as the rent payable under the lease, the percentage attributable to the sub-lease as calculated above must be multiplied by the premium received over the premium so obtainable before being applied to cost or enhancement expenditure. [*TCGA 1992, 8 Sch 4(1)(2)*].

Example

P purchases a 40-year lease of a non-wasting asset other than land in 1983 for £15,000. In 1988 he grants a sub-lease of the asset to Q for 20 years for a premium of £8,000. Had the rent under head-lease and sub-lease been the same the premium would have been £10,000. The expenditure attributable to the part disposal of the sub-lease is given by

$$£15,000 \times \frac{20}{40} \times \frac{8,000}{10,000} = 0.4 \times £15,000 = £6,000$$

Where the sub-lease is a sub-lease of part only of the asset comprised in the lease, the cost and enhancement expenditure of the head-lease must be apportioned between the sub-lease and the remainder in proportion to their respective values. [*TCGA 1992, 8 Sch 4(3)*].

59.6 LIFE INTERESTS

Life interests in settled property within 59.1 above are treated as wasting assets when the expectation of life of the life tenant is 50 years or less. The predictable life of life tenants and annuities is ascertained from actuarial tables which have Revenue approval. [*TCGA 1992, s 44(1)(d)*]. See 52.8 SETTLEMENTS for the disposal of interests in settled property generally.

Example

N is a beneficiary under a settlement. On 30 June 1983, when her actuarially estimated life expectancy was 40 years, she sold her life interest to an unrelated individual, R, for £50,000. N dies on 31 December 1996, and the life interest is extinguished.

R will have an allowable loss for 1996/97 as follows

	£	£
Disposal consideration on death of N		Nil
Allowable cost	50,000	
Deduct wasted		
$\dfrac{13\text{y } 6\text{m}}{40\text{y}} \times £50,000$	16,875	
		33,125
Allowable loss		£33,125

Note to the example
(a) The amount of the cost wasted is computed by reference to the predictable life, not the actual life, of the wasting asset.

60 Finance Act 1995–Summary of CGT Provisions

(Royal Assent 1 May 1995)

s 35	**Rates of income tax for 1995/96.** For the effect of these on rates of capital gains tax, see 2.1 ANNUAL RATES AND EXEMPTIONS and 52.1 SETTLEMENTS
ss 46, 47	**Reinvestment in shares relief.** Clarification is given on the amount of relief available where a qualifying investment is acquired by way of gift. The interests in land rule is removed, and provisions are introduced with regard to multiple claims for relief. Property development and farming are now to count as qualifying trades for relief. See REINVESTMENT IN SHARES RELIEF (45)
s 48	**Rollover relief and groups of companies.** Changes are made to rollover relief for groups. See 50.4 ROLLOVER RELIEF.
s 49	**De-grouping charges.** New provisions are added to strengthen existing anti-avoidance legislation on companies leaving groups with assets transferred to them from other group members before departure. See 13.17 COMPANIES.
s 50	**Corporate bonds.** Quoted index securities are prevented from being corporate bonds. See 44.2 QUALIFYING CORPORATE BONDS.
s 61	**Gains on retirement benefit schemes that lose their approval.** Pension schemes which lose their tax approval are deemed to have acquired their assets immediately before the date of cessation of approval. See 18.75 EXEMPTIONS AND RELIEFS.
ss 66, 67, 13 Sch	**Enterprise investment scheme.** Further changes are made to the scheme, and a new relief is introduced to allow any chargeable gain to be rolled over into a scheme. See 53.17 SHARES AND SECURITIES.
ss 68, 69	**Business expansion scheme.** The predecessor to the enterprise investment scheme is made the subject of minor modifications. See 53.18 SHARES AND SECURITIES.
ss 70–73, 14–16 Sch	**Venture capital trusts.** From 6 April 1995 a new scheme is introduced to encourage investment in unquoted trading companies through venture capital trusts. See VENTURE CAPITAL TRUSTS (58).
ss 74–76, 17 Sch	**Settlements and estates.** Various consequential amendments are made with regard to the simplification of legislation on settlements. See SETTLEMENTS (52).
s 90	**Relief for post-cessation expenditure.** Relief for expenditure that would have been deductible against the profits of a trade had it not ceased can be relieved against income tax and capital gains tax. See 35.6 LOSSES.
ss 91, 92	**Set-off of post-cessation and post-employment expenditure against income and capital gains.** Relief is available for certain types of expenditure against either income or capital gains. See 35.6 LOSSES.
ss 103–123, 20–22 Schs	**Self-assessment.** Further changes are made to existing provisions in preparation for the new regime to take effect from 1996/97. See SELF-ASSESSMENT (51).
ss 126, 127, 23 Sch	**UK representatives of non-residents.** Obligations and liabilities under self-assessment will fall upon UK representatives of non-residents carrying on a business in the UK through a branch or agency. See 51.40 SELF-ASSESSMENT.
s 154	**Short rotation coppice.** From 29 November 1994 short rotation coppice is regarded as farming and not forestry. See 18.30 EXEMPTIONS AND RELIEFS.

61 Table of Cases

Where the CIR (or, in Scotland, the Lord Advocate) are a party, the case is listed under the name of the other party only. Judicial review cases are listed under the name of the applicant and the person who is the subject of the review but again excluding the CIR etc.

61 Table of Cases

61   Table of Cases

61 Table of Cases

61   Table of Cases

62   Table of Statutes

Note. The legislation relating to capital gains tax has been divided into three sections, viz. Miscellaneous Legislation, Main Taxing Acts, and Statutory Instruments.

MISCELLANEOUS LEGISLATION
(in alphabetical order)

STATUTORY INSTRUMENTS (in date order)

Note. The bulk of Statutory Instruments mentioned in this book relate to annual exempt amounts (see 2.3; 49.2; 52.4; 52.5); double taxation treaties (see 17.2; 17.3; 47.9); exempt government securities (see 21.2); interest on overpaid tax (see 31); interest on unpaid tax (see 32); personal equity plans (see 53.20) and underwriters (see 56).

Others are as follows.

63   Index

This index is referenced to the chapter number or to the chapter and paragraph number. The entries printed in bold capitals are main subject headings in the text.